Prentice Hall

LITERATURE
Timeless Voices, Timeless Themes

Copper

Bronze

Silver

Gold

Platinum

The American Experience

The British Tradition

SERIES AUTHORS

The series authors guided the direction and the philosophy of Prentice Hall Literature: Timeless Voices, Timeless Themes. *Working closely with the development team, they contributed to the pedagogical integrity of the program and to its relevance for today's teachers and students.*

Heidi Hayes Jacobs

Department of Curriculum and Teaching
Teachers College
Columbia University
New York, New York
Heidi Hayes Jacobs has served as an educational consultant to over 1,000 schools nationally and internationally. A frequent contributor to professional journals, she has published two best-selling books through ASCD: Interdisciplinary Curriculum: Design and Implementation *and* Mapping the Big Picture: Integrating Curriculum and Assessment K–12. *She has been on the faculty of Teachers College, Columbia University, since 1981, and her years as a teacher of high-school, middle-school, and elementary-school students in Utah, Massachusetts, and New York provide the fundamental background of her experience.*

Richard Lederer

Author, speaker, columnist, and teacher
San Diego, California
Richard Lederer celebrates the English language as the best-selling author of more than ten books, including Anguished English *and* The Miracle of Language. *He writes a syndicated weekly column, "Looking at Language," and he is the* Grammar Grappler *for* Writer's Digest. *His work has also appeared in publications such as* The New York Times, Sports Illustrated, National Review, *and* Reader's Digest. *Well-known as a speaker and a presenter, Lederer has entertained and informed a wide variety of audiences, including the National Council of Teachers of English. For many years, he taught English at St. Paul's School in Concord, New Hampshire.*

Sharon Sorensen

Author, speaker, and consultant
Mt. Vernon, Indiana
An educator with more than thirty years of classroom experience, Sharon Sorensen has taught both secondary language arts and language arts methods at the university level. She has also published over eighty articles and has authored or co-authored more than twenty-five books on writing, writing process, and the teaching of writing, including How to Write Short Stories, How to Write Research Papers, *and* Webster's New World Student Writing Handbook. *She and her husband live in a self-created wildlife sanctuary in rural Indiana, where they are active in the National Audubon Society.*

PROGRAM ADVISORS

The program advisors provided ongoing input throughout the development of Prentice Hall Literature: Timeless Voices, Timeless Themes. *Their valuable insights ensure that the perspectives of teachers throughout the country are represented within this literature series.*

Diane Cappillo

Language Arts Department Chair
Barbara Goleman Senior High School
Miami, Florida
Past President of the Dade County Council of Teachers of English.

Anita Clay

English Instructor
Gateway Institute of Technology
St. Louis, Missouri
Former Middle School Team Leader; Former Chair, High School English Department.

Mary Curfman

Teacher of English
Clark County School District
Las Vegas, Nevada

Ellen Eberly

Teacher of Language Arts
Catholic Memorial
West Roxbury, Massachusetts

Nancy M. Fahner

Language Arts Instructor
Ingham Intermediate School District
Mason, Michigan
Recipient of Charlotte, Michigan, Teacher of the Year Award, 1992. Curriculum Coordinator for School-to-Work Program.

Terri Fields

Language Arts and Communication Arts Teacher, Author
Sunnyslope High School
Phoenix, Arizona
Recipient of Arizona Teacher of the Year and U.S. WEST Outstanding Arizona Teacher awards.

Susan J. Goldberg

Teacher of English
Westlake Middle School
Thornwood, New York
President, Westchester Council of English Educators. President-Elect, New York State English Council.

Prentice Hall

LITERATURE
Timeless Voices, Timeless Themes

COPPER

PRENTICE HALL
Upper Saddle River, New Jersey
Needham, Massachusetts

ACKNOWLEDGMENTS

Grateful acknowledgment is made to the following for permission to reprint copyrighted material:

Airmont Publishing Company, Inc. "Water" from *The Story of My Life* by Helen Keller. Copyright © 1965 by Airmont Publishing Company, Inc. Reprinted by permission of Airmont Publishing Company, Inc.

Ricardo E. Alegría "The Three Wishes" from *The Three Wishes: A Collection of Puerto Rican Folktales,* Selected and adapted by Ricardo E. Alegría, translated by Elizabeth Culbert. Reprinted by permission of the author.

Bantam Doubleday Dell Books for Young Readers and A.M. Heath and Company Ltd. and the author "Lob's Girl" from *A Whisper in the Night* by Joan Aiken. Copyright © 1984 by Joan Aiken. Used by permission of Bantam Doubleday Dell Books for Young Readers and A.M. Heath & Company Ltd. and the author.

Elizabeth Barnett, literary executor "The Spring and the Fall" by Edna St. Vincent Millay. From *Collected Poems,* HarperCollins. Copyright 1923, 1951 by Edna St. Vincent Millay and Norma Millay Ellis. All rights reserved. Reprinted by permission of Elizabeth Barnett, literary executor.

Susan Bergholz Literary Services, New York "Names/Nombres" by Julia Alvarez. Copyright © by Julia Alvarez 1985. First published in *Nuestro,* March, 1985. "Eleven" by Sandra Cisneros from *Woman Hollering Creek.* Copyright Sandra Cisneros 1991 by Sandra Cisneros. Published by Vintage Books, a division of Random House, Inc., New York and originally in hardcover by Random House, Inc. Reprinted by permission of Susan Bergholz Literary Services, New York. All rights reserved.

Robert Bly "Childhood and Poetry" by Pablo Neruda from *Neruda and Vallejo: Selected Poems,* edited and translated by Robert Bly, Beacon Press, 1971, 1993. Copyright © 1971, 1993 by Robert Bly. Used by permission of the translator.

Georges Borchardt, Inc. for the Estate of John Gardner "Dragon, Dragon" from *Dragon, Dragon and Other Tales* by John Gardner. Copyright © 1975 by Boskydell Artists Ltd. Reprinted by permission of Georges Borchardt, Inc. for the Estate of John Gardner.

Brandt & Brandt Literary Agents, Inc. "Wilbur Wright and Orville Wright" by Stephen Vincent Benet, from *A Book of Americans* by Rosemary and Stephen Vincent Benet (Holt, Rinehart & Winston, Inc.) Copyright © 1933 by Rosemary and Stephen Vincent Benet. Copyright renewed © 1961 by Rosemary Carr Benet. Reprinted by permission of Brandt & Brandt Literary Agents, Inc.

Gwendolyn Brooks "I'll Stay" by Gwendolyn Brooks. Used by permission of the author.

Diana Chang "Saying Yes" by Diana Chang. Copyright by Diana Chang. Reprinted by permission of the author

Clarion Books/Houghton Mifflin Company. "A Backwoods Boy," from *Lincoln: A Photobiography* by Russell Freedman. Copyright © 1987 by Russell Freedman. Reprinted by permission of Clarion Books/Houghton Mifflin Company. All rights reserved.

Cleveland Live "An Astronaut's Answers" by John Glenn, from Snappy, published online on Cleveland Live. © 1998 Cleveland Live. All rights reserved.

Don Congdon Associates, Inc. "The Sound of Summer Running" by Ray Bradbury. Published in *The Saturday Evening Post,* 2/18/56. Copyright © 1956 by the Curtis Publishing Co., renewed 1984 by Ray Bradbury. Reprinted by permission of Don Congdon Associates, Inc.

Dell Books, a division of Bantam Doubleday Dell Publishing Group, Inc. "Jeremiah's Song" by Walter Dean Myers, copyright © 1987 by Walter Dean Myers. from *Visions* by Donald R. Gallo, Editor. "The Geese" by Richard Peck, from *Sounds and Silences: Poetry For Now* by Richard Peck, Editor. Copyright © 1970, 1990 by Richard Peck. Used by permission of Dell Books, a division of Bantam Doubleday Dell Publishing Group, Inc.

Doubleday, a division of Bantam Doubleday Dell Publishing Group, Inc. "The Iron Horse" from *They Rose Above It* by Bob Considine. Copyright © 1977 by Millie Considine as Executive of the Estate of Bob Considine. "The Fun They Had" from *Earth Is Room Enough* by Isaac Asimov. Copyright © 1957 by Isaac Asimov. "Child on Top of a Greenhouse", copyright 1946 by Editorial Publications, Inc. from *The Collected Poems of Theodore Roethke* by Theodore Roethke. Used by permission of Doubleday, a division of Bantam Doubleday Dell Publishing Group, Inc.

Paul S. Eriksson, Publisher "My Papa, Mark Twain" by Susy Clemens from *Small Voices* by Josef and Dorothy Berger. © Copyright 1966 by Josef and Dorothy Berger. Published by Paul S. Eriksson. Reprinted by permission of the publisher.

Franklin Watts, a division of Grolier Publishing "How the Internet Works" from *The Internet* by Kerry Cochrane. Copyright © 1995 by Kerry Cochrane. All rights reserved. Reprinted by permission of the publisher, Franklin Watts, a division of Grolier Publishing.

Walt Disney Music Company "Circle of Life" Music by Elton John. Lyrics by Tim Rice. Copyright © 1994 Wonderland Music Company. All rights reserved. Reprinted by permission.

(Acknowledgments continue on p. 875.)

Looking at Universal Themes

Growing and Changing

Unit

2

Looking at Universal Themes

Reaching Out

Looking at Universal Themes

Proving Yourself

Unit 4

Looking at Universal Themes

Seeing It Through

Looking at Universal Themes

Mysterious Worlds

Looking at Literary Forms

Short Stories

Looking at Literary Forms

Unit 7

Nonfiction

Looking at Literary Forms

Drama

Looking at Literary Forms

Poetry

Complete Contents by Genre

SHORT STORY

DRAMA

NONFICTION

Complete Contents by Genre

NONFICTION (CONTINUED)

THE ORAL TRADITION

POETRY

Complete Contents by Genre

POETRY (CONTINUED)

Complete Contents by Theme

Complete Contents by Theme

SEEING IT THROUGH

MYSTERIOUS WORLDS

TAKING A STAND

Complete Contents by Theme

Prentice Hall

LITERATURE
Timeless Voices, Timeless Themes

In the Garden, Joseph Raphael, The Redfern Gallery

Growing and Changing

All around you the world changes in large and small ways. The tree outside has more branches than it did last year. A new building goes up on the next block. All growth involves change—especially in people. The stories, essays, and poems in this section explore the many changes—large and small—that come with growth.

Guide for Reading

Meet the Author:

Ray Bradbury (1920–   )

Athletes keep in shape by running or working out every day. Ray Bradbury exercises his mental muscles by drafting 2,000 to 3,000 words of man- uscript a day! As a boy, Bradbury nour- ished his imagination by attending circuses, watching magicians, and reading the novels of science-fiction writer Edgar Rice Burroughs. At the age of twelve, Bradbury began writing his own stories, which were mostly about space travel. Although he is most famous for his science-fiction tales, he also writes down-to-earth stories such as "The Sound of Summer Running," in addition to poetry, plays, and screenplays.

THE STORY BEHIND THE STORY

Bradbury's childhood fears and dreams fill the pages of *Dandelion Wine,* the collection of short stories from which "The Sound of Summer Running" is taken. In this story, Bradbury reaches back into his own childhood in Waukegan, Illinois, to remember how a young person feels at the beginning of summer.

◆ LITERATURE AND YOUR LIFE

CONNECT YOUR EXPERIENCE

You might associate the beginning of summer with smelling newly mowed grass or seeing heat waves rise off the hot pavement. For the boy in this story, summer and all its possibilities lie within a new pair of sneakers. New sneakers make him feel as free and happy as the children in the picture on the next page.

THEMATIC FOCUS: Growing and Changing

In this story, notice how the characters grow by pay- ing attention to what they already know.

◆ Background for Understanding

CULTURE

What you call something depends partly on where you live. In one place, you might ask for a *soda* and a *sub.* In another, you might order a *pop* and a *hoagie. Tennis shoes, sneakers,* and *running shoes* are terms used in dif- ferent parts of the United States to describe the same shoes. The boy in this story, which is set in the Midwest, calls them *tennis shoes*—even though he doesn't plan to play tennis in them.

The Sound of Summer Running

◆ Literary Focus

CHARACTERS' MOTIVES

Characters' motives are the impulses, emotions, or desires that cause them to act in a certain way. In this story, for example, Douglas's desire for a pair of sneakers motivates his actions. As you read, use a chart like the one below to make connections between the characters' actions and their motives.

Characters	Motive	Action
Douglas	Wants new sneakers	Stares in window
Mr. Sanderson		

◆ Build Vocabulary

WORD ROOTS: -meter-

In this story, Bradbury refers to a *barometer,* an instrument that measures changes in the pressure of the atmosphere. Any word with the root *meter* has something to do with measurement.

WORD BANK

Look over these words from the story. For which words do you know at least one meaning? What are the meanings you know?

seized
suspended
loam
barometer
alien
limber
revelation

Reading for Success

Literal Comprehension Strategies

When you build a house, you first construct a foundation on which the other levels are built. In reading, too, you construct a foundation. This foundation is the literal meaning—the basic facts and details the author is communicating. The following strategies will help you understand a writer's words on a literal level.

Break down long sentences.

▶ Break sentences into meaningful sections. Look at the four parts of this sentence from "The Sound of Summer Running":

> Late that night, /going home from the show / with his mother and father and his brother Tom, / Douglas saw the tennis shoes in the bright store window.

Use context clues.

Clues in the words and phrases around an unfamiliar word can help you figure out its meaning. In the following sentences, you can use the highlighted context clues to figure out that *capsize* means "to sink."

> The grass was still pouring in from the country . . . Any moment the town would capsize, go down and leave not a stir in the clover and weeds.

Use signal words to identify relationships.

Signal words show relationships, such as time or importance, among ideas.

Signal Words That Show Time	Signal Words That Show Contrast	Signal Words That Show Cause and Effect
while then next before	however although but	because consequently as a result

Reread or read ahead.

You may need to look back or ahead to clarify an idea, understand the cause of an event, or identify the relationships between people.

▶ Reread a sentence or paragraph to find connections among words or ideas.
▶ Look back to clarify relationships between characters.
▶ Read ahead to establish a context for a new idea or word.

As you read "The Sound of Summer Running," look at the notes in the boxes. The notes demonstrate how to apply these strategies to a work of literature.

The Sound of Summer Running

from Dandelion Wine

Ray Bradbury

Late that night, going home from the show with his mother and father and his brother Tom, Douglas saw the tennis shoes in the bright store window. He glanced quickly away, but his ankles were <u>seized</u>, his feet <u>suspended</u>, then rushed. The earth spun; the shop awnings slammed their canvas wings overhead with the thrust of his body running. His mother and father and brother walked quietly on both sides of him. Douglas walked backward, watching the tennis shoes in the midnight window left behind.

"It was a nice movie," said Mother.

Douglas murmured, "It was . . ."

It was June and long past time for buying the special shoes that were quiet as a summer rain falling on the walks. June and the earth full of raw power and everything everywhere in motion. The grass was still pouring in from the country, surrounding the sidewalks, stranding the houses. Any moment the town would capsize, go down and leave not a stir in the clover and weeds. And here Douglas stood, trapped on the dead cement and the red-brick streets, hardly able to move.

"Dad!" He blurted it out. "Back there in that window, those Cream-Sponge Para Litefoot Shoes . . ."

His father didn't even turn. "Suppose you tell me why you need a new pair of sneakers. Can you do that?"

"Well . . ."

It was because they felt the way it feels every summer when you take off your shoes for the first time and run in the grass. They felt like it feels sticking your feet out of the hot covers in wintertime to let the cold wind from the open window

> **Break down** this long sentence into meaningful parts at the words *because*, *when*, and *and*.

◆ **Build Vocabulary**

seized (sēzd) v.: Grabbed; taken hold of

suspended (sə spend′ id) v.: Stopped for a time

blow on them suddenly and you let them stay out a long time until you pull them back in under the covers again to feel them, like packed snow. The tennis shoes felt like it always feels the first time every year wading in the slow waters of the creek and seeing your feet below, half an inch further downstream, with refraction, than the real part of you above water.

"Dad," said Douglas, "it's hard to explain."

Somehow the people who made tennis shoes knew what boys needed and wanted. They put marshmallows and coiled springs in the soles and they wove the rest out of grasses bleached and fired in the wilderness. Somewhere deep in the soft <u>loam</u> of the shoes the thin hard sinews of the buck deer were hidden. The people that made the shoes must have watched a lot of winds blow the trees and a lot of rivers going down to the lakes. Whatever it was, it was in the shoes, and it was summer.

Douglas tried to get all this in words.

"Yes," said Father, "but what's wrong with last year's sneakers? Why can't you dig *them* out of the closet?"

Well, he felt sorry for boys who lived in California where they wore tennis shoes all year and never knew what it was to get winter off your feet, peel off the iron leather shoes all full of snow and rain and run barefoot for a day and then lace on the first new tennis shoes of the season, which was better than barefoot. The magic was always in the new pair of shoes. The magic might die by the first of September, but now in late June there was still plenty of magic, and shoes like these could jump you over

◆ Build Vocabulary

loam (lōm) *n.*: Rich soil

barometer (bə räm´ ət ər´) *n.*: Device for measuring air pressure; used to predict rain

trees and rivers and houses. And if you wanted, they could jump you over fences and sidewalks and dogs.

"Don't you see?" said Douglas. "I just *can't* use last year's pair."

For last year's pair were dead inside. They had been fine when he started them out, last year. But by the end of summer, every year, you always found out, you always knew, you couldn't really jump over rivers

> The **signal word** *But* tells you that the information in this sentence will contrast with the information in the previous sentence.

and trees and houses in them, and they were dead. But this was a new year, and he felt that this time, with this new pair of shoes, he could do anything, anything at all.

They walked up on the steps to their house. "Save your money," said Dad. "In five or six weeks—"

"Summer'll be over!"

Lights out, with Tom asleep, Douglas lay watching his feet, far away down there at the end of the bed in the moonlight, free of the heavy iron shoes, the big chunks of winter fallen away from them.

"Reason. I've got to think of reasons for the shoes."

Well, as anyone knew, the hills around town were wild with friends putting cows to riot, playing <u>barometer</u> to the atmospheric changes, taking sun, peeling like calendars each day to take more sun. To catch those friends, you must run much faster than foxes or squirrels. As for the town, it steamed with enemies grown irritable with heat, so remembering every winter argument and insult. *Find friends, ditch enemies!* That was the Cream-Sponge Para Litefoot motto. *Does the world run too fast? Want to catch up? Want to be alert, stay alert? Litefoot, then! Litefoot!*

New Shoes for H, 1973-1974, Don Eddy, The Cleveland Museum of Art

He held his coin bank up and heard the faint small tinkling, the airy weight of money there.

Whatever you want, he thought, you got to make your own way. During the night now, let's find that path through the forest. . . .

Downtown, the store lights went out, one by one. A wind blew in the window. It was like a river going downstream and his feet wanting to go with it.

In his dreams he heard a rabbit running running running in the deep warm grass.

Old Mr. Sanderson moved through his shoe store as the proprietor of a pet shop must move through his shop where are kenneled animals

> You may be confused by the sudden appearance of a "Mr. Sanderson." **Read ahead** to find out that he owns the shoe store.

from everywhere in the world, touching each one briefly along the way. Mr. Sanderson brushed his hands over the shoes in

▲ **Critical Viewing** Do you think Douglas would be drawn to any of the items in this store window? Why or why not? [Draw Conclusions]

the window, and some of them were like cats to him and some were like dogs; he touched each pair with concern, adjusting laces, fixing tongues. Then he stood in the exact center of the carpet and looked around, nodding.

There was a sound of growing thunder.

One moment, the door to Sanderson's Shoe Emporium was empty. The next, Douglas Spaulding stood clumsily there, staring down at his leather shoes as if these heavy things could not be pulled up out of the cement. The thunder had stopped when his shoes stopped. Now, with painful slowness, daring to look only at the money in his cupped hand, Douglas moved out of the bright sunlight of Saturday noon. He made careful stacks of nickels, dimes, and quarters on the counter, like someone

▲ **Critical Viewing** What feelings do you think the boy in this picture might share with Douglas? [Interpret]

playing chess and worried if the next move carried him out into sun or deep into shadow.

"Don't say a word!" said Mr. Sanderson. Douglas froze.

"First, I know just what you want to buy," said Mr. Sanderson. "Second, I see you every afternoon at my window; you think I don't see? You're wrong. Third, to give it its full name, you want the Royal Crown Cream-Sponge Para Litefoot Tennis Shoes: 'LIKE MENTHOL ON YOUR FEET!' Fourth, you want credit."

"No!" cried Douglas, breathing hard, as if he'd run all night in his dreams. "I got something better than credit to offer!" he gasped. "Before I tell, Mr. Sanderson, you got to do me one small favor. Can you re-member when was the last time you your-self wore a pair of Litefoot sneakers, sir?"

Mr. Sanderson's face darkened. "Oh, ten, twenty, say, thirty years ago. Why . . . ?"

"Mr. Sanderson, don't you think you owe it to your customers, sir, to at least try the tennis shoes you sell, for just one minute, so you know how they feel? People forget if they don't keep testing things. United Cigar Store man smokes cigars, don't he? Candy-store man samples his own stuff, I should think. So . . ."

"You may have noticed," said the old man, "I'm wearing shoes."

"But not sneakers, sir! How you going to sell sneakers unless you can rave about them and how you going to rave about them unless you know them?"

Mr. Sanderson backed off a little dis-tance from the boy's fever, one hand to his chin. "Well . . ."

"Mr. Sanderson," said Douglas, "you sell me something and I'll sell you something just as valuable."

"Is it absolutely necessary to the sale that I put on a pair of the sneakers, boy?" said the old man.

"I sure wish you could, sir!"

The old man sighed. A minute later, seated panting quietly, he laced the tennis shoes to his long narrow feet. They looked detached and <u>alien</u> down there next to the dark cuffs of his business suit. Mr. Sanderson stood up.

"How do they *feel*?" asked the boy.

"How do they feel, he asks; they feel fine." He started to sit down.

"Please!" Douglas held out his hand. "Mr. Sanderson, now could you kind of rock back and forth a little, sponge around, bounce kind of, while I tell you the rest? It's this: I give you my money, you give me the shoes, I owe you a dollar. But, Mr. Sanderson, *but*—soon as I get those shoes on, you know what *happens*?"

"What?"

"Bang! I deliver your packages, pick up packages, bring you coffee, burn your trash, run to the post office, telegraph office, library! You'll see twelve of me in and out, in and out, every minute. Feel those shoes, Mr. Sanderson, *feel* how fast they'd take me? All those springs inside? Feel all the running inside? Feel how they kind of grab hold and can't let you alone and don't like you just *standing* there? Feel how quick I'd be doing the things you'd rather not bother with? You stay in the nice cool store while I'm jumping all around town! But it's not me really, it's the shoes. They're going like mad down alleys, cutting corners, and back! There they go!"

Mr. Sanderson stood amazed with the rush of words. When the words got going the flow carried him; he began to sink deep in the shoes, to flex his toes, <u>limber</u> his arches, test his ankles. He rocked softly, secretly, back and forth in a small breeze from the open door. The tennis shoes

> The **signal word** *When* tells you that Mr. Sanderson starts to enjoy the shoes when something else happens. What happens that helps him enjoy the tennis shoes?

silently hushed themselves deep in the carpet, sank as in a jungle grass, in loam and resilient clay. He gave one solemn bounce of his heels in the yeasty dough, in the yielding and welcoming earth. Emotions hurried over his face as if many colored lights had been switched on and off. His mouth hung slightly open. Slowly he gentled and rocked himself to a halt, and the boy's voice faded and they stood there looking at each other in a tremendous and natural silence.

A few people drifted by on the sidewalk outside, in the hot sun.

Still the man and boy stood there, the boy glowing, the man with <u>revelation</u> in his face.

"Boy," said the old man at last, "in five years, how would you like a job selling shoes in this emporium?"

"Gosh, thanks, Mr. Sanderson, but I don't know what I'm going to be yet."

> The fact that Mr. Sanderson is offering Douglas a sales job is a **context clue** that helps you figure out that an *emporium* is a store.

"Anything you want to be, son," said the old man, "you'll be. No one will ever stop you."

The old man walked lightly across the store to the wall of ten thousand boxes, came back with some shoes for the boy, and wrote up a list on some paper while the boy was lacing the shoes on his feet and then standing there, waiting.

The old man held out his list. "A dozen things you got to do for me this afternoon. Finish them, we're even Stephen, and you're fired."

◆ Build Vocabulary

alien (āˊ lē ən) *adj.*: Foreign; unfamiliar

limber (limˊ bər) *v.*: Loosen up (a muscle or limb); to make easy to bend

revelation (revˊ ə lāˊ shən) *n.*: Sudden rush of understanding

"Thanks, Mr. Sanderson!" Douglas bounded away.

"Stop!" cried the old man.

Douglas pulled up and turned.

Mr. Sanderson leaned forward. "How do they *feel*?"

The boy looked down at his feet deep in the rivers, in the fields of wheat, in the wind that already was rushing him out of the town. He looked up at the old man, his eyes burning, his mouth moving, but no sound came out.

"Antelopes?" said the old man, looking from the boy's face to his shoes. "Gazelles?"

The boy thought about it, hesitated, and nodded a quick nod. Almost immediately he vanished. He just spun about with a whisper and went off. The door stood empty. The sound of the tennis shoes faded in the jungle heat.

Mr. Sanderson stood in the sun-blazed door, listening. From a long time ago, when he dreamed as a boy, he remembered the sound. Beautiful creatures leaping under the sky, gone through brush, under trees, away, and only the soft echo their running left behind.

"Antelopes," said Mr. Sanderson. "Gazelles."

He bent to pick up the boy's abandoned winter shoes, heavy with forgotten rains and long-melted snows. Moving out of the blazing sun, walking softly, lightly, slowly, he headed back toward civilization. . . .

Guide for Responding

◆ LITERATURE AND YOUR LIFE

Reader's Response Do you think most store owners would respond to Douglas's request as Mr. Sanderson did? Why or why not?

Thematic Focus In what ways do Douglas's and Mr. Sanderson's actions show that they have changed?

Journal Writing Describe three things you associate with summer.

☑ Check Your Comprehension

1. Why doesn't Douglas's father think Douglas needs new sneakers?
2. Why does Douglas feel that he does need new sneakers?
3. What does Douglas ask Mr. Sanderson to do before they discuss the sneakers?
4. Summarize Douglas's offer to Mr. Sanderson.

◆ Critical Thinking

INTERPRET

1. Why do you think last year's sneakers feel dead inside to Douglas? **[Speculate]**
2. How does Mr. Sanderson feel about his work? **[Infer]**
3. Why is Mr. Sanderson reluctant to put on the sneakers at first? **[Deduce]**
4. Why does Mr. Sanderson react as he does to wearing the sneakers? **[Draw Conclusions]**

EVALUATE

5. Do you agree with the statement: "Whatever you want, you've got to make your own way"? Explain. **[Support]**

EXTEND

6. What qualities does Douglas have that a good salesperson needs? Give examples. **[Career Link]**

Guide for Responding (continued)

◆ Reading for Success

LITERAL COMPREHENSION STRATEGIES

Review the reading strategies and the notes showing how to comprehend a writer's words and meanings. Then, apply them to answer the following:

1. What context clues near the end of the story could help you figure out what gazelles are?
2. Identify the places where you would break up the last sentence of the story into meaningful parts.
3. Identify three signal words that helped you recognize the time relationships between events.

◆ Build Vocabulary

USING THE WORD ROOT -meter-

Words dealing with measurement are often built on the word root -meter-. Match each word in Column A with what it measures in Column B.

Column A	Column B
1. thermometer	a. pressure of the atmosphere
2. barometer	b. speed
3. speedometer	c. temperature

SPELLING STRATEGY

When e and i appear together, the rule is "Use i before e except after c or when sounded like $\bar{a}$, as in neighbor and weigh." The words seized, either, leisure, weird, height, and protein are exceptions to this rule. Use the rule and the exceptions to unscramble the words in parentheses.

1. grabbed (desize)
2. accept as true (livebee)
3. deep sadness (efrig)
4. odd (wired)

USING THE WORD BANK

Write the word(s) from the Word Bank that best fit the song titles.

1. "Can't Move On" (two words)
2. "Stormy Weather"
3. "The Earth Beneath My Feet"
4. "Suddenly I Realize"
5. "Out of This World"
6. "Aerobic Workout"

◆ Literary Focus

CHARACTERS' MOTIVES

Characters' motives are the reasons or causes for the characters' actions. Impulses, emotions, and desires can be strong motives.

1. What does Douglas want?
2. What is Douglas's motive in asking Mr. Sanderson to try on the sneakers?
3. What motives do you think lead Mr. Sanderson to agree to Douglas's plan?

◆ Build Grammar Skills

NOUNS

A **noun** names a person, place, or thing. Some nouns name what can be seen, such as sneakers. Other nouns name feelings or ideas, such as happiness or memory. The chart below shows some of the many nouns people use.

People	Places	Things
Mr. Sanderson	Shoe Emporium	trees
boys	jungle	silence
Douglas	California	cement
salesperson	home	favor

Practice Copy the following sentences in your notebook, and underline the nouns.

1. Mr. Sanderson walked around the store.
2. Douglas stepped out of the sunlight.
3. The man felt a memory stir in his brain.
4. The boy and the man shared the feeling of summer.
5. The sneakers made him feel like a gazelle.

Writing Application Answer each of the following questions with a complete sentence. Underline each noun you use in your answers.

1. What is your favorite season?
2. Who is your favorite singer?
3. In what place do you and your friends like to spend time?
4. What food don't you like?

Build Your Portfolio

 Idea Bank

Writing

1. **Short Speech for a Character** As Douglas, write the words you might say to your father to convince him that you need new sneakers.

2. **Advertisement** Write an advertisement for a spectacular pair of sneakers. Include facts and descriptions of how they make a person's feet feel.

3. **Business Letter** As Douglas, outline your offer to Mr. Sanderson in a formal business letter. Look in a writing book to find the standard form for a business letter.

Speaking and Listening

4. **Role Play** With a partner, role-play the conversation between Mr. Sanderson and Douglas in the shoe store. Use words and ideas that are realistic for each character.

5. **Background Music** Choose music that captures some feelings you had as you read the story. Play the music as you read a portion of the story aloud. **[Music Link]**

Projects

6. **Collage** Create a collage that captures Douglas's feelings about the new sneakers. Include words and images that show freedom, speed, and energy. **[Art Link]**

7. **Television Commercial [Group Activity]** With a group, create a television commercial for a pair of sneakers that suit a particular sport. Divide up the following tasks: finding out the requirements of the sport; writing an explanation of how the shoes fit these needs; collecting pictures of athletes participating in the sport to use as background visuals while the commercial is being read. Present your commercial to the class and, if possible, videotape it. **[Media Link]**

 Writing Mini-Lesson

Product Description

Douglas is able to communicate the good points of a product—in this case, new sneakers. Choose a product and write a **product description**—a description that might appear in a catalog or advertisement. The description should present the product's good features so that people want to try it.

Writing Skills Focus: Use Vivid Adjectives

In product descriptions, space is limited, so make every word count. Use **vivid adjectives**—words that describe nouns and tell exactly how something looks, sounds, feels, smells, or tastes.

In "The Sound of Summer Running," Bradbury uses vivid adjectives like *blazing* sun, *resilient* clay, *tremendous* silence, and *airy* weight.

Prewriting Make a diagram or sketch of the product. Then, brainstorm for a list of vivid adjectives that describe the product in an appealing way.

Drafting Begin by telling how the product works or what it does. Then, explain the most important functions and features of the product.

Revising Have a partner review your draft and point out any places where the description might not be clear to someone unfamiliar with the product. Add details to make your description clearer.

> ◆ **Grammar Application**
>
> English sometimes offers more than one noun to name the same thing. For example, the nouns *shoe, sneaker,* and *sandal* all name things you wear on your feet. As you revise, replace general nouns with more specific ones where appropriate.

PART 1 *Finding Your Voice*

The Four Freedoms: Freedom of Speech, Norman Rockwell, © The Curtis Publishing Company

Guide for Reading

Meet the Author:

Cynthia Rylant (1954–)

When she was growing up, Cynthia Rylant really didn't think she was going to be a writer. "I always felt my life to be too limited," she says. "Nothing to write about."

A Writer Finds Her Voice At the age of twenty-four, though, Rylant went looking through the children's section of a public library and was bitten by the writer's bug. She quickly discovered that her "limited" life had in fact given her much to write about. Her first book, *When I Was Young in the Mountains,* tells of her childhood in the hill country of West Virginia.

The Story Behind the Story

When Rylant's mother went away to nursing school, Cynthia lived with her grandparents for four years in a tiny house without plumbing. Rylant's experience of hardship may be reflected in the family's situation in "Stray."

Rylant has a special attachment to her young characters. "I prefer writing about child characters," she explains, "because they have more possibilities. They can get away with more love, more anger, more fear than adult characters. . . ." Her sympathy for Doris, the child character in "Stray," is clear.

◆ Literature and Your Life

Connect Your Experience

Sometimes, you can't have what you want because there's not enough time, not enough space, or not enough money. The main character in this story knows her family can't afford a pet. Words won't change the facts, so she keeps her feelings quiet.

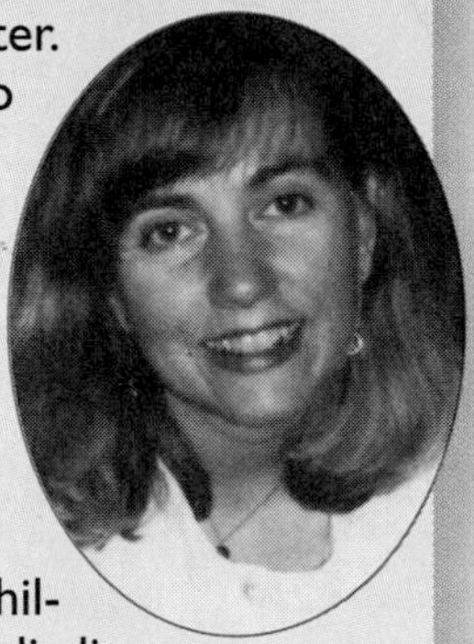

Thematic Focus: Finding Your Voice

As you read, listen to the feelings the characters in "Stray" express without words.

◆ Background for Understanding

Math

Animal shelters are overcrowded with stray animals because the number of stray animals grows exponentially—the numbers multiply in increasing proportions. Suppose one pair of stray dogs has six puppies in a year, and each of those puppies grows up to have six puppies, and so on. To find out how many puppies result in six years from that first group, multiply 6 x 6 x 6 x 6 x 6 x 6.

◆ Build Vocabulary

Suffixes: *-ly*

In "Stray," the puppy wags its tail *timidly*—in a shy and fearful way. The word *timidly* ends with the suffix *-ly.* Words ending in this suffix usually tell how or in what way an action happens. Look for another word in the story that ends with the suffix *-ly.*

Word Bank

Which word means the opposite of "notice"?

timidly
trudged
grudgingly
ignore
exhausted

◆ Stray ◆

◆ Literary Focus

SURPRISE ENDING

From looking at this picture, you'd expect this puppy to grow up to be sweet and playful. Similarly, when you read a story, the details lead you to have certain expectations about the ending. However, when a story ends differently from what you expected, it has a **surprise ending.**

Use a graphic organizer like the one below to track the reasons you expect "Stray" to end one way and the reasons it ends as it does.

◆ Reading Strategy

READ IN MEANINGFUL SECTIONS

To understand the meaning of long sentences, break them into **meaningful sections**—groups of words that each contain a chunk of information. Look for punctuation, such as commas, or connecting words, like *and* or *but,* to help you locate where one section ends and another begins. Notice how commas break up this sentence:

By the looks of it, Doris figured the puppy was about six months old, and on its way to being a big dog.

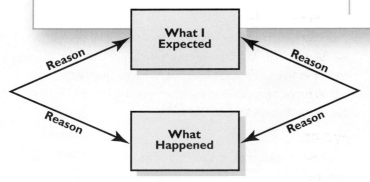

Reason → **What I Expected** ← Reason

Reason → **What Happened** ← Reason

Stray

Cynthia Rylant

In January, a puppy wandered onto the property of Mr. Amos Lacey and his wife, Mamie, and their daughter, Doris. Icicles hung three feet or more from the eaves of houses, snowdrifts swallowed up automobiles and the birds were so fluffed up they looked comic.

The puppy had been abandoned, and it made its way down the road toward the Laceys' small house, its ears tucked, its tail between its legs, shivering.

Doris, whose school had been called off because of the snow, was out shoveling the cinderblock front steps when she spotted the pup on the road. She set down the shovel.

"Hey! Come on!" she called.

The puppy stopped in the road, wagging its tail timidly, trembling with shyness and cold.

Doris trudged through the yard, went up the shoveled drive and met the dog.

"Come on, Pooch."

"Where did *that* come from?" Mrs. Lacey asked as soon as Doris put the dog down in the kitchen.

Mr. Lacey was at the table, cleaning his fingernails with his pocketknife. The snow was keeping him home from his job at the warehouse.

"I don't know where it came from," he said mildly, "but I know for sure where it's going."

Doris hugged the puppy hard against her. She said nothing.

Because the roads would be too bad for travel for many days, Mr. Lacey couldn't get out to take the puppy to the pound[1] in the city right away. He agreed to let it sleep in the basement while Mrs. Lacey grudgingly let Doris feed it table scraps. The woman was sensitive about throwing out food.

By the looks of it, Doris figured the puppy was about six months old, and on its way to being a big dog. She thought it might have some shepherd in it.

Four days passed and the puppy did not complain. It never cried in the night or howled at the wind. It didn't tear up everything in the basement. It wouldn't even follow Doris up the basement steps unless it was invited.

It was a good dog.

Several times Doris had opened the door in the kitchen that led to the basement and the puppy had been there, all stretched out, on the top step. Doris knew it had wanted some company and that it had lain against the door, listening to the talk in the kitchen, smelling

---

1. **pound**: Animal shelter.

◆ Build Vocabulary

timidly (tim´ id lē) *adv.*: In a way that shows fear or shyness

trudged (trujd) *v.*: Walked as if tired or with effort

grudgingly (gruj´ iŋ lē) *adv.*: In an unenthusiastic or resentful way

the food, being a part of things. It always wagged its tail, eyes all sleepy, when she found it there.

Even after a week had gone by, Doris didn't name the dog. She knew her parents wouldn't let her keep it, that her father made so little money any pets were out of the question, and that the pup would definitely go to the pound when the weather cleared.

Still, she tried talking to them about the dog at dinner one night.

"She's a good dog, isn't she?" Doris said,

hoping one of them would agree with her.

Her parents glanced at each other and went on eating.

"She's not much trouble," Doris added. "I like her." She smiled at them, but they continued to ignore her.

"I figure she's real smart," Doris said to her mother. "I could teach her things."

Mrs. Lacey just shook her head and stuffed a forkful of sweet potato in her mouth. Doris fell silent, praying the weather would never clear.

But on Saturday, nine days after the dog had arrived, the sun was shining and the roads were plowed. Mr. Lacey opened up the trunk of his car and came into the house.

◆ **Literary Focus**
What do you expect to happen now? Why?

Doris was sitting alone in the living room, hugging a pillow and rocking back and forth on the edge of a chair. She was trying not to cry but she was not strong enough. Her face was wet and red, her eyes full of distress.

Mrs. Lacey looked into the room from the doorway.

"Mama," Doris said in a small voice. "Please."

Mrs. Lacey shook her head.

"You know we can't afford a dog, Doris. You try to act more grown-up about this."

Doris pressed her face into the pillow.

Outside, she heard the trunk of the car slam shut, one of the doors open and close, the old engine cough and choke and finally start up.

"Daddy," she whispered. "Please."

She heard the car travel down the road, and, though it was early afternoon, she could do nothing but go to her bed. She cried herself to sleep, and her dreams were full of searching and searching for things lost.

It was nearly night when she finally woke up. Lying there, like stone, still exhausted, she wondered if she would ever in her life have anything. She stared at the wall for a while.

But she started feeling hungry, and she knew she'd have to make herself get out of bed and eat some dinner. She wanted not to go into the kitchen, past the basement door. She wanted not to face her parents.

But she rose up heavily.

◆ **Reading Strategy**
What information is presented in each section of this sentence?

Her parents were sitting at the table, dinner over, drinking coffee. They looked at her when she came in, but she kept her head down. No one spoke.

Doris made herself a glass of powdered milk and drank it all down. Then she picked up a cold biscuit and started out of the room.

"You'd better feed that mutt before it dies of starvation," Mr. Lacey said.

Doris turned around.

"What?"

"I said, you'd better feed your dog. I figure it's looking for you."

Doris put her hand to her mouth.

"You didn't take her?" she asked.

"Oh, I took her all right," her father answered. "Worst looking place I've ever seen. Ten dogs to a cage. Smell was enough to knock you down. And they give an animal six days to live. Then they kill it with some kind of a shot."

Doris stared at her father.

"I wouldn't leave an *ant* in that place," he said. "So I brought the dog back."

Mrs. Lacey was smiling at him and shaking her head as if she would never, ever, understand him.

Mr. Lacey sipped his coffee.

"Well," he said, "are you going to feed it or not?"

◆ **Build Vocabulary**

ignore (ig nôr´) *v.*: Pay no attention to

exhausted (eg zôs´ tid) *adj.*: Tired out

Guide for Responding

◆ LITERATURE AND YOUR LIFE

Reader's Response Do you think the Laceys are sensitive to Doris's feelings? Why or why not?

Thematic Focus Who has changed in this story? Explain.

Journal Writing Write a paragraph about whether you did or did not like the ending of this story.

☑ Check Your Comprehension

1. How does Doris find the dog?
2. What do her parents first decide about it?
3. Why do they wait before taking the dog away?
4. Where does Mr. Lacey take the dog?
5. What happens at the end of the story?

◆ Critical Thinking

INTERPRET

1. Contrast Mr. and Mrs. Lacey's attitude toward the dog with Doris's. **[Compare and Contrast]**
2. Explain Doris's reaction when her parents won't let her keep the dog. **[Analyze]**
3. Why does Mr. Lacey change his mind about keeping the dog? **[Analyze Cause and Effect]**
4. In the story, who shows common sense? Who shows love? Explain. **[Interpret]**

EVALUATE

5. Do you think people should always express their feelings? Explain. **[Evaluate]**

EXTEND

6. Name two benefits that people get from keeping pets. **[Health Link]**

Guide for Responding (continued)

◆ Reading Strategy

READ SENTENCES IN MEANINGFUL SECTIONS

Reading sentences in meaningful sections allows you to take in chunks of information. As you read "Stray," you may have used commas or connecting words to identify groups of words that should be read as a section. Answer each question about the following sentence from the story.

> Doris, whose school had been called off because of the snow, was out shoveling the cinderblock front steps when she spotted the pup on the road.

1. Into how many sections would you break this sentence?
2. What clues helped you decide how to break up the sentence?
3. What information did you learn in each section?

◆ Build Grammar Skills

COMPOUND NOUNS

Some nouns (words that name a person, place, or thing) are made up of more than one word. These nouns that consist of two or more words are **compound nouns.** For example, *ice cream, ten-year-old,* and *thunderstorm* are compound nouns.

Some compound nouns, such as *sunlight,* are written as one word; others, such as *mother-in-law,* have a hyphen between the words; and others, such as *pen pal,* are written as separate words.

Practice Copy the following sentences into your notebook. Underline each compound noun.
1. Doris shoveled the driveway.
2. Doris does a lot of work for an eleven-year-old.
3. She had a sweet potato, meatloaf, and a milkshake for dinner.
4. Mr. Lacey's sister is Mrs. Lacey's sister-in-law.
5. Snowdrifts covered the steps.

Writing Application Write a paragraph about the story using the following compound nouns: *grown-up, animal shelter, snowstorm.*

◆ Literary Focus

SURPRISE ENDING

To create a **surprise ending,** an author leads you to think the story will end one way, but then ends it differently.

1. Identify two facts about the family that make it unlikely they will keep the dog.
2. What details in the story make you believe that the dog is gone forever?
3. Doris's father does not tell her right away that they are keeping the dog. Explain how his way of letting her know helps make the ending a surprise.

◆ Build Vocabulary

USING THE SUFFIX -*ly*

Words that end in the suffix -*ly* usually answer the question *how* or *in what way.* Add the suffix -*ly* to each word below. Define each new word.
1. beautiful   2. sad   3. immediate

SPELLING STRATEGY

English words that sound as if they end in *j*, such as *grudge,* are actually spelled with a *ge* at the end. For each of the following phrases, write a word ending in the *j* sound that has the same meaning.
1. walk slowly   3. bravery
2. very big   4. building where cars are parked

USING THE WORD BANK

For each sentence below, write "correct" if the italicized word is used in a way that makes sense and "incorrect" if it is not. Explain your answers.
1. "Hey, buddy, I've been looking all over for you!" he said *timidly,* grabbing my hand and shaking it.
2. When I told her that Dad said we should share her favorite doll, she handed it to me *grudgingly.*
3. A good runner, he *trudged* like the wind.
4. I felt *exhausted,* so I did 100 chin-ups to relax.
5. Don't give him what he wants; just *ignore* him.

Build Your Portfolio

Idea Bank

Writing

1. **Journal Entry** Write a journal entry in which you describe a pet you have owned or have known. Compare your pet to the dog in the story.

2. **Argument** Doris has a hard time sharing her feelings about the dog. As Doris, write a letter to the Laceys explaining how you feel.

3. **Character Essay** Do you believe Mr. Lacey's explanation of why he brought the dog back? In an essay, sum up what he says, and then explain why you do or do not believe him. **[Literature Link]**

Speaking and Listening

4. **Dramatic Reenactment [Group Activity]** With two classmates, reenact the story's surprise ending. Practice what the characters say and do. Perform your scene for the class. **[Performing Arts Link]**

5. **Pet Speech** Give a speech to your class about a pet you have or would like to have. Include information about the appearance, habits, and needs of the animal. You may use video, photos, or drawings. **[Visual Arts Link; Performing Arts Link]**

Projects

6. **Presentation [Group Activity]** With a group, organize a presentation about stray animals that includes a speaker from the local animal shelter. Decide who will create charts and graphs, who will contact the shelter, who will present the information, and who will greet and introduce the speaker. **[Career Link; Social Studies Link]**

7. **Oral Report on Dogs** Dogs, descended from wolves, weren't always friendly pets! Using two library resources, find out how dogs changed from wild animals to household pets. Present your findings in an oral report. **[Science Link]**

Writing Mini-Lesson

News Report

Doris's father has strong words to say about the local animal pound. In fact, a news person reporting on the pound could grab readers' attention with a quotation from Mr. Lacey's description.

Write your own brief news report on animal shelters in your area. Start off with an effective lead.

Writing Skills Focus: Use an Effective Lead

An **effective lead paragraph** grabs readers' attention and gives the basic *who, what, where, when, why,* and *how* of the story.

Model From the Story

"I wouldn't leave an *ant* in that place," said Amos Lacey. He is speaking about Anytown's municipal animal shelter, where animals are kept in overcrowded, unhealthy conditions. Other area shelters, however, do fine work.

Prewriting Use library resources, or call or visit animal shelters to gather details that answer *who, what, where, when, why* and *how* questions.

Drafting Begin your draft with a statistic or quotation that will grab readers' attention. Follow it with a short, clear sentence that states the basic facts. Then, continue with examples and details.

> ◆ **Grammar Application**
> In your news report, try out compound nouns, such as *dog owners,* instead of longer descriptions, such as *people who own dogs*.

Revising As you revise, look for ways to make your lead more interesting. Check that you have answered the questions *who, what, where, when, why* and *how*.

More than one of the dogs you will read about in this article from *TV Guide* started out life in a pound or as a stray—just like the puppy in "Stray." These dogs were lucky that someone saw something special in them—something that could make them stars. The fact that dogs can reach superstar status shows how important these animals are in today's society.

TV's Top Dogs

Deborah Starr Seibel

The star's handlers were clearly worried. Their anxiety had been filtering through phone and fax lines for more than a week over a request for an important photo session—known in the business as a "cover try." They were interested, but would their star be on the cover? No guarantee. Would their client have to share the spotlight with other celebrities? Maybe. Publicists conferred with other handlers, including studio executives in charge of the star's next big project. Suddenly, negotiations stalled.

Elizabeth Taylor? Julia Roberts? The women of *Melrose Place*? No, that little photo-shoot nightmare involved getting Lassie—*Lassie!*—to pose.

It epitomizes, however, the new pecking order among TV's top dogs, suddenly superbig, superhot. Superdogs. New power pooches—including Comet and Barkley from *Full House*, Eddie from *Frasier*, and Murray from *Mad About You*[1]—are forcing Lassie to make room as they paw their way into the ranks of Hollywood's power players.

How powerful? Well, their newfound clout[2] is propelling the canine craze into daytime. Vinnie, a lovable one-eared mutt, has the run of ABC's new daytime talk show *Mike & Maty*. The dog often sits on Maty's lap during interviews. Another talk show is going even further by giving its bowwow top billing: On *Pet Department*, on the fX channel, Jack the Dog is—hang onto your leash—the co-host. "The other host, Steve Walker, is human," explains the show's publicist.

It's a Cinderella story for many of these dogs. Vinnie was rescued from the pound. Eddie was given up by his owners because he was too much to handle. Seeing a certain

▲ **Critical Viewing**
Why do you think people enjoy watching this dog on television? **[Speculate]**

---

1. ***Full House, . . . Frasier, . . . Mad About You:*** Television shows popular in the 1990's.

2. **clout** (klout) *n.*: Power; influence.

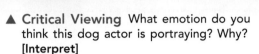

something—energy, intelligence, or an unusual personality—Hollywood animal trainers adopt these dogs, refine their skills, and take them to casting calls. If they make the cut and the show is a hit, the transformation from house dog to superdog is complete.

Two-hundred-fifty dollars a day is the standard superdog rate (roughly $31 an hour, if you're doing the math). And then there are the extras. When Lassie makes out-of-town appearances, for example, she (he, really—all eight Lassies have been males) flies first class in a reserved seat. He also has his own traveling companion, a Jack Russell[3] named Mel Gibson. At their hotel, Lassie often drinks bottled water and indulges in gourmet biscuits.

▲ **Critical Viewing** What details in this picture suggest that the dog is a celebrity? **[Support]**

Barkley, the sometimes ferocious-looking Jack Russell terrier with a two-picture deal at MGM, also flies first class, has his own director's chair, and demands ground transport worthy of a visiting dignitary.

Eddie, another scrappy Jack Russell, who regularly unnerves—and upstages—Dr. Frasier Crane with his persistent stare, sports Holiday cologne for dogs and eats "high-quality cooked chicken, hot dogs, and stew beef," according to his trainer, Mathilde deCagny. How good is the chow? "I eat it myself when I get hungry," she says, looking guilty.

3. **Jack Russell:** Small and energetic breed of dog.

▲ **Critical Viewing** What emotion do you think this dog actor is portraying? Why? **[Interpret]**

It's a glam life. But these are special animals. At the *TV Guide* photo shoot, Barkley puts Murray and Eddie—and every other canine you've ever met—to shame. He's like a little old lady, full of dignity, never making noise or changing position until asked. The setup calls for the three dogs to ape the luxe life[4] in a convertible roadster. "Can you put his hands on the steering wheel?" asks the photographer, who, like the rest of us, has quickly mistaken this animal for a human being. "He doesn't have hands," says his trainer, laughing. So she poses his paws and he stays there—forever. When Murray gets out of position, when Eddie prematurely jumps out of the car for more food . . . Barkley drives on.

"That dog is incredible," says the photographer, staring at Barkley. "Easier than most of the people I work with."

4. **ape the luxe life:** Mimic (ape) the life of luxury.

1. Name three things that top dogs have in common with human actors. **[Connect]**
2. Compare and contrast the puppy in "Stray" with one of the dogs in this article. **[Compare and Contrast]**
3. Which, if any, of the dogs in this article would you like to have as a pet? **[Relate]**

Guide for Reading

Meet the Authors:

Diana Chang (1934–   )

Diana Chang found her "voice" in other art forms as well as in poetry: fiction writing and painting. She has written novels, like *The Frontiers of Love,* and has exhibited her paintings in art galleries.

Walt Whitman (1819–1892)

Before Walt Whitman published his book *Leaves of Grass* in 1855, American poets had imitated the rhymes and regular rhythms of British poetry. With his un-rhymed verse and irregular rhythms, Whitman introduced a new voice in American poetry. He proudly declared in one poem that he was "an American, one of the roughs . . ."

This rough-and-ready poet grew up in Brooklyn, New York, and held many jobs. No matter what else he did, though, he kept bringing out new editions of *Leaves of Grass.*

THE STORY BEHIND THE POEM

Whitman loved to visit galleries and study the paintings crowded together there. In "My Picture-Gallery," you'll see how these visits influenced his poetry.

Robert Frost (1874–1963)

Frost began writing poetry as a high-school student in New England. Yet it wasn't until his book *North of Boston* became a bestseller that Frost was recognized as a major poet. He won four Pulitzer Prizes.

Before he was famous, Frost worked as a farmer in New England. The salty speech of his rural neighbors and the beauties of the New England landscape appear in his poetry.

◆ LITERATURE AND YOUR LIFE

CONNECT YOUR EXPERIENCE

In the painting on the next page, you may see black birds flying to the left, but a classmate may see white birds flying to the right. Look long enough, and you'll realize that you can see the painting in two ways. The poets in this group show that looking at the same thing in a different way can make all the difference in the world!

THEMATIC FOCUS: Finding Your Voice

As you read these poems, think about what they reveal about each poet's individual voice.

◆ Background for Understanding

LANGUAGE

Reading poetry is a little like solving a riddle. Things aren't always what they seem to be. The poem "Saying Yes," for example, seems full of questions and confusion. In fact, it is a statement of the speaker's pride in her heritage. In "My Picture-Gallery," the speaker describes an art gallery. This gallery, though, isn't quite what you might expect.

◆ Build Vocabulary

HOMOPHONES

Homophones are words that sound alike but have different meanings and are often spelled differently. When Frost says he "rued" a day, don't mistake *rued* for its homophone *rude,* meaning "impolite." *Rued* is the past tense of *rue,* meaning "to feel sorry about."

WORD BANK

Which of these words from the poems might be related to *suspense?*

| suspended |
| tableaus |
| rued |

Saying Yes ◆ My Picture-Gallery
◆ Dust of Snow ◆

Day and Night, M.C. Escher©1998, Cordon Art B.V.-Baarn-Holland

◆ Literary Focus

IMAGES IN POETRY

Poets often paint word pictures that appeal to your senses of sight, sound, smell, taste, and touch. These pictures, or **images,** help you to experience and enjoy a poem fully. By describing the "dust" of snow, for example, Robert Frost helps you to see and feel snow that is light and powdery. Look for other images as you read these poems. Jot down the details you notice on a chart like the one below.

Sight	Sound	Smell	Taste	Touch

◆ Reading Strategy

REREAD TO CLARIFY

You may need to look twice at the painting on this page to see both sets of birds. When you read poetry, you may need to look twice, or **reread,** to understand the poet's full meaning. The gallery in "My Picture-Gallery," for instance, at first appears to be an art museum. Through rereading, though, you may discover details you missed the first time. These details help you clarify Whitman's deeper meaning: The "picture gallery" may not be a room inside a building after all.

Saying Yes

Diana Chang

"Are you Chinese?"
"Yes."

"American?"
"Yes."

5   "*Really* Chinese?"
"No . . . not quite."

"*Really* American?"
"Well, actually, you see . . ."

But I would rather say
10   yes.

Not neither-nor,
not maybe,
but both, and not only

The homes I've had,
15   the ways I am

I'd rather say it
twice,
yes.

▲ **Critical Viewing**
Do you think the woman in the picture likes what she sees in the mirror? Explain. **[Infer]**

My Picture-Gallery

Walt Whitman

In a little house keep I pictures <u>suspended</u>, it is not a fix'd house,
It is round, it is only a few inches from one side to the other;
Yet behold, it has room for all the shows of the world, all memories!
Here the <u>tableaus</u> of life, and here the groupings of death;
5 Here, do you know this? this is cicerone[1] himself,
With finger rais'd he points to the prodigal[2] pictures.

---

1. **cicerone** (sis′ ə rō′ nē) *n.*: Guide who explains the history and important features of a place to sightseers.
2. **prodigal** (präd′ i gəl) *adj.*: Very plentiful.

◆ **Build Vocabulary**

suspended (sə spend′ id) *adj.*: Hung with a support from above

tableaus (ta blōz′) *n.*: Dramatic scenes or pictures

◆Guide for Responding

◆ LITERATURE AND YOUR LIFE

Reader's Response Have you ever asked or answered questions like the ones in "Saying Yes"? Explain.

Thematic Focus Did either of these poems surprise you with a new way of looking at things? Explain.

☑ Check Your Comprehension

1. What are the two strands of the speaker's heritage in "Saying Yes"?
2. To which question would the speaker rather say yes?
3. Name three qualities of the "little house" in "My Picture-Gallery."
4. What does the guide to this "house" do?

◆ Critical Thinking

INTERPRET

1. Why do the questions in lines 5 and 7 of "Saying Yes" make the poet feel uneasy? **[Infer]**
2. Explain how saying yes twice means "both, and not only." **[Interpret]**
3. In what ways is the gallery in "My Picture-Gallery" similar to and different from an art gallery or museum? **[Compare and Contrast]**
4. What is the "picture-gallery" that Whitman is describing? Support your answer. **[Interpret]**

APPLY

5. What kinds of experiences do you hope to put in your "picture-gallery"? **[Relate]**

COMPARE LITERARY WORKS

6. Explain how these two poems are both like puzzles. **[Connect]**

Dust of Snow

Robert Frost

The way a crow
Shook down on me
The dust of snow
From a hemlock tree

5   Has given my heart
A change of mood
And saved some part
Of a day I had <u>rued</u>.

◆ **Build Vocabulary**

rued (ro͞od) *v.*: Regretted (something)

Beyond Literature

Science Connection

Fingerprints: Foolproof Portraits
No two people are exactly alike, even if they share the same heritage or experiences. One of the least visible, but most reliable, marks of individuality is a fingerprint. In the 1880's, Sir Francis Galton figured out that no two people could have the same fingerprints. Then, two police officers came up with a way of classifying fingerprints based on the number and shapes of ridges. Today, computers are used to classify fingerprints.

Cross-Curricular Activity:
Fingerprint Gallery Find out how fingerprints are classified. Create a visual display that shows different categories of fingerprints and how individual fingerprints vary within these categories. If possible, use enlarged fingerprints to illustrate your points.

Guide for Responding

◆ LITERATURE AND YOUR LIFE

Reader's Response Has a small incident like the one described in "Dust of Snow" ever made you feel better?

Thematic Focus What do you think the poet would say about the way your attitude affects the way you act?

Journal Writing Make a list of things that cheer you up when you're in a bad mood.

☑ Check Your Comprehension

1. What action occurs in lines 1–4?
2. How does the speaker react to what happens in lines 1–4?

◆ Critical Thinking

INTERPRET

1. Does the crow's action make the speaker feel better or worse? Explain. **[Interpret]**
2. Why do you think the crow's action has the effect it does? **[Draw Conclusions]**

APPLY

3. What lesson do you think the speaker learned from this experience? **[Generalize]**

COMPARE LITERARY WORKS

4. Would you include in a gallery like Whitman's the experience that Frost describes? Why or why not? **[Connect]**

Guide for Responding (continued)

◆ Reading Strategy

REREAD TO CLARIFY

When you **reread to clarify,** you can find details that help you make connections between ideas. You don't always need to reread, but when you feel that you're not getting the full meaning or when something is unclear, a second look may reveal important details or connections that you missed the first time.

1. List three details in "My Picture-Gallery" that someone might miss on a first reading. In what ways do these details affect the meaning of the poem?
2. "Dust of Snow" is written as one long sentence. Reread to clarify the distinct events in the poem. Write two sentences about the two main events or ideas.

◆ Build Grammar Skills

ABSTRACT AND CONCRETE NOUNS

These poems refer to things you can't touch, like *mood,* and things you can touch, like *snow.* Words that name what is untouchable, such as *knowledge, humor,* and *beauty,* are **abstract nouns.** Words that name what is touchable, such as *snow, bird,* and *painting,* are **concrete nouns.**

Practice On your paper, explain whether each italicized word in these sentences is an abstract or a concrete noun.

1. Whitman talks about a little *house.*
2. There are many *pictures* in this *house.*
3. Whitman's *house* has *room* for all his *memories.*
4. Frost describes a *crow* on a hemlock *tree.*
5. By shaking the *snow* on him, the *crow* changes Frost's *feelings.*

Writing Application Write a brief paragraph about a scene that you remember. Use at least two abstract nouns, such as *peace, courage, beauty, hope, health,* and *life.* Use three concrete nouns in your description.

◆ Literary Focus

IMAGES IN POETRY

"My Picture-Gallery" and "Dust of Snow" have **images,** words or phrases that appeal to your senses. These images help you see a gallery and a crow on a snowy tree. They let you experience the world of the poems.

1. How do spoken words, rather than images, help you experience a scene in "Saying Yes"?
2. Using your own words, describe the image in lines 5 and 6 of "My Picture-Gallery."
3. In "Dust of Snow," how do the words "dust" and "hemlock" make it easy to see the image?

◆ Build Vocabulary

USING HOMOPHONES

Homophones sound alike but have different meanings and are often spelled differently. On your paper, write the correct homophone for each rhyme:

1. When asked who she *really* was, the poet (side, sighed). / She thought the questioner was not on her (side, sighed).
2. In my gallery, the spot is (bear, bare) / Where I placed the sketch of the (bear, bare).
3. The crow in the hemlock was (rude, rued), / But he saved a day the poet had (rude, rued).

SPELLING STRATEGY

When adding a suffix or verb tense ending to words ending in *ue,* drop the e if the added ending starts with a vowel:

rue + -ed = rued   argue + -ing = arguing

On your paper, fill in the blanks:

1. issue + -ing = _____?_____ 2. sue + -ed = _____?_____
3. cue + -ed = _____?_____ 4. glue + -ing = _____?_____

USING THE WORD BANK

Fill in each blank with a word from the Word Bank.

1. Whitman saw paintings kept _____?_____ from hooks.
2. The pictures included _____?_____ of everyday life.
3. Whitman never _____?_____ the time he spent in galleries.

Build Your Portfolio

 Idea Bank

Writing

1. **Caption** Write a caption for a picture in your mind's memory album. Tell who is in the picture, what is happening, and when it occurs.

2. **Diary Entry** As Robert Frost, write a diary entry telling what was painful about the day you rued and why the crow cheered you up.

3. **Plan for a Gallery** Suppose you could create a picture gallery to honor important people in your life. Write a plan for the gallery, telling what it would look like, whose portraits you would hang on the walls, and why. **[Career Link]**

Speaking and Listening

4. **Readers Theatre [Group Activity]** With two classmates, perform "Saying Yes" as a brief drama. Have one person ask the questions, another answer, and a third read lines 9–18. **[Performing Arts Link]**

5. **School Tour** Your school is like a gallery of your memories. Perform a speech you could give to visitors as you take them around your school. Focus on places that have been important to you. **[Career Link; Performing Arts Link]**

Projects

6. **Heritage Poster** Design a poster encouraging people to "say yes" to every strand in their heritage. Include words as well as art. If you like, use a passage from "Saying Yes." **[Art Link; Social Studies Link]**

7. **Mind Map** Whitman describes the mind as a gallery. Find an actual diagram of the brain in a science book. Use it to create your own diagram or clay sculpture, labeling the area or areas that control memory. **[Science Link; Art Link]**

 Writing Mini-Lesson

Memory Poem

Whitman had a picture gallery of memories in his mind. You may store past scenes as memory videos. Choose a memory, and write a poem about it. Your poem can be rhymed like Frost's or un-rhymed like Whitman's and Chang's.

Writing Skills Focus: Elaborate With Sensory Details

Help readers experience your memory poem by using **sensory details,** descriptions that appeal to the five senses. In "Dust of Snow," Frost uses visual details that contrast black (the crow) and white (the snow):

Model From the Poem

The way a crow
Shook down on me
The dust of snow
From a hemlock tree . . .

Prewriting Replay a brief, dramatic memory video in your mind. Jot down details of the scene that appeal to taste, smell, touch, hearing, and sight.

Drafting Draft a poem that tells a little story. Include the sensory details from your notes.

> ◆ **Grammar Application**
> Include both abstract and concrete nouns in your poem. Use abstract nouns to name your feelings or impressions. Use concrete nouns in your sensory details.

Revising As you revise, replace general statements with sensory details. If you replace *bird* with *crow*, for example, readers will see a bird with a specific shape and color.

Guide for Reading

Meet the Authors:

Walter Dean Myers (1937–)

You would expect a preschooler to prefer picture books over other kinds of reading material, but young Walter Dean Myers didn't! He was reading at age four, and by age five he was reading a newspaper every day. In spite of this impressive start with words, Myers didn't think that writing would be his career. Then, in his twenties, he won a writing contest. He hasn't stopped writing since—mostly about his heritage and his experiences growing up in Harlem, a part of New York City.

THE STORY BEHIND THE STORY

When Walter Dean Myers was three years old, his mother died. He moved to Harlem to live with foster parents. Like the child Myers, the characters in "Jeremiah's Song" must deal with feelings of love and loss.

Annie Dillard (1945–)

Annie Dillard once wrote an entire essay on a spider! Her interest in nature started in her childhood, when her parents encouraged her to draw and observe the natural world. Dillard carried into adulthood the curiosity and creativity they nurtured. While at college in Virginia, Dillard lived by a creek in a valley of the Blue Ridge Mountains. She wrote the Pulitzer Prize-winning book *Pilgrim at Tinker Creek* there.

◆ LITERATURE AND YOUR LIFE

CONNECT YOUR EXPERIENCE

You probably have at least one favorite song that captures just what you feel. Singing along is just one way you can express yourself. Maybe you write your own songs, draw, or act in plays. Whatever you do, you do it with your own special style and talent. In this story and essay, you'll see how other people express their talents.

THEMATIC FOCUS: Finding Your Voice

In "Jeremiah's Song" and "Talent," the writers explore how people can find their voices in the fields of music, art, sports, and science. What types of activities help you express yourself?

◆ Background for Understanding

HUMANITIES

The blues, the type of music played in "Jeremiah's Song," originated as folk music of African Americans. The ordinary people who "invented" the blues are not famous, but the musical form has influenced generations of musicians.

In "Talent," Dillard mentions a famous painter and a famous scientist, both of whom had an impact on the generations that followed. Paul Cezanne (1839–1906) used color and shape in bold new ways. Louis Pasteur discovered the role of germs in disease.

◆ Build Vocabulary

PREFIXES: *dis-*

When the prefix *dis-* is added to the beginning of a word, the new word means the opposite of the base word. For example, *dis-* + *infect* = *disinfect*, the opposite of *infect*.

WORD BANK

Which two words do you think you might hear in a hospital?

diagnosis
disinfect
precocious
uninspired
perpetual

Jeremiah's Song ◆ Talent

Harmonizing, 1979, Robert Gwathmey, Courtesy Terry Dintenfass Gallery, © Estate of Robert Gwathmey, Licensed by VAGA, New York, NY

◆ Literary Focus
FIRST-PERSON NARRATOR
The narrator is the person or character who tells the story. A **first-person narrator** participates in the action of the story and refers to himself or herself as "I."

The first-person narrator of "Jeremiah's Song" is a young boy. Because he participates in the action, he can tell only what *he* knows and only what *he* sees. In her essay, Annie Dillard serves as narrator. She refers to herself as "I" and shares her thoughts and feelings.

◆ Reading Strategy
CONTEXT CLUES
As you read these two pieces, you're likely to encounter unfamiliar words. When this happens, look for clues in the **context**—the surrounding words and phrases. Look at this sentence from "Talent":
...occasionally you find an American writer ... who deliberately pretended to be spontaneous and unstudied.

The word *unstudied* can provide a clue to the meaning of *spontaneous*. Paired with *spontaneous, unstudied* suggests that *spontaneous* means "unplanned" or "unpracticed." The diagram here shows you some kinds of context clues to look for when you encounter an unfamiliar word.

Synonyms	Comparisons
Unfamiliar Word	Opposites
Examples	Definitions	Restatements

JEREMIAH'S SONG

Walter Dean Myers

I knowed my cousin Ellie was gonna be mad when Macon Smith come around to the house. She didn't have no use for Macon even when things was going right, and when Grandpa Jeremiah was fixing to die I just knowed she wasn't gonna be liking him hanging around. Grandpa Jeremiah raised Ellie after her folks died and they used to be real close. Then she got to go on to college and when she come back the first year she was different. She didn't want to hear all them stories he used to tell her anymore. Ellie said the stories wasn't true, and that's why she didn't want to hear them.

I didn't know if they was true or not. Tell the truth I didn't think much on it either way, but I liked to hear them stories. Grandpa Jeremiah said they wasn't stories anyway, they was songs.

"They the songs of my people," he used to say.

I didn't see how they was songs, not regular songs anyway. Every little thing we did down in Curry seemed to matter to Ellie that first summer she come home from college. You

▲ **Critical Viewing** What does this picture suggest about the importance of music in this story? [Interpret]

couldn't do nothin' that was gonna please her. She didn't even come to church much. 'Course she come on Sunday or everybody would have had a regular fit, but she didn't come on Thursday nights and she didn't come on Saturday even though she used to sing in the gospel choir.

"I guess they teachin' her somethin' worthwhile up there at Greensboro," Grandpa Jeremiah said to Sister Todd. "I sure don't see what it is, though."

"You ain't never had no book learning, Jeremiah," Sister Todd shot back. She wiped at where a trickle of sweat made a little path through the white dusting powder she put on her chest to keep cool. "Them old ways you got ain't got nothing for these young folks."

"I guess you right," Grandpa Jeremiah said.

He said it but I could see he didn't like it none. He was a big man with a big head and had most all his hair even if it was white. All that summer, instead of sitting on the porch telling stories like he used to when I was real little, he would sit out there by himself while Ellie stayed in the house and watched the television or read a book. Sometimes I would think about asking him to tell me one of them stories he used to tell but they was too scary now that I didn't have nobody to sleep with but myself. I asked Ellie to sleep with me but she wouldn't.

"You're nine years old," she said, sounding real proper. "You're old enough to sleep alone."

I *knew* that. I just wanted her to sleep with me because I liked sleeping with her. Before she went off to college she used to put cocoa butter on her arms and face and it would smell real nice. When she come back from college she put something else on, but that smelled nice too.

It was right after Ellie went back to school that Grandpa Jeremiah had him a stroke and Macon started coming around. I think his mama probably made him come at first, but you could see he liked it. Macon had always been around, sitting over near the stuck window at church or going on the blueberry truck when we went picking down at Mister Gregory's place. For a long time he was just another kid, even though he was older'n me, but then, all of a sudden, he growed something fierce. I used to be up to his shoulder one time and then, before I could turn around good, I was only up to his shirt pocket. He changed too. When he used to just hang around with the other boys and play ball or shoot at birds he would laugh a lot. He didn't laugh so much anymore and I figured he was just about grown. When Grandpa got sick he used to come around and help out with things around the house that was too hard for me to do. I

mean, I could have done all the chores, but it would just take me longer.

When the work for the day was finished and the sows[1] fed, Grandpa would kind of ease into one of his stories and Macon, he would sit and listen to them and be real interested. I didn't mind listening to the stories when Grandpa told them to Macon because he would be telling them in the middle of the afternoon and they would be past my mind by the time I had to go to bed.

Macon had an old guitar he used to mess with, too. He wasn't too bad on it, and sometimes Grandpa would tell him to play us a tune. He could play something he called "the Delta Blues" real good, but when Sister Todd or somebody from the church come around he'd play "Precious Lord" or "Just a Closer Walk With Thee."

Grandpa Jeremiah had been feeling poorly from that stroke, and one of his legs got a little drag to it. Just about the time Ellie come from school the next summer he was real sick. He was breathing loud so you could hear it even in the next room and he would stay in bed a lot even when there was something that needed doing or fixing.

"I don't think he's going to make it much longer," Dr. Crawford said. "The only thing I can do is to give him something for the pain."

"Are you sure of your <u>diagnosis</u>?" Ellie asked. She was sitting around the table with Sister Todd, Deacon Turner, and his little skinny yellow wife.

Dr. Crawford looked at Ellie like he was surprised to hear her talking. "Yes, I'm sure," he said. "He had tests a few weeks ago and his condition was bad then."

"How much time he got?" Sister Todd asked.

"Maybe a week or two at best," Dr. Crawford said.

When he said that, Deacon Turner's wife started crying and goin' on and I give her a hard look but she just went on. I was the one

◆ **Build Vocabulary**

diagnosis (dī′ əg nō′ sis) *n*.: Explanation of or prediction about a person's medical condition

---

1. **sows** (souz) *n*.: Full-grown female pigs.

who loved Grandpa Jeremiah the most and she didn't hardly even know him so I didn't see why she was crying.

Everybody started tiptoeing around the house after that. They would go in and ask Grandpa Jeremiah if he was comfortable and stuff like that or take him some food or a cold glass of lemonade. Sister Todd come over and stayed with us. Mostly what she did is make supper and do a lot of praying, which was good because I figured that maybe God would do something to make Grandpa Jeremiah well. When she wasn't doing that she was piecing on a fancy quilt she was making for some white people in Wilmington.

Ellie, she went around asking everybody how they felt about Dr. Crawford and then she went into town and asked about the tests and things. Sister Jenkins asked her if she thought she knowed more than Dr. Crawford, and Ellie rolled her eyes at her, but Sister Jenkins was reading out her Bible and didn't make no notice of it.

Then Macon come over.

He had been away on what he called "a little piece of a job" and hadn't heard how bad off Grandpa Jeremiah was. When he come over he talked to Ellie and she told him what was going on and then he got him a soft drink from the refrigerator and sat out on the porch and before you know it he was crying.

You could look at his face and tell the difference between him sweating and the tears. The sweat was close against his skin and shiny and the tears come down fatter and more sparkly.

Macon sat on the porch, without saying a word, until the sun went down and the crickets started chirping and carrying on. Then he went in to where Grandpa Jeremiah was and stayed in there for a long time.

Sister Todd was saying that Grandpa Jeremiah needed his rest and Ellie went in to see what Macon was doing. Then she come out real mad.

"He got Grandpa telling those old stories again," Ellie said. "I told him Grandpa needed his rest and for him not to be staying all night."

He did leave soon, but bright and early the next morning Macon was back again. This time he brought his guitar with him and he went on in to Grandpa Jeremiah's room. I went in, too.

◆ **Literature and Your Life**

In what ways can music help Macon and Grandpa during this difficult time?

Grandpa Jeremiah's room smelled terrible. It was all closed up so no drafts could get on him and the whole room was smelled down with <u>disinfect</u> and medicine. Grandpa Jeremiah lay propped up on the bed and he was so gray he looked scary. His hair wasn't combed down and his head on the pillow with his white hair sticking out was enough to send me flying if Macon hadn't been there. He was skinny, too. He looked like his skin got loose on his bones, and when he lifted his arms, it hung down like he was just wearing it instead of it being a part of him.

Macon sat slant-shouldered with his guitar across his lap. He was messin' with the guitar, not making any music, but just going over the strings as Grandpa talked.

"Old Carrie went around out back to where they kept the pigs penned up and she felt a cold wind across her face. . . ." Grandpa Jeremiah was telling the story about how a old woman out-tricked the Devil and got her son back. I had heard the story before, and I knew it was pretty scary. "When she felt the cold breeze she didn't blink nary an eye, but looked straight ahead. . . ."

All the time Grandpa Jeremiah was talking I could see Macon fingering his guitar. I tried to imagine what it would be like if he was actually plucking the strings. I tried to fix my mind on that because I didn't like the way the story went

◆ **Build Vocabulary**

disinfect (dis´ in fekt´) *n.*: Dialect, or regional language, for disinfectant, a substance that kills germs

with the old woman wrestling with the Devil.

We sat there for nearly all the afternoon until Ellie and Sister Todd come in and said that supper was ready. Me and Macon went out and ate some collard greens, ham hocks,[2] and rice. Then Macon he went back in and listened to some more of Grandpa's stories until it was time for him to go home. I wasn't about to go in there and listen to no stories at night.

Dr. Crawford come around a few days later and said that Grandpa Jeremiah was doing a little better.

"You think the Good Lord gonna pull him through?" Sister Todd asked.

"I don't tell the Good Lord what He should or should not be doing," Dr. Crawford said, looking over at Sister Todd and at Ellie. "I just said that *my* patient seems to be doing okay for his condition."

"He been telling Macon all his stories," I said.

"Macon doesn't seem to understand that Grandpa Jeremiah needs his strength," Ellie said. "Now that he's improving, we don't want him to have a setback."

"No use in stopping him from telling his stories," Dr. Crawford said. "If it makes him feel good it's as good as any medicine I can give him."

I saw that this didn't set with Ellie, and when Dr. Crawford had left I asked her why.

"Dr. Crawford means well," she said, "but we have to get away from the kind of life that keeps us in the past."

She didn't say why we should be trying to get away from the stories and I really didn't

▲ **Critical Viewing** Which characters from the story could the figures in this painting portray? **[Connect]**

care too much. All I knew was that when Macon was sitting in the room with Grandpa Jeremiah I wasn't nearly as scared as I used to be when it was just me and Ellie listening. I told that to Macon.

"You getting to be a big man, that's all," he said.

That was true. Me and Macon was getting to be good friends, too. I didn't even mind so much when he started being friends with Ellie later. It seemed kind of natural, almost like Macon was supposed to be there with us instead of just visiting.

Grandpa wasn't getting no better, but he wasn't getting no worse, either.

"You liking Macon now?" I asked Ellie when we got to the middle of July. She was dishing out a plate of smothered chops for him and I hadn't even heard him ask for

◆ **Literary Focus**
Which character would be able to give the most specific information about Ellie's feelings? Why?

2. **collard greens, ham hocks:** Leafy green vegetables and joints from a pig's leg; favorite southern dishes.

anything to eat.

"Macon's funny," Ellie said, not answering my question. "He's in there listening to all of those old stories like he's really interested in them. It's almost as if he and Grandpa Jeremiah are talking about something more than the stories, a secret language."

I didn't think I was supposed to say anything about that to Macon, but once, when Ellie, Sister Todd, and Macon were out on the porch shelling butter beans after Grandpa got tired and was resting, I went into his room and told him what Ellie had said.

"She said that?" Grandpa Jeremiah's face was skinny and old looking but his eyes looked like a baby's, they was so bright.

"Right there in the kitchen is where she said it," I said. "And I don't know what it mean but I was wondering about it."

"I didn't think she had any feeling for them stories," Grandpa Jeremiah said. "If she think we talking secrets, maybe she don't."

"I think she getting a feeling for Macon," I said,

"That's okay, too," Grandpa Jeremiah said. "They both young."

"Yeah, but them stories you be telling, Grandpa, they about old people who lived a long time ago," I said.

"Well, those the folks you got to know about," Grandpa Jeremiah said. "You think on what those folks been through, and what they was feeling, and you add it up with what you been through and what you been feeling, then you got you something."

"What you got Grandpa?"

"You got you a bridge," Grandpa said. "And a meaning. Then when things get so hard you about to break, you can sneak across that bridge and see some folks who went before you and see how they didn't break. Some got bent and some got twisted and a few fell along the way, but they didn't break."

"Am I going to break, Grandpa?"

"You? As strong as you is?" Grandpa Jere-miah pushed himself up on his elbow and give me a look. "No way you going to break, boy. You gonna be strong as they come. One day you gonna tell all them stories I told you to your young'uns and they'll be as strong as you."

"Suppose I ain't got no stories, can I make some up?"

"Sure you can, boy. You make 'em up and twist 'em around. Don't make no mind. Long as you got 'em."

"Is that what Macon is doing?" I asked. "Making up stories to play on his guitar?"

"He'll do with 'em what he see fit, I suppose," Grandpa Jeremiah said. "Can't ask more than that from a man."

It rained the first three days of August. It wasn't a hard rain but it rained anyway. The mailman said it was good for the crops over East but I didn't care about that so I didn't pay him no mind. What I did mind was when it rain like that the field mice come in and get in things like the flour bin and I always got the blame for leaving it open.

When the rain stopped I was pretty glad. Macon come over and sat with Grandpa and had something to eat with us. Sister Todd come over, too.

"How Grandpa doing?" Sister Todd asked. "They been asking about him in the church."

"He's doing all right," Ellie said.

"He's kind of quiet today," Macon said. "He was just talking about how the hogs needed breeding."

"He must have run out of stories to tell," Sister Todd said. "He'll be repeating on himself like my father used to do. That's the way I *hear* old folks get."

Everybody laughed at that because Sister Todd was pretty old, too. Maybe we was all happy because the sun was out after so much rain. When Sister Todd went in to take Grandpa Jeremiah a plate of potato salad with no mayonnaise like he liked it, she told him about how people was asking for him and he told her to tell them he was doing okay and to remember him in their prayers.

Sister Todd came over the next afternoon, too, with some rhubarb pie with cheese on it, which is my favorite pie. When she took a piece into Grandpa Jeremiah's room she come right out again and told Ellie to go fetch the Bible.

It was a hot day when they had the funeral. Mostly everybody was there. The church was hot as anything, even though they had the window open. Some yellowjacks flew in and buzzed around Sister Todd's niece and then around Deacon Turner's wife and settled right on her hat and stayed there until we all stood and sang "Soon-a Will Be Done."

At the graveyard Macon played "Precious Lord" and I cried hard even though I told myself that I wasn't going to cry the way Ellie and Sister Todd was, but it was such a sad thing when we left and Grandpa Jeremiah was still out to the grave that I couldn't help it.

During the funeral and all, Macon kind of told everybody where to go and where to sit and which of the three cars to ride in. After it was over he come by the house and sat on the front porch and played on his guitar. Ellie was standing leaning against the rail and she was crying but it wasn't a hard crying. It was a soft crying, the kind that last inside of you for a long time.

Macon was playing a tune I hadn't heard before. I thought it might have been what he was working at when Grandpa Jeremiah was telling him those stories and I watched his fingers but I couldn't tell if it was or not. It wasn't nothing special, that tune Macon was playing, maybe halfway between them Delta blues he would do when Sister Todd wasn't around and something you would play at church. It was something different and something the same at the same time. I watched his fingers go over that guitar and figured I could learn that tune one day if I had a mind to.

Guide for Responding

◆ LITERATURE AND YOUR LIFE

Reader's Response What would you say to the narrator to comfort him after his grandfather's death?

Thematic Focus Being in touch with the past can sometimes help you find your own voice. Explain how.

☑ Check Your Comprehension

1. How does Ellie's reaction to Grandpa Jeremiah's stories change after her return from college?
2. After what event does Macon start visiting Grandpa Jeremiah more often?
3. What does Macon bring when he comes to visit Grandpa Jeremiah?

◆ Critical Thinking

INTERPRET

1. Why is Ellie's attitude different when she returns from college? **[Speculate]**
2. Why does the narrator like Macon? **[Synthesize]**
3. Why does Macon visit so often? **[Interpret]**
4. How does Macon feel about Grandpa and his stories? Explain. **[Draw Conclusions]**
5. Explain how you know that Ellie loves Grandpa Jeremiah. **[Support]**

EVALUATE

6. Are stories from the past valuable? Explain. **[Make a Judgment]**

EXTEND

7. What story do you know that preserves something from the past? **[Social Studies Link]**

TALENT

Annie Dillard

T here is no such thing as talent. If there are any inborn, God-given gifts, they are in the <u>precocious</u> fields of music, mathematics, and chess; if you have such a gift, you know it by now. All the rest of us, in all the other fields, are not talented. We all start out dull and weary and <u>uninspired</u>. Apart from a few like Mozart, there never have been any great and accomplished little children in the world. Genius is the product of education.

Perhaps it's a cruel thing to insist that there is no such thing as talent. We all want to believe— at least I do—that being selfless was "easy" for Albert Schweitzer,[1] that Faulkner's novels just popped into his head, that Rembrandt painted because he "had to." We want to believe all these nonsensical things in order to get ourselves off the hook. For if these people had no talent, then might the rest of us have painting or writing or great thinking as an option? We, who have no talent? I think the answer is yes, absolutely.

So I maintain that the people who have made something of their lives—the Pasteurs and Cézannes and Melvilles[2]—were neither more

---

1. **Albert Schweitzer** (shvīt´ sər) (1875–1965): Doctor and missionary famous for his selfless medical work in Africa as well as his writings.
2. **Melvilles:** Herman Melville (1819–1891) invented a new kind of novel. His most famous work is *Moby-Dick*.

◆ Build Vocabulary

precocious (prē kō´ shəs) *adj*.: Showing more abilities than is usual at one's age

uninspired [un in spīrd´] *adj*. Without bright and original ideas

▲ **Critical Viewing** What words would you use to describe this athlete's attitude? **[Infer]**

talented nor more disciplined nor more energetic nor more driven than the rest of us. They were simply better educated. Some of them did it the hard way, studying all the difficult works of their fields at home on their own. Others studied in school. But they all studied. You won't find a writer who hasn't studied the details of the works of other writers—although occasionally you find an American writer like Hemingway or Whitman who deliberately pretended to be spontaneous and unstudied, probably in order to mislead the competition. And occasionally you find a writer like Thoreau, a very well educated Harvard man whose reading was in the Greek classics[3] and in whose work most readers overlook the evidences of scholarship and effort simply because they don't want to see them.

It's hard work, doing something with your life. The very thought of hard work makes me queasy. I'd rather die in peace. Here we are, all equal and alike and none of us much to write home about—and some people choose to make themselves into physicists or thinkers or major-league pitchers, knowing perfectly well that it will be nothing but hard work. But I want to tell you that it's not as bad as it sounds. Doing something does not require discipline; it creates its own discipline.

People often ask me if I discipline myself to write, if I work a certain number of hours a day on a schedule. They ask this question with envy in their voices and awe on their faces and a sense of alienation all over them, as if they were addressing an armored tank or a talking giraffe or Niagara Falls. We all want to believe that other people are natural wonders; it

◆ **Reading Strategy**
Use the phrase "as if they were addressing an armored tank or a talking giraffe" as a context clue to figure out the meaning of "alienation."

gets us off the hook.

Now, it happens that when I wrote my first book of prose, I worked an hour or two a day for a while, and then in the last two months, I got excited and worked very hard, for many hours a day. People can lift cars when they want to. People can recite the Koran, too, and run in marathons.[4] These things aren't ways of life; they are merely possibilities for everyone on certain occasions of life. You don't lift cars around the clock or write books every year. But when you do, it's not so hard. It's not superhuman. It's very human. You do it for love. You do it for love and respect for your own life; you do it for love and respect for the world; and you do it for love and respect for the task itself.

If I had a little baby, it would be hard for me to rise up and feed that little baby in the middle of the night. It would be hard; but it certainly wouldn't be a discipline. It wouldn't be a regimen I imposed on myself out of masochism,[5] nor would it be the flowering of some extraordinary internal impulse. I would do it, grumbling, for love and because it has to be done.

Of course it has to be done. And something has to be done with your life too: something specific, something human. But don't wait around to be hit by love. Don't wait for anything. Learn something first. Then while you are getting to know it, you will get to love it, and that love will direct you in what to do. So many times when I was in college I used to say of a course like Seventeenth Century Poetry or European History, "I didn't like it at first, but

---

3. **the Greek classics:** Works of poetry, drama, history, and philosophy written in the 6th and 5th centuries B.C. in Greece; studied by generations of Europeans.

4. **. . . the Koran . . . and run in marathons:** The Koran is the holy book of Islam, the religion of Muslims; a marathon is a 26-mile race.
5. **masochism** (mas´ ə kiz´ əm): Desire to be punished.

◆ **Build Vocabulary**

perpetual (pər pech´ oo əl) *adj.*: Constant; lasting forever

now I like it." All of life is like that—a sort of dreary course which gradually gets interesting if you work at it.

I used to live in perpetual dread that I would one day read all the books that I would ever be interested in and have nothing more to read. I always figured that when that time came I would force myself to learn wildflowers, just to keep awake. I dreaded it, because I was not very interested in wildflowers but thought I should be. But things kept cropping up and one book has led to another and I haven't had to learn wildflowers yet. I don't think there's much danger of coming to the end of the line. The line is endless. I urge you to get in it, to get in line. It's a long line— but it's the only show in town.

Beyond Literature
Humanities Connection

Giants of Classical Music Wolfgang Amadeus Mozart was just one of the many classical music "superstars" that Dillard could have mentioned. Johann Sebastian Bach wrote hundreds of musical masterpieces. Ludwig van Beethoven composed many of his greatest works after he became deaf. Frederic Chopin was composing when he was nine.

Cross-Curricular Activity Create a timeline of classical music masters. Use an encyclopedia to find dates for the names mentioned above. Look under "Classical Music" to find other names to add to your timeline. Include one fact about each musician you put on the timeline.

Guide for Responding

◆ LITERATURE AND YOUR LIFE

Reader's Response Has enjoying an activity helped you improve your skill at it? Explain.

Thematic Focus: Is communicating ideas hard or easy for Dillard? Explain.

Group Discussion With a group, discuss how Dillard's essay applies to you and your efforts to reach your own goals.

☑ Check Your Comprehension

1. According to Dillard, what do most people need to do to achieve great things?
2. Identify one person Dillard presents as an example of a person who has made something of his or her life. What did that person do?
3. How do people achieve self-discipline?
4. Name Dillard's two motives for writing.
5. What advice does Dillard give to people who have not yet found an activity they love?

◆ Critical Thinking

INTERPRET
1. How would Dillard define "talent"? **[Infer]**
2. Explain Dillard's statement that great people are "simply better educated." **[Interpret]**
3. Why do people want to believe that some are naturally talented? **[Analyze]**
4. Give an example of how working on a project "creates its own discipline." **[Interpret]**
5. What job or responsibility would Dillard say all people have in life? **[Draw Conclusions]**

APPLY
6. Some say that money and fame are the main reasons people work hard. How would Dillard respond? **[Speculate]**

COMPARE LITERARY WORKS
7. What do you think Grandpa in "Jeremiah's Song" would say about Dillard's essay? **[Analyze]**

Guide for Responding (continued)

◆ Reading Strategy

USE CONTEXT CLUES

Context clues may restate the meaning of difficult or unfamiliar words. For the following sentences, give a likely meaning for the italicized word and explain the context clue or clues that you used.

1. Macon respected Grandpa and held him in high *esteem*.
2. Dillard says she doesn't *impose* a regimen on herself because she doesn't have to force herself to do something she loves.
3. She had a fear of studying wildflowers, but her greatest *dread* was running out of interesting books.

◆ Build Vocabulary

USING THE PREFIX *dis-*

The prefix *dis-* changes the meaning of a word to its opposite. In your notebook, write the opposite of each word by adding or removing *dis-* from it.

1. agree, ___?___   3. displace, ___?___
2. respectful, ___?___   4. disservice, ___?___

SPELLING STRATEGY

A prefix never changes the spelling of the original word—even when the word begins with a vowel. For example, when you add *dis-* to *infect* you write *disinfect,* not *dissinfect.*

On your paper, add *dis-* to the following words:

1. trust   2. connect   3. obey   4. interested

USING THE WORD BANK

On your paper, respond to each of the following sentences. Explain each response.

1. Who might give you a *diagnosis*?
2. Why might a doctor *disinfect* his or her hands?
3. Would a three-year-old pianist be considered *precocious*? Why or why not?
4. Why wouldn't you describe the people discussed in Dillard's essay as *uninspired*?
5. Would you enjoy *perpetual* summer? Why or why not?

◆ Literary Focus

FIRST-PERSON NARRATOR

The **first-person narrator** of "Jeremiah's Song" participates in the action of the story and refers to himself as "I." You, the reader, see all events and characters in the story through his eyes. The narrator of "Talent" doesn't tell a story, but she shares her inner thoughts and feelings.

1. Who is the narrator of "Jeremiah's Song"?
2. Identify two details that only this narrator could tell you—that Ellie or Macon would not know.
3. Identify two details revealed by the narrator of "Talent" that only she could know.

◆ Build Grammar Skills

COMMON AND PROPER NOUNS

All nouns are either common nouns or proper nouns. A **common noun** refers to any one of a group of people, places, or things. A **proper noun** is the name of one specific person, place, or thing.
Common Nouns: cousin, grandfather, guitar
Proper Nouns: Ellie, Greensboro, Koran

Proper nouns are always capitalized. A common noun is not capitalized unless it is the first word in a sentence.

Practice On your paper, write these sentences. Capitalize each proper noun, and underline each common noun.

1. Going away to college changed ellie.
2. Young macon loved to play his guitar.
3. The blues sprang up along the mississippi river.
4. As a young boy in harlem, walter dean myers read a newspaper every day.
5. The writer admires herman melville.

Writing Application Add a proper noun or a common noun to complete each of the following sentences. (Add *a, the, your,* or *my* if needed.)

1. I would like to go to (proper noun) on vacation.
2. (common noun) told me not to be late.
3. Please take (proper noun) out for a walk.

Build Your Portfolio

Idea Bank

Writing

1. **Journal Entry** Describe a talented person—a friend, relative, or celebrity. Explain his or her talent and what you know about how it grew.

2. **Classified Advertisement** Jeremiah was a good storyteller. Create a help-wanted advertisement for a good storyteller. Describe the qualifications he or she should have. **[Career Link]**

3. **Speech** At a funeral, someone might give a speech, called a *eulogy*, about the deceased person. Write a eulogy for Grandpa Jeremiah or about one of the people mentioned in Dillard's essay.

Speaking and Listening

4. **Role Play** With a partner, role-play a conversation between Ellie and Macon, in which they each explain why they feel as they do about Grandpa's stories. **[Performing Arts Link]**

5. **Presentation** Give a presentation explaining your goals in a sport or in one of the arts. Describe what steps you must take to meet your goals and, if possible, give a demonstration. **[Sports Link; Art Link]**

Projects

6. **Talent Timeline** Using library resources, construct a timeline showing important figures in a particular field. Include information about each person's most important contribution. **[Science Link; Social Studies Link]**

7. **Blues Presentation [Group Activity]** Give a group presentation on the blues. Divide up the following tasks: collecting recordings, researching the development of the blues, and preparing visual aids such as pictures of instruments and famous blues performers. **[Performing Arts Link]**

Writing Mini-Lesson

Portrait in Words

An artist might create a portrait with pencils or paint. In "Jeremiah's Song," Myers uses words to create portraits of his characters. Choose an important person in your life, and create a portrait in words that captures the person's special qualities.

Writing Skills Focus: Show, Don't Tell

An artist doesn't write across the bottom of a portrait: "This person is shy." Instead, the artist will show the subject's shyness. In the following example, Myers shows that Grandpa is old and sick.

Model From the Story

He was so gray he looked scary. His hair wasn't combed down and his head on the pillow with his white hair sticking out was enough to send me flying. . . .

Prewriting Use a cluster diagram like the one below to brainstorm for a list of your subject's qualities and actions that illustrate these qualities.

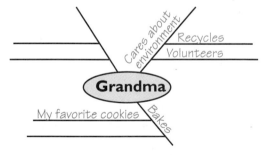

Drafting Use details to show the qualities of your subject. For example, to show height, you might write "He has to duck to avoid the ceiling fan."

Revising Look for places where you can add specific details that show rather than tell.

> ◆ **Grammar Application**
> Capitalize any proper nouns you use.

Connecting Literature to Social Studies

ANCIENT EGYPT

Mummy No. 1770 *by Patricia Lauber*

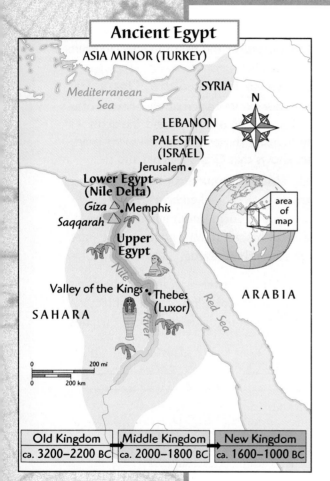

Ancient Egypt

ASIA MINOR (TURKEY)

Mediterranean Sea

SYRIA

N

LEBANON

PALESTINE (ISRAEL)

Jerusalem •

Lower Egypt (Nile Delta)

Giza △ • Memphis

Saqqarah △

area of map

Upper Egypt

Nile River

Valley of the Kings • • Thebes (Luxor)

ARABIA

SAHARA

Red Sea

0 ⎯ 200 mi
0 ⎯ 200 km

| Old Kingdom ca. 3200–2200 BC | → | Middle Kingdom ca. 2000–1800 BC | → | New Kingdom ca. 1600–1000 BC |

SOLVING ANCIENT MYSTERIES When scientists examine human remains from long ago, they act like detectives solving a murder. They want to give the "victims" a voice by finding out who they were and what happened to them.

Mummies Ancient Egyptians would have been happy to know that their dead could be identified after thousands of years. They believed that people kept their living personalities even after death. However, they thought that people could survive this way only if their bodies were preserved as mummies. This process involved treating the body with oils, removing its organs, and wrapping it in cloth bandages. The mummies of Egyptian pharaohs, or kings, were also kept in huge triangular monuments known as pyramids. Other high-born Egyptians built special tombs to protect their mummies after death.

Pharaohs Forever Maybe Egyptians believed that they would survive death because Egypt itself would always survive. Egypt had first been united around 3200 B.C. Then, it was ruled by pharaohs during three great kingdoms: Old, Middle, and New. Egyptians believed that there would be pharaohs forever.

"Mummy No. 1770" Ancient Egypt did finally vanish, but it was outlived by some of its mummies. In this essay, identifying the faceless and nameless mummy no. 1770 is a challenge for scientist-detectives.

Mummy No. 1770

Patricia Lauber

Museums have a limited number of mummies. Every time one is unwrapped, the number grows smaller, and so autopsies[1] are not often performed. But sometimes a museum has a mummy that is not important to its collection. This is a mummy it does not want to display and a mummy about which almost nothing is known. As it happened, the Manchester Museum had just such a mummy. Its wrappings were in poor condition and no one knew what period it dated from, where it was found, or who the dead person was. The mummy was known only by its museum number, 1770. This was the mummy the museum made available to a team of scientists who wanted to use modern techniques to study the wrappings and body in detail.

It was also a mummy with a mystery. X-rays taken years earlier had shown the mummy was that of a young person. The lower parts of the legs were missing, and close to the leg bones was a rounded object. The x-rays did not reveal what it was, but its shape suggested a baby's head. Was this the mummy of a mother and child? Had the mother died shortly after giving birth? Was she perhaps an unwed-mother who had been punished with a violent death? Those were questions the scientists wondered about as they began their work.

---

1. **autopsies** (ô′ täp′ sēz) n.: Examinations and dissections of dead bodies to find the causes of death or physical damage from disease.

After new x-rays were taken, the unwrapping began. Insect remains found in the bandages were carefully removed for later study. As pieces of cloth were lifted away, the lower part of the mask came into view. Beneath it were the bare bones of the neck and skull. These were in small pieces, but even so, once the pieces had been cleaned it was possible to see that the left side of the nose had been damaged by the iron hook the embalmers had used to remove the brain. The team was surprised to see red and blue paint on the skull bones. How and why had the bones been exposed?

Gently removing more cloth, the scientists found the mummy's arms were crossed on the chest and the hands had gold fingertip covers. The inner organs had been removed and the space filled with bandages and mud. The organs themselves were missing.

A small, hard object that had appeared in the x-rays proved to be a Guinea worm, a parasite that is taken in with drinking water. Within a human host, the young forms of Guinea worm develop into adults. The adults mate, and the male dies. The female, which may grow three feet long, wanders through the tissues under the skin. She generally comes to rest in the legs or feet of the host. There blisters form. They burst on contact

◆ **Build Vocabulary**

parasite (par′ ə sit′) n.: Organism, often harmful, that gets food or protection from another living thing without giving anything back

with fresh water. The female's eggs are released into the water, and the life cycle starts again. If invaded by bacteria, the blisters may form dangerous sores.

When the Manchester team unwrapped the legs of mummy 1770, they found, as the x-rays had shown, that both legs had been amputated, the left below the knee and the right above the knee. The mummy's right leg had been lengthened with a piece of wood to make it the same length as the left. The wood had been splinted to the leg bone. This meant there could not have been much, if any, flesh on the bone when the splinting was done. The feet were artificial and had gold toenail covers. The right foot was made of reeds and mud, with the ends of the reeds serving as toes. The left foot was simply a mass of reeds and mud.

By now the scientists could see that there was not even a trace of a baby. The rounded shape that had shown in the x-rays was actually a pair of beautiful slippers that had been placed on the soles of the feet.

> **Connecting Literature to Social Studies**
> What might the "beautiful slippers" reveal about the dead person's place in society?

In one way mummy 1770 was disappointing—it was very poorly preserved. No one could even be certain of its sex, although members of the team came to feel that the young person had been a girl and spoke of the mummy as female. Very little skin, muscle, or soft tissue were left, and the bones of the skull and lower trunk were broken. The scientists could not tell when the fractures had occurred. In a living person, tissue called callus forms at the place where a bone is broken. It holds the bone together until the fracture heals. Callus in a recently dead person shows that the fracture occurred during life. But callus thick enough to last thousands of years would take several weeks to form. So if there is no callus in a mummy— and there was none in 1770—there was no way to tell whether the fracture occurred after

death or shortly before. The scientists suspected, however, that the bones were broken after death. The damaged mask and the lack of jewelry and charms spoke of tomb robbers and rough handling.

In other ways, mummy 1770 was both interesting and puzzling. The evidence indicated that the body had been in a state of considerable decay when the embalmers worked on it. The wooden leg was attached to bone. All the internal organs were missing and so was the left kneecap, which suggested that the ligaments holding it in place had rotted away. The red and blue paint on the skull bones was a sign that the hair and scalp had been missing.

Why had the body decayed? Why were the legs amputated? The scientific team could think of various explanations.

One had to do with the Guinea worm. Perhaps infections had cut off the flow of blood to the legs and feet. In an effort to save the girl's life, doctors had amputated her legs, but the patient died. But if that was the case, why hadn't she been promptly embalmed?

Or perhaps the legs had been cut off in an accident, such as the collapse of a building. If the girl had been buried in rubble and not found for some time, that might explain the decay.

Or suppose the girl had drowned in the Nile, where decay would set in quickly. The body might have been attacked by a hippopotamus. Although hippos are plant eaters, they are likely to attack floating objects that appear threatening. One bite from a hippo could easily cut off a pair of legs.

A crocodile was another possibility, because it would certainly attack a floating body. The problem with this idea was that crocodiles do not usually bite through bones. They are much more likely to grasp an arm or a leg in their huge jaws and shake it until it tears loose. On the other hand, a crocodile attack might explain why the embalmers went to so much trouble over a body that was hauled out of the

Nile—why they made a face and chest mask, lengthened a leg, made artificial feet, applied gold covers to the fingers and toes. The ancient Egyptians, believing that crocodiles were earthly forms of gods, considered anyone who became food for them to be sacred.

As things turned out, there was another explanation for the state of the body and it took everyone by surprise. When the carbon-14 dating[2] was completed, it showed that the mummy was far older than its wrappings. The wrap-

Connecting Literature to Social Studies
Did the mummified person live during the Old, Middle, or New kingdom?

▲ **Critical Viewing** Why do you think scientists wanted to know what 1770 looked like? **[Speculate]**

pings dated to a time when the Romans ruled Egypt, around A.D. 260. The mummy's bones dated to around 1000 B.C. This meant that 1770 was a mummy that had been wrapped twice. It had been preserved and wrapped after the girl died, then rewrapped more than a thousand years later. Now some pieces of the puzzle began to fall into place.

There was no need to explain why the corpse had decayed, because it hadn't. Rather, it was the mummy that had been damaged by water and then had decayed. The soft tissues of the body were probably missing because they had stuck to the original wrappings.

The way the second embalmers had prepared the body made clear that they did not know whether they were dealing with a male or a female. This meant they did not know the mummy's identity. But the trouble they took shows that they thought they were dealing with someone of importance. The tomb from which the mummy came must have led them to that conclusion. At times in ancient Egypt royal mummies were moved to new tombs. If they had been damaged, they were repaired at the time of the move. Quite possibly 1770 was a person of royal or noble birth whose mummy was damaged when a tomb was flooded.

X-rays had shown that the mummy's wisdom teeth had not yet grown in, and so the girl must have been less than 20 years old. The dentist on the team now examined the roots of the second molars. Their stage of development told him that 1770 had been 13 to 14 years old. He was surprised to see that the teeth showed no sign of being worn down by sand.[3] He also found that two teeth in the upper jaw were oddly placed. A space between them near the gum formed a trap for food particles. Usually such a trap leads to infection, which damages the bone of the jaw. But this had not happened to 1770. The lack of wear and damage suggested that her diet was soft, perhaps mostly liquid. Or she may have swallowed food without trying to chew it much. Most likely she had not been very healthy.

---

2. **carbon-14 dating:** Method for figuring out approximate age by measuring the radioactive carbon-14 that is left in a fossil or other once-living thing.

---

3. **teeth showed no sign . . . sand:** Food eaten by Egyptians usually contained some sand that blew in by accident. The sand ground down their teeth.

She must also have breathed mainly through her mouth. The badly formed bones in the inner part of her nose would have made it almost impossible to breathe any other way. If a person always breathes through the mouth, the gums around the upper front teeth become irritated and the bone behind them pitted. Pits in the bones of 1770's mouth showed that she had indeed breathed through her mouth.

By this time the Manchester team had learned a great deal about 1770. She was a young person who had lived a short life with considerable suffering. She had had to breathe through her mouth, had sore gums, ate only liquid or soft food, and had been infected by Guinea worms, which cause fever and an itching rash as well as blisters. Finally, by means still not clear, she had lost her legs around the time she died.

One final step remained to be taken—to find out what 1770 had looked like. The skull had broken into about 30 pieces, some of them very small and fragile. The pieces lay in a jumbled heap and were mixed with mud and bandages. Once the pieces of bone had been cleaned, one member of the team made casts of them in plastic. When the plastic pieces were fitted together, much of the left side of the skull was still missing. A plaster cast was made to fill out the basic shape of the head. Now small pegs were placed in the plastic skull and cut to precise lengths. Each showed how thick the soft tissues of the face would be on a 13-year-old person. The face was then built up with modeling clay. First it took on a general human appearance. Then it took on an appearance of its own, shaped by the underlying bones. This model was used to cast the head in wax, so that changes could be made if more was learned about 1770. The wax head was painted, given glass eyes, a wig, and eyelashes. And there at last was 1770—an attractive teenager, perhaps of royal or noble birth, who had laughed, cried, and lived 3,000 years ago.

◆ **Build Vocabulary**
fragile (fraj´ əl) *adj.*: Easily broken

Guide for Responding

◆ LITERATURE AND YOUR LIFE

Reader's Response What is the most surprising thing about mummy 1770? Explain.

Thematic Focus In what ways do the scientists help this mummy to "speak"?

☑ Check Your Comprehension

1. Why was this mummy a "mystery"?
2. Name three ideas that scientists first suggested to explain the state of the body.

◆ Critical Thinking

INTERPRET
1. Describe three methods used by scientists who studied the mummy. **[Classify]**
2. Explain how the results from the carbon-14 dating caused scientists to rethink their ideas. **[Analyze Cause and Effect]**
3. Summarize what scientists learned about the mummy. **[Summarize]**

EVALUATE
4. Scientists put a great deal of effort into studying this mummy. Is that effort worthwhile? Why or why not? **[Make a Judgment]**

Meet the Author
Patricia Lauber (1924–   )
Patricia Lauber loves mysteries and puzzles. Her more than eighty books of fiction and nonfiction deal with such subjects as the ice age, volcanoes, the Loch Ness monster, and runaway fleas!

CONNECTING LITERATURE TO SOCIAL STUDIES

The scientists in this essay work to give the past a human face. From the bones and decayed wrappings of a mysterious mummy, they create a vivid image of a teenage girl.

Their discoveries and guesses about the girl also help you picture the land where she lived. You may know, for example, that the flooding of the Nile River gave water to the farmers of ancient Egypt. However, you may never have imagined the huge-jawed hippos and crocodiles lurking in the river!

Other discoveries reveal the health problems of ancient Egyptians and the methods of preparing mummies.

1. What problem did ancient Egyptians have with their drinking water?
2. Why did the desert surrounding the Nile give ancient Egyptians problems with their teeth?
3. Why does the double wrapping of the mummy indicate that embalming methods remained the same for at least 1,000 years?

 Idea Bank

Writing

1. **Diary Entry** Review what you know about the girl who became mummy 1770. Then, write a diary entry in which she describes an event in her life, such as receiving the slippers.

2. **Museum Plaque** Write a brief explanation to be displayed on a museum wall near mummy 1770. Tell museum visitors what this mummy is and how it relates to the history of ancient Egypt. **[Career Link]**

3. **Scientific Abstract** An abstract is a brief summary of a scientific investigation. As one of the scientists working on mummy 1770, write an abstract that tells other scientists what you've discovered. **[Career Link; Science Link]**

Speaking and Listening

4. **Museum Tour** You are a museum guide pausing with your group in front of mummy 1770. Give an interesting talk on how scientists discovered the mummy's identity. **[Performing Arts Link]**

Projects

5. **Report on Hieroglyphics** Do research on Egyptian hieroglyphics. Report your findings to the class, showing how to write hieroglyphic messages. **[Art Link]**

6. **Multimedia Mummy** Prepare a presentation in which you compare and contrast images of mummies from literature and the movies to the reality of mummies. Use models, photos, charts, and video clips. **[Media Link]**

Further Reading, Listening, and Viewing

- *The Mummy Awakes* (1993), by Megan and H. William Stine, is a novel that tells a chilling tale about a teenager and the mummy of Neshi.
- *Action Pack: Pyramid* (1994) is an interactive kit for exploring the tombs of ancient Egyptian kings.
- *King Tut: The Face of Tutankhamen* is a video documentary about the most famous Egyptian tomb.
- *Pyramid* (1975), by David McCaulay, is a nonfiction book packed with information and illustrations that bring readers inside the pyramids.

Personal Narrative

Writing Process Workshop

As you have seen in this section, everyone has a story to tell—young girls, old men, even mummies who can't talk can tell a story. One kind of story *you* can tell is a **personal narrative**—a true story about a memorable experience or event from your life. Write a personal narrative. In it, make a personal connection with your readers by including your thoughts and feelings about the event or experience.

The following skills, introduced in this section's Writing Mini-Lessons, will help you write your personal narrative.

Writing Skills Focus

▶ **Use vivid adjectives.** For instance, instead of saying "he ate an apple," you might write "he ate a crisp, red apple." (See p. 12.)

▶ Write an **effective lead,** or opening paragraph, that will capture your readers' interest. (See p. 21.)

▶ Elaborate with **sensory details** to help your readers experience the sights, sounds, smells, tastes, and feelings that you experienced. (See p. 31.)

▶ Through anecdotes and actions, **show, don't** just **tell** about people and events. (See p. 45.)

The writer of the following personal narrative uses several of these skills.

MODEL

When Peter first moved in, I thought for sure he was going to be the new bully on the street. Little did I realize that he and I were going to be best friends. ① Peter's rocky jaw and thick, black eyebrows give him a mean look. ② Even though he's the same age as I am, he has a deep, froggy voice. ③ Once, someone cut in line in front of us at the cafeteria. Peter just said, "Excuse me?" The kid took one look at him and hurried to the back of the line. ④

① This lead creates interest right away. How do Peter and the writer become friends if Peter seems like a bully?

② Vivid adjectives make a good description.

③ The writer provides a sensory detail—the sound of Peter's voice.

④ Here, the writer shows (rather than tells) how people react to Peter.

Prewriting

Choose a Topic Choose a memory that brings up strong feelings or vivid images for you. If it is important to you, then you can make it important for the reader. The following suggestions may give you some ideas to get started.

Topic Ideas

- A vacation trip
- A change in your neighborhood
- Meeting someone new

Make a List of Details to Include Jot down all the details you can remember of your experience. Taking notes will jog your memory and help you organize your story.

Cross Off Details That Will Not Interest Your Readers Think about who will read your narrative. If you are writing for your classmates, then you probably won't want to tell them every detail of your trip to your grandparents' house. Stick to the parts that will interest them.

Create a Cluster Diagram of Sensory Details For each part of your story, list the sensory details you remember:

DRAFTING/REVISING

APPLYING LANGUAGE SKILLS: Vary Tag Words in Dialogue

Include dialogue in your narrative. Dialogue is the conversation between speakers. Tag words, the words you use to indicate the speaker, can also tell how a person speaks. For example, the word *shouted* or *whispered* gives more detail than *said*.

Example:

"The last thing this house needs is another dog," George growled.

"Please let me keep him," pleaded Bella.

Practice Rewrite these sentences on your paper. Replace the word *said* to show how the words are spoken.

1. "I can't believe we're going to be late again," Dad said.
2. "Be quiet," said Martha.
3. "Pencils down," said Miss Simpson. "Time's up."

Writing Application In your personal narrative, use specific words that indicate the way each person speaks.

Writer's Solution Connection Writing Lab

View the video example of dialogue in the Drafting section of the Creative Writing tutorial.

APPLYING LANGUAGE SKILLS: Punctuating Dialogue

Follow these rules for punctuating dialogue:

• Use quotation marks before and after a speaker's exact words.

• Use a comma to separate the words identifying the speaker from the speaker's words that follow it.

• Place other punctuation marks before quotation marks.

Example:

"No way," I laughed, "are you getting me on that coaster."

Practice Rewrite the following sentences on your paper. Punctuate them correctly.

1. If we hurry we can get to the park by ten he called.

2. Do I have to go she whined.

3. If you don't want to go he replied I won't make you.

Writing Application Correctly punctuate any dialogue in your personal narrative.

Writer's Solution Connection Writing Lab

For more practice, use the Quotation Marks section of the Language Lab tutorial on Punctuation.

Drafting

Begin With an Effective Lead Start off with the most vivid sensory details or a key event. You don't have to tell your readers everything in the first paragraph, but you should tell them enough to get them curious.

Show, Don't Tell It's easy just to tell your readers what happened. Your job, though, is to help them relive your experience. Pretend you are a movie camera on the scene. What do you see? What do you hear? Incorporate details for as many senses as is appropriate.

Revising

Have a Peer Conference Have two friends or classmates review your draft. Then, ask them the following questions:

▶ Did the opening paragraph grab your attention? Why or why not?

▶ Were any details unclear or vague?

▶ At what points did you have trouble **seeing** the events?

Use your classmates' comments to determine what parts of your draft you need to strengthen when you revise.

REVISION MODEL

① I never would have guessed that Peter and I would be friends.

② on January fourteenth.

Peter came to our class ~~in the middle of the school year.~~

③ "Do you like sports?" I asked.

~~The first time I tried to talk to him, he didn't say much.~~ His only response was "Yep."

① The writer added a new first sentence that would arouse the reader's curiosity.

② The writer made the time of year more specific.

③ The writer added dialogue to show how little Peter said.

Publishing and Presenting

▶ **Album** Gather objects that illustrate or commemorate your experience—photos, drawings, advertisements, ticket stubs, dried flowers, shells, and so on. Arrange them together with your narrative in a booklet or album.

▶ **Magazine** Submit your narrative to a magazine that publishes student writing.

Strategies for Success

Every writer has a purpose, or reason, for writing. Once you understand what the author's purpose is, you will be able to read accordingly and better understand his or her work. Keep in mind that a writer may have more than one purpose.

Ask yourself the following questions to determine a writer's purpose:

Does the writer want to inform me?
If what you are reading provides only statistics and factual details that can be proven true or false, the writer's purpose is probably to inform. For example, an encyclopedia article gives facts about a topic. A news article gives facts about an event.

Does the writer want to persuade me?
Some works that contain facts and details are intended to do more than inform. If the writer offers an opinion on the facts or encourages you to think or act in a certain way, then his or her purpose is to persuade you.

For example, an advertisement for a product may present facts about the product as well as statements to persuade you to buy it.

Does the writer want to entertain me?
In some cases, the writer's purpose is to entertain you. Many works of the imagination are intended to entertain. A mystery novel entertains by keeping you in suspense. A poem can entertain you with beautiful descriptions.

Apply the Strategies

For each of the following kinds of writing, explain whether the purpose is most likely *to inform, to persuade,* or *to entertain.*

1. A newspaper announcement giving the date and place of a school event

2. The latest issue of *Cosmic Avengers Comics,* filled with fantastic stories about the future

3. An encyclopedia article that tells what newts look like, what they eat, and where they live

4. A flyer from an amusement park that tells how fast and how high "the world's most exciting coaster" travels

5. A monster story that gives you goose-bumps

✔ *Here are situations in which understanding a writer's purpose can be helpful:*
  ▶ *Finding information on a product, such as a new bicycle*
  ▶ *Looking for an entertaining book in the library*
  ▶ *Choosing sources for a research report*

Grammar Review

Nouns are words that name persons, places, things, and qualities or ideas (see page 11).

Person	character, guitarist, Doris
Place	Illinois, downtown, city
Thing	sneaker, dog, gallery
Quality or Idea	freedom, luck, knowledge

Nouns fall into these categories:

Compound (See p. 20.)	guitar-player, grandfather
Concrete (See p. 30.)	guitar, gazelle, Sanderson's Shoe Emporium
Abstract (See p. 30.)	talent, the blues, tradition
Common (See p. 44.)	tree, crow, picture
Proper (See p. 44.)	Robert Frost, Main Street, Tinker Creek

Practice 1 List the nouns in the sentences that follow. Next to each, identify the noun as common or proper.

1. Mr. Sanderson is fascinated by Douglas's speech.

2. The stray is cute, but Mrs. Lacey sees it as another mouth to feed.

3. The songs of the Mississippi Delta tell stories.

Practice 2 Identify each of the italicized nouns as abstract or concrete.

1. *Talent* is less important than hard *work*.

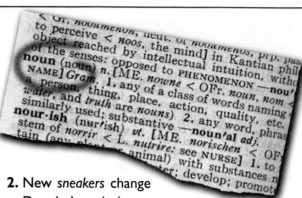

2. New *sneakers* change Douglas's *outlook*.

3. Macon's *respect* for the old man's *stories* shows his *maturity*.

Practice 3 Fill in each blank with a noun of the kind indicated.

A few different things capture the *(abstract)* ___?___ of summer for me. A brand-new pair of *(concrete)* ___?___ reminds me of summer's restless freedom. Soulful music playing on a *(concrete)* ___?___ reminds me of summer's *(abstract)* ___?___. Some songs remind me of trips to *(proper)* ___?___ , where we used to visit *(proper)* ___?___.

Grammar in Writing

✔ *A single compound noun can sometimes do the work of a whole descriptive phrase.*

Descriptive Phrase: After supper, the man playing the guitar filled the porch with music.

Compound Noun: After supper, the guitar-player filled the porch with music.

Check your writing for long phrases that you can replace with compound nouns.

PART 2 $\mathcal{Moving\ On}$

Urban Downgrade, 20th and Noe, 1988, Wayne Thiebaud, Courtesy of the artist

Guide for Reading

Meet the Author:

Jack London (1876–1916)

Jack London probably lived the most adventurous life of any American writer. By the time he was barely out of his teens, this Californian had done all of the following:

- worked twelve-hour days at a cannery.
- captained a pirate ship.
- traveled the United States as a hobo.
- served on a seal-hunting ship in the Pacific.
- prospected for gold in north-western Canada.

From Adventurer to Writer Between daring adventures, London somehow found time to read. In fact, he may have read every novel in the Oakland, California, library. His reading inspired him to write his own adventure tales. At age seventeen, he wrote a 4,000-word sea story that won $25 in a newspaper contest.

By the time he was thirty, London had written such classic adventure tales as *The Call of the Wild* and *White Fang*. Altogether, he wrote more than fifty books and earned more than a million dollars.

THE STORY BEHIND THE STORY

In 1897, London went to northwestern Canada, where gold had just been discovered. He didn't find gold, but he did have adventures on the way to Dawson City. Once, for instance, he made a boat from trees and ran the dangerous White Horse Rapids. In this story, London writes about a young gold miner who also has a thrilling trip to Dawson.

◆ LITERATURE AND YOUR LIFE

CONNECT YOUR EXPERIENCE

Recall a time when you or a friend found a dollar bill. Then, imagine a line of dollar bills stretching as far as you can see! That's the kind of easy money that the men on the next page were imagining. They were prospectors, and they believed they could dip a pan into a creek and fish out a fortune in gold.

THEMATIC FOCUS: Onward and Upward

"The King of Mazy May" tells of a young man among these prospectors who must deal with robbers. Ask yourself how a sudden threat can make a person grow up quickly.

◆ Background for Understanding

SOCIAL STUDIES

In 1896, George Carmack found gold in the Klondike region of northwestern Canada. His find began with a quarter ounce of the precious metal—equal in value to what an average worker could earn in a week! Carmack was followed by thousands of others. Most found hardship but no gold. Winter temperatures fell to −50°Fahrenheit, and dangerous outlaws preyed on gold-seekers.

◆ Build Vocabulary

SUFFIXES: -or

The word "prospectors" is built from *prospect*, "to search," and the suffix -*or*, meaning "a person or thing that does something." A *prospector* is "a person who searches for gold."

toil
endured
prospectors
liable
poising
declined
summit

WORD BANK

Which two words show an action that happened in the past?

◆ The King of Mazy May ◆

◆ Literary Focus

CONFLICT BETWEEN CHARACTERS

The glitter of gold can set off a struggle or **conflict between characters** in a story. Conflict occurs when characters battle each other to achieve their goals. As a reader, you root for one side or the other as you wait to see who wins.

In "The King of Mazy May," the glitter of gold causes a glitter of greed in some men's eyes. However, the men who are desperate for gold must battle a boy who is intent on justice.

◆ Reading Strategy

RECOGNIZE SIGNAL WORDS

Like travelers losing their way in the Klondike, you may get lost when reading unless you **recognize signal words.** These words give you directions. For example, the word *but* signals that the next idea differs from the idea you've just read.

The chart below shows signal words from "The King of Mazy May." Make a chart like it and fill in examples as you read.

Signal Word or Phrase	What Comes Next	Examples
But	Something opposite to or different from what has just been said	1. He has never had . . . shoes. . . . But he has seen the sun at midnight. . . . 2. 3.
So	A result or consequence	
On account of	A cause	
Because	A cause	

THE KING OF

MAZY MAY

Jack London

Walt Masters is not a very large boy, but there is manliness in his make-up, and he himself, although he does not know a great deal that most boys know, knows much that other boys do not know. He has never seen a train of cars nor an elevator in his life, and for that matter he has never once looked upon a cornfield, a plow, a cow, or even a chicken. He has never had a pair of shoes on his feet, nor gone to a picnic or a party, nor talked to a girl. But he has seen the sun at midnight, watched the ice jams on one of the mightiest of rivers, and played beneath the northern lights,[1] the one white child in thousands of square miles of frozen wilderness.

Walt has walked all the fourteen years of his life in suntanned, moose-hide moccasins, and he can go to the Indian camps and "talk big" with the men, and trade calico and beads with them for their precious furs. He can make bread without baking powder, yeast, or hops, shoot a moose at three hundred yards, and drive the wild wolf dogs fifty miles a day on the packed trail.

▲ **Critical Viewing** What details in the picture above suggest that these men deal with danger and hardship? **[Analyze]**

---

1. northern lights: Glowing bands or streamers of light, sometimes appearing in the night sky of the Northern Hemisphere.

Last of all, he has a good heart, and is not afraid of the darkness and loneliness, of man or beast or thing. His father is a good man, strong and brave, and Walt is growing up like him.

Walt was born a thousand miles or so down the Yukon,[2] in a trading post below the Ramparts. After his mother died, his father and he came up on the river, step by step, from camp to camp, till now they are settled down on the Mazy May Creek in the Klondike[3] country. Last year they and several others had spent much toil and time on the Mazy May, and endured great hardships; the creek, in turn, was just beginning to show up its richness and to reward them for their heavy labor. But with the news of their discoveries, strange men began to come and go through the short days and long nights, and many unjust things they did to the men who had worked so long upon the creek.

Si Hartman had gone away on a moose hunt, to return and find new stakes driven and his claim jumped.[4] George Lukens and his brother had lost their claims in a like manner, having delayed too long on the way to Dawson to record them. In short, it was the old story, and quite a number of the earnest, industrious prospectors had suffered similar losses.

But Walt Masters's father had recorded his claim at the start, so Walt had nothing to fear now that his father had gone on a short trip up the White River prospecting for quartz. Walt was well able to stay by himself in the cabin, cook his three meals a day, and look after things. Not only did he look after his father's claim, but he had agreed to keep an eye on the adjoining one of Loren Hall, who had started for Dawson to record it.

Loren Hall was an old man, and he had no dogs, so he had to travel very slowly. had been gone some time, word came u river that he had broken through the ice a Rosebud Creek and frozen his feet so badly that he would not be able to travel for a couple of weeks. Then Walt Masters received the news that old Loren was nearly all right again, and about to move on afoot for Dawson as fast as a weakened man could.

Walt was worried, however; the claim was liable to be jumped at any moment because of this delay, and a fresh stampede had started in on the Mazy May. He did not like the looks of the newcomers, and one day, when five of them came by with crack dog teams and the lightest of camping outfits, he could see that they were prepared to make speed, and resolved to keep an eye on them. So he locked up the cabin and followed them, being at the same time careful to remain hidden.

He had not watched them long before he was sure that they were professional stampeders, bent on jumping all the claims in sight. Walt crept along the snow at the rim of the creek and saw them change many stakes, destroy old ones, and set up new ones.

In the afternoon, with Walt always trailing on their heels, they came back down the creek, unharnessed their dogs, and went into camp within two claims of his cabin. When he saw them make preparations to cook, he hurried home to get something to eat himself, and then hurried back. He crept so close that he could hear them talking quite plainly, and by pushing the underbrush aside he could catch occasional glimpses of them. They had finished eating and were smoking around the fire.

◆ **Build Vocabulary**

toil (toil) *n*.: Hard work

endured (en doord´) *v*.: Suffered through

prospectors (prä´ spekt´ erz) *n*.: People who make their living searching for valuable ores, such as gold

liable (lī´ ə bəl) *adj*.: Likely (to do something or have something happen to one)

---

2. **Yukon** (yōō´ kän´): River flowing through the Yukon Territory of northwest Canada.
3. **Klondike** (klän´ dīk´): Gold-mining region along a tributary of the Yukon River.
4. **claim jumped:** A claim is a piece of land staked out by a miner (stakes are markers driven into the ground to show where the borders of the claim are). A claim that is jumped is stolen by someone else.

After Dinner Music, 1988, Scott Kennedy, Courtesy of the Greenwich Workshop Inc.

"The creek is all right, boys," a large, black-bearded man, evidently the leader, said, "and I think the best thing we can do is to pull out tonight. The dogs can follow the trail; besides, it's going to be moonlight. What say you?"

"But it's going to be beastly cold," objected one of the party. "It's forty below zero now."

"An' sure, can't ye keep warm by jumpin' off the sleds an' runnin' after the dogs?" cried an Irishman. "An' who wouldn't? The creek's as rich as a United States mint! Faith, it's an ilegant chanst to be gettin' a run fer yer money! An' if ye don't run, it's mebbe you'll not get the money at all, at all."

"That's it," said the leader. "If we can get to Dawson and record, we're rich men; and there's no telling who's been sneaking along in our tracks, watching us, and perhaps now off to give the alarm. The thing for us to do is to rest the dogs a bit, and then hit the trail as hard as we can. What do you say?"

◆ **Literary Focus**
What conflict is developing between these men and Walt?

Evidently the men had agreed with their leader, for Walt Masters could hear nothing but the rattle of the tin dishes which were being washed. Peering out cautiously, he could see the leader studying a piece of paper. Walt knew what it was at a glance—a list of all the unrecorded claims on Mazy May. Any man

▲ **Critical Viewing** What do you think it would be like to live in this cabin with only these dogs for company? [Relate]

could get these lists by applying to the gold commissioner at Dawson.

"Thirty-two," the leader said, lifting his face to the men. "Thirty-two isn't recorded, and this is thirty-three. Come on; let's take a look at it. I saw somebody had been working on it when we came up this morning."

Three of the men went with him, leaving one to remain in camp. Walt crept carefully after them till they came to Loren Hall's shaft. One of the men went down and built a fire on the bottom to thaw out the frozen gravel, while the others built another fire on the dump and melted water in a couple of gold pans. This they poured into a piece of canvas stretched between two logs, used by Loren Hall in which to wash his gold.

In a short time a couple of buckets of dirt were sent up by the man in the shaft, and Walt could see the others grouped anxiously about their leader as he proceeded to wash it. When this was finished, they stared at the broad streak of black sand and yellow gold grains on the bottom of the pan, and one of them called excitedly for the man who had remained in camp to come. Loren Hall had struck it rich and his claim was not yet recorded. It was

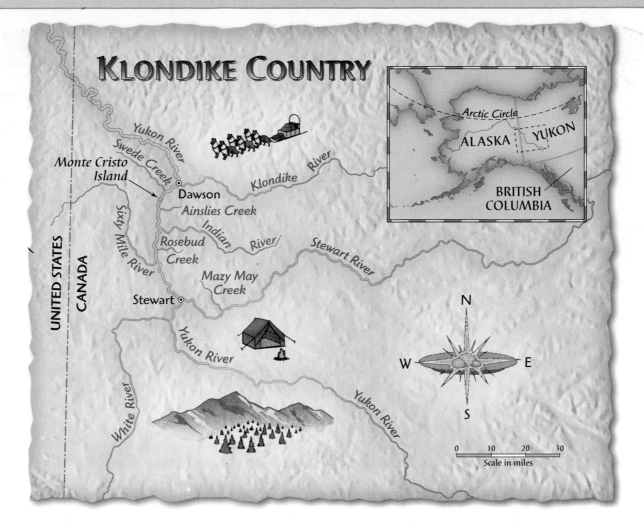

KLONDIKE COUNTRY

Yukon River

Swede Creek

Monte Cristo Island

Klondike River

Dawson

Ainslies Creek

Indian River

Rosebud Creek

Sixty Mile River

Mazy May Creek

Stewart River

UNITED STATES

CANADA

Stewart

Yukon River

White River

Yukon River

N
W   E
S

0   10   20   30
Scale in miles

Arctic Circle
ALASKA   YUKON
BRITISH COLUMBIA

▲ **Critical Viewing** Based on what you've read, why do you think so few towns are settled in this area? **[Connect]**

plain that they were going to jump it.

Walt lay in the snow, thinking rapidly. He was only a boy, but in the face of the threatened injustice to old lame Loren Hall he felt that he must do something. He waited and watched, with his mind made up, till he saw the men begin to square up new stakes. Then he crawled away till out of hearing, and broke into a run for the camp of the stampeders. Walt's father had taken their own dogs with him prospecting, and the boy knew how impossible it was for him to undertake the

> ◆ **Reading Strategy**
> What contrasting ideas are connected with the word *but*?

seventy miles to Dawson without the aid of dogs.

Gaining the camp, he picked out, with an experienced eye, the easiest running sled and started to harness up the stampeders' dogs. There were three teams of six each, and from these he chose ten of the best. Realizing how necessary it was to have a good head dog, he strove to discover a leader amongst them; but he had little time in which to do it, for he could hear the voices of the returning men. By the time the team was in shape and everything ready, the claim-jumpers came into sight in an open place not more than a hundred yards from the trail, which ran down the bed of the creek. They cried out to Walt, but instead of giving heed to them he grabbed up one of their fur sleeping robes, which lay loosely in the

▲ **Critical Viewing** Why is it difficult to tell if these men are honest stakeholders or if they are claim jumpers? [Generalize]

snow, and leaped upon the sled.

"Mush! Hi! Mush on!" he cried to the animals, snapping the keen-lashed whip among them.

The dogs sprang against the yoke straps, and the sled jerked under way so suddenly as to almost throw him off. Then it curved into the creek, <u>poising</u> perilously on the runner. He was almost breathless with suspense, when it finally righted with a bound and sprang ahead again. The creek bank was high and he could not see the men, although he could hear their cries and knew they were running to cut him off. He did not dare to think what would happen if they caught him; he just clung to the sled, his heart beating wildly, and watched the snow rim of the bank above him.

Suddenly, over this snow rim came the fly-ing body of the Irishman, who had leaped straight for the sled in a desperate attempt to capture it; but he was an instant too late. Striking on the very rear of it, he was thrown from his feet, backward, into the snow. Yet, with the quickness of a cat, he had clutched the end of the sled with one hand, turned over, and was dragging behind on his breast, swear-ing at the boy and threatening all kinds of terrible things if he did not stop the dogs; but Walt cracked him sharply across the knuckles with the butt of the dog whip till he let go.

It was eight miles from Walt's claim to the Yukon—eight very crooked miles, for the creek wound back and forth like a snake, "tying knots in itself," as George Lukens said. And because it was so crooked the dogs could not get up their best speed, while the sled ground heavily on its side against the curves, now to the right, now to the left.

Travelers who had come up and down the

Mazy May on foot, with packs on their backs, had declined to go round all the bends, and instead had made shortcuts across the narrow necks of creek bottom. Two of his pursuers had gone back to harness the remaining dogs, but the others took advantage of these shortcuts, running on foot, and before he knew it they had almost overtaken him.

"Halt!" they cried after him. "Stop, or we'll shoot!"

But Walt only yelled the harder at the dogs, and dashed around the bend with a couple of revolver bullets singing after him. At the next bend they had drawn up closer still, and the bullets struck uncomfortably near him but at this point the Mazy May straightened out and ran for half a mile as the crow flies. Here the dogs stretched out in their long wolf swing, and the stampeders, quickly winded, slowed down and waited for their own sled to come up.

Looking over his shoulder, Walt reasoned that they had not given up the chase for good, and that they would soon be after him again. So he wrapped the fur robe about him to shut out the stinging air, and lay flat on the empty sled, encouraging the dogs, as he well knew how.

At last, twisting abruptly between two river islands, he came upon the mighty Yukon sweeping grandly to the north. He could not see from bank to bank, and in the quick-falling twilight it loomed a great white sea of frozen stillness. There was not a sound, save the breathing of the dogs, and the churn of the steel-shod sled.

No snow had fallen for several weeks, and the traffic had packed the main river trail till it was hard and glassy as glare ice. Over this the sled flew along, and the dogs kept the trail fairly well, although Walt quickly discovered that he had made a mistake in choosing the

leader. As they were driven in single file, without reins, he had to guide them by his voice, and it was evident the head dog had never learned the meaning of "gee" and "haw."[5] He hugged the inside of the curves too closely, often forcing his comrades behind him into the soft snow, while several times he thus capsized[6] the sled.

There was no wind, but the speed at which he traveled created a bitter blast, and with the thermometer down to forty below, this bit through fur and flesh to the very bones. Aware that if he remained constantly upon the sled he would freeze to death, and knowing the practice of Arctic travelers, Walt shortened up one of the lashing thongs, and whenever he felt chilled, seized hold of it, jumped off, and ran behind till warmth was restored. Then he would climb on and rest till the process had to be repeated.

Looking back he could see the sled of his pursuers, drawn by eight dogs, rising and falling over the ice hummocks like a boat in a seaway. The Irishman and the black-bearded leader were with it, taking turns in running and riding.

Night fell, and in the blackness of the first hour or so Walt toiled desperately with his dogs. On account of the poor lead dog, they were continually floundering off the beaten track into the soft snow, and the sled was as often riding on its side or top as it was in the proper way. This work and strain tried his strength sorely. Had he not been in such haste he could have avoided much of it, but he feared the stampeders would creep up in the darkness and overtake him. However, he

◆ **Reading Strategy**
What do the signal words "On account of" tell you about the link between the "poor lead dog" and the "floundering" of the sled?

◆ **Build Vocabulary**
poising (poiz´ iŋ) *adj.*: Balancing
declined (di klīnd´) *v.*: Refused

---

5. **"gee" and "haw"** (jē) and (hô): Commands used to tell an animal to turn to the right or the left.
6. **capsized** (kap´ sīzd´) *v.*: Overturned.

could hear them yelling to their dogs, and knew from the sounds they were coming up very slowly.

When the moon rose he was off Sixty Mile, and Dawson was only fifty miles away. He was almost exhausted, and breathed a sigh of relief as he climbed on the sled again. Looking back, he saw his enemies had crawled up within four hundred yards. At this space they remained, a black speck of motion on the white river breast. Strive as they would, they could not shorten this distance, and strive as he would, he could not increase it.

Walt had now discovered the proper lead dog, and he knew he could easily run away from them if he could only change the bad leader for the good one. But this was impossible, for a moment's delay, at the speed they were running, would bring the men behind upon him.

When he was off the mouth of Rosebud Creek, just as he was topping a rise, the report of a gun and the ping of a bullet on the ice beside him told him that they were this time shooting at him with a rifle. And from then on, as he cleared the <u>summit</u> of each ice jam, he stretched flat on the leaping sled till the rifle shot from the rear warned him that he was safe till the next ice jam was reached.

Now it is very hard to lie on a moving sled, jumping and plunging and yawing[7] like a boat before the wind, and to shoot through the deceiving moonlight at an object four hundred yards away on another moving sled performing equally wild antics. So it is not to be wondered at that the black-bearded leader did not hit him.

After several hours of this, during which, perhaps, a score of bullets had struck about him, their ammunition began to give out and their fire slackened. They took greater care, and shot at him at the most favorable opportunities. He was also leaving them behind, the distance slowly increasing to six hundred yards.

Lifting clear on the crest of a great jam off Indian River, Walt Masters met with his first accident. A bullet sang past his ears, and struck the bad lead dog.

The poor brute plunged in a heap, with the rest of the team on top of him.

Like a flash Walt was by the leader. Cutting the traces with his hunting knife, he dragged the dying animal to one side and straightened out the team.

He glanced back. The other sled was coming up like an express train. With half the dogs still over their traces, he cried "Mush on!" and leaped upon the sled just as the pursuers dashed abreast[8] of him.

The Irishman was preparing to spring for him—they were so sure they had him that they did not shoot—when Walt turned fiercely upon them with his whip.

He struck at their faces, and men must save their faces with their hands. So there was no shooting just then. Before they could recover from the hot rain of blows, Walt reached out from his sled, catching their wheel dog by the forelegs in midspring, and throwing him heavily. This snarled the team, capsizing the sled and tangling his enemies up beautifully.

Away Walt flew, the runners of his sled fairly screaming as they bounded over the frozen surface. And what had seemed an accident proved to be a blessing in disguise. The proper lead dog was now to the fore, and he stretched low and whined with joy as he jerked his comrades along.

By the time he reached Ainslie's Creek, seventeen miles from Dawson, Walt had left his pursuers, a tiny speck, far behind. At Monte

---

7. **yawing** (yô′ iŋ) *adj.*: Swinging from side to side.

◆ Build Vocabulary
summit (sum′ it) *n.*: Highest part

---

8. **abreast** (ə brest′) *adv.*: Alongside.

◆ **Literary Focus**
Who do you think will win this conflict? Why?

Cristo Island he could no longer see them. And at Swede Creek, just as daylight was silvering the pines, he ran plump into the camp of old Loren Hall.

Almost as quick as it takes to tell it, Loren had his sleeping furs rolled up, and had joined Walt on the sled. They permitted the dogs to travel more slowly, as there was no sign of the chase in the rear, and just as they pulled up at the gold commissioner's office in Dawson, Walt, who had kept his eyes open to the last, fell asleep.

And because of what Walt Masters did on this night, the men of the Yukon have become proud of him, and speak of him now as the King of Mazy May.

Beyond Literature

Social Studies Connection

The Klondike Gold Rush On August 17, 1896, George Carmack, his wife Kate, and her relatives found gold in Bonanza Creek in the Klondike region. When news of the find reached the outside world, the rush was on. Thousands of men and women poured into the Klondike region, but few found the fortune they were seeking.

Cross-Curricular Activity:

Gold Rush Map Several areas in the United States have experienced gold rushes. While many of these areas died quickly, others, with their increased population, became permanent cities and even states. On a map of the United States, show cities and states that resulted from gold rushes.

Guide for Responding

◆ LITERATURE AND YOUR LIFE

Reader's Response Would you enjoy Walt's way of life? Why or why not?

Thematic Focus In what ways do the events in the story cause a teenager to act like an adult?

Award Dinner [Group Activity] With a group, plan an award dinner honoring Walt. Jot down ideas for gifts, decorations, menu, speeches, and entertainment.

☑ Check Your Comprehension

1. Briefly describe Walt Masters.
2. What must Walt do in the men's absence?
3. What are the stampeders planning to do?
4. How does Walt get away from the stampeders and stay ahead of them?
5. What do Walt and Loren Hall do to defeat the stampeders' plan?

◆ Critical Thinking

INTERPRET

1. In what ways is Walt like and unlike other children? **[Compare and Contrast]**
2. List three incidents in which Walt displays quick thinking. **[Classify]**
3. What three qualities in Walt's character help him defeat the stampeders? **[Analyze]**
4. Why is Walt's new title, "King of Mazy May," appropriate? **[Draw Conclusions]**

EVALUATE

5. The story suggests that "manliness" is based on strength and bravery. Explain whether you agree or disagree. **[Make a Judgment]**

EXTEND

6. What do you learn in this story about the geography and climate of the Klondike region? **[Social Studies Link]**

Guide for Responding (continued)

◆ Reading Strategy

RECOGNIZE SIGNAL WORDS

In this story, when the lead dog doesn't know the signals, the sled capsizes. However, your reading didn't capsize because you used the **signal words,** such as *but* and *so,* to know what was coming.

1. Reread the sentence beginning "Suddenly, over this snow . . ." on page 64. Explain what *but* signals in this sentence.
2. Reread the paragraph beginning "Looking over his shoulder . . ." on page 65. How do the actions that come after *So* result from the idea that comes before it?

◆ Build Vocabulary

USING THE SUFFIX *-or*

The suffix *-or* changes an action into "the person or thing that does an action." For example, a person who *edits* writing is an editor (*edit* + *-or* = *editor*). Use the suffix *-or* to name the person who does each of these jobs:

1. sails   2. advises   3. prospects   4. supervises

SPELLING STRATEGY

To spell the *oy* sound in the middle of single-syllable words, use the letters *oi*. Use *oy* at the end of words.

Middle: t*oi*l   **End:** ann*oy*

On your paper, correct only the misspelled words:

1. foyl   2. boil   3. spoyl   4. boi   5. broil

USING THE WORD BANK

Answer each question. Explain your answer.

1. Does gold mining require *toil*?
2. Was Walt a boy who had *endured* hardships?
3. Were the claim jumpers true *prospectors*?
4. Is it scary when your sled is *poising* on its runner?
5. Were Klondike claims *liable* to be jumped?
6. Had Walt *declined* to battle the claim jumpers?
7. Can you go higher on a mountain than its *summit*?

◆ Literary Focus

CONFLICT BETWEEN CHARACTERS

The **conflict between characters** in this story is a struggle between a young man and a gang of men. The boy and the men clash because their goals are directly opposite.

1. Explain how the different aims of the young man and the gang cause them to clash.
2. Using three examples, show how London keeps you guessing about who will win the conflict.
3. When do you first know who will win the conflict? Explain.

◆ Build Grammar Skills

PRONOUNS AND ANTECEDENTS

A **pronoun** is a word that takes the place of a noun or nouns appearing previously. The noun a pronoun replaces is called its **antecedent.**

In this sentence from the story, the pronoun *he* replaces *Walt*, which is its antecedent:

Walt has walked all the fourteen years of his life in suntanned, moose-hide moccasins, and *he* can go to the Indian camps. . . .

Practice On your paper, identify the pronoun and its antecedent in each sentence:

1. Although Walt was not big, he was manly.
2. Walt's father was away, but he would be back soon.
3. The camp was new, but it was comfortable.
4. After the dogs started, they ran for hours.
5. Walt's mother had died, but Walt and his father remembered her with love.

Writing Application Fill in each blank with a pronoun that can replace the antecedent:

1. Loren Hall was old, but _____?____ moved quickly.
2. When the moon rose, Walt could see _____?____ above Dawson.
3. The dogs followed the leader as _____?____ had been trained to do.

Build Your Portfolio

 Idea Bank

Writing

1. **Warning Flier** Write a flier for new prospectors warning them about the dangers of the Klondike. **[Social Studies Link]**

2. **Police Report** As a Dawson detective, write a report explaining what happened on the Mazy May Creek. Indicate what crimes were committed, who committed them, and what you'll do to catch the criminals. **[Career Link]**

3. **Proposal** In this story, the method of registering mining claims creates conflict. Write a letter to the *Klondike News* proposing a better method. Identify the problem, and suggest a solution. **[Career Link]**

Speaking and Listening

4. **Acceptance Speech** As Walt, give a speech accepting an award for courage from Dawson City. Thank the citizens, and tell them why you acted as you did. **[Performing Arts Link]**

5. **Interview** With a partner, role-play an interview between Walt and a reporter for the *Klondike News*. To get facts for a story, the reporter is asking Walt questions about his adventure. **[Career Link; Social Studies Link]**

Projects

6. **Prospecting Fair [Group Activity]** With a group, put on a fair to demonstrate old-fashioned gold mining. Group members can show how to pan for gold, point out differences between gold and fool's gold, and explain a diagram of a gold mine. **[Science Link]**

7. **Mazy May Map** Using details from the story, draw a map of the Mazy May area, including Dawson, the prospectors' claims, and the route of the sled chase. **[Art Link; Social Studies Link]**

 Writing Mini-Lesson

Narrative of a Goal Achieved

You may not have foiled stampeders, but you've had adventures that would interest readers. Write a narrative that describes how you achieved a goal or learned something important. Explain clearly how one event led to another.

Writing Skills Focus: Use Transitions to Show Causes

By using **transitions that show causes**—words signaling that one event resulted from another—you'll help readers follow your narrative. Examples of such transitions are *because, on account of, therefore*, and *so*. In this example, the word *so* indicates that Walt's actions resulted from his decision to watch the men:

Model From the Story

. . . he . . . resolved to keep an eye on them. So he locked up the cabin and followed them. . . .

Prewriting Choose a brief series of events with a clear beginning, middle, and end. Replay these events in your mind, making sure of their order and jotting down words that will help you describe them.

Drafting Record events in the right order, and vividly describe sounds and sights. Explain why these events mattered to you.

> ◆ **Grammar Application**
>
> Be sure that readers know the antecedent for every pronoun you use.

Revising Have classmates comment on any confusing parts in your narrative. To make clear how one event brought about another, add transitions to show causes.

Guide for Reading

Meet the Authors:

David McCord (1897–1997)

David McCord wrote both poems and nonfiction. He believed that poetry is rhythm, "just as the planet Earth is rhythm." "Books Fall Open" uses both rhythm and wordplay.

Robert Louis Stevenson (1850–1894)

Robert Louis Stevenson was a puzzle. He grew up a frail boy in Scotland and was troubled by poor health throughout his life. However, this sickly author wrote stirring tales of adventure, like *Treasure Island*.

Tall and thin, with a storklike walk, Stevenson looked as if he could be toppled by a gust of wind. Yet he was secretly tough and traveled all over the world.

Perhaps the puzzle of his own nature prompted him to write *The Strange Case of Dr. Jekyll and Mr. Hyde*. This thriller, whose hero has a divided personality, inspired several movies and a Broadway musical.

THE STORY BEHIND THE POEM

"O to Be Up and Doing" was a call to action that Stevenson meant partly for himself. As a boy, he wasn't up and doing at all. He wrote, "I . . . used to lie on my face on the nursery floor, chalking or painting . . . or sit up in bed . . . to play with bricks. . . ."

Charlotte Zolotow (1915–   )

Charlotte Zolotow decided to become a writer when her fourth-grade teacher praised her work. "Change" reflects her interest in how "the sounds of the words communicate the meanings of the words."

◆ LITERATURE AND YOUR LIFE

CONNECT YOUR EXPERIENCE

Maybe you've climbed mountains, like the hiker on the facing page. Perhaps you've had adventures closer to home—meeting new people or starting to play on a school team. Far or near, an adventure is anything that shakes you out of your usual ways of thinking and doing. These poems describe different kinds of adventures—reading, growing, laughing, and loving.

THEMATIC FOCUS: Onward and Upward

In what way do the adventures described in these poems involve change and movement?

◆ Background for Understanding

SCIENCE

Dendrites are tiny branches in your nervous system that reach out to gather information. Each time you try a new activity or learn a new skill, you give your dendrites a workout and make them "grow." The advice of the poets in this group is to enjoy a variety of new experiences. Follow their advice to build up your "learning muscles."

◆ Build Vocabulary

PREFIXES: *un-*

The prefix *un-* reverses the meaning of words. The poet Stevenson writes that his heart is "un-dissuaded." *Un*, which means "not," reverses the meaning of *dissuaded* ("discouraged"). *Undissuaded* means "*not* discouraged."

WORD BANK

Which of these words from the poems describes a vivid color?

delver
venture
undissuaded
summons
crimson

◆ Literary Focus

WORD CHOICE IN POETRY

A wrong word in a poem can jangle the ear like a sour note in music. That's why poets are so careful in their **word choice,** selecting words with exactly the right sound and meaning.

Notice the word choice in all these poems. For example, "Books Fall Open" begins, "Books fall open, / you fall in . . ." The word *fall* captures perfectly the way in which you tumble into a good book and lose yourself in its words.

◆ Reading Strategy

READ ACCORDING TO PUNCTUATION

Poetry may seem like strange new territory, but you can find your way around with some familiar landmarks. **Punctuation marks** are commas, periods, question marks, dashes, and other marks writers use to make their meaning clear. Respond to the punctuation in a poem in the same way you would respond to the punctuation in a story. At the same time, don't pause just because a line comes to an end. Keep reading, and let the punctuation guide you.

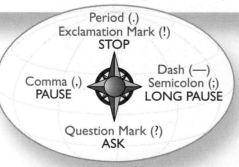

Period (.)
Exclamation Mark (!)
STOP

Comma (,)
PAUSE

Dash (—)
Semicolon (;)
LONG PAUSE

Question Mark (?)
ASK

PUNCTUATION GUIDE

Books Fall Open

David McCord

Books fall open,
you fall in,
delighted where
you've never been;
5   hear voices not once
heard before,
reach world on world
through door on door;
find unexpected
10 keys to things
locked up beyond
imaginings.
What *might* you be,
perhaps *become*,
15 because one book
is somewhere? Some
wise <u>delver</u> into
wisdom, wit,
and wherewithal
20 has written it.

True books will <u>venture</u>,
dare you out,
whisper secrets,
maybe shout
25 across the gloom
to you in need,
who hanker for
a book to read.

Land of Enchantment by Norman Rockwell on the cover of The Saturday Evening Post, The Curtis Publishing Company

◆ Build Vocabulary

delver (del´ vər): *n.*: Digger; searcher

venture (ven´ chər) *v.*: Take a chance; express a thought at the risk of criticism

O to Be Up and Doing

Robert Louis Stevenson

O to be up and doing,
Unfearing and unashamed to go
In all the uproar and the press
About my human business!
5   My <u>undissuaded</u> heart I hear
Whisper courage in my ear.
With voiceless calls, the ancient earth
<u>Summons</u> me to a daily birth,
Thou, O my love, ye, O my friends—
10   The gist[1] of life, the end of ends—
To laugh, to love, to live, to die
Ye call me by the ear and eye!

---

1. **gist** (jist) *n.*: Main point.

◆ Build Vocabulary

undissuaded (un dis swād´əd) *adj.*: Not discouraged; not persuaded to give up

summons (sum´ ənz) *v.*: Calls; orders to come

Guide for Responding

◆ LITERATURE AND YOUR LIFE

Reader's Response Do you think it's important to be "up and doing"? Why or why not?

Thematic Focus Do both of these poems express positive feelings about change and growth? Why or why not?

☑ Check Your Comprehension

1. According to lines 1–12 of "Books Fall Open," what are three experiences you might have when you read?
2. According to lines 21–28 of "Books Fall Open," what are three things books do to reach you?
3. At the end of "O to Be Up and Doing," what three things does the poet feel called to do?

◆ Critical Thinking

INTERPRET

1. In "Books Fall Open," the poet says you can "reach world on world" by reading. What does he mean? **[Interpret]**
2. Describe the kind of life the speaker in "O to Be Up and Doing" thinks is valuable. **[Draw Conclusions]**

EVALUATE

3. The first two lines of "Books Fall Open" suggest that finding good books is accidental. Do you think that is true? Why or why not? **[Make a Judgment]**

APPLY

4. Do you think that Stevenson would regard reading as a form of "doing"? Explain. **[Apply]**

Change

Charlotte Zolotow

The summer
still hangs
heavy and sweet
with sunlight
5   as it did last year.

The autumn
still comes
showering gold and <u>crimson</u>
as it did last year.

10   The winter
still stings
clean and cold and white
as it did last year.

The spring
15   still comes
like a whisper in the dark night.

It is only I
who have changed.

◆ **Build Vocabulary**

crimson (krim′ zən) *n.*: Deep red

Guide for Responding

◆ LITERATURE AND YOUR LIFE

Reader's Response How do you think you will change in the next few months?

Thematic Focus How has the speaker in this poem moved onward and upward?

Journal Writing Explain three ways you have changed in the past year.

☑ Check Your Comprehension

1. In what way is summer the same as it was last year?
2. In what way is winter the same as it was last year?
3. In what way is the speaker different from the seasons?

◆ Critical Thinking

INTERPRET

1. Why do you think the sentence in lines 17–18 of the poem is different in structure from the others in the poem? **[Analyze]**
2. What clues does the poem give about how the speaker feels about change? **[Draw Conclusions]**

EVALUATE

3. Is it good for people to change? Why or why not? **[Make a Judgment]**

COMPARE LITERARY WORKS

4. Identify two similarities and one difference among the speakers in "Books," "Up and Doing," and "Change." **[Compare and Contrast]**

Guide for Responding (continued)

◆ Reading Strategy

READ ACCORDING TO PUNCTUATION

Following **punctuation**—commas, periods, dashes, and other marks—helps you know when to pause or stop and when to keep reading.

1. Identify three places in "Books" where you paused. What punctuation mark indicated each pause?
2. Identify one place where you came to a full stop in "O to Be Up and Doing." Explain why.
3. Why didn't you pause or stop at the end of every line as you read "Change"?

◆ Build Vocabulary

USING THE PREFIX un-

Add the prefix un-, meaning "not," to three descriptive words in the following paragraph. Then, explain how the meaning of the paragraph changes.

   The student was able to get out of bed in the morning. Hearing the buzz of the alarm, she was prepared to be up and working. This attitude made people exclaim, "She's so helpful!"

SPELLING STRATEGY

When spelling most two-syllable words that contain a consonant sound in the middle, and the vowel before the consonant has a short sound, double the consonant:

   su**mm**ons   (short u sound followed by m sound)
   ra**bb**it   (short a sound followed by b sound)

Correct the words that are misspelled. Then, explain the correct spellings of every word listed.

1. ripple   2. batle   3. nuget   4. stable

USING THE WORD BANK

Match each numbered word with the lettered word or phrase that is closest to it in meaning.

1. delver	a. calls
2. undissuaded	b. dare
3. crimson	c. not discouraged
4. summons	d. searcher
5. venture	e. red

◆ Literary Focus

WORD CHOICE

Because poets are careful about **word choice,** their well-selected words create vivid pictures. In "Change," for example, Zolotow says that "autumn / still comes / showering gold and crimson." *Showering* is more active than *falling* and suggests that the many leaves are like a shower of rain.

1. Suppose McCord asked you whether the first word of line 3 of "Books Fall Open" should be *satisfied or delighted.* What would you answer? Why?
2. Why is *birth* a more dramatic word than *waking* would be in line 8 of "O to Be Up and Doing"?
3. In line 11 of "Change," why is *stings* a better word than *pinches* to describe the feeling of winter air?

◆ Build Grammar Skills

INTERROGATIVE PRONOUNS

Interrogative pronouns are words that introduce questions. The main interrogative pronouns are *who* (or *whose* or *whom*), *which*, and *what*.

Practice On your paper, identify the interrogative pronoun in each of these sentences:

1. Who posted a sign on a book saying, "Beware of falling in"?
2. What will books do to get your attention?
3. Which is the most colorful season in "Change"?
4. To what does the Earth summon the poet in "O to Be Up and Doing"?
5. To whom does the poet give credit in "O to Be Up and Doing"?

Writing Application Write a question in response to each statement. Introduce your question with an interrogative pronoun.

Example: Here are the books. Which is yours?

1. These are all the seasons.
2. The poet's heart whispers in his ear.
3. This is the book I enjoyed.

Build Your Portfolio

 ## Idea Bank

Writing

1. **Reader's Response** Choose a sentence that you especially like in one of these poems. Tell why you like it. Then, write a sentence modeled on the sentence you chose.

2. **Yearbook Sketch** For the school yearbook, describe a classmate who is adventurous and open to change. Choose your words carefully to show what you admire about this person.

3. **Song** Write song lyrics that celebrate the adventure of being "up and doing." Include a refrain—a repeated phrase or sentence—that summarizes your message. **[Music Link]**

Speaking and Listening

4. **Book Talk** Tell your classmates about a book that changed your life for the better. Explain why the book has meant so much to you.

5. **Poetry Reading** Read one of these poems aloud to the class. Don't automatically stop at the end of each line. Use punctuation to guide you, pausing for commas and stopping for end marks like periods. **[Performing Arts Link]**

Projects

6. **Reading Survey [Group Activity]** With a group, conduct a survey on favorite types of reading. Divide up the following tasks: writing questions, having schoolmates answer the questions, studying the answers, and creating a graph of the results. **[Social Studies Link; Math Link]**

7. **Biology Diagrams** Learning and growth cause changes in the nervous system. Use encyclopedia articles and science textbooks to diagram nerve cells. Show how these cells "talk" to each other. **[Science Link; Art Link]**

 ## Writing Mini-Lesson

Call to Action

Like a trumpet playing a cavalry charge, "O to Be Up and Doing" calls you to a life of participation. Write a brief essay persuading readers to take action on an issue that's important to you.

Writing Skills Focus: State Main Ideas Clearly

When writing persuasively, **state your main idea clearly,** so that readers know what you want them to do. Stevenson hammers his message home by stating it in the first line of his poem and elaborating on it in the next few lines:

Model From the Poem
O to be up and doing,
Unfearing and unashamed to go
In all the uproar and the press
About my human business!

Prewriting Choose a cause that really means something to you. Jot down your main idea—what you want readers to do—so you can express it clearly in your essay.

Drafting State your main idea early and dramatically. Then, support your call to action with examples, stories, reasons, or statistics.

> ◆ **Grammar Application**
>
> Use an interrogative pronoun in a question that gets readers thinking; for example, "*What* would it be like to live a television-free life?"

Revising Ask several classmates to read your call to action and explain it in their own words. If they have trouble, restate your message clearly at the beginning and end of your essay.

Guide for Reading

Meet the Authors:

Francisco Jiménez (1943–   )

Born in Mexico, Francisco Jiménez (hē mā´ nez) came with his family to the United States when he was four. The Jiménez family settled in California, becoming migrant workers.

In high school, Jiménez supported himself by working as a janitor. His excellent grades won him three college scholarships. He went on to become an outstanding teacher and college official. He has also won awards as a writer.

THE STORY BEHIND THE STORY

Like the young man in the story, Jiménez worked as a traveling farm worker with his dad and a brother named Roberto. Jiménez couldn't go to school before the harvest ended.

Russell Baker (1925–   )

Russell Baker grew up in Virginia, New Jersey, and Maryland. When he was in the seventh grade, he decided to become a writer. He thought that "making up stories must surely be almost as much fun as reading them."

An Award-Winning Writer As it turned out, Baker became a reporter rather than a novelist. He won a Pulitzer Prize for his newspaper column in *The New York Times*. In this selection from his book *The Good Times,* he describes his very first boss in the news business.

◆ LITERATURE AND YOUR LIFE

CONNECT YOUR EXPERIENCE

Moving to a new school or town means changing routines, changing addresses—maybe even changing friends. The main character in "The Circuit" moves with each changing season. He experiences the loneliness and sadness that are expressed on the face of the boy in the picture on the next page.

THEMATIC FOCUS: Onward and Upward

Ask yourself what this story and essay teach about the difference between moving on and growing up.

◆ Background for Understanding

SOCIAL STUDIES

"The Circuit" tells the story of a young boy and a family of migrant farm workers. Most migrant workers in the United States move frequently to follow the seasonal demands of harvesting. The entire family usually travels together, with children helping the adults work on the farms. This may mean starting school late in the fall (after the harvest season ends) and leaving early in the spring to travel to a new harvest.

◆ Build Vocabulary

COMPOUND NOUNS

In "Hard as Nails," Russell Baker tells about delivering newspapers. The word *newspaper* is a compound noun, made up of two other words: *news + paper.* Look for other compound nouns as you read.

WORD BANK

Which of these words describes doing something without thinking about it?

drone
instinctively
savoring
embedded
exhaust
sublime
drawbacks
immense

The Circuit
◆ Hard as Nails ◆

◆ Literary Focus

THEME

The **theme,** or central idea, of a story is a thought about life that the story's events suggest. Sometimes, this idea is directly stated. Other times, you must figure it out for yourself.

The themes of "The Circuit" and "Hard as Nails" are not directly stated. However, as with many stories, the titles give a clue to the theme. In reading, think about how each story's title and events point to its theme.

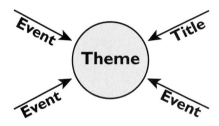

◆ Reading Strategy

BREAK DOWN LONG SENTENCES

When you read a long, difficult sentence, break it down into parts. First, identify the subject—what the sentence is about. Then, ask what the rest of the sentence tells you about the subject. Examine this sentence from "Hard as Nails":

> Watching the two of them in conversation, with Deems glancing at me now and then, I kept my shoulders drawn back. . . .

In spite of a lot of introductory words, the sentence is about "I," the teller of the story. The rest of the sentence tells you how he behaved in the circumstances.

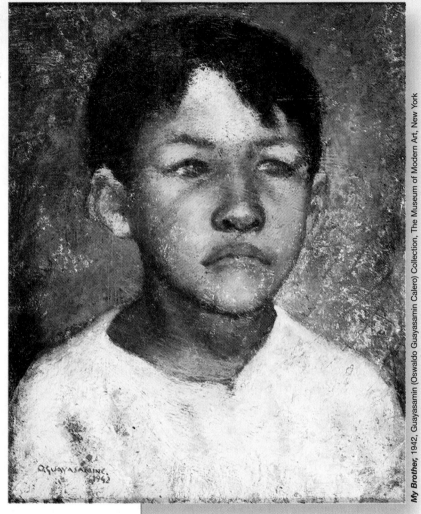

My Brother, 1942, Guayasamín (Oswaldo Guayasamín Calero) Collection, The Museum of Modern Art, New York

The Circuit

Francisco Jiménez

It was that time of year again. Ito, the strawberry sharecropper,[1] did not smile. It was natural. The peak of the strawberry season was over and the last few days the workers, most of them *braceros*,[2] were not picking as many boxes as they had during the months of June and July.

As the last days of August disappeared, so did the number of *braceros*. Sunday, only one—the best picker—came to work. I liked him. Sometimes we talked during our half-hour lunch break. That is how I found out he was from Jalisco, the same state in Mexico my family was from. That Sunday was the last time I saw him.

When the sun had tired and sunk behind the mountains, Ito signaled us that it was time to go home. "*Ya esora*,"[3] he yelled in his broken Spanish. Those were the words I waited for twelve hours a day, every day, seven days a week, week after week. And the thought of not hearing them again saddened me.

As we drove home Papá did not say a word. With both hands on the wheel, he stared at the dirt road. My older brother, Roberto, was also silent. He leaned his head back and closed his eyes. Once in a while he cleared from his throat the dust that blew in from outside.

Yes, it was that time of year. When I opened the front door to the shack, I stopped. Everything we owned was neatly packed in cardboard boxes. Suddenly I felt even more the weight of hours, days, weeks, and months of

---

1. **sharecropper** (sher′ kräp′ ər) *n*.: One who works for a share of a crop; tenant farmer.
2. *braceros* (brä ser′ os) *n*.: Migrant Mexican farm laborers who harvest crops.

3. *Ya esora* (yä es ô rä): Spanish for "It's time" (*Ya es hora*).

work. I sat down on a box. The thought of having to move to Fresno[4] and knowing what was in store for me there brought tears to my eyes.

That night I could not sleep. I lay in bed thinking about how much I hated this move.

A little before five o'clock in the morning, Papá woke everyone up. A few minutes later, the yelling and screaming of my little brothers and sisters, for whom the move was a great adventure, broke the silence of dawn. Shortly, the barking of the dogs accompanied them.

While we packed the breakfast dishes, Papá went outside to start the "Carcanchita."[5] That was the name Papá gave his old '38 black Plymouth. He bought it in a used-car lot in Santa Rosa in the winter of 1949. Papá was very proud of his little jalopy. He had a right to be

---

4. **Fresno** (frez' nō) *n.*: City in central California.
5. **Carcanchita** (kär kän chē´ tä): Affectionate name for the car.

proud of it. He spent a lot of time looking at other cars before buying this one. When he finally chose the "Carcanchita," he checked it thoroughly before driving it out of the car lot. He examined every inch of the car. He listened to the motor, tilting his head from side to side like a parrot, trying to detect any noises that spelled car trouble. After being satisfied with the looks and sounds of the car, Papá then insisted on knowing who the original owner was. He never did find out from the car salesman, but he bought the car anyway. Papá figured the original owner must have been an important man because behind the rear seat of the car he found a blue necktie.

Papá parked the car out in front and left the

motor running. "*Listo*,"[6] he yelled. Without saying a word, Roberto and I began to carry the boxes out to the car. Roberto carried the two big boxes and I carried the two smaller ones. Papá then threw the mattress on top of the car roof and tied it with ropes to the front and rear bumpers.

Everything was packed except Mamá's pot. It was an old large galvanized[7] pot she had picked up at an army surplus store in Santa María the year I was born. The pot had many dents and nicks, and the more dents and nicks it acquired the more Mamá liked it. "*Mi olla*,"[8] she used to say proudly.

I held the front door open as Mamá carefully carried out her pot by both handles, making sure not to spill the cooked beans. When she got to the car, Papá reached out to help her with it. Roberto opened the rear car door and Papá gently placed it on the floor behind the front seat. All of us then climbed in. Papá sighed, wiped the sweat off his forehead with his sleeve, and said wearily: "*Es todo*."[9]

As we drove away, I felt a lump in my throat. I turned around and looked at our little shack for the last time.

At sunset we drove into a labor camp near Fresno. Since Papá did not speak English, Mamá asked the camp foreman if he needed any more workers. "We don't need no more," said the foreman, scratching his head. "Check with Sullivan down the road. Can't miss him. He lives in a big white house with a fence around it."

When we got there, Mamá walked up to the house. She went through a white gate, past a row of rose bushes, up the stairs to the front door. She rang the doorbell. The porch light went on and a tall husky man came out. They exchanged a few words. After the man went in, Mamá clasped her hands and hurried back to the car. "We have work! Mr. Sullivan said we can stay there the whole season," she said, gasping and pointing to an old garage near the stables.

The garage was worn out by the years. It had no windows. The walls, eaten by termites, strained to support the roof full of holes. The dirt floor, populated by earthworms, looked like a gray road map.

That night, by the light of a kerosene lamp, we unpacked and cleaned our new home. Roberto swept away the loose dirt, leaving the hard ground. Papá plugged the holes in the walls with old newspapers and tin can tops. Mamá fed my little brothers and sisters. Papá and Roberto then brought in the mattress and placed it on the far corner of the garage. "Mamá, you and the little ones sleep on the mattress. Roberto, Panchito, and I will sleep outside under the trees," Papá said.

Early next morning Mr. Sullivan showed us where his crop was, and after breakfast, Papá, Roberto, and I headed for the vineyard to pick.

Around nine o'clock the temperature had risen to almost one hundred degrees. I was completely soaked in sweat and my mouth felt as if I had been chewing on a handkerchief. I walked over to the end of the row, picked up the jug of water we had brought, and began drinking. "Don't drink too much; you'll get sick," Roberto shouted. No sooner had he said that than I felt sick to my stomach. I dropped to my knees and let the jug roll off my hands. I remained motionless with my eyes glued on the hot sandy ground. All I could hear was the drone of insects. Slowly I began to recover. I poured water over my face and neck and

---

6. *Listo* (lēs to): Spanish for "Ready."
7. galvanized (gal′ və nīzd′) *adj.*: Coated with zinc to prevent rusting.
8. *Mi olla* (mē ō′ yä): Spanish for "My pot."
9. *Es todo* (es tō′ thō): Spanish for "That's everything."

watched the dirty water run down my arms to the ground.

I still felt a little dizzy when we took a break to eat lunch. It was past two o'clock and we sat underneath a large walnut tree that was on the side of the road. While we ate, Papá jotted down the number of boxes we had picked. Roberto drew designs on the ground with a stick. Suddenly I noticed Papá's face turn pale as he looked down the road. "Here comes the school bus," he whispered loudly in alarm. <u>Instinctively</u>, Roberto and I ran and hid in the vineyards. We did not want to get in trouble for not going to school. The neatly dressed boys about my age got off. They carried books under their arms. After they crossed the street, the bus drove away. Roberto and I came out from hiding and joined Papá. "*Tienen que tener cuidado,*"[10] he warned us.

After lunch we went back to work. The sun kept beating down. The buzzing insects, the wet sweat, and the hot dry dust made the afternoon seem to last forever. Finally the mountains around the valley reached out and swallowed the sun. Within an hour it was too dark to continue picking. The vines blanketed the grapes, making it difficult to see the bunches. "*Vámonos,*"[11] said Papá, signaling to us that it was time to quit work. Papá then took out a pencil and began to figure out how much we had earned our first day. He wrote down numbers, crossed some out, wrote down some more. "*Quince,*"[12] he murmured.

When we arrived home, we took a cold shower underneath a waterhose. We then sat down to eat dinner around some wooden crates that served as a table. Mamá had cooked a special meal for us. We had rice and tortillas with "*carne con chile,*"[13] my favorite dish.

The next morning I could hardly move. My body ached all over. I felt little control over my arms and legs. This feeling went on every morning for days until my muscles finally got used to the work.

It was Monday, the first week of November. The grape season was over and I could now go to school. I woke up early that morning and lay in bed, looking at the stars and <u>savoring</u> the thought of not going to work and of starting sixth grade for the first time that year. Since I could not sleep, I decided to get up and join Papá and Roberto at breakfast. I sat at the table across from Roberto, but I kept my head down. I did not want to look up and face him. I knew he was sad. He was not going to school today. He was not going tomorrow, or next week, or next month. He would not go until the cotton season was over, and that was sometime in February. I rubbed my hands together and watched the dry, acid stained skin fall to the floor in little rolls.

When Papá and Roberto left for work, I felt relief. I walked to the top of a small grade next to the shack and watched the "Carcanchita" disappear in the distance in a cloud of dust.

Two hours later, around eight o'clock, I stood by the side of the road waiting for school bus number twenty. When it arrived I climbed in. Everyone was busy either talking or yelling. I sat in an empty seat in the back.

When the bus stopped in front of the school, I felt very nervous. I looked out the bus window and saw boys and girls carrying books under their arms. I put my hands in my pant pockets and walked to the principal's office. When I entered I heard a woman's voice say: "May I

---

10. ***Tienen que tener cuidado*** (tē en´ en kā ten er´ kwē thä´ thō): Spanish for "You have to be careful."
11. ***Vamonos*** (vä´ mō nōs): Spanish for "Let's go."
12. ***Quince*** (kēn´ sā): Spanish for "fifteen."
13. **"*carne con chile*"** (kär´ nē kən chil´ ē): Dish of ground meat, hot peppers, beans, and tomatoes.

◆ Build Vocabulary

drone (drōn) *n.*: Continuous humming sound

instinctively (in stiŋk´ tiv lē) *adv.*: Done by instinct, without thinking

savoring (sā´ vər iŋ) *v.*: Enjoying with appreciation; tasting; relishing

▲ **Critical Viewing** What feelings do you think these children have as they get on the bus for school? **[Speculate]**

help you?" I was startled. I had not heard English for months. For a few seconds I remained speechless. I looked at the lady who waited for my answer. My first instinct was to answer her in Spanish, but I held back. Finally, after struggling for English words, I managed to tell her that I wanted to enroll in the sixth grade. After answering many questions, I was led to the classroom.

Mr. Lema, the sixth-grade teacher, greeted me and assigned me a desk. He then intro-

◆ **Literature and Your Life**

Have you ever felt nervous coming into a new school or class? Explain.

duced me to the class. I was so nervous and scared at that moment when everyone's eyes were on me that I wished I were with Papá and Roberto picking cotton. After taking roll,

Mr. Lema gave the class the assignment for the first hour. "The first thing we have to do this morning is finish reading the story we began yesterday," he said enthusiastically. He walked up to me, handed me an English book, and asked me to read. "We are on page 125," he said politely. When I heard this, I felt my blood rush to my head; I felt dizzy. "Would you like to read?" he asked hesitantly. I opened the book to page 125. My mouth was dry. My eyes began to water. I could not begin. "You can read later," Mr. Lema said understandingly.

For the rest of the reading period I kept getting angrier and angrier at myself. I should have read, I thought to myself.

During recess I went into the restroom and opened my English book to page 125. I began to read in a low voice, pretending I was in class. There were many words I did not know. I closed the book and headed back to the classroom.

Mr. Lema was sitting at his desk correcting papers. When I entered he looked up at me and smiled. I felt better. I walked up to him and asked if he could help me with the new words. "Gladly," he said.

The rest of the month I spent my lunch hours working on English with Mr. Lema, my best friend at school.

One Friday during lunch hour Mr. Lema asked me to take a walk with him to the music room. "Do you like music?" he asked me as we entered the building.

"Yes, I like *corridos*,"[14] I answered. He then picked up a trumpet, blew on it and handed it to me. The sound gave me goose bumps. I knew that sound. I had heard it in many *corridos*. "How would you like to learn how to play it?" he asked. He must have read my face because before I could answer, he added: "I'll teach you how to play it during our lunch hours."

That day I could hardly wait to get home to tell Papá and Mamá the great news. As I got off the bus, my little brothers and sisters ran up to meet me. They were yelling and screaming. I thought they were happy to see me, but when I opened the door to our shack, I saw that everything we owned was neatly packed in cardboard boxes.

◆ **Literary Focus**
In what way does this final scene relate to the story's title?

---

14. *corridos* (kō rē′ thōs) *n*.: Ballads.

Guide for Responding

◆ LITERATURE AND YOUR LIFE

Reader's Response How do you think Panchito felt when he saw the packed boxes? Explain.

Thematic Focus Does Panchito's constant moving interfere with his growing up? Why or why not?

Goodbye Note As Panchito, write a hurried note to Mr. Lema before you leave. Tell him what his attention has meant to you and say goodbye.

☑ **Check Your Comprehension**

1. What brings tears to Panchito's eyes at the beginning of the story?
2. Briefly describe the way of life of Panchito's family.
3. What do Panchito and Roberto do when the school bus passes?
4. Summarize Panchito's first month in school.
5. What is the best thing that happens at the end of the story? What is the worst thing that happens?

◆ Critical Thinking

INTERPRET

1. What is Panchito's mood at the beginning of the story? Why? **[Infer]**
2. How do you know that Panchito wants to make a better life for himself? **[Infer]**
3. Explain why Mr. Lema is Panchito's "best friend at school." **[Support]**
4. In what way does the final paragraph bring Panchito back to where he was at the beginning? **[Draw Conclusions]**

APPLY

5. What are the main difficulties of constantly moving and attending new schools? **[Generalize]**
6. What could you do to help a new student feel welcome in your school? **[Apply]**

EXTEND

7. If you were a television reporter doing a news story on Panchito's life, whom would you interview? Why? **[Career Link]**

Hard as Nails

Russell Baker

His My mother started me in newspaper work in 1937 right after my twelfth birthday. She would have started me younger, but there was a law against working before age twelve. She thought it was a silly law, and said so to Deems.

Deems was boss of a group of boys who worked home delivery routes for the *Baltimore News-Post*. She found out about him a few weeks after we got to Baltimore. She just went out on the street, stopped a paperboy, and asked how he'd got his job.

"There's this man Deems . . ."

Deems was short and plump and had curly brown hair. He owned a car and a light gray suit and always wore a necktie and white shirt. A real businessman, I thought the first time I saw him. My mother was talking to him on the sidewalk in front of the Union Square Methodist Church and I was standing as tall as I could, just out of earshot.

"Now, Buddy, when we get down there keep your shoulders back and stand up real straight," she had cautioned me after making sure my necktie was all right and my shirt clean.

Watching the two of them in conversation, with Deems glancing at me now and then, I kept my shoulders drawn back in the painful military style I'd seen in movies, trying to look a foot taller than I really was.

"Come over here, Russ, and meet Mister Deems," she finally said, and I did, managing to answer his greeting by saying, "The pleasure's all mine," which I'd heard people say in the movies. I probably blushed while saying it, because meeting strangers was painfully embarrassing to me.

"If that's the rule, it's the rule," my mother was telling Deems, "and we'll just have to put up with it, but it still doesn't make any sense to me."

As we walked back to the house she said I couldn't have a paper route until I was twelve. And all because of some foolish rule they had down here in Baltimore. You'd think if a boy wanted to work they would encourage him instead of making him stay idle so long that laziness got <u>embedded</u> in his bones.

That was April. We had barely finished the birthday cake in August before Deems came by the apartment and gave me the tools of the newspaper trade: an account book for keeping track of the customers' bills and a long, brown web belt. Slung around one shoulder and across the chest, the belt made it easy to balance fifteen or twenty pounds of papers against the hip. I had to buy my own wire cutters for opening the newspaper bundles the trucks dropped at Wisengoff's store on the corner of Stricker and West Lombard streets.

In February my mother had moved us down from New Jersey, where we had been living with her brother Allen ever since my father died in 1930. This move of hers to Baltimore was a step toward fulfilling a dream. More than almost anything else in the world, she wanted "a home of our own." I'd heard her talk of that "home of our own" all through those endless Depression years when we lived as poor relatives dependent on Uncle Allen's goodness. "A home of our own. One of these days, Buddy, we'll have a home of our own."

That winter she had finally saved just enough to make her move, and she came to Baltimore. There were several reasons for Baltimore. For one, there were people she knew in Baltimore, people she could go to

if things got desperate. And desperation was possible, because the moving would <u>exhaust</u> her savings, and the apartment rent was twenty-four dollars a month. She would have to find a job quickly. My sister Doris was only nine, but I was old enough for an after-school job that could bring home a few dollars a week. So as soon as it was legal I went into newspaper work.

The romance of it was almost unbearable on my first day as I trudged west along Lombard Street, then south along Gilmor, and east down Pratt Street with the bundle of newspapers strapped to my hip. I imagined people pausing to admire me as I performed this important work, spreading the news of the world, the city, and the racetracks onto doorsteps, through mail slots, and under door jambs. I had often gazed with envy at paperboys; to be one of them at last was happiness <u>sublime</u>.

◆ **Build Vocabulary**

embedded (em bed´ əd) *adj.*: Firmly fixed in a surrounding material

exhaust (ig zôst´) *v.*: Use up

sublime (sə blīm´) *adj.*: Majestic; causing awe

▼ **Critical Viewing** Would you enjoy working in a group like this one? Why or why not? **[Support]**

Very soon, though, I discovered <u>drawbacks</u>. The worst of these was Deems.

◆ **Reading Strategy**
Read the sentence that begins "Though I had. . . ." Whom is the sentence about? What does he do?

Though I had only forty customers, Deems sent papers for forty-five. Since I was billed for every paper left on Wisengoff's corner, I had to pay for the five extra copies out of income or try to hustle them on the street. I hated standing at streetcar stops yelling, "Paper! Paper!" at people getting off trolleys.[1] Usually, if my mother wasn't around to catch me, I stuck the extras in a dark closet and took the loss.

Deems was constantly baiting new traps to dump more papers on me. When I solved the problem of the five extras by getting five new subscribers for home delivery, Deems announced a competition with mouthwatering prizes for the newsboys who got the most new subscribers. Too innocent to cope with this sly master of private enterprise,[2] I took the bait.

"Look at these prizes I can get for signing up new customers," I told my mother. "A balloon-tire bicycle. A free pass to the movies for a whole year."

The temptation was too much. I reported my five new subscribers to help me in the competition.

Whereupon Deems promptly raised my order from forty-five to fifty papers, leaving me again with the choice of hustling to unload the five extras or losing money.

I won a free pass to the movies, though. It was good for a whole year. And to the magnificent Loew's Century located downtown on Lexington Street. The passes were good only for nights in the middle of the week when I usually had too much homework to allow for movies. Still, in the summer with school out, it was thrilling to go all the way downtown at night to sit in the Century's damask[3] and velvet splendor and see MGM's glamorous stars in their latest movies.

To collect my prize I had to go to a banquet the paper gave for its "honor carriers" at the Emerson Hotel. There were fifty of us, and I was sure the other forty-nine would all turn out to be slicksters wised up to the ways of the world, who would laugh at my doltish ignorance of how to eat at a great hotel banquet. My fear of looking foolish at the banquet made me lie awake nights dreading it and imagining all the humiliating mistakes I could make.

I had seen banquets in movies. Every plate was surrounded by a baffling array of knives, forks, and spoons. I knew it would be the same at the Emerson Hotel. The Emerson was one of the swankiest hotels in Baltimore. It was not likely to hold down on the silverware. I talked to my mother.

"How will I know what to eat what with?"

The question did not interest her.

"Just watch what everybody else does, and enjoy yourself," she said.

I came back to the problem again and again.

"Do you use the same spoon for your coffee as you do for dessert?"

"Don't worry about it. Everybody isn't going to be staring at you."

"Is it all right to butter your bread with the same knife you use to cut the meat?"

"Just go and have a good time."

---

3. **damask** (dam´ əsk) *adj.* Decorated with the shiny cloth called damask.

---

1. **trolleys** (träl´ ēz) *n.*: Electric passenger trains, also called streetcars, running on rails in the city streets; discontinued in many American cities after the mid-1900's.
2. **private enterprise**: Business run for profit.

◆ **Build Vocabulary**
drawbacks (drô´ baks´) *n.*: Disadvantages

Close to panic, I showed up at the Emerson, found my way to the banquet, and was horrified to find that I had to sit beside Deems throughout the meal. We probably talked about something, but I was so busy sweating with terror and rolling my eyeballs sidewise to see what silverware Deems was using to eat with that I didn't hear a word all night. The following week, Deems started sending me another five extras.

Now and then he also provided a treat.

◆ **Literary Focus**
How does this event fit in with the idea that Deems is "hard as nails"?

One day in 1938 he asked if I would like to join a small group of boys he was taking to visit the *News-Post* newsroom. My mother, in spite of believing that nothing came before homework at night, wasn't coldhearted enough to deny me a chance to see the city room[4] of a great metropolitan newspaper. I had seen plenty of city rooms in the movies. They were glamorous places full of exciting people like Lee Tracey, Edmund Lowe, and Adolphe Menjou[5] trading wisecracks and

---

4. **city room**: The office at a newspaper used by those who report on city events.

▲ **Critical Viewing** Why might it be difficult to concentrate in a room like this one? [Infer]

making mayors and cops look like saps. To see such a place, to stand, actually stand, in the city room of a great newspaper and look at reporters who were in touch every day with killers and professional baseball players—that was a thrilling prospect.

Because the *News-Post* was an afternoon paper, almost everybody had left for the day when we got there that night. The building, located downtown near the harbor, was disappointing. It looked like a factory, and not a very big factory either. Inside there was a smell compounded of ink, pulp, chemicals, paste, oil, gasoline, greasy rags, and hot metal. We took an elevator up and came into a long room filled with dilapidated[6] desks, battered telephones, and big blocky typewriters. Almost nobody there, just two or three men in shirt-sleeves. It was the first time I'd ever seen Deems look awed.

---

5. **Lee Tracey, Edmund Lowe, and Adolphe Menjou:** Actors in movies of the period.
6. **dilapidated** (də lap´ ə dāt´ əd) *adj.*: Run-down; in bad condition.

"Boys, this is the nerve center of the newspaper," he said, his voice heavy and solemn like the voice of Westbrook Van Voorhis, the *March of Time*[7] man, when he said, "Time marches on."

I was confused. I had expected the newsroom to have glamour, but this place had nothing but squalor. The walls hadn't been painted for years. The windows were filthy. Desks were heaped with mounds of crumpled paper, torn sheets of newspaper, overturned paste pots, dog-eared telephone directories. The floor was ankle deep in newsprint, carbon paper, and crushed cigarette packages. Waist-high cans overflowed with trash. Ashtrays were buried under cigarette ashes and butts. Ugly old wooden chairs looked ready for the junk shop.

It looked to me like a place that probably had more cockroaches than we had back home on Lombard Street, but Deems was seeing it through rose-colored glasses.[8] As we stood looking around at the ruins, he started telling us how lucky we were to be newsboys. Lucky to have a foot on the upward ladder so early in life. If we worked hard and kept expanding our paper routes we could make the men who ran this paper sit up and notice us. And when men like that noticed you, great things could happen, because they were important men, the most important of all being the man who owned our paper: Mr. Hearst Himself, William Randolph Hearst, founder of the greatest newspaper organization in America. A great man, Mr. Hearst, but not so great that he didn't appreciate his newsboys, who were the backbone of the business. Many of whom would someday grow up and work at big jobs on this paper. Did we realize that any of us, maybe all of us, could end up one of these days sitting right here in this vitally important room, the newsroom, the nerve center of the newspaper?

Yes, Deems was right. Riding home on the streetcar that night, I realized I was a lucky boy to be getting such an early start up the ladder of journalism. It was childish to feel let down because the city room looked like such a dump instead of like city rooms in the movies. Deems might be a slave driver, but he was doing it for my own good, and I ought to be grateful. In *News Selling*, the four-page special paper Mr. Hearst published just for his newsboys, they'd run a piece that put it almost as beautifully as Deems had.

YOU'RE A MEMBER OF THE FOURTH ESTATE was the headline on it. I was so impressed that I put the paper away in a safe place and often took it out to read when I needed inspiration. It told how "a great English orator" named Edmund Burke "started a new name for a new profession—the Fourth Estate . . . the press . . . NEWSPAPER MEN."[9]

And it went on to say:

"The Fourth Estate was then . . . and IS now . . . a great estate for HE-men . . . workers . . . those who are proud of the business they're in!"

(Mr. Hearst always liked plenty of exclamation marks, dots, and capital letters.)

"Get that kick of pride that comes from

---

7. **the *March of Time*:** The *March of Time* was a newsreel series that ran from 1935 to 1951, showing current news events along with interviews and dramatizations. Newsreels were shown between feature films at movie theaters.

8. **seeing it through rose-colored glasses:** Ignoring its unappealing features or drawbacks.

9. **Edmund Burke . . . Fourth Estate:** Edmund Burke (1729–1797) was an English political figure famous for his speeches and essays. He called the press the "Fourth Estate."

◆ **Build Vocabulary**

immense (i mens´) *adj.:* Huge

knowing you are a newspaper man. That means something!

"A newspaper man never ducks a dare. YOU are a newspaper man. A salesman of newspapers . . . the final cog[10] in the immense machine of newspaper production—a SERVICE for any man to be proud of.

"So throw back the chest. Hit the route hard each day. Deliver fast and properly. Sell every day. Add to your route because you add to the NEWSPAPER field when you do. And YOU MAKE MONEY DOING IT. It is a great life—a grand opportunity. Don't boot it—build it up. Leave it better than when you came into it."

"It is a great life." I kept coming back to that

---

10. **cog** (cäg) *n.*: Gear.

sentence as I read and reread the thing. No matter how awful it got, and it sometimes got terrible, I never quit believing it was a great life. I kept at it until I was almost sixteen, chest thrown back, delivering fast and properly, selling every day and adding to my route. At the end I'd doubled its size and was making as much as four dollars a week from it.

A few months after he took us down to see the city room, Deems quit. My mother said he'd found a better job. Later, when I thought about him, I wondered if maybe it wasn't because he hated himself for having to make life tough for boys. I hoped that wasn't the reason because he was the first newspaperman I ever knew, and I wanted him to be the real thing. Hard as nails.

Guide for Responding

◆ LITERATURE AND YOUR LIFE

Reader's Response Would you like to work for Deems? Why or why not?

Thematic Focus What did Baker's experience teach him that might help him in the future? Explain.

☑ Check Your Comprehension

1. How does Baker's mother get him started in newspaper work?
2. Why is it important for him to have an after-school job?
3. How does Deems get Baker to sell more papers?
4. What is Baker's first impression of the newsroom, and what is his later thought about it?
5. After Deems leaves the paper, what thoughts does Baker have about him?

◆ Critical Thinking

INTERPRET

1. How are Baker's dreams for himself similar to and different from his mother's dreams for him? **[Compare and Contrast]**
2. Find two examples that show the conflict between the realities of newspaper work and Baker's romantic idea of it. **[Support]**
3. At the end of the essay, why does Baker want to believe that Deems was "hard as nails"? **[Draw Conclusions]**

EVALUATE

4. Do you think that the "special paper" Hearst published "for his newsboys" was completely factual? Why or why not? **[Criticize]**

COMPARE LITERARY WORKS

5. In what ways are the young Russell Baker and the boy in "The Circuit" similar? In what ways are they different? **[Compare and Contrast]**

Guide for Responding (continued)

◆ Reading Strategy

BREAK DOWN LONG SENTENCES

Break down a long sentence by finding its subject and the key ideas about the subject.

On your paper, identify the subject and the key idea about it in these sentences:

1. Too innocent to understand Deems's tricks, Russell took the bait.
2. Still, in the summer with school out, the news boys enjoyed going to the movies.
3. No matter how awful it got, Russell never quit believing that it was a great life.

◆ Build Vocabulary

USING COMPOUND NOUNS

A compound noun is a noun made up of more than one word. Explain how the words that make up each of these compound nouns contribute to its meaning:

1. birthday
2. paperboy
3. sidewalk
4. streetcar
5. newspaper
6. newsroom

SPELLING STRATEGY

Most compound nouns, such as *textbook* and *baseball,* are written as one word. Correctly spell the compound nouns made from these pairs of words:

1. snow + flake   2. book + case   3. blood + hound

USING THE WORD BANK

On your paper, find the lettered word or phrase closest in meaning to each first word.

1. drone: (a) hum, (b) singing, (c) crash
2. instinctively: (a) wildly, (b) quietly, (c) naturally
3. savoring: (a) seasoning, (b) enjoying, (c) waiting
4. embedded: (a) asleep in, (b) upset in, (c) fixed in
5. exhaust: (a) drain, (b) save, (c) leave
6. sublime: (a) flavored, (b) distant, (c) wonderful
7. drawbacks: (a) payments, (b) problems, (c) artworks
8. immense: (a) important, (b) scary, (c) very large

◆ Literary Focus

THEME

The **theme** is the thought about life that is expressed in a story or other work of literature.

1. In what ways does the word *circuit* describe Panchito's life in "The Circuit"?
2. In Baker's essay, the words "hard as nails" could describe more than one person. Who are those people? In what way is the phrase "hard as nails" related to the theme of the essay?

◆ Build Grammar Skills

PERSONAL PRONOUNS

Writers use **personal pronouns** to refer to the person speaking, the person spoken to, or the person or topic spoken about.

	Singular	Plural
First Person (person speaking)	I, me, my, mine	we, us, our, ours
Second Person (person being spoken to)	you, your, yours	you, your, yours
Third Person (person or topic spoken about)	he, him, his, she, her, hers, it, its	they, them, theirs

Practice On your paper, identify the personal pronouns in these sentences.

1. That Sunday was the last time I saw him.
2. It was an old galvanized pot she had picked up.
3. As we drove away, I felt a lump in my throat.
4. They exchanged a few words, and Mamá clasped her hands.
5. How would you like to learn how to play it?

Writing Application Respond in a complete sentence to each question. In your response, use a personal pronoun to replace each italicized noun or pronoun.

1. Why doesn't *Panchito* want to move?
2. Why does the *family* move so much?
3. Why does *Mrs. Baker* want *Russell* to work?

Build Your Portfolio

 ## Idea Bank

Writing

1. **Movie Memo** Write a brief note to a movie director explaining which story—"The Circuit" or "Hard as Nails"—would make a better movie.

2. **Poem** Write a poem that expresses your thoughts and feelings about a kind of work you respect, including sports or the arts. **[Career Link]**

3. **Letter to a Politician** Find out about the child labor laws in your state. Write a letter to your congressperson explaining whether you think the laws are good ones. **[Social Studies Link]**

Speaking and Listening

4. **Interview** Interview an adult who works in a field that interests you. Ask questions about achieving success in that kind of work. Share the results of your interview with the class. **[Career Link]**

5. **Role Play [Group Activity]** With several classmates, act out the scene at the end of "The Circuit." Divide up the roles, and have one student act as a director who helps the others give effective performances. **[Performing Arts Link]**

Projects

6. **Circuit Dance [Group Activity]** With a few classmates, design a dance that expresses the central idea of "The Circuit"—something begun, then interrupted, then begun again. **[Performing Arts Link]**

7. **Profile of a Reporter** Use magazine articles to research a well-known television or newspaper reporter. Then, write a character sketch of this person. Include details and stories about his or her achievements, reporting style, and job history. **[Media Link; Career Link]**

 ## Writing Mini-Lesson

Letter to a Person You Admire

Russell Baker's admiration for Deems peeks through the humor of his essay "Hard as Nails." Write a personal letter to someone you admire. In your letter, explain to this person why you admire him or her.

Prewriting Choose a person who has especially impressed you. It may be a celebrity or someone you know personally.

Writing Skills Focus: Elaborate With Examples

Support with examples the points you make about the person. Recall the ways this person demonstrated the qualities you admire. Use a cluster diagram to help you come up with qualities and examples you want to include in your letter.

Drafting Remember that you write a letter to an audience of one. Keep your draft focused on your reason for writing to this person. Refer to your cluster diagram for ideas.

Revising Compare what you've actually written with the ideas in your cluster diagram. If you've left out something important, find a place to include it.

> ◆ **Grammar Application**
> Be sure that readers will know whom or what any personal pronouns refer to.

Descriptive Essay

Writing Process Workshop

When you read the stories in this section, you may find yourself speeding down a frozen river or sweating in a sunstruck field. With the magic of description, writers can whisk you to faraway places. Use this magic yourself to write a **descriptive essay**—a short piece that brings to life a thing, a place, or an experience. Use details that appeal to the senses to create an effective description. The following tips, introduced in this section's Writing Mini-Lessons, will help you.

Writing Skills Focus

▶ **Use transitions.** Words such as *behind* and *on top of* help readers see where things are located. Other transition words indicate that one event happened after or caused another. (See p. 69.)

▶ **State your main idea clearly.** Then, organize details around each main idea. For example, one main idea might be about the size of what you're describing. Write a sentence that states this idea, and then group the details that show size in one paragraph. You might state another main idea about the beauty of the place or thing. (See p. 77.)

▶ **Elaborate with sensory details.** Include details that appeal to as many senses as possible. (See p. 93.)

MODEL FROM LITERATURE

Jack London, "The King of Mazy May"

At last, ① twisting abruptly between two river islands, he came upon the mighty Yukon sweeping grandly to the north. He could not see from bank to bank, and in the quick-falling twilight it loomed a great white sea of frozen stillness. ② There was not a sound, save the breathing of the dogs, and the churn of the steel-shod sled. ③

① The transition words "At last" show that this is the final portion of the description.

② London states the main idea that the mighty Yukon sweeps grandly. Then, he groups his details around this idea.

③ London elaborates with details about sights, sounds, and feelings.

Prewriting

Choose a Topic Do you have a special keepsake? Is there an interesting place you enjoyed seeing? Choose a thing or place that is important to you. It will be easier for you to bring such a subject to life with words.

Topic Ideas

- A bird's nest I found in the woods
- A toy my uncle made for me
- My room at home

Take Notes From Memory Before you observe your subject, first work with your memories of the object or place you are going to describe. Sit in a quiet place, and jot down all the details you can remember. Use note cards, and write one detail on each card.

Revise Your Notes Visit the place or look again at the object you are describing. You may be surprised at the differences between what you remembered and what you now see. Add to or correct your note cards.

Organize Your Details Review your notes, and group your descriptive details as shown in the example below.

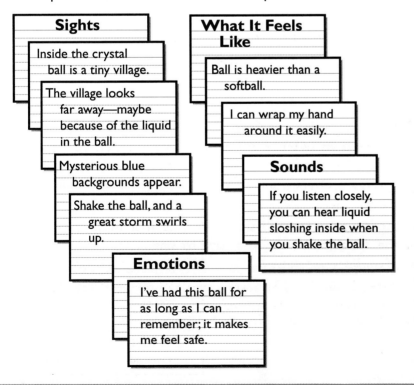

Sights
- Inside the crystal ball is a tiny village.
- The village looks far away—maybe because of the liquid in the ball.
- Mysterious blue backgrounds appear.
- Shake the ball, and a great storm swirls up.

What It Feels Like
- Ball is heavier than a softball.
- I can wrap my hand around it easily.

Sounds
- If you listen closely, you can hear liquid sloshing inside when you shake the ball.

Emotions
- I've had this ball for as long as I can remember; it makes me feel safe.

DRAFTING/REVISING

APPLYING LANGUAGE SKILLS: Using Sensory Details

Use details that appeal to the senses: specific sights, sounds, smells, feelings, and tastes. Avoid empty descriptive words, such as *nice* and *pretty*.

Enthusiastic but Empty: My tree house is really cool.

Specific Sensory Details: Shaded by a tall oak, my tree house is hidden among the rough branches and rustling leaves.

Practice Rewrite each of the following descriptions, adding one sensory detail to each.
1. He was strong.
2. The garden is pretty.
3. The full moon looks neat.

Writing Application As you reread your draft, look for places where you can add sensory details. To help you find these places, pretend that you have not named your subject anywhere in the essay. Then ask: Can my readers identify my subject, even without my naming it?

Writer's Solution Connection Writing Lab

Use the Sensory Images Word Bin activity in the Writing Lab tutorial on Description.

Applying Language Skills:
Using Commas in a Series

When you name three or more items in a sentence, one right after the other, you are making a **series.** Place a comma after each item in the series except the last one.

Examples:

  1   2   3

Papa, Mama, and Roberto had already gotten the bags packed.
             1

I like the story about the 2 prospectors, the one about the migrant workers, and the one about delivering newspapers. 3

Practice Insert commas in the series in the following sentences.

1. We harvested grapes apples and lettuce.
2. He won awards for Best Delivery Person Best Newspaper Flinger and Most Likeable Guy.
3. Francisco Jiménez Jack London and Russell Baker are three of my favorite authors.

Writer's Solution Connection
Language Lab

For additional practice using commas, complete the lesson on Commas in the Language Lab unit on Punctuation.

Drafting

See Things in Fresh Ways Concentrate on what readers would see, hear, feel, or smell if they were in the presence of what you are describing. Try to describe the details of the object or scene before you actually reveal what it is.

Organize Main Ideas Decide on the best order in which to present your main ideas. For example, you might lead your readers through the beauty of a scene and into the mystery of it. Then, group your details to illustrate your main ideas.

Use Transitions Use transition words, such as *next to* and *behind,* to make the connection between details.

Revising

Use a Peer Reviewer Ask a friend to review your draft. Then, ask him or her to draw you a picture of what you are describing.

▶ Ask yourself: What is missing from the picture? Revise to make sure you include or emphasize those missing details.

▶ Ask your friend: "Why do I care about this thing or place?" If your friend is not sure or names the wrong reasons, revise your draft to show clearly what is most important to you about the place or object.

▶ Ask your friend if any details were confusing. Review the places where such details appear. Make sure you have stated main ideas clearly and used transitions.

Publishing and Presenting

Classroom Presentation Together with your classmates, plan a series of presentations. Each of you should read your descriptive essay to the class. Then, pass around the objects described, or show photos or videos if you wrote about a place.

Art Show Have a classmate illustrate your essay. Then, show the drawing and your essay side by side.

Collage Use your essay as the centerpiece for a collage. Around your essay, arrange images and textures that capture the details you've described.

Real-World Reading Skills Workshop

Strategies for Success

Have you ever bought a gadget that didn't work, no matter what you tried, until you realized that the instructions said "Batteries required"? Written directions are important in many activities. To get the most out of directions, use the following tips:

Look Over All the Directions If you are looking at a long list of instructions, skim through them first. You will be more comfortable following the directions if you have an idea where they lead.

Read Carefully Next, go back and read the directions carefully. Each word counts, so read every one.

Identify What Each Direction Is About If you are baking a cake, some directions will explain how to make the cake. Others will tell you how to make the icing. For each direction, identify the part of the task it concerns. Note any technical words—words specific to an activity, such as baking or building—and find out what they mean.

Identify the Materials You Need For each step in the directions, identify the materials or equipment you need. Make sure you have these materials before you continue.

Look for Signal Words *Then, next, before, not,* and other signal words tell you the order of the steps or how one direction fits with others. Pay careful attention to these words.

> ✔ Here are situations in which reading directions is important:
> ▶ Assembling a model
> ▶ Using a VCR
> ▶ Making a dessert
> ▶ Installing new software

Alessandra's Extra Flaky Pie Crust

Ingredients

1 cup of flour

1/2 cup of cold water

3/4 stick of butter

1. Place the flour in a mixing bowl.
2. Add the butter to the flour in small chunks.
3. Knead the butter and flour in the bowl together.
4. When all of the butter has been mixed in with the flour, sprinkle the water onto the dough.
5. Continue kneading the dough until the flour and butter are thoroughly mixed. Collect into a ball.
6. Sprinkle flour lightly on a smooth surface.
7. Put the dough on the surface. Using a rolling pin, roll it out into a sheet less than 1/8 of an inch thick.

Apply the Strategies

Are you ready to make a pie crust? Look over the recipe. Then, answer the following questions:

1. What equipment do you need to make the pie crust?

2. In which step do you need the water?

3. What special information do you need to know about the water? Where can you find this information?

4. How much time do you think it will take to complete this recipe? Explain.

A **pronoun** is a word that takes the place of a noun or a group of words acting as a noun. The noun that the pronoun replaces is the pronoun's **antecedent.** The antecedent helps you identify the person, place, or thing to which the pronoun refers. (See page 68.)

Personal pronouns refer to the person speaking (first person), the person spoken to (second person), or the person or thing spoken about (third person). (See page 92.)

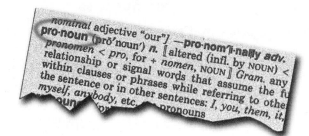

nominal adjective "our"] —pro·nom′i·nal·ly adv.
pro·noun (prō′noun′) n. [altered (infl. by NOUN) < pronomen < pro, for + nomen, NOUN] Gram. any relationship or signal words that assume the fu within clauses or phrases while referring to othe the sentence or in other sentences: I, you, them, it, myself, anybody, etc. pronouns

	Singular	**Plural**
First Person	I, me, my, mine	we, us, our, ours
Second Person	you, your, yours	you, your, yours
Third Person	he, him, his, she, her, hers, it, its	they, them, their, theirs

Interrogative pronouns introduce questions. (See page 76.) They include such words as *who, whose, whom, what,* and *which.*

Practice 1 Copy these sentences. Underline each interrogative pronoun. Circle each personal pronoun, and draw an arrow to its antecedent.

1. First, a prospector had to find gold, and then he had to guard his claim.

2. People are changed by the books they read.

3. What has changed?

4. The young migrant worker wants to play the trumpet, but his family needs him to work.

5. Deems spoke to Mrs. Baker about her son's job.

Practice 2 Rewrite the paragraph below, replacing the italicized nouns with pronouns.

Walt and Russell have very different lives. Yet *Walt and Russell* also have something in common. Walt lives on the frigid frontier, where one wrong move could land *Walt* in big trouble. Russell Baker lives in a city. *Russell's* main challenge is a new newspaper route. Mrs. Baker talks to Deems about a job for *Mrs. Baker's* son. Both Walt and Russell take on new responsibilities. These responsibilities move *Russell and Walt* onward and upward.

Grammar in Writing

✔ *Use pronouns to avoid repeating the same noun over and over. A pronoun creates confusion, though, if it can refer to more than one antecedent.*

Confusing: When the dogs chased the men down the river, they got tired.
(They could refer to the dogs or to the men.)

Clear: The dogs got tired when they chased the men down the river.

✔ **Be sure your pronouns have clear antecedents.**

Speaking, Listening, and Viewing Workshop

When you are part of a group of listeners—whether in a classroom or at a formal speech—get involved. Use the following strategies to become an active listener.

Find a Focus Note what a speaker says to introduce the topic. Identify the focus of what is being said. For example, the focus of a class presentation might be the pharaohs of Egypt.

Find a "Hook" What else have you heard about the topic? With what interests of yours does it connect? The answers to these questions can help you "hook" into the speaker's words.

Link to the Focus and Hook Identify how each key point the speaker makes ties in with the focus. Some points will give background. Points about specific details will support more general claims.

Ask Yourself Questions Do the speaker's points agree with what you have heard before on the subject? Do they shed any light on your special interests? What else would you like to know? Ask yourself questions such as these as you listen to connect your own knowledge and experiences with what you hear.

Apply the Strategies

Practice active listening. With a partner, complete these activities:

1. Listen to an audio or video recording of a famous speech. Compare your ideas about the focus of the speech.

2. Find two news articles. Read an article aloud while your partner notes the focus and links key points to it. Then, have your partner read the other article while you take notes.

3. After a presentation to your class, compare notes. Discuss how you identified the focus and used it to organize your thoughts in note form.

Tips for Active Listening

✔ *The following tips will help you get the most out of a speech:*
  ▶ *Look at the speaker. Imagine that he or she is talking right to you.*
  ▶ *Be on the lookout for a focus.*
  ▶ *Find a "hook."*
  ▶ *Link a speaker's points to the focus.*

What's Behind the Words

Vocabulary Adventures With Richard Lederer

Origins of Names

Long ago, when people lived together in small communities, the supply of names was large enough so that none had to be repeated in the same tribe or group. As groups grew larger, a system of distinguishing among people with the same first names had to be invented. Thus, people began to add descriptive information to the given name, and that's how we got last names, or surnames.

What's in a Name?

The surnames we know today originated from the places people lived, the qualities of a person, or a family relationship. The chart below shows the origins of some names.

Names From Geography	Names From Physical Qualities or Personality Traits	Names Indicating "Son of"
Churchill	Little	McCormick (son of Cormick)
Rivers	Swift	Larson, Larsen (son of Lars)
York	Reid (Red)	Fitzhugh (son of Hugh)
Underwood	Armstrong	Ivanovich (son of Ivan)
Hill	Truman (True man)	
	Wise	

Working for a Name

The largest category of surnames began as descriptions of the work people did. The village smith, who made and repaired all objects of metal, was once the most important person in the community. Today, in the telephone directories of the world's English-speaking cities, Smith is the most popular last name. International variations on Smith include Schmidt, Smed, Faber, Ferraro, Kovacs, Manx, Goff, and Gough. Other names from work include Taylor, Butler, and Archer.

ACTIVITY 1 Match each last name listed in the left column with the corresponding occupation in the right column.

1. Bailey   a. barrel maker
2. Cooper, Hooper   b. leather worker
3. Lederer   c. bricklayer
4. Mason   d. bailiff
5. Schumacher   e. shoemaker

ACTIVITY 2 The name *John* descends from the Hebrew *Yochanan*. Identify the nationality of these other versions of John:

1. Evan   3. Giovanni   5. Hans   7. Ian   9. Ivan
2. Jan   4. Jean   6. Jens   8. Juan   10. Sean

ACTIVITY 3 Do research to find out the origin of your surname. With classmates, create a chart that shows the origins of your names.

Extended Reading Opportunities

Reading about the adventures of imaginary characters can give you a new way to look at your own experiences. Following are some suggestions for reading about young people who grow and change as a result of their experiences.

Suggested Titles

The True Confessions of Charlotte Doyle
Avi

In 1832, Charlotte Doyle sets off on what should be an exciting new chapter in her life. As the only passenger on a merchant ship crossing the Atlantic, she expects to make some adjustments as she journeys toward America. To her surprise, she finds the ship full of deception, mutiny, and murder. When the journey is over, she must share in court the truth about the ship—and face the truths she has discovered about herself.

Bridge to Terabithia
Katherine Paterson

Jess's goal is to be the fastest runner in his class. Although he works all summer at running faster, he is beaten in a race on the first day of school. Jess's defeat leads to a friendship that changes his life in ways no one could have predicted. While Jess learns to deal with differences in others, great changes are taking place within him. Although he doesn't realize it, Jess is building up the strength and courage he will need to face the tragedy that comes into his life.

Sounder
William H. Armstrong

Sounder is the name of a devoted dog owned by a family of poor southern farmers in the 1800's. None of the characters except the dog is identified by name, but each character is an unforgettable personality. A young boy learns some difficult lessons about life when his father is torn away from the family and his dog disappears. The boy spends years looking for his father, and each character undergoes difficult trials in the search to be reunited with the others.

Other Possibilities

Going Home	Nicholasa Mohr
The Broccoli Tapes	Jan Slepian
A Young Painter	Zheng Zhensun and Alice Low

First Steps, Vincent Van Gogh Copyright © 1985 The Metropolitan Museum of Art, New York, New York

Reaching Out

The man in this picture reaches out to encourage the toddler to walk. In the same way, the stories, poems, and essays in this unit encourage you to move forward—to open new doors and discover new friends. By reading about the ways in which these characters and writers reach out, you will take steps toward understanding more about your world and the people in it.

Guide for Reading

Meet the Author:

Garrison Keillor (1942–)

Garrison Keillor reaches out to more than two million public radio listeners who tune in every week to hear his variety show, *A Prairie Home Companion*. Through songs, comedy sketches, and stories, Keillor nudges listeners into thinking about the really important things in life—along with the really funny ones. The highlight of the show is "The News From Lake Wobegon," Keillor's monologue about doings in an imaginary midwestern town. As you sit by the radio with your eyes closed, listening to Keillor spin his tales, it's not hard to believe Lake Wobegon is real. Keillor, whose own hometown is Anoka, Minnesota, is the author of several books of humor and a member of the Radio Hall of Fame.

THE STORY BEHIND THE STORY

Thinking about letters comes easily to Garrison Keillor. While he was growing up, his father was a railway mail clerk. Perhaps watching his father go to work every day made him wonder why people wrote to each other and how the mail was moved from town to town. Letters were and still are an effective form of communication for many people. In this essay, he outlines the reasons for keeping letters straightforward.

◆ LITERATURE AND YOUR LIFE

CONNECT YOUR EXPERIENCE

It is exciting to receive letters and birthday cards in the mail. Tearing open an envelope and reading a message written only for you can give you a wonderful feeling. Garrison Keillor discusses that wonderful feeling and other great reasons for writing letters in "How to Write a Letter."

THEMATIC FOCUS: **Reaching Out**

By writing letters, you can reach out to people who live far away. Why do you think people enjoy sending and receiving letters?

◆ Background for Understanding

MATH

Letters are among the millions of pieces of mail the United States Postal Service processes each year. Despite an increase in other methods of communication, such as e-mail, fax machines, and the Internet, the amount of mail has increased. The graph below shows the steady rise in the number of pieces of mail sent each year from 1970 to 1995, with a projection of the number for 2001.

Pieces of Mail Delivered by U.S. Postal Service

UNITED STATES POSTAL SERVICE

Year	Pieces
1970	84,882,000
1985	140,098,000
1990	166,301,000
1995	180,734,000
2001	212,300,000,000 (projected)

◆ How to Write a Letter ◆

Laurence Typing, 1952, Fairfield Porter, oil on canvas 40 x 30 1/8 inches, The Parrish Art Museum, Southampton, New York, Gift of the Estate of Fairfield Porter

◆ Literary Focus

INFORMAL ESSAY

You behave differently on a picnic with a friend than you do at a dinner party in a restaurant. In the same way, writers "behave" differently when they write different types of essays. An **essay** is a brief discussion of a topic. In an **informal essay,** like "How to Write a Letter," the writer uses casual, conversational language that creates a feeling of friendliness toward the reader.

Use an organizer like the one below to record details that create a friendly, informal feeling in "How to Write a Letter."

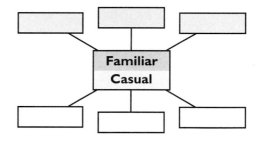

Familiar Casual

◆ Build Vocabulary

SUFFIXES: *-ory*

The suffix *-ory* means "having the quality or nature of." For example, something that is *obligatory* has the quality or nature of an *obligation*—something you are required to do.

WORD BANK

Which word is used to talk about one particular show from a weekly television series?

confidence
anonymity
obligatory
episode
sibling

Reading for Success

Literal Comprehension Strategies

The first step in understanding a work of literature is to grasp its literal meaning—the basic facts and details the author is communicating. The following strategies help you understand a writer's words on a literal level.

Apply word identification strategies.

When you come to an unfamiliar word, divide it into syllables or word parts to find familiar elements. For example, when you encounter the word *inspiration,* break it into parts:

inspiration = inspir + ation

You'll recognize the beginning as *inspire,* a word already familiar to you, so you can guess that *inspiration* means "something that inspires" or "the condition of being inspired."

Paraphrase.

As you read, restate sentences or ideas in your own words. By re-saying what you have read (even if it is just in your head), you make the meaning your own.

Keillor's Words	The burning shame you feel when you see unanswered mail makes it harder to pick up a pen and makes for a cheerless letter when you finally do.
Paraphrase	Letters that are written out of guilt aren't fun to write or to read.

Envision.

Use your imagination and details from the work to create mental pictures of
▶ people
▶ places
▶ events

Summarize.

Don't lose track of the events and ideas after you read about them. As you read, pause occasionally to think about and sum up the main points or events in the work.

As you read "How to Write a Letter," look at the notes in the boxes. The notes show you how to apply these strategies to your reading.

How to Write a Letter

Garrison Keillor

We shy persons need to write a letter now and then, or else we'll dry up and blow away. It's true. And I speak as one who loves to reach for the phone, dial the number, and talk. I say, "Big Bopper here—what's shakin', babes?" The telephone is to shyness what Hawaii is to February, it's a way out of the woods, *and yet:* a letter is better.

Such a sweet gift—a piece of hand-made writing, in an envelope that is not a bill, sitting in our friend's path when she trudges home from a long day spent among wahoos and savages, a day our words will help repair. They don't need to be immortal, just sincere. She can read them twice and again tomorrow: *You're someone I care about, Corinne, and think of often and every time I do you make me smile.*

Critical Viewing ▶ Why do you think this girl wrote a letter instead of making a phone call? **[Speculate]**

◀ **Critical Viewing** Judging from the expression on his face, who has written the letter this man is reading?

To be known by another person—to meet and talk freely on the page—to be close despite distance. To escape from anonymity and be our own sweet selves and express the music of our souls.

Same thing that moves a giant rock star to sing his heart out in front of 123,000 people moves us to take ballpoint in hand and write a few lines to our dear Aunt Eleanor. *We want to be known.* We want her to know that we have fallen in love, that we quit our job, that we're moving to New York, and we want to say a few things that might not get said in casual conversation: *Thank you for what you've meant to me, I am very happy right now.*

The first step in writing letters is to get over the guilt of *not* writing. You don't "owe" anybody a letter. Letters are a gift. The burning shame you feel when you see unanswered mail makes it harder to pick up a pen and makes for a cheerless letter when you finally do. *I feel bad about not writing, but I've been so busy,* etc. Skip this.

Few letters are obligatory, and they are *Thanks for the wonderful gift* and *I am terribly sorry to hear about George's death* and *Yes, you're welcome to stay with us next month,* and not many more than that. Write

We need to write, otherwise nobody will know who we are. They will have only a vague impression of us as A Nice Person, because, frankly, we don't shine at conversation, we lack the confidence to thrust our faces forward and say, "Hi, I'm Heather Hooten; let me tell you about my week." Mostly we say "Uh-huh" and "Oh, really." People smile and look over our shoulder, looking for someone else to meet.

So a shy person sits down and writes a letter.

◆ **Build Vocabulary**

confidence (kän´ fi dəns´) *n.*: Belief in one's own abilities

anonymity (an´ ə nim´ ə tē) *adj.*: The condition of being a stranger; not known by name

obligatory (əb lig´ ə tor´ ē) *adj.*: Required

those promptly if you want to keep your friends. Don't worry about the others, except love letters, of course. When your true love writes, *Dear Light of My Life, Joy of My Heart, O Lovely Pulsating Core of My Sensate[1] Life,* some response is called for.

Some of the best letters are tossed off in a burst of inspiration, so keep your writing stuff in one place where you can sit down for a few minutes and (*Dear Roy, I am in the middle of a book entitled* We Are Still Married *but thought I'd drop you a line. Hi to your sweetie, too*) dash off a note to a pal. Envelopes, stamps, address book, everything in a drawer so you can write fast when the pen is hot.

> You could **paraphrase** this section in the following way: Keep everything together so that when you're ready to write, it's at your fingertips.

A blank white eight-by-eleven sheet can look as big as Montana if the pen's not so hot—try a smaller page and write boldly. Or use a note card with a piece of fine art on the front; if your letter ain't good, at least they get the Matisse.[2] Get a pen that makes a sensuous[3] line, get a comfortable typewriter, a friendly word processor—whichever feels easy to the hand.

Sit for a few minutes with the blank sheet in front of you, and meditate on the person you will write to, let your friend come to mind until you can almost see her or him in the room with you. Remember the last time you saw each other and how your friend looked and what you said and what perhaps was unsaid between you, and when your friend becomes real to you, start to write.

Write the salutation—*Dear You*—and take a deep breath and plunge in. A simple declarative sentence will do, followed by another and another and another. Tell us what you're doing and tell it like you were talking to us. Don't think about grammar, don't think about lit'ry style, don't try to write dramatically, just give us your news. Where did you go, who did you see, what did they say, what do you think?

If you don't know where to begin, start with the present moment: *I'm sitting at the kitchen table on a rainy Saturday morning. Everyone is gone and the house is quiet.* Let your simple description of the present moment lead to something else, let the letter drift gently along.

The toughest letter to crank out is one that is meant to impress, as we all know from writing job applications; if it's hard work to slip off a letter to a friend, maybe you're trying too hard to be terrific. A letter is only a report to someone who already likes you for reasons other than your brilliance. Take it easy.

Don't worry about form. It's not a term paper. When you come to the end of one episode, just start a new paragraph. You can go from a few lines about the sad state of pro football to the fight with your mother to your fond memories of Mexico to your cat's urinary-tract infection to a few thoughts on personal indebtedness and on to the kitchen sink and what's in it. The more you write, the easier it gets, and when you have a True True Friend to write to, a *compadre,*[4] a soul sibling, then it's like driving a car down a country road, you just get behind the keyboard

> Using **word identification strategies,** you can discover the word *debt* when you break *indebtedness* into parts.

---

1. sensate (sen´ sāt) *adj.*: Having the power of sensory perception.
2. Matisse: Henri Matisse (än rē mə tēs´)(1869–1954), a French painter.
3. sensuous (sen´ shoo əs) *adj.*: Readily grasped by the senses.

4. *compadre* (kəm päd´ rā) *n.*: Spanish for buddy; close friend.

◆ Build Vocabulary

episode (ep´ ə sōd´) *n.*: One in a series of related events

sibling (sib´ liŋ) *n.*: Brother or sister

Envisioning the children in the attic helps you understand Keillor's statement that a letter is more lasting than a phone call.

and press on the gas.

Don't tear up the page and start over when you write a bad line — try to write your way out of it. Make mistakes and plunge on. Let the letter cook along and let yourself be bold. Outrage, confusion, love—whatever is in your mind, let it find a way to the page. Writing is a means of discovery, always, and when you come to the end and write *Yours ever* or *Hugs and kisses*, you'll know something you didn't when you wrote *Dear Pal.*

Probably your friend will put your letter away, and it'll be read again a few years from now—and it will improve with age. And forty years from now, your friend's grandkids will dig it out of the attic and read it, a sweet and precious relic of the ancient eighties that gives them a sudden clear glimpse of you and her and the world we old-timers knew. You will then have created an object of art. Your simple lines about where you went, who you saw, what they said, will speak to those children and they will feel in their hearts the humanity of our times.

You can't pick up a phone and call the future and tell them about our times. You have to pick up a piece of paper.

You can **summarize** the ideas here as follows: A letter creates a lasting record of the present, which is a gift to the future.

Guide for Responding

◆ LITERATURE AND YOUR LIFE

Reader's Response Do you like writing letters? Why or why not?

Thematic Focus Why is it sometimes important to reach out by writing?

Journal Writing Jot down a few thoughts or a piece of news you would like to share with someone in a letter.

☑ Check Your Comprehension

1. What is the reason Keillor gives for the need to write?
2. What is the first step in writing letters?
3. Why does Keillor suggest you keep your writing materials in one place?
4. According to Keillor, what should you do if you don't know where to begin when writing a letter?
5. According to this essay, what will happen after your friend puts your letter away?

◆ Critical Thinking

INTERPRET

1. How does the author feel about writing letters? **[Draw Conclusions]**
2. Why does Keillor urge people to plunge on when they make a mistake? **[Speculate]**
3. Explain how you know that the author has written many letters to friends. **[Support]**
4. Explain the message Keillor is communicating in "How to Write a Letter." **[Interpret]**

EVALUATE

5. Do you think letter writing is important in today's society? Explain. **[Make a Judgment]**
6. Which do you think is the most useful method of communication available today? **[Assess]**

EXTEND

7. What qualities does Keillor show in this essay that contribute to his successful writing career? **[Career Link]**

Guide for Responding (continued)

◆ Reading for Success

LITERAL COMPREHENSION STRATEGIES

The literal comprehension strategies you applied while reading "How to Write a Letter" can be used when reading any kind of literature.

1. Explain how you used word parts as clues to a word's meaning in "How to Write a Letter."
2. Describe a section of "How to Write a Letter" that you were able to envision.
3. Summarize the main points of Keillor's essay in a few sentences.

◆ Build Vocabulary

USING THE SUFFIX -ory

The suffix -ory indicates "having the quality or nature of." For example, obligations are obligatory. Copy the following items in your notebook. Fill in the missing words.

1. Things related to the __?__ are sensory.
2. Systems that __?__ are regulatory.
3. You might use an accusatory tone when making an __?__.

SPELLING STRATEGY

The ens sound at the end of words like confidence is often spelled ence. You may need to memorize the spelling of words that end in ence.

In your notebook, finish each word by adding ence.

1. differ__?__   2. independ__?__   3. pres__?__

USING THE WORD BANK

In your notebook, match each numbered item on the left with its definition on the right.

1. sibling	a. one happening that forms part of a whole
2. episode	
3. confidence	b. not known
4. obligatory	c. belief in one's abilities
5. anonymity	d. brother or sister
	e. required

◆ Literary Focus

INFORMAL ESSAY

An **informal essay** is a brief, casual discussion of a topic. The writer uses familiar, sometimes even humorous, words and phrases to create a relaxed, informal feeling.

1. Identify two words or phrases that Keillor probably included for a humorous touch.
2. In what way is Keillor's essay like a letter to a friend?
3. In what two ways is Keillor's essay different from the formal writing in a textbook?

◆ Build Grammar Skills

VERBS

A **verb** is a word that shows an action, a condition, or existence. Send, think, and run are verbs that show action. Was, am, become, and seem are verbs that show a condition or existence. To determine whether a word is a verb, ask yourself if it can change to show differences in time. For example, the verb sit can be changed to sat. Is can be changed to was or will be.

Practice Copy the following sentences in your notebook. Circle the verbs. (A sentence may have more than one verb.)

1. A letter brightens a friend's day.
2. Take a deep breath and plunge in.
3. A blank piece of paper seems scary.
4. The letter becomes a precious relic.
5. It is not a report.

Writing Application Answer each of the following questions with a complete sentence. Circle the verb or verbs in each answer.

1. What does Keillor want you to do?
2. What does Keillor suggest you do when a blank sheet seems too big?
3. What does Keillor say that a letter is?
4. How does Keillor feel about the telephone?

Build Your Portfolio

 ## Idea Bank

Writing

1. **Short Letter** Think about the best day you have experienced recently. Write a brief letter to a friend, describing that day in detail. Write informally.

2. **Letter to Keillor** Write a letter to Garrison Keillor. Let him know whether or not you share his enthusiasm for letter writing. Give reasons for your opinion.

3. **Comparison** Write a brief comparison of e-mail and handwritten letters. What similarities do they have that make them popular? In what ways are they different? **[Technology Link]**

Speaking and Listening

4. **Speech** Keillor's essay could be presented as an informal speech. Choose a portion of his essay, and practice delivering the ideas in the section in your own words. Use words and phrases that are familiar to you and your friends. Deliver your speech to your class. **[Performing Arts Link]**

5. **Phone Conversation [Group Activity]** With a partner, act out a telephone conversation about your day at school. When you have finished, lead a group in a discussion of how talking on the phone is different from reading or writing a letter.

Projects

6. **Visual Aid** Go to your library, and find out about the history of mail. Create a timeline, chart, or poster that shows the important milestones leading to the postal services we have today. **[Social Studies Link]**

7. **Technology Advertisement** Choose a form of technology that helps people communicate. Write an advertisement for it that includes its benefits to the user. **[Technology Link]**

 ## Writing Mini-Lesson

Postcard

Keillor advises that if a blank page seems too large, you should write on note paper or on a card with a picture. Another fun, easy way to send a message is on a postcard. Write a postcard to a friend or relative. A postcard is small, so make every word count.

Writing Skills Focus: Informal Language

Postcards are a form of informal writing, so **informal language** is acceptable. Conversational phrases, some slang, and even an occasional incomplete sentence will make your postcard lively and personal.

Model

Yesterday was the string factory tour. Not exactly a thrill a minute. Tomorrow it's off to the carnival. The water slide, the games—and the food!

Prewriting Make a list of things you want to say. If your postcard is from a vacation spot, list your three favorite things there. If your postcard is from home, list three important events of the past week.

Drafting Don't waste time or space with general statements, such as "I'm having fun." Instead, write specifics, such as, "The roller coaster here has more loops than any I've been on."

> ◆ **Grammar Application**
> Create an infomal tone by starting some statements with verbs. For example: *Went* to the carnival.

Revising Look for places where you can make your language and style more lively and personal.

PART 1   *Opening Doors*

August Afternoon, ca. 1940, Hobson Pittman, Morris Museum of Art, Augusta, Georgia

Guide for Reading

Meet the Authors:

Myron Levoy (1930–   )

You might say that Myron Levoy's jobs are "out of this world." In addition to writing, he has worked on a project involving manned spaceflight to Mars. His interest in inter-planetary travel may be the reason so many of his characters are loners—self-sufficient people who live outside of a society or group.

Helen Keller (1880–1968)

Like a sailor shipwrecked on a desert island, the young Helen Keller was cut off from the world. At age one and a half, illness left her deaf and blind. Hardly able to com-municate, Helen later explained she was "wild and unruly, . . . giggling to express plea-sure; kicking, scratching . . . to indicate the opposite."

THE STORY BEHIND THE STORY

In 1887, Helen was rescued from her island of darkness. A gifted teacher, Annie Sullivan, came to live with her. She taught Helen the manual alphabet —finger spelling. Eventually, Helen learned to speak by feeling the vibra-tions in Sullivan's throat with her hands and copying them. In "Water," from her autobiography, Keller describes her very first experience with communicating.

◆ LITERATURE AND YOUR LIFE

CONNECT YOUR EXPERIENCE

It has probably happened to you: As you struggle to push through a door, you get more and more frustrated with every push. Finally, you realize your mistake. One *pull* and the door opens easily. Aaron in "Aaron's Gift" and Helen in "Water" both struggle to push through sit-uations in their lives. They, too, discover that sometimes a new approach makes all the difference.

THEMATIC FOCUS: Opening Doors

When has trying a new approach helped you "open a door" in your life?

◆ Background for Understanding

EDUCATION

"Water" tells the story of a special experience shared by Helen Keller and her lifelong friend and teacher, Annie Sullivan. In Helen Keller's lifetime, most visually impaired or hearing impaired children lived in institutions. With Sullivan as her guide, Helen Keller lived and learned with sighted people. She attended college with sighted stu-dents, and she graduated with honors.

◆ Build Vocabulary

RELATED WORDS: FORMS OF *console*

Knowing that the word *consoled* means "comforted" will help you understand the meaning of other forms of the word. *Consolation* is the comfort given. *Inconsolable* describes someone who cannot be comforted.

WORD BANK

Which word have you heard used to refer to something that brings good luck to schools or teams?

frenzied
mascot
coaxed
consoled
drawing

Aaron's Gift
◆ Water ◆

◆ **Literary Focus**

CLIMAX

In reading a story or a nonfiction narrative, you may come to a point at which a person or character must make a choice, face a challenge, or have a showdown. This is the **climax,** or turning point. It is the high point of interest or suspense. Events have built up to this point, where the story could go one way or another. On a diagram like the one below, record events that lead to the climaxes of "Aaron's Gift" and "Water."

◆ **Reading Strategy**

REREAD

As you're reading, you may not notice every detail, or you may not understand why the writer includes certain information. It makes sense then to go back and **reread** a passage to get details clear in your mind or to see how new details fit with information provided earlier. Don't hesitate to reread to be sure that you understand what the author has written.

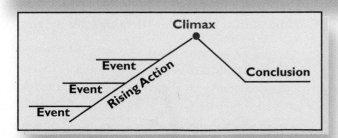

Aaron's Gift

Myron Levoy

Aaron Kandel had come to Tompkins Square Park to roller-skate, for the streets near Second Avenue were always too crowded with children and peddlers and old ladies and baby buggies. Though few children had bicycles in those days, almost every child owned a pair of roller skates. And Aaron was, it must be said, a Class A, triple-fantastic roller skater.

Aaron skated back and forth on the wide walkway of the park, pretending he was an aviator in an air race zooming around pylons, which were actually two lampposts. During his third lap around the racecourse, he noticed a pigeon on the grass, behaving very strangely. Aaron skated to the line of benches, then climbed over onto the lawn.

The pigeon was trying to fly, but all it could manage was to flutter and turn round and round in a large circle, as if it were performing a <u>frenzied</u> dance. The left wing was only half open and was beating in a clumsy, jerking fashion; it was clearly broken.

Luckily, Aaron hadn't eaten the cookies he'd stuffed into his pocket before he'd gone clacking down the three flights of stairs from his apartment, his skates already on. He broke a cookie into small crumbs and tossed some toward the pigeon. "Here pidge, here pidge," he called. The pigeon spotted the cookie crumbs and, after a moment, stopped thrashing about. It folded its wings as best it could, but the broken wing still stuck half out. Then it strutted over to the crumbs, its head bobbing forth-back, forth-back, as if it were marching a little in front of the rest of the body—perfectly normal, except for that half-open wing which seemed to make the bird stagger sideways every so often.

The pigeon began eating the crumbs as Aaron quickly unbuttoned his shirt and pulled it off. Very slowly, he edged toward the bird, making little kissing sounds like the ones he heard his grandmother make when she fed the sparrows on the back fire escape.

Then suddenly Aaron plunged. The shirt, in both hands, came down like a torn parachute. The pigeon beat its wings, but Aaron held the shirt to the ground, and the bird couldn't escape. Aaron felt under the shirt, gently, and

▲ **Critical Viewing** What do you think a bird feels when it flies? **[Speculate]**

◆ **Build Vocabulary**

frenzied (fren´ zēd) *adj.*: Wild; frantic

gently took hold of the wounded pigeon.

"Yes, yes, pidge," he said, very softly. "There's a good boy. Good pigeon, good."

The pigeon struggled in his hands, but little by little Aaron managed to soothe it. "Good boy, pidge. That's your new name. Pidge. I'm gonna take you home, Pidge. Yes, yes, *ssh*. Good boy. I'm gonna fix you up. Easy, Pidge, easy does it. Easy, boy."

Aaron squeezed through an opening between the row of benches and skated slowly out of the park, while holding the pigeon carefully with both hands as if it were one of his mother's rare, precious cups from the old country. How fast the pigeon's heart was beating! Was he afraid? Or did all pigeons' hearts beat fast?

It was fortunate that Aaron was an excellent skater, for he had to skate six blocks to his apartment, over broken pavement and sudden gratings and curbs and cobblestones. But when he reached home, he asked Noreen Callahan, who was playing on the stoop, to take off his skates for him. He would not chance going up three flights on roller skates this time.

"Is he sick?" asked Noreen.

"Broken wing," said Aaron. "I'm gonna fix him up and make him into a carrier pigeon or something."

"Can I watch?" asked Noreen.

"Watch what?"

"The operation. I'm gonna be a nurse when I grow up."

"OK," said Aaron. "You can even help. You can help hold him while I fix him up."

Aaron wasn't quite certain what his mother would say about his new-found pet, but he was pretty sure he knew what his grandmother would think. His grandmother had lived with them ever since his grandfather had died three years ago. And she fed the sparrows and jays and crows and robins on the back fire escape with every spare crumb she could find. In fact, Aaron noticed that she sometimes created

crumbs where they didn't exist, by squeezing and tearing pieces of her breakfast roll when his mother wasn't looking.

Aaron didn't really understand his grandmother, for he often saw her by the window having long conversations with the birds, telling them about her days as a little girl in the Ukraine.[1] And once he saw her take her mirror from her handbag and hold it out toward the birds. She told Aaron that she wanted them to see how beautiful they were. Very strange. But Aaron did know that she would love Pidge, because she loved everything.

To his surprise, his mother said he could keep the pigeon, temporarily, because it was sick, and we were all strangers in the land of Egypt,[2] and it might not be bad for Aaron to have a pet. *Temporarily.*

The wing was surprisingly easy to fix, for the break showed clearly and Pidge was remarkably patient and still, as if he knew he was being helped. Or perhaps he was just exhausted from all the thrashing about he had done. Two Popsicle sticks served as splints, and strips from an old undershirt were used to tie them in place. Another strip held the wing to the bird's body.

Aaron's father arrived home and stared at the pigeon. Aaron waited for the expected storm. But instead, Mr. Kandel asked, "Who *did* this?"

"Me," said Aaron. "And Noreen Callahan."

"Sophie!" he called to his wife. "Did you see this! Ten years old and it's better than Dr. Belasco could do. He's a genius!"

As the days passed, Aaron began training Pidge to be a carrier pigeon. He tied a little cardboard tube to Pidge's left leg and stuck tiny rolled-up sheets of paper with secret

---

1. **Ukraine** (yoo krān´): Country located in Eastern Europe. From 1924 to 1991, Ukraine was part of the Soviet Union.
2. **we were all . . . land of Egypt:** A reference to the biblical story of the enslavement of the Hebrew people in Egypt. Around 1300 B.C., the Hebrews were led out of Egypt by Moses.

Pigeons, John Sloan, The Hayden Collection, Courtesy, Museum of Fine Arts, Boston, Massachusetts

messages into it: THE ENEMY IS ATTACKING AT DAWN. Or: THE GUNS ARE HIDDEN IN THE TRUNK OF THE CAR. Or: VINCENT DEMARCO IS A BRITISH SPY. Then Aaron would set Pidge down at one end of the living room and put some popcorn at the other end. And Pidge would waddle slowly across the room, cooing softly, while the ends of his bandages trailed along the floor.

At the other end of the room, one of Aaron's friends would take out the message, stick a new one in, turn Pidge around, and aim him at the popcorn that Aaron put down on his side of the room.

And Pidge grew fat and contented on all the popcorn and crumbs and corn and crackers and Aaron's grandmother's breakfast rolls.

Aaron had told all the children about Pidge, but he only let his very best friends come up and play carrier-pigeon with him. But telling everyone had been a mistake. A group of older boys from down the block had a club—Aaron's

◆ **Build Vocabulary**

mascot (mas´ kät) *n.*: Any person, animal, or thing adopted by a group; meant to bring good luck
coaxed (kōkst) *v.*: Tried to persuade
consoled (kän sōld´) *v.*: Comforted

mother called it a gang—and Aaron had longed to join as he had never longed for anything else. To be with them and share their secrets, the secrets of older boys. To be able to enter their clubhouse shack on the empty lot on the next street. To know the password and swear the secret oath. To belong.

About a month after Aaron had brought the pigeon home, Carl, the gang leader, walked over to Aaron in the street and told him he could be a member if he'd bring the pigeon down to be the club <u>mascot</u>. Aaron couldn't believe it; he immediately raced home to get Pidge. But his mother told Aaron to stay away from those boys, or else. And Aaron, miserable, argued with his mother and pleaded and cried and <u>coaxed</u>. It was no use. Not with those boys. No.

Aaron's mother tried to change the subject. She told him that it would soon be his grandmother's sixtieth birthday, a very special birthday indeed, and all the family from Brooklyn and the East Side would be coming to their apartment for a dinner and celebration. Would Aaron try to build something or make something for Grandma? A present made with his own hands would be nice. A decorated box for her hairpins or a crayon picture for her room or anything he liked.

In a flash Aaron knew what to give her: Pidge! Pidge would be her present! Pidge with his wing healed, who might be able to carry messages for her to the doctor or his Aunt Rachel or other people his grandmother seemed to go to a lot. It would be a surprise for everyone. And Pidge would make up for what had happened to Grandma when she'd been a little girl in the Ukraine, wherever that was.

Often, in the evening, Aaron's grandmother

would talk about the old days long ago in the Ukraine, in the same way that she talked to the birds on the back fire escape. She had lived in a village near a place called Kishinev with hundreds of other poor peasant families like her own. Things hadn't been too bad under someone called Czar Alexander the Second,[3] whom Aaron always pictured as a tall handsome man in a gold uniform. But Alexander the Second was assassinated, and Alexander the Third, whom Aaron pictured as an ugly man in a black cape, became the Czar. And the Jewish people of the Ukraine had no peace anymore.

One day, a thundering of horses was heard coming toward the village from the direction of Kishinev. *The Cossacks! The Cossacks!* someone had shouted. The Czar's horsemen! Quickly, quickly, everyone in Aaron's grandmother's family had climbed down to the cellar through a little trapdoor hidden under a mat in the big central room of their shack. But his grandmother's pet goat, whom she'd loved as much as Aaron loved Pidge and more, had to be left above, because if it had made a sound in the cellar, they would never have lived to see the next morning. They all hid under the wood in the woodbin and waited, hardly breathing.

Suddenly, from above, they heard shouts and calls and screams at a distance. And then the noise was in their house. Boots pounding on the floor, and everything breaking and crashing overhead. The smell of smoke and the shouts of a dozen men.

The terror went on for an hour and then the sound of horses' hooves faded into the distance. They waited another hour to make sure, and then the father went up out of the cellar and the rest of the family followed. The door to the house had been torn from its hinges and every piece of furniture was broken. Every window, every dish, every stitch of clothing was totally destroyed, and one wall had been

---

3. **Czar Alexander the Second:** Leader of Russia from 1855 to 1881.

completely bashed in. And on the floor was the goat, lying quietly. Aaron's grandmother, who was just a little girl of eight at the time, had wept over the goat all day and all night and could not be <u>consoled</u>.

But they had been lucky. For other houses had been burned to the ground. And everywhere, not goats alone, nor sheep, but men and women and children lay quietly on the ground. The word for this sort of massacre, Aaron had learned, was *pogrom.* It had been a pogrom. And the men on the horses were Cossacks. Hated word. Cossacks.

And so Pidge would replace that goat of long ago. A pigeon on Second Avenue where no one needed trapdoors or secret escape passages or woodpiles to hide under. A pigeon for his grandmother's sixtieth birthday. *Oh wing, heal quickly so my grandmother can send you flying to everywhere she wants!*

But a few days later, Aaron met Carl in the street again. And Carl told Aaron that there was going to be a meeting that afternoon in which a map was going to be drawn up to show where a secret treasure lay buried on the empty lot.

♦ **Literature and Your Life**
What rewards do you look for in a friendship?

"Bring the pigeon and you can come into the shack. We got a badge for you. A new kinda membership badge with a secret code on the back."

Aaron ran home, his heart pounding almost as fast as the pigeon's. He took Pidge in his hands and carried him out the door while his mother was busy in the kitchen making stuffed cabbage, his father's favorite dish. And by the time he reached the street, Aaron had decided to take the bandages off. Pidge would look like a real pigeon again, and none of the older boys would laugh or call him a bundle of rags.

Gently, gently he removed the bandages and the splints and put them in his pocket in case he should need them again. But Pidge seemed to hold his wing properly in place.

When he reached the empty lot, Aaron

walked up to the shack, then hesitated. Four bigger boys were there. After a moment, Carl came out and commanded Aaron to hand Pidge over.

"Be careful," said Aaron. "I just took the bandages off."

"Oh sure, don't worry," said Carl. By now Pidge was used to people holding him, and he remained calm in Carl's hands.

"OK," said Carl. "Give him the badge." And one of the older boys handed Aaron his badge with the code on the back. "Now light the fire," said Carl.

"What . . . what fire?" asked Aaron.

"The fire. You'll see," Carl answered.

"You didn't say nothing about a fire," said Aaron. "You didn't say nothing to—"

"Hey!" said Carl. "I'm the leader here. And you don't talk unless I tell you that you have p'mission. Light the fire, Al."

◆ **Literary Focus**
In what way does the lighting of the fire increase the tension as the turning point approaches?

The boy named Al went out to the side of the shack, where some wood and cardboard and old newspapers had been piled into a huge mound. He struck a match and held it to the newspapers.

"OK," said Carl. "Let's get 'er good and hot. Blow on it. Everybody blow."

Aaron's eyes stung from the smoke, but he blew alongside the others, going from side to side as the smoke shifted toward them and away.

"Let's fan it," said Al.

In a few minutes, the fire was crackling and glowing with a bright yellow-orange flame.

"Get me the rope," said Carl.

One of the boys brought Carl some cord and Carl, without a word, wound it twice around the pigeon, so that its wings were tight against its body.

"What . . . what are you *doing!*" shouted Aaron. "You're hurting his wing!"

"Don't worry about his wing," said Carl. "We're gonna throw him into the fire. And

when we do, we're gonna swear an oath of loyalty to—"

"No! *No!*" shouted Aaron, moving toward Carl.

"Grab him!" called Carl. "Don't let him get the pigeon!"

But Aaron had leaped right across the fire at Carl, taking him completely by surprise. He threw Carl back against the shack and hit out at his face with both fists. Carl slid down to the ground and the pigeon rolled out of his hands. Aaron scooped up the pigeon and ran, pretending he was on roller skates so that he would go faster and faster. And as he ran across the lot he pulled the cord off Pidge and tried to find a place, *any* place, to hide him. But the boys were on top of him, and the pigeon slipped from Aaron's hands.

"Get him!" shouted Carl.

Aaron thought of the worst, the most horrible thing he could shout at the boys. "Cossacks!" he screamed. "You're all Cossacks!"

Two boys held Aaron back while the others tried to catch the pigeon. Pidge fluttered along the ground just out of reach, skittering one way and then the other. Then the boys came at him from two directions. But suddenly Pidge beat his wings in rhythm, and rose up, up over the roof of the nearest tenement, up over Second Avenue toward the park.

With the pigeon gone, the boys turned toward Aaron and tackled him to the ground and punched him and tore his clothes and punched him some more. Aaron twisted and turned and kicked and punched back, shouting "Cossacks! Cossacks!" And somehow the word gave him the strength to tear away from them.

When Aaron reached home, he tried to go past the kitchen quickly so his mother wouldn't see his bloody face and torn clothing. But it was no use; his father was home from work early that night and was seated in the living room. In a moment Aaron was surrounded by his mother, father, and grandmother, and in another moment he had told them everything that had happened, the words tumbling out between his broken sobs. Told them of the present he had planned, of the pigeon for a goat, of the gang, of the badge with the secret code on the back, of the shack, and the fire, and the pigeon's flight over the tenement roof.

And Aaron's grandmother kissed him and thanked him for his present which was even better than the pigeon.

"What present?" asked Aaron, trying to stop the series of sobs.

And his grandmother opened her pocketbook and handed Aaron her mirror and asked him to look. But all Aaron saw was his dirty, bruised face and his torn shirt.

Aaron thought he understood and then, again, he thought he didn't. How could she be so happy when there really was no present?

And why pretend that there was?

Later that night, just before he fell asleep, Aaron tried to imagine what his grandmother might have done with the pigeon. She would have fed it, and she certainly would have talked to it, as she did to all the birds, and . . .

> ◆ Reading Strategy
> Reread the passage about Grandma's experiences in Russia to clarify the connections here.

and then she would have let it go free. Yes, of course. Pidge's flight to freedom must have been the gift that had made his grandmother so happy. Her goat has escaped from the Cossacks at last, Aaron thought, half dreaming. And he fell asleep with a smile.

Guide for Responding

◆ LITERATURE AND YOUR LIFE

Reader's Response What would you have done if Carl had asked you to join his club? Explain.

Thematic Focus What doors were opened by Aaron in this story? Which doors led to positive experiences?

Journal Writing Describe a time when someone gave you a "gift" that couldn't be wrapped.

☑ Check Your Comprehension

1. Describe how Aaron finds Pidge.
2. What happened to Aaron's grandmother's goat?
3. Why does Aaron decide to give Pidge to his grandmother for her birthday?
4. What does Carl want to do with Pidge?
5. What is Aaron's grandmother's response to Pidge's escape?

◆ Critical Thinking

INTERPRET

1. Why does Aaron try to help Pidge? **[Speculate]**
2. In what ways are Aaron and his family "strangers in the land of Egypt"? **[Interpret]**
3. Why does Aaron want to be friends with the other boys? **[Infer]**
4. Why is it important to Aaron's grandmother that Pidge be set free? **[Draw Conclusions]**

APPLY

5. Both Aaron and his grandmother are the victims of cruelty. What part could you play in stopping cruelty that you have seen? **[Apply]**

EXTEND

6. Based on what you know about Aaron's interests and personality, what careers do you think he should consider? **[Career Link]**

Water

HELEN KELLER

The morning after my teacher came she led me into her room and gave me a doll. The little blind children at the Perkins Institution had sent it and Laura Bridgman had dressed it; but I did not know this until afterward. When I had played with it a little while, Miss Sullivan slowly spelled into my hand the word "d-o-l-l." I was at once interested in this finger play and tried to imitate it. When I finally succeeded in making the letters correctly I was flushed with childish pleasure and pride. Running downstairs to my mother I held up my hand and made the letters for doll. I did not know that I was spelling a word or even that words existed; I was simply making my fingers go in monkey-like imitation. In the days that followed I learned to spell in this uncomprehending way a great many words, among them *pin, hat, cup* and a few verbs like *sit, stand and walk.* But my teacher had been with me several weeks before I understood that everything has a name.

One day, while I was playing with my new doll, Miss Sullivan put my big rag doll into my lap also, spelled "d-o-l-l" and tried to make me understand that "d-o-l-l" applied to both. Earlier in the day we had had a tussle over the words "m-u-g" and "w-a-t-e-r." Miss Sullivan had tried to impress it upon me that "m-u-g" is *mug* and that "w-a-t-e-r" is *water,* but I persisted in confounding the two. In despair she had dropped the subject for the time, only to renew it at the first opportunity. I became impatient at her repeated attempts and, seizing the new doll, I dashed it upon the floor. I was keenly delighted when I felt the fragments of the broken doll at my feet. Neither sorrow nor regret followed my passionate outburst. I had not loved the doll. In the still, dark world in which I lived there was no strong sentiment or tenderness. I felt my teacher sweep the fragments to one side of the hearth,[1] and I had a sense of satisfaction that the cause of my discomfort was removed. She

▲ **Critical Viewing** In what way do the expressions on the faces of the woman and the girl show "discovery"? [**Analyze**]

---

1. **hearth** (härth) *n.*: Stone or brick floor of a fireplace, sometimes stretching out into the room.

brought me my hat, and I knew I was going out into the warm sunshine. This thought, if a wordless sensation may be called a thought, made me hop and skip with pleasure.

We walked down the path to the well-house, attracted by the fragrance of the honeysuckle with which it was covered. Some one was drawing water and my teacher placed my hand under the spout. As the cool stream gushed over one hand she spelled into the other the word *water*, first slowly, then rapidly. I stood still, my whole attention fixed upon the motions of her fingers. Suddenly I felt a misty consciousness as of something forgotten—a thrill of returning thought; and somehow the mystery of language was revealed to me. I knew then that "w-a-t-e-r" meant the wonderful cool something that was flowing over my hand. That living word awakened my soul, gave it light, hope, joy, set it free! There were barriers still, it is true, but barriers that could in time be swept away.

I left the well-house eager to learn. Everything had a name, and each name gave birth to a new thought. As we returned to the house every object which I touched seemed to quiver with life. That was because I saw everything with the strange, new sight that had come to me. On entering the door I remembered the doll I had broken. I felt my way to the hearth and picked up the pieces. I tried vainly to put them together. Then my eyes filled with tears; for I realized what I had done, and for the first time I felt repentance and sorrow.

I learned a great many new words that day. I do not remember what they all were; but I do know that *mother, father, sister, teacher* were among them—words that were to make the world blossom for me, "like Aaron's rod, with flowers." It would have been difficult to find a happier child than I was as I lay in my crib at the close of that eventful day and lived over the joys it had brought me, and for the first time longed for a new day to come.

◆ Build Vocabulary

drawing (drô´ iŋ) *v.*: Bringing forth; making flow

Guide for Responding

◆ LITERATURE AND YOUR LIFE

Reader's Response Do you think Helen should be excused for her behavior before she learned to communicate? Explain.

Thematic Focus: Explain how Annie Sullivan opens a door for Helen.

☑ Check Your Comprehension

1. What does Annie try to teach Helen, using the doll she has brought?
2. What does Helen do to the doll? Why?
3. What event helps Helen recognize the meaning of "water"?
4. What is one other word Helen learned that day?

◆ Critical Thinking

INTERPRET

1. What is Helen's life like before Annie comes? **[Interpret]**
2. Helen understands some things, even without words. Give an example. **[Support]**

EVALUATE

3. What is the most valuable part of being able to communicate? **[Evaluate]**

COMPARE LITERARY WORKS

4. In what ways are "Aaron's Gift" and "Water" about gifts that can't be held in the hand? **[Synthesize]**

Guide for Responding (continued)

◆ Reading Strategy

REREAD

By **rereading** a word, name, or idea that seems confusing, you discover meanings and ideas that you didn't know before.

1. Why might you reread the passages about Aaron's grandmother's goat?
2. Identify one person or event that you clarified through rereading. Explain what you found in your second reading that you didn't understand in your first reading.

◆ Build Vocabulary

USING FORMS OF *console*

In your notebook, match each form of *console* with its definition.

1. consolation   **a.** give comfort
2. console   **b.** unable to be comforted
3. inconsolable   **c.** comfort

SPELLING STRATEGY

When adding an ending to a word that ends in *y*, follow these rules:

If a consonant comes before the final *y*, change the *y* to *i* unless the ending begins with *i*.

    frenzy + -ed = frenzied   cry + -ing = crying

If a vowel comes before the *y*, just add the ending: play + -ed = played

There are exceptions, such as pay + -ed = paid.

In your notebook, write the correct spelling for each item that follows.

1. merry + -ment   **3.** reply + -ed
2. cry + -ed   **4.** journey + -sing

USING THE WORD BANK

On your paper, write the word from the Word Bank that belongs in each numbered space.

The boys __1__ Aaron with promises of treasure. They said a pigeon would be a good __2__. The smoke was __3__ tears from Aaron's eyes. Pidge's __4__ movements showed his fear.

◆ Literary Focus

CLIMAX

The **climax** is the moment of highest tension, when events could go one way or another.

1. Explain two different ways that "Aaron's Gift" might have turned out.
2. In "Aaron's Gift," what is the climax of the story?
3. What is the climax of "Water"?

◆ Build Grammar Skills

VERB PHRASES

A **verb phrase** is a group of words made up of a main verb and one or more helping verbs. The main verb is the most important verb. The verb phrases are in italics in the following examples:

    Aaron *had come* to Tompkins Square Park.
    Helen *was playing* with a new doll.

Common Helping Verbs	
Forms of *have*	has, have, having, had
Forms of *be*	am, is, are, was, were, being, been
Other helping verbs	do, does, did, may, might, must, can, could, will, would, shall, should

Practice Copy these sentences in your notebook. Underline each helping verb once and each main verb twice.

1. The pigeon was trying to fly.
2. The boys were waiting for Aaron.
3. You should have seen Helen's face.
4. She must have been wondering about the water.
5. Now she can communicate with the world.

Writing Application On your paper, write three sentences about Aaron or Helen using each of the following verb phrases. If you wish, you may use the word *not* between parts of the verb phrase—for example, must *not* have known.

1. must have worried   **4.** does know
2. could help   **5.** may have learned
3. should have listened

Build Your Portfolio

 ## Idea Bank

Writing

1. **Scrapbook Introduction** Aaron's grandmother tells an important story from the family's history. Write a paragraph that introduces a scrapbook illustrating this story.

2. **Helen's Description** As Helen, write a description of an object, such as a seashell or a telephone, based only on your sense of touch.

3. **Anecdote** One positive experience changed Helen Keller's life forever. Write a brief narrative about an experience of your own that opened a doorway of understanding.

Speaking and Listening

4. **Sign Language Program [Group Activity]** Today, American Sign Language is more commonly used than the manual alphabet. With a group, plan and present a program on American Sign Language. Divide the following tasks: learning and demonstrating some signs, creating a chart showing some signs, explaining the development of American Sign Language. **[Social Studies Link; Science Link]**

5. **Speech As an Animal Character** As Pidge, perform a brief monologue that explains what you think about humans. **[Performing Arts Link]**

Projects

6. **Flight Investigation** Find out what you can learn about a bird from the shape of its wings. Prepare a chart that shows different kinds of wings and what they indicate. **[Science Link; Art Link]**

7. **Helen Keller Mural** You have the job of designing a mural for the Helen Keller Memorial. Do some research into her life. Then, plan the mural by describing what will be in it or drawing a sketch. **[Art Link]**

 ## Writing Mini-Lesson

Interview

An interview is a formal conversation in which one person (the interviewer) asks questions, and the other person (the interviewee) answers them. Often, interviews are recorded in writing so that others can read the interviewee's opinions and thoughts. Write an imaginary interview with Helen Keller or another famous individual who has overcome a physical disability.

Writing Skills Focus: Anticipate Audience Questions

Avoid having too many simple questions, such as, "When were you born?" Focus instead on the kinds of things your audience will want to know. **Anticipate your audience's questions,** and ask those they would want answered. Consider questions about the most exciting moment, most admired person, and greatest fear.

Prewriting Brainstorm for a list of questions you would ask your interviewee. Then, do research to find accurate and logical answers for your questions.

Drafting Write out each complete question. Then, create an answer for each question based on your research and on what you know about the interviewee. Your interview should be consistent with the characteristics of your subject.

Revising Have a classmate comment on your draft. What questions does he or she find interesting? Which questions would he or she eliminate? Revise, based on your reviewer's suggestions.

> ◆ **Grammar Application**
> Identify the verb phrases you have used in your interview. You may find parts of a phrase separated by *not* or another adverb.

Guide for Reading

Meet the Authors:

Leslie Marmon Silko (1948–)

In addition to writing two well-received novels about Native American life (*Ceremony* and *The Almanac of the Dead*), Leslie Marmon Silko has always been a poet and a lover of poetry. In a letter to poet James Wright, she wrote about poems, "I read them the way I write them: by feeling my way to them." Her work embraces her experiences growing up on a Laguna Pueblo reservation in New Mexico, as well as her love of landscape—such as, the cold, barren region of Alaska, described in "How to Write a Poem About the Sky."

Emily Dickinson (1830–1886)

Because Emily Dickinson is one of the most outstanding poets in the English language, you might expect that she lived the life of a celebrity. In fact, she was rarely seen by anyone outside her family. She lived quietly with her father and sisters, never receiving visitors and rarely coming out of her room. She wrote more than 1,000 poems, most of which were published after her death.

Elizabeth Coatsworth (1893–1986)

Elizabeth Coatsworth was born in Buffalo, New York, but spent most of her life in Maine. As a young woman, she traveled to China, North Africa, and Europe before settling in Maine. There, she enjoyed the woods, streams, rivers, and wildlife that inspired poetry such as "Wilderness Rivers."

◆ LITERATURE AND YOUR LIFE

CONNECT YOUR EXPERIENCE

You might notice when the sky is filled with clouds or bright sunshine, but you probably take the sky for granted the rest of the time. The poets in this group describe the beauty in nature—especially the sky—that most people don't take time to appreciate.

THEMATIC FOCUS: Opening Doors

Why do you think many people spend time outdoors when they want to relax, unwind, or have fun?

◆ Background for Understanding

SCIENCE

In "I'll tell you how the Sun rose—" Emily Dickinson gives a poetic, rather than a scientific, account of a sunrise. The sun appears to "rise" and "set" as a result of the Earth's rotation. The ribbons of color that we see in sunrises and sunsets appear when sunlight hits the Earth at an angle and bounces off particles in the atmosphere.

◆ Build Vocabulary

SUFFIXES: -less

The suffix -*less* means "without" or "not able to." A cloudless sky is a sky without clouds. A flightless bird is not able to fly. The word *relentless* means "without relenting"—that is, "without a break."

WORD BANK

Which of these words might you hear in a science class?

dense
membranes
amethyst
staid
relentless
exultant

How to Write a Poem About the Sky
◆ I'll tell you how the Sun rose— ◆
Wilderness Rivers

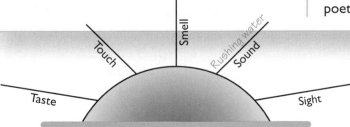

Voices of the Clouds, Jessie Lee Geiszler

◆ Literary Focus
SENSORY LANGUAGE

Sensory language describes the way things look, sound, taste, smell, and feel. In these poems, you will hear roaring rivers, feel the cold air of a frozen plain, and see the colors of a sunrise. Use a sensory language "sun" like the one below to jot down the sensory language that helps you see, hear, taste, smell, or feel what the poets describe.

◆ Reading Strategy
ENVISION

A videotape has all the images in a movie recorded on it, but you don't see the images until you pop the tape in the player and hit Play. In the same way, the words of a poem are recorded on the page, but your imagination is the player that helps you **envision,** or create a mental picture. Use the details in the poems and your imagination to create a mental movie of the scene each poet describes.

Touch · Smell · *Rushing water* · Sound · Taste · Sight

How to Write a Poem About the Sky

Leslie Marmon Silko

Left and above: *The Calm After the Storm*, Edward Moran, Private Collection

◀ **Critical Viewing**
In what ways is the sky in this picture similar to and different from the sky described in the poem? **[Compare and Contrast]**

You see the sky now
colder than the frozen river
so <u>dense</u> and white
little birds
5   walk across it.

You see the sky now
but the earth
is lost in it
and there are no horizons.
10   It is all
a single breath.

You see the sky
but the earth is called
by the same name
15   the moment
                      the wind shifts
sun splits it open
and bluish <u>membranes</u>
push through slits of skin.

20   You see the sky

◆ **Build Vocabulary**

dense (dens) *adj.*: Tightly packed; difficult to see through

membranes (mem´ brānz) *n.*: Thin, flexible layers of tissue

I'll tell you how the Sun rose—

Emily Dickinson

I'll tell you how the Sun rose—
A Ribbon at a time—
The Steeples swam in <u>Amethyst</u>—
The news, like Squirrels, ran—

5   The Hills untied their Bonnets—
The Bobolinks—begun—
Then I said softly to myself—
"That must have been the Sun!"

10   But how he set—I know not—
There seemed a purple stile
That little Yellow boys and girls
Were climbing all the while—
Till when they reached the other side,
A Dominie in Gray—
15   Put gently up the evening Bars—
And led the flock away—

◆ **Build Vocabulary**
amethyst (am´ i thist´) *n.:* Purple or violet

Guide for Responding

◆ LITERATURE AND YOUR LIFE

Reader's Response Which scene in these poems seems most familiar to you? Why?

Thematic Focus What do these poets seem to like about the outdoors?

Journal Writing Jot down your reaction to one of these poems. Explain what you do or do not like about it.

☑ Check Your Comprehension

1. What is the weather like in "How to Write a Poem About the Sky"?
2. What are two things the speaker sees in "I'll tell you how the Sun rose—"?
3. What is one thing the poet hears in "I'll tell you how the Sun rose—"?

◆ Critical Thinking

INTERPRET

1. Why can't the speaker see the horizon in "How to Write a Poem About the Sky"? **[Draw Conclusions]**
2. Describe what happens to the sky at the end of "How to Write a Poem. . . ." **[Interpret]**
3. What are the ribbons in "I'll tell you how the Sun rose—"? **[Interpret]**

EVALUATE

4. Which poem do you think more effectively captures an image of the sky? **[Make a Judgment]**

EXTEND

5. Why do meteorologists (scientists who study weather) study the sky? **[Career Link]**

Wilderness Rivers

Elizabeth Coatsworth

There are rivers
that I know,
born of ice
and melting snow,
5 with rapids,
swift to roar,
with no farms
along their shore,
with no cattle
10 come to drink
at a <u>staid</u>
and welcoming brink,
with no millwheel,
ever turning,
15 in that cold
<u>relentless</u> churning.

◆ **Build Vocabulary**

staid (stād) *adj.*: Calm; steady

relentless (ri lent´ lis) *adj.*: Never-ending

exultant (ig zult´ int) *adj.*: Joyful

▲ **Critical Viewing** What details of this scene would the speaker of "Wilderness Rivers" find appealing? **[Connect]**

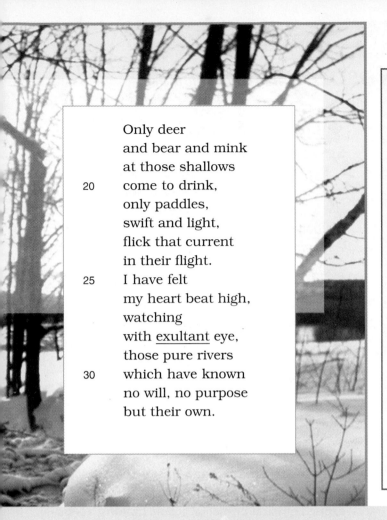

Only deer
and bear and mink
at those shallows
20 come to drink,
only paddles,
swift and light,
flick that current
in their flight.
25 I have felt
my heart beat high,
watching
with <u>exultant</u> eye,
those pure rivers
30 which have known
no will, no purpose
but their own.

Beyond Literature

Community Connection

National Parks People have long recognized the value of preserving open, natural spaces. The government of the United States has set aside more than 125,000 square miles as national parklands. National parks are managed by the National Parks Service (which also manages national monuments and historic sites). The first national park, Yellowstone National Park, was established in 1872. Today, every state except Delaware has at least one national park, in addition to state parks and nature preserves.

Cross-Curricular Activity
Map On a map of the United States, show the location of national parks, recreation areas, and national preserves managed by the National Parks Service. Create a key to identify the different locations.

Guide for Responding

◆ LITERATURE AND YOUR LIFE

Reader's Response Would you like to visit the place described in this poem? Why or why not?

Thematic Focus In what ways do rivers represent freedom?

Journal Writing Describe a scene from nature that you think would make a good subject for a poem like this one.

☑ Check Your Comprehension

1. What is the source of the water in a wilderness river?
2. What are two signs of civilization that are absent from the banks of the river?

◆ Critical Thinking

INTERPRET
1. What are the speaker's feelings about wilderness rivers? **[Infer]**
2. What does the speaker mean when she says that the rivers have known "no will, no purpose/ but their own"? **[Interpret]**

APPLY
3. What are two things people can do to protect natural resources like clean water? **[Apply]**

EXTEND
4. What are two careers open to people who enjoy working outdoors? **[Career Link; Social Studies Link]**

Guide for Responding (continued)

◆ Reading Strategy

ENVISION

When you **envision,** or create a mental movie, you enter into the experience or scene a poet describes.

1. Describe what you pictured when you read "How to Write a Poem About the Sky."
2. What details did you use to envision the sky in "I'll tell you how the Sun rose—"?
3. Identify four details in "Wilderness Rivers" that could be used in a painting of the poem.

◆ Build Vocabulary

USING THE SUFFIX -less

The suffix -less means "without" or "not able to be." On your paper, match each word that ends with the suffix -less with the person or thing it most likely describes.

1. helpless   a. garbage
2. worthless   b. baby
3. merciless   c. bully

SPELLING STRATEGY

Sometimes, as in *amethyst*, the sound of the short *i* is spelled with a *y*. On your paper, write the word with a short *i* spelled *y* that completes each part of this puzzle.

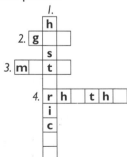

1. laughing or crying uncontrollably
2. where sports are played
3. fable or folk tale
4. a beat, tempo, or pattern

USING THE WORD BANK

In your notebook, write the word from the Word Bank that is closest in meaning to each word below.

1. skin   3. crowded   5. persistent
2. proper   4. joyful   6. gem

◆ Literary Focus

SENSORY LANGUAGE

Sensory language describes the way things look, sound, taste, smell, and feel. For example, in "I'll tell you how the Sun rose—," Dickinson's line "A Ribbon at a time" lets you *see* the sunrise. In "How to Write a Poem About the Sky," Leslie Marmon Silko's words "colder than the frozen river" help you *feel* the air.

1. Identify two words or phrases in "I'll tell you how the Sun rose—" that appeal to the sense of sight.
2. What are two words that describe how the air feels in "How to Write a Poem About the Sky"?
3. What sounds do you hear in "Wilderness Rivers"?

◆ Build Grammar Skills

ACTION AND LINKING VERBS

Verbs are either action verbs or linking verbs. **Action verbs**—such as *rose, drink,* and *shift*—express physical or mental action. **Linking verbs**—such as *is, was, become,* and *seem*—express a state of being and link the subject of the sentence to one or more words that further describe or identify it.

Action Verb: The sun rose.
Linking Verb: The sunshine felt warm.

The verb *felt* links *warm* to *sunshine*.

Practice Copy the following sentences in your notebook. Underline each action verb, and circle each linking verb. In sentences with linking verbs, draw an arrow that shows which word the verb links to the subject of the sentence. The first one is done for you.

1. The sky became bright with color.
2. The sunlight shimmered on the lake.
3. The wind blew in some clouds.
4. Then, the air seemed colder.
5. We ran into the house.

Build Your Portfolio

 Idea Bank

Writing

1. **Picture Postcard Captions** Choose a picture of a scene from nature that you would like to see as a picture postcard. Then, write a caption that describes something special about the place.

2. **Advertisement** Write an advertisement for a vacation package for one of the locations described in these poems. In your ad, describe what people will see and experience.

3. **Poems About Nature** Write a brief poem, with or without rhymes, about a scene from nature. Use sensory language in the poem's images and descriptions.

Speaking and Listening

4. **Twenty Questions [Group Activity]** Think of a beautiful or peaceful outdoor spot that is familiar to your classmates. Have your classmates ask yes-or-no questions that will help them figure out the place you have in mind. Keep a list of questions asked. Discuss which ones were most useful.

5. **Unrehearsed Speech** Based on what you've read in the poems, present a brief, unrehearsed speech that emphasizes the beauty of nature.

Projects

6. **State Park Presentation [Group Activity]** With a group, prepare a presentation on the state parks in your state. Have group members choose from these tasks: gather brochures, create maps showing locations, prepare charts showing features, illustrate attractions. **[Social Studies Link; Career Link]**

7. **Mural** Create a mural showing the kinds of animals and plants in a specific natural setting, such as a river, a meadow, or a wooded area. **[Science Link]**

 Writing Mini-Lesson

Journal Entry About Nature

The poets in this group share their personal responses to nature's beauty. Capture your own response to nature in a **journal entry,** a personal record of your experiences, thoughts, and feelings at a particular time. Most journal entries are dated. In a series of journal entries, the date helps you recall how you felt at different times.

Writing Skills Focus: Use Specific Details

Because a journal entry is a record, you should **use specific details** rather than general statements. A journal entry that tells the colors of a sunrise is a better record than one that says that the sunrise was pretty. Emily Dickinson names the specific bird whose call she hears.

Model From the Poem
The Hills untied their bonnets—
The Bobolinks—begun—

Prewriting Journals may include sketches, incomplete sentences, and lists. Before you begin recording your feelings, you may want to sketch or jot down details of what you see.

Drafting Imagine that you're writing a letter to your future self. Describe what you see, feel, and hear. Then, share your thoughts and emotional responses.

Revising Ask yourself if you will be able to recall your experience and feelings by reading this journal entry five years from now. Add details that will create a more specific record.

◆ **Grammar Application**
Use both action and linking verbs in your journal entry.

CONNECTING LITERATURE TO SOCIAL STUDIES
ANCIENT MIDDLE EAST

The Great Flood *Retold by Geraldine McCaughrean*

Ancient Middle East
- 🛕 Ancient city
- — Boundary of modern nation
- ⛰ Mountain

A WILD FRIEND A river is a wild friend to have. One day it is full of smiles and gifts. It waters the crops and sends boats full of fish on their way home. The next day, though, it may throw a reckless temper tantrum. Suddenly, it floods the land, smashing everything that gets in its way.

The Power of Floods Two rivers, the Tigris and the Euphrates, have been friends to the people of the Middle East for more than 5,000 years. Their power—for good and for ill—lies in their yearly floods.

Much of the Middle East is dry and desertlike. Every year, though, the Tigris and Euphrates swell with melting mountain snow and spill across the lowlands. The floods turn the dry plains between the rivers into rich farmland. It is not surprising that the story of Noah and the flood comes from this region.

The First Civilization By 3,500 B.C., this region, called Mesopotamia, had become a center of farming and trade. The Sumerians, ancient people living there, traveled the rivers trading goods. They built cities, invented a written language, and made laws.

For the first time in history, men and women created a settled way of life. They joined together in a group larger than a family or a tribe—a civilization.

Stories of the Flood Mesopotamia owed its farms and its trade to its rivers. Yet one ferocious flood could snatch everything away. Floods that nearly destroy the world appear in the area's early literature, including the epic poem *Gilgamesh* and the Bible story you are about to read. In this story, Noah learns that the flood is coming, and he takes on an awesome task.

THE GREAT FLOOD

Retold by Geraldine McCaughrean

As time passed, the family of Adam grew larger and larger. His children had children, their grandchildren had grandchildren. The number of people on Earth grew with every generation. But although there were more people, they were no better than Cain or wiser than Eve.[1]

Only one man was better. Noah was a good man. God and he were like friends. So God said to his friend, "Noah! The world has become a sordid, wicked place and I'm sorry I ever made it. I will wash it clean with a flood. So build a wooden ship—an ark—and daub the planks with pitch outside and in, to keep out water. Build it three stories high, and take aboard your wife and three sons—oh, and their wives, too. Then find every kind of animal—a male and a female of every bird and beast—and load them on, too. Why should they die for people's sins? Don't forget provisions, mind! Plenty of food for yourselves and the animals!"

Noah did exactly as he was told, whether or not his neighbors jeered and pointed and called him a madman, pelting him with pebbles and abuse. He set about building—right there, in the middle of dry land. He and his family went aboard, but it was seven days more before the rain came.

Then, in out of the wet came all the birds and beasts on Earth—two by two, as

---

1. **Cain . . . Eve:** In the Bible, Cain, son of Adam and Eve, killed his brother Abel. Eve had earlier been tricked into disobeying God.

lightning tore the heavens open like a ripsaw and let fall the rain in torrents.

The rising water shifted, then lifted the ark, bumping it across the ground before setting it fully afloat. Standing at the rail, Noah saw the fields silvered over, his mud house crumbling, whole cities filled to the brim with water, and everyone—every wicked living soul—run, wade, swim, scream, then sink in the mud-brown Flood. Noah, his family, his zoo—and God—watched it happen.

When, after forty days and forty nights, the rain finally stopped, water masked the face of the Earth. Nothing broke the surface—not a rock, not a tree. Then a wind sprang up; the water steamed. The ark ran aground on the peak of Mount Ararat.[2]

Noah freed a raven to fly away in search of something to eat, somewhere to perch. But the

_____

2. **Mount Ararat** (ar′ ə rat′): Mountain in Turkey, known in modern times as Agri Dagi.

raven only flew up and down, up and down, finding nowhere, nothing. Noah freed a dove, but she came back exhausted. A week later, Noah sent the dove out again. And again she came back to the ark. But to Noah's delight, there was a leaf from an olive tree in her beak. Now Noah knew that the water really was dropping. After another week, Noah's dove did not come back at all: She had found somewhere better than the ark to roost. So Noah opened up the ark and everyone climbed out: Noah, his family, and all the animals.

"Have children—lots of children!" God told the little family. "People the world all over again! But I promise you—no more floods, never again such destruction." And He wrote His oath in the sky, in the shining arc of a rainbow, His ever-lasting promise of pity.

> **Connecting Literature to Social Studies**
> Noah and his family are starting their "world all over again." What experiences of ancient Mesopotamian farmers might also fit this description?

Guide for Responding

◆ LITERATURE AND YOUR LIFE

Reader's Response What about the flood do you think was most frightening to Noah?

Thematic Focus How does the Flood open the door to a new life for Noah?

☑ Check Your Comprehension

1. What does God tell Noah to do?
2. How long does the rain last?
3. How does Noah find out that land has reappeared?

> The story of Noah comes from the Bible. The Jewish Bible (called the Old Testament by Christians) is the most important example of Hebrew literature. It contains the history, sacred laws, stories, and songs of the Hebrew people.

◆ Critical Thinking

INTERPRET

1. Why is Noah treated differently from other people? **[Interpret]**
2. Name two difficulties that Noah faces in addition to the Flood itself. **[Analyze]**
3. Describe Noah's character. Support your description with details from the story. **[Draw Conclusions]**

APPLY

4. Name two ways in which people react when they fear a disaster is coming. **[Relate]**

EXTEND

5. Identify at least one symbol of peace used by people across the world that appears in Noah's story. **[Social Studies Link]**

CONNECTING LITERATURE TO SOCIAL STUDIES

Imagine waking up one morning and looking out at the street—except that there isn't a street anymore—just water as far as the eye can see!

That kind of shock was a real possibility for an ancient Mesopotamian farmer or trader. A sudden river flood could sweep away all his belongings and ruin the work of months—destroying his world.

Noah's story expresses how uncertain life was for people at the time. It also shows how people can start over after a disaster. Even as Noah survived the flood, the civilizations of Mesopotamia survived floods and invasions for thousands of years.

1. (a) How do Noah's neighbors react when he builds the ark? (b) What do their reactions tell you about how Mesopotamians treated people whose ways they did not understand?
2. Noah sees his house crumble. Would people living by rivers have similar experiences? Explain.
3. Why might this story reassure people who live in a flood area?

 Idea Bank

Writing

1. **Diary Entry** Review the events of the story. Then, write a diary entry in which one of the people or animals on the ark describes the events of the Flood.
2. **Description of the Flood** Write a vivid description of the Flood's destructive effect on Noah's village. Using precise, vivid language, describe people's reactions, as well as the damage done.
3. **Dialogue** Noah has just spoken with God, and now he must explain to his wife what's going on. Write a dialogue in which Noah persuades his wife that they must build an ark.

Speaking and Listening

4. **Flood Farming Presentation** Give a presentation on ancient Mesopotamian farming. Use visual aids to enhance your presentation. **[Career Link; Social Studies Link]**

Projects

5. **Make a Climate Map** Make a map of the Middle East. Show the different climates in the region. Mark the areas where Noah may have started and ended his journey. **[Social Studies Link]**
6. **Ark Model** Make a model of Noah's ark, using your imagination or the account found in the Bible (Genesis 6:14–22). Write up notes about the model as they might appear on a museum card accompanying it. **[Math Link]**

Further Reading, Listening, and Viewing

- *The Earliest Farmers and the First Cities* by Charles Higham (1977) is a book that explains how the rivers contributed to farming and trade in ancient Mesopotamia.
- *Time Life's Lost Civilizations: Mesopotamia, Return to Eden* (1995) is a video exploring Mesopotamian civilization and its ruins.
- On the CD *Noah's Ark* (1990), James Earl Jones reads Peter Spier's 1977 retelling of the Noah story.

Letter to an Author

Writing Process Workshop

If you enjoyed Garrison Keillor's essay or wished "Aaron's Gift" had a different ending, you can let the author know. Many writers enjoy hearing what their readers thought of their work.

Choose a story, poem, essay, or other work you have enjoyed. Write a **letter to the author,** explaining what you liked or disliked and asking any questions you or your classmates might have.

Use the following tips to write a letter an author might enjoy receiving.

Writing Skills Focus

▶ **Use formal language,** language that is appropriate for a letter to someone you have never met. (A letter of appreciation should not be too formal, though.) (See p. 112.)

▶ **Brainstorm for good questions.** One way to come up with good questions to ask an author is to talk with others, such as classmates, who have read the author's work. (See p. 125.)

▶ **Use precise details.** Even someone who has not read the work can say, "It was great!" Be specific about the characters, events, or ideas that you liked or didn't like. (See p. 133.)

MODEL

① Dear Mr. Levoy:
I liked the story "Aaron's Gift." ② I particularly admired the way Aaron cared about his grandmother.

③ Where did you get the idea for the character of the grandmother? Is she based on someone in your family? ④ I'd appreciate any time you took to write back.
Sincerely,

Sam Weller

① Using "Mr." in the greeting is appropriately formal.

② Precise details focus the letter writer's comments.

③ These questions will interest other readers.

④ The use of the contraction "I'd" is all right in a semiformal letter. Slang and incomplete sentences are not.

Prewriting

Choose a Topic Pick a work that you found especially exciting or interesting, or one about which you have suggestions. Think of stories you retold to friends or essays that made you think. (Check with your teacher before selecting the work of an author who is no longer living.)

Topic Ideas

- A character you liked
- An event in the story that was especially exciting
- An image you found striking
- A point with which you disagree

Focus Your Topic Jot down all details that you liked, disliked, or wanted to change. Skim the chosen work to refresh your memory. Then, group these details, picking two or three main points you want to emphasize. In your letter, you can use the details as examples of each of your points.

| The Fox drives a really neat sportscar. | When the bad guys start trouble, the Fox stays cool and cracks jokes. | It was exciting when the Dark Colonel trapped the Fox inside the giant telescope. | At the last minute, the Fox used the lens to focus the sun and burn through the ropes tying his hands. |

Focus: The Fox is an exciting character.

Focus: The story is full of suspense.

Group Questions and Suggestions Around Your Focus Topics Think of questions and suggestions about the work that you found interesting.

DRAFTING/REVISING

APPLYING LANGUAGE SKILLS: Formal and Informal Language

Formal language is used in business letters, school reports, and speeches.

- Do not use contractions or slang.
- Use complete sentences.

Informal language is used in casual conversation, letters between friends, and even in some newspaper features.

- Contractions, slang, and some incomplete sentences may be used.

Practice Identify the style of each sentence as formal or informal. Then, rewrite each in the opposite style.

1. Letters are super!
2. In an emergency, one should proceed toward the door.
3. I can't wait until summer.
4. Talk about impossible!

Writing Application As you draft, use an appropriate style. Avoid slang and incomplete sentences.

Writer's Solution Connection Language Lab

For more practice, complete the Considering Audience and Purpose lesson in the Language Lab unit Composing.

APPLYING LANGUAGE SKILLS: Parts of a Letter

A letter is divided into parts, as shown on this page. At the top right is the **return address,** followed by the **date.** Next, against the left margin, appears the address of the person to whom the letter is being written. This is followed by the **greeting,** or salutation, which begins "Dear . . ." The main part is called the **body** of the letter. Letters always end with a **closing,** such as "Yours truly," followed by the writer's signature and printed name.

Practice Explain where you would expect the following information to appear:

1. Name of the person writing the letter
2. Name of the person to whom the letter is written
3. Date on which the letter was written

Writing Application As you revise, make sure your letter includes each of these basic parts.

Writer's Solution Connection Writing Lab

For additional help, use the Letter Shell in the Drafting section of the Writing Lab lesson on Expression.

Drafting

Use Proper Form Letters always contain certain information, set out in the same way:

return address	Your street address City, State, ZIP code Date
The author's name His or her street address City, State, ZIP code	**address of person to whom letter is sent**
Dear Mr./Mrs. [Author's name]: **greeting**	
[The body of your letter.]	
Best wishes, [or Regards or Sincerely,] 　　　　　　　　**closing**	
Your signature	
Your name	

Use the Appropriate Style The author is not your friend, so you should not be too informal. Write in complete sentences, and do not use slang. At the same time, use a friendly style. The use of contractions is acceptable.

Revising

Revision Checklist As you review your draft, use the following checklist to guide you:

- ▶ Have you used precise details to support your comments?
- ▶ Will your questions interest other readers?
- ▶ Did you include the basic parts of a letter, placed correctly?

Publishing and Presenting

▶ **Letter** Mail your letter to the author. Share with the class any response you receive.

▶ **Book-Jacket Display** Design and illustrate a book jacket for the story, poem, or essay that inspired your letter. Feature quotations from your letter on the back of the jacket.

Real-World Reading Skills Workshop

Judging a Writer's Purpose

Strategies for Success

Reading is a little like shopping. As a shopper, you make two judgments about each product. Before you buy, you decide whether a product is something you want or need. After you buy, you decide whether the product does what it is supposed to do. You make similar judgments about an author's purpose when you read. First, you decide whether the author's purpose fits your needs. As you read, you judge whether the author achieves his or her purpose.

Check It Out You can make some judgments even before you start to read. If you are looking for factual information on spiders, a spider folk tale that is intended to entertain will not help you. The author's purpose—to entertain— doesn't fit your needs. Titles, book jackets, and card catalogs often give information that will help you identify the author's purpose and judge whether it fits your needs.

Let Them Entertain You If you laughed, cried, or were gripped with terror while reading literature meant to entertain, then the writer was successful in achieving his or her purpose. If you had no response, identify why not. You may prefer more suspenseful writing or stories about characters your own age.

Live and Learn Sometimes the author's purpose is to inform. Judge whether the information is accurate and whether it is presented clearly.

Judge Persuasive Points When an author tries to persuade you, you must judge two things. First, judge whether the author presents logical arguments supporting his or her position. Then, decide whether those arguments sway your thinking.

Apply the Strategies

Read this article from a local newspaper. Then, answer the questions that follow:

Allendale Needs More Voters

Last Tuesday, only 30 percent of the eligible voters in Allendale bothered to vote. That's even fewer than the 40 percent who voted last year. This shameful trend must change. If Allendale is to succeed as a community, its citizens must participate. The best way to participate is to vote. Be sure to vote in the next election. It will make our town a better one.

1. What is the author's purpose? What clue could help you identify the author's purpose before you read the article?

2. On what points should you judge this author's purpose?

3. Explain why you think this writer does or does not achieve his or her purpose.

✔ Here are some other types of writing for which you may want to judge the writer's purpose:
▶ Advertisements
▶ Web sites
▶ Magazine articles

A verb is a word that shows action or being. It tells what the subject does or is. Verbs that tell what the subject *does* are **action verbs.**

Action
Verb
The bird flew.

Verbs that show *being* link the subject to one or more words that identify or describe it. These verbs are called **linking verbs.** (See page 132.)

L.V.
We are happy.

Common Linking Verbs	
Forms of *be*	am, are, is, was, were
Other linking verbs	appear, become, feel, grow, look, remain, seem, smell, sound, stay, taste, turn

A **verb phrase** is a group of words made up of a main verb and one or more helping verbs. (See page 124.)

Helping   Main
Verb   Verb
They were playing baseball.

Common Helping Verbs	
Forms of *have*	has, have, had
Forms of *be*	am, is, are, was, were, being, been
Other helping verbs	do, does, did, may, might, must, can, could, will, would, shall, should

Practice 1 Copy this paragraph in your notebook. Circle each verb.

Two of the pieces of literature in this section are about water. In "Water," Helen Keller shares an important experience. When she feels the water, she suddenly realizes that words mean something. In "The Great Flood," water washes away houses and people. Although these two works of literature are very different, they both show the power of water.

verb (verb) *n.* a word that shows action or a condition of being: some verbs are used to link a subject with words that tell about the subject, or to help other verbs show special features [In "The children ate early" and "Cactuses grow slowly," the words "ate" and "grow" are *verbs*. In "He is asleep," the word "is" is a linking *verb*. In "Where have you gone?", the word "hav~~e~~"...

Practice 2 Copy the numbered sentences on a piece of paper. Underline action verbs. Circle linking verbs. In sentences with linking verbs, draw an arrow to show which word the verb links to the subject of the sentence.

  1. The bird flapped in circles.
  2. The fire looked hot.
  3. Aaron remained calm.
  4. He skated carefully home.
  5. The bird remained quiet.

Practice 3 Copy these sentences on a piece of paper. Underline each verb phrase. Put a second line under the main verb in each verb phrase.

  1. Aaron had found a pigeon.
  2. The sky did not have a cloud in it.
  3. Helen was learning words.
  4. The elk have come here for years.
  5. I should have written that letter.

Grammar in Writing

✔ *Use a variety of action and linking verbs when you write.*

When you use an action verb, choose a strong one that shows a specific action. For example, use galloped instead of moved fast.

PART 2 *Friends in Deed*

Pushball, Kusnezov Pavel

Guide for Reading

Meet the Author:

Isaac Bashevis Singer (1904–1991)

As a boy, Singer lived in the Polish city of Warsaw, where his family struggled with poverty and illness. Singer's father was a rabbi, a teacher of the Jewish faith and laws. He gave advice to the people of the neighborhood while young Isaac listened, fascinated by the stories his father's visitors told of themselves.

A Vanished World Faced with prejudice against Jews, Singer left Poland for New York City in 1935. Soon after, World War II devastated the Jews of Eastern Europe. Villages like Leoncin and his old neighborhood in Warsaw vanished from the Earth. Yet Singer continued to write stories about such places. In literature, he said, "What happened long ago is still present." "Zlateh the Goat" helps to recapture this vanished world.

Lifelong Friends Singer loved Edgar Allan Poe's tales and the Sherlock Holmes stories. He read them in Yiddish, the language spoken by Eastern European Jews. Throughout his life, he wrote in Yiddish, translating his stories into English afterward. Storytelling and Yiddish remained his lifelong friends.

THE STORY BEHIND THE STORY

Singer wrote many stories about villages like Leoncin, the tiny Polish village where he was born. His family moved from Leoncin when he was three, but Singer always vividly remembered the pigs and other animals the peasants there brought to the village market. These childhood memories may have inspired Singer to write "Zlateh the Goat."

◆ LITERATURE AND YOUR LIFE

CONNECT YOUR EXPERIENCE

It was sunny when you left for school this morning, but now the rain is pouring down. You make a mad dash for the bus, but still you get drenched. Rain, snow, or wind can cause minor inconveniences (like getting wet), or they can create a life-and-death drama. For the boy in this story, snow becomes a deadly enemy.

THEMATIC FOCUS: Friends in Deed

In "Zlateh the Goat," a boy and a goat help each other survive in a snowstorm. Do you think their friendship is a friendship of words or of deeds?

◆ Background for Understanding

HEALTH

In "Zlateh the Goat," Aaron is lost outdoors in a winter storm. He runs the risk of frostbite and hypothermia. When frostbite occurs, ice crystals form in or just under the skin. The tissue affected may die and need to be cut out. When hypothermia occurs, the body temperature drops below the normal temperature of 98.6°F. Breathing slows, and, if the victim is not warmed, he or she becomes unconscious and may die.

◆ Build Vocabulary

PREFIXES: ex-

The prefix ex- means "out" or "away from." Knowing the meaning of ex-, you can figure out that a haystack that *exuded* the warmth of the summer sun was giving out heat.

USING THE WORD BANK

Which of these words seems to name a thing?

bound
conclusion
rapidly
exuded
trace

◆ Zlateh the Goat ◆

◆ Literary Focus
CONFLICT WITH NATURE

Stories develop around a conflict, a struggle between opposing forces. In many stories, as in "Zlateh the Goat," the force that opposes a character is an element of nature. In such stories, the characters are in **conflict with nature.** Farmers may struggle to raise crops during a drought; sailors may struggle to sail through a storm. As it is in "Zlateh the Goat," a conflict with nature is often a battle for survival.

◆ Reading Strategy
SUMMARIZE

You can better understand what is going on in a story if you pause occasionally to **summarize**— to review what has happened so far. Organize in your mind the main events, the order in which they happened, and why they happened. As you read "Zlateh the Goat," pause at the events indicated on the timeline below. Summarize what has happened up to that point by noting main events on a timeline of your own.

Aaron and Zlateh leave for the butcher

Aaron and Zlateh find the haystack

Aaron and Zlateh return home

Zlateh the Goat

Isaac Bashevis Singer

At Hanukkah[1] time the road from the village to the town is usually covered with snow, but this year the winter had been a mild one. Hanukkah had almost come, yet little snow had fallen. The sun shone most of the time. The peasants complained that because of the dry weather there would be a poor harvest of winter grain. New grass sprouted, and the peasants sent their cattle out to pasture.

For Reuven the furrier it was a bad year, and after long hesitation he decided to sell Zlateh the goat. She was old and gave little milk. Feivel the town butcher had offered eight gulden[2] for her. Such a sum would buy Hanukkah candles, potatoes and oil for pancakes, gifts for the children, and other holiday necessaries for the house. Reuven told his oldest boy Aaron to take the goat to town.

Aaron understood what taking the goat to Feivel meant, but had to obey his father. Leah, his mother, wiped the tears from her eyes when she heard the news. Aaron's younger sisters, Anna and Miriam, cried loudly. Aaron put on his quilted jacket and a cap with earmuffs, bound a rope around Zlateh's neck, and took along two slices of bread with cheese to eat on the road. Aaron was supposed to deliver the goat by evening, spend the night at the butcher's, and return the next day with the money.

While the family said goodbye to the goat, and Aaron placed the rope around her neck, Zlateh stood as patiently and good-naturedly as ever. She licked Reuven's hand. She shook

---

1. **Hanukkah** (khä´ nōō kä): Jewish festival celebrated for eight days in early winter. Hanukkah is also called the "festival of lights" because a candle is lit on each of the eight days.
2. **gulden** (gōōl´ dən) n.: Unit of money.

◆ **Build Vocabulary**

bound (bound) v.: Tied

conclusion (kən klōō´ zhən) n.: Belief or decision reached by reasoning

rapidly (rap´ id lē) adv.: Quickly

while she seemed to come to the <u>conclusion</u> that a goat shouldn't ask questions. Still, the road was different. They passed new fields, pastures, and huts with thatched roofs. Here and there a dog barked and came running after them, but Aaron chased it away with his stick.

The sun was shining when Aaron left the village. Suddenly the weather changed. A large black cloud with a bluish center appeared in the east and spread itself <u>rapidly</u> over the sky. A cold wind blew in with it. The crows flew low, croaking. At first it looked as if it would rain, but instead it began to hail as in summer. It was early in the day, but it became dark as dusk. After a while the hail turned to snow.

In his twelve years Aaron had seen all kinds of weather, but he had never experienced a snow like this one. It was so dense it shut out the light of the day. In a short time their path was completely covered. The wind became as cold as ice. The road to town was narrow and winding. Aaron no longer knew where he was. He could not see through the snow. The cold soon penetrated his quilted jacket.

At first Zlateh didn't seem to mind the change in weather. She, too, was twelve years old and knew what winter meant. But when her legs sank deeper and deeper into the snow, she began to turn her head and look at Aaron in wonderment. Her mild eyes seemed to ask, "Why are we out in such a storm?" Aaron hoped that a peasant would come along with his cart, but no one passed by.

The snow grew thicker, falling to the ground in large, whirling flakes. Beneath it Aaron's boots touched the softness of a plowed field. He realized that he was no longer on the road.

What does the goat's posture seem to indicate about her feelings? [Infer]

her small white beard. Zlateh trusted human beings. She knew that they always fed her and never did her any harm.

When Aaron brought her out on the road to town, she seemed somewhat astonished. She'd never been led in that direction before. She looked back at him questioningly, as if to say, "Where are you taking me?" But after a

snow about in eddies.[3] It looked as if white imps were playing tag on the fields. A white dust rose above the ground. Zlateh stopped. She could walk no longer. Stubbornly she anchored her cleft hooves in the earth and bleated as if pleading to be taken home. Icicles hung from her white beard, and her horns were glazed with frost.

Aaron did not want to admit the danger, but he knew just the same that if they did not find shelter they would freeze to death. This was no ordinary storm. It was a mighty blizzard. The snow had reached his knees. His hands were numb, and he could no longer feel his toes. He choked when he breathed. His nose felt like wood, and he rubbed it with snow. Zlateh's bleating began to sound like crying. Those humans in whom she had so much confidence had dragged her into a trap. Aaron began to pray to God for himself and for the innocent animal.

Suddenly he made out the shape of a hill. He wondered what it could be. Who had piled snow into such a huge heap? He moved toward it, dragging Zlateh after him. When he came near it, he realized that it was a large haystack which the snow had blanketed.

Aaron realized immediately that they were saved. With great effort he dug his way through the snow. He was a village boy and knew what to do. When he reached the hay, he hollowed out a nest for himself and the goat. No matter how cold it may be outside, in the hay it is always warm. And

▲ **Critical Viewing** Which character in this picture looks more hopeful or cheerful? [Contrast]

Maurice Sendak, HarperCollins

◆ **Literary Focus**
In what ways is the weather in conflict with Aaron and Zlateh?

He had gone astray. He could no longer figure out which was east or west, which way was the village, the town. The wind whistled, howled, whirled the

3. **eddies** (ed′ ēz) *n.:* Currents of air moving in circular motions; little whirlwinds.

◆ **Build Vocabulary**
exuded (eg zyōōd′ əd) *v.:* Gave off; oozed; radiated

hay was food for Zlateh. The moment she smelled it she became contented and began to eat. Outside, the snow continued to fall. It quickly covered the passageway Aaron had dug. But a boy and an animal need to breathe, and there was hardly any air in their hideout. Aaron bored a kind of a window through the hay and snow and carefully kept the passage clear.

Zlateh, having eaten her fill, sat down on her hind legs and seemed to have regained her confidence in man. Aaron ate his two slices of bread and cheese, but after the difficult journey he was still hungry. He looked at Zlateh and noticed her udders were full. He lay down next to her, placing himself so that when he milked her he could squirt the milk into his mouth. It was rich and sweet. Zlateh was not accustomed to being milked that way, but she did not resist. On the contrary, she seemed eager to reward Aaron for bringing her to a shelter whose very walls, floor, and ceiling were made of food.

Through the window Aaron could catch a glimpse of the chaos outside. The wind carried before it whole drifts of snow. It was completely dark, and he did not know whether night had already come or whether it was the darkness of the storm. Thank God that in the hay it was not cold. The dried hay, grass, and field flowers <u>exuded</u> the warmth of the summer sun. Zlateh ate frequently; she nibbled from above, below, from the left and right. Her body gave forth an animal warmth, and Aaron cuddled up to her. He had always loved Zlateh, but now she was like a sister. He was alone, cut off from his family, and wanted to talk. He began to talk to Zlateh. "Zlateh, what do you think about what has happened to us?" he asked.

"Maaaa," Zlateh answered.

"If we hadn't found this stack of hay, we would both be frozen stiff by now," Aaron said.

"Maaaa," was the goat's reply.

"If the snow keeps on falling like this, we may have to stay here for days," Aaron explained.

"Maaaa," Zlateh bleated.

"What does 'maaaa' mean?" Aaron asked. "You'd better speak up clearly."

"Maaaa, maaaa," Zlateh tried.

"Well, let it be 'maaaa' then," Aaron said patiently. "You can't speak, but I know you understand. I need you and you need me. Isn't that right?"

"Maaaa."

Aaron became sleepy. He made a pillow out of some hay, leaned his head on it, and dozed off. Zlateh, too, fell asleep.

When Aaron opened his eyes, he didn't know whether it was morning or night. The snow had blocked up his window. He tried to clear it, but when he had bored through to the length of his arm, he still hadn't reached the outside. Luckily he had his stick with him and was able to break through to the open air. It was still dark outside. The snow continued to fall and the wind wailed, first with one voice and then with many. Sometimes it had the sound of devilish laughter. Zlateh, too, awoke, and when Aaron greeted her, she answered, "Maaa." Yes, Zlateh's language consisted of only one word, but it meant many things. Now she was saying, "We must accept all that God gives us—heat, cold, hunger, satisfaction, light, and darkness."

Aaron had awakened hungry. He had eaten up his food, but Zlateh had plenty of milk.

For three days Aaron and Zlateh stayed in the haystack. Aaron had always loved Zlateh, but in these three days he loved her more and more. She fed him with her milk and helped him keep warm. She comforted him with her patience. He told her many stories, and she always cocked her ears and listened. When he patted her, she licked his hand and his face. Then she said, "Maaaa," and he knew it meant, I love you, too.

The snow fell for three days, though after the first day it was not as thick and the wind quieted down. Sometimes Aaron felt that there

▲ **Critical Viewing** What do you think the goat would say if she could speak? [Speculate]

brooks, and singing birds. By the third night the snow had stopped, but Aaron did not dare to find his way home in the darkness. The sky became clear and the moon shone, casting silvery nets on the snow. Aaron dug his way out and looked at the world. It was all white, quiet, dreaming dreams of heavenly splendor. The stars were large and close. The moon swam in the sky as in a sea.

On the morning of the fourth day Aaron heard the ringing of sleigh bells. The haystack was not far from the road. The peasant who drove the sleigh pointed out the way to him— not to the town and Feivel the butcher, but home to the village. Aaron had decided in the haystack that he would never part with Zlateh.

Aaron's family and their neighbors had searched for the boy and the goat but had found no <u>trace</u> of them during the storm. They feared they were lost. Aaron's mother and sisters cried for him; his father remained silent and gloomy. Suddenly one of the neighbors came running to their house with the news that Aaron and Zlateh were coming up the road.

There was great joy in the family. Aaron told them how he had found the stack of hay and how Zlateh had fed him with her milk. Aaron's sisters kissed and hugged Zlateh and gave her a special treat of chopped carrots and potato peels, which Zlateh gobbled up hungrily.

Nobody ever again thought of selling Zlateh, and now that the cold weather had finally set in, the villagers needed the services of Reuven

could never have been a summer, that the snow had always fallen, ever since he could remember. He, Aaron, never had a father or mother or sisters. He was a snow child, born of the snow, and so was Zlateh. It was so quiet in the hay that his ears rang in the stillness. Aaron and Zlateh slept all night and a good part of the day. As for Aaron's dreams, they were all about warm weather. He dreamed of green fields, trees covered with blossoms, clear

◆ **Build Vocabulary**

trace (trās) *n.*: Mark left behind by something

the furrier once more. When Hanukkah came, Aaron's mother was able to fry pancakes every evening, and Zlateh got her portion, too. Even though Zlateh had her own pen, she often came to the kitchen, knocking on the door with her horns to indicate that she was ready to visit, and she was always admitted. In the evening Aaron, Miriam, and Anna played dreidel.[4] Zlateh sat near the stove watching the children and the flickering of the Hanukkah candles.

Once in a while Aaron would ask her, "Zlateh, do you remember the three days we spent together?"

And Zlateh would scratch her neck with a horn, shake her white bearded head, and come out with the single sound which expressed all her thoughts, and all her love.

---

4. **dreidel** (drā´ dəl) *n.*: Small top with Hebrew letters on each of four sides, spun in a game played by children.

Beyond Literature

Community Connection

Farming Communities Because of the space needed to grow crops and graze livestock, homes in farming communities are usually very far from one another and from towns. Although cars and television have made farm life less isolated today than it was in Aaron's day, living in a farm community is still very different from living in a city or town.

Cross-Curricular Activity Create a pie chart that shows what percentage of the population in the United States lives on farms and what percentage lives in towns and cities.

Guide for Responding

◆ LITERATURE AND YOUR LIFE

Reader's Response What do you think is the most frightening part of Aaron's experience?

Thematic Focus Name two ways in which Zlateh and the family show they are friends.

Journal Writing Describe a time when you showed friendship through your actions rather than words.

☑ Check Your Comprehension

1. What does the father decide to do with Zlateh?
2. What does he ask Aaron to do?
3. What happens to Aaron and the goat on the way to town?
4. Explain how they are saved.
5. How does the family treat the goat in the end?

◆ Critical Thinking

INTERPRET

1. Why does the father decide to sell Zlateh? **[Interpret]**
2. How does Aaron react? **[Interpret]**
3. Find two sentences showing that Zlateh trusts her owners. **[Support]**
4. Why does their stay in the haystack change Aaron's mind about taking Zlateh to the butcher? **[Analyze]**

EVALUATE

5. Was the family's decision to sell Zlateh a good one? Explain. **[Make a Judgment]**

EXTEND

6. In what ways do weather, geography, and climate affect people's lives? **[Social Studies Link]**

Guide for Responding (continued)

◆ Reading Strategy

SUMMARIZE

When you **summarize** as you read, you can organize in your mind the order and significance of events.

1. Identify two events that occurred before Aaron and Zlateh left for the butcher.
2. Tell three things that happened in the haystack.
3. Summarize the events that led up to Zlateh's not being sold.

◆ Build Vocabulary

USING THE PREFIX ex-

Singer writes that Zlateh makes "the single sound which *expressed* all her thoughts." The prefix *ex-* means "out" or "away from." The word *expressed* means "put a thought out in the open." Using the meaning of *ex-*, define the italicized words in these sentences.

1. The damage to the house is only *external.*
2. She *extinguished* the fire with a pail of water.
3. They *exerted* a great effort to stop the fire.

SPELLING STRATEGY

Sometimes, the *s* sound at the end of a word is spelled with *ce,* as in *trace.* On your paper, unscramble each word to match the definition in parentheses.

1. ceir (a grainlike food)
2. icme (small furry animals)
3. pacle (a spot or location)
4. creag (beauty or charm)

USING THE WORD BANK

Copy the following sentences in your notebook. Supply a word from the Word Bank to complete each sentence.

1. The packages were ___?___ with string.
2. A strong smell ___?___ from the goat.
3. What ___?___ have you reached?
4. The news spread ___?___ through the town.
5. They found no ___?___ of the path.

◆ Literary Focus

CONFLICT WITH NATURE

The action in "Zlateh the Goat" revolves around a **conflict with nature.** By surviving the snowstorm with Zlateh's help, Aaron solves another problem as well.

1. What are two problems Aaron and Zlateh face in their conflict with the snowstorm?
2. Explain how the snowstorm both creates a problem and solves a problem.

◆ Build Grammar Skills

PRINCIPAL PARTS OF VERBS

Every verb (word expressing an action or state of being) has four main forms, called its **principal parts.** These parts are used to form verb tenses, the forms that show time. Regular verbs, such as *howl,* form their past tense and past participles by adding *-ed* or *-d.* Irregular verbs, such as *be,* form their past tense and/or past participles in different ways.

Base (present)	Present Participle	Past	Past Participle
look	looking	looked	(have or had) looked
howl	howling	howled	(have or had) howled
be	being	been	(have or had) been
eat	eating	ate	(has or had) eaten

Practice Copy the following chart in your notebook. Fill in the blanks.

Base (present)	Present Participle	Past	Past Participle
	walking	walked	
	keeping		(have or had) kept
go			(have or had) gone

Writing Application Write four sentences about the story. In each sentence, use a different principal part of *snow.*

Build Your Portfolio

 ## Idea Bank

Writing

1. **Weather Journal** Singer describes a fierce winter storm. In a journal entry, write your memories of a day of fierce weather—rain, wind, snow, or heat.

2. **Animal Description** Describe the animal you would want to have with you if you were trapped in a snowstorm. Explain your choice.

3. **A Place of Comfort** The haystack is a simple, warm world for Aaron and Zlateh. Describe a place—real or imaginary—where you can feel safe and protected.

Speaking and Listening

4. **Monologue** Zlateh doesn't say much in the story, but Aaron interprets her bleating to have meaning. Write and deliver a monologue in which you, as Zlateh, say what you are thinking in the haystack. **[Performing Arts Link]**

5. **Role Play** With a partner, role-play the conversation that might have taken place between Aaron and his father before Aaron took the goat to town.

Projects

6. **Storyboards** Create a storyboard showing the events in "Zlateh the Goat." You can sketch the scenes, use magazine pictures, or draw stick figures with captions. Arrange the events in order. **[Visual Arts Link]**

7. **Presentation [Group Activity]** With a group, give a presentation on the *shtetl* (the Jewish villages of Eastern Europe). Divide up the following tasks: finding out what jobs people had there; outlining the history of these villages; gathering visual materials for the presentation. **[Social Studies Link]**

 ## Writing Mini-Lesson

Persuasive Speech

Zlateh cannot talk, and nobody else speaks for her. In the end, she persuades the family to keep her through her deeds, not words. Imagine, though, that you are a neighbor who wishes to defend the goat. Write a short persuasive speech in which you explain why the family should not sell Zlateh.

Writing Skills Focus: Choose Details to Achieve Your Purpose

Not every detail about Zlateh can help you persuade Aaron's father to keep her. **Choose details to achieve your purpose.** For example, if you want Aaron's father to see Zlateh as a family member, you might use the detail that Zlateh has lived with the family for twelve years—that she and Aaron grew up together.

Prewriting Make a two-column chart. In the first column, list all the reasons you would tell Aaron's father to keep the goat. In the second column, list details you learned in the story that support those reasons.

Drafting Organize each paragraph of your speech around a single point. Include details to support each point. You might also include details that appeal to the father's emotions.

Revising Reread your speech, making sure that you focus on one main point in each paragraph and that you have supported it with at least two details.

> ◆ **Grammar Application**
> Identify the principal parts of verbs you have used in your speech.

Guide for Reading

Meet the Authors:

Charlotte Pomerantz (1930–   )

Charlotte Pomerantz has been making friends with young readers for years. She won the Jane Addams's Children's Book Award for *The Princess and the Admiral.* Her fascination with language can be seen in her books, especially *If I Had a Paka,* which is the source of "Door Number Four."

George Eliot (1819–1880)

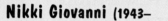

The writer George Eliot (her real name was Mary Ann Evans) grew up in the English countryside. She describes the life there vividly in her very successful novels. Eliot was a friend of many important thinkers of her time, and she thought and wrote much about the ties between people.

Nikki Giovanni (1943–   )

In her poems, Nikki Giovanni shares her thoughts and experiences. Born in Knoxville, Tennessee, and raised in Cincinnati, Ohio, she has become one of America's most popular poets.

Henry Wadsworth Longfellow (1807–1882)

Henry Wadsworth Longfellow, one of the best-loved American poets of his day, made friends throughout the world. In the late 1860's, he was invited to meet Queen Victoria of England privately—a great honor. Longfellow is still remembered for such classics as "Paul Revere's Ride."

◆ LITERATURE AND YOUR LIFE

CONNECT YOUR EXPERIENCE

The school bell rings. You fly home, throw your books down, and settle in with a nice snack. By taking a pause before homework or play, you break the day in two—you give it a rhythm. That way, time doesn't just keep a tick-tock beat. These poems explore the ways that connecting with friends and helping others add variety to the rhythm of your days.

THEMATIC FOCUS: Friends in Deed

These poems explore different kinds of friendship. What qualities do all friends have in common—regardless of age or background?

◆ Background for Understanding

LANGUAGE

These poems are like a crossroad where words from one language can drive straight into another. In "The Children's Hour," Longfellow creates a sense of adventure by using the Italian word *banditti* instead of "robbers." Charlotte Pomerantz spices her poem with the Indonesian words for *door, number, four,* and *friend.*

◆ Build Vocabulary

PREFIX: *de-*

The prefix *de-* often means "down." Knowing this, you can figure out that *descending* the stairs means "going down the stairs."

WORD BANK

Which of the words most likely means "made easier"?

eased
descending
fortress

Door Number Four ◆ Count That Day Lost ◆ The World Is Not a Pleasant Place to Be ◆ The Children's Hour

◆ Literary Focus

SPEAKER

The **speaker** is the imaginary voice a poet uses when writing a poem. There can be important differences between the poet and the poem's speaker. In "Door Number Four," for example, the poem's speaker is probably a child, even though the poet is an adult.

◆ Reading Strategy

PARAPHRASE

When you **paraphrase,** you put sentences or ideas into your own words. By "saying back" what you have read (even if you just do it in your head), you make sure you really know what's going on. You might use a diagram like the one below to help you paraphrase difficult lines from the poems.

Phrases or Lines From the Poem	My Paraphrase
"Between the dark and the daylight, / When the night is beginning to lower, . . ."	In the early evening, when it's starting to get dark, . . .
"Comes a pause in the day's occupations,/ That is known as the Children's Hour."	. . . we take a break from working, a break we call the Children's Hour.

Door Number Four

CHARLOTTE POMERANTZ

Above my uncle's grocery store
is a pintu,
is a door.
On the pintu
5   is a number,
nomer empat,
number four.
In the door
there is a key.
10   Turn it,
enter quietly.
Hush hush, diam-diam,
quietly.
There, in lamplight,
15   you will see
a friend,
teman,
a friend
who's me.

COUNT THAT DAY LOST
George Eliot

If you sit down at set of sun
And count the acts that you have done,
   And, counting, find
One self-denying[1] deed, one word
5   That <u>eased</u> the heart of him who heard,
   One glance most kind
That fell like sunshine where it went—
Then you may count that day well spent.

But if, through all the livelong day,
10   You've cheered no heart, by yea or nay—
   If, through it all
You've nothing done that you can trace
That brought the sunshine to one face—
   No act most small
15   That helped some soul and nothing cost—
Then count that day as worse than lost.

1. **self-denying** *adj.*: Opposite of selfish; done without concern for one's own interests.

◆ **Build Vocabulary**

eased (ēzd) *v.*: Comforted; freed from pain or worry

◀ **Critical Viewing** How is starting a friendship like opening a door? **[Relate]**

One Child Between Doors, (Seorang Anak di Antara Pintu Ruang) 1984, Dede Eri Supria, Courtesy of Joseph Fischer

The World Is Not a Pleasant Place to Be
NIKKI GIOVANNI

the world is not a pleasant place
to be without
someone to hold and be held by

   a river would stop
5 its flow if only
   a stream were there
   to receive it

   an ocean would never laugh
   if clouds weren't there
10 to kiss her tears

   the world is not
   a pleasant place to be without
   someone

◆ **LITERATURE AND YOUR LIFE**

Reader's Response Which of these poems would you give to your best friend? Why?

Thematic Focus In what ways is your life enriched by friends?

Journal Writing Make a list of the qualities you value in a friend.

☑ **Check Your Comprehension**

1. In "Door Number Four," where is the speaker of the poem?
2. What does the speaker of "Count That Day Lost" ask readers to count?
3. What two images does Giovanni use to show companionship in "The World Is Not a Pleasant Place to Be"?

◆ **Critical Thinking**

INTERPRET

1. At what time of day do you think "Door Number Four" takes place? **[Infer]**
2. Why do you think the speaker wants someone to visit? **[Speculate]**
3. Why does the speaker of "Count That Day Lost" say that a day is lost if you haven't helped someone? **[Interpret]**
4. Explain why you do or do not think Giovanni uses good images for friendship. **[Support]**

APPLY

5. In what ways could you apply the advice in "Count That Day Lost"? **[Relate]**
6. In what ways could the messages of these poems be applied to the relationship between groups of people or even countries? **[Social Studies Link]**

COMPARE LITERARY WORKS

7. Which two of these three poems do you think have the most similar message? Explain. **[Compare]**

Children in an Interior, Carl Holsoe

◀ Critical
Viewing
What do you
think these
children are
planning?
[Speculate]

The Children's Hour
Henry Wadsworth Longfellow

*B*etween the dark and the daylight,
    When the night is beginning to lower,
    Comes a pause in the day's occupations,[1]
    That is known as the Children's Hour.

5   I hear in the chamber above me
      The patter of little feet,
    The sound of a door that is opened,
      And voices soft and sweet.

---

1. occupations (äk´ yoo pā´ shənz) *n.*: Tasks or other
activities.

◆ **Build
Vocabulary**

descending (dē
send´ iŋ) *adj.*: Mov-
ing from a higher
to a lower place

fortress (fôr´ triss)
n.: Heavily walled
building designed
to be easily
defended against
attack

From my study I see in the lamplight,
10   Descending the broad hall stair,
    Grave Alice, and laughing Allegra,
        And Edith with golden hair.

A whisper, and then a silence:
    Yet I know by their merry eyes
15 They are plotting and planning together
    To take me by surprise.

A sudden rush from the stairway,
    A sudden raid from the hall!
By three doors left unguarded
20   They enter my castle wall!

They climb up into my turret[2]
    O'er the arms and back of my chair;
If I try to escape, they surround me;
    They seem to be everywhere.

25 They almost devour me with kisses,
    Their arms about me entwine,
Till I think of the Bishop of Bingen
    In his Mouse Tower on the Rhine![3]

Do you think, O blue-eyed banditti,[4]
30   Because you have scaled the wall,
Such an old mustache as I am
    Is not a match for you all!

I have you fast in my fortress,
    And will not let you depart,
35 But put you down into the dungeon
    In the round-tower of my heart.

And there will I keep you forever,
    Yes, forever and a day,
Till the walls shall crumble to ruin,
40   And molder in dust away!

---

2. **turret** (tŭr´ it) *n.*: Tower rising above a building, such as a castle.
3. **the Bishop of Bingen / In his Mouse Tower on the Rhine:** Bingen is a German city along the Rhine River; the Mouse Tower still stands on a rock in the river there. Legend says that in the tower, an important church official named Hatto I (the Bishop of Bingen) was bitten to death by mice for his evil deeds.
4. **banditti** (ban dǐ´ tē) *n.*: Robbers; outlaws.

Guide for Responding

◆ LITERATURE AND YOUR LIFE

Reader's Response What would you enjoy about being part of the family in the poem?

Thematic Focus Explain how the father and the children in the poem show their affection for one another.

Journal Writing Describe a childhood game you liked to play.

☑ Check Your Comprehension

1. When does the children's hour occur?
2. How many children are in the poem?
3. What do the children pretend?
4. How does the father help them pretend?

◆ Critical Thinking

INTERPRET

1. Describe three signs that let the father know what his daughters are planning. **[Analyze]**
2. How old do you think the children in this poem are? **[Infer]**
3. What is the "turret" in line 21? **[Interpret]**
4. What is happening when the father says he holds his daughters in a "fortress"? **[Infer]**
5. In what way is the father's heart like a dungeon? **[Interpret]**

EVALUATE

6. Do you think the poem gives a clear image of the game the father plays with his children? **[Evaluate]**

EXTEND

7. What details in the poem give you information about the family life of nineteenth-century Americans? **[Social Studies Link]**

Guide for Responding (continued)

◆ Reading Strategy

PARAPHRASE

While reading these poems, you may have found that **paraphrasing**—putting the poem into your own words—helped you understand sentences and ideas.

1. Paraphrase lines 8–11 of "Count That Day Lost."
2. Paraphrase lines 4–7 of "The World Is Not ..."
3. Paraphrase lines 13–16 of "The Children's Hour."
4. Paraphrase lines 33–36 of "The Children's Hour."

◆ Build Grammar Skills

VERB TENSES

Every **verb** (word expressing an action or state of being) shows when an action or state of being occurred. The **tense** of a verb shows the time of the action or being expressed by the verb. The three simple, or basic, tenses are the past, present, and future. The past tense of regular verbs is formed with -ed or -d. The past tense of irregular verbs is formed in different ways. All future tense verbs use the helping verb will.

Present	I succeed.	I run.	I am.
Past	I succeeded.	I ran.	I was.
Future	I will succeed.	I will run.	I will be.

Practice On your paper, write each of the following sentences in the past, present, and future tense.

1. He (descend).   3. You (ease).
2. They (bring).   4. I (send).

Writing Application Write two sentences in the past tense about something you did yesterday. Write two sentences in the present tense about something you are doing today. Write two sentences in the future tense about something you will do tomorrow.

◆ Literary Focus

SPEAKER

A poem's **speaker**—the person who is saying the words of the poem—is often an imaginary character. There can be important differences between the poet and the poem's speaker. In some poems, the speaker is not a character, but a "voice." The speaker may be described as "a voice of wisdom" or "a voice of the heart."

1. Describe the speaker in "Door Number Four."
2. What do you know about the age or background of the speaker in Eliot's "Count That Day Lost"?
3. What do you know about the feelings of the speaker in "The World Is Not a Pleasant Place"?
4. What do you know about the life of the speaker in "The Children's Hour"?

◆ Build Vocabulary

USING THE PREFIX de-

The prefix de- often means "down" or "lower." For each of the following words, explain what comes down or goes lower.

1. decrease
2. devalue
3. decline

SPELLING STRATEGY

In some words, like descending, an s sound is spelled with the letters sc. On your paper, add sc to each of the following groups of letters. Write the meaning of each word you create.

1. _ _enery   3. a_ _end
2. _ _ent   4. _ _ience

USING THE WORD BANK

On your paper, complete each sentence by supplying a word from the Word Bank.

1. School is to student as ___?___ is to soldier.
2. Door is to exit as stairs is to ___?___.
3. Helped is to aided as comforted is to ___?___.

Build Your Portfolio

 ## Idea Bank

Writing

1. **Definition of a Friend** Write a dictionary-style definition of a friend. Include the qualities you value in a friend.

2. **Paragraph About a Friend** Write a paragraph about a friend. Describe your friend's personality and the ways in which you and your friend are alike and different.

3. **Essay About Helping Others** Write a brief essay that explains the different ways people your age can help others. Keep your suggestions practical and realistic.

Speaking and Listening

4. **Introductions** Introductions can be the first step to a friendship. With two partners, take turns acting out how you would introduce two people to each other and how you would introduce yourself to someone else. **[Performing Arts Link]**

5. **Dance for a Day [Group Activity]** With a group, create a dance showing a day's rhythm. Divide up the following tasks: choosing music for each part of the day; organizing movements; practicing and performing the dance. **[Music Link; Performing Arts Link]**

Projects

6. **Dictionary for Friends** List ten words related to friendship. Use foreign language dictionaries to find how these words are said in at least two other languages. Use what you find to create a "dictionary for friends." Include pronunciations. **[Foreign Languages Link]**

7. **Service Presentation** Using library and community resources, research opportunities for people your age to help in the community. Present your findings to the class. **[Social Studies Link]**

 ## Writing Mini-Lesson

Thank-You Note

When a friend or relative gives you a gift or does you a big favor, you should write a thank-you note. Make your thank-you note personal—let the person who reads the note know you care.

Writing Skills Focus: Focus on Your Audience

Writing to another person doesn't mean just putting his or her name at the top of the note. It means **focusing on your audience**—thinking about who he or she is and letting that influence your words. If your Aunt Edna made you a new shirt, she'll be glad you noticed that she sewed it herself. If your best friend made you a shirt, he or she might be interested in how you like the color or where you wore it.

Prewriting Jot down a description of a gift you have recently received. Then, identify the qualities that you especially appreciated.

Drafting Begin by identifying the gift: "Thank you for the sweater you gave me for my birthday." (If someone has given you a gift of money, you can simply say "Thank you for your generous gift.") Include details about how or when you used the gift. Choose details that will interest your audience.

Revising Reread your note, imagining the person for whom you wrote it. Revise any language or details that will not be appreciated or understood by the person who receives the note.

> ◆ **Grammar Application**
> Make sure you have used the correct tenses of verbs to show when an action occurs.

Guide for Reading

Meet the Authors:

Jesse Stuart (1906–1984)

A writer for the *Chicago Tribune* once said that Jesse Stuart's stories "all have a heart." His narrative about an unusual pet—"Old Ben"—is no exception. The Kentucky-born novelist, poet, and short-story writer received a number of awards for his writing.

Arthur C. Clarke (1917–   )

When he first got his television set, noted science-fiction writer Arthur C. Clarke became the only television owner on Sri Lanka, the island off India where he lives.

THE STORY BEHIND THE STORY

Clarke holds another, more important, television "first." He was the first to think of sending television and radio signals around the world by bouncing them off satellites. If not for his own idea, his television set would have no signals to pick up! Though "Feathered Friend" is science fiction, some of Clarke's dreams about the future have become "science fact."

Pablo Neruda (1904–1973)

Pablo Neruda may be the only poet ever to write a poem to his socks! Throughout his life, he kept his ear tuned to the songs of common objects. The toy in "Childhood and Poetry," for instance, is old and tattered, but it whispers to Neruda of larger things. Neruda was also a friend of the common people, fighting for justice in Chile, his homeland. He won the 1971 Nobel Prize for Literature.

◆ LITERATURE AND YOUR LIFE

CONNECT YOUR EXPERIENCE

Mornings, you may walk the dog or feed the fish. After school, you might help a friend study for a test. *Being* a friend—whether to an animal or a person—involves responsibility. *Having* a friend, as these works show, can be well worth the effort.

THEMATIC FOCUS: Friends in Deed

As you read, think about what these works show about the rewards and responsibilities of friendship.

◆ Background for Understanding

SCIENCE

"Feathered Friend" tells of an astronaut's pet canary. A canary's small size makes it a good pet for a small place like a space capsule—or a coal mine. Years ago, miners brought these birds down into the mines. If poisonous fumes began to accumulate, the canary would pass out, well before the miners were affected. Once its cheery song had stopped, the miners knew that danger threatened.

◆ Build Vocabulary

RELATED WORDS: FORMS OF *regulate*

A *regulation* is a rule. The word *regulate* means "to govern according to a rule." The two words are related in form and meaning. Other related words are *regulator* (one who regulates) and *regulatory* (rule making).

scarce
regulation
fusing
ceased
minuscule
furtively
persecution

WORD BANK

Would you expect something that is *minuscule* to be small or large?

Old Ben ◆ Feathered Friend
◆ Childhood and Poetry ◆

◆ Literary Focus

NARRATIVES

These works all deal with friendship, but they have something else in common. Each piece is a **narrative,** that is, each piece tells a story. A narrative can be fiction (made up) or nonfiction (true). Short stories and novels are fictional narratives. Biographical and autobiographical accounts are nonfictional narratives. As you read the narratives in this group, notice which stories come from the imagination and which are true. Use a chart like the one below to keep track of the order of events in each narrative.

◆ Reading Strategy

CONTEXT CLUES

An unfamiliar or confusing word may appear to have its meaning locked up. However, you can crack it open by using **context clues**—information provided in the words and phrases around it.

In this sentence, you will find a clue to the meaning of *garbs:* "It was a skilled and difficult job, for a space suit is not the most convenient of *garbs* in which to work." Since a space suit is a type of *garb,* you can figure out that a *garb* is something you wear.

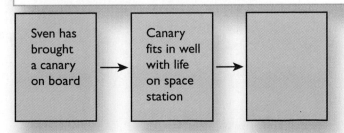

Old Ben

Jesse Stuart

One morning in July when I was walking across a clover field to a sweet-apple tree, I almost stepped on him. There he lay coiled like heavy strands of black rope. He was a big bull blacksnake. We looked at each other a minute, and then I stuck the toe of my shoe up to his mouth. He drew his head back in a friendly way. He didn't want trouble. Had he shown the least fight, I would have soon finished him. My father had always told me there was only one good snake—a dead one.

When the big fellow didn't show any fight, I reached down and picked him up by the neck. When I lifted him he was as long as I was tall. That was six feet. I started calling him Old Ben as I held him by the neck and rubbed his back. He enjoying having his back rubbed and his head stroked. Then I lifted him into my arms. He was the first snake I'd ever been friendly with. I was afraid at first to let Old Ben wrap himself around me. I thought he might wrap himself around my neck and choke me.

The more I petted him, the more affectionate he became. He was so friendly I decided to trust him. I wrapped him around my neck a couple of times and let him loose. He crawled down one arm and went back to my neck, around and down the other arm and back again. He struck out his forked tongue to the sound of my voice as I talked to him.

"I wouldn't kill you at all," I said. "You're a friendly snake. I'm taking you home with me."

I headed home with Old Ben wrapped around my neck and shoulders. When I started over the hill by the pine grove, I met my cousin Wayne Holbrook coming up the hill. He stopped suddenly when he saw me. He started backing down the hill.

"He's a pet, Wayne," I said. "Don't be afraid of Old Ben."

It was a minute before Wayne could tell me what he wanted. He had come to borrow a plow. He kept a safe distance as we walked on together.

Before we reached the barn, Wayne got brave enough to touch Old Ben's long body.

"What are you going to do with him?" Wayne asked. "Uncle Mick won't let you keep him!"

"Put him in the corncrib," I said. "He'll have plenty of delicate food in there. The cats we keep at this barn have grown fat and lazy on the milk we feed 'em."

I opened the corncrib door and took Old Ben from around my neck because he was beginning to get warm and a little heavy.

"This will be your home," I said. "You'd better hide under the corn."

Besides my father, I knew Old Ben would have another enemy at our home. He was our hunting dog, Blackie, who would trail a snake, same as a possum or mink. He had treed blacksnakes, and my father had shot them from the trees. I knew Blackie would find Old Ben, because he followed us to the barn each morning.

The first morning after I'd put Old Ben in the corncrib, Blackie followed us. He started toward the corncrib holding his head high, sniffing. He stuck his nose up to a crack in the crib and began to bark. Then he tried to tear a plank off.

"Stop it, Blackie," Pa scolded him. "What's the matter with you? Have you taken to barking at mice?"

"Blackie is not barking at a mouse," I said. "I put a blacksnake in there yesterday!"

"A blacksnake?" Pa asked, looking unbelievingly. "A blacksnake?"

"Yes, a pet blacksnake," I said.

"Have you gone crazy?" he said. "I'll move a thousand bushels of corn to get that snake!"

"You won't mind this one," I said. "You and Mom will love him."

My father said a few unprintable words before we started back to the house. After breakfast, when Pa and Mom came to the barn, I was already there. I had opened the crib door and there was Old Ben. He'd crawled up front and was coiled on a sack. I put my hand down and he crawled up my arm to my neck and over my shoulder. When Mom and Pa reached the crib, I thought Pa was going to faint.

"He has a pet snake," Mom said.

"Won't be a bird or a young chicken left on this place," Pa said. "Every time I pick up an ear of corn in the crib, I'll be jumping."

"Pa, he won't hurt you," I said, patting the snake's head. "He's a natural pet, or somebody has tamed him. And he's not going to bother birds and young chickens when there are so many mice in this crib."

"Mick, let him keep the snake," Mom said. "I won't be afraid of it."

This was the beginning of a long friendship.

Mom went to the corncrib morning after morning and shelled corn for her geese and chickens. Often Old Ben would be lying in front on his burlap sack. Mom watched

◆ **Reading Strategy**
Name one context clue that helps you figure out what it means to shell corn.

him at first from the corner of her eye. Later she didn't bother to watch him any more than she did a cat that came up for his milk.

Later it occurred to us that Old Ben might like milk, too. We started leaving milk for him. We never saw him drink it, but his pan was always empty when we returned. We know the mice didn't drink it, because he took care of them.

"One thing is certain," Mom said one morning when she went to shell corn. "We don't find any more corn chewed up by the mice and left on the floor."

July passed and August came. My father got used to Old Ben, but not until he had proved his worth. Ben had done something our nine cats couldn't. He had cleaned the corncrib of mice.

Then my father began to worry about Old Ben's going after water, and Blackie's finding his track. So he put water in the crib.

September came and went. We began wondering where our pet would go when days grew colder. One morning in early

October we left milk for Old Ben, and it was there when we went back that afternoon. But Old Ben wasn't there.

"Old Ben's a good pet for the warm months," Pa said. "But in the winter months, my cats will have to do the work. Maybe Blackie got him!"

"He might have holed up for the winter in the hayloft,"[1] I told Pa after we had removed all the corn and didn't find him. "I'm worried about him. I've had a lot of pets—groundhogs, crows and hawks—but Old Ben's the best yet."

November, December, January, February, and March came and went. Of course we never expected to see Old Ben in one of those months. We doubted if we ever would see him again.

One day early in April I went to the corncrib, and Old Ben lay stretched across the floor. He looked taller than I was now. His skin was rough and his long body had a flabby appearance. I knew Old Ben needed mice and milk. I picked him up, petted him, and told him so. But the chill of early April was still with him. He got his tongue out slower to answer the kind words I was saying to him. He tried to crawl up my arm but he couldn't make it.

That spring and summer mice got <u>scarce</u> in the corncrib and Old Ben got daring. He went over to the barn and crawled up into the hayloft, where he had many feasts. But he made one mistake.

He crawled from the hayloft down into Fred's feed box, where it was cool. Old Fred was our horse.

There he lay coiled when the horse came in and put his nose down on top of Old Ben. Fred let out a big snort and started kicking.

---

1. **hayloft** (hā′ lôft′) *n*.: Upper story in a barn or stable used for storing hay.

◆ **Literary Focus**
In what way do these events seem like a story?

He kicked down a partition,[2] and then turned his heels on his feed box and kicked it down. Lucky for Old Ben that he got out in one piece. But he got back to his crib.

Old Ben became a part of our barnyard family, a pet and darling of all. When children came to play with my brother and sisters, they always went to the crib and got Old Ben. He enjoyed the children, who were afraid of him at first but later learned to pet this kind old reptile.

Summer passed and the late days of September were very humid. Old Ben failed one morning to drink his milk. We knew it wasn't time for him to hole up for the winter.

We knew something had happened.

Pa and I moved the corn searching for him. Mom made a couple of trips to the barn lot to see if we had found him. But all we found was the rough skin he had shed last spring.

"Fred's never been very sociable with Old Ben since he got in his box that time," Pa said. "I wonder if he could have stomped Old Ben to death. Old Ben could've been crawling over the barn lot, and Fred saw his chance to get even!"

"We'll see," I said.

Pa and I left the crib and walked to the barn lot. He went one way and I went the other, each searching the ground.

Mom came through the gate and walked over where my father was looking. She started looking around, too.

"We think Fred might've got him," Pa said. "We're sure Fred's got it in for him over Old Ben getting in his feed box last summer."

"You're accusing Fred wrong," Mom said. "Here's Old Ben's track in the sand."

I ran over to where Mom had found the

---

2. **partition** (pär tish′ ən) *n*.: Something that separates or divides, such as an interior wall that separates one room from another.

track. Pa went over to look, too.

"It's no use now," Pa said, softly. "Wouldn't have taken anything for that snake. I'll miss him on that burlap sack every morning when I come to feed the horses. Always looked up at me as if he understood."

The last trace Old Ben had left was in the corner of the lot near the hogpen. His track went straight to the woven wire fence and stopped.

"They've got him," Pa said. "Old Ben trusted everything and everybody. He went for a visit to the wrong place. He didn't last long among sixteen hogs. They go wild over a snake. Even a biting copperhead can't stop a hog. There won't be a trace of Old Ben left."

We stood silently for a minute looking at the broad, smooth track Old Ben had left in the sand.

Beyond Literature

Science Connection

Facts and Fears About Snakes
Many people are afraid of *all* snakes. While all snakes should be treated with caution, only about 250 of the world's 2,700 snakes have venom that is harmful to humans. Of these "poisonous" snakes, only about twenty-five snakes can give a fatal bite.

Cross Curricular Activity
Do research to find out more about how snakes use their senses; how they move, eat, and defend themselves; and how they regulate their body temperature. Present your findings to the class.

Guide for Responding

◆ LITERATURE AND YOUR LIFE

Reader's Response Have your feelings about snakes changed as a result of reading "Old Ben"? Explain.

Thematic Focus Explain what makes Old Ben a friend.

☑ Check Your Comprehension

1. Describe Old Ben.
2. Why doesn't the narrator harm the snake when he first sees it?
3. List three examples of Ben's friendliness.
4. How did the family know something had happened to him?
5. How did Old Ben die?

◆ Critical Thinking

INTERPRET

1. How is Ben helpful to the family? **[Analyze]**
2. Why is it a "mistake" for Old Ben to crawl into Fred's feed box? **[Infer]**
3. How does Ben's trusting nature get him into trouble? **[Deduce]**
4. Friends can be found in the most unexpected places. Explain how "Old Ben" illustrates this idea. **[Support]**

EVALUATE

5. Do you think a snake would or would not be a good pet? Why? **[Support]**

APPLY

6. What is expected from farm pets? **[Synthesize]**

Feathered Friend

Arthur C. Clarke

To the best of my knowledge, there's never been a <u>regulation</u> that forbids one to keep pets in a space station. No one ever thought it was necessary—and even had such a rule existed, I am quite certain that Sven Olsen would have ignored it.

With a name like that, you will picture Sven at once as a six-foot-six Nordic giant, built like a bull and with a voice to match. Had this been so, his chances of getting a job in space would have been very slim. Actually he was a wiry little fellow, like most of the early spacers, and managed to qualify easily for the 150-pound bonus[1] that kept so many of us on a reducing diet.

Sven was one of our best construction men, and excelled at the tricky and specialized work of collecting assorted girders[2] as they floated around in free fall, making them do the slow-motion, three-dimensional ballet that would get them into their right positions, and <u>fusing</u> the pieces together when they were precisely dovetailed into the intended pattern: it was a skilled and difficult job, for a space suit is not the most convenient of garbs in which to work. However, Sven's team had one great advantage over the construction gangs you see putting up skyscrapers down on Earth. They could step back and admire their handiwork without being abruptly parted from it by gravity. . . .

Don't ask me why Sven wanted a pet, or why he chose the one he did. I'm not a psychologist, but I must admit that his selection was very sensible. Claribel weighed practically nothing, her food requirements were tiny—and she was not worried, as most animals would have been, by the absence of gravity.

I first became aware that Claribel was aboard when I was sitting in the little cubbyhole laughingly called my office, checking through my lists of technical stores to decide what items we'd be running out of next. When I heard the musical whistle beside my ear, I thought that it had come over the station intercom, and waited for an announcement to follow. It didn't; instead, there was a burst of song that made me look up with such a start that I forgot all about the angle beam just behind my head. When the stars had <u>ceased</u> to explode before my eyes, I had my first view of Claribel.

She was a small yellow canary, hanging in the air as motionless as a hummingbird—and with much less effort, for her wings were quietly

◆ Build Vocabulary

regulation (reg′ yə lā′ shən) *n.*: Rule
fusing (fyoo͞′ ziŋ) *adj.*: Joining permanently
ceased (sēsd) *v.*: Stopped

---

1. **150-pound bonus:** Extra money for being lightweight.
2. **girders** (gʉr′ dərz) *n.*: Long, thick pieces of metal.

folded along her sides. We stared at each other for a minute; then, before I had quite recovered my wits, she did a curious kind of backward loop I'm sure no earthbound canary had ever managed, and departed with a few leisurely flicks. It was quite clear that she'd already learned how to operate in the absence of gravity, and did not believe in doing unnecessary work.

Sven didn't confess to her ownership for several days, and by that time it no longer mattered, because Claribel was a general pet. He had smuggled her up on the last ferry from Earth, when he came back from leave—partly, he claimed, out of sheer scientific curiosity. He wanted to see just how a bird would operate when it had no weight but could still use its wings.

Claribel thrived and grew fat. On the whole, we had little trouble concealing our guest when VIP's from Earth came visiting. A space station has more hiding places than you can count; the only problem was that Claribel got rather noisy when she was upset, and we sometimes had to think fast to explain the curious peeps and whistles that came from ventilating shafts and storage bulkheads. There were a couple of narrow escapes—but then who would dream of looking for a canary in a space station?

We were now on twelve-hour watches, which was not as bad as it sounds, since you need little sleep in space. Though of course there is no "day" and "night" when you are floating in permanent sunlight, it was still convenient to stick to the terms. Certainly when I woke that "morning" it felt like 6:00 A.M. on Earth. I had a nagging headache, and vague memories of fitful, disturbed dreams. It took me ages to undo my bunk straps, and I was still only half awake when I joined the remainder of the duty crew in the mess. Breakfast was unusually quiet, and there was one seat vacant.

"Where's Sven?" I asked, not very much caring.

"He's looking for Claribel," someone answered. "Says he can't find her anywhere. She usually wakes him up."

Before I could retort that she usually woke me

▲ **Critical Viewing** Do you think these crew members get along with one another? Explain [**Infer**]

up, too, Sven came in through the doorway, and we could see at once that something was wrong. He slowly opened his hand, and there lay a tiny bundle of yellow feathers, with two clenched claws sticking pathetically up into the air.

"What happened?" we asked, all equally distressed.

"I don't know," said Sven mournfully. "I just found her like this."

"Let's have a look at her," said Jack Duncan, our cook-doctor-dietitian. We all waited in hushed silence while he held Claribel against his ear in an attempt to detect any heartbeat.

Presently he shook his head. "I can't hear anything, but that doesn't prove she's dead. I've never listened to a canary's heart," he added rather apologetically.

"Give her a shot of oxygen," suggested somebody, pointing to the green-banded emergency cylinder in its recess beside the door. Everyone agreed that this was an excellent idea, and Claribel was tucked snugly into a face mask that was large enough to serve as a complete oxygen tent for her.

To our delighted surprise, she revived at once. Beaming broadly, Sven removed the mask, and she hopped onto his finger. She gave her series of "Come to the cookhouse, boys" trills—then promptly keeled over again.

"I don't get it," lamented Sven. "What's wrong with her? She's never done this before."

For the last few minutes, something had been tugging at my memory. My mind seemed to be very sluggish that morning, as if I was still unable to cast off the burden of sleep. I felt that I could do with some of that oxygen—but before I could reach the mask, understanding exploded in my brain. I whirled on the duty engineer and said urgently:

"Jim!" There's something wrong with the air! That's why Claribel's passed out. I've just remembered that miners used to carry canaries down to warn them of gas."

"Nonsense!" said Jim. "The alarms would have gone off. We've got duplicate circuits, operating independently."

"Er—the second alarm circuit isn't connected up yet," his assistant reminded him. That shook Jim; he left without a word, while we stood arguing and passing the oxygen bottle around like a pipe of peace.

He came back ten minutes later with a sheepish expression. It was one of those accidents that couldn't possibly happen; we'd had one of our rare eclipses by Earth's shadow that night; part of the air purifier had frozen up, and the single alarm in the circuit had failed to go off. Half a million dollars' worth of chemical and electronic engineering had let us down completely. Without Claribel, we should soon have been slightly dead.

So now, if you visit any space station, don't be surprised if you hear a snatch of birdsong. There's no need to be alarmed; on the contrary, in fact. It will mean that you're being doubly safeguarded, at practically no extra expense.

Guide for Responding

◆ LITERATURE AND YOUR LIFE

Reader's Response Do you think it was a good idea for Sven to bring Claribel into space? Why or why not?

Thematic Focus How does Claribel prove to be a helpful friend?

☑ Check Your Comprehension

1. Where does the story take place?
2. Why do the characters hide Claribel from visitors?
3. Name one fact that shows how well Claribel fits into her new home.
4. What emergency occurs near the end of the story?
5. What event leads the narrator to discover the emergency?

◆ Critical Thinking

INTERPRET
1. Name two features of life aboard the space station that are different from life on Earth. **[Analyze]**
2. How does the crew feel about Claribel? **[Infer]**
3. By the end, how does the narrator feel about Claribel as a pet? Explain your answer. **[Draw Conclusions]**

EXTEND
4. Name three reasons that space travelers might take plants and animals into space. **[Science Link]**
5. What do you think you would like and dislike about working in a space station? **[Career Link]**

COMPARE LITERARY WORKS
6. Which story—"Old Ben" or "Feathered Friend"—interested you more? Why? **[Evaluate]**

You've Got a Friend

Carole King

When you're down and troubled
and you need some love and care
and nothin' nothin' is going right
close your eyes and think of me
and soon I will be there
to brighten up even your darkest night
and you know wherever I am
I'll come running to see you again.
Winter, spring, summer or fall,
all you have to do is call
and I'll be there.
You've got a friend.
Now ain't it good to know that
you've got a friend—when people
can be so cold? They'll hurt you,
yes, and desert you and take your soul
if you let them, oh, but don't you
let them. You just call—
If the sky above you grows dark
and full of clouds and that ol'
north wind begins to blow
keep your head together
and call my name out loud
soon you'll hear me knocking
at your door.
There, yes, I will.
You've got a friend
You've got a friend
Ain't it good to know you've
got a friend.

▲ Critical Viewing How can you tell these boys are friends? [Infer]

CHILDHOOD and Poetry

Pablo Neruda

One time, investigating in the backyard of our house in Temuco[1] the tiny objects and <u>minuscule</u> beings of my world, I came upon a hole in one of the boards of the fence. I looked through the hole and saw a landscape like that behind our house, uncared for, and wild. I moved back a few steps, because I sensed vaguely that something was about to happen. All of a sudden a hand appeared—a tiny hand of a boy about my own age. By the time I came close again, the hand was gone, and in its place there was a marvelous white sheep.

The sheep's wool was faded. Its wheels had escaped. All of this only made it more authentic. I had never seen such a wonderful sheep. I looked back through the hole but the boy had disappeared. I went into the house and brought out a treasure of my own: a pinecone, opened, full of odor and resin,[2] which I adored. I set it down in the same spot and went off with the sheep.

I never saw either the hand or the boy again. And I have never again seen a sheep like that either. The toy I lost finally in a fire. But even now, in 1954, almost 50 years old, whenever I pass a toy shop, I look <u>furtively</u> into the window, but it's no use. They don't make sheep like that any more.

I have been a lucky man. To feel the intimacy[3] of brothers is a marvelous thing in life.

---

1. **Temuco** (tay mōō′ kō): Town in Chile.

2. **resin** (rez′ ən) *n.*: Sticky substance, like sap, that oozes from some plants and trees.
3. **intimacy** (in′ tə mə sē) *n.*: Deep, personal connection.

◆ **Build Vocabulary**

minuscule (min′ ə skyōōl) *adj.*: Very small; tiny

furtively (fʉr′ tiv lē) *adv.*: In secret; in such a way as to avoid notice

To feel the love of people whom we love is a fire that feeds our life. But to feel the affection that comes from those whom we do not know, from those unknown to us, who are watching over our sleep and solitude, over our dangers and our weaknesses—that is something still greater and more beautiful because it widens out the boundaries of our being, and unites all living things.

That exchange brought home to me for the first time a precious idea: that all of humanity is somehow together. That experience came to me again much later; this time it stood out strikingly against a background of trouble and <u>persecution</u>.

It won't surprise you then that I attempted to give something resiny, earthlike, and fragrant in exchange for human brotherhood. Just as I once left the pinecone by the fence, I have since left my words on the door of so many people who were unknown to me, people in prison, or hunted, or alone.

That is the great lesson I learned in my childhood, in the backyard of a lonely house. Maybe it was nothing but a game two boys played who didn't know each other and wanted to pass to the other some good things of life. Yet maybe this small and mysterious exchange of gifts remained inside me also, deep and indestructible, giving my poetry light.

◆ **Literary Focus**
In what ways is this nonfiction narrative similar to a fictional narrative?

◆ **Build Vocabulary**

persecution (per sə kyo͞o′ shən) *n.*: Cruel and unfair treatment, often because of politics, religion, or race

*G*uide for Responding

◆ LITERATURE AND YOUR LIFE

Reader's Response Would you have responded as young Neruda did to the gift of the toy? Explain why or why not.

Thematic Focus Name one thing and one feeling that makes people feel like a friend to someone they have never met.

Journal Writing Write your recollections of the first friend you can remember meeting.

☑ Check Your Comprehension

1. What is the main incident of the story?
2. When and where does the main incident take place?
3. What gifts do the boys give each other?

◆ Critical Thinking

INTERPRET

1. What lesson does Neruda find in the exchange of gifts? **[Interpret]**
2. Neruda says giving the pinecone away is like giving his poems to the world. Name a way in which the two "givings" are alike. **[Interpret]**
3. In what way does this memory give "light" to Neruda's poetry? **[Interpret]**

APPLY

4. Describe a way in which the story of two people can be meaningful to many people. **[Apply]**

EXTEND

5. In what ways does technology bring strangers into contact with one another? **[Technology Link]**

Guide for Responding (continued)

◆ Reading Strategy

CONTEXT CLUES

Context clues can help you figure out the meaning of unfamiliar words. For each of these items, explain how context clues could be used to figure out the meaning of the italicized word.

1. We'd had one of our rare *eclipses* by Earth's shadow that night.
2. "Put him in the *corncrib*," I said. "He'll have plenty of delicate food in there."
3. To feel the *intimacy* of brothers is a marvelous thing in life.

◆ Build Vocabulary

USING FORMS OF *regulate*

In your notebook, use a form of *regulate* to fill in each blank:

regulate regulation regulator regulatory

Taisha was the ___?___ for quality control at a catcher's mitt factory. She had memorized every ___?___ in the book. One day, she received a memo from a ___?___ agency. Taisha now had to ___?___ the way workers checked gloves for holes.

SPELLING STRATEGY

When a word ends in a silent e, drop the e when adding a suffix beginning with a vowel. Do not drop the e, though, when adding a suffix beginning with a consonant. For example: *fuse + -ing = fusing*, but *scarce + -ly = scarcely*.

On your paper, add the given suffix to each word.

1. precise + -ly   2. ventilate + -ing
3. peace + -ful   4. fake + -er

USING THE WORD BANK

For each numbered word, write "true" if the word following it defines it. Otherwise, write "false."

1. precisely, exactly   4. regulation, holding
2. scarce, afraid   5. ventilating, breathing fast
3. fusing, joining   6. ceased, stopped

◆ Literary Focus

NARRATIVES

A **narrative** is a story. A narrative can be fiction, like "Feathered Friend," or nonfiction, like "Old Ben."

1. In what ways is "Old Ben" like a short story?
2. Outline the sequence of events in "Feathered Friend."
3. In what ways is "Childhood and Poetry" different from the other two narratives?

◆ Build Grammar Skills

PERFECT VERB TENSES

The **perfect tenses** of verbs combine a form of *have* with the past participle.

The **present perfect tense** shows an action that began in the past and continues into the present. It uses *have* or *has* with the past participle.

The **past perfect tense** shows a past action or condition that ended before another past action began. It uses *had* with the past participle.

The **future perfect tense** shows a future action or condition that will have ended before another begins. It uses *will have* with the past participle.

Perfect Tenses		
Present Perfect	**Past Perfect**	**Future Perfect**
have, has + past participle	*had* + past participle	*will have* + past participle
I *have been* a lucky man.	I *had never seen* such a wonderful sheep [before now].	By then, I *will have* learned.

Practice Identify the verbs and their tenses.

1. Pa had told me not to play with snakes.
2. He has noticed snakes before.
3. They have stopped making toys like that.
4. I have not seen a snake like that before.
5. By next year, he will have grown.

Writing Application Write three sentences about Old Ben. In each sentence, use a different perfect tense of the verb *slither*.

Build Your Portfolio

 ## Idea Bank

Writing

1. **Want Ad** Write a newspaper ad looking for the perfect pet. Clearly describe the kind of animal you want and the characteristics it must have.

2. **An Obituary** An obituary is an announcement in a newspaper of someone's death. Write an obituary for Old Ben. Include a summary of his main qualities.

3. **Comparison-and-Contrast Essay** Compare the pleasures and problems of having a snake as a pet to the pleasures and problems of keeping a canary. Pay special attention to the ways in which people interact with each of these pets.

Speaking and Listening

4. **A Pet Dialogue** If Old Ben or Claribel could speak, what would they say about their owners? With a friend, write and perform a dialogue between these animals, in which they compare their human friends. **[Performing Arts Link]**

5. **Multimedia Pet Narrative** Create a multimedia narrative telling about your own or someone else's experience with a pet. Use photographs, recordings, and other materials to help you tell the story to the class. **[Media Link]**

Projects

6. **Survey Pet Owners** Conduct a survey in your class about types of pets. Show your findings on a graph or chart, and present it to the class. **[Math Link]**

7. **Pet Fair [Group Activity]** Create booths giving information on different aspects of pet ownership. Small teams should each prepare one of the following subjects: choosing a pet; health needs of pets; keeping a pet happy; training a pet; getting the most enjoyment from a pet. **[Science Link]**

 ## Writing Mini-Lesson

Feature Story

If you were a reporter, your readers would love your piece on Old Ben or Claribel. They would want good reasons, called **evidence,** to believe your amazing report, though. Write a newspaper story about a special animal, actual or made up. Back up your story with evidence.

Writing Skills Focus: Provide Evidence

To keep readers' trust, reporters and other writers **provide evidence** of the following kinds:

- Direct observation
- Quotations from eyewitnesses
- Statistics reported in a reliable source
- Expert opinions

Prewriting Choose your amazing animal. Then, list information that answers these questions about its story: *How? When? Where? Who? Why?* and *What?* State clearly why this animal is amazing.

Drafting In the first paragraph, put the most important information from your list of details. In following paragraphs, give evidence, such as quotations from experts or eyewitnesses, for the facts.

Revising Ask classmates who have read your draft to answer the *how, when, where, who, why,* and *what* questions and to identify the evidence you have used. Based on their answers, revise to add or clarify necessary details.

> ◆ **Grammar Application**
> Use the past perfect tense to link past events with the events that came before.

Persuasive Letter

Writing Process Workshop

Stories and essays can influence the way people think, but you can influence people more directly through persuasion. Write a **persuasive letter,** a letter in which you try to persuade someone to think or act in a certain way. Choose an issue or event about which you have a strong opinion. Write a persuasive letter on this topic.

Use these tips to write an effective persuasive letter:

Writing Skills Focus

▶ **Choose details to achieve your purpose.** Emphasize the points that back up your arguments. (See p. 153.)

▶ **Focus on your audience.** The mayor will not be impressed by the idea that a recreation center is "a cool place to hang out." Kids will be offended by the idea that the center will "keep them out of trouble." Use the arguments to which your audience will respond. (See p. 161.)

▶ **Provide evidence.** Give your readers a reason to believe what you say. (See p. 175.) Provide facts, statistics, expert opinions, and other pieces of evidence that support your position. Make sure you use reliable sources when you gather evidence.

MODEL FROM LITERATURE

"Pa, he won't hurt you," I said, patting the snake's head. ① "He's a natural pet, or somebody has tamed him. ② And he's not going to bother birds and young chickens when there are so many mice in this crib." ③

① The boy focuses on his audience (his father) by dealing with his father's fear of the snake.

② This detail will help persuade Pa. The fact that the snake is six feet long will not, so the boy does not mention it.

③ The boy provides the evidence that the snake will not bother the birds.

Prewriting

Choose a Topic Think of issues you have heard about in school, at the dinner table, or on the news. Think of a problem a friend of yours may be facing. Choose an issue about which you have a strong opinion and for which you have sound reasons and facts to back up your opinion. If necessary, do some research to find statistics or quotations that support the point you are trying to make.

Topic Ideas

- Letter to an elected official about a law or policy
- Letter to your school principal about rules or privileges
- Letter to a friend who needs advice

Outline Points and Collect Evidence Jot down the reasons that your audience should take your side or use your suggestion.

Point	Evidence
A recreation center will be a fun place for kids to hang out.	My cousin Eddy says a lot of kids go to the rec center in his town, and they all have fun there. **(Eyewitness/Participant Report)**
A rec center will keep kids out of trouble.	In 90 towns surveyed, incidents of mischief went down an average of 45% once the town rec center opened. **(Statistical Study)**
The town ought to build a rec center.	The mayor wants to reduce mischief by kids. A rec center is a way to reduce mischief. Therefore, the mayor should build a rec center. **(Logical Argument Based on Facts)**

Drafting

Use the Proper Form Formal letters always contain certain information, set out in the same way. Refer to the Writing Process Workshop on page 138 for instructions on the correct format for a formal letter.

Keep Your Ideas Organized Each paragraph in your letter should tackle one point. State the point, and give the evidence for it.

APPLYING LANGUAGE SKILLS: Avoid Clichés

"Cold as ice," "like two peas in a pod," "a lost cause"—you have probably heard these expressions before. These common, overused expressions are known as **clichés.** Because they have been used so often, clichés have lost their power. Avoid clichés as you write. Force yourself to express your ideas in a fresh way.

Practice On your paper, rewrite each sentence in a way that avoids the cliché.

1. Her cheeks were as red as roses.
2. I'm having the time of my life.
3. We packed everything but the kitchen sink.
4. This assignment is just a drop in the bucket.
5. Thanks a million!

Writing Application Replace any clichés in your letter with fresh, interesting expressions.

Writer's Solution Connection Writing Lab

For more help drafting your letter, view writer Doug Raboy's drafting tips in the lesson on Persuasion.

APPLYING LANGUAGE SKILLS: Using *have* in Verb Phrases and Contractions

When writing verb phrases or contractions with the helping verbs *could, would,* or *should,* do not write *of* instead of *have.* Write *could've* or *could have,* not *could of.* Write *should've* or *should have,* not *should of.* Also avoid *ought to of, must of,* and *might of.*

Incorrect:

He should not of gone there.

Fred would of been frightened.

Correct:

He shouldn't have gone there.

Fred would've been frightened.

Practice On your paper, correct each sentence below.

1. He would of helped us.

2. We might of waited.

3. They should of seen it.

4. We could not of known.

5. It must of been there.

Writing Application Look over your letter. Check for and correct any incorrect uses of *have* and *of.*

Writer's Solution Connection
Language Lab

For additional practice, complete the Possessive Pronouns and Contractions lesson in the Pronouns unit.

Revising

Provide Needed Evidence Make sure you have given enough evidence for each of your points. If you cannot find evidence for a point, omit it.

Revise With Your Audience in Mind As you reread your draft, pretend you are a member of your intended audience. Would you be persuaded? If not, revise to improve your audience's response.

REVISION MODEL

July 2, 1999

To the Editor:

A new mall would provide convenient, in-town shopping opportunities.

① ~~A new mall would be a really cool place to hang out with friends~~.

② ~~No one in their right mind wants to drive all the way to Grisham.~~

Seventy-five percent of the people surveyed said they would rather have a new mall in town than continue driving forty-five minutes to Grisham.

③ Yours sincerely,
Tom Bell

① The audience for my letter will be adult newspaper readers. They would not be persuaded by these details, so I replaced them with other, more effective details.

② I provided evidence for my point.

③ I added a closing, which is a required part of a letter.

Publishing and Presenting

▶ **Reply to Letters** You and your classmates may exchange letters. Pretending to be a member of the letter's intended audience, reply to each other's letters. Were you convinced? Why or why not?

▶ **Newspaper Spread** With your classmates, assemble your letter and create two or more newspaper pages. Divide the paper between an "Advice Column," featuring those letters that give personal advice, and the "Letters to the Editor," for letters on general issues.

Strategies for Success

In every sentence or passage you read, each word has a meaning. Some words, though, are more important than others. Those are the key words—they unlock the meaning of the whole sentence. Follow these tips for recognizing key words.

Identify the Subject and the Verb Every sentence needs a subject and a verb. The subject names whom or what the sentence is about. The verb tells what the subject does or expresses a state of being. Look at the following sentence. *Ghana broke into a number of smaller states.* The subject is *Ghana,* and the verb is *broke.* Identifying the subject and verb gives you a framework on which to hang the rest of the information in the sentence.

Watch for Signal Words and Qualifiers Signal words, such as *most importantly,* get your attention when a significant fact or idea is being presented. Other signal words—such as *because, as a result,* and *nonetheless*—indicate relationships between events or ideas. Still others—such as *before, next,* and *finally*—indicate time or the order of steps. Qualifiers are words like *always, all, some,* and *never.* They qualify, or limit, the conditions of a statement. For example, *All the states participated* means something very different from *Some states participated.*

Follow Special Instructions Sentences in written instructions usually do not include the subject because the subject is understood to be you, the reader. The verb in instructions is usually an action verb: It will tell you to *print, sign, tear,* or *fold.* Verbs in instructions are key because they tell you exactly what to do. Other key words in instructions include words that tell times, places, and amounts.

Apply the Strategies

Read this notice sent to students by the principal:

Dear Students:

Please remove all books and personal items from your desks at the end of the day on Friday. Do not leave anything in your desks, because the janitor will be moving and washing all desks this weekend.

Thank you for your help.

Ms. Erickson

Ms. Erickson

1. What is the verb in the first sentence?

2. Which word or words tell you when the desks must be cleaned?

3. Which word or words signal that a reason will be given for the actions requested?

✔ Here are some other situations in which recognizing key words can be helpful:
► Reading directions for a test
► Following a recipe
► Reading the rules of a game
► Filling out a contest entry form

A **verb** is a word that shows action or being. Verbs have four basic forms, called the **principal parts.** The principal parts are the present (or base form), the present participle, the past, and the past participle.

A regular verb forms its past and past participle by adding *-ed* or *-d* to the present form. Irregular verbs form their past and past participle in different ways. (See page 152.)

a prince [the principality of Monaco] —pl. -ties
prin·ci·pal *(prin'sə pl̄e) adv.* mainly; chiefly
principal parts *pl.n. Grammar* the principal inflected forms of a verb, from which the other forms may be derived: they are the infinitive, the past tense, and the past participle [The *principal parts* of "drink" are "drink," "drank,"and "drunk."]
prin·ci·ple *(prin'sə pəl) n.* 1 a rule, truth, or belief upon which others are based [the basic *principles* of law] 2...

Base (present)	Present Participle	Past	Past Participle
look	looking	looked	(have or had) looked
howl	howling	howled	(have or had) howled
be	being	been	(have or had) been
eat	eating	ate	(has or had) eaten

The **tense** of a verb shows the time of the action or condition expressed by the verb. You form the verb tenses by using the principal parts and helping verbs. (See pages 160 and 174.)

Present: I *help.*
Past: I *helped.*
Future: I *will help.*
Present Perfect: I *have walked.*
Past Perfect: I *had walked.*
Future Perfect: I *will have walked.*

Practice 1 Name the principal part used to make each italicized verb. Then, identify the tense.

1. The canary *has fainted.*

2. It is freezing out, so they *are hiding* in a haystack.

3. The snake *cleaned* out the mice.

4. Later, he *will realize* what the toy meant.

5. I *was having* a bad day until I helped my friend.

Practice 2 On your paper, identify the tense of the verb in each sentence.

1. He *had wondered* why Ben could not be found.

2. Ben *will keep* the mice out of the corncrib.

3. By next winter, he *will have grown* a foot.

4. The mice always *eat* the corn.

5. We *have seen* snakes before.

Practice 3 Copy each of the following sentences onto your paper. Supply the form of the verb, as indicated in parentheses.

1. Stuart (see, *past*) a snake.

2. He (run, *future*) all the way home.

3. The bird (warn, *past perfect*) them of the danger.

4. He (tell, *future perfect*) them.

5. She (entertain, *present perfect*) them.

Grammar in Writing

✔ *Irregular verbs do not form the past or the past participle in the usual way, so double-check these parts when using an irregular verb.*

✔ *Use the correct part of a verb when forming tenses. For example, write I saw, not I seen.*

Introductions will help you reach out in all kinds of situations to all kinds of people. Whether you're introducing your cousin to your friend or your mother to the principal of your school, a proper introduction will give the information that allows them to connect.

Put First Things First The most important piece of information in an introduction is a name. When introducing a younger person to an older person, you give the name of the younger person to the older person first: *Mom, this is my friend Ken Zimbler.* Then, give the younger person the name of the older person: *Ken, this is my mother, Mrs. Graziano.*

Tell the Whole Story In most situations, you should give the full names or titles of the people you are introducing. Sometimes, you can introduce an adult with only a title and last name: *Mrs. Bell, Rabbi Fierstein,* or *Coach Griff.* You should also supply some identifying information about each person: *Coach Griff, this is my friend Bob Thompson. He's interested in joining the baseball team. Bob, this is Coach Griff. He's coached the team for five years.*

Tips for Making Introductions

✔ *These pointers can help you make good introductions:*

▶ Use full names and titles.
▶ Give a little extra information about each person you introduce.
▶ Speak clearly and slowly.

Apply the Strategies

In a group of three or four, role-play the following introductions:

1. Introduce a friend visiting from out of town to one of your classmates.
2. Introduce a new friend to an adult in your family.
3. Introduce an adult in your family to one of your teachers.

What's Behind the Words

Vocabulary Adventures With Richard Lederer

Words from Romance Languages

Waves of people streaming to our shores have added much variety to American English. In the period from the Revolutionary War until the mid-1840's, about 1.5 million immigrants arrived. Thereafter, the numbers were much greater—sometimes exceeding a million in a single year.

A World of Contributions

These people came from Ireland, Germany, Russia, Poland, the Scandinavian countries, Italy, France, Spain, Mexico, Africa, and Asia—from almost every nation in the world.

Unless you are Native American, the odds are three to one that your ancestors arrived in this country after 1850. The languages they brought with them found their way into American English.

The Romance of American English

Many of those who immigrated to the United States spoke a Romance language. Romance languages stem from Latin—the language of Rome. The most influential of these on American English are French, Spanish, and Italian.

The French language had a great effect on the English language following the Norman Conquest (a French victory over the English in 1066). English-speaking settlers brought the French-influenced language with them to the "New World." Spanish words, on the other hand, traveled into American English with the explorers of what is now the western United States.

The chart below shows the origins of some words from French, Spanish, and Italian that are now in English use.

Words From Romance Languages		
French	**Spanish**	**Italian**
bureau	alligator	alarm
chowder	banana	balcony
gopher	cargo	lasagna
prairie	mosquito	macaroni
pumpkin	parade	mustache
	tornado	opera
		profile
		umbrella

ACTIVITY 1 Many French phrases are in common use in American English. What do the following mean?
1. *bon voyage* 4. *hors d'oevre*
2. *cul-de-sac* 5. *papier mâché*
3. *déjà-vu*

ACTIVITY 2 The names of some Italian foods are listed on the chart. See how many other names of Italian, Spanish or French foods your class can add.

ACTIVITY 3 Look up these words in a dictionary. Explain the origin and meaning of each word.
1. fiasco   3. cache   5. patio
2. cavalier 4. depot   6. stampede

$\mathcal{E}$xtended Reading Opportunities

The characters in this unit reach out and grow by trying new experiences and discovering new friends. The following books will give you more opportunities to read about characters who reach out for adventures, discoveries, and friends.

Suggested Titles

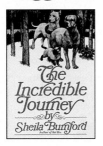

The Incredible Journey
Sheila Burnford

The adventures of two dogs and a cat in a cross-country journey show a strong bond of friendship between animals and people. Their incredible journey is filled with danger and excitement as well as humor and love. Follow the trail of these three companions as they overcome obstacles to reach the family they love.

Number the Stars
Lois Lowry

The courage of two young girls and their families is tested during World War II when the Nazis threaten to round up Danish Jews and send them to the death camps. Young Annemarie Johannsen and her best friend, Ellen Rosen, must find strength and bravery to outwit the Nazis and save Ellen's life.

The Black Stallion
Walter Farley

Stranded on a desert island, Alex struggles to survive. Help and friendship come in a most unusual form—a beautiful wild Arabian stallion. Sharing the island with the horse gives Alex a fresh look at himself and his ideas about friendship. When the time comes to return to civilization, the unusual friendship is tested. Find out how the boy and the horse meet the challenge to the bond they have formed.

Other Possibilities

The Yearling	Marjorie Kinnan Rawlings
What Hearts	Bruce Brooks
Going Home	Nicholasa Mohr

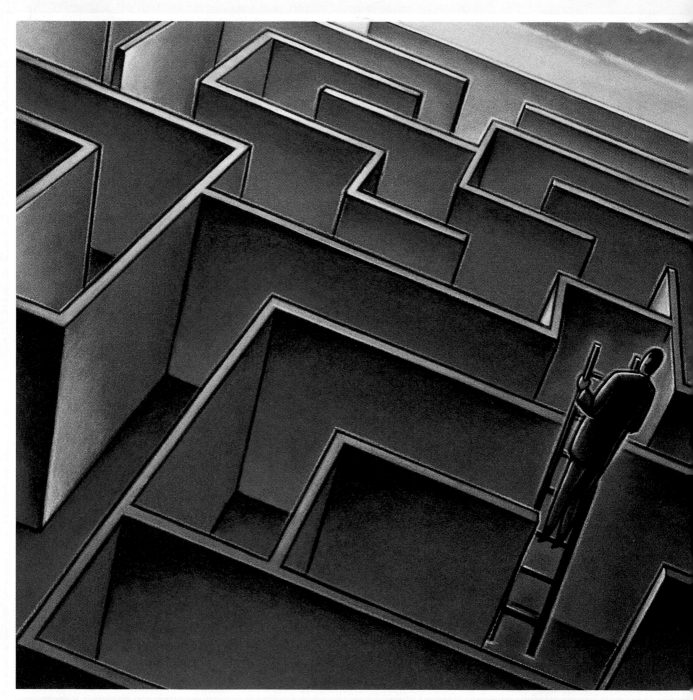

Maze at Sunset, © Garry Nichols

Proving Yourself

Life is full of twists and turns, choices and challenges. Each choice leads to a different path. Each path presents challenges that allow you to prove yourself—to test your abilities and find new strengths within yourself. Reading about the experiences of others—real people and fictional characters—allows you to see how others test their skills and prove their abilities in challenging situations.

Guide for Reading

Meet the Author:

Paul Zindel (1936–)

When he was growing up in Staten Island, New York, Paul Zindel's family moved at least fifteen times. Zindel said that he felt lonely and out of place. An English teacher made a prediction, though. Zindel says, "She was the only one to tell me I wasn't completely deranged! I was just going to be a writer!" It took Zindel a few years, though, before he proved that he really was a writer.

THE STORY BEHIND THE STORY

As they moved about Staten Island, the Zindels spent a year in the town of Travis. There, Paul met Nonno Frankie Vivona. Frankie gave him much well-meant, sometimes unusual advice. Zindel describes Frankie in loving detail in a memoir, *The Pigman & Me.*

A Proven Writer Frankie also inspired an important character in Zindel's first novel, *The Pigman.* Drawing on Zindel's own confusing teenage days, the book hit a chord with many high-school readers.

Before he wrote *The Pigman,* Zindel had spent ten years as a high-school science teacher. After the success of this book and one of his plays, he started writing full time. He had proven himself as a writer, just as his teacher had predicted he would!

◆ LITERATURE AND YOUR LIFE

CONNECT YOUR EXPERIENCE

You know that a fight doesn't prove anything. Yet when you're the new kid on the block, a fight may be hard to avoid. Other kids are picking on you. Confusion and fears are building up inside. A fight releases the pressure—fast.

In this excerpt from *The Pigman & Me,* Paul Zindel tells about a time when he felt the pressure to fight.

THEMATIC FOCUS: Proving Yourself

In what other ways, besides fighting, can a person prove himself or herself?

◆ Background for Understanding

CULTURE

Different places have different rules. Some of these rules are spelled out. They appear on signs, or people tell each other about them. In this story, trouble starts when Paul doesn't follow one of these rules in gym.

There are other rules, though, that people don't spell out. These unwritten rules can sometimes be just as important as the written ones. In *The Pigman & Me,* Paul Zindel recalls a time when, according to an unwritten rule, he was "not allowed" to back down from a fight.

◆ *from* The Pigman & Me ◆

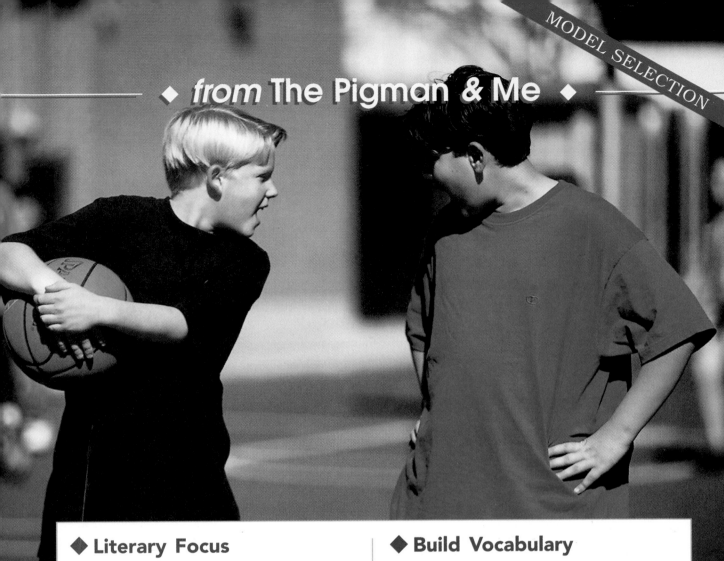

◆ Literary Focus

INTERNAL CONFLICT

A conflict is a struggle between two opposing characters or forces. An **internal conflict** takes place within a person or character. In *The Pigman & Me*, the author wants to avoid a fight, but he also wants to prove he's not afraid. The internal conflict arises because he feels he can't have it both ways. Use a chart like the one below to record the details of Paul's internal conflict.

1. Paul is ashamed to call off the fight.

1. Paul is afraid to fight.

Internal Conflict

2.

2.

3.

3.

◆ Build Vocabulary

SUFFIXES: *-tion*

In *The Pigman & Me*, a crowd boos with "condemnation." *Condemnation* ends in the suffix *-tion*, which means "the act, result, or condition of." To *condemn* is to judge someone as deserving punishment. *Condemnation* is the act of judging someone as deserving punishment.

WORD BANK

Which of these words from the story could describe a photograph that is out of focus?

exact
tactics
undulating
goading
distorted
condemnation
groveled

Reading for Success

Interactive Reading Strategies

Books don't come with plugs or batteries. To make a book work, you have to plug yourself in by interacting with the words on the page. The following strategies will help you make the connection that lights up your imagination:

Set a purpose for your reading.

Before you begin, set a purpose for reading. Are you reading for enjoyment? Are you reading to learn factual information? The details to which you pay attention will change, depending on the purpose you set.

Reading for Enjoyment	Reading for Insight
Nonno Frankie's character seems a little kooky—I want to find out more about him.	I wonder what lessons the story gives about dealing with conflicts.

Ask questions.

As you read, ask questions: *What just happened? Why did she do that?* Just by asking, you will create a new circuit in your mind. As you continue reading, the answers you find will light up the circuit.

Relate to your own experience.

Stories and poems are great inventions for letting you see things through the eyes of others. You can tune in a better picture, though, by relating what you read to experiences in your own life.

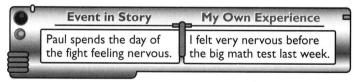

Event in Story	My Own Experience
Paul spends the day of the fight feeling nervous.	I felt very nervous before the big math test last week.

Predict.

Don't just wait to find out what will happen next. Make a prediction based on what you have read. When you do, your mind starts wiring the facts together. Your circuits are ready for maximum charge.

As you read *The Pigman & Me,* look at the notes in the boxes. The notes show how to apply these strategies to your reading.

from The Pigman & Me

Paul Zindel

When trouble came to me, it didn't involve anybody I thought it would. It involved the nice, normal, smart boy by the name of John Quinn. Life does that to us a lot. Just when we think something awful's going to happen one way, it throws you a curve and the something awful happens another way. This happened on the first Friday, during gym period, when we were allowed to play games in the school yard. A boy by the name of Richard Cahill, who lived near an old linoleum factory, asked me if I'd like to play paddle ball with him, and I said, "Yes." Some of the kids played softball, some played warball, and there were a few other games where you could sign out equipment and do what you wanted. What I didn't know was that you were allowed to sign out the paddles for only fifteen minutes per period so more kids could get a chance to use them. I just didn't happen to know that little rule, and Richard Cahill didn't think to tell me

about it. Richard was getting a drink from the water fountain when John Quinn came up to me and told me I had to give him my paddle.

"No," I said, being a little paranoid about being the new kid and thinking everyone was going to try to take advantage of me.

"Look, you *have* to give it to me," John Quinn insisted.

That was when I did something berserk. I was so wound up and frightened that I didn't think, and I struck out at him with my right fist. I had forgotten I was holding the paddle, and it smacked into his face, giving him an instant black eye. John was shocked. I was shocked. Richard Cahill came running back and he was shocked.

"What's going on here?" Mr. Trellis, the gym teacher, growled.

"He hit me with the paddle," John moaned, holding his eye. He was red as a beet, as Little Frankfurter, Conehead, Moose, and lots of the others gathered around.

"He tried to take the paddle away from me!" I complained.

"His time was up," John said.

Mr. Trellis set me wise to the rules as he took John over to a supply locker and pulled out a first-aid kit.

"I'm sorry," I said, over and over again.

Then the bell rang, and all John Quinn whispered to me was that he was going to get even. He didn't say it like a nasty rotten kid, just more like an all-American boy who knew he'd have to regain his dignity about having to walk around school with a black eye. Before the end of school, Jennifer came running up to me in the halls and told me John Quinn had announced to everyone he was going to <u>exact</u> revenge on me after school on Monday. That was the note of disaster my first week at school ended on, and I was terrified because I didn't know how to fight. I had never even been in a fight. What had happened was all an accident. It really was.

When Nonno[1] Frankie arrived on Saturday morning, he found me sitting in the apple tree alone. Mom had told him it was O.K. to walk around the whole yard now, as long as he didn't do any diggings or mutilations other than weed-pulling on her side. I was expecting him to notice right off the bat that I was white with fear, but instead he stood looking at the carvings Jennifer and I had made in the trunk of the tree. I thought he was just intensely curious about what "ESCAPE! PAUL & JEN-NIFER!" meant. Of course, the twins, being such copycats, had already added their names so the full carving away of the bark now read, "ESCAPE! PAUL & JENNIFER! & NICKY & JOEY!" And the letters circled halfway around the tree.

"You're killing it," Nonno Frankie said sadly.

"What?" I jumped down to his side.

"The tree will die if you cut any more."

---

1. **Nonno:** Italian word for "Grandpa."

I thought he was kidding, because all we had done was carve off the outer pieces of bark. We hadn't carved deep into the tree, not into the *heart* of the tree. The tree was too important to us. It was the most crucial place to me and Jennifer, and the last thing we'd want to do was hurt it.

"The heart of a tree isn't deep inside of it. Its heart and blood are on the *outside,* just under the bark," Nonno Frankie explained. "That's the living part of a tree. If you carve in a circle all around the trunk, it's like slitting its throat. The water and juices and life of the tree can't move up from the roots!" I knew about the living layer of a tree, but I didn't know exposing it would kill the whole tree. I just never thought about it, or I figured trees patched themselves up.

"Now it can feed itself from only half its trunk," Nonno Frankie explained. "You must not cut any more."

"I won't," I promised. Then I felt worse than ever. Not only was I scheduled to get beat up by John Quinn after school on Monday, I was also a near tree-killer. Nonno Frankie finally looked closely at me.

"Your first week at school wasn't all juicy meatballs?" he asked.

That was all he had to say, and I spilled out each and every horrifying detail. Nonno Frankie let me babble on and on. He looked as if he understood exactly how I felt and wasn't go-ing to call me stupid or demented or a big yellow coward. When I didn't have another word left in me, I just shut up and stared down at the ground.

> If you have a friend who makes you feel better just by listen-ing to you, then you can **relate your experience** to Paul's.

"Stab nail at ill Italian bats!" Nonno Frankie finally said.

"What?"

He repeated the weird sentence and asked me what was special about it. I guessed, "It reads the same backward as forward?"

"Right! Ho! Ho! Ho! See, you learn! You remember things I teach you. So today I will teach you how to fight, and you will smack this John Quinn around like floured pizza dough."

"But I can't fight."

"I'll show you Sicilian combat <u>tactics</u>."

"Like what?"

"Everything about Italian fighting. It has to do with your mind and body. Things you have to know so you don't have to be afraid of bullies. Street smarts my father taught me. Like 'Never miss a good chance to shut up!'"

VAROOOOOOOOOOM!

A plane took off over our heads. We walked out beyond the yard to the great field overlooking the airport.

Nonno Frankie suddenly let out a yell. *"Aaeeeeeyaaaayeeeeeh!"* It was so bloodcurdlingly weird, I decided to wait until he felt like explaining it.

"Aaeeeeeyaaaayeeeeeh!" he bellowed again. "It's good to be able to yell like Tarzan!" he said. "This confuses your enemy, and you can also yell it if you have to retreat. You run away roaring and everyone thinks you at least have guts! It confuses everybody!"

"Is that all I need to know?" I asked, now more afraid than ever of facing John Quinn in front of all the kids.

"No. Tonight I will cut your hair."

"Cut it?"

"Yes. It's too long!"

"It is?"

"Ah," Nonno Frankie said, "you'd be surprised how many kids lose fights because of their hair. Alexander the Great always ordered his entire army to shave their heads. Long hair makes it easy for an enemy to grab it and

Elephant Tree, © 1996, Robert Vickrey/Licensed by VAGA, New York, NY

▲ **Critical Viewing** What details express the way Paul feels during the first school week? **[Interpret]**

cut off your head."

"John Quinn just wants to beat me up!"

"You can never be too sure. This boy might have the spirit of Genghis Khan!"

"Who was Genghis Khan?"

"Who? He once killed two million enemies in one hour. Some of them he killed with yo-yos."

"Yo-yos?"

"See, these are the things you need to know. The yo-yo was first invented as a weapon. Of course, they were as heavy as steel pipes and had long rope cords, but they were still yo-yos!"

"I didn't know that," I admitted.

"That's why I'm telling you. You should always ask about the rules when you go to a new place."

"I didn't think there'd be a time limit on handball paddles."

"That's why you must ask."

"I can't ask everything," I complained.

"Then you *read.* You need to know all the rules wherever you go. Did you know it's illegal to hunt camels in Arizona?"

"No."

"See? These are little facts you pick up from books and teachers and parents as you grow older. Some facts and rules come in handy, some don't. You've got to be observant. Did you know that Mickey Mouse has only *four* fingers on each hand?"

"No."

"All you have to do is look. And rules change! You've got to remember that. In ancient Rome, my ancestors worshipped a god who ruled over mildew. Nobody does anymore, but it's an interesting thing to know. You have to be connected to the past and present and future. At NBC, when they put in a new cookie-cutting machine, I had to have an open mind. I had to prepare and draw upon everything I knew so that I didn't get hurt."

Nonno Frankie must have seen my mouth was open so wide a baseball could have flown into my throat and choked me to death. He stopped at the highest point in the rise of land above the airport. "I can see you want some meat and potatoes. You want to know exactly how to beat this vicious John Quinn."

"He's not vicious."

"Make believe he is. It'll give you more energy for the fight. When he comes at you, don't underestimate the power of negative thinking! You must have only positive thoughts in your heart that you're going to cripple this monster. Stick a piece of garlic in your pocket for good luck. A woman my mother knew in Palermo did this, and she was able to fight off a dozen three-foot-tall muscular Greeks who landed and tried to eat her. You think this is not true, but half her town saw it. The Greeks all had rough skin and wore backpacks and one-piece clothes. You have to go with what you feel in your heart. One of my teachers in Sicily believed the Portuguese man-of-war jellyfish originally came from England. He felt that in his heart, and he eventually proved it. He later went on to be awarded a government grant to study tourist swooning sickness in Florence."

"But how do I hold my hands to fight? How do I hold my fists?" I wanted to know.

"Like *this!*" Nonno Frankie demonstrated, taking a boxing stance with his left foot and fist forward.

"And then I just swing my right fist forward as hard as I can?"

"No. First you curse him."

"*Curse* him?"

"Yes, you curse this John Quinn. You tell him, 'May your left ear wither and fall into your right pocket!' And you tell him he looks like a fugitive from a brain gang! And tell him he has a face like a mattress! And that an espresso coffee cup would fit on his head like a sombrero. And then you just give him the big Sicilian surprise!"

"What?"

"You *kick* him in the shins!"

By the time Monday morning came, I was a nervous wreck. Nonno Frankie had gone back to New York the night before, but had left me a special bowl of pasta and steamed octopus that he said I should eat for breakfast so I'd have "gusto" for combat. I had asked him not to discuss my upcoming bout with my mother or sister, and Betty did-

> You will understand Frankie's character better if you **ask the question,** "What do his comments have to do with Paul's problem?"

> Here, you might **predict** that Paul will not do too badly in the fight.

Your **prior knowledge** might tell you that octopus is an Italian delicacy—and that Paul probably doesn't want to eat it for breakfast!

n't say anything so I assumed she hadn't heard about it.

Jennifer had offered to get one of her older brothers to protect me, and, if I wanted, she was willing to tell Miss Haines so she could stop anything from happening. I told her, "No." I thought there was a chance John Quinn would have even forgotten the whole incident and wouldn't make good on his revenge threat. Nevertheless, my mind was numb with fear all day at school. In every class I went to, it seemed there were a dozen different kids coming over to me and telling me they heard John Quinn was going to beat me up after school.

At 3 P.M. sharp, the bell rang.

All the kids started to leave school.

I dawdled.

I cleaned my desk and took time packing up my books. Jennifer was at my side as we left the main exit of the building. There, across the street in a field behind Ronkewitz's Candy Store, was a crowd of about 300 kids standing around like a big, undulating horseshoe, with John Quinn standing at the center bend glaring at me.

"You could *run,*" Jennifer suggested, tossing her hair all to the left side of her face. She looked much more than pretty now. She looked loyal to the bone.

"No," I said. I just walked forward toward my fate, with the blood in my temples pounding so hard I thought I was going to pass out. Moose and Leon and Mike and Conehead and Little Frankfurter were sprinkled out in front of me, goading me forward. I didn't even hear what they said. I saw only their faces distorted in ecstasy and expectation. They looked like the mob I had seen in a sixteenth-century etching where folks in London had bought tickets to watch bulldogs attacking water buffalo.

John stood with his black eye, and his fists up.

I stopped a few feet from him and put my fists up. A lot of kids in the crowd started to shout, "Kill him, Johnny!" but I may have imagined that part.

John came closer. He started to dance on his feet like all father-trained fighters do. I danced, too, as best I could. The crowd began to scream for blood. Jennifer kept shouting, "Hey, there's no need to fight! You don't have to fight, guys!"

If your **purpose in reading** is to be entertained, then this part is probably the high point of suspense!

But John came in for the kill. He was close enough now so any punch he threw could hit me. All I thought of was Nonno Frankie, but I couldn't remember half of what he told me and I didn't think any of it would work anyway.

"*Aaeeeeeyaaaayeeeeeh!*" I suddenly screamed at John. He stopped in his tracks and the crowd froze in amazed silence. Instantly, I brought back my right foot, and shot it forward to kick John in his left shin. The crowd was shocked, and booed me with mass condemnation for my Sicilian fighting technique. I missed John's shin, and kicked vainly again. He threw a punch at me. It barely touched me, but I was so busy kicking, I tripped myself and fell down. The crowd

◆ Build Vocabulary

undulating (un´ dyōō lā´ tiŋ) *adj.*: Moving in waves, like a snake

goading (gō´ diŋ) *v.*: Pushing a person into acting, especially by using pain or insults

distorted (di stôr´ tid) *adj.*: Twisted out of the normal shape

condemnation (kän´ dem nā´ shən) *n.*: Extreme disapproval; harsh judgment

cheered. I realized everyone including John thought his punch had floored me. I decided to go along with it. I groveled in the dirt for a few moments, and then stood up slowly holding my head as though I'd received a death blow. John put his fists down. He was satisfied justice had been done and his black eye had been avenged. He turned to leave, but Moose wasn't happy.

"Hey, ya didn't punch him enough," Moose complained to John.

"It's over," John said, like the decent kid he was.

"No, it's not," Moose yelled, and the crowd began to call for more blood. Now it was Moose coming toward me, and I figured I was dead meat. He came closer and closer. Jennifer shouted for him to stop and threatened to pull

his eyeballs out, but he kept coming. And that was when something amazing happened. I was aware of a figure taller than me, running, charging. The figure had long blond hair, and it struck Moose from behind. I could see it was a girl and she had her hands right around Moose's neck, choking him. When she let him go, she threw him about ten feet, accidentally tearing off a religious medal from around his neck. Everyone stopped dead in their tracks, and I could see my savior was my sister.

"If any of you tries to hurt my brother again, I'll rip your guts out," she announced.

Moose was not happy. Conehead and Little Frankfurter were not happy. But the crowd broke up fast and everyone headed home. I guess that was the first day everybody learned that if nothing else, the Zindel kids stick together. As for Nonno Frankie's Sicilian fighting technique, I came to realize he was ahead of his time. In fact, these days it's called karate.

◆ Build Vocabulary

groveled (grä′ vəld) *v.*: Lay or crawled about before someone in hope of mercy

Guide for Responding

◆ LITERATURE AND YOUR LIFE

Reader's Response Do you think Paul should have backed out of the fight? Explain.

Thematic Focus Do you think winning or losing a fight "proves" anything?

☑ Check Your Comprehension

1. What trouble starts on the first Friday of school?
2. Name two pieces of advice that Nonno Frankie gives Paul.
3. What does John say and do at the end of the fight?
4. Who tries to continue the fight?
5. Who prevents the fight from continuing? How?

◆ Critical Thinking

INTERPRET

1. From whom doesn't Paul ask help? Why? **[Infer]**
2. What does his tree-carving discussion with Frankie show about Paul? **[Interpret]**
3. Why does he show up for the fight? **[Deduce]**
4. If Paul had won the fight, would the other boys have left him alone? Explain. **[Speculate]**
5. What lesson does he learn? **[Draw Conclusions]**

EVALUATE

6. Do you think the fight was a good or a bad experience for Paul? Explain. **[Evaluate]**

EXTEND

7. What are some basic first-aid techniques for treating cuts and bruises? **[Health Link]**

Guide for Responding (continued)

◆ Reading for Success

INTERACTIVE READING STRATEGIES

By using **interactive strategies,** you developed your understanding of the story.

1. (a) What purpose did you set in your reading?
   (b) To what details did you pay special attention?
2. Name a question you asked right after Paul hit John. What answers did you find?
3. How did you predict the fight would end? Why?

◆ Build Vocabulary

USING THE SUFFIX *-tion*

The suffix *-tion* means "the act, condition, or result of." For instance, *condemnation* is the condition of *condemning*.

Define each of the following:

1. exploration   3. reaction   5. aggravation
2. application   4. hesitation

SPELLING STRATEGY

When spelling words that end with the *shun* sound, remember this: When the base form of the word ends with a *t* sound *(create),* use *tion* to spell the *shun* sound *(creation).* For other words, like *dimension,* spell this sound *sion.*

In your notebook, write each of the following words and its base word. Correct any misspellings.

1. correction   2. direction   3. elecsion

Check the spelling of each of the following in a dictionary.

1. porsion   2. dictionary   3. fiction   4. discution

USING THE WORD BANK

Group the following Word Bank words into three lists: those that are negative, those that are positive, and those that are neither negative nor positive.

1. distorted   4. groveled   6. exact
2. tactics   5. goading   7. condemnation
3. undulating

◆ Literary Focus

INTERNAL CONFLICT

An **internal conflict** is a struggle that takes place within a character or a person.

1. Describe Paul's internal conflict.
2. Explain how the conflict between Paul and John Quinn leads to Paul's internal conflict.
3. Is Paul's internal conflict settled by the end of the story? Explain.

◆ Build Grammar Skills

ADJECTIVES

An **adjective** is a word that describes a person, place, or thing. An adjective answers one of the following questions: *What kind? Which one? How many? How much?*

Adjective	Answers the question . . .
a *black* eye	*What kind of eye?* A *black* one.
my *right* fist	*Which one?* The *right* one.
about *300* kids	*How many?* Three hundred.
some meat and potatoes	*How much?* Some.

Practice Identify the adjectives in each of the following.

1. Nonno Frankie demonstrated, taking a boxing stance. . . .
2. I stopped a few feet from him and put my fists up.
3. Everyone stopped dead in their tracks.
4. They looked like the mob I had seen in a sixteenth-century etching.
5. The crowd froze in amazed silence.

Writing Application For each noun below, write a sentence in which the noun is modified by an adjective. Underline the adjective.

Example: *sounds:* I love the <u>rocking</u> sounds of Hairy Harry's Shoestring Jug Band.

1. cat   2. spaceship   3. tree   4. friend

Build Your Portfolio

 ## Idea Bank

Writing

1. **Letter to Paul** In a brief letter, offer Paul your suggestion about how he could have gotten out of his fight with John. Give reasons why Paul should follow your advice.

2. **Anecdote** Write an anecdote, or brief story, about a time when you, a friend, or an imaginary character went to a place where the rules were unfamiliar. Explain what happened.

3. **Essay** In a brief essay, explain why you think kids fight and how fights can be avoided.

Speaking and Listening

4. **Forum** Hold a discussion with classmates on violence in the media. Draw up a list of the points you discuss and the conclusions you reach.

5. **News Report** With others, present a news report on Paul's fight. Two students might act as anchors, while another gives a "live" report. **[Media Link]**

Projects

6. **Presentation on Being New [Group Activity]** In a group, organize and present an orientation for new kids in school. Divide up these tasks: explaining the cafeteria; explaining playground customs and rules; and providing a map of the building. **[Social Studies Link]**

7. **Self-Defense Posters** Research the ways in which people who are not trained fighters can defend themselves. Draw a series of posters illustrating each tip you discover. **[Visual Arts Link]**

 ## Writing Mini-Lesson

School Rules

If only someone had written down the rules for gym, Paul would have understood why John took the paddle from him. There would not have been a fight. Write up the rules new kids in your school need to know.

Writing Skills Focus: Be Clear and Brief

Make each rule you write **clear and brief.**

Model

Unclear: People who use paddles for fifteen minutes cannot use them anymore. (*Is this rule about a punishment or is it about taking turns?*)

Clear: After fifteen minutes, each person must return his or her paddle.

Too Long: When you return a library book, you have to pay a fine if you bent the cover or tore pages out or wrote on them.

Brief: You will be fined if you return a library book in damaged condition.

Prewriting List important rules at school. Include "unwritten" rules, such as those about which types of sneakers are cool.

Drafting Review your list of rules, and see if you can combine any. Group them according to the part of school life they concern. Number each one.

> ◆ **Grammar Application**
> Look for places in your rules where adjectives would add useful information.

Revising Make sure you have stated each rule as clearly and briefly as possible.

PART 1 *Meeting Challenges*

Jim Ryun-World Champion Miler, 1975 © Joe Wilder

Guide for Reading

Meet the Author:

Virginia Driving Hawk Sneve
(1933–   )

Virginia Driving Hawk Sneve was born on a Sioux Indian reservation in Rosebud, South Dakota. As a teacher and a writer, she devotes herself to sharing Native American life as she has experienced it. Her work includes fiction and historical articles. The 1971 Interracial Council for Minority Books for Children honored her novel *Jimmy Yellow Hawk*. She has also received awards from the Western Writers of America.

THE STORY BEHIND THE STORY

Sneve portrays Indians and their heritage from a Native American point of view. "Thunder Butte" (from the novel *When Thunders Spoke*) reflects conflicts that many Native Americans experience today. She works "to interpret history from the viewpoint of the American Indian" because she feels they have been misrepresented by historians who are not themselves Native Americans.

◆ LITERATURE AND YOUR LIFE

CONNECT YOUR EXPERIENCE

You probably have privileges now that you didn't have last year. However, you may also have had to let go of some old habits and customs. The main character in "Thunder Butte" must find a way to balance new ideas with traditions from the past.

THEMATIC FOCUS: Meeting Challenges

As you read, ask yourself how the past can help a person meet current challenges.

◆ Background for Understanding

SOCIAL STUDIES

The Sioux (soō) once lived throughout the northern plains of Minnesota, the Dakotas, and Nebraska. Today, some Sioux remain on reservations in the northern plains; others live throughout the United States. The *coup* (koō) stick in this story, like the one shown below, is a symbol of Sioux bravery and fighting skill.

◆ Build Vocabulary

RELATED WORDS: FORMS OF *vary*

The main character of "Thunder Butte" finds stones of *variegated*, or different, colors. *Variegated* is a form of a word you know: *vary*. Other words related to *vary* are *variety* and *various*. All of these related words have to do with differences.

WORD BANK

Which word on this list looks as if it might have a meaning similar to *wanderings*?

meanderings
diminutive
variegated
heathen
adamant

◆ Thunder Butte ◆

◆ Literary Focus

ATMOSPHERE

Atmosphere is the feeling or mood of a work. In the photograph above, the unusual landscape and dark shadows create a mysterious atmosphere. In "Thunder Butte," phrases such as "the ledge . . . loomed over him" and "dark, low-hanging clouds" create a serious, almost threatening, atmosphere. Use an organizer like the one below to jot down other details that contribute to the atmosphere of "Thunder Butte."

◆ Reading Strategy

ASK QUESTIONS

As you read a story, **ask questions** about what's going on. For example, ask why a character behaves as he or she does, or what causes an event to happen. Then, as you read on, search the text for answers or for details on which you can base answers. When you read "Thunder Butte," one question you might ask yourself is why each character has such a different reaction to what the main character finds.

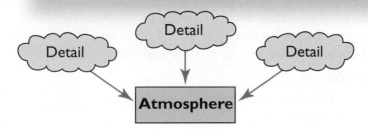

Thunder Butte

Virginia Driving Hawk Sneve

The sun was just beginning to rise when John woke Norman the next morning.

"You must get an early start if you are going to go to the west side of the butte[1] and return by supper," John said to the sleepy boy. "If you are not home by the time I get back from work, I'll come looking for you."

Norman reluctantly rose. Last night he had accepted his grandfather's command to go to the Thunder Butte without too many doubts. Yet now in the morning's chill light the boy wondered if his grandfather's dreams were the meaningless meanderings of an old mind, or if his grandfather was really worthy of the tribe's respect as one of the few remaining wise elders who understood the ancient ways.

Norman dressed in his oldest clothes and pulled on worn and scuffed boots to protect his feet from the rocks and snakes of the butte. He heard his parents talking in the other room and knew his father was telling his mother where Norman was going.

As the boy entered the room, which was kitchen and living room as well as his parents' bedroom, he heard his mother say, "What if there is a rock slide and Norman is hurt or buried on the butte? We won't know anything until you get home from work, John. I don't want Norman to go."

"The boy is old enough to have learned to be careful on the butte. He'll be all right," John answered as he tried to reassure Sarah. "Besides," he added, "my father dreamed of this happening."

Sarah grunted scornfully, "No one believes in dreams or in any of those old superstitious ways anymore."

"I'll be okay, Mom," Norman said as he sat down at the table. "I should be able to find lots of agates[2] on the west side where there is all that loose rock. Maybe I can talk the trader into giving me money for them after all." He spoke bravely despite his own inner misgivings about going to the butte.

Sarah protested no more. Norman looked at her, but she lowered her head as she set a plate of pancakes in front of him. He knew she was hiding the worry she felt for him.

John put on his hat and went to the door. "Don't forget to take the willow branch with you," he said to Norman, "and be careful."

Norman nodded and ate his breakfast. When he was finished he stood up. "Guess I'll go," he said to his mother, who was pouring hot water from the tea kettle into her dish pan. When she didn't speak Norman took the willow cane from where he had propped it by the door and his hat from the nail above it.

"Wait," Sarah called and handed him a paper bag. "Here is a lunch for you. You'll need

---

1. **butte** (byo͞ot) *n*.: Steep hill standing alone in a plain.

◆ **Build Vocabulary**

meanderings (mē an′ dər iŋz) *n*.: Aimless wanderings

---

2. **agates** (ag′ its) *n*.: Hard, semiprecious stones with striped or clouded coloring.

something to eat since you'll be gone all day." She gave him an affectionate shove. "Oh, go on. I know you'll be all right. Like your dad said, you're old enough to be careful."

Norman smiled at his mother. "Thanks," he said as he tucked the lunch into his shirt. He checked his back pocket to see if he'd remembered the salt bag to put the agates in.

He walked briskly across the open prairie and turned to wave at his mother, who had come outside to watch him leave. She waved back and Norman quickened his pace. He whistled, trying to echo the meadowlarks who were greeting the day with their happy song. He swiped the willow cane at the bushy sage and practiced spearing the pear cactus that dotted his path. The early morning air was cool, but the sun soon warmed the back of his neck and he knew it would be a hot day.

He crossed the creek south of where Matt Two Bull's tent was pitched and then he was climbing the gentle beginning slope of the butte. He stopped and studied the way before him and wondered if it wouldn't be easier to reach the west side by walking around the base of the butte even though it would be longer. Then Norman smiled as he remembered his grandfather's command to climb the south trail that wound to the top. He decided to do what the old man wanted.

The ascent sharply steepened and the sun rose with him as Norman climbed. What looked like a smooth path from the prairie floor was rough rocky terrain. The trail spiraled up a sharp incline and Norman had to detour around fallen rocks. He paused to rest about half way up and then saw how sharply the overhanging ledge of the butte protruded. Getting to the top of it was going to be a difficult struggle. He climbed on. His foot slipped and his ankle twisted painfully. Small pebbles bounced down the slope and he saw a rattlesnake slither out of the way. He tightly clutched the willow branch and leaned panting against the butte. He sighed with relief as the snake crawled out of sight. He wiggled his foot until the pain left his ankle. Then he started to trudge up the incline again.

At last only the ledge of the butte loomed over him. There appeared to be no way up. Disgusted that his laborious climb seemed dead-ended he stubbornly tried to reach the top. Remembering the courage of the ancient young men who had struggled in this same place to gain the summit and seek their visions, he was determined not to go back. His fingers found tiny cracks to hold on to. The cane was cumbersome and in the way. He was tempted to drop it, but he thought of the snake he'd seen and struggled on with it awkwardly under his arm.

Finally Norman spied a narrow opening in the ledge which tapered down to only a few feet from where he clung. He inched his way up until he reached the base of the opening and then he found a use for the cane. He jammed the stout branch high into the boulders above him. Cautiously he pulled to see if it would hold his weight. It held. Using the cane as a lever he pulled himself to the top.

This final exertion winded the boy and he lay exhausted on the summit, boots hanging over the edge. Cautiously he pulled his feet under him, stood and looked around.

He gazed at a new world. The sun bathed the eastern valley in pale yellow which was spotted with dark clumps of sage. The creek was a green and silver serpent winding its way to the southeast. His grandfather's tent was a white shoe box in its clearing, and beside it stood a <u>diminutive</u> form waving a red flag. It was Matt Two Bull signaling with his shirt, and Norman knew that his grandfather had been watching him climb. He waved his hat in reply and then walked to the outer edge of the butte.

◆ **Build Vocabulary**
diminutive (də min´ yo͞o tiv) *adj.*: Very small

The summit was not as smoothly flat as it looked from below. Norman stepped warily over the many cracks and holes that pitted the surface. He was elated that he had successfully made the difficult ascent, but now as he surveyed the butte top he had a sense of discomfort.

There were burn scars on the rough summit, and Norman wondered if these spots were where the lightning had struck, or were they evidence of ancient man-made fires? He remembered that this was a sacred place to the old ones and his uneasiness increased. He longed to be back on the secure level of the plains.

On the west edge he saw that the butte cast a sharp shadow below because the rim protruded as sharply as it had on the slope he'd climbed. Two flat rocks jutted up on either side of a narrow opening, and Norman saw shallow steps hewn into the space between. This must be the trail of which his grandfather had spoken.

▲ **Critical Viewing** What do you think the older man is saying to the younger man in this picture? **[Speculate]**

Norman stepped down and then quickly turned to hug the butte face as the steps ended abruptly in space. The rest of the rocky staircase lay broken and crumbled below. The only way down was to jump.

He cautiously let go of the willow branch and watched how it landed and bounced against the rocks. He took a deep breath as if to draw courage from the air. He lowered himself so that he was hanging by his fingertips to the last rough step, closed his eyes and dropped.

The impact of his landing stung the soles of his feet. He stumbled and felt the cut of the sharp rocks against one knee as he struggled to retain his balance. He did not fall and finally stood upright breathing deeply until the wild pounding of his heart slowed. "Wow," he said softly as he looked back up at the ledge, "that must have been at least a twenty foot drop."

He picked up the willow branch and started walking slowly down the steep slope. The trail Matt Two Bull had told him about had been obliterated by years of falling rock. Loose shale and gravel shifted under Norman's feet, and he probed cautiously ahead with the cane to test the firmness of each step.

He soon found stones which he thought were agates. He identified them by spitting on each rock and rubbing the wet spot with his finger. The dull rock seemed to come alive! Variegated hues of brown and gray glowed as if polished. They were agates all right. Quickly he had his salt bag half full.

It was almost noon and his stomach growled. He stopped to rest against a large boulder and pulled out his lunch from his shirt. But his mouth was too dry to chew the cheese sandwich. He couldn't swallow without water.

Thirsty and hungry, Norman decided to go straight down the butte and head for home.

Walking more confidently as the slope leveled out he thrust the pointed cane carelessly into the ground. He suddenly fell as the cane went deep into the soft shale.

Norman slid several feet. Loose rocks rolled around him as he came to rest against a boulder. He lay still for a long time fearing that his tumble might cause a rock fall. But no thundering slide came, so he cautiously climbed back to where the tip of the willow branch protruded from the ground.

He was afraid that the cane may have plunged into a rattlesnake den. Carefully he pulled at the stout branch, wiggling it this way and that with one hand while he dug with the other. It came loose, sending a shower of rocks down the hill, and Norman saw that something else was sticking up in the hole he had uncovered.

Curious, and seeing no sign of snakes, he kept digging and soon found the tip of a leather-covered stick. Bits of leather and wood fell off in his hand as he gently pulled. The stick, almost as long as he was tall and curved on one end, emerged as he tugged. Holding it before him, his heart pounding with excitement, he realized that he had found a thing that once belonged to the old ones.

Norman shivered at the thought that he may have disturbed a grave, which was *tehinda*,[3] forbidden. He cleared more dirt away but saw no bones nor other sign that this was a burial place. Quickly he picked up the stick and his willow cane and hurried down the hill. When he reached the bottom he discovered that in his fall the salt bag of agates had pulled loose from his belt. But he did not return to search for it. It would take most of the afternoon to travel around the base of the butte to the east side.

The creek was in the deep shade of the butte when he reached it and thirstily flopped down and drank. He crossed the shallow stream and walked to his grandfather's tent.

"You have been gone a long time," Matt Two Bull greeted as Norman walked into the clearing where the old man was seated.

"I have come from the west side of the butte, Grandpa," Norman said wearily. He sat down on the ground and examined a tear in his jeans and the bruise on his knee.

"Was it difficult?" the old man asked.

"Yes," Norman nodded. He told of the rough climb up the south slope, the jump down and finally of his fall which led him to discover the long leather-covered stick. He held the stick out to his grandfather who took it and examined it carefully.

"Are you sure there was no body in the place where you found this?"

Norman shook his head. "No, I found nothing else but the stick. Do you know what it is, Grandpa?"

"You have found a *coup*[4] stick which

---

3. **tehinda** (tā khin´ dä)
4. **coup** (ko͞o)

belonged to the old ones."

"I know that it is old because the wood is brittle and the leather is peeling, but what is—was a *coup* stick?" Norman asked.

"In the days when the old ones roamed all of the plains," the old man swept his hand in a circle, "a courageous act of valor was thought to be more important than killing an enemy. When a warrior rode or ran up to his enemy, close enough to touch the man with a stick, without killing or being killed, the action was called *coup*.

"The French, the first white men in this part of the land, named this brave deed *coup*. In their language the word meant 'hit' or 'strike.' The special stick which was used to strike with came to be known as a *coup* stick.

"Some sticks were long like this one," Matt Two Bull held the stick upright. "Some were straight, and others had a curve on the end like the sheep herder's crook," he pointed to the curving end of the stick.

"The sticks were decorated with fur or painted leather strips. A warrior kept count of his *coups* by tying an eagle feather to the crook for each brave deed. See," he pointed to the staff end, "here is a remnant of a tie thong which must have once held a feather."

The old man and boy closely examined the *coup* stick. Matt Two Bull traced with his finger the faint zig zag design painted on the stick. "See," he said, "it is the thunderbolt."

"What does that mean?" Norman asked.

"The Thunders favored a certain few of the young men who sought their vision on the butte. The thunderbolt may have been part of a sacred dream sent as a token of the Thunders' favor. If this was so, the young man could use the thunderbolt symbol on his possessions."

◆ **Build Vocabulary**

variegated (verˊ ē ə gātˊ id) *adj.*: Marked with different colors in spots or streaks

"How do you suppose the stick came to be on the butte?" Norman asked.

His grandfather shook his head. "No one can say. Usually such a thing was buried with a dead warrior as were his weapons and other prized belongings."

"Is the *coup* stick what you dreamed about, Grandpa?"

"No. In my dream I only knew that you were to find a *Wakan*,[5] a holy thing. But I did not know what it would be."

Norman laughed nervously. "What do you mean, *Wakan*? Is this stick haunted?"

Matt Two Bull smiled, "No, not like you mean in a fearful way. But in a sacred manner because it once had great meaning to the old ones."

"But why should I have been the one to find it?" Norman questioned.

His grandfather shrugged, "Perhaps to help you understand the ways—the values of the old ones."

<table>
<tr><td>◆ Reading Strategy</td></tr>
<tr><td>Ask yourself why Matt Two Bull is so respectful of the stick.</td></tr>
</table>

"But nobody believes in that kind of thing anymore," Norman scoffed. "And even if people did, I couldn't run out and hit my enemy with the stick and get away with it." He smiled thinking of Mr. Brannon. "No one would think I was brave. I'd probably just get thrown in jail."

Suddenly Norman felt compelled to stop talking. In the distance he heard a gentle rumble which seemed to come from the butte. He glanced up at the hill looming high above and saw that it was capped with dark, low-hanging clouds.

Matt Two Bull looked too and smiled. "The Thunders are displeased with your thoughts," he said to Norman. "Listen to their message."

A sharp streak of lightning split the clouds and the thunder cracked and echoed over the plains.

Norman was frightened but he answered

---

5. **Wakan** (wä kän)

with bravado, "The message I get is that a storm is coming," but his voice betrayed him by quavering. "Maybe you'd better come home with me, Grandpa. Your tent will get soaked through if it rains hard."

"No," murmured Matt Two Bull, "no rain will come. It is just the Thunders speaking." There was another spark of lightning, and an explosive reverberation sounded as if in agreement with the old man.

Norman jumped to his feet. "Well, I'm going home. Mom will be worried because I'm late now." He turned to leave.

"Wait!" Matt Two Bull commanded. "Take the *coup* stick with you."

Norman backed away, "No, I don't want it. You can have it."

The old man rose swiftly despite the stiffness of his years and sternly held out the stick to the boy. "You found it. It belongs to you. Take it!"

Norman slowly reached out his hands and took the stick.

"Even if you think the old ways are only superstition and the stick no longer has meaning, it is all that remains of an old life and must be treated with respect." Matt Two Bull smiled at the boy. "Take it," he repeated gently, "and hang it in the house where it will not be handled."

Norman hurried home as fast as he could carrying the long stick in one hand and the willow cane in the other. He felt vaguely uneasy and somehow a little frightened. It was only when he reached the security of his home that he realized the thunder had stopped and there had been no storm.

"Mom," he called as he went into the house, "I'm home."

His mother was standing at the stove. "Oh, Norman," she greeted him smiling. "I'm glad you're back. I was beginning to worry." Her

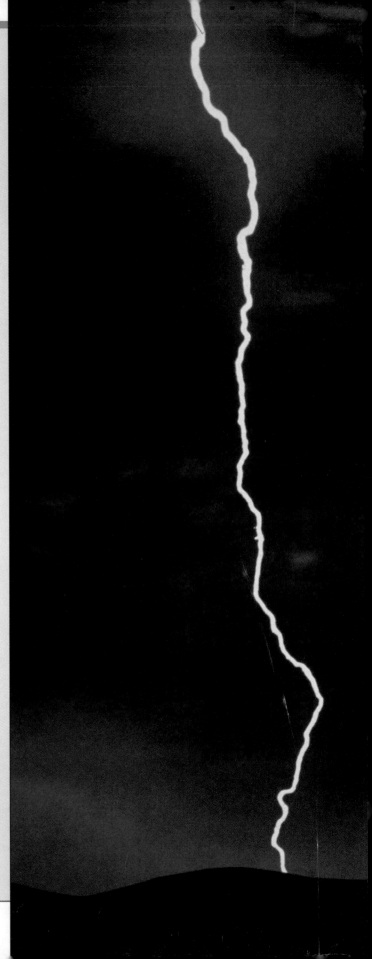

welcoming smile turned to a frown as she saw the *coup* stick in Norman's hand. "What is that?"

"Grandpa says it's a *coup* stick. Here," Norman handed it to her, "take a look at it. It's interesting the way it is made and decor—"

"No," Sarah interrupted and backed away from him. "I won't touch that <u>heathen</u> thing no matter what it is! Get it out of the house!"

"What?" Norman asked, surprised and puzzled. "There is nothing wrong with it. It's just an old stick I found up on the butte."

"I don't care," Sarah insisted. "I won't have such a thing in the house!"

"But, Mom," Norman protested, "it's not like we believe in those old ways the way Grandpa does."

But Sarah was <u>adamant</u>. "Take it out of the house!" she ordered, pointing to the door. "We'll talk about it when your dad gets home."

Reluctantly Norman took the *coup* stick outside and gently propped it against the house and sat on the steps to wait for his father. He was confused. First by his grandfather's reverent treatment of the *coup* stick as if it were a sacred object and then by Sarah's rejection of it as a heathen symbol.

He looked at the stick where it leaned against the wall and shook his head. So much fuss over a brittle, rotten length of wood. Even though he had gone through a lot of hard, even dangerous, effort to get it he was now tempted to heave it out on the trash pile.

Norman wearily leaned his head against the house. He suddenly felt tired and his knee ached. As he sat wearily rubbing the bruise

---

◀ **Critical Viewing** Why is lightning a good symbol of powerful anger? **[Support]**

◆ **Build Vocabulary**

heathen (hē′ *th*ən) *adj.*: Uncivilized

adamant (ad′ ə mənt′) *adj.*: Not flexible; not willing to give in

John Two Bull rode the old mare into the yard. Norman got up and walked back to the shed to help unsaddle the horse.

John climbed stiffly out of the saddle. His faded blue work shirt and jeans were stained with perspiration and dirt. His boots were worn and scuffed.

"Hard day, Dad?" Norman asked.

"Yeah," John answered, slipping the bridle over the mare's head. "Rustlers got away with twenty steers last night. I spent the day counting head and mending fences. Whoever the thief was cut the fence, drove a truck right onto the range and loaded the cattle without being seen." He began rubbing the mare down as she munched the hay in her manger.

"How did your day on the butte go?" John asked.

"Rough," Norman answered. "I'm beat too. The climb up the butte was tough and coming down was bad too." He told his father all that had happened on the butte, winding up with the climax of his falling and finding the old *coup* stick.

John listened attentively and did not interrupt until Norman told of Matt Two Bull's reaction to the stick. "I think Grandpa's mind has gotten weak," Norman said. "He really believes that the *coup* stick has some sort of mysterious power and that the Thunders were talking."

"Don't make fun of your grandfather," John reprimanded, "or of the old ways he believes in."

"Okay, okay," Norman said quickly, not wanting another scolding. "But Mom is just the opposite from Grandpa," he went on. "She doesn't want the *coup* stick in the house. Says it's heathen."

He walked to the house and handed the stick to his father. John examined it and then carried it into the house.

"John!" Sarah exclaimed as she saw her husband bring the stick into the room. "I told Norman, and I tell you, that I won't have that heathenish thing in the house!"

But John ignored her and propped the stick against the door while he pulled his tool box out from under the washstand to look for a hammer and nails.

"John," Sarah persisted, "did you hear me?"

"I heard," John answered quietly, but Norman knew his father was angry. "And I don't want to hear anymore."

Norman was surprised to hear his father speak in such a fashion. John was slow to anger, usually spoke quietly and tried to avoid conflict of any kind, but now he went on.

"This," he said holding the *coup* stick upright, "is a relic of our people's past glory when it was a good thing to be an Indian. It is a symbol of something that shall never be again."

Sarah gasped and stepped in front of her husband as he started to climb a chair to pound the nails in the wall above the window. "But that's what I mean," she said. "Those old ways were just superstition. They don't mean anything now—they can't because such a way of life can't be anymore. We don't need to have those old symbols of heathen ways hanging in the house!" She grabbed at the *coup* stick, but John jerked it out of her reach.

"Don't touch it!" he shouted and Sarah fell back against the table in shocked surprise. Norman took a step forward as if to protect his mother. The boy had never seen his father so angry.

John shook his head as if to clear it. "Sarah, I'm sorry. I didn't mean to yell. It's just that the old ones would not permit a woman to touch such a thing as this." He handed Norman the stick to hold while he hammered the nails in the wall. Then he hung the stick above the window.

"Sarah," he said as he put the tools away, "think of the stick as an object that could be in a museum, a part of history. It's not like we were going to fall down on our knees and pray to it." His voice was light and teasing as he tried to make peace.

But Sarah stood stiffly at the stove preparing supper and would not answer. Norman felt sick. His appetite was gone. When his mother set a plate of food before him he excused himself saying, "I guess I'm too tired to eat," and went to his room.

But after he had undressed and crawled into bed he couldn't sleep. His mind whirled with the angry words his parents had spoken. They had never argued in such a way before. "I wish I had never brought that old stick home," he whispered and then pulled the pillow over his head to shut out the sound of the low rumble of thunder that came from the west.

Guide for Responding

◆ LITERATURE AND YOUR LIFE

Reader's Response With whom do you agree—Norman's mother or his father? Explain.

Thematic Focus What are two challenges Norman meets in this story? Compare and contrast these challenges.

☑ Check Your Comprehension

1. Why does Norman climb the butte?
2. What happens to Norman on the butte after the rock slide?
3. What is a *coup* stick?
4. What happens to the *coup* stick at the end of the story?

◆ Critical Thinking

INTERPRET

1. What does the *coup* stick represent? **[Interpret]**
2. Why does Norman keep the stick? **[Analyze]**
3. Why does John think respect for tradition is valuable? **[Infer]**
4. In what ways do the past and present come into conflict in this story? **[Draw Conclusions]**

EVALUATE

5. Do you admire Norman for taking the challenge of climbing the butte? Explain. **[Evaluate]**

APPLY

6. What can you do to learn about the ways of your ancestors? **[Apply]**

Guide for Responding (continued)

◆ Reading Strategy

ASK QUESTIONS

Asking questions and looking for the answers as you read leads to a better understanding of the relationships among characters, events, and ideas.

1. (a) What questions did you ask yourself about the *coup* stick? (b) What answers did you find in the story, or what conclusions did you reach?
2. (a) What questions did you ask after Norman arrives home? (b) What answers did you find in the story, or what conclusions did you reach?

◆ Build Vocabulary

USING FORMS OF *vary*

Words related to *vary* all include the idea of *difference* in their meanings.

Fill in the blanks using each of the words listed.

variety   varied   various   variable

1. They offer a wide ____?____ of flowers.
2. The weather has been so ____?____, I don't know whether to take a parka or a bathing suit!
3. He just played one note over and over again; I like music that is more ____?____.
4. You can choose from ____?____ candies.

SPELLING STRATEGY

Pronounce a word aloud to discover how many syllables it has. For example, *variegated* has five syllables: *var i e ga ted*. Noticing the syllables will help you include all the sounds when you spell the word.

Say the following words aloud. Then, write each word in syllables.

1. meanderings 2. diminutive 3. heathen 4. adamant

USING THE WORD BANK

On your paper, identify each statement as true or false. Explain your answers.

1. Calling someone a heathen is a compliment.
2. A variegated leaf has a few different colors.
3. Adamant people are unsure of their beliefs.
4. A hut is a diminutive building.
5. Meanderings are paths in straight lines.

◆ Literary Focus

ATMOSPHERE

Atmosphere is the feeling or mood of a work of literature. The writer's choice of details helps create the atmosphere.

1. The atmosphere at the beginning of this story is mostly one of danger. Name three details that help create this atmosphere.
2. Give three details that help to create atmosphere as Norman climbs the butte. What is the atmosphere during the climb?
3. What is the atmosphere like at dinner? Why?

◆ Build Grammar Skills

POSSESSIVES AS ADJECTIVES

Adjectives are words that modify nouns or pronouns. Nouns that show possession, or ownership —such as *mother's* or *Norman's*—function as adjectives. They answer the question *whose?*

Norman's plan   Grandfather's dreams
sun's light

Possessive pronouns, such as *his, my,* and *your,* function as adjectives. These pronouns also answer the question *whose?*

his father   her voice

Practice On your paper, circle the possessives that function as adjectives. Draw an arrow to the word each possessive modifies.

1. She lowered her head.
2. My father dreamed of this.
3. Norman's grandfather spoke of the past.
4. The butte hid its secrets from Norman's eyes.
5. The stick's meaning was not understood.

Writing Application Copy the following paragraph. Add possessives to modify the italicized nouns. You may need to replace *the* with the possessive.

Grandfather spoke of the *past*. He wanted the boy to know the *traditions*. Norman wanted *grandfather* to accept the present. *Mother* was convinced that the *meaning* was outdated.

Build Your Portfolio

 ## Idea Bank

Writing

1. **Captions** Write captions—brief descriptive labels—for several landscape pictures. In each caption, capture the atmosphere of the picture.

2. **Museum Card** If Norman were to take the *coup* stick to a museum, it would be displayed with a card giving information about it. Write the text for a museum card for the *coup* stick.

3. **Essay** Write an essay in which you explain how the past and present come into conflict in this story. Support your points with passages from the story.

Speaking and Listening

4. **Conversation** With a partner, role-play the next conversation Norman has with his grandfather. **[Performing Arts Link]**

5. **Climbing Dance [Group Activity]** With a small group of classmates, plan and perform a dance showing Norman's climb up and down the butte. Divide the following tasks: choosing music, planning the motions, performing the dance. **[Performing Arts Link; Music Link]**

Projects

6. **Oral Presentation [Group Activity]** With a group, prepare an oral presentation on the Sioux Indians. Have the group members choose from among these tasks: speaking for the group; doing research; creating charts and graphs; choosing drawings, photos, models, or artifacts. **[Social Studies Link]**

7. **Diagram** Use the library or other resources to find out how a butte is formed. Create a diagram with labels. Present your diagram to the class, and explain it. **[Science Link]**

 ## Writing Mini-Lesson

Opinion Paper

Each adult member of Norman's family has an opinion about how the past and future are related to the present. Do you think people benefit more from looking back or looking forward? Write an opinion paper to explain and support your ideas.

> **Writing Skills Focus:**
> **State Main Ideas**
>
> Clearly state the three **main ideas** on which you base your opinion. These ideas are the reasons you think as you do. They are the steps that will help your readers understand your position. Use an organizer like the one shown below.
>
>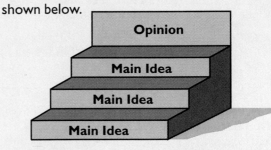

Prewriting First, write a single sentence that states your opinion. Then, list three main ideas that support your opinion.

Drafting Develop a paragraph around each of your main ideas. Include details and facts that illustrate the ideas.

Revising Ask a classmate to read your paper and restate your opinion. If necessary, revise to make your opinion clearer.

> ◆ **Grammar Application**
>
> Use possessive adjectives, such as *past's* and *people's,* and possessive pronouns, such as *our* and *your,* to give more information about the nouns you use.

Guide for Reading

Meet the Authors:

Victor Hugo (1802–1885)

Victor Hugo is considered by many to be the greatest French poet who ever lived. Yet more people know him for his novels *Les Misérables* and *The Hunchback of Notre Dame* than for his poetry.

Langston Hughes (1902–1967)

As a young man, Langston Hughes traveled to Africa and Europe as part of the crew on merchant ships. When he returned to the United States, he settled in Harlem, a section of New York City. Hughes is best known for his work during the Harlem Renaissance—a period during the late 1920's and early 1930's when African American literature, visual arts, and performing arts flourished.

Mark Twain (1835–1910)

Mark Twain was born with a much longer name—Samuel Langhorne Clemens. His pen name, Mark Twain, comes from the slang used by riverboat pilots, meaning "two fathoms deep." In his time, Twain became known as an entertaining speaker. "Stage Fright" is a record of a speech he gave after his daughter's first public singing recital.

Arnold Adoff (1935–   )

Poet, author, teacher, and lecturer Arnold Adoff has been writing poetry since he was a boy! His own memories and his experiences as a teacher and a father help him to understand the feelings and interests of young people.

◆ LITERATURE AND YOUR LIFE

CONNECT YOUR EXPERIENCE

You may have noticed that as you get older, people expect more from you. School assignments are more challenging, sports are more competitive, and friendships and other relationships are more complicated. The writers in this group offer words of encouragement for facing these everyday challenges.

THEMATIC FOCUS: Meeting Challenges

What are some challenges you have faced this year that you didn't have to confront last year?

◆ Background for Understanding

SCIENCE

In "Stage Fright," Mark Twain describes the nervous, anxious feelings that many people have when performing before a group. When your body is under stress, it produces extra adrenaline. Adrenaline increases your heart rate, your blood pressure, and the chemical reactions in your body. These heightened reactions are the reason stage fright makes your heart pound, your palms sweat, and your stomach feel uneasy.

◆ Build Vocabulary

RELATED WORDS: FORMS OF *oppose*

In "Alone in the Nets," the speaker worries about the *opposition*. Knowing that *opposition* is a form of *oppose* can help you figure out that the *opposition* is against or in contrast—it is the "other side." Another form of *oppose* is *opposite*, which means "the reverse."

WORD BANK

For which words on this list do you know at least one meaning?

slight
compulsion
opposition
evaporate

Be Like the Bird ◆ Dream Dust
Stage Fright ◆ Alone in the Nets

◆ Literary Focus

LEVELS OF MEANING

A work of literature can have more than one **level of meaning.** It's usually easy to understand the literal meaning—what the words actually say. In addition, a literary work often contains deeper meanings that relate more broadly to life in general. *Dust*, for example, is "loose dirt." In "Dream Dust," however, it has another level of meaning: It suggests dreams and experiences that are hard to hold on to.

◆ Reading Strategy

RELATE TO YOUR OWN EXPERIENCE

One of the strategies you can use to uncover levels of meaning is to **relate** the literature to your own experience. For example, in "Alone in the Nets," Arnold Adoff describes the anxiety felt by a soccer goalie. Even if you have never played soccer, you can relate the feelings described to an experience in which you felt the pressure of competition. This in turn helps you uncover a level of meaning relating to the ways in which we overcome personal fears. Use an organizer like the one at left to make connections between the literature and your own experiences.

	Topic of Poem→	Feelings Described	← My Experience
Be Like the Bird	→		←
Dream Dust	Hopes and dreams →	Hope; determination	←I really hope to make the basketball team!
Stage Fright	→		←
Alone in the Nets	→		←

Be Like the Bird
Victor Hugo

Be like the bird, who
Halting in his flight
On limb too <u>slight</u>
Feels it give way beneath him,
5 Yet sings
Knowing he hath wings.

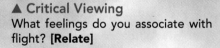

▲ **Critical Viewing**
What feelings do you associate with flight? **[Relate]**

Dream Dust
Langston Hughes

Gather out of star-dust
   Earth-dust,
   Cloud-dust,
   Storm-dust,
5 And splinters of hail,
One handful of dream-dust
   Not for sale.

◆ **Build Vocabulary**
slight (slīt) *adj.*: Light; weak

Stage Fright

Mark Twain

My heart goes out in sympathy to anyone who is making his first appearance before an audience of human beings. By a direct process of memory I go back forty years, less one month—for I'm older than I look.

I recall the occasion of my first appearance. San Francisco knew me then only as a reporter, and I was to make my bow to San Francisco as a lecturer. I knew that nothing short of compulsion would get me to the theater. So I bound myself by a hard-and-fast contract so that I could not escape. I got to the theater forty-five minutes before the hour set for the lecture. My knees were shaking so that I didn't know whether I could stand up. If there is an awful, horrible malady in the world, it is stage fright—and seasickness. They are a pair. I had stage fright then for the first and last time. I was only seasick once, too. It was on a little ship on which there were two hundred other passengers. I—was—sick. I was so sick that there wasn't any left for those other two hundred passengers.

It was dark and lonely behind the scenes in that theater, and I peeked through the little peek holes they have in theater curtains and looked into the big auditorium. That was dark and empty, too. By and by it lighted up, and the audience began to arrive.

I had got a number of friends of mine, stalwart men, to sprinkle themselves through the audience armed with big clubs. Every time I said anything they could possibly guess I intended to be funny, they were to pound those clubs on the floor. Then there was a kind lady in a box up there, also a good friend of mine, the wife of the governor. She was to watch me intently, and whenever I glanced toward her she was going to deliver a gubernatorial laugh that would lead the whole audience into applause.

At last I began. I had the manuscript tucked under a United States flag in front of me where I could get at it in case of need. But I managed to get started without it. I walked up and down—I was young in those days and needed the exercise—and talked and talked.

Right in the middle of the speech I had placed a gem. I had put in a moving, pathetic part which was to get at the hearts and souls of my hearers. When I delivered it, they did just what I hoped and expected. They sat silent and awed. I had touched them. Then I happened to glance up at the box where the governor's wife was—you know what happened.

Well, after the first agonizing five minutes, my stage fright left me, never to return. I know if I was going to be hanged I could get up and make a good showing, and I intend to. But I shall never forget my feelings before the agony left me, and I got up here to thank you for her for helping my daughter, by your kindness, to live through her first appearance. And I want to thank you for your appreciation of her singing, which is, by the way, hereditary.

◆ **Build Vocabulary**
compulsion (kəm pul′ shən) *n.*: Force

Alone in the Nets

Arnold Adoff

Alone in the Nets.

I

am

alone of course,

5   in the nets, on this cold and raining afternoon,
       and our best defending fullback
       is lying on the wet ground out of position.
       Half the <u>opposition</u> is pounding
                                down the field,
10   and their lead forward is gliding
              so fast, she can just barely keep
              the ball in front of her sliding
                                foot.
       Her cleats are expensive.
15   and her hair ᵇ ₒ ᵘ ⁿ ᶜ ᵉ ˢ
                          neatly
       like the after
              girls   in the shampoo commercials.
                     There   is   a   big   grin
20   on her face.

Now: In This Frozen Moment On This Moving World Through Space
              is the right time to ask why am I here just standing
                                in my frozen place?
       Why did I get up on time this morning?
25   Why did I get up at all?
       Why did I listen to the coach and agree to play
              this strange position in a r e a l game
              in a strange town on this wet and moving world?
       Why is it raining?
30   Why is it raining so h a r d?
       Where
              are all of ₒᵤᵣ defenders?
       Why do all of ₒᵤᵣ players
              do all of the falling
35   down?
                     Why am I here?

But Frozen Moments Can Unfreeze And I Can Stretch
       and reach for the ball flying to the corner of
                                       our
40   goal.
       I can reach and jump
              and dive into the s p a c e

▲ **Critical Viewing** What details
of this photo show the tension
of competition? **[Analyze]**

◆ **Build Vocabulary**

opposition (äp´ ə zish´ ən) *n.*:
Here, the other team

evaporate (i vap´ ə rāt´) *v.*:
Disappear like vapor

<pre>
                                        between my out
                                              stretched
                                                   hands
45   and the outside poles
                    of the nets.
        My fears evaporate like my sweat in this chilling
                                                    breeze,
50   and I can move with this moving world
        and pace my steps
        like that old
                    movie
                    high
55   noon sheriff in his just
                                        right
                                        time.
        That grinning forward gets her shot away too soon,
        and I am there, on my own time, in the air,
60   to meet the ball,
        and fall on it
        for the save.
            I wave my happy ending wave and get up.
65   The game goes on.
</pre>

Guide for Responding

◆ LITERATURE AND YOUR LIFE

Reader's Response Which piece of literature in this group do you find most encouraging? Why?

Thematic Focus What challenges do the writers and characters in this group meet?

☑ Check Your Comprehension

1. Why does the bird sing in "Be Like the Bird"?
2. In "Dream Dust," from what is dream dust gathered?
3. In "Stage Fright," what does Twain do to ensure that he will get a laugh during his first speech?
4. What happens at the end of "Alone in the Nets"?

◆ Critical Thinking

INTERPRET

1. In "Dream Dust," why shouldn't dream dust be for sale? **[Interpret]**
2. In "Stage Fright," why is Mark Twain sympathetic to anyone making his or her first appearance? **[Draw Conclusions]**

EVALUATE

3. Is "Be Like the Bird" an optimistic poem? Why or why not? **[Make a Judgment]**
4. Do you think Adoff is successful in conveying the tension of a sporting competition in "Alone in the Nets"? **[Assess]**

COMPARE LITERARY WORKS

5. Which of these works would appeal to the widest range of people? Explain. **[Assess]**

Guide for Responding (continued)

◆ Reading Strategy

RELATE TO YOUR OWN EXPERIENCE

When you **relate** a work of literature to your own experience, you'll find that it has more meaning for you.

1. What are some experiences that might cause stage fright in a person your age?
2. What emotions does the speaker express in "Alone in the Nets"?
3. What personal experiences did you relate to "Be Like the Bird" and "Alone in the Nets"?

◆ Build Vocabulary

USING FORMS OF *oppose*

Copy the following sentences on your paper. Fill in each blank with a form of *oppose: opposed, opposing, opposition,* or *opposite.*

1. The _____?_____ team was winning.
2. They did the _____?_____ of what we expected.
3. We _____?_____ a change in the schedule.
4. Next week's _____?_____ is not as strong.

SPELLING STRATEGY

Sometimes, as in *slight,* the sound of the long *i* is spelled *igh.* On your paper, unscramble the following letters to make words spelled with *igh* that rhyme with *slight.*

1. thrig 2. ghimt 3. birgth 4. thilg

USING THE WORD BANK

On your paper, write these sentences. Fill in the blank using words from the Word Bank.

1. In this heat, the water will _____?_____ quickly.
2. You've made a _____?_____ error in your math.
3. The _____?_____ to our idea was discouraging.
4. He felt a strong _____?_____ to speak.

◆ Literary Focus

LEVELS OF MEANING

To fully understand a work of literature, you may need to dig through several **levels of meaning.**

1. What does Hugo mean when he says, "be like a bird"?
2. In "Dream Dust," what might "Storm-dust, / And splinters of hail" stand for?
3. (a) What is the literal meaning of the title "Alone in the Nets"? (b) What else might the title mean?
4. What message does "Alone in the Nets" convey that can be applied to experiences not related to sports?

◆ Build Grammar Skills

ARTICLES

The **articles** *a, and,* and *the* are the most frequently used adjectives. *The* is a **definite article** because it points out a particular person, place, thing, or idea (*the* theater, *the* lecture). *A* and *an* are **indefinite articles** because they do not point out a particular person, place, thing, or idea (*a* reporter, *an* awful feeling).

Practice On your paper, identify the article in each of the following sentences, and explain whether it is definite or indefinite.

1. Be like the bird....
2. San Francisco knew me then only as a reporter....
3. A goalie must have good reflexes.
4. I got to the theater early.
5. An audience can be frightening.

Writing Application Write a paragraph about stage fright. In your paragraph, use articles with the following nouns: audience, group, nerves, entrance, exit.

Build Your Portfolio

 ## Idea Bank

Writing

1. **Advice List** Write a list of practical suggestions for what a person can do to limit the physical and emotional effects of stage fright.

2. **Article** Interview several classmates who participate in sports. Find out why they participate and what skills they need in order to do well. Write an article based on your interviews. **[Sports Link]**

3. **Speech Writing** Write a speech based on the message of one of the works of literature in this group. In your speech, use a quotation from the work.

Speaking and Listening

4. **Anecdote** Mark Twain shares an anecdote—a brief, often humorous story—about his first public appearance. Share with a small group of classmates an anecdote about a humorous experience you have had.

5. **Dramatization** Pair up with a classmate and act out the scene you imagine took place when the coach in "Alone in the Nets" asked the soccer player to play goalie for the first time. **[Sports Link]**

Projects

6. **Pantomime [Group Activity]** With a group, plan pantomimes (performances without words) that communicate the action and meaning of the literary works in this group. Perform your pantomimes for the class. **[Performing Arts Link]**

7. **Collage** Choose one of the poems from this group, and illlustrate its meaning in a collage of magazine pictures, drawings, and found objects. **[Art Link]**

 ## Writing Mini-Lesson

Poem

Three of the writers in this group respond to life's everyday challenges through poetry. Write a poem of your own that expresses how you feel about or handle challenges.

Writing Skills Focus: Choose Precise Words

Precise words—words that refer to or describe a very specific thing or action—convey more vivid images than vague or general words. Use precise words in your poem to create vivid pictures in the minds of your readers. In "Dream Dust," Hughes uses the single precise word "splinters," rather than the general and wordy "sharp little pieces."

Prewriting Use a graphic organizer like the one below to explore the feelings and ideas you have about challenges.

Drafting Write your poem in rhymed or unrhymed lines. Use line breaks and punctuation to create a pattern of sound and rhythm.

Revising Review your poem, changing vague, general words to single, precise words.

> ◆ **Grammar Application**
> Identify each definite article and each indefinite article in your poem.

CONNECTING LITERATURE TO SOCIAL STUDIES
ANCIENT ROME
The Dog of Pompeii *by Louis Untermeyer*

Ancient Pompeii
🏛 Ancient city
🌋 Mountain

N

ITALY

Adriatic Sea

•Rome

Mt. Vesuvius
Naples•• Pompeii

Mediterranean
Sea

Naples   Mt. Vesuvius
Herculaneum   Pompeii
Bay of
Naples
Destroyed by eruption   Stabiae
of Mt. Vesuvius, A.D. 79

0   150 mi
0   150 km

THE ROMAN EMPIRE The modern city of Rome is the capital of Italy. In ancient times, Rome was the center of the Western world, the capital of the Roman Empire. The Roman Empire included most of Europe and some parts of Asia and Africa. The rulers of the empire lived in the land that we now know as Italy.

Pompeii Approximately 200 miles south of Rome, near the Bay of Naples, was a city called Pompeii. The beautiful scenery and mild climate attracted many wealthy Romans to Pompeii. They built villas (homes) near the shore of the Mediterranean Sea. These typical Roman dwellings were built with rooms grouped around an atrium, or reception area. Pompeii's population was typical of the Roman Empire— landowners, artisans, shopkeepers, and slaves.

A Giant Awakes Around A.D. 62, earthquakes sent tremors through Pompeii. Seventeen years later, in A.D. 79, the volcano Mount Vesuvius awoke suddenly and violently. Hot, wet ash rained on Pompeii, burying—and preserving—the city for almost 1,700 years. When the city was excavated, archaeologists discovered that the ash had even made and preserved "molds" of people fleeing the destruction. Election slogans could still be read on the walls. Pompeii provides an amazingly detailed and accurate record of life in the Roman Empire.

History and Fiction "The Dog of Pompeii" is fiction— a story made up by its author. However, many of the details in the story are based on discoveries made by scientists who studied the ruins of Pompeii. As you read, notice the details that give clues about life in the Roman Empire.

The Dog of Pompeii

Louis Untermeyer

Tito and his dog Bimbo lived (if you could call it living) under the wall where it joined the inner gate. They really didn't live there; they just slept there. They lived anywhere. Pompeii was one of the gayest of the old Latin towns, but although Tito was never an unhappy boy, he was not exactly a merry one. The streets were always lively with shining chariots and bright red trappings;[1] the open-air theaters rocked with laughing crowds; <u>sham</u> battles and athletic sports were free for the asking in the great stadium. Once a year the Caesar[2] visited the pleasure city and the fireworks lasted for days; the sacrifices in the Forum were better than a show. But Tito saw none of these things. He was blind—had been blind from birth. He was known to everyone in the poorer quarters. But no one could say how old he was, no one remembered his parents, no one could tell where he came from. Bimbo was

another mystery. As long as people could remember seeing Tito—about twelve or thirteen years—they had seen Bimbo. Bimbo had never left his side. He was not only dog, but nurse, pillow, playmate, mother and father to Tito.

Did I say Bimbo never left his master? (Perhaps I had better say comrade, for if anyone was the master, it was Bimbo.) I was wrong. Bimbo did trust Tito alone exactly three times a day. It was a fixed routine, a custom understood between boy and dog since the beginning of their friendship, and the way it worked was this: Early in the morning, shortly after dawn, while Tito was still dreaming, Bimbo would disappear. When Tito woke, Bimbo would be sitting quietly at his side, his ears cocked, his stump of a tail tapping the ground, and a fresh-baked bread—more like a large round roll—at his feet. Tito would stretch himself; Bimbo would yawn; then they

---

1. **trappings** (trap´ iŋz) n.: Ornamental coverings.
2. **Caesar** (sē´ zər): The Roman emperor Titus. From the time of Julius Caesar until Hadrian (49 B.C.–A.D.138), all Roman emperors were called Caesar.

◆ **Build Vocabulary**

sham (sham) *adj.*: Make believe; pretended

▲ **Critical Viewing** Do you think this is a business section or a residential section of Pompeii? Why? **[Analyze]**

would breakfast. At noon, no matter where they happened to be, Bimbo would put his paw on Tito's knee and the two of them would return to the inner gate. Tito would curl up in the corner (almost like a dog) and go to sleep, while Bimbo, looking quite important (almost like a boy) would disappear again. In half an hour he'd be back with their lunch. Some-

Connecting Literature to Social Studies
What do you learn about food in the Roman Empire?

times it would be a piece of fruit or a scrap of meat, often it was noth-ing but a dry crust. But sometimes there would be one of those flat rich cakes, sprinkled with raisins and sugar, that Tito liked so much. At supper time the same thing happened, al-though there was a little less of everything, for things were hard to snatch in the evening with the streets full of people. Besides, Bimbo didn't approve of too much food before going to sleep. A heavy supper made boys too rest-less and dogs too stodgy—and it was the business of a dog to sleep lightly with one ear open and muscles ready for action.

But, whether there was much or little, hot or cold, fresh or dry, food was always there. Tito never asked where it came from and Bimbo never told him. There was plenty of rainwater in the hollows of soft stones; the old egg-woman at the corner sometimes gave him a cupful of strong goat's milk; in the grape sea-son the fat winemaker let him have drippings of the mild juice. So there was no danger of going hungry or thirsty. There was plenty of everything in Pompeii, if you knew where to find it—and if you had a dog like Bimbo.

As I said before, Tito was not the merriest boy in Pompeii. He could not romp with the other youngsters and play Hare-and-Hounds and I-spy and Follow-your-Master and Ball-against-the-Building and Jackstones and Kings-and-Robbers with them. But that did not make him sorry for himself. If he could not see the sights that delighted the lads of Pom-peii he could hear and smell things they never noticed. He could really see more with his ears and nose than they could with their eyes. When he and Bimbo went out walking he knew just where they were going and exactly what was happening.

"Ah," he'd sniff and say, as they passed a handsome <u>villa</u>, "Glaucus Pansa is giving a grand dinner tonight. They're going to have three kinds of bread, and roast pigling, and stuffed goose, and a great stew—I think bear stew—and a fig pie." And Bimbo would note that this would be a good place to visit tomorrow.

Or, "H'm," Tito would murmur, half through his lips, half through his nostrils. "The wife of Marcus Lucretius is expecting her mother. She's shaking out every piece of goods in the house; she's going to use the best clothes—the ones she's been keeping in pine-needles and camphor[3]—and there's an extra girl in the kitchen. Come, Bimbo, let's get out of the dust!"

Or, as they passed a small but elegant dwelling opposite the public baths, "Too bad! The tragic poet is ill again. It must be a bad fever this time, for they're trying smoke fumes instead of medicine. Whew! I'm glad I'm not a tragic poet!"

Or, as they neared the Forum, "Mm-m! What good things they have in the Macellum today!" (It really was a sort of butcher-grocer-market-place, but Tito didn't know any better. He called it the Macellum.) "Dates from Africa, and salt oysters from sea caves, and cuttlefish, and new honey, and sweet onions, and—ugh!—water-buffalo steaks. Come, let's see what's what in the Forum." And Bimbo, just as curious as his comrade, hurried on. Being a dog, he trusted his ears and nose (like Tito) more than his eyes. And so the two of them entered the center of Pompeii.

The Forum was the part of the town to which everybody came at least once during each day. It was the Central Square and

> **Connecting Literature to Social Studies**
> List some of the buildings in the city.

everything happened here. There were no private houses; all was public—the chief temples, the gold and red bazaars,[4] the silk shops, the town hall, the booths belonging to the weavers and jewel merchants, the wealthy woolen market, the Shrine of the Household Gods.[5] Everything glittered here. The buildings looked as if they were new—which, in a sense, they were. The earthquake of twelve years ago had brought down all the old structures and, since the citizens of Pompeii were ambitious to rival Naples and even Rome, they had seized the opportunity to rebuild the whole town. And they had done it all within a dozen years. There was scarcely a building that was older than Tito.

Tito had heard a great deal about the earthquake though, being about a year old at the time, he could scarcely remember it. This particular quake had been a light one—as earthquakes go. The weaker houses had been shaken down, parts of the outworn wall had been wrecked; but there was little loss of life, and the brilliant new Pompeii had taken the place of the old. No one knew what caused these earthquakes. Records showed they had happened in the neighborhood since the beginning of time. Sailors said that it was to teach the lazy city folk a lesson and make them appreciate those who risked the dangers of the sea to bring them luxuries and protect their town from invaders. The priests said that the gods took this way of showing their anger to those who refused to worship properly and who failed to bring enough sacrifices to the altars and (though they didn't say it in so many words) presents to the priests. The tradesmen said that the foreign merchants had corrupted the ground and it was no longer safe to traffic in imported goods that came from strange places and carried a curse with them. Everyone had a different explanation—and everyone's explanation was louder and sillier than his

---

3. **camphor** (kam´ fər) *n.*: Hard, clear substance with a strong smell. Used as a moth repellent.

◆ **Build Vocabulary**
villa (vil´ ə) *n.*: Large estate

4. **bazaars** (bə zärz´) *n.*: Streets where people sell things.
5. **Household Gods:** Gods that were said to protect the hearth, the crops, the livestock, and so on.

neighbor's.

They were talking about it this afternoon as Tito and Bimbo came out of the side street into the public square. The Forum was the favorite promenade for rich and poor. What with the priests arguing with the politicians, servants doing the day's shopping, trades-men crying their wares, women displaying the latest fashions from Greece and Egypt, children playing hide-and-seek among the marble columns, knots of soldiers, sailors, peasants from the provinces—to say nothing of those who merely came to lounge and look on—the square was crowded to its last inch. His ears even more than his nose guided Tito to the place where the talk was loudest. It was in front of the Shrine of the Household Gods that, naturally enough, the household-ers were arguing.

> **Connecting Literature to Social Studies**
> What are some occupations of people in Pompeii?

"I tell you," rumbled a voice which Tito recognized as bathmaster Rufus's, "there won't be another earthquake in my lifetime or yours. There may be a tremble or two, but earthquakes, like lightnings, never strike twice in the same place."

"Do they not?" asked a thin voice Tito had never heard. It had a high, sharp ring to it and Tito knew it as the accent of a stranger. "How about the two towns of Sicily[6] that have been ruined three times within fifteen years by the eruptions of Mount Etna?[7] And were they not warned? And does that column of smoke above Vesuvius[8] mean nothing?"

"That?" Tito could hear the grunt with which one question answered another. "That's always there. We use it for our weather guide. When the smoke stands up straight we know we'll have fair weather; when it flattens out it's sure to be foggy; when it drifts to the east—"

"Yes, yes," cut in the edged voice. "I've heard about your mountain barometer. But the column of smoke seems hundreds of feet higher than usual and it's thickening and spreading like a shadowy tree. They say in Naples—"

"Oh, Naples!" Tito knew this voice by the little squeak that went with it. It was Attilio, the cameo-cutter.[9] "*They* talk while we suffer. Little help we got from them last time. Naples commits the crimes and Pompeii pays the price. It's become a proverb with us. Let them mind their own business."

"Yes," grumbled Rufus, "and others, too."

"Very well, my confident friends," responded the thin voice which now sounded curiously flat. "We also have a proverb—and it is this: Those who will not listen to men must be taught by the gods. I say no more. But I leave a last warning. Remember the holy ones. Look to your temples. And when the smoke tree above Vesuvius grows to the shape of an umbrella pine, look to your lives."

Tito could hear the air whistle as the speaker drew his toga[10] about him and the quick shuffle of feet told him the stranger had gone.

"Now what," said the cameo-cutter, "did he mean by that?"

"I wonder," grunted Rufus, "I wonder." Tito wondered, too. And Bimbo, his head at a thoughtful angle, looked as if he had been

---

9. **cameo-cutter** (kam´ ē ō) *n.*: Person who makes cameos, carvings on gems or shells that form raised designs, usually of heads in profile.
10. **toga** (tō´ gə) *n.*: One-piece outer garment worn by people of ancient Rome.

◆ Build Vocabulary

barometer (bə räm´ ət ər) *n.*: Instrument used to forecast changes in weather

proverb (präv´ ʉrb´) *n.*: Short saying that expresses an obvious truth or familiar experience

pondering (pän´ dər iŋ) *n.*: Deep thought; careful consideration

---

6. **Sicily** (sis´ əl ē): Island off the southern coast of Italy in the Mediterranean Sea.
7. **Mount Etna** (et´ nə): Volcano in eastern Sicily.
8. **Vesuvius** (və soo͞´ vē əs): Volcano in southern Italy.

doing a heavy piece of <u>pondering</u>. By nightfall the argument had been forgotten. If the smoke had increased no one saw it in the dark. Besides, it was Caesar's birthday and the town was in holiday mood. Tito and Bimbo were among the merry-makers, dodging the charioteers who shouted at them. A dozen times they almost upset baskets of sweets and jars of Vesuvian wine, said to be as fiery as the streams inside the volcano, and a dozen times they were cursed and cuffed. But Tito never missed his footing. He was thankful for his keen ears and quick instinct—most thankful of all for Bimbo.

They visited the uncovered theater and, though Tito could not see the faces of the actors, he could follow the play better than most of the audience, for their attention wandered—they were distracted by the scenery, the costumes, the byplay, even by themselves—while Tito's whole attention was centered in what he heard. Then to the city walls, where the people of Pompeii watched a mock naval battle in which the city was attacked by the sea and saved after thousands of flaming arrows had been exchanged and countless colored torches had been burned. Though the thrill of flaring ships and lighted skies was lost to Tito, the

▲ **Critical Viewing** What details of this scene are as frightening today as they were in A.D. 79? **[Relate]**

shouts and cheers excited him as much as any and he cried out with the loudest of them.

Connecting Literature to Social Studies What do these details tell you about the location of Pompeii?

The next morning there were *two* of the beloved raisin and sugar cakes for his breakfast. Bimbo was unusually active and thumped his bit of a tail until Tito was afraid he would wear it out. The boy could not imagine whether Bimbo was urging him to some sort of game or was trying to tell him something. After a while, he ceased to notice Bimbo. He felt drowsy. Last night's late hours had tired him. Besides, there was a heavy mist in the air—no, a thick fog rather than a mist—a fog that got into his throat and scraped it and made him cough. He walked as far as the marine gate to get a breath of the sea. But the blanket of haze had spread all over the bay and even the salt air seemed smoky.

He went to bed before dusk and slept. But he did not sleep well. He had too many dreams—dreams of ships lurching in the Forum, of losing his way in a screaming crowd, of armies marching across his chest, of being pulled over every rough pavement of Pompeii.

He woke early. Or, rather, he was pulled awake. Bimbo was doing the pulling. The dog had dragged Tito to his feet and was urging the boy along. Somewhere. Where, Tito did not know. His feet stumbled uncertainly: he was still half asleep. For a while he noticed nothing except the fact that it was hard to breathe. The air was hot. And heavy. So heavy that he could taste it. The air, it seemed, had turned to powder, a warm powder that stung his nostrils and burned his sightless eyes.

Then he began to hear sounds. Peculiar sounds. Like animals under the earth. Hissings and groanings and muffled cries that a dying creature might make dislodging the stones of his underground cave. There was no doubt of it now. The noises came from underneath. He not only heard them—he could feel them. The earth twitched; the twitching changed to an uneven shrugging of the soil. Then, as Bimbo half pulled, half coaxed him across, the ground jerked away from his feet and he was thrown against a stone fountain.

The water—hot water—splashing in his face revived him. He got to his feet, Bimbo steadying him, helping him on again. The noises grew louder; they came closer. The cries were even more animal-like than before, but now they came from human throats. A few people, quicker of foot and more hurried by fear, began to rush by. A family or two—then a section—then, it seemed, an army broken out of bounds. Tito, bewildered though he was, could recognize Rufus as he bellowed past him, like a water buffalo gone mad. Time was lost in a nightmare.

It was then the crashing began. First a sharp crackling, like a monstrous snapping of twigs; then a roar like the fall of a whole forest of trees; then an explosion that tore earth and sky. The heavens, though Tito could not see them, were shot through with continual flickerings of fire. Lightnings above were answered by thunders beneath. A house fell. Then another. By a miracle the two companions had escaped the dangerous side streets and were in a more open space. It was the Forum. They rested here awhile—how long he did not know.

Tito had no idea of the time of day. He could *feel* it was black—an unnatural blackness. Something inside—perhaps the lack of breakfast and lunch—told him it was past noon. But it didn't matter. Nothing seemed to matter. He was getting drowsy, too drowsy to walk. But walk he must. He knew it. And Bimbo knew it; the sharp tugs told him so. Nor was it a moment too soon. The sacred ground of the Forum was safe no longer. It was beginning to rock, then to pitch, then to split. As they stumbled out of the square, the earth wriggled like a caught snake and all the columns of the temple of Jupiter[11] came down. It was the end of the world—or so it seemed.

To walk was not enough now. They must run. Tito was too frightened to know what to do or where to go. He had lost all sense of direction. He started to go back to the inner gate; but Bimbo, straining his back to the last inch, almost pulled his clothes from him. What did the creature want? Had the dog gone mad?

Then, suddenly, he understood. Bimbo was telling him the way out—urging him there. The sea gate of course. The sea gate—and then the sea. Far from falling buildings, heaving ground. He turned, Bimbo guiding him across open pits and dangerous pools of bubbling mud, away from buildings that had caught fire and were dropping their burning beams. Tito could no longer tell whether the noises were made by the shrieking sky or the agonized people. He and Bimbo ran on—the only silent beings in a howling world.

New dangers threatened. All Pompeii seemed to be thronging toward the marine

---

11. **Jupiter** (jōō′ pit ər): The chief Roman god, known as Zeus in Greece.

▲ **Critical Viewing** Artifacts such as this mosaic have survived from ancient Roman times to today. What details in this picture show similarities between how pets were treated then and how they are treated today? **[Draw Conclusions]**

mountain was turning itself inside out. Tito remembered a phrase that the stranger had said in the Forum two days ago: "Those who will not listen to men must be taught by the gods." The people of Pompeii had refused to heed the warnings; they were being taught now— if it was not too late.

Suddenly it seemed too late for Tito. The red hot ashes blistered his skin, the stinging vapors tore his throat. He could not go on. He staggered toward a small tree at the side of the road and fell. In a moment Bimbo was beside him. He coaxed. But there was no answer. He licked Tito's hands, his feet, his face. The boy did not stir. Then Bimbo did the last thing he could—the last thing he wanted to do. He bit his comrade, bit him deep in the arm. With a cry of pain, Tito jumped to his feet, Bimbo after him. Tito was in despair, but Bimbo was determined. He drove the boy on, snapping at his heels, worrying his way through the crowd; barking, baring his teeth, heedless of kicks or falling stones. Sick with hunger, half dead with fear and sulfur fumes,[13] Tito pounded on, pursued by Bimbo. How long he never knew. At last he staggered through the marine gate and felt soft sand under him. Then Tito fainted. . . .

Someone was dashing sea water over him. Someone was carrying him toward a boat.

"Bimbo," he called. And then louder, "Bimbo!" But Bimbo had disappeared.

Voices jarred against each other. "Hurry— hurry!" "To the boats!" "Can't you see the child's frightened and starving!" "He keeps calling for someone!" "Poor boy, he's out of his mind." "Here, child—take this!"

They tucked him in among them. The oarlocks creaked; the oars splashed; the boat rode over toppling waves. Tito was

---

gate and, squeezing among the crowds, there was the chance of being trampled to death. But the chance had to be taken. It was growing harder and harder to breathe. What air there was choked him. It was all dust now— dust and pebbles, pebbles as large as beans. They fell on his head, his hands—pumice[12] stones from the black heart of Vesuvius. The

---

12. pumice (pum´ is) *n.*: Spongy, light rock formed from the lava of a volcano.

◆ **Build Vocabulary**

vapors (vā´ pərz) *n.*: Fumes

---

13. sulfur (sul´ fer) **fumes:** Choking fumes caused by the volcanic eruption.

safe. But he wept continually.

"Bimbo!" he wailed. "Bimbo! Bimbo!"

He could not be comforted.

Eighteen hundred years passed. Scientists were restoring the ancient city; excavators were working their way through the stones and trash that had buried the entire town. Much had already been brought to light—statues, bronze instruments, bright mosaics,[14] household articles; even delicate paintings had been preserved by the fall of ashes that had taken over two thousand lives. Columns were dug up and the Forum was beginning to emerge.

It was at a place where the ruins lay deepest that the Director paused.

"Come here," he called to his assistant. "I think we've discovered the remains of a building in good shape. Here are four huge mill-

stones that were most likely turned by slaves or mules—here is a whole wall standing with shelves inside it. Why! It must have been a bakery. And here's a curious thing. What do you think I found under this heap where the ashes were thickest? The skeleton of a dog!"

"Amazing!" gasped his assistant. "You'd think a dog would have had sense enough to run away at the time. And what is that flat thing he's holding between his teeth? It can't be a stone."

"No. It must have come from this bakery. You know it looks to me like some sort of cake hardened with the years. And, bless me, if those little black pebbles aren't raisins. A raisin cake almost two thousand years old! I wonder what made him want it at such a moment?"

"I wonder," murmured the assistant.

---

14. **mosaics** (mō zā´ iks) *n*.: Pictures of designs made by inlaying small bits of colored stone in mortar.

Guide for Responding

◆ LITERATURE AND YOUR LIFE

Reader's Response What did you think of the end of this story? Why?

Thematic Focus What challenges does Bimbo help Tito face?

☑ Check Your Comprehension

1. Describe what Tito and Bimbo do on a typical day.
2. What rumors and warnings does Tito hear as he roams Pompeii?
3. How does Bimbo get Tito out of the city?
4. What happens to Bimbo?
5. What do the scientists find in Pompeii?

◆ Critical Thinking

INTERPRET

1. How does Tito "see" with his ears and his nose? **[Interpret]**
2. How does Bimbo feel about Tito? **[Infer]**
3. Why does Bimbo return to the city after getting Tito safely to the marine gate? **[Draw Conclusions]**

APPLY

4. In what ways do fire drills and other emergency plans reduce the risk of injury? **[Apply]**

EXTEND

5. To what degree has technology made it possible to predict earthquakes and volcanic eruptions? **[Science Link]**

CONNECTING LITERATURE TO SOCIAL STUDIES

Although "The Dog of Pompeii" is a fictional story, it includes many accurate details about life in the last days of the Roman Empire. These details are based on historical records and on what archaeologists have discovered in the excavated city of Pompeii. Today, visitors to Pompeii can walk the streets, go in and out of houses, and stand in the public square.

1. Name two kinds of activities that took place in the Forum.
2. (a) Name two details that show something about the connection of Pompeii with the rest of the world. (b) Describe this connection.
3. Name three kinds of things that, according to the end of the story, give historians information about life in ancient Roman cities.

 Idea Bank

Writing

1. **Warning** Write an evacuation warning to be read to the citizens of Pompeii. Include in your warning a description of what will happen to those who do not move quickly.
2. **Letter** As Tito, write a letter to a relative in Rome. Describe your experience during the eruption of Mount Vesuvius.
3. **Song** Immortalize Bimbo in a song describing the dog's bravery and loyalty. Include in your song a description of the dangers he faced for Tito's sake. **[Music Link]**

Speaking and Listening

4. **Role Play** Role-play a discussion among several citizens of Pompeii who notice odd ocurrences but have not yet realized what is happening to the city.

Projects

5. **Map** Create a color-coded map showing the growth and decline of the Roman Empire from 250 B.C. to A.D. 80. Use different colors to show the areas ruled at different times.
6. **Diorama** Create a diorama—a three-dimensional model—of a typical Roman villa, a temple, theater, or other building. Write a brief explanation of the features of your diorama. **[Art Link]**

Further Reading, Listening, and Viewing

- David Macaulay's book *City: A Story of Roman Planning and Construction* (1983) charts the planning and building of an imaginary, but typical, Roman city.
- Thomas S. Klise Company's CD-ROM *The Road to Ancient Rome* shows the ancient city through original artwork, historical photos, and interactive elements.
- Louise James's book *How We Know About the Romans* gives an illustrated history of ancient Rome based on excavations of key sites.

Summary

Writing Process Workshop

Some stories are hard to keep to yourself. When you retell a story or share the highlights of a movie with a friend, you are giving a summary. A **summary** is a brief account that includes the most important facts, events, and ideas. Write a summary of a story, book, or movie. The following tips, introduced in this section's Writing Mini-Lessons, will help you write a summary that is informative and interesting.

Writing Skills Focus

▶ **Be clear and brief.** Include enough information so that readers will understand what is happening. Leave out enough information to keep the summary short. (See page 196.)

▶ **State your main ideas.** Organize your summary around several main ideas or statements. For example, the statement *We relaxed and had fun* is the main idea for the following details: I saw my friends. We laughed a lot. We enjoyed a great pizza. (See page 211.)

▶ **Choose precise words.** A single precise word, like *butte* or *sprinted,* can communicate more information in less space than several general words, like *tall rocky hill* or *moved really fast.* (See page 219.)

MODEL

from "Thunder Butte," Virginia Driving Hawk Sneve

① Norman had a rough day at the butte. ② The climb was tough. Coming down was bad, too. On the way down, he stuck his walking stick into a hidden hole and lost his balance. ③ In the hole, he discovered an old *coup* stick.

① The statement that his day was rough is the main idea. It covers the details of falling, seeing a snake, and being hot.

② The summary includes enough information to make it clear that Norman climbed the butte and found something unusual there.

③ Coup stick is more precise than "ancient artifact."

Prewriting

Use a Memory Jogger Choose a story, movie, or book that you find exciting or interesting. Write down as many details as come to mind about the characters and setting. Write each detail on a separate note card so you can easily add, remove, and rearrange details. Then, review your notes, correcting or adding details as necessary. Organize your note cards under main ideas about characters and setting.

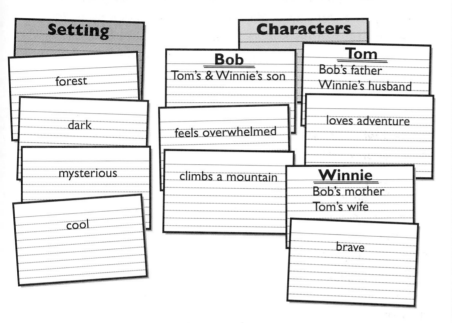

Arrange Events in Order Create a separate note card for each event that occurs in your summary. Place the notes in order, arranging them from the beginning, through the middle, to the end.

Sift Out Important Details Make sure your sequence of events is clear, complete, and in time order. As you go from one event to the next, cross out any events or details that are not needed to show how the story moves forward.

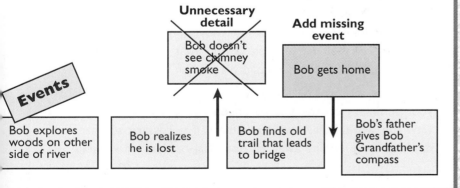

DRAFTING/REVISING

APPLYING LANGUAGE SKILLS: Avoid Run-on Sentences

A run-on sentence combines two or more sentences as if they were a single sentence.

Run-on: *John challenged me, I met him after school.*

You can fix a run-on by breaking it into separate sentences.

Correct: *John challenged me. I met him after school.*

You can also link two ideas using a comma and a connecting word, such as *and, but, or,* or *so.*

Correct: *John challenged me, so I met him after school.*

Practice Correct each run-on.
1. He taught me how to fight, Jennifer saved me.
2. The dog followed the boy all over, he saved the boy's life.
3. His mother didn't want the stick, his father said they should respect it.

Writing Application Correct run-on sentences in your summary by breaking them into separate sentences or using a connecting word.

Writer's Solution Connection Language Lab

For more practice, complete the Run-on Sentences lesson in the Language Lab unit, Sentence Errors.

APPLYING LANGUAGE SKILLS: Correct Fragments

A sentence fragment does not express a complete thought. It is not a sentence, even if it starts with a capital letter and ends with a period.

Fragment: *Because all the other kids were watching.*

You can correct a fragment by adding words to make it express a complete thought or by joining it with a sentence.

Complete Sentence: *He could not get out of the fight* **because** *all the other kids were watching.*

Practice Correct each of the following sentence fragments.

1. He fell. When he was on the cliff.
2. It's dream dust. Not for sale.
3. It made Mark Twain nervous. Making a speech.

Writing Application Correct any fragments you find in your summary.

Writer's Solution Connection Language Lab

For more practice fixing fragments, complete the Sentence Fragments lesson in the Language Lab unit Sentence Errors.

Drafting

Write a Good Beginning Begin with a general statement about the most important character or characters, the setting, and the situation. For example, you might begin a summary of "Thunder Butte" with the statement: "In this story, Norman, a young Sioux living in the desert, finds more than he bargained for when he goes looking for agates."

Follow Your Notes Lay out the details of the story or poem in a clear, straightforward way. Move from one event to the next in time order. Use words like *because* and *later* to indicate any important connections between events.

Point the Way As you mention a character or place, work in any important details. Choose only those details that will add to the readers' understanding of relationships between people, events, or places. For example, you might say, "Norman's grandfather, *who believed in the old ways*, told Norman to climb the butte." The fact that Norman's grandfather believes in the old ways affects other parts of the story. However, you would not say, "Norman's grandfather, *who had gray hair*, told Norman to climb the butte." Gray hair is not a significant detail.

Revising

Review Your Checklist As you review your draft, look for each of the items on the checklist:

▶ Clear beginning, middle, and end

▶ Words that indicate time order

▶ Information about the important characters

Also, check that your summary is clear and brief and that you have organized your significant details around main ideas and events.

Publishing and Presenting

▶ **Audio Anthology** Work with your classmates to create an audio guide to stories, books, and movies, made up of students' recordings of their summaries. Group your summaries by type. Then, have each student record his or her summary.

▶ **On-line Summaries** If your school hosts a Web site, post your summary on the site to encourage others to read or view the work. Revise your summary, if necessary, so that you don't give the ending away to potential readers or viewers.

Real-World Reading Skills Workshop

Strategies for Success

If you were walking to an appointment, you would probably move with purpose and speed. On a sightseeing tour, you would probably stroll at a more leisurely pace. The rate at which you read can also vary. It makes sense to adjust your reading rate to different situations.

Close Reading Reading to learn about a topic is like walking around to get to know an unfamiliar town. Move slowly, noticing how things fit together, and even pause to jot down notes. Go back and review anything that didn't make sense. This kind of close reading is useful for reading textbook chapters and encyclopedia articles.

Skimming Skim material that you are reviewing or previewing for main ideas. Move quickly through the text. Pause to read headings, definitions, footnotes, and highlighted material. Take in groups of words, rather than reading word for word.

Scanning Scan for specific information. Move your eyes quickly over the page, looking only for words related to what you need to know. When you find them, stop and read that paragraph or section. For example, you might find a long article on technology, but only need information about the Internet. Scan the article, looking for words like *Internet, on-line,* or *Web sites.* Scan also when looking for dates or place names.

Reading for Pleasure When you read something for enjoyment, you can read at an easy pace. Take time to appreciate the realistic details, the humor, or other special features. This kind of reading is like a leisurely stroll.

Apply the Strategies

Following is a section from a textbook chapter. Answer the questions about it before you read it word for word.

Road to Democracy Spanish colonial rule continued into the early 1800's. Then, the resentment the *criollos* felt toward the privileged class erupted into conflict. In 1810, a priest named Miguel Hidalgo called for a rebellion against Spanish rule. His cry sparked a war of independence. By 1821, the independent nation of Mexico was established. However, the gap between rich and poor remained unchanged.

1. Skim the article above. Explain your main impression of what it will be about.

2. Who inspired the revolution that began in 1810? How did you find out quickly?

3. For what reason might you read this section closely?

4. Compare and contrast the strategies you might use to read an advertisement for a running shoe and a textbook chapter.

> ✔ Here are some other situations in which you might find it helpful to adjust your reading rate:
> ▶ Reviewing for a test
> ▶ Previewing a magazine
> ▶ Reading rules or regulations
> ▶ Reading an e-mail from a friend

Adjectives

Grammar Review

An **adjective** is a word that modifies, or describes, a noun or a pronoun. (See page 195.) By answering the questions *what kind, which one, how many, how much,* and *whose,* adjectives make the words they modify more vivid and precise. An adjective may come before or after the word it modifies.

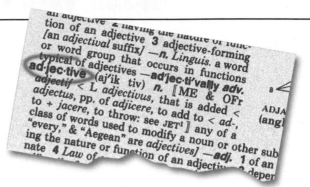

Adjective	Answers the question:
broken arm	What kind of arm? (*broken*)
twenty kids	How many kids? (*twenty*)
little trouble	How much trouble? (*little*)

Possessive Adjectives Nouns that show possession, or ownership, such as *Norman's* or *mother's,* function as adjectives. They answer the question *whose.* (See page 210.)

Grandfather's speech was inspiring.

Possessive pronouns—such as *his, my, their,* and *our*—also function as adjectives. These pronouns also answer the question *whose.*

Our ancestors had *coup* sticks.

Articles The articles *a, and,* and *the* are the most frequently used adjectives. *A* and *an* are indefinite articles. They do not indicate a specific person, place, or thing. *The* is a definite article. It indicates a particular person, place, or thing. (See page 218.)

Practice 1 Copy these sentences in your notebook. Circle the articles, underline the adjectives, and double underline the possessive adjectives and possessive pronouns that function as adjectives.

1. He carried the ancient stick to his home.

2. His mother turned her head away and called it a heathen thing.

3. The tired young man found five agates.

4. He had much work to do.

5. An agate is not worth an enormous amount.

Practice 2 Read each of the following sentences. Then, in your notebook, write the adjective that answers each question.

1. Myra went to the grocery store. (*What kind of store?*)

2. She bought eight frozen dinners. (*How many dinners? What kind of dinners?*)

3. Her life was full of modern conveniences. (*Whose life? What kind of conveniences?*)

4. She has three telephones in her business office. (*How many telephones? What kind of office? Whose business office?*)

Grammar in Writing

✔ *Some adjectives have been overused to the point of being empty, or meaningless. Empty adjectives—nice, cute, special, awful,* and *interesting, to name a few—do little to make meanings stronger or clearer. When revising, replace empty adjectives with precise adjectives.*

Part 2 *Choosing Your Own Way*

Boating in the Park, James Weeks

Guide for Reading

Meet the Author:

Rudyard Kipling (1865–1936)

Rudyard Kipling was born in India of British parents. As a young boy, he was sent to school in England. Not until 1882, at the age of seventeen, did he make his way back to India to work as a journalist. His work as a reporter, fiction writer, and poet earned him the 1907 Nobel Prize for Literature.

A Thirst for Travel In 1892, Kipling married Caroline Balestier, an American, and moved to Brattleboro, Vermont. The couple lived there until 1896, when they moved to Sussex, England. Kipling then became fascinated with South Africa. During his first visit there, in 1900, he observed war for the first time, even though he had written about soldiers in his work before that time.

THE STORY BEHIND THE STORY

When Kipling was a child in India, his Indian nurses told him many folk tales that featured talking animals. These talking animals provided inspiration for characters in many of Kipling's works, including *The Jungle Book,* in which "Mowgli's Brothers" appears.

◆ LITERATURE AND YOUR LIFE

CONNECT YOUR EXPERIENCE

When you were little, most decisions were made for you. As you get older, you take more and more responsibility for your own choices. The boy in this story faces a life-and-death choice, but it is a choice that others will make for him.

THEMATIC FOCUS: Choosing Your Own Way

As you read "Mowgli's Brothers," think about the kinds of choices Mowgli will have to make as he gets older.

◆ Background for Understanding

SCIENCE

The behavior of the animals in this story is based on the real habits of animals in the jungle. Wolves live in packs and have a social structure with a leader. While they do not have a "council," as described in the story, they do cooperate and work as a group. Tigers, on the other hand, like Shere Khan in the story, are solitary hunters.

◆ Build Vocabulary

PREFIXES: *mono-*

Rudyard Kipling describes the cry of the lead wolf as *monotonous,* which means "unchanging." The word begins with the prefix *mono-,* which means "one." A monotonous cry has one sound that does not change.

WORD BANK

Which word sounds as if it might describe an action similar to *scurried* or *scrambled?*

scuttled
quarry
fostering
veterans
monotonous
dispute
clamor

◆ Mowgli's Brothers ◆

Akela the Lone Wolf from *The Jungle Book*, Maurice and Edward Detmold, Donnell Library Center, The New York Public Library

◆ Literary Focus
ANIMAL CHARACTERS
Characters in stories can be animals as well as humans. Most of the characters you will meet in "Mowgli's Brothers" are **animal characters.** Animal characters behave according to their animal characteristics, but they also have human characteristics, such as the ability to speak.

◆ Reading Strategy
PREDICT
The details in "Mowgli's Brothers" can help you **predict,** or make logical guesses about, what characters will do and what events will occur. Making predictions involves you in the story you are reading. As you read, you may learn new information that will cause you to revise a prediction. Use a chart like the one below to make and check predictions while you read "Mowgli's Brothers." If an outcome is different from what you predicted, think about why.

Prediction	Reason(s)	What Actually Happened
The wolf pack won't accept Mowgli.	Shere Khan doesn't like Mowgli.	The wolves don't do what Shere Khan tells them to do.

MOWGLI'S BROTHERS

Rudyard Kipling

Now Chil the Kite[1] brings home the night
    That Mang the Bat sets free—
The herds are shut in byre[2] and hut
    For loosed till dawn are we.
This is the hour of pride and power,
    Talon and tush[3] and claw.
Oh hear the call!—Good hunting all
    That keep the Jungle Law!
           Night-Song in the Jungle

It was seven o'clock of a very warm evening in the Seeonee hills[4] when Father Wolf woke up from his day's rest, scratched himself, yawned, and spread out his paws one after the other to get rid of the sleepy feeling in their tips. Mother Wolf lay with her big gray nose dropped across her four tumbling, squealing cubs, and the moon shone into the mouth of the cave where they all lived. "Augrh!" said Father Wolf, "it is time to hunt again"; and he was going to spring downhill when a little shadow with a bushy tail crossed the threshold and

---

1. **Kite** (kīt) *n.*: Bird of the hawk family.
2. **byre** (bīr) *n.*: Cow barn.
3. **tush** (tush) *n.*: Tusk.
4. **Seeonee** (sē ō´ nē) **hills:** Hills in central India.

▶ **Critical Viewing** Do you think this tiger is friendly to humans? Why or why not? [Speculate]

whined: "Good luck go with you, O Chief of the Wolves; and good luck and strong white teeth go with the noble children, that they may never forget the hungry in this world."

It was the jackal[5]—Tabaqui the Dishlicker—and the wolves of India despise Tabaqui because he runs about making mischief, and telling tales, and eating rags and pieces of leather from the village rubbish-heaps. But they are afraid of him too, because Tabaqui, more than anyone else in the jungle, is apt to go mad, and then he forgets that he was ever afraid of anyone, and runs through the forest biting everything in his way. Even the tiger runs and hides when little Tabaqui goes mad, for madness is the most disgraceful thing that can overtake a wild creature. We call it hydrophobia, but they call it *dewanee*—the madness—and run.

"Enter, then, and look," said Father Wolf, stiffly; "but there is no food here."

"For a wolf, no," said Tabaqui; "but for so mean a person as myself a dry bone is a good feast. Who are we, the Gidur-log [the jackal-people], to pick and choose?" He <u>scuttled</u> to the back of the cave, where he found the bone of a buck with some meat on it, and sat cracking the end merrily.

"All thanks for this good meal," he said, licking his lips. "How beautiful are the noble children! How large are their eyes! And so young too! Indeed, indeed, I might have remembered that the children of Kings are men from the beginning."

Now, Tabaqui knew as well as anyone else that there is nothing so unlucky as to compliment children to their faces; and it pleases him to see Mother and Father Wolf look uncomfortable.

---

5. **jackal** (jak´ əl) *n.*: Wild dog, smaller than a wolf, found in Asia and northern Africa.

◆ **Build Vocabulary**

scuttled (skut´ əld) *v.*: Scurried; scampered

Tabaqui sat still, rejoicing in the mischief that he had made: then he said spitefully:

"Shere Khan, the Big One, has shifted his hunting-grounds. He will hunt among these hills for the next moon, so he has told me."

Shere Khan was the tiger who lived near the Waingunga River, twenty miles away.

"He has no right!" Father Wolf began angrily—"By the Law of the Jungle he has no right to change his quarters without due warning. He will frighten every head of game within ten miles, and I—I have to kill for two, these days."

"His mother did not call him Lungri [the Lame One] for nothing," said Mother Wolf, quietly. "He has been lame in one foot from his birth. That is why he has only killed cattle. Now the villagers of the Waingunga are angry with him, and he has come here to make *our* villagers angry. They will scour the Jungle for him when he is far away, and we and our children must run when the grass is set alight. Indeed, we are very grateful to Shere Khan!"

"Shall I tell him of your gratitude?" said Tabaqui.

"Out!" snapped Father Wolf. "Out and hunt with thy master. Thou hast done harm enough for one night."

"I go," said Tabaqui, quietly. "Ye can hear Shere Khan below in the thickets. I might have saved myself the message."

Father Wolf listened, and below in the valley that ran down to a little river, he heard the dry, angry, snarly, singsong whine of a tiger who has caught nothing and does not care if all the Jungle knows it.

"The fool!" said Father Wolf. "To begin a night's work with that noise! Does he think that our buck are like his fat Waingunga bullocks?"[6]

"H'sh! It is neither bullock nor buck he hunts tonight," said Mother Wolf. "It is Man." The whine had changed to a sort of humming purr that seemed to come from every quarter

---

6. **bullocks** (bool´ əks) *n.*: Steers.

of the compass. It was the noise that bewilders woodcutters and gypsies sleeping in the open, and makes them run sometimes into the very mouth of the tiger.

"Man!" said Father Wolf, showing all his white teeth. "Faugh! Are there not enough beetles and frogs in the tanks that he must eat Man and on our ground too!"

The Law of the Jungle, which never orders anything without a reason, forbids every beast to eat Man except when he is killing to show his children how to kill, and then he must hunt outside the hunting-grounds of his pack or tribe. The real reason for this is that man-killing means, sooner or later, the arrival of white men on elephants, with guns, and hundreds of brown men with gongs and rockets and torches. Then everybody in the jungle suffers. The reason the beasts give among themselves is that Man is the weakest and most defenseless of all living things, and it is un-sportsmanlike to touch him. They say too—and it is true—that man-eaters become mangy,[7] and lose their teeth.

The purr grew louder, and ended in the full-throated "Aaarh!" of the tiger's charge.

Then there was a howl—an untigerish howl—from Shere Khan. "He has missed," said Mother Wolf. "What is it?"

Father Wolf ran out a few paces and heard Shere Khan muttering and mumbling savagely, as he tumbled about in the scrub.

◆ **Literary Focus**
What do Father Wolf's words reveal about the character of Shere Khan?

"The fool has had no more sense than to jump at a woodcutter's campfire, and has burned his feet," said Father Wolf, with a grunt. "Tabaqui is with him."

"Something is coming up hill," said Mother

> The purr grew louder, and ended in the full-throated "Aaarh!" of the tiger's charge.

Wolf, twitching one ear. "Get ready."

The bushes rustled a little in the thicket, and Father Wolf dropped with his haunches under him, ready for his leap. Then, if you had been watching, you would have seen the most wonderful thing in the world—the wolf checked in mid-spring. He made his bound before he saw what it was he was jumping at, and then he tried to stop himself. The result was that he shot up straight into the air for four or five feet, landing almost where he left ground.

"Man!" he snapped. "A man's cub. Look!"

Directly in front of him, holding on by a low branch, stood a naked brown baby who could just walk—as soft and as dimpled a little atom[8] as ever came to a wolf's cave at night. He looked up into Father Wolf's face, and laughed.

"Is that a man's cub?" said Mother Wolf. "I have never seen one. Bring it here."

A wolf accustomed to moving his own cubs can, if necessary, mouth an egg without breaking it, and though Father Wolf's jaws closed right on the child's back not a tooth even scratched the skin, as he laid it down among the cubs.

"How little! How naked, and—how bold!" said Mother Wolf, softly. The baby was pushing his way between the cubs to get close to the warm hide. "Ahai! He is taking his meal with the others. And so this is a man's cub. Now, was there ever a wolf that could boast of a man's cub among her children?"

"I have heard now and again of such a thing, but never in our Pack or in my time," said Father Wolf. "He is altogether without hair, and I could kill him with a touch of my foot. But see, he looks up and is not afraid."

The moonlight was blocked out of the mouth of the cave, for Shere Khan's great square head and shoulders were thrust into

---

7. **mangy** (mān´ jē) *adj.*: Having the mange, a skin disease of mammals that causes sores and loss of hair.

8. **atom** (at´ əm) *n.*: Tiny piece of matter.

the entrance. Tabaqui, behind him, was squeaking: "My lord, my lord, it went in here!"

"Shere Khan does us great honor," said Father Wolf, but his eyes were very angry. "What does Shere Khan need?"

"My quarry. A man's cub went this way," said Shere Khan. "Its parents have run off. Give it to me."

Shere Khan had jumped at a woodcutter's campfire, as Father Wolf had said, and was furious from the pain of his burned feet. But Father Wolf knew that the mouth of the cave was too narrow for a tiger to come in by. Even where he was, Shere Khan's shoulders and forepaws were cramped for want of room, as a man's would be if he tried to fight in a barrel.

"The Wolves are a free people," said Father Wolf. "They take orders from the Head of the Pack, and not from any striped cattle-killer. The man's cub is ours—to kill if we choose."

"Ye choose and ye do not choose! What talk is this of choosing? By the bull that I killed, am I to stand nosing into your dog's den for my fair dues? It is I, Shere Khan, who speak!"

The tiger's roar filled the cave with thunder. Mother Wolf shook herself clear of the cubs and sprang forward, her eyes, like two green moons in the darkness, facing the blazing eyes of Shere Khan.

"And it is I, Raksha [The Demon], who answer. The man's cub is mine, Lungri—mine to me! He shall not be killed. He shall live to run with the Pack and to hunt with the Pack; and in the end, look you, hunter of little naked cubs—frog-eater—fish-killer—he shall hunt *thee*! Now get hence, or by the Sambhur that I killed (I eat no starved cattle), back thou goest to thy mother, burned beast of the Jungle, lamer than ever thou camest

> **"The cub must be shown to the Pack. Wilt thou still keep him, Mother?"**

into the world! Go!"

Father Wolf looked on amazed. He had almost forgotten the days when he won Mother Wolf in fair fight from five other wolves, when she ran in the Pack and was not called The Demon for compliment's sake. Shere Khan might have faced Father Wolf, but he could not stand up against Mother Wolf, for he knew that where he was she had all the advantage of the ground, and would fight to the death. So he backed out of the cave-mouth growling, and when he was clear he shouted:

"Each dog barks in his own yard! We will see what the Pack will say to this fostering of man-cubs. The cub is mine, and to my teeth he will come in the end, O bush-tailed thieves!"

Mother Wolf threw herself down panting among the cubs, and Father Wolf said to her gravely:

"Shere Khan speaks this much truth. The cub must be shown to the Pack. Wilt thou still keep him, Mother?"

"Keep him!" she gasped. "He came naked, by night, alone and very hungry; yet he was not afraid! Look, he has pushed one of my babies to one side already. And that lame butcher would have killed him and would have run off to the Waingunga while the villagers here hunted through all our lairs in revenge! Keep him? Assuredly I will keep him. Lie still, little frog. O thou Mowgli—for Mowgli the Frog I will call thee—the time will come when thou wilt hunt Shere Khan as he has hunted thee."

"But what will our Pack say?" said Father Wolf. The Law of the Jungle lays down very clearly that any wolf may, when he marries,

◆ Build Vocabulary

quarry (kwôr´ ē) *n.*: Prey; anything being hunted or pursued

fostering (fôs´ tər iŋ) *n.*: Taking care of

▲ Critical Viewing What qualities of Mother Wolf do you see in this wolf? **[Connect]**

withdraw from the Pack he belongs to; but as soon as his cubs are old enough to stand on

◆ **Reading Strategy** Based on Father and Mother Wolf's reactions, what do you predict the rest of the pack will say about Mowgli?

their feet he must bring them to the Pack Council, which is generally held once a month at full moon, in order that the other wolves may identify them. After that inspection the cubs are free to run where they please, and until they have killed their first buck no excuse is accepted if a grown wolf of the Pack kills one of them. The punishment is death where the murderer can be found; and if you think for a minute you will see that this must be so.

Father Wolf waited till his cubs could run a little, and then on the night of the Pack Meeting took them and Mowgli and Mother Wolf to the Council Rock—a hilltop covered with stones and boulders where a hundred wolves could hide. Akela, the great gray Lone Wolf, who led all the Pack by strength and cunning, lay out at full length on his rock, and below him sat forty or more wolves of every size and color, from badger-colored <u>veterans</u> who could handle a buck alone, to young black three-year-olds who thought they could. The Lone Wolf had led them for a year now. He had fallen twice into a wolf-trap in his youth, and once he had been beaten and left for dead; so he knew the manners and customs of men. There was very little talking at the Rock. The cubs tumbled over each other in the center of the circle where their mothers and fathers sat, and now and again a senior wolf would go quietly up to a cub, look at him carefully, and return to his place on noiseless feet. Sometimes a mother would push her cub far out into the moonlight, to be sure that he had not been overlooked. Akela from his rock would cry: "Ye know the Law—ye know the Law. Look well, O Wolves!" and the anxious mothers would take up the call: "Look—look well, O Wolves!"

At last—and Mother Wolf's neck-bristles lifted as the time came—Father Wolf pushed "Mowgli the Frog," as they called him, into the center, where he sat laughing and playing with some pebbles that glistened in the moonlight.

Akela never raised his head from his paws, but went on with the <u>monotonous</u> cry: "Look well!" A muffled roar came up from behind the rocks—the voice of Shere Khan crying: "The cub is mine. Give him to me. What have the Free People to do with a man's cub?" Akela never even twitched his ears: all he said was: "Look well, O Wolves! What have the Free People to do with the orders of any save the Free People? Look well!"

There was a chorus of deep growls, and a young wolf in his fourth year flung back Shere Khan's question to Akela: "What have the Free People to do with the man's cub?" Now the Law of the Jungle lays down that if there is any <u>dispute</u> as to the right of a cub to be accepted by the Pack, he must be spoken for by at least two members of the Pack who are not his father and mother.

"Who speaks for this cub?" said Akela. "Among the Free People who speaks?" There was no answer, and Mother Wolf got ready for what she knew would be her last fight, if things came to fighting.

Then the only other creature who is allowed at the Pack Council—Baloo, the sleepy brown bear who teaches the wolf cubs the Law of the Jungle: old Baloo, who can come and go where he pleases because he eats only nuts and roots and honey—rose up on his hind quarters and grunted.

"The man's cub—the man's cub?" he said. "*I* speak for the man's cub. There is no harm in a man's cub. I have no gift of words, but I speak the truth. Let him run with the Pack, and be entered with the others. I myself will teach him."

"We need yet another," said Akela. "Baloo has spoken, and he is our teacher for the young cubs. Who speaks besides Baloo?"

A black shadow dropped down into the circle. It was Bagheera the Black Panther, inky black all over, but with the panther marking showing up in certain lights like the pattern of watered silk. Everybody knew Bagheera, and nobody cared to cross his path; for he was as cunning as Tabaqui, as bold as the wild buffalo, and as reckless as the wounded elephant. But he had a voice as soft as wild honey dripping from a tree, and a skin softer than down.

"O Akela, and ye the Free People," he purred, "I have no right in your assembly; but the Law of the Jungle says that if there is a doubt which is not a killing matter in regard to a new cub, the life of that cub may be bought at a price. And the Law does not say who may or may not pay that price. Am I right?"

"Good! good!" said the young wolves, who are always hungry. "Listen to Bagheera. The cub can be bought for a price. It is the Law."

"Knowing that I have no right to speak here, I ask your leave."

"Speak then," cried twenty voices.

"To kill a naked cub is shame. Besides, he may make better sport for you when he is grown. Baloo has spoken in his behalf. Now to

▲ Critical Viewing How is the panther in this picture similar to and different from the tiger on page 238? [Compare and Contrast]

Baloo's word I will add one bull, and a fat one, newly killed, not half a mile from here, if ye will accept the man's cub according to the Law. Is it difficult?"

There was a <u>clamor</u> of scores of voices, saying: "What matter? He will die in the winter rains. He will scorch in the sun. What harm can a naked frog do us? Let him run with the Pack. Where is the bull, Bagheera? Let him be accepted." And then came Akela's deep bay, crying: "Look well—look well, O Wolves !"

◆ Build Vocabulary

clamor (klam´ ər) *n.*: Loud demand or complaint

Mowgli was still deeply interested in the pebbles, and he did not notice when the wolves came and looked at him one by one. At last they all went down the hill for the dead bull, and only Akela, Bagheera, Baloo, and Mowgli's own wolves were left. Shere Khan roared still in the night, for he was very angry that Mowgli had not been handed over to him.

"Ay, roar well," said Bagheera, under his whiskers; "for the time comes when this naked thing will make thee roar to another tune, or I know nothing of man."

"It was well done," said Akela. "Men and their cubs are very wise. He may be a help in time."

"Truly, a help in time of

> ◆ **Literature and Your Life**
>
> Do you think Mowgli will have more say in his own fate as he gets older? Why or why not?

need; for none can hope to lead the Pack for-ever," said Bagheera.

Akela said nothing. He was thinking of the time that comes to every leader of every pack when his strength goes from him and he gets feebler and feebler till at last he is killed by the wolves and a new leader comes up—to be killed in his turn.

"Take him away," he said to Father Wolf, "and train him as befits one of the Free People."

And that is how Mowgli was entered into the Seeonee wolf-pack at the price of a bull and on Baloo's good word.

Beyond Literature

Social Studies Connection

India Forests and jungles thrive through-out one quarter of present-day India. This vast woodland still provides a home for many types of animals, including wolves, bears, panthers, and tigers.

"Mowgli's Brothers" takes place during the last part of the nineteenth century, when India was a colony of Great Britain. India finally gained its independence in 1947, due, in part, to Mohandas Gandhi's program of peaceful noncooperation with British rule.

Cross-Curricular Activity Create a map of India, showing rivers, mountain ranges, jungles, and major cities. Accompany your map with a timeline of Indian history.

Guide for Responding

◆ LITERATURE AND YOUR LIFE

Reader's Response If you had been a member of the Council, would you have wanted Mowgli in the Pack? Why or why not?

Thematic Focus In what ways does this story show that choosing your own way can sometimes be difficult?

☑ Check Your Comprehension

1. Who finds Mowgli?
2. What are Mother Wolf and Father Wolf required to do with Mowgli?
3. Who speaks in Mowgli's favor at the Council?
4. Why is Mowgli allowed to run with the Pack?

◆ Critical Thinking

INTERPRET
1. Why do many of the younger wolves agree first with Shere Khan then with Bagheera? **[Infer]**
2. In what ways is Mowgli similar to and different from the wolves? **[Compare and Contrast]**
3. Who are Mowgli's brothers? **[Synthesize]**

EVALUATE
4. Describe the way in which the wolves in the Pack Council make decisions. Is this a good way for a group to make a decision? Explain. **[Make a Judgment]**

EXTEND
5. What do you learn about jungle habitats from this story? **[Science Link]**

Guide for Responding (continued)

◆ Reading Strategy

PREDICT

When you **predict,** you make a logical guess about what will happen in the future. As you read "Mowgli's Brothers," you made predictions based on story details. You may even have revised your predictions as you learned new details.

1. Name one prediction you made about what would happen between Shere Khan and the wolves. On what did you base your prediction?
2. What details from the story caused you to revise a prediction you had made?

◆ Build Vocabulary

USING THE PREFIX *mono-*

Use your knowledge of the prefix *mono-* (meaning "one") to answer these questions.

1. Do you think Mowgli finds life in the jungle *monotonous*? Explain.
2. What kind of speech is a *monologue*?
3. On what kind of track does a *monorail* train run?

SPELLING STRATEGY

Remember how to spell *monotonous* by noticing that it is spelled with three *o*'s in a row (then an *ous*). Fill in the blanks to discover more words that are spelled with the same vowel in three or more syllables.

1. c __ m __ t __ ry
2. s __ m __ st __ rs
3. M __ ss __ ss __ pp __
4. __ nqu __ s __ t __ ve

USING THE WORD BANK

In your notebook, match the numbered word on the left with the lettered word on the right that is closest in meaning.

1. clamor   a. experienced ones
2. dispute   b. argument
3. fostering   c. prey
4. monotonous   d. scampered
5. quarry   e. loud demand
6. scuttled   f. caring for
7. veterans   g. unchanging

◆ Literary Focus

ANIMAL CHARACTERS

The **animal characters** in "Mowgli's Brothers" act according to their animal characteristics, but they also display some human characteristics.

1. Identify two characteristics of Shere Khan that reflect his nature as a tiger.
2. What details of Shere Khan's personality seem like human characteristics?
3. In what way is the behavior of the wolves in "Mowgli's Brothers" similar to the behavior of wolves in the wild?

◆ Build Grammar Skills

ADVERBS

An **adverb** is a word that modifies—or describes—a verb, an adjective, or another adverb. Adverbs answer the questions *when, how, where,* or *to what extent.*

Adverb	Answers the question:
He spoke *spitefully*.	*How* did he speak?
The tiger hunts *now*.	*When* does the tiger hunt?
The wolf lives *here*.	*Where* does the wolf live?
Bagheera was *most* persuasive.	*To what extent* was Bagheera persuasive?

Practice Copy the following sentences in your notebook. Circle each adverb, and explain what question it answers.

1. Enter and look. There is no food here.
2. Tabaqui knew well that compliments are unlucky.
3. "I go," said Tabaqui, quietly.
4. The Council met yesterday.
5. Bagheera spoke longest.

Writing Application Rewrite this passage in your notebook. Add adverbs that answer the questions given in parentheses.

Mother Wolf growled. (*How?*) Tabaqui waited. (*Where?*) He feared Father Wolf, but he feared Mother Wolf. (*To what extent?*)

Build Your Portfolio

 ## Idea Bank

Writing

1. **Journal Entry** As Akela, write a journal entry about your thoughts after the meeting at the Council Rock.

2. **Help-Wanted Ad** Write an advertisement for a new pack leader. Include a job description and a list of the qualities an applicant should have.

3. **Letter** As Mowgli at age twelve, write a letter to your parents, explaining where you have been and why you are returning home. In your letter, include questions you have about the world you are reentering.

Speaking and Listening

4. **Speech** Imagine that you are an animal in the jungle who speaks at the Council. Take a side either for or against Mowgli's running with the Pack, and give your speech. **[Performing Arts Link]**

5. **Improvisation [Group Activity]** With one or more classmates, perform an improvisation— acting out without rehearsal—of the conversation that might have taken place among some humans who saw Father Wolf discovering Mowgli. **[Performing Arts Link]**

Projects

6. **Jungle Diorama** Create a diorama showing a jungle habitat and the animals that live there. Make labels that explain parts of your diorama. **[Science Link]**

7. **Film Review** Rent a video of *The Jungle Book*. Then, review the film for classmates. Focus on ways in which the section of the film dealing with Mowgli's early life is similar to or different from "Mowgli's Brothers." Focus especially on setting, characters, and events. **[Social Studies Link; Media Link]**

 ## Writing Mini-Lesson

Position Paper

At the Council Rock, the animals meet to state and support their positions on issues. Write a brief paper stating your position about a topic—local or global—that interests you.

Writing Skills Focus: Topic Sentence

Your position paper will contain several paragraphs. The most important sentence in a paragraph is the **topic sentence.** It expresses the main idea of the paragraph and ties together the other sentences in the paragraph.

Prewriting First, write a single statement that expresses your position. Then, use an organizer like the one below to identify the main ideas that support your position. Finally, use each main idea as the topic sentence of a paragraph.

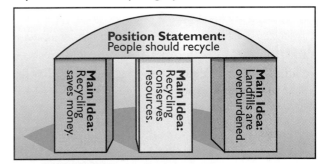

Position Statement: People should recycle

Main Idea: Recycling saves money.

Main Idea: Recycling conserves resources.

Main Idea: Landfills are overburdened.

Drafting Write one paragraph for each main idea that supports your position. In the paragraph, use examples and details to make your main idea clear.

Revising Check that you have a topic sentence in each paragraph. You may need to revise by combining paragraphs or creating two paragraphs from one.

◆ **Grammar Application**
Use adverbs in your paper to answer the questions *how, when, where,* or *to what extent.*

Guide for Reading

Meet the Authors:

Julia Alvarez (1950–)

Like many immigrants, the Alvarez family came to the United States for political reasons. Julia Alvarez's father had worked to overthrow the dictator of the Dominican Republic. After a visit from the police, though, he fled the country with his family. Julia was only ten years old when they arrived in the United States, where she discovered the world of books.

THE STORY BEHIND THE STORY

Growing up in the United States, Alvarez felt she had to "translate her experience in English." In "Names/Nombres," she shows that immigrants' names may be "translated" before they know it!

Judith Viorst (1931–)

Judith Viorst has had some practice choosing her own way. Her first job was as a model in New York City. She always wanted to be a writer, though, and she kept writing until she was successful. She is now a noted author of stories and poetry for children and adults. Her three sons—Alexander, Nick, and Anthony—sometimes pop up as characters in her books. On choosing your own way, Viorst says, " ... [You discover that] this is who you are and you trust that...."

◆ LITERATURE AND YOUR LIFE

CONNECT YOUR EXPERIENCE

Joining a group is not always easy. When you move to a new place or join a new team, others may not understand or accept you. Sometimes you adapt to fit in; sometimes the group adapts to accept you as you are. In these selections, you will read about two young people who want to fit in with a group.

THEMATIC FOCUS: Choosing Your Own Way

As you read, ask yourself how the characters choose their own ways of joining a group.

◆ Background for Understanding

SOCIAL STUDIES

Immigrants are people who settle in a country in which they were not born. Some move to find better opportunities for earning a living. Others move to escape political or religious persecution. From the 1820's to the 1920's, more than 30 million people came from other countries to live in the United States. Most were from Europe. In more recent times, large numbers of immigrants have come from Mexico, the Caribbean, Asia, India, and the Philippines.

◆ Build Vocabulary

PREFIXES: *trans-*

Alvarez writes of a relative who had to "transport" her name to a new land. The prefix *trans-* means "over, through, or across." *To transport* means "to carry over or across a distance."

WORD BANK

Which word on this list might describe a messy room?

transport
initial
inevitably
chaotic
inscribed

Names/Nombres
◆ The Southpaw ◆

◆ Literary Focus
NARRATOR'S PERSPECTIVE

The person or character who tells a story is a narrator. A narrator who is a character in the story presents his or her own **perspective** on the events—that is, the way he or she sees the events. For example, the narrator in "Names/Nombres" can tell us only what she experiences firsthand. In "The Southpaw," there are two narrators. Their two perspectives show both sides of a disagreement.

◆ Reading Strategy
SET A PURPOSE FOR READING

When you **set a purpose** for reading, you give yourself a focus as you read. For example, your purpose for reading "The Southpaw" might be to consider the contrasting perspectives of the narrators. To support your purpose, compare and contrast each character's statements and actions on a Venn diagram like the one below.

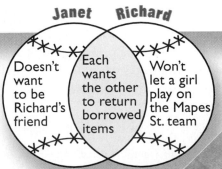

Janet   Richard

Doesn't want to be Richard's friend

Each wants the other to return borrowed items

Won't let a girl play on the Mapes St. team

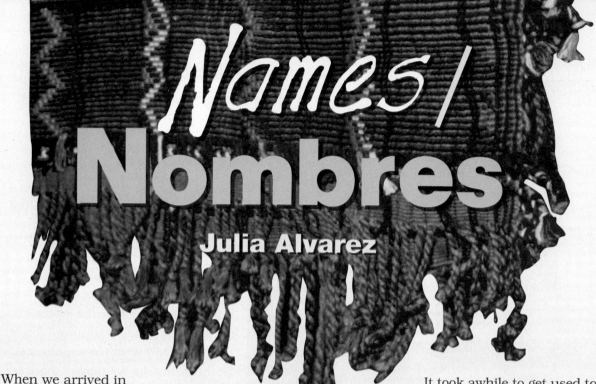

Names /
Nombres

Julia Alvarez

When we arrived in New York City, our names changed almost immediately. At Immigration,[1] the officer asked my father, *Mister Elbures,* if he had anything to declare. My father shook his head, "No," and we were waved through. I was too afraid we wouldn't be let in if I corrected the man's pronunciation, but I said our name to myself, opening my mouth wide for the organ blast of the *a,* trilling my tongue for the drumroll of the *r, All-vah-rrr-es!* How could anyone get *Elbures* out of that orchestra of sound?

At the hotel my mother was *Missus Alburest,* and I was *little girl,* as in, "Hey, little girl, stop riding the elevator up and down. It's *not* a toy."

When we moved into our new apartment building, the super[2] called my father *Mister Alberase,* and the neighbors who became mother's friends pronounced her name *Jew-lee-ah* instead of *Hoo-lee-ah.* I, her namesake, was known as *Hoo-lee-tah* at home. But at school, I was *Judy* or *Judith,* and once an English teacher mistook me for *Juliet.*

It took awhile to get used to my new names. I wondered if I shouldn't correct my teachers and new friends. But my mother argued that it didn't matter. "You know what your friend Shakespeare said, *'A rose by any other name would smell as sweet.'* " My father had gotten into the habit of calling any famous author "my friend" because I had begun to write poems and stories in English class.

By the time I was in high school, I was a popular kid, and it showed in my name. Friends called me *Jules* or *Hey Jude,* and once a group of troublemaking friends my mother forbade me to hang out with called me *Alcatraz.* I was *Hoo-lee-tah* only to Mami and Papi and uncles and aunts who came over to eat *sancocho* on Sunday afternoons—old world folk whom I would just as soon go back to where they came from and leave me to pursue whatever mischief I wanted to in America. JUDY ALCATRAZ: the name on the Wanted Poster would read. Who would ever trace her to me?

My older sister had the hardest time getting an American name for herself because *Mauricia* did not translate into English. Ironically, although she had the most foreign-sounding

---

1. **Immigration**: Government agency that processes immigrants.
2. **super**: Superintendent; the person who manages an apartment building.

name, she and I were the Americans in the family. We had been born in New York City when our parents had first tried immigration and then gone back "home," too homesick to stay. My mother often told the story of how she had almost changed my sister's name in the hospital.

After the delivery, Mami and some other new mothers were cooing over their new baby sons and daughters and exchanging names and weights and delivery stories. My mother was embarrassed among the Sallys and Janes and Georges and Johns to reveal the rich, noisy name of *Mauricia,* so when her turn came to brag, she gave her baby's name as *Maureen.*

"Why'd ya give her an Irish name with so many pretty Spanish names to choose from?" one of the women asked.

My mother blushed and admitted her baby's real name to the group. Her mother-in-law had recently died, she apologized, and her husband had insisted that the first daughter be named after his mother, *Mauran.* My mother thought it the ugliest name she had ever heard, and she talked my father into what she believed was an improvement, a combination of *Mauran* and her own mother's name, *Felicia.*

"Her name is *Mao-ree-shee-ah,*" my mother said to the group of women.

"Why that's a beautiful name," the new mothers cried. "*Moor-ee-sha, Moor-ee-sha,*" they cooed into the pink blanket. *Moor-ee-sha* it was when we returned to the States eleven years later. Sometimes, American tongues found even that mispronunciation tough to say and called her *Maria* or *Marsha* or *Maudy* from her nickname *Maury.* I pitied her. What an awful name to have to transport across borders!

My little sister, Ana, had the easiest time of all. She was plain *Anne*—that is, only her name was plain, for she turned out to be the pale, blond "American beauty" in the family. The only Hispanic thing about her was the affectionate nicknames her boyfriends sometimes gave her. *Anita,* or as one goofy guy used to sing to her to the tune of the banana advertisement, *Anita Banana.*[3]

Later, during her college years in the late '60s, there was a push to pronounce Third World names correctly. I remember calling her long distance at her group house and a roommate answering.

"Can I speak to Ana?" I asked, pronouncing her name the American way.

"Ana?" The man's voice hesitated. "Oh! you must mean *Ah-nah!*"

Our first few years in the States, though, ethnicity was not yet "in." Those were the blond, blue-eyed, bobby sock years of junior high and high school before the '60s ushered in peasant blouses, hoop earrings, serapes.[4] My initial desire to be known by my correct Dominican name faded. I just wanted to be Judy and merge with the Sallys and Janes in my class. But inevitably, my accent and coloring gave me away. "So where are you from, Judy?"

"New York," I told my classmates. After all, I had been born blocks away at Columbia Presbyterian Hospital.

"I mean, *originally.*"

"From the Caribbean," I answered vaguely, for if I specified, no one was quite sure on what continent our island was located.

"Really? I've been to Bermuda. We went last April for spring vacation. I got the worst sunburn! So, are you from Portoriko?"

"No," I sighed. "From the Dominican Republic."

◆ **Build Vocabulary**

transport (trans pôrt´) *v.*: Carry from one place to another

initial (i nish´ əl) *adj.*: Original

inevitably (in ev´ i tə blē) *adv.*: Unavoidably

---

3. **Anita Banana:** A play on the Chiquita Banana name.
4. **serapes** (sə rä´ pēz) *n.*: Colorful shawls worn in Latin America.

Collage, 1992 Juan Sanchez

"Where's that?"

"South of Bermuda."

They were just being curious, I knew, but I burned with shame whenever they singled me out as a "foreigner," a rare, exotic friend.

"Say your name in Spanish, oh please say it!" I had made mouths drop one day by rattling off my full name, which according to Dominican custom, included my middle names, Mother's and Father's surnames for four generations back.

"Julia Altagracia María Teresa Álvarez Tavares Perello Espaillat Julia Pérez Rochet González," I pronounced it slowly, a name as <u>chaotic</u> with sounds as a Middle Eastern bazaar[5] or market day in a South American village.

My Dominican heritage was never more apparent than when my extended family attended school occasions. For my graduation,

◆ **Build Vocabulary**

chaotic (kā ät′ ik) *adj.*: Completely confused

inscribed (in skrībd′) *adj.*: Written on

5. **bazaar** (bə zär′) *n.*: Marketplace; frequently, one held outdoors.

they all came, the whole lot of aunts and uncles and the many little cousins who snuck in without tickets. They sat in the first row in order to better understand the Americans' fast-spoken English. But how could they listen when they were constantly speaking among themselves in florid-sounding phrases, rococo[6] consonants, rich, rhyming vowels?

Introducing them to my friends was a further trial to me. These relatives had such complicated names and there were so many of them, and their relationships to myself were so convoluted. There was my Tía Josefina, who was not really an aunt but a much older cousin. And her daughter, Aida Margarita, who was adopted, *una hija de crianza*. My uncle of affection, Tío José, brought my *madrina* Tía Amelia and her *comadre* Tía Pilar. My friends rarely had more than a "Mom and Dad" to introduce.

---

6. **rococo** (rə kō′ kō): Fancy, ornate style of art of the early eighteenth century.

After the commencement ceremony my family waited outside in the parking lot while my friends and I signed yearbooks with nicknames which recalled our high school good times: "Beans" and "Pepperoni" and "Alcatraz." We hugged and cried and promised to keep in touch.

Our goodbyes went on too long. I heard my father's voice calling out across the parking lot, "*Hoo-lee-tah! Vamonos!*"

Back home, my *tíos* and *tías* and *primas*, Mami and Papi, and *mis hermanas* had a party for me with *sancocho* and a store-bought *pudín*, inscribed with *Happy Graduation, Julie.* There were many gifts—that was a plus to a large family! I got several wallets and a suitcase with my initials and a graduation charm from my godmother and money from my uncles. The biggest gift was a portable typewriter from my parents for writing my stories and poems.

Someday, the family predicted, my name would be well-known throughout the United States. I laughed to myself, wondering which one I would go by.

Guide for Responding

◆ LITERATURE AND YOUR LIFE

Reader's Response Which name do you think best fits the author? Why?

Thematic Focus In what ways do the names the author chooses for herself represent a bigger choice?

☑ Check Your Comprehension

1. From what country does the Alvarez family come?
2. What is their native language?
3. Describe one difficulty the author has with her name.
4. What is the author's final question to herself?

◆ Critical Thinking

INTERPRET

1. Give two reasons why Julia's name is mispronounced. [Analyze Cause and Effect]
2. Why does Julia's mother advise her not to correct people? [Interpret]

EVALUATE

3. How effectively do you think the title captures the focus of Alvarez's narrative? [Make a Judgment]

EXTEND

4. Explain how a product's name can affect what you think about that product. [Social Studies Link; Career Link]

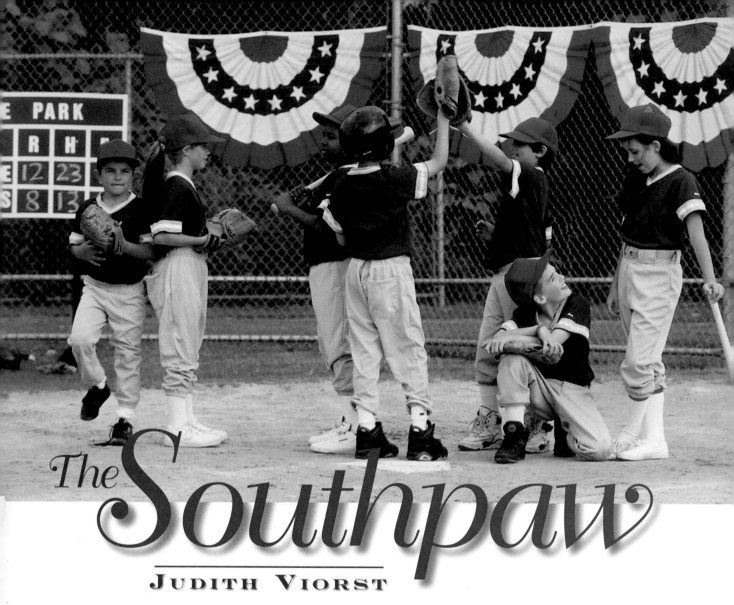

The Southpaw

JUDITH VIORST

Dear Richard,

Don't invite me to your birthday party because I'm not coming. And give back the Disneyland sweatshirt I said you could wear. If I'm not good enough to play on your team, I'm not good enough to be friends with.

Your former friend,
Janet

P.S. I hope when you go to the dentist he finds 20 cavities.

Dear Janet,

Here is your stupid Disneyland sweatshirt, if that's how you're going to be. I want my comic books now—finished or not. No girl has ever played on the Mapes Street baseball team, and as long as I'm captain, no girl ever will.

Your former friend,
Richard

P.S. I hope when you go for your checkup you need a tetanus shot.

Dear Richard,

I'm changing my goldfish's name from Richard to Stanley. Don't count on my vote for class president next year. Just because I'm a member of the ballet club doesn't mean I'm not a terrific ballplayer.

Your former friend,
    Janet

P.S. I see you lost your first game 28–0.

Dear Janet,

I'm not saving any more seats for you on the bus. For all I care you can stand the whole way to school. Why don't you just forget about baseball and learn something nice like knitting?

Your former friend,
    Richard

P.S. Wait until Wednesday.

Dear Richard,

My father said I could call someone to go with us for a ride and hot-fudge sundaes. In case you didn't notice, I didn't call you.

Your former friend,
    Janet

P.S. I see you lost your second game, 34–0.

Dear Janet,

Remember when I took the laces out of my blue-and-white sneakers and gave them to you? I want them back.

Your former friend,
    Richard

P.S. Wait until Friday.

Dear Richard,

Congratulations on your un-broken record. Eight straight losses, wow! I understand you're the laugh-ingstock of New Jersey.

Your former friend,
    Janet

P.S. Why don't you and your team forget about baseball and learn something nice like knitting maybe?

Dear Janet,

Here's the silver horseback riding trophy that you gave me. I don't think I want to keep it anymore.

Your former friend,
    Richard

P.S. I didn't think you'd be the kind who'd kick a man when he's down.

Dear Richard,

I wasn't kicking exactly. I was kicking *back*.

Your former friend,

Janet

P.S. In case you were wondering, my batting average is .345.

Dear Janet,

Alfie is having his tonsils out tomorrow. We might be able to let you catch next week.

Richard

Dear Richard,

I pitch.

Janet

Dear Janet,

Joel is moving to Kansas and Danny sprained his wrist. How about a permanent place in the outfield?

Richard

Dear Richard,

I pitch.

Janet

Dear Janet,

Ronnie caught the chicken pox and Leo broke his toe and Elwood has these stupid violin lessons. I'll give you first base, and that's my final offer.

Richard

Dear Richard,

Susan Reilly plays first base, Marilyn Jackson catches, Ethel Kahn plays center field, I pitch. It's a package deal.

Janet

P.S. Sorry about your 12-game losing streak.

Dear Janet,

Please! Not Marilyn Jackson.

Richard

Dear Richard,
   Nobody ever said that I was unreasonable. How about Lizzie Martindale instead?
Janet

Dear Janet,
   At least could you call your goldfish Richard again?
Your friend,
Richard

Math Connection

Math in Sports Math plays an important role in baseball and other sports. Team performances can be measured by comparing two teams' winning and losing averages. Batting averages and other statistics are used to compare players' performances. For example, Janet's batting average in "The Southpaw" is higher than that of most players. This indicates that she is an above-average hitter.

Cross-Curricular Activity
Sports Calculation Find out how statistics are used in a sport that you like. Using examples, demonstrate for the class how these statistics are calculated.

Guide for Responding

◆ LITERATURE AND YOUR LIFE

Reader's Response With whom do you side in this disagreement? Why?

Thematic Focus Explain whether or not Janet chooses her own way.

Journal Writing In your journal, explain why you agree with Richard or with Janet.

☑ Check Your Comprehension

1. Why won't Janet come to Richard's party?
2. What position does Janet want to play?
3. What reason does Richard give for not letting girls on the team?
4. How well does the season go for Richard's team?
5. What deal do the two make at the end?

◆ Critical Thinking

INTERPRET
1. Describe the reasons for Richard and Janet's quarrel. **[Summarize]**
2. Using two examples, explain how each friend shows anger. **[Analyze]**
3. What clues can you find that show each friend wants to make up the quarrel? **[Analyze]**
4. Explain why Richard finally changes his mind. **[Draw Conclusions]**

APPLY
5. Identify one thing Richard and Janet might have done to resolve their quarrel. **[Apply]**

COMPARE LITERARY WORKS
6. What advice do you think Julia in "Names/ Nombres" would have given to Janet in "The Southpaw"? What advice do you think Janet would have given to Julia? **[Speculate]**

Guide for Responding (continued)

◆ Reading Strategy

SET A PURPOSE FOR READING

Setting a purpose for reading helps you focus your reading and increases your understanding.

1. (a) What was your purpose for reading "Names/Nombres"? (b) What was your purpose for reading "The Southpaw"?
2. List three details in each selection that helped you achieve your purpose.
3. In what way did setting a purpose increase your appreciation of each selection?

◆ Build Vocabulary

USING THE PREFIX *trans-*

The prefix *trans-* means "over, through, or across." Use your knowledge of the meaning of this prefix to help you define the italicized words in these sentences.

1. *Transplant* that cactus into a larger pot!
2. Weather conditions can affect radio *transmission*.
3. That airplane is for *transatlantic* flights only.

SPELLING STRATEGIES

Sometimes the *k* or "hard c" sound is spelled *ch,* as it is in *chaotic.*

On your paper, unscramble the letters to spell words in which the *k* sound is spelled with *ch.*

1. heaccnim (car-fixer)   3. stemhic (works in a lab)
2. crodh (musical term)   4. rractehac (person in a story)

USING THE WORD BANK

Write these sentences on your paper. Fill in the blanks using the Word Bank words.

1. After my ___?___ visit, they invited me back.
2. The ship will ___?___ passengers as well as cargo.
3. After I baby sat for my niece, I ___?___ caught her cold.
4. Because of construction, the traffic was ___?___.
5. My initials are ___?___ on the back of my locket.

◆ Literary Focus

NARRATOR'S PERSPECTIVE

The **narrator's perspective** determines how he or she sees and presents events.

1. In "Names/Nombres," what are three different reactions the narrator has to her name and heritage? Support your answer with details from the selection.
2. Compare and contrast the two perspectives in "The Southpaw." How would the selection have been different if there were only one narrator?

◆ Build Grammar Skills

ADVERBS MODIFYING ADJECTIVES AND ADVERBS

An **adverb** modifies, or describes, a verb, an adjective (a word that modifies a noun), or another adverb. *Almost, too, so, very, quite, rather, usually, much,* and *more* are some adverbs that modify adjectives and other adverbs.

Adverb	Modifies the word:	Answers the question:
The trip is *too* long.	*long* (adjective)	*To what extent?*
He walks *very* quickly.	*quickly* (adverb)	*How?*

Practice Write these sentences on your paper. Underline each adverb, and draw an arrow to the word it modifies. Then, tell what question it answers.

1. Our names changed almost immediately.
2. Our goodbyes went on too long.
3. My Dominican heritage was never more apparent.
4. You don't think I'm good enough to play.
5. They settled their conflict, but not swiftly.

Writing Application To each sentence, add an adverb that answers the question in parentheses.

1. I was afraid we wouldn't be let in. (*How afraid?*)
2. They are crowded at the table. (*To what extent?*)
3. Janet pitched fast. (*How fast?*)

Build Your Portfolio

 Idea Bank

Writing

1. **Call for Team Players** Write a flyer describing the qualities and skills a person must have in order to join your neighborhood athletic team.

2. **Welcome Letter** Write a welcome letter to a family that is moving into your neighborhood from a different country. Tell them about the local shops, the bus stop, and anything else that would be useful to know.

3. **Newspaper Editorial** Before 1974, girls were not allowed to play with boys on Little League teams. Write a newspaper editorial explaining whether or not this rule was a good one.

Speaking and Listening

4. **Speech to the Team** As the coach of a baseball team, prepare a short pre-game pep talk to inspire your team. Deliver your talk to the class.

5. **What's in a Name?** Choose five common American first names. Learn how to pronounce the equivalent names in two different languages. Then, present them to the class. **[Social Studies Link]**

Projects

6. **Class Directory** Do research to learn the meaning or origin of your last name and those of your classmates. Make an alphabetical chart displaying the names and their meanings. **[Social Studies Link]**

7. **Immigration Visual Guide [Group Activity]** In a group, prepare a series of maps and timelines showing facts about immigration. Divide up the following tasks: finding immigration statistics; researching the history of immigration; designing maps and timelines. **[Social Studies Link; Visual Arts Link]**

 Writing Mini-Lesson

Letter About a Conflict

In "The Southpaw," Richard and Janet work out a conflict by writing letters to each other. Write a letter about a conflict, explaining why you feel about it as you do.

Writing Skills Focus: Use Words That Signal Reasons

In your letter, make clear links between your opinions and your reasons for them by **using words that signal reasons.** Such words include *because, why, so that, if . . . then,* and *in order to.*

Model From the Story
If I'm not good enough to play on your team, [*then*] I'm not good enough to be friends with.

Prewriting Decide on a conflict in the news or from a story that has two clear sides. List at least three reasons for taking each side, and list solutions that might end the conflict.

Drafting First, summarize the conflict. Then, explain each side's reasons for its actions or feelings. Finally, conclude with your own opinion or solutions—with reasons for each.

Revising Give a reason for each point you make. Clarify connections by adding words that show reasons. Follow proper letter form (see the Writing Process Workshop for Unit 2, p. 140).

◆ **Grammar Application**

Add adverbs where appropriate to make clear the type or extent of the conflict.

Guide for Reading

Meet the Authors:

Ogden Nash (1902–1971)

Ogden Nash threw away his first attempt at poetry. Luckily, he pulled it out of the trash and sent it to a magazine. It was immediately published! Nash wrote light, humorous verse. His books include *Parents Keep Out: Elderly Poems for Youngerly Readers* and *Custard and Company: Poems by Ogden Nash.*

Gwendolyn Brooks (1917–   )

By age seven, Gwendolyn Brooks had convinced her parents that she would be a writer. Brooks did become a writer—a highly successful one! She is the first African American to win the Pulitzer Prize, and she was Poet Laureate of Illinois. She has published many books of poetry and one novel.

Rosemary (1898–1962) and Stephen Vincent Benét (1898–1943)

This husband-and-wife team wrote a book of poetry entitled *A Book of Americans.* The poem "Wilbur Wright and Orville Wright" is taken from this collection. Rosemary Benét was a frequent contributor to many important magazines, including *The New Yorker.* Stephen Vincent Benét won the Pulitzer Prize for Poetry—twice!

◆ Literature and Your Life

Connect Your Experience

Some days, you may feel as if you can't do anything right. On other days, you may feel as if you could take on any challenge or solve any problem. The poems in this section celebrate the "up" days. Each poem tells of some success—real or imagined, small or large. Each one shares a triumph.

Thematic Focus: Choosing Your Own Way

Making the right choices is the first step toward success. What else is required?

◆ Background for Understanding

Social Studies

While all these poems deal with a personal success, "Wilbur Wright and Orville Wright" tells of a success that affected the course of history. The Wright brothers, who spent years experimenting with gliders, had several discouraging setbacks. Then, on December 17, 1903, near Kitty Hawk, North Carolina, they flew the first power-driven, heavier-than-air machine. The plane flew 120 feet and was in the air for twelve seconds.

◆ Build Vocabulary

Suffixes: -ous

The suffix -ous describes something as "full of" or "having the qualities of." In "Adventures of Isabel," a bear's mouth is described as *cavernous*—it has the large, dark, empty qualities of a cavern.

Word Bank

If the word *raven* can mean "eat greedily," which word on the list describes something that is greedily hungry?

ravenous
cavernous
rancor
grant

Adventures of Isabel
◆ I'll Stay ◆
Wilbur Wright and Orville Wright

WILBUR WRIGHT.

◆ Literary Focus
STANZAS

A **stanza** is a group of lines of poetry that are usually similar in length and pattern and are separated by spaces. A stanza is like a paragraph of poetry—it develops one main idea. "Adventures of Isabel" has four stanzas. As you read it and the other poems, look for the spaces that separate stanzas, and identify the main idea in each stanza.

◆ Reading Strategy
USE PRIOR KNOWLEDGE

To help you understand and connect to the main ideas in each stanza and in a poem as a whole, draw on your **prior knowledge.** Your prior knowledge is the information, experiences, and thoughts that you already have before you read a literary work. As you read these poems, use a graphic organizer like the one below to think about what you bring to each poem and what you get out of it.

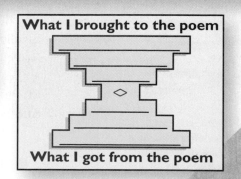

What I brought to the poem

What I got from the poem

Adventures of Isabel

Ogden Nash

Isabel met an enormous bear,
Isabel, Isabel, didn't care;
The bear was hungry, the bear was <u>ravenous</u>,
The bear's big mouth was cruel and <u>cavernous</u>.
5   The bear said, Isabel, glad to meet you,
How do, Isabel, now I'll eat you!
Isabel, Isabel, didn't worry,
Isabel didn't scream or scurry.
She washed her hands and she straightened her hair up,
10 Then Isabel quietly ate the bear up.

Once in a night as black as pitch
Isabel met a wicked old witch.
The witch's face was cross and wrinkled,
The witch's gums with teeth were sprinkled.
15 Ho ho, Isabel! the old witch crowed,
I'll turn you into an ugly toad!
Isabel, Isabel, didn't worry,
Isabel didn't scream or scurry,
She showed no rage and she showed no <u>rancor</u>,
20 But she turned the witch into milk and drank her.

Isabel met a hideous giant,
Isabel continued self-reliant.
The giant was hairy, the giant was horrid,
He had one eye in the middle of his forehead.
25 Good morning Isabel, the giant said,
I'll grind your bones to make my bread.
Isabel, Isabel, didn't worry,
Isabel didn't scream or scurry.
She nibbled the zwieback[1] that she always fed off,
30 And when it was gone, she cut the giant's head off.

Isabel met a troublesome doctor,
He punched and he poked till he really shocked her.
The doctor's talk was of coughs and chills
And the doctor's satchel bulged with pills.
35 The doctor said unto Isabel,
Swallow this, it will make you well.
Isabel, Isabel, didn't worry,
Isabel didn't scream or scurry.
She took those pills from the pill concocter,
40 And Isabel calmly cured the doctor.

1. **zwieback** (swē′ bak) *n.*: A kind of bread or biscuit that is sliced and toasted after baking.

◆ Build Vocabulary

ravenous (rav′ ə nəs′) *adj.*: Greedily hungry
cavernous (kav′ ər nəs′) *adj.*: Deep and empty
rancor (raŋ′ kər) *n.*: Bitter hate or ill will

I'll Stay

Gwendolyn Brooks

After the Storm, 1970, ©1996 Robert Vickrey/Licensed by VAGA, New York, New York

▲ **Critical Viewing** Is this girl more like Isabel or the speaker in "I'll Stay"? Why? **[Connect]**

I like the plates on the ledge
of the dining room wall (to the north)
standing on edge,
standing as if they thought they could
    stay.

5   Confident things can stand and stay!

I am confident.
I always thought there was something
    to be done about everything.
I'll stay.
I'll not go pouting and shouting out of
    the city.
10 I'll stay.

My name will be Up in Lights!
I believe it!
They will know me as Nora-the-
    Wonderful!
It will happen!
15 I'll stay.

Mother says "You rise in the morning—
You must be the Sun!
For wherever *you* are there is Light,
and those who are near you are warm,
20 feel Efficient."

I'll stay.

Wilbur Wright and Orville Wright

Rosemary and Stephen Vincent Benét

Said Orville Wright to Wilbur Wright,
"These birds are very trying.
I'm sick of hearing them cheep-cheep
About the fun of flying.
5   A bird has feathers, it is true.
That much I freely grant.
But, must that stop us, W?"
Said Wilbur Wright, "It shan't."

And so they built a glider, first,
10 And then they built another.
—There never were two brothers more
Devoted to each other.
They ran a dusty little shop
For bicycle-repairing,
15 And bought each other soda-pop
and praised each other's daring.

They glided here, they glided there,
They sometimes skinned their noses.
—For learning how to rule the air
20 Was not a bed of roses—
But each would murmur,
    afterward,
While patching up his bro,
"Are we discouraged, W?"
25 "Of course we are not, O!"

And finally, at Kitty Hawk
In Nineteen-Three (let's
    cheer it!)
The first real airplane really flew
30 With Orville there to steer it!
—And kingdoms may forget their kings
And dogs forget their bites,
But, not till Man forgets his wings,
Will men forget the Wrights.

◆ **Build Vocabulary**
grant (grant) *v.*: Admit

◆ Guide for Responding

◆ LITERATURE AND YOUR LIFE

Reader's Response Which of the people in these poems would you like to meet? Why?

Thematic Focus In what ways does each poem tell about a person choosing his or her own way?

Journal Writing Write a journal entry about a goal you have. In what ways have these poems encouraged you to reach your goal?

☑ Check Your Comprehension

1. Name three challenges Isabel faces.
2. What does the speaker in "I'll Stay" like about the plates?
3. Who compliments the speaker in "I'll Stay"?
4. What kind of shop did Wilbur and Orville Wright run?
5. What was Wilbur and Orville's achievement?

◆ Critical Thinking

INTERPRET

1. Why do you think Ogden Nash describes such unbelievable adventures for Isabel? **[Speculate]**
2. In what ways is the speaker of "I'll Stay" similar to and different from Isabel in "Adventures of Isabel"? **[Compare and Contrast]**
3. In "I'll Stay," what do the mother's words reveal about her feelings for her daughter? **[Interpret]**
4. What details in "Wilbur Wright and Orville Wright" indicate that Rosemary and Stephen Vincent Benét admire the Wright brothers? **[Support]**

APPLY

5. These poems deal with confidence and determination. In what ways are these two qualities related to success? **[Synthesize]**

COMPARE LITERARY WORKS

6. Which of these poems do you find most inspiring or encouraging? Why? **[Support]**

CONNECTIONS TO TODAY'S WORLD

Many people didn't believe that the Wright brothers would ever get a plane off the ground. If those people could have looked into the future, they would have seen that the Wright brothers' dream led to airplanes, supersonic jets, and even space travel!

John Glenn was the first American to travel around the Earth in space. On February 20, 1962, he orbited (went around) the Earth three times in the spacecraft *Friendship 7*. His return to space at age seventy-seven on board the shuttle *Discovery* makes him the oldest person ever to travel in space. In this on-line interview, he answered questions about his first space journey around the world.

An Astronaut's Answers

John Glenn

The first time you went into space, how did it feel to be all alone except for communication through radio?

In 1962, I looked down from an orbit high above our planet and saw our beautiful Earth and its curved horizon against the vastness of space. I have never forgotten that sight nor the sense of wonder it engendered. Although I was alone in Friendship 7, I did not feel alone in space. I knew that I was supported by my family, my six fellow astronauts, thousands of NASA engineers and employees, and millions of people around the world.

Why did you want to be an astronaut? How did you fly around the Earth three times? Was it hard?

I served as a fighter pilot in World War II and the Korean conflict. After Korea, I graduated from the Naval Test Pilot School and worked as a fighter test pilot. I applied for the astronaut program because I thought it was a logical career step, a challenging opportunity and one in which I could help start a new area of research that would be very valuable to everyone here on Earth. I have always considered myself very fortunate to be selected in the first group of seven astronauts.

An Atlas rocket boosted me into space and I orbited the Earth in my space capsule, the Friendship 7. It certainly was a challenge but one for which I was well prepared. The National Aeronautics and Space Administration (NASA) wanted people who were test pilots and accustomed to working under very unusual

---

◀ **Critical Viewing** Why do you think John Glenn needs a special suit and helmet for space travel? [**Draw Conclusions**]

conditions, including emergencies. During my first orbit I experienced some troubles with the automatic control system and so I had to take control of the capsule's movements by hand for the rest of the trip. Another problem developed when the signals showed that the heat shield was loose. To keep it secured during re-entry, I kept the retrorocket pack in place to steady the shield. When the Friendship 7 entered the atmosphere, the retrorocket pack burned off and flew by my window, but the heat shield stayed in place. These were problems we could not have foreseen prior to the flight.

How long was your trip around the Earth?

My trip around the Earth lasted 4 hours and 55 minutes, and I flew about 81,000 miles.

What did you eat while you were in outer space?

I took along a number of different kinds of food, such as applesauce and a mixture of meat and vegetables, all emulsified like baby food. It was packaged in containers much like toothpaste tubes so I could squeeze food into my mouth. I had no trouble eating any of it, and it tasted fine.

Why do astronauts go to the moon?

As adventurers of earlier eras crossed oceans and scaled mountains, astronauts in our time have flown to the moon and explored the heavens. The crucial hands-on experience of my flight in the Mercury program helped make the Gemini flights possible. The Gemini flights then helped make the Apollo missions to the moon a reality. Apollo gave us valuable information for the Shuttle missions, and the Shuttle/Mir program prepares us for the International Space Station. This is the nature of progress. Each of these missions has built on the knowledge gained from the previous flights.

We are a curious, questing people and our research in this new laboratory of space represents an opportunity to benefit people right here on Earth and to increase our understanding of the universe. The potential scientific, medical, and economic benefits from space are beyond our wildest dreams. That's why astronauts went to the moon, and that's why we continue to pursue our dreams of space exploration.

1. What qualities do you think are important for an astronaut to have? **[Assess]**
2. What advances in space travel have been made since John Glenn first orbited the Earth? **[Summarize]**
3. Do you think it is important for people to explore space? Why or why not? **[Make a Judgment]**

Critical Viewing ▶
What details in this picture illustrate the rocket's power? [Interpret]

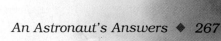

Guide for Responding (continued)

◆ Reading Strategy

USE PRIOR KNOWLEDGE

Your **prior knowledge** is the information, thoughts, and experiences you bring to a poem. It helps you make connections with what the author is saying, and it affects what you get from the poem.

1. In what ways did your prior knowledge of bears, witches, and doctors help you appreciate the humor in "Adventures of Isabel"?
2. Why would it be helpful to have some prior knowledge of the Wright brothers before reading "Wilbur Wright and Orville Wright"?

◆ Build Vocabulary

USING THE SUFFIX -ous

The suffix -ous means "having the qualities of" or "full of." In your notebook, write something that can be described by each word below, and tell why.

1. courageous   2. dangerous   3. virtuous

SPELLING STRATEGY

Even though you can't hear the o in -ous, remember to include it when you spell words ending with the suffix -ous. In your notebook, write the -ous words that answer each clue.

1. Causing outrage
2. Having the qualities of fame
3. Full of mystery
4. Full of luxury

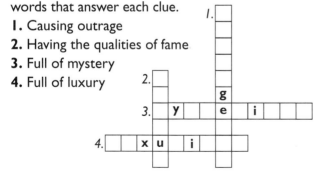

USING THE WORD BANK

In your notebook, write the opposite of each word from the Word Bank.

1. ravenous: (a) greedy, (b) full, (c) angry
2. cavernous: (a) cramped, (b) fast, (c) comfortable
3. rancor: (a) comfort, (b) exhaustion, (c) affection
4. grant: (a) spend, (b) harm, (c) deny

◆ Literary Focus

STANZAS

A **stanza** is a group of lines of poetry, usually similar in length and pattern and separated by spaces. Each stanza can usually stand alone as a single idea.

1. What is the main idea of each stanza in "Adventures of Isabel"?
2. In what ways are the stanzas of "I'll Stay" different from the stanzas of the other two poems?
3. In one or two sentences, write the main idea of the last stanza of "Wilbur Wright and Orville Wright."

◆ Build Grammar Skills

ADJECTIVE OR ADVERB?

Though many adverbs end in -ly, not all words that end in -ly are adverbs.

Adverb: *quietly* ate   **Adjective:** *ugly* toad

Sometimes, the same word may be used as either an adjective or an adverb.

Adverb: worked *hard*   **Adjective:** *hard* work

	Answer the Questions:	Modify or Describe:
Adjectives	Which? What kind? How many?	Nouns and pronouns
Adverbs	How? When? Where? To what extent?	Verbs, adjectives, and adverbs

You can tell whether a word is an adjective or an adverb by deciding which question it answers and identifying the part of speech of the word it describes.

Practice On your paper, identify each italicized word as an adjective or an adverb. Then, tell the question it answers and the part of speech of the word it modifies.

1. Isabel smiled *happily*.
2. The *silly* man left.
3. Bears move *fast!*
4. That bear is *fast*.
5. That was a *close* call.

Writing Application Write a paragraph about a confident, determined person. Use these words: confidently, early, straight, late, last. Explain whether you used each word as an adjective or an adverb.

Build Your Portfolio

 ## Idea Bank

Writing

1. **Description** In your journal, describe the ways in which someone you know shows confidence.

2. **Advertisement** Write an advertisement offering a ride on an antique airplane. Include some reasons for flying, and describe what the flight might be like.

3. **Journal Entry** Imagine that you are Isabel. Write a journal entry about each enemy that you faced. Be sure to explain what you thought as you defeated each one.

Speaking and Listening

4. **Role Play** With a partner, role-play a scene from one of these poems. **[Performing Arts Link]**

5. **Interview** With a classmate, conduct an interview with Isabel, Nora, or the Wright brothers. Prepare questions and answers based on what you've read in the poems.

Projects

6. **History of Flight** Create a timeline that shows major events in the history of flight—from the time the Wright brothers flew at Kitty Hawk to the present day. **[Social Studies Link]**

7. **Mural [Group Activity]** With a group, plan and create a mural showing people in a particular field whose achievements have improved our lives today. Divide the following tasks: choosing and researching people to include; finding models, diagrams, or other visuals showing the inventions or achievements; collecting information about how the achievements benefit people today; and drawing and painting the mural. **[Art Link]**

 ## Writing Mini-Lesson

Advice Column

Each of the people in these poems has a positive attitude about problem solving. Not everyone shares their confidence. Explore the topic of confidence by writing an advice column—a series of letters about problems followed by response letters that suggest possible solutions.

Writing Skills Focus: Elaborate With Examples

Don't just tell your readers to have confidence, to be brave, or to take a risk. **Elaborate with examples** of ways in which they can do these things. For instance, if you tell someone to use relaxation techniques before giving a speech, give examples. You might suggest deep breathing or stretching.

Prewriting Choose several problems that result from lack of confidence, such as fear of speaking in front of a group or unwillingness to try new experiences. Choose two as the subjects of letters asking for advice. Then, brainstorm for suggestions you might give in your answers.

Drafting Write your two letters asking for advice first. Then, draft your letters for giving advice. In each answer, give suggestions and examples related to the specific problem or question.

Revising Review and look for places where examples would make your advice more useful or easier to understand.

> ◆ **Grammar Application**
> After you have written your letters, identify where you have used adjectives and where you have used adverbs.

Cause-and-Effect Essay

Writing Process Workshop

"What! A little boy named Mowgli growing up with wolves! How did that happen?" This question is about the causes—the events and circumstances—that bring about a particular effect, or result. "Mowgli's Brothers" answers this question, showing the events that caused Mowgli to be adopted by wolves.

Causes and effects do not occur just in stories, though. Cause-and-effect relationships explain how the events of today lead to the events of tomorrow. In a **cause-and-effect essay,** a writer shows readers how one event leads to another.

Write a cause-and-effect essay about an event or a process. Use these tips, introduced in the section's Writing Mini-Lessons.

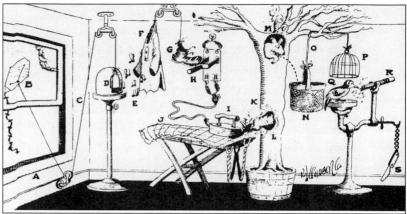

Rube Goldberg Inc., United Media/United Feature Syndicate

Writing Skills Focus

▶ **State the main idea** of each paragraph in a topic sentence. (See p. 247.)

▶ Use such words as *because of* and *therefore* to **signal the connections between causes and effects.** (See p. 259.)

▶ **Elaborate your points with examples.**
If you say that certain fertilizers cause flowers to grow better, elaborate by comparing the number of blooms on your geranium before and after you fertilized it. (See p. 269.)

MODEL FROM LITERATURE

Mowgli's Brothers, Rudyard Kipling

But [the wolves] are afraid of [Tabaqui the jackal] too, ① because Tabaqui, more than anyone else in the jungle, is apt to go mad, and then he forgets that he was ever afraid of anyone, ② and runs through the forest biting everything in his way. ③ Even the tiger runs and hides when little Tabaqui goes mad, for madness is the most disgraceful thing that can overtake a wild creature.

① Using the word *because,* Kipling clearly shows that Tabaqui's madness causes the wolves' fear.

② With the examples of behavior ("biting") and of the tiger's fear, Kipling elaborates on his main idea.

③ This topic sentence states the main idea of the paragraph.

Prewriting

Choose a Topic Think of an event or process you know, such as a change in your school or a procedure that you have studied in science class.

Make a Cause-and-Effect Diagram Write a brief description of the event or process. Note its causes and effects in a diagram like the one below. (If you are not sure about a cause or an effect, write down a question about it.)

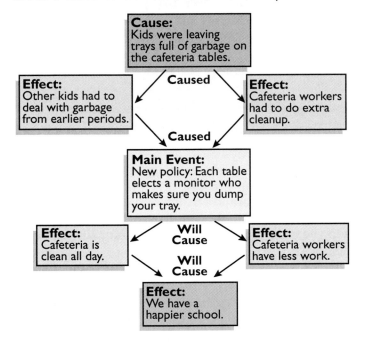

Cause: Kids were leaving trays full of garbage on the cafeteria tables.

↓ **Caused**

Effect: Other kids had to deal with garbage from earlier periods.

Effect: Cafeteria workers had to do extra cleanup.

↓ **Caused**

Main Event: New policy: Each table elects a monitor who makes sure you dump your tray.

Will Cause

Effect: Cafeteria is clean all day.

Effect: Cafeteria workers have less work.

Will Cause

Effect: We have a happier school.

Do Research Find out more about the causes or effects involved in your topic. If there is not enough information available, consider choosing another subject.

Drafting

Provide Topic Sentences For each paragraph, write a topic sentence that states a main idea—either an important cause or an effect. Then, supply the details that explain or support the idea expressed in the topic sentence.

Keep Paragraphs Focused Review your cause-and-effect diagram. As you start a paragraph, select details that go with the idea in your topic sentence.

Elaborate With Details Give examples to elaborate the points you make in your topic sentences. For instance, if you are discussing the causes of mold, you might mention the time you put wet laundry in a drawer.

APPLYING LANGUAGE SKILLS: Use the Right Conjunction

Conjunctions are words that join two words, phrases, or sentences. Common conjunctions are *and, but,* and *or.* Each tells you the relationship between the two words or ideas it joins.

and: *more of the same*

but: *different or opposite*

or: *a choice or another possibility*

Don't use just *and.* Use the conjunction that fits your meaning.

Practice Choose the right conjunction for each sentence.

1. The tiger was going to eat Mowgli, *(and, but)* the wolves saved him.
2. You may say her name the Spanish way *(or, and)* you may say it the English way.

Writing Application As you draft, use conjunctions that accurately express connections.

Writer's Solution Connection
Writing Lab

For help organizing your essay, see the instruction on different methods of organization in the Exposition tutorial.

APPLYING LANGUAGE SKILLS: Avoid Apostrophes in Plurals

The plural of most nouns is formed by adding -s or -es. Add an apostrophe only to show possession, not to form a plural.

Plural:

The cat has *kittens.*

Possessive:

The *kittens'* kittens have kittens.

Practice For each sentence, choose the plural form of the noun.

1. The (*tiger's, tigers*) scared them.
2. She chased the (*bears, bear's*).
3. The (*plane's, planes*) had strong wings.

Writing Application As you revise, check nouns ending in *s.* Unless they are possessives, make sure they do not have an apostrophe.

Writer's Solution Connection Writing Lab

For practice forming plurals, complete the Plural Nouns lesson in the Language Lab unit on Using Nouns.

Revising

Check Your Organization Ask yourself the following:

▶ Does each paragraph have a topic sentence? If not, add one.

▶ Does each topic sentence make a statement that covers all details in the paragraph? If not, consider breaking out details into separate paragraphs, each covered by an appropriate topic sentence.

Check Your Connections Check that you have made clear the connections between causes and effects. Consider using such words as *because, through, so,* and *since* to link ideas and make causal connections clear.

REVISION MODEL

Before the new cafeteria rules were invented, the situation in the cafeteria made many people unhappy.
① Kids just left their trays piled up at their tables and left. Cafeteria workers had to clean up after them. They were not happy with the extra work. ② ~~It was not like the old days when there were lunch table monitors.~~ In any case, the workers could not clean up until the end of the day. When the next group of kids came in for lunch, they had to deal with the mess. ③ Once, I couldn't find a single clean spot to sit. One chair had a squashed banana on it. Someone had piled up trays on another table, spilling soda all over. I finally sat down next to a plate of cold French fries.

① The writer added a topic sentence making a point about the situation in the cafeteria.

② This detail does not fit this paragraph.

③ The writer adds these details to elaborate on how unpleasant it was to eat in the cafeteria.

Publishing and Presenting

▶ **Panel Discussion** You and your classmates may organize a series of discussions. Students who have written on similar topics will sit on the same panel and present their essays. Through discussion with each other and the class, they can find similarities and differences between essays.

▶ **Cause-and-Effect Posters** Create a poster based on your essay showing a chain or web of causes and effects. Design and decorate the poster in a style specific to your subject. A poster about the causes and effects of elm blight, for instance, might be shaped like a tree and decorated with leaves.

Real-World Reading Skills Workshop

Strategies for Success

When reading, you often have to **make inferences,** or move from the information on the page to the story behind it. You make inferences every day. For example, you might see your neighbor's car in her driveway. Moving from what you see (the car) to the story behind it, you *infer* that your neighbor is at home.

Look for Clues Authors may not directly tell you a character's feelings or situation. Instead, they give you details or clues from which you make inferences. Read this sentence:

Emily splashed through puddles and sang to herself.

The puddles are a clue that it has just rained, and Emily's singing is a clue that she is happy.

Use Your Experience To make inferences, you must combine clues with your own knowledge. When you read the example sentence, you inferred from the puddles that it had just rained, because you know that rain collects in puddles. You inferred from Emily's singing that she is happy, because you know that people often sing when they are happy.

Apply the Strategies

Read the paragraph below, and make inferences to answer the questions that follow. For each question, list the clues in the paragraph from which you made your inference.

---

23   CHAPTER TWO

Bonita sighed as she straightened the picture on the wall. She sat down heavily in a chair. Poor Buffy! Bonita knew that she shouldn't have let Buffy off her leash, although Nick had promised to watch her. Bonita had warned him not to let her run into the street. Now, her mother wouldn't even let Bonita go with them to the veterinarian. "You've caused enough trouble for one day," Mrs. Perry had said.

---

1. How is Bonita feeling?
2. Who or what is Buffy?
3. What probably happened to Buffy?
4. How is Mrs. Perry feeling?
5. Approximately how old is Bonita?

✔ *Here are other situations in which you can make inferences:*
▶ Watching television
▶ Looking at a painting
▶ Finding your way in a new town

Adverbs

Grammar Review

An **adverb** modifies, or describes, a verb, an adjective, or another adverb (see page 246). Adverbs answer the questions *how, when, where, how often,* and *to what extent.*

Question Answered	Examples
Adverbs Modifying Verbs	
How?	The wolf *carefully* lifted the cub.
When?	They meet *early*.
Where?	The law applies *everywhere*.
How Often?	Shere Khan *usually* makes trouble.
To What Extent?	The tiger *almost* fit in the cave.
Adverb Modifying an Adjective	
To What Extent?	Akela is *most* noble.
Adverb Modifying Another Adverb	
To What Extent?	Decisions are made *very* carefully.

Though many adverbs end in *-ly*, not all words that end in *-ly* are adverbs.

Adverb: walked *quietly* **Adjective:** *ugly* toad

Sometimes, a word may be used as either an adjective or an adverb. You can tell whether a word is an adjective or an adverb by deciding which question it answers and which part of speech it modifies.

	Answer the Questions:	Modify or Describe:
Adjectives	Which? What kind? How many?	Nouns and pronouns
Adverbs	How? When? Where? To what extent?	Verbs, adjectives, and adverbs

aventuros < aventure, ADVENTURE] 1 fond of adv take chances; daring 2 full of danger; risky —
adv. —ad·ven'tur·ous·ness *n.*
ad·verb (ad'vurb') *n.* [ME *adverbe* < L *adverbi verbum,* a word] any of a class of words used gene verb, an adjective, another adverb, a phrase, or a cl ing time, place, manner, degree, cause, etc.: Engli end in *-ly* (Ex.: *fast, carefully, then*)
ad·ver·bi·al (ad vur'bē əl, ad-) *adj.* 1 of an adve nature or function of an adverb 3 used to forn *adverbial suffix*] —*n.* Linguis. a word or grammatical functi

Practice 1 Copy these sentences. Underline each adverb, and draw an arrow to the word it modifies. Identify whether the modified word is a verb, an adjective, or an adverb.

1. Isabel was quite confident.
2. She defeated her enemies easily.
3. The bear growled ravenously at the silly doctor.
4. The Wright brothers worked nearly every day.
5. They were hardly ever discouraged by difficulties.

Practice 2 Identify each italicized word as an adjective or an adverb. Explain how you know.

1. The wolf gazed at the *far* horizon.
2. The boy traveled *far*.
3. Baloo is a *good* teacher.
4. Mowgli learned *well*.
5. He met with Baloo *daily*.
6. They had *daily* meetings.

Grammar in Writing

✔ *Remember to use an adverb, not an adjective, to modify a verb.*

INCORRECT: He listened *good* to Baloo's instructions. (*Good* is an adjective.)

CORRECT: He listened *well* to Baloo's instructions. (*Well* can be used as an adverb.)

Every day, you hear and respond to many sets of directions. Your teacher might explain how to use a new computer program. Your baseball coach might tell you how to become a better hitter. It's important to listen carefully to oral directions if you want to succeed.

Notice Action Words To follow oral directions accurately, pay special attention to the action words. Notice the different action words in these two sets of directions:

Watch the dog.   *Wash the dog.*

Here are some oral directions given to a student before a fire drill. Identify the actions. *Close the doors and windows. Walk to the nearest exit. Stand with your class until your teacher counts the group.*

Think about what might happen if the student missed the action words *Close, Walk,* and *Stand.* He or she might open the windows or run to the exit, causing a fire drill disaster!

Use Visual Cues *Watch* the person giving the directions. He or she may point, use gestures, or even draw a diagram that will help you understand the directions being given.

Tips for Following Oral Directions

✔ *These pointers can help you follow oral directions successfully:*

▶ Listen closely. Pay special attention to actions.

▶ Watch the speaker at all times. If the task is physical, the speaker may demonstrate as part of the directions.

▶ Don't interrupt or distract the speaker.

▶ Review the directions with the speaker. Repeat them to yourself.

▶ Ask the speaker questions if you don't understand any part of the directions.

Apply the Strategies

With a partner, take turns giving and following oral directions for the situations listed below:

1. Going from the school library to the cafeteria

2. Preparing materials for a science experiment or another school assignment

3. Sorting baseball cards, coins, or another collection in a specific way

4. Performing a series of running, jumping, and climbing activities in the gym or on the playground

What's Behind the Words

Vocabulary Adventures With Richard Lederer

Synonyms and Their Connotations

Words that have similar meanings are called synonyms. The English language holds *lots, bunches, tons,* and *truckloads* of synonyms. (In case you haven't noticed, these words are all synonyms.) For instance, there are at least thirty synonyms for the word *beautiful* (including *pretty* and *ravishing*). What an *elegant* language!

What a Word Means

Every word has two kinds of meaning. A word's *denotation* is its basic meaning. All synonym pairs have roughly the same denotation. For instance, both *home* and *residence* mean "the place where one lives."

Words also have *connotations.* You don't tell your friends "I'm going to my residence." Instead, you say, "I'm going to my home." The reason has to do with the different connotations of each word.

Where a Word Lives

Connotations are like the habitat where the word lives, or the neighborhood where it hangs out. Just as you would be surprised to see a lion walking down Main Street, you might be surprised to find the word *giggled* in this sentence: "The football player giggled

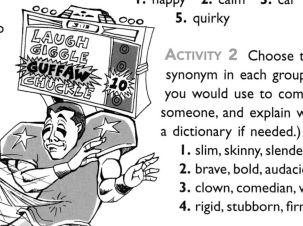

Laugh — Giggle — Guffaw

when his opponent dropped the ball."

A giggle is a kind of laugh. But it comes from the same neighborhood as *tickled* and *embarrassed.* Its connotations suggest that the person giggling is being silly. A tough football player probably *hoots* or *guffaws.*

A word's connotations add color to descriptions. The word *hoisted,* for instance, gives a more vivid sense of effort than plain old *lifted.*

Finding out more about a word's meanings is not *nosiness.* It's healthy *curiosity.*

ACTIVITY 1 Give two synonyms for each of the following words. Write a sentence using each according to its usual connotations.

    1. happy **2.** calm **3.** car **4.** food
        5. quirky

ACTIVITY 2 Choose the synonym in each group that you would use to compliment someone, and explain why. (Use a dictionary if needed.)

    1. slim, skinny, slender
    2. brave, bold, audacious
    3. clown, comedian, wit
    4. rigid, stubborn, firm

Extended Reading Opportunities

Reading about big challenges can sometimes help you face the little challenges of everyday life. These books tell of exciting adventures and the characters who must prove themselves in a challenging world.

Suggested Titles

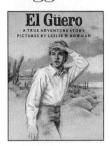

El Güero
Elizabeth Borton de Treviño

Based on the adventures of the author's ancestors, *El Güero* is the true story of a twelve-year-old boy in the late 1800's. The story follows the boy's journey from Mexico City to Ensenada, a remote outpost in Baja California. On the way, he and his family must bargain with bandits, cope with disease, and survive being stranded in the wilderness. Even then, their problems are not over. When El Güero's father is unjustly imprisoned, El Güero must find a way to save him.

Island of the Blue Dolphins
Scott O'Dell

This is the story of Karana, a twelve-year-old Native American girl who risked everything to stay with her brother, who was abandoned on the island that had been their home. Without her people, she must learn to survive on her own. In her struggle to survive, she discovers strength and serenity in her solitary life.

My Side of the Mountain
Jean Craighead George

When Sam Gribley decides to leave home to live in the wilderness of upstate New York, he has no idea of the adventures that are in store for him. Battling blizzards, hunters, loneliness, and fear, Sam learns how to live off the land. In the process, he befriends wild animals and learns a little about himself and what it means to be independent.

Other Possibilities

The Haymeadow	Gary Paulsen
Two Old Women	Velma Wallis
Mustang: Wild Spirit of the West	Marguerite Henry

Emigrants Crossing the Plains, 1867, oil on canvas, 60 x 96 in. Albert Bierstadt, National Cowboy Hall of Fame Collection, Oklahoma City

Seeing It Through

The travelers in this painting are choosing a new road. It will take all their strength and determination to see their journey through to the end. The stories, poems, and essays in this unit deal with the struggles and triumphs that people encounter when they choose a new road. Reading how fictional characters and real people find what it takes to "see it through" may help you look at some of your own experiences in a new light.

Guide for Reading

Meet the Author:
Robert Considine (1906–1975)

It all started with a mistake. The *Washington Post* misspelled Robert Considine's name in a story about a tennis tournament in which he was playing. He went to the paper and complained, "I could do a better job myself." Taking him at his word, the *Post* hired him. Considine spent the rest of his life reporting the news.

Traveling About Through much of his career, Considine wrote on sports. He also wrote about the major historical events of his day. Traveling to England and Asia during World War II and to Korea in the Korean War, he sent war news to the papers back home. His column "On the Line" appeared from 1933 all the way to 1975. He also wrote a few movie scripts, including one for the 1948 film *The Babe Ruth Story*.

Setting Records Reporters have to meet tight deadlines, and Considine could produce a news story in record speed. Fellow reporters say that once he got on a train and wrote a column about the World Series in nine minutes—finishing while the conductor was still shouting "All aboard."

THE STORY BEHIND THE STORY

Over a lifetime of reporting, Considine collected stories of ordinary people who showed extraordinary courage. These stories were published in *They Rose Above It,* from which "Lou Gehrig: The Iron Horse" comes.

◆ LITERATURE AND YOUR LIFE

CONNECT YOUR EXPERIENCE

Hit a home run or play a beautiful new tune, and people will pat you on the back. There are some days, though, when no one offers praise or encouragement. Then, doing your best must be its own reward. This selection shows baseball player Lou Gehrig doing his best, even as disease is stealing his athletic abilities.

THEMATIC FOCUS: Seeing It Through

Think about whether Lou Gehrig sees his job through as far as he can.

◆ Background for Understanding

SCIENCE

Scientists still do not know what causes the disease that killed Lou Gehrig. Named after its most famous victim, Lou Gehrig's disease gradually robs its victims of control over their movements. It affects the motor neurons—nerve cells that send commands from the brain to the muscles. The muscles governed by these neurons weaken and gradually waste away. Victims develop tremors (uncontrollable shaking). They often die two to five years after the disease takes hold.

◆ *from* Lou Gehrig: The Iron Horse ◆

◆ Literary Focus

BIOGRAPHICAL NARRATIVE

In a **biographical narrative,** a writer tells of events in someone's life as if writing a story. The narrative gives the facts, then goes beyond the facts to create a picture of people's motives and feelings. Sometimes, authors of biographical narratives may supply words and thoughts, when no one knows *exactly* what was said or thought. These small fictions help readers form a vivid picture of a person's life.

◆ Build Vocabulary

WORD ROOTS: *-chron-*

Lou Gehrig's disease, as Bob Considine notes, is "chronic." *Chronic* is formed from the word root *-chron-*, meaning "time." *Chronic* means "lasting a long time or happening time after time."

WORD BANK

Which of the words listed describes a person or thing that is well known?

renowned
contemptuous
eminent
chronic
concluded
irrepressible

Fact	Added Detail	Vivid Picture
McCarthy and Gehrig met in McCarthy's office on May 2.	Lou said, "I can't tell you how grateful I am."	An emotional meeting between Gehrig and McCarthy

Reading for Success

Strategies for Constructing Meaning

Don't let a book's quiet looks fool you. As soon as you begin reading, it becomes a busy construction site. First, you haul together words and ideas to make a foundation, the literal meaning of the work (see pages 4 and 106). Then, you begin constructing meaning, nailing information together in new ways. The following strategies can help.

Make inferences.

At a construction site, if you see a wall with a gap in it, you can make the inference that a door belongs there. As you read, nail missing parts in place. Make inferences to complete your understanding of ideas, people, and events. For example, from the details of Lou's actions, you can infer that he wants to be judged on his performance.

Inference:

Lou wants to be judged on his performance alone.

Detail:

Lou accepts a salary cut when he is not playing well.

Detail:

Lou resigns when he realizes others feel sorry for him.

Interpret.

When you interpret what you read, you explain to yourself what the author is saying and why. After you've interpreted meaning, the pieces will fit snugly in place.

Identify important ideas.

The important ideas are the author's main points. You can identify them by noticing when an author restates an idea, offers explanations, or illustrates with examples.

Compare and contrast characters and ideas.

By comparing and contrasting characters or ideas, you can find out more about how they fit together.

The fan wants Lou to quit. | Both see that Lou has a problem. | The teammate compliments a simple play.

As you read "Lou Gehrig: The Iron Horse," look at the notes in the boxes. The notes show you how to apply these strategies to your reading.

from
Lou Gehrig: The Iron Horse

Bob Considine

Henry Louis Gehrig (1903–1941) was one of baseball's brightest stars. He played his entire career (1923–1939) for the New York Yankees. He earned the nickname "The Iron Horse" by setting the record for consecutive number of games played.

Critical Viewing ▶
Name two details in this photograph that suggest that Gehrig enjoys life as a baseball player. **[Analyze]**

The first hint I had that Lou's problem was more sinister than a routine slump that year was provided by a wild-and-wooly Washington pitcher named Joe Krakauskas. After a game at Yankee Stadium he told Shirley Povich of the Washington

> You should **identify one important idea** in these opening paragraphs: Lou Gehrig is playing badly, and it is clear that something is wrong with him.

Post and me that a frightening thing had happened to him while pitching against Gehrig. Joe had uncorked his high inside fast ball with the expectation that Lou would move back and take

it, as a ball. Instead, Krakauskas said, Lou—a renowned judge of balls and strikes—moved closer to the plate.

"My pitch went between his wrists," Joe said, still shaken. "Scared the heck outta me. Something's wrong with Gehrig . . ."

> Krakauskas is "shaken" by this event. From this fact, you can **make the inference** that Gehrig was dangerously close to the plate and could have been hurt.

Lou's salary was cut three thousand dollars a year before he went South with the Yankees in 1939. There was no beef from him. He had had a bum year, for him, so the cut was deserved. He'd come back.

After all, the Babe[1] played twenty-two years without ever taking good care of himself . . .

◆ **Build Vocabulary**
renowned (ri nound′) *adj.*: Famous

1. **Babe:** George Herman Ruth (1920–1934), better known as Babe Ruth, was a noted home-run hitter and one of the greatest baseball players in history.

Joe McCarthy started Gehrig at first base on opening day of the 1939 season, <u>contemptuous</u> of a fan who, a few days before in an exhibition game at Ebbets Field, had bawled, in earshot of both of them, "Hey, Lou, why don't you give yourself up? What do you want McCarthy to do, burn that uniform off you?"

Lou hobbled as far into the 1939 season as May 2. Then, on the morning of the first game of a series against Detroit, he called McCarthy on the hotel's house phone and asked to see him.

"I'm benching myself, Joe," he said, once in the manager's suite. McCarthy did not speak.

> You can **interpret** Gehrig's offer to "bench himself" as follows: "Gehrig is not quitting because he is ashamed or because the fans are mad. He benches himself for the team. He acts unselfishly."

"For the good of the team," Lou went on. "I can't tell you how grateful I am to you for the kindness you've shown me, and your patience. . . I just can't seem to get going. The time has come for me to quit."

McCarthy snorted and told him to forget the consecutive-games-played record,[2] take a week or two off, and he'd come back strong.

Gehrig shook his head. "I can't go on, Joe," he said. "Johnny Murphy told me so."

McCarthy cursed the relief pitcher.

"I didn't mean it that way, Joe," Gehrig said. "All the boys have been swell to me. Nobody's said a word that would hurt my feelings. But Johnny said something the other day that made me know it was time for me to get out of the lineup. . .and all he meant to do was be encouraging."

McCarthy, still angry, asked for details.

"You remember the last play in that game we played at the Stadium?" Lou asked. "A ball was hit between the box and first base. Johnny fielded it, and I got back to first just in time to take the throw from him."

"So?"

"So, well, I had a hard time getting back there, Joe," Lou said. "I should have been there in plenty of time. I made the put-out, but when Johnny and I were trotting to the bench he said, 'Nice play, Lou.' I knew then it was time to quit. The boys were beginning to feel sorry for me."

At the urging of his devoted wife, Eleanor, Lou checked into the Mayo Clinic in Rochester, Minnesota. In due time he emerged with a bleak "To Whom It May Concern" document signed by the <u>eminent</u> Dr. Harold C. Harbeing:

> Compare and contrast the manager's reaction with that of Gehrig's wife. The manager doesn't want to admit Gehrig's problem is serious. Gehrig's wife suspects it is.

"This is to certify that Mr. Lou Gehrig has been under examination at the Mayo Clinic from June 13 to June 19, 1939, inclusive. After a careful and complete examination, it was found that he is suffering from amyotrophic lateral sclerosis. This type of illness involves the motor

---

2. **consecutive-games-played record:** Gehrig played in 2,130 consecutive games. His record was eventually broken, in 1995, by Cal Ripkin, Jr., who played in 2,632 consecutive games. Hardworking and dedicated, Gehrig played so many games without missing one that fans and reporters began to keep track of how many he played in a row.

pathways and cells of the central nervous system and, in lay terms, is known as a form of chronic poliomyelitis[3]—infantile paralysis.

"The nature of this trouble makes it such that Mr. Gehrig will be unable to continue his active participation as a baseball player, inasmuch as it is advisable that he conserve his muscular energy. He could, however, continue in some executive capacity."

Lou returned to the team for the remainder of the 1939 season, slowly suiting up each day, taking McCarthy's lineups to home plate to deliver to the umpires before each game. It was his only duty as captain. It was another winning season for the Yankees, but hardly for Lou. The short walk from the dugout to home plate and back exhausted him. But more exhausting was a cruel (but mostly true) story in the New York *Daily News* to the effect that some of his teammates had become afraid of drinking out of the Yankee dugout's drinking fountain after Lou used it.

"Gehrig Appreciation Day" (July 4, 1939) was one of those emotional salutes that only

---

3. **amyotrophic lateral sclerosis . . . poliomyelitis** (ā´ mī´ ō träf´ ik lat´ ər əl skli rō´ sis . . . pō´ lē ō´ mī´ ə līt´ is) An incurable illness, also called ALS or Lou Gehrig's disease, that leads to weakened muscles and eventual death. Poliomyelitis, known as polio, is a disease that paralyzes muscle groups. It, too, can be fatal.

▲ **Critical Viewing** Why do you think Gehrig has such an emotional response to "Gehrig Appreciation Day"? [Draw Conclusions]

baseball seems able to produce: packed stands, the prospect of a double-header win over the Washington Senators, a peppery speech from Mayor Fiorello LaGuardia, the presence of Yankee fan and Gehrig buff Postmaster General Jim Farley, and the array of rheumatic and fattening old teammates of yesteryear. And The Family in a sidelines box. Presents and trophies filled a table.

For Lou, now beginning to hollow out from his disease, one basic ingredient was missing. Babe Ruth

> You can make the **inference** that Gehrig cares about Babe Ruth.

wasn't there. Babe, the one he wanted to be there more than he wanted any of his old buddies, had not answered the invitations or the management's phone calls.

Then, with little warning, a great commotion and rustle and rattle in the stadium. The

◆ Build Vocabulary

contemptuous (kən temp´ cho͞o əs´) *adj.*: Lacking respect for; seeing as worthless

eminent (em´ ən ənt´) *adj.*: Outstanding in performance

chronic (krän´ ik) *adj.*: Lasting a long time or occurring again and again

---

Babe was entering. He magnetized every eye, activated every tongue. Lou wheezed a prayer of thanksgiving.

The ceremony between games of the double-header was not calculated to be anything requiring a stiff upper lip. Joe McCarthy's voice cracked as he began his prepared tribute. He promptly abandoned his script and blurted, "Don't let's cry about this . . ." which had just the opposite effect among the fans.

When Lou's turn came, he, too, pocketed the small speech he had worked on the night before. He swallowed a few times to make his voice stronger, then haltingly said:

"They say I've had a bad break. But when the office force and the groundkeepers and even the Giants from across the river, whom we'd give our right arm to beat in the World Series—when *they* remember you, that's something . . . and when you have a wonderful father and mother who worked hard to give you an education . . . and a wonderful wife . . ."

His words began to slither when he tried to say something about Jake Ruppert and Miller Huggins, dead, and McCarthy, Barrow and Bill Dickey, alive.

But nobody missed his ending.

"I may have been given a bad break," he concluded, briefly touching his nose as if to discourage a sniff, "but I have an awful lot to live for. With all this, I consider myself the luckiest man on the face of the earth."

Babe, the irrepressible, stepped forward, embraced him and blubbered, an act that turned out to be epidemic.

> Here you can **identify the important idea** that Gehrig is a champion in life as well as in baseball.

◆ Build Vocabulary

concluded (kən klŏŏ´ did) *v*.: Ended

irrepressible (ir´ ri pres´ ə bəl) *adj*.: Given to expressing feelings and ideas freely, without caution

*G*uide for Responding

◆ LITERATURE AND YOUR LIFE

Reader's Response Would you have resigned earlier than Lou Gehrig did, later, or at the same point? Explain.

Thematic Focus Explain whether Gehrig has seen his career in baseball through to the end.

Journal Writing Describe an athlete or another famous person you admire.

☑ Check Your Comprehension

1. Name two early signs that Gehrig is ill.
2. What is his employer's first response to his poor playing?
3. What assignment does McCarthy give him?
4. What event causes Gehrig to bench himself?
5. At what event does baseball say goodbye to Lou Gehrig?

◆ Critical Thinking

INTERPRET

1. Explain Gehrig's reaction to his salary cut. **[Interpret]**
2. Gehrig keeps playing despite his loss of ability. What does this show about him? **[Infer]**
3. Why does he eventually stop playing? **[Interpret]**
4. Describe his character, using your answer to the previous questions. **[Draw Conclusions]**

EVALUATE

5. Do you agree with McCarthy's decision to keep Gehrig playing? Explain. **[Evaluate]**

EXTEND

6. What are three guidelines an athlete can follow to stay in good shape? **[Sports Link; Health Link]**

Guide for Responding (continued)

◆ Reading for Success

STRATEGIES FOR CONSTRUCTING MEANING

Review the reading strategies and the notes showing how to construct meaning. Then, apply them to answer the following:

1. What inference can you make from Gehrig's increasing problems on the playing field?
2. Compare the reaction of a fan to Gehrig's early slump with the reaction of fans at his farewell.
3. Interpret Gehrig's statement that he is "the luckiest man on the face of the earth."

◆ Build Vocabulary

USING THE WORD ROOT -chron-

The word root -chron- in chronic means "time." On your paper, match the number of each -chron- word with the letter of its description.

1. chronological   **a.** history of a time period
2. chronicle   **b.** match the timing
3. synchronize   **c.** in time order

SPELLING STRATEGY

When adding endings to words that end with -ic, as chronic does, follow these guidelines:

When adding:	Guideline	Example
Endings that begin with a, such as -al or -ally	No change to spelling	chronic → chronically
Endings that begin with e, i, or y, such as -ed or -ing	Add a k to the c	picnic → picnicking panic → panicked garlic → garlicky

Practice On your paper, add the ending indicated to each word.

1. mimic (-ing)   2. picnic (-ed)   3. politic (-ally)

USING THE WORD BANK

In your notebook, write the Word Bank words that fit each description:

1. Two words having to do with time or order.
2. Two words having to do with reputation.
3. Two words describing an action and a reaction.

◆ Literary Focus

BIOGRAPHICAL NARRATIVE

A **biographical narrative** is an account of someone's life told as if it were a story. Writers sometimes supply words, thoughts, and other details. Although the writer doesn't know exactly what was said or done in these cases, the details supplied are always consistent with the subject's personality. Explain whether each of the following describes an actual event or is a detail supplied by the author.

1. Gehrig met with McCarthy in person to resign.
2. Gehrig said, "All the boys have been swell to me."
3. Mayor LaGuardia attended Gehrig's farewell.
4. Gehrig said a prayer of thanks when Ruth arrived.

◆ Build Grammar Skills

PREPOSITIONS

A **preposition** relates a noun or a pronoun following it to another word in the sentence.

Common Prepositions			
about	behind	in	to
above	below	into	toward
across	between	like	under
after	by	of	until
against	down	off	up
among	during	on	with
at	for	over	without
before	from		

Prepositions Made Up of More Than One Word	
because of in spite of instead of	next to in addition to according to

Practice On your paper, identify the preposition in each sentence.

1. In baseball, batters run around the bases.
2. Lou Gehrig hit many balls to the outfield.
3. He suffered from a terrible disease.
4. Gehrig was a good friend of Babe Ruth.
5. There is no cure for Lou Gehrig's disease.

Writing Application In your notebook, write a sentence using a preposition and the pair of nouns.

1. baseball, glove   2. doctor, disease   3. Lou, fans

Build Your Portfolio

 Idea Bank

Writing

1. **Letter** Write a letter from Gehrig to his fans explaining his decision to resign. Use details from the narrative that Gehrig might mention.

2. **Narrative** Considine vividly re-creates some of Gehrig's conversations. Choose a famous episode from history, such as the signing of the Declaration of Independence. Write a conversation the people involved might have had.

3. **Story** Write a short story about a celebrity who retires from his or her profession. Describe the person's feelings at leaving behind the fans and work.

Speaking and Listening

4. **Story Comparison** Read to the class part of another selection from Bob Considine's book *They Rose Above It.* Lead a class discussion comparing Gehrig's story with the one you have selected. **[Literature Link]**

5. **Lou's Speech** As Lou Gehrig, present to the class your farewell speech. Use Considine's descriptions and his use of punctuation to guide your delivery. **[Performing Arts Link]**

Projects

6. **Statistical Chart [Group Activity]** Lou Gehrig's consecutive-game record was broken by Cal Ripken, Jr. In a group, prepare a presentation comparing the two players. Divide the following tasks: researching and presenting their life stories, calculating and explaining their statistics, collecting and arranging visuals for display. **[Math Link]**

7. **Nervous-System Diagram** Draw a diagram showing the paths that nerve impulses take from the brain to the muscles and back. Use different color markers to show the different kinds of nerves. **[Science Link]**

 Writing Mini-Lesson

Testimonial

Bob Considine's biography shows Lou Gehrig's modesty and dignity. It is a testimonial, a speech or short written work that celebrates a person's character and highlights his or her achievements. To heighten the drama, Considine puts the most moving moment, Gehrig's farewell, at the end.

Write a testimonial to someone you admire, organizing your material so that, like "Lou Gehrig: The Iron Horse," it builds to a main point or event.

Writing Skills Focus: Build to a Main Point

To **build to a main point,** you must prepare the reader. In earlier sections of the piece, you should do the following:

- Provide all necessary background information.
- Allow readers to become familiar with your subject's character.
- Hold back enough information or details to keep readers interested in reaching the main point.

Prewriting List important details about a person you admire. Choose a main point or central event.

Drafting Work backwards. Write up your main point first. Then, add information to give background. To emphasize the exceptional main point, present related but less important details first.

Revising Have a peer review your draft. If your peer was confused by your main point, add necessary background information earlier in the draft.

◆ **Grammar Application**
Identify the prepositions in the first paragraph of your draft.

P<small>ART</small> 1 *Struggles and Triumphs*

Basketball Superstars, LeRoy Neiman

Guide for Reading

Meet the Authors:

Joan Aiken (1924–   )

Joan Aiken began her writing career early—at the age of five! By her teens, she was a published author. All this is not surprising when you consider that she comes from a family of writers. Her father is poet Conrad Aiken, and two of her sisters are also professional writers. Fans of all ages enjoy reading her tales, most of which have an unusual twist or mysterious turn of events.

James Thurber (1894–1961)

James Thurber left college to take a job as a clerk in the U.S. State Department. Thurber soon left this serious position to pursue his love of laughter through writing and cartooning. Much of his early work appeared in *The New Yorker* magazine. Although he left *The New Yorker* in 1933, he continued to contribute humorous sketches, stories, and essays. When failing eyesight forced him to give up drawing, he kept making people laugh with his writing. Some of his funny stories, such as "The Tiger Who Would Be King," have a serious point behind the humor.

Aesop (c. 620–560 B.C.)

According to tradition, Aesop was a Greek slave. He is known as the author of *Aesop's Fables*, a famous collection of short tales that teach lessons.

◆ LITERATURE AND YOUR LIFE

CONNECT YOUR EXPERIENCE

You've probably heard the expression "Experience is the best teacher." It means that you can learn something from each of your experiences. Through their experiences, the characters in these works learn—sometimes too late— important lessons about love, power, and working together.

THEMATIC FOCUS: STRUGGLES AND TRIUMPHS

As you read, ask yourself, "Do struggles bring individuals together or push them apart?"

◆ Background for Understanding

GEOGRAPHY

In "Lob's Girl" a dog travels more than 400 miles from Liverpool to Cornwall, England. Look at the map to appreciate the impressive journey this dog made.

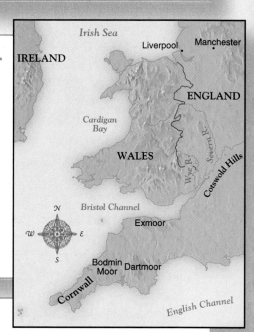

◆ Build Vocabulary

RELATED WORDS: FORMS OF *decide*

A character who speaks *decisively* has made a *decision*. Both *decisively* and *decision* are forms of *decide*.

WORD BANK

Which of these words means "decisions or intentions"? (Hint: Some people make them on New Year's Eve.)

decisively
atone
resolutions
melancholy
intimated
aggrieved
prowled
repulse
slanderous

Lob's Girl
◆ The Tiger Who Would Be King ◆
The Lion and the Bulls

◆ Literary Focus

FORESHADOWING

When James Thurber called his story "The Tiger Who Would Be King" rather than "The Tiger Who Is King," he gave you a hint about how the story ends. The use of hints suggesting events to come is called **foreshadowing.** The hints may be comments made by the narrator, experiences or feelings of characters, or events in the story. Look for hints as you read these stories, and think about what the hints foreshadow.

◆ Reading Strategy

COMPARE AND CONTRAST CHARACTERS

Characters, the people or animals in stories, have similarities and differences, just like people in life. When you examine the similarities in personalities and behaviors, you **compare characters.** When you examine the differences in personalities and behaviors, you **contrast characters.** Comparing and contrasting characters will improve your understanding of them. Use a Venn diagram like the one shown below to compare and contrast pairs of characters as you read these stories.

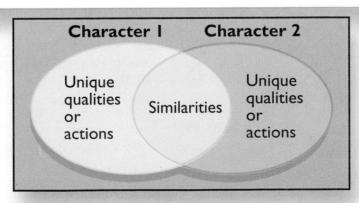

Character 1 — Character 2

Unique qualities or actions — Similarities — Unique qualities or actions

Lob's Girl

Joan Aiken

Some people choose their dogs, and some dogs choose their people. The Pengelly family had no say in the choosing of Lob; he came to them in the second way, and very decisively.

It began on the beach, the summer when Sandy was five, Don, her older brother, twelve, and the twins were three. Sandy was really Alexandra, because her grandmother had a beautiful picture of a queen in a diamond tiara and high collar of pearls. It hung by Granny Pearce's kitchen sink and was as familiar as the doormat. When Sandy was born everyone agreed that she was the living spit of the picture, and so she was called Alexandra and Sandy for short.

On this summer day she was lying peacefully reading a comic and not keeping an eye on the twins, who didn't need it because they were occupied in seeing which of them could wrap the most seaweed around the other one's legs. Father—Bert Pengelly—and Don were up on the Hard painting the bottom boards of the boat in which Father went fishing for pilchards. And Mother—Jean Pengelly—was getting ahead with making the Christmas puddings because she never felt easy in her mind if they weren't made and safely put away by the end of August. As usual, each member of the family was happily getting on with his or her own affairs. Little did they guess how soon this state of things would be changed by the large new member who was going to erupt into their midst.

Sandy rolled onto her back to make sure that the twins were not climbing on slippery rocks or getting cut off by the tide. At the same moment a large body struck her forcibly in the midriff and she was covered by flying sand. Instinctively she shut her eyes and felt the sand being wiped off her face by something that seemed like a warm, rough, damp flannel. She opened her eyes and looked. It was a tongue. Its owner was a large and bouncy young Alsatian, or German shepherd, with topaz eyes, black-tipped prick ears, a thick, soft coat, and a bushy black-tipped tail.

"*Lob!*" shouted a man farther up the beach. "Lob, come here!"

But Lob, as if trying to atone for the surprise he had given her, went on licking the sand off Sandy's face, wagging his tail so hard while he kept on knocking up more clouds of sand. His owner, a gray-haired man with a limp, walked over as quickly as he could and seized him by the collar.

"I hope he didn't give you a fright?" the man said to Sandy. "He meant it in play—he's only young."

"Oh, no, I think he's *beautiful.*" said Sandy truly. She picked up a bit of driftwood and threw it. Lob, whisking easily out of his master's grip, was after it like a sand-colored bullet. He came back with the stick, beaming, and gave it to Sandy. At the same time he gave himself, though no one else was aware of this at the time. But with Sandy, too, it was love at first sight, and when, after a lot more stick-throwing, she and the twins joined Father and Don to go home for tea, they cast many a backward glance at Lob being led firmly away by his master.

"I wish we could play with him every day." Tess sighed.

"Why can't we?" said Tim.

Sandy explained. "Because Mr. Dodsworth, who owns him, is from Liverpool, and he is only staying at the Fisherman's Arms till Saturday."

"Is Liverpool a long way off?"

"Right at the other end of England from Cornwall, I'm afraid."

It was a Cornish fishing village where the

◀ **Critical Viewing** What clue does this picture give you about the identity of "Lob" in the title? [Connect]

◆ **Build Vocabulary**

decisively (di sī´ siv lē´) *adv.*: With determination

atone (a tōn´) *v.*: Make up for a wrong

Pengelly family lived, with rocks and cliffs and a strip of beach and a little round harbor, and palm trees growing in the gardens of the little whitewashed stone houses. The village was approached by a narrow, steep, twisting hill-road, and guarded by a notice that said LOW GEAR FOR 1 ½ MILES, DANGEROUS TO CYCLISTS.

The Pengelly children went home to scones with Cornish cream and jam, thinking they had seen the last of Lob. But they were much mistaken. The whole family was playing cards by the fire in the front room after supper when there was a loud thump and a crash of china in the kitchen.

"My Christmas puddings!" exclaimed Jean, and ran out.

"Did you put TNT in them, then?" her husband said.

But it was Lob, who, finding the front door shut, had gone around to the back and bounced in through the open kitchen window, where the puddings were cooling on the sill. Luckily only the smallest was knocked down and broken.

Lob stood on his hind legs and plastered Sandy's face with licks. Then he did the same for the twins, who shrieked with joy.

"Where does this friend of yours come from?" inquired Mr. Pengelly.

"He's staying at the Fisherman's Arms—I mean his owner is."

"Then he must go back there. Find a bit of string, Sandy, to tie to his collar."

"I wonder how he found his way here," Mrs. Pengelly said, when the reluctant Lob had been led whining away and Sandy had explained about their afternoon's game on the beach. "Fisherman's Arms is right around the other side of the harbor."

Lob's owner scolded him and thanked Mr. Pengelly for bringing him back. Jean Pengelly warned the children that they had better not encourage Lob any more if they met him on the beach, or it would only lead to more trouble. So they dutifully took no notice of him the next day until he spoiled their good <u>resolutions</u> by dashing up to them with joyful barks, wagging his tail so hard that he winded Tess and knocked Tim's legs from under him.

They had a happy day, playing on the sand.

The next day was Saturday. Sandy had found out that Mr. Dodsworth was to catch the half-past-nine train. She went out secretly, down to the station, nodded to Mr. Hoskins, the stationmaster, who wouldn't dream of charging any local for a platform ticket, and climbed up on the footbridge that led over the tracks. She didn't want to be seen, but she did want to see. She saw Mr. Dodsworth get on the train, accompanied by an unhappy-looking Lob with drooping ears and tail. Then she saw the train slide away out of sight around the next headland, with a <u>melancholy</u> wail that sounded like Lob's last good-bye.

Sandy wished she hadn't had the idea of coming to the station. She walked home miserably, with her shoulders hunched and her hands in her pockets. For the rest of the day she was so cross and unlike herself that Tess and Tim were quite surprised, and her mother gave her a dose of senna.

A week passed. Then, one evening, Mrs. Pengelly and the younger children were in the front room playing snakes and ladders. Mr. Pengelly and Don had gone fishing on the

> . . . there was a loud thump and a crash of china . . .

◆ **Literary Focus**
What upcoming event might Mrs. Pengelly's question foreshadow?

◆ **Build Vocabulary**

resolutions (rez´ ə lōō´ shənz) *n.*: Intentions; things decided

melancholy (mel´ ən käl´ ē) *adj.*: Sad; gloomy

That's My Dog (German Shepard) Jim Killen, *Voyageur Art*

▲ Critical Viewing What qualities of Lob do you see in this dog? [Analyze]

the world did *he* get here?"

"He must have walked," said Sandy. "Look at his feet."

They were worn, dusty, and tarry. One had a cut on the pad.

"They ought to be bathed," said Jean Pengelly. "Sandy, run a bowl of warm water while I get disinfectant."

"What'll we do about him, Mother?" said Sandy anxiously.

Mrs. Pengelly looked at her daughter's pleading eyes and sighed.

"He must go back to his owner, of course," she said, making her voice firm. "Your dad can get the address from the Fisherman's tomorrow, and phone him or send a telegram. In the meantime he'd better have a long drink and a good meal."

evening tide. If your father is a fisherman, he will never be home at the same time from one week to the next.

Suddenly, history repeating itself, there was a crash from the kitchen. Jean Pengelly leaped up, crying, "My blackberry jelly!" She and the children had spent the morning picking and the afternoon boiling fruit.

But Sandy was ahead of her mother. With flushed cheeks and eyes like stars she had darted into the kitchen, where she and Lob were hugging one another in a frenzy of joy. About a yard of his tongue was out, and he was licking every part of her that he could reach.

"Good heavens!" exclaimed Jean. "How in

Lob was very grateful for the drink and the meal, and made no objection to having his feet washed. Then he flopped down on the hearthrug and slept in front of the fire they had lit because it was a cold, wet evening, with his head on Sandy's feet. He was a very tired dog. He had walked all the way from Liverpool to Cornwall, which is more than four hundred miles.

The next day Mr. Pengelly phoned Lob's owner, and the following morning Mr. Dodsworth arrived off the night train, decidedly put out, to take his pet home. That parting was worse than the first. Lob whined, Don walked out of the house, the twins burst out crying, and Sandy crept up to her bedroom afterward and lay with her face pressed into the quilt, feeling as if she were bruised all over.

Jean Pengelly took them all into Plymouth to see the circus on the next day and the twins cheered up a little, but even the hour's ride in the train each way and the Liberty horses and performing seals could not cure Sandy's sore heart.

She need not have bothered, though. In ten days' time Lob was back—limping this time, with a torn ear and a patch missing out of his furry coat, as if he had met and tangled with an enemy or two in the course of his four-hundred-mile walk.

Bert Pengelly rang up Liverpool again. Mr. Dodsworth, when he answered, sounded weary. He said, "That dog has already cost me two days that I can't spare away from my work—plus endless time in police stations and drafting newspaper advertisements. I'm too old for these ups and downs. I think we'd better face the fact, Mr. Pengelly, that it's your family he wants to stay with—that is, if you want to have him."

Bert Pengelly gulped. He was not a rich man; and Lob was a pedigreed dog. He said cautiously, "How much would you be asking for him?"

"Good heavens, man, I'm not suggesting I'd *sell* him to you. You must have him as a gift. Think of the train fares I'll be saving. You'll be doing me a good turn."

"Is he a big eater?" Bert asked doubtfully.

By this time the children, breathless in the background listening to one side of this conversation, had realized what was in the wind and were dancing up and down with their hands clasped beseechingly.

"Oh, not for his size," Lob's owner assured Bert. "Two or three pounds of meat a day and some vegetables and gravy and biscuits—he does very well on that."

Alexandra's father looked over the telephone at his daughter's swimming eyes and trembling lips. He reached a decision. "Well, then, Mr. Dodsworth," he said briskly, "we'll accept your offer and thank you very much. The children will be overjoyed and you can be sure Lob has come to a good home. They'll look after him and see he gets enough exercise. But I can tell you," he ended firmly, "if he wants to settle in with us he'll have to learn to eat a lot of fish."

So that was how Lob came to live with the Pengelly family. Everybody loved him and he loved them all. But there was never any question who came first with him. He was Sandy's dog. He slept by her bed and followed her everywhere he was allowed.

Nine years went by, and each summer Mr. Dodsworth came back to stay at the Fisherman's Arms and call on his erstwhile dog. Lob always met him with recognition and dignified pleasure, accompanied him for a walk or two—but showed no signs of wishing to return to Liverpool. His place, he <u>intimated</u>, was definitely with the Pengellys.

In the course of nine years Lob changed less than Sandy. As she went into her teens he became a little slower, a little stiffer, there was a touch of gray on his nose, but he was still a handsome dog. He and Sandy still loved one another devotedly.

One evening in October all the summer visitors had left, and the little fishing town looked empty and secretive. It was a wet, windy dusk. When the children came home from school—even the twins were at high school now, and Don was a full-fledged fisherman—Jean Pengelly said, "Sandy, your Aunt Rebecca says she's lonesome because Uncle Will Hoskins has gone out trawling, and she wants one of you to

◆ **Reading Strategy**
Compare Mr. Dodsworth to Mr. Pengelly. What similar quality do their actions show?

◆ **Build Vocabulary**
intimated (in´ tə māt´ id) *v*.: Hinted; made known

go and spend the evening with her. You go, dear; you can take your homework with you."

Sandy looked far from enthusiastic.

"Can I take Lob with me?"

"You know Aunt Becky doesn't really like dogs—Oh, very well." Mrs. Pengelly sighed. "I suppose she'll have to put up with him as well as you."

Reluctantly Sandy tidied herself, took her schoolbag, put on the damp raincoat she had just taken off, fastened Lob's lead to his collar, and set off to walk through the dusk to Aunt Becky's cottage, which was five minutes' climb up the steep hill.

The wind was howling through the shrouds of boats drawn up on the Hard.

"Put some cheerful music on, do," said Jean Pengelly to the nearest twin. "Anything to drown that wretched sound while I make your dad's supper." So Don, who had just come in, put on some rock music, loud. Which was why the Pengellys did not hear the truck hurtle down the hill and crash against the post office wall a few minutes later.

Dr. Travers was driving through Cornwall with his wife, taking a late holiday before patients began coming down with winter colds and flu. He saw the sign that said STEEP HILL. LOW GEAR FOR 1½ MILES. Dutifully he changed into second gear.

"We must be nearly there," said his wife, looking out of her window. "I noticed a sign on the coast road that said the Fisherman's Arms was two miles. What a narrow, dangerous hill! But the cottages are very pretty—Oh, Frank, stop, *stop!* There's a child, I'm sure it's a child—by the wall over there!"

Dr. Travers jammed on his brakes and brought the car to a stop. A little stream ran down by the road in a shallow stone culvert, and half in the water lay something that looked, in the dusk, like a pile a clothes—or was it the body of the child? Mrs. Travers was out of the car in a flash, but her husband was quicker.

"Don't touch her, Emily!" he said sharply. "She's been hit. Can't be more than a few minutes. Remember that truck that overtook us half a mile back, speeding like the devil? Here, quick, go into that cottage and phone for an ambulance. The girl's in a bad way. I'll stay here and do what I can to stop the bleeding. Don't waste a minute."

Doctors are expert at stopping dangerous bleeding, for they know the right places to press. This Dr. Travers was able to do, but he didn't dare do more; the girl was lying in a queerly crumpled heap, and he guessed she had a number of bones broken and that it would be highly dangerous to move her. He watched her with great concentration, wondering where the truck had got to and what other damage it had done.

Mrs. Travers was very quick. She had seen plenty of accident cases and knew the importance of speed. The first cottage she tried had a phone; in four minutes she was back, and in six an ambulance was wailing down the hill.

Its attendants lifted the child onto a stretcher as carefully as if she were made of fine thistledown. The ambulance sped off to Plymouth—for the local cottage hospital did not take serious accident cases—and Dr. Travers went down to the police station to report what he had done.

He found that the police already knew about the speeding truck—which had suffered from loss of brakes and ended up with its radiator halfway through the post-office wall. The driver was concussed and shocked, but the police thought he was the only person injured—until Dr. Travers told his tale.

At half-past nine that night Aunt Rebecca

Hoskins was sitting by her fire thinking aggrieved thoughts about the inconsiderateness of nieces who were asked to supper and never turned up, when she was startled by a neighbor, who burst in, exclaiming, "Have you heard about Sandy Pengelly, then, Mrs. Hoskins? Terrible thing, poor little soul, and they don't know if she's likely to live. Police have got the truck driver that hit her—ah, it didn't ought to be allowed, speeding through the place like that at umpty miles an hour, they ought to jail him for life—not that that'd be any comfort for poor Bert and Jean."

Horrified, Aunt Rebecca put on a coat and went down to her brother's house. She found the family with white shocked faces; Bert and Jean were about to drive off to the hospital where Sandy had been taken, and the twins were crying bitterly. Lob was nowhere to be seen. But Aunt Rebecca was not interested in dogs; she did not inquire about him.

"Thank the Lord you've come, Beck," said her brother. "Will you stay the night with Don and the twins? Don's out looking for Lob and heaven knows when we'll be back; we may get a bed with Jean's mother in Plymouth."

"Oh, if only I'd never invited the poor child," wailed Mrs. Hoskins. But Bert and Jean hardly heard her.

That night seemed to last forever. The twins cried themselves to sleep. Don came home very late and grim-faced. Bert and Jean sat in a waiting room of the Western Counties Hospital, but Sandy was unconscious, they were told, and she remained so. All that could be done for her was done. She was given transfusions to replace all the blood she had lost. The broken bones were set and put in slings and cradles.

"Is she a healthy girl? Has she a good constitution?" the emergency doctor asked.

"Aye, doctor, she is that," Bert said hoarsely. The lump in Jean's throat prevented her from answering; she merely nodded.

"Then she ought to have a chance. But I won't conceal from you that her condition is very serious, unless she shows signs of coming out from this coma."

But as hour succeeded hour, Sandy showed no signs of recovering consciousness. Her parents sat in the waiting room with haggard faces; sometimes one of them would go to telephone the family at home, or to try to get a little sleep at the home of Granny Pearce, not far away.

At noon next day Dr. and Mrs. Travers went to the Pengelly cottage to inquire how Sandy was doing, but the report was gloomy: "Still in a very serious condition." The twins were miserably unhappy. They forgot that they had sometimes called their elder sister bossy and only remembered how often she had shared her pocket money with them, how she read to them and took them for picnics and helped with their homework. Now there was no Sandy, no Mother and Dad, Don went around with a gray, shuttered face, and worse still, there was no Lob.

The Western Counties Hospital is a large one, with dozens of different departments and five or six connected buildings, each with three or four entrances. By that afternoon it became noticeable that a dog seemed to have taken up position outside the hospital, with the fixed intention of getting in. Patiently he would try first one entrance and then another, all the way around, and then begin again. Sometimes he would get a little way inside, following a visitor, but animals were, of course, forbidden, and he was always kindly but

◆ **Build Vocabulary**

aggrieved (ə grēvd´) *adj.*: Offended; wronged

◀ **Critical Viewing** What elements of danger do you see in this picture? **[Analyze]**

firmly turned out again. Sometimes the guard at the main entrance gave him a pat or offered him a bit of sandwich—he looked so wet and beseeching and desperate. But he never ate the sandwich. No one seemed to own him or to know where he came from; Plymouth is a large city and he might have belonged to anybody.

At tea time Granny Pearce came through the pouring rain to bring a flask of hot tea with brandy in it to her daughter and son-in-law. Just as she reached the main entrance the guard was gently but forcibly shoving out a large, agitated, soaking-wet Alsatian dog.

"No, old fellow, you can *not* come in. Hospitals are for people, not for dogs."

"Why, bless me," exclaimed old Mrs. Pearce. "That's Lob! Here, Lob, Lobby boy!"

Lob ran to her, whining. Mrs. Pearce walked up to the desk.

"I'm sorry, madam, you can't bring that dog in here," the guard said.

Mrs. Pearce was a very determined old lady. She looked the porter in the eye.

"Now, see here, young man. That dog has walked twenty miles from St. Killan to get to my granddaughter. Heaven knows how he knew she was here, but it's plain he knows. And he ought to have his rights! He ought to get to see her! Do you know," she went on, bristling, "that dog has walked the length of England—*twice*—to be with that girl? And you think you can keep him out with your fiddling rules and regulations?"

"I'll have to ask the medical officer," the guard said weakly.

"You do that, young man." Granny Pearce sat down in a determined manner, shutting her umbrella, and Lob sat patiently dripping at her feet. Every now and then he shook his head, as if to dislodge something heavy that was tied around his neck.

"It's strictly against every rule . . ."

Presently a tired, thin, intelligent-looking man in a white coat came downstairs, with an impressive, silver-haired man in a dark suit, and there was a low-voiced discussion. Granny Pearce eyed them, biding her time.

"Frankly. . . not much to lose," said the older man. The man in the white coat approached Granny Pearce.

"It's strictly against every rule, but as it's such a serious case we are making an exception," he said to her quietly. "But only *outside* her bedroom door—and only for a moment or two."

Without a word, Granny Pearce rose and stumped upstairs. Lob followed close to her skirts, as if he knew his hope lay with her.

They waited in the green-floored corridor outside Sandy's room. The door was half shut. Bert and Jean were inside. Everything was terribly quiet. A nurse came out. The white-coated man asked her something and she shook her head. She had left the door ajar and through it could now be seen a high, narrow bed with a lot of gadgets around it. Sandy lay there, very flat under the covers, very still. Her head was turned away. All Lob's attention was riveted on the bed. He strained toward it, but Granny Pearce clasped his collar firmly.

"I've done a lot for you, my boy, now you behave yourself," she whispered grimly. Lob let out a faint whine, anxious and pleading.

At the sound of that whine Sandy stirred just a little. She sighed and moved her head the least fraction. Lob whined again. And then Sandy turned her head right over. Her eyes opened, looking at the door.

"Lob?" she murmured—no more than a breath of sound. "Lobby, boy?"

The doctor by Granny Pearce drew a quick, sharp breath. Sandy moved her left arm—the one that was not broken—from below the covers and let her hand dangle down, feeling,

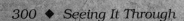

as she always did in the mornings, for Lob's furry head. The doctor nodded slowly.

"All right," he whispered. "Let him go to the bedside. But keep a hold of him."

Granny Pearce and Lob moved to the bedside. Now she could see Bert and Jean, white-faced and shocked, on the far side of the bed. But she didn't look at them. She looked at the smile on her granddaughter's face as the groping fingers found Lob's wet ears and gently pulled them. "Good boy," whispered Sandy, and fell asleep again.

Granny Pearce led Lob out into the passage again. There she let go of him and he ran off swiftly down the stairs. She would have followed him, but Bert and Jean had come out into the passage, and she spoke to Bert fiercely.

"*I* don't know why you were so foolish as not to bring the dog before! Leaving him to find the way here himself—"

"But, Mother!" said Jean Pengelly. "That can't have been Lob. What a chance to take! Suppose Sandy hadn't—" She stopped, with her handkerchief pressed to her mouth.

"Not Lob? I've known that dog nine years! I suppose I ought to know my own granddaughter's dog?"

"Listen, Mother," said Bert. "Lob was killed by the same truck that hit Sandy. Don found him—when he went to look for Sandy's schoolbag. He was—he was dead. Ribs all smashed. No question of that. Don told me on the phone—he and Will Hoskins rowed a half mile out to sea and sank the dog with a lump of concrete tied to his collar. Poor old boy. Still—he was getting on. Couldn't have lasted forever."

"*Sank him at sea?* Then what—?"

Slowly old Mrs. Pearce, and then the other two, turned to look at the trail of dripping-wet footprints that led down the hospital stairs.

In the Pengellys' garden they have a stone, under the palm tree. It says: "Lob. Sandy's dog. Buried at sea."

Guide for Responding

◆ LITERATURE AND YOUR LIFE

Reader's Response Would you have ended this story differently than the writer did? Why or why not?

Thematic Focus In what way does Lob achieve a triumph?

Journal Writing Write a journal entry about a pet you have had or would like to have.

☑ Check Your Comprehension

1. Briefly describe the events that lead up to the Pengellys' adopting Lob.
2. What happens when Sandy goes to visit her aunt?
3. How does Sandy's grandmother get Lob into the hospital room?

◆ Critical Thinking

INTERPRET

1. Why does Lob travel more than 400 miles to be with Sandy? **[Draw Conclusions]**
2. How do you think Mr. Dodsworth might have felt when Lob chose Sandy? **[Speculate]**
3. Why does hearing Lob's whine help Sandy wake up? **[Infer]**
4. What does Lob's mysterious return at the end suggest about his bond with Sandy? **[Interpret]**

APPLY

5. Why do you think that people and their pets become so attached to each other? **[Relate]**

EXTEND

6. What are some good jobs for people who like animals? **[Career Link]**

The Tiger Who Would Be King

James Thurber

One morning the tiger woke up in the jungle and told his mate that he was king of beasts.

"Leo, the lion, is king of beasts," she said.

"We need a change," said the tiger. "The creatures are crying for a change."

The tigress listened but she could hear no crying, except that of her cubs.

"I'll be king of beasts by the time the moon rises," said the tiger. "It will be a yellow moon with black stripes, in my honor."

"Oh, sure," said the tigress as she went to look after her young, one of whom, a male, very like his father, had got an imaginary thorn in his paw.

The tiger prowled through the jungle till he came to the lion's den. "Come out," he roared, "and greet the king of beasts! The king is dead, long live the king!"

Inside the den, the lioness woke her mate. "The king is here to see you," she said.

"What king?" he inquired, sleepily.

"The king of beasts," she said.

"I am the king of beasts," roared Leo, and he charged out of the den to defend his crown against the pretender.

It was a terrible fight, and it lasted until the setting of the sun. All the animals of the jungle joined in, some taking the side of the tiger and others the side of the lion. Every creature from the aardvark to the zebra took part in the struggle to overthrow the lion or to repulse the tiger, and some did not know which they were fighting for, and some fought for both, and some fought whoever was nearest, and some fought for the sake of fighting.

"What are we fighting for?" someone asked the aardvark.

"The old order," said the aardvark.

"What are we dying for?" someone asked the zebra.

"The new order," said the zebra.

When the moon rose, fevered and gibbous,[1] it shone upon a jungle in which nothing stirred except a macaw[2] and a cockatoo,[3] screaming in horror. All the beasts were dead except the tiger, and his days were numbered and his time was ticking away. He was monarch of all he surveyed, but it didn't seem to mean anything.

MORAL: You can't very well be king of beasts if there aren't any.

◆ **Build Vocabulary**

prowled (prould) *v.*: Crawled quietly and secretly

repulse (ri puls´) *v.*: Drive back; repel an attack

slanderous (slan´ der əs) *adj.*: Untrue and damaging

---

1. **gibbous** (gib´ əs) *adj.*: More than half but less than completely illuminated.
2. **macaw** (mə kô´) *n.*: Large parrot of Central or South America with bright colors and a harsh voice.
3. **cockatoo** (käk´ ə tōō´) *n.*: Crested parrot with white plumage tinged with yellow or pink.

The Lion and the Bulls Aesop

A lion often prowled about a pasture where three bulls grazed together. He had tried without success to lure one or the other of them to the edge of the pasture. He had even attempted a direct attack, only to see them form a ring so that from whatever direction he approached he was met by the horns of one of them.

Then a plan began to form in the lion's mind. Secretly he started spreading evil and <u>slanderous</u> reports of one bull against the other. The three bulls, distrustingly, began to avoid one another, and each withdrew to a different part of the pasture to graze. Of course, this was exactly what the lion wanted. One by one he fell upon the bulls, and so made easy prey of them all.

MORAL: United we stand; divided we fall.

Beyond Literature

Cultural Connection

Animal Names for Sports Teams
The writers of fables use animals to represent particular qualities. Sports teams also use animals to represent qualities, such as power or ferocity. Some teams, such as the Miami Dolphins and the University of Texas Longhorns, choose animals that live in the state or the region where the team plays.

Cross-Curricular Activity
Map of Animal Names Find at least one team (professional or college) with an animal name from each of ten states in the United States. Show the names on a map of the United States. Explain whether the animal is native to the state or if it represents a quality.

Guide for Responding

◆ LITERATURE AND YOUR LIFE

Reader's Response Which story do you think teaches a more important lesson?

Thematic Focus Do you think people learn more from their struggles or their triumphs?

Journal Writing Write a paragraph explaining what one of these fables means to you.

☑ Check Your Comprehension

1. Which two animals fight to rule in "The Tiger Who Would Be King"?
2. What is the result of the battle?
3. How does the lion in "The Lion and the Bulls" get the bulls to separate?

◆ Critical Thinking

INTERPRET
1. Some of the animals in "The Tiger Who Would Be King" fought for the sake of fighting. What does this fact suggest about the animals in the jungle? **[Interpret]**
2. What qualities of humans do Thurber and Aesop show in the animals? **[Analyze]**

APPLY
3. Is an animal fable more or less effective than one with human characters? Explain. **[Assess]**

COMPARE LITERARY WORKS
4. In what way is the moral of "The Lion and the Bulls" demonstrated in "Lob's Girl"? **[Apply]**

Guide for Responding (continued)

◆ Reading Strategy

COMPARE AND CONTRAST CHARACTERS

By **comparing and contrasting characters,** you improve your understanding of their personalities and actions.

1. In "Lob's Girl," in what ways are Sandy and Mr. Dodsworth similar and different?
2. Identify the ways in which the actions of the animals in "The Tiger Who Would Be King" are similar to and different from the actions of the bulls in "The Lion and the Bulls."

◆ Build Vocabulary

USING FORMS OF *decide*

Copy the following sentences on your paper. Fill in each blank with a form of *decide: decide, decision, decisively.*

1. Mr. Dodsworth spoke _____?_____ .
2. He had made his _____?_____ .
3. Now, Mr. Pengelly had to _____?_____ what to do.

SPELLING STRATEGY

When spelling words like *aggrieved, in* which *i* and *e* appear together, remember this rule: Use *i* before *e* except after *c* or when sounded like *a,* as in *neighbor* and *weigh.* On your paper, unscramble the letters to make words.

1. fethi   2. frige   3. lefid   4. ferind   5. lesigh

USING THE WORD BANK

On your paper, answer each of the following questions about the Word Bank.

1. Which three words name or describe unpleasant feelings or ideas?
2. Which two words indicate determined actions?
3. Which word might be the action of a person who is sorry?
4. Which word might be the action of a person with a secret?
5. Which word describes the action of a sneaky character?
6. Which word might be the action of someone defending himself or herself from attack?

◆ Literary Focus

FORESHADOWING

As you read these stories, you may have guessed what was coming. The author's use of hints that suggest what is to come is called **foreshadowing.**

1. In "Lob's Girl," what statement does the author make about the road to the village that gives a hint of an upcoming accident?
2. When Lob arrives at the hospital, he shakes his head as if to shake off something heavy. What does this mysterious detail foreshadow?
3. In "The Tiger Who Would Be King," what statement by the tiger foreshadows his hollow victory?

◆ Build Grammar Skills

PREPOSITIONAL PHRASES

A **prepositional phrase** is a group of words beginning with a preposition and ending with a noun or a pronoun. The preposition is a word like *on, between,* or *from* that shows a relationship; the noun or pronoun in the phrase is called the object of the preposition.

For example, Aiken writes "The whole family was playing cards by the fire...." *By the fire* is a prepositional phrase, introduced by the preposition *by.* The object of the preposition is *fire.*

Practice On your paper, write the prepositional phrase in each sentence. Circle the preposition. Underline the object of the preposition.

1. The tiger woke up in the jungle.
2. Greet the king of beasts!
3. Some animals fought for the tiger.
4. A plan formed in the lion's mind.
5. He fell upon the bulls.

Writing Application On your paper, complete each sentence by adding a prepositional phrase. Begin the phrase with the preposition indicated.

1. One bull stood (between)
2. They were not safe (from)
3. They didn't know (about)

Build Your Portfolio

 Idea Bank

Writing

1. **Suggestion** Write a suggestion for a peaceful way that the animals of the jungle could decide who will rule.

2. **Article** Write a newspaper article about the events at the end of "Lob's Girl." Include in your report accounts of the accident and the mysterious sighting of Lob. **[Media Link]**

3. **Speech** Write a speech based on the message of either "The Tiger Who Would Be King" or "The Lion and the Bulls." In your speech, use a summary of the tale to illustrate your point.

Speaking and Listening

4. **Storytelling** Practice telling either "The Lion and the Bulls" or "The Tiger . . ." aloud. Use your voice, gestures, and specific details to make your delivery interesting. Perform your story for the class. **[Performing Arts Link]**

5. **Skit [Group Activity]** With a group, prepare a skit of "The Tiger Who Would Be King" or "The Lion and the Bulls." Divide the following tasks: preparing dialogue, making simple costumes or masks, acting, directing the action. **[Performing Arts Link]**

Projects

6. **Big-Cat Chart** Create a chart comparing characteristics of lions and tigers. Include information about their diet, top speed, time of activity, number of offspring, and group behavior. **[Science Link]**

7. **Storyboards** Illustrate the action of one of these stories in a series of storyboards. You can draw complete scenes or create stick figures to show the action. Write a caption for each storyboard. **[Art Link]**

 Writing Mini-Lesson

Fable

"The Tiger Who Would Be King" and "The Lion and the Bulls" are fables—brief tales that teach a lesson. Write a fable of your own. Use animal characters and imaginary situations in your fable.

Writing Skills Focus: Support Points With Examples

The moral, or lesson, you want to teach is the point of your fable. **Support your point with examples** in the fable.

Model From the Fable
Moral: United we stand; divided we fall.
Example: One by one he fell upon the bulls, and so made easy prey of them all.

Prewriting Use an organizer like the one below to set up your characters and situation.

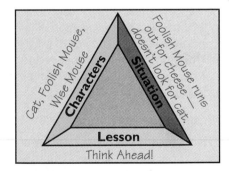

Drafting Build up to the moral of your fable by describing the events that illustrate the lesson. Write the moral at the end.

Revising Ask a partner whether the events you use support your point. Use his or her suggestions when you revise.

> ◆ **Grammar Application**
> Identify the prepositional phrases you have used in your fable.

Guide for Reading

Meet the Authors:

Maya Angelou (1928–)

Maya Angelou may have changed her childhood name, but she has never forgotten her childhood. Born Marguerite Johnson in St. Louis, Missouri, the adult Maya Angelou recalls the events and difficulties of her past in her autobiography, *I Know Why the Caged Bird Sings*. In "Life Doesn't Frighten Me," she explores the worries and concerns that a young person conquers as she moves toward adulthood.

Carl Sandburg (1878–1967)

Although he won the Pulitzer Prize for his six-volume biography of Abraham Lincoln, Carl Sandburg is best known as a "poet of the people." His jobs as a milk delivery boy, a house painter, and a newspaper reporter helped him capture in his poetry the thoughts, feelings, and experiences of everyday life. In "Arithmetic," he humorously communicates a frustration with which many students can probably identify.

May Swenson (1919–1989)

Raised and educated in Utah, May Swenson, like many poets in the second half of the twentieth century, earned a living as an editor and a teacher. She believed that poetry arises from a common desire to get through "the curtain of things as they *appear*, to things as they *are*." Her poem "Was Worm" is an example of that belief.

◆ LITERATURE AND YOUR LIFE

CONNECT YOUR EXPERIENCE

When you were little, you were probably afraid of some things that no longer frighten you. When you started school, you may have thought simple addition was very difficult—but now you use addition to work on more complicated math concepts. What once seemed like a challenge to you has now become very ordinary. These poems explore some of life's ordinary, but still challenging, struggles.

THEMATIC FOCUS: Struggles and Triumphs

Think about how the struggle described in each of these poems leads to a triumph.

◆ Background for Understanding

SCIENCE

A change in someone's personality is sometimes described as a metamorphosis. In science, this word indicates a specific type of change: a change in form, structure, or function. A caterpillar's change from a "worm" into a cocoon and then into a butterfly is a metamorphosis.

◆ Build Vocabulary

COLOR WORDS

May Swenson uses the word *saffron* to indicate the color of a butterfly's wings. The color *saffron* comes from the saffron flower, which has a bright yellow-orange center. Other color names that come from things in nature are *jade* (medium green), *ebony* (rich black), and *ocher* (pale yellow).

WORD BANK

Which word names something you could make from many little pieces of construction paper?

mosaic
saffron
weaned
metamorphosis

Life Doesn't Frighten Me
◆ Arithmetic ◆
Was Worm

◆ Literary Focus

RHYTHM

Rhythm is the sound pattern created by stressed and unstressed syllables. Stressed syllables receive more emphasis than unstressed syllables. The stressed syllables are underlined in the following lines from "Life Doesn't Frighten Me."

Shadows <u>on</u> the <u>wall</u>
Noises <u>down</u> the <u>hall</u>

The rhythm created by the pattern of stressed and unstressed syllables gives a poem a musical quality.

◆ Reading Strategy

INTERPRET POETRY

You can change a poem from a simple pattern of words and sounds into a meaningful message. To do this, you **interpret** it: You explain the meaning or significance of the poem. Ask yourself questions like the ones shown on the organizer below, to interpret each of these poems.

What does the title mean?

What emotions are described?

What connections do I make?

What scenes and events are described?

Life Doesn't Frighten Me

Maya Angelou

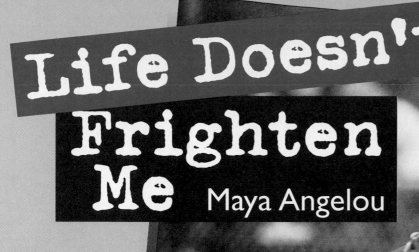

Critical Viewing ▶
Identify the details of this picture that indicate the girl is confident and determined. **[Compare and Contrast]**

Shadows on the wall
Noises down the hall
Life doesn't frighten me at all
Bad dogs barking loud
5   Big ghosts in a cloud
Life doesn't frighten me at all.

Mean old Mother Goose
Lions on the loose
They don't frighten me at all
10 Dragons breathing flame
On my counterpane[1]
That doesn't frighten me at all.

I go boo
Make them shoo
15 I make fun
Way they run
I won't cry
So they fly
I just smile
20 They go wild
Life doesn't frighten me at all.

Tough guys in a fight
All alone at night
Life doesn't frighten me at all.

25 Panthers in the park
Strangers in the dark
No, they don't frighten me at all.

That new classroom where
Boys all pull my hair
30 (Kissy little girls
With their hair in curls)
They don't frighten me at all.

Don't show me frogs and snakes
And listen for my scream,
35 If I'm afraid at all
It's only in my dreams.

I've got a magic charm
That I keep up my sleeve,
I can walk the ocean floor
40 And never have to breathe.

Life doesn't frighten me at all
Not at all
Not at all.
Life doesn't frighten me at all.

---

1. **counterpane:** Bedspread.

Arithmetic

Carl Sandburg

Arithmetic is where numbers fly like pigeons in and out of
    your head.
Arithmetic tells you how many you lose or win if you know
    how many you had before you lost or won.
5   Arithmetic is seven eleven all good children go to heaven—or
    five six bundle of sticks.[1]
Arithmetic is numbers you squeeze from your head to your
    hand to your pencil to your paper till you get the answer.
Arithmetic is where the answer is right and everything is nice
10   and you can look out of the window and see the blue sky—
    or the answer is wrong and you have to start all over and
    try again and see how it comes out this time.
If you take a number and double it and double it again and
    then double it a few more times, the number gets bigger
15   and bigger and goes higher and higher and only arithme-
    tic can tell you what the number is when you decide to
    quit doubling.
Arithmetic is where you have to multiply—and you carry the
    multiplication table in your head and hope you won't lose it.
20   If you have two animal crackers, one good and one bad, and
    you eat one and a striped zebra with streaks all over him
    eats the other, how many animal crackers will you have if
    somebody offers you five six seven and you say No no no
    and you say Nay nay nay and you say Nix nix nix?
25   If you ask your mother for one fried egg for breakfast and she
    gives you two fried eggs and you eat both of them, who is
    better in arithmetic, you or your mother?

**1. seven eleven
. . . bundle of
sticks:** This line is
a reference to
children's counting
rhymes.

Beyond Literature

Math Connection

Calculators Old and New Electronic
calculators have been in use for fewer
than fifty years, but another kind of
calculator—the abacus—has been
around since the ancient Greeks. An
abacus is a frame containing rows of
beads, used to perform calculations.

Cross-Curricular Activity
Explain the history and demonstrate the use of an abacus.
Show how the beads are used
to add, subtract, multiply,
and divide.

Was Worm

May Swenson

Was worm
swaddled in white

Now tiny queen
in sequin coat
5   peacockbright
drinks the wind
and feeds
on sweat of the leaves

Is little chinks
10 of mosaic floating
or a scatter
of colored beads

Alighting pokes
with her new black wire
15 the saffron yokes

On silent hinges
openfolds her wings'
applauding hands

Weaned
20 from coddling white
to lakedeep air
to blue and green

Is queen

Critical Viewing ▶
Why does the poet
describe the butterfly
as a queen? [Interpret]

◆ **Build Vocabulary**

mosaic (mō zā′ ik) *n.*: Colorful picture or design made
from small pieces of glass, stone, tile, or other material

saffron (saf′ rən) *adj.*: Orange-yellow

weaned (wēnd) *adj.*: Brought away from; outgrown

metamorphosis (met′ ə môr′ fə sis) *n.*: Change of form,
shape, or substance

May Swenson describes the change from caterpillar into butterfly as a beautiful triumph. Cartoonist Gary Larson creates grim humor by taking a different view of the caterpillar's struggle. In his popular cartoons from *The Far Side*, Larson often presents a unique look at a subject or a situation.

1. In what ways is this cartoon similar to and different from the poem "Was Worm"?
2. In what way does the end of this cartoon show a metamorphosis?
3. Do you think this cartoon is funny? Point out specific details to support your answer.

Metamorphosis
Gary Larson

Guide for Responding

◆ LITERATURE AND YOUR LIFE

Reader's Response Which of these poems do you find most hopeful? Why?

Thematic Focus In what ways does each of these poems show a struggle and a triumph?

☑ Check Your Comprehension

1. Name three things that don't frighten the speaker of "Life Doesn't Frighten Me."
2. According to Sandburg, what happens when your arithmetic answer is right? What happens when your answer is wrong?
3. What colors appear in "Was Worm"? What do the colors describe?

◆ Critical Thinking

INTERPRET

1. In "Life Doesn't Frighten Me," why does the speaker smile at frightening things? **[Infer]**
2. In "Arithmetic," what are the speaker's feelings about math? **[Synthesize]**
3. In "Was Worm," how is the butterfly different from the "worm"? **[Contrast]**

APPLY

4. How would you use one of these poems to cheer someone who is discouraged? **[Relate]**

COMPARE LITERARY WORKS

5. Compare the different attitudes of the speakers in these poems. **[Compare and Contrast]**

Guide for Responding (continued)

◆ Reading Strategy

INTERPRET POETRY

When you **interpret,** you explain the meaning or significance of something. For example, you can interpret the first few lines of "Arithmetic" as saying that the speaker finds arithmetic confusing.

1. In "Life Doesn't Frighten Me," how do you interpret lines 7–12?
2. What is your interpretation of the question that ends the poem "Arithmetic"?
3. Interpret these lines from "Was Worm": "Weaned/from coddling white/to lakedeep air."

◆ Build Vocabulary

USING COLOR WORDS

On your paper, describe each color and explain what in nature is the source of each color word.

1. jade   2. ocher   3. ebony
4. amethyst 5. sienna   6. turquoise

SPELLING STRATEGY

When spelling words that contain consonant blends, such as *saffron,* pronounce the word carefully before writing it to make sure you include all the letters in the blend. Write the complete word that goes with each clue below. Pronounce the word before writing it.

1. multi_ _ication (two times two)
2. con_ _ _uction (building)
3. de_ _ _ibe (tell the details of)

USING THE WORD BANK

On your paper, complete each sentence with the Word Bank word that makes the most sense.

1. The puppies were old enough to be ___?___ from their mother.
2. The tadpole's ___?___ into a frog took a long time.
3. They painted the walls ___?___.
4. The artist created a beautiful ___?___ from the multicolored tiles.

◆ Literary Focus

RHYTHM

The sound pattern of stressed and unstressed syllables in a poem forms its **rhythm.**

1. Write out lines 4–6 of "Life Doesn't Frighten Me," and underline the stressed syllables.
2. Is the rhythm of "Arithmetic" a steady beat? Explain.
3. Read "Was Worm" aloud with a partner. Experiment by stressing different syllables until you find the best rhythm. Then, read the poem to the class.

◆ Build Grammar Skills

ADJECTIVE AND ADVERB PHRASES

A prepositional phrase is a group of words that begins with a preposition and ends with a noun or a pronoun. There are two types of prepositional phrases: **adjective phrases** and **adverb phrases.**

	Adjective	**Adverb**
Modifies:	Noun or Pronoun	Verb, adjective, or adverb
Answers the questions:	What kind? Which one? How many? How much?	How? When? Where? In what way?

Adjective Phrase: tiny queen *in sequin coat* (*Which* queen?)

Adverb Phrase: numbers fly *like pigeons* (*In what way* do numbers fly?)

Practice On your paper, identify the prepositional phrases, and tell whether each phrase is an adjective or adverb and which word it modifies.

1. Panthers in the park
2. Shadows on the wall
3. . . . numbers you squeeze from your head . . .
4. swaddled in white
5. a scatter/of colored beads

Writing Application On your paper, fill in each blank with an adjective or adverb phrase. Identify the kind of phrase you've used.

The caterpillar sat ___?___ . The color ___?___ was green. He was afraid ___?___ .

Build Your Portfolio

 ## Idea Bank

Writing

1. **List Poem** Make a list of things that don't frighten you in a particular area, such as school or sports. Use your list to write a poem like "Life Doesn't Frighten Me."

2. **Nature Description** In "Was Worm," May Swenson describes something she observed in nature. Describe something in nature that you've observed.

3. **School Poem** Carl Sandburg complains about math in a poem. Write a poem about your least favorite school subject. Create humorous images as Sandburg does in "Arithmetic."

Speaking and Listening

4. **Classroom Riddles** May Swenson describes a cocoon and a butterfly without ever using those words. Describe something in your classroom, one clue at a time, without naming the thing. Allow classmates to guess after each clue. Keep a list of the clues.

5. **Group Discussion** With a group, share your likes and dislikes about different school subjects. People who like a particular subject can give helpful hints on how to enjoy the subject. Identify three main ideas discussed and write them down.

Projects

6. **Math Survey** Develop three to five survey questions about math. Conduct your survey among your classmates. Show the results in a bar graph on a poster. **[Math Link]**

7. **Anthology [Group Activity]** Create an anthology, or collection, of literature related to science or math. You can start with "Arithmetic" or "Was Worm." Group members can choose literature, illustrate or find pictures, organize the works, or write introductions. **[Math Link; Science Link]**

 ## Writing Mini-Lesson

Explanation of a Change

In "Was Worm," May Swenson describes a change she observes but does not explain how it happens. Choose a change, such as a caterpillar's metamorphosis into a butterfly, and explain how it happens.

Writing Skills Focus: Word Choice

In "Was Worm," May Swenson uses the words *worm* and *queen*. The words Swenson chooses show a more dramatic contrast than do the words *cocoon* and *butterfly*. List the qualities of your subject before the change and after. Then, choose words that show these qualities. The butterfly shows the many qualities communicated by the single word "queen."

Prewriting List the individual events that lead up to the change. Number them in order.

Drafting Write complete sentences about what happens first, next, and last. Use your list to make sure you don't leave out a step in the change.

> ◆ **Grammar Application**
> Use adjective and adverb phrases to add details to your explanation.

Revising Read your explanation aloud to a partner. Have the partner help you identify words that make the explanation clear. Substitute new words for those that are not clear.

CONNECTING LITERATURE TO SOCIAL STUDIES
CHINA
The Friends of Kwan Ming *by Paul Yee*

THE WORLD'S LONGEST WALL A wall is more than plaster or a heap of stones. Walls work hard to keep the outside out and the inside in. They make guests feel cozy and warn off strangers.

The world's longest wall stands in China. The first emperor, Shi Huangdi, began building it in 214 B.C. Stretching for 4,000 miles, the Great Wall of China protected the country from invading northern tribes.

Within the Wall Inside Shi's Great Wall, emperors ruled for 2,000 years. Chinese culture prospered. Silk cloth, the compass, and gunpowder were invented in China. Craftspeople made beautiful vases. Artists, handling brushes like musical instruments, painted graceful landscapes. Europeans visited occasionally, as Marco Polo did in 1275. For centuries, though, China restricted the activity of visitors to the country.

The Wall Begins to Crumble China's walls could not hold out change forever. In the 1800's, nations, such as Great Britain, forced China to accept more trade. A few Chinese grew rich. Most were poor, however, and many resented the foreigners. Rebellions broke out beginning in the 1850's. In 1912, the rule of the emperors ended.

Crossing the Wall During the troubled 1850's, young men often left China to find a better life. Like Kwan Ming and his friends in Paul Yee's story, thousands sailed from China to San Francisco, California, and to British Columbia, Canada. Though no walls of stone surrounded these places, the immigrants discovered other walls blocking their way—low pay, inhuman work hours, and other unfair treatment. Despite these obstacles, many succeeded in building a new life.

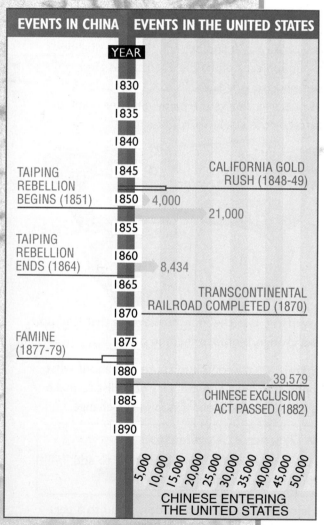

EVENTS IN CHINA	EVENTS IN THE UNITED STATES
	YEAR
	1830
	1835
	1840
TAIPING REBELLION BEGINS (1851)	1845 CALIFORNIA GOLD RUSH (1848-49)
	1850 4,000
	21,000
	1855
TAIPING REBELLION ENDS (1864)	1860
	8,434
	1865
	TRANSCONTINENTAL RAILROAD COMPLETED (1870)
	1870
FAMINE (1877-79)	1875
	1880
	39,579
	CHINESE EXCLUSION ACT PASSED (1882)
	1885
	1890

5,000 10,000 15,000 20,000 25,000 30,000 35,000 40,000 45,000 50,000

CHINESE ENTERING THE UNITED STATES

The Friends of Kwan Ming

Paul Yee

Simon Ng, Simon & Schuster

▲ **Critical Viewing** What details in this picture suggest that Kwan Ming and his friends will meet some unusual people in the "new world"? **[Analyze]**

When his father died, the peasant Kwan Ming was forced to sell his little plot of paddy[1] and the old family house to pay for the burial. After the funeral, Kwan Ming looked around at the banana trees surrounding his village, and saw that he had nothing left to his name—not even one chipped roof tile. He had just enough money to buy a steamship ticket to the New World, where he had heard jobs were plentiful.

"I can start a new life there," he told his mother. "I will send money home."

The voyage lasted six weeks, over rocky waves and through screaming storms. Kwan Ming huddled together with hundreds of other Chinese deep in the ship's hold.[2] There he became fast friends with Chew Lap, Tam Yim

and Wong Foon—men from neighboring villages. If one friend took sick, the others fetched him food and water. If one friend had bad luck gambling, the others lent him money to recover his losses. Together the three men ate, told jokes, and shared their dreams for the future.

When they arrived in the New World, everyone scattered throughout the port city to search for work. Kwan Ming hurried to the warehouse district, to the train station, and to the waterfront, but doors slammed in his face because he was Chinese. So he went to every store and laundry in Chinatown, and to every farm outside town. But there was not a job to be found anywhere, for there were too many men looking for work in a country that was

---

1. **paddy** (pad′ ē) *n.*: Rice field.
2. **ship's hold:** Inside of the ship, under the decks, where cargo is usually carried.

▲ **Critical Viewing** Why might Kwan Ming and his friends choose to buy their food at this shop? [Speculate]

still too young.

Every night Kwan Ming trudged back to the inn where he was staying with his three friends. Like him, they, too, had been searching for work but had found nothing. Every night, as they ate their <u>meager</u> meal of rice dotted with soya sauce, the friends shared information about the places they had visited and the people they had met. And every night Kwan Ming worried more and more about his mother, and how she was faring.

"If I don't find work soon, I'm going back to China," Chew Lap declared one evening.

Connecting Literature to Social Studies
How does the life the immigrants find in the New World compare to their expectations?

"What for, fool?" asked Tam Yim. "Things are worse there!"

"But at least I will be with my family!" retorted Chew Lap.

"Your family needs money for food more than they need your company," Wong Foon commented. "Don't forget that."

Then a knock was heard at the door, and the innkeeper pushed his way into the tiny attic room.

"Good news!" he cried out. "I have found a job for each of you!"

The men leapt eagerly to their feet.

"Three of the jobs are well-paying and decent," announced the innkeeper. "But the fourth job is, well . . ." He coughed sadly.

For the first time since they had met, the four men eyed one another <u>warily</u>, like four hungry cats about to pounce on a bird.

"The biggest bakery in Chinatown needs a worker," said the innkeeper. "You'll always be warm next to the oven. Who will go?"

"You go, Chew Lap," Kwan Ming said firmly. "Your parents are ill and need money for medicine."

"The finest tailor in Chinatown wants an apprentice,"[3] continued the innkeeper. "The man who takes this job will be able to throw away those thin rags you wear."

"That's for you, Tam Yim," declared Kwan Ming. "You have four little ones waiting for food in China."

"The best shoemaker in Chinatown needs an assistant," said the innkeeper. "He pays good wages. Who wants to cut leather and stitch boots?"

"You go, Wong Foon," Kwan Ming stated. "You said the roof of your house in China needs repair. Better get new tiles before the rainy season starts."

"The last job is for a houseboy."[4]

---

3. apprentice (ə pren′ tis) *n.*: Person who agrees to work for a craftsperson for a certain amount of time in exchange for instruction in the craft.
4. houseboy *n.*: Person who cleans and does other tasks for another person. (The word suggests little respect for the person so employed.)

▲ **Critical Viewing** Why do you think some of these men wear traditional Chinese clothing and some do not? [Speculate]

The innkeeper shook his head. The pay is low. The boss owns the biggest mansion in town, but he is also the stingiest man around!"

Kwan Ming had no choice but to take this job, for he knew his mother would be desperate for money. So off he went.

The boss was fatter than a cast-iron stove and as cruel as a blizzard at midnight. Kwan Ming's room was next to the furnace, so black soot and coal dust covered his pillow and blankets. It was difficult to save money, and the servants had to fight over the leftovers for their meals.

Every day Kwan Ming swept and washed every floor in the mansion. He moved the heavy oak tables and rolled up the carpets. The house was so big, that when Kwan Ming finally finished cleaning the last room, the first one was dirty all over again.

Connecting Literature to Social Studies
Why would an immigrant in the 1800's be willing to stay in such an unpleasant job?

One afternoon Kwan Ming was mopping the front porch when his boss came running out. In his hurry, he slipped and crashed down the stairs. Kwan Ming ran over to help, but the fat man turned on him.

"You turtle!" he screamed as his neck purpled and swelled. "You lazy oaf! You door-knob! You rock brain! You're fired!"

Kwan Ming stood silently for a long moment. Then he spoke. "Please, sir, give me another chance. I will work even harder if you let me stay."

The boss listened and his eyes narrowed. Then he coughed loudly. "Very well, Kwan Ming, I won't fire you," he said. "But I will have to punish you, for you have ruined this suit and scuffed my boots and made me miss my dinner."

Kwan Ming nodded miserably.

"Then find me the following things in three days' time!" the boss ordered. "Bring me a fine woolen suit that will never tear. Bring me a pair of leather boots that will never wear out. And bring me forty loaves of bread that will never go stale. Otherwise you are finished here, and I will see that you never find another job!"

Kwan Ming shuddered as he ran off. The old man's demands sounded impossible. Where would he find such items?

In despair, Kwan Ming wandered through the crowded streets of Chinatown. He sat on the raised wooden sidewalk because he had

◆ **Build Vocabulary**

meager (mē′ gər) *adj.*: Small in quantity; very little

retorted (ri tôrt′ əd) *v.*: Replied sharply; came back with

warily (wer′ ə lē) *adv.*: Carefully and cautiously

stingiest (stin′ jē əst) *adj.*: Most unwilling to spend money; cheapest

nowhere else to go.

Suddenly, familiar voices surrounded him.

"Kwan Ming, where have you been?"

"Kwan Ming, how is your job?"

"Kwan Ming, why do you never visit us?"

Kwan Ming looked up and saw his three friends smiling down at him. They pulled him up and pulled him off to the teahouse, where they ate and drank. When Kwan Ming told his friends about his predicament, the men clapped him on the shoulder.

"Don't worry!" exclaimed Tam Yim. "I'll make the woolen suit you need."

"I'll make the boots," added Wong Foon.

"And I'll make the bread," exclaimed Chew Lap.

Three days later, Kwan Ming's friends delivered the goods they had promised. An elegant suit of wool hung over a gleaming pair of leather boots, and forty loaves of fresh-baked bread were lined up in neat rows on the dining-room table.

Kwan Ming's boss waddled into the room and his eyes lit up. He put on the suit, and his eyebrows arched in surprise at how well it fit. Then he sat down and tried on the boots, which slid onto his feet as if they had been buttered.

Then the boss sliced into the bread and started eating. The bread was so soft, so sweet, and so moist that he couldn't stop. Faster and faster he chewed. He ate twelve loaves, then thirteen, then twenty.

The boss's stomach swelled like a circus tent, and his feet bloated out like balloons. But the well-sewn suit and sturdy boots held him tight like a gigantic sausage. The man shouted for help. He tried to stand up, but he couldn't even get out of his chair. He kicked his feet about like a baby throwing a tantrum.

But before anyone could do a thing, there was a shattering *Bang!*

Kwan Ming stared at the chair and blinked his eyes in astonishment. For there was nothing left of his boss.

He had exploded into a million little pieces.

Guide for Responding

◆ LITERATURE AND YOUR LIFE

Reader's Response Do you think Kwan Ming is "too nice"? Explain your answer.

Thematic Focus Name three problems against which Kwan Ming struggles. In what way does he triumph over each?

Journal Writing Write a definition of friendship, based on Kwan Ming's experiences.

☑ Check Your Comprehension

1. Why did Kwan Ming have to leave his home and family?
2. What job does he take?
3. What jobs do his friends take?
4. What goes wrong at his job?
5. In what way is Kwan Ming's problem solved?

◆ Critical Thinking

INTERPRET

1. Why does Kwan Ming allow his friends to take the better jobs? **[Infer]**
2. What do his reasons suggest about his character? **[Analyze]**
3. How does his employer treat him? **[Evaluate]**
4. How does Kwan Ming respond to his employer's treatment of him? **[Interpret]**

APPLY

5. What lesson does the story teach about friendship? **[Relate]**

EXTEND

6. What did you learn from this story about the difficulties faced by nineteenth-century immigrants from China? **[Social Studies Link]**

CONNECTING LITERATURE TO SOCIAL STUDIES

For centuries, China had put walls around itself. In the mid-1800's, though, thousands left China for the United States and Canada. In 1850, there were hardly any Chinese people in California. Two years later, one out of every ten Californians was Chinese. Many of these immigrants worked hard to build the first railroad that crossed the country.

The Chinese faced much unfairness and prejudice. They were sometimes refused work because of their nationality. Those who did find jobs were forced to work for low wages.

In 1882, Congress passed a law called the Chinese Exclusion Act. This law excluded, or barred, most Chinese from entering the United States. Until the law changed in 1945, the law was a wall few could cross.

1. When does the story take place? Explain.
2. Based on the story, what kinds of jobs were open to Chinese immigrants?
3. Kwan Ming's friends help solve his problem. What does this suggest about the way some immigrants handled the difficulties of a new life?

 Idea Bank

Writing

1. **Letter** Write a letter from Kwan Ming to his family back home, describing his experiences while traveling and after arriving in the New World.
2. **Newspaper Ad** Write a want ad in which Kwan Ming and his friends name their qualifications and ask to be hired. **[Career Link]**
3. **Script** Write a scene in which Kwan Ming, looking for a job, explains to an employer that he is a hard worker and deserves a chance.

Projects

4. **Drawing** Draw a picture of Kwan Ming and his four friends, each working at the job he got from the innkeeper. **[Art Link]**

5. **Research** Do research to learn more about two or three of the dynasties (ruling families) that governed China. Using timelines, reproductions of art, and other visual aids, deliver your report to the class.

Speaking and Listening

6. **Dramatic Reading** In a small group, assign roles, including that of narrator, and dramatically read each of the following scenes: the scene in which the innkeeper tells the friends of the four jobs and the one in which Kwan Ming's boss threatens to fire him. **[Performing Arts Link]**

Further Reading, Listening, and Viewing

- Paul Yee's book *Struggle and Hope: The Story of Chinese Canadians* (1996) is a history of the Chinese in Canada.
- Chris and Janie Filstrup's book *China, From Emperors to Communes* (1983) includes facts about Chinese history, art, traditions, and social life.
- The video *China: Ancient Rhythms and Modern Currents* (Video Visits, 1996) compares the customs and culture of ancient and modern China.

Persuasive Message

Writing Process Workshop

The stories of Lou Gehrig, Lob, and Kwan Ming show the importance of loyalty and commitment. Each story sends a **persuasive message** to the reader. Writing that tries to persuade people to adopt a belief, value, or course of action has a persuasive message.

You can send a persuasive message, too. Write a note or letter arguing for a particular choice or viewpoint. Use the following tips, introduced in this section's Writing Mini-Lessons.

Writing Skills Focus

▶ **Build to your main point.** Organize your draft so that early parts lead the way to your major point. (See p. 288.)

▶ **Support points with examples.** The right examples will get your message across clearly. For instance, support the point *you will have more fun if you stay in town* with the example *we can play baseball all day long.* (See p. 305.)

▶ **Consider word choice.** Find the words that will help others see things your way. If you want to persuade your friend not to travel to the Grand Canyon this summer, don't call the trip *an exciting adventure.* Instead, call it *a long, dusty trek.* (See p. 313.)

MODEL FROM LITERATURE

from "Lob's Girl," Joan Aiken

Lob keeps running away from his owner to be with the Pengellys. His owner says:
"That dog has already cost me two days that I can't spare away from my work ① — plus endless time ② in police stations and drafting newspaper advertisements. I'm too old for these ups and downs. I think we'd better face the fact, Mr. Pengelly, that it's your family he wants to stay with—that is, if you want to have him." ③

① These examples support the owner's point—the dog's love of the Pengellys is making him a burden.

② The choice of phrases like "endless time" makes clear that the dog has become a burden.

③ The paragraph leads dramatically to the main point—Lob's owner wants the Pengellys to take Lob.

Prewriting

Choose Your Audience Think of someone to whom you would like to send a persuasive message. It could be a friend or a family member. It could be a character in a short story or on television. Choose someone whose opinions, habits, or plans you would like to change.

Focus on Your Message Identify the main point of your message. Use a chart like the one below to note phrases, examples, and arguments you can use to persuade your audience.

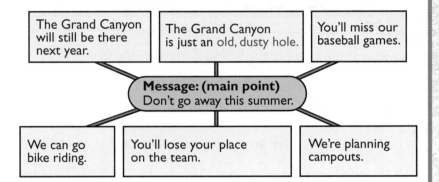

The Grand Canyon will still be there next year.

The Grand Canyon is just an old, dusty hole.

You'll miss our baseball games.

Message: (main point)
Don't go away this summer.

We can go bike riding.

You'll lose your place on the team.

We're planning campouts.

Drafting

Save the Best for Last Save your best argument or most convincing example for the end, where it will have the most impact.

Choose Words to Persuade As you draft, think about the person to whom you are writing. Remember that you are trying to be persuasive. Ask yourself: "Will my reader react better to the phrase 'You will have a lot of fun' or to the phrase 'You will have a stupendous time'? Will I have an easier time selling my bike if I call it 'my old three-speed' or if I call it 'my trusty dirt bike, which I've taken care of for years'?" Choose words and phrases that show the power behind your arguments.

Get to the Main Point As you present arguments and examples, show how each example or fact strengthens your position. Use words such as *in addition to* and *finally* to connect your ideas as you build toward your main point.

APPLYING LANGUAGE SKILLS: Connotations

Two words can mean roughly the same thing and yet have different connations. A word's connotations are the feelings and judgments associated with it.

Positive: His outfit is *classy.*

Neutral: His outfit is in *style.*

Negative: His outfit is *flashy.*

Choose words with the right connotations to add persuasive power to your writing.

Practice Identify the connotation (postive, negative, or neutral) of each underlined word. Replace it with a word of similar meaning but different connotation.

1. She is very <u>skinny</u>.
2. He is a <u>know-it-all</u>.
3. This car is an <u>antique</u>.
4. He lives in a <u>shack</u>.

Writing Application Where appropriate in your message, use words with negative or positive connotations to replace words with neutral connotations.

Writer's Solution Connection Language Lab

For more practice choosing the right words, see the Language Lab unit Choosing Words.

APPLYING LANGUAGE SKILLS: Refer to Yourself Last

When you write a sentence in which you refer to yourself as well as others, put yourself last.

My sister, my brother, and I went to the beach.

He picked Tom, Joe, and **me** for the team.

Practice Correct the order of the series in each sentence.

1. This disagreement upset me, Tom, and Seymour.
2. Life doesn't frighten me or Maya Angelou.
3. On my dream team, Lou Gehrig, I, and Jackie Robinson would play the infield.
4. Cindy, I, and Paula are as loyal to one another as Kwan Ming's friends are to him.

Writing Application If you have referred to yourself and others in your draft, make sure to refer to yourself last.

Writer's Solution Connection
Language Lab

Items in series are punctuated with commas. For practice with commas, complete the Commas lesson in the Language Lab unit Punctuation.

Revising

Use a Checklist As you review your draft, ask yourself:
▶ Have I supported each of my points with clear examples?
▶ Where might a different choice of words add energy and persuasive force?
▶ Can I build to my main point more effectively by adding more information? Should I instead take information out to create more of a surprise?

REVISION MODEL

Dear Ken,

You may think a trip to the Grand Canyon is the best way to
① *"I don't mind missing out on swimming with Joe and Phil," you are thinking. "I won't care if I'm not around for Friday night drives to the ice cream stand," you may say.*
spend your summer vacation. ~~You know, though, that you will~~

~~miss out on swimming.~~ No amount of fun can equal ~~one trip to~~
② *spending summer in the desert.*
~~the Grand Canyon.~~ I did want to mention, though, that Melanie

"Stinky Pinky" DelGrassi will be taking your place as pitcher on
② *that big, dusty hole,*
our baseball team. As you stare across ~~the canyon,~~ I am sure

you will be thinking, "I hope she is bringing the team to victory."

① The writer has added more examples for support. In addition, the writer has found a better way to build toward the main point.
② The writer has chosen new phrases with more persuasive power.

Publishing and Presenting

▶ **E-mail** If the person to whom you are writing has an e-mail account, consider e-mailing your letter to him or her. If you have chosen a fictional character, you might send your e-mail to the writer or producer responsible for the character.

Strategies for Success

The world is humming with persuasive messages. Television commercials, billboards, and advertising mail are just a few forms these messages take. These messages try to shape what we buy, think, or do. It is important to evaluate them carefully to avoid being misled.

Check the Source When a message tries to convince you to do or buy something, always ask, "Who's sending the message?" For instance, a friend might tell you a certain movie is awesome. He or she has nothing to gain if you see the movie. Your friend is an objective source. An ad might also tell you the movie is awesome. The ad comes from the producers of the movie. They make money if you go to see it. They are an interested source.

Ask Questions Once you know who is sending the message, ask questions. Often, persuasive messages leave out important information. Is the price of the product clearly listed? What ingredients does the product contain? Does the product come with a guarantee? Are the opinions expressed in the message supported by facts?

Read Carefully Sometimes, important information is found in small print. Make sure you read the entire message carefully. Ask for help if you don't understand everything clearly.

Apply the Strategies

Read the following advertisement, using the strategies for evaluating persuasive messages. Then, answer the questions.

Space Kablooie!

Kids think *Space Kablooie* is the coolest computer game ever! And now you can own it for $29.95.* Be sure to buy Space Kablooie before June 1 to get your free** Kablooie T-shirt from NerveWrackers, Inc.

* Per month for 3 months. $89.85 total.

** For each T-shirt ordered, pay $7.95 shipping and handling.

1. What does this advertisement try to persuade you to do?

2. Explain whether the source of the message is objective or interested.

3. What more do you need to know about the "kids" to evaluate the message?

4. Identify one unsupported opinion.

5. What is the total cost of the Space Kablooie game and T-shirt?

✔ Here are some other situations in which you might find it helpful to evaluate persuasive messages:
▶ Television advertisements
▶ Newspaper editorials
▶ Political speeches

Prepositions and Prepositional Phrases

Grammar Review

A **preposition** is a word or group of words that shows the relation between two or more persons, places, or things (see page 287). Here are some examples:

Common Prepositions			
about	before	from	out
above	behind	in	over
across	below	into	through
after	beside	like	to
against	between	next to	toward
ahead of	by	of	under
around	during	off	until
at	except	on	up
because of	for	on top of	with

A **prepositional phrase** (see page 304) is a phrase that begins with a preposition and ends with a noun or pronoun called the object of the preposition.

Examples of Prepositional Phrases	
Preposition	**Object of the Preposition**
from	Liverpool
to	the house
because of	illness

Prepositional phrases can act as adjectives or as adverbs. (See page 312.)

Kwan Ming lives in the *room next to the furnace. (Adjective: answers the question* Which room?)

Lou Gehrig *quit for the team's good. (Adverb: answers the question* Why?)

prep·o·si·tion (prep'ə zish'ən) *n.* [ME *preposiciou* (< *praepositus*, pp. of *praeponere* < *prae-*, before see PRE- & POSITION): transl. of Gr *prothesis*, PROT languages, a relation or function word, as English etc., that connects a lexical word, usually a noun syntactic construction, to another element of the verb (Ex.: he went *to* the store), to a noun (Ex.: music), or to an adj...

Practice 1 Copy the sentences that follow. For each prepositional phrase, underline the preposition twice and the object of the preposition once.

1. Lob escaped from his owner.

2. Because of an accident, he got into trouble.

3. Lou Gehrig set a record for the highest number of consecutive games.

Practice 2 In each sentence, identify the prepositional phrases and the word each phrase modifies. Then, tell whether the phrase acts as an adjective or an adverb.

1. Shadows on the wall don't frighten her.

2. You carry the numbers in your head.

3. The queen opens her wings on silent hinges.

Practice 3 Write three sentences using the following prepositional phrases as indicated.

1. though the woods (*adverb*)

2. over the hill (*adjective*)

3. until the end (*adverb*)

Grammar in Writing

✔ *Do not use the prepositions* at *or* to *without an object when the sentence makes sense without the preposition:*
Incorrect: Where are you going to?
Correct: Where are you going?

✔ *Do not use two prepositions when one will* do:
Incorrect: The poster fell off of the wall.
Correct: The poster fell off the wall.

PART 2 *New Roads to Follow*

Stairway, James Doolin, Courtesy of Koplin Gallery, Los Angeles, CA

Guide for Reading

Meet the Author:

Jane Yolen (1939–   )

Jane Yolen reads aloud every sentence she writes to see how it sounds. When she completes a paragraph, she reads that out loud, too! That's a lot of reading, because Jane Yolen has written more than eighty books!

Family Ties Yolen is devoted to children and family. Most of her work is written for children, and some of it is dedicated to family members. Her story "The Emperor and the Kite" was written for her father. "Owl Moon" was written for her husband.

A Modern Myth-Maker Many of Yolen's stories deal with fantastic, magical people and creatures. She has written about a girl who cries flowers instead of tears, boys who can fly, and unicorns. She has retold some of the world's most famous myths and created many award-winning tales of her own. Still, this modern myth-maker refers to herself simply as "a storyteller."

THE STORY BEHIND THE STORY

Yolen's study of the world's folklore has given her a wide range of material on which to base her stories. "Greyling" is a story from Yolen's imagination, but the main character—a selchie—comes from the folklore of Scotland and Ireland.

◆ LITERATURE AND YOUR LIFE

CONNECT YOUR EXPERIENCE

When you discover a new interest, such as in-line skating or drawing, you discover something about yourself as well. The mysterious boy in "Greyling" discovers something about himself that dramatically affects his entire future.

THEMATIC FOCUS: New Roads to Follow

As you read this story, ask yourself whether Greyling follows a new road or rediscovers an old one.

◆ Background for Understanding

CULTURE

"Greyling" is the story of a selchie. Selchies (or silkies) are common in the folk traditions of England, Ireland, Scotland, and Wales. There are many versions of selchie stories, but they all agree on one point: The selchie, who appears as a person on land, changes to a seal in the water. The legend probably has its roots in the almost human-looking eyes of the seals that are common in the seas around the countries where selchie tales are told.

◆ Build Vocabulary

RELATED WORDS: FORMS OF *grief*

The fisherman in this story hides his grief—his deep sadness. Other forms of the word *grief* also deal with sadness: *grieve* (to feel deep sadness) and *grievous* (bad enough to cause deep sadness).

WORD BANK

Which word on this list tells an action that you might have used *shears* (scissors) to do?

grief
sheared
slough
wallowed

◆ Greyling ◆

◆ **Literary Focus**

CONFLICT AND RESOLUTION

Most stories focus on a **conflict**—a struggle between two opposing forces. All the events in the story either contribute to the conflict or move it toward the **resolution**—the way the story turns out, one way or another. The resolution can be that a decision is made, a battle is won or lost, a character accepts defeat, or a character conquers an obstacle.

◆ **Reading Strategy**

PREDICT

When you **predict,** you make logical guesses about upcoming events. You base your predictions on information or details provided in the story. As you read, you may learn new information that will cause you to revise a prediction. Draw waves like the ones shown below. On each wave, write details that help you make predictions. On the crest of each wave, write a prediction.

The fisherman is kind.
The seal needs help.
The fisherman will bring the seal home.
New Details
New Details
New Details
New Prediction

One, 1986, April Gornik, Edward Thorp Gallery

Greyling

Jane Yolen

Once on a time when wishes were aplenty, a fisherman and his wife lived by the side of the sea. All that they ate came out of the sea. Their hut was covered with the finest mosses that kept them cool in the summer and warm in the winter. And there was nothing they needed or wanted except a child.

Each morning, when the moon touched down behind the water and the sun rose up behind the plains, the wife would say to the fisherman, "You have your boat and your nets and your lines. But I have no baby to hold in my arms." And again, in the evening, it was the same. She would weep and wail and rock the cradle that stood by the hearth. But year in and year out the cradle stayed empty.

Now the fisherman was also sad that they had no child. But he kept his sorrow to himself so that his wife would not know his grief and thus double her own. Indeed, he would leave the hut each morning with a breath of song and return each night with a whistle on his lips. His nets were full but his heart was empty, yet he never told his wife.

One sunny day, when the beach was a tan thread spun between sea and plain, the fisherman as usual went down to his boat. But this day he found a small grey seal stranded on the sandbar, crying for its own.

The fisherman looked up the beach and down. He looked in front of him and behind. And he looked to the town on the great grey cliffs that sheared off into the sea. But there were no other seals in sight.

So he shrugged his shoulders and took off his shirt. Then he dipped it into the water and wrapped the seal pup carefully in its folds.

"You have no father and you have no mother," he said. "And I have no child. So you shall come home with me."

And the fisherman did no fishing that day but brought the seal pup, wrapped in his shirt, straight home to his wife.

When she saw him coming home early with no shirt on, the fisherman's wife ran out of the hut, fear riding in her heart. Then she looked wonderingly at the bundle which he held in his arms.

"It's nothing," he said, "but a seal pup I

◆ Build Vocabulary

grief (grēf) *n.*: Deep sadness
sheared (shird) *v.*: Cut off sharply

found stranded in the shallows and longing for its own. I thought we could give it love and care until it is old enough to seek its kin."

The fisherman's wife nodded and took the bundle. Then she uncovered the wrapping and gave a loud cry. "Nothing!" she said. "You call this nothing?"

The fisherman looked. Instead of a seal lying in the folds, there was a strange child with great grey eyes and silvery grey hair, smiling up at him.

The fisherman wrung his hands. "It is a selchie," he cried. "I have heard of them. They are men upon the land and seals in the sea. I thought it was but a tale."

"Then he shall remain a man upon the land," said the fisherman's wife, clasping the child in her arms, "for I shall never let him return to the sea."

"Never," agreed the fisherman, for he knew how his wife had wanted a child. And in his secret heart, he wanted one, too. Yet he felt, somehow, it was wrong.

"We shall call him Greyling," said the fisherman's wife, "for his eyes and hair are the color of a storm-coming sky. Greyling, though he has brought sunlight into our home."

And though they still lived by the side of the water in a hut covered with mosses that kept them warm in the winter and cool in the summer, the boy Greyling was never allowed into the sea.

He grew from a child to a

▶ **Critical Viewing** Why might people imagine human qualities or emotions in a seal? **[Connect]**

lad. He grew from a lad to a young man. He gathered driftwood for his mother's hearth and searched the tide pools for shells for her mantel. He mended his father's nets and tended his father's boat. But though he often stood by the shore or high in the town on the great grey cliffs, looking and longing and grieving his heart for what he did not really know, he never went into the sea.

◆ **Literary Focus**
What is the conflict Greyling feels within himself?

Then one wind-wailing morning just fifteen years from the day that Greyling had been found, a great storm blew up suddenly in the North. It was such a storm as had never been seen before: the sky turned nearly black and even the fish had trouble swimming. The wind pushed huge waves onto the shore. The waters gobbled up the little hut on the beach. And Greyling and the fisherman's wife were forced to flee to the town high on the great grey cliffs. There they looked down at the roiling,[1] boiling, sea. Far from shore they spied the fisherman's boat, its sails flapping like the wings of a wounded gull. And clinging to the broken mast was the fisherman himself, sinking deeper with every wave.

The fisherman's wife gave a terrible cry. "Will no one save him?" she called to the people of the town who had gathered on the edge of the cliff. "Will no one save my own dear husband who is all of life to me?"

But the townsmen looked away. There was no man there who dared risk his life in that sea, even to save a drowning soul.

"Will no one at all save him?" she cried out again.

"Let the boy go," said one

---

1. **roiling** (roil′ in) *adj.*: Stirred up; angry.

old man, pointing at Greyling with his stick. "He looks strong enough."

But the fisherman's wife clasped Greyling in her arms and held his ears with her hands. She did not want him to go into the sea. She was afraid he would never return.

"Will no one save my own dear heart?" cried the fisherman's wife for a third and last time.

But shaking their heads, the people of the town edged to their houses and shut their doors and locked their windows and set their backs to the ocean and their faces to the fires that glowed in every hearth.

"I will save him, Mother," cried Greyling, "or die as I try."

And before she could tell him no, he broke from her grasp and dived from the top of the great cliffs, down, down, down into the tumbling sea.

"He will surely sink," whispered the women as they ran from their warm fires to watch.

"He will certainly drown," called the men as they took down their spyglasses from the shelves.

They gathered on the cliffs and watched the boy dive down into the sea.

As Greyling disappeared beneath the waves, little fingers of foam tore at his clothes. They snatched his shirt and his pants and his shoes and sent them bubbling away to the shore. And as Greyling went deeper beneath the waves, even his skin seemed to slough off till he swam, free at last, in the sleek grey coat of a great grey seal.

The selchie had returned to the sea.

But the people of the town did not see this. All they saw was the diving boy disappearing under the waves and then, farther out, a large seal swimming toward the boat that wallowed in the sea. The sleek grey seal, with no effort at all, eased the fisherman to the shore though the waves were wild and bright with foam. And then, with a final salute, it turned its back on the land and headed joyously out to sea.

The fisherman's wife hurried down to the sand. And behind her followed the people of the town. They searched up the beach and down, but they did not find the boy.

"A brave son," said the men when they found his shirt, for they thought he was certainly drowned.

"A very brave son," said the women when they found his shoes, for they thought him

---

▼ **Critical Viewing** What details suggest that this seal feels at home in the water? [Analyze]

◆ **Build Vocabulary**

slough (sluf) *v.*: Be cast off; be gotten rid of
wallowed (wäl´ ōd) *v.*: Rolled and tilted

lost for sure.

"Has he really gone?" asked the fisherman's wife of her husband when at last they were alone.

"Yes, quite gone," the fisherman said to her. "Gone where his heart calls, gone to the great wide sea. And though my heart grieves at his leaving, it tells me this way is best."

The fisherman's wife sighed. And then she cried. But at last she agreed that, perhaps, it was best. "For he is both man and seal," she said. "And though we cared for him for a while, now he must care for himself." And she never cried again.

◆ **Reading Strategy**
Which of your predictions actually happened in the story? Which were different from story events?

So once more they lived alone by the side of the sea in a new little hut which was covered with mosses to keep them warm in the winter and cool in the summer.

Yet, once a year, a great grey seal is seen at night near the fisherman's home. And the people in town talk of it, and wonder. But seals do come to the shore and men do go to the sea; and so the townfolk do not dwell upon it very long.

But it is no ordinary seal. It is Greyling himself come home—come to tell his parents tales of the lands that lie far beyond the waters, and to sing them songs of the wonders that lie far beneath the sea.

Guide for Responding

◆ LITERATURE AND YOUR LIFE

Reader's Response Do you agree that Greyling belongs in the sea? Why or why not?

Thematic Focus In what way is the "new road" Greyling chooses really an old road?

Journal Writing Write about a time when you had to choose between two things you wanted.

☑ Check Your Comprehension

1. Explain how the fisherman and his wife come to have a son.
2. Why is the son called Greyling?
3. Summarize what happens when Greyling saves his father.
4. What does Greyling do when he returns home?

◆ Critical Thinking

INTERPRET

1. Why does the fisherman feel it is wrong to keep Greyling from the sea? **[Interpret]**
2. As Greyling grows up, his heart longs and grieves for something he cannot name. What is he longing for? **[Infer]**
3. Does Greyling know what will happen when he dives into the sea? Support your answer. **[Support]**

APPLY

4. What point does this story make about loving and letting go? Do you agree? **[Make a Judgment]**

EXTEND

5. What jobs or careers, in addition to fishing, are open to people who enjoy working on, in, or near the water? **[Career Link]**

Guide for Responding (continued)

◆ Reading Strategy

PREDICT

When you **predict,** you put together clues from the story to make logical guesses about what events would occur and what characters would do.

1. (a) When you first read that the baby seal became a baby boy, what prediction did you make? Why?
   (b) Did you revise that prediction at any point? Why or why not?
2. (a) When the fisherman was caught in the storm, what prediction did you make? (b) What actually happened?

◆ Build Vocabulary

USING FORMS OF *grief*

Words related to *grief* all include the idea of deep sadness in their meaning. On your paper, respond to each numbered item.

1. Describe a *grievous* injustice in history.
2. What event almost brings *grief* to the fisherman's wife at the end of the story?
3. How does a character act when he or she *grieves*?

SPELLING STRATEGY

Slough is one of the few words in English that spells the *uff* sound with *ough*. For each clue, write a word that rhymes with slough and is spelled with *ough*.

1. plenty 2. very strong or sturdy 3. not gentle

USING THE WORD BANK

On your paper, write the word from the Word Bank that best completes each numbered item.

1. The large boat floated above the waves, but the little boat ___?___ in them.
2. The mountains rose above us, but the cliffs ___?___ away.
3. A happy person feels joy, but a sad person feels ___?___.
4. In winter I wear sweaters and coats but in spring I ___?___ off heavy clothing.

◆ Literary Focus

CONFLICT AND RESOLUTION

All the events in a story either contribute to the **conflict,** the struggle between opposing forces, or move the conflict toward a **resolution.**

1. What are the two opposing forces within Greyling?
2. What two forces are struggling against each other when the fisherman is in the sea?
3. How is the fisherman's conflict resolved?
4. In what way does the resolution of the fisherman's conflict lead to the resolution of Greyling's conflict?

◆ Build Grammar Skills

INTERJECTIONS

An **interjection** is a word or group of words that expresses emotion. A strong interjection is followed by an exclamation point.

Nothing! You call this nothing?

What! Do you expect me to believe that?

A mild interjection is followed by a comma.

Oh, you poor little thing.

Now, don't cry.

Practice On your paper, copy each sentence. Circle the interjection in each sentence.

1. Please! Won't someone help him?
2. Well, maybe the boy should go.
3. No! I won't believe it.
4. Come on, it's not that bad.
5. Wow! That was close.

Writing Application Copy the following conversation on your paper. Add at least three interjections.

"He's such a good swimmer," said the fisherman's wife.

"He sure is," replied the fisherman. "Just look at him go."

"I wish he didn't have to leave."

"We have to accept what he is. Don't worry, he'll come back for visits."

Build Your Portfolio

 ## Idea Bank

Writing

1. **Note** As Greyling, write a short note to your parents explaining why you returned to the sea.

2. **Newspaper Report** Write a newspaper report describing the events at the end of "Greyling." Include quotations from the townspeople who watched. **[Career Link; Media Link]**

3. **Follow-up** Write a few additional paragraphs to add to the end of "Greyling." Describe Greyling's thoughts as he returns to the sea.

Speaking and Listening

4. **Reply** As one of the townspeople, give a brief explanation for the reasons you can't or won't help Greyling's father. **[Performing Arts Link]**

5. **Storytelling** Jane Yolen reads aloud every sentence she writes. Practice telling this story aloud. Use your voice and gestures to increase the tension at exciting points. Then, perform your story for the class. **[Performing Arts Link]**

Projects

6. **Water-Safety Presentation** **[Group Activity]** In this story, the fisherman is saved through fantastic circumstances. In real life, people follow certain rules and guidelines to be safe around the water. With a group, prepare an oral presentation on water safety. Have group members choose from among these tasks: writing up guidelines, creating posters, and preparing demonstrations. **[Health Link]**

7. **Multimedia Presentation** Use library or other available resources to find out about selchies. Prepare a presentation on these mythical creatures. Play folk music, show art, and display some books in which selchies appear. **[Media Link; Social Studies Link]**

 ## Writing Mini-Lesson

Call to Action

The fisherman's wife calls out for volunteers to help her husband. Fortunately, most volunteer work is not as dangerous as saving the fisherman. Write a call to action, an appeal for people to do something, in which you encourage people to volunteer.

Writing Skills Focus: Appeal to Logic

In your call to action, **appeal to logic.** Give reasons why people should help, and explain the benefits they will enjoy if they do. For instance, if you ask people to help clean up the local park, point out that the park belongs to all and that a cleaner park will be more enjoyable.

Prewriting Use an organizer like the one below to jot down reasons and benefits.

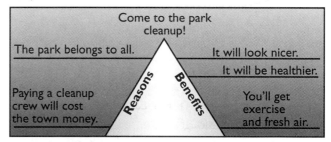

Drafting First, identify the problem or need. Then, tell readers what you want them to do. Refer to readers directly. For example, write "You can help keep our park clean" rather than "People can help."

◆ **Grammar Application**
Use interjections to add feeling to your call to action.

Revising Ask a classmate to read your call to action and identify reasons he or she would or wouldn't do what is asked. Strengthen any weak points your reviewer identifies by describing additional reasons or benefits.

*G*uide for Reading

Meet the Authors:

Sandra Cisneros (1954–   )

Growing up in a poor neighborhood in Chicago, Illinois, made for difficult times. Sandra Cisneros kept her focus, though. Drawing on her Mexican heritage, she has written short stories, poetry, and the book *The House on Mango Street*.

THE STORY BEHIND THE STORY

Cisneros believes writers must make connections between their own lives and those of others. In "Abuelito Who," she shares her feelings about her grandfather.

E.E. Cummings (1894–1962)

E. E. Cummings celebrated freedom and quirkiness. He even wrote his name with lowercase letters— "e. e. cummings"! Born in Cambridge, Massachusetts, he studied painting in Paris. It was his experiments with poetry, though, that made him famous. Cummings taught punctuation marks new tricks, using them as no one had before. He put lines on the page like a painter splashing colors or a jazz player skipping around the beat. He gave poets new roads to follow.

Walt Whitman (1819–1892)

A poet, printer, and journalist, Walt Whitman considered himself first and foremost an American. In his book *Leaves of Grass*, he created a powerful vision of what democracy means. Around the time of the Civil War—when Whitman lived—writers in the United States thought they still had much to learn from European writers. Whitman showed them that they could find everything they needed to know in themselves and their fellow citizens.

◆ LITERATURE AND YOUR LIFE

CONNECT YOUR EXPERIENCE

You might hear birds chirping in the morning and know that spring is finally here. You might watch a moving van pulling away and realize that you really are moving. As these poems show, changes announce themselves in different ways.

THEMATIC FOCUS: New Roads to Follow

Notice the different feelings about change in each of these poems.

◆ Background for Understanding

LANGUAGE

Cummings created his own rules when writing poetry. By rarely using periods or capital letters, he lets the rhythm of the words speak for itself. The phrase "sailing/away and away sailing" helps us feel the balloon's rush upward, especially since there are no commas getting in the way. The lines "always/it's/Spring" would read more easily as one line—"it's always Spring"—but Cummings makes us slow down to appreciate the idea.

◆ Build Vocabulary

COMPOUND TRANSITION WORDS

Compound transition words, like *henceforth,* are formed from two or more other words. They help readers move from one thought or event to the next. Whitman uses *henceforth* to relate present and future events. *Henceforth* combines *hence,* meaning "from this time," and *forth,* meaning "onward." *Henceforth* means "from this time on."

WORD BANK

Which word on this list means "ready to quarrel"?

henceforth
whimper
querulous

Abuelito Who
◆ who knows if the moon's ◆
The Open Road

◆ Literary Focus
FREE VERSE

A poem written in **free verse** is organized in its own unique way. Unlike formal verse, its lines do not rhyme at the end. They do not contain a set number of syllables or follow a regular rhythmic pattern. Still, the poem works with the sound, sense, and rhythm of the words. For instance, the poet may repeat words or put rhyming words close to each other. Each of the free verse poems in this group uses repeated and rhyming words.

◆ Reading Strategy
MAKE INFERENCES

To better understand what you read, you must **make inferences,** or draw conclusions, based on the information you are given. For instance, when you read that Abuelito's hair "is made of fur," you can infer that it is soft. When you read poetry, your inferences will often be based on the images the poet uses.

The illustration at the left shows two inferences you could make from details in "Abuelito Who."

Inferences
1. He is generous.
2. He calls his granddaughter a diamond.

Details
1. Abuelito throws coins like rain.
2. He loves his granddaughter.

Abuelito Who

Sandra Cisneros

Ezra Davenport, 1929, Clarence Holbrook Carter, Courtesy of the artist

▲ **Critical Viewing** Find two details in this painting that match the description of Abuelito. **[Connect]**

Abuelito[1] who throws coins like rain
and asks who loves him
who is dough and feathers
who is a watch and glass of water
5   whose hair is made of fur
is too sad to come downstairs today
who tells me in Spanish you are my diamond
who tells me in English you are my sky
whose little eyes are string
10   can't come out to play
sleeps in his little room all night and day
who used to laugh like the letter k
is sick
is a doorknob tied to a sour stick
15   is tired shut the door
doesn't live here anymore
is hiding underneath the bed
who talks to me inside my head
is blankets and spoons and big brown shoes
20   who snores up and down up and down up and down again
is the rain on the roof that falls like coins
asking who loves him
who loves him who?

---

1. **Abuelito** (ä bwe lḗ tō): In Spanish, an affectionate term for a grandfather.

Guide for Responding

◆ LITERATURE AND YOUR LIFE

Reader's Response Would you like to have Abuelito as a grandfather? Explain.

Thematic Focus The speaker must follow a new road. Explain why.

Journal Writing Write a journal entry describing someone you remember fondly.

☑ Check Your Comprehension

1. Who is Abuelito?
2. Name two of Abuelito's habits.
3. What has changed about Abuelito?

◆ Critical Thinking

INTERPRET

1. Contrast Abuelito in lines 3–5 with Abuelito in lines 10–16. **[Contrast]**
2. Why does the speaker feel as if Abuelito is "hiding underneath the bed"? **[Interpret]**
3. Name three ways in which the speaker is reminded of Abuelito. **[Interpret]**

APPLY

4. In what ways does this poem honor all grandparents? **[Relate]**

EXTEND

5. What effects of aging does Abuelito show? **[Health Link]**

who knows
if the moon's

E.E. Cummings

who knows if the moon's
a balloon, coming out of a keen[1] city
in the sky—filled with pretty people?
(and if you and i should

5   get into it, if they
should take me and take you into their balloon,
why then
we'd go up higher with all the pretty people

than houses and steeples and clouds:
10   go sailing
away and away sailing into a keen
city which nobody's ever visited, where

always
        it's
15   Spring)and everyone's
in love and flowers pick themselves

---

1. keen (kēn) *adj.:* Slang for sharp-looking. Also,
intensely felt.

THE OPEN ROAD

Walt Whitman

Afoot and light-hearted, I take to the open
   road,
Healthy, free, the world before me,
The long brown path before me, leading
   wherever I choose.

Henceforth I ask not good-fortune, I myself
   am good-fortune,
5 Henceforth I whimper no more, postpone
   no more, need nothing,
Done with indoor complaints, libraries,
   querulous criticisms,
Strong and content, I travel the open road.

◆ Build Vocabulary

henceforth (hens fôrth´) *adv.*: From now on

whimper (hwim´ pər) *v.*: Make a low, whining sound, as of fear or pain

querulous (kwer´ yōō ləs) *adj.*: Inclined to find mistakes; complaining

Guide for Responding

◆ LITERATURE AND YOUR LIFE

Reader's Response Would you like to visit the place Cummings describes? Explain.

Thematic Focus What changes for Whitman as he follows a new road?

Journal Writing What far-off country or city would you like to visit? Why?

☑ Check Your Comprehension

1. In Cummings's poem, what might happen if the moon is a balloon?
2. What is the city filled with?
3. To what place might the balloon travel?
4. At the beginning of "The Open Road," what is the speaker about to do?
5. What decision does he announce?

◆ Critical Thinking

INTERPRET

1. Name three differences between Cummings's "keen city" and the ordinary world. **[Analyze]**
2. What feelings does looking at the moon inspire in the speaker? **[Draw Conclusions]**
3. Why does the speaker in "The Open Road" feel "light-hearted"? **[Interpret]**
4. Now that he "is" good fortune, how do you think the speaker will respond when things go wrong? **[Infer]**

COMPARE LITERARY WORKS

5. Compare life in the "keen city" with life on the "open road." **[Compare and Contrast]**

EVALUATE

6. Would you prefer life in the "keen city" or life on the "open road"? Explain. **[Evaluate]**

Guide for Responding (continued)

◆ Reading Strategy

MAKE INFERENCES

You can **make inferences,** or educated guesses, about the subjects of these poems based on the images the poets used.

1. In "Abuelito Who," what images lead you to infer that Abuelito loves the speaker of the poem?
2. Would the speaker in "who knows if the moon's" like to visit the "keen city"? Which images in the poem support your answer?
3. How does the speaker of "The Open Road" feel about his journey? How can you tell?

◆ Build Vocabulary

USING COMPOUND TRANSITION WORDS

Compound transition words show a connection between ideas or events.

Fill in the blanks, using one of these compound transition words: *henceforth, nonetheless.*

1. Every day this week, I got caught in the rain. _____?_____, I will remember my umbrella.
2. The wind brought a great chill to the air. _____?_____, she did not wear a jacket.

SPELLING STRATEGY

When combined in a compound connecting word, words usually keep the same spelling. For example, hence + forth = henceforth.

Join the words in each of the following groups to spell a compound connecting word.

1. how, ever
2. mean, while
3. never, the, less
4. more, over
5. there, after
6. some, what

USING THE WORD BANK

Answer the following, explaining your answers.

1. If Sarah is always mean to you, will you spend time with her *henceforth*?
2. You have been happy all day long. Are you in a *querulous* mood?
3. The dog needs to go out. Would he *whimper*?

◆ Literary Focus

FREE VERSE

A poem written in **free verse** is not bound to a structured rhythm or rhyme pattern. Free verse seeks to capture the rhythms of speech.

1. Explain how the first six lines of "Abuelito Who" are similar to and different from one another.
2. In what way does the visual structure of "who knows if the moon's" show that it doesn't follow a regular rhythm?
3. Why do you think Whitman wrote "The Open Road" in free verse?

◆ Build Grammar Skills

CONJUNCTIONS

Conjunctions connect words, groups of words, and whole sentences. **Coordinating conjunctions** connect words or groups of words of a similar type: noun with noun, phrase with phrase, sentence with sentence, and so on. For instance, Whitman uses the coordinating conjunction *and* to connect two adjectives: "Afoot *and* light-hearted . . ." The coordinating conjunctions are *and, but, for, or, nor, so,* and *yet.*

Practice Copy the following sentences. Circle the coordinating conjunctions, and underline the words or word groups they connect.

1. Abuelito throws coins like rain and asks who loves him.
2. He is blankets and spoons and big brown shoes.
3. I ask not good-fortune, for I am good-fortune.
4. The moon is a balloon, but it is filled with pretty people.
5. On the moon, it's always spring, yet no one has ever visited.

Writing Application Join each pair of sentences with a comma followed by a coordinating conjunction.

1. I am tired. I am hungry.
2. It rained. It stopped raining after two minutes.
3. The dog is anxious. It hasn't been out to play all day.

Build Your Portfolio

 Idea Bank

Writing

1. **Journal Entry** Describe an instance when you traveled on an "open road." Explain what you learned from this experience.

2. **Postcard** Imagine that you and a friend take a trip on Cummings's "moon balloon." Write a postcard message describing your experience.

3. **Poem** Write a poem in free verse about a change of some kind. To unify your poem, repeat words and use words with similar sounds.

Speaking and Listening

4. **Monologue** As Abuelito, explain to your grand-daughter why things have changed between you and what the future holds. Deliver your mono-logue to the class. **[Performing Arts Link]**

5. **Question Exchange** With a partner, take turns asking imaginative "who knows" questions like the one in Cummings's poem. Each question should build on the one before it. Write down your five most interesting questions.

Projects

6. **Historical Maps** Prepare three maps showing the history of transportation in the United States. On one, show the routes pioneers took. On an-other, show railroads before the 1900's. On the last, show the national highway system. Present these maps, explaining how transportation—and roads—have changed. **[Social Studies Link]**

7. **Investigation Report** **[Group Activity]** In a group, prepare a multimedia presentation on the first moon landing. Divide up the following tasks: preparing a timeline on space travel; finding out about the astronauts, their vehicle, and the flight; providing background on the moon; obtaining audiovisual materials. **[Science Link]**

 Writing Mini-Lesson

Advertisement for a Vacation Spot

E. E. Cummings imagines a place where life is so easy that "flowers pick themselves." People on vacation look for this kind of place. Write an adver-tisement for a vacation place. Like Cummings, include details that will grab readers' attention and make them want to visit.

Writing Skills Focus: Choose Appropriate Details

Not every fact about a place will persuade a person to travel there. Your advertisement should include only **details** that make your va-cation spot sound unique and attactive. Answer the questions below to find those details.

- What makes this spot unlike any other?
- What unpleasant things will *not* be found there?
- What is the single most unforgettable fea-ture of the place?

Prewriting Start by choosing a vacation spot you wish to describe. Think about what the place looks like, the town or area that surrounds it, and what people do to entertain themselves there. Make a list of these details.

Drafting Begin your advertisement with a phrase that will catch a reader's eye. Put your best details first. Include basic information the reader needs.

> ◆ **Grammar Application**
> Use coordinating conjunctions to link related words or ideas in your draft.

Revising Ask a partner to read your ad and help you weed out details that are unimportant or that don't focus on your vacation spot's most attractive qualities.

Guide for Reading

Meet the Authors:

Russell Freedman (1929–   )

When Russell Freedman was growing up in San Francisco, California, his mother had a job in a bookstore and his father worked in publishing. It's not surprising, then, that Freedman eventually became a writer. After working as a reporter for the Associated Press, he went on to write more than thirty books for young readers. These include *Immigrant Kids, Children of the Wild West,* and *Cowboys of the Wild West,* all of which were named notable children's books by the American Library Association.

"A Backwoods Boy" is from Freedman's award-winning book *Lincoln: A Photobiography.*

Geoffrey C. Ward (1940–   ) and Ken Burns (1953–   )

Geoffrey C. Ward and Ken Burns work together as a creative team. Two of their famous joint efforts have been documentaries for the Public Broadcasting System. *The Civil War* is about the United States Civil War, told in the words of those who lived it—from President Abraham Lincoln to the soldier slogging through mud. *Baseball,* from which "Jackie Robinson: Justice at Last" is taken, presents the history of our national pastime.

◆ LITERATURE AND YOUR LIFE

CONNECT YOUR EXPERIENCE

Baseball players get more than one try at bat before they are called "out." Life, too, usually gives you more than once chance to succeed. Abraham Lincoln and Jackie Robinson both faced several disappointments before achieving the success of which they dreamed.

THEMATIC FOCUS: New Roads to Follow

Why is a road most challenging for the first person who travels it?

◆ Background for Understanding

HISTORY

For a brief time in the 1880's, African American baseball players played on the same professional teams as white players. Shortly afterward, the major league clubs began to exclude African Americans. African American players formed their own teams, and in the 1920's organized the Negro leagues. Although they did not become as widely known as their white counterparts, some of the best players in baseball history played on Negro leagues teams. Jackie Robinson began his professional baseball career on the Negro leagues' team the Kansas City Monarchs.

◆ Build Vocabulary

PREFIXES: *re-*

The prefix *re-* means "back," "again," or "against," as in the word *return,* meaning "give back." You can see the meaning "back" in *retaliated,* which means "got revenge" or "paid back."

WORD BANK

Which word describes a person you would not want as a friend?

aptitude
intrigued
treacherous
integrate
retaliated

◆ A Backwoods Boy ◆
Jackie Robinson: Justice at Last

◆ Literary Focus

FACTUAL ACCOUNT

Factual accounts tell about real people and events. A factual account may tell a story, but it is not always organized in time order. In addition, a factual account may offer explanations and interpretations of events and actions. For example, in "A Backwoods Boy," Russell Freedman presents facts about several places Lincoln lived as a boy and explains the reasons the Lincoln family moved.

◆ Reading Strategy

IDENTIFY MAIN IDEAS

Reading a baseball player's statistics can give you an overall impression of the player's ability. Unless you are a coach or a scout, however, you don't need to memorize the statistics. Similarly, when you read, you don't need to memorize every detail. Rather, **identify main ideas**—recognize the most important points—and use the details to help you understand these ideas. For example, the details in "Jackie Robinson" will help you identify and understand the main idea that African Americans were excluded from major league baseball on the basis of race. Use an organizer like the one below to identify main ideas.

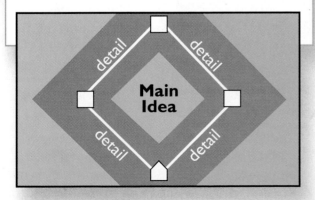

A Backwoods Boy

Russell Freedman

"It is a great piece of folly to attempt to make anything out of my early life. It can all be condensed into a simple sentence, and that sentence you will find in Gray's Elegy[1]—'the short and simple annals[2] of the poor.' That's my life, and that's all you or anyone else can make out of it."[3]

Abraham Lincoln never liked to talk much about his early life. A poor backwoods farm boy, he grew up swinging an ax on frontier homesteads in Kentucky, Indiana, and Illinois.

He was born near Hodgenville, Kentucky, on February 12, 1809, in a log cabin with one window, one door, a chimney, and a hard-packed dirt floor. His parents named him after his pioneer grandfather. The first Abraham Lincoln had been shot dead by hostile Indians in 1786, while planting a field of corn in the Kentucky wilderness.

Young Abraham was still a toddler when his family packed their belongings and moved to another log-cabin farm a few miles north, on Knob Creek. That was the first home he could remember, the place where he ran and played as a barefoot boy.

He remembered the bright waters of Knob Creek as it tumbled past the Lincoln cabin and disappeared into the Kentucky hills. Once he fell into the rushing creek and almost drowned before he was pulled out by a neighbor boy. Another time he caught a fish and gave it to a passing soldier.

Lincoln never forgot the names of his first teachers— Zachariah Riney followed by Caleb Hazel—who ran a windowless log schoolhouse two miles away. It was

19 year-old Abe Lincoln as a flatboatman on the Mississippi River, color engraving, 19th century

▲ **Critical Viewing** What does this picture show you about transporation in Lincoln's time? **[Draw Conclusions]**

1. **Elegy** (el´ ə jē) *n.:* Poem praising someone who has died.
2. **annals** (an´ əlz) *n.:* Historical records.
3. **"It is a great . . . out of it":** This is a quotation from Abraham Lincoln.

called a "blab school." Pupils of all ages sat on rough wooden benches and bawled out their lessons aloud. Abraham went there with his sister Sarah, who was two years older, when they could be spared from their chores at home. Holding hands, they would walk through scrub trees and across creek bottoms to the schoolhouse door. They learned their numbers from one to ten, and a smattering of reading, writing, and spelling.

Their parents couldn't read or write at all. Abraham's mother, Nancy, signed her name by making a shakily drawn mark. He would remember her as a thin, sad-eyed woman who labored beside her husband in the fields. She liked to gather the children around her in the evening to recite prayers and Bible stories she had memorized.

His father, Thomas, was a burly, barrel-chested farmer and carpenter who had worked hard at home-steading since marrying Nancy Hanks in 1806. A sociable fellow, his greatest pleasure was to crack jokes and swap stories with his chums. With painful effort, Thomas Lincoln could scrawl his name. Like his wife, he had grown up without education, but that wasn't unusual in those days. He supported his family by living off his own land, and he watched for a chance to better himself.

In 1816, Thomas decided to pull up stakes again and move north to Indiana, which was

▲ **Critical Viewing** Describe the kind of man you think Lincoln's father is based on this picture. **[Speculate]**

about to join the Union as the nation's nine-teenth state. Abraham was seven. He remem-bered the one-hundred-mile journey as the hardest experience of his life. The family set out on a cold morning in December, loading all their possessions on two horses. They crossed the Ohio River on a makeshift ferry, traveled through towering forests, then hacked a path through tangled un-derbrush until they reached their new homesite near the backwoods commu-nity of Little Pigeon Creek.

Thomas put up a temporary winter shelter—a crude, three-sided lean-to of logs and branches. At the open end, he kept a fire burning to take the edge off the cold and scare off the wild animals. At night, wrapped in bearskins and huddled by the fire, Abraham and Sarah listened to wolves howl and pan-thers scream.

Abraham passed his eighth birthday in the lean-to. He was big for his age, "a tall spider of a boy," and old enough to handle an ax. He helped his father clear the land. They planted corn and pump-kin seeds between the tree stumps. And they built a new log cabin, the biggest one yet, where Abraham climbed a ladder and slept in a loft beneath the roof.

Soon after the cabin was finished, some of Nancy's kinfolk arrived. Her aunt and uncle with their adopted son Dennis had decided to follow the Lincolns to Indiana. Dennis Hanks became an extra hand to Thomas and a big brother to Abraham, someone to run and wrestle with.

A year later, Nancy's aunt and uncle lay dead, victims of the dreaded "milk sickness" (now known to be caused by a poisonous plant called white snake root). An epidemic of the disease swept through the Indiana woods in the summer of 1818. Nancy had nursed her relatives until the end, and then she too came down with the disease. Abraham watched his mother toss in bed with chills, fever, and pain for seven days before she died at the age of thirty-four. "She knew she was going to die," Dennis Hanks recalled. "She called up the children to her dying side and told them to be good and kind to their father, to one another, and to the world."

Thomas built a coffin from black cherry wood, and nine-year-old Abraham whittled the pegs that held the wooden planks together. They buried Nancy on a windswept hill, next to her aunt and uncle. Sarah, now eleven, took her mother's place, cooking, cleaning, and mending clothes for her father, brother, and cousin Dennis in the forlorn and lonely cabin.

Thomas Lincoln waited for a year. Then he went back to Kentucky to find himself a new wife. He returned in a four-horse wagon with a widow named Sarah Bush Johnston, her three children, and all her household goods. Abraham and his sister were fortunate, for their stepmother was a warm and loving person. She took the motherless children to her heart and raised them as her own. She also spruced up the neglected Lincoln cabin, now shared by eight people who lived, ate, and slept in a single smoky room with a loft.

Abraham was growing fast, shooting up like a sunflower, a spindly youngster with big bony hands, unruly black hair, a dark complexion, and luminous gray eyes. He became an expert with the ax, working alongside his father, who also hired him out to work for others. For twenty-five cents a day, the boy dug wells, built pigpens, split fence rails, felled trees. "My how he could chop!" exclaimed a friend. "His ax would flash and bite into a sugar tree or a sycamore, and down it would come. If you heard him felling trees in a clearing, you would say there were three men at work, the way the trees fell."

> ◆ **Reading Strategy**
> Identify the important idea in this paragraph.

Lincoln said later that all his schooling together "did not amount to one year."

Meanwhile, he went to school "by littles," a few weeks one winter, maybe a month the next. Lincoln said later that all his schooling together "did not amount to one year." Some fragments of his schoolwork still survive, including a verse that he wrote in his homemade arithmetic book: "Abraham Lincoln/his hand and pen/he will be good but/god knows When."

Mostly, he educated himself by borrowing books and newspapers. There are many stories about Lincoln's efforts to find enough books to satisfy him in that backwoods country. Those he liked he read again and again, losing himself in the adventures of *Robinson Crusoe* or the magical tales of *The Arabian Nights*. He was thrilled by a biography of George Washington, with its stirring account of the Revolutionary War. And he came to love the rhyme and rhythm of poetry, reciting passages from Shakespeare or the Scottish poet Robert Burns at the drop of a hat. He would carry a book out to the field with him, so he could read at the end of each plow furrow, while the horse was

◆ **Literary Focus**

What facts are contained in this section of the factual account? What explanations are included?

getting its breath. When noon came, he would sit under a tree and read while he ate. "I never saw Abe after he was twelve that he didn't have a book in his hand or in his pocket," Dennis Hanks remembered. "It didn't seem natural to see a feller read like that."

By the time he was sixteen, Abraham was six feet tall—"the gangliest awkwardest feller . . . he appeared to be all joints," said a neighbor. He may have looked awkward, but hard physical labor had given him a tough, lean body with muscular arms like steel cables. He could grab a woodsman's ax by the handle and hold it straight out at arm's length. And he was one of the best wrestlers and runners around.

He also had a reputation as a comic and storyteller. Like his father, Abraham was fond of talking and listening to talk. About this time he had found a book called *Lessons in Elocution,* which offered advice on public speaking. He practiced before his friends, standing on a tree stump as he entertained them with fiery imitations of the roving preachers and politicians who often visited Little Pigeon Creek.

Folks liked young Lincoln. They regarded him as a good-humored, easy-going boy—a bookworm maybe, but smart and willing to oblige. Yet even then, people noticed that he could be moody and withdrawn. As a friend put it, he was "witty, sad, and reflective by turns. "

At the age of seventeen, Abraham left home for a few months to work as a ferryman's helper on the Ohio River. He was eighteen when his sister Sarah died early in 1828, while giving birth to her first child.

That spring, Abraham had a chance to get away from the backwoods and see something of the world. A local merchant named James Gentry hired Lincoln to accompany his son Allen on a twelve-hundred-mile flatboat voyage to New Orleans. With their cargo of country produce, the two boys floated down the Ohio River and into the Mississippi, maneuvering with long poles to avoid snags and sandbars, and to navigate in the busy river traffic.

New Orleans was the first real city they had ever seen. Their eyes must have popped as the great harbor came into view, jammed with the masts of sailing ships from distant ports all over the world. The city's cobblestone streets teemed with sailors, traders, and adventurers speaking strange languages. And there were gangs of slaves everywhere. Lincoln would never forget the sight of black men, women, and children being driven along in chains and auctioned off like cattle. In those days, New Orleans had more than two hundred slave dealers.

The boys sold their cargo and their flatboat and returned upriver by steamboat. Abraham earned twenty-four dollars—a good bit of money at the time—for the three-month trip. He handed the money over to his father, according to law and custom.

Thomas Lincoln was thinking about moving on again. Lately he had heard glowing reports about Illinois, where instead of forests there were endless prairies with plenty of rich black soil. Early in 1830, Thomas sold his Indiana farm. The Lincolns piled everything they owned into two ox-drawn wagons and set out over muddy roads, with Abraham, just turned twenty-one, driving one of the wagons himself. They traveled west to their new homesite in central Illinois, not far from Decatur. Once again, Abraham helped his father build a cabin and start a new farm.

He stayed with his family through their first prairie winter, but he was getting restless. He had met an enterprising fellow named Denton Offutt, who wanted him to take another boatload of cargo down the river to New Orleans. Abraham agreed to make the trip with his stepbrother, John Johnston, and a cousin, John Hanks.

When he returned to Illinois three months later, he paid a quick farewell visit to his father and stepmother. Abraham was twenty-two now, of legal age, free to do what he wanted. His parents were settled and could get along without him. Denton Offutt was planning to open a general store in the flourishing village of New Salem, Illinois, and he had promised Lincoln a steady job.

Lincoln arrived in New Salem in July 1831 wearing a faded cotton shirt and blue jeans too short for his long legs—a "friendless, uneducated, penniless boy," as he later described himself. He tended the counter at Denton Offutt's store and slept in a room at the back.

The village stood in a wooded grove on a bluff above the Sangamon River. Founded just two years earlier, it had about one hundred people living in one- and two-room log houses. Cattle grazed behind split-rail fences, hogs snuffled along dusty lanes, and chickens and geese flapped about underfoot. New Salem was still a small place, but it was growing. The settlers expected it to become a frontier boom town.

With his gifts for swapping stories and making friends, Lincoln fit easily into the life of the village. He showed off his skill with an ax, competed in footraces, and got along with everyone from Mentor Graham, the schoolmaster, to Jack Armstrong, the leader of a rowdy gang called the Clary's Grove boys. Armstrong was the wrestling champion of New Salem. He quickly challenged Lincoln to a match.

On the appointed day, an excited crowd gathered down by the river, placing bets as the wrestlers stripped to the waist for combat. They circled each other, then came to grips, twisting and tugging until they crashed to the ground with Lincoln on top. As he pinned Armstrong's shoulders to the ground, the other Clary's Grove boys dived in to join the scuffle. Lincoln broke away, backed against a cliff, and defiantly offered to take them all on—one at a time. Impressed, Armstrong jumped to his feet and offered Lincoln his hand, declaring the match a draw. After that, they were fast friends.

Lincoln also found a place among the town's intellectuals. He joined the New Salem Debating Society, which met once a week in James Rutledge's tavern. The first time he debated, he seemed nervous. But as he began to speak in his high, reedy voice, he surprised everyone with the force and logic of his argument. "He was already a fine speaker," one debater recalled. "All he lacked was culture."

Lincoln was self-conscious about his meager education, and ambitious to improve himself. Mentor Graham, the schoolmaster and a fellow debater, took a liking to the young man, lent him books, and offered to coach him in the fine points of English grammar. Lincoln had plenty of time to study. There wasn't much business at Offutt's store, so he could spend long hours reading as he sat behind the counter.

When the store failed in 1832, Offutt moved on to other schemes. Lincoln had to find something else to do. At the age of twenty-three, he decided to run for the Illinois state legislature. Why not? He knew everyone in town, people liked him, and he was rapidly gaining confidence as a public speaker. His friends urged him to run, saying that a bright young man could go far in politics. So Lincoln announced his candidacy and his political platform. He was in favor of local improvements, like better roads and canals. He had made a study of the Sangamon River, and he proposed that it be dredged and cleared so steamboats could call at New Salem—insuring a glorious future for the town.

Before he could start his campaign, an Indian war flared up in northern Illinois. Chief Black Hawk of the Sauk and Fox tribes had crossed the Mississippi, intending, he said, to raise corn on land that had been taken from his people thirty years earlier. The white settlers were alarmed, and the governor called for volunteers to stop the invasion. Lincoln enlisted in a militia company made up of his friends and neighbors. He was surprised and pleased when the men elected him as their captain, with Jack Armstrong as first sergeant. His troops drilled and marched, but they never did sight any hostile Indians. Years later, Lincoln would joke about his three-month stint as a military man, telling how he survived "a good many bloody battles with mosquitoes."

By the time he returned to New Salem, election day was just two weeks off. He jumped into the campaign—pitching horseshoes with voters, speaking at barbecues, chatting with farmers in the fields, joking with customers at country stores. He lost, finishing eighth in a field of thirteen. But in his own precinct,[4] where folks knew him, he received 227 votes out of 300 cast.

Defeated as a politician, he decided to try his luck as a frontier merchant. With a fellow named William Berry as his partner, Lincoln operated a general store that sold everything from axes to beeswax. But the two men showed little <u>aptitude</u> for business, and their store finally "winked out," as Lincoln put it. Then Berry died, leaving Lincoln saddled with a $1,100 debt—a gigantic amount for someone who had never earned more than a few dollars

a month. Lincoln called it "the National Debt," but he vowed to repay every cent. He spent the next fifteen years doing so.

To support himself, he worked at all sorts of odd jobs. He split fence rails, hired himself out as a farmhand, helped at the local gristmill.[5] With the help of friends, he was appointed postmaster of New Salem, a part-time job that paid about fifty dollars a year. Then he was offered a chance to become deputy to the local surveyor.[6] He knew nothing about surveying, so he bought a compass, a chain, and a couple of textbooks on the subject. Within six weeks, he had taught himself enough to start work—laying out roads and townsites, and marking off property boundaries.

As he traveled about the county, making surveys and delivering mail to faraway farms, people came to know him as an

Peculiarsome Abe, N.C. Wyeth, The Free Library of Philadelphia

▲ **Critical Viewing** Compare the attitude of young Abe Lincoln in this picture with the factual account found in this biography. **[Compare and Contrast]**

4. **precinct** (prē´ siŋkt) *n.*: Election district.

5. **gristmill** (grist´ mil´) *n.*: Place where grain is ground into flour.
6. **surveyor** (sər vā´ ər) *n.*: Person who determines the boundaries of land.

◆ **Build Vocabulary**
aptitude (ap´ tə tōōd´) *n.*: Natural ability

honest and dependable fellow. Lincoln could be counted on to witness a contract, settle a boundary dispute, or compose a letter for folks who couldn't write much themselves. For the first time, his neighbors began to call him "Abe."

In 1834, Lincoln ran for the state legislature again. This time he placed second in a field of thirteen candidates, and was one of four men elected to the Illinois House of Representatives from Sangamon County. In November, wearing a sixty-dollar tailor-made suit he had bought on credit, the first suit he had ever owned, the twenty-five-year-old legislator climbed into a stagecoach and set out for the state capital in Vandalia.

In those days, Illinois lawmakers were paid three dollars a day to cover their expenses, but only while the legislature was in session. Lincoln still had to earn a living. One of his fellow representatives, a rising young attorney named John Todd Stuart, urged Lincoln to take up the study of law. As Stuart pointed out, it was an ideal profession for anyone with political ambitions.

And in fact, Lincoln had been toying with the idea of becoming a lawyer. For years he had hung around frontier courthouses, watching country lawyers bluster and strut as they cross-examined witnesses and delivered impassioned speeches before juries. He had sat on juries himself, appeared as a witness, drawn up legal documents for his neighbors. He had even argued a few cases before the local justice of the peace.

Yes, the law <u>intrigued</u> him. It would give him a chance to rise in the world, to earn a respected place in the community, to live by his wits instead of by hard physical labor.

Yet Lincoln hesitated, unsure of himself because he had so little formal education. That was no great obstacle, his friend Stuart kept telling him. In the 1830's, few American lawyers had ever seen the inside of a law school. Instead, they "read law" in the office of a practicing attorney until they knew enough to pass their exams.

Lincoln decided to study entirely on his own. He borrowed some law books from Stuart, bought others at an auction, and began to read and memorize legal codes[7] and precedents.[8] Back in New Salem, folks would see him walking down the road, reciting aloud from one of his law books, or lying under a tree as he read, his long legs stretched up the trunk. He studied for nearly three years before passing his exams and being admitted to practice on March 1, 1837.

By then, the state legislature was planning to move from Vandalia to Springfield, which had been named the new capital of Illinois. Lincoln had been elected to a second term in the legislature. And he had accepted a job as junior partner in John Todd Stuart's Springfield law office.

In April, he went back to New Salem for the last time to pack his belongings and say good-bye to his friends. The little village was declining now. Its hopes for growth and prosperity had vanished when the Sangamon River proved too <u>treacherous</u> for steamboat travel. Settlers were moving away, seeking brighter prospects elsewhere.

By 1840, New Salem was a ghost town. It would have been forgotten completely if Abraham Lincoln hadn't gone there to live when he was young, penniless, and ambitious.

◆ **Build Vocabulary**

intrigued (in trēgd') v.: Fascinated

treacherous (trech' ər əs) adj.: Dangerous

◆ **Literature and Your Life**

What does this story about the young Lincoln suggest to you about how to look at obstacles in life?

---

7. **legal codes:** Body of laws, as for a nation or a city, arranged systematically

8. **precedents** (pres' ə dənts) n.: Legal cases that may serve as a reference.

Portrait of Lincoln

▲ **Critical Viewing** This photograph of Lincoln is by the photographer Mathew Brady. What goal do Brady and Freedman share? **[Connect]**

Beyond Literature

Media Connection

Mathew Brady, Photographer
Mathew Brady (1823–1896) was among the first photographers to use the camera to record history. Portraits like this one of Abraham Lincoln were only a small part of Brady's work. In more than 7,000 pictures, he documented different aspects of the Civil War—from bloody battles to dreary camp life.

Cross-Curricular Activity

Photo Documentary In a group, document life at your school or in your neighborhood with photographs. Decide which scenes you should include to give other people insight into your lives. Display your photographs in the classroom.

Guide for Responding

◆ LITERATURE AND YOUR LIFE

Reader's Response What was the most interesting fact you learned about young Abraham Lincoln?

Thematic Focus What are some choices Abraham Lincoln made that helped him on his road to becoming President?

Journal Writing Describe one thing you admire about Abraham Lincoln.

☑ Check Your Comprehension

1. Mention two ways eight-year-old Abraham Lincoln helped his family.
2. Identify three characteristics of Abraham Lincoln as a sixteen-year-old.
3. Why did Lincoln move to New Salem? Why did he leave?

◆ Critical Thinking

INTERPRET

1. What were some early signs that Lincoln would become a great public speaker? **[Analyze]**
2. Explain what his wrestling match with Jack Armstrong proved about Lincoln. **[Interpret]**
3. In what ways did Lincoln's early life influence the kind of man he became? **[Draw Conclusions]**

EVALUATE

4. Lincoln sums up his early life as "the short and simple annals of the poor." Do you agree with this description? Why or why not? **[Make a Judgment]**

APPLY

5. What lesson about achieving a goal do you learn from Lincoln's boyhood experiences? **[Apply]**

JACKIE ROBINSON:
JUSTICE *at Last*

Geoffrey C. Ward and Ken Burns

Critical Viewing What qualities of Jackie Robinson do you see demonstrated in this picture? [**Analyze**]

It was 1945, and World War II had ended. Americans of all races had died for their country. Yet black men were still not allowed in the major leagues. The national pastime was loved by all America, but the major leagues were for white men only.

Branch Rickey of the Brooklyn Dodgers thought that was wrong. He was the only team owner who believed blacks and whites should play together. Baseball, he felt, would become even more thrilling, and fans of all colors would swarm to his ballpark.

Rickey decided his team would be the first to integrate. There were plenty of brilliant Negro league players, but he knew the first black major leaguer would need much more than athletic ability.

Many fans and players were prejudiced—they didn't want the races to play together. Rickey knew the first black player would be cursed and booed. Pitchers would throw at him; runners would spike him. Even his own teammates might try to pick a fight.

◆ Reading Strategy
What is the main idea in this paragraph?

But somehow this man had to rise above that. No matter what happened, he must never lose his temper. No matter what was said to him, he must never answer back. If he had even one fight, people might say integration wouldn't work.

When Rickey met Jackie Robinson, he thought he'd found the right man. Robinson was 28 years old, and a superb athlete. In his first season in the Negro leagues, he hit .387. But just as importantly, he had great intelligence and sensitivity. Robinson was college-educated, and knew what joining the majors would mean for blacks. The grandson of a slave, he was proud of his race and wanted others to feel the same.

In the past, Robinson had always stood up for his rights. But now Rickey told him he would have to stop. The Dodgers needed "a man that will take abuse."

At first Robinson thought Rickey wanted someone who was afraid to defend himself. But as they talked, he realized that in this case a truly brave man would have to avoid fighting. He thought for a while, then promised Rickey he would not fight back.

Robinson signed with the Dodgers and went to play in the minors in 1946. Rickey was right—fans insulted him, and so did players. But he performed brilliantly and avoided fights. Then, in 1947, he came to the majors.

Many Dodgers were angry. Some signed a petition demanding to be traded. But Robinson and Rickey were determined to make their experiment work.

On April 15—Opening Day—26,623 fans came out to Ebbets Field. More than half of them were black—Robinson was already their hero. Now he was making history just by being on the field.

The afternoon was cold and wet, but no one left the ballpark. The Dodgers beat the Boston Braves, 5–3. Robinson went hitless, but the hometown fans didn't seem to care—they cheered his every move.

Robinson's first season was difficult. Fans threatened to kill him; players tried to hurt him. The St. Louis Cardinals said they would strike if he took the field. And because of laws separating the races in certain states, he often couldn't eat or sleep in the same places as his teammates.

Yet through it all, he kept his promise to Rickey. No matter who insulted him, he never retaliated.

◆ **Build Vocabulary**

integrate (in´ tə grāt´) v.: Remove barriers and allow access to all

retaliated (ri tal´ ē at´ id) v.: Harmed or did wrong to someone in return for an injury or wrong he or she has done

▲ **Critical Viewing** What details in this picture indicate that Jackie Robinson and his teammates shared team spirit? [Analyze]

Robinson's dignity paid off. Thousands of fans jammed stadiums to see him play. The Dodgers set attendance records in a number of cities.

Slowly his teammates accepted him, realizing that he was the spark that made them a winning team. No one was more daring on the base paths or better with the glove. At the plate, he had great bat control—he could hit the ball anywhere. That season, he was named baseball's first Rookie of the Year.

Jackie Robinson went on to a glorious career. But he did more than play the game well—his bravery taught Americans a lesson. Branch Rickey opened a door, and Jackie Robinson stepped through it, making sure it could never be closed again. Something wonderful happened to baseball—and America—the day Jackie Robinson joined the Dodgers.

◆ **Literature and Your Life**
What does Robinson's achievement show about what it takes to accomplish important goals?

Beyond Literature

Media Connection

Documentaries When Geoffrey Ward and Ken Burns told Jackie Robinson's story in the television series *Baseball*, they were not the first to use a camera to show facts. Early movie audiences in the 1890's flocked to films called "actualities," which simply showed what some faraway place looked like.

To answer the question "What was (or is) it like?" documentaries use films, photographs, and audio recordings of actual events. They may also include interviews and dramatic reenactments. Documentaries can tell about anything from endangered animals to family life in America. Unlike actualities, documentaries tell a unified story. They explain as much as they show.

Cross-Curricular Activity

Documentary Working with a group, make a video documentary of an event at school or in the community. Decide whom to interview and what to show. With the help of an adult, edit your documentary, and show it to the class.

Guide for Responding

◆ LITERATURE AND YOUR LIFE

Reader's Response Would you have accepted a place on the team if you had been in Jackie Robinson's shoes? Why or why not?

Thematic Focus How did Jackie Robinson create a new road for others to follow? Give examples.

Group Discussion In a group, think of famous people whose stories you know. Discuss the obstacles they had to overcome to meet success. What conclusions can you draw about whether talent is all that people need to succeed?

☑ Check Your Comprehension

1. Who was Branch Rickey? What was his relationship to Jackie Robinson?
2. Why did Jackie Robinson come to the attention of Branch Rickey?
3. Name three difficult situations that Jackie Robinson and the Dodgers faced in Robinson's first season.

◆ Critical Thinking

INTERPRET

1. Identify three traits that made Jackie Robinson a good choice for Rickey's plan. **[Connect]**
2. How would you describe the mood of fans and players when Jackie Robinson played on Opening Day, 1947? **[Infer]**
3. In one sentence, write a lesson that Jackie Robinson taught baseball and America. **[Synthesize]**

EVALUATE

4. This essay suggests that an integrated society is a healthy society. Explain whether you agree or disagree and why. Try to include examples from history or current events. **[Support]**

COMPARE LITERARY WORKS

5. Abraham Lincoln, Jackie Robinson, and Branch Rickey are important subjects in American history. What similarities do you find among the characteristics or personalities of these men? **[Compare]**

Guide for Responding (continued)

◆ Reading Strategy

IDENTIFY MAIN IDEAS

When you read nonfiction, it's important to identify and understand **main ideas.** The main ideas are the points the author wants you to remember.

1. List three main ideas about Abraham Lincoln that you identified while reading "A Backwoods Boy."
2. Explain two main ideas you identified in "Jackie Robinson: Justice at Last."

◆ Build Vocabulary

USING THE PREFIX *re-*

The prefix *re-*, as in *retaliate,* means "back" or "again." On your paper, explain what goes back or happens again in each of these words beginning with the prefix *re-*.

1. remember   3. reverse   5. regain
2. redesign   4. retaliate   6. reunite

SPELLING STRATEGY

The *tude* sound, as in the word *aptitude,* is spelled *tude,* not *tood.*

Write a word that ends with *tude* to complete each sentence:

1. The way you think, act, or feel reflects your _____?_____.
2. You show your _____?_____ when you feel grateful.
3. Your natural ability is your _____?_____.

USING THE WORD BANK

Answer the following questions or statements with yes or no. Then, explain your responses.

1. Did Abraham Lincoln have an *aptitude* for public speaking?
2. Did the practice of law *intrigue* Lincoln?
3. Was the Sangamon River a *treacherous* place for steamboats?
4. Did Jackie Robinson help baseball become *integrated?*
5. Did Branch Rickey convince Jackie Robinson not to *retaliate* against prejudice?

◆ Literary Focus

FACTUAL ACCOUNT

A **factual account** gives the facts and details about an event or a person. In addition, the author may explain or interpret the facts presented.

1. In New Salem, Lincoln spent much time reading. What explanation does Freedman give of this fact?
2. In "Jackie Robinson: Justice at Last," what is the authors' interpretation of Jackie Robinson's response to teammates and spectators who mistreated him?

◆ Build Grammar Skills

CONJUNCTIONS JOINING SENTENCES

A **conjunction** is a word that links other words or groups of words. When conjunctions join sentences (complete thoughts), they indicate the relationship between the ideas in the sentences they join. The conjunction *and* indicates addition. *But* and *yet* indicate a contrast between ideas. *For* and *so* indicate a cause-and-effect relationship.

Practice Copy each sentence on your paper. Underline the conjunction, and explain the connection between ideas.

1. Abraham and his sister were fortunate, for their stepmother was a warm and loving person.
2. He would carry a book out to the field with him, so he could read at the end of each plow furrow. . . .
3. Nancy had nursed her relatives until the end, and then she too came down with the disease.
4. The afternoon was cold and wet, but no one left the ballpark.
5. Branch Rickey opened a door and Jackie Robinson stepped through it. . . .

Writing Application On your paper, rewrite the following passage. Use conjunctions to combine sentences and show the relationship between ideas.

Rickey saw Robinson's talent. Rickey wanted him on his team. Robinson agreed. Robinson was worried about people's reactions.

Build Your Portfolio

 ## Idea Bank

Writing

1. **Announcement** Write a brief announcement about Jackie Robinson's joining the Dodgers. Include the date and facts about the people and circumstances involved.

2. **Book Proposal** Write a proposal for a book based on a person or event from history. In your proposal, explain why the person is worth writing about and why readers will be interested.

3. **History Report** Choose a topic from history that interests you and prepare a report about it. Make sure you choose a narrow, focused topic, such as Lincoln's Emancipation Proclamation or his assassination, rather than a big topic, such as Lincoln's life. **[Social Studies Link]**

Speaking and Listening

4. **Role Play** With a partner, role-play the first conversation between Branch Rickey and Jackie Robinson. Include what the account tells you they said, as well as what you imagine they might have said.

5. **Radio Announcement** Think of an unusual event that is "a first." Make a radio announcement about the event. You might like to tape-record the announcement and play it for the class. **[Performing Arts Link; Media Link]**

Projects

6. **Timeline [Group Activity]** With a group, create a visual timeline for the life of Abraham Lincoln. Group members can do research, find or draw pictures, or write explanations. **[Social Studies Link; Art Link]**

7. **Posters** Create a poster that advertises a political appearance by Abraham Lincoln or a baseball game in which Jackie Robinson played. **[Art Link]**

 ## Writing Mini-Lesson

Contract

When Jackie Robinson joined the Dodgers, he signed a contract—a written agreement between two parties. He promised to fulfill certain obligations to the team, and the team made promises to him in return. Write a contract that states the details of an agreement between you and a friend, a teacher, or a family member. For example, you and your teacher may have a contract about what work you will complete in a given week.

Writing Skills Focus:
State Main Points Clearly

In your contract, **state the main points clearly.** Say what each person or group is expected to do. In the following quotation, Branch Rickey clearly states the main point of his agreement with Jackie Robinson.

Model

"I want a baseball player with guts enough not to fight back."
—Branch Rickey.

Prewriting List all the points on which you and the other person must agree. Write out each person's responsibilities in a complete sentence.

Drafting Organize your points in order of importance. Begin with your most important point, and follow with less important points.

Revising Show your contract to the person for whom you wrote it. Revise to make points clearer or more accurate.

> ◆ **Grammar Application**
> Join some of your sentences with conjunctions that show how the ideas connect.

Persuasive Essay

Writing Process Workshop

Muscles and brains alone won't get the job done. When you want to build a new park or change an old law, you must first change people's minds. A **persuasive essay** presents a particular view, using arguments, examples, and vivid language. Write a persuasive essay using the following tips, introduced in this section's Writing Mini-Lessons.

Writing Skills Focus

▶ **Appeal to logic.** Show readers why your ideas make sense or how they will benefit from what you are asking them to do. (See p. 333.)

▶ **Choose appropriate details.** Present details that guide readers to your point of view. For instance, mentioning that African Americans fought for the United States in World War II helps readers see the injustice of segregation. (See p. 341.)

▶ **State your main points clearly.** Identify your main ideas, and present them clearly. "Building a new town dump will create too much traffic" clearly states a main idea, which is lost in these sentences: "The dump will force people to drive to Birch Street to get downtown. What a mess!" (See p. 357.)

MODEL FROM LITERATURE

from "Jackie Robinson: Justice at Last,"
Geoffrey C. Ward and Ken Burns

    It was 1945, and World War II had ended. Americans of all races had died for their country. ① Yet black men were still not allowed in the major leagues. ② The national pastime was loved by all America, but the major leagues were for white men only. ③

① Details like these suggest that race should not divide the country.

② This sentence clearly states one of the main ideas of the piece.

③ The writer uses logic to show that it makes no sense to exclude men who were willing to die for their country from the pleasures their country offers.

Prewriting

Choose a Topic Choose an issue that has at least two sides. Think of stories in the news, problems people are discussing, or changes in your community. Browse through news magazines for ideas.

Topic Ideas

- Should all students wear school uniforms?
- Should adults restrict kids' television viewing?
- On what items should schools spend money first?
- How can the problem of crime be solved?

Outline Main Ideas Write out a clear statement of each main idea. Then, arrange these statements in an order that makes sense: from most to least important, according to a sequence of events, or as a sequence of logical steps.

Gather Appropriate Support For each main idea, gather appropriate supporting details. These details might be statistics, facts, or expert opinions.

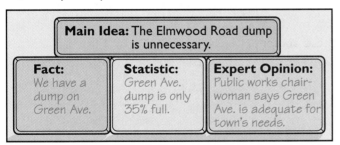

Main Idea: The Elmwood Road dump is unnecessary.

| **Fact:** We have a dump on Green Ave. | **Statistic:** Green Ave. dump is only 35% full. | **Expert Opinion:** Public works chairwoman says Green Ave. is adequate for town's needs. |

Create Effective Descriptions The words you use to describe a situation and the images you use to help readers picture it have persuasive power. A *modern refuse disposal system* sounds like the sort of thing every town should have. A *towering heap of old tires, dead batteries, and other garbage* does not. The phrase you choose to describe the new town dump depends on whether or not you support the dump.

Drafting

Start Right Begin with an attention-getting image, question, or statement that dramatizes your point of view. An essay on new rules at the public pool, for instance, might start "Twenty people run screaming, pushing their enemies into the

---

DRAFTING/REVISING

APPLYING LANGUAGE SKILLS: Avoid Exaggeration

If you emphasize positive or negative qualities to make them seem more important than they are, readers will be skeptical. State your points accurately. Avoid exaggeration, and place effective emphasis on each point you make.

Exaggeration: *A new town dump will be a bigger disaster than the sinking of the* Titanic.

Reader Response: "Oh, sure."

Effective Emphasis: *Opening a town dump will cause more problems than it solves.*

Reader Response: "I wonder what problems it will cause."

Practice Rewrite these sentences to avoid exaggeration.

1. My dog's bigger than Godzilla.
2. I'm dying of thirst!
3. It's the worst day in my life.

Writing Application Review your draft for ineffective exaggerations. Rewrite for effective emphasis.

Writer's Solution Connection Writing Lab

For instruction on other errors of persuasive style, use the section Avoiding Unreasonable Arguments in the tutorial on Persuasion.

APPLYING LANGUAGE SKILLS: Avoid Double Negatives

One negative word, such as *no, not, never,* or *hardly,* is enough to change the meaning of a sentence.

Examples:

I swim in the deep ocean.

I **never** swim in the deep ocean.

When you use two negative words to express a single negative idea, you make an error known as a double negative.

Example:

I **don't never** swim in the deep ocean.

Practice Correct the double negatives.

1. Jackie Robinson wasn't never in a fight.
2. Abe Lincoln didn't hardly ever go to the big city.
3. There isn't nobody who can keep a selchie on land forever.

Writing Application Correct any double negatives you find in your essay.

Writer's Solution Connection
Language Lab

For more on double negatives, complete the Avoiding Double Negatives lesson in the Using Modifiers unit of the Language Lab.

---

water. Is this a scene from a movie about barbarian warriors? No, it is a common sight at the local pool."

Follow Your Outline Use your outline of main ideas to organize your draft. At the appropriate points, add the supporting evidence and effective images you have chosen.

End With a Bang Make sure your readers remember your point of view. Sum up your main points and arguments in a dramatic conclusion. End with a memorable image or restatement of your point of view.

Revising

Use a Checklist As you review your draft, look for each of the items on this checklist:

▶ An effective, attention-getting introduction
▶ The use of logical arguments to make points
▶ The use of appropriate details, such as colorful descriptions and evidence

REVISION MODEL

Building a new town dump on Elmwood Road will re-route cars to Smith Road. Should a town vote for more traffic and more wasted money? That is exactly what some Town Council members might do. ∧
① If approved, the proposed Elmwood Road dump will increase taxes and increase existing traffic problems. **The traffic on**
② tangled up worse than yarn after a kitten has played with it.
Smith Road is already ∧ a problem. The new dump is not necessary, ∧ ③ since the old dump is still far from full.

① The writer has added a sentence that clearly states the main point.
② The writer has added a colorful image for stronger support.
③ The writer has added an appeal to logic.

Publishing and Presenting

▶ **Opinion Magazine** Work with your classmates to produce a magazine of opinion pieces containing your persuasive essays. Select photographs or produce illustrations or diagrams to accompany each essay.

▶ **Discussion** Work with classmates to organize a discussion. Choose two students' essays at random and distribute copies. After the class has read them, students should discuss whether they agree or disagree with each writer's viewpoint.

Strategies for Success

One good way to become involved when you read an article is to challenge the text. When readers challenge a text, they ask questions, check the writer's logic, and think of points of view other than the one presented. Often, you will find that you understand a writer's ideas better after you have challenged them.

Question Unreasonable Claims Question statements that sound unreasonable. For instance, consider the headline "Yogurt-Eaters Live to Be 150 Years Old." You might decide that the statement is unrealistic, since it is very rare for people to live 150 years. As you read the article, you should ask: "How many examples of 150-year-old yogurt-eaters does the writer provide?" You might also decide that the statement sounds unreasonable, since it suggests that a single food can prolong someone's life. You should ask: "What other health factors, such as exercise, does the article examine?"

Pony Knows Numbers

Lakeville, CA—Lightning, a Shetland pony, can add and subtract numbers up to ten. When his owner says, "Four plus four," the pony paws the ground eight times. Owner Beth Wilson says that Lightning is able to do math because his parents were so much more intelligent than other ponies. She taught him numbers by saying the word "one," and then tapping his hoof once. She would then say "two," and tap his hoof twice, and so on. Lightning must be good at math because people come from all over the area to watch him add.

Look for Support Writers should support their arguments. Support may take the form of personal experience, logical arguments, expert opinions, or statistical studies. Examine the connections between a writer's main ideas and the support he or she gives them.

Consider Another Viewpoint A writer might argue that summer tourists should be banned from town because they create a lot of litter and noise. To consider another viewpoint, you would ask: "Do tourists help the town in some ways? Are there other solutions to the problems of noise and litter?"

Apply the Strategies

Read the article "Pony Knows Numbers" in the left column. Then, respond to the following.

1. Identify one unrealistic claim in the story.

2. Which of the owner's statements are unsupported by evidence?

3. What further evidence might help you believe the story's main claim?

4. Does the writer logically support the claim that Lightning is good at math?

5. Identify another viewpoint you might take on Lightning's performance.

✔ Here are other situations in which you can use the strategies for challenging an article:
- ▶ Visiting a Web site
- ▶ Reading an advertisement
- ▶ Investigating a rumor

Grammar Review

An **interjection** is a word or a group of words that expresses emotion. It has no grammatical relation to the rest of the words in a sentence. (See page 332.) Use an exclamation point after an interjection that expresses strong feeling; use a comma after one that expresses mild emotion:

>**Strong:** *Wow!* Look at all this free stuff!

>**Mild:** *Oh,* actually that's mine.

A **coordinating conjunction** is a word that links two or more words or groups of words of the same kind. (See page 340.)

Category	Examples
Single Words	*tall* yet *slender* (two adjectives) *cars* and *bicycles* (two nouns) *ran* but *fell* (two verbs)
Phrases	We drove *over the river* and *through the woods.*
Sentences	We *ran fast,* and *we got there just in time.* I *waited for her,* but *she did not come.*

Each coordinating conjunction indicates a different kind of connection between the things, facts, or ideas it links.

Coordinating Conjunctions	Kind of Connection
and	indicates combination
but	indicates opposition
or, nor	indicates a choice or alternative
for, so	indicates cause and effect
yet	indicates the unexpected

different forms of a verb
con·junc·tion (kən juŋk'shən) *n.* 1 a joining together, combination [High winds, in conjunction with rain, made travel difficult.] 2 a word used to join other words, phrases, or clauses ["And," "but," "or," and "if" are *conjunctions.*]
con·jure (kän'jər) *v.* to practice magic or witchcraft [a strange device...]

Practice 1 Copy these sentences. Circle each interjection. Underline each coordinating conjunction.

1. Wow! Sometimes the selchie is a man and sometimes he is a seal.
2. She feels as if her grandfather still lives in the house, but he is gone.
3. Gee, I'd love to sail away in a balloon or even to take a short trip in one.
4. You know, Whitman may be the better poet, yet I prefer E. E. Cummings.
5. No way! Jackie Robinson is one of baseball's greats.

Practice 2 Use a coordinating conjunction with the appropriate meaning to combine each pair of sentences into a single sentence. (Replace the first period with a comma.)

1. Abraham Lincoln had little schooling. He succeeded anyway.
2. She wanted a son. One day her husband brought home a child.
3. The boy turned into a seal as soon as he entered the water. He still came back to visit the fisherfolk.

Grammar in Writing

✔ *Combine sentences with the right coordinating conjunction to make a clear, quick connection between ideas or events.*

If you've ever talked about music or a television show with some friends, you've participated in a group discussion. Though such discussions may seem to come naturally, there are actually a few skills that will help you get the most out of group discussions:

Keep the Dialogue Going If people in a discussion just make statements saying what they think, the discussion won't be very interesting. To keep the dialogue going, the participants should respond to one another's statements by expressing agreement or disagreement, asking for more details, or asking for clarification.

Be Clear State your points clearly. The other people in the discussion may not have had the same experiences as you have had. Give them as much information as they need to understand what you are saying.

Be Respectful Give each person in the group a chance to speak. Don't cut people off or interrupt. If you disagree with someone, explain why, giving reasons and examples. If someone in the group remains quiet, ask for his or her opinion to encourage participation.

Apply the Strategies

In a group of four or five, hold a discussion about the best movie that you've seen this year. Afterward, write an evaluation of the discussion, using the following criteria and including suggestions for improvement.

1. Did the group keep the dialogue going?
2. Was the group respectful of members' contributions?
3. Were members' contributions clear?

Tips for Participating in a Group Discussion

✔ *In a group discussion, follow these strategies:*

▶ Elect a group leader. The leader can act as "referee" and call on group members who want to speak.
▶ Elect a notetaker.
▶ Look for common ideas. If John liked everything in *Deadly Weapon 9* except the fights and Sara hated the battles in *Cosmic Pirates*, ask both if they think movies are too violent.

What's Behind the **Words**

Vocabulary Adventures With Richard Lederer

Portmanteau Words (Blends)

The Language Blender

Carroll's spirit lives on in today's inventive language. Do you need a word to express the action of splashing and spattering? How about *splatter*? What about a meal served between breakfast and lunch? Try *brunch*. Smoke plus fog? They call it *smog*. If your hotel caters to motorists, why not call it a *motel*? What should you call stairs that move in the manner of an escalading (ladder-climbing) elevator? *Escalator* will work just fine. And if your puppets look like moppets (little children), why not name them *Muppets*? Carroll would have been proud to pack these words in his portmanteau!

I n *Through the Looking Glass*, the character Humpty Dumpty says, "When *I* use a word . . . it means just what I choose it to mean." Lewis Carroll, the author of *Through the Looking Glass* and other fantasies, had great fun telling words what to do. He even invented a few of his own. He called some of his creations *portmanteau* (pôrt man´ tō´) *words*. Just as people cram clothes into a portmanteau (a kind of suitcase), Carroll scrunched two words into one to make a portmanteau word.

Carroll's most famous inventions appear in his nonsense poem "Jabberwocky"—*chortle,* which is a blend of *chuckle* and *snort,* and *galumph,* a combination of *gallop* and *triumph.* Any horse may gallop, but only a horse that feels victorious can *galumph. Chortle* has since been adopted into English as a word describing a laugh that, well, sounds like a *chuckle* with a *snort.*

ACTIVITY 1 What portmanteau words can be made from the following parts:

1. flash + gush
2. haggle + tussle
3. blow + spurt
4. flutter + hurry
5. squirm + wiggle
6. twist + whirl

ACTIVITY 2 *Time* magazine is famous for its snappy portmanteau word creations. Among the magazine's inventions is *microphonies*, people who act fake while speaking in public. Using your imagination, make up three original blends. List the meaning of each part and the definition of the entire portmanteau creation.

Extended Reading Opportunities

When you feel discouraged, a story about someone else's success can help you see through your own difficulties. The books recommended here are just a few possibilities for reading about young people who struggle to find their own way in the world.

Suggested Titles

Outcast
Rosemary Sutcliff

Beric is the only survivor of a shipwreck off the coast of Britain. The trouble is, Beric is the survivor of a Roman shipwreck, and Romans are the enemies of the British tribe who save the infant castaway. Although the tribe is willing to ignore Beric's heritage while he is still a child, the time comes when they can no longer accept him as part of their world. His life depends on finding his place in a treacherous and unfriendly world.

Tuck Everlasting
Natalie Babbitt

Winnie Foster and Mae Tuck have very different lives. Winnie is a young girl struggling to gain some independence. Mae is an older woman, with a lot of living behind her. The lives of Winnie and Mae and her family are about to come together. When Mae's son Jesse meets Winnie, a chain of events is set in motion that makes problems and solves problems. Soon, Winnie is faced with the choice of a lifetime.

Sing Down the Moon
Scott O'Dell

Fourteen-year-old Bright Morning and her friend Running Bird head out with the sheep just as they do every morning. This morning, though, will change Bright Morning's life forever. As she relaxes in the sunshine, her dog alerts her to the approach of Spanish slavers. Her struggle to keep her identity and her dignity will keep you on the edge of your seat.

Other Possibilities

Mrs. Frisby and the Rats of NIMH	Robert C. O'Brien
The Westing Game	Ellen Raskin
Amos Fortune: Free Man	Elizabeth Yates
Sadako and the Thousand Paper Cranes	Eleanor Coerr

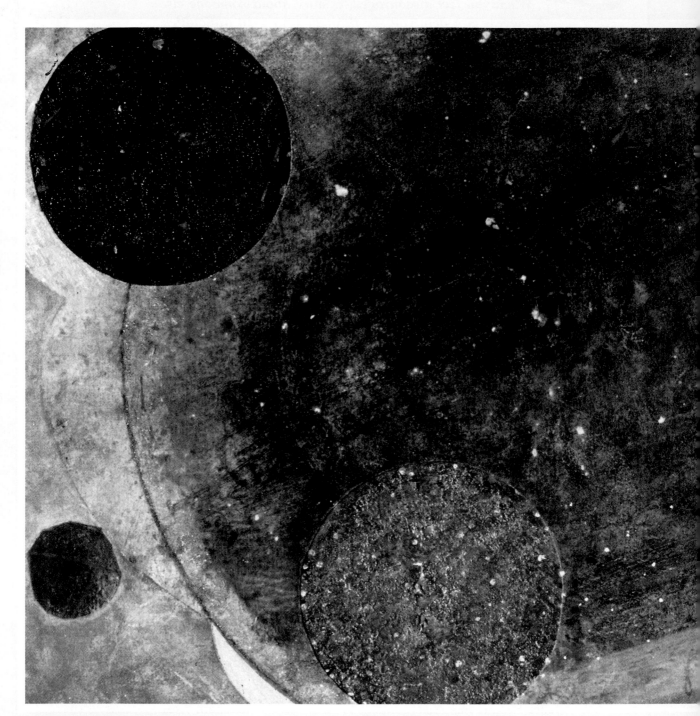

This, That, There, 1993, Pat Adams, Courtesy of Eleanor Munro

Mysterious Worlds

The picture on these pages could be a view of distant planets as seen through a telescope, or it could be a view of microorganisms as seen through a microscope. The stories, poems, and essays in this unit give you a lens through which you can examine mysteries near and far. Through the literature, you can explore the mysteries of the past, search for answers to the unexplained, and appreciate the mysteries in the everyday world around you.

Guide for Reading

Meet the Author:

Katherine B. Shippen (1892–1980)

An April Fool's Day baby, Katherine B. Shippen was born in 1892, in Hoboken, New Jersey. Before she began her writing career, she worked as a history teacher and as a curator of social studies at the Children's Museum in Brooklyn, New York.

A Late Bloomer Shippen wrote her first book, *New Found World,* when she was more than fifty years old. Her work as a teacher gave her topics and skills for writing for young people. In her book *Passage to America,* she explored the immigrant experience through the eyes of her students. She once commented, "I'm very used to talking to young people, and writing isn't very much different."

Past, Present, and Future In addition to history and biography, Shippen also wrote about medicine, aeronautics, and archaeology. She received the Newbery Honor in 1956 for her work *Men, Microscopes, and Living Things.* In this selection from *Portals to the Past,* you will learn about the many attempts to uncover the truth behind one of the world's great archaeological mysteries.

◆ LITERATURE AND YOUR LIFE

CONNECT YOUR EXPERIENCE

When you watch a mystery movie or television program, you probably find yourself searching along with the detective or hero for clues to the mystery. Similarly, scientists, historians, and archaeologists search for clues to the real-life mysteries of the past. In "The Strange Geometry of Stonehenge," you will learn about Stonehenge, a mysterious cluster of huge stones in England.

THEMATIC FOCUS: Mysterious Worlds

In reading about Stonehenge, you may notice the ways in which exploring the past is like exploring an unfamiliar world.

◆ Background for Understanding

SOCIAL STUDIES

Archaeologists are scientists who study people and lifestyles of the past. The scientists who worked to discover the origins of Stonehenge have found clues that point to a number of ancient times and cultures. The dates below will help you understand the different theories about when and by whom Stonehenge was built. Refer to these dates as you read "The Strange Geometry of Stonehenge."

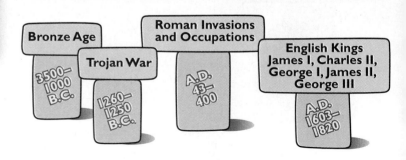

Bronze Age — 3500–1000 B.C.

Trojan War — 1260–1250 B.C.

Roman Invasions and Occupations — A.D. 43–400

English Kings James I, Charles II, George I, James II, George III — A.D. 1603–1820

The Strange Geometry of Stonehenge

Katherine B. Shippen

◀ **Critical Viewing** In what ways does this scene seem strange and mysterious? [Analyze]

In 1918 Sir Cecil Chubb of Salisbury made a unique gift to the English government. The gift was Stonehenge, a group of rough-hewn stones that stand on the chalk downs[1] of Salisbury Plain. When he presented them to England, Sir Cecil did not know exactly what he was giving. He did not know how these stones came to be in the middle of the plain, or who had dragged them there, or why they were arranged as they were. The only thing he knew was that they had stood there since time immemorial.

The huge cluster of upright stones which he had given his country stands in the center of a level circular space 300 feet wide, surrounded by a ditch and an earthwork. A grassy road which is now called "the Avenue" enters this space from the northeast and a single rough

boulder called the "Hele Stone" stands in the center of this road.

Within the outer circle the stones are carefully arranged in four series. First there is a circle of enormous "sarsen" stones, some of them 13 feet tall and weighing more than 40 tons. (The word "sarsen," which comes from "Saracen," meant anything heathenish to the people of the Middle Ages. None but the devil himself could have moved them, it was said.) Originally the sarsens in this great circle were joined by a line of lintels[2] fastened with crude stone tenons and mortises.[3]

---

2. **lintels** (lint' əlz) n.: Horizontal crosspieces over an opening.
3. **tenons** (ten' ənz) **and mortises** (môr' tis iz): Joints made by fitting extending parts (tenons) into adjoining holes (mortises).

◆ **Build Vocabulary**

immemorial (im' me môr' ē əl) adj.: Ancient; extending back before memory

---

1. **chalk downs:** Areas of open, grassy plains situated over limestone (chalky) deposits.

▲ **Critical Viewing** Identify the sarsen stones and the lintels in this picture. [**Connect**]

With the passing of time, winds and storms have blown down the lintels. Some of them still lie on the ground. The stones of the circle inside the first are somewhat smaller and of a different kind. They are "bluestones."

Inside the bluestone circle there are sarsen stones again, and here they are arranged in a big horseshoe. The stones of the horseshoe have been put up in pairs, each pair topped by a stone lintel. Each group forms a trilithon.

> These details of measurement and placement are **facts**.

The trilithons are graduated in size; the tallest one, which stands opposite the opening of the horseshoe, is more than 22 feet high, with a lintel 16 feet long and 4 feet thick. Only two trilithons are standing today; originally there were probably eleven.

ƒ Finally, inside the horseshoe there are more bluestones, but only a few of them. Enough remain, however, to show that they were once arranged in an oval pattern.

At the heart of it all is a great recumbent stone which generations of men have called the "Altar Stone." But whether or not it was an altar, or for what god it was made, no one can say.

> These questions help you recognize that part of the author's **purpose** is to communicate the mystery of Stonehenge.

What did it mean, this gigantic exercise in geometry, these circles within circles, this colossal horseshoe? Who came here in the days when the patterns of these rocks were understood? What did they do here? Once a wide road led across the down to this place, a highway broad enough for glittering processions—but processions of whom? Were they soldiers? Or priests? Unused as the ages passed, the highway nearly disappeared, obliterated by the encroaching grass. Only very recently were the vague outlines of the road found again by the penetrating eye of a camera carried in an airplane.

Rough, <u>colossal</u>, <u>inscrutable</u>, the strange geometric pattern kept its secrets through the passing centuries. Legends about it have abounded. Some said the wizard Merlin got the devil to whisk these stones from Ireland in a single night. Others said that Queen Boadicea[4] was buried here. A brave and beautiful British woman, she died leading her people in a revolt against the Roman legions. But there was nothing to prove that this was her monument.

> Most people would probably agree with Shippen's **opinion** that the stones are not easy to understand.

Again it was said that this was a monument for Hengist and Horsa,[5] who had come from Jutland to help fight off the Picts and Scots[6] and had stayed to conquer the country for

---

4. **Queen Boadicea** (bō´ ad ə sē´ ə): Queen of a tribe in ancient Britain. She died in A.D. 62.
5. **Hengist** (heŋ´ gist) **and Horsa:** Brothers who were chiefs of a tribe that had come from Jutland (now Denmark).They died in A.D. 488 and 455, respectively.
6. **Picts and Scots:** People of ancient Great Britain who were driven into Scotland by the Britons and the Romans.

themselves. But nothing remains to show that Hengist and Horsa were buried there, either.

King James I in the seventeenth century apparently wanted to have done with legends. He sent his architect Inigo Jones to examine Stonehenge. Inigo Jones announced that without any doubt it was a Roman temple.

But the theory of Roman origin for the structure did not content the patriotic English. Charles II asked John Aubrey, a noted antiquarian, to investigate further. Aubrey lived not far from Stonehenge in Avebury, where there was another large circle of standing stones. It was generally believed that those stones marked the meeting place of the Druids,[7] the mysterious bards[8] and priests who had been such a powerful influence in England at the time of the Roman occupation. Stonehenge was built by the Druids too, Aubrey announced.

The more he investigated, the more Aubrey was sure the Druids had built Stonehenge. The Roman writers with whose work he was familiar had described the Druid ceremonies; it was said the Druids were accustomed to performing human sacrifices. Did they slaughter their victims here on the Altar Stone? Examining the earth inside the great circle enclosed by the ditch and earthwork, Aubrey found a series of depressions in the ground. Undoubtedly these had been deeper holes which time had filled with silt[9] and earth. Had the Druids once burned the bodies of their victims in these holes? The "Aubrey Holes" fired the imagination of all who came to Stonehenge now, and seemed to make it more certain that Stonehenge had been built by the Druids.

William Stukely, Secretary of the Society of Antiquaries in 1718, was as sure as anyone else that the Druids had built Stonehenge. He was a doctor of medicine but he was also a minister of the Christian Church, and he was greatly interested in trying to reconcile the Druids' beliefs with the Christians'. Perhaps the Druids had not been so savage, after all, he said; the only accounts of them were those written by the Romans who wanted to eradicate them. Stukely considered the Druids poets and moral teachers, and he rehearsed all the traditions that made the oak tree and the mistletoe sacred to them. There was no doubt in his mind that they had constructed Stonehenge, as he went methodically making the first survey of the place.

Now no one thought of any other origin for Stonehenge, and when in the eighteenth century people became interested in the esoteric wisdom of the East, it was maintained that the Druids were astrologers and that Stonehenge was a stellar[10] observatory. But there was no more to prove this than that it had been Boadicea's tomb.

The years passed and Stonehenge continued to hold a fascination for antiquarians, who tried again and again to understand it. In the nineteenth century a "Mr. Cunnington" made a great effort but had no success. Sure that he would not be the last one to seek an explanation for the great stones, he hid a bottle of good port wine under the Altar Stone for the refreshment of those who came after. It was not found again till 1920. And all this time people were more and more sure that Stonehenge had been built by the Druids.

Archaeological methods took a great step

> This information about past theories will help you **evaluate** Shippen's message about the theory she believes.

---

7. **Druids** (droo′ idz): Members of an order of priests in ancient Britain who appear in legends as prophets and sorcerers.

8. **bards** (bärds) *n.*: Poets and singers.

9. **silt** (silt) *n.*: Particles of sand, rock, and so forth that accumulate on the bottom of rivers or other bodies of water.

10. **stellar** (stel′ ər): *adj.*: Of the stars.

◆ **Build Vocabulary**

colossal (kə läs′ əl) *adj.*: Huge; gigantic

inscrutable (in skroot′ ə bəl) *adj.*: Not easy to understand

eradicate (i rad′ i kāt′) *v.*: Wipe out

forward in the twentieth century, and various sciences were now joined together in investigation. Astronomy was one of these.

For some time it had been observed that if you stood behind the Altar Stone at dawn on Midsummer Day and looked straight through the great horseshoe and along the Avenue you would see the sun come up behind the Hele Stone. Scholars believed this <u>orientation</u> proved that the great design must have been made by sun worshipers. Sir Norman Lockyer, the British Royal Astronomer, was much interested in this. It was known that with the slightly irregular movement of the earth the exact point at which the sun rises on a given date each year varies slightly, and by precise calculations it is possible to determine exactly how much. If Stonehenge was oriented to the rising sun on Midsummer Day, it would be possible to find out by astronomical calculations in what year it was built.

In 1901 Sir Norman made these astronomical calculations. Stonehenge was built at a date "lying between 1900 and 1500 B.C.," he announced. But that was a thousand years before anyone ever mentioned Druids in England. If Sir Norman's conclusions were right, the whole fabric of the belief in the Druid construction of Stonehenge was destroyed. And those who looked up at the mammoth stones were more than ever at a loss to understand them.

Astronomy was not the only tool that was used to banish the idea that the Druids had built Stonehenge. While Sir Norman was working out the year in which the sun first rose over the Altar Stone, an archaeologist named Gowland began to excavate. He dug carefully at six different points so that he could compare the things he found at one place with those he found at another. As he dug he noted the exact depth of every man-made object that he found. In all six places there were coins in the first ten-inch layer—a penny of George III, a half-penny of George I, a pewter farthing of James II—and below these were coins of Roman date.

Now Gowland dug deeper. Two or three feet down he found tools of flint, then axes and hammerstones of sand-stone, and finally massive pounding hammers, or mauls—the tools that had pounded the great

> Here, Shippen reports **facts**—the items that were found.

menhirs[11] of Stonehenge into shape. But these were not all. At last, near one of the trilithons, he found a chip of sarsen stone with a small green stain of oxidized copper. This artifact indicated that the builders had lived in the Bronze Age.

Astronomy and archaeology had now confirmed each other. Stonehenge had not been built by the Druids, but a thousand years before their time. In 1950 this date was established in a third way, for charcoal dug from one of the Aubrey Holes confirmed it. Carbon-14 dating[12] placed the construction at 1847 B.C., with a possible variation of 225 years.

So the cool, precise work of the scientists put an end to legends and superstitions. There could be no more talk of Druids at Stonehenge now. Nevertheless, the ancient structure was as mysterious as it had ever been. Whence had the great stones come? Why were they of two different kinds?

> The statement that the ancient structure was as mysterious as it had ever been is an **opinion**.

Geology was another science that helped find an answer to these questions. Geological study now proved that the sarsen stones of gray sandstone must have been brought from the Marlborough Downs 24 miles away. But

---

◆ **Build Vocabulary**

orientation (ôr´ ē en tā´ shən) n.: Position in relation to the points of the compass

successive (sək ses´ iv) adj.: Following one after another in sequence

---

11. **menhirs** (men´ hirs) n.: Huge, rough, upright stones.
12. **Carbon-14 dating:** Method of dating archaeological finds by measuring the amount of radioactive carbon-14 remaining in them.

the bluestones were another matter. The nearest place that bluestone was to be found was in the Prescelly mountains in South Wales, 150 miles from Stonehenge. Why these stones were chosen, and how they were transported over the hills and valleys, and across the rivers, no one has been able to say.

Stuart Piggott, an eminent British archaeologist, started to excavate at Stonehenge in 1950. He carefully left more than half the area untouched, for he held that the diggers of the future would undoubtedly develop techniques superior to his own and he did not want to spoil their work.

After working some time Piggott announced that the earthworks and big stone circles and the horseshoe were not all put up at the same time. <u>Successive</u> groups came and went, he held, building and destroying and building up again over a period of about four hundred years. He thought the ditch and earthwork, the circle of Aubrey Holes, the Avenue, and the Hele Stone were all part of the original construction built about 1847 B.C. Another group of people made the two rings of bluestones, and later the huge sarsen circle and the trilithon horseshoe were put up. These

▲ **Critical Viewing** What can you see in this aerial photograph that you cannot see in the photographs taken on the ground? [**Compare and Contrast**]

were the last to be built, and they were made about 1500 B.C.

In all three phases the line between the center of the Altar Stone and the center of the Hele Stone was preserved, proving that all the builders had been sun worshipers and that this was not a monument or a meeting place, but a temple to the sun.

Up to 1953 no more could be found out about Stonehenge and its builders, even with the most modern scientific research. And then, by accident, a new discovery was made. It was late on a June afternoon, and the sun's rays were striking the surface of one of the sarsens obliquely. They cast small shadows wherever there were scratches or indentations on the stone's surface. One of the excavators noticed what seemed to be a pattern scratched on the stone. He looked more closely and observed that two images had been cut there. One was that of an ax. Its form was familiar enough, for many axes of this type had been uncovered in digging around the sarsens. But the other image was startling. For there, neatly etched, was a dagger—a dagger with a round handle and a long pointed blade. The English had never used daggers of this kind. This was the sort of weapon carried by the Mycenaean Greeks who influenced the culture of the Eastern Mediterranean at the time of the Trojan war. This finding seemed to indicate that the builders of Stonehenge had gone to the Eastern Mediterranean to employ an architect. Here, carved on the stone, was his symbol.

With the finding of the dagger other facts that had been casually observed became significant. There was, for instance, the shape of the sarsens; they bulged slightly, just as the pillars of the Greek temples did. And there was the technique of shaping the stone blocks. They had been banged with the heavy stone mauls which had been found in the ground near them. The granite obelisks[13] of Egypt had been fashioned in exactly the same way.

Was it an architect from the Eastern Mediterranean who was commissioned to design Stonehenge? Did the fame of the Mycenaean Greek builders extend all the way to Britain thirty-five hundred years ago? Was their reputation so great the Britons wanted a "foreigner" to design their precious temple to the sun? The sun itself, striking the stone with the slanting rays of the late afternoon, had posed new questions.

> When you **evaluate** Shippen's message, consider her thoroughness and the facts she included to support her message.

---

13. **obelisks** (äb´ ə lisks) *n.*: Tall, slender, four-sided stone pillars tapering toward their tops, which are shaped like pyramids.

Guide for Responding

◆ LITERATURE AND YOUR LIFE

Reader's Response Would you like to know more about Stonehenge after reading this article? Explain.

Thematic Focus What techniques have scientists used to discover Stonehenge's past?

☑ Check Your Comprehension

1. What are the sarsen stones?
2. Describe the bluestones.
3. What group of people was formerly believed to have built Stonehenge?
4. What evidence disproved this theory?
5. What new theory is supported by the image of the dagger on the sarsen stone?

◆ Critical Thinking

INTERPRET
1. Why is Stonehenge referred to as a "giant exercise in geometry"? **[Interpret]**
2. How did Sir Norman's new evidence add to the mystery of Stonehenge? **[Analyze]**
3. Contrast the two images that were accidentally discovered in 1953. **[Contrast]**

EVALUATE
4. Which theory about Stonehenge do you find most interesting? Why? **[Make a Judgment]**

EXTEND
5. Draw a diagram of Stonehenge. Use a scale, such as 1/2 inch to represent ten feet, to place the stones correctly. **[Math Link]**

Guide for Responding (continued)

◆ Reading for Success

STRATEGIES FOR READING CRITICALLY

Review the reading strategies and the notes showing how to read critically. Then, apply the strategies to do the following:

1. In your own words, state Shippen's purpose for writing "The Strange Geometry of Stonehenge."
2. Identify three facts and one opinion in the essay. The opinion may be the author's or one of the scientist's described in the essay.
3. Evaluate how well Shippen achieves her purpose. Give three reasons for your evaluation.

◆ Build Vocabulary

USING FORMS OF *orientation*

On your paper, use *orient, orientation,* or *disoriented* to complete each sentence.

1. Scientists considered the ___?___ of the stones.
2. They thought ancient people tried to ___?___ the stones to the sun.
3. Unable to see where they were, the scientists became ___?___.

SPELLING STRATEGY

Many words, such as *successive,* contain the sound *ses* spelled *cess.* In your notebook, write a word containing *cess* for each clue.

1. A break or time off: r_ _ _ _ _
2. Required or unavoidable: n _ _ _ _ _ a _ _
3. A method of doing something: p _ _ _ _ _ _

USING THE WORD BANK

On your paper, write the word or phrase that is most similar in meaning to the Word Bank word.

1. immemorial: (a) immature, (b) statue, (c) beyond memory
2. colossal: (a) sickening, (b) huge, (c) minor
3. eradicate: (a) break, (b) irritate, (c) wipe out
4. orientation: (a) confusion, (b) position, (c) ship
5. successive: (a) one after another, (b) certain, (c) last
6. inscrutable: (a) playful, (b) sad, (c) mysterious

◆ Literary Focus

ANALYTICAL ESSAY

Analytical essays examine a large idea or subject by breaking it into smaller parts. Looking at the parts helps you understand how they fit together and what they mean as a whole.

1. What is the big idea or subject of "The Strange Geometry of Stonehenge"?
2. What are three parts of this idea? How are they related?

◆ Build Grammar Skills

COMPLETE SUBJECTS AND PREDICATES

A sentence consists of two parts, a subject and a predicate. The **subject** is the part that tells what or whom the sentence is about. The **complete subject** is the main noun in the subject and any words that describe it. The **predicate** is the part that tells what the subject does or is. The **complete predicate** is the verb and the nouns that receive the action or further identify the subject, plus any words that describe the verb or the nouns.

Complete Subject	Complete Predicate
Sir Cecil Chubb of Salisbury	made a unique gift to the English government.

Practice Copy the following sentences onto your paper. Circle the complete subject, and underline the complete predicate.

1. The stones of the horseshoe are set in pairs.
2. The King of England did not agree.
3. The Secretary of Antiquaries had a theory.
4. The image was startling to the scientists studying Stonehenge.
5. The scientist's precise work stopped the legends.

Writing Application On your paper, add details to the following subjects and predicates. Then, circle the complete subject and underline the complete predicate.

1. Stokely believed.
2. Stonehenge stands.
3. Scientists discovered.
4. Geology helped.

The Strange Geometry of Stonehenge ◆ 377

Build Your Portfolio

 Idea Bank

Writing

1. Travel Brochure Write a pamphlet for tourists who want to visit Stonehenge. Capture their interest with mysterious questions and scientific facts.

2. Future Archaeology Describe a place you go—such as a mall or a pizza place—as if you were an archaeologist in the future discovering this "ancient" ruin.

3. Stonehenge Story Write an outline for a short story about the Stonehenge mystery. Your setting can be Stonehenge in ancient times or Stonehenge as we know it today.

Speaking and Listening

4. Explanation Review the work of one of the people described in "The Strange Geometry of Stonehenge." Give a brief explanation of the work to your class. Use note cards to remember dates and statistics, but do not read a speech. **[Performing Arts Link]**

5. Visual Interpretation Using an aerial photograph or a diagram, explain to the class the placement of the different stones at Stonehenge.

Projects

6. Timeline Archaeologists have placed the building of Stonehenge at different times in the past. On a timeline, show the different times that Stonehenge was believed to have been built. **[Social Studies Link]**

7. An Architectural Model Using clay, stones, or other materials, create a scale model of Stonehenge. Identify the parts with labels. Display your model for the class. **[Art Link]**

 Writing Mini-Lesson

Proposal for a Research Project

Write a research proposal to study Stonehenge or another mystery of the past. In a research proposal, you give an overview of what you want to study, why you want to study it, and what you will need.

Writing Skills Focus: Use an Outline

An **outline** will help you keep your proposal focused. The following example shows one way you might set up your outline:

Model

I. Reasons for studying Stonehenge
  A. To understand its purpose
  B. To know when it was built
II. What I will need
  A. Equipment
    1. Bulldozers
    2. Shovels
  B. Staff
    1. People to dig
    2. Archaeologists
    3. Astronomers

Prewriting Decide what you want to study and what questions you hope to answer. Then, prepare an outline like the one shown above.

Drafting Follow your outline as you draft your proposal. Add details to explain why each item is included in your proposal.

Revising Ask a partner to read your proposal and ask questions. Would your partner be willing to provide funding for this project? Why or why not? Revise to make your proposal more convincing.

◆ **Grammar Application**
Be sure that every sentence has both a subject and a predicate.

PART 1 *Exploring the Past*

Unnamed Clipper Ship, Claude Marks, Private Collection

Guide for Reading

Meet the Author:

Isaac Asimov (1920–1992)

Check any section of the library and you'll probably find a book by Isaac Asimov. He has written fiction, poetry, humor, autobiography, essays, a guide to Shakespeare, and science books. This multi-talented writer was born in Russia and moved to the United States with his family when he was three. Young Isaac wrote his first story when he was eleven years old.

A Passion for Science Although he was an expert in many subjects, Asimov's main interest was science. He taught biochemistry at Boston University for nine years before becoming a full-time writer in 1958. As a writer, he won many awards, including a National Science Fiction Writers Award. His love of science and his imagination prompted him to write about the wonders of robots, computers, and space travel before they became everyday realities.

THE STORY BEHIND THE STORY

When Isaac Asimov was a boy, his father did not allow him to read the science-fiction magazines in the family-owned store. Mr. Asimov thought science fiction was "trash." Finally, Isaac convinced his father that the stories were worthwhile because they were related to science. Isaac then read all of the "sci-fi" he could get his hands on. As he read, young Isaac may have had ideas of his own about what the future might hold. One of these possible futures is explored in "The Fun They Had."

◆ LITERATURE AND YOUR LIFE

CONNECT YOUR EXPERIENCE

Your grandparents, parents, aunts, and uncles once listened to records—relics of the past, which have been replaced by CDs. The children in "The Fun They Had" discover a relic of the past. However, since the story is set in the year 2155, their past is your present!

THEMATIC FOCUS: Exploring the Past

As you read this story about two schoolchildren of the future who explore the past, ask yourself why they seem so confused about the simple object they find.

◆ Background for Understanding

TECHNOLOGY

Around the middle of the twentieth century, many people did not watch, or even own, a television set. People were just beginning to acquire television sets—which showed only black-and-white images—in the late 1940's. Personal computers made their debut in 1975, and there was no World Wide Web until 1990. Technology that you take for granted was once considered "science fiction." As you read "The Fun They Had," keep in mind that it was written long before computers were used in schools.

◆ Build Vocabulary

PREFIXES: non-

The prefix non- usually indicates that something is "not" or "without." For example, nonbreakable means "not able to be broken." The prefix non- gives you a clue to the meaning of nonchalantly. When a character speaks nonchalantly, he speaks without concern.

WORD BANK

Which word on the list would you be likely to hear in a math class?

calculated
loftily
dispute
nonchalantly

◆ The Fun They Had ◆

◆ Literary Focus

SCIENCE FICTION

You can visit a different time and a different world when you read science fiction. **Science fiction** is writing that tells about imaginary events that involve science or technology. Often, these stories are set in the future. In "The Fun They Had," Asimov explores the technological advances that might affect the way students learn in the future.

◆ Reading Strategy

EVALUATE THE AUTHOR'S MESSAGE

Science-fiction stories often show the advantages or disadvantages of technology. In this way, the author communicates a message. When you **evaluate the author's message,** you make a judgment. You decide whether the author's points are logical. As you read "The Fun They Had," consider what point Asimov is making. That is his message. Then, evaluate whether his message makes sense and whether you agree or disagree. The organizer below shows some points you might consider as you evaluate Asimov's message in "The Fun They Had."

Points to Consider

I like discussing ideas with classmates.

Author's Message: Learning in a group from real people is better than learning from computers.

Computers can't explain everything.

With computers, kids learn at their own pace.

Points to Consider

The Fun They Had

Isaac Asimov

Margie even wrote about it that night in her diary. On the page headed May 17, 2155, she wrote, "Today Tommy found a real book."

It was a very old book. Margie's grandfather once said that when he was a little boy, *his* grandfather told him that there was a time when all stories were printed on paper.

They turned the pages, which were yellow and crinkly, and it was awfully funny to read words that stood still instead of moving the way they were supposed to—on a screen, you know. And then, when they turned back to the page before, it had the same words on it that it had had when they read it the first time.

"Gee," said Tommy, "what a waste. When you're through with the book, you just throw it away, I guess. Our television screen must have had a million books on it and it's good for plenty more. I wouldn't throw *it* away."

"Same with mine," said Margie. She was eleven and hadn't seen as many telebooks as Tommy had. He was thirteen.

She said, "Where did you find it?"

"In my house." He pointed without looking, because he was busy reading. "In the attic."

"What's it about?"

"School."

Margie was scornful. "School? What's there to write about school? I hate school." Margie always hated school, but now she hated it more than ever. The mechanical teacher had been giving her test after test in geography, and she had been doing worse and worse until her mother had shaken her head sorrowfully and sent for the county inspector.

He was a round little man with a red face and a whole box of tools with dials and wires. He smiled at her and gave her an apple, then took the teacher apart. Margie had hoped he wouldn't know how to put it together again, but he knew how all right, and after an hour or so, there it was again, large and ugly, with a big screen on which all the lessons where shown and the questions were asked. That wasn't so bad. The part she hated most was the slot where she had to put homework and test papers. She always had to write them out in a punch code they made her learn when she was six years old, and the mechanical teacher <u>calculated</u> the mark in no time.

The inspector had smiled after he was finished and patted her head. He said to her mother, "It's not the little girl's fault, Mrs. Jones. I think the geography sector was geared a little too quick. Those things happen sometimes. I've slowed it up to an average ten-year level. Actually, the overall pattern of her progress is quite satisfactory." And he patted Margie's head again.

◆ **Build Vocabulary**

calculated (kal´ kyo͞o lāt´ id) *v*.: Determined by using math

Margie was disappointed. She had been hoping they would take the teacher away altogether. They had once taken Tommy's teacher away for nearly a month because the history sector had blanked out completely.

So she said to Tommy, "Why would anyone write about school?"

Tommy looked at her with very superior eyes. "Because it's not our kind of school, stupid. This is the old kind of school that they had hundreds and hundreds of year ago." He added <u>loftily</u>, pronouncing the word carefully, "*Centuries* ago."

Margie was hurt. "Well, I don't know what kind of school they had all that time ago." She read the book over his shoulder for a while, then said, "Anyway, they had a teacher."

"Sure they had a teacher, but it wasn't a *regular* teacher. It was a man."

"A man? How could a man be a teacher?"

"Well, he just told the boys and girls things and gave them homework and asked them questions."

"A man isn't smart enough."

"Sure he is. My father knows as much as my teacher."

"He can't. A man can't know as much as a teacher."

"He knows almost as much I betcha."

Margie wasn't prepared to <u>dispute</u> that. She said, "I wouldn't want a strange man in my house to teach me."

◆ **Literary Focus**
How can you tell that the school of the future is different from yours?

Tommy screamed with laughter. "You don't know much, Margie. The teachers didn't live in the house. They had a special building and all the kids went there."

"And all the kids learned the same thing?"

"Sure, if they were the same age."

"But my mother says a teacher has to be adjusted to fit the mind of each boy and girl it teaches and that each kid has to be taught differently."

"Just the same, they didn't do it that way then. If you don't like it, you don't have to read the book."

"I didn't say I didn't like it," Margie said quickly.

◀ **Critical Viewing** Do you think it would be fun to go to a school of the past, such as the one shown in the picture? [Make a Judgment]

She wanted to read about those funny schools.

They weren't even half finished when Margie's mother called, "Margie! School!"

Margie looked up. "Not yet, Mamma."

"Now," said Mrs. Jones. "And it's probably time for Tommy, too."

Margie said to Tommy, "Can I read the book some more with you after school?"

"Maybe," he said, <u>nonchalantly</u>. He walked away whistling, the dusty old book tucked beneath his arm.

Margie went into the schoolroom. It was right next to her bedroom, and the mechanical teacher was on and waiting for her. It was always on at the same time every day except Saturday and Sunday, because her mother said little girls learned better if they learned at regular hours.

◆ Build Vocabulary

loftily (lôf′ tə lē) *adv.*: In a superior way

dispute (di spyoot′) *v.*: Argue; debate

nonchalantly (nän′ shə länt′ lē) *adv.*: Without concern or interest

The screen was lit up, and it said: "Today's arithmetic lesson is on the addition of proper fractions. Please insert yesterday's homework in the proper slot."

Margie did so with a sigh. She was thinking about the old schools they had when her grandfather's grandfather was a little boy. All the kids from the whole neighborhood came, laughing and shouting in the schoolyard, sitting together in the schoolroom, going home together at the end of the day. They learned the same things so they could help one another on the homework and talk about it.

◆ **Reading Strategy**
How do these details affect your evaluation of Asimov's message?

And the teachers were people. . . .

The mechanical teacher was flashing on the screen: "When we add the fractions 1/2 and 1/4 . . ."

Margie was thinking about how the kids must have loved it in the old days. She was thinking about the fun they had.

Guide for Responding

◆ LITERATURE AND YOUR LIFE

Reader's Response Would you like to go to school the way Margie and Tommy do? Why or why not?

Thematic Focus In what ways does the past seem "new" to Margie and Tommy?

☑ Check Your Comprehension

1. When does this story take place?
2. Who are the main characters in this story?
3. What kind of books do they read?
4. Who are their teachers?
5. Describe the school the children attend at this time.

◆ Critical Thinking

INTERPRET

1. Why is Margie fascinated by the book? **[Infer]**
2. What details from the "past" are familiar to you? **[Connect]**
3. Why does Margie think kids in the "old days" had fun at school? **[Interpret]**

EVALUATE

4. What do you think is the best way to learn? **[Assess]**

APPLY

5. What are some ways that computers are used in education today? **[Apply]**

Guide for Responding (continued)

◆ Reading Strategy

EVALUATE THE AUTHOR'S MESSAGE

You have an advantage when you **evaluate the author's message** in "The Fun They Had." When Asimov wrote the story, computers were not commonly used in the classroom. Now that computers are widely used in classrooms, you can make some judgments based on what you know about their uses.

1. Explain Asimov's message in your own words.
2. (a) What are some of the advantages of learning by computer shown in "The Fun They Had"? (b) What are some advantages of schools where students learn in groups?
3. Do you agree or disagree with Asimov's message? Why?

◆ Build Vocabulary

USING THE PREFIX non-

Many words contain the prefix non- (meaning "not" or "without") plus a word you already know. In your notebook, write a meaning for each word:

1. nonviolent   3. nontoxic
2. nonsense   4. nonstop

SPELLING STRATEGY

Sometimes the *sh* sound is spelled *ch*, as in *nonchalant*. For each definition below, write a word in your notebook that contains the *sh* sound spelled with *ch*.

1. a type of nut: pi _ _ _ _ _ io
2. equipment that does work: m _ _ _ ine
3. a head cook: _ _ _ _
4. a driver: _ _ au _ _ eu_

USING THE WORD BANK

Match each word in Column A with the word in Column B that best indicates its meaning.

Column A	Column B
1. calculated	a. proudly
2. loftily	b. argue
3. dispute	c. casually
4. nonchalantly	d. figured out

◆ Literary Focus

SCIENCE FICTION

Science fiction combines elements of science and technology with imagination. It is usually set in the future.

1. Identify two uses of technology that Asimov imagines for the future.
2. Which details have become more reality than fiction since Asimov wrote this story?

◆ Build Grammar Skills

SIMPLE SUBJECTS AND PREDICATES

Every sentence has a subject and a predicate. A **simple subject** is the person, place, or thing that the sentence is about. The **simple predicate** is the verb or verb phrase that tells the action or states the condition of the subject.

Look at the examples below. The complete subject is underlined once and the complete predicate twice. The simple subject is highlighted in blue. The simple predicate is highlighted in green.

Margie even wrote about it in her diary.

The mechanical teacher had been giving her tests in geography.

Practice Copy these sentences in your notebook. Underline the complete subject once, and label it *S*. Underline the complete predicate twice, and label it *P*. Circle the simple subject and the simple predicate.

1. It was a very old book.
2. They turned the pages of the book.
3. Tommy had been looking in the attic.
4. The inspector had smiled at Margie.
5. All the children learned the same thing.

Writing Application In your notebook, write four or five sentences about your school day. Draw one line under the simple subject and two lines under the simple predicate in each sentence.

Build Your Portfolio

 ## Idea Bank

Writing

1. **The Fun We Have** Write a note to Margie explaining why you would rather go to her kind of school or to yours.

2. **Journal Entry** Finish the diary entry that Margie begins on May 17, 2155. Explain your feelings about the book, schools of the past, and your learning machine.

3. **Description** Write a description of an object in your classroom from the point of view of a student of the future. Indicate the details that seem strange or outdated.

Speaking and Listening

4. **Debate** With a partner, debate the advantages and disadvantages of teacher instruction and individualized computer instruction. Jot down the arguments each side uses. **[Technology Link]**

5. **Phone Call** If you were Tommy or Margie, what would you tell a friend about the old book? With a partner, conduct a telephone conversation about this discovery. You can follow story events or develop dialogue of your own. If possible, make a recording of your conversation. **[Performing Arts Link]**

Projects

6. **Machine Design** Draw a sketch of what a teaching machine might look like. Add labels to explain how it works. **[Art Link]**

7. **Multimedia Display [Group Activity]** With classmates, create a multimedia display that shows some technological advances during the past fifty years. Group members can gather information, prepare charts and timelines, and collect images, examples, and recordings. **[Technology Link]**

 ## Writing Mini-Lesson

Product Evaluation

Sometimes products work well, but sometimes, like the mechanical teacher in "The Fun They Had," they do not. Write a product evaluation of some common form of technology, such as a computer game, a calculator, or a CD player. In a product evaluation, you judge how well a product works.

Writing Skills Focus: Support With Statistics

Support your evaluation with statistics— the numbers that demonstrate the claims you make. For example, if you say your computer game takes too long to start up, measure how long it takes in seconds or minutes. If you say most calculators of a particular brand break within a year, provide the percentage that actually does break. To get statistics, you may need to do research.

Prewriting Choose a product that you use often and with which you are familiar. List your personal observations about how it works. Then, check consumer guides to see whether others have had the same experience.

Drafting As you make your points, include the statistics that support your points. Show some statistics visually with a chart or a graph.

Revising Ask a partner to point out where you need more details or supporting data. Then, provide this information.

> ◆ **Grammar Application**
> Identify the simple subject and the simple predicate in the first three sentences of your evaluation.

Guide for Reading

Meet the Authors:

Edgar Allan Poe (1809–1849)

Edgar Allan Poe, one of America's best-known writers, led a troubled life plagued by poverty and the loss of people he loved. His father deserted him, his mother died before he was three, and his wife died while still young. Despite his problems, Poe produced a large body of work, including short stories, essays, and poems. He died in Baltimore at the age of forty, but his stories and poems live on, read by millions of readers in America and around the world.

Edna St. Vincent Millay (1892–1950)

Edna St. Vincent Millay was born in Rockland, Maine. Raised by her mother, who encouraged her creativity, she published her first poem in a children's magazine when she was only fourteen. Her first book of poetry came out when she was twenty-five. Just six years later, in 1923, she won a Pulitzer Prize for poetry. Like "The Spring and the Fall," many of Millay's lyrical poems and sonnets are about love and the loss of love.

Jack Prelutsky (1940–   )

Jack Prelutsky was born in Brooklyn, New York. His writing career began when he showed a friend some poems he had written to accompany drawings of imaginary creatures. With his friend's encouragement, Prelutsky soon published his first book of poems. He went on to write many more books and to win numerous awards for his humorous verse.

◆ Literature and Your Life

Connect Your Experience

Just when you think everything is great, a friend moves away or some other change upsets your world. No friend or experience ever completely leaves you, though. The poets in this group show that the past has a way of leaving its mark on the present.

Thematic Focus: Exploring the Past

As you read these poems, you may ask yourself what people learn from looking at the past.

◆ Background for Understanding

Science

Scientists are able to look as far as 150 million years into the past. Fossil remains reveal the lives of dinosaurs, such as the ankylosaurus in Prelutsky's poem. Ankylosaurus (aŋ´ ki lō sô´ rus) had small jaws and weak teeth suitable only for chewing soft plants. For protection, an ankylosaurus had tough, leathery skin and a heavy tail shaped like a club. Its short, stubby legs kept ankylosaurus close to the ground, protecting its soft underbelly. The picture on pages 392 and 393 shows what scientists believe an ankylosaurus looked like.

◆ Build Vocabulary

Prefixes: in-

In one of these poems, a dinosaur is described as *inedible*. The prefix *in-* is like the prefix *un-*: it means "not" or "the opposite of." Combined with *edible*, which means "fit to eat," it creates a word that means "not fit to eat."

Word Bank

Which word on this list sounds like a weapon?

deem
bough
raucous
inedible
cudgel

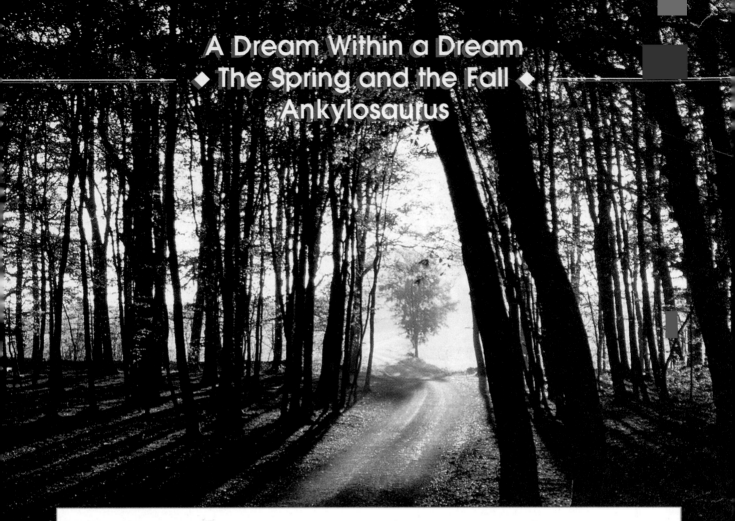

A Dream Within a Dream
◆ The Spring and the Fall ◆
Ankylosaurus

◆ Literary Focus

RHYME

Rhyme is the repetition of sounds at the ends of words. Poets use rhyme to emphasize certain words and ideas. Once a rhyme pattern has been established, you come to expect the upcoming rhymes. Many traditional poems have rhyming words at the ends of lines. For example, *seem* and *dream* provide the rhyme in these lines from "A Dream Within a Dream."

All that we see or seem

Is but a dream within a dream.

◆ Reading Strategy

MAKE INFERENCES

The poems in this group hint at past events and circumstances rather than directly stating them. However, you can use the details provided in the poems to **make inferences**— that is, to reach conclusions, about the past. The organizer below shows one inference that can be made from details in "A Dream Within a Dream."

Detail:
The speaker weeps.

Detail:
Someone is leaving.

Inference:
The speaker is sad because the person is leaving.

A Dream Within a Dream

Edgar Allan Poe

Take this kiss upon the brow!
And, in parting from you now,
Thus much let me avow—
You are not wrong, who <u>deem</u>
5   That my days have been a dream;
Yet if hope has flown away
In a night, or in a day,
In a vision, or in none,
Is it therefore the less *gone*?
10   *All* that we see or seem
Is but a dream within a dream.
I stand amid the roar
Of a surf-tormented shore,
And I hold within my hand
15   Grains of the golden sand—
How few! yet how they creep
Through my fingers to the deep,
While I weep—while I weep!
O God! can I not grasp
20   Them with a tighter clasp?
O God! can I not save
One from the pitiless wave?
Is *all* that we see or seem
But a dream within a dream?

▲ **Critical Viewing** What does the sand running through the hourglass suggest about time? [Interpret]

◆ **Build Vocabulary**
deem (dēm) *v*.: Judge
bough (bou) *n*.: Branch of a tree
raucous (rô´ kəs) *adj*.: Loud and rowdy

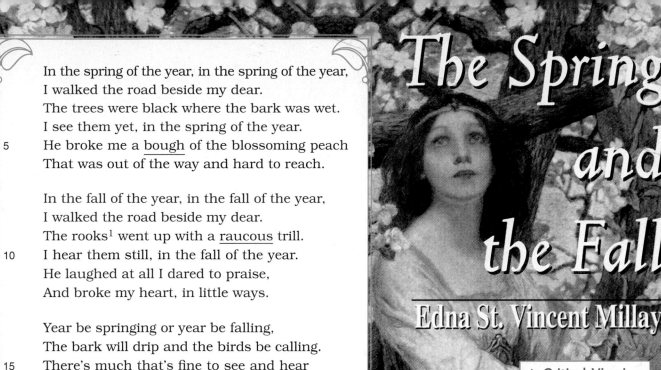

The Spring and the Fall

Edna St. Vincent Millay

In the spring of the year, in the spring of the year,
I walked the road beside my dear.
The trees were black where the bark was wet.
I see them yet, in the spring of the year.
5   He broke me a <u>bough</u> of the blossoming peach
That was out of the way and hard to reach.

In the fall of the year, in the fall of the year,
I walked the road beside my dear.
The rooks[1] went up with a <u>raucous</u> trill.
10 I hear them still, in the fall of the year.
He laughed at all I dared to praise,
And broke my heart, in little ways.

Year be springing or year be falling,
The bark will drip and the birds be calling.
15 There's much that's fine to see and hear
In the spring of a year, in the fall of a year.
'Tis not love's going hurts my days,
But that it went in little ways.

1. rooks (rŏoks) *n.:* European crows.

> ▲ **Critical Viewing**
> What emotions do
> you think this
> woman is feeling?
> **[Infer]**

Guide for Responding

◆ LITERATURE AND YOUR LIFE

Reader's Response What questions would you like to ask the speakers of these poems?

Thematic Focus In what way does memory help these poets explore the past?

Journal Writing As the speaker of one of these poems, write a journal entry about the experience on which the poem is based.

☑ Check Your Comprehension

1. What happens in the first two lines of "A Dream Within a Dream"?
2. What image does the poet describe to show how things slip away?
3. What happens to the couple in "The Spring and the Fall"?

◆ Critical Thinking

INTERPRET

1. Explain how the title "A Dream Within a Dream" indicates that the speaker's past experiences seem unreal. **[Interpret]**
2. Compare and contrast the speaker's experiences in each season of "The Spring and the Fall." **[Compare and Contrast]**

APPLY

3. What can people learn from the past? **[Apply]**

COMPARE LITERARY WORKS

4. Do you think that these two speakers would enjoy each other's company? Why or why not? **[Connect]**

Ankylosaurus

Jack Prelutsky

Clankity Clankity Clankity Clank!
Ankylosaurus was built like a tank,
its hide was a fortress as sturdy as steel,
it tended to be an <u>inedible</u> meal.

5   It was armored in front, it was armored behind,
there wasn't a thing on its minuscule mind,
it waddled about on its four stubby legs,
nibbling on plants with a mouthful of pegs.

Ankylosaurus was best left alone,
10   its tail was a <u>cudgel</u> of gristle and bone,
Clankity Clankity Clankity Clank!
Ankylosaurus was built like a tank.

◆ **Build Vocabulary**

inedible (in ed´ ə bəl) *adj.:* Not fit to be eaten
cudgel (kuj´ əl) *n.:* Short, thick stick or club

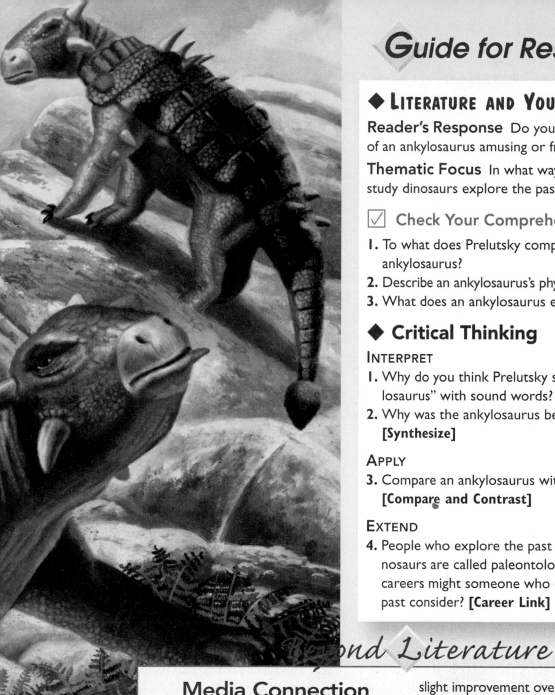

Guide for Responding

◆ LITERATURE AND YOUR LIFE

Reader's Response Do you find this description of an ankylosaurus amusing or frightening? Why?

Thematic Focus In what ways do people who study dinosaurs explore the past?

☑ Check Your Comprehension

1. To what does Prelutsky compare the ankylosaurus?
2. Describe an ankylosaurus's physical appearance.
3. What does an ankylosaurus eat?

◆ Critical Thinking

INTERPRET

1. Why do you think Prelutsky starts "Anky-losaurus" with sound words? **[Connect]**
2. Why was the ankylosaurus best left alone? **[Synthesize]**

APPLY

3. Compare an ankylosaurus with another dinosaur. **[Compare and Contrast]**

EXTEND

4. People who explore the past by studying di-nosaurs are called paleontologists. What other careers might someone who enjoys studying the past consider? **[Career Link]**

Beyond Literature

Media Connection

Dinosaurs Go to Hollywood

Except for cartoons, most early dinosaur movies were made by filming the dinosaurs in "stop action." Filming stopped and restarted each time the dinosaur model was reposi-tioned, creating a choppy motion. Occasionally, lizards were used to portray dinosaurs—not very successfully. In 1957, the first mechanical dinosaurs appeared in a movie. They were a slight improvement over stop action. Finally, computer graphics allowed movie makers to create the realistic-looking dinosaurs and dinosaur-type creatures like the ones in *Jurassic Park* (1993), *The Lost World* (1997), *Godzilla* (1998), and *T Rex* (1998).

Cross-Curricular Activity

Create a timeline of advances in technology that have improved the quality of dinosaurs in movies.

Guide for Responding (continued)

◆ Reading Strategy

MAKE INFERENCES

These poems don't directly state everything about the past on which they focus. The poets expect you to **make inferences,** to come to conclusions based on the details they do give in the poems.

1. What inferences do you make about the life of the speaker in "A Dream Within a Dream"?
2. What inference do you make about the relationship of the couple in "The Spring and the Fall"? On what do you base your inference?
3. What can you infer from "Ankylosaurus" about the world in which this dinosaur lived?

◆ Build Vocabulary

USING THE PREFIX in-

On your paper, copy the following sentences. Add the prefix in- to the italicized word to change its meaning to the opposite. Then, explain whether the rewritten sentence makes sense.

1. The speaker of "A Dream Within a Dream" feels *complete*.
2. A year is a(n) *definite* period of time.
3. Prelutsky's description of an ankylosaurus is *accurate*.

SPELLING STRATEGY

The word *bough* is one example of the *ow* sound spelled with *ough*. *Brow* is an example of the *ow* sound spelled with *ow*. On your paper, unscramble the letters to spell words that have the *ow* sound.

1. glopuh   2. dworc   3. dogruth   4. wronf

USING THE WORD BANK

On your paper, answer the following questions. Explain each answer.

1. Does Prelutsky *deem* that an ankylosaurus was thoughtful?
2. Did the ankylosaurus find plants *inedible*?
3. Would a *raucous* song be a good lullaby?
4. Would a *bough* make a good *cudgel*?

◆ Literary Focus

RHYME

Rhyme is the repetition of sounds at the end of words.

1. Identify three pairs of rhyming words used in "A Dream Within a Dream."
2. Explain which lines rhyme with one another in the first section of "The Spring and the Fall."
3. What pair of rhyming words appears twice in "Ankylosaurus"?

◆ Build Grammar Skills

COMPLETE SENTENCES

A **complete sentence** is a group of words that has at least one subject and one predicate (verb) and that expresses a complete thought. Look at the following examples.

Complete Sentence: I walked the road beside my dear.
(Contains a subject and a predicate and expresses a complete thought.)

Not a Complete Sentence: While I weep—while I weep!
(Contains a subject and a predicate but does not express a complete thought.)

Not a Complete Sentence: How few!
(Does not contain a subject and a predicate.)

Practice On your paper, explain why each numbered item is or is not a complete sentence.

1. In the spring of the year.
2. It is a dream.
3. Clankity Clankity Clankity Clank!
4. They spoke of spring.
5. Nibbling on plants.

Writing Application On your paper, add your own words to make each of the following a complete sentence.

1. walking along the road
2. if he had stayed
3. was strong and sturdy

Build Your Portfolio

Writing

1. **Message** Write a brief, encouraging message to the speaker of either "A Dream Within a Dream" or "The Spring and the Fall."

2. **Monologue** As an ankylosaurus, write a monologue (a speech for one character) about a day in your life. Describe your activities, the dangers you face, and the way you deal with the dangers.

3. **Poem** Write a stanza about summer or winter to be inserted into "The Spring and the Fall." Be sure to use the same rhyme pattern so that your stanza will fit with the rest of the poem.

Speaking and Listening

4. **Poetry Reading** **[Group Activity]** With a few classmates, stage a poetry reading featuring the work of Edgar Allan Poe and Edna St. Vincent Millay. Read several poems written by each. **[Performing Arts Link]**

5. **Choral Reading** **[Group Activity]** Plan and present a choral reading of "Ankylosaurus." Choose which parts of the poem will be read by individual speakers, groups of speakers, and the whole group. **[Performing Arts Link]**

Projects

6. **Sketch** Make a sketch or write an outline for a sketch of an ankylosaurus. Label the parts mentioned in the poem, and explain their function. **[Art Link; Science Link]**

7. **Music Video [Group Activity]** With a group, plan a music video of one of the poems. Group members can choose from the following tasks: selecting music, creating storyboards that show what will be "on-screen" as each part of the poem is read, or reading sections of the poem. If possible, record your video. **[Music Link; Media Link]**

 Writing Mini-Lesson

Letter of Advice

The speakers of "A Dream Within a Dream" and "The Spring and the Fall" are facing difficult times. Write a letter of advice to one of them. Suggest ways that he or she might handle the problem.

Writing Skills Focus: Choose Details Appropriate for Your Audience

Your letter will have the greatest impact if you **choose details appropriate for your audience.** For example, the speaker of "The Spring and the Fall" is upset because love left "in little ways." You might suggest to her that it's better to get used to a disappointment gradually, rather than be shocked by it.

Prewriting First, identify the problem. Then, use a cluster diagram like the one below to brainstorm for words of advice, comfort, or encouragement.

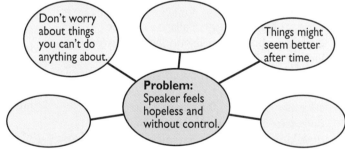

Drafting In your own words, state the problem. Suggest how the person can deal with the problem. End by offering encouragement.

Revising Ask a partner to read your letter. Would your partner find it helpful if he or she were having a problem? Add appropriate details to make your advice more meaningful.

> ◆ **Grammar Application**
> Check that each sentence has a subject and a verb and that it expresses a complete thought.

Guide for Reading

Meet the Author:
Robert Ballard (1942–)

Robert Ballard became fascinated with the ocean as a child. Although he was born in Kansas, he grew up in San Diego, California. As a teenager, he took up scuba diving and began to explore the world underwater.

A Career Under the Sea Ballard studied and worked as a marine geologist as a young man. Much of his work was done in a three-man deep-ocean submersible known as ALVIN. In ALVIN, Ballard and his crews mapped the ocean floor, studied the Earth's crust, and explored undersea mountain ranges and volcanoes.

Ocean Technology Ballard's intense curiosity about what lay under the water led him to develop a special camera called ANGUS. This camera could stay on the ocean floor for up to fourteen hours and take as many as 16,000 pictures in a single dive. Later, in the early 1980's, Ballard developed a remote-controlled robot that could move about underwater and take pictures on command.

THE STORY BEHIND THE STORY

Ballard's curiosity and inventions finally led him on one of his most remarkable expeditions. He set out to find the famous *Titanic,* a huge ship that rested more than two miles underwater on the floor of the North Atlantic Ocean. On September 1, 1985, he found this ship. After studying the famous shipwreck, he told its story and shared his findings in *Exploring the* Titanic.

◆ LITERATURE AND YOUR LIFE
CONNECT YOUR EXPERIENCE

Even if you haven't seen one of the movies made about the *Titanic,* you probably know the name spells disaster. In 1912, this luxury liner struck an iceberg in the Atlantic Ocean and sank, taking more than 1,500 people to a watery grave. The fate of the *Titanic* may not surprise you, but many facts about the ship and its voyage will!

THEMATIC FOCUS: Exploring the Past

As you read about the *Titanic,* ask yourself why a disaster from the past captures the interest of people today.

◆ Background for Understanding
HISTORY

The *Titanic* was the largest and most luxurious ocean liner of its time. According to the publicity when it was built, it was also "unsinkable." Huge watertight doors between sections and a supposedly "unbreakable" construction made the *Titanic* seem safer than other ships. Its builders never claimed it was unsinkable. Nonetheless, the owners of the *Titanic* did not supply enough lifeboats for all the passengers because they were sure lifeboats would never be needed.

◆ Build Vocabulary
COMPOUND ADJECTIVES

A compound adjective consists of two or more words linked together as one word to modify, or describe, a noun or a pronoun. For example, *watertight* consists of *water* and *tight.* It describes a thing so tight that no water can get in.

WORD BANK

Which word describes the way a queen might act?

majestically
collision
novelty
watertight

from Exploring the *Titanic*

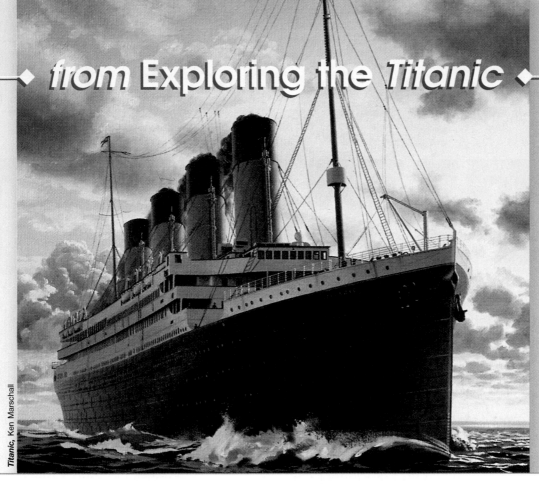

Titanic, Ken Marschall

◆ Literary Focus

SUSPENSE

Suspense is nervous anticipation about the outcome of events. Sometimes, the outcome itself is uncertain. At other times, you know *what* will happen, but not *when* or *how* it will happen. In this excerpt from *Exploring the* Titanic, you know that the *Titanic* will hit an iceberg, but you don't know when. Ballard creates suspense by constantly reminding you that icebergs are out there and keeping you wondering when the ship will hit one. Make an organizer like the one shown below. On each level of the "iceberg," write a detail that adds to the suspense.

Captain Smith doesn't see last warning.

Phillips ignores Californian's warnings.

Caronia reports icebergs.

◆ Reading Strategy

DISTINGUISH BETWEEN FACT AND OPINION

When you read nonfiction, you need to **distinguish between fact and opinion.** A fact is information that can be proved true or false. An opinion expresses a belief involving the writer's attitudes or values. It can be supported by arguments, but it can't be proved absolutely.

Fact: The *Titanic* sailed on April 10, 1912.

Opinion: The dining room was beautiful.

Some written works include both facts and opinions. Be careful not to accept opinions as if they were facts.

from
Exploring the
TITANIC
Robert D. Ballard

At noon on Wednesday, April 10, the *Titanic* cast off. The whistles on her huge funnels were the biggest ever made. As she began her journey to the sea, they were heard for miles around.

Moving <u>majestically</u> down the River Test, and watched by a crowd that had turned out for the occasion, the *Titanic* slowly passed two ships tied up to a dock. All of a sudden, the mooring ropes holding the passenger liner *New York* snapped with a series of sharp cracks like fireworks going off. The enormous pull created by the *Titanic* moving past her had broken the *New York's* ropes and was now drawing her stern toward the *Titanic*. Jack Thayer watched in

horror as the two ships came closer and closer. "It looked as though there surely would be a <u>collision</u>," he later wrote. "Her stern could not have been more than a yard or two from our side. It almost hit us." At the last moment, some quick action by Captain Smith and a tugboat captain nearby allowed the *Titanic* to slide past with only inches to spare.

It was not a good sign. Did it mean that the *Titanic* might be too big a ship to handle safely? Those who knew about the sea thought that such a close call at the beginning of a maiden voyage was a very bad omen.

Jack Phillips, the first wireless operator on the *Titanic*, quickly jotted down the message coming in over his headphones. "It's another iceberg warning," he said wearily to his young assistant, Harold Bride. "You'd better take it up to the bridge." Both men had been at work for hours in the *Titanic*'s radio room trying to get caught up in sending out a large number of personal messages. In 1912, passengers on ocean liners thought it was a real <u>novelty</u> to send postcard-style messages to friends at home from the middle of the Atlantic.

Bride picked up the iceberg message and stepped out onto the boat deck. It was a sunny but cold Sunday morning, the fourth day of the *Titanic*'s maiden voyage. The ship was steaming at full speed across a calm sea. Harold Bride was quite pleased with himself at having landed a job on such a magnificent new ship. After all, he was only twenty-two years old and had just nine months' experience at operating a "wireless set," as a ship's radio was then called. As he entered the bridge area, he could see one of the crewmen standing behind the ship's wheel steering her course toward New York.

Captain Smith was on duty in the bridge, so Bride handed the message to him. "It's from the *Caronia*, sir. She's reporting icebergs and pack ice ahead." The captain thanked him, read the message, and then posted it on the bulletin board for other officers on watch to read. On his way back to the radio room, Bride thought the captain had seemed quite unconcerned by the message. But then again, he had been told that it was not unusual to have ice floating in the sea lanes during an April crossing. Besides, what danger could a few pieces of ice present to an unsinkable ship?

Elsewhere on board, passengers relaxed on deck chairs, reading or taking naps. Some played cards, some wrote letters, while others chatted with friends. As it was Sunday, church services had been held in the morning, the first-class service led by Captain Smith. Jack Thayer spent most of the day walking about the decks getting some fresh air with his parents.

Two more ice warnings were received from nearby ships around lunch time. In the chaos of the radio room, Harold Bride only had time to take one of them to the bridge. The rest of the day passed quietly. Then, in the late afternoon, the temperature began to drop rapidly. Darkness approached as the bugle call announced dinner.

Jack Thayer's parents had been invited to a special dinner for Captain Smith, so Jack ate alone in the first-class dining room. After dinner, as he was having a cup of coffee, he was joined by Milton Long, another passenger going home to the States. Long was older than Jack, but in the easy-going atmosphere of shipboard travel, they struck up a conversation and talked together for an hour or so.

At 7:30 P.M., the radio room received three

◆ Build Vocabulary

majestically (mə jes´ tik lē) *adv.*: Grandly

collision (kə lizh´ ən) *n.*: Coming together with a sudden violent force; a crash

novelty (näv´ əl tē) *n.*: Something new or unusual

◀ **Critical Viewing** Why might an iceberg like this one be difficult to spot from far away? **[Analyze]**

more warnings of ice about fifty miles ahead. One of them was from the steamer *Californian* reporting three large icebergs. Harold Bride took this message up to the bridge, and it was again politely received. Captain Smith was attending the dinner party being held for him when the warning was delivered. He never got to see it. Then, around 9:00 P.M., the captain excused himself and went up to the bridge. He and his officers talked about how difficult it was to spot icebergs on a calm, clear, moonless night like this with no wind to kick up white surf around them. Before going to bed, the captain ordered the lookouts to keep a sharp watch for ice.

After trading travel stories with Milton Long, Jack Thayer put on his coat and walked around the deck. "It had become very much colder," he said later. "It was a brilliant, starry night. There was no moon, and I have never seen the stars shine brighter . . . sparkling like diamonds. . . . It was the kind of night that made one feel glad to be alive." At eleven

The Grand Staircase was one of the most elegant and extraordinary features of *Titanic's* interior design.

In luxurious rooms such as this, first-class passengers read, wrote letters, socialized.

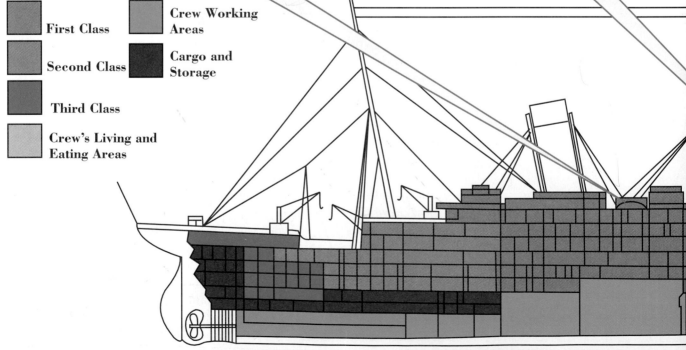

First Class

Second Class

Third Class

Crew's Living and Eating Areas

Crew Working Areas

Cargo and Storage

o'clock, he went below to his cabin, put on his pajamas, and got ready for bed.

In the radio room, Harold Bride was exhausted. The two operators were expected to keep the radio working twenty-four hours a day, and Bride lay down to take a much-needed nap. Phillips was so busy with the passenger messages that he actually brushed off the final ice warning of the night. It

◆ **Literary Focus**
What details here heighten the suspense?

was from the *Californian*. Trapped in a field of ice, she had stopped for the night about nineteen miles north of the *Titanic*. She was so close that the message literally blasted in Phillips's ears. Annoyed by the loud interruption, he cut off the *Californian's* radio operator with the words, "Shut up, shut up, I'm busy."

The radio room had received a total of seven ice warning messages in one day. It was quite clear that floating icebergs lay ahead of the *Titanic*.

The "stokers" shoveled coal to feed the huge boilers that powered the ship. When water poured into the boiler rooms, the men rushed to escape, sealing watertight doors behind them.

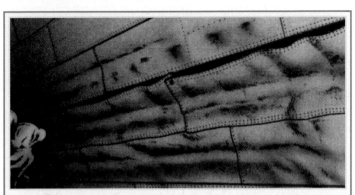

The pressure of the iceberg scraping the side of *Titanic's* hull caused the plates to buckle, allowing huge amounts of water to flow into the ship.

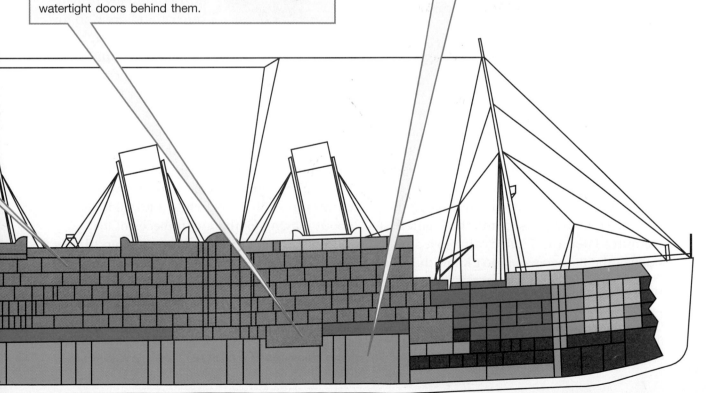

High up in the crow's nest on the forward mast, Fred Fleet had passed a quiet watch. It was now 11:40 P.M., and he and his fellow lookout were waiting to be relieved so they could head below, perhaps for a hot drink before hopping into their warm bunks. The sea was dead calm. The air bitterly cold.

Suddenly, Fleet saw something. A huge, dark shape loomed out of the night directly ahead of the *Titanic*. An iceberg! He quickly sounded the alarm bell three times and picked up the telephone.

"What did you see?" asked the duty officer.

"Iceberg right ahead," replied Fleet.

Immediately, the officer on the bridge ordered the wheel turned as far as it would go. The engine room was told to reverse the engines, while a button was pushed to close the doors to the watertight compartments in the bottom of the ship.

The lookouts in the crow's nest braced themselves for a collision. Slowly the ship started to turn. It looked as though they would miss it. But it was too late. They had avoided a head-on crash, but the iceberg had struck a glancing blow along the *Titanic*'s starboard bow.[1] Several tons of ice fell on the ship's decks as the iceberg brushed along the side of the ship and passed into the night. A few minutes later, the *Titanic* came to a stop.

Many of the passengers didn't know the ship had hit anything. Because it was so cold, almost everyone was inside, and most people had already gone to bed. Ruth Becker and her mother were awakened by the dead silence. They could no longer hear the soothing hum of the vibrating engines from below. Jack Thayer was about to step into bed when he felt himself sway ever so slightly. The engines stopped. He was startled by the sudden quiet.

Sensing trouble, Ruth's mother looked out of the door of their second-class cabin and asked a steward[2] what had happened. He told her that nothing was the matter, so Mrs. Becker went back to bed. But as she lay there, she couldn't help feeling that something was very wrong.

Jack heard running feet and voices in the hallway outside his first-class cabin. "I hurried into my heavy overcoat and drew on my slippers. All excited, but not thinking anything serious had occurred, I called in to my father and mother that I was going up on deck to see the fun."

On deck, Jack watched some third-class passengers playing with the ice that had landed on the forward deck as the iceberg had brushed by. Some people were throwing chunks at each other, while a few skidded about playing football with pieces of ice.

Down in the very bottom of the ship, things were very different. When the iceberg had struck, there had been a noise like a big gun going off in one of the boiler rooms. A couple

---

1. **starboard bow:** Right side of the front of the ship.

▲ **Critical Viewing** Based on this picture, explain why the first sign of a problem is sometimes referred to as "just the tip of the iceberg." **[Connect]**

2. **steward:** Worker on a ship who attends to the needs of the passengers.

of stokers had been immediately hit by a jet of icy water. The noise and the shock of cold water had sent them running for safety.

Twenty minutes after the crash, things looked very bad indeed to Captain Smith. He and the ship's builder, Thomas Andrews, had made a rapid tour below decks to inspect the damage. The mail room was filling up with water, and sacks of mail were floating about. Water was also pouring into some of the forward holds and two of the boiler rooms.

Captain Smith knew that the *Titanic*'s hull

◆ **Reading Strategy**
Identify three facts that do not support the opinion that the ship is unsinkable.

◆ **Build Vocabulary**

watertight *adj.*: Put together so that no water can get through

was divided into a number of watertight compartments. She had been designed so that she could still float if only the first four compartments were flooded, but not any more than that. But water was pouring into the first five compartments. And when the water filled them, it would spill over into the next compartment. One by one all the remaining compartments would flood, and the ship would eventually sink. Andrews told the captain that the ship could last an hour, an hour and a half at the most.

Harold Bride had just awakened in the radio room when Captain Smith stuck his head in the door. "Send the call for assistance," he ordered.

"What call should I send?" Phillips asked.

"The regulation international call for help. Just that." Then the captain was gone. Phillips began to send the Morse code "CQD" distress call, flashing away and joking as he did it. After all, they knew the ship was unsinkable.

*G*uide for Responding

◆ LITERATURE AND YOUR LIFE

Reader's Response If you could interview one person who was aboard the *Titanic*, who would it be? Why?

Thematic Focus In your opinion, why are people still interested in a disaster that happened in 1912?

☑ **Check Your Comprehension**

1. When did the *Titanic* begin her journey?
2. Why were the radio operators so busy and behind in their work?
3. What messages did other ships send to the *Titanic*?
4. What was the captain's reaction?
5. About how long did Thomas Andrews think it would take for the ship to go down?

◆ Critical Thinking

INTERPRET

1. Why wasn't Captain Smith concerned about the warnings he received? **[Draw Conclusions]**
2. In what way did the ship's reputation as "unsinkable" contribute to the accident? **[Analyze]**
3. Compare the scene on deck with the scene in the bottom of the ship immediately following the crash. **[Compare and Contrast]**
4. Do you think Ruth Becker and Jack Thayer survived? Explain. **[Draw Conclusions]**

APPLY

5. Why is it important to remain calm in case of an emergency? **[Apply]**

EXTEND

6. Would you rather design a ship, work as one of the crew on a ship, or be captain of a ship? Why? **[Career Link]**

Guide for Responding (continued)

◆ Reading Strategy

DISTINGUISH BETWEEN FACT AND OPINION

A **fact** can be proved true or false. An **opinion** expresses a belief that comes from the writer's attitudes or values. It's important to recognize the difference so that you don't accept an opinion as a fact.

1. Identify three facts about time or weather that Ballard includes.
2. What is Harold Bride's opinion about Smith's reaction to the *Caronia*'s warning?
3. Andrews tells the captain that the ship will sink. Is that statement a fact or an opinion? Explain.

◆ Build Vocabulary

USING COMPOUND ADJECTIVES

Sometimes, two words work together as one, like *watertight,* to modify or describe a noun or pronoun. These words are **compound adjectives.** On your paper, match each numbered compound adjective with what it probably describes.

1. head-on   **a.** ship
2. icebound   **b.** collision
3. easy-going   **c.** mood

SPELLING STRATEGY

In the word *collision,* you hear the sound *zhun,* but it is spelled *sion.* Most words that contain the sound *zhun* end in *sion.* On your paper, write a word ending in *sion* for each clue.

1. The ability to see   3. Something that intrudes
2. The end   4. Attempts to persuade

USING THE WORD BANK

On your paper, write the word from the Word Bank that belongs in each numbered space.

The *Titanic's* motion was pulling another ship toward her. She ____?____ headed out to sea. To many on board this was a ____?____. No one expected the coming ____?____, or that the ____?____ compartments would fill so rapidly.

◆ Literary Focus

SUSPENSE

Suspense is the feeling of tension you experience as you wait to find out what will happen or when something will happen.

1. What happens at the beginning of the *Titanic's* journey that suggests a disaster will occur?
2. How do the ice warnings add to the suspense?
3. Identify two other details that increase the suspense about when the collision will occur.

◆ Build Grammar Skills

KINDS OF SENTENCES

Sentences can be classified into four categories, based on what they do.

Kind of Sentence	What It Does	Punctuation
Declarative	Makes a statement	Period (.)
Imperative	Gives a command or makes a request	Period (.) or Exclamation point (!)
Interrogative	Asks a question	Question mark (?)
Exclamatory	Shows excitement or strong feeling	Exclamation point (!)

Examples

Declarative: Bride had just awakened.
Imperative: Send the call for assistance.
Interrogative: What call should I send?
Exclamatory: Let me go with them!

Practice On your paper, copy the following sentences. Then, add punctuation. Identify the kind of sentence it is.

1. Daylight shone through the glass dome
2. Did it mean that the *Titanic* was too big
3. "Shut up, shut up, I'm busy"
4. What a cold night it is
5. Imagine how frightened they were

Writing Application On your paper, write a short paragraph about the *Titanic* using at least one of each of the four kinds of sentences.

Build Your Portfolio

 Idea Bank

Writing

1. **Announcement** Write a brief announcement that a crew member might make to alert the passengers to the situation without causing them to panic.

2. **Newspaper Account** The sinking of the *Titanic* was very big news. Write a newspaper article about the tragedy. Use details from Ballard's account as well as other accounts you may know.

3. **Captain's Log** The captain of a ship keeps a detailed record, or log, of all events that occur on each day of a voyage. Create a captain's log for the *Titanic* on April 14, 1912, the day it sank. Indicate the time of each event, and what you thought about it.

Speaking and Listening

4. **Role Play** With a partner, role-play a conversation between wireless operators Jack Phillips and Harold Bride as they receive the seventh and final ice warning. **[Performing Arts Link]**

5. **Morse Code** The wireless operators sent and received messages using Morse Code. Get the key to Morse Code from an encyclopedia. Create a message using the code, and exchange messages with a partner. Each should decode the other's message and compare results.

Projects

6. **Diagram** Do research to create a diagram that shows where the *Titanic* was damaged by the iceberg, where the ship filled with water, and where it finally broke before sinking. **[Art Link]**

7. **Presentation** In any emergency, it's important to have a plan. Give a presentation to your class on emergency procedures, such as those for a fire drill. **[Health Link; Performing Arts Link]**

 Writing Mini-Lesson

Message

Write a message that might have been sent by another ship to warn the *Titanic* of the icebergs in the area.

Writing Skills Focus: State the Problem Clearly

A wireless message is very brief, so you must **state the problem clearly.** Be direct and give specific information about the danger. For example, include your location and the amount of ice you see.

Prewriting Jot down in your warning all the details that you think would help the *Titanic* avoid the ice. Include details about time of observation, location, amount of ice observed, temperature, and wind direction. For this imaginary message, you can create these details if you are not able to do research.

Drafting Set up your message as shown at right. In your message, use short, simple sentences to express the danger clearly.

> ⚓ **Message** ⚓
>
> To_____ From_____
> Time_____ Location_____
> Message_____
> _____
> _____
> _____

Revising Check that you have included the name of your ship and the time that you are sending the message. Ask a partner to suggest ways that you could make your message clearer.

◆ **Grammar Application**

Most sentences in your telegram will be declarative or imperative. Identify one of each kind that you use in your telegram.

Writer and director James Cameron is famous for the realism in his movies. When he decided to make a movie about the *Titanic,* he was determined to travel to the wreck himself and film footage of the actual ship. His passion for accuracy led to a movie that, as Cameron says, is "as close as you can get to being in a time machine and going back to the ship." The years of dedication and creative effort that went into making the movie are documented in the book *James Cameron's Titanic* by Ed Marsh and Douglas Kirkland. Cameron himself wrote the introduction to the book. In this excerpt from the introduction, Cameron explains why he created the fictional characters of Rose and Jack.

from James Cameron's
Titanic

Titanic still captures our imaginations after eighty-five years because her story is like a great novel that really happened. The story could not have been written better . . . the juxtaposition of rich and poor, the gender roles played out unto death (women first), the stoicism and nobility of a bygone age, the magnificence of the great ship matched in scale only by the folly of the men who drove her

through the darkness. And above all the lesson: that life is uncertain, the future unknowable . . . the unthinkable possible.

The tragedy has assumed an almost mythic quality in our collective imagination, but the passage of time has robbed it of its human face. Its status in our culture has become that of a morality tale, referred to more often as a metaphor in political cartoons than as an actual event. I set out to make a film that would bring the event to life, to humanize it; not a docudrama, but an experience in living history. I wanted to place the audience on the ship, in its final hours, to live out the tragic event in all its horribly fascinating glory.

The greatest challenge of writing a new film about such an oft-told subject is the very fact that the story is so well known. What to say that hasn't been said? The only territory I felt had been left unexplored in prior films was the territory of the heart. I wanted the audience to cry for *Titanic*. Which means to cry for the people on the ship, which really means to cry for any lost soul in their hour of untimely death. But the deaths of 1,500 innocents is too abstract for our hearts to grasp, although the mind can form the number easily.

To fully experience the tragedy of *Titanic*, to be able to comprehend it in human terms, it seemed necessary to create an emotional lightning rod for the audience by giving them two main characters they care about.

Jack and Rose were born out of this need, and the story of TITANIC became their story. I realized then that my film must be, first and always, a love story.

And what could be more romantic, in the dark and heart-wrenching sense of the word, than *Titanic*, with its stories of men and women torn from each other en masse by a cruel twist of fate, of widows scanning the faces of the few male survivors for their husbands and lovers, of the terrible loss and grief of the morning after . . . of so many hearts broken.

The story of *Titanic* and her fate seemed a magnificent canvas on which to paint a love story, a canvas offering the full spectral range of human emotion. The greatest of loves can only be measured against the greatest of adversities, and the greatest of sacrifices thus defined. *Titanic* in all her terrible majesty provides this as does no other historical event.

1. Why are people today still interested in the *Titanic* and in the people who sailed on the ship? **[Synthesize]**
2. What does Cameron mean when he says that "it seemed necessary to create an emotional lightning rod"? **[Interpret]**

CONNECTING LITERATURE TO SOCIAL STUDIES
ANCIENT GREECE
Orpheus by Alice Low

GODS

Zeus (zo͞os): Ruler of heaven and earth, of all gods and all mortals (humans)

Titan (tit´ ən): One of the race of giant gods who warred with the gods of Olympus

Hades (hā´ dēz): God of the underworld (also the name of the underworld)

Persephone (pər sef´ ə nē): Queen of the underworld

Charon (ker´ ən): God of the underworld who ferries the souls of the dead over the river Styx to Hades

Mnemosyne (nē mäs´ i nē): Titan mother of the Muses

Calliope (kə lī´ ə pē): One of the nine Muses

MORTALS

Orpheus (ôr´ fē əs)

Eurydice (yo͞o rid´ i sē)

Sisyphus (sis´ ə fəs),

Tantalus (tan´ tə ləs),

Ixion (iks´ ē un): Mortals who, for offending the gods, are condemned to eternal punishment in the underworld

THE BIRTH OF DEMOCRACY By 700 B.C., Greece was organized into a loose collection of independent city-states, including Athens, Sparta, and Thebes. By 508 B.C., Athens instituted a form of government that allowed all citizens a say in the government. Although "citizens" referred only to men, this form of government "by the people" was the beginning of democracy.

A Rich Legacy In addition to democracy, the Greeks left a rich heritage in the arts and sciences. Drama originated in Greece, and modern studies in medicine, astronomy, and math are often based on the pioneering work of the Greeks. Music was also very important to the ancient Greeks. They even had a god of music—Apollo. The story of Orpheus illustrates the Greek belief in the power of music.

Living on Olympus The ancient Greeks worshiped many gods and goddesses. They believed that the most important gods lived on Mount Olympus. We learn about these powerful beings and their interactions with humans in Greek mythology. "Orpheus" is one of these stories. The box at left shows some gods and humans you will need to know as you read "Orpheus."

ANCIENT GREECE

MACEDONIA
Mt. Olympus
THESSALY
Delphi
Thebes
Athens
Aegean Sea
PERSIAN EMPIRE
N
Sparta
Mediterranean Sea
Rhodes
Crete
0   100 mi
0   100 km

Orpheus

Alice Low

There were nine goddesses called Muses. Born of Zeus and a Titan named Mnemosyne, each Muse presided over a different art or science.

Calliope, one of these sisters, was the inspiration of poets and musicians. She was the mother of Orpheus (a mortal because his father was one) and gave to her son a remarkable talent for music.

Orpheus played his lyre so sweetly that he charmed all things on earth. Men and women forgot their cares when they gathered around him to listen. Wild beasts lay down as if they were tame, entranced by his soothing notes. Even rocks and trees followed him, and the rivers changed their direction to hear him play.

Orpheus loved a young woman named Eurydice, and when they were married, they looked forward to many years of happiness together. But soon after, Eurydice stepped on a poisonous snake and died.

Orpheus roamed the earth, singing sad melodies to try to overcome his grief. But it was no use. He longed for Eurydice so deeply that he decided to follow her to the underworld. He said to himself, "No mortal has ever been there before, but I must try to bring back my beloved Eurydice. I will charm Persephone and Hades with my music and win Eurydice's release."

He climbed into a cave and through a dark passage that led to the underworld. When he reached the river Styx,[1] he plucked his lyre, and Charon, the ferryman, was so charmed that he rowed him across. Then he struck his lyre again, and Cerberus, the fierce three-headed dog who guarded the gates, heard the sweet music and lay still to let him pass.

Orpheus continued to play his lyre tenderly as he made his way through the gloomy underworld. The ghosts cried when they heard his sad music. Sisyphus, who had been condemned to roll a rock uphill forever, stopped his fruitless work to listen. Tantalus, who had been sentenced to stand in a pool of receding water, stopped trying to quench his thirst. And even the wheel to which Ixion was tied as punishment stopped turning for one moment.

At last Orpheus came to the palace of Hades and Persephone, king and queen of the underworld. Before they could order him to leave, he began his gentle song, pleading for Eurydice.

When stern Hades heard Orpheus's song, he began to weep. Cold Persephone was so moved that, for the first time in all her months in the underworld, her heart melted.

> **Connecting Literature to Social Studies**
> What do these details tell you about the importance of music in ancient Greece?

◆ Build Vocabulary

inspiration (in´ spə rā´ shən) *n.*: Something that brings on creative ability; motivation

---

1. **Styx** (stiks) *n.*: River that flows around Hades.

"Oh, please, my husband," she said to Hades, "let Eurydice be reunited with Orpheus."

And Hades replied, "I, too, feel the sadness of Orpheus. I cannot refuse him."

They summoned Eurydice, and the two lovers clasped each other and turned to leave.

"Wait!" said Hades to Orpheus. "Eurydice is yours to take back to earth on one condition."

"What is that?" asked Orpheus.

"She must follow you, and you must not look back at her until you are on earth again."

"I understand," said Orpheus. "And I am forever grateful."

Orpheus and Eurydice left the underworld and made their way through the dark passage that led to the upper world. At last they reached the cave through which Orpheus had descended.

"I can see daylight ahead," called Orpheus to Eurydice. "We are almost there." But Eurydice had not heard him, and so she did not answer.

Orpheus turned to make sure that she was still following him. He caught one last glimpse of her with her arms stretched out to him. And then she disappeared, swallowed up by darkness.

"Farewell," he heard her cry as she was carried back to the underworld.

Orpheus tried to follow her, but this time the gods would not allow it. And so he wandered the earth alone. He sang his sad songs to the rocks and the trees and longed for the time when he, too, would die and be reunited with his beloved Eurydice in the underworld.

Connecting Literature to Social Studies
What do these details indicate about the way the Greeks viewed the gods?

Meet the Author

Alice Low (1926–   )

As a girl, Alice Low enjoyed making puppets and performing in plays. As an adult, she has written a musical play and many articles for magazines. She is famous for her retellings of myths and folk tales.

Guide for Responding

◆ LITERATURE AND YOUR LIFE

Reader's Response Would you have looked back to see if Eurydice was following you? Why or why not?

Thematic Focus How can myths help you explore the world of the ancient Greeks?

Journal Writing Write four or five sentences that you would say to Orpheus.

☑ Check Your Comprehension

1. Why did Orpheus go to the underworld?
2. How did Orpheus get past Cerberus?
3. Why did Orpheus turn around to look at Eurydice?
4. What happened when Orpheus turned around?

◆ Critical Thinking

INTERPRET

1. What details in the myth indicate that Orpheus had remarkable musical talent? **[Support]**
2. What do the punishments of Sisyphus, Tantalus, and Ixion suggest about the gods' attitudes toward mortals? **[Draw Conclusions]**
3. Why do you think the gods put a condition on allowing Orpheus to take Eurydice? **[Speculate]**

APPLY

4. What lesson might this story teach to people today? **[Relate]**

EXTEND

5. Why do you think we call the words to songs "lyrics"? **[Music Link]**

CONNECTING LITERATURE TO SOCIAL STUDIES

The ancient Greeks believed in gods and goddesses who controlled different things in the world. Most of the Greek myths are about humans who become involved with one or more of the divine beings. Greek mythology began as a way of explaining things about the world for which the Greeks did not have scientific answers. However, many of the stories show humans doing things that everyone can recognize. The myths are as much about human nature as they are about super-powerful beings.

That's one reason the Greek myths are still popular today.

1. What details in the myth of Orpheus help us understand what was important to the ancient Greeks?
2. What qualities does Orpheus have that can be found in people of any time period?
3. This myth has been a source of inspiration for writers, artists, and musicians throughout the ages. Why do you think the myth has been so popular?

 Idea Bank

Writing

1. **Dialogue** Write a conversation that might have taken place between Orpheus and Eurydice before they left the underworld together.
2. **Cast List** Choose performers from among today's popular actors to play the roles of Orpheus, Eurydice, Hades, and Persephone. Explain each of your choices in a paragraph.
3. **Song Lyrics** Write lyrics for a song Orpheus might have sung to convince Hades and Persephone to release Eurydice. Include praise of the gods' powers, and explain why Eurydice belongs in the world of living mortals, rather than in the underworld with Sisyphus, Tantalus, and Ixion.

Speaking and Listening

4. **Debate** Imagine that Hades and Persephone do not agree about releasing Eurydice. With a partner, role-play a discussion in which they debate whether or not she should be released.

Projects

5. **Chart** Create a chart showing the twelve gods who live on Mount Olympus. Illustrate your chart with symbols that show what the ancient Greeks believed about each god. (For example, you might draw a lyre and a sun for Apollo. He was the god of music and the sun.)
6. **Skit [Group Activity]** With a group, learn the story of another Greek myth and act it out as a skit—a brief performance using very few costumes or props.

Further Reading, Listening, and Viewing

- *The Macmillan Book of Greek Gods and Heroes* by Alice Low (1994) retells the story of Orpheus and several other popular myths from ancient Greece.
- The illustrated book *Focus on Ancient Greeks* by Anita Ganeri (1994) provides visuals and text that show you the history, social customs, language and writing, and laws of ancient Greece.
- Isaac Asimov's book *Words From the Myths* explains how names and terms from mythology have found their way into contemporary language.
- *Greek Traditional Music Collection* from FM Records features regional music and dance music played on traditional instruments.

Problem-Solution Essay

Writing Process Workshop

In "The Strange Geometry of Stonehenge," technology helped scientists solve problems. For Margie in "The Fun They Had," technology creates a problem. Suggest a solution for a problem in your own world. In a **problem-solution essay,** you identify the problem and lay out a plan for solving it.

Writing Skills Focus

▶ **Use an outline to identify and organize your ideas.** An outline will keep your ideas organized and focused. Plan the main points of your essay, and arrange supporting details around those main points. (See p. 378.)

▶ **State the problem clearly.** In the opening paragraph, tell what the problem is in a sentence or two.

▶ **Support your ideas with statistics.** Don't just say, "Many people think . . ." Give specific numbers and percentages. You may need to do research to find statistics that support your ideas. (See p. 387.)

▶ **Choose details appropriate for your audience.** Think about the people who will be reading your essay. Present facts and details that will be meaningful to these readers and easily understood by them. (See p. 395.)

MODEL

① "The dog ate it" is just one of the many excuses teachers hear when homework isn't done. ② The truth is, many students have difficulty finding a time and place to complete assignments outside of school. ③ In my math class, twelve of the twenty students say that they have turned in at least two late or incomplete assignments this year. After-school sports, clubs, and activities can last until dinner time. At home, phone calls, television, and family members can be distracting.

① This old excuse will be familiar to the writer's audience (her teacher and classmates).

② This sentence states the problem.

③ This statistic demonstrates the extent of the problem.

Prewriting

Choose a Topic Think about some of the problems you hear about in the news—either local, state, national, or world problems. You may also address a problem at your school or in your community or a personal problem. Choose a problem that can be solved and for which you have ideas for solutions. If you're having trouble coming up with an idea, consider one of the problems listed below:

Topic Ideas

- A younger brother or sister who doesn't respect your privacy
- Litter in the park
- A dog that doesn't behave
- A dangerous intersection near the school

Write an Outline Use an outline to arrange your thoughts on the problem and potential solutions.

I. Problem: Can't get homework done
  A. No time
    1. Sports
    2. Friends
    3. Favorite shows
  B. House too noisy
    1. Television
    2. Phone
    3. Rest of family talks
II. Solution: Set aside a time and place
  A. Time
    1. Leave practice on time.
    2. Make specific plans with friends instead of just hanging out.
    3. Watch only one favorite show. Tape or skip others.
    4. Set rules for when my sister can interrupt me.
  B. Place
    1. Clear off desk in room
    2. Set a family "quiet time" for using kitchen table as a desk.

DRAFTING/REVISING

APPLYING LANGUAGE SKILLS: Vary Sentence Length

As you write, use both short and long sentences. This writer revised a paragraph to create sentences that vary in length.

Draft:
There are twenty students in my math class. Twelve of them can't complete assignments. They say they don't have time. There are ways to use time wisely. Maybe they haven't thought of these ways.

Revised:
Twelve of the twenty students in my math class can't complete assignments. They say they don't have time. Maybe they haven't thought of ways they can use their time more wisely.

Practice Rewrite this passage to vary sentence length:

Students need time for activities. Students need time for homework. Students can make time for homework. They can also make time for fun.

Writing Application Vary the sentence length in your essay.

Writer's Solution Connection Language Lab

For more practice, complete the Language Lab lesson on Combining Sentences.

APPLYING LANGUAGE SKILLS: Finish With a Strong Concluding Sentence

An essay should end with a strong statement or conclusion. In the concluding sentence, restate the main idea or urge readers to take action in a memorable way.

Restatement: It's your park—keep it clean!

Call to Action: Don't wait! Join the volunteers today.

Practice On your paper, write the sentence from each pair that is the stronger conclusion. Explain why.

1. (a) I think you should find the time to volunteer.
   (b) You can make a difference if you make time to volunteer.
2. (a) We need a traffic light at Main and Barker.
   (b) Putting up a traffic light may cost money, but not putting one up may cost lives.

Writing Application Edit your essay for a strong concluding sentence.

Writer's Solution Connection Writing Lab

To evaluate your conclusion, use the Self-evaluation checklist in the Writing Lab Tutorial on Exposition.

Drafting

Write a Striking Introduction One way to catch readers' attention is to give an example of the problem through a description, a personal anecdote, or a statistic.

Tell About the Problem State the problem in a sentence or two. Explain the causes of the problem and its effects on you and on others. Use facts, examples, statistics, personal anecdotes, and other details. Refer to your outline as you draft to make sure you are not forgetting any significant points you want to make.

Revising

Use a Checklist As you review your work, use the following checklist to guide you:

▶ Have I stated the problem clearly?
▶ Did I support the ideas with statistics or details?
▶ Is my solution workable?
▶ Does my essay end with a strong concluding statement?

Revise where your essay needs more detail or support.

REVISION MODEL

Not doing homework can affect your average in a class. ① Many teachers in our school, including Ms. Paganano, Mr. Cavel, and Mr. Chen, count homework as fifteen percent of the grade for the marking period. **You can get the work done if you make a plan.** ② Set aside a special time when you will not watch television or make phone calls. Tell your friends to call you before or after that time. ~~You have to get the work done.~~ ③ Homework and fun are both important. With the right planning, you can find time for both. ~~Getting homework done is as important as having fun~~.

① The writer provides details that show how the problem affects people in her school.
② The writer adds a specific suggestion for making a plan.
③ The writer revises to create a stronger concluding statement.

Publishing and Presenting

Bulletin Board Post your problem-solution essay on a class bulletin board so classmates can read and discuss your ideas.

Letter Put your essay in letter form and send it to an elected official or "Letters to the Editor" column of a newspaper.

Strategies for Success

A walk through a shopping mall can make you feel as if you are lost in a jungle. Unlike jungles, though, most large public buildings have building maps or floor plans. With the help of the map or plan, you can find your new dentist or favorite store easily. The following pointers will help you to read a building map or floor plan.

Orient Yourself First, look at the map or floor plan for the words *You Are Here* or a symbol, such as a star. If you don't see either, then look on the map for the landmarks you can see around you—a large entrance, rows of elevators, or some clearly marked business. Once you have found where you are, you can figure out how to get where you are going.

Find the Index On the floor plan, your dentist's office may be labeled "213," not "Dr. Polansky's Office." Look for an index on the plan that lists the names of businesses and their room numbers. Match the numbers on the index with the numbers on the map.

Tips About Numbers

▶ The first numeral of an office number often tells which floor it is on. Rooms 213, 225, and 247, for example, are usually located on the second floor.

▶ In office buildings, even-numbered rooms are often on one side of a hallway, with odd-numbered rooms on the other.

Plan a Route Once you locate the store or office that you want to find, plan your route. Notice which hallways, stairways, or elevators you need to use. Select a few landmarks to look for on your way. They will help you know that you are headed in the right direction.

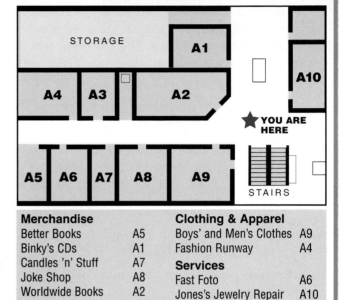

Merchandise		Clothing & Apparel	
Better Books	A5	Boys' and Men's Clothes	A9
Binky's CDs	A1	Fashion Runway	A4
Candles 'n' Stuff	A7	**Services**	
Joke Shop	A8	Fast Foto	A6
Worldwide Books	A2	Jones's Jewelry Repair	A10
Food			
Ice Cream Heaven	A3		

Apply the Strategies

1. Study this map carefully. Which stores are located nearest to you? What other landmarks are nearby?

2. Choose a store you would like to visit. List its name and number, and tell which stores are next to it.

3. You have to pick up your watch from the jewelry repair shop, buy a CD, and pick up your film. In which order will you visit the stores? Why?

✔ *You might find your building map and floor plan reading skills helpful in the following situations:*

▶ *A visit to a large library*

▶ *A trip to pick up a friend at the airport*

▶ *Your first day in a new school*

A sentence consists of two parts: the **subject** and the **predicate.** The subject states whom or what the sentence is about. The predicate tells what the subject is or does. (See page 377.)

Subject	Predicate
The luxury ship *Titanic*	sank in a collision with an iceberg.

send
sen·tence (sen'tans) *n.* **1** a group of words that is used to tell, ask, command, or exclaim something, usually having a subject and a predicate: a sentence begins with a capital letter and ends with a period, question mark, or exclamation point.

Simple Subject and Simple Predicate The simple subject is the main noun or pronoun in the complete subject. The simple predicate is the verb or verb phrase in the predicate. (See page 386.)

Simple Subject   Simple Predicate

The luxury ship *Titanic* sank in a collision with an iceberg.

Complete Sentences A **complete sentence** is a group of words that has at least one subject and one verb and that expresses a complete thought. (See page 394.)

Subject   Verb

Complete: Cerberus heard the sweet music.

Not Complete: Orpheus passing.

Kinds of Sentences Sentences may be categorized into four kinds (see page 404):

Declarative:	Makes a statement. *Orpheus wept.*
Imperative:	Gives a command or makes a request. The subject "you" is understood. *Come here.*
Interrogative:	Asks a question. *Why did Orpheus weep?*
Exclamatory:	Shows excitement or strong feeling. *I don't believe it!*

Practice 1 Copy the following sentences into your notebook. Underline the complete subject once and the complete predicate twice. Then, circle the simple subject and verb.

1. They took Tommy's teacher away for nearly a month.

2. The mechanical teacher waited patiently for the inspector's arrival.

3. The slow-witted dinosaur waddled about on its four stubby legs.

4. The huge cluster of upright stones stands in the center of a level circular space.

Practice 2 On your paper, label each of the following sentences as *declarative, imperative, interrogative,* or *exclamatory.*

1. Orpheus and Eurydice turned to leave.

2. Has Maggie read as many books as Tommy?

3. How long before computers take over?

4. Go to Stonehenge!

5. I want to go, too!

Grammar in Writing

✔ *When writing, make sure each of your sentences expresses a complete thought and contains a subject and a predicate.*

PART 2 *Meeting the Unknown*

'Sinbad the Sailor' from *Stories from the Arabian Nights*, illustrated by Edmund Dulac. Reproduced by permission of Hodder and Stoughton Limited

Guide for Reading

Meet the Author:

Laurence Yep (1948–   )

Laurence Yep was born and raised in San Francisco, California. A third-generation Chinese American, he began writing in high school, selling his first story when he was just eighteen years old. Since then, he has written many books for young people and won numerous awards and honors.

Other Worlds Yep has always been interested in other worlds. His books of science fiction and fantasy tell of strange events in mysterious lands. He is also interested in his Chinese American heritage. He has spent years researching and writing novels about the experiences of Chinese immigrants and their descendants as they struggled to survive and find an identity in a new land.

THE STORY BEHIND THE STORY

Yep's interest in Chinese folk tales was sparked by the discovery of a collection of folk tales gathered from Chinese immigrants during the 1930's. In these tales, Yep found stories of struggle and hope, loneliness, foolishness, anger, and fear. For him, they opened a window on the past, helping him to understand human nature and his own heritage better. "Breaker's Bridge" is one of those tales, retold in Yep's own words.

◆ LITERATURE AND YOUR LIFE

CONNECT YOUR EXPERIENCE

It's time to clean your room—but you can't even see the floor! You can't imagine how you'll ever accomplish this enormous task. By putting away one thing at a time, though, you finally clear away the chaos. The main character in "Breaker's Bridge" faces an enormous task set by an emperor. If he doesn't finish the job, he faces a serious penalty.

THEMATIC FOCUS: Meeting the Unknown

What might be some advantages of starting a project without a hard-and-fast plan?

◆ Background for Understanding

TECHNOLOGY

Breaker, the bridge builder in this story, faces the challenge of building supports for a bridge. Most bridges must be built on piers—columns that support the weight of the bridge. Without piers, a bridge can cover only a short distance. Even with modern equipment and technology, building piers in deep water is extremely difficult and expensive. For Breaker in ancient China, building piers in a deep, swift-moving river seems impossible.

◆ Build Vocabulary

RELATED WORDS: FORMS OF *execute*

If the main character in "Breaker's Bridge" fails to *execute,* or carry out, his orders, he will face the *executioner*—someone who carries out a death penalty. Other words related to *execute* are *executive, execution,* and *executor.*

WORD BANK

Which word describes a course on which you jump over, climb through, or crawl under things that are in your way?

obstacle
writhing
piers
executioner
immortals

◆ Breaker's Bridge ◆

◆ Literary Focus

CHARACTER TRAITS

Like real people, characters in stories have individual personalities. **Character traits** are the qualities that make up a person's or character's personality. A character's traits determine how the character acts. For example, intelligence and determination are two traits of the main character in "Breaker's Bridge." Because he has these traits, he thinks things through and doesn't give up. As you read "Breaker's Bridge," notice the traits of each of the characters.

◆ Reading Strategy

DETERMINE CAUSE AND EFFECT

The main character in this story is called Breaker because he was clumsy as a boy. His clumsiness is a **cause**—a reason why something happens. The **effect,** or result, is that people gave him a nickname. You will better understand the events in a story if you recognize the connections between causes and effects. Draw "bridges" like the ones below to show cause-and-effect relationships you discover in "Breaker's Bridge."

Breaker's Bridge

LAURENCE YEP

hunting Palace

There was once a boy who was always breaking things. He didn't do it on purpose. He just had very clumsy hands. No matter how careful he tried to be, he always dropped whatever he picked up. His family soon learned not to let him set the table or send him for eggs. Everyone in the village called him Breaker.

But Breaker was as clever as he was clumsy. When he grew up, he managed to outlive his nickname. He could design a bridge to cross any <u>obstacle</u>. No canyon was too wide. No river was too deep. Somehow the clever man always found a way to bridge them all.

Eventually the emperor heard about this clever builder and sent for him.

"There is a river in the hills," the emperor said to him. "Everyone tells me it is too swift and deep to span. So I have to go a long way around it to get to my hunting palace. But you're famous for doing the impossible."

The kneeling man bowed his head to the floor. "So far I have been lucky. But there is always a first time when you can't do something."

The emperor frowned. "I didn't think you were lazy like my other bridge builders. You can have all the workers and all the materials you need. Build the bridge and you'll have your weight in gold. Fail and I'll have your head."

There was nothing for Breaker to do but thank the emperor and leave. He went right away to see the river. He had to take a steep road that wound upward through the hills toward the emperor's hunting palace.

It was really more than a palace, for it

◄ **Critical Viewing** How do you think this old man might help Breaker solve his problem? **[Speculate]**

included a park the size of a district, and only the emperor could hunt the wildlife. The road to it had to snake through high, steep mountains. Although the road was well kept, the land became wilder and wilder. Pointed boulders thrust up like fangs, and the trees grew in twisted, <u>writhing</u> clumps.

Breaker became uneasy. "This is a place that doesn't like people very much."

The road twisted suddenly to the left when it came to a deep river gorge. On the other side of the gorge, the many trees of the palace looked like a dark-green sea. The yellow-tiled roofs looked like golden rafts floating on its top. Dark mountains, their tops capped with snow all year round, loomed behind the palace like monstrous guards.

Breaker carefully sidled to the edge of the gorge and looked down. Far below, he saw the river. When the snow melted in the distant mountains, the water flowed together to form this river. It raced faster than a tiger and stronger than a thousand buffalo. When it splashed against a rock, it threw up sheets of white spray like an ocean wave.

Breaker shook his head in dismay. "The emperor might as well have commanded me to bridge the sea."

But his failure would mean the loss of his head, so the next day Breaker set to work. The river was too wide to span with a simple bridge. Breaker would have to construct two <u>piers</u> in the middle of the river. The piers would support the bridge like miniature stone islands.

From the forests of the south came huge logs that were as tough and heavy as iron. From the quarries of the west came large, heavy stones of granite. The workers braved the cold water to sink the logs in the muddy riverbed. Breaker had to change the teams of workers often. The cold numbed anyone who stayed too long in the river.

Once the logs had been pounded into the mud, he tried to set the stones on top of the logs. But the river did not want to be tamed. It

bucked and fought like a herd of wild stallions. It crushed the piles of stones into pebbles. It dug up the logs and smashed them against the rocky sides until they were mounds of soggy toothpicks.

◆ Reading Strategy
What is the effect of the river's wild rushing?

Over the next month, Breaker tried every trick he knew; and each time the river defeated him. With each new failure, Breaker suspected more and more that he had met his match. The river flowed hard and strong and fast like the lifeblood of the earth itself. Breaker might as well have tried to tame the mountains.

In desperation, he finally tried to build a dam to hold back the river while he constructed the biggest and strongest piers yet. As he was supervising the construction, an official came by from the emperor.

"This bridge has already cost a lot of money," he announced to the wrecker. "What do you have to show for it?"

Breaker pointed to the two piers. They rose like twin towers toward the top of the gorge. "With a little luck, the emperor will have his bridge."

Suddenly, they heard a distant roar. The official looked up at the sky. "It sounds like thunder, but I don't see a cloud in the sky."

Breaker cupped his hands around his mouth to amplify his voice. "Get out," he shouted to his men. "Get out. The river must have broken our dam."

His men slipped and slid on the muddy riverbed, but they all managed to scramble out

◆ **Build Vocabulary**

obstacle (äb´ stə kəl´) n.: Something that stands in the way

writhing (rīth´ iŋ) adj.: Twisting and turning

piers (pirz) n.: Heavy structures supporting the sections of a bridge

Okasaki, Ando Hiroshige

just as a wall of water rolled down the gorge. The river swept around the two piers, pulling and tugging at the stones.

Everyone held their breath. Slowly the two piers began to rock back and forth on their foundations until they toppled over with a crash into the river. Water splashed in huge sheets over everyone, and when the spray finally fell back into the river, not one sign of the piers remained.

"All this time and all this money, and you have nothing to show for it." The official took a soggy yellow envelope from his sleeve.

Breaker and the other workers recognized the imperial color of the emperor. They instantly dropped to their knees and bowed their heads.

Then, with difficulty, Breaker opened the damp envelope and unfolded the letter. "In one month," it said, "I will have a bridge or I will have your head." It was sealed in red ink with the official seal of the emperor.

Breaker returned the letter and bowed again. "I'll try," he promised.

"You will do more than try," the official snapped. "You will build that bridge for the emperor. Or the <u>executioner</u> will be sharpening his sword." And the official left.

Wet and cold and tired, Breaker made his way along a path toward the room he had taken in an inn. It was getting late, so the

▲ **Critical Viewing** What details of this scene seem magical and mysterious? **[Analyze]**

surrounding forest was black with shadows. As he walked, Breaker tried to come up with some kind of new scheme, but the dam had been his last resort. In a month's time, he would feel the "kiss" of the executioner's sword.

"Hee, hee, hee," an old man laughed in a creaky voice that sounded like feet on old, worn steps. "You never liked hats anyway. Now you'll have an excuse not to wear them."

Breaker turned and saw a crooked old man sitting by the side of the road. He was dressed in rags, and a gourd hung from a strap against his hip. One leg was shorter than the other.

"How did you know that, old man?" Breaker wondered.

"Hee, hee, hee. I know a lot of things: the softness of clouds underneath my feet, the sounds of souls inside bodies." And he shook his gourd so that it rattled as if there were beans inside. "It is the law of the universe that all things must change; and yet Nature hates

◆ **Build Vocabulary**

executioner (ek´ si kyōō´ shən ər) *n.:* One who carries out a death penalty imposed by the courts or a ruler

change the most of all."

"The river certainly fits that description." Although he was exhausted and worried, Breaker squatted down beside the funny old man. "But you better get inside, old man. Night's coming on and it gets cold up in these mountains."

"Can't." The old man nodded to his broken crutch.

Breaker looked all around. It was growing dark, and his stomach was aching with hunger. But he couldn't leave the old man stranded in the mountains, so Breaker took out his knife. "If I make you a new crutch, can you reach your home?"

"If you make me a crutch, we'll all have what we want." It was getting so dim that Breaker could not be sure if the old man smiled.

Although it was hard to see, Breaker found a tall, straight sapling and tried to trim the branches from its sides; but being Breaker, he dropped his knife several times and lost it twice among the old leaves on the forest floor. He also cut each of his fingers. By the time he was ready to cut down the sapling, he couldn't see it. Of course, he cut his fingers even more. And just as he was trimming the last branch from the sapling, he cut the sapling right in two.

He tried to carve another sapling and broke that one. It was so dark by now that he could not see at all. He had to find the next sapling by feel. This time he managed to cut it down and began to trim it. But halfway through he dropped his knife and broke it. "He'll just have to take it as it is," Breaker said.

When he finally emerged from the forest, the moon had come out. Sucking on his cut fingers, Breaker presented the new crutch to the funny old man.

The old man looked at the branches that grew from the sides of his new crutch. "A little splintery."

Breaker angrily took his cut finger from his mouth. "Don't insult someone who's doing you a favor."

The crooked old man lifted his right arm with difficulty and managed to bring it behind his neck. "Keep that in mind yourself." He began to rub the back of his neck.

Breaker thrust the crutch at the old man. "Here, old man. This is what you wanted. "

But the old man kept rubbing the back of his neck. "Rivers are like people: Every now and then, they have to be reminded that change is the law that binds us all."

"It's late. I'm tired and hungry and I have to come up with a new plan. Here's your crutch." And Breaker laid the crutch down beside the old man.

But before Breaker could straighten, the old man's left hand shot out and caught hold of Breaker's wrist. The old man's grip was as strong as iron. "Even the least word from me will remind that river of the law."

Breaker tried to pull away, but as strong as he was, he could not break the old man's hold. "Let me go."

But the crooked old man lowered his right hand so that Breaker could see that he had rubbed some of the dirt and sweat from his skin. "We are all bound together," the old man murmured, "and by the same laws." He murmured that over and over until he was almost humming like a bee. At the same time, his fingers quickly rolled the dirt and sweat into two round little pellets.

Frightened, Breaker could only stare at the old man. "Ar-ar-are you some mountain spirit?" he stammered.

The old man turned Breaker's palm upward and deposited the two little pellets on it. Then he closed Breaker's fingers over them. "Leave one of these at each spot where you want a pier. Be sure not to lose them."

"Yes, all right, of course," Breaker promised quickly.

The old man picked up the crutch and thrust himself up from the ground. "Then you'll have what you want too." And he hobbled away quickly.

Breaker kept hold of the pellets until he reached the inn. Once he was among the inn's bright lights and could smell a hot meal, he began to laugh at himself. "You've let the emperor's letter upset you so much that you let a harmless old man scare you."

Even so, Breaker didn't throw away the pellets but put them in a little pouch. And the next morning when he returned to the gorge, he took along the pouch.

The canyon widened at one point so that there was a small beach. Breaker kept his supplies of stone and logs there. Figuring that he had nothing to lose, Breaker walked down the steep path. Then he took the boat and rowed out onto the river.

As he sat in the bobbing boat, he thought of the funny old man again. "You and I," he said to the river, "are both part of the same scheme of things. And it's time you faced up to it."

Although it was difficult to row at the same time, he got out the pouch with the two pellets. "I must be even crazier than that old man." He opened the pouch and shook one of the pellets into his hand.

When he was by the spot where the first pier should be, Breaker threw the pellet in. For a moment, nothing happened. There was only the sound of his oars slapping at the water.

And suddenly the surface began to boil. Frantically, he tried to row away, but the water began to whirl and whirl around in circles. Onshore, the workers shouted and ran to higher ground as waves splashed over the logs and stones.

From beneath the river came loud thumps and thuds and the grinding of stone on stone. A rock appeared above the surface. The water rose in another wave. On top of the wave another stone floated as if it were a block of wood. The river laid the first stone by the second.

Open-mouthed, Breaker watched the river

lay stone after stone. The watery arms reached higher and higher until the first pier rose to the top of the gorge.

As the waters calmed, Breaker eagerly rowed the boat over to the second spot. At the same time that he tried to row enough to keep himself in the right place, Breaker reached for the pouch and opened it.

But in his hurry, his clumsy fingers crushed part of the pellet. He threw the remainder of the pellet into the water and then shook out the contents of the pouch. But this time, the river only swirled and rippled.

Breaker leaned over the side and peered below. He could just make out the pale, murky shape of a mound, but that was all. Even so, Breaker wasn't upset. His workers could easily build a second pier and meet the emperor's deadline.

So Breaker finished the bridge, and that summer the emperor reached his hunting palace with ease. When the emperor finished hunting and returned to his capital, he showered Breaker with gold and promised him all the work he could ever want.

However, winter brought deep snows once again to the mountains. That spring, when the snow thawed, the river grew strong and wild again. It roared down the gorge and smashed against the first pier. But the first pier was solid as a mountain.

However, the second pier had not been built with magic. The river swept away the second pier as if it were nothing but twigs.

The bridge was repaired before the summer hunting, but the emperor angrily summoned Breaker to his hunting palace. "You were supposed to build a bridge for me," the emperor declared.

"Hee, hee, hee," laughed a creaky old voice. "He did, but you didn't say how long it was supposed to stay up."

Breaker turned around and saw it was the crooked old man. He was leaning on the crutch that Breaker had made for him. "How did you get here?" he asked the old man. But from the corner of his eye, he could see all the court officials kneeling down. And when Breaker looked back at the throne, he saw even the emperor kneeling.

"How can we serve you and the other eight <u>immortals</u>?" the emperor asked the crooked old man.

"We are all bound by the same laws," the old man croaked again, and then vanished.

And then Breaker knew the old man for what he truly was—a saint and a powerful magician.

So the emperor spared Breaker and sent him to build other projects all over China. And the emperor never regretted that he had let Breaker keep his head. But every year, the river washed away part of the bridge and every year it was rebuilt. And so things change and yet do not change.

◆ **Build Vocabulary**

immortals (im môrt′ əlz) *n.*: Beings who live forever

Beyond Literature

Technology Connection

Civil Engineering If Breaker were working today, he would probably be a civil engineer. Civil engineering involves the planning and building of large construction projects, such as highways, bridges, canals, dams, and tunnels. Engineers need skill in math and the sciences. They must be able to analyze problems systematically and logically, and they must communicate well.

Cross-Curricular Activity
Career Plan A person considering a career in engineering would need to take algebra, geometry, trigonometry, calculus, chemistry, and physics. Find out the school grade in which a person typically studies these subjects and what is studied in each of these courses. Show your findings on a chart.

Guide for Responding

◆ LITERATURE AND YOUR LIFE

Reader's Response Do you think the emperor gave Breaker a fair deal? Explain.

Thematic Focus How does Breaker react when he "meets the unknown"?

Journal Writing In your journal, describe a difficult job that you have worked on.

☑ Check Your Comprehension

1. How does Breaker get his nickname?
2. What job does the emperor give Breaker?
3. Who helps Breaker finish the job?
4. Why does the emperor feel that Breaker did not succeed?
5. Why does the emperor spare Breaker's life?

◆ Critical Thinking

INTERPRET
1. How is Breaker the man different from Breaker the boy? **[Contrast]**
2. What clues indicate that the old man is more than he at first appears to be? **[Analyze]**
3. Why do you think Breaker uses the pellets, even though he doesn't think they'll work? **[Speculate]**

APPLY
4. What do Breaker's experiences show about the importance of a positive attitude? **[Apply]**

EXTEND
5. In what way would a bridge builder use measurements of distance and weight? **[Math Link]**

Guide for Responding (continued)

◆ Reading Strategy

DETERMINE CAUSE AND EFFECT

A **cause** is what makes something happen. An **effect** is what happens.

1. What causes the piers to crumble?
2. What effect does the emperor threaten if Breaker fails to build the bridge?
3. What are two effects of Breaker's kindness to the old man?

◆ Build Vocabulary

USING FORMS OF *execute*

In your notebook, use a form of *execute* to complete each sentence. Choose from *execute, executive, execution, executioner.*

1. Breaker did not want the _____?_____ to carry out the emperor's threat.
2. An _____?_____ carries out business plans.
3. This plan is not as easy to _____?_____ as I thought it would be.
4. The _____?_____ of the plan is a little complicated.

SPELLING STRATEGY

When spelling words like *pier,* which contain an *i* and an *e,* remember this rule: Use *i* before *e* except after *c* or when sounded like *a* as in *neighbor* and *weigh.* In your notebook, complete the word for each numbered clue.

1. A strong opinion: b_l _ _f
2. To trick or lie: d_c_ _ _e
3. How heavy something is: w_ _gh_
4. Extreme sadness: g_ _ _f

USING THE WORD BANK

On your paper, write a word from the Word Bank that completes the second pair of words.

1. Bake is to baker as kill is to _____?_____.
2. Natural is to mortal as supernatural is to _____?_____.
3. Help is to assistance as problem is to _____?_____.
4. Motionless is to still as twisting is to _____?_____.
5. Table is to legs as bridge is to _____?_____.

◆ Literary Focus

CHARACTER TRAITS

Character traits are the qualities that make up a character's personality. The traits are demonstrated in the way the character acts.

1. What is one character trait of the emperor? Give an example of an action that demonstrates this trait.
2. Identify two of Breaker's character traits. Explain how these traits are shown in his actions.

◆ Build Grammar Skills

DIRECT AND INDIRECT OBJECTS

Direct and indirect objects are nouns or pronouns that receive the action of verbs.

A **direct object** is a noun or a pronoun that receives the action of the verb and answers the question *what* or *whom.*

He could design a *bridge* to cross any obstacle. (*Design what?* a bridge)

An **indirect object** is a noun or a pronoun that names the person or thing *to whom* or *for whom* an action is done. The indirect object comes immediately after the verb and before the direct object.

If I make *you* a new crutch, can you reach your home? (*Make what?* a crutch *For whom?* you)

Practice On your paper, copy the following sentences. Write D.O. over each direct object and I.O. over each indirect object.

1. The official handed Breaker the letter.
2. The old man gave him the pellets.
3. The emperor summoned Breaker.
4. Breaker found an unusual solution.
5. Breaker built the emperor a bridge.

Writing Application Write four sentences about the story. Two should include direct objects, and two should include indirect and direct objects.

Build Your Portfolio

 ## Idea Bank

Writing

1. **Help-Wanted Ad** Write a help-wanted ad that the emperor might place in a newspaper, seeking someone to build a bridge to his hunting lodge. In your ad, describe what you want done and the reward or pay you are willing to offer.

2. **Letter** As Breaker, write a letter to the emperor, explaining why you are not able to finish the bridge. Include a list of strategies you have tried.

3. **Essay** When speaking of his work, Breaker says that part of his success depends on luck. Write an essay in which you explain the factors that you think contribute to success. Support your opinion with examples from the story or from life.

Speaking and Listening

4. **Storytelling** Folk tales like "Breaker's Bridge" were originally passed along orally—by being told aloud. Familiarize yourself with the details of the story, and practice telling it aloud. Then, tell the story to your class or a small group.

5. **Role Play** With a partner, role-play a conversation in which Breaker tries to explain to the angry emperor why he cannot complete the bridge.

Projects

6. **Bridge Model [Group Activity]** With a group, build a "mini-bridge." Group members can research the parts of a bridge, gather materials, draw plans for the bridge, or complete the construction.

7. **Erosion Illustration** The river shows that "things change and yet do not change." Draw an illustration or chart to show how rivers change a landscape through erosion. **[Science Link]**

 ## Writing Mini-Lesson

Career Investigation

Breaker's "career" is building bridges. Investigate a career that interests you, and write a report on your findings. A career investigation will tell you what talents and abilities are needed for success in a chosen career, what kind of schooling or training is required, what the salary and job prospects are, and what the work is like.

Writing Skills Focus: Identify the Purpose

Focus your investigation by making a list of questions you want answered. The list will give you a **purpose** when you interview people or go to the library to do research.

Model
Career Investigation: Forest Ranger
Focus Questions:
> What do forest rangers do?
> What training is required?
> What is the average salary?
> How easy or hard is it to get a job?

Prewriting Show a librarian your focus questions, and ask him or her to help you find information. Check the Internet. If possible, interview someone who works at the job you're investigating.

Drafting Use your focus questions as headings within your written work. Using the information that you found, write a short paragraph that answers each question.

Revising Ask a partner to read your report and ask any questions he or she has about the career. Add details to answer those questions.

> ◆ **Grammar Application**
> Review your work, and identify any direct or indirect objects.

Guide for Reading

Meet the Authors:

William Shakespeare (1564–1616)

William Shakespeare is the most highly regarded poet and playwright in the English language. He was born in the English town of Stratford-on-Avon and went to London when he was a young man. There, he began writing and acting in plays. Shakespeare wrote thirty-seven plays, along with several long, narrative poems and more than one hundred and fifty shorter poems called sonnets.

"The Fairies' Lullaby" appears in *A Midsummer Night's Dream,* a comedy written around 1600. This lullaby is sung by a group of fairies to Titania, the queen of the fairies, to lull her to sleep in the forest.

Walter de la Mare (1873–1956)

Walter de la Mare attended St. Paul's Cathedral Choir School in London. After graduation, he worked as a clerk until he was given a grant by the government, which allowed him to write full time. His fascination with the magical and the mysterious shows clearly in "Someone."

Christina Rossetti (1830–1894)

Christina Rossetti came from a creative family. One brother was a successful artist, and the other was a respected author, artist, and critic. She herself is known for her poetry, especially her poetry for children. At the age of forty-one, Rossetti fell victim to a disease that left her disfigured and an invalid. She withdrew from the world and rarely received visitors, but she did continue to write.

◆ LITERATURE AND YOUR LIFE

CONNECT YOUR EXPERIENCE

If you've ever read a fairy tale or told a ghost story, then you're already acquainted with the enjoyment people get from imagining things that are difficult to explain. The poets in this group capture the delightful mystery of unseen things—both real and imaginary.

THEMATIC FOCUS: Meeting the Unknown

How do you "meet the unknown" when it is also unseen?

◆ Background for Understanding

CULTURE AND TRADITIONS

Fairies, elves, and sprites are a part of legends and myths in many cultures, especially agricultural societies. In the stories about them, fairies often act as spirits of lakes and streams or as the guardians of trees, animals, and crops. These beings are usually believed to be small and to have special magical powers. Although basically good, fairies are often portrayed as mischief makers.

◆ Build Vocabulary

OLD-FASHIONED WORDS

When you read poetry, you may come across old-fashioned words that are not commonly used today. It may be that the poem was written long ago or that the poet is trying to give a special feel to the work. In these poems, the poets use *nought*, *nigh*, and *hence,* rather than the more contemporary words *nothing, near,* and *away.*

WORD BANK

Which of these words can describe the side trying to score in a sporting competition?

nigh
hence
offense
nought

The Fairies' Lullaby ◆ Someone ◆ Who Has Seen the Wind? ◆

Illustration by Arthur Rackham. From Mother Goose. Copyright, 1913, by Arthur Rackham, 1941, by Adyth Rackham. Reproduced by permission of D. Appleton-Century Company, Inc.

◆ Literary Focus
REPETITION

A poet may repeat a word, a phrase, or a line within a poem. This **repetition** creates a musical quality and can emphasize certain words or ideas. In "The Fairies' Lullaby," repetition creates the soothing, musical sound of a child's bedtime song. Look for other uses and effects of repetition in this group of poems.

◆ Reading Strategy
PARAPHRASE

Paraphrasing means putting sentences or ideas into your own words. Paraphrasing a poem makes you think about the meaning of each line. For this reason, putting it into your own words helps you make sure you really know what's going on. Use an organizer like the one below to record your paraphrase of lines from the poems.

Lines From the Poem	My Paraphrase
Never harm, Nor spell, nor charm, Come our lovely lady nigh.	No harm, spell, or charm is allowed near our beautiful lady.

The Fairies' Lullaby

from A Midsummer Night's Dream

William Shakespeare

The Fairy Queen, Kauai, Hawaii, USA

Fairies. You spotted snakes with double tongue,
    Thorny hedgehogs, be not seen.
    Newts and blindworms,[1] do no wrong,
    Come not near our fairy Queen.
5 **Chorus.** Philomel,[2] with melody
    Sing in our sweet lullaby;
    Lulla, lulla, lullaby, lulla, lulla, lullaby.
      Never harm,
      Nor spell, nor charm,
10   Come our lovely lady <u>nigh</u>.
    So, good night, with lullaby.

    Fairies. Weaving spiders, come not here.
    <u>Hence</u>, you long-legged spinners, hence!
    Beetles black, approach not near.
15   Worm nor snail do no <u>offense</u>
    Chorus. Philomel, with melody
    Sing in our sweet lullaby;
    Lulla, lulla, lullaby, lulla, lulla, lullaby.
      Never harm
20   Nor spell nor charm,
    Come our lovely lady nigh.
    So, good night, with lullaby.

◀ **Critical Viewing** Do you think the fairy in the picture is the fairy Queen or one of the fairies singing? Why? **[Support]**

◆ **Build Vocabulary**

nigh (nī) *adv.*: Near

hence (hens) *v.*: Go away from this place

offense (ə fens´) *n.*: Harmful act

---

1. newts (noōts) **and blindworms** *n.*: Newts are salamanders, animals that look like lizards but are related to frogs. Blind-worms are legless lizards.
2. Philomel (fil´ o mel´) *n.*: Nightingale.

Guide for Responding

◆ LITERATURE AND YOUR LIFE

Reader's Response What title would you give this lullaby? Why?

Thematic Focus How do the fairies try to protect their Queen from the unknown?

Journal Writing Write a journal entry explaining what you like and do not like about this poem.

☑ Check Your Comprehension

1. What are three things the fairies do not want near their Queen?
2. Whom do the fairies ask for help in singing the lullaby?

◆ Critical Thinking

INTERPRET

1. What tone of voice do you think the fairies would use to sing or speak their lines? **[Infer]**
2. What is the meaning of the line "Hence, you long-legged spinners, hence!"? **[Interpret]**

EVALUATE

3. Is this lullaby an appropriate song to sing to a child before he or she goes to sleep? Why or why not? **[Assess]**

EXTEND

4. The first half of the poem mentions every class of vertebrate animal except fish. Identify one example of a reptile, a mammal, a bird, and an amphibian. **[Science Link]**

The Coming Storm, Isle of Wight, 1789 by George Morland, Wolverhampton Art Gallery, West Midlands, UK

SOMEONE

Walter de la Mare

Someone came knocking
   At my wee, small door;
Someone came knocking,
   I'm sure—sure—sure;
5 I listened, I opened,
   I looked to left and right,
But <u>nought</u> there was a-stirring
   In the still, dark night;
Only the busy beetle
10   Tap-tapping in the wall,
Only from the forest
   The screech owl's call,
Only the cricket whistling
   While the dewdrops fall,
15 So I know not who came knocking,
   At all, at all, at all.

◆ **Build Vocabulary**

nought (nôt) *n.*: Nothing

Who Has Seen the Wind?
Christina Rossetti

Who has seen the wind?
  Neither I nor you:
But when the leaves hang trembling,
  The wind is passing through.

5   Who has seen the wind?
  Neither you nor I:
But when the trees bow down their heads,
  The wind is passing by.

◀ **Critical Viewing** Would you like to live in this place? Why or why not? **[Relate]**

Guide for Responding

◆ LITERATURE AND YOUR LIFE

Reader's Response Do you think these poems are serious or humorous? Why?

Thematic Focus In what way does each speaker try to meet the unknown?

☑ Check Your Comprehension

1. What does the speaker hear in "Someone"?
2. What does the speaker do in response to the sound?
3. What is the answer to the question "Who has seen the wind?"
4. How do you know when the wind is passing?

◆ Critical Thinking

INTERPRET

1. In what kind of place does the speaker in "Someone" live? **[Draw Conclusions]**
2. Is the speaker in "Someone" a nervous person or a brave person? Support your answer with details from the poem. **[Support]**
3. Does the speaker of "Who Has Seen the Wind?" enjoy nature? Explain. **[Infer]**

APPLY

4. Do you need to see something to believe it? Explain. **[Relate]**

COMPARE LITERARY WORKS

5. Contrast the moods of these poems. **[Relate]**

Guide for Responding (continued)

◆ Reading Strategy

PARAPHRASE

When you **paraphrase** lines or sections of these poems, you restate them in your own words. In this way, you make the meaning your own.

1. Paraphrase the first four lines of "The Fairies' Lullaby."
2. Paraphrase the action in "Someone."
3. Write one sentence to paraphrase each of the two sections of "Who Has Seen the Wind?"

◆ Build Vocabulary

USING OLD-FASHIONED WORDS

On your paper, supply a contemporary word or phrase that is about the same in meaning for each old-fashioned word in italics.

1. Draw *nigh* and listen.
2. *Hence!* We don't want you here.
3. *Nought* was moving in the night.

SPELLING STRATEGY

In some words, such as *nought,* the *awt* sound is spelled *ought.* On your paper, unscramble the letters to make *ought* words that rhyme with *nought.*

1. thobug **2.** gruohbt **3.** thugoth **4.** ghoust

USING THE WORD BANK

On your paper, write the word from the Word Bank that fits each clue to the puzzle.

Across
1. Near
2. Insult or injury

Down
3. None
4. Away

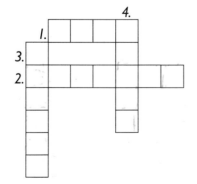

◆ Literary Focus

REPETITION

Repetition gives these poems a musical quality and emphasizes certain words and phrases.

1. In "The Fairies' Lullaby," a whole section is repeated. In what way does this make the poem similar to some songs?
2. In "The Fairies' Lullaby," what word or sound is repeated within a line?
3. Why do you think the word "knocking" is repeated in "Someone"?
4. Which words in "Someone" are repeated within a single line?
5. What question is repeated in "Who Has Seen the Wind?" In what way does this add emphasis to the question?

◆ Build Grammar Skills

DIRECT OBJECTS

A **direct object** is a noun or a pronoun that appears with an action verb and receives the action of the verb. A direct object answers the question *whom* or *what* about the verb.

D.O.
Who has seen the *wind*?

Practice On your paper, draw an arrow from the verb to the noun or pronoun that receives the action. Label the direct objects D.O.

1. Fairies sang a lullaby.
2. Spiders wove their webs.
3. I opened the door.
4. The trees bow down their heads.
5. The wind shakes the leaves.

Writing Application Add direct objects (and any other words needed) to the sentences below.

1. The poet wrote.
2. The noise frightened.
3. The man saw.

Build Your Portfolio

 Idea Bank

Writing

1. **Journal Entry** As the speaker of "Someone," write a journal entry describing your experience. Include your reactions to the event.

2. **Wind Poem** Write a short poem that answers the question "Who Has Seen the Wind?" In each line, tell one way you have "seen" the wind. For example, your first line might be "I have seen the wind in the flying leaves of autumn."

3. **Modern Verse** The lines spoken by the fairies in "The Fairies' Lullaby" refer to spotted snakes and thorny hedgehogs. These creatures probably don't affect a modern reader. Write a modern verse for the lullaby that refers to animals more familiar to you and your friends.

Speaking and Listening

4. **Choral Reading [Group Activity]** With a group, plan and perform a choral reading of "The Fairies' Lullaby." Different pairs or groups of readers should read different parts of the poem. **[Performing Arts Link]**

5. **Question-and-Answer Session** With a partner, act out the question-and-answer session between the speaker of "Someone" and a police officer sent to investigate the knocking.

Projects

6. **Shakespeare Festival [Group Activity]** With a group, plan a Shakespeare Festival for your class. Group members can choose video clips from films of his plays, make or draw costumes of the period, create posters showing his works, or make a timeline of his life. **[Social Studies Link]**

7. **Wind Diagram** Satellite pictures allow scientists who study weather to see wind patterns. Draw a diagram of a wind pattern, or use a copy of a satellite picture. Explain your visual to the class. **[Science Link; Technology Link]**

 Writing Mini-Lesson

Song

"The Fairies' Lullaby" is a song sung *by* imaginary creatures. Write your own song lyrics *about* an imaginary creature from a folk tale or a legend.

Writing Skills Focus: Use Library Resources

Use library resources to do research about the subject of your song. For example, if you choose to write a song about a dragon, find out what different cultures believe about dragons' habits and appearance.

Resources	How to find your topic
Magazines and newspapers	*Readers' Guide to Periodical Literature* CD index
Books	Card catalogs— electronic and printed
Internet	Search engines such as Yahoo and Infoseek.

If you don't know how to find information in a particular resource, ask the librarian for help.

Prewriting Jot down notes about your creature's habits and appearance. Brainstorm for a list of words you would use to describe the creature.

Drafting As you draft, use rhyme and repetition to emphasize words that describe the most important qualities of your creature.

Revising Read the words of your song to a small group. Allow time for the group to ask questions and make suggestions. Keep these questions and suggestions in mind as you revise.

◆ **Grammar Application**
Underline the direct objects in your song.

Guide for Reading

Meet the Authors:

George Laycock (1921–)

George Laycock is an avid photographer and professional writer who often illustrates his writing with his own photographs. He lives in Cincinnati, Ohio, not far from the town of Zanesville, where he was born. His interest in nature, wildlife, and the environment is evident in the books and magazine articles he writes. As a professional writer, Laycock has received many honors, including five Science Teachers of America awards for outstanding books for young people.

Chinua Achebe (1930–)

Chinua Achebe likes to retell stories that originated in his native country of Nigeria many years ago. Of African myths and legends, Achebe writes, "Our ancestors created their myths and legends and told their stories for a purpose. ... Any good story, any good novel, should have a message."

Many Messages Achebe studied broadcasting in London after graduating from college, and then he became a professional writer. Although he has written poetry, short stories, and essays, he is best known for his novels, which have won many honors and awards. His favorite topics for writing are Nigerian history and culture and African politics.

◆ LITERATURE AND YOUR LIFE

CONNECT YOUR EXPERIENCE

At one time or another, your eyes have probably played tricks on you. In the dark, a large rock can look like a threatening dog. A curtain fluttering in the wind might make you think a person has entered the room. Both "The Loch Ness Monster" and "Why the Tortoise's Shell Is Not Smooth" deal with what is seen—or thought to be seen.

THEMATIC FOCUS: Meeting the Unknown

As you read "The Loch Ness Monster" and "Why the Tortoise's Shell Is Not Smooth," ask yourself if sight alone provides enough evidence to make a judgment.

◆ Background for Understanding

SCIENCE

Some species of the world's animals have long been extinct, some have been discovered only recently, and others have not even been discovered yet. Scientists believe that the depths of the ocean hold species that have not yet been identified. Many people wonder if Loch Ness, a deep, murky lake in Scotland, may also contain an unidentified species. The picture on the next page shows the creature they wonder about.

◆ Build Vocabulary

RELATED WORDS: FORMS OF *orate*

The tortoise in "Why the Tortoise's Shell Is Not Smooth" is a great *orator*, or speaker. The word *orate* means "deliver a speech." The related noun *oration* means "a formal speech."

WORD BANK

Which of the words on the list might describe a creature that escapes, or *eludes*, notice?

elusive
abundant
famine
orator
eloquent

◆ The Loch Ness Monster ◆
Why the Tortoise's Shell Is Not Smooth

◆ Literary Focus

ORAL TRADITION

The **oral tradition** is the passing along of songs, stories, and poems by word of mouth. Eventually, these stories are set down in writing. These stories communicate the common beliefs and traditions of a culture or community. For example, for more than fourteen hundred years, people in Scotland have told the story of a creature in Loch (Lake) Ness. Today, scientists go to great lengths to discover how much of the story is true.

Stories like "Why the Tortoise's Shell Is Not Smooth" continue to be told to preserve the history of a culture.

◆ Reading Strategy

RECOGNIZE THE PURPOSE

Most stories are told for a **purpose,** or reason. You can recognize the purpose of a story by noticing the kinds of details that are included, the direct statements the author or storyteller makes, and his or her attitude toward the subject. The organizer below shows details that reveal Achebe's purpose for telling "Why the Tortoise's Shell Is Not Smooth." Make one like it to jot down details from "The Loch Ness Monster" that will help you recognize the author's purpose.

Author's Purpose: Entertain and Teach

Author's attitude is humorous. (entertains)

Specific foods are named. (teaches)

Animals talk. (entertains)

Describes Tortoise's appearance. (teaches)

Begins by describing the storyteller. (teaches)

"Why The Tortoise's Shell Is Not Smooth"

The Loch Ness Monster

George Laycock

In 1938, a tugboat captain was steering his boat across Loch Ness. Everything seemed to be in order. The sky was cloudy just as it is much of the time around Loch Ness. The water was rough from the wind. The tug plowed on mile after mile, its engines laboring normally. The captain was not thinking about monsters. He didn't believe in Nessie anyhow. He made this plain enough to anyone who asked him if he'd ever seen the beast. Then, beside the boat, a creature like nothing the captain had ever seen before stuck its long humped back out of the water. It had a long, slender neck and a little head. The monster rushed ahead, gained speed on the tug, and disappeared far out in front of the boat. This was enough to change the captain's mind. As far as he was concerned, Nessie was real, after all.

Other sightings even included an observation by a driver who saw Nessie in the beam of his headlights on a dark night as the monster crossed the highway near the loch.

These stories were told and retold. Word of Nessie spread around the world. This did a marvelous thing for Scotland. Tourists began to visit Loch Ness, hoping for a glimpse of the elusive lake monster. Tourism can be good for a country's economy. Nessie, real or not, became the most valuable animal in all Scotland.

But the lecturer who was to tell us about the Loch Ness monster that night in Oxford, Ohio, had brought scientific methods to the search for Nessie, and people were eager to hear his message. All the seats were filled and students stood around the walls and sat in the aisles to listen to the story Robert H. Rines had to tell.

Dr. Rines, president of the Boston Academy of Applied Science, led his first scientific expedition to Loch Ness in 1970. He took along modern sonar equipment and used this to "see" into the murky depths. Sonar works by sending high-intensity sound impulses into the water and measuring the echoes sent back as the sound waves bounce off the bottom or off objects between it and the bottom. It can reveal the depth of objects in the water, their size, and whether or not they are moving. That summer the sonar equipment showed the researchers important facts. There were large moving objects in the loch. Also there were abundant fish to feed monsters.

Dr. Rines meanwhile was consulting with his colleagues, searching for still better equipment for gathering information about the monster of Loch Ness. He worked with Dr. Harold E. Edgerton, who, as a professor at Massachusetts Institute of Technology, had pioneered in the development of high-speed underwater photography. Dr. Edgerton had also developed remarkable strobe lights for making pictures in dingy water. Now, he designed a system of lights Dr. Rines might use to obtain closeup pictures in Loch Ness.

Dr. Rines linked his camera to the sonar and set it so that it would begin making pictures automatically as soon as any large object passed through the sonar field. It would continue to make pictures every fifteen seconds as long as the sonar told it to.

For their first test, the crew of monster seekers chose the bay where Nessie had most often been sighted. They carefully cleaned the camera lens, then began lowering it gently toward the lake bottom. Divers checked it there and found it clean and ready to make monster pictures.

◆ **Build Vocabulary**

elusive (ē lōō′ siv) *adj.*: Always escaping
abundant (ə bun′ dənt) *adj.*: Plentiful; more than enough

◀ **Critical Viewing** Describe the "creature" you see in each of these photographs. [**Compare and Contrast**]

Another camera was suspended under the research boat and pointed downward into the dark water. All that was needed now was to wait for Nessie to come nosing around.

But a strange thing happened. The lens of the camera on the bottom of the loch was suddenly covered with sand, apparently kicked onto it by some large frightened creature. Had Nessie been there and kicked up the silt?

That camera, with its sand-covered lens, made no pictures. But the other camera, hanging beneath the boat, was still in working order. It yielded pictures that to some looked plainly like parts of a huge unknown monster swimming in the water. These color pictures were perhaps the best evidence yet that there really is a Nessie. In 1975 Dr. Rines and his crew were back in Scotland with still better photographic equipment, and the pictures they took were among those shown to the audience in Oxford.

One famous picture, believed by some to be Nessie, was made in 1934 by a noted physician who was vacationing on Loch Ness. It showed a large, dark creature swimming on the surface. Its long slender neck and small head stuck out of the water. No one was ever able to prove that this picture had been faked. Neither could anyone suggest a reason why the photographer would want to set up such a hoax. But this picture, like others made later, was rather indistinct. So, for that matter, were those made by Dr. Rines and his crew in 1972 and 1975.

But, sitting in the darkened auditorium, we saw the head of a monster in murky water as it filled the screen before us. It was lumpy and appeared to have a wide mouth where the mouth should be. It also seemed to have two small horns on the top of the head. But perhaps these were not horns. Some believe that they may, instead, have been breathing tubes. This supports the theory that Nessie is a huge reptile that must come to the surface to breathe.

Another picture revealed a large angular object that could have been a flipper, four to six feet across. It was attached to the side of what may have been the body of Nessie.

But the research team also wanted to know more about the nature of the lake deep below the surface. They hoped to learn whether there really were places where large creatures could hide.

This search was concentrated on Urquhart Bay, where Nessie has been most often reported. On the research vessel *Narwhal* the scientists cruised back and forth over the bay, taking soundings and pictures and transferring the information to a map.

For the first time they began to understand the truth about this arm of Loch Ness. Underwater, along both sides of the bay, were deep hidden ravines, rocky canyons and caves, dark recesses far below the surface. This excited the research team. The hiding places made the whole story of Nessie more believable. Nessie, it was agreed, could cruise about down there among those dark caves without sending a ripple to the surface.

This is also the area in which one earlier investigator heard strange underwater sounds the year before, tapping sounds that no biologist has yet been able to successfully identify.

These are the bits of evidence that help convince a growing number of people that there really is some "large animal" living deep in Loch Ness. Studying the accumulated evidence, Dr. George R. Zug, curator of amphibians and reptiles at the Smithsonian Institution in Washington, D.C., said, "I started as a skeptic. Now I believe there is a population of large animals in the loch. I don't have any idea of what they are." But he is convinced that research should continue and that the mystery of the Loch Ness monster should be solved.

Another scientist calling for more such research is Dr. Alfred W. Crompton, professor of biology at Harvard University. He, too, believes that the evidence points to a large aquatic animal living in Loch Ness.

What kind of animal this might be is little more than a guess. The most frequent speculation is that Nessie is an ancient reptile, a plesiosaur[1] believed extinct for fifty million years or more.

This is not the only such monster reported from deep lakes over the years. For more than half a century people around Montana's Flathead Lake have thought there might be something very large and unidentified living in the depths of that cold lake. Indians told the earliest white people about this monster. The monster of Flathead Lake is said to be at least twenty-five feet long and uniformly black, and to swim on the surface, sometimes creating huge waves even when the rest of the lake is calm.

In 1922 scientists in Argentina were choosing sides on the question of whether

---

1. **plesiosaur** (plē′ sē ō sôr′) *n.*: One of a group of large water reptiles that lived approximately 65,000,000 years ago.

there could be a similar monster in Patagonia. An American mining engineer was among those who had sighted such a creature. What he described had the size, outline, and features of the ancient plesiosaurs. But there has been little heard of this population of monsters in recent times, and if they were indeed there, they may by now have become extinct.

The mystery locked in the depths of Loch Ness may be closer to an answer than ever before. Dr. Rines and Sir Peter Scott of England have even given Nessie a proper scientific name, *Nessiteras rhombopteryx*, meaning "Ness marvel with a diamond-shaped fin." Some believe that science will soon solve the ancient mystery.

Meanwhile, officials in Scotland have taken steps to protect Nessie. They warn that their famous monsters, if they are really out there in the cold water of Loch Ness, must be among the world's most endangered wildlife. Anyone harming, or even teasing, a Loch Ness monster can be arrested.

Guide for Responding

◆ LITERATURE AND YOUR LIFE

Reader's Response How would you feel if you saw a strange creature like Nessie?

Thematic Focus What areas of the world are still unknown to people?

Journal Writing Write a list of questions about Nessie you would like to have answered.

☑ Check Your Comprehension

1. What is one reason that scientists have trouble finding Nessie?
2. What techniques have scientists used to try to prove Nessie's existence?
3. Describe what Nessie is reported to look like.

◆ Critical Thinking

INTERPRET

1. Do you think the author believes that Nessie exists? Explain. **[Draw Conclusions]**
2. Why don't people accept the photographs as evidence of Nessie's existence? **[Synthesize]**

EVALUATE

3. Does this article present a convincing case for Nessie's existence? **[Assess]**

APPLY

4. What kind of evidence would you need to be convinced that Nessie exists? **[Make a Judgment]**

Why the Tortoise's Shell Is not Smooth

Chinua Achebe

Low voices, broken now and again by singing, reached Okonkwo[1] from his wives' huts as each woman and her children told folk stories. Ekwefi[2] and her daughter, Ezinma,[3] sat on a mat on the floor. It was Ekwefi's turn to tell a story.

"Once upon a time," she began, "all the birds were invited to a feast in the sky. They were very happy and began to prepare themselves for the great day. They painted their bodies with red cam wood[4] and drew beautiful patterns on them with dye.

"Tortoise saw all these preparations and soon discovered what it all meant. Nothing that happened in the world of the animals ever escaped his notice; he was full of cunning. As soon as he heard of the great feast in the sky his throat began to itch at the very thought. There was a <u>famine</u> in those days and Tortoise had not eaten a good meal for two moons. His body rattled like a piece of dry stick in his empty shell. So he began to plan how he would go to the sky."

"But he had no wings," said Ezinma.

"Be patient," replied her mother. "That is the story. Tortoise had no wings, but he went to the birds and asked to be allowed to go with them.

"'We know you too well,' said the birds when they had heard him. 'You are full of cunning and you are ungrateful. If we allow you to come with us you will soon begin your mischief.'

"'You do not know me,' said Tortoise. 'I am a changed man. I have learned that a man who makes trouble for others is also making it for himself.'

"Tortoise had a sweet tongue, and within a short time all the birds agreed that he was a changed man, and they each gave him a feather,

---

1. **Okonkwo** (ō kōn′ kwō)
2. **Ekwefi** (e kwe′ fē)
3. **Ezinma** (e zēn′ mä)
4. **red cam** (cam) **wood**: Hard West African wood that makes a red dye.

◆ **Build Vocabulary**

famine (fa′ min) *n*.: Shortage of food

orator (ôr′ ə ter) *n*.: Speaker

eloquent (el′ ə kwint) *adj*.: Persuasive and expressive

with which he made two wings.

"At last the great day came and Tortoise was the first to arrive at the meeting place. When all the birds had gathered together, they set off in a body. Tortoise was very happy as he flew among the birds, and he was soon chosen as the man to speak for the party because he was a great <u>orator</u>.

"'There is one important thing which we must not forget,' he said as they flew on their way. 'When people are invited to a great feast like this, they take new names for the occa-

---

▼ **Critical Viewing** What details in this picture might lead to questions about a tortoise's appearance? **[Connect]**

sion. Our hosts in the sky will expect us to honor this age-old custom.'

"None of the birds had heard of this custom but they knew that Tortoise, in spite of his failings in other directions, was a widely traveled man who knew the customs of different peoples. And so they each took a new name. When they had all taken, Tortoise also took one. He was to be called *All of you.*

"At last the party arrived in the sky and their hosts were very happy to see them. Tortoise stood up in his many-colored plumage and thanked them for their invitation. His speech was so <u>eloquent</u> that all the birds were glad they had brought him, and nodded their heads in approval of all he said. Their hosts took him as the king of the birds, especially as he looked somewhat different from the others.

"After kola nuts[5] had been

---

5. **kola** (kō´ lə) **nuts**: The seeds of the African cola tree. These seeds contain caffeine and are used to make soft drinks and medicines.

presented and eaten, the people of the sky set before their guests the most delectable dishes Tortoise had ever seen or dreamed of. The soup was brought out hot from the fire and in the very pot in which it had been cooked. It was full of meat and fish. Tortoise began to sniff aloud. There was pounded yam[6] and also yam pottage[7] cooked with palm oil and fresh fish. There were also pots of palm wine. When everything had been set before the guests, one of the people of the sky came forward and tasted a little from each pot. He then invited the birds to eat. But Tortoise jumped to his feet and asked: 'For whom have you prepared this feast?'

"'For all of you,' replied the man.

"Tortoise turned to the birds and said: 'You remember that my name is *All of you.* The custom here is to serve the spokesman first and the others later. They will serve you when I have eaten.'

"He began to eat and the birds grumbled angrily. The people of the sky thought it must be their custom to leave all the food for their king. And so Tortoise ate the best part of the

▲ **Critical Viewing** What techniques might a story-teller like the one in this picture use to keep an audience interested? **[Speculate]**

food and then drank two pots of palm wine, so that he was full of food and drink and his body grew fat enough to fill out his shell.

"The birds gathered round to eat what was left and to peck at the bones he had thrown all about the floor. Some of them were too angry to eat. They chose to fly home on an empty stomach. But before they left, each took back the feather he had lent to Tortoise. And there he stood in his hard shell full of food and wine but without any wings to fly home. He asked the birds to take a message for his wife, but they all refused. In the end Parrot, who had felt more angry than the others, suddenly changed his mind and agreed to take the message.

"'Tell my wife,' said Tortoise, 'to bring out all the soft things in my house and cover the compound[8] with them so that I can jump down from the sky without very great danger.'

6. **yam** (yam) *n.*: Sweet potato.
7. **pottage** (pät' ij) *n.*: Thick soup or stew.

8. **compound** (käm' pound) *n.*: Grounds surrounded by buildings.

"Parrot promised to deliver the message, and then flew away. But when he reached Tortoise's house he told his wife to bring out all the hard things in the house. And so she brought out her husband's hoes, machetes,[9] spears, guns, and even his cannon. Tortoise looked down from the sky and saw his wife bringing things out, but it was too far to see what they were. When all seemed ready he let himself go. He fell and fell and fell until he began to fear that he would never stop falling. And then like the sound of his cannon he crashed on the compound."

"Did he die?" asked Ezinma.

"No," replied Ekwefi. "His shell broke into pieces. But there was a great medicine man in the neighborhood. Tortoise's wife sent for him and he gathered all the bits of shell and stuck them together. That is why Tortoise's shell is not smooth."

---

9. **machetes** (mə shet´ ēz) *n.*: Large heavy-bladed knives.

Beyond Literature

Science Connection

Tortoise Shells A tortoise is a turtle that lives only on land. Like other turtles, tortoises have a shell. In general, tortoises and other turtles that live on land have high, domed shells. Turtles that live in the water have flatter shells. The shell is made of two layers. The inner layer is made up of bony plates and is actually part of the skeleton. The outer layer consists of tough "scales," skin tissue called *scutes*. Because the shell is connected to the backbone, a broken or cracked shell usually means death for the turtle or tortoise.

Cross-Curricular Activity
Diagram Draw a diagram that shows the parts of a tortoise's shell and how it is attached to the rest of the skeleton. Label the skull, the backbone, the plastron, and the carapace.

Guide for Responding

◆ LITERATURE AND YOUR LIFE

Reader's Response Do you think the tortoise got what he deserved? Why or why not?

Thematic Focus What advice would you have given the birds who helped the tortoise get his wings? Explain.

☑ Check Your Comprehension

1. Why was the tortoise so eager to become a bird?
2. Why did the birds change their minds about the tortoise?
3. How did the tortoise become the one to eat first?

◆ Critical Thinking

INTERPRET
1. Why does the tortoise tell the birds he is a changed man? **[Deduce]**
2. Has the tortoise really changed? Explain. **[Analyze]**

EVALUATE
3. How do the animal characters in this folk tale reflect people's behavior? **[Assess]**

APPLY
4. How might the story have ended if the tortoise had behaved himself at the feast? **[Modify]**

Guide for Responding (continued)

◆ Reading Strategy

RECOGNIZE AUTHOR'S PURPOSE

Writers include certain details in a story for a reason. Noticing what the author includes helps you to **recognize the author's purpose.**

1. What is the author's purpose in writing about the Loch Ness monster? List three points in the selection that confirm this purpose.
2. Identify three details in "Why the Tortoise's Shell Is Not Smooth" that are probably included to entertain readers.

◆ Build Vocabulary

USING FORMS OF orate

Orate means "deliver a speech." Related forms of this word express different ideas about speaking. Complete the following sentences with the word that best completes each one.

orator   oration   oratorical

1. Tortoise's _____?_____ skills were admired by all.
2. The birds considered him a great _____?_____ .
3. He delivered an eloquent _____?_____ .

SPELLING STRATEGY

The words *eloquent* and *abundant* both end with the same sound, but their endings are spelled in two different ways. Complete the following clues to remember how to spell these two words.

1. Flue*nt* is similar in meaning (and spelling) to eloqu_e_n_t_.
2. Abund__a_n_has an *a* at the beginning and in its ending.

USING THE WORD BANK

Answer each question with Word Bank words.

1. Which two words deal with speaking?
2. Which two words could describe opposite amounts of food?
3. Which word describes something that keeps escaping?

◆ Literary Focus

ORAL TRADITION

In the **oral tradition,** stories are passed along by word of mouth.

1. In "The Loch Ness Monster," how does Laycock say that word of Nessie spread around the world? In what way does this make Nessie a part of the oral tradition?
2. What details does Achebe include at the beginning of "Why the Tortoise's Shell Is Not Smooth" to help you understand how the story was passed along before it was written down?

◆ Build Grammar Skills

SUBJECT COMPLEMENTS

A **subject complement** is a word that comes after a linking verb and identifies or describes the subject. A subject complement may be either a predicate noun or a predicate adjective.

A **predicate noun** (or pronoun) follows a linking verb and identifies or renames the subject.

I am a changed *man.* (*Man* renames *I.*)

A **predicate adjective** follows a linking verb and describes the subject.

Tortoise was very *happy* as he flew among the birds. (*Happy* describes *Tortoise.*)

Practice Copy these sentences in your notebook. Underline each subject complement, identify it as a predicate noun or predicate adjective, and draw an arrow to the word it renames or describes.

1. Tortoise is a great orator.
2. His speech was eloquent.
3. Parrot seemed a bird of great intelligence.
4. The birds felt cheated.
5. That is the reason.

Writing Application Write four sentences about Tortoise. In the first two, use predicate nouns to rename him. In the second two, use predicate adjectives to describe him.

Build Your Portfolio

 Idea Bank

Writing

1. **Postcard** Imagine that you visited Loch Ness and saw something in the water you couldn't explain. Write a postcard to a friend describing what you saw.

2. **Advice Letter** Write a letter to Tortoise. Explain how he might have avoided being tricked. Offer advice on how he should behave in the future.

3. **Mystery Creature** Describe an ordinary animal without naming it. Describe it in a way that makes it sound mysterious and new.

Speaking and Listening

4. **Debate [Group Activity]** With classmates, form two teams to debate the existence of the Loch Ness monster. Team members should review the story for points supporting their side, prepare note cards, and participate in the debate.

5. **Retelling [Group Activity]** Folk tales change slightly with each retelling. In a group, have one member write down four detailed sentences and recite them to another person. Have that person repeat the sentences to the next person (without reading), and so on. The last person should write down what he or she hears. Jot down how the original differs from the final telling. Explain why. **[Performing Arts Link]**

Projects

6. **Chart** Prepare a chart that shows how scientists would classify the Loch Ness monster's Kingdom, Phylum, Order, Family, and Genus based on the descriptions given. **[Science Link]**

7. **Storytelling Fair [Group Activity]** In a group, plan a Storytelling Fair. Group members can choose tales, practice telling the stories, or draw pictures for the storytellers to show while telling the stories. **[Performing Arts Link]**

 Writing Mini-Lesson

Comparison-and-Contrast Essay

Tortoises are similar to turtles in some ways and different in others. Write a short essay in which you compare and contrast two animals that are similar, but that are not exactly alike.

Writing Skills Focus: Organize Details by Type

Organize your essay by grouping details of the same type. For example, you can compare and contrast appearances, habits, and environments. Use an organizer like the one below to group details before you write.

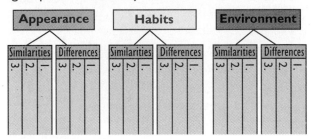

Prewriting Choose two animals that are closely related, such as dogs and wolves, alligators and crocodiles, or turtles and tortoises. Brainstorm for details about them that are similar and different. Then, do research to discover more details.

Drafting Follow your organizer as you draft. Keep related details in the same paragraph.

◆ **Grammar Application**

Use subject complements in some statements about your animals; for example, *Both the dog and the wolf are mammals.*

Revising Ask a partner to read your draft. Discuss whether your comparisons and contrasts are clear. Keep your partner's suggestions in mind as you revise.

Writing Process Workshop

In the poem "Someone," Walter de la Mare tells of hearing something—or someone—knocking at his door. When something knocks at the door of a writer's imagination, he or she must get up to find out more. The writer's reasons for writing may be as interesting as what he or she writes about.

An **I-Search report** tells about a writer's personal involvement with a topic in addition to giving information about the topic. Write an I-Search report on a topic of interest to you. Use the tips from this section's Writing Mini-Lessons:

Writing Skills Focus

▶ **Identify the purpose of your investigation.** Decide why you are researching and what you want to find out. Identifying your purpose will focus the kinds of questions you ask and the information that you find. (See p. 427.)

▶ **Use a variety of resources.** In addition to using library resources, you can interview people, visit a business or agency, and call related organizations. (See p. 435.)

▶ **Organize related details.** Organize information in categories. Write your notes on note cards, so as you narrow or broaden a category, you can easily reorganize your notes. (See p. 447.)

MODEL FROM LITERATURE

from "The Loch Ness Monster," George Laycock

① One spring evening I drove to the nearby college town of Oxford, Ohio, to hear the latest news about the search for the Loch Ness monster. ② I went as a doubter. I never said flatly that there is no such thing as the Loch Ness monster. How can one be that certain? But the probabilities seemed slender.

Those convinced, however, that this famous monster really lives appear to be closing in on it. . . . ③ In Scotland, . . . there are many who claim to have seen it.

① The writer identifies the purpose of his investigation and describes how he investigates.

② Here, the writer explains his expectations at the beginning of his search.

③ Here, the writer shares something he has learned.

Prewriting

Choose a Topic The best ideas for an I-Search report are those of interest and importance to you. Topics may come from conversations, activities, or something you read or heard. Choose a topic that is meaningful to you.

> ## Ideas for I-Search Report
>
> - How is my favorite dessert made?
> - How many students across the country play my favorite sport?
> - What would I have to do to work at the job that most interests me?

Note the Reason for Your Interest An I-Search report includes an explanation of your reasons for choosing a particular topic. Jot down a few notes explaining your interest. Examples of such reasons include a visit to a museum that sparked curiosity about a painter or your own participation in a certain sport.

Use Your Focus Questions To help direct your research, jot down a few questions to which you want answers about your subject. You may add to the list as you do your research. As you select or skim through possible sources, ask yourself: *Will this source help answer one of my focus questions?*

Take Good Notes As you research, keep three sets of note cards: one to record the sources you use, one to record information you discover from these sources, and one to record your own reactions to these discoveries.

Source Card

> A.
> www. maximumbridge.com
> (Sponsored by the Association of Bridge Engineers)

Information Card

> "The weight of the roadway is held up by many small cables, called suspender cables, which attach to the main cables running from the towers."
>
> A, p. 29

Response Cards

> On weekends, I often bike across the bridge with my friends. I've always wanted to know what all those metal ropes on it were.

> I used to think the bridge was solid and would stand forever. Now that I know more, it seems fragile! Will I dare bike across the bridge next Saturday?

DRAFTING/REVISING

APPLYING LANGUAGE SKILLS: Direct and Indirect Quotations

A **direct quotation** gives a person's exact words or thoughts within quotation marks. The first word is capitalized.

Direct:
The captain said, "I believe Nessie exists."

An **indirect quotation** reports the general meaning of someone's words or thoughts.

Indirect:
The captain said that he believes Nessie exists.

Practice On your paper, explain which of the following are direct quotations and which are indirect.

1. Most students say that they enjoy basketball.
2. Dr. Rines said, "I will investigate further."
3. The lecturer said, "This is a picture of Nessie."

Writing Application In your report, use direct quotations from your sources to support important points.

Writer's Solution Connection Writing Lab

The Writing Lab tutorial on Reports has guidelines and models for quoting and citing sources.

APPLYING LANGUAGE SKILLS: Titles of People

Capitalize the names and titles of people. Family and professional titles—such as *aunt, father, doctor,* and *professor*—are capitalized when they are used as part of a name or as a name themselves. Otherwise, they are capitalized only at the beginning of a sentence.

My cousin is Judge Wilson.
My cousin is a judge.

I like Aunt Patti very much.
I'd like you to meet my aunt.

Michael Marks is a professor of literature.
Mr. Smith spoke with Professor Marks.

Practice Write the following, correcting the capitalization if necessary.
1. mayor george clinton
2. the first president
3. president washington
4. the doctor on call

Writing Application Check for any incorrect capitalization of titles or names in your I-Search report.

Writer's Solution Connection
Language Lab

For more practice with capitalization, complete any of the lessons in the Capitalization unit.

Drafting

Organize Your Draft Begin with an introduction stating your topic and the reasons for your interest. In each paragraph in the body of your paper, focus on a specific part of your subject.

Follow Your Notes Use your note cards while drafting. Copy your information from the cards carefully. Double-check to make sure your facts and quotations are correct. Put ideas that you are not quoting in your own words.

Describe Your Experience Include personal reactions to the topic. Include explanations of how you conducted the research, what surprises you encountered, what you may have been unable to find out, and what opinions you formed or changed based on what you learned.

Revising

Use a Checklist The following checklist will help you revise:
► Have I accurately recorded my information? Double-check your notes to make sure.
► Does my paper have a clear organization? Make sure you have written an introduction and a conclusion. Read each paragraph to make sure it focuses on just one part of your topic.
► Have I included information on my own interest in the subject and reactions to my research? Include such information where appropriate.

Publishing and Presenting

Mini-Lesson Share what you've learned by using your report as the basis of a mini-lesson you present to the class. Include an activity that relates to the topic.

Documentary Create a videotape presentation of your I-Search reports in which you sum up your results and reactions. Set up the video to play in a display booth that also contains copies of the reports for interested students to read.

Magazine Article Share what you've learned with a wide audience. Send your report to a magazine that publishes student writing or to one that deals specifically with the subject of your report.

Real-World Reading Skills Workshop

Strategies for Success

It's easy to look up a friend's number in the phone book. The publishers of the book help you by listing names in alphabetical order. Some reference materials are more complex than the phone book. The following strategies can help you find specific information in reference materials.

Use Key Terms Come up with a few terms or ideas connected with the topic on which you need information. For instance, if you want to find out more about ancient Rome, you should list key terms, such as "Rome" and "Caesar."

Use Contents, Indexes, and Menus Look for your key terms in the table of contents and index of a book or on the menu of a Web site. A table of contents and a Web menu contain general information. They can tell you whether the book or site covers a topic in which you're interested. An index is an alphabetical list at the back of a nonfiction book. It lists names, events, and concepts that are included in the book, along with the pages where they appear.

Scan and Skim When you find a book that may contain the information you want, don't read it from beginning to end. First, use the index and table of contents to locate pages where material of interest might appear. List the page numbers. Then, skim the pages on your list. Do not read every single sentence. Instead, scan for your key words.

Apply the Strategies

Look over the Web site menu in the left column. Then, answer the questions about finding specific information through the menu.

1. What subject does the information on this site concern? Explain how you know.

2. Which buttons should you click on to find out which players play on which team?

3. List three items on the menu you can use to find more information about the Houston Comets.

SUSAN'S **WNBA** WEBSITE!

Team rosters—click on a team to learn about the players.

- 🏀 Charlotte Sting
- 🏀 Houston Comets
- 🏀 New York Liberty
- 🏀 Phoenix Mercury
- 🏀 Sacramento Monarchs
- 🏀 Utah Starzz

Game Schedule		All Times EDT
Saturday, June 21	New York at Los Angeles	4 p.m. (NBC)
Sunday, June 22	Charlotte at Phoenix	4 p.m. (NBC)
Monday, June 23	Los Angeles at Utah	7:30 p.m. (ESPN)
Friday, June 27	Sacramento at Los Angeles	9 p.m. (LIFETIME)
Saturday, June 28	Houston at Utah	5 p.m. (ESPN)
Monday, June 30	Los Angeles at Houston	7:30 p.m. (ESPN)

Other Sites: Click here to find out more!

- 🏀 How the WNBA started
- 🏀 Basketball rules
- 🏀 Scores and statistics

✔ Here are some other situations in which you would read to find specific information:
▶ Writing a science report
▶ Finding out where a specific movie is playing
▶ Deciding which breed of dog makes the best house pet

Grammar Review

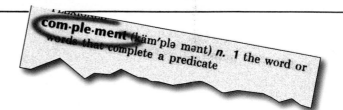

com·ple·ment (käm'plə mənt) *n.* 1 the word or words that complete a predicate

A **complement** is a word or group of words that completes the meaning of a verb. There are four kinds of complements: direct objects, indirect objects, predicate nouns, and predicate adjectives.

A **direct object** receives the action of the verb or shows the result of the action. It answers the questions *whom* or *what.* (See pages 426 and 434.)

	Direct
Verb	Object

He built a bridge.

An **indirect object** follows an action verb and **tells** *to whom* or *what* or *for whom* or *what* the action of the verb is performed. (See page 426.)

	Indirect	Direct
Verb	Object	Object

He built the emperor a bridge.

A verb can have an indirect object only if it has a direct object. The indirect object comes immediately after the verb and before the direct object.

A **predicate noun** is a noun that follows a linking verb, such as *is* or *has been,* and renames the subject. (See page 446.)

Linking	Predicate
Verb	Noun

Breaker is a bridge-builder.

A **predicate adjective** is an adjective that follows a linking verb and describes the subject. (See page 446.)

Linking	Predicate
Verb	Adjective

The bridge is very long.

Practice 1 Copy the following sentences into your notebook. Then, underline the verb in each sentence, and label the complements as indirect object, direct object, predicate noun, or predicate adjective.

1. The crooked old man gave Breaker two pellets.

2. The lecturer showed us a picture of the Loch Ness monster.

3. The monster raised its head.

4. Who has seen the wind?

5. Tortoise is a trickster.

6. Tortoise was the first one there.

Practice 2 Write a paragraph describing an imaginary creature. Use at least two sentences with direct objects, one with an indirect object, one with a predicate noun, and one with a predicate adjective.

Grammar in Writing

✔ *If you use too many sentences with predicate nouns and adjectives, your writing can become dull. For more powerful, active writing, use sentences with indirect and direct objects instead.*

Dull: *The fairy queen is safe from danger.*

Strong: *Sprites guard the fairy queen.*

Have you ever had friends urge you to do something you didn't want to do? Has a salesperson pressured you to buy something you didn't need? If you've ever been in these situations, you know that it's not always easy to say no. Doing something you don't want to do can make you feel uncomfortable. If you say no firmly and politely, most people will understand. The following guidelines will help you say no.

Be Firm When you say no, be and sound determined. If you sound as if you're not sure, it may encourage someone to ask again. You may find it helpful to give your reason for saying no. For instance, you might tell a friend, *I'm not going to the movies because I want to save my money for a bike.* Never feel, though, that you *have* to explain yourself. If you're talking to a salesperson or another stranger, your reason for saying no is none of that person's business.

Be Polite If possible, be polite when you say no. Thank people for their invitations and for wanting to include you in their plans. If someone harasses you for saying no, avoid getting into an argument. Stay calm. Repeat your answer once. If the person persists, ask why he or she is so eager to get your cooperation.

Move Away If all else fails, simply leave. Remember that what you do is up to you. You don't have to put up with someone's bullying.

Tips for Saying No

✔ *When saying no, follow these strategies:*

▶ Speak quietly and firmly.
▶ Try to change the subject after you say no. This may help stop someone from repeating the request.
▶ Remember that you, and no one else, are in charge of your choices. You have every right to say no.

Apply the Strategies

In groups of three or four, role-play these situations. First, discuss how you would say no in each situation based on the strategies above. Then, take roles and act out your suggestions. After each role play, brainstorm for other ways of handling the situation.

1. A friend wants to copy your homework.

2. A salesperson calls your house and pressures you to buy something.

3. Someone you don't know well wants to borrow your bike. You don't feel you know enough about the person to lend it to him or her.

What's Behind the Words

Vocabulary Adventures With Richard Lederer

Science-Fiction and Fantasy Vocabulary

Karel Capek, a Czechoslovakian playwright, was among the first modern science-fiction writers. In 1920, Capek wrote a play called *R.U.R.* The initials stand for "Rossum's Universal Robots." The drama centered on a group of mechanical creatures that do humans' work but then revolt against their makers. By shortening a Czech term for forced labor, *robota,* Capek invented the word *robot* to name the imaginary machine-men of his story.

The Word Spreads

The play proved a tremendous hit, and *robot* was adopted into dozens of languages. From Robbie the Robot in *Forbidden Planet* (a 1950's film) to James Cameron's *Terminator* movies to today's automated factories, Karel Capek's vision of machines in human form has taken hold of people's imaginations.

Words for "What if . . ."

Science-fiction and fantasy stories ask us to dream "What if?" They invite our imaginations to travel as far as they can into time and space and possibility. To send us on the way, writers use a few words with fascinating histories.

The movie *Star Wars* begins with the words "A long time ago, in a galaxy far, far away. . ." The root of that word *galaxy* is found in the Greek *galaxis,* from *gala,* which means "milk." The long white track of luminous stars that is our galaxy is known as the Milky Way because it resembles a splash of milk in the sky.

In Greek, *planes* meant "a wanderer or vagabond." The phrase *planetes asteres,* or "wandering stars," was applied to heavenly bodies that changed their position in relation to the stars. (In fact, planets are not stars. They do not make their own heat or light.)

Sailing the Stars

Space voyagers usually get to planets, stars, and other galaxies on board a spaceship or starship. The word *ship* comes from Old English *scip* and Middle English *schippe,* meaning "a dug-out log." Sailing ships, spaceships, starships, and passenger ships—all get their name from the primitive wooden boats that carried people across the water more than a thousand years ago.

ACTIVITY *Astrum* was the Latin word for "star," and the root *astro-* generates an astronomical number of words in English. What happens to stars in the following words?

1. astronomy   3. aster   5. disaster
2. astrology   4. asterisk

Extended Reading Opportunities

You can find mystery in imaginary worlds, in worlds of the past or future, or in the everyday world around you. The books suggested here will help you explore mysteries of many kinds—leading you to new adventures, new questions, and new ideas.

Suggested Titles

A Wrinkle in Time
Madeleine L'Engle

Meg must travel to the imaginary world of Camazotz to meet the frightening and mysterious IT. She is searching for her father, who disappeared while working on a secret government project. With the help of her genius brother Charles and her friend Calvin, Meg struggles to solve the biggest mystery of her life. In the process, she makes some unexpected discoveries about herself.

Ghosts I Have Been
Richard Peck

This story takes you into the past with its main character, fourteen-year-old Blossom Culp. Like her mother, Blossom has Gypsy blood, and it has made her able to experience the past and see the future. While that may sound like fun, Blossom doesn't think so when she is experiencing the sinking of the *Titanic* or glimpsing a terrible war coming to Europe. Her unusual ability helps her to solve some mysteries, but it also leaves her with some big questions.

The Loch Ness Monster
Elaine Landau

The author of this nonfiction book explores the theories about the mysterious lake creature. Landau explains and evaluates the evidence of Nessie's existence. The book includes folklore about Nessie, as well as the reports of actual sightings. This book is part of a "Mysteries of Science" series. If you're interested in mysterious creatures, the series also includes books about the Yeti and the Sasquatch.

Other Possibilities

America's Top Ten Curiosities	Jenny F. Tesar
The Bermuda Triangle	Jim Collins
Blackwater Swamp	Bill Wallace

The Storyteller, Adolphe Tidemand, Christie's, London

Short Stories

A short story is a doorway into another world. The world of a short story may be another town or city similar to yours, or it may be a distant planet. A short story may introduce you to new ideas or remind you of events in your own life. Although short stories cover a wide range of possibilities, they all share certain elements:

- **Plot** is the sequence of events that keeps the story moving.

- **Characters** are the people or animals in the story.

- **Setting** is the time and place in which the characters live and the events occur.

- **Theme** is the central message expressed in the story.

You will learn more about these elements as you read the short stories in this unit.

Guide for Reading

Meet the Author:

John Gardner (1933–1982)

John Gardner loved tales of heroes and other old-fashioned stories. In a few different ways, he devoted his life to keeping the old stories fresh.

A Scholar Born in upstate New York, Gardner became a professor and taught at Southern Illinois University and other universities. He made new translations of poems from the Middle Ages, such as the tales of King Arthur.

A Banjo Player! Though being a scholar is a serious job, Gardner kept a sense of humor about himself. His business card mentioned his banjo-playing abilities along with his scholarship!

THE STORY BEHIND THE STORY

Gardner brought a few old stories up to date in his own writing. His first successful novel, *Grendel*, retells the Old English story of Beowulf, one of the most famous monster-slaying heroes—but Gardner tells his legend from the monster's side! His stories for younger readers, like "Dragon, Dragon," also twist the familiar patterns of fairy tales into humorous new shapes.

◆ LITERATURE AND YOUR LIFE

CONNECT YOUR EXPERIENCE

When you are up at bat or about to go on stage, what happens next is up to you. All the good advice in the world can't change that. Yet as your nerves begin to jangle, just remembering someone's advice can help keep you steady.

In "Dragon, Dragon," John Gardner shows the power of advice—even advice that doesn't make much sense.

THEMATIC FOCUS: Working It Through

As you read "Dragon, Dragon," think about the ways in which advice helps people work through problems.

◆ Background for Understanding

CULTURE

Dating as far back as ancient Babylon, dragon stories have been told all over the world. Different cultures have different beliefs about these imaginary creatures.

Although Asian dragons are believed to be wise and good, other dragons are greedy, evil creatures. In most Western folklore, the hero who kills a dragon is rewarded with marriage to the king's daughter. Most dragon slayers are brave, strong warriors.

As you read "Dragon, Dragon," notice how the dragon and the hero are different from what you might expect.

◆ Dragon, Dragon ◆

◆ Literary Focus

PLOT

The **plot** of a story is the sequence of events that take place in it. At the heart of the plot is a problem. As characters attempt to solve the problem, events build to a climax, or turning point. The climax is followed by the resolution, or conclusion, of the story.

The diagram below shows how a story's events build up to the turning point and lead to the conclusion. As you read "Dragon, Dragon," identify the problem, significant events, turning point, and conclusion.

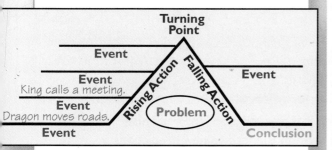

◆ Build Vocabulary

RELATED WORDS: FORMS OF *tyrant*

The king in "Dragon, Dragon" says that he is no *tyrant,* meaning "cruel, unjust ruler." Other related words are the noun *tyranny* ("a government or country run by a tyrant") and *tyrannical* ("having the qualities of a tyrant").

WORD BANK

Which of these words describe what a *savage* army might have done to a town?

plagued
ravaged
tyrant
reflecting
craned

The Reluctant Dragon, Maxfield Parrish

Reading for Success

Strategies for Reading Fiction

Fiction, which includes short stories and novels, is filled with made-up characters and events. Reading a work of fiction is like exploring a new world. As you read, your imagination creates a map of this world. The following strategies will help you find your way in a work of fiction:

Identify with a character or a situation.

When you identify with a character, you become one with that character. You put yourself in his or her place, and you share the character's thoughts, feelings, and problems.

You may identify with a character's situation if you have been in a similar one yourself. For example, to identify with the main character of "Dragon, Dragon," you might think about a time when you've faced a difficult challenge.

Predict.

A map tells you what you'll see around the next turn. As you read, make predictions about what might happen further along the "road" of the story. Base predictions on your experience

or on information in the story. In the same way that a rock in the road may cause you to choose a new path, new information can lead to new predictions.

Make inferences.

Make inferences, or logical guesses, based on details in the story. For instance, the king in "Dragon, Dragon" says that he can't "force" his knights to kill the dragon. You can make the inference that he is not a very powerful king.

Envision the action and setting.

Use details provided in the story to create a mental movie of the action and the setting. Use the following clues to help you envision:

▶ Action words
▶ Adverbs—words that describe how an action is perfomed
▶ Descriptions of how things look, sound, smell, taste, and feel

As you read "Dragon, Dragon," look at the notes in the boxes. The notes show you how to apply these strategies to your reading.

DRAGON, DRAGON

John Gardner

There was once a king whose kingdom was plagued by a dragon. The king did not know which way to turn. The king's knights were all cowards who hid under their beds whenever the dragon came in sight, so they were of no use to the king at all. And the king's wizard could not help either because, being old, he had forgotten his magic spells. Nor could the wizard look up the spells that had slipped his mind, for he had unfortunately misplaced his wizard's book many years before. The king was at his wit's end.

Every time there was a full moon the dragon came out of his lair and ravaged the country-side. He frightened maidens and stopped up chimneys and broke store windows and set people's clocks back and made dogs bark until no one could hear himself think.

He tipped over fences and robbed graves and put frogs in people's drinking water and tore the last chapters out of novels and changed house numbers around so that people crawled into bed with their neighbors.

He stole spark plugs out of people's cars and put firecrackers in people's cigars and stole the clappers from all the church bells and sprung every bear trap for miles around so the bears could wander wherever they pleased.

And to top it all off, he changed around all the roads in the kingdom so that people could not get anywhere except by starting out in the wrong direction.

"That," said the king in a fury, "is enough!" And he called a meeting of everyone in the kingdom.

Now it happened that there lived in the kingdom a wise old cobbler who had a wife and three sons. The cobbler and his family came to the king's meeting and stood way in back by the door, for the cobbler had a feeling that since he was nobody important there had probably been some mistake, and no doubt the king had intended the meeting for everyone in the kingdom except his family and him.

> Based on the preceding information about the dragon, you can **predict** that the king will look for a hero to slay the dragon.

◆ Build Vocabulary

plagued (plāgd) v.: Tormented

ravaged (rav´ ijd) v.: Violently destroyed; ruined

"Ladies and gentlemen," said the king when everyone was present, "I've put up with that dragon as long as I can. He has got to be stopped."

All the people whispered amongst themselves, and the king smiled, pleased with the impression he had made.

But the wise cobbler said gloomily, "It's all very well to talk about it—but how are you going to do it?"

And now all the people smiled and winked as if to say, "Well, King, he's got you there!"

The king frowned.

"It's not that His Majesty hasn't tried," the queen spoke up loyally.

"Yes," said the king, "I've told my knights again and again that they ought to slay that dragon. But I can't *force* them to go. I'm not a tyrant."

"Why doesn't the wizard say a magic spell?" asked the cobbler.

"He's done the best he can," said the king.

> The king has not been able to get his knights to fight the dragon. You can **make the inference** that the king is not an effective ruler.

The wizard blushed and everyone looked embarrassed. "I used to do all sorts of spells and chants when I was younger," the wizard explained. "But I've lost my spell book, and I begin to fear I'm losing my memory too. For instance, I've been trying for days to recall one spell I used to do. I forget, just now, what the deuce it was for. It went something like—

> Bimble,
> Wimble,
> Cha, cha
> CHOOMPF!

Suddenly, to everyone's surprise, the queen turned into a rosebush.

"Oh dear," said the wizard.

"Now you've done it," groaned the king.

"Poor Mother," said the princess.

"I don't know what can have happened," the wizard said nervously, "but don't worry, I'll have her changed back in a jiffy." He shut his eyes and racked his brain for a spell that would change her back.

But the king said quickly, "You'd better leave well enough alone. If you change her into a rattlesnake we'll have to chop off her head."

Meanwhile the cobbler stood with his hands in his pockets, sighing at the waste of time. "About the dragon . . . " he began.

"Oh yes," said the king. "I'll tell you what I'll do. I'll give the princess's hand in marriage to anyone who can make the dragon stop."

"It's not enough," said the cobbler. "She's a nice enough girl, you understand. But how would an ordinary person support her? Also, what about those of us that are already married?"

"In that case," said the king, "I'll offer the princess's hand or half the kingdom or both—whichever is most convenient."

The cobbler scratched his chin and considered it. "It's not enough," he said at last. "It's a good enough kingdom, you understand, but it's too much responsibility."

"Take it or leave it," the king said.

"I'll leave it," said the cobbler. And he shrugged and went home.

Frontispiece of The Boy's King Arthur, N.C. Wyeth

▲ **Critical Viewing** Contrast the king in the picture with the king in the story. [**Compare and Contrast**]

◆ **Build Vocabulary**

tyrant (tī′ rənt) *n.*: Cruel, unjust ruler

But the cobbler's eldest son thought the bargain was a good one, for the princess was very beautiful and he liked the idea of having half the kingdom to run as he pleased. So he said to the king, "I'll accept those terms, Your Majesty. By tomorrow morning the dragon will be slain."

"Bless you!" cried the king.

"Hooray, hooray, hooray!" cried all the people, throwing their hats in the air.

The cobbler's eldest son beamed with pride, and the second eldest looked at him enviously. The youngest son said timidly, "Excuse me, Your Majesty, but don't you think the queen looks a little unwell? If I were you I think I'd water her."

"Good heavens," cried the king, glancing at the queen who had been changed into a rosebush, "I'm glad you mentioned it!"

> Because heroes usually win, you might **predict** that the cobbler's eldest son will defeat the dragon. However, that would probably be the end of the story. You might predict instead that he will be defeated.

Now the cobbler's eldest son was very clever and was known far and wide for how quickly he could multiply fractions in his head. He was perfectly sure he could slay the dragon by somehow or other playing a trick on him, and he didn't feel that he needed his wise old father's advice. But he thought it was only polite to ask, and so he went to his father, who was working as usual at his cobbler's bench, and said, "Well, Father, I'm off to slay the dragon. Have you any advice to give me?"

The cobbler thought a moment and replied, "When and if you come to the dragon's lair, recite the following poem:

Dragon, dragon, how do you do?
I've come from the king to murder you.
Say it very loudly and firmly and the dragon will fall, God willing, at your feet."

"How curious!" said the eldest son. And he thought to himself, "The old man is not as wise as I thought. If I say something like that

to the dragon, he will eat me up in an instant. The way to kill a dragon is to out-fox him." And keeping his opinion to himself, the eldest son set forth on his quest.

When he came at last to the dragon's lair, which was a cave, the eldest son slyly disguised himself as a peddler and knocked on the door and called out, "Hello there!"

"There's nobody home!" roared a voice.

> **Identify** with the eldest son to understand his decision. He has just gotten advice that does not make any sense to him. Like him, you might decide to come up with your own plan.

The voice was as loud as an earthquake, and the eldest son's knees knocked together in terror.

"I don't come to trouble you," the eldest son said meekly. "I merely thought you might be interested in looking at some of our brushes. Or if you'd prefer," he added quickly, "I could leave our catalogue with you and I could drop by again, say, early next week."

"I don't want any brushes," the voice roared, "and I especially don't want any brushes next week."

"Oh," said the eldest son. By now his knees were knocking together so badly that he had to sit down.

Suddenly a great shadow fell over him, and the eldest son looked up. It was the dragon. The eldest son drew his sword, but the dragon lunged and swallowed him in a single gulp, sword and all, and the eldest son found himself in the dark of the dragon's belly. "What a fool I was not to listen to my wise old father!" thought the eldest son. And he began to weep bitterly.

"Well," sighed the king the next morning, "I see the dragon has not been slain yet."

"I'm just as glad, personally," said the princess, sprinkling the queen. "I would have had to marry that eldest son, and he had warts."

Now the cobbler's middle son decided it was his turn to try. The middle son was very strong and he was known far and wide for being able to lift up the corner of a church. He felt perfectly sure he could slay the dragon by simply laying into him, but he thought it would be only polite to ask his father's advice. So he went to his father and said to him, "Well, Father, I'm off to slay the dragon. Have you any advice for me?"

The cobbler told the middle son exactly what he'd told the eldest.

"When and if you come to the dragon's lair, recite the following poem:
Dragon, dragon, how do you do?
I've come from the king to murder you.
Say it very loudly and firmly, and the dragon will fall, God willing, at your feet."

"What an odd thing to say," thought the middle son. "The old man is not as wise as I thought. You have to take these dragons by surprise." But he kept his opinion to himself and set forth.

> Based on what happened to the first son, you can **predict** that the second son will also fail.

When he came in sight of the dragon's lair, the middle son spurred his horse to a gallop and thundered into the entrance swinging his sword with all his might.

But the dragon had seen him while he was still a long way off, and being very clever, the dragon had crawled up on top of the door so that when the son came charging in he went under the dragon and on to the back of the cave and slammed into the wall. Then the dragon chuckled and got down off the door, taking his time, and strolled back to where the man and the horse lay unconscious from the terrific blow. Opening his mouth as if for a yawn, the dragon swallowed the middle son in a single gulp and put the horse in the freezer to eat another day.

"What a fool I was not to listen to my wise old father," thought the middle son when he came to in the dragon's belly. And he too began to weep bitterly.

That night there was a full moon, and the dragon ravaged the countryside so terribly that several families moved to another kingdom.

"Well," sighed the king in the morning, "still no luck in this dragon business, I see."

"I'm just as glad, myself," said the princess, moving her mother, pot and all, to the window where the sun could get at her. "The cobbler's middle son was a kind of humpback."

Now the cobbler's youngest son saw that his turn had come. He was very upset and nervous, and he wished he had never been born. He was not clever, like his eldest brother, and he was not strong, like his second-eldest brother. He was a decent, honest boy who always minded his elders.

He borrowed a suit of armor from a friend of his who was a knight, and when the youngest son put the armor on it was so heavy he could hardly walk. From another knight he borrowed a sword, and that was so heavy that the only way the youngest son could get it to the dragon's lair was to drag it along behind his horse like a plow.

When everything was in readiness, the youngest son went for a last conversation with his father.

"Father, have you any advice to give me?" he asked.

"Only this," said the cobbler. "When and if you come to the dragon's lair, recite the following poem:
Dragon, dragon, how do you do?
I've come from the king to murder you.
Say it very loudly and firmly, and the dragon will fall, God willing, at your feet."

"Are you certain?" asked the youngest son uneasily.

"As certain as one can ever be in these matters," said the wise old cobbler.

And so the youngest son set forth on his quest. He traveled over hill and dale and at last came to the dragon's cave.

The dragon, who had seen the cobbler's youngest son while he was still a long way off, was seated up above the door, inside the cave, waiting and smiling to himself. But minutes passed and no one came thundering in. The dragon frowned, puzzled, and was tempted to peek out. However, reflecting that patience seldom goes unrewarded, the dragon kept his head up out of sight and went on waiting. At last, when he could stand it no longer, the dragon craned his neck and looked. There at the entrance of the cave stood a trembling young man in a suit of armor twice his size, struggling with a sword so heavy he could lift only one end of it at a time.

At sight of the dragon, the cobbler's youngest son began to tremble so violently that his armor rattled like a house caving in. He heaved with all his might at the sword and got the handle up level with his chest, but even now the point was down in the dirt. As loudly and firmly as he could manage, the youngest son cried—

Dragon, dragon, how do you do?
I've come from the king to murder you.

"What?" cried the dragon, flabbergasted. "You? You? Murder Me???" All at once he began to laugh, pointing at the little cobbler's son. *"He he he ho ha!"* he roared, shaking all over, and tears filled his eyes. *"He he he ho ho ho ha ha!"* laughed the dragon. He was laughing so hard he had to hang onto his sides, and

Dick Whittington on his way to London from My Nursery Story Book, Private Collection

▲ **Critical Viewing** Does the boy in this picture look like a dragon slayer? Explain. [Evaluate]

his back perfectly helpless with laughter.

"It's a good poem," said the cobbler's youngest son loyally. "My father made it up." And growing angrier he shouted, "I want you to stop that laughing, or I'll—I'll—" But the dragon could not stop for the life of him. And suddenly, in a terrific rage, the cobbler's son began flopping the sword end over end in the direction of the dragon. Sweat ran off the youngest son's forehead, but he labored on,

he fell off the door and landed on his back, still laughing, kicking his legs helplessly, rolling from side to side, laughing and laughing and laughing.

The cobbler's son was annoyed, "I *do* come from the king to murder you," he said. "A person doesn't like to be laughed at for a thing like that."

"He he he!" wailed the dragon, almost sobbing, gasping for breath. "Of course not, poor dear boy! But really, *he he*, the *idea* of it, *ha, ha, ha!* And that simply ridiculous *poem!*" Tears streamed from the dragon's eyes and he lay on

From the dragon's laughter, you can **infer** that the youngest son does not scare him one bit.

♦ **Build Vocabulary**
reflecting (ri flekt´ iŋ) *adj.*: Thinking seriously
craned (krānd) *v.*: Stretched out (one's neck) for a better view

blistering mad, and at last, with one supreme heave, he had the sword standing on its handle a foot from the dragon's throat. Of its own weight the sword fell, slicing the dragon's head off.

"*He he ho huk*," went the dragon—and then he lay dead.

The two older brothers crawled out and thanked their younger brother for saving their lives. "We have learned our lesson," they said.

Then the three brothers gathered all the treasures from the dragon's cave and tied them to the back end of the youngest brother's horse, and tied the dragon's head on behind the treasures, and started home. "I'm glad I listened to my father," the youngest son thought. "Now I'll be the richest man in the kingdom."

There were hand-carved picture frames and silver spoons and boxes of jewels and chests of money and silver compasses and maps telling where there were more treasures buried when these ran out. There was also a curious old book with a picture of an owl on the cover, and inside, poems and odd sentences and recipes that seemed to make no sense.

When they reached the king's castle the people all leaped for joy to see that the dragon was dead, and the princess ran out and kissed the youngest brother on the forehead, for secretly she had hoped it would be him.

"Well," said the king, "which half of the kingdom do you want?"

"My wizard's book!" exclaimed the wizard. "He's found my wizard's book!" He opened the book and ran his finger along under the words and then said in a loud voice, "Glmuzk, shkzmlp, blam!"

Instantly the queen stood before them in her natural shape, except she was soaking wet from being sprinkled too often. She glared at the king.

"Oh dear," said the king, hurrying toward the door.

*G*uide for Responding

◆ LITERATURE AND YOUR LIFE

Reader's Response Do you think the father is wise? Explain.

Thematic Focus The story suggests that working out a problem requires good sense as well as skill. Explain, using examples.

Journal Writing Which character in the story is your favorite? Write a few sentences explaining why.

☑ Check Your Comprehension

1. Name two reasons the king has been unable to get rid of the dragon.
2. What advice does the cobbler give his sons?
3. Summarize the way each son responds to his father's advice.

◆ Critical Thinking

INTERPRET

1. Compare the king in this story with the kings usually found in fairy tales. **[Compare and Contrast]**
2. What quality leads the two elder brothers to reject their father's advice? **[Infer]**
3. What quality leads the youngest brother to accept this advice? **[Infer]**

APPLY

4. Explain what the story teaches about the value of following advice. **[Interpret]**

EVALUATE

5. Do you think the father's advice really "worked"? Explain. **[Assess]**

Guide for Responding (continued)

◆ Reading for Success

STRATEGIES FOR READING FICTION

Review the strategies and the notes showing how to read fiction. Then, answer these questions:

1. After the first son met the dragon, what did you predict would happen? Why?
2. With which characters did you most identify? Why?
3. What inference can you make from the youngest son's trembling?
4. List three details that helped you envision the youngest son standing outside the dragon's cave.

◆ Build Vocabulary

USING FORMS OF *tyrant*

The word *tyrant* means "a cruel, unjust ruler." Other forms of the word relate to this meaning.

On your paper, define each italicized word.

1. He rules *tyrannically.*
2. The rebels tried to overthrow the *tyranny.*
3. The new law is *tyrannous.*
4. The evil king *tyrannized* the people.

SPELLING STRATEGY

Sometimes, the long *i* sound is spelled with a *y*, as in the word *tyrant*. For each of the following definitions, give a word in which the long *i* sound is spelled with a *y*.

1. A street fixture firefighters use to get water
2. Energetic
3. A doglike animal from Africa

USING THE WORD BANK

Match each numbered word with its meaning.

1. plagued   **a.** ruined
2. ravaged   **b.** stretched to get a view
3. reflecting   **c.** cruel, unjust ruler
4. tyrant   **d.** thinking seriously
5. craned   **e.** tormented

◆ Literary Focus

PLOT

A **plot** is the sequence of events in a story. Plots typically involve a problem; a series of events in which the characters try to solve the problem; a climax, or turning point; and a conclusion.

1. What is the problem in "Dragon, Dragon"?
2. Describe an event in which a character tries to solve the problem.
3. What event occurs at the climax of the story?
4. What events occur after the climax?

◆ Build Grammar Skills

CLAUSES

A **clause** is any group of words that contains a subject and a verb. An **independent clause** can stand on its own as a complete sentence. A **subordinate clause** cannot. A subordinate clause depends on an independent clause to complete its meaning.

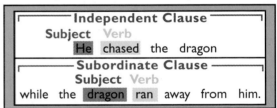

Independent Clause
Subject   Verb
He chased the dragon
Subordinate Clause
Subject   Verb
while the dragon ran away from him.

Practice Copy the sentences, and circle each clause. Identify each clause as independent or subordinate.

1. There was once a king whose kingdom was plagued by a dragon.
2. The youngest son began to tremble so violently that his armor rattled.
3. Recite a poem when you get to the dragon's lair.
4. Although the youngest brother was not strong, he was brave.
5. His hands shook when he saw the dragon.

Writing Application Use each of the following clauses in a sentence.

1. as he came near the cave
2. while the dragon laughed
3. everyone was surprised

Build Your Portfolio

 ## Idea Bank

Writing

1. **Description** Write your own vivid description of the dragon in the story. Use details of sight, sound, smell, and texture. You can use details from your imagination as well as from the story.

2. **Sequel** The treasure from the dragon's cave is about to cause some trouble! Write a brief sequel to the story, describing this problem and the way in which the youngest son solves it.

3. **Essay** Find dragon stories that come from two different cultures. Write an essay comparing the way dragons are portrayed in these stories from two different parts of the world.

Speaking and Listening

4. **Presentation** Assemble visual representations of dragons from around the world. Present them to the class, explaining the part of the world from which each comes. **[Social Studies Link; Visual Arts Link]**

5. **Group Discussion [Group Activity]** Hold a group discussion with classmates about the best ways of getting rid of dragons. Suggest alternatives to sending a single hero against the creature or to using violence at all. **[Performing Arts Link]**

Projects

6. **Dramatization [Group Activity]** With a small group, prepare and act out the scene in which the youngest son approaches the cave. Divide the following tasks: acting the parts of hero and dragon; creating sound effects; and creating a set for the cave. **[Performing Arts Link]**

7. **Dragon Comics** Create a comic strip showing the dragon's "fight" with each son. Break each episode into a few different scenes. Consider showing part of the action from the dragon's or the human's point of view. **[Visual Arts Link]**

 ## Writing Mini-Lesson

Help-Wanted Ad

A kingdom with a dragon problem needs a hero—quickly! Write a newspaper advertisement for a dragon slayer. Describe the requirements for the job, including past experience, and the benefits.

Writing Skills Focus: Focus on a Main Idea

Advertisments are limited to a small space. By focusing on **one main idea,** they can create a strong image in a reader's mind.

Model From the Story

. . . [he] began to tremble so violently that his armor rattled like a house caving in. He heaved with all his might at the sword and got the handle up level with his chest, but even now the point was down in the dirt.

  Detail: violent trembling
  +Detail: can barely lift sword
   Main Idea: The youngest son is not the standard sort of hero.

Prewriting Make a list of the characteristics your hero needs to have and the benefits of the job.

Drafting Describe the job requirements and benefits. Each of your details should be part of your main idea. For instance, asking for both strength and experience supports the main idea that your dragon slayer should be a mighty warrior.

> ◆ **Grammar Application**
> Use sentences that include more than one clause to add variety to your sentences.

Revising Add or take out details to make sure you create one main impression.

PART 1 *Plot and Character*

Nightfall (detail), 1945, N.C. Wyeth, Private Collection, Brandywine River Museum, Chadds Ford, Pennsylvania

Guide for Reading

Meet the Author:
James Berry (1925–)

In his writing, James Berry celebrates the richness of his West Indian heritage. His characters speak with the sounds and rhythms of Jamaican dialects, and many of his stories are set in his island birthplace.

A Writer and His Roots

Although he moved to England as an adult, James Berry's imagination seems to live in Jamaica. His young-adult fiction includes a novel called *Ajeemah and His Son,* the story of an African man and his son who are snatched by slave traders and taken to Jamaica. Another book, *A Thief in the Village,* is a collection of short stories about life in Jamaica. "Becky and the Wheels-and-Brake Boys" comes from this collection.

THE STORY BEHIND THE STORY

When asked why he wrote "Becky and the Wheels-and-Brake Boys," James Berry said he wanted to write about "a determined girl among boys.... Also, when I was growing up in my Jamaican village, we—myself and some other boys—did sometimes actually play with a girl like Becky."

◆ LITERATURE AND YOUR LIFE

CONNECT YOUR EXPERIENCE

A bicycle is more than just a way of getting from one place to another. You might ride a bike for exercise or just for the fun of it. Becky, the main character in "Becky and the Wheels-and-Brake Boys," sees the boys in her neighborhood enjoying the speed and freedom of riding bikes. Becky is determined to get a bike and join the fun.

THEMATIC FOCUS: Common Ground

Becky's mother can't understand why a bike is so important to Becky. As you read, notice how this mother and daughter find a common ground.

◆ Background for Understanding

LANGUAGE

People who speak the same language may come from different countries and regions, have different accents, use different words for the same thing, or have different ways of using the same words. These different forms of a single language are called dialects. Becky and her friends and family speak a West Indian dialect of English.

◆ Build Vocabulary

REGIONAL SYNONYMS

In different regions, people sometimes use regional synonyms—different words that mean the same thing. In "Becky and the Wheels-and-Brake Boys," the word used to mean "a covered area attached to a building" is *veranda.* English speakers in other regions might use the word *porch* to name the same structure.

WORD BANK

Which of the words is probably related to careless, thoughtless, and fearless?

| veranda |
| menace |
| reckless |

Becky and the Wheels-and-Brake Boys

Biking for Fun, 1992, Carlton Murrell, Courtesy of the artist

◆ Literary Focus

CONFLICT

The **conflict** in a story is a struggle between two opposing forces. The conflict is one of the most important elements of a short story because it drives the action. This organizer shows the two sides of the conflict in "Becky and the Wheels-and-Brake Boys."

◆ Reading Strategy

PREDICT

When you **predict,** you make a logical guess, based on past experience and other information you have. When you read "Becky and the Wheels-and-Brake Boys," make predictions based on details in the story and on your own experiences. As you learn new information, you might make new predictions. When you reach the end of the story, think about why your predictions did or did not match what actually happened.

Becky and the Wheels-and-Brake Boys

James Berry

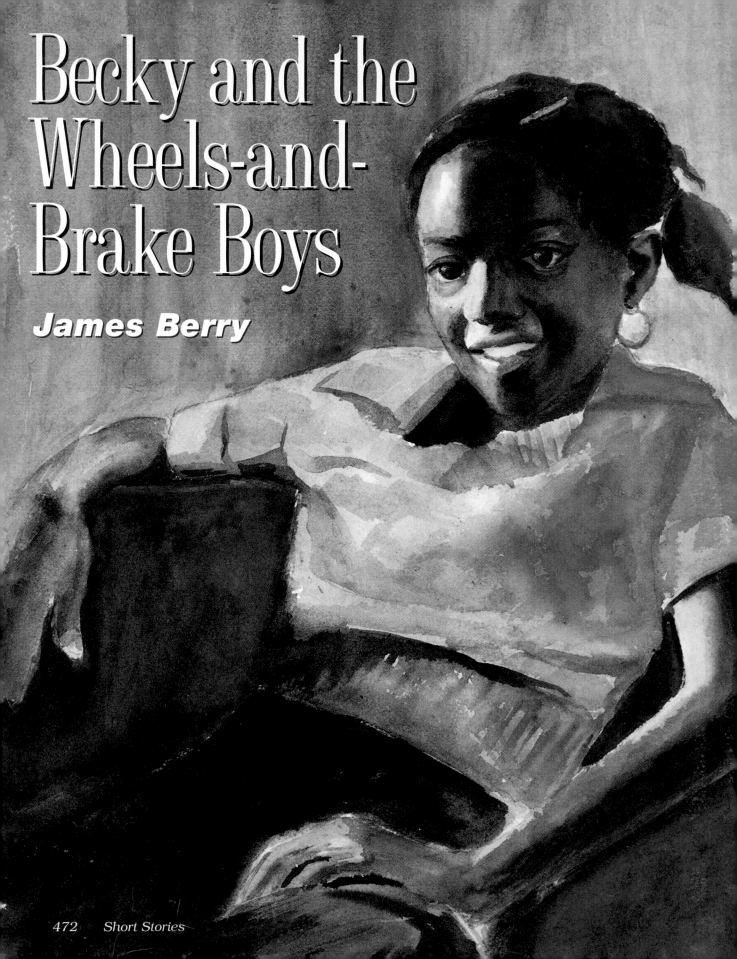

Even my own cousin Ben was there—riding away, in the ringing of bicycle bells down the road. Every time I came to watch them—see them riding round and round enjoying themselves—they scooted off like crazy on their bikes.

They can't keep doing that. They'll see!

I only want to be with Nat, Aldo, Jimmy, and Ben. It's no fair reason they don't want to be with me. Anybody could go off their head for that. Anybody! A girl can not, not, let boys get away with it all the time.

Bother! I have to walk back home, alone.

I know total-total that if I had my own bike, the Wheels-and-Brake Boys wouldn't treat me like that. I'd just ride away with them, wouldn't I?

Over and over I told my mum I wanted a bike. Over and over she looked at me as if I was crazy. "Becky, d'you think you're a boy? Eh? D'you think you're a boy? In any case, where's the money to come from? Eh?"

Of course I know I'm not a boy. Of course I know I'm not crazy. Of course I know all that's no reason why I can't have a bike. No reason! As soon as I get indoors I'll just have to ask again—ask Mum once more.

At home, indoors, I didn't ask my mum.

It was evening time, but sunshine was still big patches in yards and on housetops. My two younger brothers, Lenny and Vin, played marbles in the road. Mum was taking measurements of a boy I knew, for his new trousers and shirt. Mum made clothes for people. Meggie, my sister two years younger than me, was helping Mum on the veranda. Nobody would be pleased with me not helping. I began to help.

Granny-Liz would always stop fanning herself to drink up a glass of ice water. I gave my granny a glass of ice water, there in her rocking chair. I looked in the kitchen to find

shelled coconut pieces to cut into small cubes for the fowls' morning feed. But Granny-Liz had done it. I came and started tidying up bits and pieces of cut-off material around my mum on the floor. My sister got nasty, saying she was already helping Mum. Not a single good thing was happening for me.

With me even being all so thoughtful of Granny's need of a cool drink, she started up some botheration[1] against me.

Listen to Granny-Liz: "Becky, with you moving about me here on the veranda, I hope you dohn have any centipedes or scorpions[2] in a jam jar in your pocket."

"No, mam," I said sighing, trying to be calm. "Granny-Liz," I went on, "you forgot. My centipede and scorpion died." All the same, storm broke against me.

"Becky," my mum said. "You know I don't like you wandering off after dinner. Haven't I told you I don't want you keeping company with those awful riding-about bicycle boys? Eh?"

"Yes, mam."

"Those boys are a menace. Riding bicycles on sidewalks and narrow paths together, ringing bicycle bells and braking at people's feet like wild bulls charging anybody, they're heading for trouble."

"They're the Wheels-and-Brake Boys, mam."

"The what?"

"The Wheels-and-Brake Boys."

"Oh! Given themselves a name as well, have they? Well, Becky, answer this. How d'you always manage to look like you just escaped from a hair-pulling battle? Eh? And don't I tell

---

1. **botheration** (bäth´ ər ā´ shən) n.: Trouble.
2. **scorpions** (skôr´ pē ənz) n.: Close relatives of spiders, with a poisonous stinger at the end of their tails; found in warm regions.

◆ **Build Vocabulary**

veranda (və ran´ də) n.: Open porch, usually with a roof, along the outside of a building

menace (men´ əs) n.: Threat; a troublesome or annoying person

◀ **Critical Viewing** Based on the expression and posture of the girl in this picture, what kind of personality do you think she has? **[Analyze]**

Mother, I Love to Ride, 1992, Carlton Murrell, Courtesy of the artist

you not to break the backs down and wear your canvas shoes like slippers? Don't you ever hear what I say?"

"Yes, mam."

"D'you want to end up a field laborer? Like where your father used to be overseer?"[3]

"No, mam."

"Well, Becky, will you please go off and do your homework?"

Everybody did everything to stop me. I was allowed no chance whatsoever. No chance to

◆ **Literary Focus**
What are the two opposing forces that create the conflict in this story?

▲ **Critical Viewing** What do you think the girl in this picture would tell Becky's mother about riding a bike? **[Speculate]**

talk to Mum about the bike I dream of day and night! And I knew exactly the bike I wanted. I wanted a bike like Ben's bike. Oh, I wished I still had even my scorpion on a string to run up and down somebody's back!

I answered my mum. "Yes, mam." I went off into Meg's and my bedroom.

I sat down at the little table, as well as I might. Could homework stay in anybody's head in broad daylight outside? No. Could I keep a bike like Ben's out of my head? Not one

3. **overseer** (ō´ vər sē´ ər) *n.:* Supervisor of laborers.

bit. That bike took me all over the place. My beautiful bike jumped every log, every rock, every fence. My beautiful bike did everything cleverer than a clever cowboy's horse, with me in the saddle. And the bell, the bell was such a glorious gong of a ring!

If Dad was alive, I could talk to him. If Dad was alive, he'd give me money for the bike like a shot.

I sighed. It was amazing what a sigh could do. I sighed and tumbled on a great idea. To-morrow evening I'd get Shirnette to come with me. Both of us together would be sure to get the boys interested to teach us to ride. Wow! With Shirnette they can't just ride away!

Next day at school, everything went sour. For the first time, Shirnette and me had a real fight, because of what I hated most.

Shirnette brought a cockroach to school in a shoe-polish tin. At playtime she opened the tin and let the cockroach fly into my blouse. Pure panic and disgust nearly killed me. I crushed up the cockroach in my clothes and practically ripped my blouse off, there in open sunlight. Oh, the smell of a cockroach is the nastiest ever to block your nose! I started running with my blouse to go and wash it. Twice I had to stop and be sick.

I washed away the crushed cockroach stain from my blouse. Then the stupid Shirnette had to come into the toilet, falling about laughing. All right, I knew the cockroach treatment was for the time when I made my centipede on a string crawl up Shirnette's back. But you put fair-is-fair aside. I just barged into Shirnette.

When it was all over, I had on a wet blouse, but Shirnette had one on, too.

Then, going home with the noisy flock of children from school, I had such a new, new idea. If Mum thought I was scruffy, Nat, Aldo,

Jimmy, and Ben might think so, too. I didn't like that.

After dinner I combed my hair in the bed-room. Mum did her machining[4] on the ve-randa. Meggie helped Mum. Granny sat there, wishing she could take on any job, as usual.

I told Mum I was going to make up a quar-rel with Shirnette. I went, but my friend wouldn't speak to me, let alone come out to keep my company. I stood alone and watched the Wheels-and-Brake Boys again.

This time the boys didn't race away past me. I stood leaning against the tall coconut palm tree. People passed up and down. The nearby main road was busy with traffic. But I didn't mind. I watched the boys. Riding round and round the big flame tree, Nat, Aldo, Jimmy, and Ben looked marvelous.

◆ **Literature and Your Life**

Why do you think Becky wants to join this group of bike riders?

At first each boy rode round the tree alone. Then each boy raced each other round the tree, going round three times. As he won, the winner rang his bell on and on, till he stopped panting and could laugh and talk properly. Next, most <u>reckless</u> and fierce, all the boys raced against each other. And, leaning against their bicycles, talking and joking, the boys popped soft drinks open, drank, and ate chipped bananas.

I walked up to Nat, Aldo, Jimmy, and Ben and said, "Can somebody teach me to ride?"

"Why don't you stay indoors and learn to cook and sew and wash clothes?" Jimmy said.

I grinned. "I know all that already," I said. "And one day perhaps I'll even be mum to a boy child, like all of you. Can you cook and sew and wash clothes, Jimmy? All I want is to learn to ride. I want you to teach me."

I didn't know why I said what I said. But everybody went silent and serious.

One after the other, Nat, Aldo, Jimmy, and

◆ **Build Vocabulary**

reckless (rek´ lis) *adj*.: Not careful; taking chances

---

4. **machining** (mə shēn´ iŋ) *v*.: Sewing.

Ben got on their bikes and rode off. I wasn't at all cross with them. I only wanted to be riding out of the playground with them. I knew they'd be heading into the town to have ice cream and things and talk and laugh.

Mum was sitting alone on the veranda. She sewed buttons onto a white shirt she'd made. I sat down next to Mum. Straightaway, "Mum," I said, "I still want to have a bike badly."

"Oh, Becky, you still have that foolishness in your head? What am I going to do?"

Mum talked with some sympathy. Mum knew I was honest. "I can't get rid of it, mam," I said.

Mum stopped sewing. "Becky," she said, staring in my face, "how many girls around here do you see with bicycles?"

"Janice Gordon has a bike," I reminded her.

"Janice Gordon's dad has acres and acres of coconuts and bananas, with a business in the town as well."

I knew Mum was just about to give in. Then my granny had to come out onto the veranda and interfere. Listen to that Granny-Liz. "Becky, I heard your mother tell you over and over she cahn[5] afford to buy you a bike. Yet you keep on and on. Child, you're a girl."

"But I don't want a bike because I'm a girl."

"D'you want it because you feel like a bwoy?" Granny said.

"No. I only want a bike because I want it and want it and want it."

Granny just carried on. "A tomboy's like a whistling woman and a crowing hen, who can only come to a bad end. D'you understand?"

I didn't want to understand. I knew Granny's speech was an awful speech. I went and sat down with Lenny and Vin, who were making a kite.

By Saturday morning I felt real sorry for Mum. I could see Mum really had it hard for money. I had to try and help. I knew anything of Dad's—anything—would be worth a great

mighty hundred dollars.

I found myself in the center of town, going through the busy Saturday crowd. I hoped Mum wouldn't be too cross. I went into the fire station. With lots of luck I came face to face with a round-faced man in uniform. He talked to me. "Little miss, can I help you?"

I told him I'd like to talk to the head man. He took me into the office and gave me a chair. I sat down. I opened out my brown paper parcel. I showed him my dad's sun helmet. I told him I thought it would make a good fireman's hat. I wanted to sell the helmet for some money toward a bike, I told him.

The fireman laughed a lot. I began to laugh, too. The fireman put me in a car and drove me back home.

◆ **Reading Strategy**
What do you predict the fireman will do about the sun helmet?

Mum's eyes popped to see me bringing home the fireman. The round-faced fireman laughed at my adventure. Mum laughed, too, which was really good. The fireman gave Mum my dad's hat back. Then—mystery, mystery—Mum sent me outside while they talked.

My mum was only a little cross with me. Then—mystery and more mystery—my mum took me with the fireman in his car to his house.

The fireman brought out what? A bicycle! A beautiful, shining bicycle! His nephew's bike. His nephew had been taken away, all the way to America. The bike had been left with the fireman-uncle for him to sell it. And the good, kind fireman-uncle decided we could have the bike—on small payments. My mum looked uncertain. But in a big, big way, the fireman knew it was all right. And Mum smiled a little. My mum had good sense to know it was all right. My mum took the bike from the fireman Mr. Dean.

And guess what? Seeing my bike much, much newer than his, my cousin Ben's eyes popped with envy. But he took on the big job. He taught me to ride. Then he taught Shirnette.

---

5. **cahn:** Can't.

I ride into town with the Wheels-and-Brake Boys now. When she can borrow a bike, Shirnette comes too. We all sit together. We have patties and ice cream and drink drinks together. We talk and joke. We ride about, all over the place.

And, again, guess what? Fireman Mr. Dean became our best friend, and Mum's especially. He started coming around almost every day.

Beyond Literature

Sports Connection

Bikes, Boards, and Skates Becky and her friends enjoy riding their bikes. Bikes, boards, and skates are all popular forms of contemporary recreation, but they have been around longer than you may think. Bicycles are related to scooters—wheeled vehicles without pedals. Foot pedals were added (creating the first official bicycle) in 1839. The first in-line skates were invented in 1819. Because of poor performance, they were abandoned in favor of the easier-to-use roller skates. They were reinvented by the Chicago Roller Skate Company in 1960. The Chicago Roller Skate Company also produced the wheels for the first skateboards, which came on the scene in 1958. These "land-surfing" boards were invented by a surf-shop owner in California.

Cross-Curricular Activity
Museum Exhibit Create a timeline showing the development of bicycles, skateboards, or in-line skates. Gather maps, charts, photographs, and other materials. Label each of the visuals you gather. Then, assemble the materials you gather into a museum exhibit that you can display in the classroom.

Guide for Responding

◆ LITERATURE AND YOUR LIFE

Reader's Response Do you think Becky should have taken her father's sun helmet to sell? Why or why not?

Thematic Focus How do Becky and her mother find a common ground?

Journal Writing Write about a time when you learned to ride a bike or do some other activity that you enjoy.

☑ Check Your Comprehension

1. Why doesn't Becky's mother approve of the Wheels-and-Brake Boys?
2. What are the reasons Becky's mother says that Becky can't have a bicycle?
3. How does Becky finally get a bicycle?

◆ Critical Thinking

INTERPRET
1. What is Granny-Liz's opinion of Becky's dream of having a bike? **[Synthesize]**
2. Who in the story shares Granny-Liz's feelings? **[Connect]**
3. Why is a bike so important to Becky? **[Draw Conclusions]**
4. What qualities help Becky reach her goal? **[Analyze]**

EVALUATE
5. Who in this story do you think makes the most convincing argument? Explain. **[Assess]**

APPLY
6. How does this story demonstrate the saying "Where there's a will, there's a way"? **[Relate]**

Guide for Responding (continued)

◆ Reading Strategy

PREDICT

When you **predict,** you make a logical guess about upcoming events or actions.

1. (a) What prediction did you make at the beginning of the story about Becky's getting a bike? (b) On what details did you base your prediction?
2. Did you change your prediction as you continued reading? Why or why not?
3. What do you predict Becky will do now that she has a bike? Why?

◆ Build Vocabulary

USING REGIONAL SYNONYMS

Regional synonyms are the words used in different places to describe or name the same thing. For example, in Jamaica, Becky uses the word *veranda* to name the part of her home that a person in another area might call a porch. When you read stories that are set in different places, you will often encounter regional synonyms.

On your paper, match the regional synonyms.

1. soda   **a.** pants
2. trousers   **b.** hero
3. hoagie   **c.** soft drink

SPELLING STRATEGY

The *is* sound at the end of words is sometimes spelled with *ace*. On your paper, write a word that ends in *ace* for each clue.

1. Jewelry worn on the neck: _ _ c k _ _ _ _
2. The outer part: _ u r _ _ _ _
3. A danger: _ e _ _ _ _

USING THE WORD BANK

Complete each sentence with the Word Bank word that makes the most sense.

1. Fire is a ___?___ in dry areas.
2. The boys performed ___?___ bike stunts.
3. It is cooler on the ___?___ than it is indoors.

◆ Literary Focus

CONFLICT

The **conflict,** the struggle between opposing forces, is one of the most important parts of a story. The conflict drives the action of the story.

1. What is the conflict in "Becky and the Wheels-and-Brake Boys"?
2. Identify three events in the story that contribute to the conflict.
3. Identify one event that happens because Becky is trying to resolve the conflict.

◆ Build Grammar Skills

INDEPENDENT CLAUSES

An **independent clause** is a group of words that has a subject and a verb and that can stand on its own as a complete sentence. The independent clauses are in italics in the following examples:

Over and over she looked at me as if I was crazy.

As soon as I get indoors, *I'll just have to ask again*.

Practice Copy these sentences on your paper. Underline the independent clause in each sentence.

1. I had on a wet blouse when it was all over.
2. As he won, the winner rang his bell.
3. When she can borrow a bike, Shirnette comes too.
4. Becky was happy because she had a bike.
5. After she got her bike, she joined the group.

Writing Application On your paper, complete each of the following sentences with an independent clause.

1. When I open my book again, ___?___ .
2. After Becky talked to her mother, ___?___ .
3. ___?___ because she wanted a bike.
4. ___?___ as they rode.
5. Because she wanted a bike, ___?___ .

Build Your Portfolio

 Idea Bank

Writing Ideas

1. **Book Jacket** Book jackets often give a brief description of what a book is about. The information is intended to get readers interested enough to buy or read the book. Write a paragraph for a book jacket on a collection of stories about Becky.

2. **Letter** Write a letter to Granny-Liz explaining why you do or do not agree with her opinion that Becky should not have a bike.

3. **Story Beyond the Story** Write a continuation of the story, telling what happens next in the lives of the characters from "Becky and the Wheels-and-Brake Boys."

Speaking and Listening

4. **Role Play** With a partner, role-play a conversation between Becky and her mother about whether or not Becky can have a bike. You can use your own words, but base them on details from the story. **[Performing Arts Link]**

5. **Dialect Translation** Read a portion of the story aloud to a small group. Pause to explain expressions and words that Becky speaks in a Jamaican dialect.

Projects

6. **The Perfect Bicycle** Create a model or draw a labeled diagram of a bicycle whose design allows it to do all the things you'd like it to do. Share your design with the class, explaining the bike's special features. **[Art Link]**

7. **Jamaica-fest [Group Activity]** With a group, plan and present a celebration of Jamaica. Different group members can create maps, prepare foods, choose music, and present brief oral reports. **[Social Studies Link]**

 Writing Mini-Lesson

Journal Entry

Write a journal entry as one of the characters in "Becky and the Wheels-and-Brake Boys." In the journal entry, describe an event from the story and your own thoughts and feelings (as the character) about the event.

Writing Skills Focus: Include Thoughts and Feelings

A journal entry is like a letter to yourself. Tell yourself how you feel about the events, rather than just reporting them. Notice that Becky **includes thoughts and feelings** in the following passage:

Model From the Story

I sat down at the little table, as well as I might. Could homework stay in anybody's head in broad daylight outside? No. Could I keep a bike like Ben's out of my head? Not one bit.

Prewriting Choose a moment in the story as the topic of your journal entry. Review the story, and jot down notes about your character's reaction to the occurrences.

Drafting Write a sentence or two that tells what happened. Then, write your reactions. In a journal entry, it is not always necessary to use complete sentences.

> ◆ **Grammar Application**
> Identify where you have used independent clauses as part of a longer sentence.

Revising Ask a partner to comment on whether your journal entry reflects the feelings of the character you've chosen. Keep your partner's suggestions in mind as you revise.

Guide for Reading

Meet the Authors:

Anton Chekhov (1860–1904)

In his short lifetime, Anton Chekhov wrote more than 1,000 stories! This fact is even more surprising when you consider that he didn't even intend to be a writer.

Helping the Family Chekhov was born in the middle of a family of six children. The family lived in a small coastal town of southern Russia, where Anton's father ran a grocery business. Years later when the business failed, the family moved to Moscow. There, Chekhov enrolled in medical school. By writing short stories and humorous articles, he earned money to help support his family.

Struggling to Live Although Chekhov had tuberculosis for most of his adult life, he didn't allow his struggles against weakness and illness to limit him. He traveled to a prison island and wrote about his experiences and observations. He volunteered to work during a famine. Most important of all, he continued to write until his death at the age of forty-four.

Sandra Cisneros (1954–   )

Sandra Cisneros was born in Chicago and stayed in her hometown through college. Then, she moved to Iowa and began to write about her life, her family, and her Mexican heritage. She writes about real-life experiences—even painful ones—such as birthdays that aren't very happy.

◆ LITERATURE AND YOUR LIFE

CONNECT YOUR EXPERIENCE

Sometimes, it seems that nothing goes well, and you just have to hope that tomorrow will be better. The characters in "Overdoing It" and "Eleven" are having bad days. While reading "Overdoing It," you may find yourself amused by the character's problems. While reading "Eleven," you're more likely to feel sympathetic.

THEMATIC FOCUS: Difficult Days

As you read about these characters, ask yourself how you would react to the difficulties they face.

◆ Background for Understanding

HISTORY

In "Overdoing It," a character's fear leads him to say and do foolish things. Fear caused many problems for Russians of Chekhov's time. Because the czars (rulers of Russia) feared losing their power, they were slow to initiate policies that would bring their country into modern times. Roads were badly maintained, and many areas were plagued with poverty and crime. Fear also led the rulers to enforce harsh laws against anyone who disagreed with their policies.

◆ Build Vocabulary

PREFIXES: *fore-*

The prefix *fore-* indicates something that comes before or occurs at an earlier time. To *foresee* events is to see them before they happen.

WORD BANK

Which word might describe something that takes a long time?

prolonged
emaciated
obstructed
wry
foresee
emerged
meditated

Overdoing It ◆ Eleven

◆ Literary Focus
CHARACTERIZATION

Characterization is the art of creating and developing a character. Sometimes, a writer uses **direct characterization,** making direct statements about a character. More often, a writer uses **indirect characterization**—revealing a character's traits through the character's actions and in what other characters say and think about the character. Use a character pyramid like the one shown here to jot down details that reveal the traits of the characters in these stories.

◆ Reading Strategy
IDENTIFY WITH CHARACTERS

The girl in "Eleven" wakes up expecting a happy birthday, complete with a cake and candles. You will probably find it easy to identify with her. When you **identify with a character,** you put yourself in the character's place and share the character's thoughts and feelings. Thinking about times when you've had feelings similar to the characters' will help you to identify with the characters in "Overdoing It" and "Eleven."

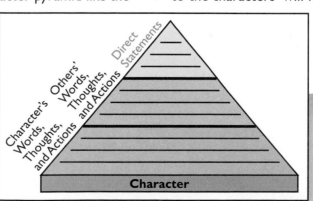

Character's Words, Thoughts, and Actions

Others' Words, Thoughts, and Actions

Direct Statements

Character

Overdoing It

Anton Chekhov

The land surveyor[1] Gleb Smirnov got off the train at Gnilushka. The station was some twenty miles from the estate he came to survey, and he had to cover that distance in a horse-drawn vehicle of some sort.

"Tell me, please, where could I find post horses and a carriage around here?" the surveyor said to the station guard.

"What kind? . . . Post horses? . . . Here for fifty miles around you couldn't even find a sled dog, let alone post horses. . . . Where are you bound for?"

"For Devkino—the estate of General Khokhotov."

"Well," the guard yawned, "try on the other side of the station. You may find some peasants over there who haul passengers."

The land surveyor made his way across from the station. After looking for some time, then after prolonged negotiations and hesitations, he engaged a husky peasant—glum, pockmarked, and dressed in a tattered gray coarse wool coat and bast-bark shoes.

"What kind of a wagon do you have here!" grumbled the surveyor as he climbed into the wagon. "You can't tell the front from the rear."

"What is there to tell? Near the horse's tail it's the front, and where your lordship is now sitting is the rear."

The horse was young but emaciated, with splayed hoofs and nicked ears. When the driver, raising himself, struck her with his hemp whip, she merely shook her head. When he cursed and struck her a second time, the wagon creaked and shook as if with a bad chill. After the third stroke, the wagon lurched and swayed from side to side, and after the fourth, it moved.

"Is this how we'll proceed all the way?" the surveyor asked, feeling a

Old Man's Head, Study, 1955, Yuri Alexeevich Dryakhlov, Courtesy of Overland Gallery of Fine Art, Scottsdale, Arizona

▲ **Critical Viewing** Does this man look brave or cowardly to you? Explain. [Speculate]

◆ **Build Vocabulary**

prolonged (prō lônŋd) *adj.*: Long and drawn out

emaciated (ē mā´ shē āt id) *adj.*: Thin and bony as a result of starvation or disease

1. **land surveyor:** One who measures land boundaries.

violent jolting and amazed at the ability of Russian drivers to combine a snail's pace with a jolting that turned one's insides upside down.

"We-e-'ll get there . . . ," the driver assured him. "The mare is a young one, and spirited. Just let her get started at her own pace, then there'll be no stopping her . . . . Giddy-up, you accursed one!"

It was dusk when the wagon drew away from the station. To the right of the surveyor stretched the dark, frozen plain—broad and endless. Try to cross it and you'll come to the end of the world. On the horizon, where the plain merged with the sky and disappeared, the autumn sun was lazily sinking in the mist. To the left of the road, in the darkening space, loomed oddly shaped mounds, and it was hard to tell whether they were last year's haystacks or the huts of a village. What there was ahead of them the surveyor could not tell because his field of vision was completely <u>obstructed</u> by the massive back of the driver. It was still, cold, frosty.

"What a God-forsaken place this is!" thought the surveyor as he tried to cover his ears with the collar of his greatcoat. "Not a man or beast in sight! Who knows what could happen in a place like this—they can attack you and rob you and no one will be the wiser for it. And this driver—he's not very reassuring. . . . Some husky back he's got! And he has the mug of a beast . . . yes, it's all very frightening."

"Tell me, my dear man," the surveyor asked, "what is your name?"

"Mine? Klim."

"Well, tell me, Klim, is it safe around here? No ruffians?"

"No, thank God! What kind of ruffians could there be here?"

"That's good that there are none. But, just the same, to play it safe, I brought along three revolvers," the surveyor lied.

"And with a gun, as you know, it's bad business to joke. I can handle ten cutthroats with them!"

It grew dark. The wagon suddenly creaked, squeaked, shook, and, as though against its will, turned left.

Old Man, 1950s, Yuri Alexeevich Dryakhlov, Courtesy of Overland Gallery of Fine Art, Scottsdale, Arizona

▲ **Critical Viewing** How is the peasant in this picture similar to and different from the peasant described in the story? [**Compare and Contrast**]

"Where is he taking me?" the surveyor thought. "He's driving straight ahead and suddenly he turns left. What is he up to? He'll take me, the wretch, into some thicket and . . . and. . . . One hears of such things happening!"

"Listen here," he called to the driver. "You say there's no danger around here? That's too bad! I like to fight off cutthroats. In appearance I'm thin, sickly looking, but I have the strength of a bull! Once three highwaymen threw themselves upon me. And what do you think happened? One of them I socked so hard that he gave up his soul to the Lord, and the other two were sentenced to Siberia to do hard labor because of me. And where I get all this power, I really couldn't tell you. I can grab a husky fellow—like you—and knock him down flat!"

Klim looked around at the surveyor, made a wry face, and struck the horse with the whip.

"Yes, brother . . . ," continued the surveyor, "may God help those who tangle with me! Not only will the cutthroat remain without arms and without legs, but he will be dragged off to court as well. I'm acquainted with every district judge and police inspector. I'm a civil servant, you know, and an important one at that. I'm in transit now, but the officials know about this journey . . . they're watching that no one does me any harm. Everywhere along the way, behind the bushes over there, are deputized village police inspectors and policemen. St-o-o-o-p!" the surveyor suddenly screamed. "Where did you drive into now? Where are you taking me?"

"Can't you see? Into the forest."

"That's right—it's a forest . . . ," thought the surveyor. "And I got scared! However, I must not show my fear. He's noticed already that I'm scared. Why has he been looking around at me so much? He's probably planning something. . . . Before he crawled along, and now look at him speed!"

"Listen, Klim, why are you hurrying your horse this way?"

"I'm not hurrying her. She is speeding of her own free will. I suppose she herself isn't pleased to have legs that make her go that fast."

"You're lying! I can see that you're lying! But I'd advise you not to rush that way. Rein in your horse! Do you hear me? Rein it in!"

"Why?"

"Because . . . because four pals of mine are joining me here . . . from the station. We must let them catch up with us. They promised to catch up with me in this forest. . . . It will be merrier to travel with them. . . . They are tough fellows, thick-set . . . each one is armed with a pistol. . . . Why do you keep looking around and fidgeting as if you were on pins and needles? Why? There is nothing to look at . . . there is nothing especially interesting about me . . . just my guns, perhaps . . . if you want me to, I'll get them out and show them to you . . . if you want . . ."

The surveyor dug into his pockets for the imaginary guns. And then something unexpected, something that he did not foresee in all his cowardice, happened. Klim suddenly rolled off the wagon and almost on all fours rushed into a thicket.

"Help!" he wailed. "Help! Take the horse and the wagon, but don't kill me! Help!"

The surveyor heard the departing steps of the driver, the crackling of the underbrush—then complete silence. Not expecting such a verbal attack, the surveyor first of all stopped the horse, then sat back more comfortably in the wagon and gave himself over to thought.

"He ran off . . . got scared, the fool! What'll I do now? I can't go on by myself because I don't know the way, and also, I might be suspected of stealing his horse. . . . What had I better do?"

"Klim! Klim!"

"Klim!" answered the echo.

The thought that he might have to spend the night sitting there in the cold dark forest, hearing only the wolves, their echo, and the neighing of the emaciated mare, sent shivers up and down the surveyor's spine, as though

◆ **Build Vocabulary**

obstructed (əb strəkt´ id) *adj.*: Blocked

wry (rī) *adj.*: Twisted

foresee (fôr sē´) *v.*: Know beforehand

it were being scraped with a cold file.

"Klimushka!" he cried. "My dear man! Where are you, Klimushka?"

The surveyor called for about two hours, and only after he became hoarse and resigned himself to spending the night in the forest, did a soft wind carry to him the sound of someone's groaning.

"Klim! Is that you, my dear man? Let's go on!"

"You'll ki-i-i-ill me!"

"I was just joking, my man! May God punish me if I wasn't joking! I have no guns! I lied because I was scared! Do me a favor, let's go on! I'm freezing to death!"

Klim, having perhaps decided that a real cutthroat would have long since got away with his horse and wagon, emerged from the thicket and hesitantly approached his passenger.

"What was there to get scared about, you fool? I . . . I was just kidding, and got scared. . . . Get in!"

"I'll have nothing more to do with you, master," Klim muttered, climbing up into the wagon. "Had I known, I wouldn't have taken you on, not for a hundred rubles. You nearly made me die of fright."

Klim struck the horse with his whip. The wagon trembled. Klim struck again, and the wagon lurched. After the fourth time, when the wagon moved, the surveyor covered his ears with his collar, and meditated. The road and Klim no longer seemed to him threatening.

◆ **Build Vocabulary**

emerged (ē merjd´) v.: Came out from; came into view

meditated (med´ i tāt id) v.: Thought deeply

*G*uide for Responding

◆ LITERATURE AND YOUR LIFE

Reader's Response What was your reaction when the driver ran into the woods?

Thematic Focus In what ways do the surveyor's own actions make his problems more difficult?

☑ Check Your Comprehension

1. What is the surveyor looking for when he gets off the train?
2. Describe the horse, wagon, and driver that the surveyor engages.
3. What does the driver do that surprises the surveyor?

◆ Critical Thinking

INTERPRET

1. Why is the surveyor so fearful? **[Speculate]**
2. Why does the surveyor brag about his bravery? **[Infer]**
3. Describe the personality of the wagon driver. **[Synthesize]**

APPLY

4. In what other ways can bragging create difficulties for the bragger? **[Relate]**

EVALUATE

5. Which of these two characters would you choose to accompany you on a dangerous journey? Why? **[Make a Judgment]**

ONNECTIONS TO TODAY'S WORLD

Anton Chekhov is known as a master of the short story. He used to say, "Conciseness [being brief or short] is the sister of talent." Snoopy, the dog writer in this comic strip, would probably agree! Created by cartoonist Charles Schulz, the "Peanuts" gang—Charlie Brown, Linus, Lucy, and, of course, Snoopy—have been making people laugh since the 1950's. In this strip, Snoopy tries to write his own short story!

PEANUTS reprinted by permission of United Feature Syndicate, Inc.

1. Compare a comic strip with a short story. **[Compare and Contrast]**
2. Snoopy thinks a short story's only requirement is to be short. What else is needed? **[Synthesize]**
3. Do you think this comic is funny? Explain. **[Assess]**

Eleven

Sandra Cisneros

What they don't understand about birthdays and what they never tell you is that when you're eleven, you're also ten, and nine, and eight, and seven, and six, and five, and four, and three, and two, and one. And when you wake up on your eleventh birthday you expect to feel eleven, but you don't. You open your eyes and everything's just like yesterday, only it's today. And you don't feel eleven at all. You feel like you're still ten. And you are—underneath the year that makes you eleven.

Like some days you might say something stupid, and that's the part of you that's still ten. Or maybe some days you might need to sit on your mama's lap because you're scared, and that's the part of you that's five. And one day when you're all grown up maybe you will need to cry like if you're three, and that's okay. That's what I tell Mama when she's sad and needs to cry. Maybe she's feeling three.

Because the way you grow old is kind of like an onion or like the rings inside a tree trunk or like my little wooden dolls that fit one inside the other, each year inside the next one. That's how being eleven years old is.

You don't feel eleven. Not right away. It takes a few days, weeks even, sometimes even months before you say eleven when they ask you. And you don't feel smart eleven, not until you're almost twelve. That's the way it is.

Only today I wish I didn't have just eleven years rattling inside me like pennies in a tin Band-Aid box. Today I wish I was one-hundred-and-two instead of eleven because if I was one-hundred-and-two I'd have known what to say when Mrs. Price put the red sweater on my desk. I would've known how to tell her it wasn't mine instead of just sitting there with that look on my face and nothing coming out of my mouth.

"Whose is this?" Mrs. Price says, and she holds the red sweater up in the air for all the class to see. "Whose? It's been sitting in the coatroom for a month."

"Not mine," says everybody. "Not me."

"It has to belong to somebody," Mrs. Price keeps saying, but nobody can remember. It's an ugly sweater with red plastic buttons and a collar and sleeves all stretched out like you could use it for a jump rope. It's maybe a thousand years old and even if it belonged to me I wouldn't say so.

Maybe because I'm skinny, maybe

▶ **Critical Viewing** What feeling or mood do you think the artist of this picture is trying to communicate? What details in the picture communicate that mood? **[Support]**

Orange Sweater, 1955, Elmer Bischoff, San Francisco Museum of Modern Art, San Francisco, California

Portrait, From the Estate of Eloy Blanco, Collection of El Museo del Barrio, New York, NY

▲ **Critical Viewing** How old do you think the girl in this painting feels? **[Speculate]**

because she doesn't like me, that stupid Felice Garcia says, "I think it belongs to Rachel." An ugly sweater like that, all raggedy and old, but Mrs. Price believes her. Mrs. Price takes the sweater and puts it right on my desk, but when I open my mouth nothing comes out.

"That's not, I don't, you're not . . . not mine," I finally say in a little voice that was maybe me when I was four.

"Of course it's yours," Mrs. Price says, "I remember you wearing it once." Because she's older and the teacher, she's right and I'm not.

Not mine, not mine, not mine, but Mrs. Price is already turning to page 32, and math problem number four. I don't know why but all of a sudden I'm feeling sick inside, like the part of me that's three wants to come out of my eyes, only I squeeze them shut tight

and bite down on my teeth real hard and try to remember today I am eleven, eleven. Mama is making a cake for me for tonight, and when Papa comes home everybody will sing happy birthday, happy birthday to you.

But when the sick feeling goes away and I open my eyes, the red sweater's still sitting there like a big red mountain. I move the red sweater to the corner of my desk with my ruler. I move my pencil and books and eraser as far from it as possible. I even move my chair a little to the right. Not mine, not mine, not mine.

In my head I'm thinking how long till lunch time, how long till I can take the red sweater and throw it over the schoolyard fence, or leave it hanging on a parking meter, or bunch it up into a little ball and toss it in the alley. Except when math period ends Mrs. Price says loud and in front of everybody, "Now, Rachel, that's enough," because she sees I've shoved the red sweater to the tippy-tip corner of my desk and it's hanging all over the edge like a waterfall, but I don't care.

"Rachel," Mrs. Price says. She says it like she's getting mad. "You put that sweater on right now and no more nonsense."

"But it's not . . ."

"Now!" Mrs. Price says.

This is when I wish I wasn't eleven, because all the years inside of me—ten, nine, eight, seven, six, five, four, three, two, and one—are all pushing at the back of my eyes when I put one arm through one sleeve of the sweater that smells like cottage cheese, and then the other arm through the other and stand there with my arms apart as if the sweater hurts me and it does, all itchy and full of germs that aren't even mine.

That's when everything I've been holding in since this morning, since when Mrs. Price put the sweater on my desk, finally lets go, and all of a sudden I'm crying in front of everybody. I wish I was invisible but I'm not.

I'm eleven and it's my birthday today and I'm crying like I'm three in front of everybody. I put my head down on the desk and bury my face in my stupid clown sweater arms. My face all hot and spit coming out of my mouth because I can't stop the little animal noises from coming out of me, until there aren't any more tears left in my eyes, and it's just my body shaking like when you have the hiccups, and my whole head hurts like when you drink milk too fast.

But the worst part is right before the bell rings for lunch. That stupid Phyllis Lopez, who is even dumber than Felice Garcia, says she remembers the red sweater is hers! I take it off right away and give it to her, only Mrs. Price pretends like everything's okay.

Today I'm eleven. There's a cake Mama's making for tonight, and when Papa comes home from work we'll eat it. There'll be candles and presents and everybody will sing happy birthday, happy birthday to you, Rachel, only it's too late.

I'm eleven today. I'm eleven, ten, nine, eight, seven, six, five, four, three, two, and one, but I wish I was one-hundred-and-two. I wish I was anything but eleven, because I want today to be far away already, far away like a tiny kite in the sky, so tiny-tiny you have to close your eyes to see it.

Guide for Responding

◆ LITERATURE AND YOUR LIFE

Reader's Response What would you like to say to Rachel? To Mrs. Price? To Felice Garcia?

Thematic Focus What circumstances create the difficult day in this story?

Journal Writing Write a paragraph describing your image of "the perfect birthday."

☑ Check Your Comprehension

1. What is special about the day in this story?
2. What article of clothing causes difficulties?
3. What must Rachel do at the end of math period?
4. How is the mix-up straightened out?
5. How does Rachel feel at the end of the story?

◆ Critical Thinking

INTERPRET

1. Explain how Rachel can be eleven, but also all her younger ages as well. **[Interpret]**
2. Why can't Rachel speak up to tell Mrs. Price the sweater is not hers? **[Infer]**
3. Why does Rachel react so strongly to being given the sweater? **[Draw Conclusions]**
4. Why does Rachel say the cake will be "too late"? **[Interpret]**

APPLY

5. In what ways do past years stay with a person through time? **[Interpret]**

COMPARE LITERARY WORKS

6. What problem do Rachel and the land surveyor share? **[Connect]**

Guide for Responding (continued)

◆ Reading Strategy

IDENTIFY WITH CHARACTERS

By **identifying with the characters** in "Overdoing It" and "Eleven," you understand their feelings and you sympathize with them.

1. Compare the land surveyor's actions in "Overdoing It" with the way you think you would have acted in his situation.
2. In what ways do you identify with Rachel in "Eleven"?

◆ Build Vocabulary

USING THE PREFIX *fore-*

On your paper, explain how each numbered word beginning with the prefix *fore-* indicates that something occurs or comes before another thing.

1. forewarned   3. forecast
2. foreshadow   4. foretell

SPELLING STRATEGY

At the beginning of some words, the *r* sound is spelled *wr*, as in *wry*. Several of these words beginning with *wr* have a homophone—another word that sounds the same but has a different meaning and spelling. For each numbered word, write a homophone that begins with *wr*. (*Be careful, the endings are not necessarily spelled the same way.*) Then, explain the difference in the meaning of the two words.

1. rap   2. ring   3. rest   4. right   5. rye

USING THE WORD BANK

On your paper, write the Word Bank word that makes the most sense in each blank space.

1. The hungry dog looked ____?____.
2. The ceremony was ____?____ by many speakers.
3. From behind the pillar, her view was ____?____.
4. He made a ____?____ face.
5. The butterfly ____?____ from its cocoon.
6. The professor ____?____ on the question.
7. I cannot ____?____ the future.

◆ Literary Focus

CHARACTERIZATION

There are two types of **characterization**—direct and indirect. In **direct characterization,** writers make direct statements about a character's appearance and personality. In **indirect characterization,** characters' traits are revealed through their own words and actions, as well as through the comments and actions of other characters.

1. Explain two things that Chekhov reveals about the land surveyor through indirect characterization.
2. In "Eleven," is Rachel's character revealed more through direct or indirect characterization? Explain.

◆ Build Grammar Skills

SUBORDINATE CLAUSES

A **subordinate clause** is a group of words that has a subject and a verb but cannot stand alone as a sentence. It is dependent on an independent clause to complete its meaning. Subordinate clauses usually begin with words like *who, which, that, after, because, before, when,* and *until.* In the following example, the subordinate clause *who haul passengers* cannot stand alone:

"You may find some peasants over there *who haul passengers.*"

Practice Copy these sentences on your paper. Underline the subordinate clause in each sentence.

1. It was dusk when the wagon left the station.
2. He's noticed already that I'm scared.
3. It takes a few days before you say eleven.
4. She wouldn't be happy until the sweater was gone.
5. After Rachel left school, she went home.

Writing Application In your notebook, complete each sentence with a subordinate clause. The first word in the clause is given in parentheses.

1. The wagon lurched (because) ____?____.
2. Klim hid (until) ____?____.
3. It was clear (that) ____?____.

Build Your Portfolio

 ## Idea Bank

Writing Ideas

1. **Notes** Write two notes to Rachel's family about what happened to her at school. Write one note as Mrs. Price. Write the other as Rachel.

2. **Explanation** Write a paragraph in which you explain why fear or insecurity makes people act differently from the way they normally would.

3. **Character Sketch** Write a description of one of the characters in "Overdoing It" or "Eleven." Use examples from the story to support the statements you make about the character.

Speaking and Listening

4. **Dialogue** With a partner, act out a dialogue between Klim and the land surveyor. Have the characters express what they are thinking and feeling, rather than hiding it as they do in the story. **[Performing Arts Link]**

5. **Interview** Interview an adult who knew you when you were three or four years old. Ask questions about what toys, foods, and activities you liked and disliked. Take notes or record your answers. Present your interview to the class, explaining how your likes and dislikes have changed or remained the same.

Projects

6. **Memento Timeline** Create a timeline of your life. Mark your birthdays on a long line. Fill the spaces between your birthdays with pictures, brief descriptions, and mementos that capture your memories of each year. **[Art Link]**

7. **Brochure [Group Activity]** With a group, create a travel brochure of Russia. Group members can collect pictures, write about the culture and climate, or arrange the text and images. **[Social Studies Link]**

 ## Writing Mini-Lesson

Letter of Complaint

As you have read in "Overdoing It," travelers had plenty to complain about. Transportation in nineteenth-century Russia was difficult and uncomfortable. Travelers might have expressed their feelings in a letter of complaint. Write your own letter of complaint—a letter in which you express your dissatisfaction with a product or a service.

Writing Skills Focus: Support With Examples

Manufacturers are usually happy to replace a product if you have a legitimate complaint. Managers, service representatives, and customer relations people will take your complaint seriously if you **support your claim with examples.**

Prewriting Brainstorm for examples that support your complaint. Use an organizer like the one that follows to jot down your ideas.

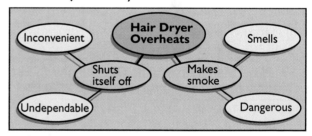

Drafting Use a business-letter format. (See p. 140.) In the body of your letter, state your complaint clearly. Then, offer examples of your complaint.

Revising Ask a partner to read your letter and offer suggestions for improving it. Keep your partner's suggestions in mind as you revise.

> ◆ **Grammar Application**
>
> If you use subordinate clauses, be sure you attach them to independent clauses. For example, the clause *after ten minutes had passed* cannot stand by itself.

CONNECTING LITERATURE TO SOCIAL STUDIES

THE UNITED STATES

Dentistry by Mark Twain

HAPPY 100TH BIRTHDAY! Where a country is concerned, one hundred years old is still pretty young. When the United States turned one hundred years old in 1876, it was an especially exciting time. The country was growing up.

1867, U.S buys Alaska

Boston, Mass., 1876, Bell patents telephone

Hartford, Conn., 1876, Mark Twain publishes *Tom Sawyer*

Promontory, Utah, 1869, transcontinental railroad completed

GREAT PLAINS

New York City, 1855, Walt Whitman publishes *Leaves of Grass*

Central Pacific R.R.

Union Pacific R.R.

Menlo Park, N.J., 1879, Edison invents light bulb

Omaha

1862, Homestead Act brings settlers west to Great Plains

Appomattox, 1865, South surrenders, Civil War ends

Sutter's Mill (Sacramento), 1848, Gold Rush starts

Philadelphia, Pa., 1876, Centennial Exposition displays recent inventions

N

United States Around Its One Hundredth Birthday

The United States Grows Up

In 1776, American colonists threw off the chains that bound them to England. Yet, people in the United States continued to look to England for examples of how to do things. Often, they viewed themselves as crude frontier people.

Over the next one hundred years, the United States built itself into a world-class economy. By the 1870's, railroads were growing fast, uniting far-flung parts of the country. Alexander Graham Bell invented his telephone in 1875. Four years later, Edison turned on the first light bulb. Americans had discovered their own original spirit of enterprise and invention—and they were proud of it.

American Literature The same spirit set a fire under American literature. Early American authors wrote just like the British. By the 1850's, writers such as Walt Whitman and Mark Twain were using "American English" to write about events and characters that belonged only in the United States.

Growing Up in the United States In 1876, Mark Twain gave the country a grand "Happy Hundredth Birthday!" present. He published his novel *The Adventures of Tom Sawyer*, from which "Dentistry" is taken. Like the young nation, Tom Sawyer is imaginative, self-reliant, and a little bit of a rascal. His adventures show the fun parts and the sad parts of growing up in the United States at the time of its one hundredth birthday.

DENTISTRY

Mark Twain

Monday morning found Tom Sawyer miserable. Monday morning always found him so—because it began another week's slow suffering in school. He generally began that day with wishing he had had no intervening holiday, it made the going into captivity and fetters again so much more <u>odious</u>.

Tom lay thinking. Presently it occurred to him that he wished he was sick; then he could stay home from school. Here was a vague possibility. He canvassed his system. No ailment was found, and he investigated again. This time he thought he could detect colicky symptoms, and he began to encourage them with considerable hope. But they soon grew feeble, and presently died wholly away. He reflected further. Suddenly he discovered something. One of his upper front teeth was loose. This was lucky; he was about to begin to groan, as a "starter," as he called it, when it occurred to him that if he came into court with that argument, his aunt would pull it out, and that would hurt. So he thought he would hold the tooth in reserve for the present, and seek further. Nothing offered for some little time, and then he remembered hearing the doctor tell about a certain thing that laid up a patient for two or three weeks and threatened to make him lose a finger. So the boy eagerly drew his sore toe from under the sheet and held it up for inspection. But now he did not know the necessary symptoms. However, it seemed well worthwhile to chance it, so he fell to groaning with considerable spirit.

But Sid slept on unconscious.

Tom groaned louder and fancied that he began to feel pain in the toe.

No result from Sid.

Tom was panting with his <u>exertions</u> by this time. He took a rest and then swelled himself up and fetched a succession of admirable groans.

Sid snored on.

Tom was aggravated. He said, "Sid, Sid!" and shook him. This course worked well, and Tom began to groan again. Sid yawned, stretched, then brought himself up on his elbow with a snort, and began to stare at Tom. Tom went on groaning. Sid said:

"Tom! Say, Tom!" (No response.) "Here, Tom! *Tom!* What is the matter, Tom?" And he shook him and looked in his face anxiously.

Tom moaned out:

"Oh don't, Sid. Don't joggle me."

"Why, what's the matter, Tom? I must call Auntie."

"No—never mind. It'll be over by and by, maybe. Don't call anybody."

"But I must! *Don't* groan so, Tom, it's awful. How long you been this way?"

"Hours. Ouch! Oh, don't stir so, Sid, you'll kill me."

"Tom, why didn't you wake me sooner? Oh Tom, *don't!* It makes my flesh crawl to hear you. Tom, what *is* the matter?"

"I forgive you everything, Sid. (Groan.) Everything you've ever done to me. When I'm gone—"

"Oh, Tom, you ain't dying, are you? Don't Tom. Oh, don't. Maybe—"

> **Connecting Literature to Social Studies**
> Explain how Tom's approach is both practical and imaginative.

◆ Build Vocabulary

odious (ō′ dē əs) *adj.*: Hateful; disgusting

exertions (eg zʉr′ shənz) *n.*: Efforts

"I forgive everybody, Sid. (Groan.) Tell 'em so, Sid. And Sid, you give my window sash and my cat with one eye to that new girl that's come to town, and tell her—"

But Sid had snatched his clothes and gone. Tom was suffering in reality, now, so handsomely was his imagination working, and so his groans had gathered quite a genuine tone.

Sid flew downstairs and said:

"Oh, Aunt Polly, come! Tom's dying!"

'Dying!"

"Yes'm. Don't wait—come quick!"

"Rubbage! I don't believe it!"

But she flew upstairs, nevertheless, with Sid and Mary at her heels. And her face grew white, too, and her lip trembled. When she reached the bedside she gasped out:

"You, Tom! Tom, what's the matter with you?"

"Oh, Auntie, I'm—"

"What's the matter with you—what *is* the matter with you, child?"

"Oh, Auntie, my sore toe's mortified!"

The old lady sank down into a chair and laughed a little, then cried a little, then did both together. This restored her and she said:

"Tom, what a turn you did give me. Now you shut up that nonsense and climb out of this."

The groans ceased and the pain vanished from the toe. The boy felt a little foolish, and he said:

"Aunt Polly, it *seemed* mortified, and it hurt so I never minded my tooth at all."

"Your tooth indeed! What's the matter with your tooth?"

"One of them's loose, and it aches perfectly awful."

"There, there, now, don't begin that groaning again. Open your mouth. Well—your tooth *is* loose, but you're not going to die about that. Mary, get me a silk thread and a chunk of fire out of the kitchen."

Tom said:

"Oh, please, Auntie, don't pull it out. It don't hurt any more. I wish I may never stir if it does. Please don't, Auntie. *I* don't want to stay home from school."

"Oh you don't, don't you? So all this row was because you thought you'd get to stay home from school and go a-fishing? Tom, Tom, I love you so, and you seem to try every way you can to break my old heart with your outrageousness."

By this time the dental instruments were ready. The old lady made one end of the silk thread fast to Tom's tooth with a loop and tied the other to the bedpost. Then she seized the chunk of fire and suddenly thrust it almost into the boy's face. The tooth hung dangling by the bedpost now.

But all trials bring their compensations. As Tom wended to school after breakfast, he was the envy of every boy he met because the gap in his upper row of teeth enabled him to expectorate in a new and admirable way. He gathered quite a following of lads interested in the exhibition; and one that had cut his finger, and had been a center of fascination and homage up to this time, now found himself suddenly without an adherent, and shorn of his glory. He heart was heavy, and he said with a disdain which he did not feel, that it wasn't anything to spit like Tom Sawyer. But another boy said, "Sour grapes!" and he wandered away a dismantled hero.

> **Connecting Literature to Social Studies**
> What conclusions can you draw about dental treatment in the nineteenth century?

Meet the Author

Mark Twain (1835–1910) is one of the most famous American writers. His real name was Samuel Clemens. He borrowed his pen name from his experiences as a riverboat pilot on the Mississippi River, where the call "mark twain" announced the depth of the river.

Twain's books were read in most parts of the world during the last years of his life. He helped people accept books written in the kind of language that Americans used every day. He also helped to popularize the idea that novels could be about ordinary people.

CONNECTING LITERATURE TO SOCIAL STUDIES

Around the time the United States turned one hundred, Americans looked at the world with a mixture of practicality and imagination. They prided themselves on getting things done—whatever it might take.

1. List two things Tom does that combine practicality and imagination.
2. Based on the speech of the characters, give two examples of distinctive ways in which nineteenth-century Americans used words.

 Idea Bank

Writing

1. **List** Make a list of three characters from television or movies that remind you of Tom. Explain why.
2. **Dialogue** Write a conversation in which Sid Sawyer tells a friend about what happened when Tom tried to skip school.
3. **Essay** As Tom Sawyer, write an essay about your tricks for fooling people. Explain how you use what people expect or want to hear to trick them into believing you.

Speaking and Listening

4. **Reading** In a small group, prepare a dramatic reading of the story. Divide the parts, and assign one or more people to read the narration. Present your reading to the class.

Projects

5. **Map** On a map of the United States, show the different places that Mark Twain lived. **[Social Studies Link]**
6. Find out more about Tom Sawyer. Then, dress as the character and tell some of your adventures to the class. **[Literature Link]**

Further Reading, Listening, and Viewing

- Jim Hargrove's book *Mark Twain: The Story of Samuel Clemens* (1984) is a biography that shows how Twain's writings reflected the events of his life.
- The video *Tom and Huck* (1995) from Disney and Buena Vista captures the adventures of two of Twain's most beloved characters.

Guide for Responding

◆ LITERATURE AND YOUR LIFE

Reader's Response What do you think of Tom's plan?

Thematic Focus How does Aunt Polly take Tom's character into account in dealing with his complaints?

☑ Check Your Comprehension

1. How does Aunt Polly react to Tom's "sore toe"?
2. What does she do about his loose tooth?

◆ Critical Thinking

INTERPRET
1. Why does Tom eventually tell Aunt Polly about his tooth? **[Interpret]**
2. Do you think Tom will try similar tricks in the future? Why or why not? **[Draw Conclusions]**

EVALUATE
3. Does Tom "win" or "lose" in the story? Explain. **[Assess]**

Response to a Short Story

Writing Process Workshop

There's only one problem with reading a short story—you do it by yourself. When you get to the exciting part, or when the ending turns out to be a big disappointment, you need to tell someone about it!

Share your reactions by writing a **response to a short story.** First, let readers know the basics of the story. Then, tell them what it was like reading the story—what you liked and didn't like. Use the following tips, presented in this section's Writing Mini-Lessons:

Writing Skills Focus

▶ **Focus on a main idea**. Write about one main subject, such as plot or character. If you discuss every detail in the story, your response will lose focus. (See p. 468.)

▶ **Include thoughts and feelings.** Spend time explaining your thoughts and feelings about the story. For instance, you might write, "I felt frustrated for Becky when her grandmother interrupted her conversations with her mother." (See p. 479.)

▶ **Support with examples.** It's easy to say, "The story was great!" but that doesn't mean much to your readers. Use examples from the story—details of the action or characters— that make the story so satisfying or so disappointing. (See p. 493.)

MODEL

James Berry's story "Becky and the Wheels-and-Brake Boys" stayed with me for a while. ① I felt sorry for Becky, the main character.

Becky wants very much to ride a bicycle with a gang called the Wheels-and-Brake boys. No one will help her, though. ② The gang is rude to her when she asks for lessons. Just as she is about to persuade her mother to buy her a bicycle, her grandmother interrupts. ③ After so much frustration, I thought Becky deserved a happy ending.

① The writer explains that the main focus will be the story's main character, Becky.

② Examples support the writer's general comments and reactions.

③ The writer shares thoughts and feelings about Becky.

Prewriting

Choose a Topic Think of a story that stands out in your memory. You don't have to remember every detail. If the story was exciting, moving, or disappointing, it will make a good topic.

Topic Ideas

- A story with a main character you'd like to be
- A story telling of adventures you'd like to have
- A story with an ending you'd like to change

Focus on a Main Idea First, jot down the details from the story that you liked or disliked, writing each detail on a separate note card. Then, group details that belong together. For instance, group together all details concerning a character or all details concerning the story's ending. Then, sum up each group with a main idea. Finally, pick one main idea as your focus.

"The Fox"

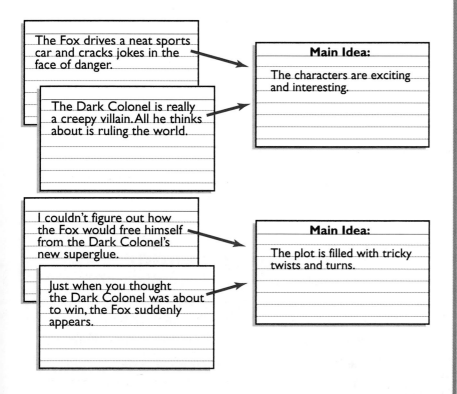

The Fox drives a neat sports car and cracks jokes in the face of danger.

The Dark Colonel is really a creepy villain. All he thinks about is ruling the world.

Main Idea:
The characters are exciting and interesting.

I couldn't figure out how the Fox would free himself from the Dark Colonel's new superglue.

Just when you thought the Dark Colonel was about to win, the Fox suddenly appears.

Main Idea:
The plot is filled with tricky twists and turns.

APPLYING LANGUAGE SKILLS: Eliminate Unnecessary Words

A strong sentence uses just the words it needs. Eliminate words that mean the same as other words or that add little meaning.

Unnecessary Words:
The dragon is a *very* fierce beast that *wrecks and* destroys whole, *entire* towns.

Revised:
The dragon is a fierce beast that destroys whole towns.

Practice Rewrite each sentence, eliminating unnecessary words:

1. He is so terrified and scared that he lies and makes up stories about himself and stuff.
2. The teacher, like, makes her put on the sweater with the awful, terrible smell.

Writing Application Look for unnecessary words in your draft and eliminate them.

Writer's Solution Connection Language Lab

For more practice, complete the Eliminating Unnecessary Words lesson in the Sentence Style unit.

Applying Language Skills: Use the Correct Homophone

Homophones are words that sound the same but are spelled differently and have different meanings. In your writing, be careful to choose the right word. The following examples show common homophones used correctly:

They're waiting there for their turn.

Two is too many to bring to her.

It's time to trim its claws.

Practice Choose the correct homophones in each sentence.

1. They should have lent her one of (they're, their, there) bicycles.
2. I'd like (to, too, two) own (to, too, two) bicycles, (to, too, two].
3. [It's, Its] not my sweater, and I hate [it's, its] smell.

Writing Application Check your draft to make sure you've used homophones correctly.

Writer's Solution Connection Writing Lab

Check your draft with the Homonyms Checker in the Writer's Tool Kit under Writing Tools, Proofreading.

Drafting

Introduce Your Response Begin by identifying the story and your focus, as in this example: "'Dragon, Dragon' by John Gardner is a funny story, but the ending was disappointing."

Summarize the Story In a paragraph, identify the main characters and their situation, and explain what happens.

Share Thoughts and Feelings Explain what your thoughts and feelings were as you read. For example: "If I were Becky, the boys' rude behavior would have made me angry."

Revising

Use a Checklist Use the following revision checklist:

▶ Have I clearly summarized the work? *Add crucial details, but cut those a reader does not need to know.*

▶ Do I focus on one main idea, or does my discussion get sidetracked? *Cut parts that distract from your focus.*

▶ Each time I write "I liked" or "I thought," do I follow with an example from the story explaining my reaction? *Add examples to clarify your reactions.*

REVISION MODEL

Simon Knight's "The Fox Fades Out" is a great adventure story ① featuring my favorite hero, the Fox. **Once again, the Fox faces death without blinking.** ② When the Dark Colonel glues him to an iceberg headed for disaster, the Fox just cracks jokes. ③ ~~The Dark Colonel's ultimate plan is to use his new super-glue to reattach South America to Africa.~~ **In the end, the Fox always gets away.** ④ When there's no way out, but the Fox still laughs, I get a big thrill. It makes me feel that no problem is too big to laugh at.

① The writer identifies the main focus, a character.
② The writer gives an example to support his or her reactions.
③ This detail was not necessary.
④ Here, the writer adds something about his feelings.

Publishing and Presenting

Panel Discussions Form a panel with classmates who responded to the same story. Discuss your responses in front of the class with members of the panel. After each panel presentation, the class may ask questions and make comments.

Two Thumbs Up In the role of a television reviewer, read your response on videotape. Then, show the video to the class.

Real-World Reading Skills Workshop

Strategies for Success

There's a novel all your friends have told you is great. You'd like to read it, but it's long. Or maybe you have to read a novel or play for one of your classes. Looking at that big, thick book can be discouraging. There are some things you can do, though, to make reading longer works easier.

Preview the Book To help plan reading time, look at the table of contents or flip through the book to see how it is set up. Depending on the way the book is divided, you might plan your reading in terms of chapters or even smaller sections.

Plan Ahead When you need to read a long book, make up a reading schedule. Do a little math. For example, imagine you have two weeks to read fifty pages. Each chapter is about ten pages long. You could read five pages every school day. Or you could set aside five blocks of time to read each chapter. To keep information fresh in your mind, do not let too much time go by between readings.

Make Predictions and Look Back When you get to the end of a chapter, make a prediction about what you will find out in the next chapter. If you start losing track of characters or events, reread earlier parts.

Take Notes If you're reading to prepare a book report, take notes only on major events and changes.

DR. MAE, ASTRONAUT!

When Dr. Mae C. Jemison, a NASA astronaut and a physician, blasted off on the space shuttle *Endeavor* in 1992, she became the first black woman to travel such a distance. On board, she pursued important research in the life sciences. Back here on Earth, she is known as one of the most daring and outspoken women of our times.

Apply the Strategies

Your teacher has assigned a book report that is due three weeks from today. Use the table of contents and cover copy for the book *Dr. Mae, Astronaut* (below) to answer the questions that follow.

Contents

1. Using a calendar, make a reading and writing schedule. (You must finish reading in time to write your report.)

2. What kind of information does the book contain?

3. How is the information organized?

4. What kind of information will you focus on as you take notes?

✔ Here are some other situations in which these strategies are useful:
▶ Reading an autobiography
▶ Reading a textbook chapter
▶ Reading a magazine story continued over several issues

A **clause** is a group of words that contains a subject and a verb. There are two kinds of clauses—independent and subordinate. (See pages 467 and 478.)

An **independent clause** contains a subject and a verb and can stand alone as a complete sentence:

Independent Clause
Over and over, she looked at me.

A **subordinate clause** also has a subject and a verb, but it does not express a complete thought, so it is not a sentence. It is part of a sentence, dependent on an independent, or main, clause to express a complete thought. Subordinate clauses usually begin with words like *who, which, that, after, because, before, when,* and *until.* (See page 492.)

Subordinate Clause   Independent Clause
As soon as I get indoors, I'll ask again.

Practice 1 Write the following clauses in your notebook. Identify each clause as independent or subordinate.

1. Becky was upset.

2. Because the boys wouldn't teach her to ride.

3. After Rachel left.

4. They waited for a long time.

5. You may find some help over there.

Grammar in Writing

✔ *Use subordinate clauses to add details to a sentence.*

✔ *Remember that a subordinate clause cannot stand alone as a sentence. If you write a subordinate clause as a sentence, you are writing a sentence fragment.*

clause (klôz or kläz) *n.* 1 a group of words that includes a subject and a verb, but that forms only part of a sentence: in the sentence "She will visit us if she can," "she will visit us" is a clause that could be a complete sentence, and "if she can" is a clause that depends on the first clause 2 a separate point or article in a law, contract, treaty, etc.

Practice 2 Copy each sentence in your notebook. Underline independent clauses once. If the sentence contains a subordinate clause, underline the subordinate clause twice.

1. She waited until the others left the room.

2. After Becky got a bike, she rode with the Wheels-and-Brake boys.

3. More and more, Becky wanted a bike.

4. The king's knights were afraid of the dragon because it was so fierce.

5. As he approached the cave, the youngest son recited a poem.

Practice 3 On your paper, add a clause to the numbered clause. Indicate whether you have added an independent clause or a subordinate clause.

1. Before the son left, _____?_____.

2. He asked his father's advice _____?_____.

3. _____?_____ because she didn't want to wear the sweater.

4. After the king held a meeting, _____?_____.

5. The king was angry _____?_____.

Part 2 *Setting and Theme*

Badlands of Dakota (detail), Thomas Moran, Spanierman Gallery, LLC, New York, NY

Guide for Reading

Meet the Authors:

Charles Dickens (1812–1870)

The stories of English author Charles Dickens have remained popular for more than one hundred years. You may be familiar with his story *A Christmas Carol* and its main character, Ebenezer Scrooge.

Dickens's early life was difficult. When he was just a boy, his father went to a prison for people who owed money. Dickens himself had to work long hours pasting labels on bottles.

At fifteen, Dickens became a law clerk. He taught himself shorthand and became a court reporter. His observations of lawyers helped him write novels like *Great Expectations*. They also helped him describe a musty, dusty lawyer's room in "The Lawyer and the Ghost."

Jean Craighead George (1919–   )

Jean Craighead George has been a reporter, illustrator, teacher, and editor. She is the author of more than thirty books, including *My Side of the Mountain* and *Julie of the Wolves*. Nearly all her books are about nature. She even calls her fiction "documentary novels" because the facts about nature they contain are scientifically accurate.

THE STORY BEHIND THE STORY

"The Wounded Wolf" is based on an incident George heard from a scientist. In retelling it, she leaves out any trace of human observation.

◆ LITERATURE AND YOUR LIFE

CONNECT YOUR EXPERIENCE

If you've been working too hard or have been sick, people may say, "You look like the ghost of yourself." Anything that worries away your healthy color can make you seem pale, frail, and ghostly.

These stories show how worry and injury make "ghosts." In one, the ghost of a lawyer frets about an old lawsuit. In the other, injury turns a wolf ghostly.

THEMATIC FOCUS: Working It Out

In each story, how does a character solve the problem of the ghost or the almost-ghost?

◆ Background for Understanding

HISTORY

For Dickens, the law was an old and haunted profession. In "The Lawyer and the Ghost," the lawyer lives in one of London's Inns of Court. Lawyers ate, slept, and studied in these centuries-old buildings. The wooden "press" in the lawyer's room is a bookcase for legal papers. It was probably called a press because of the press, or crowd, of papers it could store. Lawsuits could last for years, leaving only papers and a ghostly memory of the original complaint.

◆ Build Vocabulary

PREFIXES: *in-*

The prefix *in-*, like *un-*, is like a minus sign. It can mean "no, not, without, the lack of, or the opposite of." In "The Lawyer and the Ghost," for example, *inconsistent* means "not consistent" or "not making sense" in the circumstances.

WORD BANK

Which of these words is related to the word *spend*? How do you know?

> sufficient
> expend
> inconsistent
> massive
> stoic
> gnashes

The Lawyer and the Ghost
◆ The Wounded Wolf ◆

◆ Literary Focus

SETTING

The **setting** is the time and place of a story's events. The time can refer to a historical era, such as ancient Egypt, or the present. It can also refer to the season of the year and to the amount of time that passes during the story. Here's a sample description of a setting: *The story takes place in a modern Texas middle school, one day in June.*

You won't always be able to tell the historical era of a story. However, you'll often be able to figure out the season and the amount of time that passes. To summarize the settings of these stories, gather details of time and place from the descriptions you read.

◆ Reading Strategy

ENVISION THE ACTION AND SETTING

You can see the action and setting of a movie because the movie's director has filmed the right details. When you read, be your own director. **Envision the action and setting** by making a movie of the story in your mind. Picture the action, hear the sounds, and—going further than a movie—smell, taste, and touch the surroundings.

Use an organizer like the one below to help you envision the action and setting as you read.

Story: "The Lawyer and the Ghost"	
Details of Setting	**How I Envision Setting**
• "Old, damp, rotten" rooms • Not cheerful • "Moldering" furniture, including a wooden press	It's a gloomy old apartment that smells of mildew. A big old bookcase stands in one corner, with spiderwebs on it.
Details of Action	**How I Envision Action**
• "One of the glass doors slowly open[ed], disclos[ing] a pale and emaciated figure"	The bookcase door swings open, probably creaking. Inside there stands a thin, creepy-looking ghost.

F+

The Lawyer and the Ghost

Charles Dickens

I knew [a] man—let me see—it's forty years ago now—who took an old, damp, rotten set of chambers, in one of the most ancient Inns, that had been shut up and empty for years and years before. There were lots of old women's stories about the place, and it certainly was very far from being a cheerful one; but he was poor, and the rooms were cheap, and that would have been quite a <u>sufficient</u> reason for him, if they had been ten times worse than they really were. He was obliged to take some moldering fixtures that were on the place, and, among the rest, was a great lumbering wooden press for papers, with large glass doors, and a green curtain inside; a pretty useless thing for him, for he had no papers to put in it; and as to his clothes, he carried them about with him, and that wasn't very hard work, either.

Well, he had moved in all his furniture—it wasn't quite a truck-full—and sprinkled it about the room, so as to make the four chairs look as much like a dozen as possible, and was sitting down before the fire at night, . . . when his eyes encountered the glass doors of the wooden press. "Ah!" says he— "If I hadn't been obliged to take that ugly article at the old broker's valuation, I might have got something comfortable for the money. I'll tell you what it is, old fellow," he said, speaking aloud to the press, just because he had got nothing else to speak to— "If it wouldn't cost more to break up your old carcass, than it would ever be worth afterwards, I'd have a fire out of you, in less than no time."

He had hardly spoken the words, when a sound resembling a faint groan, appeared to issue from the interior of the case. It startled him at first, but thinking, on a moment's reflection, that it must be some young fellow in the next chambers, who had been dining out, he put his feet on the fender, and raised the poker to stir the fire. At that moment, the sound was repeated: and one of the glass doors slowly opening, disclosed a pale and emaciated figure in soiled and worn apparel,

◆ **Build Vocabulary**
sufficient (sə fish´ ənt) *adj.*: Enough; satisfactory

▶ **Critical Viewing** Does this photograph of nineteenth-century London capture the same mood as the story? Explain using details. **[Support]**

standing erect in the press. The figure was tall and thin, and the countenance expressive of care and anxiety; but there was something in the hue of the skin, and gaunt and unearthly appearance of the whole form, which no being of this world was ever seen to wear. –

"Who are you?" said the new tenant, turning very pale, poising the poker in his hand, however, and taking a very decent aim at the countenance[1] of the figure— "Who are you?"

"Don't throw that poker at me," replied the form— "If you hurled it with ever so sure an aim, it would pass through me, without resistance, and expend its force on the wood behind. I am a spirit."

"And, pray, what do you want here?" faltered the tenant.

"In this room," replied the apparition, "my worldly ruin was worked,

---

1. **countenance** (koun´ tə nəns) n.: Face; also, the look on a person's face.

◆ **Build Vocabulary**
expend (ek spend´) v.: Spend

and I and my children beggared. In this press, the papers in a long, long suit,[2] which accumulated for years, were deposited. In this room, when I had died of grief, and long-deferred hope, two wily harpies[3] divided the wealth for which I had contested during a wretched existence, and of which, at last, not one farthing was left for my unhappy descendants. I terrified them from the spot, and since that day have prowled by night—the only period at which I can re-visit the earth—about the scenes of my long-protracted misery. This apartment is mine: leave it to me."

"If you insist upon making your appearance here," said the tenant, who had had time to collect his presence of mind during this prosy statement of the ghost's— "I shall give up possession with greatest pleasure; but I should like to ask you one question, if you will allow me."

"Say on," said the apparition, sternly.

"Well," said the tenant, "I don't apply the observation personally to you, because it is equally applicable to all the ghosts I ever heard of; but it does appear to me, somewhat <u>inconsistent</u>, that when you have an opportunity of visiting the fairest spots of earth—for I suppose space is nothing to you—you should always return exactly to the very places where you have been most miserable."

"Egad, that's very true; I never thought of that before," said the ghost.

"You see, Sir," pursued the tenant, "this is a very uncomfortable room. From the appearance of that press, I should be disposed to say that it is not wholly free from bugs; and I really think you might find much more comfortable quarters: to say nothing of the climate of London, which is extremely disagreeable."

"You are very right, Sir," said the ghost, politely, "it never struck me till now; I'll try a change of air directly"—and, in fact, he began to vanish as he spoke: his legs, indeed, had quite disappeared.

"And if, Sir," said the tenant, calling after him, "if you *would* have the goodness to suggest to the other ladies and gentlemen who are now engaged in haunting old empty houses, that they might be much more comfortable elsewhere, you will confer a very great benefit on society."

▼ **Critical Viewing** What adjectives used to describe the apparition in the story could be used to describe the ghost in this picture? [**Compare and Contrast**]

---

2. **suit** (soot) *n.*: Lawsuit; a court case in which two or more persons or businesses argue over a matter.

3. **harpies** (här′ pēz) *n.*: Greedy people (originally the name of hideous mythological monsters with women's heads and birds' wings and claws).

"I will," replied the ghost; "we must be dull fellows—very dull fellows, indeed; I can't imagine how we can have been so stupid." With these words, the spirit disappeared; and what is rather remarkable, . . . he never came back again.

◆ Build Vocabulary

inconsistent (in´ kən sis´ tənt) *n.*: Contradictory; not making sense

Beyond Literature ◆

Career Connection

Lawyers and Paralegals Since Dickens's day, the legal profession has continued to expand. Lawyers do not just argue cases in front of judges and juries, but they are often called on for advice. *Corporate* and *business lawyers* advise businesses on the law and on contracts. *Personal lawyers* help individuals deal with taxes, wills, and other matters.

To qualify as a lawyer, a person must usually complete four years of college and three years of law school and pass an exam called the bar. However, many jobs in the legal profession do not require a law degree. Paralegals, for instance, complete approximately nine months of training. Then they are qualified to assist lawyers by doing research on the law and determining the facts of a case.

Cross-Curricular Activity
Pie Chart Interview a lawyer or a paralegal to find out how he or she spends a day. Create a pie chart showing the various tasks he or she might perform and the amount of time spent on each.

Guide for Responding

◆ LITERATURE AND YOUR LIFE

Reader's Response What would you have said to the ghost if it asked you to leave?

Thematic Focus What special qualities does the main character have that help him work things out with a ghost?

Journal Writing Briefly describe a place you've seen that would make a good setting for a movie about a ghost.

☑ Check Your Comprehension

1. Describe the rooms that the man rents.
2. Who is the ghost that haunts these rooms?
3. What does the ghost want?
4. What question does the man ask the ghost?
5. In what way does the ghost respond?

◆ Critical Thinking

INTERPRET
1. Why do you think the ghost returns to the scene of his "misery"? **[Speculate]**
2. What is surprising about the end of this ghost story? **[Analyze]**
3. What is humorous about the contrast between what might have happened and what actually does? **[Draw Conclusions]**

EVALUATE
4. Was the ghost in this story frightening? Why or why not? **[Assess]**

EXTEND
5. What does this story suggest about lawyers and the practice of law in Dickens's England? **[Social Studies Link]**

The Wounded Wolf

Jean Craighead George

▲ **Critical Viewing** What physical features help this wolf survive in a cold, harsh environment? **[Analyze]**

A wounded wolf climbs Toklat Ridge, a <u>massive</u> spine of rock and ice. As he limps, dawn strikes the ridge and lights it up with sparks and stars. Roko, the wounded wolf, blinks in the ice fire, then stops to rest and watch his pack run the thawing Arctic valley.

They plunge and turn. They fight the mighty caribou that struck young Roko with his hoof and wounded him. He jumped between the beast and Kiglo, leader of the Toklat pack. Young Roko spun and fell. Hooves, paws, and teeth roared over him. And then his pack and the beast were gone.

◆ **Literary Focus**
In what region of the world is the story set?

Gravely injured, Roko pulls himself toward the shelter rock. Weakness overcomes him. He stops. He and his pack are thin and hungry. This is the season of starvation. The winter's harvest has been taken. The produce of spring has not begun.

Young Roko glances down the valley. He droops his head and stiffens his tail to signal to his pack that he is badly hurt. Winds wail. A frigid blast picks up long shawls of snow and drapes them between young Roko and his pack. And so his message is not read.

A raven scouting Toklat Ridge sees Roko's signal. "Kong, kong, kong," he bells—death is coming to the ridge; there will be flesh and bone for all. His voice rolls out across the valley. It penetrates the rocky cracks where the Toklat ravens rest. One by one they hear and spread their wings. They beat their way to Toklat Ridge. They alight upon the snow and walk behind the wounded wolf.

"Kong," they toll[1] with keen excitement, for the raven clan is hungry, too. "Kong, kong"— there will be flesh and bone for all.

Roko snarls and hurries toward the shelter rock. A cloud of snow envelops him. He limps in blinding whiteness now.

A ghostly presence flits around. "Hahahaha-hahaha," the white fox states—death is coming to the Ridge. Roko smells the fox tagging at his heels.

The cloud whirls off. Two golden eyes look up at Roko. The snowy owl has heard the ravens and joined the deathwatch.

Roko limps along. The ravens walk. The white fox leaps. The snowy owl flies and hops along the rim of Toklat Ridge. Roko stops. Below the ledge out on the flats the musk-ox herd is circling. They form a ring and all face out, a fort of heads and horns and fur that sweeps down to their hooves. Their circle means to Roko that an enemy is present. He squints and smells the wind. It carries scents of thawing ice, broken grass—and earth. The grizzly bear is up! He has awakened from his winter's sleep. A craving need for flesh will drive him.

Roko sees the shelter rock. He strains to reach it. He stumbles. The ravens move in closer. The white fox boldly walks beside him. "Hahaha," he yaps. The snowy owl flies ahead, alights, and waits.

The grizzly hears the eager fox and rises on his flat hind feet. He twists his powerful neck and head. His great paws dangle at his chest. He sees the animal procession and hears the ravens' knell[2] of death. Dropping to all fours, he joins the march up Toklat Ridge.

Roko stops; his breath comes hard. A raven alights upon his back and picks the open wound. Roko snaps. The raven flies and circles back. The white fox nips at Roko's toes. The snowy owl inches closer. The grizzly bear, still dulled by sleep, stumbles onto Toklat Ridge.

Only yards from the shelter rock, Roko falls.

Instantly the ravens mob him. They scream and peck and stab at his eyes. The white fox leaps upon his wound. The snowy owl sits and waits.

---

2. **knell** (nel) *n.*: Mournful sound, like a slowly ringing bell—usually indicating a death.

◆ **Build Vocabulary**

massive (mass´ iv) *adj.*: Huge; large and impressive

---

1. **toll** (tōl) *v.*: Announce.

Young Roko struggles to his feet. He bites the ravens. Snaps the fox. And lunges at the stoic owl. He turns and warns the grizzly bear. Then he bursts into a run and falls against the shelter rock. The wounded wolf wedges down between the rock and barren ground. Now protected on three sides, he turns and faces all his foes.

The ravens step a few feet closer. The fox slides toward him on his belly. The snowy owl blinks and waits, and on the ridge rim roars the hungry grizzly bear.

Roko growls.

The sun comes up. Far across the Toklat Valley, Roko hears his pack's "hunt's end" song. The music wails and sobs, wilder than the bleating wind. The hunt song ends. Next comes the roll call. Each member of the Toklat pack barks to say that he is home and well.

"Kiglo here," Roko hears his leader bark. There is a pause. It is young Roko's turn. He cannot lift his head to answer. The pack is silent. The leader starts the count once more. "Kiglo here."—A pause. Roko cannot answer.

♦ **Reading Strategy**
Envision these sounds as if you were there. Do they have a noisy, bustling feeling or a lonely, wild one?

The wounded wolf whimpers softly. A mindful raven hears. "Kong, kong, kong," he tolls—this is the end. His booming sounds across the valley. The wolf pack hears the raven's message that something is dying. They know it is Roko, who has not answered roll call.

The hours pass. The wind slams snow on Toklat Ridge. Massive clouds blot out the sun. In their gloom Roko sees the deathwatch move in closer. Suddenly he hears the musk-oxen thundering into their circle. The ice cracks as the grizzly leaves. The ravens burst into the air. The white fox runs. The snowy owl flaps to the top of the shelter rock. And Kiglo rounds the knoll.

In his mouth he carries meat. He drops it

◀ **Critical Viewing** The wolf in the photograph is howling. Given what you learn in the story, what can you infer about the number of wolves in the area? [Infer]

close to Roko's head and wags his tail excitedly. Roko licks Kiglo's chin to honor him. Then Kiglo puts his mouth around Roko's nose. This gesture says "I am your leader." And by mouthing Roko, he binds him and all the wolves together.

The wounded wolf wags his tail. Kiglo trots away.

Already Roko's wound feels better. He gulps the food and feels his strength return. He shatters bone, flesh, and gristle and shakes the scraps out on the snow. The hungry ravens swoop upon them. The white fox snatches up a bone. The snowy owl gulps down flesh and fur. And Roko wags his tail and watches.

For days Kiglo brings young Roko food. He gnashes, gorges, and shatters bits upon the snow.

A purple sandpiper winging north sees ravens, owl, and fox. And he drops in upon the feast. The long-tailed jaeger gull flies down and joins the crowd on Toklat Ridge.

Roko wags his tail.

One dawn he moves his wounded leg. He stretches it and pulls himself into the sunlight. He walks—he romps. He runs in circles. He leaps and plays with chunks of ice. Suddenly he stops. The "hunt's end" song rings out. Next comes the roll call.

"Kiglo here."

"Roko here," he barks out strongly.

The pack is silent.

"Kiglo here," the leader repeats.

"Roko here."

Across the distance comes the sound of whoops and yipes and barks and howls. They fill the dawn with celebration. And Roko prances down the Ridge.

◆ Build Vocabulary

stoic (stō′ ik) *adj.*: Showing no reaction to good or bad events; calm and unaffected by hardship

gnashes (nash′ iz) *v.*: Bites with grinding teeth

Guide for Responding

◆ LITERATURE AND YOUR LIFE

Reader's Response Do you admire the wolves in this story? Why or why not?

Thematic Focus How do the wolves solve the problem posed by Roko's injury?

Group Activity With classmates, brainstorm for ways in which the wolves in the story are similar to and different from people. **[Science Link]**

☑ Check Your Comprehension

1. What action did Roko take that caused him to be wounded?
2. Describe the threats that Roko faces.
3. How does Kiglo help Roko?
4. What happens at the end of the story?

◆ Critical Thinking

INTERPRET

1. Why does Roko climb the ridge? **[Infer]**
2. Are there "good-guy" and "bad-guy" animals in this story? Explain. **[Analyze]**
3. What does the "celebration" at the end mean? **[Draw Conclusions]**

APPLY

4. How do the wolves demonstrate "teamwork"? **[Synthesize]**

EXTEND

5. What facts about wolves do you learn in the story? **[Science Link]**

COMPARE LITERARY WORKS

6. Which animal would make a good friend for the ghost in "The Lawyer"? Why? **[Connect]**

Guide for Responding (continued)

◆ Reading Strategy

ENVISION ACTION AND SETTING

By **envisioning** each story, you used sensory details to imagine a world and the action in it as if you were there. In "The Wounded Wolf," for example, you felt the caribou hoof "that struck . . . Roko."

1. Use sensory details to describe a scene in Dickens's story.
2. To what senses does the last paragraph of "The Wounded Wolf" appeal?
3. Use these sensory details to describe the scene.

◆ Build Vocabulary

USING THE PREFIX *in-*

Add the prefix *in-* ("no, not, without, the lack of, or the opposite of") to the first word in each phrase. Then, explain the change in meaning you've made.

1. expensive room
2. consistent reason
3. digestible food
4. efficient methods

SPELLING STRATEGY

In many words, the *shent* sound is spelled *cient:* suffi*cient.* On your paper, correct the following misspelled words.

1. profishent (skillful in doing something)
2. defishent (lacking in something)

USING THE WORD BANK

On your paper, match each Word Bank word in the first column with its lettered meaning in the second column.

1. sufficient	a. not reacting to good or bad events
2. expend	b. not making sense
3. inconsistent	c. bites with grinding teeth
4. massive	d. satisfactory; enough
5. stoic	e. large and impressive
6. gnashes	f. use up; spend

◆ Literary Focus

SETTING

Details in these stories reveal the **setting,** the place and time of the action. In "The Lawyer and the Ghost," references to the Inns of Court and London indicate the place. The narrator says the tale takes place at "night," and the fireplace suggests the fall or winter. Old furniture and the lack of a radiator hint at a time long ago.

1. Summarize the setting of "The Lawyer. . . ."
2. Find details in ". . . Wolf" that reveal the story's place and season, and the amount of time that passes.
3. Summarize the setting of ". . . Wolf."

◆ Build Grammar Skills

SIMPLE SENTENCES

A **simple sentence** contains a single independent clause:

      S   V

Weakness overcame him.

A simple sentence may have a **compound subject,** more than one subject with the same verb. It may also have a **compound verb,** more than one verb with the same subject:

Compound Subject
He and *his pack* are thin and hungry.

      Compound Verb
He *droops* his head and *stiffens* his tail.

Practice Copy each sentence on your paper. Label compound subjects or compound verbs.

1. He stops and looks.
2. The raven and the owl see Roko's signal.
3. Hooves, paws, and teeth roared over him.
4. He squints and smells the wind.
5. Roko and the other wolves call to one another.

Writing Application With five simple sentences, describe a scene from "The Wounded Wolf." Include one sentence with a compound subject and one with a compound verb.

Build Your Portfolio

 Idea Bank

Writing

1. **Annotated List** You're the stage manager of a play based on "The Lawyer. . . ." Review the story, and list the movable items and furniture you'll need, with a brief description of each.

2. **Location Report** Imagine that one of these stories will be made into a movie. Choose a location you know that would make a good setting for the picture. In a report, describe the location, and give reasons for your choice.

3. **Habitat Profile** Write a description of a wild animal's habitat—the place where it is found in nature. Describe where it hunts, sleeps, and brings up its young. As an alternative, describe the habitat of a pet. **[Science Link]**

Speaking and Listening

4. **Wolf Reunion [Group Activity]** With classmates, act out the reunion of Roko with his pack in "The Wounded Wolf." Have the wolves speak words—Roko telling what happened and the others asking questions. **[Performing Arts Link]**

5. **Storytelling** Make up and tell a funny story about a lawyer. Dickens's lawyer out-argues a ghost. Have your lawyer outwit some other challenging opponent. **[Performing Arts Link]**

Projects

6. **Illustrations of Wolf Language** Find out about the language of wolves from the story and from books about wolves. Then, draw pictures of wolves to show how they communicate with gestures. **[Science Link; Art Link]**

7. **Movie Review** Watch a movie based on a Dickens story, like *A Christmas Carol* (1951) or *Oliver Twist* (1948). Review it for classmates, describing its setting. **[Media Link; Social Studies Link]**

 Writing Mini-Lesson

Summary of a Story

A **summary** is a brief account of the story's most important events. In a summary, you show how one event leads to another. However, you leave out minor details. Write a summary of one of these stories, and notice how your memory of it improves.

Writing Skills Focus: Use Time Words

Your summary will be clearer if you **use time words** to show the order of events.
- Occurring at the same time: *as, while, meanwhile,* and *during*
- Occurring earlier: *before, prior, first,* and *earlier*
- Occurring later: *then, afterward, next,* and *later*

Prewriting Use a flowchart like this one to capture the most important events of the story.

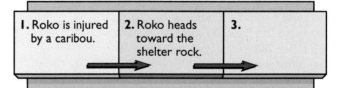

1. Roko is injured by a caribou. → 2. Roko heads toward the shelter rock. → 3.

Drafting Referring to your flowchart, summarize the most important events in your own words. Use terms like *before, while,* and *next* to indicate the order in which events occur.

Revising Compare your finished summary with your flowchart. Add missing important events, and take out minor details not in your chart. Wherever the order of events isn't clear, add a suitable time word.

◆ **Grammar Application**
Too many simple sentences in a row can create a choppy rhythm. Combine some sentences by using a compound subject or predicate.

$\mathcal{G}$uide for Reading

Meet the Authors:

Lensey Namioka (1929–   )

Namioka is a Chinese American who uses her Chinese heritage in her writing. Her novel *Who's Hu?*, the story of a Chinese girl learning the ways of Americans, is among her most popular works. The novel's heroine, Emma Hu, is a math whiz who has to battle preju- dice against girls in math.

However, Namioka con- fesses, "I don't write books primarily because I have a crusade ... I write be- cause it is fun."

THE STORY BEHIND THE STORY

Namioka's main character in "The All-American Slurp" is based on Namioka herself. Like her character, she was born in China and moved with her family to the United States as a teenager. Also like her character, she discovered big differences between Chinese and American eating habits.

Lloyd Alexander (1924–   )

Lloyd Alexander has written stories and nov- els about an imaginary kingdom called Pry- dain. Alexander found in creating this king- dom that "a writer could know and love a fantasy world as much as his real one."

Perhaps the best-known Prydain novel is *The High King* (1969), winner of a Newbery medal. "The Stone" also takes place in Prydain, where magic is part of everyday life.

◆ LITERATURE AND YOUR LIFE

CONNECT YOUR EXPERIENCE

Some pictures capture a moment of pleasure, like a photo of your favorite food or a snapshot of your friends. It's natural to want good moments to go on forever. However, it's just as natural to grow and change. These stories share insights into growth and change.

THEMATIC FOCUS: Working It Out

In each story, how do the characters deal with the problems that change brings?

◆ Background for Understanding

CULTURE

In "The All-American Slurp," Chinese coming to the United States must deal with a change in eating habits. The following are some Chinese customs concerning food that are not widely practiced in the U.S.:

- Tea is usually served during or after meals.
- Food is usually served "family style" on large platters in the center of the table.
- Food is scooped up or handled with slender sticks called chopsticks (*kuai-tzu,* "quick ones" in Mandarin Chinese).

◆ Build Vocabulary

RELATED WORDS: FORMS OF *migrate*

Some forms of the word *migrate,* "to travel from one place to another," have to do with settling in a new land. For example, *emigrated* in "The All-American Slurp" means "left one country to settle in another."

WORD BANK

Which listed word is related to *consumer,* "someone who buys or uses things"? How do you know?

emigrated
mortified
etiquette
consumption
plight
jubilation
rue
fallow

The All-American Slurp
◆ The Stone ◆

◆ Literary Focus

THEME

A story has a **theme,** a message about life. Sometimes the theme is **stated,** as when an author writes, "His experience showed that laughter is the best medicine." Often, however, the theme is **implied.** You must figure it out yourself.

To figure out the implied themes in these stories, think about the following:

- The ways in which the Lin family changes
- What Maibon learns from getting his wish

◆ Reading Strategy

MAKE INFERENCES

It's not always possible to figure out an implied theme in a single step. You have to build an understanding of the theme by **making inferences**—reaching conclusions based on evidence. Such evidence may include unusual events, as well as characters' words, actions, and reactions.

Use a flowchart like the one below to note important details, think about them, and make an inference (a sample is filled in):

Story: "The All-American Slurp"

Story Detail	My Thoughts	My Inference
The Lins sit "stiffly in a row" on the Gleasons' couch.	People sit stiffly when they feel nervous.	New to the U.S., the Lins are afraid of making a mistake.

The All-American Slurp

Lensey Namioka

"As any respectable Chinese knows, the correct way to eat your soup is to slurp."

The first time our family was invited out to dinner in America, we disgraced ourselves while eating celery. We had emigrated to this country from China, and during our early days here we had a hard time with American table manners.

In China we never ate celery raw, or any other kind of vegetable raw. We always had to disinfect the vegetables in boiling water first. When we were presented with our first relish tray, the raw celery caught us unprepared.

We had been invited to dinner by our neighbors, the Gleasons. After arriving at the house, we shook hands with our hosts and packed ourselves into a sofa. As our family of four sat stiffly in a row, my younger brother and I stole glances at our parents for a clue as to what to do next.

Mrs. Gleason offered the relish tray to Mother. The tray looked pretty, with its tiny red radishes, curly sticks of carrots, and long, slender stalks of pale green celery. "Do try some of the celery, Mrs. Lin," she said. "It's from a local farmer, and it's sweet."

Mother picked up one of the green stalks, and Father followed suit. Then I picked up a stalk, and my brother did too. So there we sat, each with a stalk of celery in our right hand.

Mrs. Gleason kept smiling. "Would you like to try some of the dip, Mrs. Lin? It's my own recipe: sour cream and onion flakes, with a dash of Tabasco sauce."

Most Chinese don't care for dairy products, and in those days I wasn't even ready to drink fresh milk. Sour cream sounded perfectly revolting. Our family shook our heads in unison.

◆ Build Vocabulary

emigrated (em′ i grāt′ id) v.: Left one country to settle in another

mortified (môrt′ ə fīd′) adj.: Ashamed; extremely embarrassed

Mrs. Gleason went off with the relish tray to the other guests, and we carefully watched to see what they did. Everyone seemed to eat the raw vegetables quite happily.

Mother took a bite of her celery. *Crunch.* "It's not bad!" she whispered.

Father took a bite of his celery. *Crunch.* "Yes, it is good," he said, looking surprised.

I took a bite, and then my brother. *Crunch, crunch.* It was more than good; it was delicious. Raw celery has a slight sparkle, a zingy taste that you don't get in cooked celery. When Mrs. Gleason came around with the relish tray, we each took another stalk of celery, except my brother. He took two.

There was only one problem: long strings ran through the length of the stalk, and they got caught in my teeth. When I help my mother in the kitchen, I always pull the string out before slicing celery.

I pulled the strings out of my stalk. *Z-z-zip, z-z-zip.* My brother followed suit. *Z-z-zip, z-z-zip, z-z-zip.* To my left, my parents were taking care of their own stalks. *Z-z-zip, z-z-zip, z-z-zip.*

Suddenly I realized that there was dead silence except for our zipping. Looking up, I saw that the eyes of everyone in the room were on our family. Mr. and Mrs. Gleason, their daughter Meg, who was my friend, and their neighbors the Badels—they were all staring at us as we busily pulled the strings of our celery.

That wasn't the end of it. Mrs. Gleason announced that dinner was served and invited us to the dining table. It was lavishly covered with platters of food, but we couldn't see any chairs around the table. So we helpfully carried over some dining chairs and sat down. All the other guests just stood there.

Mrs. Gleason bent down and whispered to us, "This is a buffet dinner. You help yourselves to some food and eat it in the living room."

Our family beat a retreat back to the sofa as

◆ **Reading Strategy**
What can you infer from this reaction of the other guests to the Lins? Explain.

if chased by enemy soldiers. For the rest of the evening, too <u>mortified</u> to go back to the dining table, I nursed a bit of potato salad on my plate.

Next day Meg and I got on the school bus together. I wasn't sure how she would feel about me after the spectacle our family made at the party. But she was just the same as usual, and the only reference she made to the party was, "Hope you and your folks got enough to eat last night. You certainly didn't take very much. Mom never tries to figure out how much food to prepare. She just puts everything on the table and hopes for the best."

I began to relax. The Gleasons' dinner party wasn't so different from a Chinese meal after all. My mother also puts everything on the table and hopes for the best.

Meg was the first friend I had made after we came to America. I eventually got acquainted with a few other kids in school, but Meg was still the only real friend I had.

My brother didn't have any problems making friends. He spent all his time with some boys who were teaching him baseball, and in no time he could speak English much faster than I could—not better, but faster.

I worried more about making mistakes, and I spoke carefully, making sure I could say everything right before opening my mouth. At least I had a better accent than my parents, who never really got rid of their Chinese accent, even years later. My parents had both studied English in school before coming to America, but what they had studied was mostly written English, not spoken.

Father's approach to English was a scientific one. Since Chinese verbs have no tense, he was fascinated by the way English verbs changed form according to whether they were in the present, past imperfect, perfect, pluperfect,[1] future, or future perfect tense. He was always making diagrams of verbs and their inflections,[2] and he looked for opportunities to show off his mastery of the pluperfect and future perfect tenses, his two favorites. "I shall have finished my project by Monday," he would say smugly.[3]

Mother's approach was to memorize lists of polite phrases that would cover all possible social situations. She was constantly muttering things like "I'm fine, thank you. And you?" Once she accidentally stepped on someone's foot, and hurriedly blurted, "Oh, that's quite all right!" Embarrassed by her slip, she resolved to do better next time. So when someone stepped on *her* foot, she cried, "You're welcome!"

In our own different ways, we made progress in learning English. But I had another worry, and that was my appearance. My brother didn't have to worry, since Mother bought him blue jeans for school, and he

dressed like all the other boys. But she insisted that girls had to wear skirts. By the time she saw that Meg and the other girls were wearing jeans, it was too late. My school clothes were bought already, and we didn't have money left to buy new outfits for me. We had too many other things to buy first, like furniture, pots, and pans.

The first time I visited Meg's house, she took me upstairs to her room, and I wound up trying on her clothes. We were pretty much the same size, since Meg was shorter and thinner than average. Maybe that's how we became friends in the first place. Wearing Meg's jeans and T-shirt, I looked at myself in the mirror. I could almost pass for an American—from the back, anyway. At least the kids in school wouldn't stop and stare at me in my white blouse and navy blue skirt that went a couple of inches below the knees.

When Meg came to my house, I invited her to try on my Chinese dresses, the ones with a high collar and slits up the sides. Meg's eyes were bright as she looked at herself in the mirror. She struck several sultry poses, and we nearly fell over laughing.

The dinner party at the Gleasons' didn't stop my growing friendship with Meg. Things were getting better for me in other ways too. Mother finally bought me some jeans at the end of the month, when Father got his paycheck. She wasn't in any hurry about buying them at first, until I worked on her. This is

◆ **Literature and Your Life**
What kinds of clothes do students wear in your school?

---

1. pluperfect (plōō′ pʉr′ fikt) *adj.*: The past perfect tense of verbs in English.
2. inflections (in flek′ shən) *n.*: The changes in the forms of words to show different tenses.
3. smugly (smug′ lē) *adv.*: In a way that shows satisfaction with oneself.

Stories

what I did. Since we didn't have a car in those days, I often ran down to the neighborhood store to pick up things for her. The groceries cost less at a big supermarket, but the closest one was many blocks away. One day, when she ran out of flour, I offered to borrow a bike from our neighbor's son and buy a ten-pound bag of flour at the supermarket. I mounted the boy's bike and waved to Mother. "I'll be back in five minutes!"

Before I started pedaling, I heard her voice behind me. "You can't go out in public like that! People can see all the way up to your thighs!"

"I'm sorry," I said innocently. "I thought you were in a hurry to get the flour." For dinner we were going to have pot-stickers (fried Chinese dumplings), and we needed a lot of flour.

"Couldn't you borrow a girl's bicycle?" complained Mother. "That way your skirt won't be pushed up."

"There aren't too many of those around," I said. "Almost all the girls wear jeans while riding a bike, so they don't see any point buying a girl's bike."

We didn't eat pot-stickers that evening, and Mother was thoughtful. Next day we took the bus downtown and she bought me a pair of jeans. In the same week, my brother made the baseball team of his junior high school, Father started taking driving lessons, and Mother discovered rummage sales.

We soon got all the furniture we needed, plus a dart board and a 1,000-piece jigsaw puzzle (fourteen hours later, we discovered that it was a 999-piece jigsaw puzzle). There was hope that the Lins might become a normal American family after all.

Then came our dinner at the Lakeview restaurant.

The Lakeview was an expensive restaurant, one of those places where a headwaiter dressed in tails conducted you to your seat, and the only light came from candles and flaming desserts. In one corner of the room a lady harpist played tinkling melodies.

Father wanted to celebrate, because he had just been promoted. He worked for an electronics company, and after his English started improving, his superiors decided to appoint him to a position more suited to his training. The promotion not only brought a higher salary but was also a tremendous boost to his pride.

Up to then we had eaten only in Chinese restaurants. Although my brother and I were becoming fond of hamburgers, my parents didn't care much for western food, other than chow mein.[4] But this was a special occasion, and Father asked his coworkers to recommend a really elegant restaurant. So there we were at the Lakeview, stumbling after the headwaiter in the murky dining room.

At our table we were handed our menus, and they were so big that to read mine I almost had to stand up again. But why bother? It was mostly in French, anyway.

Father, being an engineer, was always

▲ **Critical Viewing**
Name two details suggesting that, like the soup in the story, the soup in the picture is being served in a restaurant. **[Analyze]**

---

4. **chow mein** (chou´ mān´) *n*.: Thick stew of meat, celery, and Chinese vegetables.

systematic.[5] He took out a pocket French dictionary. "They told me that most of the items would be in French, so I came prepared." He even had a pocket flashlight, the size of a marking pen. While Mother held the flashlight over the menu, he looked up the items that were in French.

"*Pâté en croûte*,"[6] he muttered. "Let's see . . . *pâté* is paste . . . *croûte* is crust . . . hmm . . . a paste in crust."

The waiter stood looking patient. I squirmed and died at least fifty times.

At long last Father gave up. "Why don't we just order four complete dinners at random?" he suggested.

"Isn't that risky?" asked Mother. "The French eat some rather peculiar things, I've heard."

"A Chinese can eat anything a Frenchman can eat," Father declared.

> **◆ Reading Strategy**
> What does this remark suggest about Father's attitudes about fitting in with the ways of another country? Explain.

The soup arrived in a plate. How do you get soup up from a plate? I glanced at the other diners, but the ones at the nearby tables were not on their soup course, while the more distant ones were invisible in the darkness.

Fortunately my parents had studied books on western etiquette before they came to America. "Tilt your plate," whispered my mother. "It's easier to spoon the soup up that way."

She was right. Tilting the plate did the trick. But the etiquette book didn't say anything about what you did after the soup reached your lips. As any respectable Chinese knows, the correct way to eat your soup is to slurp. This helps to cool the liquid and prevent you from burning your lips. It also shows your appreciation.

We showed our appreciation. *Shloop,* went my father. *Shloop* went my mother. *Shloop, shloop,* went my brother, who was the hungriest.

The lady harpist stopped playing to take a rest. And in the silence, our family's consumption of soup suddenly seemed unnaturally loud. You know how it sounds on a rocky beach when the tide goes out and the water drains from all those little pools? They go *shloop, shloop, shloop.* That was the Lin family, eating soup.

At the next table a waiter was pouring wine. When a large *shloop* reached him, he froze. The bottle continued to pour, and red wine flooded the tabletop and into the lap of a customer. Even the customer didn't notice anything at first, being also hypnotized by the *shloop, shloop, shloop.*

It was too much. "I need to go to the toilet," I mumbled, jumping to my feet. A waiter, sensing my urgency, quickly directed me to the ladies' room.

I splashed cold water on my burning face, and as I dried myself with a paper towel, I stared into the mirror. In this perfumed ladies' room, with its pink-and-silver wallpaper and marbled sinks, I looked completely out of place. What was I doing here? What was our family doing in the Lakeview restaurant? In America?

The door to the ladies' room opened. A

---

5. **systematic** (sis´ tə mat´ ik) *adj.*: Orderly.
6. ***pâté en croûte*** (pä tā´ än kro͞ot)

◆ Build Vocabulary

etiquette (et´ i ket) *n.*: Acceptable social manners

consumption (kən sump´ shen) *n.*: Eating; drinking; using up

woman came in and glanced curiously at me. I retreated into one of the toilet cubicles and latched the door.

Time passed—maybe half an hour, maybe an hour. Then I heard the door open again, and my mother's voice. "Are you in there? You're not sick, are you?"

There was real concern in her voice. A girl can't leave her family just because they slurp their soup. Besides, the toilet cubicle had a few drawbacks as a permanent residence. "I'm all right," I said, undoing the latch.

Mother didn't tell me how the rest of the dinner went, and I didn't want to know. In the weeks following, I managed to push the whole thing into the back of my mind, where it jumped out at me only a few times a day. Even now, I turn hot all over when I think of the Lakeview restaurant.

But by the time we had been in this country for three months, our family was definitely making progress toward becoming Americanized. I remember my parents' first PTA meeting. Father wore a neat suit and tie, and Mother put on her first pair of high heels. She stumbled only once. They met my homeroom teacher and beamed as she told them that I would make honor roll soon at the rate I was going. Of course Chinese etiquette forced Father to say that I was a very stupid girl and Mother to protest that the teacher was showing favoritism toward me. But I could tell they were both very proud.

◆ **Literary Focus**
How have the Lins changed, and how have they remained the same?

The day came when my parents announced that they wanted to give a dinner party. We had invited Chinese friends to eat with

▶ **Critical Viewing**
Compare the way in which you would like these vegetables prepared with the way in which the Lins would. [**Compare and Contrast**]

us before, but this dinner was going to be different. In addition to a Chinese-American family, we were going to invite the Gleasons.

"Gee, I can hardly wait to have dinner at your house," Meg said to me. "I just *love* Chinese food."

That was a relief. Mother was a good cook, but I wasn't sure if people who ate sour cream would also eat chicken gizzards stewed in soy sauce.

Mother decided not to take a chance with chicken gizzards. Since we had western guests, she set the table with large dinner plates, which we never used in Chinese meals. In fact we didn't use individual plates at all, but picked up food from the platters in the middle of the table and brought it directly to our rice bowls. Following the practice of Chinese-American restaurants, Mother also placed large serving spoons on the platters.

The dinner started well. Mrs. Gleason exclaimed at the beautifully arranged dishes of food: the colorful candied fruit in the sweet-and-sour pork dish, the noodle-thin shreds of chicken meat stir-fried with tiny peas, and the glistening pink prawns in a ginger sauce.

At first I was too busy enjoying my food to notice how the guests were doing. But soon I remembered my duties. Sometimes guests were too polite to help themselves and you had to serve them with more food.

I glanced at Meg, to see if she needed more food, and my eyes nearly popped out at the sight of her plate. It was piled with food: the sweet-and-sour meat pushed right against the chicken shreds, and the chicken sauce ran into the prawns. She had been taking food from a second dish before she finished eating her helping from the first!

Horrified, I turned to look at Mrs. Gleason. She was dumping rice out of her bowl and putting it on her dinner plate. Then she ladled prawns and gravy on top of the rice and mixed everything together, the way you mix sand, gravel, and cement to make concrete.

I couldn't bear to look any longer, and I turned to Mr. Gleason. He was chasing a pea around his plate. Several times he got it to the edge, but when he tried to pick it up with his chopsticks, it rolled back toward the center of the plate again. Finally he put down his chopsticks and picked up the pea with his fingers. He really did! A grown man!

All of us, our family and the Chinese guests, stopped eating to watch the activities of the Gleasons. I wanted to giggle. Then I caught my mother's eyes on me. She frowned and shook her head slightly, and I understood the message: the Gleasons were not used to Chinese ways, and they were just coping the best they could. For some reason I thought of celery strings.

When the main courses were finished, Mother brought out a platter of fruit. "I hope you weren't expecting a sweet dessert," she said. "Since the Chinese don't eat dessert, I didn't think to prepare any."

"Oh, I couldn't possibly eat dessert!" cried Mrs. Gleason. "I'm simply stuffed!"

Meg had different ideas. When the table was cleared, she announced that she and I were going for a walk. "I don't know about you, but I feel like dessert," she told me, when we were outside. "Come on, there's a Dairy Queen down the street. I could use a big chocolate milkshake!"

Although I didn't really want anything more to eat, I insisted on paying for the milkshakes. After all, I was still hostess.

Meg got her large chocolate milkshake and I had a small one. Even so, she was finishing hers while I was only half done. Toward the end she pulled hard on her straws and went *shloop, shloop.*

"Do you always slurp when you eat a milkshake?" I asked, before I could stop myself.

Meg grinned. "Sure. All Americans slurp."

◆ **Literary Focus**
What is the narrator learning about differences and similarities between Chinese culture and American culture?

◀ **Critical Viewing** What details of American culture are shown in this picture? **[Analyze]**

Beyond Literature

Guide for Responding

◆ LITERATURE AND YOUR LIFE

Reader's Response What advice would you give the narrator about adjusting to life in the United States? Why?

Thematic Focus As the Lins adapt to their new life, how many of their old customs will they keep? Explain.

Group Activity With several classmates, brainstorm for customs of serving and eating food in your region.

☑ Check Your Comprehension

1. Describe the Lins' experience at the Gleasons' dinner party.
2. In what different ways do the narrator's brother, father, and mother adjust to American life?
3. How does the narrator convince her mother to buy jeans?
4. How do the Lins embarrass themselves at a restaurant?
5. Summarize what happens at the Lins' dinner party.

◆ Critical Thinking

INTERPRET
1. Describe the way in which each family member learns English. **[Analyze]**
2. What do their various ways of learning English reveal about each? **[Infer]**
3. How are the Gleasons' actions at the Lins' dinner party similar to the Lins' actions at the Gleasons' party? **[Connect]**
4. Why does Meg's remark about slurping probably seem funny and reassuring to the narrator? **[Draw Conclusions]**

EVALUATE
5. Do you think the narrator has a good sense of humor? Explain. **[Evaluate]**

EXTEND
6. What can you learn about Chinese foods and eating habits from this story? **[Social Studies Link]**
7. What agencies or services are available in your area to help recent immigrants? **[Community Link]**

The Stone

LLOYD ALEXANDER

There was a cottager named Maibon, and one day he was driving down the road in his horse and cart when he saw an old man hobbling along, so frail and feeble he doubted the poor soul could go many more steps. Though Maibon offered to take him in the cart, the old man refused; and Maibon went his way home, shaking his head over such a pitiful sight, and said to his wife, Modrona:

"Ah, ah, what a sorry thing it is to have your bones creaking and cracking, and dim eyes, and dull wits. When I think this might come to me, too! A fine, strong-armed, sturdy-legged fellow like me? One day to go tottering, and have his teeth rattling in his head, and

live on porridge, like a baby? There's no fate worse in all the world."

"There is," answered Modrona, "and that would be to have neither teeth nor porridge. Get on with you, Maibon, and stop borrowing trouble. Hoe your field or you'll have no crop to harvest, and no food for you, nor me, nor the little ones."

Sighing and grumbling, Maibon did as his wife bade him. Although the day was fair and cloudless, he took no pleasure in it. His ax-blade was notched, the wooden handle splintery; his saw had lost its edge; and his hoe, once shining new, had begun to rust. None of his tools, it seemed to him, cut or chopped or

Walk in the Country, Javran

delved[1] as well as they once had done.

"They're as worn out as that old codger I saw on the road," Maibon said to himself. He squinted up at the sky. "Even the sun isn't as bright as it used to be, and doesn't warm me half as well. It's gone threadbare as my cloak. And no wonder, for it's been there longer than I can re-member. Come to think of it, the moon's been looking a little wilted around the edges, too.

"As for me," went on Maibon, in dismay, "I'm in even a worse state. My appetite's faded, especially after meals. Mornings, when I wake, I can hardly keep myself from yawning. And at night, when I go to bed, my eyes are so heavy I can't hold them open. If that's the way things are now, the older I grow, the worse it will be!"

In the midst of his complaining, Maibon glimpsed something bouncing and tossing back and forth beside a fallen tree in a corner of the field. Wondering if one of his piglets had squeezed out of the sty and gone rooting for acorns, Maibon hurried across the turf. Then he dropped his ax and gaped in astonishment.

◆ **Reading Strategy**
What can you infer about Maibon's feelings about grow-ing old? Explain.

There, struggling to free his leg which had been caught under the log, lay a short, thick-set figure: a dwarf with red hair bristling in all directions beneath his round, close-fitting leather cap. At the sight of Maibon, the dwarf squeezed shut his bright red eyes and began holding his breath. After a moment, the dwarf's face went redder than his hair; his cheeks puffed out and soon turned purple. Then he opened one eye and blinked rapidly at Maibon, who was staring at him, speechless.

"What," snapped the dwarf, "you can still see me?"

1. **delved** (delvd) *v.*: Dug.

"That I can," replied Maibon, more than ever puzzled, "and I can see very well you've got yourself tight as a wedge under that log, and all your kicking only makes it worse."

At this, the dwarf blew out his breath and shook his fists. "I can't do it!" he shouted. "No matter how I try! I can't make myself invisible! Everyone in my family can disappear—Poof! Gone! Vanished! But not me! Not Doli! Believe me, if I could have done, you never would have found me in such a plight. Worse luck! Well, come on. Don't stand there goggling like an id-iot. Help me get loose!"

At this sharp command, Maibon began tug-ging and heaving at the log. Then he stopped, wrinkled his brow, and scratched his head, saying:

"Well, now, just a moment, friend. The way you look, and all your talk about turning yourself invisible—I'm thinking you might be one of the Fair Folk."

"Oh, clever!" Doli retorted. "Oh, brilliant! Great clodhopper! Giant beanpole! Of course I am! What else! Enough gabbling. Get a move on. My leg's going to sleep."

"If a man does the Fair Folk a good turn," cried Maibon, his excitement growing, "it's told they must do one for him."

"I knew sooner or later you'd come round to that," grumbled the dwarf. "That's the way of it with you ham-handed, heavy-footed oafs. Time was, you humans got along well with us. But nowadays, you no sooner see a Fair Folk than it's grab, grab, grab! Gobble, gobble, gobble! Grant my wish! Give me this, give me that! As if we had nothing better to do!

"Yes, I'll give you a favor," Doli went on. "That's the rule, I'm obliged to. Now, get on with it."

Hearing this, Maibon pulled and pried and chopped away at the log as fast as he could, and soon freed the dwarf.

◆ **Build Vocabulary**

plight (plīt) *n.*: Awkward, sad, or dangerous situation

Doli heaved a sigh of relief, rubbed his shin, and cocked a red eye at Maibon, saying:

◆ **Literature and Your Life**

What would you wish for if you were Maibon? Why?

"All right. You've done your work, you'll have your reward. What do you want? Gold, I suppose. That's the usual. Jewels? Fine clothes? Take my advice, go for something practical. A hazelwood twig to help you find water if your well ever goes dry? An ax that never needs sharpening? A cook pot always brimming with food?"

"None of those!" cried Maibon. He bent down to the dwarf and whispered eagerly, "But I've heard tell that you Fair Folk have magic stones that can keep a man young forever. That's what I want. I claim one for my reward."

Doli snorted. "I might have known you'd pick something like that. As to be expected, you humans have it all muddled. There's nothing can make a man young again. That's even beyond the best of our skills. Those stones you're babbling about? Well, yes, there are such things. But greatly overrated. All they'll do is keep you from growing any older."

"Just as good!" Maibon exclaimed. "I want no more than that!"

Doli hesitated and frowned. "Ah—between the two of us, take the cook pot. Better all around. Those stones—we'd sooner not give them away. There's a difficulty—"

"Because you'd rather keep them for yourselves," Maibon broke in. "No, no, you shan't cheat me of my due. Don't put me off with excuses. I told you what I want, and that's what I'll have. Come, hand it over and not another word."

Doli shrugged and opened a leather pouch that hung from his belt. He spilled a number of brightly colored pebbles into his palm, picked out one of the larger stones, and handed it to Maibon. The dwarf then jumped up, took to his heels, raced across the field, and disappeared into a thicket.

Laughing and crowing over his good fortune and his cleverness, Maibon hurried back to the cottage. There, he told his wife what had happened, and showed her the stone he had claimed from the Fair Folk.

"As I am now, so I'll always be!" Maibon declared, flexing his arms and thumping his chest. "A fine figure of a man! Oho, no gray beard and wrinkled brow for me!"

Instead of sharing her husband's jubilation, Modrona flung up her hands and burst out:

"Maibon, you're a greater fool than ever I supposed! And selfish into the bargain! You've turned down treasures! You didn't even ask that dwarf for so much as new jackets for the children! Nor a new apron for me! You could have had the roof mended. Or the walls plastered. No, a stone is what you ask for! A bit of rock no better than you'll dig up in the cow pasture!"

Crestfallen[2] and sheepish, Maibon began thinking his wife was right, and the dwarf had indeed given him no more than a common field stone.

"Eh, well, it's true," he stammered, "I feel no different than I did this morning, no better nor worse, but every way the same. That redheaded little wretch! He'll rue the day if I ever find him again!"

So saying, Maibon threw the stone into the fireplace. That night he grumbled his way to bed, dreaming revenge on the dishonest dwarf.

Next morning, after a restless night, he yawned, rubbed his eyes, and scratched his chin. Then he sat bolt upright in bed, patting his cheeks in amazement.

"My beard!" he cried, tumbling out and hurrying to tell his wife. "It hasn't grown! Not by a hair! Can it be the dwarf didn't cheat me after all?"

"Don't talk to me about beards," declared his wife as Maibon went to the fireplace,

---

2. **crestfallen** (krest′ fôl′ ən) *adj.*: Made sad or humble; disheartened.

◆ **Build Vocabulary**

jubilation (jŏō′ bə lā′ shen) *n.*: Great joy; triumph

rue (rōō) *v.*: Regret

Harvesting the Fruit Crop, Javran

▲ **Critical Viewing** Find three details that suggest the people in the painting live a life similar to that of Maibon and his wife. **[Support]**

picked out the stone, and clutched it safely in both hands. "There's trouble enough in the chicken roost. Those eggs should have hatched by now, but the hen is still brooding on her nest."

"Let the chickens worry about that," answered Maibon. "Wife, don't you see what a grand thing's happened to me? I'm not a minute older than I was yesterday. Bless that generous-hearted dwarf!"

"Let me lay hands on him and I'll bless him," retorted Modrona. "That's all well and good for you. But what of me? You'll stay as you are, but I'll turn old and gray, and worn and wrinkled, and go doddering into my grave! And what of our little ones? They'll grow up and have children of their own. And grandchildren, and great-grandchildren.

◆ **Reading Strategy**
What inference can you make about the stone's effects based on these details?

And you, younger than any of them. What a foolish sight you'll be!"

But Maibon, gleeful over his good luck, paid his wife no heed, and only tucked the stone deeper into his pocket. Next day, however, the eggs had still not hatched.

"And the cow!" Modrona cried. "She's long past due to calve, and no sign of a young one ready to be born!"

"Don't bother me with cows and chickens," replied Maibon. "They'll all come right, in time. As for time, I've got all the time in the world!"

Having no appetite for breakfast, Maibon went out into the field. Of all the seeds he had sown there, however, he was surprised to see not one had sprouted. The field, which by now should have been covered with green shoots, lay bare and empty.

"Eh, things do seem a little late these days," Maibon said to himself. "Well, no hurry. It's that much less for me to do. The wheat isn't growing, but neither are the weeds."

Some days went by and still the eggs had not hatched, the cow had not calved, the wheat had not sprouted. And now Maibon saw that his apple tree showed no sign of even the smallest, greenest fruit.

"Maibon, it's the fault of that stone!" wailed his wife. "Get rid of the thing!"

"Nonsense," replied Maibon "The season's slow, that's all."

Nevertheless, his wife kept at him and kept at him so much that Maibon at last, and very reluctantly, threw the stone out the cottage window. Not too far, though, for he had it in the back of his mind to go later and find it again.

Next morning he had no need to go looking for it, for there was the stone sitting on the window ledge.

"You see?" said Maibon to his wife. "Here it is back again. So, it's a gift meant for me to keep."

"Maibon!" cried his wife. "Will you get rid of it! We've had nothing but trouble since you brought it into the house. Now the baby's fretting and fuming. Teething, poor little thing. But not a tooth to be seen! Maibon, that stone's bad luck and I want no part of it!"

Protesting it was none of his doing that the stone had come back, Maibon carried it into the vegetable patch. He dug a hole, not a very deep one, and put the stone into it.

Next day, there was the stone above ground, winking and glittering.

"Maibon!" cried his wife. "Once and for all, if you care for your family, get rid of that cursed thing!"

Seeing no other way to keep peace in the household, Maibon regretfully and unwillingly took the stone and threw it down the well, where it splashed into the water and sank from sight.

But that night, while he was trying vainly to sleep, there came such a rattling and clattering that Maibon clapped his hands over his ears, jumped out of bed, and went stumbling into the yard. At the well, the bucket was jiggling back and forth and up and down at the end of the rope; and in the bottom of the bucket was the stone.

Now Maibon began to be truly distressed, not only for the toothless baby, the calfless cow, the fruitless tree, and the hen sitting desperately on her eggs, but for himself as well.

"Nothing's moving along as it should," he groaned. "I can't tell one day from another. Nothing changes, there's nothing to look forward to, nothing to show for my work. Why sow if the seeds don't sprout? Why plant if there's never a harvest? Why eat if I don't get hungry? Why go to bed at night, or get up in the morning, or do anything at all? And the way it looks, so it will stay for ever and ever! I'll shrivel from boredom if nothing else!"

"Maibon," pleaded his wife, "for all our sakes, destroy the dreadful thing!"

Maibon tried now to pound the stone to dust with his heaviest mallet; but he could not so much as knock a chip from it. He put it against his grindstone without so much as scratching it. He set it on his anvil and belabored it with hammer and tongs, all to no avail.

At last he decided to bury the stone again, this time deeper than before. Picking up his shovel, he hurried to the field. But he suddenly halted and the shovel dropped from his hands. There, sitting cross-legged on a stump, was the dwarf.

"You!" shouted Maibon, shaking his fist. "Cheat! Villain! Trickster! I did you a good turn, and see how you've repaid it!"

The dwarf blinked at the furious Maibon. "You mortals are an ungrateful crew. I gave you what you wanted."

"You should have warned me!" burst out Maibon.

"I did," Doli snapped back. "You wouldn't listen. No, you yapped and yammered, bound to have your way. I told you we didn't like to give away those stones. When you mortals get hold of one, you stay just as you are—but so does everything around you. Before you know it, you're mired in time like a rock in the mud. You take my advice. Get rid of that stone as fast as you can."

"What do you think I've been trying to do?" blurted Maibon. "I've buried it, thrown it down the well, pounded it with a hammer—it keeps coming back to me!"

"That's because you really didn't want to give it up," Doli said. "In the back of your mind and the bottom of your heart, you didn't want to change along with the rest of the world. So long as you feel that way, the stone is yours."

"No, no!" cried Maibon. "I want no more of it. Whatever may happen, let it happen. That's better than nothing happening at all. I've had my share of being young, I'll take my share of being old. And when I come to the end of my days, at least I can say I've lived each one of them."

"If you mean that," answered Doli, "toss the stone onto the ground, right there at the stump. Then get home and be about your business."

Maibon flung down the stone, spun around, and set off as fast as he could. When he dared at last to glance back over his shoulder, fearful the stone might be bouncing along at his heels, he saw no sign of it, nor of the redheaded dwarf.

Maibon gave a joyful cry, for at that same instant the <u>fallow</u> field was covered with green blades of wheat, the branches of the apple tree bent to the ground, so laden they were with fruit. He ran to the cottage, threw his arms around his wife and children, and told them the good news. The hen hatched her chicks, the cow bore her calf. And Maibon laughed with glee when he saw the first tooth in the baby's mouth.

Never again did Maibon meet any of the Fair Folk, and he was just as glad of it. He and his wife and children and grandchildren lived many years, and Maibon was proud of his white hair and long beard as he had been of his sturdy arms and legs.

"Stones are all right, in their way," said Maibon. "But the trouble with them is, they don't grow."

> ◆ **Literary Focus**
> What has Maibon learned from his experience with the stone?

◆ **Build Vocabulary**

fallow (fal´ ō) *adj.*: Inactive; unproductive

Guide for Responding

◆ **LITERATURE AND YOUR LIFE**

Reader's Response Would you have given up the stone? Explain.

Thematic Focus Does Modrona help Maibon solve the problem created by the stone? Explain your answer.

Journal Writing In your journal, explain whether or not the story changed your mind about the benefits of staying young forever.

☑ **Check Your Comprehension**

1. Describe how Maibon gets the stone.
2. What problems does the stone create?
3. How does Modrona feel about the stone?
4. Why can't Maibon get rid of the stone?
5. How does he feel when the stone is gone?

◆ **Critical Thinking**

INTERPRET

1. Why does Maibon choose the stone over the other gifts that Doli suggests? **[Infer]**
2. Why does he say the stone will make him "shrivel from boredom"? **[Analyze]**
3. How does the stone change his feelings about growing old? **[Draw Conclusions]**

APPLY

4. Do most people fear growing old? Why or why not? **[Speculate]**

COMPARE LITERARY WORKS

5. If the narrator of "The All-American Slurp" could ask Doli for a magical gift, what would it be? Explain. **[Hypothesize]**

Guide for Responding (continued)

◆ Reading Strategy

MAKE INFERENCES

Making inferences, reaching conclusions based on evidence, helps you understand stories. For example, Maibon's reaction to the old man in "The Stone" may have led you to infer that he fears aging.

1. What can you infer about Maibon from his relief at not meeting any more Fair Folk? Explain.
2. In "The All-American Slurp," what can you infer about the narrator from her way of getting jeans?

◆ Build Vocabulary

USING FORMS OF *migrate*

These sentences use words related to *migrate* ("travel"). On your paper, explain the meaning of each italicized word.

1. The Lins *emigrated* from their native country, China.
2. They *immigrated* to their new home, the United States.
3. Here, they were known as recent *immigrants*.

SPELLING STRATEGY

The *k* sound can be spelled *qu,* as in *plaque* and *etiquette.* Select the words that illustrate this rule:

1. cost 2. racquet 3. ache 4. kin 5. physique

USING THE WORD BANK

On your paper, answer each question true or false. Then, explain your answer.

1. People settle in the country from which they *emigrated.*
2. You don't want to repeat an experience that *mortified* you.
3. Different countries have different rules of *etiquette.*
4. Your food *consumption* affects your weight.
5. A *plight* is something you'd want to get into.
6. Winning a prize inspires people with *jubilation.*
7. A person would *rue* a great achievement.
8. A *fallow* field is ready to be harvested.

◆ Literary Focus

THEME

These stories have **themes,** or insights into life. Their themes are suggested or **implied,** rather than **stated** directly. Maibon hints at the theme of "The Stone" when he says, "Whatever may happen, let it happen."

1. Explain how "The All-American Slurp" shows this theme: Different cultures have different customs, but all people have similar feelings and needs.
2. Review the paragraph on p. 531 that begins "No, no!" Then, state what "The Stone" implies about change.

◆ Build Grammar Skills

COMPOUND SENTENCES

A **compound sentence** is made of two or more independent clauses. These clauses may be joined by a coordinating conjunction: *and, but, for, or, yet,* or *so.* In these examples, independent clauses are underlined and coordinating conjunctions are italicized:

Mother picked up one of the green stalks, *and* Father followed suit.

It was lavishly covered with platters of food, *but* we couldn't see any chairs around the table.

Practice Explain which sentences are compound sentences. Then, identify the independent clauses and coordinating conjunctions in each.

1. The old man refused, and Maibon went home.
2. Maibon cried out, for the field was covered with wheat.
3. During our first months, we had a hard time with manners.
4. The table was covered, but we couldn't see chairs around it.
5. In China we never ate celery or any other kind of vegetable raw.

Writing Application Write three compound sentences decribing American table manners.

Build Your Portfolio

 ## Idea Bank

Writing

1. **Response to a Theme** Imagine that, like Maibon in "The Stone," you could stop growing older, but that everything else would still grow. List reasons for accepting or refusing this gift.

2. **Guide to School Life** Write a guide to school life for students who are new to the country. Include tips for fitting in with others.

3. **Inference About a Theme** Many fairy tales show the problems that come with getting a magical wish. Write a paragraph explaining what inference you make from the existence of so many similar warnings.

Speaking and Listening

4. **Debate [Group Activity]** Form two teams to debate this statement: Immigrants should give up their customs and adopt those of their new country. **[Social Studies Link]**

5. **Readers Theatre [Group Activity]** With a few classmates, give a dramatic reading of "The Stone." Decide who will speak the part of each character and who will narrate. As you read, let your voice and gestures express the feelings suggested in the text. **[Performing Arts Link]**

Projects

6. **Illustrated Menu** Prepare a menu that describes and illustrates several Chinese dishes. Add notes showing how each dish follows rules called for by Chinese custom—for example, the way the food is prepared or served. **[Social Studies Link; Art Link]**

7. **Mathematics Report** "The Stone" concerns human aging. Report to your class on the mathematics of growth: how many cells in a body, how often they change in a lifetime, and similar facts. **[Math Link]**

 ## Writing Mini-Lesson

Story Suggestion

Lively stories like these might give you ideas for a story of your own. Write a suggestion for such a story. Briefly describe the setting, the characters, and the problems the characters face. Then, summarize the events of the story.

Writing Skills Focus: Identify the Central Problem

Even fascinating characters in a fascinating setting are boring if all they do is stand around. To hook readers, invent a **central problem** for characters to solve or a challenge for them to meet. Here are examples of possible central problems:

- Learning how to climb a mountain
- Earning a place on a team
- Doing better in school

Prewriting Use a story chart like the one below to gather details:

Character Profiles	Problem	Plot Summary	Setting
___	___	___	___
___	___	___	___
___	___	___	___

Drafting Refer to your story chart as you write. Remember that you are proposing a story idea, not telling a story. Just briefly note the main events.

Revising Be sure you have clearly explained the central problem that your characters face. Also, eliminate any unnecessary details.

◆ **Grammar Application**

If your draft has too many simple sentences in a row, combine some to make compound sentences.

Writing Process Workshop

A **short story** is a work of fiction presenting a sequence of events. As you read, these events may rush along like the hunting wolves in "The Wounded Wolf." They may surprise you, pulling stunts and taking tricky turns like the Wheels-and-Brake boys in James Berry's story. Yet before a short story runs on its own, it grows one word at a time from a writer's pen. The excitement of writing is watching the words come to life.

Try a taste of this excitement. Write your own short story. Start by imagining characters, setting, and a central problem for the characters to face. Use the following skills, presented in this section's Writing Mini-Lessons.

Writing Skills Focus

▶ **Use time words.** To keep the order of events clear in your story, use time words such as the following: *before, during, after, then, next, earlier, later,* and *meanwhile.* (See p. 515.)

▶ **Invent the central problem.** You may have interesting characters, but they need something interesting to do before you have a story. Invent a goal or a difficult situation for your characters. Your story will show how they achieve the goal or resolve the situation. (See p. 533.)

MODEL

Roko, the wounded wolf, finds himself alone and in danger from his enemies.

Young Roko struggles to his feet. He bites the ravens. He turns and warns the grizzly bear. ① Then, he bursts into a run and falls against the shelter rock. The wounded wolf wedges down between the rock and the barren ground. Now protected on three sides, ② he turns and faces all his foes.

① The time words *then* and *now* help the reader picture the order in which events happen when Roko finds shelter from his enemies.

② Roko's problem is clear: He is wounded, and although now sheltered, he faces a number of enemies.

Prewriting

Gather Images and Ideas Let your mind wander. Create a vivid image of a place. Then, ask yourself: *What has just happened here?* Alternatively, picture a character. Ask yourself: *How does he or she feel? Why?* As ideas begin to come, jot down notes.

Story Sparks

- A broken sword and a sack spilling jewels lie on the forest floor.
- A girl walks down the street alone, trailing her fingers through the fence railings.
- Two kids stand in the middle of a field, pointing at the sky.

Create a Central Problem Look over your notes. Think about situations that can occur in the place you have pictured. Think about what your characters want or need. From these ideas, create a central problem. Use a Problem Diagram to help come up with ideas:

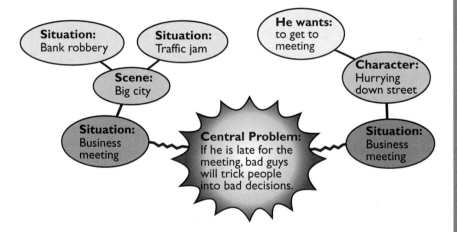

Plot the Events Now that you have a central problem, sketch a plot for your story. Ask yourself:

▶ How will the characters struggle with the problem or strive for their goal?

▶ In what way might the problem get worse or the goal get harder to reach?

▶ What will happen in the end?

APPLYING LANGUAGE SKILLS: Use Realistic Dialogue

When real people speak, they do not follow the same rules as when they write. To make your characters sound like real people, use the following elements:

Contractions:
"I can't say it's the worst idea I've ever heard," said Slim.

Colloquialisms:
"They've got tons of CDs there!"

Trailing Speech:
"Hmmm, I wonder if . . ."

Interrupted Speech:
"You can't mean it's—"

"Yes, Fred, I'm afraid it's true," he said.

Practice Write two lines of realistic dialogue for each scene:

1. One man steps on another man's toe.
2. A superhero arrives just in time to stop a villain from taking over the city.

Writing Application Use realistic dialogue in your story to bring characters to life.

Writer's Solution Connection Language Lab

For more on dialogue, complete the Writing Dialogue lesson in the Composing unit.

Applying LANGUAGE SKILLS: Capitalization of Proper Nouns

A proper noun names a particular person, place, or thing. Your name is a proper noun. The name of your state is, too. The first letter of a proper noun is always capitalized. Following are examples of other proper nouns:

Geographical Features:
Adirondacks, Missouri River

Organizations:
Boy Scouts, Yankees

Holidays:
Thanksgiving, Memorial Day

Practice Capitalize the proper nouns in the following sentences:

1. He is a lawyer in london.
2. Wolves live near the arctic circle.
3. Her brother loved the toronto blue jays.

Writing Application Make sure you've capitalized proper nouns in your draft.

Writer's Solution Connection Language Lab

For more help with capitalization, complete any lesson in the Capitalization unit.

Drafting

Draw the Reader In Begin with a sentence that makes the reader want to know more. For instance, the sentence "John Smith was late for his meeting" creates only a little curiosity. To create more curiosity, you might write: "John Smith's life didn't usually depend on whether he was on time. Today was different."

Create a Setting To help readers picture the action, include details of setting. If the action takes place on a city street, for instance, descriptions of the following details can help create a setting: traffic noises; the rush of hurrying people; the confused sounds of many conversations going on at once; litter whipping in the wind; sunlight glinting off a tall office building.

Show, Don't Tell Show readers important events, using sensory details and the reactions of characters. This sentence tells readers about an event: "The bad guys grabbed John's important papers." This sentence shows the event: "As John ran after his papers, a car came screaming around the corner. John stopped, horrified, as the car skidded to a stop. A pale hand reached through the door and scooped up the papers."

Revising

Focus on Your Central Problem Take out events that do not add to the central problem and its solution.

Check Connections Between Events Add time words to make sure the order of events is clear. Ask yourself whether the connection between the ending and the rest of the story makes sense. If not, add events or explanations to make a strong connection.

Show Important Events If an event is important to the story, make sure you show how it happened. Add sensory details, character reactions, dialogue, and other details to bring important events to life.

Publishing and Presenting

Oral Presentation Read your story to the class. Prepare by reading it aloud to another person. After your reading, ask the class which parts they liked and whether any parts need more explanation.

Internet Posting Put your story on the Web. Include an author biography explaining a little about yourself and how you came up with the story.

Real-World Reading Skills Workshop

Strategies for Success

All readers must know the difference between fact and fiction. Facts are events that really happened or situations that are true. Fiction tells of made-up events, people, and situations. Sometimes writers combine fact and fiction in their writing. A wise reader, though, can tell the difference between the two.

How to Recognize Fiction Fiction includes works such as novels and short stories. One way to recognize a work of fiction is to ask: *How did the author come to know that this or that happened?* If the author seems to know everything that happened to a character, yet nowhere explains how he or she came to know these things, the work is probably fiction. Another way to recognize fiction is to ask: *Who is telling this story?* In fiction, the person telling the story may be a character different from the author.

How to Recognize Nonfiction Books about events that actually happened, or people who actually lived, contain facts. Books of facts, such as history and science books, are also called *nonfiction*. These books generally indicate how the author came to know the facts. For instance, they may contain a bibliography listing books the author used to do research. You can always confirm whether an idea is a fact by looking it up in an encyclopedia or other reference work.

Is It Fact and Fiction? Some works, such as historical novels or science-fiction stories, include facts as well as made-up details. In some cases, common sense will help you tell the difference between fact and fiction. You can also use an encyclopedia or other reference book to find out whether a statement in a book or article is true.

Apply the Strategies

Copy the paragraphs below on a piece of paper. Circle all the sentences that are factual. Underline all the sentences that are fictional. Then, answer the questions that follow.

PRESIDENTIAL MOONWALK!

The Earth is the third planet in the solar system. It has only one moon. In 1936, a rocket ship made the first landing on the moon. The President of the United States, Susan McCarthy, was the first person to set foot on the moon's surface.

Anyone who walks on the moon needs special equipment to do so. In 1974, however, one astronaut walked on the moon with no special equipment at all. This astronaut, Julian Armstrong, spent an hour on the moon dressed only in street clothes.

1. If you do not have personal knowledge about the moon and its exploration, how can you determine which statements are true?

2. Which details make some of the fictional statements sound like facts?

✔ Here are some other situations in which these strategies are useful:
► A magazine
► A Web page
► A novel about famous people in history

Sentence Structure Grammar Review

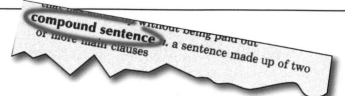

compound sentence ... without being paid out ... a sentence made up of two or more main clauses

Sentences can be classified according to the number and kinds of clauses they contain. Two sentence structures are simple and compound.

Simple Sentences Simple sentences consist of one independent clause. (See page 514.) A simple sentence can have a compound subject or compound verb and modifiers and complements, but it does not contain a subordinate clause.

S   V
Roko hears his leader.

S   V
Roko and the others *call* out.

S V   V
He lifts his head and *looks* around.

Compound Sentences A compound sentence contains two or more independent clauses. (See page 532.) The independent clauses usually are joined by a comma and a coordinating conjunction (*and, but, for, nor, or, so, yet*).

Meg got her large chocolate milkshake, *and* I had a small one.

Practice 1 Copy these sentences in your notebook. Underline the subject once and the verb twice. Identify whether the subject or the verb is compound.

1. The bear stops and sniffs the wind.

2. The owl and the raven wait patiently.

3. Maibon and his wife are old.

4. Maibon sighed and grumbled about his age.

5. Maibon pulled and pried and chopped at the tree branch.

Practice 2 In your notebook, identify each of the following sentences as either simple or compound.

1. The lawyer and the ghost came to an agreement.

2. The lawyer suggested an idea, and the ghost agreed.

3. The wolf whimpered and waited for his pack.

4. She eventually met other people, but Meg was her first real friend.

5. The girls jumped on their bikes and rode away.

Practice 3 In your notebook, combine each pair of sentences to create one sentence as indicated.

1. The lawyer spoke. The ghost spoke. (Simple sentence with a compound subject)

2. The girls rode their bikes. The girls laughed. (Simple sentence with a compound verb)

3. Maibon helped the dwarf. The dwarf gave him a wish. (Compound sentence using *and*)

4. Maibon wanted a stone. The dwarf didn't want to give him one. (Compound sentence using *but*)

Grammar in Writing

✔ If you use a comma between independent clauses, you must also use a coordinating conjunction. If you join clauses with a comma only, you will create a run-on sentence, which is an error.

People say a lot using words. They also "speak" to one another using body language. The way we move, hold ourselves, and look at others is called **body language.** A person's look, or the way he or she gestures, sits, or stands can say a great deal. Understanding body language—both your own and that of others—can help you communicate better.

Maintain Eye Contact During a conversation, the person you're speaking with may look over your shoulder or down at the floor. This might make you wonder whether the other person is really listening. You might lose interest in the conversation yourself. By maintaining good eye contact, people show interest in and respect for what the other person is saying.

Practice Good Posture When people stand straight and tall, they let others know that they feel confident and secure. If a person slumps, he or she may be insecure, tired, or simply not paying attention.

Be Aware of Your Gestures When people shrug their shoulders, make a fist, or nod their heads, they are gesturing. Some gestures, such as pointing, may be used to emphasize a point. Others show that a person is distracted: glancing at a watch, tapping a pencil, or looking out the window.

Apply the Strategies

With a partner, role-play the situations that follow. Use body language as well as words to express emotions and attitudes. Afterwards, discuss and take notes on how you might have handled the situation more effectively.

1. You meet the parents of a friend on your way to a movie. They want to know how school is. You are afraid you're going to be late for the movie.

2. An exchange student comes to stay with your family. You tell the student about school, your family, and your town.

3. A small child stops you and asks if you've seen his mother. He says he is lost. You try to reassure him.

Tips for Interpreting Body Language

✔ Follow these strategies to interpret body language:

▶ Note the person's facial expression. Is it friendly, angry, nervous, or relaxed?

▶ Evaluate the person's posture. What does it communicate?

▶ Watch carefully for hand gestures. They may be used to emphasize a point.

What's Behind the Words

Vocabulary Adventures With Richard Lederer

Geography Vocabulary

A new discovery is one important reason for inventing a new word or for borrowing an old one. When explorers mapped unfamiliar lands, they often borrowed words from Latin and Greek, the ancient languages of learning. The science of geography is filled with such words.

Geography Explored

The word *geography* itself comes from two Greek word parts. The word part *graph* means "to write," as in *autograph (auto,* "self": writing about oneself) and *photography (photo,* "light": literally, writing with light).

The word part *geo* means "earth; ground." Geography is, therefore, writing about the Earth—about its climate, continents, people, and products, as well as the mapping of its surface.

A Wide, Flat Earth

Measuring the latitude and longitude of our world is especially important for mapmakers. These words are derived from the Latin *latus,* "wide," and *longus,* "long." Ancient mapmakers used lines of latitude to indicate the length and breadth of the Earth, which they thought was flat. We still use the words *latitude* and *longitude* for the circles used to mark off distance on a globe.

A Bear of a Word

The world's most northerly region is the Arctic, from the Greek word *arktos,* meaning "bear." It is named after the constellation of the Little Bear (Ursus Minor, which includes the Little Dipper). The Little Bear contains the North Star, which is always right above the North Pole. For centuries, this star has helped explorers figure out which direction is North.

Sweaters and Hot Dogs

When explorers, traders, and other travelers returned home, they often brought strange new foods and fabrics with them. The English words for these products often come from the names of the places where they were made. A *cashmere* sweater is made from wool of a kind made in Kashmir, India. The all-American *frankfurter* looks a lot like something eaten in Frankfurt, Germany. As you explore the world of words, you will often find that what lies close to home actually comes from far away!

ACTIVITY 1 Using a dictionary, explore the origins and meanings of each of the following words: *agriculture, archipelago, boundary, climate, country, glacier, irrigation, mountain, oasis, plain, pole, region, tropic, tundra, valley, weather*

ACTIVITY 2 Identify the geographical sources of the following fabrics, clothing, and foods:

1. damask
2. denim
3. jeans
4. tuxedo
5. brussels sprouts
6. cantaloupe
7. hamburger
8. tangerine

Extended Reading Opportunities

Where do you turn when you have questions about the future? If nobody really knows what tomorrow will bring, how do you get any answers? One option is books. The titles below don't guarantee any solutions, but they're sure to give you ideas for shaping the future on your own.

Suggested Titles

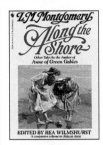

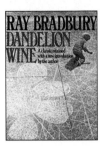

Working Days: Short Stories About Teenagers at Work
Anne Mazer, Editor

In this collection, teenagers enter a world often reserved for adults: the world of work. Whether helping their families or earning pocket money for themselves, these young people find out how it feels to be responsible and independent. As they experience the ups and downs of working, they get an early glimpse into the rewards and hardships in their futures. By reading about their experiences, you may get a glimpse into yours.

Along the Shore
Lucy Maud Montgomery

The author of *Anne of Green Gables* transports you to Prince Edward Island in this magical collection of tales of the sea. The characters invite the mysterious ocean to take part in their adventures, and it brings them treasures they never could have imagined. But the water is also dangerous, and the characters must stay calm and think like adults if they want to survive. In these stories, the sea is full of life, beauty, and danger. The sea is a story on its own.

Dandelion Wine
Ray Bradbury

In this novel, Ray Bradbury shares a series of episodes based on memories of his boyhood in Waukegan, Illinois. Each chapter is a story in itself, and all the stories work together to tell the larger story of one significant summer. "The Sound of Summer Running," on page 5, is from *Dandelion Wine*. Read the book to find out more about the main character's summer, when he encounters some unique characters and even some dangerous adventures.

Other Possibilities

Connections: Short Stories	Donald Gallo, Editor
Who Do You Think You Are? Stories of Friends and Enemies	Hazel Rochman
Baseball in April and Other Stories	Gary Soto

Desk Set, 1972, Wayne Thiebaud, Courtesy of the artist

Nonfiction

Y ou will discover in this unit that nonfiction tells true stories that are as interesting and unique as any you will find in fiction. Nonfiction is about real people and real events. In this unit, you'll read the following types of nonfiction:

- **Letters** and **journals** contain personal thoughts and reflections.

- **Biographies** and **autobiographies** are life stories. A **biography** is the life story of someone, written by someone else. An **autobiography** is a writer's own life story.

- **Media accounts** are nonfiction works written for newspapers, magazines, television, or radio.

- **Essays** are short nonfiction works about a particular subject. Types of essays include **history essays**, **persuasive essays**, **informational essays**, **narrative essays**, and **visual essays**.

Guide for Reading

Meet the Authors:

Patricia McKissack (1944–   ) and Frederick McKissack, Jr. (1939–   )

Some authors prefer to be alone when writing. Frederick and Patricia McKissack take a different approach. This husband-and-wife team works on books together.

The Making of a Team
The McKissacks first met when they were teenagers. Both were born in Nashville, Tennessee, and, later, both attended Tennessee State University. They married in 1964. Patricia McKissack taught, while her husband worked as an engineer and in construction. In 1984, they published their first book together. Currently, they live in St. Louis, Missouri.

Building With Books In books such as *Christmas in the Big House, Christmas in the Quarters,* they honor the struggles of enslaved African Americans. The McKissacks try to "build bridges with books." By showing young readers the sometimes "forgotten" parts of history, they hope to encourage understanding between different groups. As a team and individually, the McKissacks have written nearly 100 books.

◆ LITERATURE AND YOUR LIFE

CONNECT YOUR EXPERIENCE
You've probably used the expression "That's not fair!" when you feel you're being unjustly punished or made to follow a rule with which you don't agree. Sometimes, groups are treated unfairly. In "The Shutout," you'll read about the unfair situation that faced African American ballplayers in the early days of major league baseball.

THEMATIC FOCUS: Common Ground
Is baseball an experience all Americans can share?

◆ Background for Understanding

SOCIAL STUDIES
After the end of slavery, blacks and whites in the American South were segregated (kept separate) by law and custom. Blacks were not permitted to sit at the same counter as whites in restaurants. Each group went to different schools. Segregation affected every aspect of life before hard-won changes occurred in the 1950's and 1960's.

Although African Americans played alongside white players in the earliest days of baseball, segregation soon divided teams into "black" and "white." As "The Shutout" shows, though, segregation could not completely shut out African Americans from high achievements.

◆ The Shutout ◆

◆ Literary Focus

HISTORY ESSAY

A **history essay** is a short piece of nonfiction that gives facts, explanations, and insights about historical events. For instance, "The Shutout" discusses facts about baseball, such as the date the game was invented. It also explains what caused certain events. Further, it offers the insight that the story of the Negro leagues is filled with "drama and comedy."

Make a graphic organizer like the one shown below. Use it to jot down the facts, explanations, and insights you find in "The Shutout."

Facts
1. Baseball began before 1839.
2.
3.

Explanations
1. There are diary entries describing baseball games from earlier times.
2.
3.

Insights
1. There are many myths about baseball.
2.
3.

◆ Build Vocabulary

PREFIXES: *ir-*

The McKissacks call a certain decision in the history of baseball *irrational*. When you put the prefix *ir-* in front of a word, you change the word's meaning into its opposite, just as you do with the prefixes *un-* or *in-*. *Rational* means "reasonable." *Irrational* means the opposite: "without good reasons."

WORD BANK

Which of these words has some resemblance to the word *different* and describes a group of things that are *different* from each other?

anecdotes
evolved
diverse
composed
irrational

Reading for Success

Strategies for Reading Nonfiction

Nonfiction writing, such as biographies and encyclopedia articles, gives you facts and explanations concerning real people, places, and events. Don't just gobble down nonfiction. Make a nutritious "meal" by choosing the facts you need and judging the connections between them. The following strategies will help you digest nonfiction:

Set a purpose for reading.

Each fact in a nonfiction work is like an ingredient for a meal. To choose the right ingredients, decide why you are reading. You might read a work on African Americans in baseball to learn about sports history. Alternatively, you might read the same work to learn about segregation. The facts you focus on depend on your purpose.

| Baseball invented before 1839. | Blacks excluded in 1867. | Some African Americans played in major leagues. | African Americans formed their own leagues. |

Purpose: Find important baseball dates.

Purpose: Learn more about segregation.

Understand the author's purpose.

A nonfiction writer gives facts about a subject. What the writer does with the facts depends on his or her purpose. For example, a writer may present facts to provide information, to entertain you, or perhaps to persuade you of a particular viewpoint. Identify the author's purpose by considering the type of information and the way it is presented.

Identify the author's main points.

Identify main points by considering what the author wants you to remember. Look for ideas that sum up or interpret other points. For example, the following main point is made in "The Shutout": "... from the start, organized baseball tried to limit ... African American participation." This main point sums up events such as the 1867 vote to exclude African Americans.

Identify the evidence for the author's points.

The author should give evidence—facts or arguments—supporting each main point. This main point and evidence appear in "The Shutout":

Main Point: Baseball was invented before 1839.

Evidence: A diary reports George Washington's troops batting balls.

As you read "The Shutout," look at the notes in the boxes. The notes show you how to apply these strategies to your reading.

The Shutout

*Patricia C. McKissack and
Frederick McKissack, Jr.*

The history of baseball is difficult to trace because it is embroidered with wonderful anecdotes that are fun but not necessarily supported by fact. There are a lot of myths that persist about baseball—the games, the players, the owners, and the fans—in spite of contemporary research that disproves most of them. For example, the story that West Point cadet Abner Doubleday "invented" baseball in 1839 while at Cooperstown, New York, continues to be widely accepted, even though, according to his diaries, Doubleday never visited Coopers-town. A number of records and documents show that people were playing stick-and-ball games long before the 1839 date.

> If your **purpose** is to find out how baseball began, you will learn that Abner Doubleday probably did not invent the sport.

Albigence Waldo, a surgeon with George Washington's troops at Valley Forge, wrote in his diary that soldiers were "batting balls and running bases" in their free time. Samuel Hopkins Adams (1871–1958),

an American historical novelist, stated that his grandfather "played base ball on Mr. Mumford's pasture" in the 1820's.

> Waldo's diary entry and Adams's state-ment are **evidence** that baseball started before 1839.

Although baseball is a uniquely American sport, it was not in-vented by a single person. Probably the game evolved from a variety of stick-and-ball games that were played in Europe, Asia, Africa, and the Americas for centuries and brought to the colonies by the most diverse group of people ever to populate a continent. More specifically, some histori-ans believe baseball is an outgrowth of its first cousin, *rounders*, an English game. Robin Carver wrote in his *Book of Sports*

◆ **Build Vocabulary**

anecdotes (an´ ik dōts´) *n.*: Short, entertaining tales

evolved (ē vôlvd´) *v.*: Grew gradually; developed

diverse (də vʉrs´) *adj.*: Various; with differing characteristics

(1834) that "an American version of rounders called *goal ball* was rivaling cricket in popularity."

It is generally accepted that by 1845, baseball, as it is recognized today, was becoming popular, especially in New York. In that year a group of baseball enthusiasts organized the New York Knickerbocker Club. They tried to standardize the game by establishing guidelines for "proper play."

The Knickerbockers' rules set the playing field—a diamond-shaped infield with four bases (first, second, third, and home) placed ninety feet apart. At that time, the pitching distance was forty-five feet from home base and the "pitch" was thrown underhanded. The three-strikes-out rule, the three-out inning, and the ways in which a player could be called out were also specified. However, the nine-man team and nine-inning game were not established until later. Over the years, the Knickerbockers' basic rules of play haven't changed much.

> In the first section of the essay, you can see that one of the **authors' main points** is about the origins of baseball.

In 1857–1858, the newly organized National Association of Base Ball Players was formed, and baseball became a business. Twenty-five clubs—mostly from eastern states—formed the Association for the purpose of setting rules and guidelines for club and team competition. The Association defined a professional player as a person who "played for money, place or emolument (profit)." The Association also authorized an admission fee for one of the first "all-star" games between Brooklyn and New York. Fifteen hundred people paid fifty cents to see that game. Baseball was on its way to becoming the nation's number-one sport.

By 1860, the same year South Carolina seceded from the Union, there were about sixty teams in the Association. For obvious reasons none of them were from the South. Baseball's development was slow during the Civil War years, but teams continued to compete, and military records show that, sometimes between battles, Union solders chose up teams and played baseball games. It was during this time that records began mentioning African-American players. One war journalist noted that black players were "sought after as teammates because of their skill as ball handlers."

> Here the authors introduce a new **main idea:** the role of African Americans in the sport.

Information about the role of African Americans in the early stages of baseball development is slight. Several West African cultures had stick-and-ball and running games, so at least some blacks were familiar with the concept of baseball. Baseball, however, was not a popular southern sport, never equal to boxing, wrestling, footracing, or horse racing among the privileged landowners.

Slave owners preferred these individual sports because they could enter their slaves in competitions, watch the event from a safe distance, pocket

> The authors' **evidence** for the fact that slaveowners entered slaves into athletic contests is the existence of certain historical documents.

the winnings, and personally never raise a sweat. There are documents to show that slave masters made a great deal of money from the athletic skills of their slaves.

Free blacks, on the other hand, played on and against integrated[1] teams in large eastern cities and in small midwestern hamlets. It is believed that some of the emancipated[2]

---

1. **integrated** (in´ tə grā tid) *adj.*: Open to both African Americans and whites.
2. **emancipated** (ē man´ sə pā´ tid) *adj.*: Freed from slavery.

▼ **Critical Viewing** What information about the history of baseball can you learn from this picture? **[Analyze]**

Union Prisoners at Salisbury, N.C., National Baseball Library and Archive, Cooperstown, NY

slaves and runaways who served in the Union Army learned how to play baseball from northern blacks and whites who had been playing together for years.

After the Civil War, returning soldiers helped to inspire a new interest in baseball all over the country. Teams sprung up in northern and midwestern cities, and naturally African Americans were interested in joining some of these clubs. But the National Association of Base Ball Players had other ideas. They voted in December 1867 not to admit any team for membership that "may be composed of one or more colored persons." Their reasoning was as <u>irrational</u> as the racism that shaped it: "If colored clubs were

admitted," the Association stated, "there would be in all probability some division of feeling whereas, by excluding them no injury could result to anyone . . . and [we wish] to keep out of the convention the discussion of any subjects having a political bearing as this [admission of blacks on the Association teams] undoubtedly would."

So, from the start, organized baseball tried to limit or exclude African-American

◆ **Build Vocabulary**

composed (kəm pōzd´) *adj.*: Made up (of)

irrational (ir rash´ ə nəl) *adj.*: Unreasonable; not making sense

participation. In the early days a few black ball players managed to play on integrated minor league teams. A few even made it to the majors, but by the turn of the century, black players were shut out of the major leagues until after World War II. That doesn't mean African Americans didn't play the game. They did.

Black people organized their own teams, formed leagues, and competed for championships. The history of the old "Negro Leagues" and the players who barnstormed[3] on black diamonds is one of baseball's most interesting chapters, but the story is a

---

3. **barnstormed** *v.*: Went from one small town to another, putting on an exhibition.

researcher's nightmare. Black baseball was outside the mainstream of the major leagues, so team and player records weren't well kept, and for the most part, the white press ignored black clubs or portrayed them as clowns. And for a long time the Baseball Hall of Fame didn't recognize any of the Negro League players. Because of the lack of documentation, many people thought the Negro Leagues' stories were nothing more than myths and yarns, but that is not the case. The history of the Negro Leagues is a patchwork of human drama and comedy, filled with legendary heroes, infamous owners, triple-headers, low pay, and long bus rides home—not unlike the majors.

Guide for Responding

◆ LITERATURE AND YOUR LIFE

Reader's Response How might you have felt as an African American baseball player denied the chance to play in the major leagues?

Thematic Focus Give one detail showing that baseball is a common ground for all Americans, and one showing that it is not.

☑ Check Your Comprehension

1. When did baseball probably begin?
2. What did the Knickerbockers do for baseball?
3. In what part of the country did African Americans first play the sport?
4. What limits were put on their involvement in baseball?

◆ Critical Thinking

INTERPRET

1. Explain why researchers are not completely sure about the origins of baseball. **[Analyze]**
2. Name two steps by which baseball became a professional sport. **[Analyze Cause and Effect]**
3. In what way did the end of the Civil War help the growth of baseball? **[Analyze Cause and Effect]**

EVALUATE

4. Explain whether the team owners' reasons for not letting African Americans play were reasonable. **[Evaluate]**
5. Does the essay give a complete explanation of why baseball was not popular in the South? Explain. **[Assess]**

Guide for Responding (continued)

◆ Reading for Success

STRATEGIES FOR READING NONFICTION

Review the strategies and the notes showing how to read nonfiction. Then, apply those strategies to answer the following:

1. Name two facts of special interest if your reading purpose is to learn about segregation.
2. Explain the authors' purpose in writing that slave-owners won money from slave athletics but "personally never raise[d] a sweat."
3. Name the two main points of the essay.
4. What evidence do the authors give that baseball excluded African Americans from the start?

◆ Build Vocabulary

USING THE PREFIX ir-

The prefix ir- turns a word's meaning into its opposite. The prefix ir- is a variation on the spelling of the prefix in- (un-). It is always attached to a word that begins with r. Define each italicized word:

1. You broke an *irreplaceable* vase!
2. I find chocolate *irresistible*.
3. My penny fell down the well. It is *irrecoverable*.

SPELLING STRATEGY

The prefix ir- is used only with words that begin with r. When adding the prefix ir-, keep both r's. For instance, ir- + rational = irrational.

For each of the following definitions, unscramble the letters to find a word that joins the prefix ir- with a word beginning with r.

1. uneven: grularier
2. beside the point: trivelenar
3. likely to act without thinking: pironssibeler

USING THE WORD BANK

Match each numbered word from the Word Bank with its meaning.

1. anecdote   a. unreasonable
2. evolved   b. varied
3. irrational   c. grew gradually
4. diverse   d. tale
5. composed   e. made up

◆ Literary Focus

HISTORY ESSAY

History essays report a series of past events, giving facts about these events, such as dates, and evidence for the facts. History essays may also explain the causes and give insights into the meaning of events.

1. Name two facts reported in "The Shutout."
2. What evidence do the authors give for their claim that Doubleday did not invent baseball?
3. What evidence do they give that soldiers helped make baseball popular after the Civil War?
4. According to the authors, why wasn't baseball popular in the South?
5. What insight do the authors offer about information on the Negro leagues?

◆ Build Grammar Skills

SUBJECT PRONOUNS

Personal pronouns have different forms, depending on their use in a sentence. **Subject pronouns** are always used for the subject of a verb and for a subject complement following a linking verb. The subject pronouns are *I, you, he, she, it, we, you,* and *they.*

Subject: *They* tried to standardize the game.
Subject complement: It was *I* who batted last.

Practice Copy the following sentences into your notebook. Circle the subject pronoun in each, and note whether it is the subject of the sentence or a subject complement.

1. Despite setbacks, we continued to try.
2. In time, you will understand baseball.
3. He was the first African American to play major league baseball in the twentieth century.
4. It was not invented by a single person.
5. The winners are she and her sister.

Writing Application Write five sentences about a baseball game (real or imaginary) using five subject pronouns. Underline each subject pronoun.

Build Your Portfolio

 ## Idea Bank

Writing

1. **Reflection** Write a paragraph explaining why you do or do not enjoy watching or playing baseball. Give reasons for your answer.

2. **Journal Entry** Write the journal entry of an African American ballplayer on the day he learns he cannot play in the white major leagues.

3. **History Essay** Write a history essay on Jackie Robinson, the first twentieth-century African American major league baseball player. Explain why his contribution was historically important.

Speaking and Listening

4. **Speech** Read an excerpt from Martin Luther King, Jr.'s "I Have a Dream" speech to the class. Then, tell how King's ideas apply to baseball. **[Social Studies Link]**

5. **Panel Discussion [Group Activity]** With two other classmates, present a panel discussion on the effects of segregation. Divide up the following roles: spokesperson for African American players, spokesperson for white players, spokesperson for fans. **[Social Studies Link]**

Projects

6. **Flowchart** Create a flowchart that shows the possible outcomes of a player's "at bat." Begin with "Batter swings: Gets a hit?" Continue the chart by creating a branch for yes and a branch for no. Continue the chart until all the possibilities have been explored through yes-and-no questions. **[Physical Education Link]**

7. **Multimedia Report** Create a multimedia report on the Negro leagues. Include a roster of teams and any available photographs of players, uniforms, and so on. **[Visual Arts Link]**

 ## Writing Mini-Lesson

History of a Sport

"The Shutout" explains a lot about baseball, but it does not include every story or fact—that would fill many books! Write an essay on the history of a sport. Like "The Shutout," your essay should focus on a narrow topic, not on the entire history of the sport.

Writing Skills Focus: Narrowing a Topic

A good history essay focuses on a **narrow topic.** To narrow a topic, writers often start with a general idea, and then narrow it in stages:

Model

General: baseball
Includes: beginnings; ~~star players; team histories~~; records, etc.

Narrower: beginnings
Includes: invention; becomes professional; ~~early players~~

Still Narrower: invention of baseball; baseball becomes professional

Prewriting Jot down various aspects of the history of a sport. Then, narrow your topic by picking one aspect to research. As you do your research, focus only on your narrowed topic.

Drafting Write an introduction describing your narrowed topic. Then, write several paragraphs about this topic. Sum up your research in a conclusion.

Revising Take out details that have nothing to do with your narrowed topic and are not needed to explain part of that topic.

> ◆ **Grammar Application**
> Check that any pronouns you use as sentence subjects or subject complements are subject pronouns.

Part 1

Journals, Letters, and Personal Histories

Guide for Reading

Meet the Authors:

F. Scott Fitzgerald (1896–1940)

Francis Scott Key Fitzgerald was named after one of his ancestors—the author of "The Star Spangled Banner." Fitzgerald was born in St. Paul, Minnesota, educated at Princeton, and served in the army. At the age of twenty-two, he published his first novel, *This Side of Paradise,* and married Zelda Sayre. One year later, their daughter Frances (Scottie) was born.

The Fitzgeralds lived a rich, fast-paced life during the "Roaring Twenties." However, Zelda became ill, and young Scottie spent much of her childhood in boarding schools and at camps. F. Scott Fitzgerald died at the age of forty-four.

C.S. Lewis (1898–1963)

Clive Staples Lewis traveled far as a young man. He left Northern Ireland, where he was born, to attend school in the United States. He traveled even farther than that in his imagination. He is famous for his stories about the imaginary land of Narnia, beginning with *The Lion, the Witch, and the Wardrobe.* Readers around the world sent him letters, pictures, and their own stories. He answered every letter he received.

Amanda Borden (1977–   )

At age seven, this Olympic-gymnast-to-be was training two hours a day, three days a week. By ten years of age, Borden was in the gym twelve hours a week. At age nineteen, she was the captain of the gold-medal-winning 1996 U.S. Olympic gymnastic team.

◆ LITERATURE AND YOUR LIFE

CONNECT YOUR EXPERIENCE

If you want to let people know that you are thinking about them, you might send a card or a letter. When you want to sort out your own thoughts, you might keep a journal. The letters and journal entry in this group capture the thoughts and feelings that some famous people have put in writing.

THEMATIC FOCUS: Special People

Why do you think people enjoy reading the letters and journals of famous people?

◆ Background for Understanding

SPORTS

Gymnast Amanda Borden describes some of her training in "Olympic Diary." The following definitions will help you as you read "Olympic Diary."

Uneven Parallel Bars: Two parallel bars on which gymnasts perform spins and swings.

Balance Beam: A beam that is approximately four inches wide, six feet long, and four feet off the floor, on which gymnasts balance and tumble.

Floor Exercise: An event in which gymnasts combine tumbling and dance moves.

◆ Build Vocabulary

RELATED WORDS: FORMS OF *document*

In "Letter to Scottie," Fitzgerald asks for documentation, or written proof, that his daughter has been doing her work. *Documentation* is related to *document,* which means "something printed or written."

WORD BANK

Which word describes feeling curious and fascinated?

documentation
implement
intrigued
compulsory

Letter to Scottie ◆ Letter to Joan
◆ Olympic Diary ◆

◆ Literary Focus

LETTERS AND JOURNALS

A **letter** is a written communication from one person to another. In personal letters, the writer shares information, thoughts, and feelings with one other person.

A **journal** is a daily account of events and the writer's thoughts and feelings about those events.

Reading letters and journals gives you a glimpse into the personal side of a writer's life. As you read these letters and the journal, notice that the language is less formal than the language used in most other kinds of writing.

◆ Reading Strategy

UNDERSTAND THE AUTHOR'S PURPOSE

When F. Scott Fitzgerald wrote his "Letter to Scottie," one purpose, or reason, for his writing was to encourage his daughter to do her best. You will read his letter in the right frame of mind if you **understand the author's purpose** and notice how it affects the language he uses and the details he includes.

As you read "Letter to Joan" and "Olympic Diary," use a chart like the one shown to jot down notes about the author's purpose and the details he or she includes to achieve that purpose.

Woman Writing, Pierre Bonnard, Sonia Henie Collection, Oslo, Norway

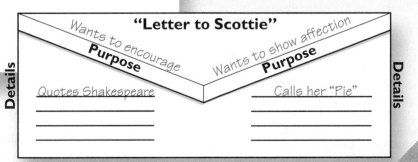

"Letter to Scottie"

Details

Wants to encourage **Purpose**

Wants to show affection **Purpose**

Details

Quotes Shakespeare

Calls her "Pie"

Letter to Scottie

F. Scott Fitzgerald

La Paix, Rodgers' Forge
Towson, Maryland
August 8, 1933

Dear Pie:[1]

I feel very strongly about you doing [your] duty. Would you give me a little more <u>documentation</u> about your reading in French? I am glad you are happy—but I never believe much in happiness. I never believe in misery either. Those are things you see on the stage or the screen or the printed page, they never really happen to you in life.

All I believe in in life is the rewards for virtue (according to your talents) and the *punishments* for not fulfilling your duties, which are doubly costly. If there is such a volume in the camp library, will you ask Mrs. Tyson to let you look up a sonnet of Shakespeare's in which the line occurs *"Lilies that fester smell far worse than weeds."*

Have had no thoughts today, life seems composed of getting up a *Saturday Evening Post*[2] story. I think of you, and always pleasantly; but if you call me "Pappy" again I am going to take the White Cat out and beat his bottom *hard, six times for every time you are impertinent.* Do you react to that?

I will arrange the camp bill.
Halfwit, I will conclude.

Things to worry about:
Worry about courage
Worry about cleanliness
Worry about efficiency
Worry about horsemanship
Worry about . . .
Things not to worry about:
Don't worry about popular opinion
Don't worry about dolls
Don't worry about the past
Don't worry about the future
Don't worry about growing up
Don't worry about anybody getting ahead of you
Don't worry about triumph
Don't worry about failure unless it comes through your own fault
Don't worry about mosquitoes
Don't worry about flies
Don't worry about insects in general
Don't worry about parents
Don't worry about boys
Don't worry about disappointments
Don't worry about pleasures
Don't worry about satisfactions
Things to think about:
What am I really aiming at?
How good am I really in comparison to my contemporaries in regard to:
(a) Scholarship
(b) Do I really understand about people and am I able to get along with them?
(c) Am I trying to make my body a useful instrument or am I neglecting it?

With dearest love,
[Daddy]

P.S. My come-back to your calling me Pappy is christening you by the word Egg, which implies that you belong to a very rudimentary state of life and that I could break you up and crack you open at my will and I think it would be a word that would hang on if I ever told it to your contemporaries. "Egg Fitzgerald." How would you like that to go through life with—"Eggie Fitzgerald" or "Bad Egg Fitzgerald" or any form that might occur to fertile minds? Try it once more and I swear I will hang it on you and it will be up to you to shake it off. Why borrow trouble?
Love anyhow.

---

1. **Pie:** Affectionate nickname for his daughter, Frances Scott Fitzgerald, also known as Scottie, who was away at summer camp.
2. ***Saturday Evening Post:*** A weekly magazine.

◆ **Build Vocabulary**

documentation (däk´ yoo mən tā´ shən) *n*.: Supporting evidence

▲ **Critical Viewing** What details in the letter indicate the affection that is shown between Fitzgerald and his daughter in this picture? **[Support]**

Letter to Joan

C. S. Lewis

The Kilns,
Headington Quarry,
Oxford

[26 June 1956]

Dear Joan—

Thanks for your letter of the 3rd. You describe your Wonderful Night v.[ery] well. That is, you describe the place & the people and the night and the feeling of it all, very well—but not the *thing* itself—the setting but not the jewel. And no wonder! Wordsworth[1] often does just the same. His *Prelude* (you're bound to read it about 10 years hence. Don't try it now, or you'll only spoil it for later reading) is full of moments in which everything except the *thing* itself is described. If you become a writer you'll be trying to describe the *thing* all your life: and lucky if, out of dozens of books, one or two sentences, just for a moment, come near to getting it across.

About *amn't I, aren't I,* and *am I not,* of course there are no right and wrong answers about the language in the sense in which there are right and wrong answers in Arithmetic. "Good English" is whatever educated people talk; so that what is good in one place or time w[oul]d not be so in another." *Amn't* was good 50 years ago in the North of Ireland where I was brought up, but bad in Southern England. *Aren't I* w[oul]d have been hideously bad in Ireland but very good in England. And of course I just don't know which (if either) is good in modern Florida. Don't take any notice of teachers and textbooks in such matters. Nor of logic. It is good to say "More than one passenger was hurt," although *more than one* equals at least two and therefore logically the verb ought to be plural *were* not singular *was!*

What really matters is:—

1. Always try to use the language so as to make quite clear what you mean and make sure y[ou]r. sentence couldn't mean anything else.
2. Always prefer the plain direct word to the long, vague one. Don't *implement* promises, but *keep* them.
3. Never use abstract nouns when concrete ones will do. If you mean "More people died" don't say "Mortality rose."
4. In writing, don't use adjectives which merely tell us how you want us to *feel* about the thing you are describing. I mean, instead of telling us that a thing was "terrible," describe it so that we'll be terrified. Don't say it was "delightful"; make *us* say "delightful" when we've read the description. You see, all those words (horrifying, wonderful, hideous, exquisite) are only like saying to your readers "Please will you do my job for me."
5. Don't use words too big for the subject. Don't say "infinitely" when you mean "very"; otherwise you'll have no word left when you want to talk about something *really* infinite.

Thanks for the photos. You and Aslan[2] both look v.[ery] well. I hope you'll like your new home.

With love,
yours
C. S. Lewis

---

1. **William Wordsworth** (1770–1850): English poet.

2. **Aslan:** The great lion in C.S. Lewis's *The Chronicles of Narnia.*

◆ Build Vocabulary

implement (im´ plə mənt´) *v.:* Carry out

Olympic Diary

Amanda Borden

March 22, 1996

Growing up, I couldn't decide which sport I liked the best. My first sport was T-ball. I wasn't very good. I had trouble hitting the ball and even more trouble catching it. So I moved on to soccer. I was pretty good at that, but I got bored when I didn't have the ball. Then came ballet. When I saw the girls leaping and jumping in beautiful tutus, I fell in love. I really enjoyed dancing and performing. But after many recitals and shows, I was ready for a new challenge.

A friend of the family suggested gymnastics. Wow, did my life change! I was 7 years old when I started and absolutely intrigued with Mary Lou Retton. I watched her in the 1984 Olympics and thought she was amazing. I never really

▲ **Critical Viewing** What qualities do you think these gymnasts share that helped them become Olympic gold medalists? **[Speculate]**

thought I could do the things she did or even have a chance to be in the Olympics like she was. All I knew is that it looked like a lot of fun.

In the beginning, I practiced one hour, one day a week. That lasted one week. My coaches moved me up to training two hours a day, three days a week. I was in the Junior Elite Testing program, where they measured physical strength and flexibility as well as basic gymnastics skills. If your scores were high enough, you qualified for a national-level training camp.

I went to Tennessee for a week. It was my first time away from home and I didn't like it.

By the time I was 10, gymnastics had become a part of me. I was in the gym 12 hours a week—and loving every minute of it. I began competing at the compulsory level, traveling

◆ Build Vocabulary

intrigued (in trēgd´) *adj.:* Fascinated

compulsory (kəm pul´ sə rē) *adj.:* Must be done; having specific requirements

around my home state of Ohio as well as Kentucky, Indiana and Michigan. My family went along. My older brother Bryan usually brought a friend to play in the hotel.

[*Amanda began training with a new coach, and soon qualified for the USA Championships.*]

I was training really hard for the biggest competition of the year. But 12 weeks before the meet, I broke my elbow. The doctors said I could compete as long as I let it heal, so I had my arm in a cast for six weeks. But when the doctor gave me the OK to start again, I pulled my hamstring. I know, it sounds like bad luck. I couldn't compete, so I began to get my body healthy again for the next year.

I was now 15 and had to compete at the Senior Elite level. That meant going up against all the big guys like Kim Zmeskal. I made the U.S. Championships and did great—finishing fifth. That qualified me for the 1992 Olympic Trials. It wasn't until that point that I realized I really had a chance to make the Olympic team. I had a really good competition and finished seventh. Seven girls make the Olympic team. So you would've thought I'd have been in Barcelona.

Well, I wasn't. There were a lot of politics involved, but to make it short and sweet they put two injured athletes, who didn't compete at the trials, on the team, and bumped Kim, Kelly and me off. It was disappointing, but life goes on. I didn't quit.

[*At the end of 1995, Amanda broke her toe and her hand. Once again, she had to stop training and competing to allow her body to heal.*]

April 12, 1996

Four weeks ago, I got the go-ahead to start practicing again and, let me tell you, I was more than ready to get back on the mat. I began training and—slowly—I got everything back. Two weeks later, I was able to compete at the Budget Gymnastics Invitational (United States vs. France). It was going to be my first

competition in a year. I was so excited I could not wait!

I flew to Miami and had a wonderful time. The women only were able to compete on bars, beam and floor—and you didn't have to compete in every event if you didn't want to.

We had four people on the team, and three had to compete in each event. I had planned on competing on the beam and floor.

The day before the competition, I was asked to compete on bars. I had only been practicing for two weeks, but I was honored to compete for the USA.

The competition was great! On bars, I got a 9.725. I had to water down my routine a little because I had not been training for my full routine, so I was pleased with that score—even with an easy dismount.

We then went to the beam. I was second up and extremely confident. I went up and rocked a set—my score was 9.775.

Our next event was the floor. I have a new routine and was excited to let everybody see it. I had to water down my tumbling passes, too, because I did not have enough time to get them ready. My first pass was a double Arabian, which is two flips in the air with a half-twist on the first flip. I had a little too much energy and ran out of bounds—but I was happy to be on my feet. My second pass was a two-and-a-half twist. That went great! I finished with a front full punch front, and that was good, too. I received a 9.512, which isn't the best score I've ever received, but I was happy to be back in competition.

I did it! I had a great meet! I felt so good! I was back, the people still remembered me and I did wonderfully!

I look back now and the injuries seem so small. When I had to deal with them, I felt like I was holding the world. After I competed, I felt I was on top of it.

Unfortunately, everyone goes through tough times, but those tough times only make the good times even better. You may think I have had my share of bad luck. I have thought that at some times, too. But when I look back on my gymnastics career, the places I've been, the people I've met and the things I've learned—the good far outweighs the bad.

Of course, I would like to never have to deal with problems, but I know that it will only make me a better person.

[Amanda's Olympic dream finally came true. In 1996, at the Olympic trials in Boston, Amanda claimed one of seven spots on the women's gymnastic team.]

July 21, 1996

What a whirlwind I've been on since the Olympic trials! We arrived in Atlanta at 1:30 p.m. and had processing, which took seven hours. We received lots of great clothes and other goodies. We were also measured for Olympic uniforms, which we will receive later. We finally got to our home at Emory University at 9 p.m. We're staying in a fraternity house until we are competing and then can move into the Olympic Village after that. Jaycie and I are rooming together, sharing a bathroom with Shannon Miller. We decorated our room to make it a little more "homey."

Training is going very well. We train at a private club, except when we have podium training. Tuesday, we had 22,000 cheering fans at our training. I was totally overwhelmed. You just can't imagine the feeling.

Here we are in the Georgia Dome and the Dream Team will be using the other side. I'm hoping to meet some of them. Too bad Michael Jordan isn't here. Oh well.

I was honored by being named captain of our team. I think we will do just great—everyone gets along so well and supports each other. Here's hoping we bring home the gold!

[Amanda Borden and her teammates did bring home the gold medal in 1996. The picture on page 559 shows the 1996 women's team after receiving their gold medals.]

*G*uide for Responding

◆ LITERATURE AND YOUR LIFE

Reader's Response Which of these writers would you like to meet? Why?

Thematic Focus How did reading these letters and the journal help you to find out something special about each writer?

Journal Writing Write a journal entry about a goal you have reached.

☑ Check Your Comprehension

1. Identify two pieces of advice that Fitzgerald gives to his daughter in "Letter to Scottie."
2. What is the subject of "Letter to Joan"?
3. In "Olympic Diary," what kinds of problems prevent Amanda from training?
4. Why didn't Amanda go to the Olympics in Barcelona?

◆ Critical Thinking

INTERPRET

1. In "Letter to Scottie," what qualities does Fitzgerald indicate are important? **[Infer]**
2. Sum up Lewis's advice about writing in "Letter to Joan." **[Summarize]**
3. Identify two places in "Olympic Diary" where Amanda shows her determination to succeed. **[Support]**

EVALUATE

4. Do you think becoming an Olympic gymnast is worth the effort? Why or why not? **[Make a Judgment]**

APPLY

5. Which observation or piece of advice in these letters and journals can you apply to your own life? Explain. **[Relate]**

Guide for Responding (continued)

◆ Reading Strategy

UNDERSTAND THE AUTHOR'S PURPOSE

Fitzgerald, Lewis, and Borden have different **purposes,** or reasons, for writing. The language they use and the details they include reveal their purposes. For example, in "Letter to Scottie," Fitzgerald uses humorous language to show his affection for his daughter while encouraging her to do her best.

1. Identify two details in "Letter to Scottie" that Fitzgerald probably includes because he wants to encourage his daughter.
2. What is C. S. Lewis's purpose in writing "Letter to Joan"?
3. What are two purposes Amanda Borden may have had for writing her "Olympic Diary"?

◆ Build Vocabulary

USING FORMS OF *document*

Words that are related to *document,* such as *documentary* and *documentation,* usually have something to do with a record, or proof. On your paper, write the form of *document* that fits each description.

1. A piece of written proof
2. A visual record of an event or time period
3. A collection of evidence

SPELLING STRATEGY

In some words, like *intrigue,* the g sound is spelled *gue.* On your paper, unscramble the letters to make words that end with *gue.*

1. conversation: doagluie
2. disease: gluape
3. unclear: vugae

USING THE WORD BANK

On your paper, write the word that is closest in meaning to the word from the Word Bank.

1. implement: (a) force, (b) do, (c) help
2. documentation: (a) paper, (b) interest, (c) proof
3. compulsory: (a) suggested, (b) interesting, (c) required
4. intrigued: (a) curious, (b) disgusted, (c) confused

◆ Literary Focus

LETTERS AND JOURNALS

By reading **letters** and **journals,** you get an insight into the personal reactions of writers to events in their lives and in the world.

1. Identify two qualities that Fitzgerald reveals about himself in "Letter to Scottie."
2. What are two opinions that C. S. Lewis shares about writing in "Letter to Joan"?
3. Identify two places in "Olympic Diary" where Amanda Borden reveals her personal reaction to an event.

◆ Build Grammar Skills

OBJECT PRONOUNS: DIRECT AND INDIRECT OBJECTS

Pronouns have different forms depending on their use in a sentence. When a pronoun is a direct object (receives the action of the verb) or an indirect object (the person to or for whom an action is done), use an **object pronoun.**

Object Pronouns:	me, you, him, her, them, us
Direct Object:	That qualified *me* for the 1992 Olympics.
Indirect Object:	. . . the doctor gave *me* the OK to start again.

Practice Copy the following sentences in your notebook. Circle each object pronoun. Then, tell whether it is an indirect object or a direct object.

1. They . . . bumped Kim, Kelly, and me off.
2. The people still remembered her.
3. Would you give me a little more documentation?
4. Don't tell them yet.
5. The doctor told her the news.

Writing Application Write a brief journal entry that uses at least four of the following object pronouns as direct or indirect objects: *me, you, him, her, it, us,* and *them.* Identify how each pronoun is used.

Build Your Portfolio

 ## Idea Bank

Writing

1. **Journal Entry** As Amanda Borden, write a journal entry expressing how you feel after your team wins the gold medal.

2. **Response** As Scottie, write a letter to Fitzgerald in which you respond to his advice and his humorous threats.

3. **Account** Write a brief account of an event. Apply C.S. Lewis's advice to Joan to your own writing. At the end of your account, explain where you have incorporated each of his suggestions.

Speaking and Listening

4. **Interview** With a partner, conduct an imaginary interview with one of the writers in this group. Base your questions and answers on information you find in the letters and the journal.

5. **Explanation** Find out about the skills and abilities on which gymnasts are judged. Explain to your class how gymnasts demonstrate these skills and abilities in one event. Define any terms that might be unfamiliar to your listeners. **[Sports Link]**

Projects

6. **Flowchart** Create a flowchart that shows what happens to a piece of mail after you drop it in the mailbox. In your flowchart, include such possibilities as a missing zip code or a wrong address. **[Art Link; Social Studies Link]**

7. **Olympic Presentation [Group Activity]** With a group, prepare a presentation on the Olympics. Group members can choose from the following tasks: researching the history of the Olympics, creating a map that shows where the Olympics have been held, or preparing posters that show the events in which athletes can compete. **[Social Studies Link; Sports Link]**

 ## Writing Mini-Lesson

Letter to a Famous Person

"Letter to Joan" is a famous writer's response to a reader's letter. You can share your thoughts, questions, and feelings with a famous writer, singer, actor, or athlete in a letter.

Writing Skills Focus: Appropriate Beginnings

Avoid beginning your letter with "Hi, my name is ..." or "I'm writing to you because ..." Write an **appropriate beginning** that gets to the point and doesn't waste words:

Model

Dear Mr. McGwire,

    I didn't think anyone would ever break Maris's record! That two people would do it in the same season is amazing!

Prewriting Decide the main reason that you are writing to this person. Then, brainstorm for details or questions related to that reason.

Drafting Write a single sentence that sums up the reason you are writing. Use this sentence as your opening. Then, elaborate on your first sentence by providing examples and details. Ask any questions that are related to your reason for writing. For example, if you're telling a songwriter how much you like his or her lyrics, you might ask where he or she gets ideas.

Revising Ask a partner to help you eliminate any unnecessary details or empty words.

> ◆ **Grammar Application**
>
> Whether you use a pronoun as a direct or an indirect object, be sure you have used the object form of the pronoun.

Guide for Reading

Meet the Authors:

Susy Clemens (1872–1896)

Susy Clemens was the oldest of Mark Twain's three daughters. She grew up in a luxurious home in Hartford, Connecticut, where her parents entertained some of the most prominent people of the time. As a girl, Susy adored her father, but as she grew older, she began to resent his showy public image. She died at the age of twenty-four.

THE STORY BEHIND THE ESSAY

Susy wrote this biographical account in her journal when she was only thirteen years old. When Mark Twain read the account, he said, "I have had no compliment, no praise, no tribute from any source that was so precious to me as this one was and still is."

Gary Soto (1952–)

This popular writer of poetry and prose was once a farm worker in California's San Joaquin Valley. Some of his work—including the poetry collection *The Elements of San Joaquin*—explores the lives of migrant farm workers.

Other books—such as the collection of essays *Living Up the Street,* which won an American Book Award, and *Baseball in April*—focus on his family and friends and the large and small events of their lives. Today, Gary Soto lives and teaches in Berkeley, California.

◆ LITERATURE AND YOUR LIFE

CONNECT YOUR EXPERIENCE

Your best childhood memories—such as a favorite aunt or a picnic at the beach—probably center on the people and events that were important to you at the time. In "My Papa, Mark Twain" and "The Drive-In Movies," the writers share important scenes from their childhood memories.

THEMATIC FOCUS: Working It Out

Both of these works show a humorous side to the way people work things out.

◆ Background for Understanding

CULTURE

Gary Soto fondly remembers going to a drive-in movie. In the 1950's and 1960's, many people saw movies at the "drive-in." There, people parked their cars in front of a large outdoor screen, hooked up a listening box, and enjoyed the show. Since many drive-in theaters charged admission by the car rather than by the person, the drive-in was an economical way for families to see a movie.

◆ Build Vocabulary

WORD ROOT: -sequi-

The Latin root -sequi-, meaning "follow," is found in the word *consequently,* which means "following as a result." It also appears in *sequence,* which means "a series in which one thing follows another," and *sequel,* which means "the story that follows."

WORD BANK

Which word is sometimes used to describe the shape of the moon?

incessantly
consequently
consumed
prelude
crescent
pulsating
vigorously

My Papa, Mark Twain
◆ The Drive-In Movies ◆

◆ Literary Focus

BIOGRAPHY AND AUTOBIOGRAPHY

A **biography** is the story of someone's life written by another person. An **autobiography** is a person's own account of his or her life.

"My Papa, Mark Twain" is biographical. In it, Susy Clemens shares a portion of her father's life story. As in all biography, we see the subject through the writer's eyes.

"The Drive-In Movies" is autobiographical. Gary Soto tells a story from his own childhood. Because he is telling his own story, he can include his thoughts and feelings about his experiences.

◆ Reading Strategy

AUTHOR'S EVIDENCE

When a detective solves a crime, he or she provides evidence in the form of fingerprints, lab reports, or eyewitnesses. When an author tells the story of someone's life (including his or her own life), the author provides **evidence** to back up the points he or she makes about the subject. The evidence may be examples of the subject's behavior, observations by people who knew the subject, or details from the author's own memory. As you read "My Papa, Mark Twain" and "The Drive-In Movies," use a chart like the one at right to jot down the evidence that supports the author's points.

Point	✔ Evidence
	✔ Evidence
	✔ Evidence
	✔ Evidence
Point	✔
	✔
	✔

My Papa,
Mark Twain

Susy Clemens

We are a very happy family. We consist of Papa, Mamma, Jean, Clara and me. It is papa I am writing about, and I shall have no trouble in not knowing what to say about him, as he is a *very* striking character.

Papa's appearance has been described many times, but very incorrectly. He has beautiful gray hair, not any too thick or any too long, but just right; a Roman nose which greatly improves the beauty of his features; kind blue eyes and a small mustache. He has a wonderfully shaped head and profile. He has a very good figure—in short, he is an extrodinarily fine looking man. All his features are perfect exept that he hasn't extrodinary teeth. His complexion is very fair, and he doesn't ware a beard. He is a very good man and a very funny one. He has got a temper, but we all of us have in this family. He is the loveliest man I ever saw or ever hope to see—and oh, so absentminded.

Papa's favorite game is billiards, and when he is tired and wishes to rest himself he stays up all night and plays billiards, it seems to rest his head. He smokes a great deal almost incessantly. He has the mind of an author exactly, some of the simplest things he can't understand. Our burglar alarm is often out of order, and papa had been obliged to take the mahogany room off from the alarm altogether for a time, because the burglar alarm had been in the habit of ringing even when the mahogany-room window was closed. At length he thought that perhaps the burglar alarm might be in order, and he decided to try and see; accordingly he put it on and then went down and opened the window; consequently the alarm bell rang, it would even if the alarm had been in order. Papa went despairingly upstairs and said to mamma, "Livy the

◀ **Critical Viewing** What details in the picture show that the Clemens family enjoy spending time together? [**Analyze**]

mahogany room won't go on. I have just opened the window to see."

"Why, Youth," mamma replied. "If you've opened the window, why of course the alarm will ring!"

"That's what I've opened it for, why I just went down to see if it would ring!"

Mamma tried to explain to papa that when he wanted to go and see whether the alarm would ring while the window was closed he *mustn't* go and open the window—but in vain, papa couldn't understand, and got very impatient with mamma for trying to make him believe an impossible thing true.

Papa has a peculiar gait we like, it seems just to suit him, but most people do not; he always walks up and down the room while thinking and between each coarse at meals.

Papa is very fond of animals particularly of cats, we had a dear little gray kitten once that he named "Lazy" (papa always wears gray to match his hair and eyes) and he would carry him around on his shoulder, it was a mighty pretty sight! the gray cat sound asleep against papa's gray coat and hair. The names that he has give our different cats are really remarkably funny, they are named Stray Kit, Abner, Motley, Fraeulein, Lazy, Buffalo Bill, Soapy Sall, Cleveland, Sour Mash, and Pestilence and Famine.

Papa uses very strong language, but I have an idea not nearly so strong as when he first married mamma. A lady acquaintance of his is rather apt to interrupt what one is saying, and papa told mamma he thought he should say to the lady's husband "I am glad your wife wasn't present when the Deity said Let there be light."

◆ **Reading Strategy**
What evidence does the author provide to support her statement that Twain is fond of animals?

◆ **Build Vocabulary**

incessantly (in ses´ ənt lē) *adv.*: Never ceasing
consequently (kän´ si kwent´ lē) *adv.*: As a result

Papa said the other day, "I am a mugwump[1] and a mugwump is pure from the marrow out." (Papa knows that I am writing this biography of him, and he said this for it.) He doesn't like to go to church at all, why I never understood, until just now, he told us the other day that he couldn't bear to hear anyone talk but himself, but that he could listen to himself talk for hours without getting tired, of course he said this in joke, but I've no dought it was founded on truth.

One of papa's latest books is "The Prince and the Pauper" and it is unquestionably the best book he has ever written, some people want him to keep to his old style, some gentleman wrote him, "I enjoyed Huckleberry Finn immensely and am glad to see that you have returned to your old style." That enoyed me,

---

1. **mugwump** (mug´ wump´) n.: A Republican who refused to support the candidates of the party in the 1884 election.

▲ **Critical Viewing** Susy is observing her two sisters in this picture. What do you think she might write about them in her journal? **[Speculate]**

that enoyed me greatly, because it trobles me to have so few people know papa, I mean realy know him, they think of Mark Twain as a humorist joking at everything; "And with a mop of reddish brown hair which sorely needs the barbar brush, a roman nose, short stubby mustache, a sad care-worn face, with maney crows' feet" etc. That is the way people picture papa, I have wanted papa to write a book that would reveal something of his kind sympathetic nature, and "The Prince and the Pauper" partly does it. The book is full of lovely charming ideas, and oh the language! It is *perfect*. I think that one of the most touching scenes in it is where the pauper is riding on horseback with his nobles in the "recognition procession" and he sees his mother oh and then what followed! How she runs to his side, when she sees him throw up his hand palm outward, and is rudely pushed off by one of the King's officers, and then how the little pauper's conscience troubles him when he remembers the shameful words that were falling from his lips when she was turned from his side "I know you not woman" and how his grandeurs were stricken valueless and his pride <u>consumed</u> to ashes. It is a wonderfully beautiful and touching little scene, and papa has described it so wonderfully. I never saw a man with so much variety of feeling as papa has; now the "Prince and the Pauper" is full of touching places, but there is always a streak of humor in them somewhere. Papa very seldom writes a passage without some humor in

◆ Build Vocabulary

consumed (kən soomd´) *v.*: Destroyed

it somewhere and I don't think he ever will.

Clara and I are sure that papa played the trick on Grandma about the whipping that is related in "The Adventures of Tom Sawyer": "Hand me that switch." The switch hovered in the air, the peril was desperate—"My, look behind you Aunt!" The old lady whirled around and snatched her skirts out of danger. The lad fled on the instant, scrambling up the high board fence and disappeared over it.

> ### ◆ Literary Focus
> What details about Twain's life do you learn in this section of the biographical account?

We know papa played "Hookey" all the time. And how readily would papa pretend to be dying so as not to have to go to school! Grandma wouldn't make papa go to school, so she let him go into a printing office to learn the trade. He did so, and gradually picked up enough education to enable him to do about as well as those who were more studious in early life.

Guide for Responding

◆ LITERATURE AND YOUR LIFE

Reader's Response What questions would you still like answered about Mark Twain?

Thematic Focus Describe the way Mark Twain works out a problem or puzzle.

Journal Writing Describe someone about whom you would like to write a biography.

☑ Check Your Comprehension

1. List three physical features that Susy includes in her description of her father.
2. Compare Susy's view of her father with the view she says the public sees.
3. Summarize Susy's feelings about *The Prince and the Pauper*.

◆ Critical Thinking

INTERPRET

1. How does Susy feel about her father's lack of formal education? Explain. **[Deduce]**
2. This essay contains many misspelled words. Why do you think it was published without correcting the errors? **[Speculate]**
3. What are three words you would use to describe Mark Twain? **[Synthesize]**

APPLY

4. Which of your traits would you want to have included in a biography about you? **[Make a Decision]**

EXTEND

5. In what jobs could Susy use her skills at observing people? **[Career Link]**

THE DRIVE-IN MOVIES

GARY SOTO

For our family, moviegoing was rare. But if our mom, tired from a week of candling eggs,[1] woke up happy on a Saturday morning, there was a chance we might later scramble to our blue Chevy and beat nightfall to the Starlight Drive-In. My brother and sister knew this. I knew this. So on Saturday we tried to be good. We sat in the cool shadows of the TV with the volume low and watched cartoons, a <u>prelude</u> of what was to come.

One Saturday I decided to be extra good. When she came out of the bedroom tying her robe, she yawned a hat-sized yawn and blinked red eyes at the weak brew of coffee I had fixed for her. I made her toast with strawberry jam

spread to all the corners and set the three boxes of cereal in front of her. If she didn't care to eat cereal, she could always look at the back of the boxes as she drank her coffee.

I went outside. The lawn was tall but too wet with dew to mow. I picked up a trowel and began to weed the flower bed. The weeds were really bermuda grass, long stringers that ran finger-deep in the ground. I got to work quickly and in no time <u>crescents</u> of earth began rising under my fingernails. I was sweaty

◆ Build Vocabulary

prelude (prel´ yōōd´) *n.*: An introduction to a main event or action coming later

crescent (kres´ ənt) *n.*: Anything shaped like the moon in its first or last quarter

---

1. **candling eggs:** Examining eggs for freshness by placing them in front of a candle.

*El Auto Cinema*, 1985, Roberto Gil de Montes, Courtesy of Jan Baum Gallery

▲ **Critical Viewing** What are some reasons people might enjoy watching a movie from their car? [Speculate]

hot. My knees hurt from kneeling, and my brain was dull from making the trowel go up and down, dribbling crumbs of earth. I dug for half an hour, then stopped to play with the neighbor's dog and pop ticks from his poor snout.

I then mowed the lawn, which was still beaded with dew and noisy with bees hovering over clover. This job was less dull because as I pushed the mower over the shaggy lawn, I could see it looked tidier. My brother and sister watched from the window. Their faces were fat with cereal, a third helping. I made a face at them when they asked how come I was working. Rick pointed to part of the lawn. "You missed some over there." I ignored him and kept my attention on the windmill of grassy blades.

While I was emptying the catcher, a bee stung the bottom of my foot. I danced on one leg and was ready to cry when Mother showed her face at the window. I sat down on the grass and examined my foot: the stinger was <u>pulsating</u>. I pulled it out quickly, ran water over the sting and packed it with mud, Grandmother's remedy.

Hobbling, I returned to the flower bed where I pulled more stringers and again played with the dog. More ticks had migrated to his snout. I swept the front steps, took out the garbage, cleaned the lint filter to the dryer (easy), plucked hair from the industrial wash basin in the garage (also easy), hosed off the patio, smashed three snails sucking paint from the house (disgusting but fun), tied a bundle of newspapers, put away toys, and, finally, seeing that almost everything was done and the sun was not too high, started waxing the car.

My brother joined me with an old gym sock, and our sister watched us while sucking on a cherry Kool-Aid ice cube. The liquid wax drooled onto the sock, and we began to swirl the white slop on the chrome. My arms ached from buffing, which though less boring than weeding, was harder. But the beauty was evident. The shine, hurting our eyes and glinting like an armful of dimes, brought Mother out. She looked around the yard and said, "Pretty good." She winced[2] at the grille and returned inside the house.

◆ Literary Focus
What autobiographical details would only the writer know about his own childhood?

We began to wax the paint. My brother applied the liquid and I followed him rubbing hard in wide circles as we moved around the car. I began to hurry because my arms were hurting and my stung foot looked like a water balloon. We were working around the trunk when Rick pounded on the bottle of wax. He squeezed the bottle and it sneezed a few more white drops.

We looked at each other. "There's some on the sock," I said. "Let's keep going."

We polished and buffed, sweat weeping on our brows. We got scared when we noticed that the gym sock was now blue. The paint was coming off. Our sister fit ice cubes into our mouths and we worked harder, more intently, more dedicated to the car and our mother. We ran the sock over the chrome, trying to pick up extra wax. But there wasn't enough to cover the entire car. Only half got waxed, but we thought it was better than nothing and went inside for lunch. After lunch, we returned outside with tasty sandwiches.

◆ Literature and Your Life
For what outing or entertainment would you be willing to work this hard?

Rick and I nearly jumped. The waxed side of the car was foggy white. We took a rag and began to polish <u>vigorously</u> and nearly in tears, but the fog wouldn't come off. I blamed Rick and he blamed me. Debra stood at the window, not wanting to get involved. Now, not only would we not go to the movies, but Mom would surely snap a branch from the plum tree and chase us around the yard.

Mom came out and looked at us with hands on her aproned hips. Finally, she said, "You boys worked so hard." She turned on the garden hose and washed the car. That night we did go to the drive-in. The first feature was about nothing, and the second feature, starring Jerry Lewis,[3] was *Cinderfella*. I tried to stay awake. I kept a wad of homemade popcorn in my cheek

---

2. **winced** (winst) *v.*: Drew back slightly, as if in pain.

3. **Jerry Lewis:** Comedian who starred in many movies during the 1950's and 1960's.

and laughed when Jerry Lewis fit golf tees in his nose. I rubbed my watery eyes. I laughed and looked at my mom. I promised myself I would remember that scene with the golf tees and promised myself not to work so hard the coming Saturday. Twenty minutes into the movie, I fell asleep with one hand in the popcorn.

◆ Build Vocabulary

pulsating (pul′ sāt′ iŋ) *v.*: Beating or throbbing in rhythm

vigorously (vig′ ər əs lē) *adv.*: Forcefully; powerfully

Beyond Literature

Media Connection

Motion Pictures Moving pictures— more commonly known as movies—have been around in one form or another for a long time. The first successful "motion pictures" were taken in 1877 by Eadweard Mybridge, a British photographer. He set up a row of cameras to take a series of pictures of a horse running. Inventors around the world began trying to develop ways of recording and reshowing moving pictures. One of these inventors was Thomas Alva Edison. His company exhibited the first motion picture machine at the World's Fair of 1893. Only one viewer at a time could watch the motion picture through Edison's "kinetoscope." In 1896, Edison adapted a French inventor's device and showed the first movies to be projected onto a screen in the United States.

Cross-Curricular Activity
Diagram Create a diagram that shows how a movie projector uses light to create images on a screen.

Guide for Responding

◆ LITERATURE AND YOUR LIFE

Reader's Response How would you have felt if you had worked so hard and then had fallen asleep at the movies? Explain.

Thematic Focus If you were to give young Gary Soto an award for working out his problem that day, what sentence would you write on the certificate?

☑ Check Your Comprehension

1. Why did the boys wax only one side of the car?
2. What two things does the narrator promise himself to remember?
3. Why doesn't the narrator see the end of the movie?

◆ Critical Thinking

INTERPRET
1. Explain why the narrator's mother does not get angry with the boys for making a mess of the car. **[Draw Conclusions]**
2. Do you think the narrator is older or younger than his brother and sister? Use evidence from the story to support your answer. **[Deduce]**

APPLY
3. Do people work only when they are being rewarded? Do people ever work for other reasons? Explain. **[Relate]**

COMPARE LITERARY WORKS
4. In what ways are biography and autobiography similar? How are they different? Use details from these two works to illustrate your points. **[Compare and Contrast]**

Guide for Responding (continued)

◆ Reading Strategy

AUTHOR'S EVIDENCE

In these works, the authors use **evidence** in the form of examples and observations to support their points.

1. List three details or examples in "My Papa, Mark Twain" that support Susy Clemens's statement "We are a very happy family."

2. What evidence in "The Drive-In Movies" supports the statement that the narrator does not easily give up on a goal he has set for himself?

◆ Build Vocabulary

USING THE WORD ROOT -sequi-

When you see the root -sequi- in a word, you can guess that the word's meaning has something to do with "following" or "coming after." On your paper, explain the meaning of each italicized word.

1. The alarm didn't ring; consequently, I was late.
2. We liked the sequel better than the original.
3. In the sequence for this pattern, a blue dot follows three red dots.

SPELLING STRATEGY

Many words contain the letter sequence cess. Remember that this group of letters has one c and two s's.

Write the word that fits each of the following definitions. Each answer contains the letters cess.

1. A period of time when children leave their classrooms to play outside
2. Too much
3. Something that is needed and essential

USING THE WORD BANK

On your paper, write a word from the Word Bank that could be used as a synonym for each word below.

1. steadily
2. curved shape
3. used up
4. energetically
5. therefore
6. throbbing
7. introduction

◆ Literary Focus

BIOGRAPHY AND AUTOBIOGRAPHY

In a **biography,** a writer tells about someone else's life. In an **autobiography,** the writer tells about his or her own life.

1. Identify two details that Susy Clemens includes in "My Papa, Mark Twain" that Twain might not tell about himself.

2. What are three details in "The Drive-In Movies" that an author other than Soto would not know and therefore would not include.

◆ Build Grammar Skills

OBJECT PRONOUNS: OBJECTS OF PREPOSITIONS

In the two essays in this group, you'll find prepositional phrases that contain pronouns. When the object of a preposition is a pronoun, use an object pronoun form. Object pronouns are *me, him, her, them,* and *us.* In the following sentences, the prepositional phrase appears in italics, and the object of the preposition is in green.

I made a face *at them.*

What did you say *about him?*

Practice On your paper, write the pronoun form in parentheses that correctly completes each sentence.

1. The essay was written by (she, her) when she was thirteen years old.
2. Their mother took all of (they, them) to the drive-in movies.
3. For (he, him), the essay presents a memory from childhood.
4. She went to the movies with (we, us).
5. There is enough popcorn for you and (I, me).

Writing Application Write a paragraph about Mark Twain using at least three of the following prepositions with an object pronoun: *about, for, with, to,* and *by.*

Build Your Portfolio

 Idea Bank

Writing

1. **Top-Five List** Create a list of five people you would want to write a biography about. For each one, write a sentence to tell why this person appears on your top-five list.

2. **Biographical Sketch** Using Susy Clemens's journal entry as a model, write a brief biographical sketch of someone you know. Include examples of the person's actions and words to bring your subject to life.

3. **Autobiography** Write your "future" auto-biography. Describe events and accomplishments that you would like to achieve during the next twenty years.

Speaking and Listening

4. **Readers Theatre [Group Activity]** With a group, perform "The Drive-In Movies" as a Readers Theatre. Assign parts (including someone to read narration between dialogue) to each group member, rehearse the script, and perform it for the class. **[Performance Link]**

5. **Radio Interview** Use information in "My Papa, Mark Twain" to create interview questions and responses for a radio interview. Perform it live or make a recording and play it.

Projects

6. **Media Update** Do research to learn about the most recent developments in storing and playing back sound and pictures. Explain your findings to the class. **[Science Link]**

7. **Character Parade [Group Activity]** With a group, prepare a parade of some of Mark Twain's most famous characters. Group members can choose to research the characters, create cos-tumes, write words for the characters to say, or perform as the characters. **[Performing Arts Link]**

 Writing Mini-Lesson

Introduction of a Speaker

Imagine that Mark Twain, Gary Soto, or another famous person is coming to speak to your class. Write a brief introduction of the speaker that out-lines his or her accomplishments.

Writing Skills Focus
Use a KWL Chart

You may need to do some research to get information to use in your introduction. To prepare to do research, use a **KWL chart** like the one shown below. In the *K* column, write what you already know. Then, in the *W* column, write what you want to know. Leave the *L* column blank to jot down unexpected facts that you learn as you research.

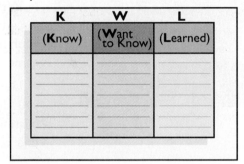

K	W	L
(**K**now)	(**W**ant to **K**now)	(**L**earned)

Prewriting Review your chart and notes. Make sure you have notes on basic information, such as full name, current work, and a few accomplishments.

Drafting Keep your introduction brief. Include only the most interesting and important details.

Revising Read your introduction aloud to a partner. Ask your partner to suggest changes that would make your introduction more interesting.

 Grammar Application

Make sure that objects of prepositions that are pronouns are written in the object form.

Letter to Request Information

Writing Process Workshop

Much information is available in the library or on the Internet, but sometimes you need to talk to an expert or someone you especially trust. When Joan wanted to learn more about "Good English," for instance, she wrote a letter to the scholar and novelist C. S. Lewis.

In a **letter to request information,** a writer asks someone with special knowledge for a specific piece of information. An effective letter is addressed to the right person and identifies the information the writer needs. Write a letter requesting information on a topic of special interest. Use the following tips, presented in this section's Writing Mini-Lessons.

Writing Skills Focus

▶ **Narrow your topic.** Focus on a particular aspect of your topic. Asking for too much information may mean you don't get any. (See p. 552.)

▶ **Write an appropriate beginning.** Identify your reason for writing at the very beginning of the letter. Don't waste your reader's time with roundabout introductions like "My name is . . ." (See p. 563.)

▶ **Use a KWL chart.** To ask a good question, review what you already know to determine what information you are missing. Use a **K**now-**W**ant to Know-**L**earned chart like the one on the next page to focus your questions. (See p. 575.)

MODEL

Dear ① County Clerk,

② We have just gotten a new puppy, and I wanted to find out about licensing the animal.

③ I would like to know at what age an animal must be licensed and what shots it must have. I also need to know how to prove that it has had these shots.

Thank you for any information you are able to provide.

① The writer addresses an official who probably has the information needed.

② The writer gets to the point right away, clearly stating the request.

③ The writer reviews what he or she already knows to determine what information is still needed.

Prewriting

Choose a Topic Think of subjects about which you want to learn more. Think also of problems that you might need to solve at some future time, such as finding the best route between two towns, licensing a dog, or getting into college.

> ## Topic Ideas
> - What changes have taken place in your town in the last ten years
> - How to start a comic-book collection
> - What a person needs to do to become a doctor

Identify an Expert Your letter should go to a person, company, or government office that has information about your subject. Use the phone book, library resources, or the advice of librarians and others to identify possible experts.

Prepare a KWL Chart Use a KWL chart to focus your questions. In the *K* column, list what you already know about the subject. Review the list. Then, jot down what you want to know in the *W* column. Use the *L* column to jot down the useful information you learn when your letter is answered.

KWL Chart

Know	Want to Know	Learned
• Comic books started taking off in the 1940's and 1950's.	• How much do comics from this time period cost?	
• I'm the only one of all my friends that has Issue 1 of *Green Gook*.	• Are there ways to find old comics besides through specialty shops?	
• Sometimes you can see really old comics on display in specialty shops.	• How can you tell whether a comic you own is really valuable?	
	• Is it better to collect comics that are already valuable or to save new comics and hope they will become valuable later?	

Narrow Your Topic Decide exactly what it is you want to know. Don't ask someone to tell you all about your favorite baseball team. Instead, ask for information on a specific player or season.

DRAFTING/REVISING

APPLYING LANGUAGE SKILLS: Business-Letter Format

A business letter always contains certain information, set out in the same way. (See the example on page 578.)

The Heading: Your address and the date appear in the upper right-hand corner.

The Inside Address: The name and address of the person to whom you are writing the letter appear on the left side.

Salutation: Under the inside address is the greeting. It begins with the word *Dear,* followed by the person's title and name, and ends with a colon.

Closing: End the letter with a phrase such as "Yours sincerely" on a line by itself, followed by a comma.

Signature: Sign the letter with your full name. On the following line, type out your name.

Writing Application Check your draft to make sure you have included each element of a business letter.

Writer's Solution Connection Writing Lab

For help formatting a letter, use the Business Letter Shell in the Writer's Toolkit under Writing Tools, Drafting.

APPLYING LANGUAGE SKILLS: Commonly Confused Words

Choose words thoughtfully. Do not be tricked into using an incorrect word that happens to sound like the word you need:

Incorrect:

Please except my apology.

That doesn't effect me.

Correct:

Please accept my apology.

That doesn't affect me.

Practice Write each sentence, choosing the correct word:

1. Turning the lights on had a great (affect, effect) on everyone's mood.
2. I'd like to go, (accept, except) that I need to go shopping with my Dad.
3. (Besides, Beside) my bed sits a letter.

Writing Application Check your draft to make sure you've chosen the correct words.

Writer's Solution Connection
Language Lab

For help focusing questions in your lesson, complete the Narrowing a Topic lesson in the Composing unit.

Drafting

Follow the Proper Form Letters written for business follow a certain standard form, containing the same parts in the same order.

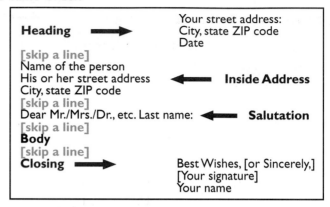

Introduce Your Request Clearly state your reason for writing. If you have more than one question to ask, summarize the topic about which you are writing.

Focus Your Questions Ask specific questions, such as, "Is collecting current first issues of comic books a good idea?" If you ask a general question, such as, "Can you tell me more about collecting comics?" you may not get the information you want. Use your KWL chart to focus your questions.

Revising

Use a Checklist For revising, use the following checklist:

▶ Have I stated my request for information in the opening paragraph? (Cut any unnecessary introductory material, and summarize your topic of interest.)

▶ Do my questions concern what I need to know, or are they unfocused? (Make questions more specific.)

▶ Have I followed proper business-letter format? (Check each part of your letter against the model above.)

Publishing and Presenting

Class Presentation Mail your letter to your expert. When a reply arrives, fill out the "Learned" column in your KWL chart. Read your letter, the reply, and the KWL chart to the class. Discuss your letter and any changes you could have made to it to make it more successful.

Real-World Reading Skills Workshop

Strategies for Success

There are many kinds of maps. Some maps show whole countries; other maps show highways that get you from one place to another; and still other maps show you the streets and landmarks in a city or town. The strategies here will help you read maps effectively:

Identify Your Purpose Know why you are looking at the map. A map of the United States is not going to help you find your way around Houston, but a map of Houston is not going to tell you which states border Texas. Choose the map that fits your purpose.

Check Out the Key Most maps have keys or legends that explain any symbols used on the map. A scale tells you the distance represented by a quarter inch or a half inch. Although most maps are drawn so that north is at the top of the map, a map will usually have a compass on it to confirm the directions. Use all these aids to help you read the map.

Make Connections Locate the cities, landmarks, or street names on the map, and make connections between them. If you are using a city map to find your way around, identify where you are. Then, choose the route that will get you where you want to go. If you are looking at a map of a country, use the scale to calculate distances between countries.

✔ Here are some situations in which reading maps is useful:
▶ Reading a social studies textbook
▶ Finding your way around a strange city on vacation
▶ Finding out how far away a city or a country is

Apply the Strategies

Use the two maps on this page to answer the questions that follow.

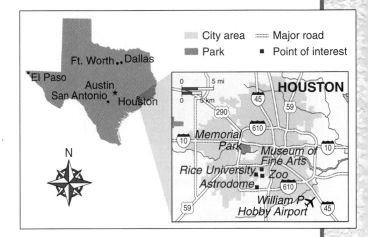

1. Which map would you use if you were trying to identify major cities in Texas?

2. Which map would help you get to the Astrodome?

3. What are three points of interest in Houston?

4. In which direction would you travel to go from Houston to Ft. Worth?

5. If you were on Route 10, approximately how many miles would you travel to get from the west boundary of Houston to the east boundary?

Grammar Review

Personal pronouns have different forms depending on their use in a sentence. Notice the different forms of subject and object pronouns:

nominal adjective "our"] —pro·nom'i·nal·ly *adv.* **pro·noun** (prō'noun') *n.* [altered (infl. by NOUN) < *pronomen* < pro, for + *nomen*, NOUN] *Gram.* any relationship or signal words that assume the fu within clauses or phrases while referring to othe the sentence or in other sentences: *I, you, them, it, myself, anybody, etc.* pronouns

Subject Pronouns	I	he	she	they	we
Object Pronouns	me	him	her	them	us
No Change	it	you			

Subject pronouns are always used for the subject of a verb and for a subject complement (a pronoun or a noun that renames or gives more information about the subject) following a linking verb. (See page 551.)

Subject: *She* wrote a letter.
Subject Complement: The letter writer was *she.*

An object pronoun is used when the pronoun is a direct object (receives the action of a verb), an indirect object (the noun to or for whom an action is done), or the object of a preposition. (See pages 562 and 574.)

Direct Object: The letter encouraged *me.*
Indirect Object: The letter gave *me* encouragement.
Object of a Preposition: She talked about *him.*

Grammar in Writing

✔ *When you use pronouns, remember to use the subject form for subjects and subject complements. Use the object form for direct and indirect objects and objects of prepositions.*

Practice 1 Copy the following sentences into your notebook. Circle each pronoun. Then, identify the pronoun as a subject, a subject complement, an indirect object, a direct object, or the object of a preposition.

1. After the war, they weren't allowed to play.

2. The coach helped them win.

3. She spoke about baseball.

4. The speakers are Tom and she.

5. When Amanda won the gold, the coach congratulated her.

Practice 2 For each of the following sentences, choose the correct form of the pronoun. Give the part of speech for each pronoun.

1. It belongs to Mark and (he, him).

2. (She, Her) and the team won the gold.

3. The coach expected (they, them) to win.

4. She spoke to Amanda and (I, me).

5. The team gave the award to (she, her).

6. The team gave (he, him) a round of applause.

PART 2 *Essays, Speeches, and Media Accounts*

Retroactive I, 1964, Robert Rauschenberg, Wadsworth Atheneum, Hartford, © Robert Rauschenberg/Licensed by VAGA, New York, NY

Guide for Reading

Meet the Authors:

William Harwood (1952–   )

William Harwood's first article about the space program was written for his school newspaper at the University of Tennessee. Since then, he has covered more than eighty-five shuttle flights, working for United Press International, CBS News, and the *Washington Post*. In addition to writing about the space program, Harwood has written astronomy articles for *Ciel et Espace* (a French astronomy magazine) and *Astronomy Now*.

John Updike (1932–   )

John Updike got his start on *The New Yorker* magazine. His frequent contributions to this magazine helped him earn fame as a writer. ("Central Park" is one of the pieces he contributed.)

Updike writes poetry, short stories, essays, and novels. He has won two Pulitzer Prizes for his novels.

Charles Kuralt (1934–1997)

Charles Kuralt discovered unusual places and faces all around the United States. He traveled from place to place in a motor home, reporting on such unique subjects as a unicycling school, a 104-year-old entertainer, and a gas station/poetry factory. His feature about Noah Webster's dictionary was inspired by a visit to a Connecticut spelling bee.

◆ LITERATURE AND YOUR LIFE

CONNECT YOUR EXPERIENCE

When you call a friend to tell about a game or concert you attended, you share what you observed and probably what you thought about it as well. You can experience places and events that others observe by reading articles and transcripts like those in this group.

THEMATIC FOCUS: A Different View

As you read, ask yourself what makes each writer's view of an event or a place unique.

◆ Background for Understanding

TECHNOLOGY

The space shuttle *Challenger* was the twenty-fifth shuttle launched by the United States. On board were seven crew members, including Christa McAuliffe. Because she was the first teacher ever chosen to travel in space, public interest in and excitement about the launch was greater than usual. Seventy-three seconds after its launch, as the nation watched, the *Challenger* exploded, killing the seven people on board.

◆ Build Vocabulary

HOMOPHONES

Homophones are words that sound alike but have different meanings and, usually, different spellings. For example, *cite* ("to give as an example") is pronounced the same way as *sight* ("the ability to see") and *site* ("a place").

WORD BANK

Which word on the list could describe an event that is a catastrophe?

monitoring
occasionally
accumulations
moot
peripheral
catastrophic
cite
atrocious

Space Shuttle *Challenger*
◆ Central Park ◆
Noah Webster's Dictionary

◆ Literary Focus
MEDIA ACCOUNTS

Much of what you learn about the world comes to you through **media accounts**—reports, explanations, opinions, or descriptions written for television, radio, newspapers, and magazines. Some media accounts report only facts; others include the writer's thoughts and reflections. Media accounts bring the world to you, allowing you to experience and consider a wide range of events and ideas.

◆ Reading Strategy
SET A PURPOSE

You usually have a purpose when you go into a store—to buy clothes or to get school supplies. Similarly, you should **set a purpose** before "going in" to a work of literature. Decide *why* you are reading, and then "shop" for the details that help you achieve your purpose. One purpose you might have for reading the works in this group is to broaden your experience. The graphic organizer at left shows details that might help you broaden your experience as you read "Central Park." Make an organizer like it to complete as you read the other works in this group.

Purpose: Broaden Experience

Central Park

Descriptions	Skater falls	Pigeons	Slush
Writer's Reactions	Enjoyment		
My Impression	Busy place	Lots to do	
My Reaction	I'd like to go there		

Space Shuttle *Challenger*

William Harwood

I witnessed the launch from the Kennedy Space Center press site just 4.2 miles from pad 39B. It was my 19th shuttle launch but my first without the comforting presence of UPI Science Editor Al Rossiter Jr., a space veteran with all of the experience I lacked. He was in Pasadena, California, at the Jet Propulsion Laboratory covering *Voyager 2*'s flyby of Uranus.

I arrived at the UPI trailer around 11:30 p.m. Monday night, January 27. I always came to work before the start of fueling on the theory that anytime anyone loaded a half-million gallons of liquid oxygen and liquid hydrogen into anything it was an event worth staffing.

It was bitterly cold that night. I remember cranking up the drafty UPI trailer's baseboard heaters in a futile attempt to warm up while I started banging out copy. I was writing for afternoon, or PM, newspapers that would hit the streets the following afternoon. Because *Challenger*'s launch was scheduled for that morning, the PM cycle was where the action was, the closest thing to "live" reporting that print journalists ever experience. . . . I had written my launch copy the day before and as usual, I spent most of the early morning hours tweaking the story, checking in periodically with NASA public affairs and <u>monitoring</u> the chatter on the bureau's radio scanner. I would <u>occasionally</u> glance toward the launch pad where *Challenger* stood bathed in high power spotlights, clearly visible for dozens of miles around. Off to the side, a brilliant tongue of orange flame periodically flared in the night as excess hydrogen was vented harmlessly into the atmosphere. Back in the UPI trailer, radio reporter Rob Navias rolled in around 4 a.m. A veteran shuttle reporter with an encyclopedic memory for space trivia, Rob and I had covered 14 straight missions together. In keeping with long-standing launch-day tradition, Rob's first comment after stomping into the trailer was "Will it go?" to which I would respond: "Or will it blow?" It was a grim little charade we carried out to mask our constant fear of catastrophe.

As night gave way to day, the launch team was struggling to keep the countdown on track. Problems had delayed fueling and launch—originally scheduled for 9:38 a.m.—for two hours to make sure no dangerous

<u>accumulations</u> of ice had built up on *Challenger*'s huge external tank. Finally, all systems were "go" and the countdown resumed at the T-minus nine-minute mark for a liftoff at 11:38 a.m. Battling my usual pre-launch jitters, I called UPI national desk editor Bill Trott in Washington about three minutes before launch. I had already filed the PM launch story to UPI's computer and Trott now called it up on his screen. We shot the breeze. I reminded him not to push the SEND button until I confirmed vertical motion; two previous launches were aborted at the last second and we didn't want to accidentally "launch" a shuttle on the wire when it was still firmly on the ground. But there were no such problems today. *Challenger*'s three main engines thundered to life on schedule, belching blue-white fire and billowing clouds of steam. Less than seven seconds later, the shuttle's twin boosters ignited with a ground-shaking roar

◆ Build Vocabulary

monitoring (män´ i tər iŋ) *adj.*: Watching or listening to
occasionally (ō kā´ zhən ə lē´) *adv.*: Now and then
accumulations (ə kyōōm´ yōō lā´ shənz) *n.*: Buildups occurring over a period of time

and the spacecraft vaulted skyward.

"And liftoff . . . liftoff of the 25th space shuttle mission, and it has cleared the tower!" said NASA commentator Hugh Harris.

"OK, let it go," I told Trott when Harris started talking. He pushed the SEND button and my story winged away on the A-wire.

◆ **Reading Strategy**
What details help you appreciate the experience of witnessing a launch?

Four miles away, *Challenger* was climbing majestically into a cloudless blue sky. We could not see the initial puffs of smoke indicating a fatal booster flaw. A few seconds later, the crackling roar of those boosters swept over the press site and the UPI trailer started shaking and rattling as the ground shock arrived. I marveled at the view, describing it to Trott in Washington. We always kept the line open for the full eight-and-a-half minutes it took for a shuttle to reach orbit; should disaster strike, the plan went, I would start dictating and Trott would start filing raw copy to the wire.

But for the first few seconds, it was a <u>moot</u> point. The roar was so loud we couldn't hear each other anyway. But the sound quickly faded to a dull rumble as *Challenger* wheeled about and arced over behind its booster exhaust plume, disappearing from view. NASA television, of course, carried the now-familiar closeups of the orbiter, but I wasn't watching television. I was looking out the window at the exhaust cloud towering into the morning sky.

"Incredible," I murmured.

And then, in the blink of an eye, the exhaust plume seemed to balloon outward, to somehow thicken. I recall a fleeting <u>peripheral</u> impression of fragments, of debris flying about, sparkling in the morning sunlight. And then, in that pregnant instant before the knowledge that something terrible has happened settled in, a single booster emerged from the cloud, corkscrewing madly through the sky.

I sat stunned. I couldn't understand what I was seeing.

"Wait a minute . . . something's happened . . ." I told Trott. A booster? Flying on its own? "They're in trouble," I said, my heart pounding. "Lemme dictate something!"

"OK, OK, hang on," Trott said. He quickly started punching in the header material of a one-paragraph "story" that would interrupt the normal flow of copy over the wire and alert editors to breaking news.

I still didn't realize *Challenger* had actually exploded. I didn't know what had happened. For a few heartbeats, I desperately reviewed the crew's options: Could the shuttle somehow have pulled free? Could the crew somehow still be alive? Had I been watching television, I would have known the truth immediately and my copy would have been more final.

But I wasn't watching television.

"Ready," Trott said.

The lead went something like this: "The space shuttle *Challenger* apparently exploded about two minutes after launch today (pause for Trott to catch up) and veered wildly out of control. (pause) The fate of the crew was not known."

"Got it . . ." Trott said, typing as I talked. Bells went off seconds later as the story started clattering out on the bureau's A-wire printer behind me.

Out in Pasadena, Rossiter had watched the launch on NASA television. He ran to his computer, checked the wire and urgently called the bureau. He wanted to know why we had "apparently" blown up the shuttle in the precede. On television, there was no "apparently" about it.

Trott and I quickly corrected the time of the accident (my sense of time was distorted all day) and clarified that *Challenger* had, in fact, suffered a <u>catastrophic</u> failure. While we did not yet know what had happened to the crew, we all knew the chances for survival were virtually zero and the story began reflecting that belief.

For the next half hour or so, I simply dictated my impressions and background to Trott, who would file three or four paragraphs of "running copy" to the wire at a time. At one point, I remember yelling "Obits! Tell somebody to refile the obits!" Before every shuttle mission, I wrote detailed profiles of each crew member. No one actually printed these stories; they were written to serve as instant obits in the event of a disaster. Now, I wanted to refile my profiles for clients who had not saved them earlier. At some point—I have no idea when—I put the phone down and started typing again, filing the copy to Washington where Trott assembled all the pieces into a more-or-less coherent narrative. Dozens of UPI reporters swung into action around the world, later funneling reaction and quotes into the evolving story.

For the next two hours or so I don't remember anything but the mad rush of reporting. Subconsciously, I held the enormity of the disaster at bay; I knew if I relaxed my guard for an instant it could paralyze me. I was flying on some kind of mental autopilot. And then, around 2 p.m. or so, I recall a momentary lull.

My fingers dropped to the keyboard and I stared blankly out the window toward the launch pad. I saw those seven astronauts. I saw them waving to the photographers as they headed for the launch pad. I remembered Christa McAuliffe's smile and Judy Resnik's flashing eyes. Tears welled up. I shook my head, blinked rapidly and turned back to my computer. I'll think about it all later, I told myself. I was right. I think about it every launch.

◆ **Literary Focus**
Why do you think Harwood includes his personal reactions in this media account?

◆ **Build Vocabulary**

moot (mo͞ot) *adj.*: Not worthy of thought or discussion because it has already been resolved

peripheral (pə rif′ ər əl) *adj.*: Lying on the outside edge

catastrophic (kat′ ə sträf′ ik) *adj.*: Causing a complete disaster

Guide for Responding

◆ LITERATURE AND YOUR LIFE

Reader's Response Would you want to keep reporting on the space program after this event? Why or why not?

Thematic Focus In what ways did Harwood's view differ from the view of people who saw the *Challenger* launch on tape?

Journal Writing Jot down your reactions to Harwood's description of this event.

☑ Check Your Comprehension

1. From where did Harwood watch the launch?
2. Why wasn't Harwood certain that the shuttle had exploded?
3. What does Harwood think about when he has finished his reporting?

◆ Critical Thinking

INTERPRET

1. Why do you think Harwood has "pre-launch" jitters? **[Infer]**
2. What do you think Harwood felt when he saw the booster come out of the cloud from the explosion? **[Speculate]**
3. Why do you think Harwood thinks about the *Challenger* at every launch he covers? **[Draw Conclusions]**

EVALUATE

4. Do you think space exploration is worth the risk? **[Make a Judgment]**

EXTEND

5. Would you like to be an astronaut or report on space travel? Why? **[Career Link]**

Central Park

John Updike

On the afternoon of the first day of spring, when the gutters were still heaped high with Monday's snow but the sky itself was swept clean, we put on our galoshes and walked up the sunny side of Fifth Avenue to Central Park. There we saw:

Great black rocks emerging from the melting drifts, their craggy skins glistening like the backs of resurrected brontosaurs.

A pigeon on the half-frozen pond strutting to the edge of the ice and looking a duck in the face.

A policeman getting his shoe wet testing the ice.

Three elderly relatives trying to coax a little boy to accompany his father on a sled ride down a short but steep slope. After much balking, the boy did, and, sure enough, the sled tipped over and the father got his collar full of snow. Everybody laughed except the boy, who sniffled.

Four boys in black leather jackets throwing snowballs at each other. (The snow was ideally soggy, and packed hard with one squeeze.)

Seven men without hats.

Twelve snowmen, none of them intact.

Two men listening to the radio in a car parked outside the Zoo; Mel Allen was broadcasting the Yanks-Cardinals game from St. Petersburg.

A tahr (*Hemitragus jemlaicus*) pleasantly squinting in the sunlight.

An aoudad absently pawing the mud and chewing.

A yak with its back turned.

Empty cages labeled "Coati," "Orang-outang," "Ocelot."

A father saying to his little boy, who was annoyed almost to tears by the inactivity of the seals, "Father (Father Seal, we assumed) is very tired; he worked hard all day."

Most of the cafeteria's out-of-doors tables occupied.

A pretty girl in black pants falling on them at the Wollman Memorial Rink.

"BILL & DORIS" carved on a tree. "REX & RITA" written in the snow.

Two old men playing, and six supervising, a checkers game.

The Michael Friedsam Foundation Merry-Go-Round, nearly empty of children but overflowing with calliope music.

A man on a bench near the carrousel reading, through sunglasses, a book on economics.

Crews of shinglers repairing the roof of the Tavern-on-the-Green.

A woman dropping a camera she was trying to load, the film unrolling in the slush and exposing itself.

A little boy in aviator goggles rubbing his ears and saying, "He really hurt me." "No, he didn't," his nursemaid told him.

The green head of Giuseppe Mazzini staring across the white softball field, unblinking, though the sun was in his eyes.

Water murmuring down walks and rocks and steps. A grown man trying to block one rivulet with snow.

Things like brown sticks nosing through a plot of cleared soil.

A tire track in a piece of mud far removed from where any automobiles could be.

Footprints around a KEEP OFF sign.

Two pigeons feeding each other.

Two showgirls, whose faces had not yet thawed the frost of their makeup, treading indignantly through the slush.

A plump old man saying "Chick, chick" and feeding peanuts to squirrels.

Many solitary men throwing snowballs at tree trunks.

Many birds calling to each other about how little the Ramble has changed.

One red mitten lying lost under a poplar tree.

An airplane, very bright and distant, slowly moving through the branches of a sycamore.

◆ **Literature and Your Life**
Which details in this scene do you think you would have noticed first?

Guide for Responding

◆ LITERATURE AND YOUR LIFE

Reader's Response Does Central Park remind you of any place you've been?

Thematic Focus In what way is Updike's description different from what you normally notice in a park?

Journal Writing Describe a scene near your home. Include many details, as Updike does.

☑ Check Your Comprehension

1. What season does Updike describe?
2. Name three things he sees.
3. Name one thing he hears.

◆ Critical Thinking

INTERPRET

1. Why do you think Updike lists details in no particular order of importance? **[Speculate]**
2. Describe the weather on the day Updike describes. **[Draw Conclusions]**

EVALUATE

3. How well does Updike's description help you "see" Central Park? **[Assess]**

APPLY

4. Why is it valuable for towns and cities to provide recreational parks? **[Apply]**

Noah Webster's Dictionary

Charles Kuralt

▲ Critical Viewing How can you tell that the man on the cover of the dictionary is interested in language and words? **[Infer]**

◆ Build Vocabulary

cite (sīt) *v.*: Refer to as an example

atrocious (ə trō′ shəs) *adj.*: Very bad; outrageous

West Hartford, Connecticut. I watched students of West Hartford's Bridlepath School compete in that vanishing standby of American education, the spelling bee. The spelling bee was held in Noah Webster's kitchen. That was a good place for it, because if it hadn't been for Noah Webster, we might never have had spelling bees or even much spelling. Before this Yankee schoolmaster came along, Americans spelled poorly or not at all; George Washington, to <u>cite</u> one <u>atrocious</u> example, spelled pretty much as he pleased. After Noah Webster, Americans spelled the way Noah told them to.

The kids in the spelling bee came from all kinds of backgrounds and from all over the country. That they speak the same language—that a kid from Maine can meet a kid from Oregon and understand him right from the start—that is Noah Webster's gift to us. His little Blue-Backed Speller sold nearly 100 million copies in his lifetime. It wore out printing presses. It was read by nearly every American who could read.

And then, working for twenty-five years, alone and by hand, Noah Webster produced his dictionary— seventy thousand words, including a lot of American words that had never been in a dictionary before:

applesauce, bullfrog, chowder, hickory, skunk. It was the most valuable piece of scholarship any American ever did.

Noah Webster, from this old house in West Hartford, created American style and American manners. It is not too much to say that he created American education. He was the first teacher of American history, the first influential American newspaper editor.

"What rubbed Mr. Webster's fur the wrong way," West Hartford historian Nelson Burr told me, "was that even after the Revolution, most of America's books and most of America's ideas still came from England. He wanted to put a stop to that. He wanted to create Americanism—not in the sense of jingoistic patriotism,[1] but in the sense of a new literature, a new language."

In the Italy of Noah Webster's day, there were so many dialects that many Italians couldn't talk to one another. The same thing, to a lesser degree, was true in Great Britain. America's common language, with more or less agreed-upon rules for spelling and punctuation, was the work of Noah Webster. He wanted us to be one nation, a new nation, and he showed us how.

---

1. **jingoistic** (jin´ gō is´ tik) **patriotism** (pā´ trē ə tiz´ əm): Blind, uncritical love of one's country.

Guide for Responding

◆ LITERATURE AND YOUR LIFE

Reader's Response Estimate how often you use a dictionary in a year.

Thematic Focus In what way did Webster's view of language influence future generations?

☑ Check Your Comprehension

1. What is the location of Kuralt's broadcast?
2. How long did it take Webster to produce the first dictionary?
3. What is one other "first" that Kuralt credits to Webster?

◆ Critical Thinking

INTERPRET

1. How does Kuralt feel about Webster? **[Infer]**
2. Why did Webster invest so much time in producing a dictionary? **[Draw Conclusions]**
3. Explain the statement that Webster "created American style and American manners." **[Interpret]**

EVALUATE

4. Explain why it is important to use correct spelling. **[Support]**

APPLY

5. Identify two reasons that you or a classmate might consult a dictionary. **[Relate]**

Beyond Literature

Cultural Connection

Dictionaries and Our Changing Language The dictionary that carries Noah Webster's name has been revised many times. American English, like other languages, is constantly changing. Words that were once slang may become so commonly used that they are eventually considered almost standard. For example, today's dictionaries include entries that say that *cool* means "very good." Technological advances create the need for whole sets of new words. When Noah Webster created his dictionary, no one needed a word for *camcorder*. Today, a dictionary would not be complete without this entry.

Cross-Curricular Activity
Specialized Words Create dictionary entries for at least ten words from math, music, science, or another subject. Include correct pronunciation and a definition for each word.

Guide for Responding (continued)

◆ Reading Strategy

SET A PURPOSE

When you have a **purpose for reading,** your purpose helps you to focus on what to remember. If your purpose for reading these works was to broaden your experience, then you would focus on details and impressions that helped you achieve this purpose.

1. Describe the main impression you have of Central Park after reading "Central Park."
2. Identify three things you learned as you read "Noah Webster's Dictionary."

◆ Build Vocabulary

USING HOMOPHONES

On your paper, match the homophones. Explain the meaning of each word.

1. way   **a.** knead
2. scent   **b.** weigh
3. need   **c.** sent

SPELLING STRATEGY

Some words, like *occasionally,* contain doubled consonants as well as single consonants. Patterns can help you remember which is which. For example, notice that in *occasionally,* two single consonants come between two doubles. For each of the following words, the pattern is two singles, a double, then a single. On your paper, write a word for each clue.

1. lines that don't intersect: p _ _ _ _ _ _ l
2. made of metal: m _ _ _ _ _ _ c
3. huge: c _ _ _ _ _ _ l

USING THE WORD BANK

On your paper, match each word from the Word Bank with the word closest in meaning.

1. monitoring   **a.** watching
2. moot   **b.** sometimes
3. peripheral   **c.** on the outskirts
4. catastrophic   **d.** give as an example
5. cite   **e.** not worth discussing
6. occasionally   **f.** buildups
7. accumulations   **g.** disastrous
8. atrocious   **h.** outrageous

◆ Literary Focus

MEDIA ACCOUNTS

In a **media account**—writing done for newspapers, magazines, television, or radio, you can learn about people, places, and events around the world.

1. Why do you think Harwood included feelings as well as facts in "Space Shuttle *Challenger*"?
2. Why might people be interested in reading a magazine article about Central Park?
3. What details in "Noah Webster's Dictionary" indicate that it was written to be read aloud on television or radio?

◆ Build Grammar Skills

APOSTROPHES

Apostrophes have two uses:

• An apostrophe is used with singular or plural nouns to show a relationship or possession.

Voyager 2's flyby of Uranus (the flyby that *Voyager 2* made)

Webster's Dictionary (the dictionary that Webster wrote)

• Apostrophes indicate missing letters in a contraction (a word or a combination of words written in shortened form).

Something's happened! (*Something has* happened!)

Practice On your paper, write each numbered item, placing an apostrophe where it is needed.

1. the bureaus radio scanners
2. He didnt know.
3. West Hartfords Bridlepath School
4. the cafeterias tables
5. the *Challengers* tanks

Writing Application On your paper, write each group of words in a shorter way. Use apostrophes in your shortened version.

1. the snow that fell on Monday
2. He had written
3. the gift Noah Webster gave to us
4. We would not have

Build Your Portfolio

 Idea Bank

Writing

1. **Detailed List** Prepare a detailed list of the things that are happening around you in the classroom. Give the list a title.

2. **Journal Entry** In your journal, respond to "Noah Webster's Dictionary." Explain whether or not you agree that Webster's accomplishment was as important as Kuralt says.

3. **Reflection** Write a media account like Kuralt's that starts with a small event and leads to your thoughts and feelings about a larger issue.

Speaking and Listening

4. **Television Script** Read "Noah Webster's Dictionary" as if you were the one to read it on the air. If possible, record your reading on audio- or videotape.

5. **Spelling Bee [Group Activity]** With a group of classmates, plan a mini spelling bee. Each group member should contribute ten words and explain why they are difficult to spell. Make a list of the words and the reasons they are included.

Projects

6. **Dictionary [Group Activity]** With a group of classmates, choose at least twenty slang words that you and your friends use. Create a dictionary of these words. Group members can write definitions, illustrate the definitions, create a cover, or arrange the words in alphabetical order.

7. **Space Exploration Timeline** Create a timeline that shows important dates and events in the history of space exploration. Annotate your timeline with facts and statistics about each event.

 Writing Mini-Lesson

Eyewitness Account

Think of an event or a situation that you saw and experienced as it happened. Write about the event, telling what happened and what your reactions were.

Writing Skills Focus: Time Order

Because you are telling about an event, the most logical order is **time order.** Put details in order of what happened first, next, and last.

Prewriting Use a sequence-of-events chart like the one shown below to organize details of the event in the order in which they happened:

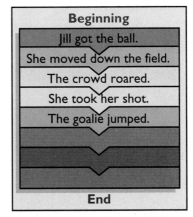

Drafting Write complete sentences about each of the details on your chart. Use words that show time order to indicate when things happened.

Revising Have a partner read your draft and comment on whether he or she was able to form a clear mental picture of the event. Use any suggestions your partner may have to make your account more vivid.

> ◆ **Grammar Application**
>
> Check that you have correctly used apostrophes to show contractions, relationships, and possession. Do not use apostrophes with plurals.

Guide for Reading

Meet the Authors:

Joseph Bruchac (1942–)

This successful writer was once told by a writing instructor "Give it up. You'll never write a good poem." Since that awful prediction, Bruchac has written and edited many collections of poetry, winning numerous writing awards. His poems, stories, and essays have been translated into Russian, Italian, Polish, German, and many other languages. As you will read in "Restoring the Circle," Bruchac is committed to preserving and celebrating his Native American heritage.

Henry David Thoreau (1817–1862)

At the age of twenty-eight, Thoreau built a cabin on Walden Pond, in Concord, Massachusetts, and lived there by himself for two years. He wrote about his daily experiences in *Walden*, a book that changed the way many Americans viewed their place in the world. Although Thoreau did not advise everyone to live alone in nature, he did encourage people to strive to live a simple life.

Bailey White (1950–)

As a first-grade teacher in the town where she was born and raised, Bailey White didn't expect to become famous. Radio, though, brought her voice and observations into homes across the country. Although she is now a best-selling author, she continues to live a simple life in the pine woods of Georgia.

Kerry Cochrane (1956–)

Kerry Cochrane has taught classes and written books on using the Internet. She is Head of Reference at Loyola University's library.

◆ LITERATURE AND YOUR LIFE

CONNECT YOUR EXPERIENCE

Outside your own home, where do you find connections between your own experience and the rest of the world? Each of the essays in this group shows how people make connections between themselves and the world around them.

THEMATIC FOCUS: The Living Earth

What do these writers have to say about humans' place in the world?

◆ Background for Understanding

SOCIAL STUDIES

Three of these essays deal with the subject of conserving nature. People were not always as aware of the need to care for natural resources as they are today. Conservation became an issue in the United States in the early 1900's. President Theodore Roosevelt established the first federal wildlife refuge at Pelican Island in Florida and set aside more than 140 million acres to be national forest reserves. He also held a national conference on conservation that led leaders in individual states to establish conservation groups.

◆ Build Vocabulary

RELATED WORDS: FORMS OF *tolerate*

Joseph Bruchac encourages tolerance in his essay. The word *tolerance* means "recognition and respect for something you may not agree with." It is a form of *tolerate,* "the action of respecting something you don't necessarily agree with."

WORD BANK

Which of these words names the result of something being diluted, or made weaker?

tolerance
detrimental
imparted
dilution
demise
vigilance

Restoring the Circle
◆ *from* In Wildness Is the Preservation of the World ◆
Turkeys ◆ How the Internet Works

Paradise #1, Suzanne Duranceau, Illustratrice

◆ Literary Focus

TYPES OF ESSAYS

An essay is a short nonfiction work about a particular subject. There are many kinds of essays:

- "Restoring the Circle" is a **persuasive essay:** It attempts to convince a reader to act or think in a certain way.
  - "In Wildness Is the Preservation of the World" is a **visual essay:** It conveys its point through photographs as well as text.
    - "Turkeys" is a **narrative essay:** It tells a story about a real-life experience.
    - "How the Internet Works" is an **informational essay:** It explains or informs.

◆ Reading Strategy

IDENTIFY AUTHOR'S MAIN POINTS

On a walk through the woods, you would identify a tree or an animal by its main features. Similarly, to understand the message of an essay, you would **identify the author's main points.** The main points are probably those for which the author provides examples or explains in great detail. As you read these essays, make a tree graphic organizer like the one shown. On the branches, write the main points and the examples that illustrate the points.

Example
Example
Example
Example
Example
Example
Main point
Main point
Main point

Message of Essay

Restoring the Circle:

Native American Literature as a Means of Preserving Cultural Traditions

JOSEPH BRUCHAC

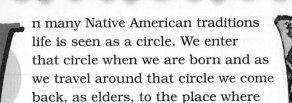

In many Native American traditions life is seen as a circle. We enter that circle when we are born and as we travel around that circle we come back, as elders, to the place where we began. The elders, who have spent a lifetime learning their cultural traditions, are the ones who are supposed to be the closest to the children, passing on their traditions through the teaching to be found in stories. As long as that circle remains unbroken, the people will survive.

Imagine what it would be like if someone who never met you and knew nothing about the circle of your life wrote a story about you. Even if that person was a good writer, you probably would not agree with what he wrote. As interesting as imagination may be, it cannot take the place of experience and firsthand knowledge. In a similar way, imaginative portrayals of Native American people and Native American cultures became painful stereotypes and distorted history. Native American men were pictured as savage and dangerous people who were aggressive for no good reason. Yet it is historically true that none of America's so-called "Indian wars" were ever begun by the Indians. Native American women were pictured as nothing more than beasts of burden. Yet in many Native American cultures, such as that of the Iroquois, the women were the heads of families, the owners of the houses, and the ones who chose the chiefs. Details of Native cultures were badly confused. For example, the famous poem *Hiawatha* by Henry Wadsworth Longfellow actually tells the story of Managozho, a trickster hero of the Chippewa people. The real Hiawatha was a political leader of the Iroquois people. It would be like calling the hero of the Anglo-Saxon epic *Beowulf* Julius Caesar. More than 400 different languages are spoken by the various Native American nations of North America, but instead of showing the complexity and variety of Native American cultures, much of the literature by non-Native people made all Indians look and sound alike.

◆ **Literary Focus** What example does Bruchac use to persuade you that Native American cultures are rich and valuable?

Many Native Americans chose to become writers because they wanted to restore the circle through more accurate portrayals of themselves and their people. In many cases, too, they hoped to restore a sense of pride in their own heritage. Because of the inaccurate and unpleasant ways Native Americans have been portrayed in books by non-Indian authors, Native children have sometimes felt ashamed of themselves and decided that it would be better for them to forget their own cultures and try to be "just like everyone else." Today, because of the writing of such Native American authors as Michael Dorris or Linda Hogan, young Native people can read stories and poems in which Native Americans are presented as fully-rounded characters from accurately described tribal traditions. As portrayed by Native American authors, Indians are sometimes good, sometimes not so good, but no longer one-dimensional stereotypes.

In the period between 1850 and 1950, many Native American children were sent away to Indian boarding schools where they were not allowed to speak their own Native languages. Whether they wanted to or not, they were expected to no longer "be Indian" and, removed completely from the circle of their families, denied contact with their elders. It was felt by many well-meaning people in the United States government that the only way to "help the Indians" was by making them be more like European Americans. Today, of course, we see

◀ **Critical Viewing** What are these children doing to celebrate their Native American heritage? **[Identify]**

◀ **Critical Viewing** Based on the essay and this picture of Bruchac, explain whether you think Bruchac enjoys nature. **[Speculate]**

Kiowa Indian ancestry. His first novel, *House Made of Dawn,* tells the story of a young Native American man who returns home after fighting as an American soldier in a foreign war. He feels divided between the white world and the Indian world, and that division in himself makes him sick. It is only by understanding his own traditions and returning to them that he is able to restore his health and self-respect. That novel, which won a Pulitzer Prize in 1969, is a good example of the kind of Native American writing which helps preserve cultural traditions. It contains authentic and very well-written descriptions of Native American life around the time of the late 1940's and early 1950's. Many Native Americans who have read this book have felt deeply inspired by it because its main character, caught between the white and Indian worlds, experiences some of the confusion and pain which they have also felt. It is hard to be a stranger in your own country, but that is the way many Native Americans sometimes feel. By reading Momaday's novel, they gained a better understanding of their own feelings, and it strengthened their convictions about the importance of preserving their own traditions.

Native American literature, like all literatures, is also a way to speak to the world. In some cases, novels by Native American writers are now being used as textbooks in college courses in history and sociology. Writing can become a window into another reality, offering

things differently. In a multicultural world we understand how important cultural traditions are in maintaining a sense of self-worth. It is now believed that whoever you are, whether you are Jewish American, African American, Italian American, or Native American, knowing about your own history and culture can make you a stronger person. Today, many Native American people are discovering that Native American literature can help them find their way back to that old circle of knowledge. In some cases, people who were not taught their tribal languages as children are learning those languages again through literature. In Arizona, a successful project helped Pima and Papago children learn their native O'odham language by reading traditional songs in O'odham and then writing poems in O'odham. Those songs, which had been preserved as literature, and the new poems worked together to help strengthen traditions.

One of the most prominent Native American writers is N. Scott Momaday, who is of

◆ **Literature and Your Life**
How could connecting with your history make you a stronger person?

to non-Natives the opportunity to authentically experience something of Native American culture. If you read a book about another culture, you may be more likely to have understanding and <u>tolerance</u> for that culture. When you have respect for another culture, then you are much less likely to do things which will be <u>detrimental</u> to that culture and to the people of that culture. Perhaps, because of the cultural understanding offered through Native American literature, the circle of Native American cultural traditions will be less threatened in the generations to come.

◆ **Build Vocabulary**

tolerance (täl´ ər əns) *n.*: Respect for something different

detrimental (de´ trə ment´ əl) *adj.*: Harmful

Beyond Literature

Social Studies Connection

Native Americans of the Eastern Woodlands Joseph Bruchac is part Abenaki, a Native American group in the northeastern United States. The name Abenaki is an Algonquian word for easterner. Eastern Woodland Indians, of which the Abenaki are a part, at first welcomed the European settlers. The growing European population, though, decreased the game supply and made it difficult for these Native Americans to continue their traditional lifestyles. Eventually, the hunters became farmers, and by 1800, the Abenaki, who had once ranged over much of the Northeast, found themselves limited to Maine.

Cross-Curricular Activity
Find out more about the traditional and contemporary culture of another group of Native Americans from the Eastern Woodlands. Explain your findings to the class.

Guide for Responding

◆ LITERATURE AND YOUR LIFE

Reader's Response What questions would you like to ask Joseph Bruchac about his heritage?

Thematic Focus Why do you think Americans tend to link Native American cultures so strongly to nature?

☑ **Check Your Comprehension**

1. Describe how some Native Americans use a circle to explain life.
2. What are two examples of ways in which Native American people have been misunderstood by those who are not Native American?

◆ Critical Thinking

INTERPRET
1. Explain the title "Restoring the Circle." **[Interpret]**
2. In what ways do Native American writers help to restore the circle? **[Support]**
3. Why is it important to Bruchac that Native American culture be acknowledged and respected? **[Synthesize]**

EVALUATE
4. Do you think an understanding of one's heritage makes a person stronger? Explain. **[Make a Judgment]**

APPLY
5. Identify three resources you could use to gather accurate information about Native American culture. **[Social Studies Link]**

from In WILDNESS Is the PRESERVATION of the WORLD

Henry David Thoreau and Eliot Porter

Time is but the stream I go a-fishing in. I drink at it; but while I drink I see the sandy bottom and detect how shallow it is. Its thin current slides away, but eternity remains. I would drink deeper; fish in the sky, whose bottom is pebbly with stars. I cannot count one. I know not the first letter of the alphabet. I have always been regretting that I was not as wise as the day I was born.

Sabbaday Brook with Yellow Leaves, Passaconaway, New Hampshire, 1956, Eliot Porter, Amon Carter Museum, Fort Worth, Texas

Who taught the oven-bird to conceal her nest? It is on the ground, yet out of sight. What cunning there is in nature! No man could have arranged it more artfully for the purpose of concealment.

Only the escape of the bird betrays it.

Ovenbird, Ely, Minnesota, June 30, 1961, Eliot Porter, Amon Carter Museum, Fort Worth, Texas

Early in May, the oaks, hickories, maples, and other trees, just putting out amidst the pine woods around the pond, imparted a brightness like sunshine to the landscape, especially in cloudy days, as if the sun were breaking through mists and shining faintly on the hill-sides here and there.

Maple, Oak and Beech, Conway, New Hampshire, 1957, Eliot Porter, Amon Carter Museum, Fort Worth, Texas

Every day a new picture is painted and framed, held up for half an hour, in such lights as the Great Artist chooses, and then withdrawn, and the curtain falls.

And then the sun goes down, and long the afterglow gives light.

And then the damask curtains glow along the western window.

And now the first star is lit, and I go home.

◆ **Build Vocabulary**

imparted (im pärt´ id) *v.:* Gave; revealed

Sunset Clouds, Tesuque, New Mexico, 1959, Eliot Porter, Amon Carter Museum, Fort Worth, Texas

Guide for Responding

◆ LITERATURE AND YOUR LIFE

Reader's Response Which of Thoreau's ideas about nature interests you most? Why?

Thematic Focus Thoreau describes nature at Walden Pond during May. What is nature like in May where you live?

Sketch Draw a picture of nature in May in your community.

☑ Check Your Comprehension

1. Where is an oven-bird's nest found?
2. To what does Thoreau compare a newly painted and framed picture?

◆ Critical Thinking

INTERPRET

1. According to Thoreau, why is May special? **[Analyze]**
2. Why is time like a stream, according to Thoreau? **[Draw Conclusions]**
3. What appears in the new picture Thoreau describes as an everyday event? **[Interpret]**

APPLY

4. Based on your own ideas and what you may have discovered about nature from Thoreau's observations, how would you define the importance of nature in a person's life? **[Define]**

TURKEYS

Bailey White

Something about my mother attracts ornithologists. It all started years ago when a couple of them discovered she had a rare species of woodpecker coming to her bird feeder. They came in the house and sat around the window, exclaiming and taking pictures with big fancy cameras. But long after the red cockaded woodpeckers had gone to roost, the ornithologists were still there. There always seemed to be three or four of them wandering around our place and staying for supper.

In those days, during the 1950's, the big concern of ornithologists in our area was the wild turkey. They were rare, and the pure-strain wild turkeys had begun to interbreed with farmers' domestic stock. The species was being degraded. It was extinction by <u>dilution</u>, and to the ornithologists it was just as tragic as the more dramatic <u>demise</u> of the passenger pigeon or the Carolina parakeet.

One ornithologist had devised a formula to compute the ratio of domestic to pure-strain wild turkey in an individual bird by comparing the angle of flight at takeoff and the rate of acceleration. And in those sad days, the turkeys were flying low and slow.

It was during that time, the spring when I was six years old, that I caught the measles. I had a high fever, and my mother was worried about me. She kept the house quiet and dark and crept around silently, trying different methods of cooling me down.

Even the ornithologists stayed away—but not out of fear of the measles or respect for a household with sickness. The fact was, they had discovered a wild turkey nest. According to the formula, the hen was pure-strain wild—not a taint of the sluggish domestic bird in her blood—and the ornithologists were camping in the woods, protecting her nest from predators and taking pictures.

◀ **Critical Viewing** Why would scientists be interested in saving this species of bird? [Speculate]

One night our phone rang. It was one of the ornithologists. "Does your little girl still have measles?" He asked.

"Yes," said my mother. "She's very sick. Her temperature is 102."

"I'll be right over," said the ornithologist.

In five minutes a whole carload of them arrived. They marched solemnly into the house, carrying a cardboard box. "A hundred and two, did you say? Where is she?" they asked my mother.

They crept into my room and set the box down on the bed. I was barely conscious, and when I opened my eyes, their worried faces hovering over me seemed to float out of the darkness like giant, glowing eggs. They snatched the covers off me and felt me all over. They consulted in whispers.

"Feels just right, I'd say."

"A hundred two—can't miss if we tuck them up close and she lies still."

I closed my eyes then, and after a while the ornithologists drifted away, their pale faces bobbing up and down on the black wave of fever.

The next morning I was better. For the first time in days I could think. The memory of the ornithologists with their whispered voices was like a dream from another life. But when I pulled down the covers, there staring up at me with googly eyes and wide mouths were sixteen fuzzy baby turkeys, and the cracked chips and caps of sixteen brown speckled eggs.

I was a sensible child. I gently stretched myself out. The eggshells crackled, and the turkey babies fluttered and cheeped and snuggled

---

◀ **Critical Viewing** Compare and contrast the wild turkey with a wild bird from your area. [Compare and Contrast]

◆ **Build Vocabulary**

vigilance (vij´ ə ləns) *n.*: Watchfulness

against me. I laid my aching head back on the pillow and closed my eyes. "The ornithologists," I whispered. "The ornithologists have been here."

It seems the turkey hen had been so disturbed by the elaborate protective measures that had been undertaken on her behalf that she had abandoned her nest on the night the eggs were due to hatch. It was a cold night. The ornithologists, not having an incubator on hand, used their heads and came up with the next best thing.

The baby turkeys and I gained our strength together. When I was finally able to get out of bed and feebly creep around the house, the turkeys peeped and cheeped around my ankles, scrambling to keep up with me and tripping over their own big spraddle-toed feet. When I went outside for the first time, the turkeys tumbled after me down the steps and scratched around in the yard while I sat in the sun.

Finally, in late summer, the day came when they were ready to fly for the first time as adult birds. The ornithologists gathered. I ran down the hill, and the turkeys ran too. Then, one by one, they took off. They flew high and fast. The ornithologists made Vs with their thumbs and forefingers, measuring angles. They consulted their stopwatches and paced off distances. They scribbled in their tiny notebooks. Finally they looked at each other. They sighed. They smiled. They jumped up and down and hugged each other. "One hundred percent pure wild turkey!" they said.

Nearly forty years have passed since then. Now there's a vaccine for measles. And the woods where I live are full of pure wild turkeys. I like to think they are all descendants of those sixteen birds I saved from the vigilance of the ornithologists.

Guide for Responding

◆ LITERATURE AND YOUR LIFE

Reader's Response How would you have reacted if you woke up surrounded by newly hatched turkeys?

Thematic Focus How does Bailey White help care for the living Earth?

Journal Writing Make a list of five things you can do to preserve nature.

☑ Check Your Comprehension

1. Why are the ornithologists studying the wild turkeys around White's home?
2. Why do the ornithologists want to know young White's temperature?
3. How do the ornithologists know that the turkeys are 100 percent wild?

◆ Critical Thinking

INTERPRET

1. What is White's opinion of the ornithologists' personalities? **[Infer]**
2. How do you think White feels about animals? **[Draw Conclusions]**
3. How do you think young White felt when she watched the turkeys take off? **[Speculate]**

EVALUATE

4. How important is the survival of one species, such as the wild turkey, in the balance of nature? **[Assess]**

EXTEND

5. What are some factors that can contribute to the extinction of a species? **[Science Link]**

How the Internet Works

Kerry Cochrane

The central problem in designing the Internet was finding a way for different kinds of computers all over the country to talk to one another. ARPA solved this problem with Internet protocols. Protocols are sets of rules that standardize how something is done, so that everyone knows what to expect. For example, think of any game you've played and the rules that went with that game. The rules of the game tell you how many players you can have, what order you play in, what's allowed and what's not allowed, and how to keep score. Once you know the rules, you can play with people very different from you. Internet protocols are like game rules: they set up standard procedures for computers to follow so that they can communicate with each other.

The Internet is often compared to the postal service. They both seem to work like one big organization, but are actually made up of smaller parts that work together. There are local post offices in small towns, regional postal systems in big cities, and national postal services for countries. They all use different machinery to handle the mail, and different equipment to deliver it

from bicycles to trucks to airplanes. Postal workers all over the world speak hundreds of different languages. But they all manage to work together because of certain rules, or protocols. Postal protocols say that mail must be in envelopes or packages, there must be postage, and every piece of mail must have an address. As long as you know these rules, you can send mail to anyone in the world.

The Internet works in a similar way. As long as everyone knows the protocols, information can travel easily between machines and the people using them worldwide. The basic group of protocols that governs the Internet is the TCP/IP set of protocols. This stands for Transmission Control Protocol (TCP) and Internet Protocol (IP). Internet Protocol says that every computer connected to the Internet must have a unique address. These addresses consist of four sets of numbers separated by periods. For example, the IP address for one of the computers at the University of Illinois at Urbana-Champaign is **128.174.5.49.** Once you have the IP address of a computer, you know where to send messages or other information. Transmission Control Protocol manages the information you send out by computer. TCP breaks each message into manageable chunks and numbers each chunk in order. Then the numbered groups of information are marked with the IP address of the other computer and are sent out to it. When they arrive on the other end, TCP software checks to see that all the pieces are there and puts them back in order, ready to use.

When you drop a letter into a mailbox, it gets collected and sorted with hundreds of other pieces of mail. Your local post office sorts and routes the mail according to its destination and then sends it on to the next post office. Information is sorted and routed on the Internet in the same way. Computers on the Internet called routers, or packet switchers, read the IP addresses on each packet of information, and direct the packets to their destination. The information can be sent from one computer to another on phone lines, by satellite networks, on fiber-optic cables, or even through radio transmissions.

IP addresses are made up of numbers, which can be hard to remember and use. So computers usually have alphabetical addresses as well. Like IP addresses, these alphabetical addresses have several parts separated by periods, although they may have fewer or more than four parts. So a computer at the University of Iowa with the IP address **128.255.40.201** also has the alphabetical address **panda.uiowa.edu,** which is easier to remember. The first part of this address, **panda,** is the name of the *host* computer. The rest of this address, **uiowa.edu,** is called a domain name, because each part of the name refers to a domain. Each domain gives information about

the Internet site, such as where it's located, who's responsible for the computer, and what kind of institution it's connected to. Moving from right to left, the domains give more specific information about the location of the host computer. In the domain name **uiowa.edu,** for example, the domain **edu** tells you that the host computer is run by an educational institution, because **edu** is the domain attached to all United States educational sites. The domain **uiowa** stands for the University of Iowa, which is the specific educational institution where the host computer named panda is located.

In the United States, there are six domains that are used at the end of domain names, and each one refers to the type of site that's running the computer.

Countries outside the United States do not use these domains. Instead, they have two-letter country domains at the end of their names, such as **nz** for New Zealand, **br** for Brazil, or **ca** for Canada.

Every person with an Internet *account* has a personal address, too. Individual Internet addresses are made up of a unique *user ID* (sometimes called a user name) for each person, which is attached to an alphabetical address by an "at" symbol (@). User IDs are usually taken from your name. My full Internet address is **kcochra@orion.it.luc.edu.** Reading this address from left to right, you see that my user ID is **kcochra** (from Kerry Cochrane), and I'm at the address **orion.it.luc.edu. Orion** is the name of the host machine running this account. The office of Information Technologies runs the computer named orion, so the first domain is called **it.** Information Technologies is an office of Loyola University Chicago, so the next domain is **luc.** Because this is an educational institution, the final domain is **edu.** The President of the United States even has an Internet address at the White House: **president@ whitehouse.gov.** Although they may seem complicated at first, Internet addresses make sense when you know how they work.

A few years ago the Internet was not available to the general public. Most people with Internet accounts got them through universities or companies where they were students or employees. As interest in the Internet has grown, however, ways to connect have increased, and they are improving all the time. One of the fastest-growing groups of Internet users is students and teachers in kindergarten through 12th grade.

Schools around the world are getting access to the Internet so children can benefit from the immense resources available on-line.

There are several ways for schools to connect to the Internet. Many states or regions have developed their own networks to link schools together and get them on-line. Some universities and colleges provide guest accounts for local schools. Also, companies called Internet providers have begun to market Internet accounts to schools, companies, and private individuals. Your school may already be connected to the Internet, or someone in your family may have an account at work or at home.

Guide for Responding

◆ LITERATURE AND YOUR LIFE

Reader's Response Did the comparison to a post office help you understand how the Internet works? Explain.

Thematic Focus In what way does the Internet bring you closer to the rest of the world?

Journal Writing Jot down an e-mail message you'd like to send to a friend.

☑ Check Your Comprehension

1. What are Internet protocols?
2. What does TCP/IP stand for?
3. What is the Internet address of the President of the United States? Explain each part of the address.
4. What is the fastest growing group of Internet users ?

◆ Critical Thinking

INTERPRET

1. What does the author mean when she mentions computers talking to one another? **[Infer]**
2. How does the Internet operate in a way similar to and different from a postal service? **[Compare and Contrast]**
3. How are these two Internet addresses related: 123.666.12.878 and marv.utexas.edu? **[Distinguish]**
4. What do you know about this person from the Internet address: chairman@computerinc.dom? **[Draw Conclusions]**

APPLY

5. What kind of address could you create for yourself at your school? Explain each part. **[Apply]**

EXTEND

6. In what ways does a good understanding of math help you to use and work with a computer? **[Mathematics Link]**

CONNECTIONS TO TODAY'S WORLD

The addressing system described in "How the Internet Works" allows Internet users to access hundreds of thousands of sites, or places, on the Internet. Once you arrive at a site, you can navigate through its levels. This page has many levels, dealing with all kinds of sports.

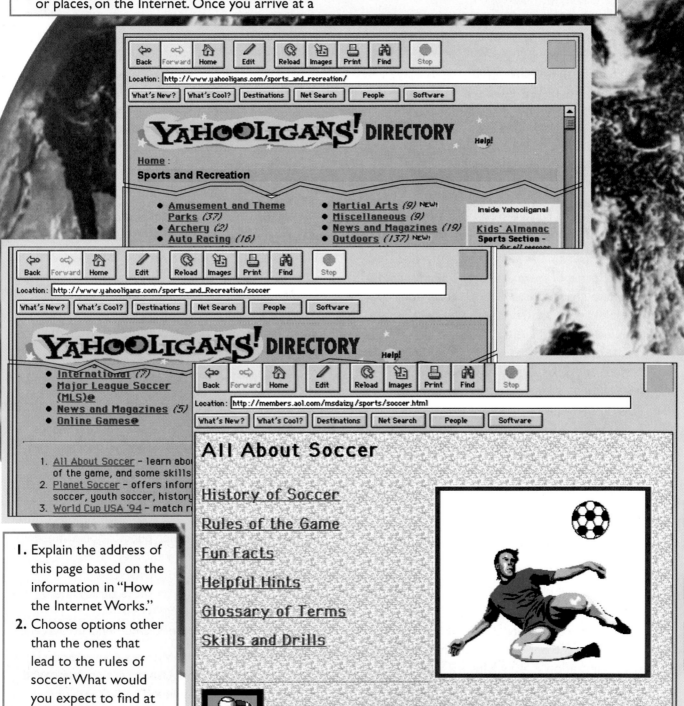

YAHOOLIGANS! DIRECTORY

Location: http://www.yahooligans.com/sports_and_recreation/

What's New? | What's Cool? | Destinations | Net Search | People | Software

Home :
Sports and Recreation

- **Amusement and Theme Parks** *(37)*
- **Archery** *(2)*
- **Auto Racing** *(16)*
- **Martial Arts** *(9)* NEW!
- **Miscellaneous** *(9)*
- **News and Magazines** *(19)*
- **Outdoors** *(137)* NEW!

Inside Yahooligans!

Kids' Almanac Sports Section — *for all seasons*

YAHOOLIGANS! DIRECTORY

Location: http://www.yahooligans.com/sports_and_Recreation/soccer

What's New? | What's Cool? | Destinations | Net Search | People | Software

- **International** *(7)*
- **Major League Soccer (MLS)@**
- **News and Magazines** *(5)*
- **Online Games@**

1. All About Soccer – learn abo[ut] of the game, and some skills
2. Planet Soccer – offers infor[mation] soccer, youth soccer, history
3. World Cup USA '94 – match r[esults]

Location: http://members.aol.com/msdaizy/sports/soccer.html

What's New? | What's Cool? | Destinations | Net Search | People | Software

All About Soccer

History of Soccer

Rules of the Game

Fun Facts

Helpful Hints

Glossary of Terms

Skills and Drills

---

1. Explain the address of this page based on the information in "How the Internet Works."

2. Choose options other than the ones that lead to the rules of soccer. What would you expect to find at each level?

Guide for Responding (continued)

◆ Reading Strategy

IDENTIFY AUTHOR'S MAIN POINTS

To understand an author's message, you must identify the **author's main points.**

1. In "Restoring the Circle," what are two of Bruchac's main points about the way Native American culture has been viewed in the past?
2. Identify the main point made by each photo-and-text combination in "In Wildness Is the Preservation of the World."
3. What are the main points Bailey White makes about wild turkeys in "Turkeys"?
4. What point does Cochrane make by comparing the Internet to a post office?

◆ Build Vocabulary

USING FORMS OF *tolerate*

The forms of *tolerate* all deal with respect for a view or a group that is different from your own. Complete each sentence with one of these words: *tolerated, tolerance, tolerant.*

1. The baby turkeys were ___?___ of the sick little girl.
2. White's mother ___?___ the unusual habits of the scientists.
3. Thoreau's ___?___ made him open to many ideas.

SPELLING STRATEGY

When changing the ending of a word from *ant* or *ent* to *ance* or *ence*, remember to keep the same vowel in the ending. For example, *tolerant* becomes *tolerance*. *Reverent* becomes *reverence*. On your paper, change the ending of each of the following words to *ance* or *ence*.

1. resistant   2. insistent   3. defiant   4. resident

USING THE WORD BANK

On your paper, write the word from the Word Bank that is the opposite of each numbered word.

1. concentration   4. helpful
2. rejection   5. held back
3. carelessness   6. success

◆ Literary Focus

TYPES OF ESSAYS

An **essay** is a short nonfiction work about a particular subject. Each work in this group is a different kind of essay.

1. What does Bruchac try to persuade you to think in "Restoring the Circle"?
2. What do the pictures in the visual essay "In Wildness..." illustrate about nature?
3. What do you learn from the informational essay "How the Internet Works"?
4. In what ways is the narrative essay "Turkeys" like a short story?

◆ Build Grammar Skills

QUOTATION MARKS

Quotation marks enclose the exact words of a speaker. A comma, question mark, or exclamation point separates the speaker's words from the words that indicate who said them. Punctuation marks at the end of a quotation go inside the closing quotation marks.

"I'll be right over," said the ornithologist.

"Does your little girl still have measles?" he asked.

"One hundred percent wild turkey!" they said.

The comma at the end of the introductory words comes before the opening quotation marks.

She asked, "Why do you want to know?"

Practice On your paper, copy each sentence. Insert quotation marks and other punctuation as needed.

1. What do you want my mother asked.
2. Feels just right, the scientists said.
3. She thought Why are all these turkeys here
4. Look I yelled.
5. The scientists called out One hundred percent

Writing Application Write a conversation between you and a friend. Use quotation marks and other punctuation as needed.

Build Your Portfolio

 ## Idea Bank

Writing Ideas

1. **Journal Entry About an Animal** Write a brief description of an animal. You can describe the turkey pictured on page 602, a pet, or another animal you have observed.

2. **Nature Poems** Write a four-line nature poem. In the first line, identify the color and texture of your subject. In the second line, tell something surprising about that same thing from nature. In the third and fourth lines, compare or contrast your subject with something else.

3. **Essay** Write a brief comparison-contrast essay in which you explore the similarities and differences between the Internet and a post office.

Speaking and Listening

4. **Conversation** With a partner, role-play the conversation that may have taken place between Bailey White's mother and an ornithologist. If possible, make an audiotape of the conversation.

5. **Nature Game [Group Activity]** Assume that you are an animal or object in nature. Tell five significant details about yourself, but do not give away your name. Allow other students to guess what you are. Jot down the details that you give, and have the person who guesses correctly explain which two clues were most helpful. **[Science Link]**

Projects

6. **Picture Books** Create a beginning readers' picture book about something in nature. Create an illustration and related sentence for each page. **[Art Link; Science Link]**

7. **Native American Fair [Group Activity]** With a group, prepare a Native American celebration that shows the unique food, music, and clothing of a particular Native American group. **[Social Studies Link]**

 ## Writing Mini-Lesson

Explanation of a Game

In "How to Use the Internet," Kerry Cochrane explains how to create an e-mail address. It is important that explanations or instructions be clear and complete. Choose a simple game like checkers, Simon Says, or tag. Write a step-by-step explanation of how the game is played.

Writing Skills Focus: Relationships Among Steps

Make your explanation clear by identifying the **relationships among the steps.** Indicate the game's penalty or reward for a particular action. Explain when two things must happen together. In "How the Internet Works," Cochrane indicates conditions and time relationships:

Model From the Essay

As long as you know these rules, you can send mail to anyone in the world. . . .

When you drop a letter in the mailbox, it gets collected and sorted. . . .

Prewriting List all the steps in your game. Then, number them in the order in which they should be followed.

Drafting Use words and phrases that link one action or step with another. For example, *If* you get tagged by someone on the other team, *then* you must freeze *until* someone on your team tags you again.

Revising Read your instructions to a younger person who does not know how to play the game. Use the child's questions as a guide to where you need to revise.

> ◆ **Grammar Application**
> Use quotation marks around any words that are said during the game, such as "You're it!"

CONNECTING LITERATURE TO SOCIAL STUDIES

INDIA

Eulogy for Gandhi *by Jawaharlal Nehru*

A GREAT IDEA An idea is a flimsy thing, wispier than a breath or flame. Yet when it spreads, it can grow into a roaring fire. Mohandas K. Gandhi (1869–1948) had an idea powerful enough to free India from the mighty British Empire.

British Rule In the 1700's, the British began controlling India. They grew rich trading in Indian crops, such as tea. They taxed Indians heavily, but gave them limited say in government.

Gandhi's Idea A mild, thin man, Gandhi worked to end the injustices of British rule. He asked Indians to trust in the truth of their cause and to act without fear, violence, or hatred. He called his idea *satyagraha* (sut´ yə gru´ hə), "clinging to the truth." Beginning in 1919, he led the people in marches and in nonviolent disobedience to unjust laws. One of these was the "March to the Sea," shown on the map at left. When he was jailed by the British, Gandhi accepted the punishment as part of the struggle and continued to lead.

Gandhi's March to the Sea, 1930

- ····· Approx. route of Gandhi's March to the Sea
- —— Modern nation
- ▦ Territory ruled by Britain
- ▦ Territory controlled by Britain; ruled by Indian nobles

Uniting India British India was patched together from many kingdoms and states. People spoke any of 723 languages or dialects. Some followed Hinduism; some, Islam. No one person could overcome all of these differences. Gandhi reached out to all Indians, though, and brought many together. Many loved him, calling him *Mahatma* ("great soul").

The Fire Spreads In 1947, England accepted Gandhi's demands. India became independent. Months later, Gandhi was assassinated. In his "Eulogy," given at Gandhi's funeral, Jawaharlal Nehru suggests that not even death could put out Gandhi's fire. Indeed, Gandhi's idea inspired Martin Luther King, Jr., who led nonviolent protests in the United States in the 1960's.

Eulogy¹ for Gandhi

Jawaharlal Nehru

A glory has departed and the sun that warmed and brightened our lives has set and we shiver in the cold and dark. Yet he would not have us feel this way. After all, that glory that we saw for all these years, that man with the divine fire, changed us also—and such as we are, we have been molded by him during these years; and out of that divine fire many of us also took a small spark which strengthened and made us work to some extent on the lines that he fashioned. And so if we praise him, our words seem rather small, and if we praise him, to some extent we also praise ourselves. Great men and eminent men have monuments in bronze and marble set up for them, but this man of divine fire managed in his lifetime to become enshrined in millions and millions of hearts so that all of us became somewhat of the stuff that he was made of, though to an infinitely lesser degree. He spread out in this way all over India, not in palaces only, or in select places or in assemblies, but in every hamlet and hut of the lowly and those who suffer. He lives in the hearts of millions and he will live for immemorial ages.

What, then, can we say about him except to feel humble on this occasion? To praise him we are not worthy—to praise him whom we could not follow adequately and sufficiently. It is almost doing him an injustice just to pass him by with words when he demanded work and labor and sacrifices² from us; in a large measure he made this country, during the last thirty years or more, attain to heights of sacrifice which in

▲ **Critical Viewing** Why do you think so many people admired this man? **[Speculate]**

Connecting Literature to Social Studies Why might Gandhi's nonviolent approach have made him especially beloved by "those who suffer"?

---

1. **eulogy** (yoo′ lə jē): Speech praising a person who has died.

2. **sacrifices** (sak′ rə fīs′ əs): Things of value given up for a cause or a person.

that particular domain have never been equaled elsewhere. He succeeded In that. Yet ultimately things happened which no doubt made him suffer tremendously, though his tender face never lost its smile and he never spoke a harsh word to anyone. Yet, he must have suffered—suffered for the failing of this generation whom he had trained, suffered because we went away from the path that he had shown us. And ultimately the hand of a child of his—for he, after all, is as much a child of his as any other Indian—the hand of a child of his struck him down. . . .

He was perhaps the greatest symbol of the India of the past, and may I say, of the India of the future, that we could have had. We stand on this perilous edge of the present, between the past and the future to be, and we face all manner of perils. And the greatest peril is sometimes the lack of faith which comes to us, the sense of frustration that comes to us, the sinking of the heart and of the spirit that comes to us when we see ideals go overboard, when we see the great things that we talked about somehow pass into empty words, and life taking a different course. Yet, I do believe that perhaps this period will pass soon enough.

He has gone, and all over India there is a feeling of having been left <u>desolate</u> and forlorn. All of us sense that feeling and I do not know when we shall be able to get rid of it. And yet together with that feeling there is also a feeling of proud thankfulness that it has been given to us of this generation to be associated with this mighty person. In ages to come, centuries and maybe millennia after us, people will think of this generation when this man of God trod on earth, and will think of us who, however small, could also follow his path and tread the holy ground where his feet had been. Let us be worthy of him.

◆ **Build Vocabulary**

perils (per´ əlz) *n.*: Situations full of dangers
desolate (des´ ə lit) *adj.*: Lonely or abandoned

Meet the Author
Jawaharlal Nehru (1889–1964) was India's first prime minister, taking office after independence. He became a supporter of Gandhi in 1920.

Guide for Responding

◆ LITERATURE AND YOUR LIFE

Reader's Response After reading Nehru's speech, do you feel you know Gandhi? Explain why or why not.

Thematic Focus Name three special characteristics that a leader of a people must have.

☑ **Check Your Comprehension**

1. When did Nehru make this speech?
2. What does he say Gandhi has done for India?
3. What does Nehru believe future citizens of India will remember about his generation?

◆ Critical Thinking

INTERPRET

1. Contrast the way Gandhi will be remembered and the way other important people are remembered. **[Compare and Contrast]**
2. Why does Nehru call the man who killed Gandhi "a child of his"? **[Interpret]**
3. What responsibility does Nehru believe his audience has? **[Interpret]**

APPLY

4. Describe another situation in which Gandhi's ideas could be helpful. **[Apply]**

CONNECTING LITERATURE TO SOCIAL STUDIES

Mohandas Gandhi's idea of *satyagraha* had roots in ancient traditions. Hinduism, an Indian religion founded thousands of years ago, teaches the importance of spirit over things like money. Gandhi himself was raised in Jainism, a religion that came from Hinduism. Jainism teaches respect for all life.

Gandhi also had modern ideas. Indians, he said, should depend only on themselves. To this end, he asked them to spin their own cloth. He himself used a spinning wheel. In 1930, he led a march to the sea to protest the British tax on salt. (See the map on page 612.) At the sea, the marchers made their own sea salt. Thousands followed their example and were jailed by the British.

1. Explain why Gandhi's connection with Hinduism makes him a "symbol of India's past."
2. In what way does Gandhi's idea of self-reliance help explain Nehru's idea that "He lives in the hearts of millions"?

 Idea Bank

Writing

1. **List** Repetition is one of the most effective ways to make a speech memorable. Make a list of words and phrases that Nehru repeats in the first paragraph of his speech. Next to each, write a paragraph explaining the ideas it brings to mind.
2. **Letter** Imagine that you are a Gandhi supporter listening to Nehru's eulogy. Write a letter to a friend or relative telling how you reacted to the speech.
3. **Newspaper Article** You are a newspaper reporter covering Nehru's speech. Write an article that summarizes the speech and mentions its main points.

Speaking and Listening

4. **Oral Interpretation** Choose a paragraph from the eulogy and, as Nehru, read it for the class. Use expression and gesture to convey Nehru's feelings.

Projects

5. **Oral Report** Do research on British rule in India and the movement for independence. Report your findings to the class.
6. **Art** Draw a portrait of Gandhi from photographs. In your drawing, feature three symbols of his campaign and life—such as the spinning wheel—that you find through research.

Further Reading, Listening, and Viewing

- Montgomery Rider's book *Gandhi: Peaceful Fighter* (1970) tells about the Indian leader and his campaign of nonviolence.
- Lila Fincke and John P. Hayes's *Jawaharlal Nehru* (1987) is a biography of India's first prime minister.
- The Columbia film *Gandhi,* starring Ben Kingsley, is available for rental on videotape.

How-to Essay

Writing Process Workshop

Wild turkeys, dictionaries, and space shuttles all have something in common. You can learn about them (and about everything from India to the Internet) by reading nonfiction works.

One kind of nonfiction essay, a **how-to essay,** gives you step-by-step instructions that guide you through a particular task or from one place to another. Write a how-to essay on an activity with which you are familiar. Use the following tips, presented in this section's Writing Mini-Lessons.

Writing Skills Focus

▶ **Present events in the order in which they occur.** To help your readers follow your instructions, start with the first step they must take. Follow with what comes next, and end with what comes last. (See p. 593.)

▶ **Identify relationships between events.** Each event you discuss is connected with others. Some events come before others; some cause or prevent others. Identify these relationships to help your reader understand what is going on. Use phrases such as "first . . . , then . . . ," "if you don't . . . , then . . . ," and "by doing this . . . , you will cause . . ." (See p. 611.)

MODEL

Installing a program on your computer is not difficult if you take the following steps:

① First, read the part of the manual called "System Requirements." Check the hard-disk space and memory that the program requires. ② Then, check your machine to make sure you have enough free space and memory. ③ If you try to install software on a machine that doesn't meet these requirements, you may run into trouble.

① The writer follows time order. The first step given is the first step the reader must take.

② The words *first* and *then* signal relationships between events.

③ The writer identifies the relationship between not meeting requirements and possible trouble.

Prewriting

Choose a Topic Think of activities you know or perform well, in which events follow a certain order. If you need help getting started, consider the suggestions below:

> ### Topic Ideas
> - Playing a video game
> - Building a model car
> - Baking a cake
> - Getting from your house to school

Identify the Steps Once you've chosen a topic, list the steps involved. Write each step on a separate note card.

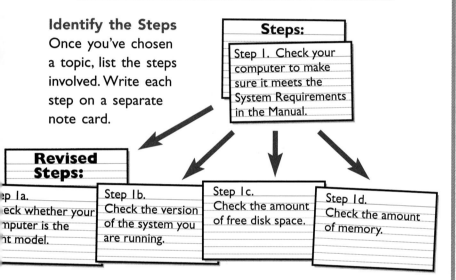

Steps:

Step 1. Check your computer to make sure it meets the System Requirements in the Manual.

Revised Steps:

Step 1a. Check whether your computer is the right model.

Step 1b. Check the version of the system you are running.

Step 1c. Check the amount of free disk space.

Step 1d. Check the amount of memory.

Identify the Materials For each step you have noted, identify any materials, equipment, or ingredients that are needed.

Analyze the Steps For each step, ask yourself: Can I break this down into two or more separate steps? For instance, the step, "Attach the two boards" could be broken down into these steps: "Drill holes in one board 3/4 inch from the top. Line up the edge of the other board with the top. Then, screw the boards together." Make a new set of note cards showing the new steps.

Drafting

Introduce Your Topic Let your readers know exactly what task or activity you will be telling them about. Then, list any materials, equipment, and ingredients the reader may need.

DRAFTING/REVISING

APPLYING LANGUAGE SKILLS: Use Synonyms for Variety

Synonyms are words that have similar meanings. Sometimes you can use synonyms when referring to the same thing. In this way, you can add variety to your writing.

Repetitive:

Before you hammer *the nail, make sure it is straight. Hold the nail while you* hammer *it. Let go of the nail, and* hammer *it a few more times.*

More Varied:

Before you hammer *the nail, make sure it is straight. Hold the nail while you* hit *it. Let go of the nail, and* pound *it a few more times.*

Practice Give a synonym for each word or phrase:

1. novel
2. device
3. turn on
4. connect
5. drive to

Writing Application Find places in your essay where you might use synonyms for variety.

Writer's Solution Connection Language Lab

For more help choosing words, complete any lesson in the Choosing Words unit.

APPLYING LANGUAGE SKILLS: Subject and Verb Agreement

The subject of a sentence is singular when it names one person or thing and plural when it names more than one. Verbs change form to agree with a singular or a plural subject. Notice the forms of the verbs with singular and plural subjects in the following examples:

Singular:

Sally runs.
Dave's team was there.

Plural:

Sally and her sister run.
All the teams were there.

Practice For each sentence, pick the correct form of the verb:

1. Most space launches (is, are) successful.
2. Central Park (smell, smells) wonderful in summer.
3. Bailey and her mother (help, helps) the ornithologist.

Writing Application Check your draft to make sure your verbs agree with their subjects.

Writer's Solution Connection Language Lab

For more practice with subject and verb agreement, complete any lesson in the Subject-Verb Agreement unit.

Follow Time Order Set down in the proper order each step required by the process. Refer to your note cards to ensure that you put the steps in the right order.

Indicate the Relationships Between Events Use words such as *first, next, before,* and *then* to show the order of events. Use words such as *because* and *in order* to indicate reasons. Use words such as *if . . . , then . . .* to show causes and effects.

Revising

Check Your Organization Make sure that you have listed all materials at the beginning and that steps appear in the right order.

Simplify the Steps If a step really takes two or more steps to complete, explain each step separately.

Show Relationships Between Events Add words and phrases to show the relationships between events.

REVISION MODEL

To install software, you must have the ① installation
First, read
disks. ② ~~Read~~ the system requirements part of the manual.
manual and
③ Then, check to make sure you have enough free space
~~and memory~~ .

by looking in the File Manager or in Explorer. Next, check the
memory in the Program Manager or the System Control Panel.

① Because the manual is mentioned later in the instructions, it should be listed with the materials.

② The writer added a word to show the relationship between the steps.

③ The writer broke this step into two steps.

Publishing and Presenting

Web Site With other members of your class, post your how-to essays on a Web site. Add useful diagrams or illustrations. Organize essays by category, and create an index to the site.

Demonstration Use your "how-to" essay as the basis of an in-class demonstration. Make copies available for your classmates to follow along as you demonstrate.

Real-World Reading Skills Workshop

Strategies for Success

Not all information comes in sentences. There will be times when you need to read a chart or a graph to get information. You might have to check the times of a train schedule, find out the percentage of an ingredient in a recipe, or calculate the increase in a population.

Check the Labels When you must read a chart or a graph, first look at the categories into which information is sorted. Read the labels to see what each part of the graph is telling you. Sometimes small explanations at the bottom of a chart or graph explain symbols. For example, on the weather graph for São Paulo, the labels tell you that the numbers on the left of the graph indicate temperature and the numbers on the right side show inches. The explanation on the bottom gives more information. By looking at the dots or bars above each month, you can read the temperature and rainfall for the month.

Know What You Need Charts are a way to present a great deal of information in a limited space. Most charts will contain more information than you need. For example, a train schedule will list the destinations, departure points, and times of many different trains on weekdays, weekends, and holidays. Be clear about what you need to find before you dive into a chart.

✔ Here are some situations in which reading charts and graphs is useful:
  ▶ Reading informational articles in newspapers, textbooks, or nonfiction books
  ▶ Reading advertisements or consumer reports

Apply the Strategies

The graph below shows the average temperature and precipitation in São Paulo, Brazil. Use it to answer the following questions.

1. What is the average temperature in São Paulo, Brazil, in February? How many inches of precipitation does the city have?

2. What is the temperature in São Paulo in September? How much precipitation does the city have?

3. Create a chart or graph to show average temperature in your town or city for each month of the year.

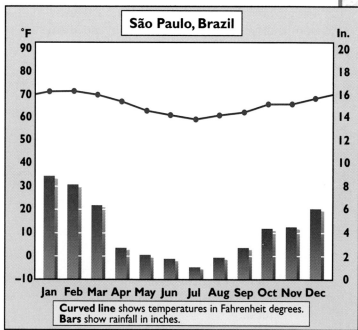

Curved line shows temperatures in Fahrenheit degrees.
Bars show rainfall in inches.

Grammar Review

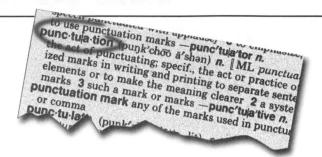

Apostrophes have two uses:

• An apostrophe is used with singular or plural nouns to show a relationship or possession:

> Harwood's account (The account Harwood gave)
>
> The class's computers (The computers belonging to the class)

• Apostrophes indicate missing letters in a contraction (a word or a combination of words written in shortened form). (See page 592.)

> Something's strange. (Something is strange.)
> We're waiting. (We are waiting.)

Quotation marks enclose the exact words of a speaker. A comma, question mark, or exclamation point separates the speaker's words from the words that indicate who said them. Other punctuation marks at the end of a quotation go inside the closing quotation marks:

> "My mother loved birds," she said.
> "Do you see that bird?" I asked.
> "Wow!" they yelped.

The comma at the end of the introductory words comes before the opening quotation marks. (See page 610.)

> She asked, "Why are you so interested?"

Grammar in Writing

✔ When writing dialogue, use contractions to make the speaker's words sound natural.

✔ Use quotation marks to set off each speaker's words.

✔ Start a new paragraph each time the speaker changes.

Practice 1 On your paper, write each group of words in a shortened way. Use apostrophes in your shortened version.

1. The booster for the *Challenger*

2. They are playing checkers.

3. The dictionary written by Webster

4. The rain that fell on Tuesday

5. I would have remembered.

Practice 2 On your paper, copy each sentence. Insert quotation marks and other punctuation where needed.

1. What do you see the ornithologist asked.

2. I don't believe it she cried.

3. They said Please help us with these birds.

4. Wait he warned.

5. Why he asked

Practice 3 Rewrite the following passage as a conversation in the present. Use apostrophes and quotation marks where appropriate.

My mother said that I had the measles. The ornithologists asked what my temperature was. My mother said my temperature was one hundred and two.

Being a good public speaker is a real skill. The best speakers know how to keep an audience's attention. Read the following strategies for making successful oral presentations. Apply them the next time you speak in front of a group.

Make It Clear A good oral presentation starts with a clear, confident speaking voice. Practice your presentation before you present it. Speak in a clear, strong voice. There is no need to shout, but be sure not to mumble, either.

Don't Speak Too Fast Sometimes people making an oral presentation become nervous and rush through their speech. Speaking too quickly makes it difficult for others to understand what you are saying. Pause for a moment before you begin speaking. As you begin, pay attention to the speed at which you are speaking. Speak at a moderate pace, and listeners will be able to take in everything you have to say.

Maintain Eye Contact Make good eye contact with your audience. If you are using notes, try to look up from time to time. If you look interested in the audience, the audience will be interested in what you have to say.

Apply the Strategies

Working in a group, practice giving different types of oral presentations. Each member of the group should prepare and present one of the assignments that follow.

After each presentation, the group should discuss the good aspects of the presentation and any points for improvement. Each member may then do another assignment, applying the group's suggestions. The group may then comment on improvements.

1. A news report about an event that took place in your town or neighborhood
2. A speech explaining why you should be class president
3. A short talk about a book you've read or a movie you've seen

Tips for Making Oral Presentations

✔ *Follow these strategies when giving an oral presentation to a group:*

▶ Stand up straight and speak clearly.

▶ Focus your attention on your presentation. If you seem bored, your listeners will be bored, too.

▶ Keep your voice upbeat and lively.

What's Behind the Words

Vocabulary Adventures With Richard Lederer

Mathematics (Measurement) Vocabulary

One of the ways that we describe and identify our neighborhood, community, nation, world, and universe is through the skill of numbers. Our vocabulary numbers many words for shapes, boundaries, and measurements.

It All Adds Up

When we put 2 and 2 together, we do exactly what the Latin *addo* tells us to do, "to put." Indeed, we turn to Latin for most of our mathematical terms. *Subtractus,* for example, is cobbled from the Latin *sub,* "away," and *tractus,* "taken." When we subtract, we "take away."

The word *multiply* claims *multiplico* as its ancestor—*multus,* "many," and *plico,* "fold." To multiply, then, is to make manifold, that is, to increase many times. But when you divide, you "split apart." *Divido* is just that, *di-,* "apart," and *vid,* "separate."

Getting Your Vocabulary in Shape

Circumference, from the Latin *circumferencia,* takes its form from the elements *circum,* "around," and *fero,* "carry." When you have carried something around an area, you have traveled its circumference.

Diameter harks back to the Greek term *dia-* "across" or "through," and *metros,* "measure." In the same pattern, we have *perimeter,* from the Greek *peri,* "around." Hence, to calculate a perimeter, you "measure around."

Measuring Metrically

The metric system is becoming more universal. As you have just seen, the root *metros* means "measure," which lies at the heart of *meter,* a measurement of 39.37 inches. A *centimeter* is a hundredth of a meter, a *millimeter* is a thousandth of a meter, and a *kilometer* is a thousand meters.

With the word *infinity,* we leave all measures behind. *Infinity* could be called "no-end-ity," as it comes originally from the Latin *infinitas,* which owes its being to *in-,* "not," and *finis,* "end." Infinity designates time and space "without end."

ACTIVITY 1 Explain the meanings and origins of the following measurement words:

1. acre
2. fathom
3. furlong
4. hectare
5. pound
6. knot
7. mile
8. ounce
9. radius
10. ton

ACTIVITY 2 Explain what each of the following devices measures:

1. barometer
2. pedometer
3. speedometer
4. chronometer
5. seismometer
6. thermometer
7. voltmeter

Extended Reading Opportunities

As they grow, people develop different ways to handle challenging or difficult times. Whether writing in a diary, talking to trusted friends, or simply looking at things from a new angle, the characters in the books discussed below find ways to overcome the obstacles that life presents.

Suggested Titles

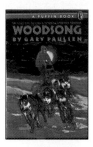

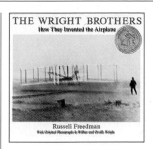

Keeping Secrets: The Girlhood Diaries of Seven Women Writers
Mary E. Lyons

Take a journey through time as you read the girlhood diaries of some famous female authors. How did Louisa May Alcott come up with the character of Jo in *Little Women*? What made Kate Chopin think it was hard to be a woman? As you read their private thoughts, you will begin to see what life was like for these writers—what they feared, hoped for, and loved. You will find out what events inspired stories that are still popular.

Woodsong
Gary Paulsen

This funny, moving book tells the story of Gary Paulsen and his adventures with the Minnesota wilderness and his team of sled dogs. As he prepares to race in the grueling Iditarod—a snowy trek across Alaska—Paulsen faces incredible obstacles. He learns to rely on his knowledge of nature, his inner strength, and, most importantly, his loyal dogs! This book is not only an adventure; it is a tale of friendship and survival. In addition, it is full of interesting facts about dog training and the great outdoors.

The Wright Brothers: How They Invented the Airplane
Russell Freedman, With Original Photographs by Wilbur and Orville Wright

For years, people laughed at the idea of a flying machine. This book introduces you to the Wright brothers—two men who ignored the naysayers and devoted their lives to building an airplane. The stories and photos in this book let you travel along with the Wrights on their journey from tinkering around with paper airplanes to shocking the world with their first successful flight.

Other Possibilities

The Abracadabra Kid: A Writer's Life	Sid Fleischman
Amos Fortune: Free Man	Elizabeth Yates
53 ½ Things That Changed the World: And Some That Didn't	Steve Parker

Theatre Scene, Edgar Degas

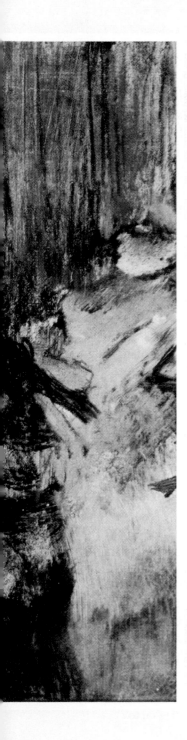

Drama

Drama is different from other forms of literature—
it is written to be performed. When you read a drama,
you should imagine that you see and hear the action of
the performance. The following elements help readers
and performers create the magic of drama:

- **Dialogue** is the conversation among characters.

- **Stage directions** are the words that tell readers
  and performers about the action, the sets, and the
  way in which the dialogue should be spoken.

- **Scenery, costumes, props, sound effects,**
  and **lighting** help create the world in which the
  actors perform. Playwrights usually give directions
  about these elements in the stage directions.

As you read the dramas in this unit, notice these features
that make drama a unique form of literature.

Reading for Success

Strategies for Reading Drama

The story of a drama is told mostly through performance—the actors speak and move as the characters. When you read a drama, keep in mind that it was written to be performed. The following strategies will help you as you read a drama:

Envision the setting and the action.

Use your imagination and the information the author provides to create a picture in your mind of the setting and the action. To envision the setting and the action, pay attention to the stage directions and the dialogue.

▶ Stage directions often describe the setting and the way characters look, sound, and move.

▶ Dialogue gives clues about the action. For example, a character might say "This is for you" to another character. The dialogue gives a clue that one character is handing something to the other.

Predict.

As you read, make educated guesses, or predictions, about what you think will happen. Look for hints in the dialogue and the action that seem to suggest an outcome. Rethink your predictions as you learn new details.

Question.

Don't accept everything the characters do and say at face value. Ask yourself questions like the following:

▶ Why did the character do or say that?

▶ Is the character speaking sincerely or sarcastically?

▶ What does the character mean by that?

▶ What caused this to happen?

Summarize.

Dramas are frequently broken into parts called acts, which may be broken into smaller parts called scenes. At the end of an act or a scene, pause to summarize what has happened so far. If the play is not broken into acts or scenes, pause to summarize when an incident or an event is over.

As you read the plays in this unit, apply these strategies. They will enable you to better understand and enjoy the plays.

Part 1 *Humorous Characters*

Finishing the Hat, Bill Nelson, Courtesy of the artist

Guide for Reading

Meet the Authors:

Norton Juster (1923–   )

Norton Juster's first career was as an architect. He went on to teach design to college students and eventually took up writing. As an architect and a designer, he creates by putting lines and shapes together in unusual ways. As a writer, he puts words and ideas together in creative and unusual ways. Juster designed clever word constructions in *The Phantom Tollbooth*, the novel on which this play is based.

Susan Nanus

Susan Nanus writes scripts of all kinds—scripts for stage performances, for television, and for movies. She has written dialogue for stars like Cher, Sissy Spacek, and Meryl Streep. Her writing skill has earned her several awards. Like other screenwriters, Nanus sometimes adapts novels to create screenplays for movies and scripts for stage plays. Her script for *The Phantom Tollbooth* is an adaptation of Norton Juster's novel *The Phantom Tollbooth*.

◆ LITERATURE AND YOUR LIFE

CONNECT YOUR EXPERIENCE

Boredom: Everyone experiences it at some time or another. So what's the cure for boredom? That's a question that *The Phantom Tollbooth* explores through the adventures of its main character, Milo.

THEMATIC FOCUS: A Different View

Milo's adventures help him to look at ordinary events and ideas in some new and exciting ways.

◆ Background for Understanding

LANGUAGE

The names of some characters and places in *The Phantom Tollbooth* describe their qualities. The following list explains the words from which these names come. Refer to the list as you read the play.

Lethargarians (leth´ ər jer´ ē ənz): From *lethargy*, which means "sluggish; without energy."

Digitopolis (dǐ´ ji täp´ ə les): From *digit*, which is a numeral from 0 to 9.

Kakafonous (ka ka´ fən əs) **A. Dischord:** From *cacophonous*, which means "having harsh, jarring sounds" and *discord*, which means "unpleasant combination of sounds."

Terrible Trivium (trǐ´ vē um): From *trivium* (the singular of *trivia*), which is an unimportant fact or thing.

◆ Build Vocabulary

PREFIXES: *pre-*

The boy in *The Phantom Tollbooth* is warned to take precautionary steps. The prefix *pre-*, meaning "before," is a clue that precautionary steps are cautionary measures he must take before something happens.

WORD BANK

Which word on the list means "misunderstanding" or "mistake"?

> ignorance
> precautionary
> misapprehension

◆ The Phantom Tollbooth, Act I ◆

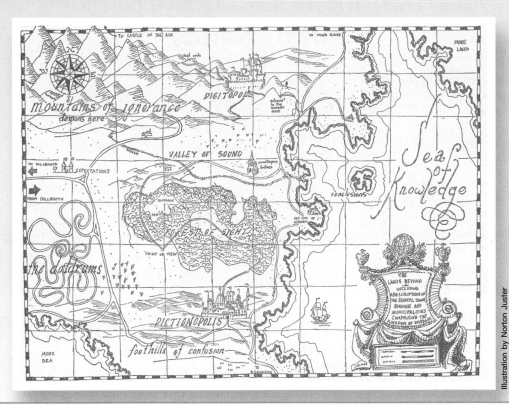

Illustration by Norton Juster

◆ Literary Focus

ELEMENTS OF DRAMA

A **drama** is a story written to be performed by actors. Drama contains some of the same elements as a story or a novel—characters, settings, and a plot. However, in a drama, the plot is told through dialogue and the action is performed by actors who pretend to be the characters. Dialogue is the words spoken by the actors. The action is often indicated in the stage directions. The element of representing the story is what makes drama different from other forms of literature.

◆ Reading Strategy

SUMMARIZE

To **summarize** is to restate something briefly in your own words. A good summary includes all the important details and events, and makes clear the order in which the events occurred. Related ideas and events may be grouped, and the connections between them indicated. As you read Act I of *The Phantom Tollbooth*, pause at the signposts indicated on the "road map" below to summarize what you have read so far. Make a "road" of your own to jot down details along the way.

The Phantom Tollbooth
Based on the book by Norton Juster
Susan Nanus

CAST (in order of appearance)

- THE CLOCK
- MILO, A BOY
- THE WHETHER MAN
- SIX LETHARGARIANS
- TOCK, THE WATCHDOG (SAME AS THE CLOCK)
- AZAZ THE UNABRIDGED, KING OF DICTIONOPOLIS
- THE MATHEMAGICIAN, KING OF DIGITOPOLIS
- PRINCESS SWEET RHYME
- PRINCESS PURE REASON

- GATEKEEPER OF DICTIONOPOLIS
- THREE WORD MERCHANTS
- THE LETTERMAN (FOURTH WORD MERCHANT)
- SPELLING BEE
- THE HUMBUG
- THE DUKE OF DEFINITION
- THE MINISTER OF MEANING
- THE EARL OF ESSENCE
- THE COUNT OF CONNOTATION
- THE UNDERSECRETARY OF UNDERSTANDING

- A PAGE
- KAKAFONOUS A. DISCHORD, DOCTOR OF DISSONANCE
- THE AWFUL DYNNE
- THE DODECAHEDRON
- MINERS OF THE NUMBERS MINE
- THE EVERPRESENT WORDSNATCHER
- THE TERRIBLE TRIVIUM
- THE DEMON OF INSINCERITY
- SENSES TAKER

THE SETS

1. MILO'S BEDROOM—WITH SHELVES, PENNANTS, PICTURES ON THE WALL, AS WELL AS SUGGESTIONS OF THE CHARACTERS OF THE LAND OF WISDOM.

2. THE ROAD TO THE LAND OF WISDOM—A FOREST, FROM WHICH THE WHETHER MAN AND THE LETHARGARIANS EMERGE.

3. DICTIONOPOLIS—A MARKETPLACE FULL OF OPEN AIR STALLS AS WELL AS LITTLE SHOPS. LETTERS AND SIGNS SHOULD ABOUND.

4. DIGITOPOLIS—A DARK, GLITTERING PLACE WITHOUT TREES OR GREENERY, BUT FULL OF SHINING ROCKS AND CLIFFS, WITH HUNDREDS OF NUMBERS SHINING EVERYWHERE.

5. THE LAND OF IGNORANCE—A GRAY, GLOOMY PLACE FULL OF CLIFFS AND CAVES, WITH FRIGHTENING FACES. DIFFERENT LEVELS AND HEIGHTS SHOULD BE SUGGESTED THROUGH ONE OR TWO PLATFORMS OR RISERS, WITH A SET OF STAIRS THAT LEAD TO THE CASTLE IN THE AIR.

Act 1

Scene i

[*The stage is completely dark and silent. Suddenly the sound of someone winding an alarm clock is heard, and after that, the sound of loud ticking is heard.*]

[*LIGHTS UP on the* CLOCK, *a huge alarm clock. The* CLOCK *reads 4:00. The lighting should make it appear that the* CLOCK *is suspended in mid-air (if possible). The* CLOCK *ticks for 30 seconds.*]

CLOCK. See that! Half a minute gone by. Seems like a long time when you're waiting for something to happen, doesn't it? Funny thing is, time can pass very slowly or very fast, and sometimes even both at once. The time now? Oh, a little after four, but what that means should depend on you. Too often, we do something simply because time tells us to. Time for school, time for bed, whoops, 12:00, time to be hungry. It can get a little silly, don't you think? Time is important, but it's what you do with it that makes it so. So my advice to you is to use it. Keep your eyes open and your ears perked. Otherwise it will pass before you know it, and you'll certainly have missed something!

Things have a habit of doing that, you know.

Being here one minute and gone the next. In the twinkling of an eye. In a jiffy. In a flash!

I know a girl who yawned and missed a whole summer vacation. And what about that caveman who took a nap one afternoon, and woke up to find himself completely alone. You see, while he was sleeping, someone had invented the wheel and everyone had moved to the suburbs. And then of course, there is Milo. [*LIGHTS UP to reveal* MILO's *Bedroom. The* CLOCK *appears to be on a shelf in the room of a young boy—a room filled with books, toys, games, maps, papers, pencils, a bed, a desk. There is a dartboard with numbers and the face of the* MATHEMAGICIAN, *a bedspread made from* KING AZAZ'S *cloak, a kite looking like the* SPELLING BEE, *a punching bag with the* HUMBUG'S *face, as well as records, a television, a toy car, and a large box that is wrapped and has an envelope taped to the top. The sound of FOOTSTEPS is heard, and then enter* MILO *dejectedly. He throws down his books and coat, flops into a chair, and sighs loudly.*] Who never knows what to do with himself—not just sometimes, but always. When he's in school, he wants to be out, and when he's out, he wants to be in. [*During the following speech,* MILO *examines the various toys, tools, and other possessions in the room, trying them out and rejecting them.*] Wherever he is, he wants to be somewhere else—and when he gets there, so what. Everything is too much trouble or a waste of time. Books—he's already read them. Games—boring. T.V.—dumb. So what's left? Another long, boring afternoon. Unless he bothers to notice a very large package that happened to arrive today.

MILO. [*Suddenly notices the package. He drags himself over to it, and disinterestedly reads the*

◆ Build Vocabulary

ignorance (igʹ ner ens) *n.*: Lack of knowledge, education, or experience

precautionary (prē kôʹ shən erʹ ē) *adj.*: Taking care beforehand to prevent danger

label.] "For Milo, who has plenty of time." Well, that's true. [*Sighs and looks at it.*] No. [*Walks away.*] Well . . . [*Comes back. Rips open envelope and reads.*]

A VOICE. "One genuine turnpike tollbooth, easily assembled at home for use by those who have never traveled in lands beyond."

MILO. Beyond what? [*Continues reading.*]

A VOICE. "This package contains the following items:" [MILO *pulls the items out of the box and sets them up as they are mentioned.*] "One (1) genuine turnpike tollbooth to be erected according to directions. Three (3) precautionary signs to be used in a precautionary fashion. Assorted coins for paying tolls. One (1) map, strictly up to date, showing how to get from here to there. One (1) book of rules and traffic regulations which may not be bent or broken. Warning! Results are not guaranteed. If not perfectly satisfied, your wasted time will be refunded."

MILO. [*Skeptically.*] Come off it, who do you think you're kidding? [*Walks around and examines tollbooth.*] What am I supposed to do with this? [*The ticking of the* CLOCK *grows loud and impatient.*] Well . . . what else do I have to do. [MILO *gets into his toy car and drives up to the first sign.*]

VOICE. "HAVE YOUR DESTINATION IN MIND."

MILO. [*Pulls out the map.*] Now, let's see. That's funny. I never heard of any of these places. Well, it doesn't matter anyway. Dictionopolis. That's a weird name. I might as well go there. [*Begins to move, following map. Drives off.*]

CLOCK. See what I mean? You never know how things are going to get started. But when you're bored, what you need more than anything is a rude awakening.

[*The ALARM goes off very loudly as the stage darkens. The sound of the alarm is transformed into the honking of a car horn, and is then joined by the blasts, bleeps, roars and growls of heavy highway traffic When the lights come up,*

MILO'S *bedroom is gone and we see a lonely road in the middle of nowhere.*]

Scene ii *The Road to Dictionopolis*

[*ENTER* MILO *in his car.*]

MILO. This is weird! I don't recognize any of this scenery at all. [*A SIGN is held up before* MILO, *startling him.*] Huh? [*Reads.*] WELCOME TO EXPECTATIONS. INFORMATION, PREDICTIONS AND ADVICE CHEERFULLY OFFERED. PARK HERE AND BLOW HORN. [MILO *blows horn.*]

◆ **Reading Strategy**
Summarize what has happened so far.

WHETHER MAN.
[*A little man wearing a long coat and carrying an umbrella pops up from behind the sign that he was holding. He speaks very fast and excitedly.*] My, my, my, my, my, welcome, welcome, welcome, welcome to the Land of Expectations, Expectations, Expectations! We don't get many travelers these days; we certainly don't get many travelers. Now what can I do for you? I'm the Whether Man.

MILO. [*Referring to map.*] Uh . . . is this the right road to Dictionopolis?

WHETHER MAN. Well now, well now, well now, I don't know of any *wrong* road to Dictionopolis, so if this road goes to Dictionopolis at all, it must be the right road, and if it doesn't, it must be the right road to somewhere else, because there are no wrong roads to anywhere. Do you think it will rain?

MILO. I thought you were the Weather Man.

WHETHER MAN. Oh, no, I'm the Whether Man, not the weather man. [*Pulls out a SIGN or opens a FLAP of his coat, which reads: "WHETHER."*] After all, it's more important to know whether there will be weather than what the weather will be.

MILO. What kind of place is Expectations?

WHETHER MAN. Good question, good question! Expectations is the place you must always go to before you get to where you are going. Of course, some people never go beyond Expectations, but my job is to hurry them along whether they like it or not. Now what else can I do for you? [*Opens his umbrella.*]

MILO. I think I can find my own way.

WHETHER MAN. Splendid, splendid! Whether or not you find your own way, you're bound to find some way. If you happen to find my way, please return it. I lost it years ago. I imagine by now it must be quite rusty. You did say it was going to rain, didn't you? [*Escorts* MILO *to the car under the open umbrella.*] I'm glad you made your own decision. I do so hate to make up my mind about anything, whether it's good or bad, up or down, rain or shine. Expect everything, I always say, and the unexpected never happens. Goodbye, goodbye, goodbye, good . . .

[*A loud CLAP of THUNDER is heard.*] Oh dear! [*He looks up at the sky, puts out his hand to feel for rain, and RUNS AWAY.* MILO *watches puzzledly and drives on.*]

MILO. I'd better get out of Expectations, but fast. Talking to a guy like that all day would get me nowhere for sure. [*He tries to speed up, but finds instead that he is moving slower and slower.*] Oh, oh, now what? [*He can barely move. Behind* MILO, *the* LETHARGARIANS *begin to enter from all parts of the stage. They are dressed to blend in with the scenery and carry small pillows that look like rocks. Whenever they fall asleep, they rest on the pillows.*] Now I really am getting nowhere. I hope I didn't take a wrong turn. [*The car stops. He tries to start it. It won't move. He gets out and begins to tinker with it.*] I wonder where I am.

LETHARGARIAN 1. You're . . . in . . . the . . . Dol . . . drums . . . [MILO *looks around.*]

LETHARGARIAN 2. Yes . . . the . . . Dol . . . drums . . . [*A YAWN is heard.*]

MILO. [*Yelling.*] WHAT ARE THE DOLDRUMS?

LETHARGARIAN 3. The Doldrums, my friend, are where nothing ever happens and nothing ever changes. [*Parts of the Scenery stand up or Six People come out of the scenery colored in the same colors of the trees or the road. They move very slowly and as soon as they move, they stop to rest again.*] Allow me to introduce all of us. We are the Lethargarians at your service.

MILO. [*Uncertainly.*] Very pleased to meet you. I think I'm lost. Can you help me?

LETHARGARIAN 4. Don't say think. [*He yawns.*] It's against the law.

LETHARGARIAN 1. No one's allowed to think in the Doldrums. [*He falls asleep.*]

LETHARGARIAN 2. Don't you have a rule book? It's local ordinance 175389-J. [*He falls asleep.*]

MILO. [*Pulls out rule book and reads.*] Ordinance 1175389-J: "It shall be unlawful, illegal and unethical to think, think of thinking, surmise, presume, reason, meditate or speculate while in the Doldrums. Anyone breaking this law shall be severely punished." That's a ridiculous law! Everybody thinks.

ALL THE LETHARGARIANS. We don't!

LETHARGARIAN 2. And most of the time, you don't, that's why you're here. You weren't thinking and you weren't paying attention either. People who don't pay attention often get stuck in the Doldrums. Face it, most of the time, you're just like us. [*Falls, snoring, to the ground.* MILO *laughs.*]

LETHARGARIAN 5. Stop that at once. Laughing is against the law. Don't you have a rule book? It's local ordinance 574381-W.

MILO. [*Opens rule book and reads.*] "In the Doldrums, laughter is frowned upon and smiling is permitted only on alternate Thursdays." Well, if you can't laugh or think, what can you do?

LETHARGARIAN 6. Anything as long as it's nothing, and everything as long as it isn't anything. There's lots to do. We have a very busy schedule . . .

LETHARGARIAN 1. At 8:00 we get up and then we spend from 8 to 9 daydreaming.

LETHARGARIAN 2. From 9:00 to 9:30 we take our early midmorning nap . . .

LETHARGARIAN 3. From 9:30 to 10:30 we dawdle and delay . . .

LETHARGARIAN 4. From 10:30 to 11:30 we take our late early morning nap . . .

LETHARGARIAN 5. From 11:30 to 12:00 we bide our time and then we eat our lunch.

LETHARGARIAN 6. From 1:00 to 2:00 we linger and loiter . . .

LETHARGARIAN 1. From 2:00 to 2:30 we take our early afternoon nap. . .

LETHARGARIAN 2. From 2:30 to 3:30 we put

off for tomorrow what we could have done today . . .

LETHARGARIAN 3. From 3:30 to 4:00 we take our early late afternoon nap . . .

LETHARGARIAN 4. From 4:00 to 5:00 we loaf and lounge until dinner . . .

LETHARGARIAN 5. From 6:00 to 7:00 we dilly-dally . . .

LETHARGARIAN 6. From 7:00 to 8:00 we take our early evening nap and then for an hour before we go to bed, we waste time.

LETHARGARIAN 1. [*Yawning.*] You see, it's really quite strenuous doing nothing all day long, and so once a week, we take a holiday and go nowhere.

LETHARGARIAN 5. Which is just where we were going when you came along. Would you care to join us?

MILO. [*Yawning.*] That's where I seem to be going, anyway. [*Stretching.*] Tell me, does everyone here do nothing?

LETHARGARIAN 3. Everyone but the terrible watchdog. He's always sniffing around to see that nobody wastes time. A most unpleasant character.

MILO. The Watchdog?

LETHARGARIAN 6. THE WATCHDOG!

ALL THE LETHARGARIANS. [*Yelling at once.*] RUN! WAKE UP! RUN! HERE HE COMES! THE WATCHDOG! [*They all run off and ENTER a large dog with the head, feet, and tail of a dog, and the body of a clock, having the same face as the character THE CLOCK.*]

◆ **Literary Focus**
How do the stage directions help you here?

WATCHDOG. What are you doing here?

MILO. Nothing much. Just killing time. You see . . .

WATCHDOG. KILLING TIME! [*His ALARM RINGS in*

fury.*] It's bad enough wasting time without killing it. What are you doing in the Doldrums, anyway? Don't you have anywhere to go?

MILO. I think I was on my way to Dictionopolis when I got stuck here. Can you help me?

WATCHDOG. Help you! You've got to help yourself. I suppose you know why you got stuck.

MILO. I guess I just wasn't thinking.

WATCHDOG. Precisely. Now you're on your way.

MILO. I am?

WATCHDOG. Of course. Since you got here by not thinking, it seems reasonable that in order to get out, you must *start* thinking. Do you mind if I get in? I love automobile rides. [*He gets in. They wait.*] Well?

MILO. All right. I'll try. [*Screws up his face and thinks.*] Are we moving?

WATCHDOG. Not yet. Think harder.

MILO. I'm thinking as hard as I can.

WATCHDOG. Well, think just a little harder than that. Come on, you can do it.

MILO. All right, all right. . . . I'm thinking of all the planets in the solar system, and why water expands when it turns to ice, and all the words that begin with "q," and . . . [*The wheels begin to move.*] We're moving! We're moving!

WATCHDOG. Keep thinking.

MILO. [*Thinking.*] How a steam engine works and how to bake a pie and the difference between Fahrenheit and Centigrade. . .

WATCHDOG. Dictionopolis, here we come.

MILO. Hey, Watchdog, are you coming along?

TOCK. You can call me Tock, and keep your eyes on the road.

MILO. What kind of place is Dictionopolis, anyway?

TOCK. It's where all the words in the world

come from. It used to be a marvelous place, but ever since Rhyme and Reason left, it hasn't been the same.

MILO. Rhyme and Reason?

TOCK. The two princesses. They used to settle all the arguments between their two brothers who rule over the Land of Wisdom. You see, Azaz is the king of Dictionopolis and the Mathemagician is the king of Digitopolis and they almost never see eye to eye on anything. It was the job of the Princesses Sweet Rhyme and Pure Reason to solve the differences between the two kings, and they always did so well that both sides usually went home feeling very satisfied. But then, one day, the kings had an argument to end all arguments. . . .

[*The LIGHTS DIM on* TOCK *and* MILO, *and come up on* KING AZAZ *of Dictionopolis on another part of the stage.* AZAZ *has a great stomach, a grey beard reaching to his waist, a small crown and a long robe with the letters of the alphabet written all over it.*]

AZAZ. Of course, I'll abide by the decision of Rhyme and Reason, though I have no doubt as to what it will be. They will choose *words,* of course. Everyone knows that words are more important than numbers any day of the week.

[*The* MATHEMAGICIAN *appears opposite* AZAZ. *The* MATHEMAGICIAN *wears a long flowing robe covered entirely with complex mathematical equations, and a tall pointed hat. He carries a long staff with a pencil point at one end and a large rubber eraser at the other.*]

MATHEMAGICIAN. That's what you think, Azaz. People wouldn't even know what day of the week it is without *numbers.* Haven't you ever looked at a calendar? Face it, Azaz. It's numbers that count.

AZAZ. Don't be ridiculous. [*To audience, as if leading a cheer.*] Let's hear it for WORDS!

MATHEMAGICIAN. [*To audience, in the same manner.*] Cast your vote for NUMBERS!

AZAZ. A, B, C's!

MATHEMAGICIAN. 1, 2, 3's! [*A FANFARE is heard.*]

AZAZ AND MATHEMAGICIAN. [*To each other.*] Quiet! Rhyme and Reason are about to announce their decision.

[RHYME *and* REASON *appear.*]

RHYME. Ladies and gentlemen, letters and numerals, fractions and punctuation marks— may we have your attention, please. After careful consideration of the problem set before us by King Azaz of Dictionopolis [AZAZ *bows.*] and the Mathemagician of Digitopolis [MATHEMAGICIAN *raises his hands in a victory salute.*] we have come to the following conclusion:

REASON. Words and numbers are of equal value, for in the cloak of knowledge, one is the warp and the other is the woof.

RHYME. It is no more important to count the sands than it is to name the stars.

RHYME AND REASON. Therefore, let both kingdoms, Dictionopolis and Digitopolis, live in peace.

[*The sound of CHEERING is heard.*]

AZAZ. Boo! is what I say. Boo and Bah and Hiss!

MATHEMAGICIAN. What good are these girls if they can't even settle an argument in anyone's favor? I think I have come to a decision of my own.

AZAZ. So have I.

AZAZ AND MATHEMAGICIAN. [*To the* PRINCESSES.] You are hereby banished from this land to the Castle-in-the-Air. [*To each other.*] And as for you, KEEP OUT OF MY WAY! [*They stalk off in opposite directions.*]

[*During this time, the set has been changed to the Market Square of Dictionopolis. LIGHTS come UP on the deserted square.*]

TOCK. And ever since then, there has been

neither Rhyme nor Reason in this kingdom. Words are misused and numbers are mismanaged. The argument between the two kings has divided everyone and the real value of both words and numbers has been forgotten. What a waste!

MILO. Why doesn't somebody rescue the Princesses and set everything straight again?

TOCK. That is easier said than done. The Castle-in-the-Air is very far from here, and the one path which leads to it is guarded by ferocious demons. But hold on, here we are. [*A Man appears, carrying a Gate and a small Tollbooth.*]

GATEKEEPER. AHHHHREMMMM! This is Dictionopolis, a happy kingdom, advantageously located in the foothills of Confusion and caressed by gentle breezes from the Sea of Knowledge. Today, by royal proclamation, is Market Day. Have you come to buy or sell?

MILO. I beg your pardon?

GATEKEEPER. Buy or sell, buy or sell. Which is it? You must have come here for a reason.

MILO. Well, I . . .

GATEKEEPER. Come now, if you don't have a reason, you must at least have an explanation or certainly an excuse.

MILO. [*Meekly.*] Uh . . . no.

GATEKEEPER. [*Shaking his head.*] Very serious. You can't get in without a reason. [*Thoughtfully.*] Wait a minute. Maybe I have an old one you can use. [*Pulls out an old suitcase from the tollbooth and rummages through it.*] No . . . no . . . no . . . this won't do . . . hmmm . . .

MILO. [*To* TOCK.] What's he looking for? [TOCK *shrugs.*]

GATEKEEPER. Ah! This is fine. [*Pulls out a Medallion on a chain. Engraved in the Medallion is: "WHY NOT?"*] Why not. That's a good reason for almost anything . . . a bit used, perhaps, but still quite serviceable. There you are, sir. Now I can truly say: Welcome to Dictionopolis.

[*He opens the Gate and walks off.* CITIZENS *and* MERCHANTS *appear on all levels of the stage, and* MILO *and* TOCK *find themselves in the middle of a noisy marketplace. As some people buy and sell their wares, others hang a banner which reads:* WELCOME TO THE WORD MARKET.]

MILO. Tock! Look!

MERCHANT 1. Hey-ya, hey-ya,

hey-ya, step right up and take your pick. Juicy tempting words for sale. Get your fresh-picked "ifs" "and's" and "but's!" Just take a look at these nice ripe "where's" and "when's."

MERCHANT 2. Step right up, step right up, fancy, best-quality words here for sale. Enrich your vocabulary and expand your speech with such elegant items as "quagmire," "flabbergast," or "upholstery."

MERCHANT 3. Words by the bag, buy them over here. Words by the bag for the more talkative customer. A pound of "happy's" at a very reasonable price . . . very useful for "Happy Birthday," "Happy New Year," "happy days," or "happy-go-lucky." Or how about a package of "good's," always handy for "good morning," "good afternoon," "good evening," and "goodbye."

MILO. I can't believe it. Did you ever see so many words?

TOCK. They're fine if you have something to say. [*They come to a Do-It-Yourself Bin.*]

MILO. [*To* MERCHANT 4 *at the bin.*] Excuse me, but what are these?

MERCHANT 4. These are for people who like to make up their own words. You can pick any assortment you like or buy a special box complete with all the letters and a book of instructions. Here, taste an "A." They're very good. [*He pops one into* MILO'S *mouth.*]

MILO. [*Tastes it hesitantly.*] It's sweet! [*He eats it.*]

MERCHANT 4. I knew you'd like it. "A" is one of our best-sellers. All of them aren't that good, you know. The "Z," for instance—very dry and sawdusty. And the "X"? Tastes like a trunkful of stale air. But most of the others aren't bad at all. Here, try the "I."

MILO. [*Tasting.*] Cool! It tastes icy.

MERCHANT 4. [*To* TOCK.] How about the "C" for you? It's as crunchy as a bone. Most people are just too lazy to make their own words, but take it from me, not only is it more fun, but it's also *de*-lightful, [*Holds up a "D."*] *e*-lating, [*Holds up an "E."*] and extremely *u*seful! [*Holds up a "U."*]

MILO. But isn't it difficult? I'm not very good at making words.

[*The* SPELLING BEE, *a large colorful bee, comes up from behind.*]

SPELLING BEE. Perhaps I can be of some assistance . . . a-s-s-i-s-t-a-n-c-e. [*The Three turn around and see him.*] Don't be alarmed . . . a-l-a-r-m-e-d. I am the Spelling Bee. I can spell anything. Anything. A-n-y-t-h-i-n-g. Try me. Try me.

MILO. [*Backing off,* TOCK *on his guard.*] Can you spell goodbye?

SPELLING BEE. Perhaps you are under the misapprehension . . . m-i-s-a-p-p-r-e-h-e-n-s-i-o-n that I am dangerous. Let me assure you that I am quite peaceful. Now, think of the most difficult word you can, and I'll spell it.

MILO. Uh . . . o.k. [*At this point,* MILO *may turn to the audience and ask them to help him choose a word or he may think of one on his own.*] How about . . . "Curiosity"?

SPELLING BEE. [*Winking.*] Let 's see now . . . uh . . . how much time do I have?

MILO. Just ten seconds. Count them off, Tock.

SPELLING BEE. [*As* TOCK *counts.*] Oh dear, oh dear. [*Just at the last moment, quickly.*] C-u-r-i-o-s-i-t-y.

MERCHANT 4. Correct! [ALL *Cheer.*]

MILO. Can you spell anything?

SPELLING BEE. [*Proudly.*] Just about. You see, years ago, I was an ordinary bee minding my own business, smelling flowers all day, occasionally picking up part-time work in people's bonnets. Then one day, I realized that I'd never amount to anything without an education, so I decided that . . .

HUMBUG. [*Coming up in a booming voice.*] BALDERDASH! [*He wears a lavish coat, striped pants, checked vest, spats and a derby hat.*] Let me repeat . . . BALDERDASH! [*Swings his cane and clicks his heels in the air.*] Well, well, what have we here? Isn't someone going to introduce me to the little boy?

SPELLING BEE. [*Disdainfully.*] This is the Humbug. You can't trust a word he says.

HUMBUG. NONSENSE! Everyone can trust a Humbug. As I was saying to the king just the other day . . .

◆ **Build Vocabulary**

misapprehension (mis′ ap rē hen′ shən) *n.*: Misunderstanding

SPELLING BEE. You've never met the king. [*To* MILO.] Don't believe a thing he tells you.

HUMBUG. Bosh, my boy, pure bosh. The Humbugs are an old and noble family, honorable to the core. Why, we fought in the Crusades with Richard the Lionhearted, crossed the Atlantic with Columbus, blazed trails with the pioneers. History is full of Humbugs.

SPELLING BEE. A very pretty speech . . . s-p-e-e-c-h. Now, why don't you go away? I was just advising the lad of the importance of proper spelling.

HUMBUG. BAH! As soon as you learn to spell one word, they ask you to spell another. You can never catch up, so why bother? [*Puts his arm around* MILO.] Take my advice, boy, and forget about it. As my great-great-great-grandfather George Washington Humbug used to say. . .

SPELLING BEE. You, sir, are an impostor i-m-p-o-s-t-o-r who can't even spell his own name!

HUMBUG. What? You dare to doubt my word? The word of a Humbug? The word of a Humbug who has direct access to the ear of a King? And the king shall hear of this, I promise you . . .

VOICE 1. Did someone call for the King?

VOICE 2. Did you mention the monarch?

VOICE 3. Speak of the sovereign?

VOICE 4. Entreat the Emperor?

VOICE 5. Hail his highness?

[*Five tall, thin gentlemen regally dressed in silks and satins, plumed hats and buckled shoes appear as they speak.*]

MILO. Who are they?

SPELLING BEE. The King's advisors. Or in more formal terms, his cabinet.

MINISTER 1. Greetings!

MINISTER 2. Salutations!

MINISTER 3. Welcome!

MINISTER 4. Good Afternoon!

MINISTER 5. Hello!

MILO. Uh . . . Hi.

[*All the* MINISTERS, *from here on called by their numbers, unfold their scrolls and read in order.*]

MINISTER 1. By the order of Azaz the Unabridged . . .

MINISTER 2. King of Dictionopolis . . .

MINISTER 3. Monarch of letters . . .

MINISTER 4. Emperor of phrases, sentences, and miscellaneous figures of speech . . .

MINISTER 5. We offer you the hospitality of our kingdom . . .

MINISTER 1. Country

MINISTER 2. Nation

MINISTER 3. State

MINISTER 4. Commonwealth

MINISTER 5. Realm

MINISTER 1. Empire

MINISTER 2. Palatinate

MINISTER 3. Principality.

MILO. Do all those words mean the same thing?

MINISTER 1. Of course.

MINISTER 2. Certainly.

MINISTER 3. Precisely.

MINISTER 4. Exactly.

MINISTER 5. Yes.

MILO. Then why don't you use just one? Wouldn't that make a lot more sense?

MINISTER 1. Nonsense!

MINISTER 2. Ridiculous!

MINISTER 3. Fantastic!

MINISTER 4. Absurd!

MINISTER 5. Bosh!

MINISTER 1. We're not interested in making sense. It's not our job.

MINISTER 2. Besides, one word is as good as another, so why not use them all?

MINISTER 3. Then you don't have to choose which one is right.

MINISTER 4. Besides, if one is right, then ten are ten times as right.

MINISTER 5. Obviously, you don't know who we are. [*Each presents himself and* MILO *acknowledges the introduction.*]

MINISTER 1. The Duke of Definition.

MINISTER 2. The Minister of Meaning.

MINISTER 3. The Earl of Essence.

MINISTER 4. The Count of Connotation.

MINISTER 5. The Undersecretary of Understanding.

ALL FIVE. And we have come to invite you to the Royal Banquet.

SPELLING BEE. The banquet! That's quite an honor, my boy. A real h-o-n-o-r.

HUMBUG. DON'T BE RIDICULOUS! Everybody goes to the Royal Banquet these days.

SPELLING BEE. [*To the* HUMBUG.] True, everybody does go. But some people are invited and others simply push their way in where they aren't wanted.

HUMBUG. HOW DARE YOU? You buzzing little upstart, I'll show you who's not wanted . . . [*Raises his cane threateningly.*]

SPELLING BEE. You just watch it! I'm warning w-a-r-n-i-n-g you! [*At that moment, an ear-shattering blast of TRUMPETS, entirely off-key, is heard, and a* PAGE *appears.*]

PAGE. King Azaz the Unabridged is about to begin the Royal banquet. All guests who do not appear promptly at the table will automatically lose their place. [*A huge Table is carried out with* KING AZAZ *sitting in a large chair, carried out at the head of the table.*]

AZAZ. Places. Everyone take your places. [*All the characters, including the* HUMBUG *and the* SPELLING BEE, *who forget their quarrel, rush to take their places at the table.* MILO *and* TOCK *sit near the* KING. AZAZ *looks at* MILO.] And just who is this?

MILO. Your Highness, my name is Milo and this is Tock. Thank you very much for inviting us to your banquet, and I think your palace is beautiful!

MINISTER 1. Exquisite.

MINISTER 2. Lovely.

MINISTER 3. Handsome.

MINISTER 4. Pretty.

MINISTER 5. Charming.

AZAZ. SILENCE! Now tell me, young man, what can you do to entertain us? Sing songs? Tell stories? Juggle plates? Do tumbling tricks? Which is it?

MILO. I can't do any of those things.

AZAZ. What an ordinary little boy. Can't you do anything at all?

MILO. Well . . . I can count to a thousand.

AZAZ. AARGH, numbers! Never mention numbers here. Only use them when we absolutely have to. Now, why don't we change the subject and have some dinner? Since you are the guest of honor, you may pick the menu.

MILO. Me? Well, uh . . . I'm not very hungry. Can we just have a light snack?

AZAZ. A light snack it shall be!

[AZAZ *claps his hands. Waiters rush in with*

Covered trays. When they are uncovered, Shafts of Light pour out. The light may be created through the use of battery-operated flashlights which are secured in the trays and covered with a false bottom. The Guests help themselves.]

HUMBUG. Not a very substantial meal. Maybe you can suggest something a little more filling.

MILO. Well, in that case, I think we ought to have a square meal . . .

AZAZ. [*Claps his hands.*] A square meal it is! [*Waiters serve trays of Colored Squares of all sizes. People serve themselves.*]

SPELLING BEE. These are awful. [HUMBUG *Coughs and all the Guests do not care for the food.*]

AZAZ. [*Claps his hands and the trays are removed.*] Time for speeches. [*To* MILO.] You first.

MILO. [*Hesitantly.*] Your Majesty, ladies and gentlemen, I would like to take this opportunity to say that . . .

AZAZ. That's quite enough. Mustn't talk all day.

MILO. But I just started to . . .

AZAZ. NEXT!

HUMBUG. [*Quickly.*] Roast turkey, mashed potatoes, vanilla ice cream.

SPELLING BEE. Hamburgers, corn on the cob, chocolate pudding p-u-d-d-i-n-g. [*Each Guest names two dishes and a dessert.*]

AZAZ. [*The last.*] Pate de fois gras, soupe a l'oignon, salade endives, fromage et fruits et demi-tasse. [*He claps his hands. Waiters serve each Guest his Words.*] Dig on. [*To* MILO.] Though I can't say I think much of your choice.

MILO. I didn't know I was going to have to eat my words.

AZAZ. Of course, of course, everybody here does. Your speech should have been in better taste.

MINISTER 1. Here, try some somersault. It improves the flavor.

MINISTER 2. Have a rigamarole. [*Offers bread-basket.*]

MINISTER 3. Or a ragamuffin.

MINISTER 4. Perhaps you'd care for a synonym bun.

MINISTER 5. Why not wait for your just desserts?

AZAZ. Ah yes, the dessert. We're having a special treat today . . . freshly made at the half-bakery.

MILO. The half-bakery?

AZAZ. Of course, the half-bakery! Where do you think half-baked ideas come from? Now, please don't interrupt. By royal command, the pastry chefs have . . .

MILO. What's a half-baked idea?

[AZAZ *gives up the idea of speaking as a cart is wheeled in and the Guests help themselves.*]

HUMBUG. They're very tasty, but they don't always agree with you. Here's a good one. [HUMBUG *hands one to* MILO.]

MILO. [*Reads.*] "The earth is flat."

SPELLING BEE. People swallowed that one for years. [*Picks up one and reads.*] "The moon is made of green cheese." Now, there's a half-baked idea.

[*Everyone chooses one and eats. They include: "It Never Rains But Pours," "Night Air Is Bad Air," "Everything Happens for the Best," "Coffee Stunts Your Growth."*]

AZAZ. And now for a few closing words. Attention! Let me have your attention! [*Everyone leaps up and Exits, except for* MILO, TOCK, *and the* HUMBUG.] Loyal subjects and friends, once again on this gala occasion, we have . . .

MILO. Excuse me, but everybody left.

AZAZ. [*Sadly.*] I was hoping no one would notice. It happens every time.

HUMBUG. They're gone to dinner, and as soon as I finish this last bite, I shall join them.

MILO. That's ridiculous. How can they eat dinner right after a banquet?

AZAZ. SCANDALOUS! We'll put a stop to it at once. From now on, by royal command, everyone must eat dinner before the banquet.

MILO. But that's just as bad.

HUMBUG. Or just as good. Things which are equally bad are also equally good. Try to look at the bright side of things.

MILO. I don't know which side of anything to look at. Everything is so confusing, and all your words only make things worse.

AZAZ. How true. There must be something we can do about it.

HUMBUG. Pass a law.

AZAZ. We have almost as many laws as words.

HUMBUG. Offer a reward. [AZAZ *shakes his head and looks madder at each suggestion.*] Send for help? Drive a bargain? Pull the switch? Lower the boom? Toe the line?

[*As* AZAZ *continues to scowl, the* HUMBUG *loses confidence and finally gives up.*]

MILO. Maybe you should let Rhyme and Reason return.

AZAZ. How nice that would be. Even if they were a bother at times, things always went so well when they were here. But I'm afraid it can't be done.

HUMBUG. Certainly not. Can't be done.

MILO. Why not?

HUMBUG. [*Now siding with* MILO.] Why not, indeed?

AZAZ. Much too difficult.

HUMBUG. Of course, much too difficult.

MILO. You could, if you really wanted to.

HUMBUG. By all means, if you really wanted to, you could.

AZAZ. [*To* HUMBUG.] How?

MILO. [*Also to* HUMBUG.] Yeah, how?

HUMBUG. Why . . . uh, it's a simple task for a brave boy with a stout heart, a steadfast dog and a serviceable small automobile.

AZAZ. Go on.

HUMBUG. Well, all that he would have to do is cross the dangerous, unknown countryside between here and Digitopolis, where he would have to persuade the Mathemagician to release the Princesses, which we know to be impossible because the Mathemagician will never agree with Azaz about anything. Once achieving that, it's a simple matter of entering the Mountains of Ignorance from where no one has ever returned alive, an effortless climb up a two thousand foot stairway without railings in a high wind at night to the Castle-in-the-Air. After a pleasant chat with the Princesses, all that remains is a leisurely ride back through those chaotic crags where the frightening fiends have sworn to tear any intruder from limb to limb and devour him down to his belt buckle. And finally after doing all that, a triumphal parade! If, of course, there is anything left to parade . . . followed by hot chocolate and cookies for everyone.

AZAZ. I never realized it would be so simple.

MILO. It sounds dangerous to me.

TOCK. And just who is supposed to make that journey?

AZAZ. A very good question. But there is one far more serious problem.

MILO. What's that?

AZAZ. I'm afraid I can't tell you that until you return.

MILO. But wait a minute, I didn't . . .

AZAZ. Dictionopolis will always be grateful to you, my boy, and your dog. [AZAZ *pats* TOCK *and* MILO.]

TOCK. Now, just one moment, sire . . .

AZAZ. You will face many dangers on your journey, but fear not, for I can give you something for your protection. [AZAZ *gives* MILO *a box.*] In this box are the letters of the alphabet. With them you can form all the words you will ever need to help you overcome the obstacles that may stand in your path. All you must do is use them well and in the right places.

MILO. [*Miserably.*] Thanks a lot.

AZAZ. You will need a guide, of course, and since he knows the obstacles so well, the Humbug has cheerfully volunteered to accompany you.

HUMBUG. Now, see here . . . !

AZAZ. You will find him dependable, brave, resourceful and loyal.

HUMBUG. [*Flattered.*] Oh, your Majesty.

MILO. I'm sure he'll be a great help. [*They approach the car.*]

TOCK. I hope so. It looks like we're going to need it.

[*The lights darken and the* KING *fades from view.*]

AZAZ. Good luck! Drive carefully! [*The three get into the car and begin to move. Suddenly a thunderously loud NOISE is heard. They slow down the car.*]

MILO. What was that?

TOCK. It came from up ahead.

HUMBUG. It's something terrible, I just know it. Oh, no. Something dreadful is going to happen to us. I can feel it in my bones. [*The NOISE is repeated. They all look at each other fearfully as the lights fade.*]

Guide for Responding

◆ LITERATURE AND YOUR LIFE

Reader's Response Does any character in this play remind you of someone you know?

Thematic Focus How has this act affected the way you think about words and numbers?

☑ Check Your Comprehension

1. Which characters does Milo meet before meeting Tock?
2. Who will accompany Milo as he continues his journey?
3. Where do Milo and his friends have to go to rescue the princesses?

◆ Critical Thinking

INTERPRET

1. Why is it necessary that Milo rescue the banished princesses? **[Infer]**
2. What has Milo learned from his adventures in Dictionopolis? **[Synthesize]**

EVALUATE

3. Did you find Act I of *The Phantom Tollbooth* entertaining? Explain. **[Assess]**

APPLY

4. What are three strategies you have for using time well? **[Apply]**

Guide for Responding (continued)

◆ Literary Focus

ELEMENTS OF DRAMA

The **elements of drama** are a story, action, dialogue, and characters represented by actors. Dramas are often divided into acts and scenes.

1. Which character opens the play?
2. What action would help an actor portray a Lethargarian?
3. Why do you think the playwright starts a new scene when Milo goes through the tollbooth?

◆ Reading Strategy

SUMMARIZE

A good summary identifies the main characters, includes significant events, and indicates the order in which they happen. **Summarize** what has happened to Milo since he went through the tollbooth.

◆ Build Grammar Skills

SUBJECT AND VERB AGREEMENT

The verb in a sentence must **agree** in number with the subject. Singular subjects refer to one person, place, or thing. Plural subjects refer to more than one. Verbs in the present tense change form to agree with a singular or plural subject. Singular verbs end in s, while plural verbs do not:

Singular: The car moves. **Plural:** The cars move.

Practice On your paper, write the verb that agrees with the subject.

1. The Lethargarians (take, takes) an evening nap.
2. The spelling bee (spell, spells) words.
3. They (know, knows) the princesses.
4. The merchants (sell, sells) words and letters.
5. Milo (give, gives) several reasons.

Writing Application For the sentences below, change the singular subjects and verbs to plural and the plural to singular. Write the new sentences on your paper.

1. The man likes numbers.
2. The Lethargarians sleep in a tree.

◆ Build Vocabulary

USING THE PREFIX *pre-*

Knowing that the prefix *pre-* means "before" can help you figure out the meaning of words with *pre-*. On a piece of paper, write a definition for each italicized word.

1. Milo takes *precautionary* measures.
2. I'd like to *preview* the second act.

SPELLING STRATEGY

The letters *tion* and *sion* can both be used to spell the sound *shun*. Following are clues for the two *shun* words in the Word Bank. On your paper, write the word that matches each clue.

1. It is spelled with an s in the prefix and in the suffix.
2. The *pre-* in this word rhymes with the *t* in the *shun* sound.

USING THE WORD BANK

On your paper, fill in each blank with the appropriate word from the Word Bank.

The __?__ directions helped Milo avoid danger. He had the __?__ that the Humbug could be trusted. He soon regretted his __?__ .

Idea Bank

Writing

1. **Proclamation** Write a proclamation, or announcement, that tells why Princesses Rhyme and Reason are banished to the Castle-in-the-Air.

2. **Speech** Write a brief speech that Milo might have delivered at the banquet.

Project

3. **Board Game** Create a board game based on Act I of *The Phantom Tollbooth*. Make some squares "bonus spots," where players can move ahead for spelling a word or adding a sum correctly. Make other squares penalties, such as "stuck in the Doldrums." **[Art Link]**

Guide for Reading

◆ Literary Focus

STAGING

Staging is the art of putting a play on the stage and making it come to life for the audience. It includes the use of sets and scenery, costumes, props (objects that are used as part of the play, such as a book or a pencil), lighting, sound effects, and special effects. For example, the first act of *The Phantom Tollbooth* requires three different sets: Milo's bedroom, the road to Dictionopolis, and the city of Dictionopolis. In addition, the play requires numerous props—objects that are used by actors during the production of the play.

◆ Reading Strategy

ENVISION

The main characteristic of drama is the performance of a story. When you read a drama, use the dialogue and descriptions in the stage directions to **envision,** or picture in your mind, the action in the scene. Create a diagram like the one shown below. On it, jot down details about sets and props that help you envision the characters and the action.

Scene	Change of Set	Use of Prop
Act II Scene i	Milo is on the road. Digitopolis is in the background, and a wagon is nearby.	1. Dischord pours liquid into a special bottle. 2. _____
Scene ii		

◆ Build Vocabulary

WORD ROOTS: *-son-*

In Act II, Milo meets a Doctor of "Dissonance." Words formed from the root *-son-* include the idea of sound in their meaning. *Dissonance* means "a harsh or disagreeable combination of sounds." Other words built from the root *-son-* are *sonic* ("having to do with sound") and *sonnet* ("a poem arranged to make a musical sound").

WORD BANK

Which word on the list would the Greek goddess Iris use to describe her shining, many-colored rainbow?

dissonance
admonishing
iridescent
malicious

Act II

Scene i

The set of Digitopolis glitters in the background, while Upstage Right near the road, a small colorful Wagon sits, looking quite deserted. On its side in large letters, a sign reads:
"KAKAFONOUS A. DISCHORD
Doctor of <u>Dissonance</u>"
Enter MILO, TOCK and HUMBUG, fearfully. They look at the wagon.

TOCK. There's no doubt about it. That's where the noise was coming from.

HUMBUG. [To MILO.] Well, go on.

MILO. Go on what?

HUMBUG. Go on and see who's making all that noise in there. We can't just ignore a creature like that.

MILO. Creature? What kind of creature? Do you think he's dangerous?

HUMBUG. Go on, Milo. Knock on the door. We'll be right behind you.

MILO. O.K. Maybe he can tell us how much further it is to Digitopolis.

[MILO tiptoes up to the wagon door and KNOCKS timidly. The moment he knocks, a terrible CRASH is heard inside

◆ Build Vocabulary

dissonance (dis´ ə nəns) n.: Harsh combination of sounds

the wagon, and MILO and the others jump back in fright. At the same time, the Door Flies Open, and from the dark interior, a Hoarse VOICE inquires.]

VOICE. Have you ever heard a whole set of dishes dropped from the ceiling onto a hard stone floor? [The Others are speechless with fright. MILO shakes his head. VOICE happily.] Have you ever heard an ant wearing fur slippers walk across a thick wool carpet? [MILO shakes his head again.] Have you ever heard a blindfolded octopus unwrap a cellophane-covered bathtub? [MILO shakes his head a third time.] Ha! I knew it. [He hops out, a little man, wearing a white coat, with a stethoscope around his neck, and a small mirror attached to his forehead, and with very huge ears, and a mortar and pestle in his hands. He stares at MILO, TOCK and HUMBUG.] None of you looks well at all! Tsk, tsk, not at all. [He opens the top or side of his Wagon, revealing a dusty interior resembling an old apothecary shop, with shelves lined with jars and boxes, a table, books, test tubes and bottles and measuring spoons.]

MILO. [Timidly.] Are you a doctor?

DISCHORD. [VOICE.] I am KAKAFONOUS A. DISCHORD, DOCTOR OF DISSONANCE! [*Several small explosions and a grinding crash are heard.*]

HUMBUG. [*Stuttering with fear.*] What does the "A" stand for?

DISCHORD. *AS LOUD AS POSSIBLE!* [*Two screeches and a bump are heard.*] Now, step a little closer and stick out your tongues. [DISCHORD *examines them.*] Just as I expected. [*He opens a large dusty book and thumbs through the pages.*] You're all suffering from a severe lack of noise. [DISCHORD *begins running around, collecting bottles, reading the labels to himself as he goes along.*] "Loud Cries." "Soft Cries." "Bangs, Bongs, Swishes. Swooshes." "Snaps and Crackles." "Whistles and Gongs." "Squeeks, Squacks, and Miscellaneous Uproar." [*As he reads them off, he pours a little of each into a large glass beaker and stirs the mixture with a wooden spoon. The concoction smokes and bubbles.*] Be ready in just a moment.

> ◆ **Literary Focus**
> What sets, props, and sound effects are needed for the staging of this scene?

MILO. [*Suspiciously.*] Just what kind of doctor are you?

DISCHORD. Well, you might say, I'm a specialist. I specialize in noises, from the loudest to the softest, and from the slightly annoying to the terribly unpleasant. For instance, have you ever heard a square-wheeled steamroller ride over a street full of hard-boiled eggs? [*Very loud CRUNCHING SOUNDS are heard.*]

MILO. [*Holding his ears.*] But who would want all those terrible noises?

DISCHORD. [*Surprised at the question.*] Everybody does. Why, I'm so busy I can hardly fill all the orders for noise pills, racket lotion, clamor salve and hubbub tonic. That's all people seem to want these days. Years ago, everyone wanted pleasant sounds and business was terrible. But then the cities were built and there was a great need for honking horns, screeching trains, clanging bells and all the rest of those wonderfully unpleasant sounds we use so much today. I've been working overtime ever since and my medicine here is in great demand. All you have to do is take one spoonful every day, and you'll never have to hear another beautiful sound again. Here, try some.

HUMBUG. [*Backing away.*] If it's all the same to you, I'd rather not.

MILO. I don't want to be cured of beautiful sounds.

TOCK. Besides, there's no such sickness as a lack of noise.

DISCHORD. How true. That's what makes it so difficult to cure. [*Takes a large glass bottle from the shelf.*] Very well, if you want to go all through life suffering from a noise deficiency, I'll just give this to Dynne for his lunch. [*Uncorks the bottle and pours the liquid into it. There is a rumbling and then a loud explosion accompanied by smoke, out of which* DYNNE, *a smog-like creature with yellow eyes and a frowning mouth, appears.*]

DYNNE. [*Smacking his lips.*] Ahhh, that was good, Master. I thought you'd never let me out. It was really cramped in there.

DISCHORD. This is my assistant, the awful Dynne. You must forgive his appearance, for he really doesn't have any.

MILO. What is a Dynne?

DISCHORD. You mean you've never heard of the awful Dynne? When you're playing in your room and making a great amount of noise, what do they tell you to stop?

MILO. That awful din.

DISCHORD. When the neighbors are playing their radio too loud late at night, what do you wish they'd turn down?

TOCK. That awful din.

DISCORD. And when the street on your block is being repaired and the drills are working all day, what does everyone complain of?

HUMBUG. [*Brightly.*] The dreadful row.

DYNNE. The Dreadful Rauw was my grandfather. He perished in the great silence epidemic of 1712. I certainly can't understand why you don't like noise. Why, I heard an explosion last week that was so lovely, I groaned with appreciation for two days. [*He gives a loud groan at the memory.*]

DISCORD. He's right, you know! Noise is the most valuable thing in the world.

MILO. King Azaz says words are.

DISCORD. NONSENSE! Why, when a baby wants food, how does he ask?

DYNNE. [*Happily.*] He screams!

DISCORD. And when a racing car wants gas?

DYNNE. [*Jumping for joy.*] It chokes!

DISCORD. And what happens to the dawn when a new day begins?

DYNNE. [*Delighted.*] It breaks!

DISCORD. You see how simple it is? [*To* DYNNE.] Isn't it time for us to go?

MILO. Where to? Maybe we're going the same way.

DYNNE. I doubt it. [*Picking up empty sacks from the table.*] We're going on our collection rounds. Once a day, I travel throughout the kingdom and collect all the wonderfully horrible and beautifully unpleasant sounds I can find and bring them back to the doctor to use in his medicine.

DISCORD. Where are you going?

MILO. To Digitopolis.

DISCORD. Oh, there are a number of ways to

get to Digitopolis, if you know how to follow directions. Just take a look at the sign at the fork in the road. Though why you'd ever want to go there, I'll never know.

MILO. We want to talk to the Mathemagician.

HUMBUG. About the release of the Princesses Rhyme and Reason.

DISCORD. Rhyme and Reason? I remember them. Very nice girls, but a little too quiet for my taste. In fact, I've been meaning to send them something that Dynne brought home by mistake and which I have absolutely no use for. [*He rummages through the wagon.*] Ah, here it is . . . or maybe you'd like it for yourself. [*Hands* MILO *a Package.*]

MILO. What is it?

DISCORD. The sounds of laughter. They're so unpleasant to hear, it's almost unbearable. All those giggles and snickers and happy shouts of joy, I don't know what Dynne was thinking of when he collected them. Here, take them to the Princesses or keep them for yourselves, I don't care. Well, time to move on. Goodbye now and good luck! [*He has shut the wagon by now and gets in. LOUD NOISES begin to erupt as* DYNNE *pulls the wagon offstage.*]

MILO. [*Calling after them.*] But wait! The fork in the road . . . you didn't tell us where it is . . .

TOCK. It's too late. He can't hear a thing.

HUMBUG. I could use a fork of my own, at the moment. And a knife and a spoon to go with it. All of a sudden, I feel very hungry.

MILO. So do I, but it's no use thinking about it. There won't be anything to eat until we reach Digitopolis. [*They get into the car.*]

HUMBUG. [*Rubbing his stomach.*] Well, the sooner the better is what I say.
[*A SIGN suddenly appears.*]

VOICE. [*A strange voice from nowhere.*] But which way will get you there sooner? That is the question.

TOCK. Did you hear something?

MILO. Look! The fork in the road and a signpost to Digitopolis! [*They read the Sign.*]

DIGITOPOLIS

5	Miles
1,600	Rods
8,800	Yards
26,400	Feet
316,800	Inches
633.600	Half Inches

AND THEN SOME

HUMBUG. Let's travel by miles, it's shorter.

MILO. Let's travel by half inches. It's quicker.

TOCK. But which road should we take? It must make a difference.

MILO. Do you think so?

TOCK. Well, I'm not sure, but . . .

HUMBUG. He could be right. On the other hand, he could also be wrong. Does it make a difference or not?

VOICE. Yes, indeed, indeed it does, certainly, my yes, it does make a difference.
[*The* DODECAHERON *Appears, a 12-sided figure with a different face on each side, and with all the edges labeled with a small letter and all the angles labeled with a large letter. He wears a beret and peers at the others with a serious face. He doffs his cap and recites:*]

DODECAHERON.

> *My angles are many.*
> *My sides are not few.*
> *I'm the Dodecahedron.*
> *Who are you?*

MILO. What's a Dodecahedron?

DODECAHERON. [*Turning around slowly.*] See for yourself. A Dodecahedron is a mathematical shape with 12 faces. [*All his faces appear as he turns, each face with a different expression. He*

points to them.] I usually use one at a time. It saves wear and tear. What are you called?

MILO. Milo.

DODECAHERON. That's an odd name. [*Changing his smiling face to a frowning one.*] And you have only one face.

MILO. [*Making sure it is still there.*] Is that bad?

DODECAHERON. You'll soon wear it out using it for everything. Is everyone with one face called Milo?

MILO. Oh, no. Some are called Billy or Jeffery or Sally or Lisa or lots of other things.

DODECAHERON. How confusing. Here everything is called exactly what it is. The triangles are called triangles, the circles are called circles, and even the same numbers have the same name. Can you imagine what would happen if we named all the twos Billy or Jeffery or Sally or Lisa or lots of other things? You'd have to say Robert plus John equals four, and if the fours were named Albert, things would be hopeless.

MILO. I never thought of it that way.

DODECAHERON. [*With an* admonishing *face.*] Then I suggest you begin at once, for in Digitopolis, everything is quite precise.

MILO. Then perhaps you can help us decide which road we should take.

DODECAHERON. [*Happily.*] By all means. There's nothing to it. [*As he talks, the three others try to solve the problem on a Large Blackboard that is wheeled onstage for the occasion.*] Now, if a small car carrying three people at 30 miles an hour for 10 minutes along a road 5 miles long at 11:35 in the morning starts at the same time as 3 people who have been traveling in a little automobile at 20 miles an hour for 15 minutes on another road exactly twice as long as half the distance of the other, while a dog, a bug, and a boy travel an equal distance in the same time or the same distance in an equal time along a third road in mid-October, then which one arrives first and which is the best way to go?

HUMBUG. Seventeen!

MILO. [*Still figuring frantically.*] I'm not sure, but . . .

DODECAHERON. You'll have to do better than that.

MILO. I'm not very good at problems.

DODECAHERON. What a shame. They're so very useful. Why, did you know that if a beaver 2 feet long with a tail a foot and a half long can build a dam 12 feet high and 6 feet wide in 2 days, all you would need to build Boulder Dam is a beaver 68 feet long with a 51 foot tail?

HUMBUG. [*Grumbling as his pencil snaps.*] Where would you find a beaver that big?

DODECAHERON. I don't know, but if you did, you'd certainly know what to do with him.

MILO. That's crazy.

DODECAHERON. That may be true, but it's completely accurate, and as long as the answer is right, who cares if the question is wrong?

TOCK. [*Who has been patiently doing the first problem.*] All three roads arrive at the same place at the same time.

DODECAHERON. Correct! And I'll take you there myself. [*The blackboard rolls off, and all four get into the car and drive off.*] Now you see how

◆ **Build Vocabulary**

admonishing (ad män´ ish iŋ) *adj.*: Disapproving

important problems are. If you hadn't done this one properly, you might have gone the wrong way.

MILO. But if all the roads arrive at the same place at the same time, then aren't they all the right road?

DODECAHERON. [*Glaring from his upset face.*] Certainly not! They're all the wrong way! Just because you have a choice, it doesn't mean that any of them has to be right. [*Pointing in another direction.*] That's the way to Digitopolis and we'll be there any moment. [*Suddenly the lighting grows dimmer.*] In fact, we're here. Welcome to the Land of Numbers.

HUMBUG. [*Looking around at the barren landscape.*] It doesn't look very inviting.

MILO. Is this the place where numbers are made?

DODECAHERON. They're not made. You have to dig for them. Don't you know anything at all about numbers?

MILO. Well, I never really thought they were very important.

DODECAHERON. NOT IMPORTANT! Could you have tea for two without the 2? Or three blind mice without the 3? And how would you sail the seven seas without the 7?

MILO. All I meant was . . .

DODECAHERON. [*Continues shouting angrily.*] If you had high hopes, how would you know how high they were? And did you know that narrow escapes come in different widths? Would you travel the whole world wide without ever

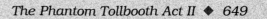

knowing how wide it was? And how could you do anything at long last without knowing how long the last was? Why numbers are the most beautiful and valuable things in the world. Just follow me and I'll show you. [*He motions to them and pantomimes walking through rocky terrain with the others in tow. A Doorway similar to the Tollbooth appears and the* DODECA-HERON *opens it and motions the others to follow him through.*] Come along, come along. I can't wait for you all day. [*They enter the doorway and the lights are dimmed very low, as to simulate the interior of a cave. The SOUNDS of scrapings and tapping, scuffling and digging are heard all around them. He hands them Helmets with flashlights attached.*] Put these on.

◆ **Reading Strategy**
What details help you envision this scene?

MILO. [*Whispering.*] Where are we going?

DODECAHERON. We're here. This is the numbers mine. [*LIGHTS UP A LITTLE, revealing Little Men digging and chopping, shoveling and scraping.*] Right this way and watch your step. [*His voice echoes and reverberates.* Iridescent *and glittery numbers seem to sparkle from everywhere.*]

MILO. [*Awed.*] Whose mine is it?

VOICE OF MATHEMAGICIAN. By the four million eight hundred and twenty-seven thousand six hundred and fifty-nine hairs on my head, it's mine, of course! [*ENTER* THE MATHEMAGICIAN, *carrying his long staff which looks like a giant pencil.*]

HUMBUG. [*Already intimidated.*] It's a lovely mine, really it is.

MATHEMAGICIAN. [*Proudly.*] The biggest number mine in the kingdom.

◆ Build Vocabulary

iridescent (ir´ ə des´ ənt) *adj.*: Showing different colors when seen from different angles

MILO. [*Excitedly.*] Are there any precious stones in it?

MATHEMAGICIAN. *Precious stones!* [*Then softly.*] By the eight million two hundred and forty-seven thousand three hundred and twelve threads in my robe, I'll say there are. Look here. [*Reaches in a cart, pulls out a small object, polishes it vigorously and holds it to the light, where it sparkles.*]

MILO. But that's a five.

MATHEMAGICIAN. Exactly. As valuable a jewel as you'll find anywhere. Look at some of the others. [*Scoops up others and pours them into* MILO'S *arms. They include all numbers from 1 to 9 and an assortment of zeros.*]

DODECAHERON. We dig them and polish them right here, and then send them all over the world. Marvelous, aren't they?

TOCK. They are beautiful. [*He holds them up to compare them to the numbers on his clock body.*]

MILO. So that's where they come from. [*Looks at them and carefully hands them back, but drops a few which smash and break in half.*] Oh, I'm sorry!

MATHEMAGICIAN. [*Scooping them up.*] Oh, don't worry about that. We use the broken ones for fractions. How about some lunch?
[*Takes out a little whistle and blows it. Two miners rush in carrying an immense cauldron which is bubbling and steaming. The workers put down their tools and gather around to eat.*]

HUMBUG. That looks delicious! [TOCK *and* MILO *also look hungrily at the pot.*]

MATHEMAGICIAN. Perhaps you'd care for something to eat?

MILO. Oh, yes, sir!

TOCK. Thank you.

HUMBUG. [*Already eating.*] Ummm . . . delicious! [*All finish their bowls immediately.*]

MATHEMAGICIAN. Please have another portion. [*They eat and finish.* MATHEMAGICIAN *serves them again.*] Don't stop now. [*They finish.*] Come on, no need to be bashful. [*Serves them again.*]

MILO. [*To* TOCK *and* HUMBUG *as he finishes again.*] Do you want to hear something strange? Each one I eat makes me a little hungrier than before.

MATHEMAGICIAN. Do have some more. [*He serves them again. They eat frantically, until the* MATHEMAGICIAN *blows his whistle again and the pot is removed.*]

HUMBUG. [*Holding his stomach.*] Uggghhh! I think I'm starving.

MILO. Me, too, and I ate so much.

DODECAHERON. [*Wiping the gravy from several of his mouths.*] Yes, it was delicious, wasn't it? It's the specialty of the kingdom . . . subtraction stew.

TOCK. [*Weak from hunger.*] I have more of an appetite than when I began.

MATHEMAGICIAN. Certainly, what did you expect? The more you eat, the hungrier you get, everyone knows that.

MILO. They do? Then how do you get enough?

MATHEMAGICIAN. Enough? Here in Digitopolis, we have our meals when we're full and eat until we're hungry. That way, when you don't have anything at all, you have more than enough. It's a very economical system. You must have been stuffed to have eaten so much.

DODECAHERON. It's completely logical. The more you want, the less you get, and the less you get, the more you have. Simple arithmetic, that's all. [TOCK, MILO *and* HUMBUG *look at him blankly.*] Now, look, suppose you had something and added nothing to it. What would you have?

MILO. The same.

DODECAHERON. Splendid! And suppose you had something and added less than nothing to it? What would you have then?

HUMBUG. Starvation! Oh, I'm so hungry.

DODECAHERON. Now, now, it's not as bad as all that. In a few hours, you'll be nice and full again . . . just in time for dinner.

MILO. But I only eat when I'm hungry.

MATHEMAGICIAN. [*Waving the eraser of his staff.*] What a curious idea. The next thing you'll have us believe is that you only sleep when you're tired.
[*The mine has disappeared as well as the Miners.*]

HUMBUG. Where did everyone go?

MATHEMAGICIAN. Oh, they're still in the mine. I often find that the best way to get from one place to another is to erase everything and start again. Please make yourself at home.

[*They find themselves in a unique room, in which all the walls, tables, chairs, desks, cabinets and blackboards are labeled to show their heights, widths, depths and distances to and from each other. To one side is a gigantic notepad on an artist's easel, and from hooks and strings hang a collection of rulers, measures, weights and tapes, and all other measuring devices.*]

MILO. Do you always travel that way? [*He looks around in wonder.*]

MATHEMAGICIAN. No, indeed! [*He pulls a plumb line from a hook and walks.*] Most of the time I take the shortest distance between any two points. And of course, when I have to be in several places at once . . . [*He writes $3 \times 1 = 3$ on the notepad with his staff.*] I simply multiply. [THREE FIGURES *looking like the* MATHEMAGICIAN *appear on a platform above.*]

MILO. How did you do that?

MATHEMAGICIAN AND THE THREE. There's nothing to it, if you have a magic staff. [THE THREE

FIGURES *cancel themselves out and disappear.*]

HUMBUG. That's nothing but a big pencil.

MATHEMAGICIAN. True enough, but once you learn to use it, there's no end to what you can do.

MILO. Can you make things disappear?

MATHEMAGICIAN. Just step a little closer and watch this. [*Shows them that there is nothing up his sleeve or in his hat. He writes:*]

4 + 9 − 2 x 16 + 1 = 3 x 6 − 67 + 8 x 2 − 3 + 26 − 1 − 34 + 3 − 7 + 2 − 5 = [*He looks up expectantly.*]

HUMBUG. Seventeen?

MILO. It all comes to zero.

MATHEMAGICIAN. Precisely. [*Makes a theatrical bow and rips off paper from notepad.*] Now, is there anything else you'd like to see? [*At this point, an appeal to the audience to see if any-one would like a problem solved.*]

MILO. Well . . . can you show me the biggest number there is?

MATHEMAGICIAN. Why, I'd be delighted. [*Opening a closet door.*] We keep it right here. It took four miners to dig it out. [*He shows them a huge "3" twice as high as the* MATHEMAGICIAN.]

MILO. No, that's not what I mean. Can you show me the longest number there is?

MATHEMAGICIAN. Sure. [*Opens another door.*] Here it is. It took three carts to carry it here. [*Door reveals an "8" that is as wide as the "3" was high.*]

MILO. No, no, that's not what I meant either. [*Looks helplessly at* TOCK.]

TOCK. I think what you would like to see is the number of the greatest possible magnitude.

MATHEMAGICIAN. Well, why didn't you say so? [*He busily measures them and all other things as he speaks, and marks it down.*] What's the

greatest number you can think of? [*Here, an appeal can also be made to the audience or* MILO *may think of his own answers.*]

MILO. Uh . . . nine trillion, nine hundred and ninety-nine billion, nine hundred ninety-nine million, nine-hundred ninety-nine thousand, nine hundred and ninety-nine [*He puffs.*]

MATHEMAGICIAN. [*Writes that on the pad.*] Very good. Now add one to it. [MILO *or audience does.*] Now add one again. [MILO *or audience does so.*] Now add one again. Now add one again. Now add . . .

MILO. But when can I stop?

MATHEMAGICIAN. Never. Because the number you want is always at least one more than the number you have, and it's so large that if you started saying it yesterday, you wouldn't finish tomorrow.

HUMBUG. Where could you ever find a number so big?

MATHEMAGICIAN. In the same place they have the smallest number there is, and you know what that is?

MILO. The smallest number . . . let's see . . . one one-millionth?

MATHEMAGICIAN. Almost. Now all you have to do is divide that in half and then divide that in half and then divide that in half and then divide that . . .

MILO. Doesn't that ever stop either?

MATHEMAGICIAN. How can it when you can al-ways take half of what you have and divide it in half again? Look. [*Pointing offstage.*] You see that line?

MILO. You mean that long one out there?

MATHEMAGICIAN. That's it. Now, if you just follow that line forever, and when you reach the end, turn left, you will find the Land of Infinity. That's where the tallest, the shortest, the biggest, the smallest and the most and the least of everything are kept.

MILO. But how can you follow anything forever? You know, I get the feeling that everything in Digitopolis is very difficult.

MATHEMAGICIAN. But on the other hand, I think you'll find that the only thing you can do easily is be wrong, and that's hardly worth the effort.

MILO. But . . . what bothers me is . . . well, why is it that even when things are correct, they don't really seem to be right?

MATHEMAGICIAN. [*Grows sad and quiet.*] How true. It's been that way ever since Rhyme and Reason were banished. [*Sadness turns to fury.*] *And all because of that stubborn wretch Azaz!* It's all his fault.

MILO. Maybe if you discussed it with him . . .

MATHEMAGICIAN. He's just too unreasonable! Why just last month, I sent him a very friendly letter, which he never had the courtesy to answer. See for yourself. [*Puts the letter on the easel. The letter reads:*]

4738 1919,

667 394107 5841 62589
85371 14 39588 7190434 203
27689 57131 481206.

5864 98053,
62179875073

MILO. But maybe he doesn't understand numbers.

MATHEMAGICIAN. Nonsense! Everybody understands numbers. No matter what language you speak, they always mean the same thing. A seven is a seven everywhere in the world.

MILO. [*To* TOCK *and* HUMBUG.] Everyone is so sensitive about what he knows best.

TOCK. With your permission, sir, we'd like to rescue Rhyme and Reason.

MATHEMAGICIAN. Has Azaz agreed to it?

TOCK. Yes, sir.

MATHEMAGICIAN. THEN I DON'T! Ever since they've been banished, we've never agreed on anything, and we never will.

MILO. Never?

MATHEMAGICIAN. NEVER! And if you can prove otherwise, you have my permission to go.

MILO. Well then, with whatever Azaz agrees, you disagree.

MATHEMAGICIAN. Correct.

MILO. And with whatever Azaz disagrees, you agree.

MATHEMAGICIAN. [*Yawning, cleaning his nails.*] Also correct.

MILO. Then, each of you agrees that he will disagree with whatever each of you agrees with, and if you both disagree with the same thing, aren't you really in agreement?

MATHEMAGICIAN. I'VE BEEN TRICKED! [*Figures it over, but comes up with the same answer.*]

TOCK. And now may we go?

MATHEMAGICIAN. [*Nods weakly.*] It's a long and dangerous journey. Long before you find them, the demons will know you're there. Watch out for them, because if you ever come face to face, it will be too late. But there is one other obstacle even more serious than that.

MILO. [*Terrified.*] What is it?

MATHEMAGICIAN. I'm afraid I can't tell you until you return. But maybe I can give you something to help you out. [*Claps hands. ENTER the DODECAHERON, carrying something on a pillow. The MATHEMAGICIAN takes it.*] Here is your own magic staff. Use it well and there is nothing it can't do for you. [*Puts a small, gleaming pencil in MILO's breast pocket.*]

HUMBUG. Are you sure you can't tell about that serious obstacle?

MATHEMAGICIAN. Only when you return. And now the Dodecahedron will escort you to the road that leads to the Castle-in-the-Air. Farewell, my friends, and good luck to you. [*They shake hands, say goodbye, and the DODECAHERON leads them off.*] Good luck to you! [*To himself.*] Because you're sure going to need it. [*He watches them through a telescope and marks down the calculations.*]

DODECAHERON. [*He re-enters.*] Well, they they're on their way.

MATHEMAGICIAN. So I see. . . [DODECAHERON *stands waiting.*] Well, what is it?

DODECAHERON. I was just wondering myself, your Numbership. What actually is the serious obstacle you were talking about?

MATHEMAGICIAN. [*Looks at him in surprise.*] You mean you really don't know?

BLACKOUT

Scene ii

The Land of Ignorance

LIGHTS UP on RHYME *and* REASON, *in their*

castle, looking out two windows.

RHYME.

> *I'm worried sick, I must confess*
> *I wonder if they'll have success*
> *All the others tried in vain,*
> *And were never seen or heard again.*

REASON. Now, Rhyme, there's no need to be so pessimistic. Milo, Tock, and Humbug have just as much chance of succeeding as they do of failing.

RHYME.

> *But the demons are so deadly smart*
> *They'll stuff your brain and fill your heart*
> *With petty thoughts and selfish dreams*
> *And trap you with their nasty schemes.*

REASON. Now, Rhyme, be reasonable, won't you? And calm down, you always talk in couplets when you get nervous. Milo has learned a lot from his journey. I think he's a match for the demons and that he might soon be knocking at our door. Now come on, cheer up, won't you?

RHYME. I'll try.

[*LIGHTS FADE on the* PRINCESSES *and COME UP on the little Car, traveling slowly.*]

MILO. So this is the Land of Ignorance. It's so dark. I can hardly see a thing. Maybe we should wait until morning.

VOICE. They'll be mourning for you soon enough. [*They look up and see a large, soiled, ugly* BIRD *with a dangerous beak and a* malicious *expression.*]

MILO. I don't think you understand. We're looking for a place to spend the night.

BIRD. [*Shrieking.*] It's not yours to spend!

MILO. That doesn't make any sense, you see . . .

BIRD. Dollars or cents, it's still not yours to spend.

MILO. But I don't mean . . .

BIRD. Of course you're mean. Anybody who'd spend a night that doesn't belong to him is very mean.

TOCK. Must you interrupt like that?

BIRD. Naturally, it's my job. I take the words right out of your mouth. Haven't we met before? I'm the Everpresent Wordsnatcher.

MILO. Are you a demon?

BIRD. I'm afraid not. I've tried, but the best I can manage to be is a nuisance. [*Suddenly gets nervous as he looks beyond the three.*] And I don't have time to waste with you. [*Starts to leave.*]

TOCK. What is it? What's the matter?

MILO. Hey, don't leave. I wanted to ask you some questions. . . . Wait!

BIRD. Weight? Twenty-seven pounds. Bye-bye. [*Disappears.*]

MILO. Well, he was no help.

MAN. Perhaps I can be of some assistance to you? [*There appears a beautifully-dressed* MAN, *very polished and clean.*] Hello, little boy. [*Shakes* MILO's *hand*] And how's the faithful dog? [*Pats* TOCK.] And who is this handsome creature? [*Tips his hat to* HUMBUG.]

HUMBUG. [*To others.*] What a pleasant surprise to meet someone so nice in a place like this.

MAN. But before I help you out, I wonder if first you could spare me a little of your time, and help me with a few small jobs?

HUMBUG. Why, certainly.

TOCK. Gladly.

MILO. Sure, we'd be happy to.

MAN. Splendid, for there are just three tasks.

◆ **Build Vocabulary**

malicious (mə lish´ əs) *adj.:* Showing evil intentions

First, I would like to move this pile of sand from here to there. [*Indicates through pantomime a large pile of sand.*] But I'm afraid that all I have is this tiny tweezers. [*Hands it to* MILO, *who begins moving the sand one grain at a time.*] Second, I would like to empty this well and fill that other, but I have no bucket, so you'll have to use this eyedropper. [*Hands it to* TOCK, *who begins to work.*] And finally, I must have a hole in this cliff, and here is a needle to dig it. [HUMBUG *eagerly begins. The* MAN *leans against a tree and stares vacantly off into space. The* LIGHTS *indicate the passage of time.*]

MILO. You know something? I've been working steadily for a long time, now, and I don't feel the least bit tired or hungry. I could go right on the same way forever.

MAN. Maybe you will. [*He yawns.*]

MILO. [*Whispers to* TOCK.] Well, I wish I knew how long it was going to take.

TOCK. Why don't you use your magic staff and find out?

MILO. [*Takes out pencil and calculates. To* MAN.] Pardon me, sir, but it's going to take 837 years to finish these jobs.

MAN. Is that so? What a shame. Well then you'd better get on with them.

MILO. But . . . it hardly seems worthwhile.

MAN. WORTHWHILE! Of course they're not worthwhile. I wouldn't ask you to do anything that was worthwhile.

TOCK. Then why bother?

MAN. Because, my friends, what could be more important than doing unimportant things? If you stop to do enough of them, you'll never get where you are going. [*Laughs villainously.*]

MILO. [*Gasps.*] Oh, no, you must be . . .

MAN. Quite correct! I am the Terrible Trivium, demon of petty tasks and worthless jobs, ogre of wasted effort and monster of habit. [*They start to back away from him.*] Don't try to leave, there's so much to do, and you still have 837 years to go on the first job.

MILO. But why do unimportant things?

MAN. Think of all the trouble it saves. If you spend all your time doing only the easy and useless jobs, you'll never have time to worry about the important ones which are so difficult. [*Walks toward them. whispering.*] Now do come and stay with me. We'll have such fun together. There are things to fill and things to empty, things to take away and things to bring back, things to pick up and things to put down . . . [*They are transfixed by his soothing voice. He is about to embrace them when a* VOICE *screams.*]

VOICE. Run! Run! [*They all wake up and run with the Trivium behind. As the* VOICE *continues to call out directions, they follow until they lose the Trivium.*] RUN! RUN! This way! This way! Over here! Over here! Up here! Down there! Quick, hurry up!

TOCK. [*Panting.*] I think we lost him.

VOICE. Keep going straight! Keep going straight! Now step up! Now step up!

MILO. Look out! [*They all fall into a Trap.*] But he said "up!"

VOICE. Well, I hope you didn't expect to get anywhere by listening to me.

HUMBUG. We're in a deep pit! We'll never get out of here.

VOICE. That is quite an accurate evaluation of the situation.

MILO. [*Shouting angrily.*] Then why did you help us at all?

VOICE. Oh, I'd do as much for anybody. Bad advice is my specialty. [*A Little Furry Creature appears.*] I'm the demon of Insincerity. I don't mean what I say; I don't mean what I do; and I don't mean what I am.

MILO. Then why don't you go away and leave us alone!

INSINCERITY. (voice) Now, there there's no need to get angry. You're a very clever boy and I have complete confidence in you. You can certainly climb out of that pit . . . come on, try. . .

MILO. I'm not listening to one word you say! You're just telling me what you think I'd like to hear, and not what is important.

INSINCERITY. Well, if that's the way you feel about it . . .

MILO. That's the way I feel about it. We will manage by ourselves without any unnecessary advice from you.

INSINCERITY. [*Stamping his foot.*] Well, all right for you! Most people listen to what I say, but if that's the way you feel, then I'll just go home. [*Exits in a huff.*]

HUMBUG. [*Who has been quivering with fright.*] And don't you ever come back! Well, I guess we showed him, didn't we?

MILO. You know something? This place is a lot more dangerous than I ever imagined.

TOCK. [*Who's been surveying the situation.*] I think I figured a way to get out. Here, hop on my back. [MILO *does so.*] Now, you, Humbug, on top of Milo. [*He does so.*] Now hook your umbrella onto that tree and hold on. [*They climb over* HUMBUG, *then pull him up.*]

HUMBUG. [*As they climb.*] Watch it! Watch it, now. Ow, be careful of my back! My back! Easy, easy . . . oh, this is so difficult. Aren't you finished yet?

TOCK. [*As he pulls up* HUMBUG.] There. Now, I'll lead for a while. Follow me, and we'll stay out of trouble. [*They walk and climb higher and higher.*]

HUMBUG. Can't we slow down a little?

TOCK. Something tells me we better reach the Castle-in-the-Air as soon as possible, and not stop to rest for a single moment. [*They speed up.*]

MILO. What is it, Tock? Did you see something?

TOCK. Just keep walking and don't look back.

MILO. You *did* see something!

HUMBUG. What is it? Another demon?

TOCK. Not just one, I'm afraid. If you want to see what I'm talking about, then turn around. [*They turn around. The stage darkens and hundreds of Yellow Gleaming Eyes can be seen.*]

HUMBUG. Good grief! Do you see how many there are? Hundreds! The Overbearing Know-it-all, the Gross Exaggeration, the Horrible Hopping Hindsight, . . . and look over there! The Triple Demons of Compromise! Let's get out of here! [*Starts to scurry.*] Hurry up, you two! Must you be so slow about everything?

MILO. Look! There it is, up ahead! The Castle-in-the-Air! [*They all run.*]

HUMBUG. They're gaining!

MILO. But there it is!

HUMBUG. I see it! I see it!
[*They reach the first step and are stopped by a little man in a frock coat, sleeping on a worn ledger. He has a long quill pen and a bottle of ink at his side. He is covered with ink stains over his clothes and wears spectacles.*]

TOCK. Shh! Be very careful. [*They try to step over him, but he wakes up.*]

SENSES TAKER. [*From sleeping position.*] Names? [*He sits up.*]

HUMBUG. Well, I . . .

SENSES TAKER. *NAMES?* [*He opens book and begins to write, splattering himself with ink.*]

HUMBUG. Uh . . . Humbug, Tock and this is Milo.

SENSES TAKER. Splendid, splendid. I haven't had an "M" in ages.

MILO. What do you want our names for? We're sort of in a hurry.

SENSES TAKER. Oh, this won't take long. I'm the official Senses Taker and I must have some information before I can take your sense. Now if you'll just tell me: [*Handing them a form to fill. Speaking slowly and deliberately.*] When you were born, where you were born, why you were born, how old you are now, how old you were then, how old you'll be in a little while . . .

MILO. I wish he'd hurry up. At this rate, the demons will be here before we know it!

SENSES TAKER. . . . Your mother's name, your father's name, where you live, how long you've lived there, the schools you've attended, the schools you haven't attended . . .

HUMBUG. I'm getting writer's cramp.

TOCK. I smell something very evil and it it's getting stronger every second. [*To* SENSES TAKER.] May we go now?

SENSES TAKER. Just as soon as you tell me your height, your weight, the number of books

you've read this year . . .

MILO. We have to go!

SENSES TAKER. All right, all right, I'll give you the short form. [*Pulls out a small piece of paper.*] Destination?

MILO. But we have to . . .

SENSES TAKER. *DESTINATION?*

MILO, TOCK AND HUMBUG. The Castle-in-the-Air! [*They throw down their papers and run past him up the first few stairs.*]

SENSES TAKER. Stop! I'm sure you'd rather see what I have to show you. [*Snaps his fingers; they freeze.*] A circus of your very own. [*CIRCUS MUSIC is heard.* MILO *seems to go into a trance.*] And wouldn't you enjoy this most wonderful smell? [TOCK *sniffs and goes into a trance.*] And here's something I know you'll enjoy hearing . . . [*To* HUMBUG. *The sound of CHEERS and APPLAUSE for* HUMBUG *is heard, and he goes into a trance.*] There we are. And now, I'll just sit back and let the demons catch up with you.

[MILO *accidentally drops his package of gifts. The Package of Laughter from* DR. DISCHORD *opens and the Sounds of Laughter are heard. After a moment,* MILO, TOCK *and* HUMBUG *join in laughing and the spells are broken.*]

MILO. There was no circus.

TOCK. There were no smells.

HUMBUG. The applause is gone.

SENSES TAKER. I warned you I was the Senses Taker. I'll steal your sense of Purpose, your sense of Duty, destroy your sense of Proportion—and but for one thing, you'd be helpless yet.

MILO. What's that?

SENSES TAKER. As long as you have the sound of laughter, I cannot take your sense of Humor. Agh! That horrible sense of humor.

HUMBUG. HERE THEY COME! LET'S GET OUT OF HERE!

[*The demons appear in nasty slithering hordes, running through the audience and up onto the stage, trying to attack* TOCK, MILO *and* HUMBUG. *The three heroes run past the* SENSES TAKER *up the stairs toward the Castle-in-the-Air with the demons snarling behind them.*]

◆ **Literary Focus**
What is needed to stage this scene?

MILO. Don't look back! Just keep going! [*They reach the castle.* THE TWO PRINCESSES *appear in the windows.*]

PRINCESSES. Hurry! Hurry! We've been expecting you.

MILO. You must be the Princesses. We've come to rescue you.

HUMBUG. And the demons are close behind!

TOCK. We should leave right away.

PRINCESSES. We're ready anytime you are.

MILO. Good, now if you'll just come out. But wait a minute—there's no door! How can we rescue you from the Castle-in-the-Air if there's no way to get in or out?

HUMBUG. Hurry, Milo! They're gaining on us.

REASON. Take your time, Milo, and think about it.

MILO. Ummmn all right . . . just give me a second or two. [*He thinks hard.*]

HUMBUG. I think I feel sick.

MILO. I've got it! Where's that package of presents? [*Opens the package of letters.*] Ah, here it is. [*Takes out the letters and sticks them on the door, spelling:*] E-N-T-R-A-N-C-E. Entrance. Now, let's see. [*Rummages through and spells in smaller letters:*] P-u-s-h. Push. [*He pushes and a door opens. The* PRINCESSES *come out of the castle. Slowly, the demons ascend the stairway.*]

HUMBUG. Oh, it's too late. They're coming up and there's no other way down!

MILO. Unless . . . [*Looks at* TOCK.] Well . . . Time flies, doesn't it?

TOCK. Quite often. Hold on, everyone, and I'll take you down.

HUMBUG. Can you carry us all?

TOCK. We'll soon find out. Ready or not, here we go!

[*His alarm begins to ring. They jump off the platform and disappear. The demons, howling with rage, reach the top and find no one there. They see the* PRINCESSES *and the heroes running across the stage and bound down the stairs after them and into the audience. There is a mad chase scene until they reach the stage again.*]

HUMBUG. I'm exhausted! I can't run another step.

MILO. We can't stop now . . .

TOCK. Milo! Look out there! [*The armies of* AZAZ *and* MATHEMAGICIAN *appear at the back of the theater, with the Kings at their heads.*]

AZAZ. [*As they march toward the stage.*] Don't worry, Milo, we'll take over now.

MATHEMAGICIAN. Those demons may not know it, but their days are numbered!

SPELLING BEE. Charge! C-H-A-R-G-E! Charge! [*They rush at the demons and battle until the demons run off howling. Everyone cheers. The* FIVE MINISTERS *of* AZAZ *appear and shake*

MILO's *hand.*]

MINISTER 1. Well done.

MINISTER 2. Fine job.

MINISTER 3. Good work!

MINISTER 4. Congratulations!

MINISTER 5. CHEERS! [*Everyone cheers again. A fanfare interrupts. A PAGE steps forward and reads from a large scroll:*]

PAGE.

> Henceforth, and forthwith,
> Let it be known by one and all,
> That Rhyme and Reason
> Reign once more in Wisdom.

[*The PRINCESSES bow gratefully and kiss their brothers, the Kings.*]

> And furthermore,
> The boy named Milo,
> The dog known as Tock,
> And the insect hereinafter referred to
>   as the Humbug
> Are hereby declared
> to be Heroes of the Realm.

[*All bow and salute the heroes.*]

MILO. But we never could have done it without a lot of help.

REASON. That may be true, but you had the courage to try, and what you can do is often a matter of what you *will* do.

AZAZ. That's why there was one very important thing about your quest we couldn't discuss until you returned.

MILO. I remember. What was it?

AZAZ. Very simple. It was impossible!

MATHEMAGICIAN. *Completely* impossible!

HUMBUG. Do you mean . . . ? [*Feeling faint.*] Oh . . . I think I need to sit down.

AZAZ. Yes, indeed, but if we'd told you then, you might not have gone.

MATHEMAGICIAN. And, as you discovered, many things are possible just as long as you don't know they're impossible.

MILO. I think I understand.

RHYME. I'm afraid it's time to go now.

REASON. And you must say goodbye.

MILO. To everyone? [*Looks around at the crowd. To TOCK and HUMBUG.*] Can't you two come with me?

HUMBUG. I'm afraid not, old man. I'd like to, but I've arranged for a lecture tour which will keep me occupied for years.

TOCK. And they do need a watchdog here.

MILO. Well, O.K., then. [*MILO hugs the HUMBUG.*]

HUMBUG. [*Sadly.*] Oh, bah.

MILO. [*He hugs TOCK, and then faces everyone.*] Well, goodbye. We all spent so much time together, I know I'm going to miss you. [*To the PRINCESSES.*] I guess we would have reached you a lot sooner if I hadn't made so many mistakes.

REASON. You must never feel badly about making mistakes, Milo, as long as you take the trouble to learn from them. Very often you learn more by being wrong for the right reasons than you do by being right for the wrong ones.

MILO. But there's so much to learn.

RHYME. That's true, but it's not just learning that's important. It's learning what to do with what you learn and learning why you learn things that matters.

MILO. I think I know what you mean, Princess. At least, I hope I do. [*The car is rolled forward and MILO climbs in.*] Goodbye! Goodbye! I'll be back someday! I will! Anyway, I'll try. [*As MILO drives the set of the Land of Ignorance begins to move offstage.*]

AZAZ. Goodbye! Always remember. Words! Words! Words!

MATHEMAGICIAN. *And* numbers!

AZAZ. Now, don't tell me you think numbers are as important as words?

MATHEMAGICIAN. Is that so? Why I'll have you know . . . [*The set disappears, and* MILO'S *Room is seen onstage.*]

MILO. [*As he drives on.*] Oh, oh, I hope they don't start all over again. Because I don't think I'll have much time in the near future to help them out. [*The sound of loud ticking is heard.* MILO *finds himself in his room. He gets out of the car and looks around.*]

THE CLOCK. Did someone mention time?

MILO. Boy, I must have been gone for an awful long time. I wonder what time it is. [*Looks at* CLOCK.] Five o'clock. I wonder what day it is.

[*Looks at calendar.*] It's still today! I've only been gone for an hour! [*He continues to look at his calendar, and then begins to look at his books and toys and maps and chemistry set with great interest.*]

CLOCK. An hour, Sixty minutes. How long it really lasts depends on what you do with it. For some people, an hour seems to last for ever. For others, just a moment, and so full of things to do.

MILO. [*Looks at clock.*] Six o'clock already?

CLOCK. In an instant. In a trice. Before you have time to blink. [*The stage goes black in less than no time at all.*]

Guide for Responding

◆ LITERATURE AND YOUR LIFE

Reader's Response Of all the senses that the Senses Taker wants to steal, which do you think is the most important? Why?

Thematic Focus In what way has Milo changed his view of time?

Journal Writing Describe something you do that makes the time pass quickly.

☑ Check Your Comprehension

1. What city do Milo and his companions visit?
2. What kind of knowledge is important to the Mathemagician?
3. Describe two dangers that Milo faces in the Land of Ignorance.
4. Summarize Milo, Tock, and Humbug's rescue of the two Princesses.

◆ Critical Thinking

INTERPRET

1. In what way is the Mathemagician like King Azaz? **[Compare and Contrast]**
2. What does the Terrible Trivium show Milo about using time? **[Interpret]**
3. What does the Senses Taker show Milo about a sense of humor? **[Draw Conclusions]**

APPLY

4. The Mathemagician says that "many things are possible" if you don't know they're impossible. Give an example illustrating this idea. **[Apply]**

EVALUATE

5. Do you agree with the Clock that the way time passes depends on what you are doing? Explain. **[Evaluate]**

Guide for Responding (continued)

◆ Reading Strategy

ENVISION

To **envision** a work of literature, use details in the stage directions and dialogue. Explain which details help you envision the following scenes or actions.

1. Milo's meeting with the Mathemagician
2. Milo and Dodecahedron entering the number mine
3. The demons chasing Milo and the others

◆ Build Grammar Skills

VERB AGREEMENT WITH SPECIAL SUBJECTS

The **verb** in a sentence must always **agree** with its subject in number (singular or plural). Some pronouns are always singular (even though the meaning may be plural). They require the singular form of the verb. The following pronouns are always singular: *everybody, everyone, everything, each, anybody, nobody,* and *somebody.*

Everybody *understands* numbers.

Anybody who'd spend a night that doesn't belong to him *is* very mean.

Although the words *everybody* and *anybody* refer to more than one person, they take a singular verb.

Practice Choose the correct form of the verb in each of the following sentences:

1. Then, each of you (agree, agrees) that he will disagree. . . .
2. Nobody (understand, understands) the king.
3. (Are, Is) everyone with one face called Milo?
4. Here everything (is, are) called exactly what it is.
5. Somebody (help, helps) Milo.

Writing Application Write five sentences describing the inhabitants of Dictionopolis and Digitopolis. In each, use a pronoun that is always singular.

◆ Literary Focus

STAGING

Staging a play includes the use of sets, scenery, costumes, props, lighting, sound, and special effects.

1. List a sound effect, a special bit of costume, and a prop needed for the scene with Dischord.
2. Describe the scenery for the numbers mine.
3. (a) In what way might staging the Terrible Trivium's three tasks present a problem? (b) How does the author solve that problem?
4. Why might the author have the demons run through the audience to reach the stage?

◆ Build Vocabulary

USING THE WORD ROOT -son-

The word root *-son-* in *dissonant* means "sound." Using this information, fill in the blanks on your paper to match each definition:

1. A letter that is not a vowel: c _ _ _ _ _ _ n t
2. Vibrate with sound: r e _ _ _ _ t e
3. Sounding unpleasant: dis_ _ _ a _t

SPELLING STRATEGY

The sound *sh*əs at the end of a word is often spelled *cious,* as in *malicious* and *suspicious.* On your paper, unscramble the following letters and add *cious* to make a word that matches the definition.

1. Valuable: rep
2. Well-mannered: rag
3. Roomy: aps

USING THE WORD BANK

On your paper, write out this paragraph. Fill in the blanks using words from the Word Bank.

Your tollbooth, while painted with beautiful, ____?____ colors, makes a noise of unbelievable ____?____ . Only a ____?____ person would drive through it in the middle of the night. I am tired of ____?____ you; please get rid of the contraption now!

Build Your Portfolio

 Idea Bank

Writing

1. **Letter** Milo starts out very bored. Write a letter to him explaining three productive things he might do to keep from getting bored.

2. **Article** As a reporter, write a ten-question interview with Milo. Find out what news he brings from the Land of Wisdom. Would he do anything differently if he went back?

3. **Essay** Write a brief essay explaining the theme, or central lesson, of *The Phantom Tollbooth,* using examples. Pay special attention to the speeches made by the Clock at the beginning and the end.

Speaking and Listening

4. **Sounds** As Dr. Dischord, play a tape or CD of sound effects. After each sound, lead a class discussion of the qualities that help you recognize the sound. Jot down lists of these qualities. **[Science Link]**

5. **Debate [Group Activity]** With a group, debate the following idea: Numbers are more important and more fun than words. Divide into two teams, one speaking for numbers and one for words. **[Performing Arts Link]**

Projects

6. **Stage a Scene [Group Activity]** With a group, select a scene from the play to act out. Divide the following tasks: making scenery, assembling props, playing various roles, and helping actors figure out where to stand and how to speak their parts. **[Performing Arts Link]**

7. **Big Numbers** Do research into the idea of infinity and of the biggest and the smallest number. Using diagrams and other aids, present what you learn to the class. **[Math Link]**

 Writing Mini-Lesson

Setting Description

The setting of *The Phantom Tollbooth*, the Land of Wisdom, is a wildly fantastical place. To help people stage the play, the author provides descriptions of places such as the number mine. Write a description of the setting for a scene of a play. To make your description clear, organize your details in spatial order.

Writing Skills Focus: Spatial Organization

When using **spatial organization,** writers explain the location of each detail ("to the left," "further back," and so on). They present details in order, going from left to right or top to bottom, to help readers understand the description.

Model From the Play

The set of Digitopolis glitters in the background, while Upstage Right [away from the audience, on their right] near the road, a small colorful Wagon sits, looking quite deserted.

Prewriting Think of a few places where exciting events might occur. Choose one of these places. Then, jot down specific details a reader needs in order to understand where the play is set.

Drafting Use spatial order to present your setting. Then, describe each detail in order.

Revising Have a peer review your draft. Ask: "Where does this scene take place? How do you know? What is unclear in this description?" Refer to your peer's comments as you revise.

> ◆ **Grammar Application**
> When using a pronoun such as *everyone* or *everybody* as a subject, make sure the verb is singular.

CONNECTING LITERATURE TO SOCIAL STUDIES
CANADA

Anne of Green Gables *Adapted by Donald Harron*

ORPHANS IN THE WILDERNESS When early European settlers arrived in Canada, they found a huge wilderness. Ancient forests, mighty rivers, and icy plains stretched for miles without a road in sight. Like the orphan Anne of Green Gables from Lucy M. Montgomery's novels, Canada's early settlers faced life on their own.

Furs and Farms In the 1600's, adventurers arrived from France to trap beavers for their valuable fur. They led lonely lives filled with hardship. British settlers arrived later to farm the land. In 1763, after the Seven Years War with France, Britain gained control of Canada. The French who stayed there were now truly "orphans": Their parent country, France, no longer ruled them.

More Orphans Soon, they were joined by more "orphans," colonists who had fought on the British side during the American Revolution. After George Washington led the Patriots to victory, many of these Loyalists fled to Canada. They were no longer welcome in the United States.

Making a New Home Canadians now made their land into a home of their own. In 1867, Canada won the right to govern itself. It became fully independent of Britain in 1982.

Finding a Name Canada today has a government much like Britain's. Both French and English are official languages. Yet the people are neither French nor English. They are Canadians. Just as the English and French settlers invented new identities, Anne invents stories about herself and the land. This spirit explains why Anne's story is so popular and why the musical from which the selection comes is performed every year on Prince Edward Island, her Canadian home.

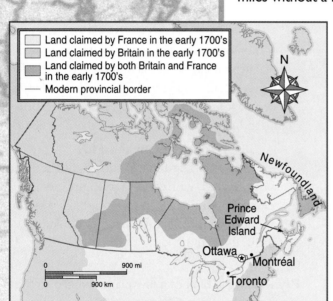

Land claimed by France in the early 1700's
Land claimed by Britain in the early 1700's
Land claimed by both Britain and France in the early 1700's
Modern provincial border

N

Newfoundland

Prince Edward Island

Ottawa
Montréal
Toronto

0   900 mi
0   900 km

Anne of Green Gables
Adapted by Donald Harron from the novel by L. M. Montgomery

Matthew Cuthbert and his sister Marilla need someone to help out on their farm on Prince Edward Island in Canada. They have requested an orphan boy, but the orphanage has sent Anne instead. In this scene, Matthew arrives at the train station expecting to pick up the boy.

from Act I, Scene 2.

ANNE. I suppose you are Mr. Matthew Cuthbert. Mrs. Spencer told me what you looked like. I was beginning to be afraid you weren't coming for me. The stationmaster said the train was early because they had a new engineer on and he wasn't very experienced.

MATTHEW. There must be some mistake.

ANNE. Yes. He said usually the 5:30 train is half an hour late, regular as clockwork. If you hadn't come for me I was going to walk down the track to that big wild cherry tree. . . . See it? (*Points. He looks obediently.*)

MATTHEW. Oh yes.

ANNE. And I was going to climb into that beautiful tree and stay all night. Wouldn't that be lovely? Am I talking too much? People are always telling me I do. Mrs. Spencer said my tongue must be hung in the middle, it flaps so. If you say so, I'll stop. I *can* stop when I make up my mind, although it's awfully difficult.

MATTHEW. No, you can talk all you want. I don't mind.

ANNE. Oh, I'm so glad. It seems so wonderful that I'm going to live with you and belong to you.

MATTHEW. I'll let Marilla do it.

ANNE. I beg your pardon?

MATTHEW. Oh . . . ah . . . let me help you with your bag.

ANNE. Oh, I can carry it. It isn't heavy. It's an excruciatingly old bag. Thank goodness I'll never have to use it again. Mr. Cuthbert, which would you rather be if you had your wish? Divinely beautiful? or dazzlingly clever? or angelically good?

MATTHEW. Well now, I don't rightly know. (*Exits.*)

ANNE. Oh, neither do I. But it would be nice to think you had a choice. (*Exits.*)

(*DROP CURTAIN.* ANNE *and* MATTHEW *reappear riding in a buggy.* [*Horse optional.*] *It crosses the stage during the course of the song.*)

> **Connecting Literature to Social Studies**
> During what period in Canada's history do you think this scene takes place? Explain.

SONG: Gee I'm Glad I'm No One Else
But Me

ANNE.

*Once I thought I'd like to be
A blossom growing on a tree,
White and pink and lazy as can be.
But I'd be king just in the spring.
So now I think it over,
Gee, I'm glad I'm no one else but me.
If you sit around and find the world is
gloomy
And it isn't just your cup of tea
It's easy to imagine that it's rose-in-
bloomy,
You can be the things you want to be.
So when all is said and done
Imagining's a lot of fun,
But when there are battles to be won
Be what you are, it's best by far
And soon you'll be in clover.
Gee, I'm glad I'm no one else but me*

Mr. Cuthbert!

MATTHEW. (*Pulls on the reins, the buggy
stops.*) Ho, Pearl!

ANNE. Your roads! They're red! Oh, I'm so
sorry!

MATTHEW. Don't you like them?

ANNE. Mr. Cuthbert, what color would you
say this is?

MATTHEW. Why, it's red, ain't it?

ANNE. Yes. Red hair and freckles have
been my lifelong sorrows. But why are
your roads red?

MATTHEW. Well now . . . I remember a fellow
telling me once it was the iron in the soil
getting rusty. But I don't think he could
have meant it.

ANNE.

*Do you suppose
that it could be
The wounds of tragic destiny
Dripping from a bloodstained family tree?
An evil spell that did compel
The founders of this island
To meet their doom and perish horribly.*

*Picture now the vicious strife that started
raging
Way back in the olden days of yore . . .
Family with family in feuds engaging,
Drenching all your local soil with gore!*

*There! As far as I can see
I've just cleared up the mystery
Of why your roads are red perpetually!*

> **Connecting Literature
> to Social Studies**
> What historic events
> might Anne's song
> suggest?

Guide for Responding

◆ LITERATURE AND YOUR LIFE

Reader's Response If you were Matthew,
how would you feel about meeting Anne? Why?

Thematic Focus In what way is Anne's view
of the world different from that of others?

☑ Check Your Comprehension

1. Who is Matthew expecting to meet?
2. Who is waiting there for him instead?
3. What reason does Matthew give for the
color of the roads?

◆ Critical Thinking

INTERPRET

1. Describe Matthew's reaction to Anne. **[Infer]**
2. Contrast Matthew and Anne, using details
from the selection. **[Compare and Contrast]**

APPLY

3. Can imagination help someone fight gloom?
Give an example from your own life. **[Apply]**

Meet the Author

Donald Harron (1924–   ) is an actor and an
award-winning playwright.

MATTHEW.

The answer's found
Not in the ground . . .
In your imagination!

Gee up, Pearl!

(Buggy starts again.)

ANNE.

Gee, I'm glad I'm no one else!
Gee, I'm glad I'm no one else!
Gee, I'm glad I'm no one else but me!

(Buggy disappears off stage.)

◆ **Build Vocabulary**

gore (gôr): Blood spilled from a wound

CONNECTING LITERATURE TO SOCIAL STUDIES

Like the orphan Anne, settlers in Canada needed to make a new home for themselves. To natural resources and their own hard work, the settlers added imagination. They created a fresh picture of who they were—neither British nor French, but Canadians. Under British rule, Canada was just a group of separate colonies. In 1864, colonial leaders met on Prince Edward Island, Anne's home. There, they imagined a union of all Canadian colonies. In 1867, Britain agreed to their plan, and the nation of Canada was born.

1. Name two details from the play that show the changes people made to the land. **[Support]**
2. Explain which of Anne's characteristics would be useful for settlers in a new land. **[Analyze]**

 Idea Bank

Writing

1. **Letter** Write a letter to a friend in which you describe Anne's character. Use details from the script to illustrate your points.
2. **Dialogue** Write a continuation of the dialogue between Anne and Matthew.
3. **Song** Add a verse to Anne's song in which you suggest another historic reason that the roads might be red.

Speaking and Listening

4. **Dramatic Reading** With a partner, rehearse and perform this scene.

Projects

5. **Geology Report** Find out what factors can influence the color of soil. Present your findings to the class using diagrams and illustrations. **[Science Link]**
6. **Map** Create a map of Prince Edward Island. On the map, show population, farmland, and railroads. **[Social Studies Link]**

Further Reading, Listening, and Viewing

- *Anne of Green Gables* (Walt Disney Home Video, 1987) is a dramatic adaptation of Anne's story in film.
- *Confederation: A New Nationality* (Grolier, 1981), a book by Michael Bliss, explains the way in which Canada was transformed from a group of separate colonies into a united nation.

Dramatic Scene

Writing Process Workshop

Using just a painted screen and a few chairs, doors, or other props, actors performing a play bring viewers into another world. An audience watching Milo in the clutches of the Senses Taker would squirm in their seats, wondering how Milo is going to escape.

Before a play reaches the stage, though, it starts as words on a page. These words are shaped into **dramatic scenes.** The action in a scene occurs in one place. For instance, Milo's adventure in the Land of Ignorance is one scene in *The Phantom Tollbooth.* Using the following tips, write a dramatic scene.

Writing Skills Focus

▶ **Use stage directions.** Stage directions identify and describe the place where a scene is set. They also tell about characters' actions, expressions, and tone of voice. (See page 662.)

▶ **Use spatial organization.** In your stage directions, present details in spatial order—from left to right or top to bottom—to help readers picture the scene clearly. (See page 663.)

▶ **Develop conflict.** Though it is not the whole play, a scene should relate to the play's central conflict. For instance, a scene might show the hero planning to defeat the "bad guys."

Notice how the writer uses these skills in this model:

MODEL FROM LITERATURE

---

from *The Phantom Tollbooth* by Susan Nanus

Humbug. What is it? Another demon?
Tock. Not just one, I'm afraid. If you want to see what I'm talking about, then turn around. ① [*They turn around. The stage darkens and hundreds of Yellow Gleaming Eyes can be seen.*]
Humbug. ② Good grief! Do you see how many there are? Hundreds! . . . Let's get out of here! ③ [*Starts to scurry.*] Hurry up, you two! Must you be so slow about everything?

① These stage directions help readers (and directors) imagine the scene.

② The conflict in this scene is between the demons and Milo's group.

③ This stage direction shows what the Humbug is doing as he speaks.

Prewriting

Picture a Scene Let your mind wander. Picture two or more people in a place. As ideas begin to come, answer the following questions:

- ▶ Who are these people?
- ▶ What are their names?
- ▶ How old is each one?
- ▶ What does each one look like?
- ▶ What is their connection with each other?
- ▶ Where are they?
- ▶ What are they doing?

Scene Seeds

- A mother and children stand beside the road.
- One man hides behind a rock near the place where two others are talking.
- Two kids look at each other in shock as they realize that the door is locked.

Create a Conflict Once you know who your characters are, think about their conflicts, or problems. For instance, two runners might each want to win a race. There is a conflict between them. A group of people might be trapped in a landslide and need to escape. They have a problem to solve.

Focus Your Scene Decide which part of the story you will show in your scene. For instance, your scene would not show an emergency from beginning to end. Instead, you might show one level-headed person in the situation trying to persuade panicking people to follow a plan.

Think About Dialogue Once you know who your characters are and what conflict or problem they have, think about the dialogue. Answer the following questions for each character:

- ▶ What is this character's most important characteristic?
- ▶ In what way would someone with this characteristic speak? What expressions would he or she use?
- ▶ What does this character want to say to other characters? For instance, does he or she need to get someone's cooperation? Someone's understanding? Does he or she need to trick someone?

APPLYING LANGUAGE SKILLS: Plurals and Possessives

The letter *s* is added to the end of most nouns to form a plural (a word naming more than one person or thing). An apostrophe and an *s* are added to form a possessive (a word showing to whom or what another thing belongs). Use an apostrophe only with a possessive, not with a plural.

Plural: The cats walked home. (more than one cat)

Possessive: The cat's whiskers tickled. (whose whiskers?)

Practice Choose the correct word in each sentence. Then, tell whether it is plural or possessive.

1. Two (Lethargarians, Lethargarian's) slept there.
2. (Milos, Milo's) car brought him to Dictionopolis.
3. There were many (numbers, number's) in the mine.

Writing Application Check your draft to make sure you use apostrophe and *s* correctly.

Writer's Solution Connection Language Lab

For more practice, complete the Possessive Nouns lesson in the Using Nouns unit.

APPLYING LANGUAGE SKILLS:
Write Contractions Correctly

A contraction is a word or a combination of words written in a shortened form. An apostrophe is used to show where one or more letters have been left out:

could not = couldn't
(*o* is left out)

is not = isn't (*o* is left out)

I will = I'll (*wi* is left out)

he is = he's (*i* is left out)

Practice In each sentence, change the italicized words into a contraction.

1. Milo *could not* avoid the Terrible Trivium.
2. I *have not* had a chance to read the ending.
3. It *is not* far to Dictionopolis from here.

Writing Application Check contractions in your draft to make sure the apostrophe is placed properly.

Writer's Solution Connection
Language Lab

For more practice, complete the Using Apostrophes and Hyphens lesson in the Punctuation unit.

Drafting

Write Dialogue Suited to the Characters As you draft, refer to your notes about your characters. The words you give them to say should reflect who they are. A tough crook would not say, "May I please have your wallet?" Instead, he might say, "Gimme your cash." (When writing a play, you may use slang to imitate people's speech.)

Use Stage Directions Include stage directions that help readers visualize the location of the scene and the actions of characters. Stage directions appear italicized within brackets, as in this example:

Lethargarian 1. You're . . . in . . . the . . . Dol . . .drums . . . [*Milo looks around.*]

Organize Descriptions of Setting Spatially In stage directions describing the setting, list details in spatial order—from top to bottom, left to right, or back to front.

Revising

Make Dialogue Consistent With the Characters Read your scene aloud. For each character, ask yourself: Would this kind of character use these words? Adding slang can help make certain characters more realistic.

Add Helpful Stage Directions Add stage directions to let readers know where the scene is set, what the characters do, and the characters' tone of voice.

REVISION MODEL

Fred. [*Raising his voice.*] We ① ~~must~~ *gotta* keep calm.

Panicking will not get us out of this jam.

[*Sarcastically.*]
Susan. ② Like you have something better for us to do?

① The writer replaces one word with an expression that the character is likely to use.
② The writer adds a stage direction to help readers and actors understand how Susan sounds.

Publishing and Presenting

Stage Your Scene With your classmates, stage each other's scenes. Create simple backgrounds, gather props, and assign roles. Rehearse each scene. Then, perform the scenes for the class.

Real-World Reading Skills Workshop

Understanding an Internet Web Page

Strategies for Success

No matter what kind of information you are looking for, you can find it on the Internet. But there's so much information out there that searching the Internet can be difficult. Knowing how an Internet Web page works can help you to find the information you need quickly and easily.

Check the Home Page

The Internet is broken down into many different subject areas. Each subject can have hundreds—or even thousands—of Internet Web pages devoted to it. The first "page" of any Internet site is called the *Home Page*. A Home Page lets you know how that Web site works and what information you can find on it.

Make Links
Internet Web pages often contain *links* that let you "travel" around the Internet. When you click on a link, you travel immediately to another section of that Web site—or to a whole new site. Links are usually underlined or printed in a color that stands out.

Read the Menu
Most Internet Web pages have a *menu* somewhere on their Home Page. The menu tells you what information a site has to offer. Each of the items on a menu is usually a link directly to that information.

Menus might also link you to other Internet Web pages.

Apply the Strategies

Look at the Web page below. Then, answer the questions that follow:

> ### REPTILE FAN CLUB
> ### HOME PAGE
>
> ► <u>About This Site</u>
> ► <u>Reptile Bulletin Board</u>
> ► <u>Fan Club Membership Info</u>
> ► <u>Photo Gallery</u>
> ► <u>Links to Other Reptile Sites</u>
>
> Here's the place to visit if you're interested in:
> **Snakes:** Information about snakes from around the world, including the Eastern diamondback rattlesnake, the cobra, the king snake, and the boa constrictor. You'll also find a special photograph gallery.
>
> **Lizards:** Ever wanted a pet iguana? How about something a little smaller, like a chameleon? We've got tips for choosing and caring for the lizard that's right for you. Go to the Reptile Bulletin Board for more information.
>
> **Turtles:** Come out of your shell for a picture tour of the Galapagos islands. Meet a 200-year-old turtle named Elizabeth!
>
> **Dinosaurs:** So what if none of these are alive today? Check out some cool fossils. Then connect to the Colorado Dinosaur Society Home Page to listen to a speech about the brontosaurus by Professor Helen Moriarity.

1. Name the links that might be useful to a person doing a report on snakes.

2. Explain two ways to get to the Photograph Gallery from the Home Page.

3. Name two organizations you can investigate using this Web page as your starting point.

> ✔ Here are some situations in which you might use an Internet Web page:
> ► Researching a history project
> ► Finding a place to buy computer equipment
> ► Looking for information about your favorite musician

Grammar Review

The **subject** and **verb** in a sentence must **agree** in number. (See page 643.) Singular subjects refer to one person, place, or thing. Plural subjects refer to more than one. Verbs in the present tense change form to agree with a singular or a plural subject. Singular verbs end in s, but plural verbs do not.

Singular: The clock ticks.

Plural: The clocks tick.

Special Subjects Some pronouns are singular, even though their meanings may be plural. When these pronouns are the subject of a sentence, they require the singular form of the verb. (See page 662.) The following pronouns are always singular: *everybody, everyone, everything, each, anybody, nobody,* and *somebody.*

Each *needs* to think for himself.

Nobody *likes* to go to the Doldrums.

Even though the words *each* and *nobody* refer to more than one person, they take a singular verb.

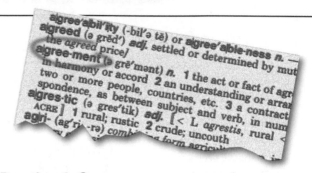

Grammar in Writing

✔ *Make sure you use singular verbs with singular subjects.*

✔ *Read your work aloud after you write it. Often, you can catch an error in subject and verb agreement because of the way it sounds.*

Practice 1 On your paper, write each sentence below, using the corrrect form of the verb.

1. Milo (meet, meets) the Lethargarians.

2. The Lethargarians (sleep, sleeps) much of the time.

3. The king (invite, invites) Milo to a banquet.

4. The guests (make, makes) speeches.

5. The Spelling Bee (spell, spells) his words.

Practice 2 For the sentences below, change the singular subjects and verbs to plural, and change the plural subjects and verbs to singular.

1. The boys open the package.

2. The king eats the honey.

3. The princesses settle the argument.

4. The word sounds interesting.

5. The names describe the place.

Practice 3 Choose the correct form of the verb in each of the following sentences:

1. Somebody (know, knows) the answers.

2. Everybody (spell, spells) correctly.

3. They (enter, enters) the new land.

4. Anybody (love, loves) to take a trip.

5. We (feel, feels) a lot like Milo.

PART 2 *Powerful Voices*

Speech (detail), Paul S. Sample

Guide for Reading

Meet the Author:
Arthur Miller (1915–)

Arthur Miller has known good times and bad. Today, he is one of the most respected and influential American playwrights. As a teenager, though, Miller had to leave school so he could work full time to help with family finances.

The Script of a Lifetime The "script" Miller was writing for his own life did not include failure or defeat. Even though he did not have a high-school diploma, Miller convinced the University of Michigan to accept him as a student. He began writing while in college. Though he held a variety of jobs after graduation, he continued to write. In 1949, he won a Pulitzer Prize for his play *Death of a Salesman.* Other works include *A View From the Bridge* and *The Crucible.*

◆ LITERATURE AND YOUR LIFE

CONNECT YOUR EXPERIENCE

Even if you've never visited the Statue of Liberty, you've probably seen it in a movie, a book, or on a postcard. This play tells a story from Lady Liberty's early days, when the only way to see her was "in person."

THEMATIC FOCUS: Common Ground

In what way does the Statue of Liberty represent common ground?

◆ Background for Understanding

HISTORY

In 1865, a French politician proposed the construction of a shared French-American monument celebrating the idea of liberty. Joseph Pulitzer, a famous newspaper publisher, launched a huge fund-raising campaign in the United States to raise money for the pedestal. Rich and poor were eager to contribute. Within five months, enough money was collected to complete the pedestal.

◆ Build Vocabulary

WORD ROOTS: -scrib-

In *Grandpa and the Statue,* the people on Grandpa's street want to be 100 percent *subscribed* to the fundraiser. Words with the root *-scrib-* (or *-scrip-*) come from the Latin word *scribere,* which means "to write." To *subscribe* to something means to write your name to show agreement, usually agreement to pay.

stingiest
subscribed
peeved
uncomprehending
tempest

WORD BANK

Which word on the list describes a miser?

◆ Grandpa and the Statue ◆

◆ Literary Focus

DIALOGUE

Grandpa and the Statue was written as a radio play—a play to be listened to but not watched. (Radio plays were very popular in the past, when few people had television sets, but most had radios.) Even in a drama that is written to be watched, not every action occurs "onstage" or "onscreen." What characters are doing or plan to do is often revealed in **dialogue**—the conversations among characters. Dialogue also reveals the characters' thoughts and feelings about events and other characters.

◆ Reading Strategy

PREDICT

When you watch a scary movie, you probably have a good idea when the villain is about to show up. As you get involved in the action, you wait to see if what you *think* will happen *does* happen. You can become actively involved in what you read by **predicting,** or making logical guesses, based on clues. As you read *Grandpa and the Statue,* use a chart like the one below to jot down clues that lead you to predict upcoming events. When you get new information, revise your predictions.

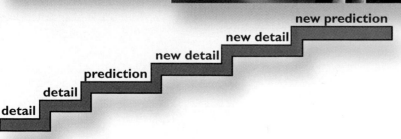

GRANDPA AND THE STATUE

Arthur Miller

[*Music: Theme*]

ANNOUNCER. The scene is the fourth floor of a giant army hospital overlooking New York Harbor. A young man sitting in a wheel chair is looking out a window—just looking. After a while another young man in another wheel chair rolls over to him and they both look.

[*Music out*]

AUGUST. You want to play some checkers with me, Monaghan?

MONAGHAN. Not right now.

AUGUST. Okay. [*Slight pause*] You don't want to go feeling blue, Monaghan.

MONAGHAN. I'm not blue.

AUGUST. All you do most days is sit here looking out this window.

MONAGHAN. What do you want me to do, jump rope?

AUGUST. No, but what do you get out of it?

MONAGHAN. It's a beautiful view. Some companies make millions of dollars just printing that view on postcards.

AUGUST. Yeh, but nobody keeps looking at a postcard six, seven hours a day.

MONAGHAN. I come from around here, it reminds me of things. My young days.

AUGUST. That's right, you're Brooklyn, aren't you?

MONAGHAN. My house is only about a mile away.

AUGUST. That so. Tell me, are you looking at just the water all the time? I'm curious. I don't get a kick out of this view.

MONAGHAN. There's the Statue of Liberty out there. Don't you see it?

AUGUST. Oh, that's it. Yeh, that's nice to look at.

MONAGHAN. I like it. Reminds me of a lot of laughs.

AUGUST. Laughs? The Statue of Liberty?

MONAGHAN. Yeh, my grandfather. He got all twisted up with the Statue of Liberty.

AUGUST. [*Laughs a little*] That so? What happened?

MONAGHAN. Well. My grandfather was the stingiest man in Brooklyn. "Mercyless" Monaghan, they used to call him. He even

---

◀ **Critical Viewing** In what way does the angle of this picture make the statue look very impressive? [Analyze]

◆ **Build Vocabulary**

stingiest (stin′ jē est) *adj*.: Most unwilling to spend any money

used to save umbrella handles.

AUGUST. What for?

MONAGHAN. Just couldn't stand seeing anything go to waste. After a big windstorm there'd be a lot of broken umbrellas laying around in the streets.

AUGUST. Yeh?

MONAGHAN. He'd go around picking them up. In our house the closets were always full of umbrella handles. My grandma used to say that he would go across the Brooklyn Bridge on the trolley just because he could come back on the same nickel. See, if you stayed on the trolley they'd let you come back for the same nickel.

AUGUST. What'd he do, just go over and come back?

MONAGHAN. Yeh, it made him feel good. Savin' money. Two and a half cents.

AUGUST. So how'd he get twisted up with the Statue of Liberty?

MONAGHAN. Well, way back in 1887 around there they were living on Butler Street. Butler Street, Brooklyn, practically runs right down to the river. One day he's sitting on the front porch, reading a paper he borrowed from the neighbors, when along comes this man Jack Sheean who lived up the block.

[*Music: Sneak into above speech, then bridge, then out*]

SHEEAN. [*Slight brogue*[1]] A good afternoon to you, Monaghan.

MONAGHAN. [*Grandfather*] How're you, Sheean, how're ya?

SHEEAN. Fair, fair. And how's Mrs. Monaghan these days?

---

1. **brogue** (brōg) *n*.: Irish accent.

MONAGHAN. Warm. Same as everybody else in summer.

SHEEAN. I've come to talk to you about the fund, Monaghan.

MONAGHAN. What fund is that?

SHEEAN. The Statue of Liberty fund.

MONAGHAN. Oh, that.

SHEEAN. It's time we come to grips with the subject, Monaghan.

MONAGHAN. I'm not interested, Sheean.

SHEEAN. Now hold up on that a minute. Let me tell you the facts. This here Frenchman has gone and built a fine statue of Liberty. It costs who knows how many millions to build. All they're askin' us to do is contribute enough to put up a base for the statue to stand on.

MONAGHAN. I'm not . . . !

SHEEAN. Before you answer me. People all over the whole United States are puttin' in for it. Butler Street is doin' the same. We'd like to hang up a flag on the corner saying—"Butler Street, Brooklyn, is one hundred per cent behind the Statue of Liberty." And Butler Street *is* a hundred per cent <u>subscribed</u> except for you. Now will you give us a dime, Monaghan? One dime and we can put up the flag. Now what do you say to that?

MONAGHAN. I'm not throwin' me good money away for somethin' I don't even know exists.

SHEEAN. Now what do you mean by that?

MONAGHAN. Have you seen this statue?

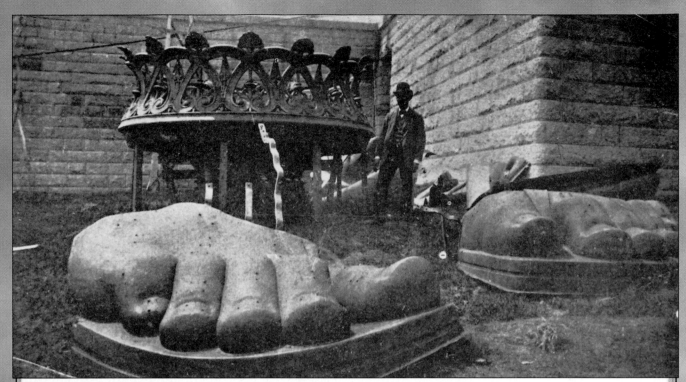

▲ **Critical Viewing** Why might Grandpa be unwilling to contribute after seeing these pieces of the statue? [Infer]

SHEEAN. No, but it's in a warehouse. And as soon as we get the money to build the pedestal they'll take it and put it up on that island in the river, and all the boats comin' in from the old country will see it there and it'll raise the hearts of the poor immigrants to see such a fine sight on their first look at this country.

MONAGHAN. And how do I know it's in this here warehouse at all?

SHEEAN. You read your paper, don't you? It's been in all the papers for the past year.

MONAGHAN. Ha, the papers! Last year I read in the paper that they were about to pave Butler Street and take out all the holes. Turn around and look at Butler Street, Mr. Sheean.

SHEEAN. All right. I'll do this: I'll take you to the warehouse and show you the statue. Will you give me a dime then?

MONAGHAN. Well . . . I'm not sayin' I would, and I'm not sayin' I wouldn't. But I'd be more *likely* if I saw the thing large as life, I would.

SHEEAN. [*Peeved*] All right, then. Come along.

[*Music up and down and out*]

[*Footsteps, in a warehouse . . . echo . . . they come to a halt.*]

Now then. Do you see the Statue of Liberty or don't you see it?

MONAGHAN. I see it all right, but it's all broke!

SHEEAN. *Broke!* They brought it from France on a boat. They had to take it apart, didn't they?

MONAGHAN. You got a secondhand statue, that's what you got, and I'm not payin' for new when they've shipped us something that's all smashed to pieces.

SHEEAN. Now just a minute, just a minute. Visualize what I'm about to tell you, Monaghan, get the picture of it. When this statue is put together it's going to stand ten stories high. Could they get a thing ten stories high into a four-story building such as this is? Use your good sense, now Monaghan.

MONAGHAN. What's that over there?

SHEEAN. Where?

MONAGHAN. That tablet there in her hand. What's it say? July Eye Vee (IV) MDCCLXXVI . . . what . . . what's all that?

SHEEAN. That means July 4, 1776. It's in Roman numbers. Very high class.

MONAGHAN. What's the good of it? If they're going to put a sign on her they ought to put it: Welcome All. That's it. Welcome All.

SHEEAN. They decided July 4, 1776, and July 4, 1776, it's going to be!

MONAGHAN. All right, then let them get their dime from somebody else!

SHEEAN. Monaghan!

MONAGHAN. No, sir! I'll tell you something. I didn't think there was a statue but there is. She's all broke, it's true, but she's here and maybe they can get her together. But even if they do, will you tell me what sort of a welcome to immigrants it'll be, to have a gigantic thing like that in the middle of the river and in her hand is July Eye Vee MCDVC . . . whatever it is?

SHEEAN. That's the date the country was made!

MONAGHAN. The divil with the date! A man comin' in from the sea wants a place to stay, not a date. When I come from the old country I git off at the dock and there's a feller says to me, "Would you care for a room for the night?" "I would that," I sez, and he sez, "All right then, follow me." He takes me to a rooming house. I no sooner sign me name on the register—which I was able to do even at that time—when I look around and the feller is gone clear away and took my valise[2] in the bargain. A statue anyway can't move off so fast, but if she's going to welcome let her say welcome, not this MCDC. . . .

SHEEAN. All right, then, Monaghan. But all I can say is, you've laid a disgrace on the name of Butler Street. I'll put the dime in for ya.

MONAGHAN. Don't connect me with it! It's a swindle, is all it is. In the first place, it's broke; in the second place, if they do put it up it'll come down with the first high wind that strikes it.

SHEEAN. The engineers say it'll last forever!

▼ **Critical Viewing** What tools and equipment might be needed to reassemble the statue? [Draw Conclusions]

---

2. **valise** (və lēs´) *n.*: Small suitcase.

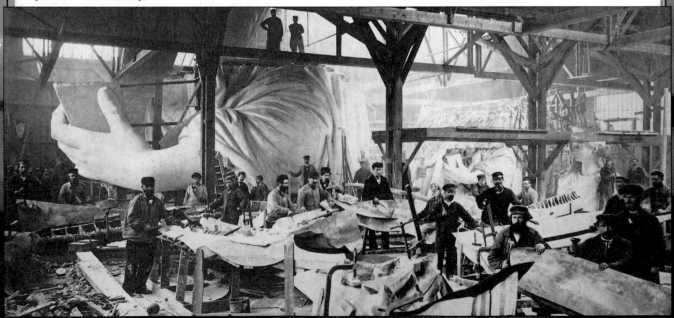

MONAGHAN. And I say it'll topple into the river in a high wind! Look at the inside of her. She's all hollow!

SHEEAN. I've heard everything now, Monaghan. Just about everything. Good-bye.

MONAGHAN. What do you mean, good-bye? How am I to get back to Butler Street from here?

SHEEAN. You've got legs to walk.

MONAGHAN. I'll remind you that I come on the trolley.

SHEEAN. And I'll remind you that I paid your fare and I'm not repeating the kindness.

MONAGHAN. Sheean? You've stranded me!

[*Music up and down*]

YOUNG MONAGHAN. That was Grandpa. That's why I have to laugh every time I look at the statue now.

AUGUST. Did he ever put the dime in?

YOUNG MONAGHAN. Well—in a way. What happened was this: His daughters got married and finally my mom . . . put *me* out on Butler Street. I got to be pretty attached to Grandpa. He'd even give me an umbrella handle and make a sword out of it for me. Naturally, I wasn't very old before he began working on me about the statue.

[*High wind*]

CHILD MONAGHAN. [*Softly, as though* GRANDPA *is in bed*] Grampa?

MONAGHAN. [*Awakened*] Heh? What are you doin' up?

CHILD MONAGHAN. Ssssh! Listen!

[*Wind rising up and fading. Rising higher and fading*]

MONAGHAN. [*Gleefully*] Aaaaaaaah! Yes, yes.

This'll do it, boy. This'll do it! First thing in the morning we'll go down to the docks and I'll bet you me life that Mr. Sheean's statue is smashed down and layin' on the bottom of the bay. Go to sleep now, we'll have a look first thing.

[*Music up and down*]

[*Footsteps*]

◆ **Reading Strategy**
Predict whether the statue will fall.

CHILD MONAGHAN. If it fell down, all the people will get their dimes back, won't they, Grampa? Slow down, I can't walk so fast.

MONAGHAN. Not only will they get their dimes back, but Mr. Sheean and the whole crew that engineered the collection are going to rot in jail. Now mark my words. Here, now, we'll take a short cut around this shed . . .

[*Footsteps continue a moment, then gradually . . . disappointedly they come to a halt.*]

CHILD MONAGHAN. She's . . . she's still standing, Grampa.

MONAGHAN. She is that. [*Uncomprehending*] I don't understand it. That was a terrible wind last night. Terrible.

CHILD MONAGHAN. Maybe she's weaker though. Heh?

MONAGHAN. Why . . . sure, that must be it. I'll wager she's hangin' by a thread. [*Realizing*] Of course! That's why they put her out there in the water so when she falls down she won't be flattening out a lot of poor innocent people. Hey—feel that?

CHILD MONAGHAN. The wind! It's starting to blow again!

MONAGHAN. Sure, and look at the sky blackening over!

◆ **Build Vocabulary**

uncomprehending (ən cäm prē hend´ iŋ) *adj.*: Not understanding

[*Wind rising*]

Feel it comin' up! Take your last look at the statue, boy. If I don't mistake me eyes she's takin' a small list[3] to Jersey already!

[*Music up and down*]

YOUNG MONAGHAN. It was getting embarrassing for me on the block. I kept promising the other kids that when the next wind came the statue would come down. We even had a game. Four or five kids would stand in a semicircle around one kid who was the statue. The statue kid had to stand on his heels and look right in our eyes. Then we'd all take a deep breath and blow in his face. He'd fall down like a stick of wood. They all believed me and Grampa . . . until one day. We were standing around throwing rocks at an old milk can . . .

[*Banging of rocks against milk can*]

GEORGE. [*Kid*] What're you doin'?

CHILD MONAGHAN. What do we look like we're doin'?

GEORGE. I'm going someplace tomorrow.

CHARLEY. [*Kid*] I know, church. Watch out, I'm throwin'.

[*Can being hit*]

GEORGE. I mean after church.

JACK. Where?

GEORGE. My old man's going to take me out on the Statue of Liberty boat.

[*Banging against can abruptly stops.*]

CHILD MONAGHAN. You're not going out on the statue, though, are you?

GEORGE. Sure, that's where we're going.

CHILD MONAGHAN. But you're liable to get killed. Supposing there's a high wind tomorrow?

GEORGE. My old man says that statue couldn't fall down if all the wind in the world and John L. Sullivan[4] hit it at the same time.

CHILD MONAGHAN. Is that so?

GEORGE. Yeh, that's so. My old man says that the only reason your grandfather's saying that it's going to fall down is that he's ashamed he didn't put a dime in for the pedestal.

CHILD MONAGHAN. Is that so?

GEORGE. Yeh, that's so.

CHILD MONAGHAN. Well, you tell your old man that if he gets killed tomorrow not to come around to my grandfather and say he didn't warn him!

JACK. Hey, George, would your father take me along?

GEORGE. I'll ask him, maybe he—

CHILD MONAGHAN. What, are you crazy, Jack?

MIKE. Ask him if he'd take me too, will ya, George?

CHILD MONAGHAN. Mike, what's the matter with you?

JOE. Me too, George, I'll ask my mother for money.

CHILD MONAGHAN. Joe! Didn't you hear what my grampa said?

JOE. Well . . . I don't really believe that any more.

CHILD MONAGHAN. You don't be . . .

MIKE. Me neither.

JACK. I don't really think your grampa knows what he's talkin' about.

---

3. **list** (list) *n*.: Lean; tilt.

4. **John L. Sullivan:** American prizefighter at the time of the play's action.

CHILD MONAGHAN. He don't, heh? [*Ready to weep*] Okay . . . Okay. [*Bursting out*] I just hope that wind blows tomorrow, boy! I just hope that wind blows!

[*Music up and down*]
[*Creaking of a rocking chair*]

Grampa . . . ?

MONAGHAN. Huh?

CHILD MONAGHAN. Can you stop rocking for a minute?

[*Rocking stops*]

Can you put down your paper?

[*Rustle of paper*]

I—I read the weather report for tomorrow.

MONAGHAN. The weather report . . .

CHILD MONAGHAN. Yeh. It says fair and cool.

MONAGHAN. What of it?

CHILD MONAGHAN. I was wondering. Supposing you and me we went on a boat tomorrow. You know, I see the water every day when I go down to the docks to play, but I never sat on it. I mean in a boat.

MONAGHAN. Oh. Well, we might take the ferry on the Jersey side. We might do that.

CHILD MONAGHAN. Yeh, but there's nothing to see in Jersey.

MONAGHAN. You can't go to Europe tomorrow.

CHILD MONAGHAN. No, but couldn't we go toward the ocean? Just . . . *toward* it?

MONAGHAN. Toward it. What—what is it on your mind, boy? What is it now?

CHILD MONAGHAN. Well, I . . .

MONAGHAN. Oh, you want to take the Staten

Welcome, Christian Montone, Artwork from the permanent collection of THIRTEEN/WNET's Student Arts Festival, 1978-1993

▲ **Critical Viewing** How do you think the artist feels about the Statue of Liberty? [Speculate]

Island ferry. Sure, that's in the direction of the sea.

CHILD MONAGHAN. No, Grampa, not the Staten Island ferry.

MONAGHAN. You don't mean—[*Breaks off*] Boy!

CHILD MONAGHAN. All the kids are going tomorrow with Georgie's old man.

MONAGHAN. You don't believe me any more.

CHILD MONAGHAN. I do, Grampa, but . . .

MONAGHAN. You don't. If you did you'd stay clear of the Statue of Liberty for love of your life!

CHILD MONAGHAN. But, Grampa, when is it going to fall down? All I do is wait and wait.

MONAGHAN. [*With some uncertainty*] You've got to have faith.

CHILD MONAGHAN. But every kid in my class went to see it and now the ones that didn't are going tomorrow. And they all keep talking about it and all I do . . . Well, I can't keep telling them it's a swindle. I—I wish we could see it, Grampa. It don't cost so much to go.

MONAGHAN. As long as you put it that way I'll have to admit I'm a bit curious meself as to how it's managed to stand upright so long. Tell you what I'll do. Barrin' wind, we'll chance it tomorrow!

CHILD MONAGHAN. Oh, Gramp!

MONAGHAN. But! if anyone should ask you where we went you'll say—Staten Island. Are y' on?

CHILD MONAGHAN. Okay, sure. Staten Island.

MONAGHAN. [*Secretively*] We'll take the early boat, then. Mum's the word, now. For if old man Sheean hears that I went out there I'll have no peace from the thief the rest of m' life.

[*Music up and down*]

[*Boat whistles*]

CHILD MONAGHAN. Gee, it's nice ridin' on a boat, ain't it, Grampa?

MONAGHAN. Never said there was anything wrong with the boat. Boat's all right. You're sure now that Georgie's father is takin' the kids in the afternoon.

CHILD MONAGHAN. Yeh, that's when they're going. Gee, look at those two sea gulls. Wee!—look at them swoop! They caught a fish!

MONAGHAN. What I can't understand is what all these people see in that statue that they'll keep a boat like this full makin' the trip, year in year out. To hear the newspapers talk, if the statue was gone we'd be at war with the nation that stole her the followin' mornin' early. All it is is a big high pile of French copper.

CHILD MONAGHAN. The teacher says it shows us that we got liberty.

MONAGHAN. Bah! If you've got liberty you don't need a statue to tell you you got it; and if you haven't got liberty no statue's going to do you any good tellin' you you got it. It was a criminal waste of the people's money. [*Quietly*] And just to prove it to you I'll ask this feller sitting right over there what he sees in it. You'll see what a madness the whole thing was. Say, mister?

ALF. Hey?

MONAGHAN. I beg your pardon. I'm a little strange here, and curious. Could you tell me why you're going to the Statue of Liberty?

ALF. Me? Well, I tell ya. I always wanted to take an ocean voyage. This is a pretty big boat—bigger than the ferries—so on Sundays, sometimes, I take the trip. It's better than nothing.

MONAGHAN. Thank you. [*To the kid*] So much for the great meaning of that statue, me boy. We'll talk to this lady standing at the rail. I just want you to understand why I didn't give Sheean me dime. Madam, would you be good enough to . . . Oh pardon me. [*To the kid*] Better pass her by, she don't look so good. We'll ask that girl there. Young lady, if you'll pardon the curiosity of an old man . . . could you tell me in a few good words what it is about that statue that brings you out here?

GIRL. What statue?

MONAGHAN. Why, the Statue of Liberty up 'head. We're coming up to it.

GIRL. Statue of Liberty! Is this the Statue of Liberty boat?

MONAGHAN. Well, what'd you think it was?

GIRL. Oh, my! I'm supposed to be on the Staten Island ferry! Where's the ticket man? [*Going* *away*] Ticket man! Where's the ticket man?

CHILD MONAGHAN. Gee whiz, nobody seems to want to see the statue.

MONAGHAN. Just to prove it, let's see this fellow sitting on this bench here. Young man, say . . .

YOUNG MAN. I can tell you in one word. For four days I haven't had a minute's peace. My kids are screaming, my wife is yelling, upstairs they play the piano all day long. The only place I can find that's quiet is a statue. That statue is my sweetheart. Every Sunday I beat it out to the island and sit next to her, and she don't talk.

CHILD MONAGHAN. I guess you were right, Grampa. Nobody seems to think it means anything.

MONAGHAN. Not only doesn't mean anything, but if they'd used the money to build an honest roomin' house on that island, the immigrants would have a place to spend the night, their valises wouldn't get robbed, and they—

MEGAPHONE VOICE. *Please keep your seats while the boat is docking. Statue of Liberty—all out in five minutes!*

CHILD MONAGHAN. Look down there, Gramp! There's a peanut stand! Could I have some?

MONAGHAN. I feel the wind comin' up. I don't think we dare take the time.

▶ **Critical Viewing** Using details from this picture, explain whether or not you think this statue is a good symbol of liberty. **[Assess]**

[*Music up and down*]

CHILD MONAGHAN. Sssssseuuuuuww! Look how far you can see! Look at that ship way out in the ocean!

MONAGHAN. It is, it's quite a view. Don't let go of me hand now.

CHILD MONAGHAN. I betcha we could almost see California.

MONAGHAN. It's probably that grove of trees way out over there. They do say it's beyond Jersey.

CHILD MONAGHAN. Feels funny. We're standing right inside her head. Is that what you meant . . . July IV, MCD . . . ?

MONAGHAN. That's it. That tablet in her hand. Now shouldn't they have put Welcome All on it instead of that foreign language? Say! Do you feel her rockin'?

CHILD MONAGHAN. Yeah, she's moving a little bit. Listen, the wind!

[*Whistling of wind*]

MONAGHAN. We better get down, come on! This way!

CHILD MONAGHAN. No, the stairs are this way! Come on!

[*Running in echo. Then quick stop*]

MONAGHAN. No, I told you they're the other way! Come!

VETERAN. [*Calm, quiet voice*] Don't get excited, pop. She'll stand.

MONAGHAN. She's swayin' awful.

VETERAN. That's all right. I been up here thirty, forty times. She gives with the wind, flexible. Enjoy the view, go on.

MONAGHAN. Did you say you've been up here forty times?

VETERAN. About that many.

MONAGHAN. What do you find here that's so interesting?

VETERAN. It calms my nerves.

MONAGHAN. Ah. It seems to me it would make you more nervous than you were.

VETERAN. No, not me. It kinda means something to me.

MONAGHAN. Might I ask what?

VETERAN. Well . . . I was in the Philippine War . . . back in '98.[5] Left my brother back there.

MONAGHAN. Oh, yes. Sorry I am to hear it. Young man, I suppose, eh?

VETERAN. Yeh. We were both young. This is his birthday today.

MONAGHAN. Oh, I understand.

VETERAN. Yeh, this statue is about the only stone he's got. In my mind I feel it is anyway. This statue kinda looks like what we believe. You know what I mean?

MONAGHAN. Looks like what we believe . . . I . . . I never thought of it that way. I . . . I see what you mean. It does look that way. [*Angrily*] See now, boy? If Sheean had put it that way I'd a give him me dime. [*Hurt*] Now, why do you suppose he didn't tell me that! Come down now. I'm sorry, sir, we've got to get out of here.

[*Music up and down*]

---

5. **back in '98:** 1898.

[*Footsteps under*]

Hurry now, I want to get out of here. I feel terrible. I do, boy. That Sheean, that fool. Why didn't he tell me that? You'd think . . .

CHILD MONAGHAN. What does this say?

[*Footsteps halt*]

MONAGHAN. Why, it's just a tablet, I suppose. I'll try it with me spectacles, just a minute. Why, it's a poem, I believe . . . "Give me your tired, your poor, your huddled masses yearning to breathe free, the wretched refuse of your teeming[6] shore. Send these, the homeless, tempest-tost to me, I lift . . . my lamp beside . . . the golden door!" Oh, dear. [*Ready to weep*] It had Welcome All on it all the time. Why didn't Sheean tell me? I'd a given him a quarter! Boy . . . go over there and here's a nickel and buy yourself a bag of them peanuts.

CHILD MONAGHAN. [*Astonished*] Gramp!

MONAGHAN. Go on now, I want to study this a minute. And be sure the man gives you full count.

CHILD MONAGHAN. I'll be right back.

[*Footsteps running away*]

MONAGHAN. [*To himself*] "Give me your tired, your poor, your huddled masses . . ."

[*Music swells from a sneak to full, then under to background*]

YOUNG MONAGHAN. [*Soldier*] I ran over and got my peanuts and stood there cracking them open, looking around. And I happened to glance over to Grampa. He had his nose right up to that bronze tablet, reading it. And then he reached into his pocket and kinda spied around over his eyeglasses to see if anybody was looking,

◆ **Literature and Your Life**
Explain what beliefs the Statue of Liberty appears to represent.

---

6. **teeming** (tēm´ in) *adj.*: Swarming with life.

and then he took out a coin and stuck it in a crack of cement over the tablet.

[*Coin falling onto concrete*]

It fell out and before he could pick it up I got a look at it. It was a half a buck. He picked it up and pressed it into the crack so it stuck. And then he came over to me and we went home.

[*Music: Change to stronger, more forceful theme*]

That's why, when I look at her now through this window, I remember that time and that poem, and she really seems to say, Whoever you are, wherever you come from, Welcome All. Welcome Home.

[*Music: Flare up to finish*]

◆ **Build Vocabulary**

tempest (tem´ pist) *n.*: Violent storm with high winds

Guide for Responding

◆ LITERATURE AND YOUR LIFE

Reader's Response What does the Statue of Liberty mean to you?

Thematic Focus What finally helped Grandpa recognize that the Statue of Liberty belongs to everyone?

Journal Writing In your own words, write a brief definition of liberty.

☑ Check Your Comprehension

1. Where is Monaghan when the play opens?
2. What makes him think of his grandfather?
3. What does Sheean want Grandpa to do?
4. What does Grandpa tell his grandson will happen to the statue?
5. What convinces Grandpa that his fears are unfounded?

◆ Critical Thinking

INTERPRET
1. Explain why Grandpa is called "stingy." **[Support]**
2. What problem does Grandpa's decision about the Statue of Liberty cause for his grandson, Child Monaghan? **[Connect]**
3. How do Grandpa's feelings change over the course of the play? **[Compare and Contrast]**

APPLY
4. What do the words Grandpa reads at the base of the Statue of Liberty mean to you? **[Interpret]**

EXTEND
5. What public monument or memorial is most meaningful to you? Why? **[Social Studies Link]**

Guide for Responding (continued)

◆ Reading Strategy

PREDICT

You can make **predictions,** or logical guesses, based on clues in what you read. Answer the following questions about predictions you made while reading *Grandpa and the Statue.*

1. What prediction did you make about Grandpa and the fund-raiser for the statue's base?
2. What did you predict about Grandpa's visiting the statue? Did you ever revise that prediction? Why?

◆ Build Vocabulary

USING THE WORD ROOT -scrib-

The word roots *-scrib-* and *-scrip-* come from the Latin word *scribere,* which means "to write." On your paper, explain the way writing contributes to the meaning of each numbered item below:

1. A child's *scribble*
2. The *script* for a play
3. Initials *inscribed* on a locket

SPELLING STRATEGY

When adding *er* or *est* to an adjective that ends in *y,* change the *y* to *i* before adding the ending:

stingy + -est = stingiest

On your paper, add the ending indicated to each word.

1. happy (er) **2.** silly (est) **3.** mighty (est) **4.** stingy (er)

USING THE WORD BANK

On your paper, complete each sentence with a word from the Word Bank.

1. A surprise makes a person pleased, but a disappointment makes a person __?__.
2. The volunteer was the most generous person in the group, but the miser was the __?__.
3. We joined the club, and we __?__ to the magazine.
4. A scientist would be informed by a lecture, but a toddler would be __?__.
5. We picnicked in the sunshine, but we took shelter during the __?__.

◆ Literary Focus

DIALOGUE

Dialogue is the conversation that takes place among characters in a drama. Dialogue can reveal events, actions, and settings, as well as the characters' thoughts and feelings.

1. Identify two places in *Grandpa and the Statue* where dialogue indicates what a character is doing.
2. Identify two places where dialogue indicates a character's feelings.
3. Identify one place where dialogue indicates where the characters are.

◆ Build Grammar Skills

PRONOUN AND ANTECEDENT AGREEMENT

Pronouns help writers avoid repeating the same nouns over and over. For a pronoun to make sense, however, it must **agree** with its antecedent (the noun or pronoun it replaces) in gender (masculine or feminine) and number (singular or plural).

My *grandfather* was the stingiest man.... *He* even used to save umbrella handles.

The singular masculine pronoun *he* agrees with its antecedent, *grandfather,* which is also masculine and singular.

All the *people* will get *their* dimes back.

The plural pronoun *their* agrees with its antecedent, *people,* which is plural.

Practice On your paper, fill in each blank with a pronoun that agrees with its antecedent.

1. All the kids said that __?__ believe me.
2. Each man must make __?__ own decision.
3. My sister said __?__ might go with us.
4. Each girl in the class gave __?__ dime.
5. All the visitors felt the statue belonged to them; it was __?__.

Writing Application Write five sentences about famous people. Use a pronoun and an antecedent in each sentence.

Build Your Portfolio

 ## Idea Bank

Writing

1. **Invitation** Write an invitation to the public to attend the grand opening of the Statue of Liberty in New York Harbor in 1887.

2. **Journal Entries** As Grandpa or the Child Monaghan, write a journal entry just before you visit the Statue of Liberty and an entry just after the visit.

3. **Essay** Write an essay explaining why the Statue of Liberty is an important symbol of freedom.

Speaking and Listening

4. **Sound Effects** Prepare a sound-effects tape to be used in a radio production of this play. Experiment with different ways of making wind sounds, creaking sounds, and other sounds needed for the play. Use the best results on your tape.

5. **Readers Theatre [Group Activity]** With a group, practice a portion of the play as a Readers Theatre. Perform your scene for the class. If possible, make a video or audio recording of the scene. **[Performing Arts Link]**

Projects

6. **Liberty Island Information Fair [Group Activity]** With a group, create a Liberty Island in your classroom. Group members can choose to make diagrams of the island, prepare charts giving facts about and a history of the statue, or create posters showing a view of the area. **[Social Studies Link]**

7. **Liberty Math** Review Liberty's numbers, such as height, weight, and stairs to the top. Create a chart showing comparisons that will help others to appreciate Liberty's statistics. For example, compare her height to a famous building in your area. (See p. 687.) **[Math Link]**

 ## Writing Mini-Lesson

Opinion

Grandpa and Sheean had very different opinions about the importance of the Statue of Liberty. Write your opinion on a current topic in school, local, or national news.

Writing Skills Focus: Support

Provide **support** for each point of your opinion. Give facts, details, and reasons that will help your opinion stand up under examination. In the following example, Sheean gives Grandpa examples (other people contributing to the fund) and a reason (the street wants to put up a flag).

Model From the Play

People all over the whole United States are puttin' in for it. Butler Street is doin' the same. We'd like to hang up a flag on the corner saying—"Butler Street, Brooklyn, is one hundred per cent behind the Statue of Liberty."

Prewriting Write out your opinion in a single sentence. Then, jot down the reasons why you feel as you do.

Drafting Include examples or details that illustrate your views. For example, if your opinion is that people spend too much time watching television, give examples of better ways to spend time.

Revising Ask a partner to answer the following questions: "Is the opinion clearly stated? Where could I use more support? Do you agree with my opinion? Why or why not?" Use your partner's answers to determine what you need to revise.

> ◆ **Grammar Application**
> Make sure any pronouns you have used agree with their antecedents in number and gender.

CONNECTIONS TO TODAY'S WORLD

Immigrants in the late nineteenth and early twentieth centuries passed the Statue of Liberty on their way to Ellis Island. The government began using Ellis Island as an immigration station in 1892. Although it remained open until 1954, its large-scale use ended in 1924. The island was reopened to the public in 1990. The following brochure is available to visitors to Ellis Island.

Ellis Island

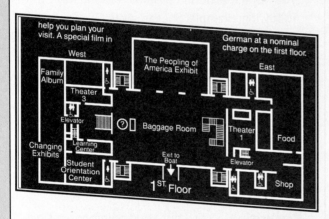

Ellis Island Immigration Museum Directory

The Ellis Island Museum is self-guided. A video presentation on the first floor gives an overview of the exhibits to help you plan your visit. A special film in the first and second floor theaters along with four major exhibits brings the immigrant experience to life. Please inquire about access for the disabled at the information desk. Taped audio tours are available in English, French, Spanish, and German at a nominal charge on the first floor.

Museum Highlights

- More than thirty separate galleries filled with artifacts, historic photos, posters, maps, oral histories, and ethnic music, all telling the story of what happened at the Ellis Island depot and to the newcomers who helped settle America.
- Two theaters featuring *Island of Hope, Island of Tears*, an award-winning film documenting the Ellis Island experience.
- An innovative learning center with state-of-the-art technology that teaches schoolchildren of all ages about their cultural heritage. Use of the center is by reservation only.

- Treasures From Home, a collection of priceless family heirlooms brought to America by immigrants.
- More than two thousand artifacts including personal papers, jewelry, tools, religious articles, and clothing are on display in the museum.

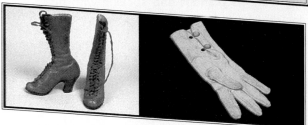

Great Hall

Now magnificently restored, the Great Hall was once the focal point of the immigrant processing. Here newcomers underwent questioning and were either given permission to land or denied entry into the country.

Wall of Honor

With 420,000 entries, the memorial is the largest wall of names in the world. For information, inquire at reception desk on the first floor.

Ellis Island is one of the country's most important historic sites. It is also one of our most heavily visited monuments. Careful planning will make your trip more enoyable. The Circle Line–Statue of Liberty Ferry provides transportation to Ellis Island from Battery Park in New York and Liberty State Park in New Jersey from 9:00 A.M. to 5:00 P.M. daily, with extended hours in the summer. For ticket rates and schedule information, call (212) 269 5755.

For further information

Contact the Superintendent, Statue of Liberty National Monument, Liberty Island, New York, NY 10004.

1. Which exhibit would you visit first? Why?
2. How do the pictures and map help you get an overview of the island's buildings and exhibits?
3. How could you get more information about Ellis island?

Critical Response

Writing Process Workshop

Reading *Grandpa and the Statue,* you may have felt surprise when Grandpa Monaghan changed his mind about the Statue of Liberty. Your surprise is a kind of response to the play. You might think about the reasons for your response. You might decide, for instance, that this surprise shows how powerful the message of the Statue of Liberty can be.

In a **critical response,** a writer examines the reasons for his or her responses to a book, a movie, or a play. A critical response includes a summary of the work, an evaluation of the work's strengths and weaknesses, and a recommendation to readers. Write a critical response to *Grandpa and the Statue* or another work, using the following tips:

Writing Skills Focus

▶ **Analyze your responses.** Explain which features of the work caused your responses. For instance, "I felt bad for Child Monaghan" is a response. "The play showed that he was torn between sticking with his grandpa and sticking with his friends" explains the reasons for that response.

▶ **Support your points.** Give examples from the work to support each point you make. (See p. 689.)

Notice how the writer uses these skills in this model:

MODEL

① *Grandpa and the Statue* is about a man who lives at the time the Statue of Liberty is being built. He will not contribute money for the statue's pedestal because he is stingy and mistrustful.

② The play is interesting as it shows people reacting to the statue when it is new. ③ Some, like the man on the ferry, see it as a place to escape from worries. ④ However, the author does not clearly show why Grandpa suddenly stops being a stingy man and supports the statue. ⑤ In spite of this one weakness, *Grandpa and the Statue* is worth reading.

① The writer gives a brief summary.

② The writer points out one of the play's strengths.

③ The writer supports the point with an example.

④ Here, the writer analyzes a response, explaining where the author did not succeed.

⑤ The writer makes a recommendation.

Prewriting

Choose a Topic If you choose not to write about *Grandpa and the Statue*, think about stories you have read or movies or plays you have seen. Choose a work to which you had a strong reaction (even if that reaction was strong dislike).

Clarify Your Opinion Once you've chosen a work, review your thoughts about it. Create a chart like the one below to list what you liked about the work and what you didn't like.

LIKED/DISLIKED	
I Liked . . .	**I Disliked . . .**
I liked the character of the kid.	I disliked the character of Grandpa.
I liked the part where Grandpa asks people why they are going to the statue.	I disliked that Grandpa changes his mind so quickly.

Analyze Your Responses For each item you list on your chart, think about your reasons for reacting as you did. Create a chart like the one below to identify what your reactions tell you about the play.

ANALYZE RESPONSES		
Response	**Reasons**	**Conclusion About the Play**
I liked the character of the kid.	He tries hard to stay loyal to his grandpa.	The play has some likeable characters.
I disliked the character of Grandpa.	He is needlessly rude to people.	The writer fails to make Grandpa appealing to me.
I liked the part where Grandpa asks people why they are going to the statue.	It gave me a real sense of how people lived at this time.	The writer is good with realistic details.

Decide on Your Evaluation Look over your two charts. Decide whether you think the work has more strengths or weaknesses and whether you will recommend it to your readers.

Drafting

Include Required Parts Using the details you've gathered, draft your critical response. Introduce your response by explaining your general evaluation of the work. Then, give a brief summary of what the work is about and what happens in it. Next, explain what you liked and disliked about the work. Conclude by restating your evaluation and offering a recommendation to readers.

APPLYING LANGUAGE SKILLS: Vary Sentence Beginnings

By using different kinds of beginnings for your sentences, you will make your writing more interesting for the reader. Here are some ways to begin a sentence:

Begin with the subject (a noun or a pronoun): They rode the ferry to the statue.

Begin with a phrase or a single word: With Grandpa, he rode the ferry to the statue.

Later, they returned.

Practice Rewrite the following sentences, changing the way each begins.

1. Grandpa does not believe at the time they are building the Statue of Liberty that it will keep standing.
2. He changes his mind in the meantime.
3. At the end of the play, he realizes the statue is a good thing.

Writing Application As you draft, vary the way in which you begin sentences.

Writer's Solution Connection Language Lab

For more help with sentence style, complete a lesson in the Sentence Style unit.

APPLYING LANGUAGE SKILLS: Use the Correct Verb Form

Every verb has more than one form. Some verb forms require a helping verb; others are never used with helping verbs. Be careful to choose the correct form.

Incorrect:
I seen the statue.

Correct:
I have seen the statue.
I saw the statue.

Incorrect:
He has did his homework.

Correct:
He has done his homework.
He did his homework.

Practice In each sentence, select the correct form of the verb.

1. Grandpa (been, had been) stingy.
2. He (do, does) not want to give money for the statue.
3. He (come, had come) to this country.

Writing Application Check your draft to make sure that you have used the correct verb forms.

Writer's Solution Connection
Language Lab
For more practice with verbs, complete the lesson on the Principal Parts of Verbs in the Using Verbs unit.

Support Points With Examples For each reaction you describe, provide a specific example. For instance, if you liked the characters in the play, you might write: "I liked Arthur Miller's characters. Grouchy old Grandpa was funny because of his ridiculous stinginess. I liked Young Monaghan because he stuck with his grandpa, even when that caused problems with his friends."

Use Precise Adjectives In a critical response, your job is to share your opinions with readers. To express your opinions as clearly as possible, choose adjectives that express precisely what you mean. Here are some examples:

PRECISE ADJECTIVES	
Positive	**Negative**
The author wrote a *well-crafted* story, in which the pieces fit together well.	The character is *grouchy*.
The character is *cheerful*.	The speech was *pointless* to start with.

Revising

Use a Checklist Use the following checklist:
- ▶ Have you included all the elements of a critical response? *Make sure you provide a summary of the work, make an evaluation, and give a recommendation.*
- ▶ Have you clearly expressed your opinion of the work? *To clarify your opinion, use precise adjectives.*
- ▶ Have you provided enough supporting details? *Wherever you express an opinion, make sure you give a detail from the work to support it.*

Publishing and Presenting

Newspaper Review Section With a group of classmates, assemble your critical responses in newspaper format. If possible, incorporate photographs of each reviewer (just like the byline photos in a newspaper). For each review, invent a catchy headline and pull out a quotation (a phrase or sentence from the review set in large type in a box outside the review). You can even make up funny advertisements to fill out each page!

Real-World Reading Skills Workshop

Using Headings and Text Structure

Strategies for Success

Articles in magazines, newspapers, textbooks, and other nonfiction works often contain large amounts of detailed information. The way the text is presented on the page can help you read the information in manageable chunks. The following features can help you do this:

- ▶ Headings or section titles
- ▶ Sections set off in boxes or lists
- ▶ Special fonts

Preview Headings Skim through an article, looking for section headings. These headings will give you an idea of what is explained in the section. Knowing the main topics and the general organization will give you a framework for understanding the details.

Identify Relationships The size of a section heading can give you a clue about how the information is related to other parts of the article. For instance, a large heading shows a main idea or topic. The sections with smaller headings that follow support or explain the idea in the larger heading.

Read the Extras Material that is set off in boxes or lists may give examples or definitions that will help you understand the topic. Set off in this way, it is easy to find the material when you need to refer to it.

✔ Here are other situations in which using headlines and text structure can be helpful:
- ▶ Reading a magazine or newspaper
- ▶ Reading an entry in an encyclopedia or atlas

Apply the Strategies

Read the textbook article below. Then, answer the questions that follow.

Latin America: Physical Geography

Latin America is located in the Western Hemisphere, south of the United States. It includes all the nations from Mexico to the tip of South America. It also includes the islands that dot the Caribbean Sea.

Landforms of Latin America

Geographic features divide Latin America into three smaller regions.

Mexico and Central America Mexico and Central America stretch 2,500 miles from the U.S. border to South America. Mountains dominate this region. Between the mountains in Mexico lies Mexico's central plateau. This central plateau makes up more than half of the country's area. Most of Mexico's people live here. Central America, located south of Mexico, is an isthmus. Narrow plains run along Central America's coast. Between these plains are rugged, steep mountains. More than a dozen of these mountains are active volcanoes.

The Caribbean The Caribbean is made up of two types of islands. The smaller islands are made of coral. The larger islands are the tops of huge underwater mountains.

South America South America is so large it is classifed as a continent. It contains may types of landforms, including mountains, plains, and tropical rain forests. The rain forests cover more than a third of the continent.

Geographic Terms

plateau Large raised area of mostly level land

isthmus Narrow strip of land that has water on both sides and connects two larger bodies of land

plains Large area of flat or gently rolling land

tropical rain forest Dense, evergreen forest having abundant rainfall throughout the year

1. What is the main subject of the article?

2. (a) Why is it broken into three sections? (b) What are the sections? (c) How can you tell that the sections are of equal importance?

3. Why is it helpful to have the geographic terms pulled out into a separate box?

ante-ced-ent (an'tə sēd″nt) 4 Gram. the word, phrase, or clause to which a pronoun refers ["man" is the antecedent of "who" in "the man who spoke"] 5 Logic the part of a conditional proposition that

Pronouns help writers avoid repeating the same nouns over and over. For a pronoun to make sense, however, it must agree with its antecedent (the noun or pronoun it replaces) in gender (masculine or feminine) and number (singular or plural). (See page 688.)

Use a singular pronoun to agree with a singular antecedent:

> *Mother* always opens *her* windows.

The singular feminine pronoun *her* agrees with its antecedent, *mother*, which is also singular and feminine.

Use a plural pronoun to agree with a plural antecedent:

> *People* sometimes share *their* thoughts.

> When *people* visit the statue, *they* are inspired.

The plural pronouns *they* and *their* agree with their antecedent, *people*, which is also plural.

Practice 1 On your paper, fill in each blank with a pronoun that agrees with its antecedent.

1. The man put ___?___ hand on the statue.

2. The people want ___?___ money's worth.

3. The girls said ___?___ wanted to go.

4. The girls paid ___?___ admission fee.

5. Grandpa said ___?___ would not contribute.

6. Carla contributed ___?___ dime.

7. Young Monaghan went with ___?___ grandfather.

Practice 2 On your paper, write an ending for each sentence. In the ending, use a pronoun that agrees with the noun that is in italics.

Example: My *father* told . . .

Answer: My father told me about his childhood.

1. The people on the boat ___?___.

2. Lady Liberty holds a torch ___?___.

3. My grandfather changed ___?___.

4. The children said ___?___.

5. Mr. Monaghan told us that ___?___.

Grammar in Writing

✔ *Avoid using a pronoun that could refer to more than one antecedent.*

Unclear: *Grandpa told Young Monaghan that he could see the statue. (Who could see the statue—Grandpa or Young Monaghan?)*

Clear: *Grandpa told Young Monaghan that the boy could see the statue. OR Grandpa could see the statue, and he told Young Monaghan.*

✔ *Remember that a pronoun must reflect the gender and number of its antecedent.*

Speaking, Listening, and Viewing Workshop

Evaluating a Performance

On Monday, you may give a friend your opinion of a new movie. On Tuesday, you may give a classmate feedback on a presentation. On both days, you are evaluating a performance. When you evaluate a performance, you judge the presentation, interest level, and delivery:

Evaluate the Presentation Presentation is the most basic level of the performance. When you judge presentation, evaluate whether the performer seems skilled and prepared for the performance.

Judge the Interest Level Judging the interest level doesn't mean judging whether or not it's your favorite subject. Consider whether the material is appropriate for and appeals to its intended audience.

Consider the Delivery When you judge the delivery, consider whether you could see and hear the performance, whether it moved at an appropriate pace, and whether you found the performance believable, informative, or moving.

The questions on the chart below show the kinds of questions you should ask yourself when you evaluate different types of performances:

Apply the Strategies

With a partner, choose and evaluate an example of each of the following:

1. A play or a movie
2. The performance of a song by a popular singer
3. A speech at an assembly or an oral report

	Presentation	Interest Level	Delivery
Recitation	Does the speaker speak confidently and smoothly?	Is the material appropriate for the audience?	Does the speaker vary tone of voice, volume, and speed to reinforce the meaning of the words?
Dramatic Performance	Do the performers know their lines?	Is the plot interesting?	Can you see and hear the performers? Are the performers believable?
Oral Report	Does the presenter seem knowledgeable about the topic?	Does the presenter give you a reason to care about the topic?	Does the presenter use appropriate visual aids?
Musical Performance	Is the performer skilled?	Does the music appeal to the audience?	Does the performer communicate a feeling or an idea?

Tips for Evaluating a Performance

✔ *When evaluating a performance, follow these strategies:*

▶ *Be objective and fair. Judge the performance in each of the key areas, not just on one actor or detail.*

▶ *Be specific. Explain how the parts you didn't rate highly could be improved.*

What's Behind the Words

Vocabulary Adventures With Richard Lederer

Antonyms

Words that have opposite meanings are called antonyms. The word *antonym* is formed from the Greek *anti-*, "opposite of," and *-onymaa*, "word or name." The opposite, or antonym, of *day* is *night*. *Near* and *far* are antonyms, as are *high* and *low* and *sweet* and *sour*.

Antonyms are the opposite of synonyms. For example, some synonyms of *happy* are *cheerful, content, glad, joyful,* and *pleased.* Antonyms of *happy* include *dejected, depressed, downhearted, forlorn, glum, melancholy,* and *sad.*

Many words form their antonyms with a prefix or a suffix. Thus, *guilty* can be turned into the antonym *guiltless,* and *coordinated* can be turned into the antonym *uncoordinated.* Other antonyms are not related in form. An antonym of *guilty* could be *innocent,* and an antonym of *coordinated* could be *clumsy.*

From a study of synonyms and antonyms, you will become more accurate in expressing ideas.

ACTIVITY 1 Do the two words in each pair have similar or opposite meanings? On your paper, indicate your answer with an *S* if they are synonyms and an *A* if they are antonyms:

1. quick, rapid
2. wordy, long-winded
3. beautiful, attractive
4. honest, sincere
5. clumsy, awkward
6. kind, cruel
7. stationary, mobile
8. wise, foolish
9. bored, amused
10. awkward, graceful

ACTIVITY 2 Provide as many antonyms as you can for each word:

1. ask
2. cautious
3. polite
4. careful
5. irritable
6. brave
7. enduring
8. wise
9. tidy
10. generous

ACTIVITY 3 Write the following list in your notebook. Fill in each blank with a word that is an antonym of the words listed on both the left and the right:

New Word

1. loud _____?_____ hard
2. young _____?_____ new
3. wrong _____?_____ left
4. tall _____?_____ short
5. smooth _____?_____ gentle
6. even _____?_____ normal
7. sharp _____?_____ interesting
8. win _____?_____ find
9. past _____?_____ absent
10. costly _____?_____ enslaved

Extended Reading Opportunities

Reading or performing a play lets you assume a new identity for a while. In the selections below, you can become part of a cast of characters different from your friends. Join them, learn from them, and enjoy your brief stay.

Suggested Titles

Anne of Green Gables, Adapted for the Stage
Donald Harron

This musical adaptation of Lucy Maude Montgomery's classic tale is so popular it is performed every year on Prince Edward Island—the setting of the drama. It tells the story of Anne, an independent and spirited orphan. Her thoughts and experiences are captured in dialogue and song. You will enjoy the many scrapes Anne gets herself into and out of as she learns and grows.

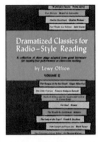

Escape to Freedom
Ossie Davis

The early life of Frederick Douglass is dramatized in this play, which includes songs, narrative, dialogue, and dance. In 1824, seven-year-old Frederick Douglass was taken to Baltimore to be young Thomas Auld's personal slave. Although Thomas's mother attempts to teach him to read, her husband soon puts a stop to her efforts. As you will discover in this inspirational play, young Frederick was not so easily stopped. He found a way to teach himself to read, and he found a way to freedom.

Dramatized Classics for Radio-Style Reading
Lewy Olfson

This collection of short plays contains works adapted from great literature. In this book, you will find adaptations of "The Masque of the Red Death" by Edgar Allan Poe, "The Little Princess" by Frances Hodgsen Burnett, and many other favorites. They are written with the student performer in mind: Sets are not needed and, since they are adapted as radio plays, no memorization of lines is required!

Other Possibilities

When the Rattlesnake Sounds   Alice Childress

Mystery Plays: 8 Plays for the Classroom Based

  on Stories by Famous Writers   Tom Conklin

Waves of Matsushima, Edo period, early 18th century, six-panel folding screen, Korin Ogata, Courtesy, Museum of Fine Arts, Boston, MA

Poetry

Poetry is a type of literature in which sound is just as important as meaning. Through the use of sound devices such as rhyme, poets give their works a musical quality. Through the use of images, or word pictures, they paint vivid portraits in our minds. There are many types of poetry. Following are just a few:

- **Narrative** poetry tells a story.

- **Lyric** poetry expresses thoughts and feelings.

- **Concrete** poems are shaped to look like their subjects.

- **Haiku** and **limericks** are short and follow strict syllable patterns.

Guide for Reading

Meet the Author:

T.S. Eliot (1888–1965)

T. S. Eliot was a poet who made poetry sound more like ordinary spoken language. He also gave poetry the nervous rhythms of the early twentieth century, a time of rapid change.

Over a period of many generations, Eliot's family had moved from England to New England and then to St. Louis, Missouri. In his own life, Eliot reversed this pattern. He was born in St. Louis and went to college in New England. Then, he traveled to England, settling there and becoming a citizen of that country.

For many years, he worked at a publishing house in London, gaining a reputation as a poet and critic. In 1948, he received the Nobel Prize for Literature.

Eliot's poetry is often very serious. However, he also wrote the humorous poems in *Old Possum's Book of Practical Cats*. This book, which includes "The Naming of Cats," inspired the Broadway musical *Cats*.

THE STORY BEHIND THE POEM

Before Eliot published "The Naming of Cats" and other cat poems, he mailed them to friends as a joke. The poems were unsigned, but his friends always knew who sent them!

◆ LITERATURE AND YOUR LIFE

CONNECT YOUR EXPERIENCE

You may have noticed that cats are not the friendly go-getters that many dogs are. Cats are independent. They keep to themselves. This behavior gives them an air of mystery—whether they're licking themselves clean or staring thoughtfully into space.

T. S. Eliot was fascinated by the behavior of cats. In this poem, he considers how to name an animal that often seems to be somewhere else even when it's here.

THEMATIC FOCUS: Finding the Humor

How does Eliot make the naming of cats sound very serious and very funny at the same time?

◆ Background for Understanding

SOCIAL STUDIES

Maybe thoughtful-looking cats are remembering their mysterious past in ancient Egypt. Thousands of years ago, wild cats came to Egypt from elsewhere in Africa. By 1500 B.C., the Egyptians had tamed these cats and were using them to protect their supplies of grain from rodents.

Sometime between 2465 and 2150 B.C., ancient Egyptians began to worship the cat. They honored cats by mummifying them, preserving their dead bodies. Beside them, they put mouse mummies for food!

◆ The Naming of Cats ◆

◆ Literary Focus

RHYTHM IN POETRY

When you listen to songs, you beat out and feel their rhythm. Poems also have a **rhythm,** based on a pattern of stressed and unstressed syllables.

Here's the pattern in the first line of "The Naming of Cats":

The NAM ing of CATS is a DIF fi cult MAT ter

The pattern may vary a bit as the poem goes on. However, you'll often hear a rhythm like this one: da da DA. Listen for it, and think about how it adds to the poem's humor.

◆ Build Vocabulary

RELATED WORDS: FORMS OF *scrutiny*

The word *scrutiny* means "close observation." Different forms of this word relate to the idea of observing or knowing. Eliot, for example, calls a cat's secret name *inscrutable,* meaning "not able to be known."

WORD BANK

Which of these words from the poem are nouns? How do you know? Check the Build Vocabulary box on page 706 to see if you were correct.

perpendicular
meditation
contemplation
inscrutable

Reading for Success

Strategies for Reading Poetry

Poetry is different from other types of writing. Even plain, everyday words seem different, or strange, in poems. Instead of getting lost in a paragraph, these words stand out in a poem's lines and seem to mean more than they usually do. Also, these usually quiet words can chime with other words, making rhymes like *same–name*. Poetry can make words act in strange ways. However, these tips will help you figure out what's happening in a poem:

Read lines according to punctuation.

Don't sound like a stiff computer voice by automatically stopping after each line. Read according to the punctuation: Pause briefly for commas and semicolons and longer for end marks:

> Thrust against the metal sky, (brief pause)
> Somehow it survives and even thrives. (longer pause)

Identify the speaker.

The voice that "says" a poem is its speaker, but the speaker isn't necessarily the poet. The speaker can be a character in an imaginary situation. When you read a poem, use clues to figure out who the speaker is:

| My father was the first to hear | *Who is the speaker?* |
| The passage of the geese each fall | The speaker is the son or daughter speaking about his or her father. |

Use your senses.

A poem isn't just words on a page. It's an introduction to a world. However, you must use your senses to experience this world as you read. For example, the line "It laughs a lovely whiteness" from "Cynthia in the Snow" appeals to your senses of hearing and sight.

Paraphrase the lines.

To be sure what a line, a passage, or a whole poem is saying, restate it in your own words:

| The Naming of Cats is a difficult matter, | *Paraphrase:* |
| It isn't just one of your holiday games; | Naming a cat isn't as easy as playing a game. |

As you read "The Naming of Cats," look at the notes in the boxes that show how to apply these strategies to a work of literature.

The Naming of Cats

T. S. Eliot

The Naming of Cats is a difficult matter,
    It isn't just one of your holiday games;
You may think at first I'm as mad as a hatter
When I tell you, a cat must have THREE DIFFERENT NAMES.
5 First of all, there's the name that the family use daily,
    Such as Peter, Augustus, Alonzo or James,
Such as Victor or Jonathan, George or Bill Bailey—
    All of them sensible everyday names.
There are fancier names if you think they sound sweeter,
10   Some for the gentlemen, some for the dames:
Such as Plato, Admetus, Electra, Demeter—
    But all of them sensible everyday names.

The **speaker** seems to be an expert on the naming of cats.

Follow the punctuation when reading line 11. Pause slightly after each comma and for a longer time after the dash.

You can **paraphrase** the beginning of the poem by saying: It's not easy to name cats because each cat needs three different names, starting with the name the family will call the cat.

Illustration from *Old Possum's Book of Practical Cats*, Edward Gorey

◀ **Critical Viewing** Explain how the humor of this picture is similar to the humor of the poem. [Connect]

But I tell you, a cat needs a name that's particular,
    A name that's peculiar, and more dignified,
15 Else how can he keep up his tail perpendicular,
    Or spread out his whiskers, or cherish his pride?
Of names of this kind, I can give you a quorum,[1]
    Such as Munkustrap, Quaxo, or Coricopat,
    Such as Bombalurina, or else Jellylorum—
20   Names that never belong to more than one cat.
But above and beyond there's still one name left over,
    And that is the name that you never will guess;
The name that no human research can discover—
    But THE CAT HIMSELF KNOWS, and will never confess.
25 When you notice a cat in profound meditation,
    The reason, I tell you, is always the same:
His mind is engaged in a rapt contemplation
    Of the thought, of the thought, of the thought of his name:
      His ineffable effable
30   Effanineffable[2]
Deep and inscrutable singular Name.

> **Use your sense of sight** to picture a cat with a perpendicular tail and spread-out whiskers.

1. **quorum** (kwôr´ əm) *n.*: Minimum number of members necessary for an organization to carry on with business.

2. **ineffable** (in ef´ ə bəl) *adj.*: . . . **Effanineffable:** *Ineffable* means "inexpressible." *Effable* has the opposite meaning. In line 30, Eliot playfully combines both words.

◆ **Build Vocabulary**

perpendicular (pʉr´ pən dik´ yōō lər) *adj.*: At a right angle to something else

meditation (med ə tā´ shən) *n.*: Deep thought

contemplation (kän´ təm plā´ shən) *n.*: Thoughtful study

inscrutable (in skrōōt´ə bəl) *adj.*: Not easily understood

Guide for Responding

◆ LITERATURE AND YOUR LIFE

Reader's Response What name would you choose for a cat? Why?

Thematic Focus In what way do phrases like "profound meditation" and "rapt contemplation" add to the poem's humor?

Journal Writing Briefly note an experience you've had recently with a cat or another type of pet.

☑ Check Your Comprehension

1. According to the speaker, how many names must a cat have?
2. Briefly describe each different type of name.
3. Which name is the cat thinking about when it is in "rapt contemplation"?

◆ Critical Thinking

INTERPRET

1. Explain how Eliot uses exaggeration in lines 1–4 to create humor. **[Analyze]**
2. Choose three of the names Eliot mentions, and tell what is funny about them. **[Analyze]**
3. In what way is the conclusion of the poem mysterious as well as funny? **[Draw Conclusions]**

EVALUATE

4. Could you have included even funnier cats' names than Eliot did? Explain. **[Evaluate]**

APPLY

5. Explain the process you go through when choosing a name for anything—a pet, a team, a club, or a person. **[Connect]**

Guide for Responding (continued)

◆ Reading for Success

STRATEGIES FOR READING POETRY

Review the reading strategies and the notes in the boxes showing how to read poetry. Then, use them to answer these questions:

1. Explain where and for how long you would pause in reading lines 9–12.
2. Is the speaker of the poem very educated? How can you tell?
3. What sense can you use in reading line 25? Explain.
4. Review lines 13–16. Then, restate them in your own words.

◆ Build Vocabulary

USING FORMS OF *scrutiny*

Explain how each form of *scrutiny* relates to its meaning (close observation):

As a *scrutinizer,* he wouldn't just accept what anyone told him. After hearing a woman say that cats were *inscrutable,* he *scrutinized* the history of cats to check her statement.

SPELLING STRATEGY

When the sound *shun* appears at the end of words, it is often spelled *tion,* as in *meditation* and *contemplation.* On your paper, replace the italicized *shun* sound in each word with the correct spelling:

1. na*shun*   3. sta*shun*   5. rela*shun*
2. ela*shun*   4. infla*shun*

USING THE WORD BANK

On your paper, answer each question *yes* or *no.* Then, explain your answer.

1. Is a building usually *perpendicular* to the street?
2. Will *meditation* on an idea help you to see all sides of it?
3. Is someone lost in *contemplation* very noisy?
4. Would you call an open, honest person *inscrutable?*

◆ Literary Focus

RHYTHM IN A POEM

The **rhythm** of "The Naming of Cats" is its pattern of stressed and unstressed syllables. The poem's rolling beat comes from the repetition of two unstressed syllables followed by a stressed syllable:

When you NO tice a CAT in proFOUND med i TA tion

1. Use capital and lowercase letters to show the rhythm of lines 27–28.
2. Explain how the rhythm of the poem changes in lines 30 and 31.

◆ Build Grammar Skills

COMPARISON OF ADJECTIVES AND ADVERBS

Most adjectives and adverbs have different forms —the positive (fancy), the comparative (fancier), and the superlative (fanciest). Eliot uses the comparative form of *fancy* and *sweet* in this line: "There are *fancier* names if you think they sound *sweeter.*"

Short adjectives and adverbs form the comparative by adding *-er* to the positive. They form the superlative with *-est* (slow, slow*er*, slow*est*). Use the comparative form when comparing two items and the superlative form when comparing more than two.

Practice On your paper, change the adjective or adverb in parentheses from the positive to the comparative form:

1. She wants her cat to be (quiet) than theirs.
2. The cat named Peter is (crazy) than the one named Plato.
3. No other cat is (happy) than Jellylorum.
4. I can run (rapidly) than Bombalurina.
5. No cat owner dressed (fashionably) than T. S. Eliot.

Writing Application Using the comparative form of an adjective and an adverb, compare the behavior of two pets you've seen.

Build Your Portfolio

 ## Idea Bank

Writing

1. **Paraphrase of a Song** Reread the lyrics of your favorite song. Then, in your own words, restate what they're saying.

2. **Cat Caricature** Create a verbal caricature of a cat or other pet animal. Exaggerate qualities for a humorous effect.

3. **Quaxo's Poem** Suppose that the cat Quaxo has just read Eliot's "The Naming of Cats" and has seen his own name mentioned. Write the poem that he might compose in response.

Speaking and Listening

4. **Rhythm Exchange** Read a line of "The Naming of Cats" to a partner. Then, ask your partner to tap out the rhythm on a desk. Represent the rhythm visually. **[Music Link]**

5. **Presentation of the Show *Cats*** Bring in a CD of the musical *Cats,* and play one or two songs for your classmates. Hand out the words of the songs. Then, lead a discussion on similarities and differences between the songs and Eliot's poem. **[Music Link]**

Projects

6. **Tableau of Cats [Group Activity]** In a tableau, a group of people "freeze" in certain positions to make a "picture." With several classmates, create a tableau of different cats to illustrate Eliot's poem. **[Performing Arts Link]**

7. **Multimedia Report on Egyptian Cats** Use reproductions of art, clips from classic films, drawings, diagrams, and models to report on the role of cats in ancient Egypt. **[Media Link; Social Studies Link; Art Link]**

 ## Writing Mini-Lesson

Observation of an Animal

In "The Naming of Cats," Eliot shares some observations about these furry, independent creatures. You, too, may have looked carefully at cats or some other animals. Use what you've seen to write an observation of an animal's behavior and appearance. In an observation, you describe something so that readers can almost experience it for themselves.

Writing Skills Focus: Sensory Details

You'll make readers feel they're right there with the animal by using **sensory details.** In "The Naming of Cats," for instance, Eliot appeals to your sense of sight:

Model From the Poem
Else how can he *keep up his tail*
perpendicular,
Or *spread out his whiskers,* or cherish
his pride?

Prewriting Jot down details about how the animal looks and sounds. If you are observing an animal "up-close" you might also record details of how it smells and what its fur or skin feels like.

Drafting Make clear how you're observing the animal—face to face in an apartment, from outside its zoo cage, or through binoculars. Also, include sensory details to describe the animal's behavior and appearance.

Revising Ask classmates if your observation gives them a vivid picture of the animal. If it does not, include more sensory details.

◆ **Grammar Application**

Use the comparative form of adjectives and adverbs when you compare your subject to one other thing.

PART **1** *Types and Forms*

Synchromie Cosmique, 1913–1914, Morgan Russel, Munson–Williams–Proctor Institute Museum of Art, Utica, New York

Guide for Reading

Meet the Authors:

Lewis Carroll (1832–1898)

Lewis Carroll is the pen name of Englishman Charles Lutwidge Dodgson, a math professor. Under his pen name, he wrote two famous books: *Alice's Adventures in Wonderland* and *Through the Looking Glass,* which contains "The Walrus and the Carpenter." As you'll see from this poem, Carroll's work sparkles with imagination and wordplay.

Shel Silverstein (1932–)

Chicago-born Shel Silverstein grew up wanting to become a dancer or a baseball player. Instead, he became a cartoonist and a writer. He is best known for his books of poetry, *Where the Sidewalk Ends* and *A Light in the Attic*.

Sara Teasdale (1884–1933)

Teasdale had a very protected childhood in St. Louis, Missouri. Perhaps that's why her highly musical poems seem so delicate. Her book *Love Songs* (1917) received a Columbia Poetry Prize, now known as the Pulitzer Prize.

Richard Peck (1934–)

Richard Peck is known not only for his poetry, but also for his young-adult novels. These include *Ghosts I Have Been, Dreamland Lake,* and *Secrets of the Shopping Mall*.

◆ LITERATURE AND YOUR LIFE

CONNECT YOUR EXPERIENCE

The tone of your voice and the words you say express who you are and what you're thinking and feeling. There's a voice behind each of these poems, too, a voice you "hear" as you read. Some may sound like a comedian in a funny-face mask. Others may sound like a sad ballad singer.

THEMATIC FOCUS: A Different View

What unique idea is expressed in each poem?

◆ Background for Understanding

LITERATURE

Some of the poems in this group are lyric poems. (See Literary Focus, p. 711.) The word *lyric* is a gift from the past. In ancient Greece, poets accompanied their recitations with a stringed instrument called a lyre (līr). This instrument had three to twelve strings that were plucked or strummed to create background music.

◆ Build Vocabulary

MULTIPLE MEANINGS

You can make poetry more understandable if you realize that some words have more than one meaning. The word *lean* in "Jimmy Jet and His TV Set" can mean "thin" or "rest against." Test each meaning to see which one applies.

WORD BANK

Which of these words is almost sure to come from the poem "Jimmy Jet and His TV Set"? Why?

| beseech |
| lean |
| antennae |

The Walrus and the Carpenter
◆ February Twilight ◆
Jimmy Jet and His TV Set ◆ The Geese

◆ Literary Focus
NARRATIVE AND LYRIC POETRY

Narrative poetry tells a story using devices you'll find in fiction: plot, characters, and dialogue. **Lyric poetry** musically expresses a speaker's personal thoughts and feelings. "The Walrus and the Carpenter" and "Jimmy Jet and His TV Set" are narratives. Notice how they relate a sequence of events—even if those events are silly. "February Twilight" and "The Geese" are lyrics. As you read them, listen for the music of a speaker's observations and feelings.

◆ Reading Strategy
IDENTIFY THE SPEAKER IN A POEM

The imaginary character that says the words of a poem is the **speaker.** Identifying a poem's speaker is important, because the speaker's feelings and attitudes often affect how the events and details in a poem are presented and can play a key role in shaping the poem's meaning. To identify the speakers in these poems, answer questions like the ones on the diagram below.

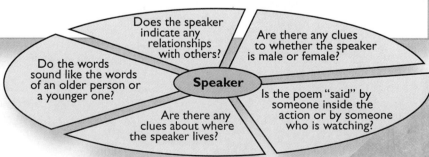

Does the speaker indicate any relationships with others?

Are there any clues to whether the speaker is male or female?

Do the words sound like the words of an older person or a younger one?

Speaker

Is the poem "said" by someone inside the action or by someone who is watching?

Are there any clues about where the speaker lives?

The Walrus and the Carpenter

Lewis Carroll

▼ **Critical Viewing** How does the picture help you predict that this poem will be funny? [Connect]

From *Alice Through the Looking Glass* by Lewis Carroll, Illustration by John Tenniel

The sun was shining on the sea,
　　Shining with all his might:
He did his very best to make
　　The billows smooth and bright—
5　And this was odd, because it was
　　The middle of the night.

The moon was shining sulkily,
　　Because she thought the sun
Had got no business to be there
10　After the day was done—
"It's very rude of him," she said,
　　"To come and spoil the fun!"

The sea was wet as wet could be,
　　The sands were dry as dry.
15　You could not see a cloud, because
　　No cloud was in the sky:
No birds were flying overhead—
　　There were no birds to fly.

The Walrus and the Carpenter
20　Were walking close at hand:
They wept like anything to see
　　Such quantities of sand:
"If this were only cleared away,"
　　They said, "it would be grand!"

25　"If seven maids with seven mops
　　Swept it for half a year,
Do you suppose," the Walrus said,
　　"That they could get it clear?"
"I doubt it," said the Carpenter,
30　And shed a bitter tear.

"O Oysters, come and walk with us!"
　　The Walrus did <u>beseech</u>.
"A pleasant walk, a pleasant talk,
　　Along the briny beach:
35　We cannot do with more than four,
　　To give a hand to each."

The eldest Oyster looked at him,
　　But never a word he said:
The eldest Oyster winked his eye,
40　And shook his heavy head—
Meaning to say he did not choose
　　To leave the oyster-bed.

But four young Oysters hurried up,
　　All eager for this treat:
45　Their coats were brushed, their faces
　　　washed,
　　Their shoes were clean and neat—
And this was odd, because, you know,
　　They hadn't any feet.

Four other Oysters followed them,
50　And yet another four;
And thick and fast they came at last,
　　And more, and more, and more—
All hopping through the frothy waves,
　　And scrambling to the shore.

55　The Walrus and the Carpenter
　　Walked on a mile or so,
And then they rested on a rock
　　Conveniently low:
And all the little Oysters stood
60　And waited in a row.

"The time has come," the Walrus said,
　　"To talk of many things:
Of shoes—and ships—and sealing wax—
　　Of cabbages—and kings—
65　And why the sea is boiling hot—
　　And whether pigs have wings."

"But wait a bit," the Oysters cried,
　　"Before we have our chat;
For some of us are out of breath,
70　And all of us are fat!"
"No hurry!" said the Carpenter.
　　They thanked him much for that.

◆ **Build Vocabulary**

beseech (bi sēch´) *v.*: Beg

▲ **Critical Viewing** Explain how this picture tells a story
by itself. [Interpret]

"A loaf of bread," the Walrus said,
　"Is what we chiefly need:
75　Pepper and vinegar besides
　Are very good indeed—
　Now, if you're ready, Oysters dear,
　We can begin to feed."

"But not on us!" the Oysters cried,
80　Turning a little blue.
"After such kindness, that would be
　A dismal thing to do!"
"The night is fine," the Walrus said.
　"Do you admire the view?"

85　"It was so kind of you to come!
　And you are very nice!"
The Carpenter said nothing but
　"Cut us another slice.
I wish you were not quite so deaf—
90　I've had to ask you twice!"

"It seems a shame," the Walrus said,
　"To play them such a trick.
After we've brought them out so far,
　And made them trot so quick!"
95　The Carpenter said nothing but
　"The butter's spread too thick!"

"I weep for you," the Walrus said:
　"I deeply sympathize."
With sobs and tears he sorted out
100　Those of the largest size,
Holding his pocket-handkerchief
　Before his streaming eyes.

"O Oysters," said the Carpenter,
　"You've had a pleasant run!
105　Shall we be trotting home again?"
　But answer came there none—
And this was scarcely odd, because
　They'd eaten every one.

Beyond Literature

Science Connection

The Food Chain Although readers may feel sympathy for the poor unsuspecting oysters in "The Walrus and the Carpenter," the oysters are fulfilling their function as one of the lowest levels of the food chain. The food chain describes the way energy moves through various stages in the form of food. In any food chain, plants are the primary producers because they can make their own food. In a real-life food chain involving oysters, small plants called plankton (primary producers) are eaten by oysters (primary consumers). Oysters are eaten by sea gulls, which are in turn eaten by walruses. (Sea gulls and walruses are secondary consumers.) When the walrus dies, it decomposes, providing food for another level of the food chain.

Cross-Curricular Activity

Diagram Draw a diagram showing a sample food chain or food web. Include producers, primary consumers, secondary consumers, and decomposers.

Guide for Responding

◆ LITERATURE AND YOUR LIFE

Reader's Response What do you think is the silliest passage in this poem? Why?

Thematic Focus Most of the children's literature written in Carroll's time had a serious message. In what way is "The Walrus and the Carpenter" different from this literature?

Journal Writing Look at John Tenniel's pictures on pages 712 and 714. These illustrations appeared with the poem from the time it was first published. Jot down what you like or dislike about them. **[Art Link]**

☑ Check Your Comprehension

1. Where does this poem take place?
2. Why is it "odd" that the sun is shining?
3. What do the Walrus and the Carpenter ask the Oysters to do?
4. What happens to the Oysters?

◆ Critical Thinking

INTERPRET

1. Find two passages in which silly ideas are expressed seriously. Then, explain your choices. **[Support]**
2. At what point did you realize that the Walrus and the Carpenter might want to harm the Oysters? Why? **[Analyze]**
3. How is this poem both funny and a tiny bit sad? **[Draw Conclusions]**

EVALUATE

4. Do you think this poem should have a different ending? Why or why not? **[Make a Judgment]**

APPLY

5. Lewis Carroll is one of the most famous writers of nonsense verse. Using this poem, write a definition of nonsense verse. **[Define]**

February Twilight

Sara Teasdale

I stood beside a hill
    Smooth with new-laid snow,
A single star looked out
    From the cold evening glow.

5 There was no other creature
    That saw what I could see—
I stood and watched the evening star
    As long as it watched me.

Jimmy Jet and His TV Set

Shel Silverstein

I'll tell you the story of Jimmy Jet—
And you know what I tell you is true.
He loved to watch his TV set
Almost as much as you.

5 He watched all day, he watched all night
Till he grew pale and <u>lean</u>,
From *The Early Show* to *The Late Late Show*
And all the shows between.

He watched till his eyes were frozen wide,
10 And his bottom grew into his chair.
And his chin turned into a tuning dial,
And <u>antennae</u> grew out of his hair.

And his brains turned into TV tubes,
And his face to a TV screen.
15 And two knobs saying "VERT." and "HORIZ."
Grew where his ears had been.

And he grew a plug that looked like a tail
So we plugged in little Jim.
And now instead of him watching TV
20 We all sit around and watch him.

◆ Build Vocabulary

lean (lēn) *adj.:* Thin

antennae (an ten´ ē) *n.:* Metal rods that receive TV or radio signals

---

Guide for Responding

◆ LITERATURE AND YOUR LIFE

Reader's Response How do you react to Silverstein's poem? Why?

Thematic Focus Did either of these poems change the way you look at something? Explain.

Journal Writing In your journal, describe a television program you feel is worth the time people spend watching it.

☑ Check Your Comprehension

1. Where is the speaker of "February Twilight"?
2. What does the speaker see?
3. How much time does Jimmy Jet spend watching his television set?
4. What happens to him as a result?

◆ Critical Thinking

INTERPRET

1. Why do you think the speaker in "February Twilight" pauses outdoors on such a cold night? **[Speculate]**
2. Does the speaker enjoy the experience she describes? **[Draw Conclusions]**
3. What is funny about Jimmy's name and his behavior? **[Interpret]**
4. What does the story of Jimmy Jet suggest about the effects of watching television? **[Draw Conclusions]**

EXTEND

5. Identify one way television viewing could contribute to a person's physical fitness and one way it could interfere with a person's physical fitness. **[Health Link]**

COMPARE LITERARY WORKS

6. Do you think Jimmy Jet and the speaker of "February Twilight" would enjoy spending time together? Explain. **[Assess]**

The Geese

Richard Peck

My father was the first to hear
The passage of the geese each fall,
Passing above the house so near
He'd hear within his heart their call.

5   And then at breakfast time he'd say:
"The geese were heading south last night,"
For he had lain awake till day,
Feeling his earthbound soul take flight.

Knowing that winter's wind comes soon
10   After the rushing of those wings,
Seeing them pass before the moon,
Recalling the lure of faroff things.

▲ **Critical Viewing** Why might a sight like this one cause someone to think of the past or the future? [Infer]

Narrative poetry tells a story, while lyric poetry expresses a speaker's feelings. Sometimes, however, lyrics can help tell a story, too. These song lyrics from the movie *The Lion King* set up the context in which the story events must be considered.

Circle of Life

Lyrics by Tim Rice

As Performed by Elton John

From the day we arrive on the planet
And blinking, step into the sun
There's more to be seen than can ever be seen
More to do than can ever be done

5 Some say eat or be eaten
Some say live and let live
But all are agreed as they join the stampede
You should never take more than you give

10 In the circle of life
It's the wheel of fortune
It's the leap of faith
It's the band of hope
Till we find our place
15 On the path unwinding
In the circle, the circle of life

Some of us fall by the wayside
And some of us soar to the stars
And some of us sail through our troubles
20 And some have to live with the scars

There's far too much to take in here
More to find than can ever be found
But the sun rolling high through the
    sapphire sky
Keeps great and small on the endless round

© 1994 Wonderland Music Company, Inc.
All Rights Reserved. Reprinted by Permission

1. Which words suggest that the singer of these lyrics views life with a sense of wonder? Explain.
2. What do you think is the main message of this song?

Guide for Responding

◆ LITERATURE AND YOUR LIFE

Reader's Response Have you ever felt "the lure of faroff things"? Explain.

Thematic Focus In what ways does the speaker in this poem seem more thoughtful than many people?

☑ Check Your Comprehension

1. What is it that the father is the first to hear?
2. What do the geese recall for the father?

◆ Critical Thinking

INTERPRET

1. What feelings does hearing the passage of the geese stir up in the father? **[Analyze]**
2. What might have been on the father's mind when he recalled "the lure of faroff things"? **[Speculate]**

EXTEND

3. How do you think geese know when to migrate? **[Science Link]**

Guide for Responding (continued)

◆ Reading Strategy

IDENTIFY THE SPEAKER IN A POEM

Details in a poem help you **identify the speaker,** the imaginary character who says the poem's words. In "The Geese," for example, the words "My father" show that the speaker is a son or a daughter.

1. Find a detail in "The Geese" that shows that the speaker knew the father well. Explain.
2. In "February Twilight," which details suggest that the speaker loves nature? Explain.

◆ Build Vocabulary

USING MULTIPLE MEANINGS

A number of words, like *lean* and *mean,* have more than one meaning. On your paper, explain how each sentence shows multiple meanings.

1. The lean Carpenter leaned on the rock.
2. What do you mean when you say he is mean?
3. You might discover that his might is greater than yours.
4. The sun was bright, but the Oysters were not bright.

SPELLING STRATEGY

The long *e* sound is spelled in different ways, including *ee* and *ea.* On your paper, write the words from the Word Bank that the clues below can help you remember how to spell.

1. You do this when you need something. This word and *need* are both spelled with *ee.*
2. You want your team to be _____ and mean. This word, *team,* and *mean* are all spelled with *ea.*

USING THE WORD BANK

On your paper, respond to each numbered item by writing a sentence that includes a Word Bank word. Don't use the same word twice.

1. Tell how the Oysters might beg the Walrus to spare them.
2. Why will Jimmy Jet have trouble with haircuts?
3. Describe the Carpenter's physical appearance.

◆ Literary Focus

NARRATIVE AND LYRIC POETRY

Narrative poems show the actions of characters in a connected sequence of events. **Lyric poems** put less emphasis on actions and more on a speaker's observations and feelings.

1. In your own words, retell the story of one of the narrative poems—"The Walrus . . ." or "Jimmy Jet . . ."
2. On which person or moment does each poem focus?

◆ Build Grammar Skills

IRREGULAR COMPARISONS

In "The Walrus and the Carpenter," the Walrus says, "Pepper and vinegar besides / Are very good indeed." If he wanted to compare salt with pepper, he might say pepper is *better* than salt. A few modifiers, like *good* and *bad,* are **irregular.** You must learn their comparative and superlative forms:

Positive	Comparative	Superlative
good	better	best
bad	worse	worst
well	better	best
little	less	least
many	more	most

Practice On your paper, change the positive form of the modifier to the correct comparative or superlative form:

1. The Walrus is a (good) eater than the Carpenter.
2. Of all the characters, the Oysters got the (bad) deal.
3. Your problems are (little) serious than Jimmy Jet's.
4. Jimmy gets the (well) reception of any television set.
5. He can see (many) stars than the speaker in the lyric.

Writing Application Write a series of sentences in which you use three irregular modifiers to compare several characters in Carroll's poem.

Build Your Portfolio

 Idea Bank

Writing

1. **Refrain** A refrain is a repeated section that sums up the feeling of a song or a poem. Rewrite "February Twilight" or "The Geese," adding a refrain for it. Remember that the speaker will "say" the refrain after each stanza.

2. **Birthday Card** The father in "The Geese" is having a birthday. Write a message for the speaker in the poem to include in a birthday card.

3. **Essay About a Poem's Speaker** Choose one of the poems in the group. Then, write an essay in which you identify the poem's speaker, tell what you learn about him or her from the details in the poem, and explain his or her feelings about the details and the events in the poem.

Speaking and Listening

4. **Choral Reading [Group Activity]** Perform "The Walrus and the Carpenter" with a small group. Assign individual roles (Narrator, Walrus, and Carpenter), and have a group recite the Oysters' part. **[Performing Arts Link]**

5. **Singing Poetry** Perform one of the lyric poems as a song. Choose a familiar melody, or make up one of your own. **[Performing Arts Link]**

Projects

6. **Pantomime** With a small group, perform the action in "Jimmy Jet" without using words. Show what's happening through gestures, movements, and facial expressions. **[Performing Arts Link]**

7. **Model of a Lyre [Group Activity]** With several classmates, build a model of an ancient Greek lyre. Research lyres in an encyclopedia. Then, use materials like string or wire and wood or papier-mâché to build your model. **[Social Studies Link; Art Link; Music Link]**

 Writing Mini-Lesson

Monologue As a Person or an Animal

A lyric poem like "February Twilight" is similar to a monologue, a brief speech delivered by a single character. Write a monologue in which an imaginary character expresses thoughts and feelings about a person, place, or problem. Your character can be a human or an animal.

Writing Skills Focus: Choose Language Appropriate for the Speaker

Use language that is suitable for the speaker. In "The Geese," the speaker is remembering his or her father. The memory is special. That's why it is **appropriate for the speaker** to use language that is formal and poetic:

Model From the Poem
For he had lain awake till day,
Feeling his earthbound soul take flight.

Prewriting Choose a character and a subject for the character to discuss.

Drafting Review your prewriting notes. Then, act the part of your character by making up a speech. Use words and phrases suitable to the character and situation. Record your speech as you give it.

Revising Be sure your character uses language suitable to his or her personality and to the situation. A sly fox should not speak like an angry gorilla. A person should not describe a lovely twilight in the same way as a nasty toothache.

◆ **Grammar Application**
Check that you have used the right comparative and superlative forms for irregular modifiers.

Guide for Reading

Meet the Authors:

Lillian Morrison (1917–   )

Lillian Morrison spent nearly forty years working in the New York Public Library. She has also written a number of poetry books, including *The Sidewalk Racer and Other Poems of Sports and Motion*. Morrison says, "I love rhythms, the body movement implicit in poetry, explicit in sports . . ." You'll find plenty of rhythm in her poem "The Sidewalk Racer."

Dorthi Charles (1960–   )

Charles was a student when she wrote "Concrete Cat."

Matsuo Bashō (1644–1694)

Bashō was born into a landowning Japanese family. However, his father died when he was only twelve. Bashō then entered the service of a local lord and began to write poetry.

THE STORY BEHIND THE POEM

Bashō wrote "An old silent pond" in the spring of 1686. The Japanese have erected a monument in the place where people believe he wrote it. Famous as it is, this poem went through several revisions. In his first draft, for example, Bashō used the past tense: "A frog jumped . . ." Later, he changed "jumped" to "jumps."

MusoSoseki (1275–1351)

MusoSoseki was one of the most important religious leaders of his time in Japan. He was also a respected poet. Many people consider his haiku to be among his best work.

◆ LITERATURE AND YOUR LIFE

CONNECT YOUR EXPERIENCE

One of the first things people notice when they look at something is its shape. Some of these poets give their poems a shape that imitates the subject. Others use a poetic form that shapes the experience they describe.

THEMATIC FOCUS **A Different View**

Notice how these poets create a different view of their subjects by arranging words in unique ways.

◆ Background for Understanding

SCIENCE

"The Sidewalk Racer" is a poem that's shaped like a skateboard. Scientists design skateboards, airplanes, or speedboats to be streamlined because they have discovered that objects move faster when shaped with a narrow, rounded front and a body that widens as it curves back.

◆ Build Vocabulary

WORD GROUPS: *homophones*

Homophones are words that sound alike but differ in meaning and often in spelling. A limerick you'll read has fun with the homophones *flee* and *flea*. The first means "run away," and the second is a "little insect."

WORD BANK

Which of these words from the poems would be a tongue twister if you said them together?

skimming
flue
flee
flaw

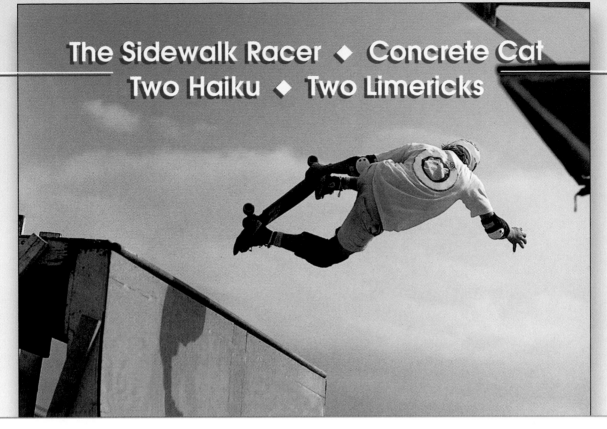

The Sidewalk Racer ◆ Concrete Cat
Two Haiku ◆ Two Limericks

◆ Literary Focus
SPECIAL FORMS OF POETRY

Poets use **special forms** to streamline poems so they move quickly to your mind or heart or funny bone:

• In a **concrete poem,** words are arranged in a shape that reflects the subject of the poem.

• A **haiku** is a Japanese verse form with three lines of five, seven, and five syllables each.

• A **limerick** is a short, funny poem five lines long. The first, second, and fifth lines rhyme, as do the third and fourth. The lines that rhyme have the same rhythm.

In this group, you will explore these forms.

◆ Reading Strategy
USE YOUR SENSES

Poems speak not only to your mind and heart, but also to your senses. That's why you'll get more from poems if you **use your senses** to experience them. Look at the shape the words make on the page. Also, imagine seeing, hearing, tasting, smelling, and touching what the words describe.

Use a chart like the one below to help you read with your senses.

Sight	Hearing	Smell	Touch	Taste

The Sidewalk Racer
or On the Skateboard

Lillian Morrison

Skimming
an asphalt sea
I swerve, I curve, I
sway; I speed to whirring
5 sound an inch above the
ground; I'm the sailor
and the sail, I'm the
driver and the wheel
I'm the one and only
10 single engine
human auto
mobile.

◆ **Build Vocabulary**

skimming (skim´ iŋ) *adj.*: Gliding; moving swiftly and lightly over a surface

CONCRETE CAT

Dorthi Charles

```
       A        A
    e  r     e  r
                          stripestripestripestripe
    eYe    eYe               stripestripestripe           t
 whisker        whisker   stripestripestripestripe    a i l t a i l
 whisker  m  h whisker       stripestripestripe
              o    t          stripestripestripe
              U
                         stripestripestripestripe

         paw paw        paw paw              ǝsnoɯ

     dishdish                         litterbox
                                      litterbox
```

Guide for Responding

◆ LITERATURE AND YOUR LIFE

Reader's Response Could you feel "The Sidewalk Racer" in your muscles? Explain.

Thematic Focus How do the shapes of the poems help create a different view of the subjects?

Pantomime Using movement and facial expressions but not words, act out either one of these poems.

☑ Check Your Comprehension

1. What is the speaker in "The Sidewalk Racer" doing?
2. Identify three things that the speaker in "The Sidewalk Racer" says that he or she is.
3. Name four features of a cat created and named by the words in "Concrete Cat."
4. Which three words in "Concrete Cat" are things related to cats but not part of them?

◆ Critical Thinking

INTERPRET

1. How is the speaker in "The Sidewalk Racer" both "the sailor / and the sail"? **[Interpret]**
2. In "The Sidewalk Racer," what overall feeling does the speaker express? Explain. **[Draw Conclusions]**
3. In "Concrete Cat," why is the word *mouse* upside down? **[Infer]**

EVALUATE

4. Would "The Sidewalk Racer" be more or less effective with a different shape? Explain. **[Evaluate]**

EXTEND

5. Is "Concrete Cat" a work of art, a poem, or both? Explain. **[Art Link]**

COMPARE LITERARY WORKS

6. For which of these poems is the shape more important? Why? **[Compare and Contrast]**

Haiku
Bashō

An old silent pond . . .
A frog jumps into the pond,
splash! Silence again.

Frog, 1814, Meika Gafu, British Museum

Haiku
Musо̄ Soseki

Over the wintry
forest, winds howl in a rage
with no leaves to blow.

Beyond Literature

Humanities Connection

Ink Painting Ink painting is an art form that became popular in Japan in the early 1300's. These paintings, created with black ink and diluted grays, are similar to haiku in their simple, understated style. As in the ink painting of a frog above, a whole animal or scene could be suggested with just a few lines or shapes. Another feature shared by ink painting and haiku is the frequent focus on nature.

Cross-Curricular Activity
Painting Find examples of Japanese ink paintings in art reference books. After viewing several paintings, create your own painting using only black ink, water, and a paintbrush. You can use black watercolor paint if ink is unavailable.

Two Limericks
Anonymous

A flea and a fly in a <u>flue</u>
Were caught, so what could they do?
    Said the fly, "Let us <u>flee</u>."
    "Let us fly," said the flea.
5   So they flew through a <u>flaw</u> in the flue.

There was a young fellow named Hall,
Who fell in the spring in the fall;
    'Twould have been a sad thing
    If he'd died in the spring,
5   But he didn't—he died in the fall.

◆ Build Vocabulary

flue (flo͞o) *n.*: A tube for the passage of smoke, as in a chimney
flee (flē) *v.*: To run or escape from danger
flaw (flô) *n.*: Break; crack

Guide for Responding

◆ LITERATURE AND YOUR LIFE

Reader's Response Do you think the limericks are funny? Why or why not?

Thematic Focus Explain how these poets give you different views of their subjects.

Five-Second Video Briefly describe the camera shots and sound track for a five-second video inspired by one of the haiku. **[Media Link]**

☑ Check Your Comprehension

1. Where does Bashō's haiku take place?
2. Where does Musō Soseki's haiku take place?
3. In your own words, summarize the action described in each limerick.

◆ Critical Thinking

INTERPRET
1. When Bashō revised his haiku, why do you think he changed "jumped" to "jumps"? **[Speculate]**
2. Describe the overall feeling associated with each haiku. **[Draw Conclusions]**
3. Explain how double meanings of words adds humor to each limerick. **[Analyze]**

APPLY
4. Why are brief descriptions, like those in haiku, sometimes more effective than long descriptions? **[Generalize]**

COMPARE LITERARY WORKS
5. Explain how you might turn one of the haiku or the limericks into a concrete poem. **[Connect]**

*G*uide for Responding *(continued)*

◆ Reading Strategy

USE YOUR SENSES

When you **use your senses,** you not only read these poems but experience them. For example, you see how the words of "The Sidewalk Racer" form a skateboard that is ready to roll. You also use your own memories of skateboards to hear the "whirring / sound" that the poet describes.

1. Explain how you can use three different senses to experience lines 1–5 of "The Sidewalk Racer."
2. What word can you add to "Concrete Cat" to help readers "hear" the poem?
3. What are the two most important senses for experiencing the haiku? Why?

◆ Build Vocabulary

USING HOMOPHONES

Homophones are words that sound the same but have different meanings and are often spelled differently. On your paper, choose the homophones that best complete each sentence:

1. Pursued by a (flee, flea), he had to (flea, flee) the room.
2. The fly and the flea (flue, flew) speedily up the (flew, flue).

SPELLING STRATEGY

The *oo* sound in words can be spelled differently, as in f*lue, do, zoo, new,* and as*sume.* Remember that the *u* spelling usually occurs with a consonant and a silent *e.* On your paper, list another example for each spelling of this sound.

USING THE WORD BANK

On your paper, replace each italicized word or phrase with a word from the Word Bank:

A fly and a flea were *gliding* along when a frog jumped out of a pond to chase them. The fly said to the flea, "We don't have to *escape* from the *chimney-tube* to get away from this beast." Turning to the frog, the fly said calmly, "There's a *mistake* in your thinking. You're in the wrong poem!"

◆ Literary Focus

SPECIAL FORMS OF POETRY

These poems illustrate the special forms that poets use to shape their work: **concrete poems,** in which words are arranged into a picture; **haiku,** poems about a moment or scene in three lines of five, seven, and five syllables; and **limericks,** in which lines 1, 2, and 5 have the same rhythm and rhyme as do lines 3 and 4.

1. Would either "The Sidewalk Racer" or "Concrete Cat" work as a regular poem? Explain.
2. Show how each haiku is successful in capturing a moment or a scene in nature.
3. Do you think it would be possible to write a serious limerick? Why or why not?

◆ Build Grammar Skills

COMPARISONS WITH *more* AND *most*

To form the comparative and the superlative of longer adjectives and most adverbs, add **more** or **most** to the positive:

Positive	Comparative	Superlative
dignified	more dignified	most dignified
frightened	more frightened	most frightened
roughly	more roughly	most roughly
carefully	more carefully	most carefully

Practice On your paper, change the positive form of each modifier to the comparative or superlative.

1. She is a (confident) skateboarder than her sister.
2. I am the (experienced) skateboarder in my neighborhood.
3. This is the (threatening) wind I have ever heard.
4. The frog jumps (clumsily) than the flea.
5. Of all insects, the flea makes up its mind the (speedily).

Writing Application Using five comparisons with *more* or *most,* describe a debate between a fly and a flea.

Build Your Portfolio

 Idea Bank

Writing

1. **Inscription for a Monument** A monument marks the spot where Bashō wrote "An old silent pond." Write a statement honoring Bashō that will be carved on this monument. Tell what he achieved with his haiku.

2. **Sports Haiku** Write a haiku on your favorite athlete. Refer to the time of year in your first line of five syllables. Then, in lines of seven and five syllables, describe something the athlete does. Use words that appeal to your readers' senses.

3. **Concrete Poem** Write a poem in which the words on the page form a picture of your subject—whether it's a telephone receiver or a roller coaster. Also, use a rhythm that will make readers think of your subject.

Speaking and Listening

4. **"Concrete" Recital** With a group, form the shape of a skateboard or a cat. Then, recite "The Sidewalk Racer" or chant the words of "Concrete Cat." **[Performing Arts Link]**

5. **Poetry Performance** Perform "The Sidewalk Racer" by acting out its movements as you recite it. **[Performing Arts Link]**

Projects

6. **Poetry Masquerade Party** Hold a class party to which students come dressed as poetic forms. For example, someone can be a limerick by dressing up as a clown and reciting a limerick. Another can dress in the shape of a concrete poem. **[Performing Arts Link]**

7. **Poetry, Inc. [Group Activity]** With several classmates, design and market a new poetic form. It can be brief, but it should be funny. Then, create a few models to show how it works.

 Writing Mini-Lesson

Limerick

A limerick tells a funny little story with a surprise twist at the end. Write your own limerick. Use the following tips to help you.

Writing Skills Focus: Use the Right Rhythm

No matter what kind of poem you write, **rhythm** is an important factor. The rhythm for limericks is created by using a specific number of syllables in each line. The natural rhythm of speech creates groups of syllables that usually have two unstressed syllables followed by a stressed one.

Prewriting Make a list of names and words that rhyme with them. Choose the words that suggest the funniest situation.

Drafting In the first line or two, introduce your character. Then, describe a situation. In the last line or two, give the situation a twist. Use the framework below when you write your limerick. Each dash represents a syllable. The lines marked by matching letters should end with words that rhyme with each other.

__ __ _____**a**

_____**a**

_____**b**

_____**b**

_____**a**

Revising Read your limerick out loud to check for rhymes and syllable counts.

◆ **Grammar Application**

Be sure you've used *more* or *most* in comparisons with longer adjectives and most adverbs.

Writing Process Workshop

Poems help us discover hidden beauties and secret connections in the world. In "The Geese," for instance, we hear a connection between the coming winter winds and "the rushing" of geese wings. Poets discover such connections by listening carefully to the meaning and sound of words. As they write poems with a pattern of syllables and rhymes, they pay close attention to the words they choose.

See what you can discover by listening to words. Write your own **poem,** using the form of "The Geese" (p. 718) or by following haiku form (p. 726). Use the following tips introduced in this section's Writing Mini-Lessons:

Writing Skills Focus

▶ **Use sensory details.** Describe the look, feel, sound, smell, and taste of things using vivid, precise words. (See p. 708.)

▶ **Choose appropriate language.** If your poem describes a sad sight, formal language is appropriate. If your poem describes a funny event, words that sound a little wacky may fit better. (See p. 721.)

▶ **Use the right rhythm.** As you write, read the lines back to yourself. Clap once for each stressed syllable to make sure the accents fall in the right place. (See p. 729.)

Notice how the writer uses these skills in this model:

MODEL FROM LITERATURE

from "The Geese" by Richard Peck

Knowing that winter's wind comes
    soon ①
After the rushing ② of those wings,
Seeing them pass before the moon,
Recalling ③ the lure of faroff things.

① Each line has eight or nine syllables with four stresses.

② The rushing of wings appeals to your sense of hearing.

③ The poem is about a beautiful, slightly sad memory, so formal words such as *recalling* and *lure* are suitable.

Prewriting

Choose a Type of Poem Decide whether you want to write a lyric poem about a season and the feelings it calls to mind, or two haiku, each about a scene in nature.

Learn the Form If you write a lyric poem, use the form of Robert Peck's "The Geese" (p. 718). Each stanza has four lines with four stressed syllables (for example, da-DUM, da-DUM, da-DUM, da-DUM or DA-dum, DA-dum, DA-dum, DA-dum). The first and third lines rhyme, as do the second and fourth lines. You can review haiku form on page 726. Read the model for your poem aloud, clapping your hands once for each stressed syllable and listening for accents.

Choose a Topic If you are writing a lyric, choose a season about which to write. If you are writing two haiku, think of two sights, creatures, or other scenes from nature.

Brainstorm for Images and Feelings Look at your topic from various sides. For instance, winter may be snow and wind, but it may also be hot chocolate and peppermint candy canes. Jot down memories and images in a graphic organizer like the one below.

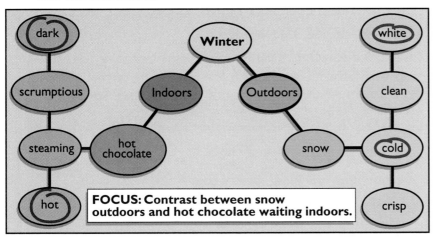

FOCUS: Contrast between snow outdoors and hot chocolate waiting indoors.

Test Your Words As you brainstorm, say words aloud to get a feeling of them. For example, *branch* and *bough* name a part of a tree, but *bough,* with its long, round *o* sound, suggests something gentle, graceful, and curving. A *branch,* with its sharp *a* and crunchy *ch,* might *snap, crack,* or *crunch* if you *crashed* into it. Jot down good words in your graphic organizer.

Find a Focus Review your graphic organizer for a central image, contrast, or idea. You might choose the contrast between the cold snow outdoors and the steaming cocoa indoors.

DRAFTING/REVISING

APPLYING LANGUAGE SKILLS: Vivid Nouns and Verbs

A word is said to be vivid if it creates a sharp picture of a thing or an action.

Vivid Nouns	General Nouns
lilac	flower
superhighway	road
orchard	farm
mansion	house

Vivid Verbs	General Verbs
to simmer	to cook
to trudge	to walk
to reek	to smell
to dash	to run

Practice Replace each italicized word with a vivid noun or verb.

When the winds start *blowing,* and *birds* fill the air with lonely *noises,* winter is near. It is time to bundle up in warm *clothing, gather* by the fire, and *warm* yourself.

Writing Application Replace general or dull words in your draft with vivid ones.

Writer's Solution Connection Language Lab

For more practice, complete the lesson on Vivid and Precise Verbs in the Choosing Words unit.

APPLYING LANGUAGE SKILLS: Punctuating Poetry

Sentences in a poem are typically punctuated just as ordinary sentences are. Each begins with a capital letter and ends with a period or other end mark.

Poetry is divided into lines. A sentence in a poem can stretch over more than one line. It usually begins with a capital letter and ends with an end mark.

Practice Add end punctuation to the following poem.

If I were in charge of the world
You wouldn't have lonely
You wouldn't have clean
You wouldn't have bedtimes

Writing Application Check that the punctuation of your poem indicates where you want readers to stop or to pause.

Writer's Solution Connection
Language Lab

For more practice with punctuation, complete the lesson on End Marks in the Punctuation unit.

Drafting

Paint a Picture As you draft, use the images in your graphic organizer. Choose the following kinds of words:

▶ **Precise nouns,** such as *branch,* rather than general nouns, such as *stick.*

▶ **Vivid adjectives,** such as *leafy,* rather than empty adjectives, such as *pretty.*

▶ **Precise verbs,** such as *cracked,* rather than dull verbs, such as *broke.*

Writing Tip If you are writing a lyric, use a rhyming dictionary from the library to help find words that rhyme.

Use Appropriate Language Use formal words, such as *strode,* if your subject is serious, but use casual or quirky words, such as *boogied,* if your subject is humorous.

Stick to Form Make sure that each line has the correct number of syllables and accents, and that it rhymes if required.

Revising

Review Your Word Choices Ask yourself: Does the poem bring to mind specific pictures, or could many different pictures fit the same words? Replace general, empty, or dull words with precise, vivid words.

Check the Rhythm Read the poem aloud, clapping for each stressed syllable. Make sure each line follows the correct pattern.

REVISION MODEL

① *trudged*
I ~~walked~~ through miles of snow,
② *dazzling*
A crunching, crackling, ~~pretty~~ rug.

But all I saw as I did go
③ *mug.*
Was steam from chocolate in a

① *Trudged* is more vivid and precise than *walked.*
② *Dazzling* is more vivid than *pretty.*
③ *Mug* fits the rhyme pattern, rhyming with *rug.*

Publishing and Presenting

Multimedia Poetry Reading With a group, read your poem to the class. Choose slides, posters, or other visual aids that will add to the enjoyment of the reading. Others in the group can help readers set up these aids.

Real-World Reading Skills Workshop

Strategies for Success

Like poets, songwriters want to communicate a message with the words they write. The following points will help you interpret the lyrics of songs—that is, understand the message in the words.

Find a Clue in the Music Song lyrics are written to go with music. The mood, or feeling, of the music can give you your first clue to the meaning of the words. If the music has a sad or mournful quality, then the lyrics probably tell a sad story.

Identify the Speaker Like a poem, a song has a speaker. The speaker may be an individual, a group, or two people in conversation. Identify who the character or characters are that are supposed to be saying the words. Remember that the speaker may not be the same as the singer or songwriter.

Listen to the Refrain Many songs have a chorus or a refrain—lines that are repeated after each section of the song. The refrain often includes the main idea of the lyrics.

Look for Symbols Songwriters often use symbols—things that stand for something else. Sunshine can stand for happiness. An outstretched hand can stand for friendship. Look for symbols, and think about what they mean.

✔ Here are situations in which interpreting song lyrics can be helpful:
- ► Listening to a new song on the radio
- ► Understanding a folk song
- ► Appreciating a style of music you don't usually listen to

Apply the Strategies

Read the portion of song lyrics below. Then, answer the questions that follow.

YOU'VE GOT A FRIEND
Carole King

When you're down and troubled
and you need a helping hand
and nothin', nothin' is going right
close your eyes and think of me
and soon I will be there
to brighten up even your darkest night

You just call out my name
and you know wherever I am
I'll come running to see you again
Winter, spring, summer or fall
all you have to do is call
and I'll be there
You've got a friend

1. What do you think would be the mood of the music played with these lyrics?

2. What do you think the songwriter means by the "darkest night"?

3. The section that begins "You just call out my name . . ." is the refrain. In your own words, restate the main idea of the refrain.

Comparison of Adjectives and Adverbs

Grammar Review

com·par·i·son (kəm per′i sən) *n.* **1** the listing of the positive, comparative, and superlative forms of an adjective or adverb (Examples: long, longer, longest; slowly, more slowly, most slowly) **—in comparison with** compared with

Adjectives and adverbs can be used to compare two or more items. There are three forms of adjectives and adverbs:

Positive: Describes one thing

Comparative: Compares one thing to one other thing

Superlative: Compares one thing to two or more other things

An **adjective** is used to compare nouns. One-syllable adjectives and many two-syllable adjectives, like *fancy,* take an *-er* ending for the comparative form and an *-est* ending for the superlative. (The final *y* becomes *i.*)

My cat's name is *fancier* than your cat's name.

My cat's name is the *fanciest* of all names.

An **adverb** is used to compare actions, adjectives, or other adverbs. Most adverbs use *more* or *less* for the comparative and *most* or *least* for the superlative.

To form the comparative and superlative of longer adjectives and most adverbs, add *more* or *most* to the positive.

Positive	Comparative	Superlative
dignified	more dignified	most dignified
roughly	more roughly	most roughly
carefully	more carefully	most carefully

A few modifiers, like *good* and *bad,* are irregular. You must learn their comparative and superlative forms.

Positive	Comparative	Superlative
good	better	best
bad	worse	worst
well	better	best
little	less	least
many	more	most

Practice 1 On your paper, write each sentence. Change the adjective or adverb in parentheses to the comparative or superlative form.

1. His cat is (smart) than ours.

2. This lyric poem is the (long) of any I have read.

3. I read the first poem (carefully) than I read the second one.

4. I found the first poem (enjoyable) than the second one.

5. I thought this poem was (good) of all.

Practice 2 On your paper, use the positive, comparative, or superlative form of the adjective or adverb in parentheses.

1. I am a (skilled) skateboarder.

2. He is the (big) frog in the pond.

3. This pond has (many) frogs than that one.

4. The Walrus was (tricky), but the Oysters were not.

5. The youngest Oyster had the (little) sense of all of them.

Grammar in Writing

✔ *Use the comparative form when comparing two things to each other.*

✔ *Use the superlative form when comparing one thing to two or more other things.*

PART 2   *Elements of Poetry*

Zinnias, 1937, John Hollis Kaufmann, Private Collection

Guide for Reading

Meet the Authors:

Rachel Field (1894–1942)

Field couldn't read until she was ten. However, this late reader became a well-known writer of books for adults and children. She also became the first woman to receive a Newbery medal for children's literature. One reason for her success as a writer was her "camera memory," which stored up details. You'll see—and hear—some of these details in "Parade."

Gwendolyn Brooks (1917–)

Brooks has written many poems about her neighbors and neighborhood in Chicago. She has lived most of her life in that large midwestern city.

When she was only seven, Brooks started writing poetry. As a teenager, she had her poetry published in a well-known magazine. Her poems were also published in a local newspaper, the *Chicago Defender.*

Eventually, she became a well-respected poet. She received the Pulitzer Prize for her second book, *Annie Allen* (1949).

THE STORY BEHIND THE POEM

Brooks included "Cynthia in the Snow" in a book entitled *Bronzeville Boys and Girls* (1956). Bronzeville refers to an African American community in Chicago. Written for young readers, the poems in this book are about young African Americans living in Bronzeville.

◆ LITERATURE AND YOUR LIFE

CONNECT YOUR EXPERIENCE

Stop for a moment and listen to the world's music all around you: a cough, a clock ticking, a palm rubbing a cotton sleeve, the seat of a chair squeaking and complaining. These poets also stopped and listened to the world's music. They stored it up in words on a silent page. However, if you listen as you read, you can hear what they heard.

THEMATIC FOCUS: Memorable Days

What makes the experience described in each of these poems memorable?

◆ Background for Understanding

HISTORY

"Parade" describes a circus tradition more than 100 years old: Imagine that it's circus day in your small town, sometime in the 1840's. There's no television or radio, so you've learned about the coming of the circus from posters. You know that the whole circus is going to march down Main Street in a free parade. Here it is, a large-as-life advertisement for the performances to come: beautiful women on horses, clowns on stilts, chariots, cages of wild animals. It ends with a giant calliope, thirty-two steam whistles hooting favorite tunes.

◆ Build Vocabulary

SUFFIXES: *-ly*

The suffix *-ly* can be used to create a word that tells how something happens. For example, the word *leisurely* in "Parade" is made up of *leisure* ("freedom and relaxation") and *-ly* ("in what way"). It means "in a relaxed way."

WORD BANK

Which of these words is related to the word *gold*? How do you know?

gilded
leisurely

◆ Parade ◆
Cynthia in the Snow

◆ Literary Focus

SOUND DEVICES

A poem is like a parade of sounds through your ears. That's why poets use **sound devices,** ways of adding music to poetry. The most obvious sound device is rhyme. However, another device is **onomatopoeia** (än′ ō mat′ ō pē′ ə), the use of words that sound like what they mean, such as *hush*. Still another device is **alliteration,** the repetition of sounds at the beginning of words or in stressed syllables: "*whitely whirs.*"

Both poets use all these sound devices. However, listen for the way they use them differently. Brooks makes them whisper the whiteness of snow. Field makes them blare like trumpets in a bold parade.

◆ Reading Strategy

READ ACCORDING TO PUNCTUATION

Punctuation keeps the words marching at the right pace through a poem. If you read **according to punctuation,** you'll keep the parade of the poem in good order:

- Pause slightly for commas and a bit longer for semicolons or dashes.
- Stop longest for end marks like periods and question marks.
- Don't stop at the ends of lines where there is no punctuation.

.?! STOP .?!

,;- PAUSE ,;-

PARADE

Rachel Field

◀ **Critical Viewing** To what senses do parades like this one appeal? [Analyze]

This is the day the circus comes
With blare of brass, with beating drums,
And clashing cymbals, and with roar
Of wild beasts never heard before
5   Within town limits. Spick and span
Will shine each <u>gilded</u> cage and van;
Cockades at every horse's head
Will nod, and riders dressed in red
Or blue trot by. There will be floats
10 In shapes like dragons, thrones and boats,
And clowns on stilts; freaks big and small,
Till <u>leisurely</u> and last of all
Camels and elephants will pass
Beneath our elms, along our grass.

Cynthia in the Snow

Gwendolyn Brooks

It SUSHES.
It hushes
The loudness in the road.
It flitter-twitters,
5 And laughs away from me.
It laughs a lovely whiteness,
And whitely whirs away,
To be
Some otherwhere,
10 Still white as milk or shirts.
So beautiful it hurts.

Guide for Responding

◆ LITERATURE AND YOUR LIFE

Reader's Response Does "Parade" remind you of any procession that you have seen? Why or why not?

Thematic Focus Why do you think these poets want to remember these experiences?

☑ Check Your Comprehension

1. List four attractions you'd see if you were watching the circus procession in "Parade."
2. What comes at the end of the procession in "Parade"?
3. Name two things to which Brooks compares the snow's whiteness in "Cynthia in the Snow."

◆ Critical Thinking

INTERPRET

1. Is the speaker in "Parade" an adult or a child? Explain. **[Infer]**
2. In what way is the procession in "Parade" an extraordinary event in ordinary surroundings? **[Support]**
3. How is snow something that the speaker can't hold or keep in "Cynthia in the Snow"? **[Analyze]**

COMPARE LITERARY WORKS

4. In what way do both poems deal with unusual, magical events? **[Compare and Contrast]**

Guide for Responding (continued)

◆ Reading Strategy

READ ACCORDING TO PUNCTUATION

Reading according to punctuation helps keep the meaning of the poem clear. Pause slightly for commas, longer for semicolons, and longest for periods.

1. Explain how the punctuation guides your reading of lines 1–3 of "Cynthia in the Snow."
2. How does the punctuation in line 10 help emphasize line 11?
3. Explain how the punctuation in lines 5–11 of "Parade" helps you "see" each attraction in turn.

◆ Build Vocabulary

USING THE SUFFIX -ly

The suffix -ly often turns adjectives into adverbs telling *when, how,* or *in what way.* Use it in a "Wanted" poster for a monkey that ran away from the circus parade: Add -ly to each adjective. Then, use the new word to describe the monkey's behavior.

1. clever   3. affectionate   5. quick
2. stubborn   4. sly

SPELLING STRATEGY

This rule explains whether e or i goes first: i goes before e except after c (*ceiling*) and in words with a long a sound (*weigh*). Among the exceptions to the rule are *leisure, weird, seize, height,* and *neither.* On your paper, choose the correct spelling of these words and explain your choice:

1. freight, frieght   3. nieghbor, neighbor
2. wierd, weird

USING THE WORD BANK

On your paper, answer each statement true or false, and explain your answer:

1. A gilded circus wagon would have a dull appearance.
2. If Cynthia played leisurely with the snow, she'd look calm.

◆ Literary Focus

SOUND DEVICES

Both poets use **sound devices,** ways of making writing musical. In "Cynthia in the Snow," Brooks writes, "It *SUSHES.*" This word is an example of **onomatopoeia** because it imitates the soft, hushing sound of snowfall. In "Parade," Field uses **alliteration,** the repetition of sounds at the beginning of words: "*Sp*ick and *sp*an . . ."

1. Find two examples of onomatopoeia in line 3 of "Parade." Describe the effect of each example.
2. Find two examples of alliteration in lines 6–7 of "Cynthia in the Snow."

◆ Build Grammar Skills

DOUBLE NEGATIVES

Only one negative word is needed to give a negative meaning. Sometimes people mistakenly use **double negatives**—two negatives together. Notice that Rachel Field writes in "Parade," "Of wild beasts *never* heard before . . ." She avoids a double negative like "*not never* heard before."

Other negative words are *barely, hardly, neither, no, nobody, none, no one, nothing, nowhere,* and *scarcely.* Contractions sometimes indicate negatives with *n't.*

Practice On your paper, tell which sentences have double negatives. Then, correct them.

1. Cynthia has not never seen snow.
2. In the snowstorm, she couldn't hardly hear the cars.
3. I don't expect to see no elephants this year.
4. There are many wild beasts I've never heard before.
5. Nobody nowhere remembers seeing a real circus.

Writing Application Invent a comic character called Mr. No-No, who incorrectly speaks in double negatives. Write three sentences he would use to describe the snow.

Build Your Portfolio

 ## Idea Bank

Writing

1. License-Plate Phrase Using alliteration, write a phrase that will appear on your state's license plates. Not only should it be brief and memorable, but it should highlight something important about your state. **[Career Link]**

2. Analysis of a Commercial Find a television or radio commercial that uses alliteration, onomatopoeia, or both. Write down the examples you find. Then, explain whether or not they make the commercial easier to remember. **[Media Link]**

3. Comparison and Contrast Write a brief essay comparing and contrasting the two poems. Focus on similarities and differences in the events described and in the use of sound devices.

Speaking and Listening

4. All-out, Alliterative Parade With a group, create a parade of alliterative circus attractions. One person might start with "*lordly lion*," another could invent an alliterative phrase for another attraction, and so on. Make a list of your alliterations.

5. Radio Reading Choose one of these poems to read over a local radio station. Copy the poem, and indicate where and how long you'll pause for punctuation. After practicing, record your reading. **[Performing Arts Link; Media Link]**

Projects

6. Diorama Build a model of a circus parade. Use papier-mâché, pipe cleaners, wood, spangles, or other materials. **[Art Link]**

7. Crazy Comics [Group Activity] With a few classmates, design a comic strip in which some characters speak using onomatopoeia and others use alliteration. Tell an interesting story. **[Art Link]**

 ## Writing Mini-Lesson

Advertising Jingle

Sound devices like rhyme, alliteration, and onomatopoeia help you remember poems. The same devices can keep an advertising jingle—a brief song used to sell a product—going around in your mind. Have some fun by writing a catchy jingle for a real or an imaginary product.

Writing Skills Focus: Use of Rhyme

Use **rhyme,** the chiming of word sounds, to make your jingle memorable. Notice the rhymes at the ends of lines 7 and 8 of "Parade":

> ***Model From the Poem***
> Cockades at every horse's *head*
> Will nod, and riders dressed in *red*
> Or blue trot by. . . .

Prewriting Use a diagram like the one below to note the features of your product and possible rhymes you can use.

Features	Rhymes		
blue	true	do	new
fast	past	last	
power	hour	shower	

Drafting Write two sentences about the best features of your product. Then, use ideas from your chart to create rhyming sentences. You may need to use a word order you wouldn't use when speaking. For example, you might write "Blue is the shirt" instead of "The shirt is blue."

Revising Sing or read your jingle to a partner. Revise to incorporate your partner's suggestions for how to make the jingle more memorable.

> ◆ **Grammar Application**
> Check to see that you haven't used any double negatives in your jingle.

Guide for Reading

Meet the Authors:

Eve Merriam (1916–1992)

This poet was bitten by the word bug early in life, falling in love with the music of language. Among her many books of poems is the award-winning *Family Circle*.

Emily Dickinson (1830–1886)

Dickinson published only seven poems during her lifetime. However, together with Walt Whitman, she's considered a founder of American poetry. Her poems are a kind of lifelong diary of her deepest guesses and wonderings. The daughter of a lawyer in Amherst, Massachusetts, she lived quietly in her family's home all her life. All the while, she was writing and saving away her 1,775 brief lyrics.

Langston Hughes (1902–1967)

Langston Hughes brought the rhythms of African American music and speech to American poetry. Raised in the Midwest, he traveled the world on merchant ships as a young man. Then, he settled in New York City's African American community of Harlem. There, he felt the influence of musical styles like jazz and the blues. Among his best-known collections of poetry are *The Weary Blues* (1926) and *The Dream Keeper* (1932).

THE STORY BEHIND THE POEM

Hughes kept a childlike sense of wonder throughout his life. It's not surprising therefore that he published his first poems in a magazine for African American children. "April Rain Song," with its youthful wonder at the rain, appeared in the April 1921 issue.

◆ LITERATURE AND YOUR LIFE

CONNECT YOUR EXPERIENCE

Trees, bees, and rain—they don't, at first, sound very exciting. However, these poets use imagination to put wings on their words. The comparisons they make will surprise you into seeing things in a new way.

THEMATIC FOCUS: Special Individuals

As you read, ask yourself how these poets show that each individual and each experience are unique.

◆ Background for Understanding

SCIENCE

Willow trees and ginkgo trees are very different from each other. You can compare and contrast them by looking at the willow on  page 743 and the ginkgo branch pictured here.

◆ Build Vocabulary

WORD GROUPS: MUSICAL WORDS

"Simile: Willow and Ginkgo" uses several words from the world of music. One of these is *soprano*, which means "the highest singing voice."

WORD BANK

Which of these words comes from the Latin word *supra*, meaning "higher"? How do you know?

| soprano |
| chorus |

◆ Literary Focus

FIGURATIVE LANGUAGE

Figurative language is language that uses comparisons to help you see or feel things in a new way:

- **Simile**—uses *like* or *as* to compare apparently unlike things: *Reading poems is like eating candy.*
- **Metaphor**—compares apparently unlike things by describing one as if it were the other, without using *like* or *as*: *The poems are candy.*
- **Personification**—compares apparently unlike things by describing something non-human as if it were human: *The candies whispered to one another.*

Find the similes in "Simile: Willow and Ginkgo," the metaphor in "Fame Is a Bee," and the personification in "April Rain Song."

◆ Reading Strategy

RESPOND

A poem is an invitation. **Respond** to this invitation by bringing your thoughts and feelings to the poem's word celebration. Tap out its rhythms, agree or disagree with its comparisons, and enrich its descriptions with your memories. The more you bring, the more you'll enjoy the party!

To get started responding to these poems, make a tree branch like the one shown below. On the "leaves" of your chart, write answers to these questions:

"Simile"
If I could be one of these trees, which one would I choose?

"Fame Is a Bee"
When have I seen fame sting someone?

"April Rain Song"
When have I seen rain kiss someone?

Simile:

Willow and Ginkgo

Eve Merriam

The willow is like an etching,[1]
Fine-lined against the sky.
The ginkgo is like a crude sketch,
Hardly worthy to be signed.

5 The willow's music is like a soprano,
Delicate and thin.
The ginkgo's tune is like a chorus
With everyone joining in.

The willow is sleek as a velvet-nosed calf;
10 The ginkgo is leathery as an old bull.
The willow's branches are like silken thread;
The ginkgo's like stubby rough wool.

The willow is like a nymph[2] with streaming hair;
Wherever it grows, there is green and gold and fair.
15 The willow dips to the water,
Protected and precious, like the king's favorite
    daughter.

The ginkgo forces its way through gray concrete;
Like a city child, it grows up in the street.
Thrust against the metal sky,
20 Somehow it survives and even thrives.

My eyes feast upon the willow,
But my heart goes to the ginkgo.

◆ Build Vocabulary

soprano (sə pran′ ō) *n.*: The highest singing voice of women, girls, or young boys

chorus (kôr′ əs) *n.*: The part of a song sung by many voices at once

1. **etching** (ech′ iŋ) *n.*: A print of a drawing or design made on metal, glass, or wood.
2. **nymph** (nimf) *n.*: Goddess of nature thought of as a beautiful maiden.

Fame Is a Bee

Emily Dickinson

Fame is a bee.
It has a song—
It has a sting—
Ah, too, it has a wing.

April Rain Song

Langston Hughes

Let the rain kiss you.
Let the rain beat upon your head with silver liquid drops.
Let the rain sing you a lullaby.

The rain makes still pools on the sidewalk.
5   The rain makes running pools in the gutter.
The rain plays a little sleep-song on our roof at night—

And I love the rain.

▲ **Critical Viewing** Which line from the poem would you use as a caption for this picture? **[Connect]**

Beyond Literature

Music Connection

Vivaldi's *The Four Seasons* Langston Hughes responds to a season through poetry. Others might respond through art; still others, in music. Antonio Vivaldi (1678–1741) was an Italian composer who wrote one of the world's most famous pieces of music about the seasons. It is called *The Four Seasons,* and it is a collection of four violin concertos—one for each season. (A concerto is a musical composition written for a single instrument. It usually has three movements, or main sections.)

Cross-Curricular Activity
Musical Art Listen to one of the concertos in Vivaldi's *The Four Seasons.* After listening, create a picture that captures the feelings in the music and portrays the season for which the concerto was named.

Guide for Responding

◆ LITERATURE AND YOUR LIFE

Reader's Response Which of these poems seems closest to your experience? Explain.

Thematic Focus What unique quality did each poet find in his or her subject?

Journal Writing Describe your favorite season.

☑ Check Your Comprehension

1. List all the things to which the willow is compared in "Simile: Willow and Ginkgo."
2. List all the things to which the ginkgo is compared.
3. In "Fame Is a Bee," what three things does fame have?
4. What three things does the speaker of "April Rain Song" tell you to let the rain do?
5. What does the rain do on the sidewalk, in the gutter, and on the roof?

◆ Critical Thinking

INTERPRET

1. Contrast the general impression you get of the willow and the ginkgo in "Simile: Willow and Ginkgo." **[Compare and Contrast]**
2. Explain the meaning of lines 21–22 of "Simile: Willow and Ginkgo." **[Interpret]**
3. What is fame's "song"? **[Interpret]**

EVALUATE

4. Do you think a bee is a good image to suggest fame? Explain. **[Assess]**
5. How would "April Rain Song" be different if it were about a late autumn rain in a cold climate? **[Hypothesize]**

COMPARE LITERARY WORKS

6. Would the speaker in "April Rain Song" prefer the willow or the ginkgo in "Simile: Willow and Ginkgo"? Why? **[Connect]**

Guide for Responding (continued)

◆ Reading Strategy

RESPOND

You **respond** to these poems with your own ideas and feelings. In fact, you may disagree with them, just as you sometimes disagree with friends.

1. Was there a comparison in "Simile: Willow and Ginkgo" that you didn't think was accurate? Why or why not?
2. Has someone you know been stung by fame? Explain.
3. What memories of rain did lines 4–6 of "April Rain Song" bring to mind?

◆ Build Vocabulary

USING MUSICAL WORDS

Like many fields, music has its own terms. A *chorus*, for example, is "a singing group." On your paper, write these terms for the singers in a chorus in order (highest voice on top, lowest on bottom).

bass	alto
soprano	tenor

SPELLING STRATEGY

When a consonant precedes a final *o,* you usually add *-es* to form the plural. Exceptions include all musical terms, as *sopranos.* On your paper, find and correct the italicized words that are misspelled:

The *altoes* sang to the accompaniment of *banjoes* and *pianos* while the audience ate *potatoes.*

USING THE WORD BANK

On your paper, answer these questions. Then, explain your answer.

1. Would you cast a woman or a man to sing a soprano part?
2. Would a bass, a chorus, or a songbird sing the loudest?

◆ Literary Focus

FIGURATIVE LANGUAGE

These poems use **figurative language,** language based on comparisons, to surprise you into new ways of seeing:

	Simile	Metaphor	Personification
Definitions	Comparison using *like* or *as*	Describes one thing as if it were another	Refers to the non-human with human qualities
Examples	"The willow is *like* an etching …" ("Willow and Ginkgo")	"It [Fame] has a sting—" ("Fame Is a Bee")	"Let the rain kiss you." ("April Rain Song")

1. On your paper, complete the chart with another example of each figure of speech.
2. For each example, state what things are being compared and how they are similar.

◆ Build Grammar Skills

CORRECT USE OF *its* AND *it's*

Its is the possessive form of the pronoun *it.* However *it's* is a contraction of *it is* or *it has:*

The ginkgo forces *its* way through gray concrete. (possessive—The *way* belongs to *it.*)

It's true that the ginkgo is "a city child." (contraction—*It's* stands for *It is.*)

Practice On your paper, choose the right form of *it* to complete each sentence correctly.

1. (Its, It's) clear that Merriam likes both trees.
2. Do you think (it's, its) easy to be a ginkgo?
3. Dickinson says that fame has (it's, its) sting.
4. (It's, Its) sweet to be kissed by the April rain.
5. The April rain has (its, it's) own lullaby to play.

Writing Application Restate in your own words what Dickinson is saying about fame. Correctly use *its* and *it's.*

Build Your Portfolio

 ## Idea Bank

Writing

1. **Personified Machine** Name a machine, and then briefly describe it as if it were human.

2. **Contrast Poem** Imitate "Simile: Willow and Ginkgo" by writing a poem that contrasts two things: plants, animals, people, or places. Use figurative language to make your contrasts more lively.

3. **Extended Definition** Write a definition of fame. Begin by putting a dictionary definition into your own words. Then, using examples and stories, show how fame has "a song," "a sting," and "a wing."

Speaking and Listening

4. **Partner Reading** With a partner, perform "Simile: Willow and Ginkgo." One of you will read the lines about the willow, and the other, the lines about the ginkgo. Let your reading express the qualities of your tree. **[Performing Arts Link]**

5. **Reading to Music** Find a piece of music to accompany "April Rain Song." Be sure it reflects the mood of the poem. Then, read the poem aloud as you play this piece of music in the background. **[Music Link; Performing Arts Link]**

Projects

6. **Collage** Copy one of these poems and use it as the centerpiece of a collage. Around the poem, paste pictures and found objects that reflect the poem's meaning. **[Art Link]**

7. **Multimedia Report on Trees [Group Activity]** Use these materials to compare the willow and the ginkgo: drawings of leaves or actual leaves, timelines showing the origin of the trees, slides, diagrams, quotations from scientists. Present your comparison to the class. **[Science Link]**

 ## Writing Mini-Lesson

Descriptive Postcard

The wonderfully descriptive "April Rain Song" could fit on a postcard. Write your own descriptive postcard about an ordinary experience you enjoy.

Writing Skills Focus: Use Similes

Enliven your description with **similes,** comparisons using *like* or *as*. A good simile—in poetry or in prose—should surprise readers by comparing things that seem to be unlike. However, it should also convince readers that the two things share a similar quality. This simile from "Simile: Willow and Ginkgo" is both surprising and convincing:

Model From the Poem
The ginkgo is like a crude sketch,
Hardly worthy to be signed.

Prewriting Use a chart like the one below to gather ideas for similes:

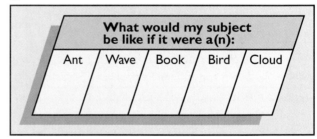

What would my subject be like if it were a(n):				
Ant	Wave	Book	Bird	Cloud

Drafting Write four or five sentences about the main qualities you want to capture. Use your chart to create a simile that highlights one of the qualities of your subject.

Revising Have several classmates read your postcard. Ask them if your similes surprised them into seeing something familiar in a new way. If not, replace your similes with other suggestions from your chart.

> ◆ **Grammar Application**
> Check to see that you've correctly used *its* and *it's* in your description.

Exclamation *and* Wind and water and stone, *Octavio Paz*

In his poem "Wind and water and stone," Paz tells how these three elements play a never-ending game with one another. This game is more than a poetic idea. The imaginary hands of these elements have shaped the land of Mexico.

The Invisible Hand of Wind Wind's invisible hands block or bring the rain. Counterclockwise winds create a dry climate in the north of Mexico. Yet hurricanes drench the eastern and western coasts from August through October. In the south, air masses bring heavy rains in late spring and summer.

Fingers of Water Mexico has a few large rivers that reach through the land like fingers. The largest in the dry north is the Río Bravo del Norte, known in the United States as the Rio Grande. The Balsas River, southwest of Mexico City, generates much electric power. Starting west of Mexico City, the Lerma River flows northward to form enormous Lake Chapala.

The Supporting Palm Most Mexicans live in the center of the country, on a raised, open plain. This region is part of a larger plain that stretches like an open palm from the north to the Isthmus of Tehuantepec. Mountains rise up on either side.

Colliding Knuckles Beneath Mexico, giant stone "plates" collide like opposing knuckles. These collisions have created earthquakes and formed volcanoes like Popocatépetl (pô pô′ kä te′ pet′ əl) in central Mexico. This tongue-twister name means "smoking mountain" in a Native American language.

"Wind and water and stone" As you read this poem, remember that it's about natural forces, not just words.

Exclamation

Octavio Paz

Stillness
        not on the branch
in the air
        not in the air
5   in the moment
            hummingbird

WIND AND WATER AND STONE

Octavio Paz

The water hollowed the stone,
the wind dispersed the water,
the stone stopped the wind.
Water and wind and stone.

5 The wind sculpted the stone,
the stone is a cup of water,
the water runs off and is wind.
Stone and wind and water.

10 The wind sings in its turnings,
the water murmurs as it goes,
the motionless stone is quiet.
Wind and water and stone.

One is the other, and is neither:
among their empty names
15 they pass and disappear,
water and stone and wind.

Guide for Responding

◆ LITERATURE AND YOUR LIFE

Reader's Response Which element is your favorite—earth, water, air, or fire? Why?

Thematic Focus How can poems such as these enhance your appreciation of the natural world?

☑ Check Your Comprehension

1. What is the bird that Paz describes in "Exclamation"?
2. Name one way in which each element interacts with another in "Wind and water and stone."

◆ Critical Thinking

INTERPRET

1. How could the hovering bird in "Exclamation" create a stillness "in the moment"? **[Analyze]**
2. In what way is "Wind and water and stone" a poem about constant change? **[Analyze]**
3. In "Wind and water and stone," the last line of each stanza is similar but different. How does this repetition with change support the main idea of the poem? **[Draw Conclusions]**

EXTEND

4. What changes have wind, water, and stone created in your region? **[Science Link]**

CONNECTING LITERATURE TO SOCIAL STUDIES

"Wind and water and stone" describes the changes and interchanges of these elements. This movement shapes not only the land of Mexico, but also the lives of Mexicans. For example, weather and climate help determine where and how people live. Lack of rainfall in northern Mexico and a tropical climate in the southern part cause fewer people to live in these regions.

1. Do you think the same kinds of plants and animals live in Mexico's dry north and its tropical south? Explain.
2. Like Mexico City, the capital of the ancient Aztec Indians was built in central Mexico. Why?

 Idea Bank

Writing

1. **Stanza** Write another four-line stanza for "Wind and water and stone." In the first three lines, tell what each of these elements does to another element. Then, in the last line, combine the words wind, water, and stone.
2. **Description** Write a description of your region for an atlas. Include information about climate and weather; rivers, streams, and lakes; and mountains, valleys, and plains.
3. **Mexico's Poem** Write a poem in which the country of Mexico speaks about the forces that shaped it.

Speaking and Listening

4. **Oral Interpretation** Read both of these poems aloud to the class. Capture the hovering stillness of "Exclamation" and the sense of movement in "Wind and water and stone."

Projects

5. **Hummingbird Routes** Many hummingbirds migrate south in the winter. Make a map showing hummingbird migratory routes into or through Mexico. Focus on Allen's, calliope, rufous, and ruby-throated hummingbirds. **[Science Link; Art Link]**
6. **Map** Draw or trace a map of Mexico. On it, indicate the locations of major rivers, mountains, volcanoes, and canyons.

Meet the Author

Octavio Paz (äk tä´ vē ō päz) (1914–1998) Mexican poet Octavio Paz probably traveled to more unusual places and saw more interesting things than any other modern poet. His wide-ranging travel was matched by the freedom of his imagination.

Further Reading, Listening, and Viewing

• Juliet Piggott's book *Mexican Folk Tales* contains "Popocatepetl and Ixtlaccihuatl," a legend about these volcanoes.
• Jack Rummel's book *Mexico (Places and Peoples of the World)* has a wealth of information about our southern neighbor.

Guide for Reading

Meet the Authors:

William Wordsworth (1770–1850)

Instead of fancy poetic words, the Englishman William Wordsworth used everyday language to talk about everyday things. He showed that what is ordinary is really extraordinary. His ideas about poetry were inspired by his experiences in the beautiful Lake District in northwestern England, where he grew up and lived much of his life.

Theodore Roethke (1908–1963)

This poet's father grew and sold flowers in Saginaw, Michigan. That's probably why Roethke's most famous poems seem to speak of roses and carnations as if they were his sisters and brothers. Many of these flower poems appear in *The Lost Son* (1948).

John Ciardi (1916–1986)

Ciardi wrote and translated poems for adults. He also wrote books of children's poetry, like *The Reason for the Pelican* and *The Man Who Sang the Sillies*.

Ian Serraillier (1912–1994)

Ian Serraillier was born in London, England, and spent much of his life there as a teacher.

Mary Austin (1868–1934)

Austin spent years living with Native Americans in the Southwest, translating Native American poetry and writing poems, articles, and stories of her own.

◆ LITERATURE AND YOUR LIFE

CONNECT YOUR EXPERIENCE

Sometimes, your eyes play tricks on you. Other times, your vision is so crisp that you can pick out details on a baseball speeding toward you.

Some of these poems give you pictures that shift and change as you try to guess what they are. Others give you pictures that are clear and unforgettable.

THEMATIC FOCUS: **A Different View**

Ask yourself how these poets fool your mind's eye before revealing the whole picture in the poem.

◆ Background for Understanding

CULTURE

Theodore Roethke's poem vividly describes a "Child on Top of a Greenhouse." In the past, it was very common for a family with a large house and lots of property to have a greenhouse made of glass and an elaborate framework—much like the one pictured on page 757. The greenhouse was used to grow shrubs and plants for the grounds.

◆ Build Vocabulary

SUFFIXES: *-est*

The ending *-est* indicates that the word it's attached to is the *most* of something. For example, one riddle in this group refers to "the *swiftest* railroad train."

WORD BANK

Which of these words from the poems sounds like *pray* but has a different spelling and meaning?

withered
prey
feats
devours
swiftest

754 ◆ *Poetry*

The Kitten at Play
◆ Child on Top of a Greenhouse ◆
The Shark ◆ Two Riddles

Florence in the Garden, c. 1986, Peter Kuhfield, Bonhams, London, UK

◆ Literary Focus

POETIC IMAGE AND RIDDLE POEM

A **poetic image** is a description that helps you see something. It may also help you smell, taste, hear, or touch it. For example, Emily Dickinson writes, "How soft a Caterpillar steps— / I find one on my Hand." Her image helps you *feel* a caterpillar as well as see it! An image can also help you solve a **riddle poem.** You can use the details the poet describes to guess what he or she does not name.

◆ Reading Strategy

PARAPHRASE

The images or words in a poem can sometimes seem to rush by in a confusing blur. To make sense of the lines, you can slow down and **paraphrase**—restate the meaning in your own words. The chart below shows a paraphrase of lines 17–18 of "The Kitten at Play." Create a chart like it to jot down your paraphrases of other lines from the poems.

Poem	Paraphrase
Yet were gazing thousands there; What would little Tabby care?	This kitten wouldn't mind if thousands of people were staring at it.

The Kitten at Play

William Wordsworth

See the kitten on the wall,
Sporting with the leaves that fall,
<u>Withered</u> leaves, one, two and three
Falling from the elder tree,
5   Through the calm and frosty air
Of the morning bright and fair.

See the kitten, how she starts,
Crouches, stretches, paws and darts;
With a tiger-leap half way
10   Now she meets her coming <u>prey</u>.
Lets it go as fast and then
Has it in her power again.

Now she works with three and four,
Like an Indian conjurer;
15   Quick as he in <u>feats</u> of art,
Gracefully she plays her part;
Yet were gazing thousands there;
What would little Tabby care?

◆ **Build Vocabulary**

withered (with´ərd) *adj.*: Dried up

prey (prā) *n.*: Animals hunted or killed for food by other animals

feats (f ēts) *n.*: Remarkable deeds or acts

Child on Top of a Greenhouse

Theodore Roethke

The wind billowing out the seat of my britches,
My feet crackling splinters of glass and dried putty,
The half-grown chrysanthemums staring up like accusers,
Up through the streaked glass, flashing with sunlight,
5   A few white clouds all rushing eastward,
A line of elms plunging and tossing like horses,
And everyone, everyone pointing up and shouting!

THE SHARK

John Ciardi

My dear, let me tell you about the shark.
Though his eyes are bright, his thought is dark.
He's quiet—that speaks well of him.
So does the fact that he can swim.
5   But though he swims without a sound,
Wherever he swims he looks around
With those two bright eyes and that one dark thought.
He has only one but he thinks it a lot.
And the thought he thinks but can never complete
10   Is his long dark thought of something to eat.
Most anything does. And I have to add
That when he eats his manners are bad.
He's a gulper, a ripper, a snatcher, a grabber.
Yes, his manners are drab. But his thought is drabber.
15   That one dark thought he can never complete
Of something—anything—somehow to eat.

Be careful where you swim, my sweet.

Riddle
Ian Serraillier

In the dripping gloom I see
A creature with broad antlers,
Motionless. It turns its head;
One gleaming eye <u>devours</u> the dark.
5   I hear it cough and clear its throat;
Then, with a hungry roar, it charges
     into the night
And is swallowed whole.

(A motorcycle)

◆ Build Vocabulary

devours (di vourz´) *v.:* Swallows whole
swiftest (swift´ est) *adj.:* The most rapid; the fastest

Riddle
Mary Austin

I come more softly than a bird,
And lovely as a flower;
I sometimes last from year to year
And sometimes but an hour.

5   I stop the <u>swiftest</u> railroad train
Or break the stoutest tree.
And yet I am afraid of fire
And children play with me.

(Snow)

Guide for Responding

◆ LITERATURE AND YOUR LIFE

Reader's Response Which of the poems in this group would you like to share with someone else? Why?

Thematic Focus Which poem created the most curious picture in your mind?

☑ Check Your Comprehension

1. Briefly summarize the action in "The Kitten at Play" and "Child on Top of a Greenhouse."
2. What is the shark's "one dark thought"?
3. What is the answer to each riddle?

◆ Critical Thinking

INTERPRET

1. What images does the poet use to contrast life and death in "Kitten at Play"? **[Analyze]**
2. In "The Shark," why is the shark's one dark thought never satisfied? **[Infer]**
3. In "…Greenhouse," why is everyone pointing and shouting? **[Draw Conclusions]**
4. Explain the first riddle's metaphor. **[Interpret]**

COMPARE LITERARY WORKS

5. Which poem presents the most unforgettable picture? Explain. **[Compare and Contrast]**

◆ Guide for Responding (continued)

◆ Reading Strategy

PARAPHRASE

You understood confusing passages in these poems by **paraphrasing** them, restating them in your own words. A paraphrase can't capture the music of a poem. However, it can give you a better sense of its meaning.

1. Paraphrase lines 13–16 of "The Kitten at Play."
2. Paraphrase lines 3–4 of "The Shark." Find your own words for expressions like "speaks well of."
3. Retell Serraillier's riddle in your own words.

◆ Build Vocabulary

USING THE WORD ENDING -est

Use the word ending -est ("the most of something") in a sentence with each of these adjectives:

1. swift   2. stout   3. sweet   4. calm   5. smart

SPELLING STRATEGY

Sometimes the *ay* sound is spelled *ey*, as in *prey*. On your paper, complete the word that fits each definition. Be sure the word has the *ey* spelling of the *ay* sound.

1. A word you might yell to get someone's attention: ___?___ ey
2. What you do when you follow orders: ___?___ ey

USING THE WORD BANK

On your paper, choose the word from the Word Bank that best answers each question.

1. Which adjective usually suggests that something is old?
2. Which noun refers to anything that is hunted?
3. Which adjective describes something with the greatest speed?
4. Which verb describes a greedy way of eating?
5. Which noun refers to remarkable deeds?

◆ Literary Focus

POETIC IMAGE AND RIDDLE POEMS

These poems have many **images,** descriptions that appeal to one or more senses. As you read lines 1–2 of "Child on Top of a Greenhouse," you see and feel the wind "billowing" the child's pants. You also hear the "crackling" of glass.

Serraillier's image of a motorcycle includes sounds and sights.

1. Find three images in these poems that appeal to a different one of these senses—sight, touch, hearing.
2. Do the images in the riddles hide something as well as reveal it? Explain.

◆ Build Grammar Skills

CORRECT USE OF *good* AND *well*

Good is an adjective, which modifies a noun. *Well* is most often an adverb that modifies a verb and answers the question *how*. In "The Shark," Ciardi writes, "He's quiet—that speaks *well* of him." Here, the adverb *well* modifies the verb *speaks*. *Good* would be incorrect because it is an adjective and can't modify a verb.

Practice On your paper, choose *good* or *well* to complete each sentence correctly. Then, underline the word it modifies.

1. How (good, well) that little cat plays!
2. Would a (good, well) boy climb to the top of a greenhouse?
3. For the shark, swimming (well, good) is the key to eating.
4. In her riddle, Austin describes the snow (good, well).
5. I am (well, good) at solving riddles.

Writing Application As an aquarium manager, write a job advertisement for a shark. Correctly use the words *good* and *well*.

Build Your Portfolio

 ## Idea Bank

Writing

1. **Advertising Image** Describe a kitten to be used on a poster that encourages people to adopt a pet from an animal shelter.

2. **Poetry Postcard** Write a postcard to one of these poets. Tell the poet what you liked or disliked about an image in his or her poem.

3. **Newspaper Story** Write a newspaper story to explain "Child on Top of a Greenhouse." Readers will want to know when and where this occurred, who the child was, how he or she climbed the greenhouse, whether the child was hurt, and what finally happened.

Speaking and Listening

4. **Retelling** Review "The Shark." Then, using your own words, retell it as a scary story. Pretend you are speaking to an audience of younger children, and remember to include the warning at the end. **[Performing Arts Link]**

5. **Poetry Slam [Group Activity]** With several classmates, stage a poetry-reading contest, called a slam. See who can read "Child on Top of a Greenhouse" and "The Shark" with the most drama. The rest of the class can serve as judges. **[Performing Arts Link]**

Projects

6. **Cover Art** Use an image from one of these poems to draw or paint a picture for the cover of a book of poetry. **[Art Link]**

7. **Report on the Greenhouse Effect** Read about the greenhouse effect in a science magazine or an encyclopedia. Then, give an oral report on it to the class. Use diagrams to explain how the whole Earth can resemble a greenhouse. **[Science Link]**

 ## Writing Mini-Lesson

Riddle

Imitate Ian Serraillier and Mary Austin by writing your own riddle. You can do this by describing something familiar in a different and surprising way.

Writing Skills Focus: Identify Main Qualities

Include the main qualities of the item you're describing, even if you disguise them slightly. Notice, for example, how lines 7–8 of Austin's riddle refer to two important qualities of snow: It melts in fire, and it can make snowballs and snowmen.

Model From the Poem
And yet I am afraid of fire
And children play with me.

Prewriting Choose an object, a person, a structure, or even a type of weather. Then, list the main qualities of the item that you will disguise slightly in your description.

Drafting Here are two ways of disguising the item's qualities:

• Talk about the item as if it were something else: Describe raindrops as if they were a crowd of people.

• Describe the item's opposite qualities: Rain blankets whole cities but can be captured in a cup.

Revising Have classmates guess the answer to your riddle. If they guess it too easily, disguise your item's qualities. If they can't guess it, include more of your item's main qualities.

> ◆ **Grammar Application**
> Be sure that you haven't incorrectly used the adjective *good* to modify a verb.

You hear poetry every day. Poetry is rocking the kid's radio on the corner. Poetry is even in your house—on your television set. You might say, "That's not poetry, it's music!" Popular music, though, uses **lyrics,** words set to music. Like poems, song lyrics rhyme and follow a beat. Like poems, song lyrics use words in powerful ways to spark thought and emotion.

Write your own song lyrics. (You may write them to fit a tune you know.) Your lyrics should stick to a pattern of rhyme and rhythm. Use the following tips introduced in this section's Writing Mini-Lessons.

Writing Skills Focus

▶ **Use rhyme.** Rhyme occurs when words chime. Rhyming words usually fall at the end of lines. Use a pattern of end rhymes, such as rhyming every other line. (See p. 741.)

▶ **Use similes and metaphors.** A simile compares two unlike things using *like* or *as.* A metaphor compares unlike things without using *like* or *as.* By comparing unlike things, similes and metaphors highlight the quality that is shared by the two things being compared. These figures of speech can vividly describe a person, place, or thing. (See p. 749.)

▶ **Identify main qualities.** Capture the most important qualities of your subject in vivid descriptions. (See p. 761.)

Notice how the writer uses these skills in this model:

MODEL FROM LITERATURE

from "You've Got a Friend" by Carole King

When you're down and troubled,
And you need some love and care, ①
And nothin', nothin' is going right
Close your eyes and think of me
② And soon I will be there
③ To brighten up even your darkest night.

① The writer rhymes *care* with *there* three lines later, and *right* with *night,* to create a pattern of end rhymes.

② The writer identifies a main quality of a friend: to be there during difficult times.

③ This metaphor compares a friend's company to a bright light, and a bad mood to a dark night.

Prewriting

Choose a Topic Love, birthdays, hurt feelings, superheroes, world peace, and many other subjects have been the topic of popular songs. Choose a topic from among the things about which you care or which you find funny.

> ### Topic Ideas
> - Something or someone you love
> - A funny nonsense phrase
> - A happy occasion

Identify Your Subject's Main Qualities Using a diagram like the one below, jot down ideas and feelings that your topic brings to mind. Review these notes. Then, identify those qualities and feelings that are most important.

Main Qualities Diagram

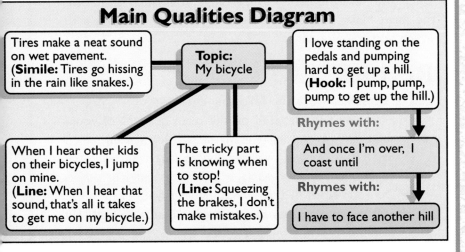

Tires make a neat sound on wet pavement. (**Simile:** Tires go hissing in the rain like snakes.)

Topic: My bicycle

I love standing on the pedals and pumping hard to get up a hill. (**Hook:** I pump, pump, pump to get up the hill.)

When I hear other kids on their bicycles, I jump on mine. (**Line:** When I hear that sound, that's all it takes to get me on my bicycle.)

The tricky part is knowing when to stop! (**Line:** Squeezing the brakes, I don't make mistakes.)

Rhymes with: And once I'm over, I coast until

Rhymes with: I have to face another hill

Find a "Hook" In most song lyrics, certain ideas, lines, phrases, or words are repeated throughout. Look over your Main Qualities Diagram. Then, come up with lines, phrases, or words that express these qualities. Make the lines and phrases catchy, so that they will sound good if repeated. (See also the next section, "Use Similes and Metaphors.")

Use Similes and Metaphors Review your Main Qualities Diagram to create similes and metaphors that describe your subject. A simile is a comparison of unlike things using *like* or *as*. "Talking to you is like hugging a porcupine" is a simile. "Your eyes flash with fireworks" is a metaphor. If your figure of speech is catchy, use it as a "hook."

Choose a Tune Choose a tune to which to set your lyrics. Using an existing tune will help you structure your words.

Applying Language Skills: Spelling Plurals

To form the plural of most words, simply add *-s*. With some words, however, you must follow other rules to form the plural:

Words ending in *-s*, *-ss*, *-x*, *-sh*, or *-ch*: add *-es*

lunches   boxes
dresses   wishes
buses

Words ending in *-y* or preceded by a consonant: change the *y* to *i* and add *-es*

daisies   ponies

Words ending in *-o* preceded by a consonant: usually add *-es*

tomatoes   heroes

Practice Write the plurals of the following nouns. Explain which rule each plural follows.

1. tax   **5.** pastry
2. bakery   **6.** patch
3. dish   **7.** silo
4. potato   **8.** pass

Writing Application Check your draft to make sure you have spelled plurals correctly.

> ### Writer's Solution Connection
> ### Language Lab
> For more help with spelling plurals, complete the Plural Nouns lesson in the Using Nouns unit.

APPLYING LANGUAGE SKILLS: Figurative Language

Figurative language includes the use of similes, metaphors, and personification. It creates new ways of looking at things.

Simile Comparison of unlike things using *like* or *as*.

He eats like a bear.

Metaphor Comparison of unlike things without using *like* or *as*.

My day has been a rollercoaster ride.

Personification Giving human characteristics to an animal, thing, or idea.

The slice of pie across the table leaned over, smiled, and said, "C'mon, take a bite."

Practice Describe each item using figurative language.

1. Good food
2. An annoying laugh
3. A kitten playing

Writing Application Spice up your draft by using figurative language.

Writer's Solution Connection
Writing Lab

For help writing your lyrics, complete the interactive instructions on sound devices in the Creative Writing tutorial.

Drafting

Catch the Beat! Sing or listen to the tune you are using as your model. Snap your fingers to the beat. Once you have the song's patterns in your mind, draft lines for the song. Refer to your Main Qualities Diagram for ideas.

Use Rhymes Write a few lines with rhyming words at the end. Once you have a few rhyming lines, you are ready to think about the structure of the song.

Establish a Form When you have a few rhyming lines, hooks, and other ideas, decide on the form of your song. For instance, each verse might be four lines long, with rhymes at the end of lines two and four. Alternatively, you can rhyme the first two lines, then the next two. The chorus (a section that is repeated at a number of points in the song) might be made up of one of your hooks, repeated four times in a row. Once you have the basic form, arrange your ideas to match the form. Make sure the form you choose fits the tune with which you are working.

Revising

Use a Checklist Use the following checklist:
▶ Have you concentrated on the main qualities of your subject? *Take out uninteresting details. Add similes, metaphors, or other vivid descriptions that show what's most important, or most loveable, or funniest about your subject.*
▶ Do your lyrics fit the tune? *Sing your lyrics along with your model song. They do not have to match perfectly, but they should fit the rhythms of the song.*
▶ Do your lyrics follow a consistent pattern? *Check the rhythm of your lines and the patterns of your rhymes. Make sure that each verse follows the same pattern.*

Publishing and Presenting

Record Record your song on an audio- or videotape. For musical backup, you can accompany yourself on an instrument; ask a musical classmate, friend, or family member to help; or use a karaoke recording of your model song if one is available.

Bulletin Board With classmates, post your song lyrics—along with appropriate photographs, drawings, and other illustrations—on a class bulletin board.

Real-World Reading Skills Workshop

Strategies for Success

The world is full of symbols and icons—visual images that stand for something. In order to understand what you read in literature or see in the media, it is important to recognize symbols and icons. The following strategies will help you:

Analyze Your First Impression The qualities of what is represented are usually captured in the symbol. Often, your first impression of an image conveys the qualities it is meant to represent. For example, when you see an outstretched hand in an advertisement, you probably don't need to read the text to know that the hand represents help or support. When you stop to think about your first impression, it usually leads you in the right direction.

Look for the Hidden Messages Often, a symbol is used because people associate it with certain feelings. When a writer wants to create these feelings in a reader, the writer may use that image. For example, a picture of a fireplace might give a feeling of warmth and security. Advertisers, especially, use symbols and icons that are meant to convey a particular feeling. For example, an advertment for sports equipment may feature a picture of a cheetah. Even though a cheetah has nothing to do with the sport, it suggests speed. Examine symbols and icons to recognize the hidden messages.

Know the Signs Some of the most common symbols and icons are found on signs. You would probably recognize a red hexagon as a stop sign, even without the word *stop*. Similarly, any symbol with a red circle around it and a diagonal line through it means the action is prohibited.

Apply the Strategies

Read the following advertisement. Then, answer the questions that follow.

SUPER SNEAKERS

Athletic shoes for a new generation!

Life is a race—you need footwear that can help you keep up.

Super Sneakers make you look good and keep you on the move. They're not the same old sneaker. Space Age polymers and special air pockets carry your feet on clouds. A cool design gives them fashion flair.

GET SUPER SNEAKERS—MOVE WITH THE TIMES

1. What is your first impression when you look at the advertisement?

2. (a) What visual symbols and icons do you see? (b) What do they say?

3. What connections do you think the writer wants you to make between text and images?

✔ Here are situations in which recognizing symbols and icons can be helpful:
▶ Navigating a Web page
▶ Interpreting poetry
▶ Evaluting advertisements

Correct Usage

Grammar Review

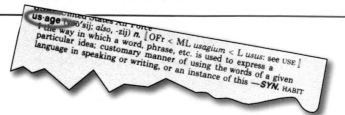

us·age (yoo'sij; *also*, -zij) *n.* [OFr < ML *usagium* < L *usus*: see USE] the way in which a word, phrase, etc. is used to express a particular idea; customary manner of using the words of a given language in speaking or writing, or an instance of this —**SYN.** HABIT

Errors in usage often occur when one word is mistaken for another or when a word is used where it is not needed. Many of these problems can be easily solved by learning rules of correct usage.

▶ Only one negative word is needed to give a sentence a negative meaning. Do not use a double negative.

Incorrect: She *never* told us *nothing*.
Correct: She *never* told us anything.
Other negative words are *barely, hardly, neither, no, nobody, none, no one, not, nowhere,* and *scarcely.*

▶ *Its* is the possessive form of the pronoun *it.* However, *it's* is a contraction of *it is* or *it has.*
Its sound is pleasant.
(possessive—the sound belongs to *It.*)
It's a beautiful tree.
(contraction—*It's* stands for *It is.*)

▶ *Good* is an adjective that modifies a noun. *Well* is most often an adverb that modifies a verb and answers the question *how.*
A *good* poem can make you think.
(The adjective *good* modifies the noun *poem.*)
She plays that sport *well.*
(The adverb *well* modifies the verb *plays.*)

Practice 1 The following sentences contain double negatives. On your paper, underline the negative words and correct the sentences.

1. They didn't want to see none of it.

2. I saw hardly no birds in the sky.

3. There were scarcely no balloons left.

4. Nobody had no homework.

5. Cynthia hardly never gets cold.

Practice 2 On your paper, choose the correct word to complete each sentence.

1. The tree lost (its, it's) leaves.

2. Do you know (its, it's) secret?

3. (Its, It's) a small but powerful animal.

4. I wonder if (its, it's) raining outside.

5. Whatever it is, (its, it's) loud!

Practice 3 On your paper, choose the correct word to complete each sentence, and underline the word it modifies.

1. Greenhouses are (good, well) for gardening.

2. She solves riddles (good, well).

3. A shark would not make a (good, well) pet.

4. It was a (good, well) day for a parade.

5. Donna spoke (good, well).

Grammar in Writing

✔ *It's important to observe correct usage in writing for clarity and to create a good impression.*

✔ *When in doubt about usage, consult a grammar and usage handbook.*

The point of leaving a telephone message is to get information to someone. You will achieve that purpose if you use the following strategies when you must leave a phone message:

Keep It Short When you leave a message, you usually expect the receiver of the message to call you back. For that reason, you don't need to include every detail that you want to discuss with the person. Instead, leave a brief message with only the most important information:

- Your name
- Your phone number
- The purpose of your call
- Any deadline you may have for a return call
- What you want the receiver of the message to do

Here is a good example:

This is Pam. My number is 555-5555. I'm calling to see if Mrs. Lynch still needs me to baby sit on Friday night. Please call me by Wednesday to let me know.

Talk to the Machine Many of the messages you leave will probably be on an answering machine. A machine can't ask you to repeat a name or number that isn't clear, so get it right the first time. Speak clearly and slowly, enunciating every word and number carefully. If you are calling someone who doesn't know you, you may want to spell your name.

Apply the Strategies

Practice the following telephone messages. Then, deliver them to the class.

1. Leave a message on the answering machine of a new neighbor whom you've called to introduce yourself.

2. Leave a message with the assistant of a person you've called to interview for a school project.

3. Leave a message on your best friend's machine, asking if you can get a ride to play practice that night.

Tips for Leaving a Telephone Message

✔ *Follow these strategies when leaving a phone message:*

▶ Speak slowly and clearly.

▶ If you're leaving a message with a person, not a machine, ask the person to read back your phone number to check for accuracy.

What's Behind the Words

Vocabulary Adventures With Richard Lederer

Animal Idioms

Many children's magazines have picture puzzles in which readers are asked to identify a number of hidden animals. In a cloud may lurk a cow, in the leaves of a tree may be concealed a fish, and on the side of a house may be a soaring eagle.

The English language is like those pictures. Take a gander at the expressions in our language, and you will discover a menagerie of creatures hidden in our sentences. (Did you catch one of them in the last sentence?)

Our Beastly Language

Some of our wildlife words and phrases simply transfer a distinctive animal characteristic to human activities, such as *eagle-eyed, antsy, crabby, slothful,* and *pigheaded.* We often compare people to animals by using the conjunction *as—busy as a bee (or beaver), dead as a dodo, healthy as a horse, hungry as a bear, nervous as a kitten, quiet as a mouse, sick as a dog, slippery as an eel, sly as a fox,* and *strong as an ox (or bull).*

Horsing Around With English

Other beastly expressions are not so obvious. For example, high-strung racehorses are sometimes given goats as stable mates to calm them, and the two animals can become inseparable friends. Certain gamblers have been known to steal the goat that is the friend of a particular horse in order to make that horse run poorly the next day. That's why, when someone upsets you, he or she *gets your goat.*

English Is for the Birds

English is not just a beastly language. In our vocabulary, words of a feather flock together. Some of us are *larks* because we like to get up early in the morning; others are owls who stay up late. On Wall Street, *bulls* and *bears* compete to make money. In Congress, *hawks* and *doves* fight like cats and dogs about matters of going to war.

ACTIVITY 1 Complete each common expression with the name of an animal. Explain whether the comparison is appropriate.

1. blind as a ____?____
2. free as a ____?____
3. gentle as a ____?____
4. happy as a ____?____
5. proud as a ____?____
6. stubborn as a ____?____
7. wise as an ____?____

ACTIVITY 2 Another kind of zoological English is the transferring of animal nouns into common verbs without any basic change of form. For example, to take more than you deserve is to *hog* it. To imitate someone is to *ape* or *parrot* that person. To get out of a task or difficult situation is to *worm* or *weasel* your way out. With your classmates, identify at least three more animal verbs.

Extended Reading Opportunities

Poetry can make you laugh or make you think; it can help you see new places, meet new people, and consider new ideas. The collections presented here give you a variety of types of poetry to read.

Suggested Titles

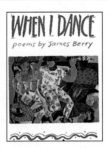

A Light in the Attic
Shel Silverstein

Highly imaginative and funny, these poems are entertaining for both children and adults. Limericks, ballads, ridiculous situations, and a clever way with words are only some the tricks Shel Silverstein uses to amuse his audience. Spend a few rainy afternoons and read about the Dragon of Grindly Grun, Thumb Face, the Homework Machine, and many other entertaining characters.

Appreciating Poetry
Prentice Hall

A gathering of poets from the past and present will help you discover the many adventures to be found in poetry. Poems from Gary Soto, Langston Hughes, and Emily Dickinson will illustrate the variety of techniques poets use to turn ordinary words into poetry. Whether you like humorous poetry, thought-provoking poetry, or beautifully descriptive poetry, you're sure to find something you like in this collection.

When I Dance
James Berry

Fifty-nine poems form a musical link between inner-city and rural life. Images of urban back streets, open-air markets, bright sunshine, and strong personal bonds merge the realities of the city and the country into one. Common experiences ranging from sorrow and loneliness to friendship and joy will touch people of all nationalities and experiences.

Other Possibilities

Best Loved Poems to Read Again and Again — Mary Sanford Laurence, Editor

The Place My Words Are Looking For — Paul B. Janeczko

Poetry in Motion — Molly Peacock, Editor

A Time to Talk — Myra Cohn Livingston, Editor

The Story of the War Robe, Joseph H. Sharp, 0137.321, ©Gilcrease Museum, Tulsa, Oklahoma

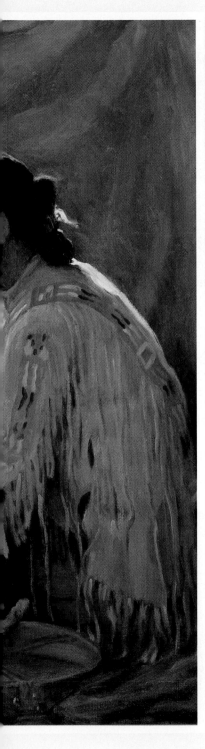

The Oral Tradition

Long before there were books, there were stories—stories that were passed along from one generation to the next by being told aloud. The passing along of stories in this way is called the oral tradition. The oral tradition includes the following types of stories:

- **Folk Tales** are stories told by and about ordinary people. These tales communicate the shared ideas of a culture.

- **Myths** are stories of gods, goddesses, and heroes. Myths often explain things in nature or teach lessons about how to behave.

- **Fables** are stories that usually feature animals that speak and act like humans. A fable usually has a moral, a lesson about how to live.

The myths and folk tales in this unit have been written down after being retold for many generations. They provide a sampling of literature from oral traditions around the world.

Guide for Reading

Meet the Author:
Hans Christian Andersen
(1805–1875)

Although Hans Christian Andersen is most famous as a writer of children's fairy tales, his stories often have a message for adults as well. "The Emperor's New Clothes" teaches a lesson for people of all ages. In addition to his famous fairy tales, Andersen wrote plays, novels, and accounts of his travels.

Many Places, Many Friends Andersen traveled widely and was acquainted with other famous writers and artists of his time, including the composer Franz Liszt, Swedish singer Jenny Lind, and the writers Victor Hugo and Charles Dickens.

THE STORY BEHIND THE STORY

The story of Andersen's own life sounds like one of his fairy tales. Andersen, born in Odense, Denmark, was the son of a poor shoemaker. His father died when Hans was eleven years old. At the age of fourteen, the boy left his hometown to seek his fortune as a performer. He struggled through hard times, but then made the acquaintance of Jonas Collin. Collin arranged a scholarship for Andersen, which permitted him to continue his education. Andersen later became a well-known and popular writer. By the age of thirty, the poor shoemaker's son had achieved fame and fortune.

◆ LITERATURE AND YOUR LIFE
CONNECT YOUR EXPERIENCE

Somtimes it's hard to hold on to your own opinion. You see a pair of jeans in a store window that you really like, but when your friend says they're goofy looking, you decide not to buy them. In "The Emperor's New Clothes," Andersen shows that although it's human nature to worry about the opinions of others, it's more important to make up your own mind.

THEMATIC FOCUS: A Different View

As you read, ask yourself why each character is willing to pretend to see something that isn't there.

◆ Background for Understanding
SOCIAL STUDIES

Most of the characters in this story are part of a royal court. The head of a royal court is the ruler—an emperor, king, queen, or regent. The court consists of the ruler's family, advisors, ministers, statesmen, and attendants. Each position within the court has a particular rank or importance, and many of the positions, especially of the advisors and ministers, are appointed by the ruler. To displease or insult the ruler could result in the loss of the position.

The Emperor's New Clothes

Drawing by Henry J. Ford for "The Emperor's New Clothes" by Hans Christian Andersen

◆ Literary Focus

CHARACTERS IN FOLK LITERATURE

You will notice as you read "The Emperor's New Clothes" that the characters don't have a great deal of individuality. **Characters in folk literature** usually represent qualities rather than real people. Readers are meant to focus more on the results of characters' actions (and usually to learn from them) than on the characters themselves. Make a crown like the one shown below. In each section, write the quality that each character in "The Emperor's New Clothes" represents.

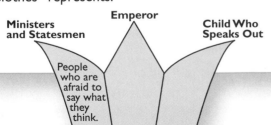

Ministers and Statesmen / **Emperor** / **Child Who Speaks Out**

People who are afraid to say what they think.

◆ Build Vocabulary

SUFFIXES: *-ful*

In "The Emperor's New Clothes," something dreadful happens to the emperor. The suffix *-ful* indicates that something is "full of" or "characterized by" the word to which the suffix is attached. A *dreadful* event, for example, is characterized by dread, or extreme fear.

WORD BANK

For which of these words do you know at least one meaning?

exquisite
property
dreadful
rogues
becoming

Reading for Success

Strategies for Reading Folk Literature

You've probably enjoyed fairy tales since you were a small child. The fairy tales you know connect you to others who know those same stories. Folk literature includes all the stories shared and passed along by people of a country or culture. Folk literature can take the form of a myth, a legend, a fairy tale, a folk tale, or a tall tale. The following strategies will help you understand and appreciate the different types of folk literature you will read in this unit:

Understand the cultural background.

Since folk literature is the literature of the people, it often incorporates cultural elements that are important to and commonly understood by the people who tell the story. For example, in Denmark, where the government is a monarchy (ruled by a single royal ruler), the people are familiar with the ways of the royal courts. They know that displeasing the ruler could have serious consequences. They also know that not all monarchs are wise.

Recognize the storyteller's purpose.

As you read folk literature, look for the reason the writer or storyteller is sharing the story. The chart below shows some common purposes for folk literature:

Purpose	Explain	Teach	Entertain
Type of Folk Literature	• Myths • Folk Tales • Legends	• Myths • Folk Tales • Fairy Tales	• Tall Tales • Folk Tales • Fairy Tales • Legends

Predict.

Make predictions while you read. Folk literature has a predictable pattern: Good deeds are usually rewarded, and foolish or selfish actions usually create problems. When a character does something good or selfish, you can easily predict what might happen to that character.

As you read "The Emperor's New Clothes," look at the notes in the boxes. The notes show how to apply these strategies to your reading.

The Emperor's New Clothes

Danish Tale

Hans Christian Andersen

Many years ago there was an emperor who was so fond of new clothes that he spent all his money on them. He did not give himself any concern about his army; he cared nothing about the theater or for driving about in the woods, except for the sake of showing himself off in new clothes. He had a costume for every hour in the day, and just as they say of a king or emperor, "He is in his council chamber," they said of him, "The emperor is in his dressing room."

> These details help you **understand the culture** from which this folk tale comes.

Life was merry and gay in the town where the emperor lived, and numbers of strangers came to it every day. Among them there came one day two rascals, who gave themselves out as weavers and said that they knew how to weave the most <u>exquisite</u> stuff imaginable. Not only were the colors and patterns uncommonly beautiful, but the clothes that were made of the stuff had the peculiar <u>property</u> of becoming invisible to every person who was unfit for the office he held or who was exceptionally stupid.

"Those must be valuable clothes," thought the emperor. "By wearing them I should be able to discover which of the men in my empire are not fit for their posts. I should distinguish wise men from fools. Yes, I must order some of the stuff to be woven for me directly." And he paid the swindlers a handsome sum of money in advance, as they required.

As for them, they put up two looms and pretended to be weaving, though there was nothing whatever on their shuttles. They called for a quantity of the finest silks and of the purest gold thread, all of which went into their own bags, while they worked at their empty looms till late into the night.

"I should like to know how those weavers are getting on with the stuff," thought the emperor. But he felt a little queer when he reflected that those who were stupid or unfit

◆ Build Vocabulary

exquisite (eks kwi′ zit) *adj.*: Very beautiful or lovely

property (präp′ ər tē) *n.*: Trait; characteristic

for their office would not be able to see the material. He believed, indeed, that he had nothing to fear for himself, but still he thought it better to send someone else first, to see how the work was coming on. All the people in the town had heard of the peculiar property of the stuff, and everyone was curious to see how stupid his neighbor might be.

"I will send my faithful old prime minister to the weavers," thought the emperor. "He will be best capable of judging this stuff, for he is a man of sense and nobody is more fit for his office than he."

So the worthy old minister went into the room where the two swindlers sat working the empty looms. "Heaven save us!" thought the old man, opening his eyes wide. "Why, I can't see anything at all!" But he took care not to say so aloud.

Both the rogues begged him to step a little nearer and asked him if he did not think the patterns very pretty and the coloring fine. They pointed to the empty loom as they did so, and the poor old minister kept staring as hard as he could — without being able to see anything on it, for of course there was nothing there to see.

"Heaven save us!" thought the old man. "Is it possible that I am a fool! I have never thought it, and nobody must know it. Is it true that I am not fit for my office? It will never do for me to say that I cannot see the stuff."

"Well, sir, do you say nothing about the cloth?" asked the one who was pretending to go on with his work.

"Oh, it is most elegant, most beautiful!" said the dazed old man, as he peered again through his spectacles. "What a fine pattern, and what fine colors! I will certainly tell the emperor how pleased I am with the stuff."

"We are glad of that," said both the weavers; and then they named the colors and pointed out the special features of the pattern. To all of this the minister paid great attention, so that he might be able to repeat it to the emperor when he went back to him.

And now the cheats called for more money, more silk, and more gold thread, to be able to proceed with the weaving, but they put it all into their own pockets, and not a thread went into the stuff, though they went on as before, weaving the empty looms.

After a little time the emperor sent another honest statesman to see how the weaving was progressing, and if the stuff would soon be ready. The same thing happened with him as with the minister. He gazed and gazed, but as there was nothing but empty looms, he could see nothing else.

"Is not this an exquisite piece of stuff?" asked the weavers, pointing to one of the looms and explaining the beautiful pattern and the colors which were not there to be seen.

"I am not stupid. I know I am not!" thought the man, "so it must be that I am not fit for my good office. It is very strange, but I must not let it be noticed." So he praised the cloth he did not see and assured the weavers of his delight in the lovely colors and the exquisite pattern. "It is perfectly charming," he reported to the emperor.

Everybody in the town was talking of the splendid cloth. The emperor thought he should like to see it himself while it was still on the loom. With a company of carefully selected men, among whom were the two worthy officials who had been there before, he went to visit the crafty impostors, who were working as hard as ever at the empty looms.

"Is it not magnificent?" said both the honest statesmen. "See, Your Majesty, what splendid colors, and what a pattern!" And they pointed to the looms, for they believed that others, no doubt, could see what they did not.

◆ **Build Vocabulary**

dreadful (dred´ fəl) *adj.*: Very bad; disagreeable
rogues (rōgz) *n.*: Rascals; scoundrels

"What!" thought the emperor. "I see nothing at all. This is terrible! Am I a fool? Am I not fit to be emperor? Why nothing more <u>dreadful</u> could happen to me!"

"Oh, it is very pretty! It has my highest approval," the emperor said aloud. He nodded with satisfaction as he gazed at the empty looms, for he would not betray that he could see nothing.

His whole court gazed and gazed, each seeing no more than the others, but, like the emperor, they all exclaimed, "Oh, it is beautiful!" They even suggested to the emperor that he wear the

◆ Reading Strategy
What do you **predict** will happen during the procession? Why?

splendid new clothes for the first time on the occasion of a great procession which was soon to take place.

"Splendid! Gorgeous! Magnificent!" went from mouth to mouth. All were equally delighted with the weavers' workmanship. The emperor gave each of the impostors an order of knighthood to be worn in their buttonholes, and the title Gentleman Weaver of the Imperial Court.

Before the day on which the procession was to take place, the weavers sat up the whole night, burning sixteen candles, so that people might see how anxious they were to get the emperor's new clothes ready. They pretended to take the stuff from the loom, they cut it out in the air with huge scissors, and they stitched away with needles that had no thread in them. At last they said, "Now the clothes are finished."

The emperor came to them himself with his grandest courtiers, and each of the <u>rogues</u>

Illustration by Arthur Rackham for "The Emperor's New Clothes" by Hans Christian Andersen

▲ **Critical Viewing** What details in the picture indicate that the story takes place in the past? **[Analyze]**

lifted his arm as if he held something, saying, "See! Here are the trousers! Here is the coat! Here is the cloak," and so on. "It is as light as a spider's web. One would almost feel as if one had nothing on, but that is the beauty of it!"

"Yes," said all the courtiers, but they saw nothing, for there was nothing to see.

"Will Your Majesty be graciously pleased to take off your clothes so that we may put on the new clothes here, before the great mirror?"

The emperor took off his clothes, and the

rogues pretended to put on first one garment and then another of the new ones they had pretended to make. They pretended to fasten something round his waist and to tie on something. This they said was the train, and the emperor turned around and around before the mirror.

"How well his Majesty looks in the new clothes! How becoming they are!" cried all the courtiers in turn. "That is a splendid costume!"

"The canopy that is to be carried over Your Majesty in the procession is waiting outside," said the master of ceremonies.

"Well, I am ready," replied the emperor. "Don't the clothes look well?" and he turned around and around again before the mirror, to appear as if he were admiring his new costume.

The chamberlains, who were to carry the train, stooped and put their hands near the floor as if they were lifting it. Then they pretended to be holding something in the air. They would not let it be noticed that they could see and feel nothing.

So the emperor went along in the procession, under the splendid canopy, and everyone in the streets said: "How beautiful the emperor's new clothes are! What a splendid train! And how well they fit!"

No one wanted to let it appear that he could see nothing, for that would prove him not fit for his post. None of the emperor's clothes had been so great a success before.

"But he has nothing on!" said a little child.

"Just listen to the innocent," said its father. And one person whispered to another what the child had said. "He has nothing on. A child says he has nothing on!"

"But he has nothing on," cried all the people. The emperor was startled by this, for he had a suspicion that they were right. But he thought, "I must face this out to the end and go on with the procession." So he held himself more stiffly than ever, and the chamberlains held up the train that was not there at all.

◆ **Build Vocabulary**

becoming (bē kum´ in) *adj.*: Suitable to the wearer

Guide for Responding

◆ LITERATURE AND YOUR LIFE

Reader's Response What would you have said to the emperor if you were sent to check the cloth?

Thematic Focus In what ways do you think the opinions of others shape your view of events or circumstances?

Journal Writing Why is it sometimes difficult to express a different view?

☑ Check Your Comprehension

1. What do the weavers promise?
2. What do the weavers actually do?
3. How is the truth finally revealed?

◆ Critical Thinking

INTERPRET

1. For what purpose do the weavers say that people who are stupid or unfit for their office can't see the cloth? **[Infer]**
2. Why is the child unafraid to reveal the truth? **[Draw Conclusions]**

APPLY

3. Why is it important to form your own opinions rather than be influenced by the opinions of others? **[Apply]**

EVALUATE

4. Should a person be truthful if it might hurt someone's feelings? **[Make a Judgment]**

Guide for Responding (continued)

◆ Reading for Success

STRATEGIES FOR READING FOLK LITERATURE

Review the reading strategies and the notes showing how to read folk literature. Then, apply the strategies to answer the following questions:

1. What do you think is Andersen's purpose in telling this story?
2. What details in this story indicate that it takes place in a country or culture different from your own?
3. Explain how a reader could probably predict that someone would finally speak out about the emperor's "new clothes."

◆ Build Vocabulary

USING THE SUFFIX -ful

On your paper, match the word that ends with the suffix -ful with the person, place, or thing it best decribes:

1. dreadful   **a.** a tightrope walker
2. careful   **b.** a happy person
3. cheerful   **c.** a terrible storm

SPELLING STRATEGY

In the word exquisite, the z sound is spelled with an s. On your paper, write a word that contains the z sound for each numbered clue. Use an s to spell the z sound.

1. Want: de_ _ _ _
2. Make changes: rev_ _ _
3. Give advice: a _ _ _ _ _

USING THE WORD BANK

On your paper, write the word or phrase that is most similar in meaning to the Word Bank word:

1. exquisite: (a) expensive, (b) large, (c) beautiful
2. property: (a) quality, (b) person, (c) color
3. dreadful: (a) horrible, (b) irritated, (c) sleeping
4. becoming: (a) waiting, (b) arrival, (c) attractive
5. rogues: (a) villains, (b) rascals, (c) heroes

◆ Literary Focus

CHARACTERS IN FOLK LITERATURE

Characters in folk literature represent qualities of people. For example, the weavers represent dishonesty in people.

1. What quality does the emperor represent?
2. What quality do the ministers and statesmen represent?
3. What quality does the child represent?

◆ Build Grammar Skills

COMMAS IN COMPOUND SENTENCES

One major use of a **comma** is to separate two simple sentences that are joined in a compound sentence. The two parts of a **compound sentence** are usually joined by a coordinating conjunction, such as but, and, for, or, so, or yet. The following example shows how a compound sentence is punctuated:

> I have never thought it, and nobody must know it.

Practice Copy the following sentences in your notebook, putting commas where needed:

1. They pointed to the looms and the king smiled.
2. It is very strange but I must not let it be noticed.
3. The courtiers all agreed for they were foolish.
4. The child saw no clothes so he spoke his mind.
5. The emperor stopped yet he didn't turn.

Writing Application On your paper, combine a sentence from Column A with a sentence from Column B. Use a comma and a coordinating conjunction between the two simple sentences. The coordinating conjunction you use will depend on which two sentences you combine.

Column A	Column B
1. The emperor stared.	**a.** He saw nothing.
2. The child spoke.	**b.** Everyone was silent.
3. The weavers worked.	**c.** The people were amazed.

Build Your Portfolio

 ## Idea Bank

Writing

1. **Advertisement** Write an advertisement for the "cloth" the weavers make. Describe the qualities the weavers claim the cloth has.

2. **Proclamation** As the emperor, write a proclamation explaining why you pretended to see the cloth that was not there. Explain to the people of the kingdom what you have learned from your experience.

3. **Weaver's Defense** Write a short speech explaining why the emperor and his ministers share responsibility for what happened to the emperor.

Speaking and Listening

4. **Skit [Group Activity]** With a group of classmates, perform "The Emperor's New Clothes" as a skit—a short play that uses few costumes and little or no scenery. If possible, make a video recording of your skit. **[Performing Arts Link]**

5. **Procession Music** Choose music for the emperor's procession. Then, choose the part of the music that sounds like a place where the child might announce that the emperor is not wearing any clothes. Play the music for the class and explain why you chose it. **[Music Link]**

Projects

6. **Weaving** Make a simple loom with cardboard, or use a store-bought loom and weave yarn, fabric strips, or string on it. Make a simple pattern using different colors. If you cannot make or use a loom, weave a pattern from strips of construction paper. **[Art Link]**

7. **Hans Christian Andersen Posters** Make posters illustrating some of Andersen's famous fairy tales. Display your posters in class. **[Art Link]**

 ## Writing Mini-Lesson

Description of Clothing

If the weavers wanted to sell you clothing, they would describe the clothes that most appeal to you. Think about the colors, features, and styles of clothing that you like. Choose one item, and describe it.

Writing Skills Focus: Use Vivid Adjectives

To show the beauty, comfort, or usefulness of the clothing you describe, be specific. Use **vivid adjectives** that tell exactly how the fabric feels or the precise shade of a color. For example, don't just say a sweater is comfortable; tell in what way it is comfortable:

> The sweater is soft and cozy.

Prewriting Use an organizer like the one below to brainstorm for the specific features of your subject and the vivid adjectives that will describe it.

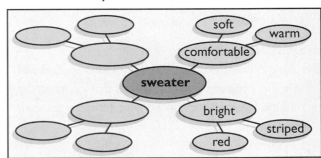

Drafting Use complete sentences to describe the details you want to include. Group related details in the same paragraph.

Revising Ask a partner to read your description and answer the following questions. Does the description help you form a mental picture of the clothing? What other information would you like to know?

◆ **Grammar Application**
Use some compound sentences in your description. Punctuate these sentences correctly.

PART **1** *Tales That Amaze and Amuse*

The Owl and the Birds, 1912, Arthur Rackham, Arthur Rackham Collection, Columbia University, New York, NY

Guide for Reading

Meet the Authors:

Leo Tolstoy (1828–1910)

Leo Tolstoy was born to live a life of luxury. His family was wealthy, and he inherited the family estate at the age of nineteen. After attending law school and serving in the army, Tolstoy turned to writing. His novels *War and Peace* and *Anna Karenina* are among the most famous literary works in the world.

Tolstoy married when he was thirty-four. Then, when he was about fifty, he began to question his lifestyle. He became a vegetarian, surrendered the rights to many of his published works, gave his property to his family, and moved off the estate. This world-famous writer died alone in an obscure train station in Russia.

Virginia Hamilton (1936–   )

Virginia Hamilton comes from Yellow Springs, Ohio, a town famous as a stop on the Underground Railroad before the Civil War. Hamilton was lucky to come from a family of storytellers who passed along tales of their family experience and heritage. Although she focuses her writing mainly on African American subjects and characters, the themes in her books are meaningful to all people.

I.G. Edmonds (1917–   )

I. G. Edmonds is a collector of folk tales. As a soldier in the South Pacific during World War II, Edmonds decided to collect folk tales after he heard a native chief's story about how his island was created. The tales Edmonds collected are published in his book *Trickster Tales*.

◆ LITERATURE AND YOUR LIFE

CONNECT YOUR EXPERIENCE

Cartoons on television often make you laugh at animal characters acting like humans. Like cartoons, the folk tales "He Lion, Bruh Bear, and Bruh Rabbit" and "Señor Coyote and the Tricked Trickster" use animal characters that seem like people. These folk tales, however, are not only humorous; they're instructive as well.

THEMATIC FOCUS: Our Living World

As you read, ask yourself how these animal characters fit into the worlds in which they live.

◆ Background for Understanding

CULTURE

"Señor Coyote and the Tricked Trickster" is, as the title suggests, a trickster tale. Many cultures contain trickster tales—folk stories about a clever character who outwits other characters through sly thinking and tricky maneuvering. Although the tricksters are usually not people you would want to associate with in real life, their adventures make entertaining stories.

◆ Build Vocabulary

RELATED WORDS: FORMS OF *dignity*

In "Señor Coyote and the Tricked Trickster," Coyote responds *indignantly* to Mouse's accusations. He feels that Mouse's accusations are unfair or not respectful. The word *indignantly* is related to *dignity*, which means "being worthy of respect."

WORD BANK

Which word might describe someone who "starts up" in surprise?

startled
lair
cordial
gnaw
ungrateful
reproachfully
indignantly

The Ant and the Dove
◆ He Lion, Bruh Bear, and Bruh Rabbit ◆
Señor Coyote and the Tricked Trickster

◆ Literary Focus
FOLK TALES

Folk tales are stories shared by a people—the "folk." The tales usually do not originate from a single author. They are passed down from generation to generation. Today, many authors write down folk tales for all to enjoy. Besides entertaining, folk tales may teach a lesson or explain something in nature. Often, different cultures have folk tales that teach a similar lesson. For example, the Russian folk tale "The Ant and the Dove" teaches a lesson about kindness. A similar story can be found in other cultures around the world.

◆ Reading Strategy
RECOGNIZE THE STORYTELLER'S PURPOSE

Like other forms of literature, folk tales have a purpose. You will better understand the tale if you **recognize the purpose.** Many folk tales have a combination of purposes. For example, the purpose of "He Lion ..." is to teach a lesson, but it also intends to entertain while it teaches. For each tale in this group, make a chart like the one below. Jot down details from the tale. Then, note whether the details entertain, teach, or both.

	Detail	Entertains	Teaches
He Lion . . .	Humorous description of animals	X	
	He Lion stops bragging so much		X

The Ant and the Dove

RUSSIAN FOLK TALE

Leo Tolstoy

A thirsty ant went to the stream to drink. Suddenly it got caught in a whirlpool and was almost carried away.

At that moment a dove was passing by with a twig in its beak. The dove dropped the twig for the tiny insect to grab hold of. So it was that the ant was saved.

A few days later a hunter was about to catch the dove in his net. When the ant saw what was happening, it walked right up to the man and bit him on the foot. Startled, the man dropped the net. And the dove, thinking that you never can tell how or when a kindness may be repaid, flew away.

◆ **Build Vocabulary**

startled (stärt´ əld) *adj.*: Surprised

He Lion, Bruh Bear, and Bruh Rabbit

African American Folk Tale

Virginia Hamilton

Say that he Lion would get up each and every mornin. Stretch and walk around. He'd roar, ME AND MYSELF, ME AND MYSELF, like that. Scare all the little animals so they were afraid to come outside in the sunshine. Afraid to go huntin or fishin or whatever the little animals wanted to do.

"What we gone do about it?" they asked one another. Squirrel leapin from branch to branch, just scared. Possum[1] playin dead, couldn't hardly move him.

He Lion just went on, stickin out his chest and roarin, "ME AND MYSELF, ME AND MYSELF."

The little animals held a sit-down talk, and one by one and two by two and all by all, they decide to go see Bruh[2] Bear and Bruh Rabbit.

---

1. Possum (päs´ əm): Colloquial for "opossum," a small tree-dwelling mammal that pretends to be dead when it is trapped.
2. Bruh (bru): Early African American dialect for "brother."

▲ **Critical Viewing** Why do you think a lion might be used to represent someone who has a high opinion of himself or herself? **[Draw Conclusions]**

For they know that Bruh Bear been around. And Bruh Rabbit say he has, too.

So they went to Bruh Bear and Bruh Rabbit. Said, "We have some trouble. Old he Lion, him scarin everybody, roarin every mornin and all day, ME AND MYSELF, ME AND MYSELF, like that.

"Why he Lion want to do that?" Bruh Bear said.

"Is that all he Lion have to say?" Bruh Rabbit asked.

"We don't know why, but that's all he Lion can tell us and we didn't ask him to tell us that," said the little animals. "And him scarin the children with it. And we wish him to stop it."

"Well, I'll go see him, talk to him. I've known he Lion a long kind of time," Bruh Bear said.

"I'll go with you," said Bruh Rabbit. "I've known he Lion most long as you."

That bear and that rabbit went off through the forest. They kept hearin somethin. Mumble, mumble. Couldn't make it out. They got farther in the forest. They heard it plain now. "ME AND MYSELF. ME AND MYSELF."

"Well, well, well," said Bruh Bear. He wasn't scared. He'd been around the whole forest, seen a lot.

"My, my, my," said Bruh Rabbit. He'd seen enough to know not to be afraid of an old he lion. Now old he lions could be dangerous, but you had to know how to handle them.

The bear and the rabbit climbed up and up

the cliff where he Lion had his <u>lair</u>. They found him. Kept their distance. He watchin them and they watchin him. Everybody actin <u>cordial</u>.

"Hear tell you are scarin everybody, all the little animals, with your roarin all the time," Bruh Rabbit said.

"I roars when I pleases," he Lion said.

"Well, might could you leave off the noise first thing in the mornin, so the little animals can get what they want to eat and drink?" asked Bruh Bear.

"Listen," said he Lion, and then he roared: "ME AND MYSELF. ME AND MYSELF. Nobody tell me what not to do," he said. "I'm the king of the forest, *me and myself.*"

"Better had let me tell you something," Bruh Rabbit said, "for I've seen Man, and I know him the real king of the forest."

He Lion was quiet awhile. He looked straight through that scrawny lil Rabbit like he was nothin atall. He looked at Bruh Bear and figured he'd talk to him.

"You, Bear, you been around," he Lion said.

"That's true," said old Bruh Bear. "I been about everywhere. I've been around the whole forest."

"Then you must know something," he Lion said.

"I know lots," said Bruh Bear, slow and quiet-like.

"Tell me what you know about Man," he Lion said. "He think him the king of the forest?"

"Well, now, I'll tell you," said Bruh Bear, "I been around, but I haven't ever come across Man that I know of. Couldn't tell you nothin about him."

◆ Build Vocabulary

lair (lār) *n.*: Cave or den

cordial (kôr′ jəl) *adj.*: Warm and friendly

◀ **Critical Viewing** How well does this bear fit the image of Bruh Bear? [**Assess**]

So he Lion had to turn back to Bruh Rabbit. He didn't want to but he had to. "So what?" he said to that lil scrawny hare.

"Well, you got to come down from there if you want to see Man," Bruh Rabbit said. "Come down from there and I'll show you him."

He Lion thought a minute, an hour, and a whole day. Then, the next day, he came on down.

He roared just once, "ME AND MYSELF. ME AND MYSELF. Now," he said, "come show me Man."

So they set out. He Lion, Bruh Bear, and Bruh Rabbit. They go along and they go along, rangin the forest. Pretty soon, they come to a clearin. And playin in it is a little fellow about nine years old.

"Is that there Man?" asked he Lion.

"Why no, that one is called Will Be, but it sure is not Man," said Bruh Rabbit.

So they went along and they went along. Pretty soon, they come upon a shade tree. And sleepin under it is an old, olden fellow, about ninety years olden.

"There must lie Man," spoke he Lion. "I knew him wasn't gone be much."

"That's not Man," said Bruh Rabbit. "That fellow is Was Once. You'll know it when you see Man."

So they went on along. He Lion is gettin tired of strollin. So he roars, "ME AND MYSELF. ME AND MYSELF." Upsets Bear so that Bear doubles over and runs and climbs a tree.

"Come down from there," Bruh Rabbit tellin him. So after a while Bear comes down. He keepin his distance from he Lion, anyhow. And they set out some more. Goin along quiet and slow.

In a little while they come to a road. And comin on way down the road, Bruh Rabbit sees Man comin. Man about twenty-one years old. Big and strong, with a big gun over his shoulder.

"There!" Bruh Rabbit says. "See there,

▲ **Critical Viewing** In what ways does Bruh Rabbit represent opposite qualities from Bruh Bear's? [Compare and Contrast]

he Lion? There's Man. You better go meet him."

"I will," says he Lion. And he sticks out his chest and he roars, "ME AND MYSELF. ME AND MYSELF." All the way to Man he's roarin proud, "ME AND MYSELF. ME AND MYSELF!"

"Come on, Bruh Bear, let's go!" Bruh Rabbit says.

"What for?" Bruh Bear wants to know.

"You better come on!" And Bruh Rabbit takes ahold of Bruh Bear and half drags him to a thicket. And there he makin the Bear hide with him.

For here comes Man. He sees old he Lion real good now. He drops to one knee and he takes aim with his big gun.

Old he Lion is roarin his head off: "ME AND MYSELF. ME AND MYSELF!"

The big gun goes off: PA-LOOOM!

He Lion falls back hard on his tail.

The gun goes off again. PA-LOOOM!

He Lion is flyin through the air. He lands in the thicket.

"Well, did you see Man?" asked Bruh Bear.

"I seen him," said he Lion. "Man spoken to me unkind, and got a great long stick him keepin on his shoulder. Then Man taken that stick down and him speakin real mean. Thunderin at me and lightnin comin from that stick, awful bad. Made me sick. I had to turn around. And Man pointin that stick again and thunderin at me some more. So I come in here, cause it seem like him throwed some stickers at me each time it thunder, too."

"So you've met Man, and you know zactly what that kind of him is," says Bruh Rabbit.

"I surely do know that," he Lion said back.

Awhile after he Lion met Man, things were some better in the forest. Bruh Bear knew what Man looked like so he could keep out of his way. That rabbit always did know to keep out of Man's way. The little animals could go out in the mornin because he Lion was more peaceable. He didn't walk around roarin at the top of his voice all the time. And when he Lion did lift that voice of his, it was like, "Me and Myself and Man. Me and Myself and Man." Like that.

Wasn't too loud at all.

◆ Reading Strategy
What is the **purpose** of showing that he Lion becomes humble?

Guide for Responding

◆ LITERATURE AND YOUR LIFE

Reader's Response Which character do you think is most amusing? Why?

Thematic Focus What do these characters learn about living with others in the world?

☑ Check Your Comprehension

1. In "The Ant and the Dove," what does the dove do for the ant?
2. How does the ant repay the dove?
3. In "He Lion . . ." why do the little animals seek help from Bruh Bear and Bruh Rabbit?
4. Why does he Lion want to see Man?
5. What happens to he Lion when he sees Man?

◆ Critical Thinking

INTERPRETING

1. Why does the dove help the ant, even when she doesn't think the ant can ever help her? **[Infer]**
2. Why isn't Bruh Rabbit afraid of he Lion? **[Infer]**
3. Describe he Lion before and after he meets Man. **[Compare and Contrast]**

EVALUATE

4. Are human qualities effectively shown in the characters in "He Lion . . ."? Explain. **[Assess]**

APPLY

5. Why do some people feel the need to "roar" about themselves, as he Lion does? **[Relate]**

SEÑOR COYOTE AND THE TRICKED TRICKSTER

MEXICAN FOLK TALE
I. G. Edmonds

One day long ago in Mexico's land of sand and giant cactus *Señor*[1] Coyote and Señor Mouse had a quarrel.

None now alive can remember why, but recalling what spirited *caballeros*[2] these two were, I suspect that it was some small thing that meant little.

Be that as it may, these two took their quarrels seriously and for a long time would not speak to each other.

Then one day Mouse found Señor Coyote caught in a trap. He howled and twisted and fought, but he could not get out. He had just about given up when he saw Señor Mouse grinning at him.

---

1. *Señor* (sen yôr´): Spanish title used like "mister."
2. *caballeros* (kä bä yer´ ôs): Spanish for "gentlemen."

▼ **Critical Viewing** What qualities does folk art share with folk tales? **[Connect]**

Coyotes, detail from hand-painted wood desk, Maureen Mahoney-Barraclough

"Mouse! *Mi viejo amigo*[3]—my old friend!" he cried. "Please gnaw this leather strap in two and get me out of this trap."

"But we are no longer friends," Mouse said. "We have quarreled, remember?"

"Nonsense!" Señor Coyote cried. "Why I love you better than I do Rattlesnake, Owl, or anybody in the desert. You must gnaw me loose. And please hurry for if the *peon*[4] catches me I will wind up a fur rug on his wife's kitchen floor."

Mouse remembered how mean Señor Coyote had been to him. He was always playing tricks on Mouse and his friends. They were very funny to Señor Coyote for he was a great trickster, but often they hurt little Mouse.

"I'd like to gnaw you free," he said, "but I am old and my teeth tire easily."

---

3. **Mi viejo amigo** (mē vē ä′ hō ä mē′ gō)
4. **peon** (pē′ ən): Spanish for "worker"—an unskilled laborer.

"Really, Señor Mouse, you are ungrateful," said Señor Coyote reproachfully. "Remember all the nice things I have done for you."

"What were they?"

"Why—" Coyote began and stopped. He was unable to think of a single thing. There was a good reason for this. He had done nothing for Mouse but trick him.

But Señor Coyote is a sly fellow. He said quickly, "Oh, why remind you of them. You remember them all."

"I fear my memory of yesterday is too dim," Mouse said, "but I could remember very well what you could do for me tomorrow."

"Tomorrow?" Coyote asked.

"Yes, tomorrow. If I gnaw away the leather rope holding you in the trap, what will you do for me tomorrow, and the day after tomorrow and the day after the day after tomorrow and the day—"

"Stop!" Señor Coyote cried. "How long is this going on?"

Mouse and Owl, detail from hand-painted wood desk, Maureen Mahoney-Barraclough

"A life is worth a life. If I save your life, you should work for me for a lifetime. That is the only fair thing to do."

◆ **Literary Focus**
What details in this **folk tale** indicate the culture from which it comes?

"But everyone would laugh at a big, brave, smart fellow like me working as a slave for a mere mouse!" Señor Coyote cried.

"Is that worse than feeling sad for you because your hide is a rug in the peon's kitchen?"

Señor Coyote groaned and cried and argued, but finally agreed when he saw that Mouse would not help him otherwise.

"Very well," he said tearfully, "I agree to work for you until either of us dies or until I have a chance to get even by saving your life."

Mouse said with a sly grin, "That is very fine, but I remember what a great trickster you are. So you must also promise that as soon as I free you that you will not jump on me, threaten to kill me, and then save my life by letting me go!"

"Why, how can you suggest such a thing!" Coyote cried <u>indignantly</u>. And then to himself he added, "This mouse is getting *too* smart!"

"Very well, promise," Mouse said.

"But I am not made for work," Señor Coyote said tearfully. "I live by being sly."

"Then be sly and get out of the trap yourself," Mouse retorted.

◀ **Critical Viewing** What do you think Mouse is telling Owl about Coyote? [Speculate]

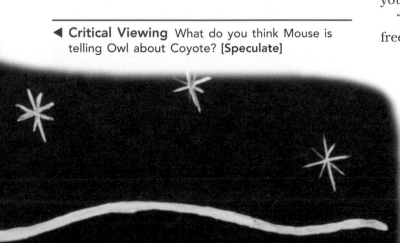

"Very well," Señor Coyote said sadly. "I will work for you until I can pay back the debt of my life."

And so Mouse gnawed the leather strap in two and Coyote was saved. Then for many days thereafter Señor Coyote worked for Mouse. Mouse was very proud to have the famous Señor Coyote for a servant. Señor Coyote was greatly embarrassed since he did not like being a servant and disliked working even more.

There was nothing he could do since he had given his promise. He worked all day and dreamed all night of how he could trick his way out of his troubles. He could think of nothing.

Then one day Baby Mouse came running to him. "My father has been caught by Señor Snake!" he cried. "Please come and save him."

"Hooray!" cried Coyote. "If I save him, I will be released from my promise to work for him."

He went out to the desert rocks and found Señor Rattlesnake with his coils around Señor Mouse.

"Please let him go and I will catch you two more mice," Coyote said.

"My wise old mother used to tell me that a bird in the hand is worth two in the bush," Snake replied. "By the same reasoning, one mouse in Snake's stomach is worth two in Coyote's mind."

"Well, I tried, Mouse," Coyote said. "I'm sorry you must be eaten."

"But you must save me, then you will be free from your promise to me, " Mouse said.

"If you're eaten, I'll be free anyway," Coyote said.

"Then everyone will say that Coyote was not smart enough to trick Snake," Mouse said quickly. "And I think they

◆ **Build Vocabulary**

gnaw (nô) *v.*: To bite and wear away bit by bit with the teeth

ungrateful (un grāt′ fəl) *adj.*: Not thankful

reproachfully (ri prōch′ fəl lē) *adv.*: With blame

indignantly (in dig′ nənt lē) *adv.*: Angrily

will be right. It makes me very sad for I always thought Señor Coyote the greatest trickster in the world."

This made Coyote's face turn red. He was very proud that everyone thought him so clever. Now he just *had* to save Mouse.

So he said to Snake, "How did you catch Mouse anyway?"

"A rock rolled on top of him and he was trapped," Mouse said. "He asked me to help him roll it off. When I did he jumped on me before I could run away."

"That is not true," Snake said. "How could a little mouse have the strength to roll away a big rock. There is the rock. Now you tell me if you think Mouse could roll it."

It was a very big rock and Coyote admitted that Mouse could not possibly have budged it.

"But it is like the story *Mamacita*[5] tells her children at bedtime," Mouse said quickly. "Once there was a poor burro who had a load of hay just as large as he could carry. His master added just one more straw and the poor burro fell in the dirt. Snake did not have quite enough strength to push the rock off himself. I came along and was like that last straw on the burro's back and together we rolled the rock away."

"Maybe that is true," Snake said, "but by Mouse's own words, he did only a very little of the work. So I owe him only a very little thanks. That is not enough to keep me from eating him."

"Hmmm," said Coyote. "Now you understand, Snake, that I do not care what happens myself. If Mouse is eaten, I will be free of my bargain anyway. I am only thinking of your own welfare, Snake."

"Thank you," said Señor Rattlesnake, "but I do enough thinking about my welfare for both of us. I don't need your thoughts."

"Nevertheless," Coyote insisted, "everyone is going to say that you ate Mouse after he was kind enough to help you."

"I don't care," Snake said. "Nobody says anything good of me anyway."

"Well," said Coyote, "I'll tell you what we should do. We should put everything back as it was. Then I will see for myself if Mouse was as much help as he said he was or as little as you claim. Then I can tell everyone that you were right, Snake."

"Very well," said Señor Snake. "I was lying like this and the rock was on me—"

"Like this?" Coyote said, quickly rolling the rock across Snake's body.

"Ouch!" said Snake. "That is right."

"Can you get out?" Coyote asked.

"No," said Snake.

"Then turn Mouse loose and let him push," said Coyote.

This Snake did, but before Mouse could push, Coyote said, "But on second thought if Mouse pushes, you would then grab him again and we'd be back arguing. Since you are both as you were before the argument started, let us leave it at that and all be friends again!"

Then Coyote turned to Mouse. "So, my friend, I have now saved your life. We are now even and my debt to you is paid."

"But mine is such a *little* life," Mouse protested. "And yours is so much *larger*. I don't think they balance. You should still pay me part."

"This is ridiculous!" Coyote cried. "I—"

"Wait!" Snake put in hopefully. "Let me settle the quarrel. Now you roll the rock away. I'll take Mouse in my coils just the way we were when Coyote came up. We'll be then in a position to decide if—"

"Thank you," said Mouse. "It isn't necessary to trouble everyone again. Señor Coyote, we are even."

---

5. *Mamacita* (mä mə sē´ tä): Spanish for "mommy."

Beyond Literature

Media Connection

Tricksters on Television Folk tales aren't the only place you'll meet clever tricksters. In modern times, many television characters use their wits to escape almost any situation. Cartoon characters such as the Road Runner and Bugs Bunny outwit their enemies with a combination of crafty planning and intelligent mischief. Trickster characters appear in situation comedies as well. One such character is Lucy Ricardo on the old "I Love Lucy" show. She uses trickery to get out of trouble in almost every episode.

Cross-Curricular Activity Make a chart or poster showing trickster characters from several different cultures. Include on your poster some modern tricksters from current television programs.

Guide for Responding

◆ LITERATURE AND YOUR LIFE

Reader's Response Which character do you think is most clever? Why?

Thematic Focus What qualities help these characters survive in the world?

Journal Writing Write a paragraph explaining what you think is the lesson of this folk tale.

☑ Check Your Comprehension

1. Why is Mouse reluctant to help the trapped Coyote?
2. Why does Coyote work as Mouse's servant?
3. Summarize the events that lead to Coyote's being freed from being Mouse's servant.

◆ Critical Thinking

INTERPRETING

1. Why is Coyote surprised that Mouse can outwit him? **[Infer]**
2. To which of Coyote's characteristics does Mouse appeal in persuading Coyote to save him from Snake? **[Draw Conclusions]**
3. What common failing do Mouse and Coyote share that makes them easy to trick? **[Compare and Contrast]**

APPLY

4. Trickster tales appear in folk literature all over the world. Why do you think tricksters are such popular characters? **[Generalize]**

EXTEND

5. Explain how prey animals (animals that are hunted) like mice protect themselves in the wild. **[Science Link]**

Guide for Responding (continued)

◆ Reading Strategy

RECOGNIZE THE STORYTELLER'S PURPOSE

Folk tales are told for many reasons. Recognizing the **storyteller's purpose** gives you insight into both the tale and the culture from which it comes.

1. What are two details in "The Ant and the Dove" that indicate that its purpose is to teach?
2. Identify one detail that entertains and one that is meant to teach in "He Lion . . ."
3. Identify three details that indicate that the purpose of "Señor Coyote . . ." is to entertain.

◆ Build Vocabulary

USING FORMS OF *dignity*

Match each form of *dignity* with its definition:

1. dignity   **a.** angrily
2. dignitary   **b.** something that insults one's worth
3. indignity   **c.** a person worthy of respect
4. indignantly   **d.** the quality of being worthy

SPELLING STRATEGY

Sometimes, as in *cordial,* the sound *j* is spelled with *di.* For each clue, write a word that contains the *j* sound spelled with *di.*

1. Someone who serves in the army: s_ _ _ _ er
2. Pleasant and friendly: c _ _ _ _ al

USING THE WORD BANK

On your paper, write the word from the Word Bank that matches each definition.

1. In an insulted way
2. Surprised
3. Cave or den
4. Friendly
5. As if blaming
6. Chew
7. Not thankful

◆ Literary Focus

FOLK TALES

Folk tales are the stories that the people (or "folk") of a country or culture have told from generation to generation. Today, many folk tales have been written down so that people around the world can read and enjoy them.

1. Why do you think several cultures have a folk tale similar to "The Ant and the Dove"?
2. How does Virginia Hamilton preserve the feeling that "He Lion, Bruh Bear, and Bruh Rabbit" is a story being told aloud?
3. What details from Mexican culture do you find in "Señor Coyote and the Tricked Trickster"?

◆ Build Grammar Skills

COMMAS IN A SERIES

Sometimes a sentence lists a number of items. When three or more items are listed, the list is called a **series.** The items in the series are separated by **commas.** The items in a series may be single words or groups of words. Notice the commas after the items in the series in this sentence:

Why do I love you better than I do Rattlesnake, Owl, or anybody in the desert?

Practice On your paper, copy each sentence. Insert commas where needed to separate items in a series.

1. He Lion thought a minute an hour and a whole day.
2. Coyote Mouse and Owl have a problem.
3. Coyote watched waited and hoped.
4. Everyone would laugh at a big brave smart fellow like me working for you.
5. You must not jump on me threaten to kill me and then save my life by letting me go.

Writing Application Use each of the following series in a sentence. Add commas where needed.

1. past the rock past the tree and behind the cactus
2. promised to work begged for help and yelled in anger

Build Your Portfolio

 Idea Bank

Writing

1. **Rules** Write a list of rules that Coyote and Mouse should follow to avoid further conflict.

2. **Story Continuation** Write a few paragraphs that tell what happens the next time Coyote and Mouse meet.

3. **Brief Fable** Using "The Ant and the Dove" as a model, write a similar fable with different characters in a similar situation. Your fable should communicate the same lesson that is communicated in "The Ant and the Dove."

Speaking and Listening

4. **Role Play [Group Activity]** With two classmates, role-play the scene between Snake, Coyote, and Mouse after Snake is retrapped or the scene between Bruh Bear, Bruh Rabbit, and he Lion after he Lion meets Man.

5. **Group Discussion [Group Activity]** With a group, discuss how the lesson in "The Ant and the Dove" can be applied to situations in your own lives. Make a list of three situations, and jot down a brief explanation of how the lesson applies.

Projects

6. **Pantomime [Group Activity]** With a group, plan pantomimes (performances without words) that communicate the action and meaning of one of the folk tales in this group. Perform your pantomimes for the class. **[Performing Arts Link]**

7. **Mural** Illustrate the events in one of these folk tales by drawing a mural. Begin on the left side of a long sheet of paper, and draw early events in the tale. As you move to the right, illustrate events that follow. **[Art Link]**

 Writing Mini-Lesson

Animal Dialogue

Each of these folk tales contains dialogue—the conversation between characters. Write a dialogue for two of the animal characters in these folk tales.

Writing Skills Focus: Identify Qualities of a Character

To write dialogue that sounds like a character, you must **identify qualities of a character.** For example, Bruh Bear is patient and calm. His words show that he speaks slowly and with great thought:

> "I know lots," said Bruh Bear, slow and quiet-like. . . .
>
> "Well, now, I'll tell you," said Bruh Bear, "I been around, but I haven't ever come across Man that I know of. Couldn't tell you nothin about him."

Prewriting First, choose your characters. Then, choose characteristics from the list below or come up with some of your own.

excitable	irritable	thoughtful
patient	kind	generous
impatient	boastful	greedy
tricky	talkative	quiet

Drafting Write each character's part in words that reflect his or her qualities. Refer to the qualities list as you draft.

Revising Review your draft, looking for places where you can make each character's personality clearer through dialogue.

> ◆ **Grammar Application**
>
> If you use any series, separate the items in the series with commas.

Guide for Reading

Meet the Authors:

Anne Terry White (1896–1980)

Anne Terry White was born in Russia. She worked as a teacher, a social worker, and a translator of Russian literature. The subjects of her writing are as varied as her interests: stars, rocks, rivers, mountains, American history, and ancient civilizations. She has become most famous, however, for her collection of Greek myths, from which "The Gorgon's Head" comes.

Gail Robinson (1935–)
and Douglas Hill (1935–)

Gail Robinson and Douglas Hill are Canadian. They lived among Native Americans for many years and heard the stories of the Crow people first-hand. One character who appears in many Native American myths is Coyote. He is a hero of great cunning and resourcefulness. Coyote is so prominent in Native American folk literature that Robinson and Hill published an entire book of stories about him. The book is entitled *Coyote the Trickster.*

◆ LITERATURE AND YOUR LIFE

CONNECT YOUR EXPERIENCE

The hero of an action movie is usually tough, strong, resourceful, and intelligent. Such heroes existed long before movies portrayed them. The heroes of ancient myths are similar to the movie heroes of today. They solve problems through a combination of wit, strength, and daring.

THEMATIC FOCUS: Working It Out

As you read these myths, ask yourself whether the strategies these heroes use are strategies that could help someone work out everyday problems.

◆ Background for Understanding

CULTURE

The ancient Greeks believed in oracles, or people who had great knowledge and could see into the future. The oracle at Delphi was the most famous of these prophets. Any prediction made was also called an oracle. Many Greek myths, including "The Gorgon's Head," tell of adventures that arise from a prediction made by an oracle.

◆ Build Vocabulary

SUFFIXES: -ous

The suffix *-ous* means "having" or "full of." Something *perilous,* for example, is "full of peril or danger." Something *venomous* is "full of venom"; a *valorous* person has "valor, or courage."

WORD BANK

Which word might describe someone who feels embarrassed or bashful after being corrected?

evade
perilous
venomous
abashed
valorous
rivulets

◆ The Gorgon's Head ◆
How Coyote Stole Fire

◆ Literary Focus

MYTHS

A **myth** is an ancient story that relates the actions of gods or heroes or explains events in nature. One of the most popular Greek myths tells the adventures of the hero Perseus. His brave deeds are the subject of "The Gorgon's Head."

"How Coyote Stole Fire" is a Native American myth that explains how ancient peoples came to have the fire that helped them survive.

◆ Reading Strategy

UNDERSTAND CULTURAL BACKGROUND

To appreciate a myth, you must understand the **culture** from which it comes. In ancient Greece, strength and bravery in battle were the most valued qualities. You will see these qualities in Perseus, the hero of "The Gorgon's Head."

For the Native Americans who told the stories of Coyote, bravery and cunning were important. You will see these qualities in the hero of "How Coyote Stole Fire." Draw a graphic organizer like the one shown below. On each point of the flame, jot down a detail that shows what each culture valued in a hero.

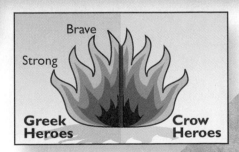

The Gorgon's Head

Greek Myth
ANNE TERRY WHITE

Medusa (Laura Dreyfus Barney), 1982, Alice Pike Barney, The National Museum of American Art, Smithsonian Institution, Washington, DC

Acrisius,[1] King of Argos,[2] came home from Delphi with a heavy heart, for he had received a dreadful oracle.

"No sons shall be born to you," the priestess had told him. "But you shall have a grandson, and by his hand you shall die."

Now the king had an only daughter, who was yet a maiden. So in his distress he thought: "I will evade my fate. I will shut Danae[3] up away from the sight of men in a house of bronze all sunk underground." And he carried out his cruel plan.

But Acrisius forgot to take the gods into account. Part of the roof of the house was open to the sky. And one day, as lovely Danae sat sadly looking up at the passing clouds, Zeus[4] beheld the maiden. Changing himself into a shower of gold, he stormed into her chamber.

When afterwards a son was born to Danae, she hid him from her father's sight. Nevertheless, the king discovered the baby and was more than ever filled with fear. He dared not kill the little Perseus[5] directly lest the gods avenge the murder. Instead, he had a great chest built, placed Danae and her boy in it, and set them adrift upon the sea.

All day and all night the chest tossed upon the waves. Danae lulled her child with song, and he slept. But when dawn came, a great wave picked up the chest and carried it close to the tiny island of Seraphos.[6]

It happened that a fisherman, Dictys[7] by name, saw the chest bobbing on the waves close to the shore. He dragged the box to land and opened it. When he beheld the pitiful mother with the helpless little child, his heart was moved. He took them both to his wife, for

Dictys was childless, and there in the kindly fisherfolk's humble home Perseus grew up.

Now Danae had been a beautiful maiden. And when Perseus was grown into a fine tall youth, she was still beautiful. So it was not strange that King Polydectes,[8] who was Dictys' brother, fell in love with her and made her his wife. But the King hated the youth—just because Danae doted on him—and sought some way to be rid of him.

At last Polydectes said to his stepson, "The time has come, Perseus, for you to win glory for yourself in some bold adventure."

Young Perseus thought so, too. But what should the adventure be?

"I think," the wily Polydectes said, "it would be a good idea for you to cut off the Medusa's[9] head. That would bring you the greatest fame."

All unsuspecting, Perseus set off to find the Medusa, not knowing in the least how perilous an adventure he had undertaken. For the Medusa was one of the three Gorgons, terrible winged monsters who lived alone on an island. They had teeth like the tusks of a boar, hands of brass, and snakes instead of hair. Perseus did not know where to look for the Gorgons. Nor did he know which of them was Medusa. And this was important, for Medusa was the only one of the three that could be slain.

From place to place the prince went in his quest, getting more and more discouraged. Then one day he beheld a young man of great beauty, wearing winged sandals and a winged cap, and carrying in his hand a wand around which two golden serpents twined. Perseus knew at once that this was Hermes and was overjoyed when the god said:

"Perseus, I approve the high adventure you have in mind. But you must be properly

---

1. **Acrisius** (ə kris´ ē əs)
2. **Argos** (är´ gōs): A city in Greece.
3. **Danae** (dan´ ä ē): Daughter of Acrisius.
4. **Zeus** (zōōs)
5. **Perseus** (per´ sē us)
6. **Seraphos** (sə ri´ fōs): An island in the Aegean Sea.
7. **Dictys** (dik´ tis)

◀ **Critical Viewing** What words would you use to describe Medusa as she appears in the picture? **[Analyze]**

---

8. **Polydectes** (päl ē dək´ tēz)
9. **Medusa's** (mə dōō´ säz)

◆ **Build Vocabulary**

evade (i vād´) v.: Avoid; escape

perilous (per´ el es) adj.: Dangerous

equipped for it. Without the winged sandals, the magic wallet, and the helmet of invisibility which the Nymphs[10] of the North possess, you can never succeed. Now, I cannot tell you where the Nymphs live, but I will take you to the Gray Women.[11] You can find out from them."

"And will they indeed tell me?" Perseus asked.

"Not willingly," Hermes replied. "But you can make them do it. They have but one eye among the three. Snatch it from them as they pass it from one to another and none can see. And do not give it back till they tell you what you want to know."

With that, Hermes gave Perseus a magnificent curved sword.

"You will need it," he said, "for the Medusa's scales are hard as metal."

Perseus had just taken the sword when there was a sudden brightness in the sky, and he beheld the goddess Athene[12] descending toward them.

"Of what use will be your sword, my brother," she said to Hermes, "when none may look on the Gorgons and live? The sight of them, as you well know, turns men to stone. Take my bright shield, Perseus. Look into it instead of at the monster as you approach to do battle, and you will see the Medusa reflected as in a mirror."

So saying, the goddess disappeared, and the brightness with her.

On and on with his god-companion Perseus journeyed, farther than man had ever been. At last they came to the end of the earth. There the weird Gray Women sat, passing their eye from one to another just as Hermes had said. Danae's son knew what to do. He left the god and crept quietly towards them, waited till one had taken the eye from her forehead, and

snatched it away as she passed it to her sister.

The Gray Women raised a fearful clamor when they realized that a stranger had their eye. They howled and they threatened. But without the eye they were helpless, and in the end they grudgingly told Perseus the way to the Nymphs of the North.

So again Perseus went on, this time to find the happy beings who possessed the three priceless things he needed.

And when the Nymphs heard the reason he wanted them, they were willing to give him the winged shoes, the helmet that would make him invisible, and the magic wallet that would become the right size for whatever he wished to carry.

Fully equipped now, Perseus lightly sped through the air over land and over sea to the fearful island of the Gorgons. As he approached, he could see, scattered in the fields and along the roads, statues of men and beasts whom the sight of the Gorgons had turned to stone. And, at last, from high above, he beheld the monsters themselves reflected in his shield. Their scale-covered bodies glistened in the sun, their great wings were folded, the snakes that were their hair lay hideously coiled and intertwined. The Gorgons were asleep.

But which of the three was Medusa? Perseus could see no difference among them.

Suddenly he heard Athene's voice:

"Descend, Perseus, and strike! The Gorgon nearest the shore is Medusa."

Perseus swept down, and still gazing into the shield, boldly swung his blade. With one stroke he cut off the grisly head. Then, springing into the air, he thrust his prize, all writhing and hissing, into the magic wallet.

Up leaped the Gorgon sisters, for they heard the rattle of Medusa's scales as the severed body thrashed about. They turned their snaky heads and when they saw Perseus, they roared with fury. Flapping their great wings, they set off in pursuit. But they could not outstrip the winged sandals.

Over lands and peoples the hero flew, on and on. He had lost his way now, for Hermes

---

10. **Nymphs** (nimfz): Minor nature goddesses, thought of as beautiful maidens living in rivers, trees, and so on.
11. **Gray Women:** Also called Graeae (grē´ ē´): Three old sisters who act as guards for the Gorgons and have only one eye and one tooth to share among them.
12. **Athene** (ə thē´ nä): Goddess of wisdom, skills, and warfare.

Perseus, under the protection of Minerva, turns Phineus to stone by brandishing the head of Medusa, Jean-Marc Nattier, Musée des Beaux-Arts, Tours

had left him. Below, the Lybian desert stretched endlessly. Perseus did not know what those sands were, nor did he guess that the ruby drops falling from Medusa's head were turning into <u>venomous</u> snakes that would inhabit the desert forever. But now he saw a sight that made his heart beat fast with excitement and wonder.

Fastened by chains to a cliff by the sea was a beautiful maiden. Had it not been that a slight breeze stirred her hair and that tears flowed from her eyes, he would have thought her a statue. Perseus almost forgot to keep his winged sandals moving, so struck was he by her rare beauty.

"Lovely maiden, you should not wear such chains as these," he stammered out, "but rather those which bind the hearts of lovers. I pray you, tell me your name and why you are bound like this."

At first the girl made no reply, so <u>abashed</u>

◆ Build Vocabulary

venomous (ven´ əm əs) *adj.*: Poisonous
abashed (ə basht´) *adj.*: Ashamed

▲ **Critical Viewing** What evidence in this painting shows that Medusa's head has terrible power? [Analyze]

was she before the youth. But when he urged her again and again to speak, she told him all her story.

"I am Andromeda,"[13] she said, "daughter of Cepheus,[14] King of the Ethiopians. The beautiful Cassiopeia[15] is my mother. It is her beauty that has chained me here. For the gods are jealous, and in nothing may we mortals surpass them. Woe, woe the day my mother vaunted[16] herself fairer than the daughters of Nereus![17] The sea god has sent a serpent to prey upon our people, and my death alone can appease his anger. So says the oracle."

She had scarcely finished speaking when the loud roaring of the waves announced that the monster was on his way. Andromeda

---

13. **Andromeda** (an dräm´ ə dä)
14. **Cepheus** (sē´ fē us)
15. **Cassiopeia** (kas ē ō pē´ ä)
16. **vaunted** (vänt´ əd) *v.*: Boasted or bragged.
17. **Nereus** (nē´ rē us): A god of great kindliness; also called the Old Man of the Sea and Nereus the Truthful. The father of the Nereids, the nymphs of the sea.

shrieked. At her cry, her frantic father and mother came running. They clung to their daughter and lamented.

"Enough of tears!" Perseus said to them sternly. "I am Perseus, son of Zeus and Danae. Now I will make this contract with you—that Andromeda shall be mine if I save her from the serpent."

"Indeed, indeed, valorous youth, she shall be yours! Only save her from the monster, and you shall have our kingdom as well as our daughter."

The monster was coming on, his breast parting the waves like a swift ship. Suddenly Perseus sprang into the air and shot high up in the clouds. Seeing the youth's shadow upon the sea, the monster attacked it in fury. Then Perseus swooped like an eagle from the sky and buried his sword up to the hilt in the beast's right shoulder. The creature reared upright, then plunged beneath the water, and turned around and around like some fierce wild boar in the midst of baying hounds.

Nimbly avoiding the snapping jaws, Perseus dealt blow after blow wherever he had the chance to strike. Red blood poured from the monster's mouth. The air was so filled with spray that the hero's winged sandals grew heavy. He dared not trust himself to them longer. Spying a rock over which the waves were breaking, he braced himself against it with his left hand, and four times he drove his sword into the monster's side.

As the creature sank to its death, Perseus heard shouts of joy from the shore. And when he looked, Andromeda already stood free beside her parents.

"I will take this fair maiden without dowry," Perseus said.

And that very day the wedding was celebrated. Torches were tossed in the air, incense was thrown on the flames. Garlands were hung from the palace roof. And everywhere the sound of lyres and pipes and singing was heard.

Now while the marriage feast was at its height, the door of the banquet hall was suddenly flung open, and in burst a mob of shouting, riotous men. Foremost stood Andromeda's uncle, Phineas,[18] javelin in hand.

"Behold, I am here!" he cried. "I have come to avenge the theft of my promised bride."

"What are you doing, brother?" the father cried. "Do you, who stood by and watched while Andromeda was put in chains and did nothing to help her, dare to be indignant because another has snatched the prize? Let the man who rescued her have the reward he was promised! He has not been chosen in preference to you, but in preference to certain death."

Phineas said not a word. He looked from the king to Perseus, undecided at which to aim his weapon, then hurled it at the hero. The spear struck in Perseus' couch.

Perseus leaped up from the cushions, wrenched out the spear, and hurled it back at his foe. Had Phineas not taken refuge behind the altar, he would have perished. As it was, one of his followers received the weapon full in his forehead.

Then the rioters went wild. Weapons were hurled, and the feast turned into a battle. Thick as hail, javelins sped by Perseus' ears. He set his shoulders against a great stone column and struck down one man after another. But at last he realized that valor could not withstand the numbers against him.

"If I have any friends here, let them hide their faces!" he shouted.

With this he drew Medusa's head out of the wallet. One of the attackers was just preparing to cast his javelin, but before he could cast, he was turned to stone. Another, who was about to thrust his sword through Perseus, stood frozen with it in his hand. A third was turned to stone even as he uttered a taunt. Two hun-

◆ Build Vocabulary

valorous (val´ er əs) *adj.*: Brave

---

18. **Phineas** (fin´ ē us)

dred men became stony statues before Phineas yielded, crying:

"Put away your horrible weapon. Hide it! Grant me only my life and may the rest be yours!"

"What I can give you, most cowardly Phineas, I will!" Perseus replied. "You shall be a lasting monument here in the palace of my father-in-law."

The unhappy Phineas tried to turn away his eyes, but even as he did so, his flesh turned to stone.

When at the year's end, Perseus sailed home with Andromeda, Polydectes' hatred had in no way lessened. The King was furious that his stepson had returned, and refused to believe that he had actually slain the Medusa. With scornful taunts he upbraided the young man for having come home empty-handed.

It was more than Perseus could bear.

"I shall prove to you that what I say is true!" he cried. "Hide your eyes, all you who are my friends!" And he showed the Gorgon's head to cruel Polydectes.

That was the last time Perseus ever used the horrible head. He gave it most willingly to Athene, who kept it ever after.

Now that Polydectes was dead, Danae yearned to go home again and be reconciled to her father. So Perseus made the fisherman Dictys king of the island and sailed with his mother and Andromeda to Greece.

But it happened that when they came to Argos, King Acrisius was away from home. Games were being held in Larissa, and Perseus, hearing of them, decided to go there and take part. And there at the games it was that the oracle which Acrisius had received at Delphi was strangely fulfilled. For when it came Perseus' turn to throw the discus, he threw it so that it swerved to one side. It landed among the spectators and killed an old man. That old man was King Acrisius, who had gone to such cruel lengths to avoid the fate which the gods had ordained.

Guide for Responding

◆ LITERATURE AND YOUR LIFE

Reader's Response Do you find the story of Perseus exciting? Why or why not?

Thematic Focus What qualities help Perseus work out the problems that he faces?

☑ Check Your Comprehension

1. What is the "dreadful oracle" that is delivered to King Acrisius?
2. What goal does Polydectes set for Perseus?
3. List three perilous encounters that Perseus experiences during his adventure.
4. How does the oracle finally come true?

◆ Critical Thinking

INTERPRET

1. What is Polydectes' true motive in sending Perseus to kill Medusa? **[Analyze]**
2. What message about fate does the myth seem to express through the death of Acrisius? **[Interpret]**
3. Describe the kind of person Perseus is. **[Synthesize]**

APPLY

4. Explain the purpose you think heroes serve in a society. **[Support]**

EXTEND

5. Name three real-life occupations that require courage. **[Career Link]**

How Coyote Stole Fire

Native American Myth
Gail Robinson and Douglas Hill

Long ago, when man was newly come into the world, there were days when he was the happiest creature of all. Those were the days when spring brushed across the willow tails, or when his children ripened with the blueberries in the sun of summer, or when the goldenrod bloomed in the autumn haze.

But always the mists of autumn evenings grew more chill, and the sun's strokes grew shorter. Then man saw winter moving near, and he became fearful and unhappy. He was afraid for his children, and for the grandfathers and grandmothers who carried in their heads the sacred tales of the tribe. Many of these, young and old, would die in the long, ice-bitter months of winter.

Coyote, like the rest of the People, had no need for fire. So he seldom concerned himself with it, until one spring day when he was passing a human village. There the women were singing a song of mourning for the babies and the old ones who had died in the winter. Their voices moaned like the west wind through a buffalo skull, prickling the hairs on Coyote's neck.

"Feel how the sun is now warm on our backs," one of the men was saying. "Feel how it warms the earth and makes these stones hot to the touch. If only we could have had a small piece of the sun in our teepees during the winter."

Coyote, overhearing this, felt sorry for the men and women. He also felt that there was something he could do to help them. He knew of a faraway mountaintop where the three Fire Beings lived. These Beings kept fire to themselves, guarding it carefully for fear that man might somehow acquire it and become as strong as they. Coyote saw that he could do a good turn for man at the expense of these selfish Fire Beings.

So Coyote went to the mountain of the Fire Beings and crept to its top, to watch the way that the Beings guarded their fire. As he came near, the Beings leaped to their feet and gazed searchingly round their camp. Their eyes glinted like bloodstones, and their hands were clawed like the talons of the great black vulture.

"What's that? What's that I hear?" hissed one of the Beings.

"A thief, skulking in the bushes!" screeched another.

The third looked more closely, and saw Coyote. But he had gone to the mountaintop on all-fours, so the Being thought she saw only an ordinary coyote slinking among the trees.

"It is no one, it is nothing!" she cried, and the other two looked where she pointed and also saw only a gray coyote. They sat down

---

▶ **Critical Viewing** Does Coyote look as if he has the qualities necessary to steal fire? **[Assess]**

again by their fire and paid Coyote no more attention.

So he watched all day and night as the Fire Beings guarded their fire. He saw how they fed it pine cones and dry branches from the sycamore trees. He saw how they stamped furiously on runaway <u>rivulets</u> of flame that sometimes nibbled outwards on edges of dry grass. He saw also how, at night, the Beings took turns to sit by the fire. Two would sleep while one was on guard; and at certain times the Being by the fire would get up and go into their teepee, and another would come out to sit by the fire.

Coyote saw that the Beings were always jealously watchful of their fire except during one part of the day. That was in the earliest morning, when the first winds of dawn arose on the mountains. Then the Being by the fire would hurry, shivering, into the teepee calling, "Sister, sister, go out and watch the fire." But the next Being would always be slow to go out for her turn, her head spinning with sleep and the thin dreams of dawn.

Coyote, seeing all this, went down the mountain and spoke to some of his friends among the People. He told them of hairless man, fearing the cold and death of winter. And he told them of the Fire Beings, and the warmth and brightness of the flame. They all agreed that man should have fire, and they all promised to help Coyote's undertaking.

Then Coyote sped again to the mountain-top. Again the Fire Beings leaped up when he came close, and one cried out, "What's that? A thief, a thief!"

But again the others looked closely, and saw only a gray coyote hunting among the bushes. So they sat down again and paid him no more attention.

Coyote waited through the day, and watched as night fell and two of the Beings went off to the teepee to sleep. He watched as they changed over at certain times all the night long, until at last the dawn winds rose.

Then the Being on guard called, "Sister, sister, get up and watch the fire."

And the Being whose turn it was climbed slow and sleepy from her bed, saying, "Yes, yes, I am coming. Do not shout so."

But before she could come out of the teepee, Coyote lunged from the bushes, snatched up a glowing portion of fire, and sprang away down the mountainside.

Screaming, the Fire Beings flew after him. Swift as Coyote ran, they caught up with him, and one of them reached out a clutching hand. Her fingers touched only the tip of the tail, but the touch was enough to turn the hairs white, and coyote tail-tips are white still. Coyote shouted, and flung the fire away from him. But the others of the People had gathered at the mountain's foot, in case they were needed. Squirrel saw the fire falling, and caught it, putting it on her back and fleeing away through the tree tops. The fire scorched her back so painfully that her tail curled up and back, as squirrels' tails still do today.

The Fire Beings then pursued Squirrel, who threw the fire to Chipmunk. Chattering with fear, Chipmunk stood still as if rooted until the Beings were almost upon her. Then, as she turned to run, one Being clawed at her, tearing down the length of her back and leaving three stripes that are to be seen on chipmunks' backs even today. Chipmunk threw the fire to Frog, and the Beings turned towards him. One of the Beings grasped his tail, but Frog gave a mighty leap and tore himself free, leaving his tail behind in the Being's hand—which is why frogs have had no tails ever since.

As the Beings came after him again, Frog

◆ Build Vocabulary

rivulets (riv´ yoo litz) *n.*: Little streams

flung the fire on to Wood. And Wood swallowed it.

The Fire Beings gathered round, but they did not know how to get the fire out of Wood. They promised it gifts, sang to it and shouted at it. They twisted it and struck it and tore it with their knives. But Wood did not give up the fire. In the end, defeated, the Beings went back to their mountaintop and left the People alone.

But Coyote knew how to get fire out of Wood. And he went to the village of men and showed them how. He showed them the trick of rubbing two dry sticks together, and the trick of spinning a sharpened stick in a hole made in another piece of wood. So man was from then on warm and safe through the killing cold of winter.

Beyond Literature

Cultural Connection

Canine Companions Through History

Dogs, like coyotes, are canines. Canines were the first animals to be tamed. Approximately 12,000 years ago, they began living among humans, eventually becoming companions, workers, and protectors. At first, most dogs were kept to assist with the herding of animals or to protect property. Today, most dogs in the United States are kept as pets, but there are many who continue to work in specialized areas such as herding, search and rescue, and assisting people with disabilities.

Cross-Curricular Activity
Graph Make a graph that shows the approximate proportions of companion dogs to working dogs. Divide working dogs into separate categories.

Guide for Responding

◆ LITERATURE AND YOUR LIFE

Reader's Response Which of the explanations in this myth did you find most interesting or surprising?

Thematic Focus What qualities help these heroes work out the challenges they face?

Journal Writing Describe the qualities you associate with a hero.

☑ **Check Your Comprehension**

1. Why do the humans need fire?
2. How do the Fire Beings keep the fire going?
3. How does Coyote steal fire?
4. Who helps Coyote?

◆ Critical Thinking

INTERPRET
1. Why does Coyote help the humans? **[Speculate]**
2. What human characteristics do the animals show? **[Compare and Contrast]**
3. Why do you think the Crow people included Chipmunk, Squirrel, and Frog in the story? **[Infer]**

APPLY
4. Aside from warmth, what other benefits has fire given to humans? **[Synthesize]**

EXTEND
5. Identify two natural resources that are used to heat buildings. **[Science Link]**

Characters from myths have inspired a number of television programs. Some of the heroes, such as Hercules and Sinbad, are based on actual figures from traditional myths. The scriptwriters use the myths as a springboard and create new adventures for the heroes. Others, such as Xena, are inventions from the minds of scriptwriters. This popular television program features a female hero—a warrior princess. Like other heroes, she is strong, brave, and resourceful. Xena's adventures often include famous characters from myths, such as Orpheus, Hercules, and Odysseus. In this adventure, Xena and her friend Gabrielle rescue their bumbling companion Joxer. The creation of programs such as "Xena: Warrior Princess" demonstrate the enduring appeal of mythical heroes.

XENA:
WARRIOR PRINCESS

Adam Armus and Nora Kay Forster

4 EXT. WOODS—ALL SURREAL ANGLES—DAY

In the woods. All looks quiet.

We see WOLVES, *in pursuit of the* UNKNOWN MAN.

GABRIELLE. [*Off Screen*] Driven by an unquenchable thirst for blood, they track their intended victim relentlessly . . .

The UNKNOWN MAN *leaps a small boulder, barely ahead of the pursuing* WOLVES. *In his arms he carries a* BAG.

GABRIELLE. [O.S.] . . . until they corner him, and tear him limb from limb.

As the WOLVES *close in on his heels, the* UNKNOWN MAN *runs for all he's worth, crashing through the undergrowth, as we:*

CUT TO:

5 EXT. PATH IN WOODS—DAY

All is quiet as XENA *and* GABRIELLE *continue down the path.*

GABRIELLE. If you ask me, the stories are exaggerated. You know, made up to give people a good scare—

Suddenly, the Unknown Man, JOXER, *bursts out of the woods,* CRASHING INTO *Gabrielle and knocking her to the ground.*

JOXER. Help! Wolves!

He sprints past XENA *and* UP A TREE. *Just then, the* WOLVES *bound out of the woods after him.*

XENA *pulls* GABRIELLE *behind her as* TWO *of the* WOLVES *surround them. A* THIRD WOLF *rushes to* JOXER, *now up the tree.*

XENA *grabs her* BULL WHIP—

XENA. [*to* GABRIELLE] Stay behind me.

The WOLVES *close in on* XENA, *baring their teeth. They circle, poised to strike. Meanwhile . . .*

JOXER, *just out of reach, looks down at the* WOLF *who is barking and snarling.*

JOXER. Ha! Outsmarted you! You brainless flea-bitten mutt . . .

—*In the middle of which, the branch he's on starts to* BEND, *dangling him dangerously close to the* WOLF! *It leaps, grabbing onto his boot.*

JOXER. [*panicky*] Uh . . . Good doggy. Nice doggy . . .

As he tries to shake himself free . . .

XENA *snaps her whip at the* LEAD WOLF, *backing him off, but the* OTHER WOLF *advances. She counters with another whip snap, then finally lands a stinging blow to the* LEAD WOLF's *snout. He whimpers, and the* WOLVES *quickly scuttle off into the forest.*

The THIRD WOLF, *realizing he's alone, lets go of* JOXER *and follows the others.*

XENA *and* GABRIELLE *cross to* JOXER *as he climbs down from the tree.*

GABRIELLE. Joxer!? Are you all right?

JOXER. Me? Never better. Why do you ask?

XENA. Could've been that cry for help.

JOXER. Oh that? All an act. The secret to fighting a wolf pack is wearing 'em down. I appeared defenseless to keep them on the hunt. Actually, I had those mongrels right where I wanted 'em.

▲ **Critical Viewing** In what ways does Xena resemble a hero from mythology? [**Connect**]

1. What qualities does this adventure share with a myth?
2. (a) In what way do the writers incorporate humor into the adventure? (b) Why do you think they do so?
3. In what way is Xena different from the hero in a traditional myth?

▼ **Critical Viewing** Why do you think wolves hunt in packs? [**Deduce**]

Guide for Responding (continued)

◆ Reading Strategy

UNDERSTAND CULTURAL BACKGROUND

The details in a myth reflect the culture from which the myth comes. To appreciate the myth, you must understand the **cultural background.**

1. What are two details in "The Gorgon's Head" that show that ancient Greeks valued strength and bravery?
2. Why do you think early Native Americans would have admired a hero who could move quietly and undetected?
3. What detail in "How Coyote Stole Fire" shows that early Native Americans valued teamwork?

◆ Build Vocabulary

USING THE SUFFIX -ous

Match each word that ends in -ous with the person or thing it most likely describes:

1. perilous   **a.** knight
2. venomous   **b.** gymnasium
3. valorous   **c.** snake
4. spacious   **d.** sword

SPELLING STRATEGY

When spelling words that end with *ous,* remember to include the *o,* even though you don't hear it. On your paper, write a word that ends in *ous* for each clue:

1. Very well known
2. Funny
3. Filled with mystery

USING THE WORD BANK

On your paper, complete each sentence with a word from the Word Bank:

1. Mountain is to hills as stream is to ____?____.
2. Uncover is to reveal as hide is to ____?____.
3. Coward is to fearful as hero is to ____?____.
4. Mouse is to timid as snake is to _____.
5. Security is to safe as danger is to ____?____.
6. Pride is to confident as shame is to ____?____.

◆ Literary Focus

MYTHS

Myths are ancient stories that tell about the actions of gods or heroes or that explain events or circumstances in nature.

1. What two details make the hero Perseus seem like a "superhero"?
2. Why do you think early Native Americans needed an explanation for fire?

◆ Build Grammar Skills

COMMAS WITH INTERRUPTERS

Interrupters are words, phrases, or clauses that interrupt a sentence to add information not essential to the meaning of the sentence. The commas indicate that these words could be left out and the sentence would still make sense. In the following sentence, the phrase *King of Argos* interrupts the sentence.

Acrisius, *King of Argos,* came home from Delphi.

The following chart shows examples of common kinds of interrupters:

Using Commas With Interrupting Words and Phrases	
The name of a person being addresssed:	Please, Squirrel, help me!
Phrases or clauses that rename or describe a noun:	Chipmunk, who was waiting by the tree, took the fire.
Common expressions:	Coyote, of course, escaped from the Fire Beings.

Practice On your paper, copy each sentence. Insert commas where needed to set off interrupting words.

1. It happened that a fisherman Dictys by name saw the chest bobbing.
2. Polydectes who was Dictys' brother fell in love.
3. Many of these both young and old would die.
4. No Coyote I don't believe you.
5. Coyote it is said is the greatest trickster of all time.

Writing Application Write three sentences about Coyote. In each sentence, use a different kind of interrupter.

Build Your Portfolio

 Idea Bank

Writing

1. **Comparison** Write a paragraph comparing Perseus or Coyote to a contemporary action hero.

2. **Help-Wanted Ad** Write a help-wanted ad that describes the kind of hero needed to solve the problem in either "The Gorgon's Head" or "How Coyote Stole Fire." Describe what the hero will have to do and the qualities needed to accomplish the task.

3. **Movie Suggestion** Imagine that you are a director planning a movie. Write a few paragraphs explaining why you think one of these myths would make a good movie. Suggest any changes you would make, and describe a few key scenes.

Speaking and Listening

4. **Storytelling** Myths come from the oral tradition—they are passed along by being told aloud. Practice telling one of these myths, and then tell it to a small group. If possible, make a video or audio recording of your storytelling session.

5. **Interview** With a partner, conduct an interview with either Coyote or Perseus. Plan your questions ahead of time, and create answers based on the details in these myths.

Projects

6. **Hero Display [Group Activity]** With a group, create a display of heroes of different times and cultures. Group members can do research to find information about heroes; illustrate heroes; or gather stories, pictures, or video clips showing the heroes in action. **[Social Studies Link]**

7. **Myth Collection [Group Activity]** With a group, create an anthology, or collection, of myths. Group members can choose myths, illustrate them, or write introductions to the myths.

 Writing Mini-Lesson

Portrait of a Modern Hero

Coyote and Perseus are heroes from a particular time and culture. Create a verbal portrait—a picture with words—of a hero from modern culture. Your hero can be fictional or real.

Writing Skills Focus: Order of Importance

To create the strongest impression, organize the qualities of your hero in **order of importance.** For example, you can start with the least important qualities and build toward the most important. Or, you may start with qualities that your hero shares with other heroes and build toward the quality that makes your hero unique.

Prewriting Choose your hero, and brainstorm for a list of words to describe him or her. Then, organize the hero's qualities in order of importance.

Drafting In your draft, include examples of the hero's actions that illustrate each of the qualities that you describe. If you say your hero is brave, describe something brave the hero has done. Arrange your details to emphasize the most important quality.

Revising Ask a partner to review your draft and to answer these questions: Would you change the order of the details? Where would you add details or examples to create a clearer picture? Keep your partner's suggestions in mind as you revise.

> ◆ **Grammar Application**
> Use commas to set off any words or phrases you use that interrupt the main thought in your sentences.

Comparison-and-Contrast Essay

Writing Process Workshop

Characters in folk tales and myths often represent qualities—good and evil, bravery and cowardice. You can learn more about characters, places, or things by comparing and contrasting them, that is, identifying their similarities and differences. Write a comparison-and-contrast essay. The following strategies will help you effectively show similarities and differences.

Writing Skills Focus

▶ **Use vivid adjectives.** Vivid adjectives tell exactly how something looks, feels, tastes, sounds, or smells. (See p. 780.)

▶ **Identify qualities.** Focus on the main qualities that make your subjects what they are. For instance, if you are comparing and contrasting two characters, do not try to describe everything about each character. Focus on three or four qualities that the characters share and three or four qualities that make each character unique. (See page 795.)

▶ **Use appropriate organization.** Choose a logical organization that will most clearly demonstrate the similarities and differences. You might want to group all the similarities together and follow with differences; you might want to organize details in order of importance; or you might want to organize your similar and different details point by point: by appearance, personality, and actions. (See page 811.)

MODEL

Two characters work together in "He Lion, Bruh Bear, and Bruh Rabbit" to solve the problem of he Lion's roaring. ① While these two characters share the qualities of intelligence, they are different in personality and appearance.

Bruh Bear is thoughtful and careful. His speech, movements, and thoughts are slow and deliberate. ② Bruh Rabbit is quick and sharp. He moves, speaks, and thinks in a hurry.

③ The appearances of the two characters are as different as their personalities. Bruh Bear is huge and powerful-looking. Bruh Rabbit is small and fragile-looking.

① The writer identifies the qualities on which the essay will focus.

② The writer uses vivid adjectives such as *thoughtful, careful,* and *deliberate.*

③ The writer organizes point by point. First, the personalities of the animals are contrasted. Then, differences in appearance are shown.

Prewriting

Choose a Topic Choose two things that have enough in common to make it worthwhile exploring their similarities and differences. If you are having trouble coming up with a topic, consider some of the suggestions below:

Topic Ideas

- Compare and contrast two cities as possible locations for a movie.
- Compare and contrast two characters in a story you enjoyed.
- Compare and contrast two amusement park rides.
- Compare and contrast two athletes.

Brainstorm for Qualities Use a Venn diagram like the one shown below to identify the similarities and differences of your subjects. On the space where the ovals overlap, write the qualities your subjects share. On the parts of the ovals that do not overlap, write the qualities that your subjects do not share.

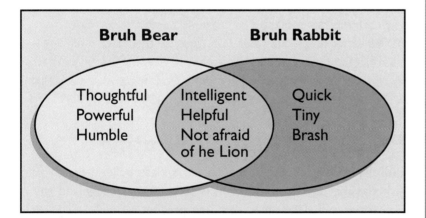

Bruh Bear   **Bruh Rabbit**

Thoughtful
Powerful
Humble

Intelligent
Helpful
Not afraid
of he Lion

Quick
Tiny
Brash

Drafting

Describe With Vivid Adjectives When you show the differences between your subjects, use adjectives that capture the qualities that make each character unique. For instance, don't just say "Bruh Bear is bigger than Bruh Rabbit." Instead, help your readers see how different their sizes are by using such vivid adjectives as *huge* and *tiny* or *looming* and *minuscule*.

DRAFTING/REVISING

APPLYING LANGUAGE SKILLS: Words That Show Comparison and Contrast

Make it clear when you are showing shared qualities and when you are showing unique qualities. To show comparisons, use words such as *similarly* or *in the same way*. To show contrast, use words such as *on the other hand, but,* or *in contrast*.

Draft:
Bruh Rabbit is tiny but quick. Bruh Bear is large and deliberate.

Revised:
Bruh Rabbit is tiny but quick. On the other hand, Bruh Bear is large and deliberate.

Practice On your paper, rewrite by adding words to indicate comparisons and contrasts:

Bruh Rabbit is the liveliest animal in the forest. He moves lightning fast. He is intelligent, and he thinks fast. Bruh Bear is intelligent. He thinks slowly.

Writing Application Add words that clarify comparisons and contrasts in your essay.

Writer's Solution Connection Language Lab

To help you identify points to compare and contrast, use the interactive Venn diagram in the Exposition: Making Connections unit.

APPLYING LANGUAGE SKILLS: Commas

Use commas correctly in your essay. Too few commas make your writing confusing. Too many commas will make your writing jumpy. Use commas in the following situations:

To separate items in a series:
Bruh Bear is thoughtful, gentle, and slow.

To set off interrupting words:
Bruh Rabbit, on the other hand, is quick and jumpy.

To separate clauses in a compound sentence:
Bruh Rabbit is impatient, but Bruh Bear is methodical.

Practice On your paper, write the following sentences, adding commas where needed.

1. He Lion doesn't know Man but the other animals do.
2. Why the animals wondered did he have to roar?
3. Possum Squirrel Rabbit and Bear had a meeting.

Writing Application Add commas to your essay where they are needed.

Writer's Solution Connection
Language Lab

For more help with commas, complete the Commas lesson in the Language Lab.

Follow Your Organization Stick to the organization you have chosen. Place related details together, or place similarities and differences together.

Revising

Use a Checklist As you review your work, use the following checklist to guide you:
▶ Have I focused on a few significant qualities?
▶ Do I use vivid adjectives when I describe qualities?
▶ Do I stick to my organization?

Revise where your essay needs more vivid adjectives or a more consistent organization.

REVISION MODEL

Bruh Bear and Bruh Rabbit share the quality of intelligence.
① ~~Bruh Bear is smart. Bruh Rabbit is smart.~~ Bear
     deliberate   ,but
shares his intelligent thoughts in a ~~slow~~ way. ②
Rabbit's ideas and speech are quick.
③ Both   and   have
  Bruh Bear ~~has seen a lot.~~ Bruh Rabbit ~~has~~ seen a lot.

① The writer revises this sentence to indicate that intelligence is a main focus point.
② The writer uses the word *but* to show that two qualities are being contrasted.
③ The writer revises to show that the animals share a quality.

Publishing and Presenting

Bulletin Board Post your essay on a class bulletin board. Ask classmates to comment on whether they recognized the similarities and differences that you presented.

Book Report Create a unique book report by comparing and contrasting the characters in the report.

Poster Mount your essay at the center of a poster. Around the essay, paste pictures and images that capture the features of your subjects that you have compared and contrasted.

Strategies for Success

On any given issue or topic, there are bound to be several different opinions or viewpoints. When you read to find information, you should read from several sources. In each of the sources, the writer will write about the idea or topic from his or her own viewpoint in his or her own words. It's up to you to compare the same idea expressed in different words and to create a balanced picture.

Choose Your Sources In order to create a balanced picture, choose sources that are likely to express different viewpoints, rather than two that express the same viewpoint. For example, if you are learning about a political candidate, read something written by a member of the candidate's party and something by a member of a different party. Do not read a speech by the candidate and a press release that his party has prepared.

Identify Key Points Identify which points are discussed in both works. Then, think about what each work says about the point. Look for places where the ideas overlap and where they differ dramatically. Evaluate the support that each side provides for the key points. The balanced picture usually lies somewhere between the two opposite viewpoints.

✔ Here are situations in which you may need to compare the same idea in different words:
  ▶ Researching a historical person or event
  ▶ Reading political material
  ▶ Reading about current events
  ▶ Evaluating a product

Apply the Strategies

Read over the two editorials about the proposed closing of a neighborhood park. Then, answer the questions that follow.

To the editor:
How long will our taxes pay for a park that is not being properly used? The Wilson Memorial Park on Smith Street is infrequently used during the day, but after dark the park is full of teens just hanging out. The equipment is run down and dangerous, and the night crowds make the neighborhood unpleasant. I hope others will join me in urging Mayor Blinn and the council to close the park.

To the editor:
Lately, many people have complained about the Wilson Memorial Park on Smith Street, and there is the possibility that it will be closed. The park is the only outdoor area left in which people in our neighborhood can escape the noise of traffic and the bustle on our congested streets. I have taken advantage of the park on many summer evenings. As a senior citizen who has lived in the area for more than twenty years, I would be sorry to see it closed. I hope others will join me in urging Mayor Blinn and the council to keep the park open and to make plans to repair the broken equipment.

---

1. (a) What is the main topic of each letter? (b) What are the key points discussed in both letters?
2. On which point do both writers agree?
3. On which points do the writers disagree?
4. What is your opinion after reading both letters?

Grammar Review

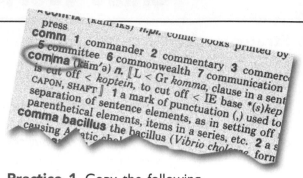

Commas are used to help make your meaning clear. The following are some common uses of commas:

Use commas in compound sentences.
Separate the two simple sentences in a compound sentence with a coordinating conjunction and a comma. (See page 779.)

> The ministers lied, but the child told the truth.

Use commas to separate items in a series.
When three or more items are listed, the list is called a series. The items in the series are separated by commas. The items in a series may be single words or groups of words. (See page 794.)

> They described the beauty, richness, and color of the cloth.

> They bought the loom, gathered supplies, and wove the cloth.

Use commas to set off interrupters.
Interrupters are words, phrases, or clauses that interrupt a sentence to add information that is not essential to the meaning of the sentence. The commas indicate that these words could be left out and the sentence would still make sense. (See page 810.)

> Coyote, who was very clever, stole the fire.

> Acrisius, of course, couldn't have known.

Grammar in Writing

✔ *Leaving out commas in places where they belong will create confusion. Using too many commas, however, will make your writing choppy and slow.*

Practice 1 Copy the following compound sentences into your notebook. Place commas where they are needed.

1. Coyote played many tricks and these tricks hurt Mouse.

2. The emperor saw nothing but he was afraid to say so.

3. The child spoke out for he was not afraid.

4. The advisor was worried so he didn't tell the truth.

5. Coyote ran quickly yet he was scorched.

Practice 2 Copy the following sentences into your notebook. Add commas where they are needed to separate items in a series or to set off interrupters.

1. He Lion Bruh Bear and Bruh Rabbit set off to find Man.

2. The emperor who was very vain believed them.

3. Coyote ran to the fire grabbed a branch and dashed off.

4. Coyote Chipmunk and Squirrel worked together.

5. They waited freezing for the gift of fire.

PART 2 *Lessons and Legacies*

The Lesson, Sharon Wilson, © Felix Rosenstiel's Widow & Son Ltd, 1993

Guide for Reading

Meet the Authors:

Julius Lester (1939–   )

Julius Lester had a successful career in music when he turned to writing books on subjects related to his African American background. He has been a runner-up for the Newbery Medal and a finalist for the National Book Award.

Olivia E. Coolidge (1908–   )

As a teacher of English, Latin, and Greek, as well as a writer, Olivia E. Coolidge has lived in both the United States and Europe. She has written stories, myths, and biographical sketches for young readers.

Tran My-Van

Tran My-Van left her native land and moved to Australia because of the Vietnam War, but she never abandoned her cultural heritage. She received a medal for her service to Australian-Asian relations.

Ricardo E. Alegría (1921–   )

A native of San Juan, Ricardo Alegría has held many important positions related to education, archaeology, and culture in Puerto Rico. As director of the Center for Advanced Studies of Puerto Rico and the Caribbean, he has said, "Culture is the way mankind expresses itself to live and live collectively."

◆ LITERATURE AND YOUR LIFE

CONNECT YOUR EXPERIENCE

People make wishes in many ways. They wish on stars, throw pennies in a fountain, blow out the candles on a birthday cake. "The Three Wishes" and "A Crippled Boy" tell of people whose wishes came true—sometimes with unexpected results.

THEMATIC FOCUS: Our Living World

As you read, ask yourself whether the characters are better off when their wishes are granted or when they must work for their dreams.

◆ Background for Understanding

CULTURE

There are versions of "The Three Wishes" in several cultures around the world. Because folk tales are passed along orally, they can "migrate" from one place to another. Each storyteller adds details from his or her own experience or culture. After a number of tellings, a whole new version of the tale emerges. It teaches the same lesson and has the same basic plot, but key details reflect the beliefs and customs of that particular culture.

◆ Build Vocabulary

WORD ROOTS: -mort-

The myth "Arachne" tells about mortals and immortals. The root -mort-, which means "death," appears in the words *mortal* and *immortal*. Mortals can die, and immortals cannot die.

WORD BANK

Which word describes an action?

> obscure
> immortal
> mortal
> obstinancy
> foliage
> embraced
> covetousness

Why Monkeys Live in Trees ◆ Arachne
◆ A Crippled Boy ◆ The Three Wishes ◆

◆ Literary Focus
ORAL TRADITION

The stories in these selections were originally told orally in the cultures from which they come. They were later written down for us to read. Stories handed down orally from generation to generation reflect the traditions, beliefs, and values of the common people. Myths and tales like these from the **oral tradition** were and still are honored teaching tools.

◆ Reading Strategy
PREDICT

When you read the beginning of each of these myths or tales, can you **predict,** or state, what you think will happen? A prediction is more than a guess, though. When you predict, you use what you already know, based on your past reading and life experiences. Folk tales are very predictable. They usually follow a formula in which cleverness and bravery are rewarded. Undesirable qualities, such as arrogance, are punished.

After you read each story beginning, write your prediction on a chart like the one below. After you complete the story, note its outcome.

Prediction	What Actually Happened

WHY MONKEYS LIVE IN TREES

AFRICAN FOLK TALE

JULIUS LESTER

One day Leopard was looking at his reflection in a pool of water. Looking at himself was Leopard's favorite thing in the world to do. Leopard gazed, wanting to be sure that every hair was straight and that all his spots were where they were supposed to be. This took many hours of looking at his reflection, which Leopard did not mind at all.

Finally he was satisfied that nothing was disturbing his handsomeness, and he turned away from the pool of water. At that exact moment, one of Leopard's children ran up to him.

"Daddy! Daddy! Are you going to be in the contest?"

"What contest?" Leopard wanted to know. If it was a beauty contest, of course he was going to be in it.

"I don't know. Crow the Messenger just flew by. She said that King Gorilla said there was going to be a contest."

Without another word, Leopard set off. He went north-by-northeast, made a right turn at the mulberry bush and traveled east-by-south-by-west until he came to a hole in the ground. He went around in a circle five times, and headed north-by-somersault until he came to a big clearing in the middle of the jungle and that's where King Gorilla was.

King Gorilla sat at one end of the clearing on his throne. Opposite him, at the other side of the clearing, all the animals sat in a semicircle. In the middle, between King Gorilla and the animals, was a huge mound of what looked like black dust.

Leopard looked around with calm dignity. Then he strode regally over to his friend, Lion.

"What's that?" he asked, pointing to the mound of black dust.

"Don't know," Lion replied. "King Gorilla said he will give a pot of gold to whoever can eat it in one day. I can eat it in an hour."

Leopard laughed. "I'll eat it in a half hour."

It was Hippopotamus's turn to laugh. "As big as my mouth is, I'll eat that mound in one gulp."

◀ **Critical Viewing** For what reason might monkeys need extraordinary climbing ability? **[Deduce]**

The time came for the contest. King Gorilla had the animals pick numbers to see who would go in what order. To everybody's dismay, Hippopotamus drew Number 1.

Hippopotamus walked over to the mound of black dust. It was bigger than he had thought. It was much too big to eat in one gulp. Nonetheless, Hippopotamus opened his mouth as wide as he could, and that was very wide indeed, and took a mouthful of the black dust.

He started chewing. Suddenly he leaped straight into the air and screamed. He screamed so loudly that it knocked the ears off the chickens and that's why to this day chickens don't have ears.

Hippopotamus screamed and Hippopotamus yelled. Hippopotamus roared and Hippopotamus bellowed. Then he started sneezing and crying and tears rolled down his face like he was standing in the shower. Hippopotamus ran to the river and drank as much water as he could, and that was very much, indeed, to cool his mouth and tongue and throat.

The animals didn't understand what had happened to Hippopotamus, but they didn't care. They were happy because they still had a chance to win the pot of gold. Of course, if they had known that the mound of black dust was really a mound of black pepper, maybe they wouldn't have wanted the gold.

Nobody was more happy than Leopard because he had drawn Number 2. He walked up to the black mound and sniffed at it.

"AAAAAAAACHOOOOOOO!" Leopard didn't like that but then he remembered the pot of gold. He opened his mouth wide, took a mouthful and started chewing and swallowing.

Leopard leaped straight into the air, did a back double flip and screamed. He yelled and he roared and he bellowed and, finally, he started sneezing and crying, tears rolling down his face like a waterfall. Leopard ran to the river and washed out his mouth and throat and tongue.

Lion was next, and the same thing happened to him as it did to all the animals. Finally only Monkey remained.

Monkey approached King Gorilla. "I know I can eat all of whatever that is, but after each mouthful, I'll need to lie down in the tall grasses and rest."

King Gorilla said that was okay.

Monkey went to the mound, took a tiny bit of pepper on his tongue, swallowed, and went into the tall grasses. A few minutes later, Monkey came out, took a little more, swallowed it, and went into the tall grasses.

Soon the pile was almost gone. The animals were astonished to see Monkey doing what they had not been able to do. Leopard couldn't believe it either. He climbed a tree and stretched out on a sturdy limb to get a better view. From his limb high in the tree Leopard could see into the tall grasses where Monkey went to rest. Wait a minute! Leopard thought something was suddenly wrong with his eyes because he thought he saw a hundred monkeys hiding in the tall grasses.

He rubbed his eyes and looked another look. There wasn't anything wrong with his eyes. There were a hundred monkeys in the tall grasses and they all looked alike!

Just then, there was the sound of loud applause. King Gorilla announced that Monkey had won the contest and the pot of gold.

Leopard growled a growl so scary that even King Gorilla was frightened. Leopard wasn't thinking about anybody except the monkeys. He took a long and beautiful leap from the tree right smack into the middle of the tall grasses where the monkeys were hiding.

The monkeys ran in all directions. When the other animals saw monkeys running from the grasses, they realized that the monkeys had tricked them and started chasing them. Even King Gorilla joined in the chase. He wanted his gold back.

The only way the monkeys could escape was to climb to the very tops of the tallest trees where no one else, not even Leopard, could climb.

And that's why monkeys live in trees to this very day.

Arachne

GREEK MYTH
Olivia E. Coolidge

Arachne[1] was a maiden who became famous throughout Greece, though she was neither wellborn nor beautiful and came from no great city. She lived in an <u>obscure</u> little village, and her father was a humble dyer of wool. In this he was very skillful, producing many varied shades, while above all he was famous for the clear, bright scarlet which is made from shellfish, and which was the most glorious of all the colors used in ancient Greece. Even more skillful than her father was Arachne. It was her task to spin the fleecy wool into a fine, soft thread and to weave it into cloth on the high, standing loom within the cottage. Arachne was small and pale from much working. Her eyes were light and her hair was a dusty brown, yet she was quick and graceful, and her fingers, roughened as they were, went so fast that it was hard to follow their flickering movements. So soft and even was her thread, so fine her cloth, so gorgeous her embroidery, that soon her products were known all over Greece. No one had ever seen the like of them before.

At last Arachne's fame became so great that people used to come from far and wide to watch her working. Even the graceful nymphs[2] would steal in from stream or forest and peep shyly through the dark doorway, watching in wonder the white arms of Arachne as she stood at the loom and threw the shuttle from hand to hand between the hanging threads, or drew out the long wool, fine as a hair, from the distaff[3] as she sat spinning. "Surely Athene[4] herself must have taught her," people would murmur to one another. "Who else could know the secret of such marvelous skill?" Arachne was used to being wondered at, and she was immensely proud of the skill that had brought so many to look on her. Praise was all she lived for, and it displeased her greatly that people should think anyone, even a goddess, could teach her anything. Therefore when she heard them murmur, she would stop her work and turn round indignantly to say, "With my own ten fingers I gained this skill, and by hard practice from early morning till night. I never had time to stand looking as you people

---

1. **Arachne** (ä räk´ nē)

◆ Build Vocabulary

obscure (əb skyoor´) *adj.*: Not well known

---

2. **nymphs** (nimfz) *n.*: Minor nature goddesses, thought of as beautiful maidens living in rivers, trees, and so on.
3. **distaff** (dis´ taf) *n.*: A stick on which flax or wool is wound for use in spinning.
4. **Athene** (ə thē´ nə): Greek goddess of wisdom, skills, and warfare.

Arachne (detail), Arvis Stewart. Reprinted with the permission of Macmillan Publishing Company from The Macmillan Book of Greek Gods and Heroes by Alice Low, illustrated by Arvis Stewart. Copyright © 1985 by Macmillan Publishing Company

▲ **Critical Viewing** How can you tell that the characters in this picture are in conflict? **[Draw Conclusions]**

do while another maiden worked. Nor if I had, would I give Athene credit because the girl was more skillful than I. As for Athene's weaving, how could there be finer cloth or more beautiful embroidery than mine? If Athene herself were to come down and compete with me, she could do no better than I."

One day when Arachne turned round with such words, an old woman answered her, a gray old woman, bent and very poor, who stood leaning on a staff and peering at Arachne amid the crowd of onlookers. "Reckless girl," she said, "how dare you claim to be equal to the <u>immortal</u> gods themselves? I am an old woman and have seen much. Take my advice and ask pardon of Athene for your words. Rest content with your fame of being the best spinner and weaver that <u>mortal</u> eyes have ever beheld."

"Stupid old woman," said Arachne indignantly, "who gave you a right to speak in this way to me? It is easy to see that you were never good for anything in your day, or you would not come here in poverty and rags to gaze at my skill. If Athene resents my words, let her answer them herself. I have challenged her to a contest, but she, of course, will not come. It is easy for the gods to avoid matching their skill with that of men."

At these words the old woman threw down her staff and stood erect. The wondering onlookers saw her grow tall and fair and stand clad in long robes of dazzling white. They were terribly afraid as they realized that they stood in the presence of Athene. Arachne herself flushed red for a moment, for she had never really believed that the goddess would hear her. Before the group that was gathered there she would not give in; so pressing her pale lips together in <u>obstinacy</u> and pride, she led the goddess to one of the great looms and set herself before the other. Without a word both began to thread the long woolen strands that

hang from the rollers, and between which the shuttle[5] moves back and forth. Many skeins lay heaped beside them to use, bleached white, and gold, and scarlet, and other shades, varied as the rainbow. Arachne had never thought of giving credit for her success to her father's skill in dyeing, though in actual truth the colors were as remarkable as the cloth itself.

Soon there was no sound in the room but the breathing of the onlookers, the whirring of the shuttles, and the creaking of the wooden frames as each pressed the thread up into place or tightened the pegs by which the whole was held straight. The excited crowd in the doorway began to see that the skill of both in truth was very nearly equal, but that, however the cloth might turn out, the goddess was the quicker of the two. A pattern of many pictures was growing on her loom. There was a border of twined branches of the olive, Athene's favorite tree, while in the middle, figures began to appear. As they looked at the glowing colors, the spectators realized that Athene was weaving into her pattern a last warning to Arachne. The central figure was the goddess herself competing with Poseidon[6] for possession of the city of Athens; but in the four corners were mortals who had tried to strive with gods and pictures of the awful fate that had overtaken them. The goddess ended a little before Arachne and stood back from her marvelous work to see what the maiden was doing.

Never before had Arachne been matched against anyone whose skill was equal, or even nearly equal to her own. As she stole glances from time to time at Athene and saw the goddess working swiftly, calmly, and always a

---

5. shuttle (shut´ əl) *n.*: An instrument used in weaving to carry the thread back and forth.
6. Poseidon (pō sī´ dən): Greek god of the seas and of horses.

little faster than herself, she became angry instead of frightened, and an evil thought came into her head. Thus as Athene stepped back a pace to watch Arachne finishing her work, she saw that the maiden had taken for her design a pattern of scenes which showed evil or unworthy actions of the gods, how they had deceived fair maidens, resorted to trickery, and appeared on earth from time to time in the form of poor and humble people. When the goddess saw this insult glowing in bright colors on Arachne's loom, she did not wait while the cloth was judged, but stepped forward, her gray eyes blazing with anger, and tore Arachne's work across. Then she struck Arachne across the face. Arachne stood there a moment, struggling with anger, fear, and pride. "I will not live under this insult," she cried, and seizing a rope from the wall, she made a noose and would have hanged herself.

◆ **Reading Strategy**
Predict what will happen to Arachne.

The goddess touched the rope and touched the maiden. "Live on, wicked girl," she said. "Live on and spin, both you and your descendants. When men look at you they may remember that it is not wise to strive with Athene." At that the body of Arachne shriveled up, and her legs grew tiny, spindly, and distorted. There before the eyes of the spectators hung a little dusty brown spider on a slender thread.

All spiders descend from Arachne, and as the Greeks watched them spinning their thread wonderfully fine, they remembered the contest with Athene and thought that it was not right for even the best of men to claim equality with the gods.

◆ **Build Vocabulary**

immortal (i môr´ təl) *adj.*: Living forever

mortal (môr´ təl) *adj.*: Referring to humans, who must eventually die

obstinacy (äb´ stə nə sē) *n.*: Stubbornness

Guide for Responding

◆ **LITERATURE AND YOUR LIFE**

Reader's Response If you were Arachne, would you have challenged the goddess Athene? Why or why not?

Thematic Focus What do these tales explain about our living world?

Journal Writing Write a paragraph in which you explain why you like or dislike the way each of these stories ended.

☑ **Check Your Comprehension**

1. Describe Arachne's skills.
2. Who is the "gray old woman" who appears in the crowd? What advice does she offer Arachne?
3. What is the contest in "Why Monkeys Live in Trees"?
4. How do the monkeys win the contest?

◆ **Critical Thinking**

INTERPRET

1. Why does Arachne refuse to accept the advice from the old woman? **[Draw Conclusions]**
2. In "Why Monkeys Live in Trees," what information about the black powder would help the animals prepare better to be in the contest? **[Deduce]**

EVALUATE

3. Summarize the "sentence" Athene imposes on Arachne at the end of the myth. What lesson might the Greeks have learned from this myth? **[Assess]**

APPLY

4. Pride and confidence can be both helpful and harmful. Give examples from these stories that show both possibilities. **[Interpret]**

Red Tree, 1910, Piet Mondrian, Municipal Museum, The Hague

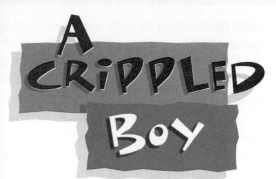

A CRIPPLED BOY

Vietnamese Folk Tale

Tran My-Van

Long, long ago there was a boy called Theo. He was crippled in both legs and could hardly walk. Since he could not work, he had no choice but to live on rice and vegetables which kind people gave him.

Often he sat watching other children play and run about. Unable to join them, he felt very miserable. To amuse himself Theo practiced throwing pebbles at targets. Hour after hour he would spend practicing his aim. Having nothing else to do he soon learned to hit all his targets. Other children took pity on him and gave him more pebbles to throw. Besides this, Theo could also make all sorts of shapes with stones on the ground.

One hot day Theo sat under a big banyan tree[1] which provided him with a delightful, cool shade under its thick leaves. He aimed stones at the thick <u>foliage</u> and managed to cut it into the outlines of animal forms. He was very pleased at what he could do and soon forgot his loneliness.

One day Theo was under his favorite banyan tree. To his surprise, he heard a drumbeat. Soon he saw many men in official clothes. It happened that the King was out for a country walk with some of his officials and was passing by Theo's tree.

The King's attention was caught by the unusual shadow of the tree. He stopped and was very surprised to see little crippled Theo sitting there all alone.

Theo was very frightened and tried to get away; but he could not crawl very far. The King asked Theo what he had been doing. Theo told the King his story.

Then the King asked Theo to demonstrate his skill at pebble throwing. Theo was happy to do so. The King was impressed and asked Theo to return with him to the palace where the King said:

"I have a little job for you to do."

The following day, before the King had a meeting with his mandarins,[2] he ordered Theo to sit quietly behind a curtain. The King had ordered a few holes to be made in the curtain so that Theo could see what was going on.

"Most of my mandarins talk too much," the King explained. "They never bother to listen to me or let me finish my sentence. So if anybody opens his mouth to speak while I am talking,

just throw a pebble into his mouth. This will teach him to shut up."

Sure enough, just as the meeting was about to start one mandarin opened his big mouth, ready to speak.

Oops! Something got into his mouth and he quickly closed it.

Another mandarin opened his mouth to speak but strangely enough he, too, shut his mouth without saying a word.

A miracle had happened. Throughout the whole meeting all the mandarins kept their silence.

For once the King could speak as much as he wanted without being interrupted. The King was extremely pleased with his success and the help that Theo had given him.

After that he always treasured Theo's presence and service. So Theo remained happily at the palace, no longer needing to beg for food and no longer always sitting alone under the banyan tree.

Beyond Literature

Community Connection

Handicap Access You probably recognize the signs on parking spaces that indicate they are reserved for people with disabilities. These parking spots that are close to a building are just one of the ways communities make sure that all people have equal access to public buildings and facilities. Other accommodations include ramps, automatic doors, hand rails, braille dots on printed signs, special phones, and sign language interpretations of performances.

Cross-Curricular Activity
Report Card Give your community a report card on its accommodations for the physically disabled. Visit several public buildings in your community, and rate them on whether a person with a disability could use the building or facility. Report your findings to the class.

Guide for Responding

◆ LITERATURE AND YOUR LIFE

Reader's Response How do you feel about what the king did to his mandarins?

Thematic Focus How is a king different from other people in a society?

Role Play With your classmates, role-play a conversation in which you tell the king what you think.

☑ Check Your Comprehension

1. Why does Theo begin to throw stones?
2. How does the king become aware of Theo?
3. What does the king ask Theo to do?
4. What is the result of the plan made by the king and Theo?

◆ Critical Thinking

INTERPRET
1. In what ways does Theo benefit from developing his talent? **[Analyze]**
2. How is Theo different from the mandarins in the king's court? **[Distinguish]**

APPLY
3. Explain why this folk tale can be enjoyed by people from many cultures. **[Relate]**

EXTEND
4. Which government jobs in the United States remind you of mandarins or the king? What skills and traits do you think people in these positions should have? **[Social Studies Link; Career Link]**

The Three Wishes

PUERTO RICAN FOLK TALE
Ricardo E. Alegría

any years ago, there lived a woodsman and his wife. They were very poor but very happy in their little house in the forest. Poor as they were, they were always ready to share what little they had with anyone who came to their door. They loved each other very much and were quite content with their life together. Each evening, before eating, they gave thanks to God for their happiness.

One day, while the husband was working far off in the woods, an old man came to the little house and said that he had lost his way in the forest and had eaten nothing for many days. The woodsman's wife had little to eat herself, but, as was her custom, she gave a large portion of it to the old man. After he had eaten everything she gave him, he told the woman that he had been sent to test her and that, as a reward for the kindness she and her husband showed to all who came to their house, they would be granted a special grace. This pleased the woman, and she asked what the special grace was.

The old man answered, "Beginning

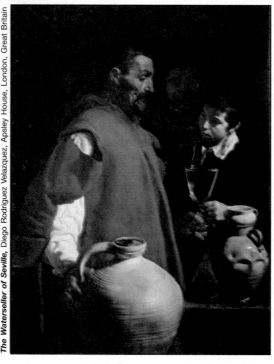

The Waterseller of Seville, Diego Rodriguez Velazquez, Apsley House, London, Great Britain

immediately, any three wishes you or your husband may wish will come true."

When she heard these words, the woman was overjoyed and exclaimed, "Oh, if my husband were only here to hear what you say!"

The last word had scarcely left her lips when the woodsman appeared in the little house with the ax still in his hands. The first wish had come true.

The woodsman couldn't understand it at all. How did it happen that he, who had been cutting wood in the forest, found himself here in his house? His wife explained it all as she <u>embraced</u> him. The woodsman just stood there, thinking over what his wife had said. He looked at the old man who stood quietly, too, saying nothing.

Suddenly he realized that his wife, without stopping to think, had used one of the three wishes, and he became very annoyed when he remembered all of the useful things she might have asked for with the first wish. For the first time, he became angry with his wife. The desire for riches had turned his head, and he scolded his wife, shouting at her, among other

---

▲ **Critical Viewing** What details indicate that this man doesn't make very much money? **[Analyze]**

things, "It doesn't seem possible that you could be so stupid! You've wasted one of our wishes, and now we have only two left! May you grow ears of a donkey!"

He had no sooner said the words than his wife's ears began to grow, and they continued to grow until they changed into the pointed, furry ears of a donkey.

When the woman put her hand up and felt them, she knew what had happened and began to cry. Her husband was very ashamed and sorry, indeed, for what he had done in his temper, and he went to his wife to comfort her.

The old man, who had stood by silently, now came to them and said, "Until now, you have known happiness together and have never quarreled with each other. Nevertheless, the mere knowledge that you could have riches and power has changed you both. Remember, you have only one wish left. What do you want? Riches? Beautiful clothes? Servants? Power?"

The woodsman tightened his arm about his wife, looked at the old man, and said, "We want only the happiness and joy we knew before my wife grew donkey's ears."

No sooner had he said these words than the donkey ears disappeared. The woodsman and his wife fell upon their knees to ask forgiveness for having acted, if only for a moment, out of covetousness and greed. Then they gave thanks for all their happiness.

The old man left, but before going, he told them that they had undergone this test in order to learn that there can be happiness in poverty just as there can be unhappiness in riches. As a reward for their repentance, the old man said that he would bestow upon them the greatest happiness a married couple could know. Months later, a son was born to them. The family lived happily all the rest of their lives.

◆ Build Vocabulary

embraced (em brāsd´) *v.*: Clasped in the arms, usually as an expression of affection

covetousness (kuv´ ət əs nəs) *n.*: Envy; wanting what another person has

Guide for Responding

◆ LITERATURE AND YOUR LIFE

Reader's Response Do you agree with the last wish? If not, what wish do you think the woodsman and his wife should have made?

Thematic Focus Why do you think the disguise of an old man is used to test the woodsman and his wife?

☑ Check Your Comprehension

1. Describe the life of the woodsman and his wife before they had the opportunity to make three wishes.
2. What situation made it possible for the woodsman and his wife to make three wishes?

◆ Critical Thinking

INTERPRET

1. What did the old man hope to find as an answer to the test he gave the woodsman and his wife? **[Infer]**
2. How does the saying "Be careful what you wish for" apply to the woodsman and his wife? **[Interpret]**

COMPARE THE LITERATURE

3. Would you consider all or some of these tales as good tools for learning how to live? Explain. **[Relate]**

Guide for Responding (continued)

◆ Reading Strategy

PREDICT

When you **predict** the outcome of a folk tale, you make a statement based on the formula folk tales usually follow.

1. Explain why the ending of "Why Monkeys ..." is predictable.
2. What undesirable quality is punished in "Arachne"?
3. What quality is rewarded in "A Crippled Boy"?
4. What did you predict about the outcome of "The Three Wishes"? Why?

◆ Build Vocabulary

USING THE WORD ROOT -mort-

The root -mort- that appears in *mortal* and *immortal* means "death." On your paper, write the meaning of the words containing the root -mort-.

1. The *mortician* prepared the body for burial.
2. The *mortality* rate lowers when the very sick receive good medical treatment and live.

SPELLING STRATEGY

The letters *cy* and *sy* often appear at the ends of words. Both spellings have the same pronunciation. One clue you can use is that -*cy* is a suffix that creates nouns meaning "the quality or state of." The suffix -*sy* forms other kinds of nouns and adjectives. Complete the word in each sentence with the letters *cy* or *sy*:

1. Athene did not appreciate Arachne's obstina_ _.
2. King Gorilla learned of the monkeys' trick through the courte_ _ of Leopard.

USING THE WORD BANK

Complete the paragraph with the Word Bank word that makes the most sense in each blank.

Some rarely told, _____ folk tales are among the most entertaining. They may tell tales of those who are _____ and _____. Usually, characters are punished for character flaws such as _____ and _____. Clever characters, like the monkeys who hide in the _____ usually do well. It seems they are _____ by good fortune.

◆ Literary Focus

ORAL TRADITION

The **oral tradition** refers to folk tales and myths that were handed down by word of mouth from one generation to the next before they were eventually written down for people to read. These tales express the history, values, and beliefs of a culture.

1. Oral tales survive because they are appealing in some way. Why do you think "Why Monkeys Live in Trees" has survived so many centuries?
2. What does "The Three Wishes" tell us about the values of people in Puerto Rico?

◆ Build Grammar Skills

VARIETY IN SENTENCE BEGINNINGS

Words may be arranged in several ways to form sentences. You don't always have to start with the subject. Sometimes you can start with a phrase or an adverb. Notice the beginnings in these examples:

Subject: "Crow the Messenger just flew by."
Prepositional Phrase: "To everybody's dismay, Hippopotamus drew Number 1."
Adverb: "Suddenly he leaped straight into the air and screamed."

Practice Each of the following sentences begins with a subject, verb, preposition, or modifier. Identify the way each sentence begins.

1. Excitedly, Arachne and Athene began to weave.
2. Without thinking clearly, the woodsman made a wish.
3. Leopard leapt when the black dust touched his tongue.
4. Boast little and keep the gods happy.
5. In an instant, the monkeys reached the trees.

Writing Application Rewrite the following sentences so that each uses a different kind of beginning:

1. Between them, Athene and Arachne wove two beautiful pieces of cloth.
2. In the meantime, Arachne thought angry thoughts.
3. The monkeys reached the trees in the nick of time.

Build Your Portfolio

 Idea Bank

Writing

1. **Make a Wish** Write three wishes you would make for your class as a whole.

2. **Story Blurb** Using one of the stories, write one or two sentences that would catch the attention of readers and make them want to read the story.

3. **Tale [Group Activity]** With a small group, write a tale that explains how and why children first went to school.

Speaking and Listening

4. **Contest Broadcast** Imagine that the contest between Arachne and Athene is being broadcast on radio. Create and perform a "play-by-play" commentary for the event. **[Performing Arts Link]**

5. **Myth and Tale Tellers' Circle [Group Activity]** In your own words, tell a myth or a folk tale you know to a group of classmates. If the story comes from another culture, tell about that culture. **[Social Studies Link]**

Projects

6. **Myth and Tale Mural [Group Activity]** With a small group of classmates, create a mural that illustrates something these myths and tales teach readers or listeners. **[Art Link]**

7. **Myth or Tale Performance [Group Activity]** Create a dance or a pantomime (acting without words) based on a myth or a tale that interests you. Prepare a written introduction, and read it aloud prior to the performance.

 Writing Mini-Lesson

Explanation

If a young child asked you how computers came into being, you could explain the facts that led to this invention, or you could use your imagination and create a story like "Why Monkeys Live in Trees." Choose a modern invention, and create a fictional story about how it came to be.

Writing Skills Focus: Narrow Your Topic

If you want to write your explanation about how electronics came into being and changed people's lives, the topic may be too broad, with too many parts. Television, computers, fax machines, among other inventions, are all a part of electronics. You could **narrow the topic** of your focus, and choose just one invention to explain.

For example, the story "Why Monkeys Live in Trees" focuses on just one aspect of monkeys. It does not try to explain everything about monkeys. As the title suggests, the folk tale focuses on explaining why monkeys live in trees. The last line, in fact, wraps up the tale by saying "And that's why monkeys live in trees to this very day."

Prewriting Choose a broad topic, like "electronics." Then, list subtopics related to it. Choose a subtopic, and see if you can narrow it even further.

Drafting Present your explanation like a story, with detailed events in the order in which they occurred.

Revising Check to make sure you've included enough details to make the explanation clear and understandable.

> ◆ **Grammar Application**
> Vary the way you begin sentences. Sometimes start with an adverb or a prepositional phrase.

THE PLACE WHERE I LIVE Look out the window, and think about what you see. Perhaps you see mountains and apple trees, or skyscrapers and traffic jams. Such things make the place where you live the place that it is. They help answer the question "Where am I?"

Where Am I? Geographers study the characteristics of places and regions, including weather patterns, mountains, and rivers. Geographers have invented systems for identifying location, such as longitude and latitude. They help people answer the question, "Where am I?"

Before people made maps or put up road signs, though, they answered this question in other ways. One of the ways was by inventing myths. A myth is a story that explains the origin of natural events or features. By explaining features of the land, myths help explain what makes "here" *here*.

The Nisqually Indians The Nisqually, a Native American tribe, tell myths about their home in what is now Washington State. In "Loo-Wit, the Fire-Keeper," they tell the story of two neighboring tribes and of how three mountains in the area came to be. Looking at what we call Mount St. Helens, a Nisqually might say, "I am near Loo-Wit."

Where the Good Heart Lives "Loo-Wit" also teaches a lesson about selfishness. Looking at the mountain and thinking of Loo-Wit, a Nisqually might say, "I am in a land where selfishness nearly destroyed us all." By telling us where we are, Loo-Wit's story also makes us think about how we should act.

CANADA

Columbia River

• Seattle

Washington

★ Olympia

Mount St. Helens

Mount Adams

N

Portland •

The Dalles

Mount Hood

0   100 mi

0   100 km

Willamette River

Oregon

Loo-Wit, the Fire-Keeper

Native American Myth   Joseph Bruchac

When the world was young, the Creator gave everyone all that was needed to be happy.

The weather was always pleasant. There was food for everyone and room for all the people. Despite this, though, two brothers began to quarrel over the land. Each wanted to control it. It reached the point where each brother gathered together a group of men to support his claim. Soon it appeared there would be a war.

The Creator saw this and was not pleased. He waited until the two brothers were asleep one night and then carried them to a new country. There a beautiful river[1] flowed and tall mountains rose into the clouds. He woke them just as the sun rose, and they looked out from the mountaintop to the land below. They saw what a good place it was. It made their hearts good.

> **Connecting Literature to Social Studies**
> Judging from this description, how do the Nisqually feel about this land?

"Now," the Creator said, "this will be your land." Then he gave each of the brothers a bow and a single arrow. "Shoot your arrow into the air," the Creator said. "Where your arrow falls will be the land of your people, and you shall be a great chief there."

The brothers did as they were told.

The older brother shot his arrow. It arched over the river and landed to the south in the valley of the Willamette River. There is where he and his people went, and they became the Multnomahs.[2] The younger brother shot his arrow. It flew to the north of the great river. He and his people went there and became the Klickitats.[3]

Then the Creator made a Great Stone Bridge across the river. "This bridge," the Creator said, "is a sign of peace. You and your peoples can visit each other by crossing over this bridge. As long as you remain at peace, as long as your hearts are good, this bridge will stand."

For many seasons the two peoples remained at peace. They passed freely back and forth across the Great Stone Bridge. One day, though, the people to the north looked south toward the Willamette and said, "Their lands are better than ours." One day, though, the people to the south looked north toward the Klickitat and said, "Their lands are more beautiful than ours." Then, once again, the people began to quarrel.

The Creator saw this and was not pleased.

The people were becoming greedy again. Their hearts were becoming bad. The Creator darkened the skies and took fire away. Now the people grew cold. The rains

---

1. **a beautiful river:** Columbia River, which flows between the present-day states of Oregon and Washington.

2. **Multnomahs:** Native American people who were nearly killed off by disease in the 1800's.
3. **Klickitats:** A Native American tribe of Washington; now part of the Yakima Nation.

of autumn began and the people suffered greatly.

"Give us back fire," they begged. "We wish to live again with each other in peace."

Their prayers reached the Creator's heart. There was only one place on Earth where fire still remained. An old woman name Loo-Wit had stayed out of the quarreling and was not greedy. It was in her <u>lodge</u> only that fire still burned. So the Creator went to Loo-Wit.

"If you share your fire with all the people," the Creator said, "I will give you whatever you wish. Tell me what you want."

"I want to be young and beautiful," Loo-Wit said.

"That is the way it will be," said the Creator. "Now take your fire to the Great Stone Bridge above the river. Let all the people come to you and get fire. You must keep the fire burning there to remind people that their hearts must stay good."

The next morning, the skies grew clear and the people saw the sun rise for the first time in many days. The sun shone on the Great Stone Bridge, and there the people saw a young woman as beautiful as the sunshine itself. Before her, there on the bridge, burned a fire. The people came to the fire and ended their quarrels. Loo-Wit

◆ Build Vocabulary

lodge (läj) *n.*: Small house or other dwelling

gave each of them fire. Now their homes again became warm and peace was everywhere.

One day, though, the chief of the people to the north came to Loo-Wit's fire. He saw how beautiful she was and wanted her to be his wife. At the same time, the chief of the people to the south also saw Loo-Wit's beauty. He, too, wanted to marry her. Loo-Wit could not decide which of the two she liked better. Then the chiefs began to quarrel. Their peoples took up the quarrel, and fighting began.

When the Creator saw the fighting, he became angry. He broke down the Great Stone Bridge. He took each of the two chiefs and changed them into mountains. The chief of the Klickitats became the mountain we now know as Mount Adams. The chief of the Multnomahs became the mountain we now know as Mount Hood. Even as mountains, they continued to quarrel, throwing flames and stones at each other. In some places, the stones they threw almost blocked the river between them. That is why the Columbia River is so narrow in the place called The Dalles today.

Loo-Wit was heartbroken over the pain caused by her beauty. She no longer wanted to be a beautiful young woman. She could no longer find

> **Connecting Literature to Social Studies**
> What might the Great Stone Bridge look like today?

◀ ▶ **Critical Viewing** Why are these two Native Americans shown in stone? **[Connect]**

peace as a human being.

The Creator took pity on her and changed her into a mountain also, the most beautiful of the mountains. She was placed so that she stood between Mount Adams and Mount Hood, and she was allowed to keep the fire within herself which she had once shared on the Great Stone Bridge. Eventually, she became known as Mount St. Helens and she slept peacefully.

Though she was asleep, Loo-Wit was still aware, the people said. The Creator had placed her between the two quarreling mountains to keep the peace, and it was intended that humans, too, should look at her beauty and remember to keep their hearts good, to share the land and treat it well. If we humans do not treat the land with respect, the people said, Loo-Wit will wake up and let us know how unhappy she and the Creator have become again. So they said long before the day in the 1980's when Mount St. Helens woke again.

> **Connecting Literature to Social Studies**
> Judging from Loo-Wit's story, what kind of mountain is Mount St. Helens?

Meet the Author

Joseph Bruchac (1942–   )

When he was growing up, Joseph Bruchac was strongly influenced by his grandfather, a member of the Abenaki people. That influence led Bruchac to devote much of his time to writing about Native Americans. He has written more than sixty books about Native American culture. He and his wife founded Greenfield Review Press, a publishing company that specializes in multicultural works.

Guide for Responding

◆ LITERATURE AND YOUR LIFE

Reader's Response Were you surprised by the behavior of the brothers after the Creator returned fire to them? Explain.

Thematic Focus What lessons does this myth teach?

☑ Check Your Comprehension

1. What method does the Creator use to divide the land between the two brothers?
2. Why does the Creator take fire away from the brothers?
3. Why is Loo-Wit the only person allowed to have fire?

◆ Critical Thinking

INTERPRET

1. Give two details showing that the Creator is kind and forgiving. **[Support]**
2. What actions of Loo-Wit make her different from the two brothers? **[Distinguish]**
3. (a) What do the brothers share successfully? (b) What do they share with difficulty? **[Analyze]**
4. How do you think the Nisqually would treat a selfish person? Explain. **[Draw Conclusions]**

EXTEND

5. Tell what you know about the scientific explanation of volcanic eruptions. **[Science Link]**

CONNECTING LITERATURE TO SOCIAL STUDIES

Myths and folk tales answer the question "Where is this place where I live?" They also teach lessons about how people should act.

The Klickitats and the Multnomahs, the groups about whom the Nisqually tell this tale, lived along the Columbia River, near the Cascade Mountains. This range includes volcanos. Most are inactive, but Mount St. Helens has erupted as recently as the 1980's. Temperatures in the region can reach 100°F in the summer, but can drop below 0°F in the winter.

"Loo-Wit . . ." tells of the land where the Klickitats and Multnomahs lived. It also tells of the selfishness that causes people to quarrel over lands and of the need for fire that all people share.

1. Name four features of the region in this tale.
2. How would the Nisqually Indians explain an eruption of Mount St. Helens?
3. Do the Nisqually Indians think people should share the land? Do they think people are *able* to share the land? Explain.

 Idea Bank

Writing

1. **Character Description** Write a short description of Loo-Wit based on details from the story. Add details that are not in the story. For example, you might tell of an incident that shows a quality that Loo-Wit has.
2. **Dialogue** Write a conversation between two people who have just learned that there is no more fire. Include details describing ways in which their lives will be affected.
3. **Invent a Myth** Select some geographical feature of the place where you live—a lake, a city, a mountain, or some other feature. Make up a myth explaining how this feature was created.

Speaking and Listening

4. **Role Play** In the voice of the Creator, speak to the two brothers after they have quarreled with each other about who has the better land. **[Performing Arts Link]**

Projects

5. **Art** Using a map of Washington State, draw a "mythological map." Replace Mount Hood, Mount Adams, and Mount St. Helens with figures based on the characters in Loo-Wit. **[Art Link; Science Link]**
6. **Oral Presentation** Learn more about the Native Americans of the Pacific Northwest. Using slides and other materials, report your findings to the class. **[Social Studies Link]**

Further Reading, Listening, and Viewing

- Joseph Bruchac and Michael J. Caduto's book *Keepers of the Earth: Native American Stories and Environmental Activities for Children* (1988) includes "Loo-Wit, the Fire-Keeper" and other folk tales.
- Nancy Luenn's book *Miser on the Mountain: A Nisqually Legend of Mount Rainier* (1997) is a story about a man who climbs one of the Cascade Mountains and learns an important lesson.
- The video *Mount Rainier* explains more about the geology and the history of the Cascade Mountains.

Research Report

Writing Process Workshop

Maybe you want to find out more about the country from which one of the myths or folk tales comes. Perhaps you want to find out the scientific explanation for how volcanoes are formed. To learn more about a topic, you do research. You can share what you've learned in a **research report**—a written presentation of factual information that you've gathered on a particular topic. The following skills will help you write an informative, well-organized research paper.

Writing Skills Focus

▶ **Choose a narrow topic.** Choose a topic that is narrow enough to cover in the length of the report you plan to write. If, for instance, you are interested in Ancient Greece, you could narrow your topic to the government of ancient Greece or a particular hero from Greek mythology. (See p. 831.)

▶ **Use a clear and logical organization.** You might choose to present your facts in order of importance, time order, or by type. The organization you choose depends on the topic of your research.

▶ **Have a clear, consistent purpose.** Know before you even start writing what you hope to show or demonstrate. Gather details that will help you achieve your purpose.

MODEL

The area that is now southern Mexico was once home to the Mayas, ① one of the most advanced civilizations in the Western Hemisphere. ② By A.D. 400, the Mayas had developed a complex system of writing and had made advances in ③ science, mathematics, architecture, and the arts.

① The author clearly states the purpose of the research report: to show the advanced civilization of the Mayas.

② The writer provides support for the statement that the Mayas were advanced.

③ The writer can organize details by type under advances in these areas.

Prewriting

Choose a Topic A research report can be about anything that interests you and for which you can find factual information. Choose a topic that is narrow enough to cover in the length of the report you plan to write. The chart below shows some topics that have been narrowed.

Broad	Narrow	Narrower
Sports	Football	The History of Football
Animals	Animals of Africa	Endangered Species in Africa
Environment	Conserving Resources	Recycling

Get Ready to Research Before you begin researching, make a list of what you know and what you want to find out. Then, take your list to the library and use the resources there to gather information. You can use encyclopedias (usually available in text and on CD), nonfiction books, the *Readers' Guide to Periodical Literature,* and on-line information services.

Take Notes Put each fact on a separate note card. Doing this will make it easy to reorganize details if necessary. Make a source card for each source you use. The sample cards below show the best way to make note cards and source cards.

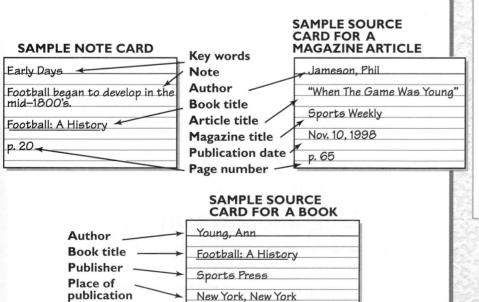

SAMPLE NOTE CARD

Early Days

Football began to develop in the mid–1800's.

Football: A History

p. 20

Key words
Note
Author
Book title
Article title
Magazine title
Publication date
Page number

SAMPLE SOURCE CARD FOR A MAGAZINE ARTICLE

Jameson, Phil

"When The Game Was Young"

Sports Weekly

Nov. 10, 1998

p. 65

SAMPLE SOURCE CARD FOR A BOOK

Author
Book title
Publisher
Place of publication
Copyright date

Young, Ann

Football: A History

Sports Press

New York, New York

1994

APPLYING LANGUAGE SKILLS: Crediting Sources

You must indicate the source of your information when you use someone else's exact words, when you include someone else's idea or opinion, when you use a statistic, or when you include a little-known fact.

In most research papers, you can credit your source in parentheses:

More than 14,000 high schools in the United States have football teams. (Young, p. 225)

Sometimes, you might credit your sources in footnotes:

More than 14,000 high schools in the United States have football teams. (Young, p. 225)

1. Ann Young, *Football: A History* (New York: Sports Press, 1994), p. 225.

Practice Write a parenthetical credit and a footnote for information that comes from page 65 of *Sports Weekly.* (See source card on this page.)

Writing Application Credit sources in your research paper.

Writer's Solution Connection Writing Lab

For help with note cards and source cards, use the note-card activity in the Reports tutorial.

APPLYING LANGUAGE SKILLS:
Formatting a Bibliography

A bibliography is an alphabetical list of the sources you consulted for your report. Look at these examples to see how to format entries in your bibliography:

Interview: Nelson, Frank, Interview. November 13, 1999.

Encyclopedia Entry: "Football." World Book. Vol.7, pp. 365, 366.

Full-Length Book: Carpenter, Albert. Football, Now and Then. Upper Saddle River, NJ: Prentice Hall, 1997.

Magazine Article: Taylor, Beth. "Glory Days." Football Journal, July 1995, pp. 40–45.

CD-ROM: "Early Days." Football. Lanon Digital: 1999.

Practice Write a bibliography entry for each of the sources on the source cards on the previous page.

Writing Application Create a bibliography for your research report. Use the correct format.

Writer's Solution Connection
Writing Lab

For more help formatting a bibliography, use the Interactive Bibliography Model in the tutorial on Reports.

Drafting

Write the Introduction Begin your report with an introduction in which you present your main idea, grab your readers' interest, and make a transition to the body of your report.

Develop Your Main Idea Develop the main idea in the body of your report. Focus each paragraph on a single key point stated in a topic sentence that supports or explains the main idea. Use facts, examples, statistics, and expert opinions to illustrate the key point in your topic sentence.

Sum It Up In your conclusion, restate your main idea and sum up key points. Look at the following example of a conclusion:

MODEL

The introduction to this library research report stated that the Mayan culture was one of the most advanced in this part of the world. Notice that the conclusion restates the main idea. It also summarizes the key points that support the main idea.

The ancient Mayas show that a society does not have to be modern to be advanced. They made great achievements in mathematics, science, architecture, and the arts. The Mayas were one of the most advanced civilizations of our time.

Revising

Use a Checklist As you review your work, use the following checklist to guide you:
- ▶ Do I state my main idea in the introduction?
- ▶ Do I provide support for my main idea in the body?
- ▶ Is each paragraph focused on a single key point?
- ▶ Do I credit sources of information.

If you have answered no to any of these questions, revise so that you can answer yes.

Publishing and Presenting

Bulletin Board Post your research report on a class bulletin board so classmates can learn more about your topic.

Mini-Lesson Use your report as the basis of a mini-lesson on your topic. Present your mini-lesson to the class.

Real-World Reading Skills Workshop

Strategies for Success

When you do research, you should use a variety of sources. Evaluate each source, however, before using the information in it.

Consider the Source When you evaluate a source, begin by asking yourself two questions:

- Is this a reliable source of factual information?
- Is the information in this source directly related to my topic?

For example, if you are writing a research report on the space shuttle *Challenger,* you may find a science-fiction story about space travel in a magazine and an article on the history of space travel. The science-fiction story is not a reliable source of factual information. The article on the history of space travel is not directly related to the topic of the space shuttle *Challenger.*

Check the Date Some areas, such as science or social studies, are constantly changing. New information replaces old. For this reason, you should look for sources that have been published recently. Magazines usually have the publication date right on the cover. Books usually put the publication date on the page following the title page.

> ✔ Here are situations in which it is important to evaluate sources of information:
> ▶ Reading newspaper articles
> ▶ Reading two articles on the same topic
> ▶ Researching to write a report

Apply the Strategies

Look at the following sources. Then, answer the questions that follow.

> *World Book Encylopedia,* Volume S, 1997.
>
> *Strange Stories of Outer Space,* Larry Stein, 1975, Roan Publishing.
>
> *Neil Armstrong: Space Pioneer,* Kathy Simpson, Milford Press, 1999.
>
> "Space Travel in the Twentieth Century," *Astronomy Now,* February 23, 1969.
>
> *A History of Space Travel,* George Rigby, Technology Press, 2000.

1. Which source or sources would be most useful and reliable if you were writing a research report on space travel? Explain your choices.

2. Which source or sources would be least useful and reliable if you were writing a research report on space travel? Explain your choices.

If you wore your favorite color every day, it wouldn't be your favorite color for long. You would soon tire of it. In the same way, readers can tire of reading the same kind of sentence over and over again. For this reason, you should use a variety of sentence structures and beginnings when you write.

Vary Sentence Beginnings You don't always have to start a sentence with the subject. Sometimes, you can start with a prepositional phrase or an adverb. (See page 830.)

> Hippopotamus slowly opened his jaws.
> Slowly, Hippopotamus opened his jaws.

> The monkeys waited in the trees.
> In the trees, the monkeys waited.

Combine Sentences Combine some of your short sentences so that your writing will include sentences of various lengths.

Use a compound subject:

> The hippo tried to eat the pepper.
> The leopard tried to eat the pepper.
> The hippo and the leopard tried to eat the pepper.

Use a compound verb:

> Arachne looked.
> Arachne saw that Athene's weaving was beautiful.
> Arachne looked and saw that Athene's weaving was beautiful.

Form a compound sentence:

> They were poor. They were happy.
> They were poor, but they were happy.

SEND

sen·tence (sen'təns) *n.* 1 a group of words that is used to tell, ask, command, or exclaim something, usually having a subject and a predicate; a sentence begins with a capital letter and ends with a period, question mark, or exclamation point

Practice 1 On your paper, write each sentence with a different beginning.

1. Arachne silently prepared the loom.

2. On the loom was the most beautiful weaving.

3. I gained this skill with my own ten fingers.

4. She would not yield before the group.

5. Angrily, she shook her head.

Practice 2 On your paper, combine each pair of sentences in the way indicated.

1. He realized his wife had used one of the wishes. He became annoyed. (compound sentence)

2. He was angry. He scolded his wife. (compound verb)

3. The woodsman was sorry. His wife was sorry. (compound subject)

4. The old man appeared. He told them it was a test. (compound verb)

5. They loved each other very much. They were happy with their lives. (compound sentence)

Grammar in Writing

✔ *You can also combine sentences with appositive phrases.*
  Arachne was a skilled weaver.
  She became famous throughout Greece.
  Arachne, who was a skilled weaver, became famous throughout Greece.

Not all research is done in a library. One way to gather valuable information is to conduct an interview. The strategies below will help you conduct a mature, informative interview.

Prepare. Prepare your interview questions well ahead of time. Allow yourself time to think them over and discuss them with a partner. Review and revise any questions before you go into the interview. Carefully prepared questions will avoid wasted time in the interview.

If possible, supply the person you will interview with a copy of the questions. Allowing your subject to see the questions ahead of time means that he or she can think about the answers and give you a clear, detailed response.

Be Specific. Ask a series of questions rather than one big question. For example, rather than asking, "What was life like when you were young?" break the question into a series of questions about school, activities, rules, music, and clothes.

Take Notes. Take careful notes. You might take written notes on a chart or an outline you prepare based on your questions, or you might ask your subject if he or she will allow you to tape-record the interview.

Don't Interrupt. Allow your subject to finish speaking before asking another question. If a question occurs to you while your subject is speaking, jot it down. That way you won't forget it and can wait until your subject is finished with his or her thought.

Apply the Strategies

Practice interviewing by conducting each of the following interviews. Share the results of your interviews with the class.

1. Interview the manager of a local business or store about what jobs are available and the requirements for each.

2. Interview a friend or family member who is at least twenty years older than you are to find out how music today is different from when he or she was young.

3. Interview an adult who works in a field that interests you to find out what he or she does at work.

Tips for Conducting an Interview

✔ *Be on time. Don't waste your subject's time by keeping him or her waiting.*

✔ *Listen attentively. When you are not jotting down a note, look at your subject to show your interest in what he or she is saying.*

What's Behind the Words

Vocabulary Adventures With Richard Lederer

Words From Myths

Of all the literary sources that feed into our English language, ancient mythology is one of the richest. You frequently speak, hear, and write the names of ancient gods, goddesses, and heroes—even if you don't always know it.

Echoes of Mythology

Echo, for example, is an echo of a story that is more than two millenniums old. Echo was a beautiful nymph who angered Hera, wife of Zeus. Hera punished the nymph by taking away Echo's power to start a conversation. As a result, Echo could only repeat the last words of anything she heard.

Later, Echo fell madly in love with a very handsome Greek boy named Narcissus. Because of Echo's peculiar disability, Narcissus would have nothing to do with her. So deeply did the nymph grieve for her unreturned love, that she wasted away to nothing—until all that was left was her voice, always repeating the last words she heard.

The fate that befell Narcissus explains why his name has been transformed into the word *narcissism,* meaning "extreme self-love." One day, Narcissus looked into a still forest lake and beheld his own face in the water, although he did not recognize himself. He at once fell in love with the beauty of the face he saw, and he, like Echo, pined away for a love that could never be returned.

A Tantalizing Story

Tantalus, King of Lydia, was such an evil villain that the gods banished him to Hades, the underworld. There, he is condemned to stand in a sparkling pool of water with branches of luscious fruit above his head. When he stoops to drink, the water drains away through the bottom of the pool. When he reaches up to take some fruit, the branches sway just beyond his grasp. Today, when something presents itself temptingly to our view but seems just out of reach, we say it *tantalizes* us.

ACTIVITY A Greek herald in Homer's *Iliad* was a human public-address system, for his voice could be heard all over camp. Today, the adjective *stentorian* means "loud-voiced; bellowing." Locate the sources of the following words that come down to us from mythology. Explain how the origin of the word relates to the meaning of the word today.

1. flora	**8.** mentor
2. fauna	**9.** nemesis
3. fury	**10.** phobia
4. hermetic	**11.** titanic
5. martial	**12.** jovial
6. chaotic	**13.** panic
7. lethal	**14.** Olympics

Extended Reading Opportunities

In many folk tales, the main character faces the challenge of his or her life. Very often, some unknown force surfaces to help this character succeed. Whether it is a wise elder, a magical power, or something from within, these heroes find ways to learn and to win.

Suggested Titles

Patakin: World Tales of Drums and Drummers
Nina Jaffe

You may be surprised by the important role of drums in various cultures since the beginning of time. In these tales from Ireland, India, and many other countries, the beating of drums inspires men and women, for their sound reflects and excites the beating of their hearts. The rhythm of drums has a magical way of moving people and keeping their spirits up during difficult times. Drums have been used for a lot more than just rock music!

Aladdin and Other Tales From the Arabian Nights
W. Heath Robinson

The brilliant Scheherazade fears for her life: Will her fate be the same as the other wives of her cruel husband? In a clever attempt to prolong her life, Scheherazade tricks her husband by telling him irresistible stories full of suspense—and makes him wait until tomorrow to find out what happens next. As you read, you will be entranced by both Scheherazade's tales and the story of her own fascinating and troubled life.

Flying With the Eagle, Racing the Great Bear: Stories From Native North America
Told by Joseph Bruchac

Imagine having to fight off a huge, hungry beast before being considered an adult. In this collection of Native American tales, young boys undertake challenging quests to learn what it means to be a man in their culture. They learn lessons about courage, respect, and the value of life, as they prove to others and to themselves that they can handle anything the world throws their way.

Other Possibilities

The Canary Prince	Eric Jon Nones
The Farthest Away Mountain	Lynne Reid Banks
The Mermaid's Twin Sister: More Stories From Trinidad	Lynn Joseph

GLOSSARY

abashed (ə basht´) *v.*: Ashamed

abundant (ə bun´ dənt) *adj.*: Plentiful; more than enough

accumulations (ə kyōōm´ yōō lā´ shənz) *n.*: Buildup occurring over a period of time

adamant (ad´ ə mənt) *adj.*: Not flexible; not willing to give in

admonishing (ad män´ ish iŋ) *adj.*: Disapproving

aggrieved (ə grēvd´) *adj.*: Offended; wronged

alien (ā´ lē ən) *adj.*: Foreign; unfamiliar

amethyst (am´ i thist´) *n.*: Purple or violet

anecdotes (an´ ik dōts´) *n.*: Short, entertaining tales

anonymity (an´ ə nim´ ə tē) *adj.*: The condition of being a stranger; not known by name

antennae (an ten´ ē) *n.*: Metal rods that receive TV or radio signals

aptitude (ap´ tə tōōd´) *n.*: Natural ability

atone (a tōn´) *v.*: Make up for a wrong

atrocious (ə trō´ shəs) *adj.*: Very bad; outrageous

barometer (bə räm´ ət ər) *n.*: Device for measuring air pressure; used to predict rain

becoming (bē kum´ iŋ) *adj.*: Suitable to the wearer

beseech (bi sēch´) *v.*: Beg

bough (bou) *n.*: Branch of a tree

bound (bound) *v.*: Tied

calculated (kal´ kyōō lāt´ id) *v.*: Determined by using math

catastrophic (kat´ ə straf´ ik) *adj.*: Causing a complete disaster

cavernous (kav´ ər nəs´) *adj.*: Deep and empty

ceased (sēsd) *v.*: Stopped

chaotic (kā ät´ ik) *adj.*: Completely confused

chorus (kôr´ əs) *n.*: The part of a song sung by many voices at once

chronic (krän´ ik) *adj.*: Lasting a long time or occurring again and again

cite (sīt) *v.*: Refer to as an example

clamor (klam´ ər) *n.*: Loud demand or complaint

coaxed (kōkst) *v.*: Tried to persuade

collision (kə lizh´ ən) *n.*: Coming together with a sudden violent force; a crash

colossal (kə läs´ əl) *adj.*: Huge; gigantic

composed (kəm pōzd´) *adj.*: Made up (of)

compulsion (kəm pul´ shən) *n.*: Force

compulsory (kəm pul´ sə rē) *adj.*: Must be done; having specific requirements

conclusion (kən klōō´ zhən) *n.*: Belief or decision reached by reasoning

condemnation (kän´ dem nā´ shən) *n.*: Extreme disapproval; harsh judgment

confidence (kän´ fi dəns´) *n.*: Belief in one's own abilities

consequently (kän´ si kwent´ lē) *adj.*: As a result

consoled (kän sōld´) *v.*: Comforted

consumed (kən sōōmd´) *v.*: Destroyed

consumption (kən sump´ shen) *n.*: Eating; drinking; using up

contemptuous (kən temp´ chōō əs´) *adj.*: Lacking respect for; seeing as worthless

cordial (kôr´ jəl) *adj.*: Warm and friendly

covetousness (kuv´ ət əs nəs) *n.*: Envy; wanting what another person has

craned (krānd) *v.*: Stretched out (one's neck) for a better view

crescent (kres´ ənt) *n.*: Anything shaped like the moon in its first or last quarter

crimson (krim´ zən) *n.*: Deep red

cudgel (kuj´ əl) *n.*: Short, thick stick or club

decisively (di sī´ siv lē) *adv.*: With determination

declined (di klīnd´) *v.*: Refused

deem (dēm) *v.*: Judge

delver (del´ vər) *n.*: Digger; searcher

demise (dē mīz´) *n.*: Death

dense (dens) *adj.*: Tightly packed; difficult to see through

descending (də send´ iŋ) *v.*: Moving from a higher to a lower place

desolate (des´ ə lit) *adj.*: Lonely or abandoned

detrimental (de´ trə ment´ əl) *adj.*: Harmful

devours (di vourz´) *v.*: Swallows whole

diagnosis (dī əg nō´ sis) *n.*: Explanation of or prediction about a person's medical condition

dilution (di lōō´ shən) *n.*: Process of weakening by mixing with something else

diminutive (də min´ yōō tiv) *adj.*: Very small

disinfect (dis´ in fekt´) *n.*: Dialect, or regional language, for disinfectant, a substance that kills germs

dispute (di spyōōt´) *n.*: Argument; debate; quarrel

dissonance (dis´ ə nəns) *n.*: Harsh combination of sounds

distorted (di stôr´ tid) *adj.*: Twisted out of the normal shape

diverse (də vurs´) *adj.*: Various; with differing characteristics

documentation (däk´ yōō mən tā´ shən) *n.*: Supporting evidence

drawbacks (drô´ baks´) *n.*: Disadvantages

drawing (drô´ iŋ) *v.*: Bringing forth; making flow

dreadful (dred´ fəl) *adj.*: Very bad; disagreeable

drone (drōn) *n.*: Continuous humming sound

eased (ēzd) *v.*: Comforted; freed from pain or worry

eloquent (el´ ə kwint) *adj.*: Persuasive and expressive

elusive (ē lōō´ siv) *adj.*: Always escaping

emaciated (ē mā´ shē āt id) *adj.*: Thin and bony as a result of starvation or disease

embedded (em bed´ əd) *adj.*: Firmly fixed in a surrounding material

embraced (em brāsd´) *v.*: Clasped in the arms, usually as an expression of affection

emerged (ē merjd´) *v.*: Came out from; came into view

emigrated (em´ i grāt id) *v.*: Left one country to settle in another

eminent (em´ ən ənt) *adj.*: Outstanding in performance

endured (en dòord´) *v.*: Suffered through

episode (ep´ ə sōd´) *n.*: One in a series of related events

eradicate (i rad´ i kāt´) *v.*: Wipe out

etiquette (et´ i ket) *n.*: Acceptable social manners

evade (i vād´) *v.*: Avoid; escape

evaporate (i vap´ ə rāt´) *v.*: Disappear like vapor

evolved (ē vôlvd´) *v.*: Grew gradually; developed

exact (eg zakt´) *v.*: Take using force or authority

executioner (ek´ si kyōō´ shən ər) *n.*: One who carries out a death penalty imposed by the courts or a ruler

exertions (eg zur´ shənz) *n.*: Efforts

exhaust (ig zôst´) *v.*: Use up

exhausted (eg zôs´ tid) *adj.*: Tired out

expend (ek spend´) *v.*: Spend

exquisite (eks kwi´ zit) *adj.*: Very beautiful or lovely

exuded (eg zyōōd´ əd) *v.*: Gave off; oozed; radiated

exultant (ig zult´ int) *adj.*: Joyful

fallow (fal´ ō) *adj.*: Inactive; unproductive

famine (fa´ min) *n.*: Shortage of food

feats (fēts) *n.*: Remarkable deeds or acts

flaw (flô) *n.*: Break; crack

flee (flē) *v.*: To run or escape from danger

flue (flōō) *n.*: A tube for the passage of smoke, as in a chimney

foliage (fō´ lē ij) *n.*: Leaves of trees and bushes

foresee (fôr sē´) *v.*: Know beforehand

fortress (fôr´ triss) *n.*: Heavily walled building designed to be easily defended against attack

fostering (fôs´ tər iŋ) *n.*: Taking care of

fragile (fraj´ əl) *adj.*: Easily broken

frenzied (fren´ zēd) *adj.*: Wild; frantic

furtively (fur´ tiv lē) *adv.*: In secret; in such a way as to avoid notice

fusing (fyōō´ ziŋ) *v.*: Joining permanently

gilded (gild´ id) *adj.*: Coated with a thin layer of gold

gnashes (nash´ iz) *v.*: Bites with grinding teeth

gnaw (nô) *v.*: To bite and wear away bit by bit with the teeth

goading (gō´ diŋ) *v.*: Pushing a person into acting, especially by using pain or insults

gore (gôr) *n.*: Blood spilled from a wound

grant (grant) *v.*: Admit

grief (grēf) *n.*: Deep sadness

groveled (grä´ vəld) *v.*: Lay or crawled about before someone in hope of mercy

grudgingly (gruj´ iŋ lē) *adv.*: In an unenthusiastic or resentful way

heathen (hē´ thən) *adj.*: Uncivilized

henceforth (hens fôrth´) *adv.*: From now on

ignorance (ig´ ner əns) *n.*: Lack of knowledge, education, or experience

ignore (ig nôr´) *v.*: Pay no attention to

immemorial (im´ me môr´ ē əl) *adj.*: Ancient; extending back before memory

immense (i mens´) *adj.*: Huge

immortal (i môr´ təl) *adj.*: Living forever

immortals (im môrt´ əlz) *n.*: Beings who live forever

imparted (im pärt´ id) *v.*: Gave; revealed

implement (im´ plə mənt´) *v.*: Carry out

incessantly (in ses´ ənt lē) *adj.*: Never ceasing

indignantly (in dig´ nənt lē) *adv.*: Angrily

inedible (in ed´ ə bəl) *adj.*: Not fit to be eaten

inevitably (in ev´ i tə blē) *adv.*: Unavoidably

initial (i nish´ əl) *adj.*: Original

inscribed (in skrībd´) *adj.*: Written on

inscrutable (in skrōōt´ ə bəl´) *adj.*: Not easy to understand

inspiration (in´ spə rā´ shən) *n.*: Something that brings on creative ability; motivation

instinctively (in stiŋk´ tiv lē) *adv.*: Done by instinct, without thinking

integrate (in´ tə grāt´) *v.*: Remove barriers and allow access to all

intimated (in´ tə māt´ id) *v.*: Hinted; made known

intrigued (in trēgd´) *v.*: Fascinated

iridescent (ir´ ə des´ ənt) *adj.*: Showing different colors when seen from different angles

irrational (ir rash´ ə nəl) *adj.*: Unreasonable; not making sense

jubilation (jōō′ bə lā′ shən) *n.*: Great joy; triumph

lair (lār) *n.*: Cave or den

lean (lēn) *adj.*: Thin

leisurely (lē′ zhər lē) *adj.*: In an unhurried way

liable (lī′ ə bəl) *adj.*: Likely (to do something or have something happen to one)

limber (lim′ bər) *v.*: Loosen up (a muscle or limb); to make easy to bend

loam (lōm) *n.*: Rich soil

lodge (läj) *n.*: Small house or other dwelling

loftily (lof′ tə lē) *adv.*: In a superior way

majestically (mə jes′ tik lē) *adv.*: Grandly

malicious (mə lish′ əs) *adj.*: Showing evil intentions

mascot (mas′ kät) *n.*: Any person, animal, or thing adopted by a group; meant to bring good luck

massive (mass′ iv) *adj.*: Huge; large and impressive

meager (mē′ gər) *adj.*: Small in quantity; very little

meanderings (mē an′ dər inz) *n.*: Aimless wanderings

meditated (med′ i tāt id) *v.*: Thought deeply

melancholy (mel′ ən käl′ ē) *adj.*: Sad; gloomy

membranes (mem′ brānz) *n.*: Thin, flexible layers of tissue

menace (men′ əs) *n.*: Threat; a troublesome or annoying person

metamorphosis (met′ ə môr′ fə sis) *n.*: Change of form, shape, or substance

minuscule (min′ ə skyōōl) *adj.*: Very small; tiny

misapprehension (mis′ ap rē hen′ shən) *n.*: Misunderstanding

monotonous (mə nät′ ən əs′) *adj.*: Tiresome because it does not vary

monitoring (män′ i tər iŋ) *v.*: Watching or listening to

moot (mōōt) *adj.*: Not worthy of thought or discussion because it has already been resolved

mortal (môr′ təl) *adj.*: Referring to humans, who must eventually die

mortified (môrt′ ə fīd′) *v.*: Ashamed; extremely embarrassed

mosaic (mō zā′ ik) *n.*: Colorful picture or design made from small pieces of glass, stone, tile, or other material

nonchalantly (nän′ shə lant′ lē) *adv.*: Without concern or interest

nought (nôt) *n.*: Nothing

novelty (näv′ əl tē) *n.*: Something new or unusual

obligatory (əb lig′ ə tor′ ē) *adj.*: Required

obscure (əb skyoor′) *adj.*: Not well known

obstacle (äb′ stə kəl) *n.*: Something that stands in the way

obstinacy (äb′ stə nə sē) *n.*: Stubbornness

obstructed (əb strəkt′ id) *adj.*: Blocked

occasionally (ō kā′ zhən ə lē) *adv.*: Now and then

odious (ō′ dē əs) *adj.*: Hateful; disgusting

opposition (äp′ ə zish′ ən) *n.*: Here, the other team

orator (ôr′ ə tər) *n.*: Speaker

orientation (ôr′ ē en tā′ shən) *n.*: Position in relation to the points of the compass

parasite (par′ ə sīt′) *n.*: Organism, often harmful, that gets food or protection from another living thing without giving anything back

peeved (pēvd) *v.*: Made bad-tempered or annoyed

perilous (per′ el əs) *adj.*: Dangerous

perils (per′ əlz) *n.*: Situations full of dangers

peripheral (pə rif′ ər əl) *adj.*: Lying on the outside edge

perpetual (ər pech′ ōō əl) *adj.*: Constant; lasting forever

persecution (per sə kyōō′ shən) *n.*: Cruel and unfair treatment, often because of politics, religion, or race

piers (pirz) *n.*: Heavy structures supporting the sections of a bridge

plagued (plāgd) *v.*: Tormented

plight (plīt) *n.*: Awkward, sad, or dangerous situation

poising (poiz′ iŋ) *v.*: Balancing

pondering (pän′ dər iŋ) *n.*: Deep thought; careful consideration

precautionary (prē kô′ shən er′ ē) *adj.*: Taking care beforehand to prevent danger

precocious (prē kō′ shəs) *adj.*: Showing more abilities than is usual at one's age

prelude (prel′ yōōd′) *n.*: An introduction to a main event or action coming later

prey (prā) *n.*: Animals hunted or killed for food by other animals

prolonged (prō lôŋd′) *adj.*: Long and drawn out

property (präp′ ər tē) *n.*: Trait; characteristic

prospectors (prä′ spekt′ erz) *n.*: People who make their living searching for valuable ores, such as gold

proverb (präv′ ʉrb′) *n.*: Short saying that expresses an obvious truth or familiar experience

prowled (prould) *v.*: Crawled quietly and secretly

pulsating (pul′ sāt′ iŋ) *v.*: To beat or throb in rhythm

quarry (kwôr′ ē) *n.*: Prey; anything being hunted or pursued

querulous (kwer′ yōō ləs) *adj.*: Inclined to find mistakes; complaining

rancor (raŋ′ kər) *n.*: Bitter hate or ill will

rapidly (rap′ id lē) *adv.*: Quickly

raucous (rô′ kəs) *adj.*: Loud and rowdy

ravaged (rav′ ijd) *v.*: Violently destroyed; ruined

ravenous (rav′ ə nəs′) *adj.*: Greedily hungry

reckless (rek′ lis) *adj.*: Not careful; taking chances

reflecting (ri flekt′ iŋ) *adj.*: Thinking seriously

regulation (reg′ yə lā′ shən) *n.*: Rule

relentless (ri lent′ lis) *adj.*: Never ending

renowned (ri nound′) *adj.*: Famous

reproachfully (ri prōch′ fəl lē) *adv.*: With blame

repulse (ri puls′) *v.*: Drive back; repel an attack

resolutions (rez′ ə lōō′ shənz) *n.*: Intentions; things decided

retaliated (ri tal′ ē at′ id) *v.*: Harmed or did wrong to someone in return for an injury or wrong he or she has done

retorted (ri tôrt′ əd) *v.*: Replied sharply; came back with

revelation (rev′ ə lā′ shən) *n.*: Sudden rush of understanding

rivulets (riv′ yoo litz) *n.*: Little streams

rogues (rōgz) *n.*: Rascals; scoundrels

rue (rōō) *v.*: Regret

saffron (saf′ rən) *adj.*: Orange-yellow

savoring (sā′ ver iŋ) *v.*: Enjoying with appreciation; tasting; relishing

scarce (skers) *adj.*: Few in number or infrequent; not common

scuttled (skut′ əld) *v.*: Scurried; scampered

seized (sēzd) *v.*: Grabbed; taken hold of

sham (sham) *adj.*: Make believe; pretended

sheared (shird) *v.*: Cut off sharply

sibling (sib′ liŋ) *n.*: Brother or sister

skimming (skim′ iŋ) *v.*: Gliding; moving swiftly and lightly over a surface

slanderous (slan′ der əs′) *adj.*: Untrue and damaging

slight (slīt) *adj.*: Light; weak

slough (sluf) *v.*: Be cast off; be gotten rid of

soprano (sə pran′ ō) *n.*: The highest singing voice of women, girls, or young boys

staid (stād) *adj.*: Calm; steady

startled (stärt′ əld) *adj.*: Surprised

stingiest (stin′ jē əst) *adj.*: Most unwilling to spend money; cheapest

stoic (stō′ ik) *adj.*: Showing no reaction to good or bad events; calm and unaffected by hardship

sublime (sə blīm′) *adj.*: Majestic; causing awe

subscribed (səb skrībd′) *adj.*: Signed up to give money

successive (sək ses′ iv) *adj.*: Following one after another in sequence

sufficient (sə fish′ ənt) *adj.*: Enough; satisfactory

summit (sum′ it) *n.*: Highest part

summons (sum′ ənz) *v.*: Calls; orders to come

suspended (sə spend′ id) *adj.*: Hung with a support from above

suspended (sə spend′ id) *v.*: Stopped for a time

swiftest (swift′ est) *adj.*: The most rapid; the fastest

tableaus (ta blōz′) *n.*: Dramatic scenes or pictures

tactics (tak′ tiks) *n.*: Methods used for a particular purpose; tricks

tempest (tem′ pist) *n.*: Violent storm with high winds

timidly (tim′ id lē) *adv.*: In an unenthusiastic or resentful way

toil (toil) *n.*: Hard work

tolerance (täl′ ər əns) *n.*: Respect for something different

trace (trās) *n.*: Mark left behind by something

transport (trans pôrt′) *v.*: Carry from one place to another

treacherous (trech′ ər əs) *adj.*: Dangerous

trudged (trujd) *v.*: Walked as if tired or with effort

tyrant (tī′ rənt) *n.*: Cruel, unjust ruler

uncomprehending (ən cäm prē hend′ iŋ) *adj.*: Not understanding

undissuaded (un dis swād′ əd) *adj.*: Not discouraged; not persuaded to give up

undulating (un′ dyoo lā′ tiŋ) *adj.*: Moving in waves, like a snake

ungrateful (un grāt′ fəl) *adj.*: Not thankful

uninspired (un in spīrd′) *adj.*: Without bright and original ideas

valorous (val′ er əs) *adj.*: Brave

vapors (vā′ pərz) *n.*: Fumes

variegated (ver′ ē ə gāt′ id) *adj.*: Marked with different colors in spots or streaks

venomous (ven′ əm əs) *adj.*: Poisonous

venture (ven′ chər) *v.*: Take a chance; express a thought at the risk of criticism

veranda (və ran′ də) *n.*: Open porch, usually with a roof, along the outside of a building

veterans (vet′ ər enz′) *n.*: Those having experience

vigilance (vij′ ə ləns) *n.*: Watchfulness

vigorously (vig′ ər əs lē) *adv.*: Forcefully; powerfully

villa (vil′ ə) *n.*: Large estate

wallowed (wäl′ ōd) *v.*: Rolled and tilted

warily (wer′ ə lē) *adv.*: Carefully and cautiously

watertight (wôt′ ər tīt′) *adj.*: Put together so that no water can get through

weaned (wēnd) *adj.*: Brought away from; outgrown

whimper (hwim′ pər) *v.*: Make a low, whining sound, as of fear or pain

withered (with′ ərd) *adj.*: Dried up

writhing (rīth′ iŋ) *adj.*: Twisting and turning

wry (rī) *adj.*: Twisted

LITERARY TERMS HANDBOOK

ACT See *Drama.*

ALLITERATION *Alliteration* is the repetition of initial consonant sounds. Writers use alliteration to draw attention to certain words or ideas, to imitate sounds, and to create musical effects. In "Parade," on page 738, Rachel Field's use of alliteration creates the feeling and excitement of circus activity.

ANECDOTE An *anecdote* is a brief story about an interesting, amusing, or strange event. Writers tell anecdotes to entertain or to make a point. For example, in "The Drive-In Movies," on page 570, Gary Soto tells several anecdotes about his activities one Saturday. He tells these anecdotes to create a feeling of anticipation for the ending.

ANTAGONIST An *antagonist* is a character or a force in conflict with a main character, or protagonist. In "The King of Mazy May," on page 60, the five men who plan to jump the claims of Loren Hall are the antagonists. They are in conflict with Walt, who intends to protect Loren's claim. See *Conflict* and *Protagonist.*

ATMOSPHERE *Atmosphere,* or *mood,* is the feeling created in the reader by a literary work or passage. Writers use many devices to create atmosphere, including images, dialogue, setting, and plot. For example, the atmosphere of "Thunder Butte," on page 200, is serious and threatening. The writer's choice of details helps to create this atmosphere.

AUTOBIOGRAPHY An *autobiography* is the story of the writer's own life, told by the writer. Autobiographical writing may tell about the person's whole life or only a part of it. Gary Soto's autobiographical account "The Drive-In Movies," on page 570, tells about a Saturday when he was a boy.

Because autobiographies are about real people and events, they are a form of nonfiction. Most autobiographies are written in the first person.
See *Biography, Nonfiction,* and *Point of View.*

BIOGRAPHY A *biography* is a form of nonfiction in which a writer tells the life story of another person. Most biographies are written about famous or admirable people. Although biographies are nonfiction, the most effective ones share the qualities of good narrative writing. In "My Papa, Mark Twain," on page 566, Susy Clemens writes a personal biographical account of Mark Twain from the intimate perspective of a daughter.
See *Autobiography* and *Nonfiction.*

CHARACTER A *character* is a person or an animal that takes part in the action of a literary work. The main, or *major,* character is the most important character in a story, poem, or play. A *minor* character is one who takes part in the action but is not the focus of attention.

Characters are sometimes classified as flat or round. A *flat character* is one-sided and often stereotypical. A *round character,* on the other hand, is fully developed and exhibits many traits—often both faults and virtues. Characters can also be classified as dynamic or static. A *dynamic character* is one who changes or grows during the course of the work. A *static character* is one who does not change.

Characters can be animals as well as humans. Animal characters behave according to their animal characteristics, but they also have human characteristics, such as the ability to speak. For example, most of the characters in "Mowgli's Brothers," on page 238, are animals.
See *Characterization, Hero/Heroine,* and *Motive.*

CHARACTERIZATION *Characterization* is the act of creating and developing a character. Authors use two major methods of characterization—*direct* and *indirect.* When using *direct* characterization, a writer states the *characters' traits,* or characteristics. For example, in "Overdoing It" on page 482, Anton Chekhov uses direct characterization to describe the wagon driver as a "husky peasant—glum, pockmarked, and dressed in a tattered gray coarse wool coat and bast-bark shoes."

When describing a character indirectly, a writer depends on the reader to draw conclusions about the character's traits. Sometimes the writer tells what other participants in the story say and think about the character. The reader then draws his or her own conclusions.
See *Character* and *Motive.*

CLIMAX See *Conflict* and *Plot.*

CONCRETE POEM A *concrete poem* is one with a shape that suggests its subject. The poet arranges the letters, punctuation, and lines to create an image, or picture, on the page. "The Sidewalk Racer," on page 724, is an example of a concrete poem.

CONFLICT A *conflict* is a struggle between opposing forces. Conflict is one of the most important elements of stories, novels, and plays because it causes the action. There are two kinds of conflict: external and internal.

An *external conflict* is one in which a character struggles against some outside force, such as another person. In "The King of Mazy May," on page 60, greed causes the men who are desperate for gold to battle a boy who is intent on justice. The *climax* is the turning point, the point at which events will go one way or the other. In, "The King of Mazy May," the climax is the chase. This is the point at which Walt will either be caught or escape.

Another kind of external conflict, a *conflict in nature*, may occur between a character and some force in nature, as in "Zlateh the Goat," on page 146, when Aaron and Zlateh face the snowstorm.

An *internal conflict* is one that takes place within the mind of a character. The character struggles to make a decision, take an action, or overcome a feeling. For example, in "The Pigman & Me," on page 189, the author struggles to avoid a fight but also wants to prove he's not afraid.

The *resolution* of a conflict is the way the conflict is solved, the final outcome.
See *Plot*.

DEVELOPMENT See *Plot*.

DIALECT *Dialect* is the form of a language spoken by people in a particular region or group. Dialects differ in pronunciation, grammar, and word choice. The English language is divided into many dialects. British English differs from American English. The English spoken in Boston differs from that spoken in Charleston, Chicago, Houston, or San Francisco. This variety adds richness to the language.

The story "He Lion, Bruh Bear, and Bruh Rabbit," on page 785, is an example of writing in a dialect.

DIALOGUE A *dialogue* is a conversation between characters. In poems, novels, and short stories, dialogue is usually set off by quotation marks to indicate a speaker's exact words.

In a play, dialogue follows the names of the characters, and no quotation marks are used.

DRAMA A *drama* is a story written to be performed by actors. Although a drama is meant to be performed, one can also read the *script*, or written version, and imagine the action. The script of a drama is made up of dialogue and stage directions. The *dialogue* are the words spoken by the actors. The *stage directions*, usually printed in italics, tell how

the actors should look, move, and speak. They also describe the setting, sound effects, and lighting.

Dramas are often divided into parts called *acts*. The acts are often divided into smaller parts called *scenes*. *The Phantom Tollbooth*, on page 630, is a two-act drama. The first act has two scenes, and the second act has two scenes.

DYNAMIC CHARACTER See *Character*.

ESSAY An *essay* is a short nonfiction work about a particular subject. Most essays have a single major focus and a clear introduction, body, and conclusion.

There are many types of essays. An *informal essay*, like "How to Write a Letter," on page 107, uses casual, conversational language that creates a feeling of friendliness toward the reader. A *history essay*, such as "The Shutout," on page 547, gives facts, explanations, and insights about historical events. An *analytical essay*, such as "The Strange Geometry of Stonehenge," on page 371, explains a great idea to the reader by breaking it down into parts. A *narrative essay*, like "Turkeys," on page 602, tells a story about a real-life experience. An *informational* essay, such as "How the Internet Works," on page 606, presents facts, discusses ideas, or explains a process. A *persuasive essay*, like "Restoring the Circle," on page 596, offers an opinion and supports it with strong arguments, or reasons. A *visual essay*, such as "In Wildness Is the Preservation of the World," on page 600, conveys its point through images as well as text.
See *Exposition, Narration,* and *Persuasion*.

EXPOSITION *Exposition* is writing or speech that explains a process or presents information. This Literary Terms Handbook is an example of exposition. So are the introductions to the selections in this text. In the plot of a story or a drama, the *exposition*, or introduction, is the part of the work that introduces the characters, setting, and basic situation.
See *Plot*.

EXTERNAL CONFLICT See *Conflict*.

EXTENDED METAPHOR In an *extended metaphor*, as in a regular metaphor, a subject is spoken or written of as though it were something else. However, extended metaphor differs from regular metaphor in that several comparisons are made. "My Picture-Gallery," by Walt Whitman, on page 27, is an extended metaphor. In it, the speaker's world of memories is described in terms of a museum which is full of pictures.
See *Metaphor*.

FABLE A *fable* is a brief story or poem, usually with animal characters, that teaches a lesson, or moral. The moral is usually stated at the end of the fable.

' "The Lion and the Bulls," on page 303, is one of Aesop's fables. James Thurber, the twentieth-century American humorist, called his works fables for our time, and many of them have surprise endings. "The Tiger Who Would Be King," on page 302, is a fable by James Thurber.
See *Irony* and *Moral*.

FANTASY A *fantasy* is highly imaginative writing that contains elements not found in real life. Examples of fantasy include stories that involve supernatural elements, stories that resemble fairy tales, stories that deal with imaginary places and creatures, and science-fiction stories.
See *Science Fiction*.

FICTION *Fiction* is prose writing that tells about imaginary characters and events. Short stories and novels are works of fiction. Some writers base their fiction on actual events and people, adding invented characters, dialogue, settings, and plots. Other writers of fiction rely on imagination alone to provide their materials.
See *Narration, Nonfiction,* and *Prose*.

FIGURATIVE LANGUAGE *Figurative language* is writing or speech that is not meant to be taken literally. The many types of figurative language are known as *figures of speech*. Common figures of speech include metaphor, personification, and simile. Writers use figurative language to state ideas in vivid and imaginative ways.
See *Metaphor, Personification, Simile,* and *Symbol*.

FIGURE OF SPEECH See *Figurative Language*.

FLAT CHARACTER See *Character*.

FOLK TALE A *folk tale* is a story composed orally and then passed from person to person by word of mouth. Folk tales originated among people who could neither read nor write. These people entertained one another by telling stories aloud—often dealing with heroes, adventure, magic, or romance. Eventually, modern scholars collected these stories and wrote them down.

Folk tales reflect the cultural beliefs and environments from which they come. Notice the setting and characters in "Why Monkeys Live in Trees," on page 820, and "A Crippled Boy," on page 826.
See *Fable, Legend, Myth,* and *Oral Tradition*.

FOOT See *Meter*.

FORESHADOWING *Foreshadowing* is the author's use of clues to hint at what might happen later in the story. Writers use foreshadowing to build their readers' expectations and to create suspense. For example, in "Lob's Girl," on page 292, the description of the dangerous, steep road and Lob's ability to find Sandy are both elements of foreshadowing.

FREE VERSE *Free verse* is poetry not written in a regular, rhythmical pattern, or meter. The poet is free to write lines of any length or with any number of stresses, or beats. Free verse is therefore less constraining than *metrical verse,* in which every line must have a certain length and a certain number of stresses.

"Cynthia in the Snow," on page 739, is written in free verse.
See *Meter*.

GENRE A *genre* is a division or type of literature. Literature is commonly divided into three major genres: poetry, prose, and drama. Each major genre is, in turn, divided into lesser genres, as follows:

1. *Poetry:* lyric poetry, concrete poetry, dramatic poetry, narrative poetry, epic poetry
2. *Prose:* fiction (novels and short stories) and nonfiction (biography, autobiography, letters, essays, and reports)
3. *Drama:* serious drama and tragedy, comic drama, melodrama, and farce

See *Drama, Poetry,* and *Prose*.

HAIKU The haiku is a three-line Japanese verse form. The first and third lines of a haiku each have five syllables. The second line has seven syllables. A writer of haiku uses images to create a single, vivid picture, generally of a scene from nature. See the examples of haiku by Bashō and Soseki on page 726.

HERO/HEROINE A *hero* or *heroine* is a character whose actions are inspiring, or noble. Often heroes and heroines struggle mightily to overcome the obstacles and problems that stand in their way. Note that the term *hero* was originally used only for male characters, while heroic female characters were always called *heroines*. However, it is now acceptable to use *hero* to refer to females as well as to males.

IMAGES *Images* are words or phrases that appeal to one or more of the five sense. Writers use images to describe how their subjects look, sound, feel, taste, and smell.

Poets often paint images, or word pictures, that appeal to your senses. These pictures help you to experience the poem fully.

IMAGERY See *Image*.

INTERNAL CONFLICT See *Conflict*.

IRONY *Irony* is the general name given to literary techniques that involve surprising, interesting, or amusing contradictions.

JOURNAL A *journal* is a daily, or periodic, account of events and the writer's thoughts and feelings about those events. Personal journals are not normally written for publication, but sometimes they do get published later with permission from the author or the author's family. "Olympic Diary," on page 559, is an example of a journal.

LEGEND A *legend* is a widely told story about the past—one that may or may not have a foundation in fact. Every culture has its own legends—its familiar, traditional stories.
See *Folk Tale, Myth,* and *Oral Tradition*.

LETTERS A *letter* is a written communication from one person to another. In personal letters, the writer shares information and his or her thoughts and feelings with one other person or group. F. Scott Fitzgerald's letter to his daughter appears on page 556. Although letters are not normally written for publication, they sometimes do get published later with the permission of the author or the author's family.

LIMERICK A *limerick* is a humorous, rhyming, five-line poem with a specific meter and rhyme scheme. Most limericks have three strong stresses in lines 1, 2, and 5 and two strong stresses in lines 3 and 4. Most follow the rhyme scheme *aabba*. Two limericks are shown on page 727.

LYRIC POEM A *lyric poem* is a highly musical verse that expresses the observations and feelings of a single speaker. It creates a single, unified impression. "February Twilight," on page 716, is a lyric poem.

MAIN CHARACTER See *Character*.

MEDIA ACCOUNTS *Media Accounts* are reports, explanations, opinions, or descriptions written for television, radio, newspapers, and magazines. While some media accounts report only facts, others include the writer's thoughts and reflections. Media reports, such as "Space Shuttle *Challenger*," on page 584, can be about major events or they can cover seemingly insignificant topics, such as those in "Central Park," on page 588.

METAPHOR A *metaphor* is a figure of speech in which something is described as though it were something else. A metaphor, like a simile, works by pointing out a similarity between two unlike things. In "Ankylosaurus," on page 392, Jack Prelutsky describes the subject by comparing it to a tank. While describing the ankylosaurus, he says it was "armored in front" and "armored behind."
See *Extended Metaphor* and *Simile*.

METER The *meter* of a poem is its rhythmical pattern. This pattern is determined by the number of *stresses,* or beats, in each line. To describe the meter of a poem, read it emphasizing the beats in each line. Then, mark the stressed and unstressed syllables, as follows:

My fáth | er was | the fírst | to hear |

As you can see, each strong stress is marked with a slanted line (´) and each unstressed syllable with a horseshoe symbol (˘). The weak and strong stresses are then divided by vertical lines (|) into groups called *feet*.

MINOR CHARACTER See *Character*.

MOOD See *Atmosphere*.

MORAL A *moral* is a lesson taught by a literary work. A fable usually ends with a moral that is directly stated. For example, Aesop's fable "The Lion and the Bulls," on page 303, ends with the moral "United we stand; divided we fall." A poem, novel, short story, or essay often suggests a moral that is not directly stated. The moral must be drawn by the reader, based on other elements in the work.
See *Fable*.

MOTIVATION See *Motive*.

MOTIVE A *motive* is a reason that explains or partially explains a character's thoughts, feelings, actions, or speech. Writers try to make their characters' motives, or motivations, as clear as possible. If the motives of a main character are not clear, then the character will not be believable.

Characters are often motivated by needs, such as food and shelter. They are also motivated by feelings, such as fear, love, and pride. Motives may be obvious or hidden. In "Aaron's Gift," on page 116, Aaron is motivated by concern for the injured pigeon, desire to belong to a gang, and love for his grandmother.

MYTH A *myth* is a fictional tale that explains the actions of gods or heroes or the origins of elements of nature. Myths are part of the oral tradition. They are composed orally and then passed from generation to generation by word of mouth. Every ancient culture has its own mythology,

or collection of myths. Greek myths, such as "Arachne," on page 822, are known collectively as *classical mythology*.
See *Oral Tradition*.

NARRATION *Narration* is writing that tells a story. The act of telling a story is also called narration. Each piece is a *narrative*. A story told in fiction, nonfiction, poetry, or even in drama is called a narrative.
See *Narrative, Narrative Poem,* and *Narrator*.

NARRATIVE A *narrative* is a story. A narrative can be either fiction or nonfiction. Novels and short stories are types of fictional narratives. Biographies and autobiographies are nonfiction narratives. "Old Ben," on page 164, is an example of a narrative. In it, Jesse Stuart tells the story of how a snake became a family pet.

Poems that tell stories are also narratives.
See *Narration* and *Narrative Poem*.

NARRATIVE POEM A *narrative poem* is a story told in verse. Narrative poems often have all the elements of short stories, including characters, conflict, and plot. An example of a narrative poem is "The Walrus and the Carpenter," on page 712.

NARRATOR A *narrator* is a speaker or a character who tells a story. The narrator's perspective is the way he or she sees things. A *third-person narrator* is one who stands outside the action and speaks about it. A *first-person narrator* is one who tells a story and participates in its action. For example, the first-person narrator of "Jeremiah's Song," on page 34, is a young boy.
See *Point of View*.

NONFICTION *Nonfiction* is prose writing that presents and explains ideas or that tells about real people, places, objects, or events. Autobiographies, biographies, essays, reports, letters, memos, and newspaper articles are all types of nonfiction.
See *Fiction*.

NOVEL A *novel* is a long work of fiction. Novels contain such elements as characters, plot, conflict, and setting. The writer of novels, or novelist, develops these elements. In addition to its main plot, a novel may contain one or more subplots, or independent, related stories. A novel may also have several themes.
See *Fiction* and *Short Story*.

ONOMATOPOEIA *Onomatopoeia* is the use of words that imitate sounds. *Crash, buzz, screech, hiss, neigh, jingle,* and *cluck* are examples of onomatopoeia. *Chickadee, towhee,* and *whippoorwill* are onomatopoeic names of birds.

Onomatopoeia can help put the reader in the activity of a poem. In "Cynthia in the Snow," on page 739, Gwendolyn Brooks uses words such as "sushes" and "whirs" to describe the sounds of the snow on the ground and in the wind.

ORAL TRADITION *Oral tradition* is the passing of songs, stories, and poems from generation to generation by word of mouth. Folk songs, folk tales, legends, and myths all come from the oral tradition. No one knows who first created these stories and poems. For example, in "Why the Tortoise's Shell Is Not Smooth," on page 442, Chinua Achebe tells a story from the oral tradition of Nigeria. Notice how he begins with people telling stories to each other.
See *Folk Tale, Legend,* and *Myth*.

PERSONIFICATION *Personification* is a type of figurative language in which a nonhuman subject is given human characteristics. For example, in "April Rain Song," on page 746, Langston Hughes gives the rain the ability to "kiss you," "beat upon your head," and "sing you a lullaby."

PERSPECTIVE See *Narrator* and *Point of View*.

PERSUASION *Persuasion* is used in writing or speech that attempts to convince the reader or listener to adopt a particular opinion or course of action. Newspaper editorials and letters to the editor use persuasion. So do advertisements and campaign speeches given by political candidates. In his persuasive essay "Restoring the Circle," Joseph Bruchac writes about the need to accurately recognize Native American cultures.
See *Essay*.

PLOT *Plot* is the sequence of events in which each event results from a previous one and causes the next. In most novels, dramas, short stories, and narrative poems, the plot involves both characters and a central conflict. The plot usually begins with an *exposition* that introduces the setting, the characters, and the basic situation. This is followed by the *inciting incident,* which introduces the central conflict. The conflict then increases during the *development* until it reaches a high point of interest or suspense, the *climax*. The climax is followed by the *falling action,* or end, of the central conflict. Any events that occur during the falling action make up the *resolution* or *denouement*.

Some plots do not have all of these parts. Some stories begin with the inciting incident and end with the resolution. In some, the inciting incident has occurred before the opening of the story.
See *Conflict*.

POETRY *Poetry* is one of the three major types of literature, the others being prose and drama. Most poems make use of highly concise, musical, and emotionally charged language. Many also make use of imagery, figurative language, and special devices of sound such as rhyme. Major types of poetry include *lyric poetry, narrative poetry,* and *concrete poetry.* See *Concrete Poem, Genre, Lyric Poem,* and *Narrative Poem.*

POINT OF VIEW *Point of view* is the perspective, or vantage point, from which a story is told. It is either a narrator outside the story or a character in the story. *First-person point of view* is told by a character who uses the first person pronoun "I." "Becky and the Wheels-and-Brake Boys," on page 472, is told in the first person by the main character of the story.

The two kinds of *third-person point of view,* limited and omniscient, are called "third person" because the narrator uses third-person pronouns such as *he* and *she* to refer to the characters. There is no "I" telling the story.

In stories told from the *omniscient third-person point of view,* the narrator knows and tells about what each character feels and thinks. "The Wounded Wolf," on page 510, is written from the omniscient third-person point of view.

In stories told from the *limited third-person point of view,* the narrator relates the inner thoughts and feelings of only one character, and everything is viewed from this character's perspective. In "Overdoing It," on page 482, Anton Chekhov uses the limited third-person point of view by telling the story from the surveyor's perspective.
See *Narrator.*

PROSE *Prose* is the ordinary form of written language. Most writing that is not poetry, drama, or song is considered prose. Prose is one of the major genres of literature and occurs in two forms—fiction and nonfiction.
See *Fiction, Genre,* and *Nonfiction.*

PROTAGONIST The *protagonist* is the main character in a literary work. Often, the protagonist is a person, but sometimes it can be an animal. In "The Wounded Wolf," on page 510, the protagonist, or main character, is an animal. See *Antagonist* and *Character.*

REFRAIN A *refrain* is a regularly repeated line or group of lines in a poem or a song. In the poem "The Fairies' Lullaby," by William Shakespeare, on page 430, the lines labeled "Chorus" are the refrain.

REPETITION *Repetition* is the use, more than once, of any element of language—a sound, word, phrase, clause, or sentence. Repetition is used in both prose and poetry. See *Alliteration, Meter, Plot, Rhyme,* and *Rhyme Scheme.*

RESOLUTION See *Plot.*

RHYME *Rhyme* is the repetition of sounds at the ends of words. Poets use rhyme to lend a songlike quality to their verses and to emphasize certain words and ideas. Many traditional poems contain *end rhymes,* or rhyming words at the ends of lines. "A Dream Within a Dream," on page 390, contains end rhyme that causes it to flow musically.

Another common device is the use of *internal rhymes,* or rhyming words within lines. Internal rhyme also emphasizes the flowing nature of a poem, as in "The Spring and the Fall," by Edna St. Vincent Millay, on page 391.
See *Rhyme Scheme.*

RHYME SCHEME A *rhyme scheme* is a regular pattern of rhyming words in a poem. To indicate the rhyme scheme of a poem, one uses lowercase letters. Each rhyme is assigned a different letter, as follows in the first stanza of "Dust of Snow," on page 28, by Robert Frost:

The way a crow	*a*
Shook down on me	*b*
The dust of snow	*a*
From a hemlock tree	*b*

Thus, the stanza has the rhyme scheme *abab.*

RHYTHM *Rhythm* is the pattern of stressed and unstressed syllables in spoken or written language.
See *Meter.*

ROUND CHARACTER See *Character.*

SCENE See *Drama.*

SCIENCE FICTION *Science fiction* combines elements of fiction and fantasy with scientific fact. Many science-fiction stories are set in the future. "The Fun They Had," on page 382, is a science-fiction story that takes place in the year 2155.

SENSORY LANGUAGE *Sensory language* is writing or speech that appeals to one or more of the five senses. For example, in "How to Write a Poem About the Sky," on page 128, Leslie Marmon Silko's words "colder than the frozen river" help you *feel* the air.
See *Image.*

SETTING The *setting* of a literary work is the time and place of the action. The setting includes all the details of a place and time—the year, the time of day, even the weather. The place may be a specific country, state, region, community, neighborhood, building, institution, or home.

Details such as dialects, clothing, customs, and modes of transportation are often used to establish setting. In most stories, the setting serves as a backdrop—a context in which the characters interact. Setting can also help to create a feeling, or atmosphere. In "The Lawyer and the Ghost," on page 506, the writer's description of the room as "old, damp, rotten" and the furniture as "moldering" creates a mood of gloom.
See *Mood*.

SHORT STORY A *short story* is a brief work of fiction. Like a novel, a short story presents a sequence of events, or plot. The plot usually deals with a central conflict faced by a main character, or protagonist. Like a lyric poem, a short story is concise and creates a single effect, or dominant impression, on its reader. The events in a short story usually communicate a message about life or human nature. This message, or central idea, is the story's theme.
See *Conflict, Plot,* and *Theme*.

SIMILE A *simile* is a figure of speech that uses *like* or *as* to make a direct comparison between two unlike ideas. Everyday speech often contains similes, such as "pale as a ghost," "good as gold," "spread like wildfire," and "clever as a fox."

In her poem "Simile: Willow and Ginkgo," on page 744, Eve Merriam uses simile in each stanza to describe and compare a willow tree with a ginkgo tree.

SPEAKER The *speaker* is the imaginary voice a poet uses when writing a poem. The speaker is the character who tells the poem. This character, or voice, often is not identified by name. There can be important differences between the poet and the poem's speaker. In "Door Number Four," on page 156, the poem's speaker is probably a child, even though the poet is an adult.
See *Narrator*.

STAGE DIRECTIONS *Stage directions* are notes included in a drama to describe how the work is to be performed or staged. Stage directions are usually printed in italics and enclosed within parentheses or brackets. Some stage directions describe the movements, costumes, emotional states, and ways of speaking of the characters.

STAGING *Staging* includes the setting, the lighting, the costumes, special effects, music, dance, and so on that go into putting on a stage performance of a drama.
See *Drama*.

STANZA A *stanza* is a group of lines of poetry that are usually similar in length and pattern and are separated by spaces. A stanza is like a paragraph of poetry—it states and develops a single main idea. For example, "Adventures of Isabel," on page 262, has four stanzas, each with its own main idea.

STATIC CHARACTER See *Character*.

SURPRISE ENDING A *surprise ending* is a conclusion that is unexpected. The reader has certain expectations about the ending based on details in the story. For example, in "Stray," on page 16, Doris's father does not tell her right away that they are keeping the dog, thus making the story ending a surprise. Often, a surprise ending is *foreshadowed*, or subtly hinted at, in the course of the work.
See *Foreshadowing* and *Plot*.

SUSPENSE *Suspense* is a feeling of anxious uncertainty about the outcome of events in a literary work. Writers create suspense by raising questions in the minds of their readers. For example, in "Lob's Girl," on page 292, Joan Aiken builds suspense with uncertainty about Sandy's condition in the hospital.

SYMBOL A *symbol* is anything that stands for or represents something else. Symbols are common in everyday life. A dove with an olive branch in its beak is a symbol of peace. A blindfolded woman holding a balanced scale is a symbol of justice. A crown is a symbol of a king's status and authority.

THEME The *theme* is a central message, concern, or purpose in a literary work. A theme can usually be expressed as a generalization, or a general statement, about human beings or about life. The theme of a work is not a summary of its plot. The theme is the central idea that the writer communicates.

Although a theme may be stated directly in the text, it is more often presented indirectly. When the theme is stated indirectly, or implied, the reader must figure out what the theme is by looking carefully at what the work reveals about people or about life. For example, the theme of "The Circuit," on page 80, is not directly stated, but the title is a clue to the theme.

WRITING HANDBOOK

THE WRITING PROCESS

The writing process can be roughly divided into a series of stages: prewriting, drafting, revising, editing, proofreading, and publishing. It's important to remember that the writing process is one that moves backward as well as forward. Even while you are moving forward in the creation of your composition, you may still return to a previous stage—to rethink or rewrite.

Following are stages of the writing process with key points to address during each stage.

Prewriting

In this stage, you plan out the work to be done. You prepare to write by exploring ideas, gathering information, and working out an organization. Following are the key steps to take at this stage.

Step 1: Analyze the writing situation. Before writing, analyze the writing assignment. To do this, ask yourself the following questions about each element:

- *Topic (the subject you will be writing about)*: What exactly are you going to write about? Can you state your subject in a sentence? Is your subject too broad or too narrow?
- *Purpose (what you want your writing to accomplish)*: Do you want your writing to explain? To describe? To persuade? To tell a story? To entertain? What do you want your audience to learn or to understand?
- *Audience (the people who will read or listen to your writing)*: Who is your audience? What might they already know about your subject? What basic facts will you have to provide for them?

Step 2: Gather ideas and information. After thinking about the writing situation, you may find that you need more information. If so, you must decide how to gather this information. On the other hand, you may find that you already have too much information—that your topic is too broad. If this is the case, then you must decide how to narrow your topic.

There are many ways to gather information, to narrow a topic. Cnsider these strategies:

- *Brainstorm.* Discuss the topic with a group of people. Try to generate as many ideas as possible. Not all of your brainstormed ideas will be useful or

suitable. You'll need to evaluate them later.
- *Consult other people about your topic.* Speaking with others may suggest an idea or approach you did not see at first.
- *Make a list of questions about your topic.* Begin your questions with words like who, what, where, when, why, and how. Then find the answers to your questions.

Step 3: Organize your notes. Once you have gathered enough information, you will have to organize it. Sort your ideas and notes; decide which points are most important. You can make an outline to show the order of ideas, or you can use some other organizing plan that works for you.

There are many ways to organize and develop your material. Careful organization will make your writing easy to read and understand. The following are common methods of organizing information:

- *Time Order or Chronological Order* Events are organized in order of occurrence (from earliest to latest, for example)
- *Spatial Order* Details are organized by position in space (from left to right, for example)
- *Degree Order* This order is organization by size, amount, or intensity (from coldest to warmest, for example)
- *Priority Order* This is organization by importance, value, usefulness, or familiarity (from worst to best, for example)

Drafting

Drafting follows prewriting and is the second stage in the writing process. Working from your prewriting notes and your outline or plan, you develop and present your ideas in sentences and paragraphs. The following are important points to remember about drafting:

- Do not try to make your rough draft perfect. Concentrate on getting your ideas on paper. Once this is done, you can make improvements in the revision and proofreading stages.
- Keep your audience and purpose in mind as you write. This will help you determine what you say and how you say it.
- Don't be afraid to set aside earlier ideas if later

ones work better. Some of the best ideas are those that were not planned at the beginning.

Most papers, regardless of the topic, are developed with an introduction, a body, and a conclusion. Here are tips for developing these parts of a paper:

Introduction In the introduction to a paper, you want to engage your readers' attention and let them know the purpose of your paper. You may use the following strategies in your introduction.

- State your main idea.
- Take a stand.
- Use an anecdote.
- Quote someone.
- Startle your readers.

Body of the paper In the body of your paper, you present your information and make your points. Your organization is an important factor in leading readers through your ideas. Your elaboration on your main ideas is also important. Elaboration is the development of ideas to make your written work precise and complete. You can use the following kinds of details to elaborate your main ideas:

- Facts and statistics
- Anecdotes
- Sensory details
- Examples
- Explanation and definition
- Quotations

Conclusion The ending of your paper is the final impression you leave with your readers. Your conclusion should give readers the sense that you have pulled everything together. Following are some effective ways to end your paper:

- Summarize and restate.
- Ask a question.
- State an opinion.
- Tell an anecdote.
- Call for action.

Revising

Once you have a draft, you can look at it critically or have others review it. This is the time to make changes on many levels. *Revising* is the process of reworking what you have written to make it as good as it can be. You many changes some details so that your ideas flow smoothly and are clearly supported. You may discover that some details don't work and you'll need to discard them. Try these strategies:

- Read your work aloud. This is an excellent way to catch any ideas or details that have been left out and to notice errors in logic.
- Ask someone else to read your work. Choose someone who can point out how to improve it.

How do you know what to look for and what to change? Here is a checklist of major writing issues. If the answer to any of these questions is No, then that is an area that needs revision.

1. Does the writing achieve my purpose?
2. Does the paper have unity? That means, does it have a single focus, with all details and information contributing to that focus?
3. Is the arrangement of information clear and logical?
4. Have I elaborated enough to give my audience adequate information?

Editing

When you *edit,* you look more closely at the language you have used so that the way you express your ideas is most effective.

- Replace dull language with vivid, precise words.
- Cut or change redundant expressions (unnecessary repetition).
- Check passive voice; active voice is more effective.
- Replace wordy expressions with shorter, more precise ones.

Proofreading

After you finish your final draft, the last step is to *proofread* the draft to make it ready for a reader. You may do this on your own or with the help of a partner.

It's useful to have handy both a dictionary and ausage handbook to help you check for correctness. Here are the tasks in proofreading:

- Correct errors in grammar and usage.
- Correct punctuation and capitalization.
- Correct errors in spelling.

Publishing and Presenting

These are some of the many ways in which you can share your work:

- Share your writing in a small group by reading it aloud or by passing it around for others to read.
- Read your work aloud to the class
- Display your work on a classroom bulletin board.
- Submit your writing to the school literary magazine, or start a literary magazine for your school or for your class.
- Submit your writing to your school or community newspaper.
- Enter your writing in literary contests for student writers.
- Submit your writing to a magazine that publishes work by young people.

THE MODES OF WRITING

Expression

Expression is writing that captures your thoughts, feelings, and experiences. Some expressive writing is private, written only for yourself. Some is written to be shared with an audience—friends, family, or other interested readers. Through expressive writing, you can share your experiences and emotions and reflect on memorable moments in your life. Expressive writing takes many forms. Here are a few of them:

Personal Journal Entry A personal journal entry is usually written for you alone. In a journal entry, you might use single words and sentence fragments. A series of journal entries allows you to record your feelings, thoughts, and observations over a period of time.

Postcard Message A postcard is a way to send a brief message when there is no need for privacy. A postcard message is written in informal language. Sentence fragments are acceptable on a postcard, where space is tight and it is necessary to keep the message brief.

Personal Letter Writing a personal letter is a good way to share your thoughts and experiences with a friend or a family member. A personal letter may contain factual news as well as the writer's feelings and opinions.

Description

Description is writing that brings a person, an animal, a scene, or an experience to life for the readers. When you write a description, you use words to capture how something looks, smells, tastes, feels, or sounds. A description may stand on its own or be part of a longer work, such as a short story.

When you write a description, bring it to life with sensory details, which tell you how your subject looks, smells, sounds, tastes, or feels. Choose your details carefully so that you create a single main impression of your subject. You should avoid language and details that don't contribute to this main impression. Keep these guidelines in mind whenever you are assigned one of the following types of description:

Remembrance A remembrance is a description of a memorable person or place from your past. When writing a remembrance, include details that help convey your feelings about the person or place you're describing. Include sensory details to capture the character of the time and the people.

Observation In an observation, you describe an event that you have witnessed firsthand, often over an extended period of time.

Narration

Narration is the process of telling a story. Every time you tell a friend what you did over the weekend or describe a family vacation, you are using narration. Narratives can be true-life stories based on actual events or they can be made up. Most narratives share certain elements—characters, a setting, a sequence of events (or plot, in fiction), and, often, a theme. Usually, you meet the main characters near the beginning of the story, follow them as events unfold, and learn what happens to them at the end. You might be asked to write one of these types of narration:

Personal Narrative A personal narrative is autobiographical. It is a true story about a significant event that happened to you. When writing a personal narrative, include your thoughts and feelings about the event.

Firsthand Biography In a firsthand biography, you tell about the life of a person you know personally. You can use your close relationship with the person to help you include personal insights not found in biographies based solely on research.

Short Story Short stories are brief fictional narratives in which a main character faces a conflict that is resolved by the end of the story. In planning a short story, focus on developing the plot, setting, and characters.

Exposition: Giving Information

Exposition to give information is writing that informs or explains. Here are some types of exposition that give information that you may be asked to write:

Definition and Classification A definition explains something by describing its main features. When you classify, you group items into categories based on the things they have in common.

Summary To write a summary, or synopsis, use as few words as possible to communicate the basic information of plot, setting, characters, and the connections between and the significance of events.

How-to Essay In a how-to essay, you provide detailed, step-by-step directions that explain a process or activity.

Letter to Request Information When writing to request information, you must be clear and specific about the information you need.

Exposition: Making Connections

Exposition can make connections by comparing and contrasting two subjects, by explaining cause-and-effect relationships, or by showing potential solutions to a problem. Here are some types of exposition that make connections:

Comparison-and-Contrast Essay Comparison-and-contrast essays explain the similarities and differences between two or more people, places, objects, or events.

Written Solution for a Problem Writers use exposition to present or explain a problem and to provide a solution. In a written solution to a problem, you define a specific problem and suggest one or more solutions, supported with facts and examples.

Cause-and-Effect Essay In a cause-and-effect essay, you show how one or more events are related as the cause or result of the other.

Persuasion

Persuasion is writing or speaking that tries to convince people to agree with a position or to take a desired action. Here are a few forms your persuasive writing may take:

Persuasive Letter In a persuasive letter, you attempt to convince an individual or a group to think or act in a certain way. Examples of persuasive letters include a letter to the editor or a letter to an elected official.

Advertisement The purpose of an advertisement is to persuade people to buy something, accept an idea, vote for someone, or support a cause. When you write an advertisement, include imaginative, lively writing that will catch your readers' or viewers' attention.

Essay Supporting an Opinion In writing an essay to support an opinion, you build an argument and support your opinions with a variety of evidence: facts, statistics, examples, and statements from experts.

Reports

A report is writing based on research. People write reports to present information and ideas, to share findings and research, and to explain subjects. Here are some types of reports:

Biographical Sketch A biographical sketch gives a picture of an individual's personality and character by describing achievements and actions. When writing a biographical sketch, include details that illustrate your subject's qualities, rather than trying to tell the person's entire life story.

I-Search Report An I-Search report is a personal, in-depth exploration of a topic that especially interests you. You tell the story of how you became interested in the topic, how you went about exploring it, and what you learned during your exploration.

Library Research Report When you write a library research report, put together information from books and other library sources. Include details from the research to support your main idea. Credit your sources in footnotes or parenthetical credits.

Creative Writing

Creative writing blends imagination, ideas, and emotions, allowing you to present your own unique view of the world. Poems, plays, short stories, dramas, and television programs are examples of creative writing. All are represented in this anthology and may provide inspiration for you to create your own works, such as the following:

Song Lyrics In writing lyrics, or words, for a song, you use many elements of poetry—rhyme, rhythm, repetition, and imagery. Song lyrics convey emotions and make the reader think.

Poem In writing poems, use figurative language and sensory images. You might also use rhyme and rhythm to create a musical effect.

Monologue A monologue is a dramatic speech spoken by one character. In writing a monologue, choose a subject, and write the details from the point of view of your subject or from your own point of view.

Dramatic Scene In a dramatic scene, use dialogue and stage directions to indicate the feelings and actions of the characters.

Response to Literature

In a *response to literature,* you express your thoughts and feelings about a work. Often, this leads you to a better understanding of the work. Here are two ways you might respond in writing to literature:

Reader's Response Journal Entry Your reader's response journal is a record of your feelings about works you've read. Use it to remind yourself of works that you have liked or disliked and the reasons why.

Letter to an Author or a Character You can respond to a work of literature by writing a letter to the author, explaining why you liked or disliked the work. You can also explore your responses by writing a letter to a character, explaining your feelings about his or her situation or actions.

Grammar and Mechanics Handbook

Nouns A **noun** is the name of a person, place, or thing. A **common noun** names any one of a class of people, places, or things. A **proper noun** names a specific person, place, or thing.

Common Nouns	Proper Nouns
writer	Francisco Jiménez
city	Los Angeles

Pronouns A **pronoun** is a word that stands for a noun or for a word that takes the place of a noun.

A **personal pronoun** refers to (1) the person speaking, (2) the person spoken to, or (3) the person, place, or thing spoken about.

	Singular	Plural
First Person	I, me, my, mine	we, us, our, ours
Second Person	you, your, yours	you, your, yours
Third Person	he, him, his, she, her, hers, it, its	they, them, their, theirs

"If we allow you to come with us, you will soon begin your mischief."

—"Why the Tortoise's Shell Is Not Smooth," Achebe, p. 442

A **demonstrative pronoun** directs attention to a specific person, place, or thing.

this lamp   *these* rugs   *that* chair   *those* tables

An **interrogative pronoun** is used to begin a question.

Who is the author of "Jeremiah's Song"?

An **indefinite pronoun** refers to a person, place, or thing, often without specifying which one.

Many of the players were tired.

Everyone bought something.

Verbs A **verb** is a word that expresses time while showing an action, a condition, or the fact that something exists.

An **action verb** indicates the action of someone or something.

"I listened, I opened,
I looked to left and right, . . ."

—"Someone," De la Mare, p. 432

A **linking verb** connects the subject of a sentence with a noun or a pronoun that renames or describes the subject.

I am a changed man.

—"Why the Tortoise's Shell Is Not Smooth," Achebe, p. 442

A **helping verb** can be added to another verb to make a single verb phrase.

We had invited Chinese friends to eat with us before, but this dinner was going to be different.

—"The All-American Slurp," Namioka, p. 523

Adjectives An **adjective** describes a noun or a pronoun or gives a noun or a pronoun a more specific meaning. Adjectives answer these questions:

What kind?	*red* rose, *small* bowl
Which one?	*this* spoon, *those* pots
How many?	*four* hours, *many* tomatoes
How much?	*no* rain, *little* money

The articles *the, a,* and *an* are adjectives. *An* is used before a word beginning with a vowel sound.

A noun may sometimes be used as an adjective.

family home   *science* fiction

Adverbs An **adverb** modifies a verb, an adjective, or another adverb. Adverbs answer the questions *where, when, in what way,* or *to what extent.*

Close the window *quickly.* (modifies verb *close*)

We were *very* sad. (modifies adjective *sad*)

They left *too* suddenly. (modifies adverb *suddenly*)

Prepositions A **preposition** relates a noun or a pronoun following it to another word in the sentence.

across the road   *near* the corner

except me   *during* the show

Conjunctions A **conjunction** connects other words or groups of words.

A **coordinating conjunction** connects similar kinds or groups of words.

lions *and* tigers   small *but* strong

Correlative conjunctions are used in pairs to connect similar words or groups of words.

both Grandpa *and* Dad   *neither* they *nor* I

Interjections An **interjection** is a word that expresses feeling or emotion and functions independently of a sentence.

"Ah!" says he—

— "The Lawyer and the Ghost,"
Dickens, p. 506

Sentences A **sentence** is a group of words with two main parts: a complete subject and a complete predicate. Together, these parts express a complete thought.

The surveyor dug into his pockets for the imaginary guns.

— "Overdoing It," Chekhov, p. 485

A **fragment** is a group of words that does not express a complete thought.

"Not right away."

— "Eleven," Cisneros, p. 488

Subject-Verb Agreement To make a subject and a verb agree, make sure that both are singular or both are plural. Two or more singular subjects joined by *or* or *nor* must have a singular verb. When singular and plural subjects are joined by *or* or *nor*, the verb must agree with the closest subject.

He *is* at the door.

They *drive* home every day.

Both *pets are* hungry.

Either the *chairs* or the *table is* on sale.

Phrases A **phrase** is a group of words, without a subject and a verb, that functions in a sentence as one part of speech.

A **prepositional phrase** is a group of words that includes a preposition and a noun or a pronoun that is the object of the preposition.

near the town   with them

An **adjective phrase** is a prepositional phrase that modifies a noun or a pronoun by telling *what kind* or *which one.*

Mr. Sanderson brushed his hands over the shoes *in the window. . . .*

— "The Sound of Summer Running,"
Bradbury, p. 7

An **adverb phrase** is a prepositional phrase that modifies a verb, an adjective, or an adverb by pointing out *where, when, in what manner,* or *to what extent.*

The trees were black *where the bark was wet.*

— "The Spring and the Fall,"
St. Vincent Millay, p. 391

An **appositive phrase** is a noun or a pronoun with modifiers, placed next to a noun or a pronoun to add information and details.

Calliope, *one of these sisters*, was the inspiration of poets and musicians.

— "Orpheus," Low, p. 409

A **participial** phrase is a participle modified by an adjective or an adverb phrase or accompanied by a complement. The entire phrase acts as an adjective.

Dropping to all fours, he joins the march.

— "The Wounded Wolf,"
George, p. 511

An **infinitive phrase** is an infinitive with modifiers, complements, or a subject, all acting together as a single part of speech.

At first I was too busy enjoying my food *to notice how the guests were doing.*

— "The All-American Slurp,"
Namioka, p. 523

Clauses A **clause** is a group of words with its own subject and verb.

An **independent clause** can stand by itself as a complete sentence.

"I think it belongs to Rachel."

— "Eleven," Cisneros, p. 490

A **subordinate clause** has a subject and a verb but cannot stand by itself as a complete sentence; it can only be part of a sentence.

An **adjective clause** is a subordinate clause that modifies a noun or a pronoun by telling *what kind* or *which one.*

The field, *which by now should have been covered with green shoots,* lay bare and empty.

— "The Stone," Alexander, p. 529

An **adverb clause** modifies a verb, an adjective, or an adverb by telling *where, when, in what way, to what extent, under what condition,* or *why.*

Once the logs had been pounded into the mud, he tried to set the stones on top of the logs.

— "Breaker's Bridge," Yep, p. 421

Summary of Capitalization and Punctuation

Capitalization

Capitalize the first word of a sentence.

> Young Roko glances down the valley.
> > —"The Wounded Wolf,"
> > Jean Craighead George, p. 511

Capitalize all proper nouns and adjectives.

> Mark Twain   Amazon River   Thanksgiving Day
> Montana   October   Italian

Capitalize a person's title when it is followed by the person's name or when it is used in direct address.

> Doctor   General Khokhotov   Mrs. Price

Capitalize titles showing family relationships when they refer to a specific person, unless they are preceded by a possessive noun or pronoun.

> Granny-Liz   Margie's mother

Capitalize the first word and all other key words in the titles of books, periodicals, poems, stories, plays, paintings, and other works of art.

> from *Tom Sawyer*   "Grandpa and the Statue"
> "Breaker's Bridge"   "The Spring and the Fall"

Capitalize the first word and all nouns in letter salutations and the first word in letter closings.

> Dear Willis,   Yours truly,

Punctuation

End Marks Use a **period** to end a declarative sentence, an imperative sentence, and most abbreviations.

> The fisherman's wife hurried down to the sand.
> > —"Greyling," Yolen, p. 330

> "Find a bit of string, Sandy, to tie to his collar."
> > —"Lob's Girl," Aiken, p. 294

Use a **question mark** to end a direct question or an incomplete question in which the rest of the question is understood.

> Is *all* that we see or seem
> But a dream within a dream?
> > —"A Dream Within a Dream,"
> > Poe, p. 390

Use an **exclamation mark** after a statement showing strong emotion, an urgent imperative sentence, or an interjection expressing strong emotion.

> "Then find me the following things in three days' time!"
> > —"The Friends of Kwan Ming,"
> > Yee, p. 317

> "No! *No!*" shouted Aaron, moving toward Carl.
> > —"Aaron's Gift," Levoy, p. 120

Commas Use a **comma** before the conjunction to separate two independent clauses in a compound sentence.

> At Hanukkah time the road from the village to the town is usually covered with snow, but this year the winter had been a mild one.
> > —"Zlateh the Goat," Singer, p. 146

Use commas to separate three or more words, phrases, or clauses in a series.

> November, December, January, February, and March came and went.
> > —"Old Ben," Stuart, p. 166

> The old man walked lightly across the store to the wall of ten thousand boxes, came back with some shoes for the boy, and wrote up a list on some paper while the boy was lacing the shoes on his feet and then standing there, waiting.
> > —"The Sound of Summer
> > Running," Bradbury, p. 9

Use commas to separate adjectives of equal rank. Do not use commas to separate adjectives that must stay in a specific order.

> It would have been forgotten completely if Abraham Lincoln hadn't gone there to live when he was young, penniless, and ambitious.
> > —"A Backwoods Boy,"
> > Freedman, p. 350

Use a comma after an introductory word, phrase, or clause.

> Still, she tried talking to them about the dog at dinner one night.
> > —"Stray," Rylant, p. 18

> In the afternoon, with Walt always trailing on their heels, they came back down the creek. . . .
> > —"The King of Mazy May,"
> > London, p. 61

> When I heard the musical whistle beside my ear, I thought that it had come over the station intercom. . . .
> > —"Feathered Friend," Clarke, p. 168

Use commas to set off parenthetical and nonessential expressions.

> "Come to think of it, the moon's been looking a little wilted around the edges, too."
>
> —"The Stone," Alexander, p. 527

> "Well, in that case, I think we ought to have a square meal . . ."
>
> —"The Phantom Tollbooth,"
> Nanus, p. 640

Use commas with places and dates made up of two or more parts.

> Ray Bradbury was born in Waukegan, Illinois.

> On July 20, 1969, American astronauts first set foot on the moon.

Use commas after items in addresses, after the salutation in a personal letter, after the closing in all letters, and in numbers of more than three digits.

> Sturbridge Place, Allentown, PA   My dear Cal,
>
> Sincerely yours,   1,372,597

Use a comma to set off a direct quotation.

> "Gladly," he said.
>
> —"The Circuit," Jiménez, p. 85

Semicolons Use a **semicolon** to join independent clauses that are not already joined by a conjunction.

> Doing something does not require discipline; it creates its own discipline.
>
> —"Talent," Dillard, p. 42

Use a semicolon to join independent clauses or items in a series that already contain commas.

> The Pengelly family had no say in the choosing of Lob; he came to them in the second way. . . .
>
> —"Lob's Girl," Aiken, p. 293

Colons Use a **colon** before a list of items following an independent clause.

> Mrs. Gleason exclaimed at the beautifully arranged dishes of food: the colorful candied fruit in the sweet-and-sour pork dish, the noodle-thin shreds of chicken meat stir-fried with tiny peas, and the glistening pink prawns. . . .
>
> —"The All-American Slurp,"
> Namioka, p. 523

Use a colon in numbers giving the time, in salutations in business letters, and in labels used to signal important ideas.

> 4:30 A.M.   Dear Pie:
>
> Danger: Landslide Area Ahead

Quotation Marks A **direct quotation** represents a person's exact speech or thoughts and is enclosed in quotation marks.

> Robin Carver wrote in his *Book of Sports* (1834) that "an American version of rounders called *goal ball* was rivaling cricket in popularity."
>
> —"The Shutout," McKissack, p. 547

An **indirect quotation** reports only the general meaning of what a person said or thought and does not require quotation marks.

> Mrs. Gleason announced that dinner was served and invited us to the dining table.
>
> —"The All-American Slurp,"
> Yolen, p. 519

Always place a comma or a period inside the final quotation mark of a direct quotation.

Place a question mark or an exclamation mark inside the final quotation mark if the end mark is part of the quotation; if it is not part of the quotation, place it outside the final quotation mark.

> "Couldn't you borrow a girl's bicycle?" complained Mother.
>
> —"The All-American Slurp,"
> Namioka, p. 521

> Does that poem by Robert Frost start with the line, "The way a crow"?
>
> —"Dust of Snow," Frost, p. 29

Underline or italicize the titles of long written works, movies, television and radio shows, lengthy works of music, paintings, and sculptures.

> Anne of Green Gables   *The Mona Lisa*

Use quotation marks around the titles of short written works, episodes in a series, songs, and titles of works mentioned as parts of collections.

> "Parade"   "Lob's Girl"
>
> "You've Got a Friend"   "A Dream Within a Dream"

Hyphens Use a **hyphen** with certain numbers, after certain prefixes, with two or more words used as one word, and with a compound modifier that comes before a noun.

> fifty-four   self-employed
>
> daughter-in-law   happy-go-lucky friend

Apostrophes Add an **apostrophe** and s to show the possessive case of most singular nouns.

    the author's story   Dickens's novels   Aesop's Fables

Add an apostrophe to show the possessive case of plural nouns ending in s and es.

    the wolves' hooves   the Knickerbockers' rules

Add an apostrophe and s to show the possessive case of plural nouns that do not end in s or es.

    the women's hats   the mice's whiskers

Use an apostrophe in a contraction to indicate the position of the missing letter or letters.

    "Couldn't you borrow a girl's bicycle?" complained Mother.

                —"All-American Slurp," Namioka, p. 521

GLOSSARY OF COMMON USAGE

accept, except
Accept is a verb that means "to receive" or "to agree to." *Except* is a preposition that means "other than" or "leaving out." Do not confuse these two words.

    Aaron sadly *accepted* his father's decision to sell Zlateh.

    Everyone *except* the fisherman and his wife had children.

affect, effect
Affect is normally a verb meaning "to influence" or "to bring about a change in." *Effect* is usually a noun, meaning "result."

    The thought of having to move to Fresno *affects* Panchito.

    The wizard's spell had an immediate *effect* on the queen. She turned into a rosebush.

among, between
Among is usually used with three or more items. *Between* is generally used with only two items.

    "Stray" was *among* the stories Lisha liked best.

    A conflict developed *between* the men and Walt in "The King of Mazy May."

amount, number
Amount refers to a mass or a unit, whereas *number* refers to individual items that can be counted. Therefore, *amount* generally appears with singular nouns, and *number* appears with plural nouns.

    A great *amount* of information could fit on a telebook.

    A *number* of letters were in the package.

bad, badly
Use the predicate adjective *bad* after linking verbs such as *feel, look,* and *seem.* Use *badly* whenever an adverb is required.

    Mouse does not feel *bad* about tricking Coyote.

    In the myth, Athene treats Arachne *badly.*

beside, besides
Do not confuse these two prepositions, which have different meanings. *Beside* means "at the side of" or "close to." *Besides* means "in addition to."

    Sitting *beside* his parents, Greyling sings songs of the wonders that lie beneath the sea.

    Besides "April Rain Song," what other poems did you like this year?

can, may
The verb *can* generally refers to the ability to do something. The verb *may* generally refers to permission to do something.

    Maibon replies that he *can* still see the dwarf.

    Norman's mother tells him he *may* not bring the coup stick in the house.

compare, contrast
The verb *compare* can involve both similarities and differences. The verb *contrast* always involves differences. Use *to* or *with* after compare. Use *with* after contrast.

    Rena *compared* Lewis's "Letter to Joan" to Fitzgerald's "Letter to Scottie."

    In many works of science fiction, elements of fantasy *contrast* with the reality of the everyday world.

different from, different than
Different from is generally preferred over *different than.*

farther, further
Use *farther* when you refer to distance. Use *further* when you mean "to a greater degree or extent" or "additional."

    As the snow continued to fall, Aaron and Zlateh could not travel any *farther,* and they had to seek shelter.

    Walt wants to prevent any *further* hardships for Loren Hall.

fewer, less

Use *fewer* for things that can be counted. Use *less* for amounts or quantities that cannot be counted.

> Which poem has *fewer* rhyming lines: "April Rain Song" or "Ankylosaurus"?

> Because Walt had to harness the team quickly, he had *less* time than he needed to choose a good lead dog.

good, well

Use the predicate adjective *good* after linking verbs such as *feel, look, smell, taste,* and *seem.* Use *well* whenever you need an adverb.

> Most people feel *good* when they receive letters from friends.

> In "The Dog of Pompeii," Louis Untermeyer describes the eruption of the volcano especially *well.*

hopefully

You should not loosely attach this adverb to a sentence, as in "*Hopefully,* the rain will stop by noon." Rewrite the sentence so *hopefully* modifies a specific verb. Other possible ways of revising such sentences include using the adjective *hopeful* or a phrase like "everyone *hopes* that."

> The author of "The All-American Slurp" writes *hopefully* about her family's adjustment to America.

> Tom Sawyer *hopes* that his complaining will keep him home from school.

its, it's

Do not confuse the possessive pronoun *its* with the contraction *it's,* standing for "it is" or "it has."

> The jackal is known for *its* mischief.

> *It's* a shame that life is sometimes cruel.

lay, lie

Do not confuse these verbs. *Lay* is a transitive verb meaning "to set or put something down." Its principal parts are *lay, laying, laid, laid. Lie* is an intransitive verb meaning "to recline." Its principal parts are *lie, lying, lay, lain.*

> Aaron *lays* some popcorn on the floor for Pidge.

> The boy makes a pillow out of some hay and *lies* down to sleep.

leave, let

Be careful not to confuse these verbs. *Leave* means "to go away" or "to allow to remain." *Let* means "to permit."

> Even in the hospital, the dog did not want to *leave* Sandy's side.

> She opened the door and *let* the moth fly out.

like

Like is a preposition that usually means "similar to" or "in the same way as." *Like* should always be followed by an object. Do not use *like* before a subject and a verb. Use *as* or *that* instead.

> Myths *like* "Arachne" explain the origins of things.

> "Stray" did not end *as* Tara expected.

loose, lose

Loose can be either an adjective (meaning "unattached") or a verb (meaning "to untie"). *Lose* is always a verb (meaning "to fail to keep, have, or win").

> Today, many Native Americans are sad due to the *loose* connection their children have to the past.

> The fisherman's wife feared she would someday *lose* her son to the sea.

many, much

Use *many* to refer to a specific quantity. Use *much* for an indefinite amount or for an abstract concept.

> *Many* people prefer stories with animal characters.

> Chinese American authors have *much* to say about the clash of their two worlds.

of, have

Do not use *of* in place of *have* after auxiliary verbs like *would, could, should, may, might,* or *must.*

> Maibon realizes that he *should have* destroyed the stone.

raise, rise

Raise is a transitive verb that usually takes a direct object. *Rise* is intransitive and never takes a direct object.

> During the whole time they *raised* Greyling, the fisherman and his wife never allowed the child to go into the sea.

> Before the students *rise* for the lunch bell, Phyllis Lopez remembers that the sweater is hers.

set, sit

Do not confuse these verbs. *Set* is a transitive verb meaning "to put (something) in a certain place." Its principal parts are *set, setting, set, set. Sit* is an intransitive verb meaning "to be seated." Its principal parts are *sit, sitting, sat, sat.*

> The Walrus *sets* a loaf of bread and some pepper and vinegar on the rocks.

> I would like to read "The Fairies' Lullaby" while I *sit* on a beautiful beach and watch the sunset.

than, then

The conjunction *than* is used to connect the two parts of a comparison. Do not confuse *than* with the adverb *then,* which usually refers to time.

> Rudyard Kipling lived longer *than* Jack London.

> The water in the public fountains boils, and *then* the streets of Pompeii start to crumble.

that, which, who

Use the relative pronoun *that* to refer to things or people. Use *which* only for things and *who* only for people.

> The ancient coup stick *that* Norman finds might have been buried with a dead warrior.

> The theme, *which* is the central message of a literary work, is often not directly stated.

> Robert Frost is a poet *who* writes vividly about nature.

their, there, they're

Do not confuse the spelling of these three words. *Their* is a possessive adjective and always modifies a noun. *There* is usually used either at the beginning of a sentence or as an adverb. *They're* is a contraction for "they are."

> In Thurber's fable, some of the beasts did not even know what *their* fight was about.

> *There* was nothing that could frighten Isabel in Ogden Nash's poem.

> Limericks are short, and *they're* usually humorous.

to, too, two

Do not confuse the spelling of these words. *To* is a preposition that begins a prepositional phrase or an infinitive. *Too,* with two *o's,* is an adverb and modifies adjectives and other adverbs. *Two* is a number.

> Panchito spoke *to* Mr. Lema about some difficult English words.

> Rob thought that his essay about the Internet was *too* long, so he revised it.

> *Two* poems that Laurie especially liked were Walt Whitman's "My Picture-Gallery" and Sara Teasdale's "February Twilight."

when, where, why

Do not use *when, where,* or *why* directly after a linking verb such as *is.* Reword the sentence.

> **Faulty:** Suspense is *when* an author increases the reader's tension.

> **Revised:** An author uses suspense to increase the reader's tension.

> **Faulty:** A biography is *where* a writer tells the life story of another person.

> **Revised:** In a biography, a writer tells the life story of another person.

who, whom

In formal writing, remember to use *who* only as a subject in clauses and sentences and *whom* only as an object.

> Maya Angelou, *who* wrote "Life Doesn't Frighten Me," often expresses her concern for the black community.

> One poet *whom* Chris especially liked was Langston Hughes.

Speaking, Listening, and Viewing Handbook

Communication is the way in which people convey their ideas and interact with one another. The literature in this book is written, which is one form of communication, but much of your personal communication is probably oral or visual. Oral communication involves both speaking and listening. Visual communication involves both conveying messages through physical expression or pictorial representations and interpreting images. Developing strong communication skills can benefit your school life and your life outside of school.

Many of the assignments accompanying the literature in this textbook involve speaking, listening, viewing, and representing. This handbook identifies some of the terminology related to the oral and visual communication you experience every day and the assignments you may do in conjunction with the literature in this book.

Communication

You use many different kinds of communication every day. When you communicate with your friends, your teachers, or your parents, or when you interact with a cashier in a store, you are communicating orally. In addition to ordinary conversation, oral communication includes class discussions, speeches, interviews, presentations, and debates. When you communicate face to face, you usually use more than your voice to get your message across. If you communicate by telephone, however, you must rely solely on your verbal skills. At times, you may use more visual communication than any other kind. For example, when you paint a picture, participate in a dance recital, or prepare a multimedia presentation, you use strategies of visual communication.

The following terms will give you a better understanding of the many elements that are a part of oral and visual communication:

BODY LANGUAGE refers to the use of facial expressions, eye contact, gestures, posture, and movement to communicate a feeling or an idea.

CONNOTATION is the set of associations a word calls to mind. The connotations of the words you choose influence the message you send. For example, most people respond more favorably to being described as "slim" rather than as "skinny." The connotation of *slim* is more appealing than that of *skinny.*

EYE CONTACT is direct visual contact with another person's eyes.

FEEDBACK is the set of verbal and nonverbal reactions that indicate to a speaker that a message has been received and understood.

GESTURES are the movements made with arms, hands, face, and fingers to communicate.

LISTENING is understanding and interpreting sound in a meaningful way. You listen differently for different purposes.
Listening for key information: For example, when a teacher gives an assignment, or when someone gives you directions to a place, you listen for key information.
Listening for main points: In a classroom exchange of ideas or information, or while watching a television documentary, you listen for main points.
Listening critically: When you evaluate a performance, a song, or a persuasive or political speech, you listen critically, questioning and judging the speaker's message.

MEDIUM is the material or technique used to present a visual image. Common media include paint, clay, and film.

NONVERBAL COMMUNICATION is communication without the use of words. People communicate nonverbally through gestures, facial expressions, posture, and body movements. Sign language is an entire language based on nonverbal communication.

VIEWING is observing, understanding, analyzing, and evaluating information presented through visual means. You might use the following questions to help you interpret what you view:
- What subject is presented?
- What is communicated about the subject?
- Which parts are factual? Which are opinion?
- What mood, attitude, or opinion is conveyed?
- What is your emotional response?

VOCAL DELIVERY is the way in which you present a message. Your vocal delivery involves all of the following elements:
Volume: the loudness or quietness of your voice
Pitch: the high or low quality of your voice
Rate: the speed at which you speak; also called pace
Stress: the amount of emphasis placed on different syllables in a word or on different words in a sentence

All of these elements individually, and the way in which they are combined, contribute to the meaning of a spoken message.

Speaking, Listening, and Viewing Situations

Here are some of the many types of situations in which you apply speaking, listening, and viewing skills:

AUDIENCE Your audience in any situation refers to the person or people to whom you direct your message. An audience can be a group of people sitting in a classroom or auditorium observing a performance or just one person to whom you address a question or a comment. When preparing for any speaking situation, it's useful to analyze your audience, learning what you can about their backgrounds, interests, and attitudes so that you can tailor your message to them.

CHARTS AND GRAPHS are visual representations of statistical information. For example, a pie chart might indicate how the average dollar is spent by government, and a bar graph might compare populations in cities over time.

DEBATE A debate is a formal public-speaking situation in which participants prepare and present arguments on opposing sides of a question, stated as a **proposition.**

The two sides in a debate are the *affirmative* (pro) and the *negative* (con). The affirmative side argues in favor of the proposition, while the negative side argues against it. The affirmative side begins the debate, since it is seeking a change in belief or policy. The opposing sides take turns presenting their arguments, and each side has an opportunity for *rebuttal,* in which they may challenge or question the other side's argument.

DOCUMENTARIES are nonfiction films that analyze news events or other focused subjects. You can watch a documentary for the information on its subject.

GROUP DISCUSSION results when three or more people meet to solve a common problem, arrive at a decision, or answer a question of mutual interest. Group discussion is one of the most widely used forms of interpersonal communication in modern society.

INTERVIEW An interview is a form of interaction in which one person, the interviewer, asks questions of another person, the interviewee. Interviews may take place for many purposes: to obtain information, to discover a person's suitability for a job or a college, or to inform the public of a notable person's opinions.

MAPS are visual representations of the Earth's surface. Maps may show political boundaries or physical features. They can also provide information on a variety of other topics. A map's title and its key identify the content of the map.

ORAL INTERPRETATION is the reading or speaking of a work of literature aloud for an audience. Oral interpretation involves giving expression to the ideas, meaning, or even the structure of a work of literature. The speaker interprets the work through his or her vocal delivery. **Storytelling,** in which a speaker reads or tells a story expressively, is a form of oral interpretation.

PANEL DISCUSSION is a group discussion on a topic of interest common to all members of a panel and to a listening audience. A panel is usually composed of four to six experts on a particular topic who are brought together to share information and opinions.

PANTOMIME is a form of nonverbal communication in which an idea or a story is communicated completely through the use of gesture, body language, and facial expressions, without any words at all.

POLITICAL CARTOONS are drawings that comment on important political or social issues. Often, these cartoons use humor to convey a message about their subject. Viewers use their own knowledge of events to evaluate the cartoonist's opinion.

READERS THEATRE is a dramatic reading of a work of literature in which participants take parts from a story or a play and read them aloud in expressive voices. Unlike a play, however, sets and costumes are not part of the performance, and the participants remain seated as they deliver their lines.

ROLE PLAY To role-play is to take the role of a person or character and, as that character, act out a given situation, speaking, acting, and responding in the manner of the character.

SPEECH A speech is a talk or an address given to an audience. A speech may be **impromptu**—delivered on the spur of the moment with no preparation—or formally prepared and delivered for a specific purpose or occasion.

- *Purposes*: The most common purposes of speeches are to persuade (for example, political speeches), to entertain, to explain, and to inform.
- *Occasions*: Different occasions call for different types of speeches. Speeches given on these occasions could be persuasive, entertaining, or informative, as appropriate. The following are common occasions for speeches:

Introduction: Introducing a speaker at a meeting
Presentation: Giving an award or acknowledging the contributions of someone
Acceptance: Accepting an award or a tribute
Keynote: Giving an inspirational address at a large meeting or convention
Commencement: Honoring the graduates of a school

Test Preparation Handbook

Contents
Test Preparation Workshops

Test Preparation Handbook

Test Practice Bank

Reading Comprehension: Using Context Clues

Reading Comprehension: Identifying Related Details

Reading Comprehension: Identifying the Main Idea

Reading Comprehension: Identifying Cause-and-Effect Relationships

Reading Comprehension: Drawing Inferences and Conclusions

Reading Comprehension: Arranging Details in Sequential Order

Reading Comprehension: Making Generalizations

Reading Comprehension: Recognizing Author's Point of View and Purpose

Reading Comprehension: Distinguishing Fact and Opinion

Reading Comprehension: Describing Plot, Setting, Character, and Mood

Combined Reading and Literary Skills

Writing Skills Sentence Construction

Writing Skills Identifying Appropriate Usage

Writing Skills Spelling, Capitalization, and Punctuation

Writing Tasks

Test Preparation Workshop 1

Reading Comprehension | Using Context Clues

Strategies for Success

The reading sections of standardized tests ask you to read a passage and answer questions about word meanings. Some questions require you to figure out the meanings of words by using context clues. Use the following strategies to help you answer test questions on word meanings:

Use Context Clues The words and phrases around a word are the word's context. Sometimes, even if you don't recognize a word, you can figure out its meaning from the overall sense of the passage in which it appears. To use context clues, first read for the general meaning of the whole passage. Then, ask yourself what the unfamiliar word must mean in order for the passage to make sense. Sometimes substituting each answer choice for the unfamiliar word will make it clear which one is correct. Look at the following example:

Lou counted the change in her purse. Just fifty cents more and she could buy the perfect present for her dad. Perhaps her brother would lend her the money. He was **parsimonious,** but perhaps he would be willing to do it for a good cause and her promise to pay it back with interest.

In this passage, the word **parsimonious** means—

  A quiet   **C** stingy
  B happy   **D** helpful

A and **B** have nothing to do with lending money. The word *but* implies that lending money would be in contrast to being *parsimonious,* so **D** is not correct. The correct answer has to be **C**.

Multiple-Meaning Words Context clues help to determine the correct meaning of a word that has several meanings. When you are asked to identify the meaning of a word with multiple meanings, be sure to read the word in context before answering the question. Read this example.

Sean's mother had asked him to clean out the garage, and he was happy to do it. As he put the tools away, he thought about how hard his mother worked at the electronics **plant** to support the family.

The word **plant** in this passage means—

  A factory   **C** hotel
  B leaf   **D** flower

A person would not work at **B** or **D**. An electronics hotel does not make sense. Thus, the answer has to be **A**.

Apply the Strategies

Answer these test questions based on the following passage.

The squad had been ordered to subdue the village with as little violence as possible. Unexpectedly, the villagers had resisted savagely. It was a **signal** accomplishment that the sergeant was able to prevent the angry soldiers from **wasting** the entire village.

1 In this passage, the word **signal** means—
  A regrettable   **C** remarkable
  B sign   **D** time

2 The word **wasting** in this passage means—
  A feeding   **C** squandering
  B destroying   **D** charging

Test Preparation Workshop 2

Reading Comprehension

Identifying Related Details

Strategies for Success

The reading sections of standardized tests require you to read a passage and answer multiple-choice questions about details in a passage. Use the following strategies to help you answer test questions about details:

Identify Related Details Some test questions ask you to select the facts and details that support a main idea. Read the question carefully to identify the main idea. Then, read the answer choices to see if you can eliminate any answer that is not related to the main idea. If you need to, skim the passage looking for one or more details that support the main idea. Look at the following example:

> A strong breeze made the leaves rustle. A twig snapped beneath his foot and Martin jumped. He had never walked the woodsy path between his house and Andy's alone at night. The sounds made him nervous. An owl's hoot didn't exactly scare him, but it did contribute to the eerie feeling of the walk.

What details made Martin's walk eerie?

A rustling leaves, snapping twig, hooting owl
B being alone, hooting owl, howling wind
C darkness, cold, snapping twig
D quietness, darkness, trees

The passage does not mention howling wind, cold, or quietness. **B**, **C**, and **D** are incorrect. The answer is **A**.

Separate Fact From Opinion When identifying facts and details that support a main idea, it is important to separate fact from opinion. A *fact* is a statement that can be proved. An *opinion* is a person's feelings or beliefs. Look at this example:

> The builders of the Great Pyramid of Giza took elaborate precautions to prevent robbers from finding the royal tomb. They constructed false passages and fake burial chambers. They used stones to seal off the real burial chamber from the Grand Gallery. Then, they sealed the entrance to the Grand Gallery with enormous blocks of stone. The design of the Great Pyramid reveals the creativity of ancient Egyptians.

Which of these details does *not* support the main idea—that the builders of the Great Pyramid wanted to keep robbers from the tomb?

A false passages   **C** creativity of builders
B sealed entrances   **D** fake burial chambers

A, **B**, and **D** support the main idea. **C** is an opinion and does not support the main idea.

Apply the Strategies

Answer the questions based on this passage.

> The destruction of the world's tropical rain forests must stop. These forests are filled with treasures more valuable than gold or jewels. Rain forests include many varieties of fruits, thousands of species of animals, and many plants with healing properties. The trees give off oxygen, which is necessary to humans. Rubber trees yield natural rubber, necessary for many products. The sap of one kind of tree is pure diesel oil.

1 Treasures of the rain forests include—
   A oxygen, fruits, gold
   B medicine, rubber, oxygen
   C diesel fuel, animals, jewels
   D fruits, medicine, wheat

2 Which is a FACT expressed in the passage?
   A Rain forests have treasures of gold and jewels.
   B Rain forest trees give off oxygen.
   C Few animals can survive in the rain forests.
   D Destruction of the rain forests must stop.

Test Preparation Workshop 3

Reading Comprehension
Identifying Main Idea

Strategies for Success

The reading sections of standardized tests require you to read a passage and answer multiple-choice questions about main ideas.

Identify the Stated Main Idea A main idea is often stated in a topic sentence that summarizes the passage. The topic sentence may be located anywhere in the passage. In a test question, the correct answer choice sometimes restates the topic sentence in different words. Look at the following passage and question:

> Every year hundreds of powwows are held all over the United States and Canada. A powwow is a celebration of Native American heritage. With drummers setting the rhythm, dancers compete in various categories, including fancy dances, grass dances, and jingle dances. Between the contests, dances called intertribals are open to anyone.

What is the main idea of this passage?

A Dancers compete in different categories.
B A powwow celebrates Native American heritage.
C Every year hundreds of powwows are held.
D Intertribals are open to anyone.

A and **D** are details. **C** is a general comment, not the main idea. **B** is the main idea.

Identify the Implied Main Idea If a main idea is not stated, it is implied, or suggested. To identify an implied main idea, look for the answer choice that best summarizes the details in the passage. Look at this example:

> Most powwow dancers make their own outfits. In the past, the jingle in jingle dancers' dresses came from animal teeth, bones, or shells. Today, these dresses are decorated with cones shaped from tin-can lids. Grass dancers used to braid sweet grass to decorate their outfits. Now they use strands of colorful wool.

What is the implied main idea of this passage?

A Grass dancers decorate their outfits with strands of wool instead of grass.
B Some Native American dancers have adapted their traditional styles of dress with new materials.
C Only women do jingle dances.
D Jingle dancers and grass dancers are the only dancers who make their own clothing.

A is a detail. **C** and **D** do not summarize the passage. **B** is the implied main idea.

Apply the Strategies

Answer the questions based on this passage.

> While Maria's neighbors were on vacation, she went to their apartment every morning to take care of the cats. First, she put out fresh food and water. Next, she cleaned the litter box. Then, Maria played with the cats. Taking care of cats was the best job she ever had.

> Maria hoped to convince her parents to let her have a cat. "Cats are clean," she argued. "They're quiet and cuddly. I can take care of a cat." Still, their answer was no.

1 What is the main idea of the first paragraph?
   A Maria went to her neighbor's apartment.
   B She put out food and water for the cats.
   C Taking care of cats was the best job Maria had ever had.
   D Maria played with the cats.

2 What is the main idea of the second paragraph?
   A Maria wanted a cat.
   B Maria's parents could not be convinced to let her have a cat.
   C Cats are clean and easy to take care of.
   D Cats make good pets.

Test Preparation Workshop 4

Reading Comprehension — Cause-and-Effect Relationships

Strategies for Success

The reading sections of both national and Texas standardized tests require you to read a passage and answer multiple-choice questions about cause and effect. Use the following strategies to help you answer such questions:

Look for Signal Words A *cause* is an event or condition that makes something happen. An *effect* is what happens or results from the cause. Certain words signal cause-and-effect relationships, including *because, why, the reason for, as a result of, in order to,* and *so that.* Look at the following example:

> "Sheila went to bed because she was tired."

In the example, going to bed is the *effect* and being tired is the *cause.* The word "because" is a signal word for the *cause* part of the sentence.

Ask Yourself Questions Test items about cause-and-effect relationships may be worded in different ways, for example, "Why did. . . ?" or "What happened as a result of. . . ?" Other test items may be sentence stems, for example, "Some birds migrate because. . . " or "As a result of the accident, Hector. . . ."

To answer a cause-and-effect test item, ask yourself, "Why did something happen?" or "What happened as a result of something?" Look at the following passage and questions:

> The Cabrera children liked their new home in the United States. Their parents had good jobs, the neighbors were friendly, and their house was pleasant. Still, they missed their relatives in the Dominican Republic, and looked forward to a long summer vacation on the island.

I Why were the Cabrera children happy in the United States?

A The neighbors were friendly.
B They could go to the Dominican Republic for the summer.
C Their mother didn't have to work.
D Their new house was like their old one.

2 The children missed their relatives, so they—
A planned to move back to the Dominican Republic
B asked their parents to quit their jobs
C looked forward to summer vacation
D sold their new home in the United States

I **C** and **D** are not stated. **B** is not the reason they were happy. **A** is the answer.

2 **A** and **B** are not stated. **D** does not make sense in the sentence. **C** is the answer.

Apply the Strategies

Answer the questions based on this passage.

> Immigrants have come to the United States for many reasons. Some have come to escape war, famine, or religious persecution. Others have wanted to make a better life for their families.
>
> In the early twentieth century, millions of immigrants came from southern and eastern Europe. Many of them stayed in the coastal cities where they landed. As a result, these cities experienced growth and overcrowding.

I Immigrants came to the United States to—
A lose their old identity
B escape war, famine, and persecution
C avoid persecution in their old country
D escape political conditions

2 What contributed to the growth of cities in the United States in the early twentieth century?
A overcrowding   **C** immigration
B famine   **D** progress

Test Preparation Workshop 5

Reading Comprehension | Draw Inferences and Conclusions

Strategies for Success

The reading sections of standardized tests require you to read a passage and answer multiple-choice questions about inferences and conclusions. Use the following strategies to help you answer such questions:

Draw Inferences Writers don't always state everything directly. Sometimes you must infer the writer's meaning by "reading between the lines." To draw inferences, combine information from the text with your own knowledge. If the answer to a question is not stated in the passage, look for facts and details that could help you arrive at a logical answer. Look at this example:

> Sam checked his backpack once again. He didn't want to arrive too early at the bus stop to stand with kids he didn't know. After fidgeting for five more minutes, Sam said goodbye to his mother and walked out the front door. Seven or eight boys and girls were waiting at the corner. "Hi," said one of them. "Are you new in town?"

Which word best describes Sam?

A cheerful   **C** relaxed
B nervous   **D** sloppy

There are no details to support choices **A**, **C**, or **D**. Answer **B** is correct.

Draw Conclusions When you draw a conclusion, you use evidence in the text to reach a general understanding about the topic. The conclusion should follow logically from the information that you read in the text or infer from the text. Review the passage above and answer the following question.

I The passage gives you reason to believe that—

A Sam is unfriendly
B Sam and his mother don't communicate well
C Sam lives near his new school
D this is Sam's first day at a new school

There is no evidence to support choices **A** or **B**. Sam is taking a bus, so **C** is not correct. **D** is the correct answer.

Apply the Strategies

Use the strategies you have learned to answer the questions based on this passage.

> For years, people have dreamed of having robots to do household chores. While this has not happened, robots are doing many important jobs. Surgeons use robots to make precise movements that are difficult for a human hand. Robots pick apples from the tops of trees without bruising them. Security robots warn of fires and intruders. Scientists have used robots to explore places too dangerous for humans, for example inside active volcanoes, on the ocean floor, and on the surface of Mars.

1 Information in the passage suggests that—
   A robots are cheaper than human surgeons
   B Mars is too cold for humans
   C robots are not as reliable as humans
   D robots can survive higher temperatures than humans

2 From this passage, you can conclude that—
   A robots will never do household chores
   B robots have expanded scientific knowledge
   C the idea for robots came from science fiction
   D robots would not be useful in schools

Test Preparation Workshop 6

Reading Comprehension — Describing Plot, Setting, Character, and Mood

Strategies for Success

The reading sections of standardized tests require you to read a passage and answer multiple-choice questions about such literary elements as plot, setting, character, and mood. Use the following strategies to help you answer such questions:

Describe Plot and Setting *Plot* is the series of events that make up the action of a story. A plot usually revolves around one or more conflicts. When you are asked a question about the plot, choose the answer that most accurately tells what happens in the story or passage. *Setting* is the time and place of the action. When you are asked about setting, you may have to infer the time and place based on other information in the story.

Describe Character and Mood *Character* refers to the person(s) or animal(s) in the story. Questions about character may ask you to draw inferences about characters' actions and words or what others say about the characters. *Mood* refers to the feeling, or emotions, you get from reading a passage. The descriptive details in a passage help establish the mood. Read this example:

> With a deep sigh, Dulcie drifted toward the window. In the fading light, she could barely see the figure riding up the path. As soon as he sprang from his horse and strode to the front door, Dulcie knew it was Lance. Quickly, she thrust the letter she had been reading into her dress pocket. The door to the drawing room swung open.
>
> "What have you done with our son?" Lance bellowed, his face distorted with rage.
>
> "He is in a safe place," Dulcie replied, and with a sudden movement, she yanked at the bell cord to summon the servant.

1 Before Lance arrived, Dulcie had been—
A waiting for him
B saying goodbye to their son
C reading a letter
D staring out the window

2 This story takes place—
A early in the morning   **C** mid-morning
B late at night   **D** late afternoon

3 Dulcie can be described as—
A passive   **C** careless
B courageous   **D** unfaithful

4 At the end of the passage, the mood is—
A tense   **C** mysterious
B humorous   **D** calm

For question 1: The text supports choice **C**.
For question 2: The text supports choice **D**.
For question 3: The text supports choice **B**.
For question 4: The text supports choice **A**.

Apply the Strategies

Use the strategies you have learned to answer these questions on the passage above.

1 Dulcie and Lance are in conflict over—
A their home   **C** the servant
B their son   **D** money

2 The story takes place—
A in a foreign country   **C** in the past
B in the United States   **D** in the present

3 Lance can be described as—
A angry   **C** supportive
B unhappy   **D** distant

4 At the beginning of the passage, the mood is—
A eerie   **C** quiet
B energetic   **D** romantic

Test Preparation Workshop 7

Reading Comprehension

Distinguishing Fact and Opinion

Strategies for Success

The reading sections of standardized tests require you to read a passage and answer multiple-choice questions about distinguishing fact and opinion. Use the following strategies to help you answer such questions:

Recognize Facts A *fact* is a statement that can be proved by consulting a reliable source, such as a book or an expert on the topic. When you are asked to identify a statement as a fact, ask yourself, "Could this statement be proved?" Look at this example:

"Be careful," warned the dealer. "That's the most valuable stamp in the shop. It's the prettiest, too. You'll never see another one of those. There are only five in the world. I never get tired of telling the story of how I found that stamp. It happened when I was traveling in North Africa. Stamp collecting is a hobby for the adventurous."

Which of these is a FACT in the passage?

A You'll never see another one of those.
B That's the most valuable stamp in the shop.
C It's the prettiest one, too.
D I never get tired of telling how I found that stamp.

A, **C**, and **D** cannot be proved. The answer is **B**.

Recognize Opinions An opinion may sound like a fact, but cannot be proved. An opinion is a statement of the writer's belief. A writer's opinion may be supported by reliable facts, but that does not make the writer's statement a fact. Look at this question based on the passage above:

Which is an OPINION expressed in the passage?

A There are only five in the world.
B I never get tired of telling the story of how I found the stamp.

C It happened when I was traveling in North Africa.
D Stamp collecting is a hobby for the adventurous.

A, **B**, and **C** can be proved. **D** is the dealer's opinion.

Apply the Strategies

Read the passage and answer the questions.

It is illegal to hunt and sell wild chimpanzees. Captured chimps often get sick in captivity. Then, their owners give them up. Concerned people have set up sanctuaries to shelter chimps who cannot be returned to the wild. Some wildlife experts think the money used to run the sanctuaries should be spent on enforcing the hunting laws instead. Famous chimpanzee specialist Jane Goodall says, "I cannot turn my back on an individual."

1 Which of these statements is an OPINION?
   A It is illegal to hunt chimpanzees.
   B Sick chimps' owners give them up.
   C Money spent on sanctuaries should be used to enforce the hunting laws.
   D Goodall cannot turn her back on chimps.

2 Which is a FACT expressed in the passage?
   A Captured chimps often get sick.
   B Goodall is the most famous chimpanzee expert.
   C Freed chimps are better off in the wild.
   D Money should be used to enforce laws.

Test Preparation Workshop 8

Writing Skills | Sentence Construction

Strategies for Success

The writing sections of standardized tests require you to read a passage and answer multiple-choice questions about sentence construction. Use the following strategies to help you answer such questions:

Recognize Incomplete Sentences and Run-on Sentences An incomplete sentence is lacking a subject or a predicate or both. It is not a complete thought. An incomplete sentence can be made into a complete thought by adding words to it or by combining it with another sentence or part of a sentence. Run-on sentences are two or more sentences without the correct punctuation. A run-on sentence can be corrected by making shorter sentences, by adding punctuation, and/or by including a conjunction to separate sentences.

Combine Sentences Sometimes two short, closely related sentences can be combined into one sentence. When you are given this option as a test answer choice, make sure the answer you choose is a complete sentence. Look at the following sample test item:

According to Thomas Edison, genius is one percent inspiration and ninety-nine percent perspiration. (1) By his own definition, he certainly qualified during his lifetime he patented 1,093 inventions.

Choose the best way to write the underlined section. If it needs no change, choose "Correct as is."

A He certainly qualified by his own definition during his lifetime he patented 1,093 inventions.

B By his own definition, he certainly qualified.

During his lifetime, he patented 1,093 inventions.

C By his own definition. He certainly qualified during his lifetime he patented 1,093 inventions.

D Correct as is

A is a run-on sentence. **C** contains incomplete and run-on sentences. **B** is correct. It turns a run-on sentence into two complete sentences.

Apply the Strategies

Choose the best way to write the underlined section. If it needs no change, choose "Correct as is."

(1) Scientists have been studying bubbles. The bubbles were trapped in Antarctic ice for thousands of years. Studies show a connection between the amount of carbon dioxide in the air and the temperature. (2) This is important for people today. Because the amount of carbon dioxide in the air is increasing yearly.

1 **A** Scientists have been studying bubbles in Antarctic ice for thousands of years.

B Scientists have been in Antarctic ice for thousands of years.

C Bubbles were trapped in Antarctic ice.

D Correct as is

2 **A** This is important for people today because the amount of carbon dioxide in the air is increasing yearly.

B This is important. For people today because carbon dioxide is increasing yearly.

C This is important for people today the amount of carbon dioxide in the air increasing yearly.

D Correct as is

Test Preparation Workshop 9

Reading Comprehension

Strategies for Success

The writing sections of standardized tests require you to read a passage and answer multiple-choice questions about appropriate usage. Use the following strategies to help you answer such questions:

Use the Correct Form of a Word Some test questions ask you to choose the correct part of speech, the appropriate form of an adjective or adverb, the correct pronoun, or the correct form of a negative. Look at these examples:

1 Get the teacher's _____ for your topic.
   A approve   **C** approval
   B approving   **D** approved

A noun is needed, so **C** is correct.

2 The first problem is _____ than the second.
   A simple   **C** more simpler
   B simply   **D** simpler

Two things are compared, so the comparative form of the adjective is needed. **D** is correct.

3 Bill asked Matt and _____ to go skating.
   A I   **C** myself
   B me   **D** mine

The correct answer is **B**, a direct object.

4 I _____ forget my tenth birthday.
   A will barely never   **C** will not never
   B will probably never **D** will hardly never

A, **C**, and **D** are double negatives. **B** is correct.

Use Correct Agreement A verb must agree with its subject in number. A pronoun agrees with its antecedent (the word it stands for) in person, number, and gender. Look at these examples:

1 The blossoms on the rose bush _____ red.
   A is   **C** are
   B has been   **D** was

The verb must agree with the plural subject *blossoms*. **C** is correct.

2 Every cup has _____ matching saucer.
   A its   **C** your
   B their   **D** his

The antecedent, *cup,* is third person singular, so **A** is correct.

Use Correct Verb Tense and Form Some test questions ask you to choose the correct tense or form of a verb. Look at this example:

When Elisa _____ the sign, she turned left.
   A saw   **C** had seen
   B see   **D** seeing

The sentence describes a simple past action, so **A** is correct.

Apply the Strategies

Read the passage and choose the word or words that belong in each space.

Christopher Wolfe __(1)__ believe his eyes. Sticking out of a hillside __(2)__ dinosaur horns! Chris and his dad, who is a paleontologist, __(3)__ up the fossils and took __(4)__ to a museum. Imagine their __(5)__ when they learned that the fossils were a ninety-million-year-old dinosaur!

1 **A** couldn't hardly   **C** could never hardly
  B could hardly   **D** didn't hardly

2 **A** has been   **C** were
  B was   **D** is

3 **A** dug   **C** had digged
  B dugged   **D** digged

4 **A** it   **C** themselves
  B him   **D** them

5 **A** excitement   **C** exciting
  B excite   **D** excitedly

Test Preparation Workshop 10

Writing Skills

Spelling, Capitalization, Punctuation

Strategies for Success

The writing sections of standardized tests require you to read a passage and answer multiple-choice questions about spelling, capitalization, and punctuation. Use the following strategies to help you answer such questions:

Recognize Spelling Errors Check the spelling of each word in the passage. Pay special attention to words with double medial consonants, (*reach*, not *reech*), suffix endings (*-ful*, not *-full*), verb endings (*cried*, not *cryed*), and words that are homophones (*to, too, two*).

Recognize Capitalization Errors Make sure that the first word in a sentence is capitalized, that all proper nouns are capitalized, and that no words are capitalized unnecessarily. All the words in a compound proper noun should be capitalized (*New York City*).

Recognize Punctuation Errors Check end punctuation. Make sure that a question ends with a question mark, a sentence with a period, and an exclamation with an exclamation mark. Be sure that all necessary commas are included. Check for complete quotation marks. Look at this example:

Read the passage and decide which type of error, if any, appears.

(1) If you think relay races are fun imagine one on horseback! (2) At United States Pony club rallies, (3) horses and there riders compete in ten different relay races.

1 **A** Spelling error   **C** Punctuation error
   B Capitalization error   **D** No error

2 **A** Spelling error   **C** Punctuation error
   B Capitalization error   **D** No error

3 **A** Spelling error   **C** Punctuation error
   B Capitalization error   **D** No error

For question 1: Use a comma after an introductory adverb clause (*fun,*). **C** is correct.

For question 2: *United States Pony Club* is a compound proper noun. **B** is correct.

For question 3: *There* is a homophone for *their*. **A** is correct.

Apply the Strategies

Read the passage and decide which type of error, if any, appears.

(1) While Rick set the table, Carol strung the streamers over the dining room table (2) Suddenly, they herd a click at the door. The children quickly assembled in the dining room. (3) their parents walked in. "Happy Anniversary!" the children shouted.

1 **A** Spelling error   **C** Punctuation error
   B Capitalization error   **D** No error

2 **A** Spelling error   **C** Punctuation error
   B Capitalization error   **D** No error

3 **A** Spelling error   **C** Punctuation error
   B Capitalization error   **D** No error

Test Preparation Workshop 11

Research Skills | Using Information Resources

Strategies for Success

Some tests require you to review a packet of information resources, and to respond to questions about how you would use these resources to gather information and plan a report on a given subject. Use these strategies:

Review the Packet of Information Skim through the packet to see what types of material are included, such as articles from encyclopedias and computer information.

Scan the Questions Look through the questions to see which types of information are required to answer the questions. Focus on each question separately. The questions are not necessarily related to each other. Locate the best example or piece of information in the packet to answer each question.

Use Correct Sentence Form Write responses to the short-answer questions in complete sentences and include key words. Look at these examples:.

Directions: Suppose that you are writing a report on the life and times of Thomas Alva Edison (1847–1931). Edison is one of the world's most important inventors.
This packet includes several information resources about Thomas Alva Edison:

- an excerpt from an encyclopedia article, "Inventions of the Nineteenth Century"
- a biographical dictionary entry
- *Thomas Alva Edison*, a biography of the inventor: a short excerpt, table of contents, and a list of key dates in Edison's life and career
- Computer screen: on-line index of library books about Thomas Edison

Excerpt from Encyclopedia Article: "Inventions of the Nineteenth Century"

A flood of inventions swept the United States in the late 1800's. By the 1890's Americans were patenting 21,000 new inventions a year. These inventions helped industry to grow and become more efficient. New devices also made daily life easier in many American homes.

Advanced Communication Some remarkable new devices filled the need for faster communication. The telegraph speeded communication within the United States. It still took weeks, however, for news from Europe to arrive by boat. In 1866, Cyrus Field ran an underwater telegraph cable across the Atlantic Ocean, bringing the United States and Europe closer together.

Thomas Edison In an age of invention, Thomas Edison was right at home. In 1876, he opened a research laboratory in Menlo Park, New Jersey. There, Edison boasted that he and his 15 co-workers set out to create "minor" inventions every 10 days and "a big thing every 6 months or so."

Biographical Dictionary

Edison, Thomas Alva A poor student, Thomas Edison grew up to invent the light bulb, the phonograph, and dozens of other devices. Edison once went without sleep for three days working on his phonograph. At last, he heard his own voice reciting "Mary Had a Little Lamb." Edison said, "Genius is one percent inspiration and ninety-nine percent perspiration."

Table of Contents from *Thomas Alva Edison*

Test Preparation Workshop 11

Research Skills | Using Information Resources (cont.)

Short Excerpt from *Thomas Alva Edison*

The key to Edison's success was his approach. He turned inventing into a system. Teams of experts refined Edison's ideas and turned them into practical inventions. Menlo Park became an "invention factory." The results were amazing. Edison became knows as the "Wizard of Menlo Park" for inventing the light bulb, the phonograph, and hundreds of other devices.

Lists of Key Dates
from *Thomas Alva Edison*

1847: Born in Milan, Ohio

1852: Moved to Port Huron, Michigan

1869: Was paid $40,000 for improvements to the stock ticker. Opened his first workshop in Newark, New Jersey

1874: Improved the typewriter

1877: Invented the phonograph

1879: Perfected the electric light

1887: Moved to West Orange, New Jersey. Worked on such inventions as the motion picture, a storage battery, a cement mixer, the Dictaphone, and a duplicating machine.

1931: Died at 84 in West Orange, New Jersey

Computer Screen

Library Online Catalog

Subject Search: Thomas Alva Edison

Line	Titles	Subjects
1	2	Edison, Thomas: Early Life
2	4	Edison, Thomas: Bibliography
3	1	Edison, Thomas: Biography

Sample Questions and Explanations

1 Which information given in the encyclopedia article would be LEAST useful for your report?
 A the number of patents in the 1890's
 B the date Edison opened his laboratory
 C Cyrus Field's contributions to communication
 D the description of Edison's workshop

The correct answer is **C.** Cyrus Field's contributions are not important to a report on Edison.

2 In which chapter of *Thomas Alva Edison* would you find information about Edison's schooling? ("Early Years" would provide the information.)

3 Which of these sources would you use to find books written about Thomas Alva Edison?
 A the encyclopedia article
 B the biographical dictionary article
 C computer screen
 D the biography *Thomas Alva Edison*

The correct answer is **C.** The other sources do not reference other books about Edison.

Apply the Strategies

4 Suppose you are going to write an outline of your report on the life of Thomas Alva Edison. What three main topics would you include?

5 State the main idea of your report.

6 In which source would you find detailed information about Edison's marriage?
 A the encyclopedia article
 B the biographical dictionary entry
 C the main body of the biography
 D the list of key dates from the biography

Test Preparation Workshop 12

Writing Skills — Proofreading

Strategies for Success

The writing sections of some standardized tests assess your ability to edit, proofread, and use other writing processes. You are required to look for mistakes in passages and then to choose the best way to correct them.

Check for Incorrect Verb Tense and Errors in Subject-Verb Agreement Check to see that the correct verb tense is used and make the verb agree in number with its subject. If the parts of the subject name more than one thing, use a plural verb. If the parts of the subject refer to the same thing, use a singular verb.

Correct Run-on Sentences Use an end mark and a capital letter to separate main clauses. Use a semicolon between clauses.

Correct Sentence Fragments Add a subject or verb to make a sentence fragment a complete sentence.

Use Supporting Details Effectively Avoid the use of details that interrupt the flow of the passage, and that do not support the main idea.

Sample Passage and Questions:

Directions: A student wrote a paper about Alaska. There are mistakes that need correcting.

(1) Susan Butcher win the Iditarod dog-sled race several times. (2) A large strip of mountains cross Alaska. (3) Despite its challenges, the race attracts more and more racers every year. (4) In the years ahead, racers may come from such far-off countries as Sweden Norway and Denmark.

1 Select the best way to write sentence 1.
  A Susan Butcher won the Iditarod dog-sled race several times.
  B Susan Butcher will win the Iditarod dog-sled race several times.

  C Susan Butcher would have won the Iditarod dog-sled race several times.
  D Best as it is

The correct answer is **A.** *Won* is the past tense of the irregular verb *win*.

2 Select the best way to write sentence 2.
  A A large strip of mountains crosses Alaska.
  B A large strip of mountains do cross Alaska.
  C A mountainous strip crosses Alaska.
  D Best as it is.

The correct answer is **A.** A large strip of mountains crosses Alaska. The subject is singular and requires a singular verb.

Apply the Strategies

(1) Secretary of State Seward bought Alaska from Russia the deal was mocked as "Seward's Folly." (2) Seward's $7.2 million purchase proved to be a bargain; gold deposits were discovered there three decades later. (3) My uncle told me about a trip he took to Alaska when he was only 12 years old. (4) Prospectors first struck gold in 1889.

1 Which is the best way to write the underlined section in sentence one?
  A Secretary of State Seward bought Alaska from Russia. The deal was mocked as "Seward's Folly."
  B Secretary of State Seward bought Alaska from Russia, and the deal was mocked.
  C Secretary of State Seward bought Alaska. The deal was "Seward's Folly."
  D Best as it is

2 Which is the correct way to fix the flow of the passage?
  A Delete sentence 3
  B Move sentence 4 to the beginning.
  C Switch sentences 1 and 2
  D Move sentence 1 to the end.

Test Preparation Workshop 13

Writing Skills — Responding to Writing Prompts

Strategies for Success

The writing sections of many standardized tests require you to write an essay based on a writing prompt. Your essay usually is evaluated as a whole, on a 1–6 point scale from *outstanding* to *deficient,* and assessed for focus, content, organization, grammar, usage, and mechanics. Use the following strategies to help you with a writing assessment:

Read the writing prompt The writing prompt consists of two parts. The first part explains the topic you are asked to write about, or the writing situation. The second part provides specific instructions on how to respond to the prompt.

Look for Key Words As you examine the writing prompt, look for key words such as *define, explain, classify,* and *contrast.* These words indicate the purpose of your essay. It is essential that you keep these key words in mind as you develop your essay.

Budget Your Time When writing for a test, you need to be aware of how much time you have. Allow one quarter of your time for gathering ideas, half your time for writing your first draft, and one quarter of your time for revising.

Collect Your Ideas Before you begin writing, jot down key ideas and details that you plan to include. Then, review your ideas and decide on the best organization.

Draft Carefully Because you'll have less time to revise than you might in other writing situations, take care in the words and sentences you use as you draft your essay. Begin with an introduction that presents your main point. Follow with body paragraphs, each focusing on a single subtopic. Then, end with a conclusion restating your point.

Use Transitions As you draft, use transitional words to indicate the connections between ideas. The following words show comparison-and-contrast relationships: *however; nevertheless; yet; likewise; in like manner; on the contrary; similarly; instead;* and *nonetheless.*

Proofread Make sure your descriptions are clear. Check that there are no errors in spelling, grammar, usage, or mechanics.

Key Strategies:

- Focus on the topic and do not include unnecessary information.
- Present the material in an organized manner.
- Provide supporting ideas.
- Write with sentence variety.
- Proofread your work.

Apply the Strategies

Practice the preceding strategies by writing an essay in response to the following prompt.

Sample Writing Prompt

Everyone looks forward to weekends and a break from the weekday routine. Think about one thing that you like to do on weekends and why. It could be a community activity, an opportunity to be by yourself to play video games or watch television, or it could be sharing time with family members and friends.

Now explain in an essay why this event or activity is important to you. Support your ideas with examples and details.

Test Practice Bank

Reading Comprehension

Using Context Clues

Read the passage, and then answer the questions that follow. Mark the letter of your answer on a bubble sheet if your teacher provides one; otherwise, number from 1 to 6 on a separate sheet of paper, and write the letter of the correct answer next to each number.

> Garrison Keillor reaches out to more than 2 million public radio listeners who tune in every week to hear his variety show, *A Prairie Home Companion*. Through songs, comedy sketches, and stories, Keillor nudges listeners into thinking about the really important things in life—along with the really funny ones. The highlight of the show is "The News From Lake Wobegon," Keillor's monologue about doings in an imaginary midwestern town. As you sit by the radio with your eyes closed, listening to Keillor spin his tales, it's not hard to believe Lake Wobegon is real.

1 The *word* tune in this passage means—
   A melody
   B air
   C listen
   D prepare

2 In this passage, the word *sketches* means—
   F cartoons
   G designs
   H funny drawings
   J short plays

3 The word *nudges* in this passage means—
   A prods
   B shouts
   C shows
   D hurries

4 In this passage, the word *highlight* means—
   F longest part
   G musical part
   H most suspenseful part
   J part of special interest

5 In this passage, the word *monologue* means—
   A instructions for someone
   B make-believe place
   C play with different characters
   D speech by one person

6 The word *spin* in this passage means
   F ride
   G sew
   H copy
   J tell

Reading Comprehension

Identifying Related Details

Read each passage, and then answer the questions that follow. Mark the letter of your answer on a bubble sheet if your teacher provides one; otherwise, number from 1 to 6 on a separate sheet of paper, and write the letter of the correct answer next to each number.

Spending time with a pet can improve your health. Research shows that the relaxation gained from petting a cat or dog or watching fish swim can actually lower blood pressure. Walking a dog each day is good for you, too, because the fresh air and exercise help you relax. A pet can help you emotionally as well; a pet's companionship can keep a person from becoming lonely or depressed. Though pets require a lot of care and can sometimes be costly, most pet owners will tell you the benefits outweigh the costs.

1 Pets can improve your health by—
A keeping you company
B helping you sleep
C protecting your home
D teaching you responsibility

2 How are watching a fish swim and walking a dog ALIKE?
F They help a person relax.
G They're nice to people.
H They help you get fresh air.
J They help people exercise.

3 According to the passage, which is a disadvantage of owning a pet?
A time required   **C** watching it
B the costs   **D** exercising it

Most people don't remember learning to walk, but if you want an idea of what it was like, try skiing. You try to stand, but you can't. You feel that you have no control over your body because you keep falling. Most people don't hurt themselves when they learn to walk. But when you ski, you fall again and again until your entire body aches. You have to learn to fall the right way, too, or you can hurt yourself. Many people are seriously injured skiing, especially when they are learning to ski. But learning to ski is worth the trouble. Gliding down a mountain is a terrific thrill and worth all the bumps and bruises!

4 Which of these details does NOT support the idea that skiing for the first time is difficult?
A falling over and over again
B having no control
C twisting a limb
D gliding down a mountain

5 Which of these statements is a FACT in the passage?
F Skiing is difficult.
G Many people injure themselves when learning to ski.
H Skiing is fun.
J You feel as though you have no control when walking.

6 How is learning to ski MOST similar to learning to walk?
A You have to learn how to fall.
B You can injure yourself.
C They are both thrilling.
D They both involve falling often.

Reading Comprehension

Identifying the Main Idea

Read each passage, and then answer the questions that follows. Mark the letter of your answer on a bubble sheet if your teacher provides one; otherwise number from 1 to 4 on a separate sheet of paper, and write the letter of the correct answer next to each number.

Saguaro National Park in Arizona is home to many giant and beautiful saguaro cacti. The park was set aside to protect the cacti from human destruction, which began to be a problem as more people moved to the area.

1 What is the main idea of this passage?
  A Saguaro National Park is home to saguaro cacti.
  B Saguaro cacti are giant plants.
  C People threaten saguaro cacti.
  D Saguaro National Park is in Arizona.

While many people know Abraham Lincoln as the sixteenth president of the United States, they know little about the person. At six feet four inches tall, Lincoln was the tallest President. He often carried letters under his stovepipe hat. Despite his serious appearance, Lincoln loved listening to and telling stories and jokes.

2 What is the main idea of this passage?
  F President Lincoln loved jokes.
  G People know little about Lincoln.
  H Lincoln was the sixteenth president.
  J Lincoln looked serious.

Diana Chang is a native New Yorker, though she spent part of her childhood in China. Her mother is Eurasian, and her father is Asian. Chang's poetry, novels, and artwork often draw on her Asian and American background.

3 What is the main idea of this passage?
  A Diana Chang is a New Yorker.
  B Chang spent time in China.
  C Diana Chang's mother is Eurasian.
  D Chang's writing reflects her Asian and American background.

When he was barely out of his teens, American writer Jack London was captain of a pirate ship. He traveled throughout the United States and prospected for gold in northwestern Canada. Once, he made a boat from trees and used the boat to run the dangerous White Horse Rapids.

4 What is the main idea in this passage?
  F Jack London led an adventurous life.
  G Jack London liked to travel.
  H Riding the White Horse Rapids was a thrill for Jack London.
  J Prospecting for gold was fun.

Reading Comprehension

Identifying Cause-and Effect-Relationships

Read the passage, and then answer the questions that follow. Mark the letter of your answer on a bubble sheet if your teacher provides one; otherwise, number from 1 to 6 on a separate sheet of paper, and write the letter of the correct answer next to each number.

Sonny sat on his front porch and sighed. His best friend Rick wasn't at home, and his mother was busy cooking supper. A cool breeze made him shiver. He zipped up his jacket. He put his chin in his hands and watched the wind blow leaves on the sidewalk. A big clump of leaves blew down the steps of an abandoned house across the street. Sonny noticed, however, that the clump didn't sail into the air like the other leaves. He walked across the street to investigate. As he approached, he heard a soft cry. Sonny realized that what he had thought was a clump of leaves was actually a small gray and brown kitten. The kitten meowed, and Sonny noticed that it was wet and shivering. When the kitten tried to walk toward Sonny, it fell over onto its side. Sonny noticed that something was wrong with its leg. He took off his jacket and gently wrapped it around the kitten. He picked the kitten up and headed home.

1 Sonny is watching the leaves blow on the sidewalk because—
A he has nothing else to do
B his mother is cooking supper
C he is looking for his kitten
D he is collecting leaves

2 Why does Sonny cross the street?
F He is looking for Rick.
G He sees something odd.
H He has lost his kitten.
J He is going to the library.

3 What is one reason Sonny wraps the kitten in his jacket?
A The kitten is purring loudly.
B The kitten is trying to get away.
C The kitten is cold and hurt.
D The kitten is unconscious.

4 The kitten can't walk because—
F it is injured
G it is too young to walk
H Sonny has wrapped it in his jacket
J the porch steps are icy

5 Why did Sonny zip his jacket?
A The wind blew leaves onto the sidewalk.
B A cool breeze made him shiver.
C The kitten was shivering.
D His mother told him to zip it.

6 The clump of leaves Sonny sees does not sail into the air because—
F it is really a kitten
G it is too wet
H it is actually Sonny's jacket
J it is a big clump

Reading Comprehension

Drawing Inferences and Conclusions

Read the passage, and then answer the questions that follow. Mark the letter of your answer on a bubble sheet if your teacher provides one; otherwise, number from 1 to 6 on a separate sheet of paper, and write the letter of the correct answer next to each number.

Melanie stuffed the little box into her backpack and ran into the house. "Hi, Mom!" she shouted as she bolted up the stairs to her room. Quickly, she shut the door and took the little box out of her backpack. She opened it and smiled at the ring inside. Just the other day, she had seen her mother admiring the ring in a store window. Buying the ring had taken all the allowance money Melanie had saved and money she had borrowed from her father, but she had done it. Her father had assured her that her mother would love the present. Melanie planned to give the ring to her mother for her birthday the next day. Melanie turned when she heard a knock on her bedroom door.

"Are you okay, honey?" her mother asked.

"I'm fine, Mom. I'll be right there," Melanie replied as she stuffed the ring box under her pillow.

1 Which word best describes Melanie?
   A excited
   B sloppy
   C forgetful
   D content

2 This passage gives you reason to believe that Melanie is—
   F unable to keep a secret
   G throwing her mother a party
   H generous
   J shy

3 From this passage, you can conclude that Melanie—
   A thinks her mother will like the ring
   B wants her father to give her mother the ring
   C thinks her mother will scold her
   D wants to keep the ring for herself

4 This passage suggests that Melanie—
   F wants the ring to be a surprise
   G is afraid she has bought the wrong ring
   H is going to put the ring in another box
   J will hide the ring from her father

5 Which word best describes Melanie's mother?
   A thrilled
   B tidy
   C concerned
   D annoyed

6 From this passage you can conclude that—
   F Melanie's mother knows about the ring
   G Melanie's father knows about the ring
   H Melanie will buy her mother another present
   J Melanie will show the ring to her friends

Reading Comprehension

Arranging Details in Sequential Order

Read the passage, and then answer the questions that follow. Mark the letter of your answer on a bubble sheet if your teacher provides one; otherwise, number from 1 to 5 on a separate sheet of paper, and write the letter of the correct answer next to each number.

Jill lay back on the cool grass at the park and watched the squirrels play in the oak trees. She had found this spot last month and had been coming here almost every day after school to sit and think. Yesterday it had rained, and so she hadn't come. She thought about all the things that had happened to make this day go wrong. First, she had misplaced her homework assignment and spent fifteen minutes searching the house in a panic. Just as she found her homework, she heard the bus outside. When she ran downstairs and out the front door, the bus was already two blocks away. She finally got a ride with her neighbors. In the lunchroom, she dropped her tray, and her lunch went all over the floor. She had really been looking forward to lunch, since she hadn't had time to eat breakfast. Suddenly, she was startled by a nut hitting her arm. A squirrel on the limb above her looked down at her, chattering. Jill thought it sounded like laughter, and she managed a small chuckle. It was the same squirrel that had stolen a piece of sandwich from another squirrel the day before! "I think I'll call you Mischief," Jill said to the squirrel.

1 What was Jill doing when the bus arrived at the stop?
   A lying on the grass in the park
   B watching squirrels play
   C finding her homework
   D eating breakfast

2 Which of these did Jill do first?
   F go to the park
   G miss the bus
   H misplace her homework
   J look around the house in a panic

3 When did Jill discover the spot she visited after school?
   A last month
   B yesterday
   C when she missed the bus
   D when she rode with her neighbor

4 What happened before Jill got a ride with neighbors?
   F She named the squirrel.
   G She missed the bus.
   H She dropped her tray.
   J She was startled by the squirrel.

5 What did Jill do last in the story?
   A think about her day
   B look forward to lunch
   C search for her homework
   D name the squirrel

Reading Comprehension

Making Generalizations

Read each passage, and then answer the question that follows it. Mark the letter of your answer on a bubble sheet if your teacher provides one; otherwise, number from 1 to 4 on a separate sheet of paper, and write the letter of the correct answer next to each number.

Writer Paul Zindel and his family spent a year in Travis, a town on Staten Island, New York. Zindel wanted to find a place where he could find some inspiration for his writing. While in Travis, Zindel met Nonno Franki Viona, who gave him a great deal of advice. In his memoir *The Pigman & Me,* Zindel describes his relationship with Viona in great detail.

1 Which of these statements is a generalization about the passage?
   A Writers are inspired by the people in their lives.
   B Living in Travis helps a writer think of things to write about.
   C A friend gives advice.
   D Zindel and his family moved to Travis.

The beautiful scenery and mild climate of Pompeii attracted many wealthy Romans to the city. They built large villas there on the shores of the Mediterranean Sea. The villas were designed to take advantage of this warm climate. They usually had large outdoor patios that were used as reception areas.

2 Which of these statements is a generalization about the passage?
   F The Romans designed their villas according to the local climate.
   G The Romans in Pompeii were all wealthy people.
   H Pompeii was located near the Mediterranean Sea.
   J The climate in Pompeii was usually mild and warm.

Lindsey's palms were sweating and her hands were trembling. As she reviewed the notes for her speech one last time, she worried her voice would crack when she tried to speak. She took a deep breath and tried to calm the butterflies in her stomach. She was next.

3 Which of these statements is a generalization about the passage?
   A Lindsey did not memorize her speech.
   B Lindsey is afraid to speak.
   C Lindsey's voice will tremble when she speaks.
   D Lindsey's palms are sweaty.

There have been many successful husband-and-wife writing teams. The husband-and-wife team of Rosemary and Stephen Vincent Benét wrote a book of poetry entitled *A Book of Americans.* Rosemary Benét was a frequent contributor to many important magazines. Stephen Vincent Benét won the Pulitzer Prize for poetry—twice!

4 Which of these statements is a generalization about the passage?
   F Stephen Vincent Benét won two Pulitzer prizes.
   G Rosemary Benét wrote for magazines.
   H A husband can be more famous than his wife.
   J Rosemary and Stephen Vincent Benét were a successful team.

Reading Comprehension

Recognizing Author's Point of View and Purpose

Read the passage, and then answer the questions that follow. Mark the letter of your answer on a bubble sheet if your teacher provides one; otherwise, number from 1 to 6 on a separate sheet of paper, and write the letter of the correct answer next to each number.

Deems was short and plump and had curly brown hair. He owned a car and a light gray suit and always wore a necktie and white shirt. A real businessman, I thought the first time I saw him. My mother was talking to him on the sidewalk in front of the Union Square Methodist Church and I was standing as tall as I could, just out of earshot.

"Now, Buddy, when we get down there keep your shoulders back and stand up real straight," she had cautioned me after making sure my necktie was all right and my shirt clean.

Watching the two of them in conversation, with Deems glancing at me now and then, I kept my shoulders drawn back in the painful military style I'd seen in movies, trying to look a foot taller than I really was.

—"Hard as Nails" by Russell Baker

---

1 The author of this passage thinks Deems is—
A nervous
B selfish
C successful
D thoughtful

2 The author's main purpose is to—
F tell a story about a businessman
G describe his appearance as a child
H describe his first meeting with Deems
J show readers how to behave

3 What is another purpose the author might have had for writing this passage?
A to remind children to listen to their elders
B to illustrate the importance of good posture
C to protest the rules children are expected to follow

D to entertain readers

4 The author includes the last paragraph of the passage to—
F show Deems's effect on him
G give more information about Deems
H summarize the previous information
J indicate his wish to become a soldier

5 The author thinks the way Deems dresses is—
A careless
B impressive
C odd
D old-fashioned

6 What type of person does the author believe Deems to be?
F a role model
G a true friend
H a greedy thief
J a strict teacher

Reading Comprehension

Distinguishing Fact and Opinion

Read each passage, and then answer the questions that follow. Mark the letter of your answer on a bubble sheet if your teacher provides one; otherwise, number from 1 to 4 on a separate sheet of paper, and write the letter of the correct answer next to each number.

> Robinson signed with the Dodgers and went to play in the minors in 1946. Rickey was right—fans insulted him, and so did players. But he performed brilliantly and avoided fights. Then, in 1947, he came to the majors.
>
> Many Dodgers were angry. Some signed a petition demanding to be traded. But Robinson and Rickey were determined to make their experiment work. . . .
>
> Robinson's first season was difficult. Fans threatened to kill him; players tried to hurt him. . . .
>
> —"Jackie Robinson: Justice at Last" by Geoffrey C. Ward and Ken Burns

1 Which of these statements is a FACT in the passage?
  A Robinson was determined to succeed.
  B Robinson faced the anger of other players.
  C Robinson signed with the Dodgers in 1946.
  D Robinson performed brilliantly.

2 Which of these is an OPINION expressed in the passage?
  F Robinson's first season in the major leagues was difficult.
  G In 1947, Robinson came to the Dodgers' Major League team.
  H Players attempted to hurt Robinson.
  J Some Dodgers signed a petition.

> When Isaac Asimov was a boy, his father did not allow him to read the science-fiction magazines in the family-owned store. Mr. Asimov thought science fiction was "trash." Finally, Isaac convinced his father that the stories were worthwhile because they were related to science. Isaac then read all the "sci-fi" he could get his hands on. As Isaac read, he formed ideas about what the future might hold.
>
> Isaac began writing his first science-fiction story when he was seventeen. He planned to mail the story to the magazine *Astounding Science Fiction*. He was shocked at his father's suggestion that he submit it in person. Isaac took his father's suggestion.

3 Which of these is an OPINION expressed in the passage?
  A Isaac may have foreseen the future as he read.
  B Isaac's father did not allow him to read science fiction.
  C Isaac delivered his first story.
  D Isaac took his father's suggestion.

4 Which of these is a FACT in the passage?
  F Mr. Asimov shocked his son.
  G Science stories are worthwhile.
  H Mr. Asimov did not read sci-fi.
  J Isaac began writing at seventeen.

Reading Comprehension

Describing Plot, Setting, Character, and Mood

Read the passage, and then answer the questions that follow. Mark the letter of your answer on a bubble sheet if your teacher provides one; otherwise, number from 1 to 6 on a separate sheet of paper, and write the letter of the correct answer next to each number.

On this summer day [Sandy] was lying peacefully reading a comic and not keeping an eye on the twins, who didn't need it because they were occupied in seeing which of them could wrap the most seaweed around the other one's legs. . . .

Sandy rolled onto her back to make sure that the twins were not climbing on slippery rocks or getting cut off by the tide. At the same moment a large body struck her forcibly in the midriff and she was covered by flying sand. Instinctively she shut her eyes and felt the sand being wiped off her face by something that seemed like a warm, rough, damp flannel. She opened her eyes and looked. It was a tongue. Its owner was a large and bouncy young Alsatian, or German shepherd, with topaz eyes, black-tipped prick ears, a thick, soft coat, and a bushy black-tipped tail.

"*Lob!*" shouted a man farther up the beach. "Lob, come here!"

But Lob, as if trying to atone for the surprise he had given her, went on licking the sand off Sandy's face, wagging his tail so hard while he kept on knocking up more clouds of sand. His owner, a gray-haired man with a limp, walked over as quickly as he could and seized him by the collar.

"I hope he didn't give you a fright?" the man said to Sandy. "He meant it in play—he's only young."

"Oh, no, I think he's *beautiful*," said Sandy truly. . . .

—"Lob's Girl" by Joan Aiken

1 Before Lob arrived, Sandy had been—
  A reading a book
  B talking to the twins
  C playing with a puppy
  D talking to her father

2 This story takes place—
  F on a boat **H** on a beach
  G in the woods **J** in a house

3 Lob can be described as—
  A mean **C** intelligent
  B cautious **D** playful

4 At the beginning of the passage, the mood is—
  F mysterious **H** romantic
  G calm **J** tense

5 The gray-haired man is worried about Sandy because—
  A his dog jumped on her
  B she tripped and fell
  C the wind blew sand in her eyes
  D she was cut off by the tide

6 When Lob jumps on her, Sandy—
  F is angry **H** is confused
  G gets hurt **J** knows it's a dog

Combined Reading and Literary Skills

Read the passage, and then answer the questions that follow. Mark your answers to questions 1–9 on a bubble sheet if your teacher provides one; otherwise, number from 1 to 9 on a separate sheet of paper, and write the letter of the correct answer next to each number. Answer number 10 on a separate sheet of paper.

We shy persons need to write a letter now and then, or else we'll dry up and blow away. It's true. And I speak as one who loves to reach for the phone, dial the number, and talk. I say, "Big Bopper here—what's shakin', babes?" The telephone is to shyness what Hawaii is to February, it's a way out of the woods, *and yet:* a letter is better.

Such a sweet gift—a piece of handmade writing, in an envelope that is not a bill, sitting in our friend's path when she trudges home from a long day spent among wahoos and savages, a day our words will help repair. They don't need to be immortal, just sincere. She can read them twice and again tomorrow: *You're someone I care about, Corinne, and think of often and every time I do you make me smile.*

We need to write, otherwise nobody will know who we are. They will have only a vague impression of us as A Nice Person, because, frankly, we don't shine at conversation, we lack the confidence to thrust our faces forward and say, "Hi, I'm Heather Hooten; let me tell you about my week." Mostly we say "Uh-huh" and "Oh, really." People smile and look over our shoulder, looking for someone else to meet.

So a shy person sits down and writes a letter. To be known by another person— to meet and talk freely on the page—to be close despite distance. To escape from anonymity and be our own sweet selves and express the music of our souls.

Same thing that moves a giant rock star to sing his heart out in front of 123,000 people moves us to take ballpoint in hand and write a few lines to our dear Aunt Eleanor. *We want to be known.* We want her to know that we have fallen in love, that we quit our job, that we're moving to New York, and we want to say a few things that might not get said in casual conversation: *Thank you for what you've meant to me, I am very happy right now.*

—"How to Write a Letter" by Garrison Keillor

1 The word *immortal* in this passage means—
A brief
B dreary
C timeless
D vague

2 In this passage, the word *anonymity* means—
F being selfish
G being unknown
H feeling comfortable
J knowing too much

3 What does the author mean when he says "the telephone is to shyness what Hawaii is to February"?

A Shy people find relief by going to Hawaii in February.

B Shy people who go to Hawaii in February can use the telephone easily.

C Being in Hawaii in February helps shy people.

D Using the telephone is a relief for shy people just as Hawaii is a relief in February.

4 You can conclude from the passage that the narrator—

F gives up easily

G has few friends

H is sometimes shy

J is often unhappy

5 The author's main purpose is to—

A describe the types of letters he has written

B teach readers simple rules for writing letters

C explain why shy people like to write letters

D contrast letters with telephone conversations

6 What is the main idea of the second paragraph?

F Letters should be handwritten.

G Envelopes rarely contain letters.

H A letter can be read many times.

J Receiving a letter is a nice surprise.

7 What is the main idea of the last paragraph?

A Writing a letter is like performing in a rock concert.

B People write letters because they want to be known.

C Having a casual conversation is similar to writing a letter.

D People should write letters to those who have helped them.

8 The word *giant* in this passage means—

F imaginary   **H** strong

G popular   **J** tall

9 The author believes shy people say little about themselves because—

A they have no stories to tell

B they do not have confidence

C they are often misunderstood

D they do not know many people

10 Why does Garrison Keillor believe that shy people can benefit from writing letters? Support your answer with evidence from the text.

Writing Skills

Sentence Construction

Read the passage, and then answer the questions that follow. Mark the letter of your answer on a bubble sheet if your teacher provides one; otherwise, number from 1 to 4 on a separate sheet of paper, and write the letter of the correct answer next to each number.

Saturday morning cartoons are quite difficult to make. (1) Cartoons are a form of animation. Animation is a process in which a series of drawings is recorded and played back. (2) The earliest cartoons were drawn and colored by hand, then each scene in the cartoon, called a frame, was filmed. (3) When the film was played. The characters looked as if they were moving. (4) Although computers can now be used for each stage in animation, many cartoonists still prefer to draw each frame by hand. Next, a soundtrack is recorded for the cartoon. The soundtrack consists of dialogue and music. Then, the cartoon undergoes editing, during which final changes are made.

---

1 What is the BEST way to write section 1?

A Cartoons are a form of animation. A series of drawings is recorded.

B Cartoons are a form of animation, a process in which a series of drawings is recorded and played back.

C Cartoons are a form of animation, a series of drawings is recorded and played back.

D Correct as is

2 What is the BEST way to write section 2?

F The first cartoons were drawn and colored by hand. Then each scene in the cartoon, called a frame, was filmed.

G The first cartoons were drawn and colored by hand, each scene called a frame, was filmed.

H Cartoons were drawn and colored by hand, each scene was filmed.

J Correct as is

3 What is the BEST way to write section 3?

A The film was played; and the characters looked as if they were moving.

B When the film was played, characters looked as if they were moving.

C The film was played when the characters were moving.

D Correct as is

4 What is the BEST way to write section 4?

F Although computers can now be used for each stage in animation.

G Computers can now be used for each stage in animation, and many cartoonists still prefer to draw each frame by hand.

H Because computers can be used for animation, many cartoonists still draw by hand.

J Correct as is

Writing Skills

Identifying Appropriate Usage

Read the passage, and choose the word or group of words that belongs in each space. Mark the letter of your answer on a bubble sheet if your teacher provides one; otherwise, number from 1 to 8 on a separate sheet of paper, and write the letter of the correct answer next to each number.

When my brother and (1) asked our parents for a pet, we were hoping

for a dog, so we (2) disappointed when our father bought us a hamster.

We weren't sad for long, however. Sammy, our hamster, is very cute. He spends

much of his time digging in (3) cage. Sammy probably does this because

hamsters (4) burrows in the wild. Sammy is the (5) hamster I have ever

seen. He loves to come out of his cage and be (6) . Sometimes he crawls

onto my shoulder and (7) my ear. No dog can (8) that!

---

1   **A** him
     B I
     C me
     D we

2   **F** are
     G had been
     H was
     J were

3   **A** her
     B his
     C its
     D their

4   **F** dig
     G digged
     H digging
     J digs

5   **A** lovable
     B lovablest
     C more lovable
     D most lovable

6   **F** held
     G hold
     H holded
     J holding

7   **A** nuzzle
     B nuzzled
     C nuzzles
     D nuzzling

8   **F** did
     G do
     H does
     J done

Writing

Spelling, Capitalization, and Punctuation

Read the passage, and decide which type of error, if any, appears in each underlined section. Mark the letter of your answer on a bubble sheet if your teacher provides one; otherwise, number from 1 to 6 on a separate sheet of paper and write the letter of the answer next to each number.

Stained glass consists of windows or sheets of glass made up of small dyed

or painted panels held together, by strips of lead. Most stained-glass windows
<u>(1)</u>

contain colored pictures that glimmer when sunlight shines through them. No
<u>(2)</u>

one knows for certain who made the first stained-glass window, although it is

believed the technique was first used to make jewelery. Stained glass was used
<u>(3)</u>

in church windows in France, and Germany as early as the tenth century;
<u>(4)</u>   <u>(5)</u>

Some English homes also had stained-glass windows. They were also common
<u>(6)</u>

in Roman cathedrals built during the twelfth century.

---

1 **A** Spelling error
       B Capitalization error
       C Punctuation error
       D No error

2 **F** Spelling error
       G Capitalization error
       H Punctuation error
       J No error

3 **A** Spelling error
       B Capitalization error
       C Punctuation error
       D No error

4 **F** Spelling error
       G Capitalization error
       H Punctuation error
       J No error

5 **A** Spelling error
       B Capitalization error
       C Punctuation error
       D No error

6 **F** Spelling error
       G Capitalization error
       H Punctuation error
       J No error

Writing Tasks

The following activity is designed to assess your writing ability. The prompts will ask you to explain something. You may think of your audience as being any reader other than yourself.

In "How to Write a Letter," Garrison Keillor says that the telephone is a way for shy people to communicate, but a letter is better.

Do you agree or disagree? Write a response that expresses your views on Keillor's statement. Explain your reasons for agreeing or disagreeing. You may use examples from real life, books you have read, movies, or television shows.

"We want to be known." That is what Garrison Keillor believes is the reason that people write letters.

Write an essay to explain how writing letters is a way for people to make themselves known. You may use examples from real life, books you have read, movies, or television shows.

Writing a letter, calling a person on the telephone, and sending electronic mail by computer are ways to communicate.

Write an essay comparing and contrasting these forms of communication. You may use examples from real life, books you have read, movies, or television shows.

Index of Authors and Titles

INDEX OF SKILLS

Complete predicates, 377
Complete sentences, 394, 395, 416
Complete subjects, 377
Compound nouns, 20, 21, 56
Compound sentences, 532, 533, 538, 779, 780
Compound subject, 514
Compound verb, 514
Concrete nouns, 30, 31, 56
Conjunctions, 340, 341, 362
  joining sentences, 356, 357
Contractions, 748, 766
Coordinating conjunctions, 340, 341, 362
Declarative sentence, 404, 405, 416
Definite article, 218, 219
Direct objects, 426, 427, 434, 435, 452, 562, 580
Double negatives, 740, 741, 766
Exclamatory sentence, 404, 416
Helping verbs, 124, 142
Imperative sentence, 404, 405, 416
Indefinite article, 218, 219
Independent clauses, 467, 478, 479, 502
Indirect objects, 426, 427, 452, 562, 580
Interjections, 332, 333, 362
Interrogative pronouns, 76, 77, 98
Interrogative sentence, 404, 416
Irregular comparisons, 720, 721
Linking verbs, 132, 133, 142
Nouns, 11, 12
  abstract, 30, 31, 56
  common, 44, 56
  compound, 20, 21, 56
  concrete, 30, 31, 56
  predicate, 446, 452
  proper, 44, 45, 56
Object pronouns, 562, 563, 574, 575, 580
Objects of prepositions, 574, 580
Personal pronouns, 92, 93, 98, 580
Plural verbs, 643
Positive comparisons, 707, 720, 734
Possessive adjectives, 210, 211, 234
Possessives, 748, 766
Predicate adjectives, 446, 447, 452
Predicate nouns, 446, 447, 452
Predicates, 377, 378, 386, 416
Prepositional phrases, 304, 305, 324
Prepositions, 287, 288, 324
Pronouns, 68, 98, 580
  antecedent agreement with, 688, 689, 696
  interrogative, 76, 77, 98
  object pronouns, 562, 574, 580
  personal, 92, 93, 98, 580
  subject, 551, 552, 580
Proper nouns, 44, 45, 56
Quotation marks, 610, 611, 620
Sentences, 356, 394, 404, 416, 514, 532, 538, 779
Sentence variety, 830, 831, 842
Simple predicates, 386, 387, 416
Simple sentences, 514, 515, 538
Simple subjects, 386, 387, 416
Singular verbs, 643
Subject complements, 446, 447, 551, 552, 580
Subject pronouns, 551, 580
Subjects, 377, 378, 386, 416, 446, 514, 643, 662, 672
Subject and verb agreement, 643, 662, 672
Subordinate clauses, 467, 492, 493, 502
Superlatives, 707, 720, 721, 728, 729, 734
Usage, 748, 766
Verb phrase, 124, 125, 142
Verbs, 111, 112, 180, 514
  action, 132, 133, 142

helping, 124, 142
linking, 132, 133, 142
plural, 643
principle parts of, 152, 153, 180
singular, 643
special subjects, agreement with, 662, 663, 672
subjects, agreement with, 643, 672
Verb tenses, 160, 161, 174, 175, 180

VOCABULARY

Adjectives, 404, 698
Animal idioms, 768
Antonyms, 696
Color words, 306, 312
Comparison word ending,
  -er, 754, 760
  -est, 754, 760
Compound adjectives, 396, 404
Compound nouns, 78, 92
Compound transition words, 334, 340
Fantasy vocabulary, 454
Geography vocabulary, 540
Homophones, 24, 30, 582, 592, 722, 728
Mathematics (measurement) words, 622
Multiple meanings, 710, 720
Musical words, 742, 748
Myths, words from, 844
Names, origins of, 100
Old-fashioned words, 428, 434
Portmanteau words (blends), 364
Prefixes:
  de-, 154, 160
  dis-, 32, 44
  ex-, 144, 152
  fore-, 480, 492
  in-, 388, 394, 504, 514
  ir-, 545, 551
  mono-, 236, 246
  non-, 380, 386
  pre-, 628, 643
  re-, 342, 356
  trans-, 248, 258
  un-, 70, 76
Regional synonyms, 470, 478
Related words:
  forms of console, 114, 124
  forms of decide, 290, 304
  forms of dignity, 782, 794
  forms of document, 554, 562
  forms of execute, 418, 426
  forms of grief, 326, 332
  forms of migrate, 516, 532
  forms of oppose, 212, 218
  forms of orate, 436, 446
  forms of orientation, 369, 377
  forms of regulate, 162, 174
  forms of scrutiny, 703, 707
  forms of tolerate, 594, 610
  forms of tyrant, 459, 467
  forms of vary, 198, 210
Romance language words, 182
Science-fiction vocabulary, 454
Suffixes:
  -ful, 773, 779
  -less, 126, 132
  -ly, 14, 20, 736, 740
  -or, 58, 68
  -ory, 105, 111
  -ous, 260, 268, 796, 810
  -tion, 187, 195
Synonyms and their connotations, 276
Transition words, 334, 340
Word roots:
  -chron-, 281, 287

-meter-, 3, 11, 622
-mort-, 818, 836
-scrib-, 674, 688
-sequi-, 564, 574
-son-, 644, 662

CRITICAL THINKING AND VIEWING

Analyze, 19, 43, 60, 67, 75, 122, 136, 151, 167, 170, 209, 216, 222, 253, 255, 257, 283, 295, 299, 303, 315, 318, 330, 339, 351, 352, 354, 371, 376, 383, 399, 403, 422, 425, 445, 473, 477, 509, 510, 513, 521, 524, 525, 531, 549, 550, 567, 601, 667, 677, 706, 715, 719, 727, 738, 739, 752, 759, 799, 801, 803, 827, 828, 836
Analyze cause and effect, 19, 50, 159, 253, 550
Apply, 73, 85, 121, 131, 173, 209, 228, 257, 303, 351, 385, 391, 403, 425, 589, 608, 614, 642, 661, 666, 778
Assess, 110, 217, 267, 303, 385, 431, 441, 445, 466, 477, 487, 497, 509, 550, 589, 605, 642, 685, 717, 739, 747, 786, 788, 804, 825, 831
Classify, 50, 67
Compare, 157, 355
Compare and contrast, 19, 23, 27, 67, 75, 91, 128, 244, 245, 265, 267, 308, 311, 339, 349, 375, 391, 393, 403, 439, 462, 466, 484, 487, 508, 523, 573, 604, 608, 614, 661, 666, 687, 725, 727, 739, 747, 759, 787, 788, 793, 807
Connect, 23, 27, 29, 37, 63, 123, 130, 242, 263, 293, 329, 336, 351, 355, 372, 385, 391, 393, 402, 443, 477, 491, 513, 525, 687, 705, 712, 727, 746, 747, 789, 809, 835
Contrast, 148, 311, 337, 376, 425
Criticize, 91
Deduce, 10, 167, 194, 284, 445, 569, 573, 809, 820, 825
Define, 601, 715
Distinguish, 608, 827, 837
Draw conclusions, 7, 10, 29, 39, 43, 67, 73, 75, 85, 91, 110, 121, 129, 136, 170, 194, 209, 217, 227, 228, 257, 266, 285, 286, 301, 339, 344, 351, 403, 410, 433, 441, 477, 491, 497, 509, 513, 525, 531, 573, 587, 589, 591, 601, 605, 608, 661, 680, 706, 715, 717, 725, 727, 752, 759, 778, 785, 793, 823, 825, 836
Evaluate, 19, 123, 159, 170, 194, 209, 286, 318, 339, 465, 525, 550, 661, 706, 725
Generalize, 29, 64, 85, 727, 752, 793
Hypothesize, 531, 747
Identify, 597
Infer, 10, 26, 27, 41, 43, 85, 89, 121, 131, 147, 157, 159, 167, 169, 170, 171, 194, 209, 228, 245, 286, 301, 311, 318, 331, 339, 355, 385, 391, 431, 433, 466, 486, 491, 512, 513, 525, 531, 561, 587, 590, 591, 605, 608, 642, 666, 679, 718, 725, 739, 759, 788, 793, 807, 829
Interpret, 8, 19, 23, 27, 29, 34, 39, 43, 73, 110, 118, 121, 123, 129, 131, 136, 151, 157, 159, 173, 191, 194, 209, 217, 228, 253, 265, 267, 286, 301, 303, 310, 318, 331, 337, 339, 351, 376, 385, 390, 391, 407, 431, 466, 491, 497, 591, 599, 601, 614, 661, 687, 714, 717, 725, 747, 759, 778, 803, 825, 829
Make a decision, 569
Make a judgment, 39, 50, 67, 73, 75, 110, 129, 151, 217, 245, 253, 267, 331, 351, 376, 384, 441, 486, 561, 587, 599, 715, 778

oral, 621, 840
Procession music, 780
Question-and-answer session, 435
Radio announcement, 357
Radio interview, 575
Radio reading, 741
Readers Theatre, 31, 533, 575, 689
Reading, 497, 749
Reply, 333
Retelling, 447
Retelling review, 761
Rhythm exchange, 708
Riddles, 313
Role play, 12, 45, 93, 153, 211, 229, 269,
    357, 405, 427, 479, 611, 795, 867
School tour, 31
Sign language program, 125
Singing poetry, 721
Skit, 305, 411, 780
Sound effects, 663, 689
Speech, 112
    as an animal character, 125
    "I Have a Dream", excerpt from, 552
    jungle animal, 247
    by Lou Gehrig, 288
    to a team, 259
    unrehearsed, 133
Spelling bee, 593
Stage a scene, 670
Story comparison, 288
Storytelling, 305, 333, 427, 515, 811
Telephone message, 767
Television script, 593
Twenty questions, 133
Visual interpretation, 378
Wolf reunion, 515

LIFE AND WORK SKILLS

Abstract writing, 51
Architecture, 687
Animal health careers, 21, 301
Astronaut, 266, 587
Canine companions, 807
Career choice, 93, 121, 425
Civil engineering, 425
Classical music, 43, 747
Compare ideas across texts, 815
Courageous careers, 803
Documentaries, 355
Employment credentials, 319
Evaluating sources of information, 841
Farming communities, 151
Flood farming, 137
Fingerprints, 29
Food service career, 525
Friends and friendship, 171
Government jobs, 827
Ink painting, 726
Internet, 609
Interview, 69, 843
Legal career, 509
Maps, reading, 46, 67, 134, 220, 408, 494,
    612, 664, 750, 832
Math in sports, 257
Meteorology, 129
Motion pictures, 573
Movie realism, 406
Museum plaque writer, 51
National parks, 131
Newspaper reporter, 69, 93, 333
Observing people, 569
Paleontology, 393
Pet ownership, 19
Photography, 351
Police report writing, 69

Product names, 253
Proposal writing, 69
Recognizing symbols and icons, 765
Salesperson, 10
Ship-related careers, 403
Telephone message, 767
Television reporter, 85, 93
Timeline, reading, 314
Tour guide, 31
Water-related careers, 331
Web page, understanding, 671
Wilderness careers, 131
Writer, 110

PROJECTS

Advice column, 178, 269
Album, 54
Anthology, 313
Architecture, 687
Architectural model, 378
Ark model, 137
Art, 96, 615, 837
Big-cat chart, 305
Big numbers, 663
Biology diagrams, 77
Board game, 643
Bridge model, 427
Brochure, 493
Character parade, 575
Chart, 288, 305, 411, 447, 552, 563, 793
Circuit dance, 93
Class directory, 259
Climate map, 137
Collage, 96
    of poetry meaning, 219, 749
    of sneakers, 12
Comics, 468, 741
Cover art, 761
Crazy comics, 741
Diagram, 77, 211, 288, 405, 435
Dictionary, 161, 593
Diorama, 229, 247, 741
Dragon comics, 468
Dramatization, 468, 497
Drawing, 319
Erosion illustration, 427
Film review, 247
Flight investigation, 125
Flowchart, 552, 563
Geology report, 667
Helen Keller mural, 125
Hero display, 811
Historical maps, 341
Hummingbird routes, 753
Illustrated menu, 533
Illustrations of wolf language, 515
Immigration visual guide, 259
Investigation report, 341
Jamaica-fest, 479
Liberty Island information fair, 689
Liberty math, 689
Machine design, 387
Magazine submission, 54
Maps, 31, 69, 137, 229, 341, 497, 667, 753
Mathematics report, 533
Math survey, 313
Mazy May map, 69
Media update, 575
Memento timeline, 493
Mind map, 31
Model:
    of an ark, 137
    architectural, 378
    of a lyre, 721
    of a bridge, 427

Movie review, 515
Multimedia display, 387
Multimedia mummy, 51
Multimedia report, 333, 552, 708, 749
Mural, 125, 133, 269, 795, 831
Music video, 395
Myth collection, 811
Myth and tale mural, 831
Myth or tale performance, 831
Native American fair, 611
Nervous-system diagram, 288
Newspaper reporter, 93
Olympic presentation, 563
Oral presentation, 21, 211, 615, 837
Panel discussion, 272
Pantomime, 219, 721, 795
Perfect bicycle, 479
Pet fair, 175
Picture book, 611
Poetry, Inc., 729
Poetry masquerade party, 729
Poster, 357
    on cause-and-effect, 272
    of Hans Christian Andersen tales, 780
    on heritage, 31
    on self-defense, 196
Presentation, 21, 96
    on being new, 196
    on the blues, 45
    to the class, 578
    on community service, 161
    on emergency plan, 405
    multimedia, 333
    on the Olympics, 563
    oral, 211, 615, 837
    on the shtetl, 153
    on a state park, 133
    on water safety, 333
Prospecting fair, 69
Reading survey, 77
Report,
    on dogs, 21
    on greenhouse effect, 761
    on hieroglyphics, 51
Research, on Chinese dynasties, 319
Shakespeare festival, 435
Sketch, 395
Skit, 411
Stage a scene, 663
Statistical chart, 288
Statistics, of Statue of Liberty, 689
Storyboards, 153, 305
Storytelling fair, 447
Survey:
    math, 313
    of pet owners, 175
    reading, 77
Tableau of cats, 708
Technology advertisement, 112
Television commercial, 12
Timeline:
    on Abraham Lincoln's life, 357
    on history of flight, 269
    on space exploration, 593
    of Stonehenge, 378
    talent, 45
    of your life, 493
Visual aid, 112
Water-safety presentation, 333
Weaving, 780
Wind diagram, 435

STAFF CREDITS

The people who made up the *Prentice Hall Literature: Timeless Voices, Timeless Themes* team—representing design services, editorial, editorial services, managing editor, manufacturing and inventory planning, market research, marketing services, on-line services/multimedia development, permissions, product marketing, production services, and publishing processes—are listed below. Bold type denotes core team members.

Laura Bird, Betsy Bostwick, Pam Cardiff, **Megan Chill,** Rhett Conklin, Carlos Crespo, Gabriella Della Corte, Ed de Leon, Donna C. DiCuffa, **Amy E. Fleming, Holly Gordon, Rebecca Z. Graziano, William J. Hanna, Rick Hickox,** Jim Jeglikowski, John Kingston, **Perrin Moriarty, James O'Neill, Jim O'Shea, Maureen Raymond,** Rob Richman, Doris Robinson, Gerry Schrenck, Ann Shea, Melissa Shustyk, Annette Simmons, **Rita M. Sullivan, Elizabeth Torjussen**

Additional Credits

Ernie Albanese, Robert H. Aleman, Diane Alimena, Michele Angelucci, Rosalyn Arcilla, Penny Baker, Anthony Barone, Rui Camarinha, Tara Campbell, Amy Capetta, Lorena Cerisano, Kam Cheng, Elizabeth Crawford, Mark Cryan, Paul Delsignore, Robert Dobaczewski, Irene Ehrmann, Kathryn Foot, Joe Galka, Catalina Gavilanes, Elaine Goldman, Joe Graci, Stacey Hosid, Leanne Korszoloski, Jan Kraus, Gregory Lynch, Mary Luthi, Vickie Menanteaux, John McClure, Frances Medico, Omni-Photo Communications, Inc., Photosearch, Inc., Linda Punskovsky, David Rosenthal, Laura Ross, Rose Sievers, Gillian Speeth/Picture This, Cindi Talocci, Mark Taylor, Lashonda Williams, Jeff Zoda

Houghton Mifflin Company "The Shark" from *Fast and Slow* by John Ciardi. Copyright © 1975 by John Ciardi. "Rhyming Riddle 1(Snow)" from *The Children Sing In the Far West* by Mary Austin. Copyright 1928 by Mary Austin, © renewed 1956 by Kenneth M. Chapman and Mary C. Wheelwright. "Arachne" by Olivia Coolidge from *Greek Myths*. Copyright © 1949, © renewed 1977 by Olivia E. Coolidge. Reprinted by permission of Houghton Mifflin Company. All rights reserved.

International Creative Management "Grandpa and the Statue" by Arthur Miller. Copyright 1945 by Arthur Miller.

Francisco Jiménez "The Circuit" by Francisco Jiménez, *The Arizona Quarterly* (Autumn 1973). Reprinted by permission of the author.

Alfred A. Knopf, Inc. "Dream Dust" and "April Rain Song" from *Collected Poems* by Langston Hughes. Copyright © 1994 by the Estate of Langston Hughes. "Justice at Last" from *25 Great Moments* by Geoffrey C. Ward, Ken Burns and S. A. Kramer. Copyright © 1994 by Baseball Enterprises International, Inc. "Central Park" from *Assorted Prose* by John Updike. Copyright © 1965 by John Updike. "He Lion, Bruh Bear and Bruh Rabbit" from *The People Could Fly* by Virginia Hamilton. Copyright © 1985 by Virginia Hamilton. Reprinted by permission of Alfred A. Knopf, Inc.

Barbara S. Kouts for Joseph Bruchac "Loo-Wit, the Fire-Keeper" a Nisqually myth, retold by Joseph Bruchac, from *Keepers of the Earth: Native American Stories and Environmental Activities for Children* by Michael J. Caduto and Joseph Bruchac. Copyright © 1988 by Joseph Bruchac. Used by permission of Barbara S. Kouts for Joseph Bruchac.

The Lazear Agency "Turkeys" from *Mama Makes Up Her Mind* by Bailey White, published by Addison-Wesley, copyright © 1993 by Bailey White. Used by permission of The Lazear Agency.

Lescher & Lescher, Ltd., Authors Representatives "The Southpaw" by Judith Viorst. Copyright © 1974 by Judith Viorst. From *Free to Be...You and Me*. Used by permission of Lescher & Lescher, Ltd., Authors Representatives.

Ellen Levine Literary Agency "How to Write a Letter" from *We Are Still Married* by Garrison Keillor. Published by Viking Penguin Inc. Copyright © 1987 by International Paper Company, copyright © Garrison Keillor 1989. Used by permission of International Paper Company (originally titled "How To Write A Personal Letter.")

Little, Brown and Company "Books Fall Open" from *One At a Time* by David McCord. Copyright © 1965, 1966 by David McCord. From *Adventure of Isabel* by Ogden Nash. Copyright © 1936 by Ogden Nash. Used by permission of Little, Brown and Company.

Liveright Publishing Corporation "who knows if the moon's," copyright 1923, 1925, 1951, 1953, © 1991 by the Trustees for the E. E. Cummings Trust. Copyright © 1976 by George James Firmage, from *Complete Poems: 1904–1962* by E. E. Cummings, Edited by George J. Firmage. Reprinted by permission of Liveright Publishing Corporation.

Los Angeles Times Syndicate "TV's Top Dogs" by Deborah Starr Seibel, published in *TV Guide*, June 18, 1994. Used by permission of the Los Angeles Times Syndicate.

Literary Trustees of Walter de la Mare, and the Society of Authors as their representative "Someone" from *The Complete Poems of Walter de la Mare*, copyright 1969, 1970. Used by permission of the Literary Trustees of Walter de la Mare, and the Society of Authors as their representative.

Joan C. McIntosh "The Fairies' Lullaby" from "A Midsummer Night's Dream" from *Shakespeare: Major Plays and the Sonnets*, by G. B. Harrison. Copyright 1948 by Harcourt Brace & Company, © renewed by Joan C. McIntosh. Used by permission of Joan C. McIntosh.

McIntosh & Otis, Inc "Overdoing It" from *Shadows and Light: Nine Stories* by Anton Chekhov, edited and translated by Miriam Morton, originally published by Doubleday & Company, Inc. Copyright © 1968 by Miriam Morton. Reprinted by permission of McIntosh & Otis, Inc.

Margaret K. McElderry Books, an imprint of Simon & Schuster Children's Publishing Division, and Orion Publishing Group Ltd. "Noah and the Flood" (retitled "The Great Flood") is reprinted with the permission of Margaret K. McElderry Books, an imprint of Simon & Schuster Children's Publishing Division, and Orion Publishing Group Ltd. from *God's People* by Geraldine McCaughrean. Text copyright © 1997 Geraldine McCaughrean.

William Morrow & Company, Inc. "Hard As Nails" from *The Good Times* by Russell Baker. Copyright © 1989 by Russell Baker. "The World is Not a Pleasant Place To Be" from *My House* by Nikki Giovanni. Copyright © 1972 by Nikki Giovanni. Used by permission of William Morrow & Company, Inc. Reprinted by permission of William Morrow & Company, Inc.

Lensey Namioka "The All-American Slurp" by Lensey Namioka. Copyright © 1987, from *Visions*, edited by Donald R. Gallo. Reprinted by permission of Lensey Namioka. All rights are reserved by the Author.

New Directions Publishing Corp. "Exclamation" by Octavio Paz, translation by Mark Strand, from *Collected Poems 1957–1987*. Copyright © 1968 by Octavio Paz and Charles Tomlinson. "Wind and Water and Stone" by Octavio Paz, translation by Mark Strand, from *Collected Poems 1957–1987*. Copyright © 1979 by The New Yorker Magazine. Reprinted by permission of New Directions Publishing Corp.

Orchard Books, a Division of Franklin Watts, Inc. and Hamish Hamilton, a division of Penguin Books UK "Becky and the Wheels-and-Brake Boys" from *A Thief in the Village and Other Stories* by James Berry. Copyright © 1987 by James Berry. All rights reserved. Used by permission.

Philomel Books, an imprint of the Putnam Berkley Group Inc. *Greyling* by Jane Yolen, text copyright © 1968 by Jane Yolen. Reprinted by permission of Philomel Books, an imprint of the Putnam Berkley Group Inc.

Prentice Hall, Inc. "Restoring the Circle" by Joseph Bruchac, from *The Writers Solution Sourcebook, Bronze*, copyright © 1996 Prentice Hall, Inc. Used by permission of the publisher.

Random House, Inc. "Life Doesn't Frighten Me" from *And Still I Rise* by Maya Angelou. Copyright © 1978 by Maya Angelou. Reprinted by permission of Random House, Inc.

Marian Reiner for the author "The Sidewalk Race," originally titled "The Sidewalk Racer or on the Skateboard" by Lillian Morrison, from *The Sidewalk Racer and Other Poems of Sports and Motion* by Lillian Morrison. Copyright © 1968, 1977 by Lillian Morrison. Reprinted by permission of Marian Reiner for the author.

Marian Reiner, Literary Agent Haiku by Bashō and Soseki from *Cricket Songs: Japanese Haiku*, translated by Harry Behn. Copyright © 1964 by Harry Behn. © renewed 1992 Prescott Behn, Pamela Behn Adam and Peter Behn. "Simile: Willow and Gingko" by Eve Merriam., from *A Sky Full of Poems*. Copyright © 1964, 1970, 1973 by Eve Merriam; © renewed 1992 Eve Merriam. Reprinted by permission of Marian Reiner, Literary Agent. All rights reserved.

Scholastic, Inc. "Why Monkeys Live in Trees" by Julius Lester, from *How Many Spots Does A Leopard Have? and Other Tales* by Julius Lester. Copyright © 1989 by Julius Lester. "The Shutout" from *Black Diamond: The Story of the Negro Baseball Leagues* by Patricia C. McKissack and

ART CREDITS

Cover: Luis Casteneda/The Image Bank **vii: t.** Silverstre Machado/Tony Stone Images **b.** Philip & Karen Smith/Tony Stone Images **viii: t.** Jane Burton/Bruce Coleman, Inc. **b.** *Voices of the Clouds,* Jessie Lee Geiszler, Courtesy of the artist **ix: t.** *Elephant Tree,* ©1996 Robert Vickrey/Licensed by VAGA, New York NY **b.** Lou Jones/The Image Bank **x: t.** image© Copyright 1997 PhotoDisc, Inc. **b.** Corel Professional Photos CD-ROM™ **xi: t.** ©1997, Michael Simpson/FPG International Corp. **b.** Benelux Press/H. Armstrong Roberts **xii: t.** *Daddy's Girl,* 1992, Carlton Murrell, Courtesy of the artist, photo by John Lei/Omni-Photo Communications, Inc.; **b.** Tom and Pat Leeson/Photo Researchers, Inc. **xiii: t.** AP/Wide World Photos **b.** David Ball/Tony Stone Images **xiv: t.** *Finishing the Hat,* Bill Nelson, Courtesy, Bill Nelson **b.** Grace Davies/Omni-Photo Communications, Inc. **xv: t.** Vicki Silbert/PhotoEdit **b.** Corel Professional Photos CD-ROM™ **xvi: t.** *Coyotes:* detail from hand-painted wood desk, Maureen Mahoney Barraclough **b.** image©Copyright 1997 PhotoDisc, Inc. **1:** *In the Garden,* Joseph Raphael, The Redfern Gallery **2:** Thomas Victor **3:** Harold Sond/The Image Bank **7:** *New Shoes for H,* Don Eddy, The Cleveland Museum of Art, Don Eddy, American, b. 1944. New Shoes for H, 1973–1974. Acrylic on canvas, 111.7 x 121.9 cm.© the Cleveland Museum of Art, 1998, Purchase with a grant from the National Endowment for the Arts and matched by gifts from members of The Cleveland Society for Contemporary Art, 1974.53 **8:** Silverstre Machado/Tony Stone Images **13:** *The Four Freedoms: Freedom of Speech,* Norman Rockwell, © The Curtis Publishing Company. Printed by permission of the Norman Rockwell Family Trust Copyright © 1943 the Norman Rockwell Family Trust **15:** ©Zig Leszczynski/Animals Animals **16:** Corel Professional Photos CD-ROM™ **18:** ©Margot Conte/Animals Animals **22 t.:** NASA **22 b.:** ©1996 Paramount Pictures. All Rights Reserved. **23:** Everett Collection **24 t.:** Rollie McKenna **24 m.:** Courtesy of the Library of Congress **24 b.:** Dimitri Kessel/Life Magazine; **25:** M.C. Escher, *Day and Night* ©1998, Cordon Art B.V.-Baarn-Holland. All rights reserved. **26:** University of Washington Press, Photo by Gordon Robotham **28 & 29:** David Macias/ Photo Researchers, Inc. **32 t.:** John Craig Photo **32 b.:** Thomas Victor **33:** Robert Gwathmey, Courtesy Terry Dintenfass Gallery **34:** Frank Orel/Tony Stone Images **37:** *Springtime Rain,* 1975, Ogden M. Pleissner, Ogden M. Pleissner Estate Marion G. Pleissner Trust, Bankers Trust Company. Photo by Grace Davies/Omni-Photo Communications, Inc.; **40–41:** Kathy Ferguson/PhotoEdit **46 & 49:** The Manchester Museum, The University of Manchester, England **52:** Mary Kate Denny/PhotoEdit **55:** Tony Freeman/PhotoEdit **57:** *Urban Downgrade, 20th and Noe,* 1988, Wayne Thiebaud, Courtesy of the artist **58:** Corbis-Bettmann **59:** The Granger Collection, New York **60:** Special Collections Division, University of Washington Libraries, E. A. Hegg, 578 **62:** © 1988, Greenwich Workshop Inc. Courtesy of the Greenwich Workshop Inc. **64:** Special Collections Division, University of Washington Libraries, E.A. Hegg, 181 **70 t.:** Thomas Garland/Fay Foto Service, Inc. **70 m:** Culver Pictures, Inc. **71:** Philip & Karen Smith/Tony Stone Images **72:** © The Curtis Publishing Company **74 & 75:** Corel Professional Photos CD-ROM™ **78 t.:** Charles G. Barry **78 b.:** Corbis-Bettmann **79:** *My Brother,* 1942, Guayasamin (Oswaldo Guayasamin Calero), Oil on wood, 15 7/8 x 12 3/4", Collection, The Museum of Modern Art, New York, Inter-American Fund **81:** Marc Solomon/The Image Bank **84:** Charles Feil/Stock, Boston **87:** ©Anthony Potter Collections/Archive Photos **89:** ©Levick/Archive Photos **94:** Corel Professional Photos CD-ROM™ **99:** Will Hart **102–103:** Copyright © 1985 The Metropolitan Museum of Art, Gift of George N. and Helen M. Richard, 1964. (64.165.2) Photograph by Malcolm Varon **104:** Minnesota Public Radio, photo by Carmen Quesada **105:** *Laurence Typing,* 1952, Fairfield Porter, oil on canvas 40 x 30 1/8

inches, The Parrish Art Museum, Southampton, New York, Gift of the Estate of Fairfield Porter1980.10.112 **107:** Richard Hutchings/Photo Researchers, Inc. **108:** ©Jim Cummings/FPG International Corp. **113:** *August Afternoon,* ca. 1940, Hobson Pittman, Morris Museum of Art, Augusta, Georgia **114 b.:** American Foundation for the Blind **115:** ©The Stock Market/ Marco Cristofori **116:** Jane Burton/Bruce Coleman, Inc. **118:** *Pigeons,* John Sloan, Oil on canvas, 26 x 32", The Hayden Collection, Courtesy, Museum of Fine Arts, Boston, Massachusetts **122:** Photofest **126 t.:** Thomas Victor **126 m.:** The Granger Collection, New York **126 b.:** Macmillan, Inc. Photo by R.C. Frampton **127:** *Voices of the Clouds,* Jessie Lee Geiszler, Courtesy of the artist **128:** *The Calm After the Storm,* Edward Moran, Private Collection/Superstock, Inc. **129:** Corel Professional Photos CD-ROM™ **130:** Corel Professional Photos CD-ROM™ **135:** Reprinted with the permission of Margaret K. McElderry Books, an imprint of Simon & Schuster Children's Publishing Division from GOD'S PEOPLE by Geraldine McCaughrean, illustrated by Anna C. Leplar. Illustrations copyright © 1997 Anna C. Leplar **138:** Lynn Saville **143:** *Pushball,* Kusnezov Pavel, Art Resource, NY **144:** Thomas Victor **145:** Corel Professional Photos CD-ROM™ **147–150:** from "Zlateh the Goat and Other Stories" by Isaac Bashevis Singer, illustrations by Maurice Sendak © 1966, HarperCollins, Publishers, Inc. **154 t.:** Hearst Books, Photo by Daniel Pomerantz. **154 m.t.:** Hulton Getty Images/Tony Stone Images **154 m.b.:** Courtesy of the author **154 b.:** Henry Wadsworth Longfellow (detail), Thomas B. Read, The National Portrait Gallery, Smithsonian Institution, Washington, D.C./Art Resource, New York; **155:** Michelle Bridwell/PhotoEdit **156–157:** Courtesy of Joseph Fischer **158:** Children in an Interior, Carl Holsoe, Christie's Images **162 t.:** Jesse Stuart Foundation **162 m.:** Corbis-Bettmann **162 b.:** Sergio Larrain/Magnum Photos, Inc.; **163:** image © Copyright 1997 PhotoDisc, Inc. **164:** M.P. Kahl/Photo Researchers, Inc. **165:** J.L. Lepore/ Photo Researchers, Inc. **166–167:** J.L. Lepore/Photo Researchers, Inc. **168:** image©Copyright 1997 PhotoDisc, Inc. **169:** NASA **171:** Robert E. Daemmrich/Tony Stone Images **172–173:** Harald Sund/The Image Bank **176:** M.P. Kahl/Photo Researchers, Inc. **181:** Michael Newman/ PhotoEdit **184–185:** *Maze at Sunset,* © Garry Nichols, The Stock Illustration Source Inc. **186:** Harper Collins **187:** David Young-Wolff/PhotoEdit **189:** Mary Kate Denny/PhotoEdit **191:** *Elephant Tree,* ©1996 Robert Vickrey/Licensed by VAGA, New York NY **192–193:** ©David Burnett/Contact Press Images **197:** *Jim Ryun - World Champion Miler,* 1975, Joe Wilder, © Joe Wilder **198: t.** Courtesy of the author **198 b.:** Shelburne Museum, Shelburne, Vermont (46.5.1-2), Photograph by Ken Burris. **199:** Corel Professional Photos CD-ROM™ **200–201:** Corel Professional Photos CD-ROM™ **203:** ©The Stock Market/Bob Shaw **206–207:** Corel Professional Photos CD-ROM™ **212 t.:** Courtesy of the Library of Congress **212 m.t.:** New York Public Library **212 m.b.:** The Mark Twain House, Hartford, CT **212 b.:** Virginia Hamilton **213:** David Young-Wolff/ PhotoEdit **214:** Corel Professional Photos CD-ROM™ **216–217:** ©The Stock Market/Bob Woodward **221–223:** Scala/Art Resource, NY **224–227:** Corel Professional Photos CD-ROM™ **227 t.l.:** Cave Canem, Roman Mosaic, Pompeii, Italy, Scala/Art Resource, NY **228:** Scala/Art Resource, NY **230:** Corel Professional Photos CD-ROM™ **235:** *Boating in the Park,* James Weeks, Courtesy of Jerry I. Speyer, photo by Greg Heins **236:** Courtesy of the National Portrait Gallery, London **237:** *Akela the Lone Wolf,* 1913, Illustration by Maurice and Edward Detmold from The Jungle Book by Rudyard Kipling, The Century Company, The Central Children's Room, Donnell Library Center, The New York Public Library **238:** Renne Lynn/Tony Stone Images **242:** © Tom McHugh/Photo Researchers, Inc.; **244:** Corel Professional Photos CD-ROM™ **239–245:** border Renne

Lynn/Tony Stone Images **248 t.:** Prentice Hall **248 b.:** Atheneum Books, photo by Didi Cutler **249:** Rhoda Sidney/Stock, Boston **250:** Corel Professional Photos CD-ROM™ **252:** *Collage*, 1992, Juan Sanchez, Courtesy of Juan Sanchez and Guarighen, Inc. NYC **254–257:** Lou Jones/The Image Bank **260 t.:** UPI/Corbis-Bettmann **260 m.:** Corbis-Bettmann **260 b.:** Courtesy of Thomas Benét **261:** Culver Pictures, Inc. **263:** *After the Storm*, 1970, ©1996 Robert Vickrey/Licensed by VAGA, New York, NY **264–265:** The Granger Collection, New York **266t:** NASA; **266b:** AP/Wide World Photos **267:** NASA **270:** Rube Goldberg Inc., United Media/United Feature Syndicate **275:** Corel Professional Photos CD-ROM™ **278–279:** *Emigrants Crossing the Plains*, 1867, Albert Bierstadt, oil on canvas, 60 x 96 in., A.011.1T, National Cowboy Hall of Fame, Oklahoma City **280:** AP/Wide World Photos **281–285:** Corbis **289:** Basketball Superstars by LeRoy Neiman Copyright © LeRoy Neiman, Inc. All Rights Reserved. **290 m.:** Corbis-Bettmann **290 b.:** The Granger Collection, New York **291:** Renee Lynn/Photo Researchers, Inc. **292:** Corel Professional Photos CD-ROM™ **295:** *That's My Dog* (German Shepard), Jim Killen, Voyageur Art **298:** Brian Yarvin/Photo Researchers, Inc. **302:** Renee Lynn/Photo Researchers, Inc. **303:** Mickey Gibson/ANIMALS ANIMALS **306 t.:** Henry McGee/Globe Photos **306 m.:** *Carl Sandburg*, Miriam Svet, The National Portrait Gallery, Smithsonian Institution, Washington, D.C./Art Resource, New York; **306 b.:** Photo by Dorothy Alexander **307:** Corel Professional Photos CD-ROM™ **308:** ©Jeffery A. Salter **310:** image © Copyright 1997 PhotoDisc, Inc. **311:** THE FAR SIDE © 1982 FARWORKS, INC. Used by permission of UNIVERSAL PRESS SYNDICATE. All rights reserved. **315:** Reprinted with the permission of Simon & Schuster for Young Readers, an imprint of Simon & Schuster Children's Publishing Division from TALES FROM GOLD MOUNTAIN by Paul Yee, paintings by Simon Ng. Illustration copyright (c) 1989 Simon Ng. **316:** Culver Pictures, Inc. **317:** Courtesy, The Bancroft Library 1905.5278.234 **320:** John Running /Black Star **325:** *Stairway*, James Doolin, Courtesy of Koplin Gallery, Los Angeles, CA **326:** Prentice Hall **327:** *One*, 1986, April Gornik, Edward Thorp Gallery **328–329:** border Jeremy Walker/Tony Stone Images **329:** inset Corel Professional Photos CD-ROM™ **330:** Corel Professional Photos CD-ROM™ **334 t.:** AP/Wide World Photos **334 m.:** *E. E. Cummings* (detail), 1958, Self Portrait, The National Portrait Gallery, Smithsonian Institution, Washington, D.C./Art Resource, New York; **334 b.:** Courtesy of the Library of Congress **335:** Corel Professional Photos CD-ROM™ **336:** *Ezra Davenport*, 1929, Clarence Holbrook Carter, Oil on canvas, Courtesy of the artist **338–339:** image © Copyright 1997 PhotoDisc, Inc. **342 t.:** Russell Freedman, Photograph by Charles Osgood, Copyrighted 5/23/88, Chicago Tribune Company, All rights reserved, Used with permission; **342 m.:** Villard Books, photo © John Isaac **342 b.:** Florentine Films. Photo by Pam Tubridy Baucom **343:** UPI/Corbis-Bettmann **344:** The Granger Collection, New York **345:** Lincoln Boyhood National Memorial, Photo by John Lei/Omni-Photo Communications, Inc.; **349:** *Peculiarsome Abe*, N. C. Wyeth, The Free Library of Philadelphia **351:** Courtesy of the Library of Congress **352 & 354:** UPI/Corbis-Bettmann **358:** Deborah Davis/PhotoEdit **363:** Lynn Saville **364:** Illustration from Alice Through the Looking Glass by Lewis Carroll, John Tenniel **366–367:** *This, That, There*, 1993, Pat Adams, Courtesy of the Eleanor Munro Collection /Zabriskie Gallery **368:** New York Public Library **369:** Lawrence Migdale/Photo Researchers, Inc. **371:** ©Uniphoto, Inc. **372:** Robin Scagell/Science Photo Library/Photo Researchers, Inc. **375:** Lawrence Migdale/Photo Researchers, Inc. **379:** *Unnamed Clipper Ship*, Claude Marks, Private Collection/The Bridgeman Art Library, London/New York **380:** Thomas Victor **381:** David Crosier/Tony Stone Images **382:** ©1997, Michael Simpson/FPG International Corp. **384:** Benelux Press/H. Armstrong Roberts **388 t.:** Corbis-Bettmann **388 m.:** Nationwide News Service **389:** Maurice Huser/Tony Stone Images **390 & 391:** image © Copyright 1997 PhotoDisc, Inc. **396:** Woods Hole Oceanographic Institution **397:** Courtesy of Ken Marschall **400 l.:** Courtesy of the Library of Congress **400 r.:** Courtesy

of Ken Marschall **401 l.:** Photo by Brown Bros./Ken Marschall **401 r.:** Courtesy Madison Press, Illustrated by Pronk and Associates **402:** Courtesy Madison Press, Illustrated by Pronk and Associates **406 & 407:** Everett Collection **412:** Lynn Saville **417:** 'Sinbad the Sailor' from *Stories from the Arabian Nights*, illustrated by Edmund Dulac, Reproduced by permission of Hodder and Stoughton Limited **418:** BridgeWater Books **419:** *The Kintai Bridge in Springtime*, (detail) Kawase Hasui, The Bridgeman Art Library, London **420:** *The Immortal*, 1990, Chi-Fong Lei, Courtesy of the artist; **422:** Corel Professional Photos CD-ROM™ **428 t.:** *William Shakespeare*, (detail), Artist unknown, by courtesy of the National Portrait Gallery, London; **428 m.:** ©Faber & Faber Ltd; **428 b.:** *Christina Rossetti* (1830-1894), english poet, wood engraving after Dante Gabriel Rossitti, The Granger Collection, New York **429:** Illustration by Arthur Rackham. From Mother Goose. Copyright, 1913, by Arthur Rackham, 1941, by Adyth Rackham. Reproduced by permission of D. Appleton-Century Company, Inc. **430:** Corel Professional Photos CD-ROM™ **432:** *The Coming Storm, Isle of Wight*, 1789 by George Morland (1763-1804) Wolverhampton Art Gallery, West Midlands, UK/Bridgeman Art Library, London/New York **436 t.:** Photo by Darr Bass **436 b.:** AP/Wide World Photos **437:** ©Popperfoto/Archive Photos **438:** inset ©Susan Greenspan/Archive Photos **438:** © Popperfoto/Archive Photos **442–443:** Frans Lanting/Photo Researchers, Inc. **444:** M & E Bernheim/ Woodfin Camp & Associates **448:** Corel Professional Photos CD-ROM™ **453:** Tony Freeman/PhotoEdit **456–457:** *The Storyteller*, Adolphe Tidemand, Chritie's, London , SuperStock **458:** ©1979 R.E. Potter III **459:** Photo Courtesy of the Archives of the American Illustrators Gallery, New York City © Copyright 1998, by ASAP of Holderness, NH, 03245, USA. Authorized by The Maxfield Parrish Family Trust **462:** Reprinted with the permission of Atheneum Books for Young Readers, an imprint of Simon & Schuster Children's Publishing Division from THE BOY'S KING ARTHUR by Sidney Lanier, illustrated by N.C. Wyeth. Copyright © 1917 Charles Scribner's Sons; copyrights renewed 1945 N.C. Wyeth and 1952 John Lanier, David Lanier and Sterling Lanier. **465:** Dick Whittington on his way to London from "My Nursery Story Book", published by Blackie and Son (book illustration) by Frank Adams, Private Collection/The Bridgeman Art Library, London **469:** *Nightfall* (detail), N.C. Wyeth, Private Collection, Brandywine River Museum **470:** Camera Press/Globe Photos; **471:** *Biking for Fun*, 1992, Carlton Murrell, Courtesy of the artist, photo by John Lei/Omni-Photo Communications, Inc.; **472:** *Daddy's Girl*, 1992, Carlton Murrell, Courtesy of the artist, photo by John Lei/Omni-Photo Communications, Inc.; **474:** *Mother, I Love to Ride*, 1992, Carlton Murrell, Courtesy of the artist, photo by John Lei/Omni-Photo Communications, Inc.; **480 t.** Corbis-Bettmann **480 b.:** AP/Wide World Photos **481:** © Elizabeth Simpson/FPG International Corp. **482–483:** Corel Professional Photos CD-ROM™ **483:** *Old Man's Head, Study*, 1955, Yuri Alexeevich Dryakhlov, Courtesy of Overland Gallery of Fine Art, Scottsdale, AZ **484:** *Old Man*, 1950s, Yuri Alexeevich Dryakhlov, Courtesy of Overland Gallery of Fine Art, Scottsdale, Az. **484–485:** border Corel Professional Photos CD-ROM™ **486:** Corel Professional Photos CD-ROM™ **487:** PEANUTS reprinted by permission of United Feature Syndicate, Inc. **487:** NASA **489:** *Orange Sweater*, 1955, Elmer Bischoff, San Francisco Museum of Modern Art, Gift of Mr. and Mrs. Mark Schorer **490:** *Portrait*, From the Estate of Eloy Blanco, Collection of El Museo del Barrio, New York, NY **498:** Dorothy Littel/Stock, Boston/PNI **503:** *Badlands of Dakota* (detail), Thomas Moran, Spanierman Gallery, LLC, New York City **504 t.:** Corbis-Bettmann **504 b.:** Prentice Hall **505:** UPI/Corbis-Bettmann **507:** Hulton Getty/Tony Stone Images **508:** UPI/Corbis-Bettmann **510:** ©Stephen J. Krasemann/Peter Arnold, Inc. **512:** Tom and Pat Leeson/Photo Researchers, Inc. **516 t.:** Courtesy of the author. Photo by Don Perkins. **516 b.:** Alexander Limont **517:** Ralph Cowan/ Tony Stone Images **518 & 519:** Corel Professional Photos CD-ROM™ **520 & 521:** Anthony Johnson/The Image Bank : Anthony Johnson/The Image Bank **524:** David Young-Wolff/Tony Stone Images **526:** *Walk in the Country*, Javran,

Superstock; **529:** *Harvesting the Fruit Crop,* Javran, Superstock **534:** Corel Professional Photos CD-ROM™ **539:** Tony Freeman/PhotoEdit **542–543:** *Desk Set,* 1972, Wayne Thiebaud, Courtesy of the artist **544:** Scholastic, Inc **545:** National Baseball Library and Archive, Cooperstown, N.Y. **549:** National Baseball Library and Archive, Cooperstown, N.Y. **553:** *Still Life,* Anonymous, Private Collection/The Bridgeman Art Library, London/New York **554 m.:** Marion E. Wade Center, Wheaton College, Wheaton, IL **554 t.:** Culver Pictures, Inc. **554 b.:** William Sallaz/Duomo Photography, Inc. **555:** *Woman Writing,* Pierre Bonnard, Sonia Henie Collection, Oslo, Norway/The Bridgeman Art Library, London **557:** Culver Pictures, Inc. **559:** Steven E. Sutton/Duomo Photography, Inc. **564 t.:** The Mark Twain House, Hartford, CT **564b.:** Diane Trejo **565, 566, & 568:** The Mark Twain House, Hartford, CT **571:** *El Auto Cinema,* 1985, Roberto Gil de Montes, Oil on wood, Courtesy of Jan Baum Gallery, Collection of Patricia Storace; **576:** Barrie Fanton/Omni-Photo Communications, Inc. **581:** *Retroactive I,* Robert Rauschenberg, 1964, Wadsworth Atheneum, Hartford, Connecticut, Gift of Susan Morse Hilles, © Robert Rauschenberg/Licensed by VAGA, New York, NY; **582 m.:** Thomas Victor **582 b.:** AP/Wide World Photos **583–587:** AP/Wide World Photos **588–589:** Bernard Boutrit/ Woodfin Camp & Associates **590:** The Granger Collection, New York **594 b.:** Spencer **594 t.:** Prentice Hall **594 m.:** Corbis-Bettmann **595:** *Paradise #1* , Suzanne Duranceau, Illustratrice **596:** David Ball/Tony Stone Images **598:** Prentice Hall **600 t.:** *Sabbaday Brook with Yellow Leaves, Passaconaway, New Hampshire,* 1956, dye transfer print, Eliot Porter, P1990.51.4065.1, © 1990, Amon Carter Museum, Fort Worth, Texas, Bequest of Eliot Porter **600 b.:** *Ovenbird, Ely, Minnesota, June 30, 1961,* Eliot Porter, P1990.52.471.2, © 1990, Amon Carter Museum, Fort Worth, Texas, Bequest of Eliot Porter **601 r.:** *Sunset Clouds, Tesuque, New Mexico,* 1959, Eliot Porter, P1990.51.1829.1, © 1990, Amon Carter Museum, Fort Worth, Texas, Bequest of Eliot Porter **601 l.:** *Maple, Oak and Beech, Conway, New Hampshire,* 1957, Eliot Porter, P1990.51.4108.1, © 1990, Amon Carter Museum, Fort Worth, Texas, Bequest of Eliot Porter **602–603:** Leonard Le Rue III/Tony Stone Images **604:** ©Joe Mc Donald/Animals Animals **609:** NASA **613:** Courtesy Information Service of India **616:** Prentice Hall **621:** Lynn Saville **624:** Garcia/Stills/Retna, LTD **624–625:** *Theatre Scene,* Edgar Degas/The Bridgeman Art Library, London/New York **627:** *Finishing the Hat,* Bill Nelson, Courtesy, Bill Nelson **628:** Photo, John Martin **629:** Illustration by Norton Juster **643:** Jon Ortner/Tony Stone Images **665:** Corel Professional Photos CD-ROM™ **673:** *Speech* (detail), Paul S. Sample **674:** Garcia/Stills/Retna, LTD; **675:** Jon Ortner/Tony Stone Images; **676:** Grace Davies/Omni-Photo Communications, Inc. **679:** Courtesy of the Library of Congress **680:** Musée Bartholdi, Colmar, France **683:** *Welcome,* Christian Montone, Artwork from the permanent collection of THIRTEEN/WNET's Student Arts Festival, 1978-1993 **685:** Ron Watts/Black Star **690t:** NASA **690–691:** Ellis Island Immigration Museum **692:** Grace Davies/Omni-Photo Communications, Inc. **697:** Corel Professional Photos CD-ROM™ **700–70:** *Waves of Matsushima,* Edo period, early 18th century, six-panel folding screen, Korin Ogata, Courtesy, Museum of Fine Arts, Boston, Fenollosa-Weld Collection **702 t.:** *T. S. Elliot* (detail), 1888-1965, Sir Gerald Kelly, National Portrait Gallery, Smithsonian Institution, Art Resource, New York; **702 b.:** Yoav Levy/Phototake/PNI703 P. Proehl/The Image Bank **705:** Illustration from Old Possum's Book of Practical Cats by T. S. Eliot, illustration copyright ©1982 by Edward Gorey, reproduced by permission of Harcourt Brace & Company **709:** Morgan Russel, *Synchromie Cosmique,* 1913–1914, oil on canvas, 16 1/2 x 13 1/4, Munson-Williams-Proctor Institute Museum of Art, Utica, New York, 57.26 **710 t.:** New York Public Library Picture Collection **710 m.t.:** AP/Wide World Photos **710 m.b.:** Corbis-Bettmann **710 b.:** Don Lewis Photography; **711:** Corel Professional Photos CD-ROM™ **712:** Illustration from Alice Through the Looking Glass by Lewis Carroll, John Tenniel, Photography by John Lei/Omni-Photo Communications, Inc.; **714:** Illustration from Alice Through the

Looking Glass by Lewis Carroll, John Tenniel, Photography by John Lei/Omni-Photo Communications, Inc.; **718:** Corel Professional Photos CD-ROM™ **722 t.:** Photo by Isidro Rodriguez **722 b.:** The Granger Collection, New York **723 & 724:** © Mike & Elvan Habicht/ Animals Animals **726:** *Frog,* 1814, Meika Gafu, Reproduced by Courtesy of the Trustees of the British Museum; **730:** Corel Professional Photos CD-ROM™ **735:** *Zinnias,* 1937, John Hollis Kaufmann, Private Collection/SuperStock **736 t.:** Courtesy of Simon & Schuster, Children's Publishing Division **736 b.:** Corbis-Bettmann **737:** Vicki Silbert/PhotoEdit **738 & 739:** Corel Professional Photos CD-ROM™ **742 t.:** Photo by Bachrach **742 m.:** The Granger Collection, New York **742 m.r.:** Maurice Nimmo/A-Z Botanical Collection **742 b.:** New York Public Library **743 & 744:** Debra P. Hershkowitz/Bruce Coleman, Inc. **746:** Steve Satushek/The Image Bank **751:** Corel Professional Photos CD-ROM™ **752:** Robert Frerck/ Odyssey Productions/Chicago **754 t.:** The Granger Collection, New York **754 m.t.:** AP/Wide World Photos **754 m.m.:** Thomas Victor **754 m.b.:** Courtesy of the author **754 b.:** The Huntington Library, San Marino, California **755:** *Florence in the Garden,* c. 1986, Peter Kuhfield, Bonhams, London, UK/The Bridgeman Art Library, London/New York **756:** Jane Burton/Bruce Coleman, Inc. **757:** Greenhouse and Bothy, Charles Neal/SuperStock **758:** inset Carney House, 1998, Corel Professional Photos CD-ROM™ **758:** Corel Professional Photos CD-ROM™ **759:** Corel Professional Photos CD-ROM™ **759:** Stanley R. Shoneman/Omni-Photo Communications, Inc. **762:** Tony Freeman/PhotoEdit **770–771:** *The Story of the War Robe,* oil on canvas, 30 x 36", Joseph H. Sharp, 0137.321, © Gilcrease Museum, Tulsa, Oklahoma **772:** The Granger Collection, New York **773:** The Granger Collection, New York **777:** The Granger Collection, New York **781:** *The Owl and the Birds,* 1912, Arthur Rackham, Arthur Rackham Collection, Rare Book and Manuscript Library, Columbia University. Arthur Rackham illustration reproduced with the kind permission of his family **782 t.:** L. N. Tolstoi, I. E. Repin, Sovfoto/Eastfoto; **782 b.:** Prentice Hall **783:** Coyote at Sunset: detail from hand-painted wood bird house, Maureen Mahoney-Barraclough **785 & 786:** Corel Professional Photos CD-ROM™ **787:** © John Gerlach/Animals Animals **789:** Coyotes: detail from hand-painted wood desk, Maureen Mahoney-Barraclough **790-791:** Mouse and Owl: detail from hand-painted wood desk, Maureen Mahoney-Barraclough **793:** Coyotes: detail from hand-painted wood desk, Maureen Mahoney-Barraclough **797:** The Granger Collection, New York **798:** *Medusa* (Laura Dreyfus Barney), 1982, Alice Pike Barney, The National Museum of American Art, Smithsonian Institution, Washington, DC/Art Resource, NY **801:** *Perseus, under the protection of Minerva, turns Phineus to stone by brandishing the head of Medusa,* Jean-Marc Nattier, Musee des Beaux-Arts, Tours/ The Bridgeman Art Library, London **805:** © The Stock Market/Tom Brakefield **808:** NASA **809 t.:** Photofest **809 b.:** © The Stock Market/Ron Stafford and Mike Agliolo **812 t.:** Corel Professional Photos CD-ROM™ **812 b.:** © John Gerlach/Animals Animals **817:** *The Lesson,* Sharon Wilson, © Felix Rosenstiel's Widow & Son Ltd, 1993 **818 t.:** Scholastic Art and Writing Awards **818 b.:** Courtesy, Houghton Mifflin Company **819:** Nigel Dennis/Photo Researchers, Inc. **820:** Philip van den Berg/HPH Photography **822–823:** Myrleen Ferguson/PhotoEdit **822:** image © Copyright 1997 PhotoDisc, Inc. **823:** Arachne (detail), Arvis Stewart, Reprinted with the permission of Macmillan Publishing Company from The Macmillan Book of Greek Gods and Hereos by Alice Low, illustrated by Arvis Stewart, Copyright © 1985 by Macmillian Publishing Company; **824:** image © Copyright 1997 PhotoDisc, Inc. **824–825:** Myrleen Ferguson/PhotoEdit **826:** *Red Tree,* 1910, Piet Mondrian, Municipal Museum, The Hague **828:** *The Waterseller of Seville,* Diego Rodriguez Velazquez, Apsley House, London, Great Britain, Art Resource, NY; **834:** © Wolfgang Kaehler; **834–835:** David Weintraub/Photo Researchers, Inc. **835r.:** Bobbi Lane/Tony Stone Images **838.:** Tony Freeman/Photo Edit **841:** NASA **843:** Michael Newman/Photo Edit